# BURKE'S
## Presidential Families
## of the United States of
## America

BURKE'S GENEALOGICAL SERIES

*Founded in London 1826 by John Burke and Sir Bernard Burke CB LLD*
*(Ulster King of Arms 1853-1892)*
*Editorial Director: Hugh Montgomery-Massingberd*

THE BOOKPLATE OF GEORGE WASHINGTON
(*upon whose armorial bearings the "Stars and Stripes" were based*)

THE WHITE HOUSE

The White House, the official residence of the President of the United States of America, is situated on Pennsylvania Avenue, Washington, DC. The site was chosen by President Washington and the engineer Pierre Charles L'Enfant; and the architect, Thomas Hoban, is said to have loosely based his design on Leinster House in Dublin (originally the town house of the Dukes of Leinster and now the Irish Parliament). The cornerstone was laid October 13 1792 and President John Adams took up residence November 1 1800. Writing to his wife next day he said "I pray Heaven to bestow the best of blessings on this house and all that shall hereafter inhabit it. May none but wise and honest men ever rule under this roof." President Franklin D. Roosevelt had these words inscribed on the mantel of the State Dining Room.

The house was burnt by the British in 1814 and the sandstone exterior was painted white during the course of reconstruction. Officially designated the "Executive Mansion", the popular name by which it came to be known was made official by President Theodore Roosevelt. The Executive Office was added at the west end of the White House in 1902 and other additions were made in 1942 and 1948, the interior being completely reconstructed between 1943 and 1952. The White House contains 132 rooms.

# BURKE'S
# Presidential Families
# of the
# United States of
# America

FIRST EDITION

LONDON

## Burke's Peerage Limited

MCMLXXV

*Distributed in North America by Arco Publishing Company Inc, 219 Park Avenue South, New York, NY 10003, USA*

PUBLISHERS' NOTE

Every care has been taken to check the information supplied for this book but the Publishers cannot
accept responsibility for mis-statements, omissions or other inaccuracies which may appear in
this work

ISBN 0 85011 017 3
LCCC 74-25177

R
929.2

This book has been set in Linotron Imprint, display headings in Perpetua
by T. and A. Constable Ltd, Edinburgh
for the Publishers, Burke's Peerage Ltd
Registered Office: 42 Curzon Street, London W1)
Publishing and Editorial Offices: 56 Walton Street, London SW3 1RB

Book Designer: Humphrey Stone (The Compton Press Ltd, Wiltshire)

MADE AND PRINTED IN GREAT BRITAIN

*Distributed in North America by Arco Publishing Company Inc, 219 Park Avenue South, New York,
NY 10003, USA*

# Contents

# List of Illustrations

# Preface

WHAT DO the following have in common? Joseph and Stewart Alsop; the composer of *Anchors Aweigh*; Francis Bacon; the Princes Cantacuzene; Salmon P. Chase; Edmund "Crouchback"; Sir Winston Churchill; Richard Henry Dana; David I of Scotland; the late Duke of Devonshire; Edwards I and III of England; Faye Emerson; Professor M. R. D. Foot; Stephen Foster; John of Gaunt; Owen Glendower; Henri I of France; Henry III of England; Jameses II, III and IV of Scotland; Peter Lawford; General Robert E. Lee; The Macneil of Barra; Chief Justice Marshall; Pierpont Morgan; Aristotle Onassis; Princess Pocahontas; General Israel Putnam; The Queen Mother; Paul Revere; Ted Schroeder; Vicomte de Spoelberch; John Strachey; Rhys ap Tewdwr; and Brigham Young. The answer is that they all appear in the pedigrees in this book devoted to the PRESIDENTIAL FAMILIES.

Some of the names are featured in genealogical tables in the APPENDICES where a limited selection of Royal descents (many more could certainly be worked out) of the Presidents is given. Royal descents, called "vainglorious boasts" by those without a sense of history, are a further illustration of the truly universal cousinship of man. For example, Mr David Williamson, who has compiled the major part of this book, discovered in the course of his researches that he and Mr Nixon share the same line of direct descent from King Edward III of England. Both are twentieth in descent from that chivalrous monarch, often described as the ancestor of the British upper-middle class. Similar claims can be made by thousands of others (including the present writer, 22nd in descent from Edward III).

Amusing (and really quite simple) exercises though they may be, Royal descents are not the *raison d'être* of genealogy or, for that matter, this book. When BURKE'S started in 1826 (the United States of America is not the only institution to be celebrating an important anniversary in 1976) the nineteenth-century appetite for bogus medieval romanticism was approaching its height and, alas, our books were in the van of those trying to satisfy that appetite. Countless family histories would begin with the dread phrase "The origins of this ancient family are lost in the mists of antiquity . . ."; whereas it was often more likely that the origins were lost in the dust thrown up by their carriage wheels. By the time BURKE'S came to its senses the damage had been done—the stigma of snobbery had firmly attached itself to genealogy. This was a tragedy with repercussions against which we are still fighting. To re-establish genealogy for what it is—a serious and scholarly pursuit of objective truth and an invaluable tool of Social History—has been a long struggle. It is one thing to eradicate the hoary old myths from pedigrees that appear in our books. It is quite another to persuade people to *read* and enjoy them as interesting history books (as well as to use them for reference) without prejudice and without being somehow apologetic about their "snobbery" in doing so. One hopes it will not be too long before the study of family history—a preferable description to "genealogy" which implies merely the bare bones of the subject rather than the fascinating flesh-and-blood—is accepted as an admirable way of learning History. The reflection of wars and great national events on a set of individual families can sometimes tell one much more than the wide-ranging generalizations of a theorizing politico-economic historian. Similarly how much deeper an understanding of Social History can be derived from reading the plain facts about families without having them "interpreted", analyzed and put on a statistical graph by a sociologist. And in modern educational terms what better project for a classroom of children than for them to go about tracing their family histories? We all have ancestors and to a genealogist every family history is of value. Those who claim to have no interest in these matters and pride themselves on having nothing to do with such "outdated snobbery", etc, etc, are often secretly ashamed of what they might find. It is thus they who are the real snobs in thinking that any unsavory revelation might do them some curious harm—whereas, if one is objective about it, coming across an unpleasant twig in one's family tree adds to the enjoyment. The only reason the undersigned can establish the identity of his earliest recorded ancestor is the existence of a document showing that Lambert Massyngberd was up for grievous bodily harm in 1288. So let us forget about snobbery, about the fashions of the age we live in and remember, whether we like it or not, that every one of us is a tiny part of a continuing line—stretching backwards and (hopefully) forwards.

To help achieve objectivity in our books it might be imagined that they are put together in an Ivory Tower, as it were. During the time this book has been prepared for publication, however, the stream of significant events affecting its contents has threatened to become a torrent. The Presidency of the United States of America has been constantly in the news and the historic resignation of Mr Nixon, and the events before and after, are of course still sensitive matters of debate. It would therefore be out of place in this Preface to indulge in any personal or editorial views on the position of the Presidency and the political and constitutional situation in the United States over the last few years. That is not to say that there are no opinions expressed in this book. There certainly are plenty and they will be found controversial and thought-provoking. But opinions have been left to those qualified to give them: Professor Sir Denis Brogan, Professor Marcus Cunliffe and his American wife Lesley Hume Cunliffe. Although it is true that Professors Brogan and Cunliffe were not Americans by birth the great weight of their distinguished historical scholarship has been produced on or in the United States and there can be no question that they have been regarded as two of the leading writers and commentators on the Presidency and the Presidents.

For the beginning of this book we commissioned a special essay by Sir Denis Brogan on the Presidency. Unfortunately Sir Denis died shortly after delivering his typescript but we are proud to be able to publish his lively discussion of THE OFFICE AND THE MAN. As he was a perceptive and far-seeing observer there was little that needed to be added or changed before publication, but we are indebted to Mr Hugh Brogan, the author's son and another American historian, who kindly revised the article for press.

The main body of the work dealing with THE PRESIDENTS AND THEIR FAMILIES has its own Introduction (*see p 23*) and there is not much more that needs to be said here. The biographies of the Presidents by Marcus and Lesley Hume Cunliffe are of especial importance and can be highly recommended to the general reader. We are deeply grateful to Professor and Mrs Cunliffe for their contribution and for the valuable help and advice they have generously given us.

Much of the credit for this work must go to David Williamson who first mentioned this project to us seven years ago and with whom we have developed it through to the final product. The factual accounts of the Presidents' careers, their ancestry, their descendants and their brothers and sisters, which he has compiled, are the main contribution to what is hoped will be recognized as a definitive work of reference. For this and for the other things Mr Williamson has done in connection with the book, we thank him very warmly indeed.

It would be foolish to pretend that the genealogy in this work is complete—no genealogy ever is, ever has been or ever will be—but we have aimed at absolute accuracy. We tried to make contact with everyone we could but we are conscious that we failed in some instances and therefore we shall be delighted to hear from anyone with informed additions, corrections and present addresses of members of the families so that we can revise their entries for a future edition. It is ironical, incidentally, that when compiling books of this nature one always hears too much from the people who have least to contribute and not nearly enough from the people who have most. Advance notices of this work have been appearing in the press since the spring of 1972 and we have been overwhelmed with letters from persons claiming to be "direct descendants" of every President under the sun—including Benjamin Franklin (who was never President), Presidents who had no descendants and even President Buchanan (who was unmarried). In some cases these claimants turned out to be remote collaterals; in others no relation at all. A considerable amount of confusion seems to exist as to what a "direct descendant" really is. Put simply, a direct descendant of a President can trace his or her ancestry back through male or female lines straight to that President and his wife. A "collateral descendant" of a President can trace his or her ancestry back through male or female lines direct to a brother or a sister (and their spouses) of that President.

Inevitably there will be some people who will be disappointed at not being included but we are pleased to announce that this book is only the first in an exciting new American Series. We shall shortly be starting work on BURKE'S *Distinguished Families of America.* This will be published in several regional volumes. We would be very interested to hear from those families who wish to be considered for inclusion. Other books in the American Series are being planned and those wishing to be kept informed of our future program should write to us or to our North American distributors, Arco Publishing Company Inc of 219 Park Avenue South, New York, NY 10003, USA.

Apart from the genealogical tables already touched upon, the APPENDICES at the end of the book include the Vice-Presidents, the Declaration of Independence (shortly to be celebrated in the Bi-Centennial), the Constitution, a list of the Presidential Election results and a color feature of the Presidential Insignia. Many regard Jefferson Davis, the one and only President of the Confederate States of America, as a legitimate Head of State and therefore he has been dealt with in an Appendix in exactly the same way as the Presidents of the Union earlier in the book.

Also at the end of the book there is a GUIDE TO THE READER. An elderly reader once told us that he had just been spending the morning teaching his young grandson "how to read BURKE'S" and one admired his splendid assumption that this was a natural and essential part of a civilized education. For too long, perhaps, BURKE'S has imagined that it would be an insult to the readers to explain to them how and why we set out family histories the way we do. We are pleased to remedy this with the innovation of a GUIDE, as we are not ashamed of our style of setting out a narrative pedigree which we believe is the clearest, most logical and satisfactory that has been found!

The LIST OF ILLUSTRATIONS preceding this Preface sets out the documentation of all the pictures included in the book and the captions in the text have accordingly been kept as simple as possible. We are obliged to all those institutions and individuals who kindly gave us their permission to reproduce copyright material. We have already mentioned something of our gratitude to the Brogans, the Cunliffes and David Williamson. The Introduction to the PRESIDENTS AND THEIR FAMILIES acknowledges certain genealogical contributions. It remains to thank Ms Elizabeth Simonds Cook and Mr Kelvin Smith who both did useful work for us in America. Mss Cook and Wendy Regina Moore undertook the picture research. Behind the name BURKE'S there is a team—not one-tenth the size one might think but including Mss Suzanna Osman Jones, Rona Segal and Isobel Clive-Ponsonby-Fane (to name but a few)—and the way this has pulled together, both inside and outside the office, to create this book on a tight schedule amid spiralling production costs is deserving of our sincere and heartfelt thanks.

HUGH MONTGOMERY-MASSINGBERD

Editorial Director Burke's Peerage Ltd
London
*October 1974*

# The Presidency
# of the United States:
# the Office and the Man

Denis Brogan

THE HISTORY of the Presidency of the United States of America illustrates
the truth of the maxim "stoning the prophets is ancient news". For in that
very remarkable body, the Constitutional Convention of 1787, there were
several schemes for the concentration of executive power under the new
Constitution which did not involve giving all final decisions to one man or
see in that one man "We, the People of the United States". It is probable
that if George Washington had not been available to be the first President,
the office would have been less important and might, indeed, have been a
failure. But Washington brought to this new and untried institution the
immense prestige of his career in the American Revolution. Of course, it
was not only a question of past military services that enabled Washington
to reinforce the prestige and power of the Presidency: it was his
fundamental sagacity, courage, and Roman virtue. Perhaps no political
leader could have been quite as virtuous as Parson Weems made the first
President of the United States seem, but we can see in the growth and
power of the Presidency something like an invisible hand, to quote from
Adam Smith, driving, or leading, the American people to their prodigious
destiny.

The office of President was in part a corrected version of the English
monarchy. President George Washington was to be a superior version of
King George III, not only because he was presumed to be more

intelligent, but because the new Constitution was to tie his hands and prevent some of the follies that had marked the careers of so many English monarchs. The colonial experience accounts for the character of the new constitutional system: the final decision to concentrate executive power in one man instead of dividing it as had been done in the Republic of Venice and in the Dutch Republic, or a mixed royal, aristocratic, and popular government system such as was appearing in eighteenth-century Britain. But it very soon became evident in the practical working of the new system set up in 1787 that the Presidency would have no real parallel in the English system and was destined to be either a great success or a great failure.

On the whole, the Presidency has been a great success. The concentration in one man of the power of the executive created by the new Constitution was far more fruitful than the members of the Convention can have foreseen. An obvious reason the Presidency was to acquire its prestige, was the fact that the first President *was* George Washington, and it was not a mere snobbish imitation of English society that led people to talk of "the Republican Court" or to refer to Mrs Washington as "Lady Washington". Other reasons for the rapid growth in power and prestige of the brand new office were the same pressing necessities that had led to the adoption of the new constitution and finally forced the recalcitrant states of Rhode Island and North Carolina to join their brethren. The colonial experience had given monarchical powers to the governors, whether they were appointed by "proprietors" like the Calverts in Maryland or the Penns in Pennsylvania, or like various British nominees who often delegated their responsibilities (but not all their salaries) to "capable Scots". Indeed, two colonies, Rhode Island and Connecticut, actually elected their governors. The American people in 1787 were accustomed to seeing one man, possibly with his hands partly tied by councils or assemblies, as the chief executive in a way King George III had ceased to be and which the younger Pitt had not yet become.

We must also notice that the Constitution of the United States not only has been reinterpreted by Congress, by the courts, by public opinion, by Presidents, like Andrew Jackson, with immense personal prestige, but has grown like a tree, increasingly deeper rooted, increasingly casting its shadow over the whole of American life. In a comparatively short time, the office of President of the United States acquired the sacred character of the Roman consulate or the papal throne. From the beginning of the institution, the American people, even if bitter partisans, noted the difference between the man who held the office of President and the officer who *was* the President. Within the generation of the revolutionary epoch, the Presidency had acquired religious aspects for which no modern European country has been able to find a substitute, combining, as it did, the office of a monarch, a semi-priestly office embodying remote history, and the practical effectiveness of the command of executive power of the new state in a symbiotic relationship which has no parallel in any other living political institution.

The new United States might not have survived if it had had to endure in its infant years Presidents like Franklin Pierce and James Buchanan, but a cynical saying that "God looks after fools, children, and the United States" has some justification. "*Novus ordo seclorum*", it now combines both novelty and antiquity. It owed a great deal to its first four Presidents. George Washington was both a semi-divine hero, a man of probity, and a man of very sound political intelligence. His successor but one, Thomas Jefferson, was a man of genius and of great political talents, including some talents which were not of the purest ethical quality. More than that, Jefferson was successful in "selling" to the American people the prestige of the Presidency even when it was not helped by Washington, and reinforcing the habit of looking to the President for a kind of national leadership that no other Federal official could display.

John Adams, the second President, was elected with no enthusiasm, defeating Jefferson, who made no serious campaign, and who devoted himself to organizing the parliamentary habits of Congress as well as what was far more important, organizing the first effective American party, known originally as the Republican Party and then as the Democratic Party which is now the oldest effective political party in the world. John Adams's temperament was complicated by the fact that he liked to spend much of his time in remote Quincy away from the current capital, Philadelphia. Yet Adams was able to impose his will against the artful, ambitious, and possibly wrongly thwarted Alexander Hamilton. If only in a negative sense, by ending the "quasi war with France", Adams affected the history of the United States very seriously. And if Jefferson's greatest contribution was on one side the creation of the American party system and on the other the annexation through the deal with First Consul Bonaparte of a third of the present American territory by the purchase of Louisiana, he also gave to the President the role of a political leader which he has never fully lost, even when the President was extremely incompetent or idle.

The fourth President, James Madison, was the most learned and in many ways politically acute holder of the office, but he lacked effective political talent and had to see a great deal of the presidential power accumulated by Washington and Jefferson slip out of his hands in the War of 1812 with Britain. It was a war with no great military though considerable naval success, in which the only great land victory, General Andrew Jackson's at New Orleans, occurred after peace had been signed at Ghent in 1814. The importance of Madison was not as a President, and yet the Presidency as an office was in a large sense his creation since he was among the chief authors of the Constitution.

The next President was the only person who was elected almost unanimously as Washington had been: only one vote was cast against re-electing James Monroe although this amiable but unimpressive man owed his place in history, and the doctrine which bears his name, to his cabinet, notably to John Quincy Adams who succeeded him as President. But the Presidency was still a reward given or homage paid to heroes of the Revolution. The first President elected for more recent services was the formidable Andrew Jackson who not only defeated, with ignominious ease, the Peninsular veterans of Wellington (under the highly inefficient leadership of the Duke's brother-in-law, General Pakenham) but created a large part of the modern presidential mystique by setting himself up as peculiarly the spokesman of "We, the People of the United States". The strong Bonapartist element in the practical Constitution of the United States owes more to General Andrew Jackson than to anyone else. He was a successful First Consul and also made the political system of the United States far more democratic than even President Jefferson had tried to make it. Jackson was able to leave the Presidency to that extremely adroit, intelligent and on the whole effective President, Martin Van Buren; even under the economic disasters which fell on his nearly innocent head, Van Buren was able to preserve the basic powers to the office made so potent by Washington, Jefferson and Jackson.

One of the legendary episodes of American politics was the defeat of President Van Buren by a very pale imitation of General Andrew Jackson, General William Henry Harrison. Perhaps fortunately for the United States, General Harrison lived only a month after his inauguration and was succeeded, in what was a precedent-making interpretation of the Constitution, by the Vice-President John Tyler, an ambitious if not terribly impressive Virginian politician whose estimation of his own merits was not widely shared. Yet it was under President Tyler, and owing largely to his aggressive and pathologically ambitious Secretary of State, John Caldwell Calhoun, that Texas was joined to the Union by treaty, not by conquest or purchase.

A more significant President was James Knox Polk, who not only began the Mexican War but conducted it with marked success and showed in victory a degree of moderation which, when all things are considered, was remarkable. The moderation was often not approved of. Captain U. S. Grant, who was the Quartermaster General in the Army of Occupation in Mexico City, wrote to his wife (displaying a sense of humor otherwise occulted) declaring that the Army (by which he meant the regular West Point officers) was unanimous on one point: the Mexicans must be forced to take back Texas! Instead of that, President Polk acquired about a third of the present territory of the United States; above all, he annexed California with immediate and long term results whose final effect on American life we cannot yet assess.

The professional soldier, Zachary Taylor, who was elected in 1848, was a man of courage, great independence of views, and considerable if lately developed political wisdom. But he died a year after inauguration, and was succeeded by Millard Fillmore, a President almost as dim as William Henry Harrison, although not as mischievous as his own successors, Franklin Pierce and James Buchanan. The first successor had some minor claims to being a war hero. He was a college class-mate and patron of Nathaniel Hawthorne to whom he gave the political prize of the consulate at Liverpool, a useful reward for a President to confer on a friend. He was also a heavy drinker and lacking in political or any other character. Under his misguided sway, the Presidency began to go downhill as an institution. The *glissade* continued with the election of one of the most professional of politicians and one of the least effective of Presidents, James Buchanan. He had been Minister to the Tsar, he had been Minister to King William IV of England, he had been Senator, he had been Secretary of State, but, as Frederick the Great said, there was not much point appointing a General because he had been in many campaigns: that was a qualification equally visible in an old army mule. Buchanan was possibly the most mischievous President of the United States because of his character, because of his vanity, and because of his lack of courage. It would be absurd to suggest that it was the faults of Buchanan's character that led to the outbreak of the Civil War, but certainly he did nothing to prevent the Civil War, and it was fortunate for the United States that it did not break out while he was President for he undoubtedly would not have won it. The Presidency was never at a lower moral, intellectual and political level than under this eminent Pennsylvanian politician. He had, however, a high notion of himself and of his office and told the real leader of the Democratic Party, Senator Stephen Douglas, that he should remember the fate of those who had opposed General Jackson. Douglas could only reply that General Jackson was dead. Yet it was Buchanan's action and inaction that helped to precipitate the Civil War, and accidentally made way for Abraham Lincoln.

There has been some dispute about the first "dark horse" who attained the White House. The favorite candidate has been James Knox Polk, but at the very worst he was merely grey. He had been Speaker of the House of Representatives; he had been leader in the contorted and quarrelsome politics of Tennessee and a representative of the Jacksonian tradition. In the drab and confused politics that followed the defeat of Martin Van Buren in 1840, he rose more easily than he would have done at a later time, but Henry Clay, Daniel Webster, and John Caldwell Calhoun, all men of much greater eminence and apparently of greater ability, in various ways cancelled each other out. Perhaps the Republican nominated and elected in 1860, Abraham Lincoln of Illinois, was more truthfully a dark horse than Polk. He had served only one term in the House of Representatives with no very marked distinction. He was, it is true an important figure in the Whig Party of Illinois, but the Whig Party of Illinois, like the Whig Party elsewhere, was rapidly collapsing "in shallows and in miseries". He was not obviously a serious rival to either William H. Seward or Salmon P. Chase, and he owed more to the ingenious manipulation of friends and patrons like Judge David Davis than he owed to any American popular backing. He was remarkably ugly, clumsy, and quite lacking in the social graces which, if not essential in the White House, were still an asset. It is no wonder that he was underestimated by his rivals, notably by the eminent New York politician, Senator Seward who had expected (and had been expected) to be the successful nominee and who had reluctantly accepted the office of Secretary of State from the President-elect largely because he expected to be, in fact, the President in power, inspiring the policies of this rustic statesman.

It was some time before the public, Congress, and the new cabinet appreciated the fact that the "rail splitter" from Illinois was a man of remarkable abilities and of remarkable political talent. One of the first to appreciate the special merits of the new President was William H. Seward, who soon discovered that the effective President was the legal occupant of the White House. The egregiously vain Salmon Portland Chase never realized it, but went to his grave convinced that the United States had made a fatal mistake in not choosing him for the Presidency. A jest which, whether true or not, illustrates the increasing reputation of the underestimated President, tells of a cabinet meeting at which a motion was proposed (in the days when cabinets voted on points of policy) and President Lincoln announced the result: "Nays, seven; ayes, one, The ayes have it".

We have to avoid the mistake of reading history backwards and attributing to the Lincoln of 1861 the hard-earned sagacity and wisdom of the Lincoln of 1865. Lincoln was a man of appreciable self-confidence and self-esteem, but he had pride, not vanity, and he handled his enemies, who were numerous, his rivals who were also numerous, with adroitness, and learned as he exercised his office the realities of the American political system. As one of his successors, Woodrow Wilson, was to say, a President was as great as he wanted to be and was fit to be. Again and again in his four terrible years of office, Lincoln displayed the highest statesmanship, often in a happy combination with the lowest cunning.

Lincoln was faced with a situation whose importance and alarming character he underestimated. He could not believe that the South would be so reckless as to break out in rebellion or, if it did, that the rebellion would last for more than a few weeks or months. Not all the same illusions were dominant in the new rebel capital of Richmond as in the beleaguered capital of Washington. For no government was less prepared for a great military effort than the Government of the United States. Its Army barely mustered 16,000 men. Its Navy consisted almost entirely of obsolete wooden ships. Most of the world expected to see the aggressive embodiment of democracy get its come-uppance.

The Lincoln Administration began by an ignominious disaster at Bull Run (also knows as Manassas) where the confident and complaisant amateur Army of the United States broke down in panic instead of marching on Richmond. The Federal Government had difficulty in holding on to Washington, and at times the new President wondered if it could do even that. But Lincoln was what actors call "a quick study". Fortunately for Lincoln—a good fortune that produced the legend that he had provoked the attack on Fort Sumter which opened the Civil War—the aggression of the South at once produced an explosion of loyalty to the Constitution of the United States and to the nascent nationality of the United States, a loyalty which finally the formidable South attacked in vain.

Lincoln soon discovered that not only was much of the militia, "the National Guard", almost worthless as a fighting force, but that the great new democracy with a population of thirty millions was almost totally disarmed. Federal authority had to be constructed from the ground up, and it is reasonable to speculate that if the South had exploited the victory of Bull Run, it might have occupied Washington which might and probably would have provoked a recognition of the Confederacy by the only two important powers whose decision could affect the United States, Great Britain and France. And the Civil War, if it had lasted for only a short time, would have ended in the dissolution of the United States. But the favour of God, or the folly of the South, saved the day for the time being.

One of the first discoveries made in the terrible year from April 1861 till the Battle of Antietam in September 1862, was that the superiority of the North was not merely its much greater wealth, its much greater technical resources, or even its legal position as the government which was still recognized by all the powers, large and small, as the heir of the authority of the once over-vaunting United States, but the political superiority of the leadership of the North. It was not only, of course, the leadership provided by President Lincoln whose authority grew even in disaster. It was the superiority of some members of Lincoln's cabinet, notably the loyal Secretary of the Navy, Gideon Welles, and the energetic if often detestable Secretary of War, Edwin Stanton.

But it was not the abilities or even the loyalty of cabinet officers, like Welles, like Seward, or like some competent State governors, that saved the United States at times it seemed in danger of collapsing in ruin. It was the immense and visibly increasing political sagacity of the once despised President. Lincoln in his famous speech at the Gettysburg military cemetery showed himself (as H. L. Mencken was later to put it) the only American rival of Thomas Jefferson as a political master of English prose; he had also a profound understanding of human nature, especially of the very human nature displayed in Congress and in his own cabinet.

Lincoln above all knew the virtues of patience and the still greater virtue of courage. There were moments in which he, unlike the Roman consul, despaired of the republic, especially in the summer of 1864. There were times in which the danger of foreign intervention, notably of British and French intervention, threatened total collapse. There were times when the vanity of people like Chase, like Senator Sumner, like General Benjamin Butler, threatened the survival of the Union. The superiority in military organization and military aptitude of the rebel South imposed humiliating defeats on the legal Government of the United States. The fact that the South was fighting for its life, whereas the North was fighting for victory, made the contest much more equal than the disparity of resources would suggest, although we must remember that the territory controlled by the rebel Confederacy was as large as all western Europe. Great victories like Gettysburg and the capture of Vicksburg, greater victories like Chattanooga, dramatic but not immensely important triumphs like the sinking of the Confederate raider CSS *Alabama* by the USS *Kearsarge* kept the North in the war despite very effective propaganda for a negotiated peace which would have ended the union of the United States. More important was the political sagacity which Lincoln displayed.

He knew when to give way, as he did by turning over the captured Confederate envoys who had been seized by the truculent Captain Wilkes of the United States Navy, by avoiding the ostentatious use of the United States naval power, by keeping on good terms with the liberating Tsar of Russia, Alexander II. He knew how to be silent. When he had already decided to use his power as Commander-in-Chief to abolish slavery (a very great strain on the Constitution of the United States) he kept his decision to himself while enduring the sermons of Horace Greeley; and when he did finally issue the emancipation proclamation, it was after the victory of Antietam.

Lincoln's non-dogmatic patience had its reward. It was the nerve of the high command of the rebel states that broke. Jefferson Davis, a man of limited political talent though probably the best the South had, unwisely removed one of the best of his generals, General Joe Johnston, replacing him by the belligerent Texan John B. Hood. The result was the triumph of General William Tecumseh Sherman who marched into the heart of the Confederacy. The young, small, aggressive officer, Philip Sheridan, made it possible to clear out the Shenandoah Valley and at last remove all danger to Washington. By the beginning of the year 1865, the issue of the war was not in doubt, although Jefferson Davis in 1865, like Hitler in 1945, still nursed the unreal hope of ultimate victory. The wisdom and patience and political skill of President Lincoln were triumphing at last. Southern military and economic power was crumbling and Lincoln, coming back from the capture of Richmond, could quote from his favorite writer's *Macbeth:*

> Duncan is in his grave;
> After life's fitful fever he sleeps well;
> Treason has done his worst; nor steel nor poison,
> Malice domestic, foreign levy, nothing,
> Can touch him further.

In one of the best authenticated premonitions of history, Lincoln had a dream which he had had before, of some portentous approaching event. The event, in fact, was not only the victory of the Union, but his own death. When his body was taken from Ford's Theater on Good Friday 1865, exactly four years since the fall of Fort Sumter, it was, of all people, the unamiable Stanton who found the appropriate words: "Now he belongs to the ages". The first President to be a martyr to his office, which has become increasingly dangerous in the ugly modern world, was also the greatest President; and in so far as the United States has had one single savior, it has been this self-educated son of ambiguous parentage to whom the higher powers gave the destiny of saving what Lincoln himself had called "the last best hope of earth".

The Romans worshipped the Fortune of Roma. The Americans worship the Fortune of America. With the surrender of the Southern rebels, the world began to look with a new respect, a new dislike, a new envy at the astonishing spectacle of this republic facing, successfully, a terrible crisis. The new prestige was important in these two bloody centuries, for without military success, mere political success would have been fruitless. (When Lincoln made his famous speech at Gettysburg on November 19 1863, he was already not quite certain, but rightfully hopeful, that the experiment which he described had changed, decisively, modern history all over the known world).

Of course, the good fortune of the United States has not been simply the work of great Presidents, and the occasional disasters of American history have not been simply the result of weak Presidents, for institutions like the Supreme Court and the Senate, have played an important part. But from the point of view of the average American, the President is psychologically more impressive even than the Chief Justice of the United States, and even an incompetent President is more important than a highly competent Senator. The strength of the Presidency was paradoxically manifested at a time when the Presidency itself was most under attack and most handicapped by congressional jealousy or hatred. What is significant about the impeachment of President Andrew Johnson, Lincoln's unhappy successor, was not that it was attempted, but that it failed. Even at that moment of the lowest ebb of Presidential fortune, the Presidency kept its basic rights and could not be ignored or effectively emasculated.

None of the Presidents who followed Lincoln, down at any rate to Theodore Roosevelt, were what can be called exceptional Presidents, nor would American history probably have been seriously altered if *X* had been President rather than *Y*. Some of the Presidents were men of ability and strength of character, like Grover Cleveland, but the United States, until the beginning of the twentieth century, got along with a much more feeble executive power than had been exercised by Washington, Jefferson, Jackson or Lincoln. What *is* to be noted is that even at this low ebb, the tide never totally ran out. Even Presidents of extravagant incompetence were important American figures because of the office they held. Even Presidents as tepid in their anxiety to rule the United States as Calvin Coolidge could not help increasing the power of the White House. Every President in this century could have said, whatever he had promised before he became President, "no winter shall abate this spring's increase". It may be that the tide has turned, and that presidential power is being limited and the power of Congress has been revived. But the President is still at the center of the American political system, and however much a President may be disliked or despised, he is *the* President, and has no rival in the American political system.

What the Presidency would have been after the Civil War if Lincoln had not been assassinated, we do not know. He was so masterly a politician that he might have been able to preserve for the Presidency some of the power he had seized during the great Civil War. *Dis aliter visum.* Only Cleveland in the last half of the nineteenth century could, by even the most flattering theory, have been called a great President, and the United States had to settle, with some relief, for merely adequate Presidents. Yet the tide of history, with all its ebbs and flows, flooded in the not very long run, towards a revival of presidential power. Politicians, even very competent politicians like Speaker Reed, coveted the Presidency with an almost sexual lust, for the President might be incompetent, he might be slothful, he might, like Grant, be a victim of crooks, but he was still the embodiment of "the People of the United States". A famous story dating from the time when the Presidency was far from being a predominant institution reflects the basic perdurability of the office. Chester Arthur, who had been Vice-President, became, by the assassination of President Garfield, and to the general surprise, an effective President of the United States. What the office had become was illustrated by the story of an old friend's slapping the new President on the back at the Newport Yacht Club, and the President doing nothing but turning and looking at him. The presumptuous friend blushed and shuffled away, and never dared to speak to his old pal Chet Arthur again.

Theodore Roosevelt did much to revive the monarchical character of the White House. He was a patron of the arts, an exponent of somewhat arrogant nationalism, a party leader of great adroitness, and one whose pull on the American voter was far more than that of a mere resourceful politician. Even his successor, generally regarded as an unsuccessful President, William Howard Taft, was yet in many ways an effective President, and of course his next successor, Woodrow Wilson, was a great President, at any rate for the first six years of his office. The "Republican Court" of General Washington's time was in all senses revived by Theodore Roosevelt. And it was not unimportant that the city of Washington became more and more visibly a capital.

The great catastrophe of the economic collapse of 1929 threw the burden of holding the United States together on the only office capable of giving a national lead, for few Congresses have been less edifying or impressive than those which frustrated even such inert Presidents as Coolidge and Harding. Hoover, one of the ablest men who ever held the presidential office, was thwarted by politicians like Senator Watson of Indiana, to name one of the less attractive of the "Solons" who thought they had taken over the United States with the collapse of the Wilson régime. President Hoover was, in many ways, simply unlucky; he was inheriting the absence of policy which had marked the Administrations of President Harding and President Coolidge. Had either of these Presidents been self-critical, he might have imitated Louis XV and given an American equivalent of that king's alleged criticism of his own reign, "*Après moi, le déluge*".

The international situation, of course, increased the power of the Presidency almost automatically. From 1929, the concentration of power, the concentration of publicity, the concentration of the court function of "representing" the United States to the American people and to the world, fell to remarkable Presidents: to Franklin Delano Roosevelt who accumulated power by formally dissipating it, and to Harry Truman who accumulated power by accepting, candidly and openly, the responsibilities which his predecessor had often dodged or evaded. There have been few more revealing presidential comments on the office than President Truman's famous motto, "the buck stops here!" No man has more effectually defended the presidential prerogatives than the obscure Middle Western politician who dismissed a national hero, General MacArthur, with the same decisiveness that Cromwell got rid of the Long Parliament. The buck *did* stop in the office of President Truman, and the American people began to realize how unusual a President Mr Truman was, and to notice how innocently he did not overestimate his own importance and knew very well the distinction between the President of the United States and Harry S. Truman of Independence, Missouri.

There is a paradox in what the Romans would have called the *cursus honorum* in the United States. A good many ambitious generals have in fact been elected to the Presidency. We can guess (although it is not a very plausible guess) that General Douglas MacArthur would have been an impressive or at any rate a prominent President. Pershing was tempted to cash in on his service in the First World War by ending his career in the White House, and several Presidents, including remarkable Presidents, have been soldiers although not strictly speaking professional soldiers. But although West Point has high prestige and has produced some outstanding public servants, it has produced only two Presidents and neither of these men can be classed among the great Presidents or even among the good Presidents. The first case is that of a soldier who was a dismally unsatisfactory President, Ulysses S. Grant. The faults of character which had been commented on in the old regular Army were suddenly discovered to be unimportant when he was faced with the tests of war. Grant was, in fact, a man fit only for one thing: to command a big army, and by a fault of judgement and an institutional fault of the American political system, he was projected into the White House where the most one can say is that he did not disgrace himself quite as much as gossip, Democrats, and jealous Republicans believed. But Grant's glory ended at Appomattox when Lee surrendered, and the rest of his career was quite simply a story of decline. It might be suggested that Harding was at least as well qualified to be President as the former successful commander of one of the largest armies in history.

Soldiers, and in the case of Admiral Dewey, at least one sailor, assumed that the White House was a legitimate reward for their services. Grant was notoriously jealous of the lavish way in which the British governing class rewarded Wellington compared with the miserable rewards offered to a former President. At the "Point" and in the Army, Dwight David Eisenhower's career was respectable and promising if not overwhelmingly brilliant. And again, although his service in the Army was not disastrous as Grant's had been, but for his role in the Second World War Eisenhower would simply have been one of the generals of that West Point class "on which the stars fall". It was the wise decision of Franklin D. Roosevelt and the disciplined competence of George Marshall that gave the *beau rôle* to Marshall's protégé, General Eisenhower.

What was needed when the United States entered the European war with the North African landings was political sagacity more than military genius, and General Eisenhower's achievements in North Africa, in the basket-of-snakes atmosphere of Algiers, showed that he had what was above all necessary, a natural political instinct. Very few great soldiers have been conspicuously unselfish characters. Eisenhower certainly was not one of them. He learned a good deal about life as a young lobbyist to Congress for Douglas MacArthur, and of course still more from his brutally sudden education in the North African landings in the autumn of 1942; and since, as Clausewitz put it, war is the continuation of policy by different means, Eisenhower had the one thing necessary, a political sagacity which enabled him to understand that the winner in any contest among the French pretenders to authority was bound to be Charles de Gaulle. He had the great asset of not making a fool of himself as Franklin D. Roosevelt did and of not losing his temper and sometimes his judgement as Churchill did.

The role of President Eisenhower in some ways was very like the role of General Eisenhower. He was a moderator; he was a diplomat. And political education was available to him in the White House. Eisenhower, although he spent a lot of his time with politicians and had many political talents, had to realize that republics are still ungrateful. The regular politicians of the Republican Party were not willing to give the ultimate prize to a man like Eisenhower who had hardly more political background than Grant. Again, what was in some ways an asset to Eisenhower, made him difficult to understand and difficult to assess. Was he an innocent at a loss in the political world, or was he in fact an artful dodger? Both these roles could be attributed to him. What was certain about him was only that, next to his sense of duty to the United States and the United States Army, his chief sense of duty was to himself, as he showed in what some people thought was at least the ungrateful, and others thought was the disgraceful treatment of General George Marshall to whom he owed so much.

It is still debatable whether the apparent innocence of President Eisenhower was a genuine innocence. But it seems more likely that he had at least as much natural political talent as Senator Robert Taft, and what he had to learn he learned quickly. What he learned was not always edifying, but there is no country in which politics are really edifying, and if there is such a country, it is not the United States. And, although it is not true that the new President had no principles, he was less dogmatic not only than Senator Taft, but than President Truman. His temperament suited the time. The United States was tired of the war which had officially ended in victory in 1945, only to break out again in the form of the Korean War, and to break out yet again towards the end of Eisenhower's presidential career in the more disastrous war in Vietnam. Frederick the Great is supposed to have asked of one of his generals, "Is he lucky?" General Eisenhower was lucky.

If he was naïvely surprised to discover the unimpressive ethical character of many of the leading Republican Senators, he very quickly learned all the necessary tricks of the trade, and when he made up his mind, he made it up decisively and since the immediate climate of opinion in the United States was deeply pacific, what was politically wise was also politically expedient. He avoided decisions, if not nearly as much as

President Coolidge did. But General Eisenhower was above criticism, could not topple from his place in the national esteem, and consequently could disregard, if he chose, the not very serious risks of being both bold and wise. If the United States needed an intelligent policy of inaction (as perhaps it did), if many people in modern American political history were better qualified for the job than General Eisenhower, and if some of his wisest decisions were in fact made by his subordinates, like General Bedell Smith, the ability to pick wise assistants is itself a political asset.

John F. Kennedy was conscious of the immense psychological hold of Eisenhower on the American people, and conscious also that his narrow victory did not give him as effective a political authority as he would have liked and needed. It was quite common in Washington in his Administration to find important members of it looking forward to what they could do when the young President began his second term, by which time he would have accumulated enough political authority to carry out a policy of his own without looking backwards to his predecessor.

Whether there was a policy on the way is of course a matter for speculation. When Kennedy was assassinated there was still a good chance of keeping out of the swamps of Indo-China in what turned out to be a hopeless endeavor to impose an American solution. President Kennedy had learned a great deal from his experience in the White House. He learned from the failures and the follies of the invasion of Cuba in the spring of 1961. He learned a great deal from his encounter with Khrushchev in Vienna, and he learned even more when faced with a showdown (which he won) when Khrushchev attempted to move into the American sphere of influence.

Then Kennedy also learned that much needed to be done at home, and he was forced or chose to go to the left to an increasing degree. His political prestige was enhanced by the ending of the Cuba crisis, and he had assets which he could have used and probably would have used in his second term if he had been re-elected. The President was maturing as much as the American people, and the education was in some ways an education in the "illusion of American omnipotence".

Kennedy's assassination brought to the White House an extraordinary politician who yet was lacking in adequate knowledge of the outside world. Texas and Washington were not quite a sufficient preparation for a fluid and dangerous world situation. Yet Lyndon Johnson had many assets. The Kennedy Administration had not been notably successful in the manipulation of Congress. The young President was handicapped by the survival in positions of great congressional power of veterans who had their own ideas of their own importance. Lyndon Johnson was what, in the Elizabethan age, was called an "undertaker". His career in the Senate had been that of a political manager who often was more helpful to President Eisenhower than were the leaders of Eisenhower's own party.

The American public, deeply affected by the assassination, was willing to follow the firm lead given by Lyndon Johnson after his overwhelming victory in 1964. Perhaps the victory was too overwhelming, the defeat of Barry Goldwater too complete. Yet the parliamentary talents of Johnson were used effectively for at any rate two years before they were made more and more irrelevant by the impact of the Vietnam War which was as much a disaster for Johnson as "the Spanish ulcer" was for Napoleon. There was a steady ebbing away of confidence in Washington and in the country as the apparently endless, bloody, and expensive war continued. Victory was always just over the hill or round the corner. More than that, by this time it was not clear what victory really meant. There was an increasingly mutinous spirit in Congress, above all in the Senate, where it was largely embodied in the personality of Senator Fulbright. Lyndon Johnson was conscious of this ebbing of authority and yet could not provide the decisive victory which would have allowed him to end the Vietnam War in a glorious or even a moderately satisfactory way.

Yet President Johnson, on the domestic side at any rate, had many achievements to his credit, and this was in a sense reflected in the very narrow victory of Mr Nixon in 1968 and the belated realization by eminent Democrats that if they had believed that Mr Humphrey, the Vice-President who ran as Democratic candidate, could be elected, he *would* have been elected.

The experience of President Nixon was equally disconcerting and equally threatening for the prestige and power of the Presidency, although his decline in power had different sources and was of a different character. Although Mr Nixon had been a Congressman and a Senator, and as Vice-President under Eisenhower had, formally at any rate, presided over the Senate, he had not acquired, or he disdained to use, a political technique which would have kept Congress more than sulkily willing to follow his lead.

Mr Nixon more and more shut himself up in the White House, in San Clemente, in Camp David, and was a less than effective leader of the Republican Party which had certainly not acquired the popular support that innocent or naïve young Republican ideologists assumed would flow from the formal victory of 1968. A lesson that all American Presidents, even the most successful, have to learn is that political victory, like military victory, does not keep, and Mr Nixon did not manage to identify his fortunes with those of the Congressmen and Senators. In the autumn of 1972, the Nixon campaign was run with almost complete indifference to the interests and assets of congressional candidates. Congressmen noticed this, and did not like it. There was no equivalent in the Nixon Administration of political undertakers like James A. Farley or Lawrence O'Brien or Mark Hanna. President Nixon behaved, too much for his own good, like an hereditary monarch; because of the 1951 amendment of the

Constitution, he could not run for a third term, and so he had not the interest in the general fortunes of the Republican Party which would have linked his interests with those of Congress.

This was reflected in the ambiguous role of the White House staff. For one thing, the people closest to President Nixon had, with hardly any exception, no political weight of their own. The fact that, like President Nixon, most of his cabinet came from Southern California was not necessarily an advantage in the rest of the United States. President Harding suffered from the increasingly disastrous reputation of "the Ohio gang". Harding died before his balloon burst, whereas Nixon was to become deeply involved in the greatest scandals of American political history since the Civil War. The bright young men around President Nixon were cashing in on a victory which proved, even more than most presidential victories, to be "a garland briefer than a girl's". Since President Nixon was notably lacking in what the French call *doigté* and did not devote much—certainly not enough—time to cultivating the men on whom he could have depended in the Senate, he was peculiarly vulnerable to faults in his own carefully chosen staff.

The scandals of the Harding régime were scandals of graft and even of sheer mismanagement, but they were human weaknesses with which practical politians could sympathize. The young men around the White House or President Nixon's San Clemente citadel were politically arrogant and politically naïve. That a new Republican President should try and fail to succeed in nominating two very mediocre lawyers for the Supreme Court of the United States was an omen of things to come. It was perhaps important that the White House under Nixon became less and less the center of presidential power, and that Mr Nixon felt more at home in his native state of California, or even in Florida, than he did in Washington. More and more practising Republican politicians who had, perhaps, never shared the illusions of the Nixon general staff, repented their involvement in what became from the end of 1972 onwards, a disaster area. It was ominous for *any* President, and especially for a President who was not notorious for his power of attracting people, that there was no personal devotion which could be exploited to cover up growing political weakness. And the vulnerability of the chief supporters of the Nixon White House was bound, however wrongly, to reflect on the judgement and perhaps on the character of the President who had chosen such men for important jobs for which their qualifications now seemed miserably inadequate.

The history of the Presidency is not merely a history of Presidents, but of an institution that has grown more and more in size, in power, and in cost. Twentieth century Washington, with the growth of the immense Federal civil service, is very different from the absurdly understaffed and, in many ways, impotent bureaucracy of the nineteenth century; and this has meant that there has been a permanent center of power not officially recognized, a vast Federal bureaucracy which can thwart and can change the policy of even very activist Presidents. Presidents who were themselves extremely industrious and competent, like Harry Truman, discovered how hard it was to get the great Federal machine to work at all or to deliver any very effective administrative support. And as the Federal Government became the greatest center of economic power in the United States, it became more and more unmanageable.

It had been, of course, an old enough tradition of the Presidency that an unofficial White House grew up beside, and was perhaps more important than, the official hierarchy. It was not only Andrew Jackson who had a "kitchen cabinet". But there were very great vicissitudes in the history of the Presidency as an office, and the power was often ineffectively exercised or lost in the labyrinths of the growing bureaucracy. President Truman lived up to his own motto, but in fact the buck often stopped long before it got to the President's desk.

This has meant that the traditional breaking down of the Presidency into specific administrative departments conceals a great deal of the realities of American government. This has worked in two ways. Some of the powers seized, for example, in the First World War by Woodrow Wilson, were never lost for, whatever the victorious Republicans of 1920 said and perhaps believed, the Federal Government could not be cut down to size again. In the very dangerous modern world, some powers accrued to the President and to no one else, and these were powers of the greatest moment. It was no trivial matter that the command of the atom bomb and the system of putting it into action (if this dreadful necessity ever arose) were entirely in the presidential hands. Here the President—any President—was in the strictest sense *the* Commander-in-Chief, with a power of destruction unparalleled in history. And the President, notably President Nixon, was able to thwart Congress by not using all the resources provided for him or by misusing powers he got by the constitution, by statute law, and by mere tradition. The Presidency was still monarchical and still overwhelmingly important even in the increasingly clumsy hands of Richard Nixon.

It retained its very important psychological weight. There, and nowhere else, the average American saw the power of "We, the People of the United States". The President could be manifestly incompetent, but he could not be bypassed as a source of final decision. And it was a monarchical power, for a President could do or not do some of the most important things that the American Government was concerned with. The power to use the atom bomb was the most dramatic of these, but it was only the most important and the most dramatic—and the least used of the powers inherent by the Constitution, by law, by tradition in the White House.

Presidential power was far from being omnipotent. But often what the President did not do or could not do was what needed to be done, and if it was not done by his orders, it was not done at all. How far the accumulation of power in the hands of "the Presidency" rather than simply in the hands of the President is to go, is as yet undecided, but one can guess that however disastrous a given Presidency may be, the power of the Presidency, if not that of a specific office holder, will remain almost decisive. Congress may act up to Dunning's famous resolution in the eighteenth century House of Commons; the power of the Presidency "has increased, is increasing and ought to be diminished", but an office which has survived the assaults on Andrew Johnson can survive the assaults on Richard Nixon.

It is worth noting that what has been the most effective exercise of presidential power has, oddly enough in a country which thinks of itself as formally pacific, been in the fields of foreign affairs and of war. President Polk was not a popular figure and is little remembered by the average American, but it was he who ended the Mexican War and whose Treaty of Guadelupe Hidalgo added to the United States the single greatest territorial accession in American history. The decision to manufacture the atom bomb, and to use it in April 1945, was finally a presidential decision alone. A great deal of American history since then has been the history of foreign policy and of two other bloody wars, and this foreign policy has been almost entirely the result of presidential decisions although, of course, the effectiveness of these decisions has depended quite often on skilful management of congressional support.

In domestic affairs, the President has never been so effective as in foreign affairs. Perhaps the most important event of Jefferson's two Administrations was the Louisiana Purchase. The foreign policy of President Eisenhower, even when it was deliberately negative, was decisive for the particular issues he took an interest in, whereas in domestic affairs, an inbuilt jealousy between Congress and White House can thwart both Congress and the White House. But there is still no substitute for presidential power, and there is not much sign of Congress's examining its own sins of omission and commission adequately, so as to fight with any President on equal terms.

The office of President of the United States is a much greater office than that to which George Washington was elected, 'and not only because of the character of modern government which has left so many overwhelmingly important decisions in practice to one man, whether as President or as Commander-in-Chief. This has been the central institution and the central achievement of American government. It is not accidental that the congressional equivalent of the parliamentary mace is the Roman *fasces*, and any President is the heir of Caesar as much as of any feudal monarch.

The monarchical character of the Presidency which owed so much to the Presidency of General Washington was never quite lost. True, John Adams spent a great deal of time out of Philadelphia and Jefferson was a widower. The modern social life of the White House really began with Dolley Madison, wife of his Secretary of State (later himself President). The charming Mrs Madison created precedents which were not always followed but were often aimed at.

The role of women in the new presidential palace (long popularly called "the White House" before it was so named officially by President Theodore Roosevelt) was, by European standards, inconspicuous, and the social life of the Executive Mansion in the period after the ending of the term of President Madison down to the outbreak of the Civil War was erratic. The two most important Presidents, Jefferson and Jackson, were both widowers. The hospitality offered in the White House varied in attractiveness, and it was a basis of attack on Presidents John Quincy Adams and Martin Van Buren that they wasted public money in decorating the White House or importing such European instruments of vice as billiard tables. The White House provided a number of official celebrations for members of the cabinet, foreign ministers, and distinguished guests; but the court life of Washington, although the little city was itself, as Henry Adams testified, very attractive, was lacking in glamor.

It has also to be noted that presidential wives were not always assets to their husbands. Mrs Lincoln had a great many faults and not many social virtues. She was morbidly jealous. She was extravagant. She spent a good deal more money on the decoration of the White House than Congress had voted. (The great Glasgow carpet firm of Templeton which she called on to adorn the White House was not paid for its services till the end of the nineteenth century). During the Administration of Andrew Johnson, the White House was under siege by the angry politicians of the Republican Left, and under President Grant it had to suffer the activities of the President's not very creditable family. Indeed, even as a working office the White House suffered from inadequate space and inadequate staff. A President of great ability like Grover Cleveland was not provided with secretarial or stenographic support that would have been thought adequate by a small town banker.

The first President to restore some of the glamor of President Jefferson and Dolley Madison was Theodore Roosevelt. He realized the importance of giving to the residence of the President of the United States something more than merely political prestige. He was a slightly bogus polymath, but he was also in fact a man of genuine intellectual energy and curiosity. He had a charming family, and he managed to attract to the White House a host of people who were not mere politicians. This was not always admired by the politicians, and the quarrel over the social life of the White

House as against the social ambitions of Congress has continued to the present day.

The first Mrs Woodrow Wilson was very much admired and very much liked; the second Mrs Woodrow Wilson, especially after the physical collapse of her husband, was regarded as a usurper—in fact as a kind of President of the United States without any genuine legal or political authority. But by the end of the First World War the power of the United States was so great that the social defects of the Harding Administration had to be ignored; and if few Presidents have been more somnolently charmless than Calvin Coolidge, Mrs Coolidge was beautiful, intelligent, and almost able to carry out the functions that her husband ignored. And it was perhaps characteristic that it was Herbert Hoover, who imposed a more rigorous social discipline on the White House and its guests than Lincoln or Theodore Roosevelt had thought fit to attempt.

By the outbreak of the Second World War, the question was decided: the social center of Washington, the social center of the United States, was now the White House. The nearest equivalent of Dolley Madison (in fact, much more than an equivalent of Dolley Madison), Eleanor Roosevelt, combined with her immense energy, social, political, philanthropical and ideological authority. She became as much part of the Presidency as her husband. (Whether she would have done so if her husband had not been crippled is problematic.) And even though the White House food was notoriously bad, there was no doubt any longer that the White House was the center of Washington socially as well as politically.

What was begun by the Roosevelts was continued by the Kennedys. Indeed, it was John Kennedy and his wife who really re-created the Republican Court of General Washington, and they did it by replacing the desperately stiff Virginian etiquette of the first President with the most dazzling and attractive and, formally at least, "democratic" social life that the White House had ever known. The new Dolley Madison was President John F. Kennedy's beautiful and sophisticated wife. True, she ignored some of the social duties of her rank and cultivated her own friends, many of whom were not politically minded at all, rather than the jealous spouses of Senators and Congressmen; but the young matrons not only of Washington but of the whole country admired the dazzling social skills of Jackie Kennedy as they had admired, in a very different way, the tireless social energy of Eleanor Roosevelt. The history of the cooking at the White House became a political issue of some importance, especially after the Senate had rashly tried to rival in its restaurant, the culinary hospitality of the Kennedys at the White House.

But of course the White House, to use the generic term, had far more important aspects than providing better food and drink than had been provided for a very long time in the "Executive Mansion", and even

Presidents and their wives lacking in some of the more obvious graces, like the Lyndon Johnsons and the Nixons, were yet the heads of society *ex officio*. History has made a complete circle, and President and Mrs Ford now have many of the social duties and social assets of the first President and his wife. The Nixon Administration, however, recalled Louis XIV as much as General Washington. For it was soon clear that President Nixon very much preferred residence at San Clemente in his native State of California where a great deal of Federal money was spent in providing a Western White House. Louis XIV had moved the Government of France from Paris to the then fairly remote suburb of Versailles. San Clemente and, to a less degree, Camp David, which had been Franklin D. Roosevelt's Shangri-La, were modern equivalents of Versailles. Versailles suffered from being twenty odd miles from the Tuileries. San Clemente suffered from being three thousand miles from the White House. Some historically minded critics thought that the isolation of the President away from the center of the government machine was not only an obstacle to efficiency but a revelation of the attitude of President Nixon to the East and to the Eastern establishment. As he had displayed a possibly excessive trust in his fellow Californians in composing his staff, so he showed an excessive devotion to the social life and to the climate of Southern California. Historically minded critics could recall that the move to Versailles was the first sign of the approaching collapse of the French monarchy.

# The Presidents
# and Their Families

---

## Biographies of the Presidents
### by *Marcus and Lesley Hume Cunliffe*

## The Families
### compiled by *David Williamson*

### *INTRODUCTION*

THIS THE main part of the book comprises thirty-seven chapters, one for each of the thirty-seven men who have filled the office of President of the United States of America from its inception in 1789 to the present day. There have in fact been thirty-eight Presidencies as (Stephen) Grover Cleveland (the 22nd and 24th President) held the office for two non-consecutive terms. The chapters are divided into the following sections: (a) *Biography*; (b) *Portraits*; (c) *Chronology*; (d) *Writings*; (e) *Lineage*; (f) *Descendants*; (g) *Brothers and Sisters*; and (h) *Notes*.

The *Biographies* of the Presidents by Professor Marcus Cunliffe of the University of Sussex and his wife Lesley Hume Cunliffe are both character sketches and historical assessments. The personal temperament of each President and how he responded to major difficulties is discussed; and the differences of opinion that have been held about him are summarized. The views expressed are, of course, those of Professor and Mrs Cunliffe and are not necessarily shared by the Editor and Publishers. The biographies are accompanied by *Portraits* of the Presidents and their wives. Pictures of all the wives have been included whether or not they have actually been "First Lady". In the case of Mrs Jefferson, for whom no conventional portrait is on record, we have illustrated a silhouette (from the collection of one of her descendants) which is accepted as representing her. The

*Chronologies* cover the principal events in the Presidents' careers and as a factual breakdown of their lives year by year these will be found useful for reference. The *Writings* list the published works of the Presidents and also mention the progress of publication of the Presidents' major papers.

David Williamson, with the assistance of other members of BURKE'S Genealogical team, has compiled all the genealogy and the biographical entries for members of the Presidential Families. In the *Lineages* of the Presidents the direct male line ancestry of each President is traced back to the earliest recorded origins of the family. A straight "father-to-son" descent is shown and the collateral lines stemming from the brothers and sisters of the Presidents' ancestors have been excluded. A detailed account is then furnished of all the *Descendants*, living and dead, in male and female lines, of the Presidents. Stepchildren and adopted children of Presidents and their descendants are also included. The *Brothers and Sisters* of the Presidents are in a separate section and, in cases where Presidents had no issue or issue which has become extinct, the descendants of his brothers and sisters are given in as much detail as possible. The pedigrees are set out in BURKE'S usual narrative style and readers unfamiliar with this are strongly advised to refer to the end of the book where they will find a brief GUIDE TO THE READER, as well as a LIST OF ABBREVIATIONS used and an INDEX of surnames appearing in the pedigrees.

The *Notes* mention various points of interest and often contain references to the APPENDICES which include genealogical tables showing a selection of Royal descents and some remarkable kinships. Inter-presidential relationships have been shown in the Notes under the name of the first President, *e.g.* the relationship between Presidents Grant and Franklin D. Roosevelt will be found set out under Grant, and the relationships between Presidents Van Buren and Theodore Roosevelt are in the Notes to the Van Buren chapter.

Acknowledgment must be made to two pioneer works in the same field: *Genealogies of the Families of the Presidents*, by Reginald Buchanan Henry, MD (1935); and *The Descendants of the Presidents of the United States of America*, by Walter Lewis Zorn (1954). The former by Dr Henry (himself a collateral descendant of President Buchanan) gave no exact dates, very few biographical details and has many gaps. Mr Zorn's privately printed work dealt with its subject in more detail but ignored the Presidents' siblings (brothers and sisters). It can therefore be claimed that BURKE's *Presidential Families of the United States of America* is the first book to cover the character, career, ancestry, descendants and siblings of all the American Presidents in so comprehensive a manner.

It has never been BURKE'S practice over the last 150 years to cite the authority for every statement made in its pages and a full bibliography of the numerous printed books, genealogies, periodicals, and material in our own records which have been used in the compilation of these chapters would run to many pages. Among books which have been invaluable are: *Who's Who in America; Who Was Who in America*; the *Dictionary of American Biography; Notable American Women 1607-1950* (edited by Edward T. James); *The Abridged Compendium of American Genealogy*, by Frederick A. Virkus; A. M. Burke's *Prominent Families of America*; and the Supplement to the 1939 BURKE'S *Landed Gentry* which was entitled "American Families with British Ancestry" (this was later re-issued as a separate book called the *Distinguished Families of America*, by which it is referred to in the pedigrees that follow, but it should *not* be confused with our forthcoming new work, announced in the PREFACE, under the same title). We have also had the benefit of the result of much private genealogical research, which was generously made available to us, notably that of: Professor Raymond M. Bell, of Washington and Jefferson College; Mr Ernesto Caldeira, of Woodville, Mississippi; Mr Hugh B. Johnston, Jr, of Wilson, North Carolina; Dr R. Whitney Tucker, of Charlotte, South Carolina; Mr George S. H. L. Washington, of Cambridge, England; and Mr John A. Washington, of Chevy Chase, Maryland. Finally we must express our debt of gratitude to the Presidents' descendants who have played their part by completing, correcting and promptly returning the draft entries sent out to them and without whom, naturally, this work would not have been possible.

# George Washington
## 1732-1799

———

1st President of the
United States of America
1789-1797

GEORGE WASHINGTON, 1ST PRESIDENT

# George Washington

## 1732-1799

## *1st President of the United States of America*
## *1789-1797*

IN 1788 the previous year's new federal Constitution was ratified by eleven
of the thirteen states. The next stage was to put it into operation. This
entailed among other things the creation of the brand-new office of
President. There was no agreement among Americans as to what the Chief
Executive would actually do, or how the post might evolve. Pessimists
feared that the Presidency would turn into a monarchy, and possibly a
despotism. In fact Thomas Jefferson, absent in France at the time, wrote
home to express his uneasiness over what he took to be a serious flaw in the
Constitution. It ignored the good democratic principle of compulsory
"rotation" by allowing the President to stand for re-election when his first
four-year term was up—indeed, to be re-elected indefinitely. Even
optimists confessed they did not know how the new Constitution would
turn out.

Almost everyone, though, took comfort from the belief that there was
already one ideal incumbent, and one only: General Washington. There
was another hero of comparable fame, Benjamin Franklin, but Franklin
was eighty years old and in poor health. So Washington was the universal
candidate. He had served the nation as Commander-in-Chief for over
eight years without salary. When American independence was secured he
had resigned his commission and gone back to his planter's life at Mount
Vernon with obvious pleasure. He was clearly no Caesar or Cromwell.
The only comparison Americans could discover was with the legendary
Roman, Cincinnatus, who having delivered his people from military
danger resumed his ordinary routine as a farmer. Washington was a man
to trust. He was a gentleman, rumored to be richer than he actually was,
but no aristocrat on the European model. He was strong-willed and
dignified, a natural leader in appearance and in temperament. Unlike

some of his contemporaries he placed the national interest above those of the individual states. He had made no secret of his belief that America needed a more effective Federal Government than that provided by the Articles of Confederation, which the Philadelphia Constitution was designed to replace. Chosen by his fellow Virginians to act as a delegate at Philadelphia, he had then been picked unanimously to chair the Convention. Fifty-six years old in 1788, George Washington was the perfect, the indispensable President.

There was one snag: he did not want the post. Mount Vernon was his favorite place on earth. He had been forced to neglect his plantations for years at a stretch. Running them was a full-time as well as a deeply congenial task. Might he not be accused of "inconsistency and ambition" if he re-entered public life after having announced his final retirement in 1783? Where would his honor be if the Electoral College rejected him? The voting system, as yet untried, seemed likely to divide preferences among a large number of candidates. How and where would he live, when the seat of the new Federal Government had not been decided? If he served again without salary, which pride inclined him to do, could he afford the expense? Was the post itself within his capabilities? He was a farmer and a soldier, not a philosopher-statesman. As a result he would make no public declaration, for he did not regard himself as a "candidate" in the modern sense.

The lightning did strike. After months of wretched unease Washington received the inevitable summons. "My movements to the chair of Government", he confided to his old friend Henry Knox, "will be accompanied by feelings not unlike those of a culprit who is going to the place of his execution: so unwilling am I . . . to quit a peaceful abode for an Ocean of difficulties. . . ". Nor, as far as we can tell, did he ever enjoy being President. In 1789 James Madison and other correspondents held out to him the inducement that perhaps he need not stay at the helm for the full term. They used the same seductive arguments in 1792, when Washington was being called upon to offer himself for re-election. It was fortunate for the young republic that Washington did not set a precedent by resigning (no President in fact was to resign until 1974). The Constitution did not explicitly cover such a situation, and Vice-President John Adams would probably have been treated as merely a stopgap replacement.

Other precedents were set, deliberately or unwittingly. One of these was Washington's firm decision that nothing would lure him into standing for a third term. Again America was fortunate. If he had been another sort of man who relished being Chief Executive, he might have set in motion the tendency that worried critics of the Constitution. In yet another respect early circumstances helped the infant nation. Washington was childless: there was no blood-heir to arouse suspicion. Even so, fervent

MARTHA DANDRIDGE CUSTIS, MRS WASHINGTON

democrats grumbled that Washington's style was too much that of a monarch. He was cold and stiff, they said. Official entertainments were encumbered with ritual. He resented criticism, whether from Congress or from the press. He thought himself above reproach. And his Administration became increasingly partisan, while denying that the "Republican" opposition had a right to exist. Suspicious Americans, while admitting that Martha Washington was amiable and unaffected, complained of the tendency to address her as "Lady Washington". Perhaps there was some jealousy; Martha was a young widow with a sizeable estate when Washington courted and won her.

It must be conceded that Washington was not a breezy person, still less a brilliant conversationalist. He did take offence at newspaper stories. He never quite realized that a party system was beginning to emerge in the 1790s, and that it might be a legitimate development. But then he was the first President, feeling his way forward in the dark. To the extent that his office symbolized the whole United States, he was convinced that he ought to maintain a fairly high style. He also thought that constitutionally he ought to keep a polite distance from Congress. Basically he was wise to act as he did, though subsequent Presidents would tend to be somewhat less formal. He never dreamed of making himself a king, as some of his wilder critics alleged. He soon ran into problems not of his own making, as the French Revolution became more extreme, enlarged into a wholesale war, and bitterly divided Americans. He found his own cabinet at loggerheads. He was accused of heading a pro-British Government. These antagonisms hurt and angered him. Certain of his actions may have been ill-advised. He was so conscious of his own integrity that he could not see others might think he was proclaiming himself perfect—or any rate that his reputation made a convenient fortress for Alexander Hamilton and other "Federalists" to shelter behind. Even those who greatly admired him could be forgiven for wondering whether he was not too closely identified in the popular mind with the very fibre of American being. Some of course were jealous, or cynical. George Washington, they insisted was a man and not a demigod.

Washington himself never claimed otherwise. Being only human, he was no doubt gratified to have stood at the head of events, and to have won such recognition from his countrymen. He knew he was less clever and less sophisticated than a Hamilton or a Jefferson. Part of his immense celebrity was a matter of being in the right place at the right moment. But he was also uniquely the right man in the right place. He was steadfast and sensible. Authority flowed naturally from him. Hero-worshipping biographers, especially Mason Weems with the story of little George and the cherry-tree, made him sound too good to be true. Yet even debunking writers have failed to tarnish his image. We must conclude that the clichés are justified after all. Washington was to an extraordinary degree *the*

Founding Father, "first in war, first in peace, first in the hearts of his countrymen". He did not live to see the Government move to its new home, "Federal City", in the autumn of 1800. He was aware, though, that it was to be named Washington. The man deserved the honor. Sceptics of a later age might ask: has the city always been equally deserving?

# Chronology

1732    Born at Pope's Creek, Westmoreland County, Virginia 22 Feb (11 Feb 1731/2 *os*).

1738    Family moved to Ferry Farm on the Rappahannock River 1 Dec.

1743    Inherited Ferry Farm and other property on the death of his father.

1748    Accompanied surveying party to chart western estate of Lord Fairfax beyond Blue Ridge Mountains 11 March-13 April.

1749    Received Surveyor's licence from William and Mary College 5 May; appointed Official Surveyor of Culpeper County, Virginia 20 July.

1751    Accompanied his half-brother Lawrence Washington on voyage to Barbados 28 Sept; ill with smallpox in Bardados Nov-Dec.

1752    Returned to Virginia 28 Jan; initiated into Fraternal Order of Free and Accepted Masons at Fredericksburg 4 Nov; appointed District Adjutant of Virginia (with rank of Major) by Governor Robert Dinwiddie 6 Nov.

1753    Degree of Master Mason conferred by Fredericksburg Lodge No 4 at Fredericksburg 4 Aug; left for NW Pennsylvania to deliver ultimatum from Governor Dinwiddie ordering the French Commandant of Fort Le Boeuf (now Waterford) to withdraw 31 Oct.

1754    Returned to Virginia with message that the French were prepared to fight to hold the Ohio Valley 16 Jan; commissioned Lt-Col Virginia Regt 15 March; commanded militia force sent to build forts and defend outposts 2 April; defeated French scouting party 28 May; built Fort Necessity at Great Meadows (east of present Uniontown), Pennsylvania 30 May-3 June; surrendered Fort Necessity to superior combined force of French and Indians 4 June; resigned commision 5 Nov after being offered reduced rank of Capt on division of Virginia Regt into companies; acquired Mount Vernon estate on lease from Col George Lee (who had married his half-brother Lawrence's widow) 17 Dec.

1755    Appointed ADC to Major-Gen Edward Braddock, Commander of all British Forces in America 10 May; escaped injury in ambuscade by French and Indians nr Turtle Creek on the Monongahela River, Pennsylvania (in which Braddock was mortally wounded) 9 July; appointed Col and C-in-C of Virginia Regt 13 Aug.

1756        Travelled to Philadelphia, New York and Boston Feb-April.

1758        Elected Member from Fredericksburg County to the House of Burgesses in Virginia Assembly 24 July; commanded expedition against Fort Duquesne (renamed Fort Pitt) 14-27 Nov; resigned commission 5 Dec.

1759        Took seat in House of Burgesses at Williamsburg 22 Feb.

1761        Inherited Mount Vernon estate on the death of his former sister-in-law Mrs George Lee (*see* BROTHERS AND SISTERS OF PRESIDENT WASHINGTON, *p 48*) 14 March.

1769        Introduced non-importation resolutions stating that Virginians could be taxed only by Virginians and condemning British threat to ship accused Americans to England for trial 16 May.

1770        Made exploratory trip to junction of Ohio and Great Kanawha Rivers 5 Oct-1 Dec.

1772        Began operating ferry across the Potomac 5 June.

1773        Attended testimonial dinner for General Thomas Gage in New York 27 May.

1774        Attended first Virginia Provincial Convention at Williamsburg 1 Aug; chosen one of seven Virginia Delegates to First Continental Congress 5 Aug; attended First Continental Congress at Philadelphia 5 Sept-26 Oct.

1775        Attended Second Continental Congress at Philadelphia 10 May-23 June; accepted commission as commanding General of the Continental Army 16 June; took command of Continental Army at Cambridge, Massachusetts 3 July; commissioned Capt Nicholas Broughton, of Marblehead, Massachusetts, as first naval officer 2 Sept; authorized Col John Glover, of Massachusetts, to arm fishing vessels 13 Oct; had first town named in his honour (formerly Forks of Tar River, N Carolina) 5 Nov; Congress adopted rules for regulation of the Navy 28 Nov.

1776        Raised flag of the United Colonies at Cambridge, Massachusetts 1 Jan; occupied and fortified Dorchester Heights, Massachusetts 4-5 March; Gen Howe evacuated Boston 17 March; entered Boston 20 March; awarded Congressional Medal for capture of Boston 25 March; received honorary degree of Doctor of Laws from Harvard 3 April; proceeded to New York City 4-13 April; conferred with Congress at Philadelphia 23 May-5 June; ordered Declaration of Independence to be read to the Army in New York City 9 July; refused to accept letter from Adm Howe, the British naval commander, offering the King's pardon to colonists withdrawing from the rebellion 12 July; fought Battle of Long Island with British and Hessian troops and retreated to Brooklyn Heights after suffering heavy losses and many wounded 27 Aug; withdrew Army to Manhattan 29-30 Aug; decided to evacuate New York City 12 Sept; repulsed British attack below Harlem Heights 16 Sept; withdrew Army to White Plains, New York 21-28 Oct; fought Battle of White Plains and was again forced to retreat 28 Oct; withdrew Army to North Castle Heights 31 Oct-1 Nov; inspected Fort Washington 14-15 Nov; Fort Washington captured by the British 16 Nov; retreated across New Jersey into Pennsylvania 20 Nov-8 Dec; fought Battle of Trenton, gaining first major victory 25-26 Dec; returned to south bank of the Delaware 27 Dec; re-crossed the Delaware and re-occupied Trenton 30-31 Dec.

1777        Fought Battle of Princeton 3 Jan; established winter HQ at Morristown, New Jersey 6 Jan; ordered all British supporters to take oath of allegiance to United States within thirty days or withdraw behind British lines 25 Jan; maintained

HQ at Middlebrook, New Jersey 29 May-3 July; conferred with members of Second Continental Congress at Philadelphia 1 Aug; marched Army through Philadelphia 24 Aug; fought Battle of Brandywine Creek 11 Sept; Congress fled to Lancaster, Pennsylvania 19 Sept; Philadelphia occupied by the British 26 Sept; Congress moved to York, Pennsylvania 30 Sept; fought Battle of Germantown, losing about 1,000 men 4 Oct; over 5,700 British and Hessian troops under Gen John Burgoyne surrendered at Saratoga 17 Oct; informed Congress that the British had control of the Delaware River and firm possession of Philadelphia 23 Nov; established winter HQ at Valley Forge, Pennsylvania 19 Dec.

1778    Commercial and Military Treaty with France signed 6 Feb (ratified by Congress 4 May); British evacuated Philadelphia 18 June and marched towards New York City pursued by the American troops; fought Battle of Monmouth, New Jersey 28 June; British retreated to Sandy Hook 30 June; British reached New York City 5 July; American Army moved to White Plains, New York 20 July; to Fredericksburg, New York 16 Sept; set out for winter HQ at Middlebrook, New Jersey 28 Nov; arrived 11 Dec; went to Philadelphia to confer with Congress 22 Dec; Savannah fell to British 29 Dec.

1779    Suggested defensive campaign adopted by Congress 15 Jan; returned to Middlebrook 5 Feb; ordered expedition against Indians of Six Nations 31 May; moved Army to Smith's Clove, New York 2-7 June; established HQ at New Windsor, New York 21 June; granted general pardon on Independence Day to all American soldiers under sentence of death 4 July; Gen Wayne took Stony Point 15-16 July; established HQ at West Point 21 July; British evacuated Newport, Rhode Island 25 Oct; established winter HQ at Morristown, New Jersey 1 Dec.

1780    Ordered raid, which proved unsuccessful, on British post on Staten Island 14 Jan; first town incorporated in his honor (Washington, Georgia, now a city) 23 Jan; received commission as Lt-Gen and Vice-Adm of France 10 May; British captured Charleston, S Carolina 12 May; British landed at Elizabethtown Point 6 June; American Army retreated to Short Hills, south-east of Morristown 7 June; moved Army to North River 21 June; to Ramapo, New Jersey 27 June; established HQ at Preakness, New Jersey 1 July; French fleet arrived off Newport, Rhode Island 10 July; moved Army to King's Ferry, New York 1 Aug; established HQ at Tappan, New Jersey 8 Aug; Southern Army defeated nr Camden, S Carolina by British under Cornwallis 16 Aug; moved south to Teaneck, New Jersey 23 Aug; moved Army to base nr Hackensack, New Jersey 4 Sept; left for conference in Connecticut with French leaders, Lt-Gen Rochambeau and Adm Ternay 18 Sept; ordered back to Tappan 20 Sept; conferred with Rochambeau and Ternay at Hartford, Connecticut 21-22 Sept; moved army to Paramus, New Jersey 7 Oct; major victory over the British gained at the Battle of King's Mountain, S Carolina 7 Oct; established winter HQ at New Windsor, New York 6 Dec.

1781    Mutiny of Pennsylvania troops nr Morristown 1 Jan; satisfactory agreement with mutineers concluded at Trenton 11 Jan; British Army defeated at Cowpens, S Carolina by Gen Daniel Morgan 17 Jan; New Jersey troops mutinied 20 Jan; order restored by New England troops 23 Jan; Congress ratified Articles of Confederation 1 March and adopted title of *The United States in Congress Assembled* 2 March; left New Windsor for Newport to confer with Rochambeau 2 March; arrived at Newport 6 March; left 13 March; arrived back in New Windsor 20 March; British won Battle of Guilford Court House, N Carolina 4

April; received honorary degree of Doctor of Laws from Yale 24 April; conferred with Rochambeau at Wethersfield, Connecticut 21-22 May; joined Army at Peekskill encampment 25 June; reviewed combined American and French Armies with Rochambeau 7 July; American and French armies crossed Hudson River 20-25 Aug; arrived in Philadelphia 30 Aug; left Philadelphia for Head of Elk, Maryland 5 Sept; arrived at Mount Vernon 9 Sept; arrived at Williamsburg, Virginia 14 Sept; combined armies moved to Williamsburg 14-24 Sept; Yorktown surrounded 28-29 Sept; British Army surrendered 19 Oct; *communiqué* with news of British surrender read to Congress in Philadelphia 24 Oct; left Yorktown 5 Nov; visited mother at Fredericksburg 12 Nov; arrived at Mount Vernon 13 Nov; left for Philadelphia 20 Nov; arrived 26 Nov; received congratulations of Congress 28 Nov.

1782    Circulated letter to State Governors urging that sums requisitioned by Congress be paid 22 Jan; circulated second letter to State Governors urging completion of troop quotas as requested by Congress 31 Jan; issued proclamation offering pardons to all deserters who returned to the Army by 1 June 8 Feb; left Philadelphia 22 March; established HQ at Newburgh, New York 31 March; Washington College chartered at Chestertown, Maryland in his honour 15 June; visited posts in upper New York State 24 June-2 July; British evacuated Savannah 11 July; conferred with Rochambeau in Philadelphia 15 July; instituted Badge of Military Merit 7 Aug; moved Army to Verplanck's Point 26 Oct; established HQ at Newburgh, New York 28 Oct; visited by Rochambeau at Newburgh 7-14 Dec; British evacuated Charleston, S Carolina 14 Dec; French Army sailed from Boston 24 Dec.

1783    Peace treaty signed in Paris 20 Jan; *communiqué* arrived in Philadelphia 23 March; conferred with British C-in-C Sir Guy Carleton at Dobbs Ferry, New York 6 May; received with military honors aboard British sloop 8 May; circulated letter to State Governors urging stronger union of States 8 June; elected President-General of the Society of the Cincinnati at Newburgh 19 June; received honorary degree of Doctor of Laws from University of Pennsylvania 4 July; toured upper New York State 18 July-5 Aug; issued last orders as C-in-C 17 Aug; left Newburgh for Princeton 18 Aug; issued farewell address to Army at Rocky Hill, New Jersey 2 Nov; Army disbanded by general order of Congress 3 Nov; took possession of New York City 25 Nov; visited Philadelphia 8-15 Dec; arrived at Annapolis, Maryland 19 Dec; resigned commission as C-in-C at Annapolis 23 Dec; left for Mount Vernon 24 Dec.

1784    Attended first general meeting of the Society of the Cincinnati at Philadelphia 4-18 May.

1785    Elected President of Potomac Company, Alexandria, Virginia 17 May; received the gift of a jackass (subsequently named *Royal Gift*) from King Carlos III of Spain 5 Dec.

1785-86 Managed his plantation.

1786    Appointed one of seven Virginia delegates to proposed convention of States.

1787    Left Mount Vernon for Philadelphia 9 May; arrived 13 May; unanimously elected President of the Federal Convention 25 May; Convention adjourned 26 July; reassembled 6 Aug; charter granted to Washington Academy, Washington, Pennsylvania (later Washington College and now Washington and Jefferson College) Sept; signed Constitution 17 Sept; left Philadelphia 18 Sept; arrived at Mount Vernon 22 Sept.

1788     Elected Chancellor of William and Mary College, Williamsburg 18 Jan; accepted office 30 April.

1789     Cast vote for Presidential Elector from his district, Alexandria, Virginia 7 Jan; cast vote for Congressman from his district 2 Feb; Presidential Electors cast their ballots in New York 4 Feb; paid last visit to his mother in Fredericksburg 7-9 March; first quorum of House of Representatives in New York 1 April; first quorum of the Senate and first session of the 1st Congress 6 April; ballots cast by the Presidential Electors officially counted and Washington and Adams officially declared elected as President and Vice-President; officially notified of election 14 April; left Mount Vernon for New York 16 April; arrived 23 April; inaugurated as 1st President of the United States of America on the balcony of the Senate Chamber, Federal Hall, New York City 30 April; attended inaugural ball 7 May; signed first Act of Congress 1 June; received honorary degree of Doctor of Laws from Washington College, Chesterton, Maryland 24 June; signed Act placing duty on imports 4 July; signed Act establishing Department of Foreign Affairs 27 July; signed Act giving President power to remove any officer of Government except a member of the judiciary and Act establishing Department of War 7 Aug; signed Act establishing Treasury Department 2 Sept; signed Act establishing Executive Department and judicial salaries 11 Sept; signed Act temporarily establishing the Post Office and creating the office of Postmaster General under the Secretary of the Treasury; signed Judiciary Act of 1789 24 Sept; twelve proposed amendments to the Constitution submitted to the States for ratification 28 Sept; signed first Appropriation Act 29 Sept; issued proclamation establishing Thanksgiving Day 3 Oct; toured New England States 15 Oct-13th Nov; Fort Washington completed, Cincinnati, Ohio 29 Dec.

1790     Delivered first annual address to Congress 8 Jan; moved to Broadway from Cherry Street 23 Feb; signed Act providing for first federal census 1 March; signed first Patent Act 10 April; conferred with Senators regarding Foreign Service Bill 7 May; signed first Copyright Act 31 May; signed Act establishing temporary and permanent seats of government 16 July; left for Rhode Island 15 Aug; returned to New York 22 Aug; moved from New York to Philadelphia 30 Aug-2 Sept; received honorary degree of Doctor of Laws from Brown University 1 Sept; left for Mount Vernon 6 Sept; arrived 11 Sept; left for Philadelphia 22 Nov; arrived 27 Nov; delivered second State of the Union address to Congress 8 Dec.

1791     Initiated custom of New Year's Day reception 1 Jan; issued Federal District Proclamation 24 Jan; signed Act providing for admission of Vermont as State (as from 4 March) 18 Feb; signed Act granting charter to Bank of the United States 25 Feb; signed first Internal Revenue Act 2 March; signed Act providing for defense of frontiers 3 March; issued proclamation delineating boundaries of Federal District; visited Mount Vernon 31 March-7 April; toured Southern States 7 April-12 June; at Mount Vernon 12-27 June; visited Georgetown, Federal District 29 June; returned to Philadelphia 6 July; left for Mount Vernon 15 Sept; returned 21 Oct; delivered third State of the Union address to Congress 25 Oct; received first Minister from Great Britain (George Hammond) 11 Nov; held first cabinet meeting 26 Nov; ten of twelve proposed amendments to the Constitution declared ratified 15 Dec.

1792     Signed Act detailing provisions for permanent Post Office 20 Feb; signed Presidential Succession Act 1 March; received Indian Chiefs of the Six Nations and presented silver medal to Red Jacket, Chief of the Senecas 23 March; signed Act establishing the Mint 2 April; vetoed Apportionment Bill 5 April; left for

Mount Vernon 10 May; returned to Philadelphia 1 June; Kentucky admitted as 15th State 1 June; left for Mount Vernon 18 July; issued proclamation warning citizens not to resist excise tax 15 Sept; returned to Philadelphia 13 Oct; delivered fourth State of the Union address to Congress 6 Nov; Presidential Electors cast ballots 5 Dec, re-electing him for second term.

1793    Electoral votes tabulated by Congress and Washington and Adams officially declared re-elected as President and Vice-President 13 Feb; officially notified of re-election 15 Feb; inaugurated for second term in the Senate Chamber, Federal Hall, Philadelphia 4 March; left for Mount Vernon 27 March; returned to Philadelphia 17 April; issued Proclamation of Neutrality 22 April; left for Mount Vernon 24 June; returned to Philadelphia 11 July; left for Mount Vernon 10 Sept; laid cornerstone of the Capitol Building in Federal District 18 Sept; returned to Germantown, nr Philadelphia 1 Nov; delivered fifth State of the Union address to Congress 3 Dec.

1794    Signed Flag Act, adding two additional stars and stripes (for Vermont and Kentucky) to the flag 13 Jan; eleventh amendment to the Constitution submitted to the States for ratification 5 March; issued proclamation imposing embargo on ships bound for foreign ports 26 March; signed Neutrality Act 5 June; left for Mount Vernon 17 June; returned to Philadelphia 7 July; moved to Germantown 30 July; issued proclamation ordering Whiskey Rebellion rioters to disperse 7 Aug; returned to Philadelphia 20 Sept; issued second proclamation ordering suppression of Whiskey Rebellion 25 Sept; left for Carlisle, Pennsylvania to superintend proposed military action (which proved unnecessary) against the rioters; returned to Philadelphia 28 Oct; delivered sixth State of the Union address to Congress 19 Nov.

1795    Signed first Naturalization Act (requiring five years residence and renunciation of titles of nobility and allegiance to foreign sovereigns) 29 Jan; eleventh amendment to the Constitution ratified 7 Feb (not declared until 8 Jan 1798); submitted Jay's Treaty (signed in London 19 Nov 1794) to special session of the Senate 8 March; left for Mount Vernon 14 April; returned to Philadelphia 2 May; Jay's Treaty conditionally ratified by the Senate 24 June; issued proclamation pardoning all those involved in the Whiskey Rebellion who gave assurance of submission to the law 10 July; left for Mount Vernon 15 July; conferred with Federal District Commissioners 20 July; returned to Philadelphia 11 Aug; conferred with cabinet regarding Jay's Treaty 12 Aug; signed Treaty 18 Aug; left for Mount Vernon 8 Sept; returned to Philadelphia 20 Oct; delivered seventh State of the Union address to Congress 8 Dec.

1796    Issued proclamation calling Jay's Treaty law of the land 29 Feb; refused to release Jay's Treaty papers to House of Representatives 30 March; Tennessee admitted as 16th State 1 June; left for Mount Vernon 13 June; visited Federal District 15 June and 18 Aug; returned to Philadelphia 21 Aug; issued Farewell Address 17 Sept; left for Mount Vernon 19 Sept; returned to Philadelphia 31 Oct; delivered eighth (and last) State of the Union address to Congress 7 Dec.

1797    Vetoed Bill to reduce cavalry contingent of the Army 28 Feb; retired from office and attended the inauguration of his successor John Adams 4 March; left Philadelphia 9 March; arrived at Mount Vernon 15 March.

1798    Washington Academy (formerly Liberty Hall Academy and later Washington College and Washington and Lee University) established at Lexington, Virginia 19 Jan; nominated Lt-Gen and C-in-C of the Armies by President Adams 2 July (confirmed by the Senate 3 July); accepted commission 13 July; arrived in

Philadelphia 10 Nov; attended joint session of Congress 8 Dec; left Philadelphia 14 Dec; arrived at Mount Vernon 19 Dec.

1799    Made his will 9 July; taken ill with sore throat 12 Dec; died of pneumonia at Mount Vernon 14 Dec; buried there 18 Dec.

# The Writings of President Washington

George Washington was the author of one small book published in his lifetime, *The Journal of Major George Washington* (1754)

His *Diary*, edited by John C. Fitzpatrick, has been published in 4 vols (1925)

His *Letters and Papers*, edited by John C. Fitzpatrick, have been published in 39 vols (1931-44). This collection will eventually be superseded by a new, even more comprehensive and scholarly edition

# Lineage of President Washington

It is highly probable that the Washingtons descend in direct male line from Crinan, Hereditary Lay Abbot of Dunkeld, and his wife Bethoc, dau of Malcolm II, King of Scots (*see* BURKE'S *Guide to the Royal Family, p 313*), through Gospatric, 1st Earl of Dunbar, son of Maldred, Lord of Allerdale, son of Crinan. Gospatric *alias* Sir Patric of the Hirsel and Patric de Offerton, a yr son of Gospatric, 3rd Earl of Dunbar, was probably the father of Sir William de Hertburn (Hartburn) *alias* de Wessington, from whom the Washingtons undoubtedly stem.

WILLIAM DE WASHINGTON, who had a grant of the manor of Washington, nr Sunderland, co Durham, in exchange for that of Hartburn, in the parish of Stockton, from Hugh du Puiset, Bishop of Durham *ca* 1180, witnessed charters in Durham as *William de Wessington* from *ca* 1180 to *ca* 1190, and had issue (with an elder son, Walter, who *dsp ca* 1210),

WILLIAM DE WASHINGTON, of Washington, *m* 1211, Alice de Lexington, and *d* in or *post* 1239, leaving issue,

SIR WALTER DE WASHINGTON, of Washington, acquired lands in Northumberland *jure uxoris*, named among the Durham Knights at the Battle of Lewes 1264, *b ca* 1212, *m* Joan (or Juliana) (living as his widow 1266), sister and heiress of Sir Roger de Whitchester, Keeper of the Rolls, and was probably *k* at the Battle of Lewes 14 May 1264, leaving, with other issue,

SIR WILLIAM DE WASHINGTON, of Washington, *m* Margaret, sister and co-heiress of Sir Robert de Morville, of Helton Flecket, Westmorland, and *d* between 1288 and 1290, leaving, with other issue, a yr son,

ROBERT DE WASHINGTON, acquired lands in Kendal, Westmorland, and half the manor of Carnforth, in the parish of Warton, Lancs, *m* Joan, dau of Sir William de Stirkeland (Strickland), of Sizergh Castle, Westmorland (*see* BURKE'S *LG*, HORNYOLD-STRICKLAND *of Sizergh*), and *d* 1324, leaving issue,

ROBERT DE WASHINGTON, of Carnforth, *m* Agnes, only dau and heiress of Ranulf le Gentyl, and *d* between 1346 and 1348, leaving issue, with two other sons (of whom the elder, Robert, was a witness for Sir Robert Grosvenor in the celebrated Scrope-Grosvenor controversy about the coats-of-arms of the two families 1386), a yst son,

JOHN DE WASHINGTON, *m* 1st 1363, Eleanor (or Alina) (*d* 1370), widow of Sir William de Lancaster, of Howgill, Westmorland, and dau of — Garnet. He *m* 2ndly 1382, Joan, dau and heiress of John de Croft, of Tewitfield in Warton, Lancs, and *d* 1407/8, having by her had issue,

JOHN DE WASHINGTON, to whom his mother Joan surrendered the manor of Tewitfield and other lands 1408, *b ca* 1385, *m*, and *d* 1423, leaving issue,

ROBERT WASHINGTON, of Tewitfield, *m* Margaret, widow of John Lambertson, of Warton, and *d* 7 Dec 1483, leaving, with other issue, a 2nd son,

ROBERT WASHINGTON, of Warton, *b ca* 1455, *m* 1st, —, dau of John Westfield, of Overton, Lancs, and had issue. He *m* 2ndly, —, dau of Myles Whittington, of Borwick, Lancs; and 3rdly, Agnes Bateman, of Heversham, Westmorland, and *d* 1528 (will dated 6 Sept). His son (by his 1st wife),

JOHN WASHINGTON, of Warton, *b ca* 1478, *m* Margaret, dau of Robert Kytson, of Warton[1], and *dvp ante* 1528, leaving, with other issue, an eldest son,

LAWRENCE WASHINGTON, of Sulgrave Manor, Northants, which he built, having received the manor of Sulgrave, formerly the property of the Priory of St Andrew in Northampton, by grant from the King 10 March 1539, Mayor of Northampton 1532 and 1545, *b ca* 1500, *m* 1st, Elizabeth (*dsp*), widow of William Gough, mercer, of Northampton; and 2ndly, Amy (*d* 6 Oct 1564), 3rd dau of Robert Pargiter, of Greatworth, nr Sulgrave, and *d* 19 Feb 1584 (*bur* Sulgrave), having by her had, with other issue, an eldest son,

ROBERT WASHINGTON, of Sulgrave Manor (which he surrendered to his eldest son Lawrence 1 May 1601), purchased the manor of Nether Boddington from his son-in-law Alban Wakelyn 1600, *b* 1544, *m* 1st 1565, Elizabeth (*d* 1599), dau and heiress of Walter Light, of Radway Grange, Warwicks, and had issue. He *m* 2ndly, Anne Fisher (*bur* at East Haddon, Northants 16 March 1652), and *d* 1620 (will dated 7 Feb 1620, *pr* 3 Jan 1621), having by her had issue. His eldest son (by his 1st wife),

LAWRENCE WASHINGTON, of Sulgrave Manor, sold the demesne lands to Thomas Atkins, of Over Winchendon, Bucks 20 Aug 1605, but retained the Manor House and 7 acres of land until 1 March 1610, when (with the consent of his father) he sold the reversion to his cousin Lawrence Makepeace, *b ca* 1568, *m* at Aston-le-Walls, Northants 3 Aug 1588, Margaret (*d* 1652), dau of William Butler, of Tyes Hall, Cuckfield, Sussex[2], and *dvp* 13 Dec 1616 (*bur* Brington, Northants), having had, with other issue, a 5th son,

THE REVEREND LAWRENCE WASHINGTON, Rector of Purleigh, Essex 1633-43, ejected from his living as a Royalist, later Rector of Little Braxted, Essex, *b* at Sulgrave Manor *ca* 1602, *educ* Brasenose Coll Oxford (BA 1623, Fell 1624, MA 1626, Proctor and Lector 1631, BD 1634), *m* 1632, Amphyllis (*bur* Tring, Herts 12 Jan 1655), dau and co-heiress of John Twigden, of Little Creaton, Northants, by his wife Anne (later wife of Andrew Knowling, of Tring), dau of William Dickens, of Great Creaton, by his wife Anne, sister of Thomas Thornton, of Brockhall, Northants (*see* BURKE'S *LG*), and was *bur* at Maldon, Essex 21 Jan 1653, leaving, with other issue, an eldest son,

COLONEL JOHN WASHINGTON, of Washington Parish, Westmoreland County, Virginia, where he settled 1656, Col cmdg Virginian Forces in the Indian War 1675, mem Virginia House of Burgesses for Westmoreland County, acquired over 6,000 acres of land in Virginia including the nucleus of the Wakefield and Mount Vernon estates, *b* 1633, *m* 1st Dec 1658, Anne, dau of Lt-Col Nathaniel Pope, JP, of The Cliffs, Westmoreland County, and had, with other issue[3], an elder son (LAWRENCE, *of whom presently*). Col John Washington *m* 2ndly, Frances (who *m* 2ndly, Capt William Hardidge, and had issue, *see p 48*), and *d* 1677. His elder son,

CAPTAIN LAWRENCE WASHINGTON, of Westmoreland County, Virginia, mem Virginia House of Burgesses 1685, High Sheriff 1692, *b* Sept 1659, *m ca* 1689, Mildred (who *m* 2ndly 16 May 1700, George Gale, of Whitehaven, Cumberland, and was *bur* there 26 March 1701), dau and co-heiress of Col Augustine Warner, of Warner Hall, Gloucester County, Virginia, Speaker Virginia House of Burgesses and mem Gov's Council, by his wife Mildred, dau of Hon George Reade, Actg Gov of Virginia[4], and *d* Feb 1697, having had, with other issue, a yr surv son,

CAPTAIN AUGUSTINE WASHINGTON, of Wakefield, Westmoreland County, Virginia, JP, High Sheriff 1727, had the estate of Epsewasson (later called Mount Vernon) transferred to him by his sister Mildred 26 May 1726, managed plantation at Hunting Creek and owned and directed the working of an iron mine at Fredericksburg, *b* in Westmoreland County *ca* 1694, *educ* Appleby Sch, England, *m* 1st 20 April 1715, Jane (*b* in Westmoreland County 24 Dec 1699; *d* probably at Pope's Creek, Westmoreland County 24 Nov 1729), dau and heiress of Major Caleb Butler, JP, of Westmoreland County, and had issue (*see p 48*). He *m* 2ndly 6 March 1731, Mary (*b* in Lancaster County, Virginia 1708/9; *d* at Fredericksburg, Virginia 25 Aug 1789), only dau of Col Joseph Ball, of Epping Forest, Lancaster County, Virginia[5], by his 2nd wife Mary Johnson, and *d* at Ferry Farm, King George County, Virginia 12 April 1743, having by her had, with other issue (*see* BROTHERS AND SISTERS OF PRESIDENT WASHINGTON, *p 51*),

GEORGE WASHINGTON, **1st President of the United States of America.**

# President Washington's Wife and Stepchildren

GEORGE WASHINGTON *m* in New Kent County, Virginia 6 Jan 1759, Martha (*b* in New Kent County 21 June 1731; *d* at Mount Vernon, Virginia 22 May 1802, *bur* there), widow of Col Daniel Parke Custis, and eldest dau of Col John Dandridge, of New Kent County[6], by his wife Frances, dau of Orlando Jones.

There were no children of the marriage and thus President Washington has *no descendants*. However, he had step-children through his wife's 1st marriage.

Mrs Washington *m* 1st June 1749, Col Daniel Parke Custis, of The White House, New Kent County, Virginia (*d* there 8 July 1757), and had issue,

1 Daniel Parke CUSTIS, *b* 19 Nov 1751; *d* 19 Feb 1754 (*bur* first at Marston Church, later removed to Bruton Churchyard, Williamsburg, Virginia).

2 Frances Parke CUSTIS, *b* 12 April 1753; *d* 1 April 1757 (*bur* first at Marston Church, later removed to Bruton Churchyard, Williamsburg, Virginia).

3 John (Jack) Parke CUSTIS, fought in the Revolutionary War, *b* at the White House, Virginia Nov 1754, *educ* King's Coll, New York (now Columbia Univ), *m* at Mount Airy, Maryland 3 Feb 1774, Eleanor (Nelly) (*b* at Mount Airy 1757; *m* 2ndly 1783, Dr David Stuart, of Abingdon, Virginia, and Hope Park, Fairfax County, Virginia; *d* 28 Sept 1811), 2nd dau of Benedict Calvert, of Mount Airy (illegitimate son of Charles Calvert, 6th Baron Baltimore — *see* BURKE'S *Dormant and Extinct Peerages*), by his wife Elizabeth, dau of Charles Calvert, Gov of Maryland, and *d* at Eltham, New Kent County, Virginia 5 Nov 1781 (*bur* there), having had issue,

  1 A dau, *b ca* Aug 1775; *d* an inf.

  2 Elizabeth Parke CUSTIS, *b* at Abingdon, Virginia 21 Aug 1776, *m* 20 March 1796 (*m* diss by div 1811), Thomas Law, of Georgetown, DC (*b* in England 23 Oct 1756; *d* at Washington, DC 31 July 1834), son of Rt Rev Edmund,Law, DD, Bishop of Carlisle, by his wife Mary Christian (and brother of 1st Baron Ellenborough — *see* BURKE'S *Peerage*), and *d* 1 Jan 1832 (*bur* Mount Vernon), having had issue,

    Eliza Parke Custis LAW, *b* 19 Jan 1797, *m* 5 April 1817, as his 1st wife, Nicholas Lloyd Rogers[7], of Druid Hill, Baltimore, Maryland (*b ca* 1787; *d* at Baltimore 22 Nov 1860, *bur* Druid Hill Park, Baltimore), son of Nicholas Rogers, by his wife Eleanor Buchanan, and *d* nr Baltimore 9 Aug 1822, leaving issue,

      1*a* Edmund Law ROGERS, *b* at Baltimore 22 Jan 1818, *educ* Harvard, *m* at Baltimore, Charlotte Matilda Leeds (*d post* 1898), dau of John Rousby Plater, by his wife Charlotte Matilda Edmondson, and *d* at Baltimore 24 Jan 1896, having had issue,

        1*b* Edmund Law ROGERS, Jr, *b* at Baltimore 1 July 1852; *dunm* at New York 19 Dec 1893.

        2*b* Charlotte Plater ROGERS, *m* 1st at Baltimore 8 June 1893, Frank Kirby Flower Smith (*b* at Pawlet, Vermont 1862; *d* 6 Dec 1918), son of Henry H. Smith, by his wife Julia M. Flower, and had issue,

          1*c* ● Edmund Law Rogers SMITH [*230 Stoney Run Lane, Apt 2-A, Baltimore, Maryland 21210, USA*], *b* 1897, *educ* Johns Hopkins Univ, *m* 1918, ● Katherine Powell, dau of Cuthbert Powell

Noland, by his wife Rosalie Haxall, and has issue,

    1*d* ● Charlotte H. N. SMITH, *b* 1922, *m* 1941, ● Ross Ransom Williams, and has issue,

      ● Ross Ransom WILLIAMS, Jr (brought up by his maternal grandparents and uses the name of (Ross) Ransom Williams SMITH), *b* 1942, *m* 1965, ● Eva Haekkerup.

    2*d* ● Katherine Powell Noland SMITH, *b* 1924, *m* 1st 1943, Lieut Richard Maddox Combs, US Army (*ka* 1944). She *m* 2ndly 1948, ● Rev Van Santvoord Merlesmith, Jr [*54 East Church, Bethlehem 18, Pennsylvania, USA*], son of Van Santvoord Merlesmith, by his wife Kate G. Fowler, and has issue,

      1*e* ● Van Santvoord MERLESMITH III, USN [*25 Beekman Place, New York, NY, USA*], *b* 1949, *m* at Middleburg, Virginia 28 June 1969, ● Mia C., dau of Robinson McIlvaine, of Washington, DC, by his wife Alice W. Nicolson.

      2*e* ● Edmund Law MERLESMITH, *b* 1950, *m* 27 June 1970, ● Barbara A., dau of John P. Rudolph.

      3*e* ● Katherine P. MERLESMITH, *b* 1952, *educ* Wells.

      4*e* ● Grosvenor F. MERLESMITH, *b* 1954, *educ* Columbia.

      5*e* ● Barton N. MERLESMITH, *b* 1956, *educ* Hill.

    2*c* Geoffrey Flower SMITH, *d* an inf 1900.

    3*c* Eleanor Rosamund Flower SMITH, *b* 1902, *m* 1927, Robert Hazlehurst Plant McCaw, of Cincinnati, Ohio, and *d* 1950, leaving issue,

      1*d* ● R. Plant MCCAW.

      2*d* ● Kirby Custis MCCAW, *m* ● Louis F. Wade.

    Charlotte Plater Rogers, *m* 2ndly 5 Aug 1921, Prof Wilfred Pirt Mustard (*b*. at Uxbridge, Ontario, Canada 18 Feb 1864; *d* 30 July 1932).

    2*a* Eliza Law ROGERS, *b* at Baltimore *ca* 1820; *d* young.

    3*a* Eleanor Agnes ROGERS, *b* at Baltimore 28 May 1822, *m* there 5 Jan 1862, George Robins Goldsborough (*b* at Myrtle Grove, Maryland 11 April 1821; *d* at Ashby, Maryland 18 Aug 1899), son of Hon Robert Henry Goldsborough, by his wife Henrietta Maria Nichols, and *d* 30 Jan 1906, having had issue,

      Eleanor GOLDSBOROUGH, *d* an inf 26 May 1863.

3 Martha Parke CUSTIS, *b* 31 Dec 1777, *m* 6 Jan 1795, Thomas Peter, of Georgetown, DC (*b* 4 Jan 1769; *d* 16 April 1834), son of Robert Peter, Mayor of Georgetown (*see* BURKE'S *Distinguished Families of America*), by his wife Elizabeth Scott, and *d* 13 July 1854, having had issue,

(1) Martha Eliza Angela (or Martha Eliza Eleanor) PETER, *b* 20 Jan 1796; *d* at Georgetown 20 Sept 1800.

(2) Columbia Washington PETER, *b* 2 Dec 1797; *dunm* 3 Dec 1820.

(3) John Parke Custis PETER, *b* 14 Nov 1799, *m* 2 Feb 1830, Elizabeth Jane Henderson (*b* in Orange County, Virginia 17 March 1812; *d* 1877), and *d* 19 Jan 1848, having had issue,

1*a* Sarah Elizabeth PETER, *b* 11 Feb 1831, *m* 26 May 1858, as his 3rd wife, William Daniel Slaymaker (*b* 22 July 1797; *d* 28 May 1868), and had issue,

1*b* Walter Custis SLAYMAKER, *b* 15 May 1860; *dunm* 21 Sept 1887.

2*b* John Edmund SLAYMAKER, *b* 23 Jan 1862, *m* 5 Jan 1893, his 1st cousin, Sarah Freeland (*b* 1867), 2nd dau of Thomas Peter (*see below*), and had issue,

Elizabeth Scott SLAYMAKER, *m* Harry Kimball.

2*a* Thomas PETER, *b* 6 March 1833, *m* 3 Dec 1856, his 1st cousin once removed Elizabeth (*b* 26 Feb 1838; *d* 20 June 1914), dau of George Peter, by his 3rd wife Sarah Norfleet Freeland, and had issue,

1*b* George PETER, *b* 5 Feb 1858, *m* Laura Magruder, and had issue,

1*c* Allan Magruder PETER.

2*c* Norman Phillips PETER.

2*b* John Parke Custis Henderson PETER, *b* 5 June 1859, *m* Emma Bartlett.

3*b* James Henderson PETER, *b* 28 Dec 1860, *m* Mary Hodges.

4*b* Margaret Gibson PETER, *b* 18 Dec 1863, *m* Henry P. Walton.

5*b* Thomas PETER, *b* 16 April 1865, *m* Minnie Fisher, and *d* 1953.

6*b* Sarah Freeland PETER, *b* 1867, *m* 5 Jan 1893, her 1st cousin, John Edmund Slaymaker, and had issue (*see above*).

7*b* Elizabeth PETER, *b* 6 July 1868, *m* Harry N. Carter.

8*b* Edith PETER, *b* 10 Sept 1869; *dunm*.

3*a* Martha Custis PETER, *b* 13 Sept 1836, *m* 18 Jan 1855, as his 2nd wife, Archibald Chisholm Gibbs, of West River, Maryland (*b* 1807; *d* 6 Nov 1892), and *d* 1910, having had issue,

1*b* Charles Howard GIBBS, *b* 13 Nov 1856, *m* 28 Jan 1892, Emily Thompson, and *d* 3 June 1927, leaving issue,

Virginia Lee GIBBS, *m* Dolfin Austin Davis.

2*b* Archibald Henderson GIBBS, *b* 24 Sept 1859; *dunm* 15 Oct 1900.

3*b* Elizabeth Jane GIBBS, *b* 17 Oct 1861.

4*b* Nannie Lee GIBBS, *b* 18 Sept 1868.

4*a* David PETER, *b* 11 July, *d* 15 Aug 1837.

5*a* John Parke Custis PETER, Jr, *b* in Virginia 5 March 1839, *m* 20 Feb 1866, Lucy Pollard Roberts (*b* in Orange County, Virginia 17 March 1846; *d* at Culpeper, Virginia 10 Dec 1884), and *d* 5 March 1904, having had issue,

1*b* John Parke Custis PETER III, *b* at Culpeper, Virginia 4 Dec 1867, *m* 15 Sept 1895, Gertrude Landon Pile (*b* at Gladspring, Virginia 24 Dec 1874; *d* at Radford, Virginia 13 July 1934), and *d* at Radford, Virginia 1 May 1952, having had issue,

1*c* Eleanor Custis PETER, *b* 1896; *d* Nov 1905.

2*c* John Parke Custis PETER IV, *b* 23 Dec 1898, *m* Minnie Catherine Heider, and *d* 1953, leaving issue,

1*d* ●Elizabeth PETER, *b* 7 July 1928, *m* 1948, ●John C. Cissell.

2*d* ●Eleanor Parke Custis PETER, *b* 21 Jan 1932, *m* ●Rayburn Neil Munson, and has issue,

●Pamela Ann MUNSON, *b* 2 Nov 1954.

3*c* ●Annie Lucy PETER, *b* 1 Sept 1901, *m* ●Thomas Kyle Glasgow (*b* 10 Sept 1900).

4*c* ●James Beverley PETER.

5*c* ●Gertrude Elizabeth PETER, *b* at Radford, Virginia 17 June 1907, *m* 19 Sept 1935, ●Clayton

Wallace Mills (*b* at Whitinsville, Mass 26 Aug 1903) [*5 Ovington Road, Morrisville, Pennsylvania 19067, USA*], and has issue,

●Elizabeth Wallace MILLS [*Apt B, 1535 North 1st Street, San Jose, California 95112, USA*], *b* 14 July 1943.

6*c* ●Laura Gordon PETER, *b* 28 Jan 1909, *m* ●James Patterson Cannon (*b* 2 Dec 1904), and has issue,

1*d* ●Martha Custis CANNON, *b* 11 July 1942.

2*d* ●Jane Patterson CANNON, *b* 21 Sept 1947.

7*c* ●Randolph Tucker PETER, *b* 7 Feb 1920.

2*b* William Henderson PETER, *b* 13 April 1870.

3*b* Nellie Henderson PETER, *b* 15 June 1872; *dunm* 14 Dec 1898.

4*b* James Minnigerode PETER, *b* 17 July 1876; *dunm* 31 Jan 1909.

5*b* Beverley Stanard PETER, *b* 28 June 1880, *m* March 1906, Nora Lee Thorne (*d* Nov 1918), and had issue,

●Beverley Kennon PETER, MD [*Beckley, W Virginia, USA*], *b* 13 Jan 1907, *m* 8 Feb 1941, ●Mary Keyes Shanklin, and has issue,

1*d* ●Lelia Maude PETER, *b* 13 April 1942.

2*d* ●Mary Lee PETER, *b* 13 Sept 1943.

6*a* James Henderson PETER, *b* 24 Jan 1841; *d* young.

7*a* Jane PETER, *b* 24 July 1842, *m* James H. McMurran, and *d* 24 April 1905, leaving issue,

1*b* John Parke MCMURRAN, *m*, and had issue,

John Parke Custis MCMURRAN, *m*, and had issue,

●John Parke Custis MCMURRAN, Jr.

2*b* William T. MCMURRAN, *b* 18 Aug 1867, *m* Nellie McClung.

3*b* Charles Henry MCMURRAN, *m*, and *dsp*.

4*b* Gertrude MCMURRAN, *m* William O. Blakey, and had issue,

1*c* Dandridge BLAKEY, *m* John Parks Boylin, and had issue,

1*d* ●Eleanor Custis BOYLIN.

2*d* ●John Parks BOYLIN, Jr.

2*c* William O. BLAKEY, Jr, *m*, and *dsp*.

3*c* Madeleine Calvert BLAKEY, *m* Alan Street, and had issue,

●Jane Peter STREET, *m* ●James Forrest Scott Oldacre.

4*c* Gertrude McMurran BLAKEY, *m*, and *d ante* 1955.

5*b* George Custis MCMURRAN, *m*, and *d* 25 Nov 1908, leaving issue,

Lucille MCMURRAN, *m* John Park Boyd, and had issue, one son.

6*b* Jean Henderson MCMURRAN, *m* Robert McLean, and *dsp*.

7*b* John Holmes MCMURRAN, *m* Rosamond Patzell, and *dsp*.

8*b* Anna Lee MCMURRAN, *m* Allan Street.

9*b* Martha Custis MCMURRAN, *m* William Hayes Chapman.

8*a* Britannia Kennon PETER, *b* 8 April 1844, *m* Major John B. Stanard, and *dsp*.

9*a* Daniel Parke Custis PETER, *b* 31 Oct 1846, *m* Elizabeth S. Calvert, and had issue,

1*b* Eugene PETER.

2*b* Britannia Wellington PETER.

(4) George Washington Parke Custis PETER, of Howard County, Maryland, *b* 18 Nov 1801, *m* 6 Feb 1840, Jane Boyce (*b* 8 April 1813; *d* 31 Jan 1882), and *d* 10 Dec 1877, having had issue,

1*a* Mary PETER, *b* 11 March 1841; *dunm* 8 July 1877.

2*a* Gabriella PETER, *b* 22 April 1844, *m* James Mackubin, of MacAlpine, Howard County, Maryland, Attorney-at-law (*b* 1830; *d* 1904), son of George Mackubin, by his wife Eleanor MacCubbin, and *d* 25 Feb 1920, having had issue,

1*b* Ella MACKUBIN, *b* 17 Aug 1870.

2*b* George MACKUBIN, of Baltimore, Maryland, investment banker, *b* in Howard County, Maryland 30 Aug 1872, *m* 17 Oct 1900, Maud Tayloe (*b* in Gloucester County, Virginia 15 Oct 1876), dau of John Tayloe Perrin, by his wife Maud Tabb, and *d* at Baltimore 14 March 1964, leaving issue,

1*c* ●George MACKUBIN, Jr [*Gloucester, Virginia,*

*USA*], *b* in Howard County, Maryland 24 Sept 1901, *m*●Olita Landry, and has issue,
●Mildred Lee MACKUBIN.
2*c*●Eleanor Parke Custis MACKUBIN [*Zanoni PO, Gloucester County, Virginia, USA*], *b* at Baltimore 18 July 1903.
3*c*●Elizabeth Tayloe Perrin MACKUBIN, *b* at Baltimore 18 July 1903 (twin with Eleanor Parke Custis), *m* 1929, ●Charles Frederick Lyman, Jr, and has issue,
  1*d*●Eleanor Mackubin LYMAN.
  2*d*●Joan F. LYMAN.
  3*d*●Charles Frederick LYMAN III.
3*b* Parke Custis MACKUBIN, *b* 11 Nov 1873; *dunm* 20 March 1903.
4*b* Emily Boyce MACKUBIN, *b* 17 March 1876; *dunm* 1946.
5*b* Mildred Lee MACKUBIN, *b* 28 Sept 1881, *m* 14 Oct 1925, Arthur Gordon, and *dsp.*
3*a* Parke Custis PETER, *b* 16 Aug 1845; *d* 22 April 1861.
4*a* William Boyce PETER, *b* 29 Nov 1846, *m* 1878, Ella H. Mercer (who *m* 2ndly, Edwin J. Farber, of Baltimore), and *d* 15 April 1907, leaving issue,
  1*b* Mary PETER, *b* 20 Feb 1879, *m* 1904, Augustus John Philbin Gallagher, of Baltimore, and had issue,
    1*c*●Martha Mercer GALLAGHER.
    2*c*●John GALLAGHER.
  2*b* Emily Margaret PETER, *b* 28 Sept 1881, *m* 27 Feb 1910, Leon Marié, and had issue,
    1*c* Leon Peter MARIÉ, *b* 9 Oct 1912; *d* 1 Dec 1920.
    2*c*●Camille Stewart MARIÉ, *b* 29 April 1918.
(5) America Pinckney PETER, *b* 12 Oct 1803, *m* 22 June 1826, Capt William George Williams, US Army (*b* in S Carolina 1801; *d* at Monterey, Mexico 21 Sept 1846), and *d* 25 April 1842, leaving issue,
1*a* Martha Custis (Markie) WILLIAMS, *b* 28 March 1827, *m post* 1875, as his 2nd wife, Adm Samuel Powhatan Carter (*b* 6 Aug 1819; *d* 26 May 1891), and *dsp* 31 Oct 1899.
2*a* Lawrence WILLIAMS, Major US Army, *b* 1832, *m* Sarah Law, of New York, and *d* 1879, having had issue,
  1*b* Anna Wright (Nannie) WILLIAMS, *m* 25 April 1894, her 2nd cousin, Armistead Peter, Jr, of Tudor Place, Washington, DC (*b* 30 Nov 1870; *d* 25 July 1960), 2nd son of Dr Armistead Peter, by his wife Martha Custis Kennon, and had issue (*see below, p* 43).
  2*b* George WILLIAMS, *d* young.
3*a* Katharine Alicia WILLIAMS, *b* 1834, *m* 1851, as his 1st wife, Rear-Adm John Henry Upshur, USN (*b* in Northampton County, Virginia 5 Dec 1823; *d* 30 May 1917), son of John E. Nottingham, by his wife Elizabeth Parker Upshur (which surname he legally adopted), and *d* 22 Aug 1862, leaving issue,
  1*b* Custis Parke UPSHUR, of Washington, DC, sometime USN, served in Spanish-American War, *b* 21 Aug 1852, *m* 5 Dec 1876, Margaret Louise (*b* 1 April 1858), dau of Dr Curtis James Trenchard, of Astoria, Oregon, by his wife Marian, and *d* at Norfolk, Virginia 9 Oct 1920, having had issue,
    1*c* Kate Marion UPSHUR, *b* 3 March 1878, *m* 31 Dec 1901, Dr Alexander Gustavus Brown, Jr, of Richmond, Virginia (*b* at Ashland, Virginia 31 Aug 1873; *d* 16 Sept 1953), son of Rev Alexander Gustavus Brown, of Ashland, Virginia, by his wife Frances Cooksey, and had issue,
      1*d*●Margaret Upshur BROWN, *b* 1 Dec 1902, *m* 20 Oct 1927, James Pleasant Massie (*b* 1899; *d* 9 Oct 1954), son of Col Eugene C. Massie, of Richmond, Virginia, and has issue,
        1*e*●Margaret Brown MASSIE, *b* 17 Oct 1928.
        2*e*●James Pleasant MASSIE, Jr, *b* 31 Aug 1931.
        3*e*●Kate Rey MASSIE, *b* 31 July 1942.
      2*d*●Alexander Gustavus BROWN III, MD [*Richmond, Virginia, USA*], *b* 1907.
    2*c* John Parke Custis UPSHUR, of Oakland, California, *b* 9 April 1880, *m* 27 June 1915, Claire (*b* 9 Aug 1889), dau of William Justin Harsha, by his wife Sarah Hockenhull, and *dsp* 1952.
    3*c* Arthur Littleton UPSHUR, *b* 1883; *d* an inf.
    4*c* Margaret Gertrude UPSHUR, *b* 16 May 1887, *m*

25 Sept 1913, Simon Willard Sperry (*b* 13 Nov 1883), and had issue,
  1*d*●Simon Willard SPERRY, Jr, *b* 9 Nov 1915, *m* 26 Sept 1943, ●Elizabeth Jean Parlee.
  2*d*●Margaret Upshur SPERRY, *b* 4 Nov 1918, *m*●— Davenport.
  3*d*●Richard Parke SPERRY, *b* 12 June 1922.
5*c* Lawrence Lewis UPSHUR, *b* 1 Aug 1889, *m* 16 Sept 1933, Ivy Ruth (*b* 15 March 1893), dau of Walter Augustus Hill, by his wife Stella Lenore Secrest.
6*c* Henry Custis UPSHUR, *b* 2 June 1892, *m* ●Elinor — (who *m* 2ndly, —), and had issue,
  1*d*●Elinor UPSHUR (legally adopted by her stepfather and now bears his name).
  2*d*●John Henry UPSHUR (legally adopted by his stepfather and now bears his name).
2*b* George Littleton (or Lyttleton) UPSHUR, *b* at Washington Navy Yard 8 Feb 1856, *m* 24 March 1885, Minnie (*b* 20 Feb 1863), dau of David Milliken, of New York, and *dsp* at New York 24 April 1938.
3*b* Katherine (Kate) UPSHUR, *b* 12 March 1861, *m* 6 Feb 1883, Frank Turner Moorhead, of Pittsburgh, Pennsylvania (*b* 23 Sept 1857), son of John Moorhead, by his wife Anna Catherine, and had issue,
  1*c* Martha Custis Williams MOORHEAD, *b* 11 Dec 1883; *d* 18 Aug 1884.
  2*c* John Upshur MOORHEAD, of Red Bank, New Jersey, and Washington, DC, *b* 3 March 1885, *m* 2 Feb 1910, Lillian Chew, of Washington (*b* 15 May 1889), and *d* 28 March 1919, leaving issue,
    1*d*●John Upshur MOORHEAD, Jr [*Rumson, New Jersey, USA*], *b* 20 Oct 1910, *m*●Christine, dau of Edgar A. Knapp, of Rumson, and has issue,
      ●Suzanne Custis MOORHEAD, *b* 27 Dec 1939.
    2*d*●Thomas Chew MOORHEAD, *b* 26 Feb 1914, *m*●Claire Fahnstock, and has issue,
      1*e*●Thomas Chew MOORHEAD, Jr, *b* 22 May 1947.
      2*e*●John Upshur MOORHEAD II, *b* 10 May 1952.
      3*e*●Margaret Fahnstock MOORHEAD, *b* 10 Aug 1954.
    3*d*●Henry Parke Custis MOORHEAD, *b* 14 Jan 1918, *m* ●Doris Bushman, and has issue,
      1*e*●Cynthia Chew MOORHEAD, *b* 17 Aug 1951.
      2*e*●Martha Coffey MOORHEAD, *b* 10 Dec 1953.
4*b* Gertrude UPSHUR, *b* 23 July 1862, *m* 31 Aug 1882, William Henry Hunt, Gov of Puerto Rico 1901-04, Fed Judge 1904-28 (*b* at New Orleans 5 Nov 1857; *d* at Charlottesville, Virginia 4 Feb 1949), son of William Henry Hunt, Sec of the Navy (1881-82) and sometime Min to Russia, by his wife Elizabeth Augusta Ridgely, and *d* 2 July 1944, leaving issue,
  1*c* Elizabeth Ridgely HUNT, *b* at Fort Benton, Montana 22 July 1883, *m* 1st 18 Sept 1906 (*m* diss by div), George Washington Thompson (*b* 7 April 1878; *d* 11 July 1931), and had issue,
    1*d*●George Washington THOMPSON, Jr, *b* 12 July 1907, *m* 10 Nov 1934, ●Sara Sayles Smith, and has issue,
      1*e*●Jonathan THOMPSON, *b* 12 Oct 1936.
      2*e*●William Hunt THOMPSON, *b* 15 Nov 1937.
      3*e*●Sara Sayles THOMPSON, *b* 12 Dec 1938.
      4*e*●Susan Ridgely THOMPSON, *b* 14 Sept 1950.
    2*d*●Elizabeth Ridgely THOMPSON, *b* 12 July 1909, *m* 14 Oct 1932, ●John S. Wise (*b* 11 Nov 1906), son of Henry A. Wise, and has issue,
      1*e*●John S. WISE, Jr, *b* 1 Oct 1934.
      2*e*●Henry A. WISE, *b* 17 Feb 1937.
      3*e*●Edward Tayloe WISE, *b* 21 Oct 1945.
  Elizabeth Ridgely Hunt, *m* 2ndly 1913, Edward Tayloe Dickinson, of Edgehill, Charlottesville, Virginia, and *d* 3 Oct 1954.
  2*c* William Henry HUNT, Jr, *b* 3 April 1886; *dunm* 17 Dec 1955.

3c Helen Upshur HUNT, b at Helena, Montana 28 Feb 1889, m 22 May 1915, Barnaby Conrad, of San Francisco (b 19 Oct 1887), and had issue,
  1d●William Hunt CONRAD, b 2 Oct 1916, m 28 Jan 1950, ●Marion Kitchin, and has issue,
    ●William Hunt CONRAD, Jr, b 14 Nov 1955.
  2d●Barnaby CONRAD, Jr, author and illustrator, b at San Francisco 27 March 1922, m 1st 19 March 1949, Dale Cowgill, and has issue,
    1e●Barnaby CONRAD III, b 17 April 1952.
    2e●Tani CONRAD, b 20 June 1954.
    3e●Winston Stuart CONRAD, b 1956.
  Barnaby Conrad, Jr m 2ndly 18 May 1962, ●Mary Slater, and by her has issue,
    4e●Kendall CONRAD.
4c●Gertrude Livingston HUNT, m 19 Nov 1920, ●Nelson Rulison Knox, and has issue,
  1d●Nelson Rulison KNOX, Jr, b 6 May 1921, m 20 Aug 1955, ●Pamela Fitzgerald Craig.
  2d●Peter Gaillard KNOX, b 5 Aug 1924, m 4 March 1951, ●Lilla Thorne Davison, and has issue,
    1e●Sarah Davison KNOX, b 9 Feb 1952.
    2e●Peter Gaillard KNOX, Jr, b 29 June 1954.
    3e●Robin Hunt KNOX, b 29 Nov 1955.
5b Henry N. UPSHUR, b 1862; d 1865.
4a Columbia W. (Lum) WILLIAMS, m Abel Brown Upshur, and dsp.
5a William Orton WILLIAMS, Col CSA, b 7 July 1839; hanged as a spy 9 June 1863, unm.
(6) Robert Thomas PETER, b 7 Nov 1806; d 5 Oct 1807.
(7) Martha Custis Castania PETER, b 5 Oct 1808; d 5 April 1809.
(8) Britannia Wellington PETER, b at Washington, DC 28 Jan 1815, m 8 Dec 1842, as his 2nd wife, Cdre Beverley Kennon, USN (b in Mecklenburg County, Virginia 17 April 1793; accidentally k by the explosion of a gun on board USS *Princeton* on the Potomac River, nr Washington, DC 28 Feb 1844), son of Gen Richard Kennon, Continental Army, first Gov of Louisiana, by his wife Elizabeth Beverley Munford, and d at Washington, DC 27 Jan 1911, having had issue,
  Martha Custis KENNON, b 18 Oct 1843, m 23 April 1867, her 1st cousin once removed, Dr Armistead Peter, of Washington, DC (b 23 Feb 1840; d 28 Jan 1902), son of George Peter (yr brother of Thomas Peter — see p 41) by his 3rd wife Sarah Norfleet Freeland (and brother of Elizabeth Peter, Mrs Thomas Peter — see above, p 41), and d 8 Sept 1886, leaving issue,
  1b Walter Gibson PETER, of Washington, DC, Fell American Inst of Arch, mem Soc of the Cincinnati, b 24 June 1868, educ Mass Inst of Technology, m 1st 16 March 1907, Ellen Marbury (b at Washington, DC 18 Oct 1874; d 3 June 1932), widow of Albert E. S. Greene, and dau of Dr James Shields Beale, by his wife Fannie Sawyer Marbury, and had issue,
    Walter Gibson PETER, Jr, architect, b at Washington, DC 11 Dec 1908, m 16 Aug 1939, ●Evelyn (b 20 Jan 1911) [*3024 Dumbarton Avenue NW, Washington, DC 20007, USA*], dau of Naomon Wesley Booth, by his wife Maud Mildred Lyon, and d at Washington, DC 4 Feb 1971, leaving issue,
    1d●Walter Gibson PETER III [*1345 30th Street NW, Washington, DC, USA*], b 24 Feb 1943, m ●Charlotte Martin Ecker, and has issue,
      ●Robert Dunlop PETER, b 1971.
    2d●Martha Custis PETER [*3024 Dumbarton Avenue NW, Washington, DC 20007, USA*], b 17 June 1952.
  Walter Gibson Peter, Sr m 2ndly 14 May 1935, Grace Glasgow (b 31 July 1878; d at Chevy Chase, Maryland 31 March 1974), widow of John Beard Ecker, and dau of George Thomas Dunlop, by his wife Emily Redin Kirk.
  2b Armistead PETER, Jr, of Tudor Place, Washington, DC, b at Tudor Place 30 Nov 1870, m 25 April 1894, his 2nd cousin, Anna Wright, dau of Major Lawrence Williams (see above, p 42), and d 25 July 1960, leaving issue,
    ●Armistead PETER III, Lt-Cmdr USN (ret)

[*Tudor Place, 1644 31st Street NW, Washington, DC, USA*], b 19 July 1896, m 24 Feb 1921, Caroline Ogden (b at Paris, France 26 Dec 1894; d 2 Oct 1965), dau of Mahlon Ogden Jones, by his wife Susan Frisbie Tilghman Earle, and has issue,
    ●Anne Custis PETER, b 12 Sept 1922, m ●Dr Douglas Worthington Pearre [*1670 31st Street, Washington, DC, USA*], and has issue,
    1e●Louise H. C. PEARRE, b 1954.
    2e●Worthington P. PEARRE, b 1956.
3b Beverley Kennon PETER, b at Tudor Place 21 June 1872; d unm at Washington, DC 15 Feb 1922.
4b George Freeland PETER (Rev), STB, DD, sometime Canon and Chancellor of Washington Cathedral, b at Tudor Place 12 June 1875, educ Univ of the South, Gen Theological Seminary, New York City, and Oxford Univ, m at Cobham Park, Cobham, Virginia 20 July 1916, ●Lulie (b at Richmond Virginia 15 June 1882) [*Cobham Park, Cobham, Virginia, USA*], widow of W. Otto Nolting, of Richmond, Virginia, and dau of Charles Evans Whitlock, by his wife Elizabeth Brockenbrough Aiken, and d at Charlottesville, Virginia 22 Feb 1953, leaving issue,
  ●George Freeland PETER, Jr, Lieut US Marine Corps, served in World War II, partner accounting firm of Wilkinson and Peter, Charlottesville [*Cobham Park, Cobham, Virginia*], b at Richmond, Virginia 6 Nov 1919, educ St Alban's Washington, Episcopal High Sch, Alexandria, and Univ of Virginia (BA), m 1st 11 Oct 1947 (m diss by div), Elizabeth, formerly wife of W. Haggin Perry, and dau of Capt Richard Crofton. He m 2ndly at Rockville, Maryland 14 June 1952, ●Virginia Mary (b at Roanoke, Virginia 28 June 1917), dau of Louis James San, by his wife Eleanor Brophy.
5b Agnes PETER, served with American and French Armies in World War I, had French Medal of Honour, b at Tudor Place 3 Feb 1880, m at Washington, DC 28 July 1953, as his 2nd wife, Rev Dr John Raleigh Mott, Chm Internat Missionary Council 1910-41, hon Pres World Council of Churches (b at Livingston Manor, New York 25 May 1865; d 31 Jan 1955), son of John S. Mott, by his wife Elmira Dodge, and dsp 6 Oct 1957.
4 Eleanor (Nelly) Parke CUSTIS, b at Abingdon, Virginia 31 March 1779, m at Mount Vernon 22 Feb 1799, as his 2nd wife, Lawrence Lewis (b 4 April 1767; d at Arlington, Virginia 20 Nov 1839), 9th son of Col Fielding Lewis, of Kenmore, Fredericksburg, Virginia, by his 2nd wife Betty, sister of Pres Washington (see p 51), and d at Audley, Clarke County, Virginia 15 July 1852, having had issue,
  (1) Frances Parke LEWIS, b at Mount Vernon 27 Nov 1799, m at Woodlawn, Fairfax County, Virginia 4 April 1826, Col Edward George Washington Butler, 3rd Drags, US Army (b 22 Feb 1800; d 5 Sept 1888), son of Edward Butler, by his wife Isabella Fowler, and d at Pass Christian, Mississippi 30 June 1875, having had issue,
    1a Edward George Washington BUTLER, b 4 Dec 1826; d 23 Sept 1827.
    2a and 3a Twin daus, b and d 29 Feb 1828.
    4a Edward George Washington BUTLER, sometime Sec of Legation at Berlin, Offr CSA, b at Woodlawn 4 June 1829, educ Univ of Virginia, and Harvard, ka at the Battle of Belmont, Missouri 7 Nov 1861, unm.
    5a Eleanor Angela Isabella BUTLER, b in Louisiana 7 Feb 1832, m 9 (or 12?) May 1854, as his 1st wife, Col George McWillie Williamson, of Shreveport, Louisiana, sometime US Min to Central America (b 22 Sept 1829; d 29 Jan 1882), son of Thomas Taylor Williamson, by his wife Tirzah Ann McWillie, and d 9 Jan 1867, leaving issue,
    1b Isabel Butler WILLIAMSON, b 4 Nov 1855, m 1881, Arthur Hodge, and d 1909, having had issue,
      Evelyn Angela Isabel HODGE, b 24 July 1884; drowned in Twelve-Mile Bayou, nr Shreveport, Louisiana 3 May 1903, unm.
    2b George McWillie WILLIAMSON, Jr, of DeSoto Parish, Louisiana, b 1857, m 1882, Adine Eatman (b 1859; d 1912), and had issue,
      1c George McWillie WILLIAMSON III, b 14 April 1884.
      2c Isabel Butler WILLIAMSON, b in DeSoto Parish,

Louisiana 21 March 1888, *m* James Cummings, or Cumming.

3*c* Sarah Leigh WILLIAMSON, *b* 19 Sept 1892, *m* Joseph A. Becker, of Brookhaven, Mississippi, and had issue,
  ● Mary Adine BECKER, *m* ● Chester W. Hill, and has issue,
    1*e* ● Mary Lee HILL, *b ca* 1947.
    2*e* ● Jackson Becker HILL, *b ca* 1950.
4*c* ● Mary Alice WILLIAMSON, *b* 10 Jan 1898.
5*c* ● Caro Butler WILLIAMSON, *b* 3 July 1900.
3*b* Evelyn Angela WILLIAMSON (Sister Marie Angela), teacher at Port of Spain, Trinidad 1905, *b* 22 Feb 1859 (?).
4*b* William McWillie WILLIAMSON, *b* 17 March 1861, *m* Nannie Lemon, and *d* in Central America May 1894, having had issue,
  Matelle WILLIAMSON, *d* an inf.
5*b* Anne McWillie WILLIAMSON, *b ca* 1863, *m* 1900, George Herbert Freeman.
6*b* Caroline Butler WILLIAMSON, *b* at Shreveport, Louisiana 11 June 1865, *m* 1887, Philip Bernard Frierson, of Frierson, Louisiana (*b* 1859; *d* 1903), son of Gen Philip Frierson, of S Carolina, and *d ante* 1909, leaving issue,
  1*c* ● Anne Leigh FRIERSON, *b* 12 June 1891, *m* 1st, Thomas B. Wilson; and 2ndly, ● John A. Sewall, Jr [*656 Herndon Avenue, Shreveport, Louisiana, USA*].
  2*c* ● George Philip FRIERSON, *b* 16 Nov 1893.
  3*c* ● Dorothy Witten FRIERSON, *b* 3 Feb 1896.
  4*c* ● Edward Butler FRIERSON, *b* 3 Dec 1898.
  5*c* ● Mary Eleanor FRIERSON, *b* 9 March 1900.
6*a* Caroline Swanwick BUTLER, *b* 21 Aug 1834, *m* 9 May 1853, William Barrow Turnbull, of Turnbull Island, nr Simmesport, Louisiana, sugar cane planter (*b* 8 Aug 1829; drowned 11 Nov 1856), and *d* 1876 (*bur* Pass Christian, Mississippi), leaving issue,
  1*b* William Butler TURNBULL, of S Dakota and later of Boston, Mass, *b* 8 April 1854, *m* 1st *post* 1889 (*m* diss by div), Sarah, formerly wife of — Barrow, and dau of Col Robert H. Barrow, by his wife — Barrow. He *m* 2ndly, Sarah (?) Hill, of New York City, and *d post* 1935, having by her had issue,
    1*c* ● Caro TURNBULL, *m*, and has issue.
    2*c* ● Thelma TURNBULL.
  2*b* Daniel Parke TURNBULL, of Mandan, N Dakota, attorney, *b* 25 May 1856, *educ* Washington and Lee Univ, *m post* 1889 —, a widow, and had issue,
    Daniel Parke TURNBULL, Jr, *b* 1898; *dunm* 5 Feb 1920.
7*a* Lawrence Lewis BUTLER, Major CSA, *b* 10 March 1837, *m* 1st 11 March 1869, Mary Susan (*b* 1847; *d* at St Louis, Missouri 26 March 1882), dau of Edward J. Gay, and had issue,
  1*b* Frances Parke BUTLER, *b* 27 Dec 1869, *m* 28 Aug 1895, John Ewens, of Vicksburg, Mississippi, and *d* 21 April 1929, leaving issue,
    ● Frances Butler EWENS, *b* 19 Dec 1898, *m* 1922, ● Major Edward Francis Twiss, and has issue,
      1*d* ● Nan Betty TWISS, *b* 4 May 1923.
      2*d* ● Edward Francis TWISS, Jr, *b* 7 Oct 1925.
  2*b* Edward Gay BUTLER, of Boyce, Virginia, *b* 18 June 1872, *m* 7 June 1898, Emily Mansfield (*b* 18 Jan 1874; *d* 26 Aug 1952), and *dsp* 8 Feb 1953.
  3*b* Lavinia Hynes BUTLER, *b* 30 May 1875, *m* 28 Oct 1896, Wyatt Shallcross, of Kirkwood, St Louis, Missouri (*b* 5 March 1865), and had issue,
    1*c* ● Eleanor Custis SHALLCROSS, *b* 7 Dec 1898.
    2*c* ● Nan Butler SHALLCROSS, *b* 5 April 1901, *m* 18 Oct 1933, ● Cyril C. Clemens [*841 N Kirkwood Road, Montana, USA*].
    3*c* ● Lawrence Butler SHALLCROSS, *b* 10 Nov 1907.
    4*c* ● Wyatt SHALLCROSS, Jr, *b* 2 May 1910.
    5*c* ● Mary Sue SHALLCROSS, *b* 20 April 1919.
  4*b* Anna Gay BUTLER, *b* 1 Aug 1877, *m* 30 Nov 1904, Richard Cheatham Plater, of Nashville, Tennessee, later of New York City (*b* 4 Feb 1872), and had issue,
    1*c* ● Richard Cheatham PLATER, Jr, *b* 20 May

1908, *m* 1st June 1931, Eleanore Leake, and has issue,
      1*d* ● Richard Ormonde PLATER, *b* 6 Sept 1933.
      2*d* ● David Dunboyne PLATER, *b* 1935 (?).
    Richard Cheatham Plater, Jr, *m* 2ndly, ● Pamela Quarles, dau of R. G. Robinson.
    2*c* ● Louise PLATER, *b* 31 Jan 1910, *m* 1934, ● Robert Walter Hale, Jr [*Mount Lake Club, Lake Wales, Florida, USA*], son of Robert Walter Hale, and has issue,
      ● Robert Walter HALE III [*2208 Tyne Boulevard, Nashville, Tennessee, USA*], *m* ● Janice L. Sinclair.
5*b* Mary Suzanne BUTLER, *b* at St Louis, Missouri 19 Oct 1880, *m* there 12 Feb 1901, George Armistead Whiting, of Roland Park, Baltimore, Maryland (*b* at Baltimore 3 Nov 1879; *d* there 7 Sept 1947), son of Clarence Carlyle Whiting, by his wife Marian Gordon Armistead, and had issue,
  1*c* Eleanor Custis WHITING, *b* at Baltimore 3 Jan 1902, *m* 1st 1923 (*m* diss by div), William Francis FitzGerald, Jr, son of William Francis FitzGerald, by his wife Mary E. O'Leary, and had issue,
    ● Mary Carlyle FITZGERALD, *b* 4 Oct 1925.
  Eleanor Custis Whiting *m* 2ndly at Jackson, Wyoming 8 Aug 1949, ● Baron Leopold Ludwig James Wulff Mogens von Plessen (*b* at Darmstadt 13 June 1894), 3rd son of Ludwig Mogens Gabriel, Count von Plessen-Cronstern, by his wife Countess Leopoldine Hoyos, and *d* at San Francisco 1 Sept 1949.
  2*c* Lawrence Lewis Butler WHITING, of Baltimore, orthopaedic surg, *b* at Catonsville, Maryland 9 April 1906, *educ* Johns Hopkins Univ (MD), *m* 26 Oct 1931, Katherine Ahern (*b* at Chestertown, Maryland 7 March 1912; *d* at Baltimore 5 Sept 1948), dau of David Ford, by his wife Anna Ahern, and *d* at Pensacola, Florida 26 Jan 1950, having had issue,
    1*d* George Armistead WHITING, *b* 23 Jan 1935; *d* 5 Sept 1948.
    2*d* ● Suzanne Lewis WHITING, *b* 13 June 1936.
    3*d* ● Lewis Butler WHITING, *b* 3 Aug 1940.
    4*d* David Ford WHITING, *b* 8 June, *d* 13 June 1941.
  3*c* ● Betty Washington WHITING [*4221 Greenway, Baltimore, Maryland, USA*], *b* at Elkridge, Maryland 4 Oct 1912.
Major Lawrence Lewis Butler *m* 2ndly 1886, Sue Martin (*d* 1893), and *d* at St Louis, Missouri 3 June 1898.
(2) Martha Betty LEWIS, *b* at Mount Vernon 19 Aug 1801; *d* there 17 June 1802.
(3) Lawrence Fielding LEWIS, *b* and *d* at Western View, Culpeper County, Virginia 5 Aug 1802.
(4) Lorenzo LEWIS, *b* at Woodlawn 13 Nov 1803, *m* 6 June 1827, Esther Maria (*b* 1804; *d* at Audley, Clarke County, Virginia 23 June 1885), dau of Dr John Redman Coxe, of Philadelphia, and *d* at Audley, Clarke County, Virginia 27 Aug 1847, leaving issue,
  1*a* George Washington LEWIS, Cadet VMI, Commissary Offr CSA, *b* at Philadelphia 12 Feb 1829, *m* at Baltimore 25 March 1852, Emily Contee (*b* 31 July 1832; *d* 8 April 1909), dau of Reverdy Johnson, of Baltimore, by his wife Mary Mackall Bowie, and *d* at Monterey, Clarke County, Virginia 5 Feb 1885, having had issue,
    1*b* Lorenzo LEWIS, *b* at Baltimore 11 March 1853, *m* 28 Feb 1885, Rose Ellzey (*b* 21 July 1855; *d* 21 Feb 1948), dau of Col Francis McCormick, of Berryville, Virginia, by his wife Rosanna Mortimer Ellzey, and *d* at Frankford, Clarke County, Virginia 27 Feb 1887, leaving issue,
      George Washington LEWIS, of Alexandria, Virginia, lawyer, *b* 22 July 1886, *m* 12 Dec 1916, Sylvia Ishbel De Beck, of New York, and *d* 1918, leaving issue,
        ● Lorenzo Custis LEWIS, *b* at Braddock, Clarke County, Virginia 18 Nov 1917.
    2*b* Reverdy Johnson LEWIS, *b* at Audley, Clarke County, Virginia 25 April, *d* there 1 May 1854.
    3*b* Mary Bowie LEWIS, *b* at Monterey, Clarke County, Virginia 17 July 1855; *dunm* at Hoboken, New Jersey

25 April 1886.
4*b* Esther Maria LEWIS, *b* at Monterey, Clarke County, Virginia 6 Aug 1856, *m* at Berryville, Virginia 7 Dec 1882, Samuel McCormick, of Berryville (*b* at Frankford, Clarke County, Virginia 5 July 1849; *d* 17 Feb 1937), son of Col Francis McCormick, by his wife Rosanna Mortimer Ellzey (and brother of Mrs Lorenzo Lewis — *see p 44*), and *d* at Four Winds, Berryville 28 July 1931, having had issue,
  1*c* Emily Contee McCORMICK, *b* at Monterey, Clarke County, Virginia 15 Sept 1885; *dunm.*
  2*c* Mary Lewis McCORMICK, *b* at Norwood, Clarke County, Virginia 11 Oct 1887; *d* there 17 July 1888.
  3*c* Edward Lewis McCORMICK, *b* at Berryville 22 May 1895; *dunm.*
5*b* Emily Contee LEWIS, *b* at Monterey, Clarke County, Virginia 29 Dec 1857, *m* at Berryville 28 Oct 1879, Col Edwin Augustus Stevens, Jr, of Castle Point, Hoboken, New Jersey (*b* at Philadelphia 14 March 1858; *d* at Washington, DC 8 March 1918), son of Edwin Augustus Stevens (son of Col John Stevens, founder of Hoboken, New Jersey), by his wife Martha Bayard Dod, and *d* at Bedminster, New Jersey 25 Oct 1931, having had issue,
  1*c* John STEVENS VI, *b* 28 Jan 1881; *dunm* 27 Aug 1932.
  2*c* Edwin Augustus STEVENS III, *b* 15 Aug 1882; *dunm* at Hoboken, New Jersey 1 Dec 1954.
  3*c* Washington Lewis STEVENS, *b* 26 Sept 1883, *educ* Princeton (AB 1905) *m* 28 Oct 1905 (*m* diss by div 1916), Nannie Nye Jackson, and *dsp* 5 March 1946.
  4*c* Bayard STEVENS, *b* 20 July 1885, *m* at Berryville, Virginia 11 Oct 1910, Mary Green (*b* at Anchorage, Kentucky 9 March 1887; *d* at Berryville Jan 1966), dau of William Naylor McDonald, of Berryville, Virginia, by his wife Catherine S. Gray, and *d* 15 Nov 1927, leaving issue,
    1*d* John STEVENS VII, *b* at Hoboken, New Jersey 8 Jan 1912; *dunm* 16 April 1941.
    2*d* ●Bayard McDonald STEVENS [*73 Goetze Street, Bay Head, New Jersey, USA*], *b* at Hoboken, New Jersey 9 March 1916, *educ* Princeton (AB 1939), and New York Univ (AM), *m* at Morristown, New Jersey 24 May 1940, ●Mary Louise Whitney (*b* 30 Sept 1918), and has issue,
      1*e* ●Elizabeth Alexander STEVENS, *b* at New York 10 April 1942, *m* 20 May 1972, ●Benjamin Bergstein.
      2*e* ●Bayard McDonald STEVENS, Jr [*206 East 34th Street, New York, NY, USA*], *b* at New York 27 June 1945.
    3*d* ●Nancy Gray STEVENS, *b* at Short Hills, New Jersey 29 May 1925, *m* at Berryville 25 Aug 1945, ●Douglas Brooke Allen (*b* 1 Oct 1923), and has issue,
      1*e* ●Catherine MacDonald ALLEN.
      2*e* ●Nancy Bayard ALLEN, *b* 1 Dec 1951.
5*c* Martha Bayard STEVENS, *b* at Castle Point, Hoboken, New Jersey 30 Dec 1886; *d* there 3 April 1888.
6*c* Basil Martiau STEVENS, a US Commr for Dist of New Jersey 1932-36, Special Master in Chancery of New Jersey 1933-47, Commr of the Supreme Court of New Jersey 1933-47, Lt-Col Inf NGNJ, *b* at Castle Point, Hoboken, New Jersey 28 Dec 1888, *m* at Newcastle, Pennsylvania 28 Oct 1913, Helen Clendenin (*b* at Newcastle 5 March 1891; *d* 2 Dec 1943), dau of Edward Hatnett Ward, by his wife Mary Clendenin, and *d* 7 Nov 1957, leaving issue,
    1*d* ●Emily Custis Lewis STEVENS, *b* at Hoboken, New Jersey 22 May 1915, *m* 3 July 1948, ●James Vincent de Paul Tully, formerly Britt (*b* at Bayonne, New Jersey 21 Sept 1910) [*16 Prospect Avenue, Montclair, New Jersey 07042, USA*], son of John Britt, by his wife Emma Hall.
  2*d* Edwin Augustus STEVENS IV, *b* at Bernardsville, New Jersey 8 March 1917, *educ* Colorado Univ (AB, BEd 1941), and Univ of S

California (MS, PhD), *m* at Beverly Hills, California 14 Aug 1954, ●Mary Susanne Leake (*b* 9 July 1928), and *d* at Whittier, California 26 Sept 1959, leaving issue,
    1*e* ●Edwin Augustus STEVENS V [*316 19th Street, Santa Monica, California, USA*], *b* 17 July 1955.
    2*e* ●Mary Stuyvesant STEVENS, *b* 9 Feb 1957.
    3*e* ●William Leake STEVENS, *b* 5 July 1959.
7*c* Lawrence Lewis STEVENS, *b* at Castle Point, Hoboken, New Jersey 29 Nov 1889, *m* at Philadelphia 2 April 1913, Anne D. Malpass (*b* at Philadelphia 22 Aug 1890; *d* May 1974), and had issue,
    ●Lawrence Lewis STEVENS, Jr [*462 Montgomery Avenue, Heverford, Pennsylvania, USA*], *b* at Philadelphia 29 July 1915, *educ* Pennsylvania Univ, *m* ●Dorothy A. Poole, and has issue,
      1*e* ●Edward M. STEVENS [*370 East 76th Street, New York, NY, USA*].
      2*e* ●Mark L. STEVENS, *educ* Susquehanna.
8*c* Emily Custis Lewis STEVENS, *b* at Bernardsville, New Jersey 27 June 1896; *dunm* 8 May 1963.
6*b* Reverdy Johnson LEWIS, *b* at Monterey, Clarke County, Virginia 3 June 1859, *m* Alice Powers (*b* 23 Feb 1854; *d* 12 Oct 1934), and *dsp* at Berryville, Virginia 14 Dec 1928.
7*b* Louise Travers LEWIS, *b* at Monterey, Clarke County, Virginia 3 March 1861; *d* 17 Aug 1863.
8*b* Charles Conrad LEWIS, *b* at Monterey, Clarke County, Virginia 14 June 1862, *m* 1st 14 Feb 1895, Alice Maud Hough (*b* 1 Oct 1865; *d* 4 April 1902). He *m* 2ndly at Cranford, New Jersey 4 Sept 1912, Mabel Eleanor (*b* 30 July 1876), dau of William Henry Boyer, by his wife Sally Coxe, and *d* at Fielding, Clarke County, Virginia 7 March 1930, having by her had issue,
  ●Charles Conrad LEWIS, Jr, *b* at Fielding, Clarke County, Virginia 9 Feb 1918.
9*b* Louise Travers LEWIS, *b* at Monterey, Clarke County, Virginia 10 Oct 1863; *dunm* at Rome, Italy 20 Jan 1912.
10*b* William Travers LEWIS, lawyer, Commonwealth Attorney of Clarke County, Virginia, *b* at Monterey, Clarke County, Virginia 14 March 1865, *m* Dec 1902, Maria Garnett McGuire (*b* 11 March 1867), and *d* 17 May 1929, having had issue,
  William Travers LEWIS, Jr, *b* 17 July, *d* 31 July 1904.
11*b* Ella Johnson LEWIS, *b* at Monterey, Clarke County, Virginia 16 May 1868, *m* 1 June 1898, James McKenney White (*b* 4 Dec 1873), and *dsp* 18 May 1941.
12*b* Robert Edward Lee LEWIS, of New York, lawyer, *b* at Monterey, Clarke County, Virginia 17 Sept 1869, *m* 24 Nov 1896, Johanna Elizabeth Mathilde Gossler (*b* 24 May 1870; *d* 1952), and *d* 19 Oct 1946, leaving issue,
  1*c* ●Edwin Stevens LEWIS [*Skyhill, Delaplane, Virginia, USA*], *b* 1898.
  2*c* ●Robert Edward Lee LEWIS, Jr [*Twyford, Old Tavern Road, Farmingdale, New Jersey, USA*], *b* 10 May 1903, *m* 4 June 1928, ●Alice McKim Voss (*b* 28 April 1903), and has issue,
    1*d* ●Eleanor Custis LEWIS.
    2*d* ●Sandra V. LEWIS, *b* 1933.
13*b* Maude LEWIS, *b* at Monterey, Clarke County, Virginia 4 March 1871, *m* 31 Aug 1891, Fenton Peterkin Whiting, of Berryville, Virginia (*b* 19 Dec 1853; *d* 6 June 1921), son of Francis Henry Whiting, and *dsp* 18 April 1925.
14*b* Eleanor Parke Custis LEWIS, *b* at Monterey, Clarke County, Virginia 25 May, *d* there 23 Aug 1872.
2*a* John Redman Coxe LEWIS, went with Cdre Perry's expdn to Japan 1853, Offr in US Revenue Cutter Service, Col CSA, *b* at Audley, Clarke County, Virginia 18 April 1834, *m* at Richmond, Virginia 12 Dec 1863, Maria Bradfute (*b* at Lynchburg, Virginia 24 May 1838; *d* 1920), dau of John Freeland, of Richmond, Virginia, by his wife Rose Bradfute (and sister of Mrs Henry Llewellyn Daingerfield Lewis — *see below, p 47*), and *d*

1898, leaving issue,
1*b* Lawrence Fielding LEWIS, *b* at Richmond, Virginia 7 Oct 1864, *m* 9 June 1891, Jane Hollins Nicholas, and had issue,
  ●Janet Hollins LEWIS, *b* at Baltimore 27 April 1895, *m* ●Harry Manvell, and has issue,
    1*d*●Harry MANVELL, Jr.
    2*d*●Jean MANVELL.
2*b* John Redman Coxe LEWIS, Jr, *b* at Richmond, Virginia 13 June 1870; *dunm* at Virginia Univ 26 Feb 1905.
3*b* Marie Stuart LEWIS, *b* at Richmond, Virginia 25 Jan 1875, *m* at Lexington, Virginia 24 Nov 1908, St Julien Ravenel Marshall, of New York (*b* at Portsmouth, Virginia 23 Nov 1881), and had issue,
  1*c*●St Julien Ravenel MARSHALL, Jr, *b* 24 July 1910, *m* ●—, dau of Col Harold C. Fiske, and has issue,
    1*d*●Louise Ravenel MARSHALL, *m* 1962, ●Carleton Francis Rosenburgh, Jr [*Scarsdale, New York, USA*], son of Carleton Francis Rosenburgh.
    2*d*●Virginia Fiske MARSHALL.
  2*c* John Lewis MARSHALL, *b* at Washington, DC 23 June 1912; *d* at New York 25 May 1927.
4*b* Duncan Freeland LEWIS, *b* at Richmond, Virginia 18 Feb 1876; *dunm* at Washington, DC 12 Feb 1914.
3*a* Lawrence Fielding LEWIS, *b* at Audley, Clarke County, Virginia 18 April 1834 (twin with John Redman Coxe); *dunm* 25 Jan 1857.
4*a* Edward Parke Custis LEWIS, Col CSA, sometime US Min to Portugal, *b* at Audley, Clarke County, Virginia 7 Feb 1837, *m* 1st 23 March 1858, Lucy Belmain (*b* 1839; *d* at Audley 28 Aug 1866), dau of Josiah William Ware, by his wife Frances Toy Glassell, and had issue,
  1*b* Eleanor Angela LEWIS, *b* 25 July 1859; *d* 18 Feb 1860.
  2*b* Lawrence Fielding LEWIS, *b* 1861; *d* an inf.
  3*b* John Glassell LEWIS, *b* 1862; *d* an inf.
  4*b* Edward Parke Custis LEWIS, *b* Aug 1864; *d* 22 March 1866.
  5*b* Lucy Ware LEWIS, *b* at Audley, Clarke County, Virginia 26 Aug 1866, *m* 31 Dec 1893, Charles Treadwell Ayres McCormick, of Berryville, Virginia (*b* 11 March 1861; *d* 16 March 1932), and *d* 8 Nov 1944, having had issue,
    1*c* Charles Treadwell Ayres McCORMICK, Jr, US Marine Corps, served in World War I, *ka* at the Battle of Soissons 1918, *unm*.
    2*c* Mary Elizabeth McCORMICK, *b* 6 Aug 1899; *d* 16 Aug 1908.
Edward Parke Custis Lewis *m* 2ndly at Baltimore 1 June 1869, Mary Picton (*b* at Philadelphia 19 May 1840; *d* at Bernardsville, New Jersey 21 Sept 1903), widow of Gen Muscoe Russell Hunter Garnett, and dau of Edwin Augustus Stevens (and half-sister of Col Edwin Augustus Stevens, Jr, — *see above, p 45*), and *d* at Hoboken, New Jersey 3 Sept 1892, having by her had issue,
  6*b* Edwin Augustus Stevens LEWIS, *b* at Pau, France 15 March 1870, *m* 7 Jan 1899, Alice Stuart (*b* at New York 24 Nov 1877; *d* at Baltimore 22 Nov 1973), dau of Gen Henry Harrison Walker, CSA, by his wife Mary Stuart Mercer, and *d* 5 Sept 1906, leaving issue,
    1*c* Edward Parke Custis LEWIS; *d* at Hoboken, New Jersey 13 Feb 1900; *dunm* at Baltimore 21 July 1973.
    2*c*●Henry Harrison Walker LEWIS, lawyer [*103 St John's Road, Baltimore, Maryland, USA; Burnside Farm, Eccleston, Maryland, USA*], *b* at Hoboken, New Jersey 10 Feb 1904, *m* 7 Oct 1938, ●Eleanor Randall (*b* at Pottsville, Pennsylvania 3 Oct 1914), dau of John Marbury Nelson, Jr, by his wife Ellen Cheston McIlvaine, and has issue,
      1*d*●Edwin Augustus Stevens LEWIS, *b* at Baltimore 4 March 1940, *m* 27 Jan 1968, ●Mary Ann (*b* 15 July 1938), dau of Donald Glasgo, and has issue,
        1*e*●Catherine Bell LEWIS, *b* at Hartford, Conn 7 Feb 1970.
        2*e*●Walker LEWIS, *b* at Schenectady, New York 23 Nov 1972.
      2*d*●John Nelson LEWIS, *b* at Baltimore 16 March 1942, *m* 11 Aug 1973, ●Jo Deweese (*b* 21 Dec 1945).
      3*d*●Fielding LEWIS, *b* at Pasadena, California 11 march 1945.
    4*d*●Henry McIlvaine LEWIS, *b* at Baltimore 10 March 1947, *m* 22 Nov 1969, ●Deborah Ann (*b* 13 June 1949), dau of Charles B. Sanders, and has issue,
      ●Kelly Lynn LEWIS, *b* at Princeton, New Jersey 21 Nov 1971.
7*b* Esther Maria LEWIS, *b* at Geneva, Switzerland 17 June 1871, *m* 19 May 1894, Charles Merrill Chapin, of Cleveland, Ohio, and New York City (*b* 19 April 1871; *d* 1932), and had issue,
  1*c* Mary Stevens CHAPIN, *b* 10 Nov 1895, *m* 1 July 1916, Dr Shepard Krech, of New York City (*b* at St Paul, Minnesota 22 Feb 1891), son of Alvin William Krech, by his wife Caroline Shepard, and *d* 23 Sept 1967, leaving issue,
    1*d*●Shepard KRECH, Jr, MD [*Whitehouse Farm, Widgeon Point, Easton, Maryland, USA*], *b* at New York 24 April 1918, *educ* Yale, and Cornell Univs, *m* 14 Aug 1940, ●Nora Potter, and has issue,
      ●Shepard KRECH III [*Southern Avenue, Essex, Maryland, USA*], *m* ●Minette D. Grand.
    2*d*●Merrill Chapin KRECH [*2209 Alhambra Circle, Coral Gables, Florida 33134, USA*], *b* 18 Sept 1919, *educ* Yale Univ, *m* at East Hampton, New York 27 July 1946, ●Cynthia Smathers Haynes.
    3*d*●Mary Esther KRECH, *b* 12 Dec 1921, *m* 1st 26 July 1941, William Brinckelhoff Jackson, and has issue,
      1*e*●Mary Stevens JACKSON.
      2*e*●Barbara JACKSON.
    Mary Esther Krech *m* 2ndly 21 June 1947, ●Lyttleton Bowen Purnell Gould, Jr [*Bamboo Brook House, Pottersville, New Jersey, USA*], son of Lyttleton Bowen Purnell Gould, and has further issue,
      3*e*●Lyttleton Bowen Purnell GOULD III [*1330 Massachusetts Avenue, Washington, DC, USA*], *b* 6 March 1948.
      4*e*●Isabel Cynthia GOULD, *b* 28 Oct 1950.
    4*d*●Alvin William KRECH, *b* 10 Jan 1925, *educ* Goddard Coll, *m* at Thomasville, Georgia 16 June 1948, ●Virginia Groover, dau of William Thomas Mardre, of Boston, Georgia.
  2*c*●Charles Merrill CHAPIN, Jr, *b* 27 May 1898, *m* 1st 7 July 1925, Cynthia Meldrum Robinson (*d* 1934). He *m* 2ndly, ●Katherine, formerly wife of Charles Huntington Erhart, and dau of George Edward Kent, of Jericho, New York.
8*b* Julia Stevens LEWIS, *b* at Hoboken, New Jersey 4 March 1874, *m* 4 June 1898, James Millar Cumming, of Newark, New Jersey (*b* at Kilmarnock, Scotland 28 March 1876), son of Robert Cumming, of Ayrshire, Scotland, by his wife Elizabeth Aitken Millar, and had issue,
  1*c*●Robert A. CUMMING, MD, *b* at Bernardsville, New Jersey 5 July 1900, *educ* Edin Univ, *m* Feb 1929, ●Elizabeth Jean (*b* 17 April 1901), dau of William Knox, of Edinburgh, Scotland, and has issue,
    1*d*●Grace Kirk CUMMING, *b* 11 April 1931.
    2*d*●Julia Stevens Lewis CUMMING.
    3*d*●Robert CUMMING.
  2*c*●Edward Parke Custis Lewis CUMMING [*Rock Hill, Oyster Bay, Long Island, New York, USA*], *b* at Newark, New Jersey 25 June 1905, *educ* Emmanuel Coll Camb, *m* 4 June 1927 (*m* diss by div), Lucy Barney, dau of Walter Gurnee, and has issue,
    ●Edward Parke Custis Lewis CUMMING, Jr, *m* 16 April 1955, ●Kerrin Bartlett Gjellerup.
9*b* Elinor Parke Custis LEWIS, *b* 28 March 1876, *m* 1st 14 Jan 1905 (*m* diss by div) Thomas Bloodgood Peck,

Jr, of New York (*b* 22 Feb 1875), son of Thomas Bloodgood Peck. She *m* 2ndly, Dr Baron Zdenko von Dworzak, of Florence, Italy (*b* 1875), and *dsp.*

5*a* Charles Conrad LEWIS, *b* at Audley, Clarke County, Virginia 28 Oct 1839; *dunm* at Virginia Univ 7 March 1859.

6*a* Henry Llewellyn Daingerfield LEWIS, on staff of Gov Fitzhugh Lee of Virginia, *b* at Audley, Clarke County, Virginia 25 April 1843, *m* 26 April 1871, Carter Penn (*b* at Richmond, Virginia 11 March 1853; *d* at Charlotte, N Carolina 3 Dec 1915), dau of John Freeland, of Richmond, Virginia, by his wife Rosalie Warwick Bradfute (and sister of Mrs John Redman Coxe Lewis — *see above, p* 45), and *d* at Audley 17 Dec 1893, having had issue,

  1*b* Rosalie Warwick LEWIS, *b* at Berryville, Virginia 21 July 1872, *m* there 21 June 1893, as his 1st wife, Frank Vincit Tilford, of Washington, DC (*b* at New York 30 Nov 1871; *d* 1932), son of John Boyle Tilford, by his wife Florinda Jones Hammond, and *dsp* at Berryville 28 Sept 1895.

  2*b* Lorenzo Conrad LEWIS, *b* 18 July 1874; *d* 20 Nov 1879.

  3*b* James Freeland LEWIS, of St Petersburg, Florida, *b* 31 Oct 1875, *m* 1907, Page Ellyson, of Newport News, Virginia (*b* 31 Aug 1886), and *d* Aug 1952, leaving issue,

    1*c* ● James Freeland LEWIS, Jr [*2214 River Road, Maumee, Ohio, USA*], *m*, and has issue,
      ● Moaste Fielding LEWIS.
    2*c* ● Page Ellyson LEWIS.

  4*b* Henry Llewellyn Daingerfield LEWIS, Jr, of Hewlett, Long Island, New York, *b* at Richmond, Virginia 17 June 1877, *m* 1st, Lucy Reis; and 2ndly 2 May 1925, Jessie Somerville Knox Voss, and *dsp.*

  5*b* Edward Parke Custis LEWIS, *b* 2 May 1879; *d* at Lexington, Virginia 10 March 1896.

  6*b* Esther Maria LEWIS, *b* at Audley, Clarke County, Virginia 26 March 1881, *m* at Winchester, Virginia 3 Oct 1906, Dr Alexander Wylie Moore, of Charlotte, N Carolina (*b* at Chester, S Carolina 23 Feb 1878), son of Eli Peyton Moore, by his wife Annie Wylie, and *dsp.*

  7*b* Mary Picton LEWIS, *b* 27 May 1883; *dunm* 17 Jan 1905.

  8*b* Carter Penn LEWIS, *b* at Audley, Clarke County, Virginia 2 July 1885, *m* William Henry Wiley, of Hackensack, New Jersey, and *d* at Wilmington, Delaware 4 July 1963, leaving issue,

    1*c* ● Carter Penn WILEY, *m* ●— Desbernine.
    2*c* ● Mary Patricia WILEY, *m* ● Harold G. Brown [*Chad's Ford, Pennsylvania, USA*].

  9*b* John Freeland LEWIS, *b* 18 March 1887; *d* 15 June 1894.

  10*b* Margaret LEWIS, *b* 1889, *m* 27 Oct 1917, as his 1st wife, Thomas Bolling Byrd, of Winchester, Virginia (*b* 4 Sept 1889), son of Richard Evelyn Byrd, by his wife Elinor Bolling Flood, and *d* 1920, leaving issue,

    ● Margaret Lewis BYRD, *b* at Charlotte, N Carolina 13 April 1920, *m* ● Harry F. Stimpson, Jr, son of Harry F. Stimpson.

  11*b* Fielding LEWIS, of Charlotte, N Carolina, and Tampa, Florida, *b* at Audley, Clarke County, Virginia 28 Oct 1890; *dunm.*

  12*b* William McGuire LEWIS, *b* 14 March 1892; *d* 14 April 1893.

(5) Eleanor Agnes Freire LEWIS, *b* at Woodlawn 8 Aug 1805; *d* at Philadelphia 28 Aug 1820.

(6) Fielding Augustine LEWIS, *b* at Woodlawn 12 July 1807; *d* 27 March 1809.

(7) George Washington Custis LEWIS, *b* at Woodlawn 14 Feb 1810; *d* 16 Dec 1811.

(8) Mary Eliza Angela LEWIS, *b* at Woodlawn 1 April 1813, *m* there 30 July. 1835, Charles Magill Conrad (*b* at Winchester, Virginia 24 Dec 1804; *d* at New Orleans 11 Feb 1878), son of Frederick Conrad, by his wife Frances Thruston, and *d* at Pass Christian, Mississippi 21 Sept 1839, having had issue,

  1*a* Angela Lewis CONRAD, *b* at New Orleans 17 March 1836; *d* 25 March 1837.

  2*a* Charles Angelo Lewis CONRAD, *b* at Bay St Louis 14 Aug 1837, *m* 1867, Norma (*d* 28 Sept 1915), dau of Alfred Penn, of Lynchburg, Virginia, by his wife Evelyn Bradfute, and *dsp* at New Orleans 23 Sept 1892.

  3*a* Lawrence Lewis CONRAD, *b* at Pass Christian, Mississippi 3 July 1839, *m* Sallie Howard Worthington, of Baltimore, Maryland (*b* 26 April 1842; *d* 2 June 1917), and *d* 7 Aug 1883, leaving issue,

    1*b* Charles Angelo Lewis CONRAD, *b* 8 Jan 1873; *dunm* 1 March 1911.

    2*b* Marie W. CONRAD, *b* 4 April 1884, *m* as his 1st wife, Dr Louis C. Lehr, of Baltimore, Maryland (*b* 19 Feb 1876; *d* 20 Feb 1930), and *dsp* 6 June 1921.

5 and 6 Twin children, *b* and *d* 1780.

7 George Washington Parke CUSTIS, brought up at Mount Vernon by the Washingtons, *b* at Mount Airy, Maryland 30 April 1781, *m* 7 July 1804, Mary Lee (*b* 22 April 1788; *d* 23 April 1853), dau of William Fitzhugh, by his wife Anne Randolph, and *d* 10 Oct 1857, having had issue,

  (1) A child, *b* and *d* 15 May 1805.

  (2) Martha Elizabeth Ann CUSTIS, *b* 15 May 1806; *d* 10 March 1807.

  (3) Mary Anna Randolph CUSTIS, *b* 1 Oct 1807, *m* at Arlington, Virginia 30 June 1831, Gen Robert Edward Lee, the celebrated C-in-C of the Confederate Armies (*b* at Stratford, Westmoreland County, Virginia 19 Jan 1807; *d* at Lexington, Virginia 12 Oct 1870), son of Major-Gen Henry Lee, thrice Gov of Virginia, by his 2nd wife Anne Hill, dau of Charles Carter, of Shirley, Virginia, and *d* 5 Nov 1873, having had issue,

    1*a* George Washington Custis LEE, of Lexington, Virginia, Major-Gen CSA, *b* at Fort Monroe, Virginia 16 Sept 1832; *dunm* 18 Feb 1913.

    2*a* Mary Custis LEE, *b* 12 July 1835; *dunm* at Ravensworth, Virginia 22 Nov 1918.

    3*a* William Henry Fitzhugh LEE, Major-Gen CSA, mem Virginia State Senate 1875-79, mem House of Reps 1887-91, *b* at Arlington, Virginia 30 May 1837, *educ* Harvard, *m* 1st 23 March 1859, Charlotte Georgiana (*d* 26 Dec 1863), dau of Carter Wickham, and had issue,

      1*b* Robert Edward LEE, *b* ca Dec 1860; *d* ante Dec 1862.

      2*b* A dau, *d* an inf. Dec 1862.

    Gen William Lee *m* 2ndly at Petersburg, Virginia 28 Nov 1867, Mary Tabb (*b* 27 Aug 1846; *d* at Richmond, Virginia 24 May 1924), dau of George Washington Bolling, of Petersburg, Virginia, by his wife Martha Stith Nicholas, and *d* in Fairfax County, Virginia 15 Oct 1891, having by her had issue,

      3*b* Robert Edward LEE III, *b* at Petersburg, Virginia 11 Feb 1869, *m* 2 July 1919, Mary Wilkinson (*d* at Asheville, N Carolina 19 May 1959), widow of Gustavus Memminger Pinckney, and dau of Ralph Izard Middleton, of Charleston, S Carolina, by his wife Sarah Virginia Memminger, and *dsp* 7 Sept 1922.

      4*b* Mary Tabb LEE, *b* 1870; *d* Dec 1871.

      5*b* George Bolling LEE, MD, of New York, *b* 21 Aug 1872, *m* 21 April 1920, Helen Madeline Keeney, of San Francisco (*b* 26 Sept 1895; *d* 8 July 1968), and *d* 13 July 1948, leaving issue,

        1*c* ● Mary Walker LEE, *b* 10 June 1921, *m* 25 Nov 1960, as his 2nd wife, ● A. Smith Bowman, Jr [*Sunset Hills, Fairfax County, Virginia, USA*], son of A. Smith Bowman.

        2*c* ● Robert Edward LEE IV, *b* 25 Dec 1924, *m* ● Marjorie Tracy, and has issue,
          1*d* ● Tracy LEE, *b* 1960.
          2*d* ● Robert Edward LEE V, *b* 1964.

      6*b* Annie Agnes LEE, *d* an inf 1874.

      7*b* William Henry Fitzhugh LEE, *d* an inf 1875.

    4*a* Anne Carter LEE, *b* at Arlington, Virginia 18 June 1839; *dunm* at White Sulphur Springs, Warren County, N Carolina 20 Oct 1862.

    5*a* Eleanor Agnes LEE, *b* at Arlington, Virginia 27 Feb 1841; *dunm* at Lexington, Virginia 15 Oct 1873.

    6*a* Robert Edward LEE, Jr, Capt CSA, later in business in Washington, DC, and farming in Virginia, *b* at Arlington, Virginia 27 Oct 1843, *educ* Univ of Virginia, *m* 1st 16 Nov 1871, Charlotte Taylor (*b* 23 Oct 1848; *d* 22 Sept 1872), dau of Richard Barton Haxall, of Orange County, Virginia, by his wife Octavia Robinson. He *m* 2ndly 8 March 1894, Anne Juliet (*b* 6 April 1860; *d* 17 Nov 1915), dau of Col Thomas Hill Carter, of

Pampatike, nr Richmond, Virginia, by his wife Susan Elizabeth Roy, and *d* in Fauquier County, Virginia 19 Oct 1914, having by her had issue,
    1*b●*Anne Carter LEE, *b* 22 July 1897, *m* 3 Sept 1921, Hanson Edward Ely, Jr (*b* 31 March 1896; *d* 29 Sept 1938), son of Hanson Edward Ely, and has issue,
        1*c●*Hanson Edward ELY III, *b* 20 Oct 1923.
        2*c●*Anne Carter Lee ELY, *b* 10 June 1927, *m* ●Fred Zimmer.
    2*b●*Mary Custis LEE, *b* 23 Dec 1900, *m* 1 Oct 1925, ●William Hunter de Butts (*b* 23 Oct 1899), and has issue,
        1*c●*Robert Edward Lee DE BUTTS [*402 Virginia Avenue, Alexandria, Virginia, USA*], *b* 10 Nov 1927, *m* 1955, ●Adeline Ray, and has issue,
           1*d●*Robert Edward Lee DE BUTTS, Jr, *b* 1957.
           2*d●*William Fitzhugh DE BUTTS, *b* 1959.

           3*d●*Rosaline Burnham DE BUTTS, *b* 1962.
           4*d●*Hasseltine Ray DE BUTTS, *b* 1964.
        2*c●*William Hunter DE BUTTS, Jr, *b* 22 Oct 1929, *m* 28 Feb 1953, ●Jane Sprague, and has issue,
           1*d●*Jane Sprague DE BUTTS, *b* 1954.
           2*d●*Helen Forest DE BUTTS, *b* 1955.
           3*d●*William Hunter DE BUTTS III, *b* 1958.
        3*c●*Mary Custis Lee DE BUTTS, *b* 20 June 1932, *m* ●Frederick Leonard Spencer, and has issue,
           1*d●*Mary Custis Lee SPENCER, *b* 1956.
           2*d●*Martha Richardson SPENCER, *b* 1962.
  7*a* Mildred Childe LEE, *b* 10 Feb 1846; *dunm* nr New Orleans 27 March 1905.
  (4) Edward Hill Carter CUSTIS, *b* 14 Aug 1809; *d* 19 Oct 1810.
**4** Martha (Patsy) Parke CUSTIS, *b ca* Dec 1755; *d* at Mount Vernon 19 June 1773.

# The Brothers and Sisters of President Washington

*President Washington had nine siblings. His father married twice (see* LINEAGE OF PRESIDENT WASHINGTON, *p 39 for full details) and by his first marriage had issue, three sons and one dau (who were thus half-siblings to the President); and by his second marriage, four sons (including the President) and two daus.*

## A: HALF-BROTHERS AND SISTER OF PRESIDENT WASHINGTON

**1** Butler WASHINGTON, *b* at Bridge's Creek, Virginia 1716; *d ante* 1729.
**2** Lawrence WASHINGTON, of Mount Vernon, Virginia, Adjt-Gen of Virginia, Burgess for Fairfax County, Pres of Ohio Co, served under Adm Vernon in W Indies 1740-42, as 2 i/c and afterwards as Cmdr of the Virginia Forces, *b* at Bridge's Creek, Virginia 1718, *m* 19 July 1743, Anne (*b* 1728; *m* 2ndly 16 Dec 1752, Col George Lee, of Mount Pleasant, nephew of Hon Thomas Lee, Actg Gov of Virginia, and *d* 14 March 1761), eldest dau of Hon William Fairfax, of Belvoir, Pres of the Gov's Council in Virginia, by his 1st wife Sarah Walker, and half-sister of Bryan, 8th Baron Fairfax (*see* BURKE'S *Peerage*), and *d* at Mount Vernon 22 July 1752, having had issue,
  1 Jane WASHINGTON, *b* at Mount Vernon 27 Sept 1744; *d* there Jan 1745/6.
  2 Fairfax WASHINGTON, *b* at Mount Vernon 22 Aug, *d* there Oct 1747.
  3 Mildred WASHINGTON, *b* at Mount Vernon 28 Sept 1748; *d* there 1749.
  4 Sarah WASHINGTON, *b* at Mount Vernon 7 Nov 1750; *d* there autumn 1752.
**3** Augustine WASHINGTON, of Wakefield, Virginia, Col Virginia Militia, mem Virginia Assembly, *b* at Bridge's Creek, Virginia 1720, *m* 1743, Anne (*b* 1726; *d* Wakefield Dec 1773), dau and co-heiress of Col William Aylett, Burgess for King William County, by his 1st wife Anne, dau of Col Henry Ashton, of Nominy, and co-heiress of his 1st wife Elizabeth, dau and heiress of Capt William Hardidge, by his wife Frances, widow of Col John Washington, the emigrant (*see p 39*), and *d* 1762, having had issue,
  1 Lawrence WASHINGTON, *b ca* 1745; *d* an inf.
  2 Augustine WASHINGTON, *b ca* 1747; *d* an inf.
  3 Elizabeth WASHINGTON, *b* at Wakefield 15 Nov 1749, *m* 15 Feb 1769, Brig-Gen Alexander Spotswood, Virginia Militia, of Nottingham, Spotsylvania County, Virginia (*b* at New

Post, Virginia 16 Oct 1746; *d* at Nottingham 20 Dec 1818), son of John Spotswood, by his wife Mary Dandridge, and grandson of Gen Alexander Spotswood, Gov of Virginia (*see* BURKE'S *LG*, 1952 *Edn*, SPOTTISWOODE *of Spottiswoode*), and *d* 20 Oct 1814, having had issue, six sons and seven daus (of whom the 6th, Henrietta Brayne, *m* her 1st cousin Bushrod Washington — *see below, p* 49).
**4** Anne WASHINGTON, *b* at Wakefield 2 April 1752, *m* 19 Dec 1768, as his 1st wife, Col Burdett Ashton, of Chestnut Hill, Westmoreland County, Virginia, mem Virginia Convention 1788, and mem Virginia Assembly (*b* 21 Nov 1747; *d* in King George County 8 March 1814), son of Charles Ashton, by his wife Sarah Butler, and *d* 3 June 1777, having had issue, two sons and two daus.
**5** Jane WASHINGTON, *b* at Wakefield April 1756, *m* Milbank, King George County, Virginia 1784 Col John Thornton (*b* in Spotsylvania County *ca* 1747; *d* in Culpeper County 20 Jan 1822), son of Francis Thornton, by his wife Frances, dau of Roger Gregory, by his wife Mildred Washington, and *d* at Thornton Hill, Rappahannock County, Virginia Oct 1833, having had issue, two sons and three daus.
**6** William Augustine WASHINGTON, of Wakefield, Westmoreland County, Virginia, Lt-Col 3rd Dragoons, Brig-Gen US Army, *b* at Wakefield 25 Nov 1757, *m* 1st 25 Sept 1777, his half 1st cousin Jane (*b* in Westmoreland County, Virginia 20 June 1759; *d* at Sweet Springs 16 Aug 1791), eldest dau of John Augustine Washington (*see below, p* 55), and had issue,
  (1) Hannah Bushrod WASHINGTON, *b* 7 Aug 1778; *dunm* May 1797.
  (2) Augustine WASHINGTON, *b* 15 June 1780; *d* 9 Feb 1798.
  (3) Ann Aylett WASHINGTON, *b* at Haywood, Westmoreland County 11 Feb 1783, *m* in Westmoreland County 8 Oct 1800, as his 1st wife, her 5th cousin, William

Robinson, of Bunker Hill, Westmoreland County, Virginia (*b* 1 June 1782; *d* 17 Aug 1857), son of William Robinson, by his wife Margaret, dau of Dr Walter Williamson, by his wife Mildred Washington (widow of Langhorne Dade), and *d* at Alexandria, Virginia 12 Sept 1804, having had issue, three children (who all *d* in infancy).
(4) Bushrod WASHINGTON, of Mount Zephyr, *b* at Haywood 4 April 1785, *educ* Harvard, *m* 14 Aug 1806, his 1st cousin Henrietta Brayne (*b* in Spotsylvania County 29 Aug 1786; *d* at Baltimore, Maryland 10 Aug 1869), 6th dau of Gen Alexander Spotswood, by his wife Elizabeth, eldest dau of Augustine Washington (*see above, p 48*), and *d* at Mount Eagle, Fairfax County 16 April 1831, leaving issue.
  1*a* Ann Eliza WASHINGTON, *b* at Mount Zephyr, Fairfax County, Virginia 17 Sept 1807, *m* at Washington, DC 15 March 1831, Rev William Philander Chase Johnson (*b* in Bucks County, Pennsylvania 5 Nov 1806; *d* at Clinton, Louisiana Nov 1852), son of James Johnson, and *d* at Jackson, Mississippi 18 April 1851, having had issue, eight sons and two daus.
  2*a* Jane Mildred WASHINGTON, *b* at Mount Zephyr 25 Nov 1809; *dunm* in Fairfax County, Virginia 19 Sept 1839 (*bur* Mount Vernon).
  3*a* Spotswood Augustine WASHINGTON, of Watseka, Iroquois County, Illinois, *b* at Mount Zephyr 17 July 1811, *m* at Kalamazoo, Michigan 9 April 1837 Evaline Fletcher (*b* at Romney, W Virginia 6 Dec 1815; *d* at Watseka, Illinois 28 Dec 1877) and *d* at Watseka 25 Aug 1865, leaving issue,
    1*b* Bushrod DeLaneau WASHINGTON, of Chicago, Illinois *b* at Kalamazoo, Michigan 20 Sept 1841, *m* at Chicago 12 Aug 1866, Martha Jane (*b* at Macon, Georgia 31 May 1842; *d* at Chicago Oct 1912), dau of Daniel McRae, by his wife Anne Adams, and *d* at Chicago 21 Dec 1918, leaving issue,
      Estella Evaline WASHINGTON, *b* at Chicago 28 Aug 1867, *m* 1st *ca* 1896, Lewis Nieman (*d* at Pittsburgh, Pennsylvania 1913), and had issue, one dau (who *d* young). She *m* 2ndly 22 Feb 1916, John Rudisill Withers (*b* at Chicago; *d* there 25 April 1927), and *d* at Chicago *ca* 1931.
    2*b* James Fletcher WASHINGTON, of Chicago, Illinois, *b* at Kankakee, Illinois 4 July 1846, *m* 1st at Carthage, Jasper County, Illinois 25 Nov 1871, Caroline (*b* in Newton County, Missouri; *d* at Chicago *ca* 1890), dau of Daniel McRae, by his wife Anne Adams, and sister of Mrs Bushrod DeLaneau Washington (*see above*), and had issue,
      1*c* Martha Ella WASHINGTON, *b* at Watseka 17 March 1873, *m* at Chicago Aug 1896, Charles Halden Barnard (*b* at Lafayette, Indiana 12 Oct 1866; *d* at Chicago 10 Oct 1926), and *d* at Pittsburgh, Pennsylvania 12 Jan 1951, having had issue, three sons and two daus.
      2*c* Orra May WASHINGTON, *b* at Chicago 18 Feb 1881; *d* at Watseka 15 July 1883
    James Fletcher Washington *m* 2ndly 29 Dec 1896, Mary R. Bryant, widow of — Horne (*b* in Canada 1859; *d* at Chicago 31 July 1926) and by her had issue,
      3*c* Lee Richardson WASHINGTON, *b* at Chicago 29 July 1897, *m* 1st 1 May 1919 (*m* diss by div 1950), Lucienne Audette (*b* in Ontario, Canada 21 April 1897; *d* 1963), and had issue,
        ●Odelle Lee WASHINGTON, *b* 20 April 1921, *m* 1st 28 Nov 1940 (*m* diss by div 1947), Charles Ketchel. She *m* 2ndly 28 April 1948, ●Ernest Chrest Hanson (*b* 8 Dec 1917) [*111, 145th Avenue, Madeira Beach, Florida, USA*], and has issue,
          1*e* ●Brynda Leigh HANSON, *b* 3 Dec 1948, *m* 23 Dec 1972, ●Michael Kelly.
          2*e* ●Victoria Louise HANSON, *b* 28 March 1954.
      Lee Richardson Washington *m* 2ndly *ca* 1957, Mary Kelly, widow of — English, and *d* at Olma, Florida *ca* 1970
    3*b* William Augustine WASHINGTON, of Kankakee, Illinois, attorney, *b* at Watseka, Illinois July 1849, *m* there 3 July 1872 Louise Jane (*b* in Fountain County, Indiana 14 March 1852; *d* at Kankakee 30 Aug 1927), dau of Ebenezer Hooker, by his wife Marie Hastings,

and *d* at Kankakee 24 March 1913, having had issue
      1*c* Inez Louisa WASHINGTON, *b* at Watseka 18 March 1873, *m* 1st at Kankakee 1894 (*m* diss by div), Dr James Guthrie; and 2ndly at Kankakee 28 June 1905, Thomas Akers Beebe (*b* 12 Oct 1862; *d* Aug 1920), and *dsp* at Kankakee 9 Aug 1955.
      2*c* Evaline Edna WASHINGTON, *b* at Danville, Vermilion County, Illinois 17 Aug 1874; *d* 14 March 1875.
      3*c* Spotswood Corbin WASHINGTON, of Kankakee, Illinois, carpenter and decorator *b* at Danville Illinois 1 Feb 1876, *m* 12 April 1905, Bertha Wilhelmina (*b* at Bonfield, Illinois 7 April 1878; *d* at Quincy, Illinois 16 June 1974), dau of Ludwig Nowack, by his wife Johannah Haase, and *d* at Kankakee 13 May 1948, leaving issue,
        1*d* ●William Augustine WASHINGTON, tool and die and model maker, only surv male line descendant of Augustine Washington's 1st marriage [*Box 243, Aroma Park, Illinois 60910, USA*], *b* at Kankakee 28 Jan 1906, *m* there 11 Nov 1927, Hazel Marie (*b* at Fairmount, Illinois 13 June 1910), dau of Albert A. Craver, by his wife Mary Zettie Myers, and has issue,
          1*e* ●Joyce Eileen WASHINGTON, *b* at Kankakee 26 Oct 1928, *m* there 25 June 1950, ●John C. De Valk (*b* at Chicago 26 Dec 1926) [*Bradley, Illinois, USA*], son of Corneil De Valk, by his wife Florence Brewer, and has issue,
            1*f* ●John C. DE VALK, Jr, *b* 4 Oct 1953.
            2*f* ●Daniel Wayne DE VALK, *b* 19 May 1955.
            3*f* ●Lana Joyce DE VALK, *b* 6 July 1966.
          3*e* ●Inez Gay WASHINGTON, *b* at Kankakee 21 Feb 1934, *m* 27 Sept 1953, ●Ewald Kunde (*b* at Kankakee 30 Aug 1930) [*Bonfield, Illinois, USA*], son of Ewald E. Kunde, by his wife Elsie Pearl Yancey, and has two adopted children,
            1*f* ●Julie Ann KUNDE, *b* 27 July 1963.
            2*f* ●Steven Lee KUNDE, *b* 15 April 1967.
        2*d* ●Florence Evaline WASHINGTON, *b* at Kankakee 14 Aug 1909, *m* at Peotone, Illinois 21 Aug 1930, ●Frederick Henry Nemitz (*b* at Kankakee 14 Dec 1905), son of Frank Nemitz, by his wife Bertha Doberstein, and has issue,
          1*e* ●Gerald Frederick NEMITZ, certified public acct, *b* at Kankakee 26 Dec 1931, *m* ●Janet Hicks.
          2*e* ●Beverly Ann NEMITZ, *b* at Kankakee 10 April 1933, *m* 1st, —; and 2ndly, ●Dale R. Irps [*St Anne, Illinois, USA*].
          3*e* ●William Corbin NEMITZ, *b* at Kankakee 15 Nov 1935, *m* ●Phyllis Lehnus.
      4*c* Fannie Evaline WASHINGTON, *b* at Danville Illinois 22 June 1878, *m* 12 Feb 1904, Robert Gregory Morris (*b* at St. Louis, Missouri 31 Dec 1936), and *dsp* at St Louis, Missouri 26 April 1931.
      5*c* A child, *b* 19 April, *d* 15 Sept 1880.
      6*c* Julia Henrietta WASHINGTON, *b* 17 March, *d* 27 Sept 1884.
      7*c* A child, *d* an inf.
      8*c* A child, *d* an inf.
    4*b* Estella Henrietta WASHINGTON, *b* at Watseka 27 Sept 1852, *m* there 12 Sept 1871, Delbert Brooks Kice (*b* in Illinois 24 March 1851; *d* at Chicago 13 Feb 1892), and *d* at Chicago 18 Feb 1892, having had issue, four sons and three daus.
    5*b* A child, *d* an inf.
    6*b* A child, *d* an inf.
  4*a* Bushrod Corbin WASHINGTON, *b* at Mount Zephyr 14 Dec 1813; *d* ante 1826.
  5*a* George William WASHINGTON, *b* at Mount Zephyr 4 Sept 1816, *educ* West Point, *m* —, and *dsp* between 1850 and 1869
  6*a* John WASHINGTON, *b* at Mount Zephyr 15 Jan 1818; *dunm* between 1839 and 1850.
  7*a* Mary Randolph WASHINGTON, *b* at Mount Zephyr Jan 1819; *d* an inf *ante* 1824.

8*a* Martha D. WASHINGTON, *b* at Mount Zephyr 1821; *d* an inf *ante* 1831 (*bur* at Mount Vernon).
9*a* Mary Henrietta WASHINGTON, *b* 10 May 1824; *dunm* at Watseka, Illinois 30 March 1863.
10*a* Corbin WASHINGTON, *b* 20 April 1826; *dunm* at Georgetown, DC 27 Nov 1871.
11*a* Frances Louisa Augusta WASHINGTON, *b* 17 Feb 1828, *m* 1st 8 Oct 1856, as his 2nd wife, Rev Daniel Motzer (*b* in Pennsylvania *ca* 1818; *d* 1 Nov 1864). She *m* 2ndly 24 April 1872, Myron L. Finch, of Brooklyn, New York (*d ca* 1880), and *dsp* at Georgetown, DC 15 March 1900.
12*a* Hannah Bushrod WASHINGTON, *b* 6 June 1830; *d* an inf (*bur* Mount Vernon).
(5) Corbin Aylett WASHINGTON, *b* at Haywood 11 May 1787; *d* Nov 1788.
(6) George Corbin WASHINGTON, of Wakefield, and later of Dumbarton House, Georgetown, DC, mem Maryland legislature, mem House of Reps, Pres Chesapeake and Ohio Canal Co, *b* at Haywood 20 Aug 1789, *educ* Harvard, *m* 1st at Dumbarton 1 Sept 1807, Elizabeth Ridgely (*b* 22 Nov 1786; *d* Georgetown 1 July 1820), dau and co-heiress of Col Thomas Beall, of Rock of Dumbarton, by his wife Anne Orme, and had issue,
1*a* Thomas Beall Augustine WASHINGTON, *b* 7 June 1808; *d* 2 Feb 1809.
2*a* George Thomas Beall WASHINGTON, *b* 26 Feb 1810; *d* young.
3*a* Augustine Bushrod WASHINGTON, *b* 10 June 1811; *d* 12 Feb 1812.
4*a* Lewis William WASHINGTON, of Beall Air, Jefferson County, Virginia, Col US Army, captured by John Brown during his famous raid on Harper's Ferry, *b* at Georgetown 30 Nov 1812, *m* 1st at Baltimore, Maryland 17 May 1836, Mary Ann (*b* 19 Oct 1817; *d* at Beall Air 16 Nov 1844), dau of James Barroll, of Baltimore, Maryland, by his wife Mary Ann Crockett, and had issue,
  1*b* George Corbin WASHINGTON, *b* at Baltimore 20 March 1837; *d* there 20 Sept 1843.
  2*b* James Barroll WASHINGTON, Major CSA, *b* at Baltimore 26 Aug 1839, *m* at Montgomery, Alabama 23 Feb 1864, Jane Bretney (*b* 15 Feb 1842; *d* at Atlantic City, New Jersey 1 June 1901), widow of Dr Powhatan Bolling Cabell, and dau of Major William Lewis Lanier, by his wife Lucy Elizabeth Virginia Armistead, and *d* at Pittsburgh, Pennsylvania 6 March 1900, having had issue,
    1*c* William Lanier WASHINGTON, Pres and Gen Man Pittsburgh Sheet Steel Mfrg Co, *b* at Montgomery, Alabama 30 March 1865, *m* 1st New York 6 June 1906 (*m* diss by div), May Bruce, (*b* at Louisville, Kentucky 28 June 1873), formerly wife of Lewis Jane Shallcross, and dau of Thomas Brennan, of Louisville, Kentucky, by his wife Anna Virginia Bruce. He *m* 2ndly 7 July 1919 (*m* diss by div), Ida Alice Holland, and by her had issue,
      Winston Lanier WASHINGTON, *b* 6 May 1920; *d* 17 Sept 1921.
    William Lanier Washington *m* 3rdly at St Louis, Missouri 3 July 1923, Augusta Adeline (*b* 18 April 1895), dau of William Koblank, by his wife Elizabeth von Heiser, and *d* 11 Sept 1933.
    2*c* Benjamin Cabell WASHINGTON, *b* at Baltimore 16 Nov 1866; *d* Allegheny, Pennsylvania 23 Sept 1881.
    3*c* Lewis William WASHINGTON, *b* at Baltimore 20 Nov 1869, *m* in London, England 12 Nov 1904 Anne Raymond Cox, and *dsp* at Nice, France 15 May 1906.

4*c* Mary WASHINGTON, *b* at Baltimore 4 Oct 1871; *d* there 25 Aug 1872.
3*b* Mary Ann WASHINGTON, *b* at Baltimore 1 June 1841, *m* there 17 Nov 1864, Henry Irvine Keyser, of Baltimore, Maryland (*b* 17 Dec 1837; *d* 7 May 1916), son of Samuel S. Keyser, by his wife Elizabeth Wyman, and *d* 8 Dec 1931, having had issue, five sons and one dau.
4*b* Eliza Ridgely Beall WASHINGTON, *b* Beall Air 16 Nov 1844, *m* at Baltimore 25 April 1865, Elias Glenn Perine (*b* 14 June 1829; *d* 15 June 1922), son of David Maulden Perine, by his wife Mary —, and *d* 28 Jan 1919, having had issue, six sons and seven daus.
Col Lewis William Washington *m* 2ndly at Clover Lea, Hanover County, Virginia 6 Nov 1860, Ella More (*b* at Eltham, New Kent County, Virginia 7 Sept 1834; *d* at New York 17 Jan 1898), 5th dau of George Washington Bassett, by his wife Betty Burnett, 4th dau of Robert Lewis, 8th son of Col Fielding Lewis, by his wife Betty Washington (*see below, p 51*), and *d* in Jefferson County, Virginia 1 Oct 1871, having by her had issue,
  5*b* Betty Lewis WASHINGTON, *b* at Clover Lea 26 Aug 1861; *d* 25 July 1862.
  6*b* William de Hertburn WASHINGTON, *b* at Clover Lea 29 June 1863; *dunm* at New York 30 Aug 1914.
5*a* Bushrod WASHINGTON, *b* Dec 1814; *d* Aug 1815.
6*a* Harriet Ann Bushrod WASHINGTON, *b* 16 March 1816; *d* 4 Dec 1817.
7*a* Cornelia Adelaide WASHINGTON, *b* March 18—; *d* young.
George Corbin Washington *m* 2ndly 25 Oct 1821, Ann Thomas Beall (*b* at Georgetown 1 May 1800; *d* there 3 Feb 1861), dau of Col John Peter, by his wife Eleanor Orme, and *d* at Georgetown 17 July 1854, having by her had issue,
8*a* Eleanor Ann WASHINGTON, *b* at Georgetown 30 Oct 1822; *dunm* at Georgetown 13 April 1849.
William Augustine Washington *m* 2ndly in Westmoreland County 10 July 1792, his half 1st cousin, Mary (*b* 28 July 1764; *dsp* 2 Nov 1795), eldest dau of Richard Henry Lee, by his 1st wife Anne Aylett. He *m* 3rdly 11 May 1799, Sarah (*b* 5 March 1765; *d* at Princeton, New Jersey 3 Sept 1834), dau of Col John Tayloe, of Mount Airy, Virginia, by his wife Rebecca Plater, and *d* at Georgetown 2 Oct 1810, having by her had issue,
(7) Sarah Tayloe WASHINGTON, *b* at Haywood 14 April 1800, *m* there 26 Oct 1819, Lawrence Washington, of Westmoreland County, Virginia (*b* in Westmoreland County 26 Feb 1791; *d* 15 March 1875), son of Henry Washington, by his wife Sarah West Ashton, and *d* 20 Dec 1886, having had issue, eight sons and three daus.
(8) A son, *b* and *d* 12 April 1803.
(9) William Augustine WASHINGTON, *b* at Haywood 30 Aug 1804, *m* 7 Oct 1823, Juliet Elizabeth (*b* 4 March 1806; *d* 16 Dec 1865), dau of Samuel J. Bayard, of Princeton, New Jersey, and *d* at Haywood 26 June 1830, having had issue,
  1*a* A child, *b* at Washington, DC 28 July, *d* there 30 July 1824.
  2*a* Martha WASHINGTON, *b* 2 Jan 1826; *d* 21 Feb 1828.
  3*a* William Augustine WASHINGTON, *b* 15 April 1828; *d* 21 Feb 1833.
  4*a* Julia Augusta WASHINGTON, *b* at Princeton, New Jersey 1 Sept 1830, *m* 19 Nov 1855, Dabney Carr Wirt (*b* in Richmond County, Virginia 2 March 1817; *d* in Westmoreland County 27 March 1893), son of William Wirt, and *dsp* 24 April 1888.
7 George WASHINGTON, *b* at Wakefield *ca* 1760; *dunm* March 1781.
4 Jane WASHINGTON, *b* at Bridge's Creek, Virginia 1722; *d* 17 Jan 1734/5.

**B:** FULL BROTHERS AND SISTERS OF PRESIDENT WASHINGTON

**5** Betty WASHINGTON, *b* at Wakefield, Westmoreland County, Virginia 20 June 1733, *m* 7 May 1750, as his 2nd wife, Col Fielding Lewis, of Kenmore, Fredericksburg, Virginia (*b* at Warner Hall, Gloucester County, Virginia 7 July 1725; *d* at Fredericksburg, Virginia Dec 1781), son of John Lewis, by his wife Frances Fielding, and *d* at Western View, Culpeper County, Virginia 31 March 1797, having had issue, nine sons and two daus. Her 4th son, Major George Lewis, of Marmion, King George County (1757-1821), *m* Catherine Daingerfield, and had, with other issue, Mary Willis Lewis (1781-1834), who *m* Col Byrd Charles Willis (1781-1846), and had, with other issue, Catherine Daingerfield Willis (1803-1867), who *m* 1st, Atchison Gray, and 2ndly 1826, Napoléon-Achille Murat (1801-1847), the eldest son of Joachim Murat, King of Naples, and nephew of Napoléon. Betty Washington Lewis's 7th son, Lawrence Lewis (1767-1839), *m* Eleanor Parke Custis, the grand-dau of Martha Washington, and had issue (*see above, p 43*); and her 8th son, Robert Lewis (1769-1829), was the grandfather of Ella More Bassett, the 2nd wife of Lewis William Washington (*see above, p 50*).

**6** Samuel WASHINGTON, of Harewood, Jefferson County, Virginia, Col Virginia Militia, JP and High Sheriff, *b* at Wakefield, Westmoreland County, Virginia 16 Nov 1734, *m* 1st *ca* 1754, Jane (*dsp ca* 1755), dau of Col John Champe, of Lamb's Creek, King George County, Virginia. He *m* 2ndly *ca* 1756, Mildred (*b ca* 1741; *d ca* 1762), dau of Col John Thornton, of Caroline County, Virginia, by his wife Mildred, dau and co-heiress of Roger Gregory, by his wife Mildred, dau of Capt Lawrence Washington (*see above, p 39*), and by her had issue,

  **1** Thornton WASHINGTON, *b* in Stafford County *ca* 1758, *m* 1st in Charles County, Maryland 26 Dec 1779, his 4th cousin, Mildred (*b ca* 1760; *d ca* 1785), dau of Thomas Berry, by his wife Elizabeth Washington, and had issue,

    (1) Thomas Berry WASHINGTON, *b ca* 1780; *d* 1794.

    (2) John Thornton Augustine WASHINGTON, of Cedar Lawn, Jefferson County, Virginia, *b* in Berkeley County 20 May 1783, *m* at Shepherdstown 24 Sept 1810, Elizabeth Conrad (*b* at Shepherdstown 27 Sept 1793; *d* at Cedar Lawn 21 Oct 1837), dau of Major Daniel Bedinger, by his wife Sarah Rutherford, and sister of Hon Henry Bedinger, US Min to Denmark, and *d* at Cedar Lawn 9 Oct 1841, having had issue,

      1*a* Lawrence Berry WASHINGTON, lawyer, author and poet, served as Lieut Virginia Militia in Mexican War, *b* at Cedar Lawn 26 Nov 1811; *dunm* in Missouri 21 Sept 1856.

      2*a* Daniel Bedinger WASHINGTON, Col CSA, *b* at Cedar Lawn 8 Feb 1814, *m* at Harper's Ferry, Virginia 24 Oct 1843, his 1st cousin Lucy Anne (*b* 9 Dec 1811; *d* 22 Aug 1885), widow of Dr John James Wharton, and dau of Samuel Washington (*see below, p 52*), and *d* 28 Dec 1887, having had issue,

        1*b* Samuel Thornton WASHINGTON, *b* at Cedar Lawn 23 Dec 1844; *d* at Buffalo, Putnam County, W Virginia 15 Nov 1850.

        2*b* Catharine Townsend WASHINGTON, *b* at Cedar Lawn 11 Sept 1846; *dunm* at Garden City, Cass County, Missouri 27 Oct 1919.

        3*b* Elizabeth Bedinger WASHINGTON, *b* at Red House, Putnam County, W Virginia 3 Sept 1848, *m* at Index, Cass County, Missouri 26 May 1881, Clark Craig (*b* at Buffalo, Putnam County, W Virginia 20 Oct 1837; *d* there 15 May 1904), and *d* at Poca, Putnam County, W Virginia 28 Oct 1931, leaving issue, one son and two daus.

        4*b* Thornton Augustine WASHINGTON, of St Louis, Missouri, *b* at Buffalo, Putnam County, W Virginia 23 April 1854; *dunm* at Garden City, Missouri 10 Aug 1935.

        5*b* Marian Wallace WASHINGTON, *b* at Otterville, Johnson County, Missouri 17 June 1856; *dunm* in Cass County, Missouri 18 July 1948.

      3*a* Virginia Thornton WASHINGTON, *b* at Cedar Lawn 22 May 1816; *dunm* in Jefferson County, Virginia 13 Nov 1838.

      4*a* Sarah Eleanor WASHINGTON, *b* at Cedar Lawn 7 April 1818; *dunm* in Cass County, Missouri 21 Jan 1858.

      5*a* Benjamin Franklin WASHINGTON, author, Collector of the Port of San Francisco, *b* at Cedar Lawn 17 April 1820, *m* at Charles Town, Virginia 22 Oct 1845, Georgianna Hite (*b* in Jefferson County *ca* 1822; *d* at San Francisco, California 3 Dec 1860), dau of James Lackland Ransom, by his wife Frances Madison Hite, niece of President Madison (*see p 140*), and *d* at San Francisco, California 22 Jan 1872, having had issue,

        1*b* John Thornton WASHINGTON, *b* at Charles Town 26 July 1846; *dunm* at San Francisco 22 Feb 1929.

        2*b* Franklin Bedinger WASHINGTON, *b* at Charles Town 13 June 1848, *m* at Mill Valley, California 14 June 1898, Alice Maria Bacon (*b* at San Francisco 30 Oct 1858; *d* at Palo Alto, California 25 April 1939), and *d* at Oakland, California 12 May 1915, leaving issue,

          ●Lawrence WASHINGTON, *present senior representative of President George Washington [Palo Alto, California, USA]*, *b* at San Francisco, California 30 May 1899, *m* at Berkeley, California 24 Jan 1942, ●Eileen Louise McCall (*b* at Portland, Oregon 6 Sept 1907), and has issue,

            ●Margot Elise WASHINGTON, *b* at Berkeley, California 9 Nov 1942, *m* 22 Nov 1962, ●David Clarence Hall (*b* 18 May 1939), and has issue,

              1*e*●Daniel Lawrence Washington HALL, *b* 14 June 1963.

              2*e*●Wendy Lynn HALL, *b* 24 Feb 1965.

              3*e*●Timothy David HALL, *b* 29 March 1966.

        3*b* Fanny Madison WASHINGTON, *b* at San Francisco 13 Aug 1853, *m* there 8 April 1876, Capt Daniel Delehany, USN (*b* 12 Dec 1845; *d* 2 Feb 1918), and *d* 4 June 1930, having had issue, three sons and four daus (*see* ADDENDUM).

        4*b* Lillian WASHINGTON, *b* at San Francisco 12 July 1856; *d* at Charlestown 26 March 1857.

        5*b* Bertha James WASHINGTON, *b* at San Francisco 2 March 1858, *m* 1st 8 Sept 1880, Sherwood Callaghan (*d* in London, England *ca* 1890), and had issue, four daus. She *m* 2ndly in London, England *ca* 1891, William Robert Sullivan (*b* 14 Dec 1860; *d* at Los Angeles Feb 1916), and *d* 29 June 1935.

  6*a* Georgeanna Augusta WASHINGTON, *b* at Cedar Lawn 3 March 1822, *m* there 20 Nov 1851, Col John Wheeler Smith, US Army (*b* 14 May 1825; *d* 23 Dec 1892), son of Samuel Mansfield Smith, by his wife Eliza —, and *d* at Little Rock, Arkansas 26 Oct 1895, leaving issue, two sons and three daus.

  7*a* Mary Elizabeth WASHINGTON, *b* at Cedar Lawn 11 March 1824, *m* in Johnson County, Missouri 17 Aug 1858, Squire Asbury (*b* 16 March 1821; *d* 10 March 1896), and *d* at Pleasant Grove, Arkansas 3 March 1898, having had issue, one son and two daus.

  8*a* Thornton Augustine WASHINGTON, Major and Assist Adjt-Gen CSA, *b* at Cedar Lawn 22 Jan 1826, *m* at San Antonio, Texas 8 March 1860, Olive Ann (*b* at Detroit, Michigan 8 Sept 1839; *d* at Washington, DC 1 April 1922), dau of Enoch Jones, by his wife Olive Ann —, and *d* at Washington, DC 10 July 1894, leaving issue,

      1*b* Flora Mary WASHINGTON, *b* at Indianola, Texas 1 May 1861; *dunm* at Washington, DC 17 June 1927.

      2*b* George Thornton WASHINGTON, *b* at San Antonio, Texas 13 April 1863, *m* 13 Dec 1889, Catherine La Vallee (*b* at New Orleans, Louisiana 24 Feb 1865; *d* there Nov 1953), and *dsp* at New Orleans 11 Oct 1938.

      3*b* Lee Howard WASHINGTON (dau), *b* at San Antonio, Texas 17 April 1865; *dunm* at Washington, DC 3 Oct 1930.

      4*b* Sarah WASHINGTON, *b* at San Antonio, Texas 12 April 1867; *dunm* 27 Dec 1909.

      5*b* Lawrence Berry WASHINGTON, *b* at San Antonio, Texas 23 July 1869, *m* 8 Oct 1908, Ruth Bird, and *dsp* at Tulsa, Oklahoma 16 Aug 1919.

      6*b* Olive Ann WASHINGTON, *b* at Galveston, Texas 12 Sept 1875, *m* at Washington, DC 5 Sept 1905, Frank Coburn (*b* 21 May 1862; *d* June 1954), having had issue, one son and one dau.

      7*b* Elizabeth WASHINGTON, *b* 17 March 1877, *m* at

Washington, DC 8 Oct 1902, Vernon Goldsborough Owen (*b* at Gaithersburg, Maryland 1 May 1879; *d* at Washington, DC 20 Feb 1944), and *d* at Washington, DC 8 May 1963, having had issue, one son and one dau.

9*a* Mildred Berry WASHINGTON, *b* at Cedar Lawn 3 Sept, *d* there 12 Sept 1827.

10*a* Mildred Berry WASHINGTON, *b* at Cedar Lawn 28 March 1829, *m* there 8 Feb 1854, Solomon Singleton Bedinger (*d* 8 Feb 1873), son of Henry Clay Bedinger, by his 2nd wife Judith Singleton, and *d* at Lewisburg, Conway County, Arkansas 8 Nov 1871, having had issue, three sons and two daus.

11*a* George WASHINGTON, Judge of Johnson County, Missouri, *b* at Cedar Lawn 9 Dec 1830, *m* at Otterville, Johnson County, Missouri 11 April 1871, Mary Virginia (*b* in Cooper County, Maryland 23 May 1844; *d* 1931), dau of William Rowland Dempsey, by his wife Mahala —, and *d* 20 Nov 1890, having had issue,

   1*b* Robert WASHINGTON, *b* at Centerview, Johnson County, Missouri 17 March 1872; *d* an inf.

   2*b* Mary Virginia WASHINGTON, *b* at Centerview 14 July 1873; *d* there 24 April 1882.

   3*b* Vernon de Hertburn WASHINGTON, *b* at Centerview 27 July 1876; *dunm* at Eldorado Springs, Missouri 23 Aug 1941.

12*a* Susan Ellsworth WASHINGTON, *b* at Cedar Lawn 1 April 1833, *m* 22 May 1857, Henry Clay Bedinger, of Lewis County, Kentucky (*b* 5 Sept 1832; *d* 27 July 1908), son of Henry Clay Bedinger, by his 2nd wife Judith Singleton, and *d* 28 July 1893, having had issue, three sons and five daus.

13*a* Henrietta Gray WASHINGTON, *b* at Cedar Lawn 10 Sept 1835; *d* 18 Dec 1838.

Thornton Washington *m* 2ndly in King George County 2 April 1786, his 4th cousin Frances Townshend (*b* 18 April 1767; *m* 2ndly in King George County 14 June 1788, Col Griffin Stith, and *d ante* 1808), dau of Lawrence Washington, by his wife Elizabeth Dade and *d* in Berkeley County 1787, having by her had issue,

   (3) Samuel WASHINGTON, of Delraine, Culpeper County, Virginia, and Newport, Kentucky, *b* in Berkeley County 14 Feb 1787, *m* his 2nd cousin Catherine Townshend (*b* 25 Aug 1790; *d* at Delhi, Hamilton County, Ohio 4 Sept 1869), dau of John Washington, by his wife Martha Massey, and *d* at Delhi, Hamilton County, Ohio 18 March 1867, leaving issue,

   1*a* Lucy Anna WASHINGTON, *b* in Culpeper County, Virginia 9 Dec 1811, *m* 1st in Culpeper County 2 April 1834, Dr John James Wharton, of Greenville, Culpeper County (*b* in London, England 1807; *d* at St Louis, Missouri *ca* 1839), son of Dr John Wharton, by his wife Ann — (widow of — Abbott), and had issue, one son and one dau. She *m* 2ndly 24 Oct 1843, Daniel Bedinger Washington (*b* 8 Feb 1814; *d* 28 Dec 1887), 2nd son of John Thornton Augustine Washington, by his 1st wife Elizabeth Conrad Bedinger, and *d* at Index, Cass County, Missouri 22 Aug 1885, having had further issue (*see above, p* 51).

   2*a* John Thornton Augustine WASHINGTON, commission merchant in Memphis, Tennessee and Newport, Kentucky, *b* in Virginia 1812, *m* at Lexington, Fayette County, Kentucky 20 Jan 1839, Adelaide Josephine (*b ca* 1822; *d* at Newport, Kentucky 13 April 1893), dau of Thomas Tibbatts, of Lexington, and *d* at Newport, Kentucky 8 May 1888, having had issue,

   1*b* Mary Elizabeth WASHINGTON, *b* 23 Nov 1839; *dunm* post 1866.

   2*b* Elizabeth WASHINGTON, *b* at Newport, Kentucky 15 March 1842, *m* in Campbell County, Kentucky 18 June 1862, Col John Barry Taylor, of Newport, Kentucky (*b ca* 1837; *d* at Newport 22 Dec 1914), and *dsp* at Newport 22 May 1917.

   3*b* Francis Townsend WASHINGTON, *b* 14 Oct 1844(?), *m* Josephine Russell (*d* at Englewood, New Jersey 7 July 1930), and *dsp* 6 Nov 1917.

   4*b* John Thornton WASHINGTON, of St Louis, Missouri, *b* 14 Oct 1852, *m* 1886, Agatha (*b* at Baltimore, Maryland *ca* 1863; *d* at Cincinnati, Ohio 17 Dec 1941), dau of Jerome Bonaparte Timmonds, by his wife Kathryn Ayers, and *d* at London Bridge,

Princess Anne County, Virginia 30 Jan 1910, having had issue,

   1*c* ● Betty WASHINGTON, *b* at St Louis, Missouri 23 May 1892, *m* at Newport, Kentucky, her 2nd cousin Dr Herbert Hoffman Truesdell (*b* in Campbell County, Kentucky 8 Feb 1873; *d* at Newport, Kentucky 9 June 1963), son of George Fletcher Truesdell, by his wife Lucy Ella, dau of George Washington Carmack, by his wife Martha Dandridge Washington, and has issue,

   ● Patricia TRUESDELL, *b* 20 Feb 1922, *m* ● Kenneth Davis, and has issue,

   ● A dau.

   2*t* John Taylor WASHINGTON, *d* aged 18.

   3*c* Adelaide Estelle WASHINGTON, *b* at St Louis, Missouri 16 Oct 1906; *dunm* 14 March 1942.

   5*b* Florence May WASHINGTON, *b* at Newport, Kentucky 8 May 1856; *dunm* 15 July 1926.

3*a* Frances T. WASHINGTON, *b ca* 1813; *dunm* at Delraine, Culpeper County, Virginia June 1830.

4*a* George WASHINGTON, of Newport, Kentucky, steamboat captain, *b* at Culpeper Courthouse, Virginia 2 Jan 1815(?), *m* 1st 28 Sept 1837, Mary Elizabeth (*b* 4 March 1814; *d* at Covington, Kentucky 12 Jan 1839), dau of Benjamin Wharton, by his wife Elizabeth Finney Gray, and had issue,

   1*b* Thomas Wharton WASHINGTON, *b* 1 Jan, *d* 20 Aug 1839.

Capt George Washington *m* 2ndly in Campbell County, Kentucky 10 May 1842, Martha Ann (*b* in Ohio *ca* 1823; *d* 1876), dau of John Doxon, by his wife Elizabeth Nolan, and *d* at Newport, Kentucky 1857, having by her had issue,

   2*b* George WASHINGTON, lawyer, of Knoxville, Tennessee and Newport, Kentucky, Chm of Kentucky Constitutional Convention of 1890, *b* at Newport, Kentucky 25 Dec 1843, *m* at Memphis, Tennessee 1867, Jane Todd (*b* in Tennessee 6 Oct 1847; *d* in Texas 29 Oct 1924), dau of Dr Francis Alexander Ramsey, by his wife Anne Maria Breck, and *d* at Newport, Kentucky 23 Aug 1905, having had issue,

   1*c* Ramsey WASHINGTON, County Attorney of Campbell, Newport, Kentucky, *b* at Memphis, Tennessee 4 Feb 1869, *m* 1st 27 Dec 1897, Eunice E. Barbee, of Ohio. He *m* 2ndly, Ida M. Hughes, and *dsp* 19 Sept 1923.

   2*c* Bushrod WASHINGTON, *b* May(?) 1870; *d ante* 1877.

   3*c* Anne Lee WASHINGTON, *b* at Knoxville, Tennessee 6 Oct 1872, *m* 14 Sept 1904, Ezekiel Field Clay, Jr, of Lexington, Kentucky (*b* 16 June 1871; *d* 1915), son of Col Ezekiel Field Clay, by his wife Mary Letitia Woodford (and great-great-great-grandson of Gen William Woodford and Mary Thornton, his wife, who was dau of John Thornton and Mildred Gregory, dau of Roger Gregory and Mildred Washington), and *d* 1922, leaving issue, one son.

   4*c* Alfred Rogers WASHINGTON, *b* at Knoxville, Tennessee 24 Feb 1876, *m* 17 March 1904, Katherine Montgomery Lucas, of Paris, Kentucky, and *dsp* at San Francisco 1925.

   5*c* William Morrow WASHINGTON (Rev), Rector of St Thomas's Episcopal Church, Detroit, Michigan, *b* at Knoxville, Tennessee 7 June 1877, *m* in Texas 25 June 1902, Janet Margaret Thomas (*b* at Newport, Kentucky 25 June 1877; *d* at Washington, DC 21 April 1954), and *d* 6 Feb 1942, having had issue,

   1*d* Janet WASHINGTON, *b* 1907; *d* an inf 1907 or 1908.

   2*d* Judge George Thomas WASHINGTON, Prof of Law, Cornell Univ, Ithaca, New York, Assist Solicitor-Gen of USA, Judge US Circuit Court of Appeals for Dist of Columbia, *b* in Ohio 24 June 1908, *educ* Yale, and Oxford Univ (Rhodes Scholar), *m* 18 July 1953, ● Helen Goodner (*b* 17 June 1909), and *dsp* at Santa Barbara, California 21 Aug 1971.

   3*d* Katherine Elizabeth WASHINGTON, *b* in

Ohio 10 Oct 1909, *m* ● Donald Bertram Scheurer [*204 Garden Court, Falls Church, Virginia, USA*], and has issue,

    1*e* ● Janet Washington SCHEURER, *b* 12 Feb 1942.

    2*e* ● Andrea M. SCHEURER, *b* 16 July 1947.

6*c* Elizabeth Taylor WASHINGTON, *b* at Knoxville, Tennessee 17 Sept 1878; *dunm* 4 May 1895.

7*c* John WASHINGTON, *d* an inf.

3*b* Alice WASHINGTON, *b* 17 July 1846, *m* Gettys Scott, Prin of Sch for Deaf Mutes, Austin, Texas, and *d* 1901, leaving issue, six children.

4*b* Ernest WASHINGTON, *b* 14 May 1849; *d* 23 June 1852.

5*a* Martha Dandridge WASHINGTON, *b* in Virginia Aug 1817, *m* 1st in Culpeper County, Virginia 1832, Allen Thomas Johnson, and had issue, one son. She *m* 2ndly, in Campbell County, Kentucky, 14 May 1838, George Washington Carmack (*b* nr Knoxville, Tennessee June 1812; *d* at Alexandria, Campbell County, Kentucky April 1895), and *d* 18 May 1881, having had further issue, five sons and two daus.

6*a* Marion W. WASHINGTON, *b* in Culpeper County, Virginia 19 March 1819, *m* in Hamilton County, Ohio 11 May 1854, Dr John M. Mackenzie (*b* in Columbiana County, Ohio 14 March 1816; *d* at Delhi, Ohio 20 April 1891), son of James Mackenzie, by his wife Ellen Burrowes, and *dsp* at Delhi, Ohio 15 Jan 1889.

7*a* Maria WASHINGTON, *b* 1823, *m* in Campbell County, Kentucky 17 March 1847, James E. Perry, of Newport, Kentucky, and *d* at Newport 1901, having had issue two sons and five daus.

8*a* John Francis WASHINGTON, of Memphis, Tennessee, *b* in Virginia *ca* 1826, *m* in Hamilton County, Ohio 28 June 1854, Eleanor B. Mackenzie (*b* in Ohio *ca* 1837; *d* at Memphis, Tennessee 5 Oct 1878), and *d* at Memphis, Tennessee 23 Sept 1897, having had issue,

    1*b* Mary WASHINGTON, *b* at Alexandria, Campbell County, Kentucky 7 April 1855, *m* William M. Carr (*b* *ca* 1849; *d* 16 March 1900), and *d* 31 Oct 1937, having had issue, two daus.

    2*b* George WASHINGTON, *b* in Kentucky *ca* 1857; *dunm* 3 Nov 1888.

    3*b* Vernon Delraine WASHINGTON, *d* an inf.

9*a* Catherine Townshend WASHINGTON, *b* in Culpeper County, Virginia 20 April 1834, *m* at Newport, Kentucky 23 April 1855, James Bausman Duke (*b* *ca* 1827; *d* *ca* 1866), son of Dr Alexander Duke, by his wife Mary Mackall Broome, and *d* at St Louis, Missouri 30 Nov 1916, leaving issue one son and two daus.

10*a* Ella WASHINGTON, *d* young.

11*a* A child, *d* young.

12*a* A child, *d* young.

13*a* A child, *d* young.

2 Tristram WASHINGTON, *b* *ca* 1760; *d* ante 1768.

Col Samuel Washington *m* 3rdly *ca* 1762, Louisa (*b* 29 June 1743; *dsp* *ca* 1763), dau of Nathaniel Chapman, of Fairfax County, Virginia by his wife Constantia Pearson. He *m* 4thly 24 March 1764, Anne (*b* 10 Oct 1737; *d* at Harewood 14 March 1777), widow of Willoughby Allerton, of The Narrows, and dau of Col James Steptoe, of Homing Hall, by his 1st wife, and by her had issue,

3 Ferdinand WASHINGTON, *b* in Stafford County, Virginia 15 July 1767, *m* —, and *dsp* in Lancaster County, Virginia Feb 1788.

4 Frederick Augustus WASHINGTON, *b* in Stafford County, Virginia 4 June 1768; *d* there 23 April 1770.

5 Lucinda WASHINGTON, *b* in Stafford County, Virginia 29 Nov 1769; *d* at Harewood 3 Nov 1770.

6 George Steptoe WASHINGTON, of Harewood, *b* at Harewood 17 Aug 1771, *m* at Philadelphia 20 May 1793, Lucy (*b* in Hanover County, Virginia *ca* 1772; *m* 2ndly at the White House, Washington, DC 29 March 1812, Hon Thomas Todd, Assoc Justice, US Supreme Court; *d* at Megwillie, Jefferson County 29 Jan 1846), dau of John Payne, of Philadelphia, by his wife Mary Coles, and sister of Mrs James Madison (*see p 138*), and *d* at Augusta, Georgia 10 Jan 1809, having had issue,

    (1) George WASHINGTON, *b* at Harewood *ca* 1795; *d* an inf.

    (2) Samuel Walter WASHINGTON, MD, of Harewood, *b* at Harewood 20 March 1797, *m* at Philadelphia 3 Aug 1820, Louisa (*b* 4 Sept 1805; *d* 14 Feb 1882), dau of Thomas Green Clemson, of Philadelphia, by his wife Elizabeth Baker, and *d* at Harewood 12 Oct 1831, having had issue,

    1*a* A son, *b* and *d* 23 Jan 1822.

    2*a* Lucy Elizabeth WASHINGTON, *b* at Harewood 2 July 1823, *m* at Baltimore, Maryland 3 March 1840, John William Bainbridge Packett (*b* 18 Feb 1817; *d* at Locust Hill, Jefferson County 18 Nov 1872), son of John Packett, by his wife Fanny Hammond, and *d* 14 April 1881, having had issue, three sons and three daus.

    3*a* George Lafayette WASHINGTON, of Harewood, Jefferson County, W Virginia, and of Claymont, Delaware *b* at Harewood 12 Jan 1825, *m* at Claymont, Delaware 29 April 1859, Anna Bull (*b* 18 June 1833; *m* 2ndly, Samuel Roberts; *d* 28 June 1914), dau of Rev John Baker Clemson, by his 1st wife Margaretta Jacobs Bull, and *d* at Siegfried's Bridge, Pennsylvania 7 Feb 1872, having had issue,

        1*b* Margaretta WASHINGTON, medical artist, illustrator of medical textbooks, *b* 11 June 1860; *dunm* 11 Jan 1917.

        2*b* Louisa Clemson WASHINGTON, *b* 29 April 1862; *d* June 1864.

        3*b* John Clemson WASHINGTON, *b* 5 Jan 1865; *d* 1 Oct 1881.

        4*b* Martha WASHINGTON, of Philadelphia, Herald of Plantagenet Soc, *b* 29 Aug 1867; *dunm* 13 Aug 1956.

        5*b* Anne Harewood WASHINGTON, *b* 26 Nov 1869, *m* 6 June 1906, as his 2nd wife Edwin Fairfax Naulty (*b* 16 March 1869), and *d* 3 Jan 1951, leaving issue, one dau.

        6*b* Elizabeth Fisher WASHINGTON, artist, painter of miniatures and landscapes, Regent Gen of National Soc of Magna Carta Dames, *b* 20 Dec 1871; *dunm* 30 Aug 1953.

    4*a* Christian Maria WASHINGTON, *b* at Harewood 16 Dec 1826, *m* at Philadelphia 20 Nov 1844, Richard Scott Blackburn Washington (*b* 12 Nov 1822; *d* at Charlestown 15 Oct 1910), yst son of John Augustine Washington, of Mount Vernon, by his wife Jane Charlotte Blackburn, and *d* 10 June 1895, having had issue (*see below, p 57*).

    5*a* Annie Steptoe Clemson WASHINGTON, *b* at Harewood 8 Sept 1831, *m* at Philadelphia 17 Oct 1854, Thomas Augustus Brown, of Charlestown, W Virginia (*b* at Charlestown 20 Dec 1822; *d* 23 May 1909), son of William Brown, by his wife Elizabeth Forrest, and *d* 19 July 1911, having had issue, one son and five daus.

(3) William Temple WASHINGTON, of Megwillie, Jefferson County, and of Inglewood, Stafford County *b* at Harewood 16 July 1800, *m* at Lexington, Kentucky 3 Aug 1821, Margaret Calhoun (*b* at Lexington 1805; *d* at Falmouth, Stafford County, Virginia 9 Jan 1865), dau of Gen Thomas Fletcher (son of Charles-François-Joseph, Comte de Fléchir), by his wife Margaret Calhoun, and *d* in Stafford County 20 April 1877, having had issue,

    1*a* Lucy WASHINGTON, *b* at Lexington, Kentucky 8 Oct 1822; *d* 17 Oct 1825.

    2*a* Millissent Fowler WASHINGTON, *b* in Bath County, Kentucky 4 Aug 1824, *m* at Megwillie, Jefferson County 10 Dec 1840, Robert Grier McPherson (*b* in Maryland 26 March 1819; *d* 13 Nov 1899), son of Robert Grier McPherson, by his wife Maria —, and *d* 17 Nov 1893, having had issue, four sons and four daus.

    3*a* William Temple WASHINGTON, *b* at Lexington, Kentucky 7 Jan 1827, *m* 1846, Lucy Herndon (*b* *ca* 1829; *d* in Indiana 1850), and *dsp*.

    4*a* Thomas West WASHINGTON, *b* at Megwillie 17 March 1829; *dunm* in Missouri 12 April 1849.

    5*a* Jean Charlotte WASHINGTON, *b* at Megwillie 29 June 1834, *m* at Falmouth, Stafford County 12 April 1868, Thomas Gascoigne Moncure (*b* at Fork 26 Feb 1837; *d* 5 July 1906), son of Richard Cassius Lee Moncure, by his wife Mary Butler Washington Conway, and *d* 2 Aug 1916, having had issue, three sons and one dau.

    6*a* Eugenia Scholay WASHINGTON, First Mem and Registrar-Gen DAR *b* at Megwillie 24 June 1838; *dunm* at Washington, DC 30 Nov 1900.

    7*a* Ferdinand Steptoe WASHINGTON, *b* at Megwillie 22 Jan 1843; *dunm* in Arkansas 22 Aug 1912.

(4) George Steptoe WASHINGTON, *b* at Harewood 15 Oct 1806, *m* at Frankfort, Kentucky 2 May 1827, Gabriella Augusta (*b* in Bourbon County, Kentucky 25 Jan 1810; *m* 2ndly, Col Leo Tarleton; *d post* 1898), dau of Thomas Wyatt Hawkins, by his wife Ann Eleanor Gerrard, and *dsp* at Belvidere, Jefferson County 13 Oct 1831.

7 Lawrence Augustine WASHINGTON, *b* at Harewood 11 April 1774, *m* at Winchester 6 Nov 1797, Mary Dorcas (*b* 6 Nov 1781; *d* in Ohio County, (W) Virginia 9 Nov 1835), dau of Robert Wood, by his wife Comfort Welch, and *d* in Ohio County 15 Feb 1824, leaving issue,

(1) Robert Wood WASHINGTON, *b* at Winchester, Frederick County, Virginia 1808; *dunm* in Ohio County 1843.

(2) Emma Tell WASHINGTON, *b* at Red House Shoals, Mason County, Virginia 22 Sept 1812; *dunm* 1838.

(3) Lawrence Augustine WASHINGTON, MD, *b* at Red House Shoals, Mason County, Virginia 3 Dec 1814, *m* at Charleston, Kanawha County, Virginia 21 Nov 1839, Martha Dickinson Shrewsbury (*b* at Charleston, Kanawha County, Virginia 16 March 1820; *d* at Denison, Texas 29 July 1891), and *d* at Denison, Texas 11 Aug 1882, having had issue,

1*a* Lawrence Augustine WASHINGTON, *b* in Kanawha County, Virginia 21 March 1841; *d* at Denison, Texas 20 Aug 1852.

2*a* Walter Good WASHINGTON, *b* in Mason County, (W) Virginia 21 Feb 1843, *m* at Silver Cliff, Colorado 4 March 1885, Olive Eleanor Lawrence (*b* at Rock Island, Illinois 10 July 1857; *d* at Pueblo, Colorado 14 Sept 1894), and *d* at Guerida, Colorado 2 April 1904, having had issue,

1*b* A son, *d* an inf.

2*b* A dau, *d* an inf.

3*b* ● Winifred Lee WASHINGTON [*469 Lucas Avenue, Los Angeles, California, USA*], *b* at Silver Cliff, Colorado 6 Aug 1889, *m* 1st 10 Jan 1906 (*m* diss by div 1915), William Charles Falkenberg (*b* 25 July 1870), and has had issue,

Walter Washington FALKENBERG, *b* 8 Oct 1907; *dunm* 25 Dec 1929.

She *m* 2ndly 24 Feb 1931, Robert Scott Wheatley (*b* 21 April 1889).

4*b* ● Anna Louise WASHINGTON [*469 Lucas Avenue, Los Angeles, California, USA*], *b* 27 April 1891, *m* 1st 1915, James Henry Fitzpatrick (*b* 1880; *d* 11 Nov 1928); and 2ndly 15 June 1941, Albert Henry Lybarger (*b* 12 Nov 1887; *d* 31 Jan 1947).

3*a* John Shrewsbury WASHINGTON, *b* at Mason County, W Virginia 27 April 1845; *dunm* at Denison, Texas 1 Aug 1898.

4*a* James Turner WASHINGTON, of Proctor, Texas, *b* in Mason County, W Virginia 3 March 1847, *m* at Brownwood, Brown County, Texas 29 Nov 1874, Josephine Clara (*b* in Indiana 4 Feb 1857; *d* at Procter, Texas 1 Nov 1943), dau of — Burroughs, by his wife Mary Jane Hines, and *d* at Procter, Texas 1 May 1926, having had issue,

1*b* Martha WASHINGTON, *b* in Comanche County, Texas 6 Nov 1875, *m* 1st 22 July 1896, William Edgar McCampbell (*b* 12 Aug 1865; *d* 28 Feb 1904), and had issue, one son and one dau. She *m* 2ndly 12 June 1917, Richard Francis Moore (*b* 1 March 1861; *d* 6 May 1921), and *d* at Dallas, Texas 1961.

2*b* A son, *b* and *d* 19 May 1878.

3*b* Mary Estelle WASHINGTON, *b* at Denison, Texas 21 July 1879, *m* 1st 23 March 1902, Dr John Wilson Roark (*b* in Tennessee 29 May 1872; *d* 17 Dec 1938), and had issue, one child who *d* an inf. She *m* 2ndly 22 Oct 1947, James S. Hair (*b* at Bartlett, Texas 15 June 1878; *d* April 1954).

4*b* Wood Elliot WASHINGTON, *b* at Procter, Texas 23 Feb 1882, *m* 1st 2 July 1904 (*m* diss by div *ca* 1917), Amos Hardin Plummer (*b* 14 March 1873), and had issue, one son and one dau. She *m* 2ndly 15 May 1944, Charles Kincaid (*b* at Wallace, Harris County, W Virginia, 8 Feb 1875; *d* Feb 1951), and *d* at Abilene, Texas 1955.

5*b* Frances Marion WASHINGTON, *b* at Procter, Texas 23 March, *d* there 12 Nov 1885.

6*b* James Turner WASHINGTON, of Procter, Texas, *b*

there 20 May 1887; *dunm* there 1950.

7*b* George Patrick WASHINGTON, of Denton, Texas, *b* at Procter, Texas 7 Oct 1890, *m* at Dallas, Texas 6 June 1920, ● Arlee Myrtle (*b* at Lewisville, Texas 8 June 1897) [*649 Elm Street, Hurst, Texas, USA*], dau of Isaac Emery, by his wife Annette Ratliff, and *d* at Hurst, Texas 1965, leaving issue,

1*c* ● Shirley Annette WASHINGTON, *b* at Roanoke, Texas 2 Aug 1921, *m* 14 Feb 1941 (*m* diss by div), Jack Scott (*b* 1 March 1921), and has issue,

1*d* ● Suzanne SCOTT, *b* 29 June 1944, *m*, and has issue, one dau.

2*d* ● John SCOTT, *b* 1946.

2*c* ● Mary George WASHINGTON, *b* at Denton, Texas 7 April 1923, *m* 4 Dec 1944, ● William Alec Southwell (*b* 13 Feb 1920) [*RR2, 308 Highland Lake Drive, Lewisville, Texas, USA*], and has issue,

1*d* ● William Alec SOUTHWELL, Jr, *b* 12 Dec 1945, *m*.

2*d* ● Steven C. SOUTHWELL, *b* 1952.

3*c* ● Paul Emery WASHINGTON, Man William Cameron & Co, Corpus Christi, Texas [*6122 Boca Raton, Corpus Christi, Texas 78413, USA*], *b* at Santa Maria, Texas 2 Aug 1926, *educ* Baylor Univ (BS 1951), *m* at Denton, Texas 22 Aug 1948, ● Jo Delle (*b* at Groesbeck, Texas 27 Aug 1927), dau of Ernest Robertson Trotter, by his wife Esther Lurline Webb, and has issue,

1*d* ● Julianne WASHINGTON, *b* at Waco, Texas 6 July 1949, *m* at San Antonio, Texas 5 Nov 1967, ● Gary Robert Spencer (*b* at Indianapolis, Indiana 3 Nov 1933), son of Sylvester Spencer, by his wife Viola McNay, and has issue,

● Shelley SPENCER, *b* at San Antonio, Texas 6 Feb 1970.

2*d* ● Richard Trotter WASHINGTON, Man Chess King Store, San Antonio, Texas, *b* at Waco, Texas 16 April 1952.

3*d* ● Bill Emery WASHINGTON, *b* at Corpus Christi, Texas 29 Dec 1953, *educ* San Antonio Coll.

4*d* ● Jack Webb WASHINGTON, *b* at Corpus Christi, Texas 1 Aug 1956, *m* at San Antonio, Texas 22 Nov 1972, ● Winona Carol (*b* at Wiesbaden, Germany 11 April 1956), dau of William Charles Herm, by his wife Marilyn Joan Bruce, and has issue,

● David Michael WASHINGTON, *b* at Corpus Christi, Texas 14 April 1973.

4*c* ● Carolyn Sue WASHINGTON, *b* at Handley, Texas 5 Oct 1932, *m* (*m* diss by div), William Yates, and has issue,

● Mark YATES, *b* 1963.

8*b* ● Elizabeth Bryan WASHINGTON [*6149 Prospect Avenue, Dallas, Texas 75214, USA*], *b* at Procter, Texas 3 July 1893, *m* 16 June 1918, Edward Campbell Kean (*b* at Abilene, Texas 24 May 1888), and has issue,

● Dr James Edward KEAN [*Colorado Springs, Colorado, USA*], *b* at Austin, Texas 5 June 1922, *m* 1st 6 Sept 1947 (*m* diss by div), Mary Ella Denning (*b* at Bryson, Texas 7 Aug 1925), and has issue,

1*d* ● Mary Elizabeth KEAN, *b* at Austin, Texas 16 Dec 1948, *m*.

Dr James Edward Kean *m* 2ndly, and by her has issue,

2*d* ● Michelle KEAN.

3*d* ● James KEAN.

9*b* Paul Gray WASHINGTON, served in World War I with 9th Field Art US Inf, *b* at Procter, Texas 6 March 1898; *dunm* 1 Oct 1923.

5*a* Emma Tell WASHINGTON, *b* in Mason County, W Virginia 27 Sept 1848, *m* at Eagle Lake, Colorado County, Texas 16 Sept 1865, George Lewis Patrick (*b* at Springville, Alabama; *d* 1914), son of George Washington Patrick, by his wife Margaret —, and *d* 18 Dec 1907, having had issue, three sons and six daus.

6*a* Julia Wood WASHINGTON, *b* at Columbus, Colorado County, Texas 29 May 1850, *m* there 19 June 1873, Sydney Thruston Fontaine, of Houston, Texas (*b* at

Houston 28 Nov 1838; *d* at Galveston, Texas 5 Sept 1912), son of Judge Henry Whiting Fontaine, by his wife Susan Elizabeth Bryan, and *d* at New York 1 Oct 1936, having had issue, four sons and two daus.

7*a* Mary Wood WASHINGTON (changed name to Cecil Wood WASHINGTON), *b* in Colorado County, Texas 1 Jan 1858, *m* 1st 1877, Capt Richard Saunders (*d* at Denison, Texas July (?) 1878) and had issue, one son. She *m* 2ndly at Sherman, Texas 29 Sept 1885 (*m* diss by div), Joshua E. Howard, of Denison, Texas. She *m* 3rdly at Sherman, Texas 7 March 1897, as his 1st wife, George McLagan, of Pueblo, Colorado, and Los Angeles, California (*b* 9 Oct 1859; *d* at Hollywood, California 26 June 1945), and *d* at San Diego, California 16 Dec 1916, leaving further issue, one dau.

(4) Mary Dorcas WASHINGTON, *b* in Mason County, Virginia 10 April 1817; *dunm* in Colorado County, Texas 15 Nov 1861.

8 Harriott WASHINGTON, *b* at Harewood 2 Aug 1776, *m* at Richmond, Virginia 15 July 1796, Col Andrew Parks, of Baltimore and Fredericksburg, later of Kanawha Salines, Virginia (now Malden, W Virginia) (*b* 10 Aug 1773; *d* in Kanawha County 1836), son of John Parks, by his wife Margaret Gibson, and *d* in Kanawha County 3 Jan 1822, having had issue, five sons and three daus.

Col Samuel Washington *m* 5thly *ca* 1778, Susannah (*b* 27 June 1753; *d* at Harewood 5 March 1783), widow of George Holden, and dau of John Ferrin, of Gloucester County, Virginia and *d* at Harewood 26 Sept 1781, having by her had issue,

9 John Perrin WASHINGTON, *b* at Harewood *ca* 1779; *d* there 1783.

**7** John Augustine WASHINGTON, of Bushfield, Westmoreland County, Virginia, Col Virginia Militia, mem Virginia Conventions 1775-76, *b* in Stafford County, Virginia 13 Jan 1735/6, *m* in Westmoreland County 14(?) April 1756, Hannah (*b* at Bushfield *ca* 1738; *d* there 1801), elder dau and co-heiress of Col John Bushrod, of Bushfield, JP and Burgess, and only dau by his 1st wife Jane, dau of Hon Gawin Corbin, Pres of Gov's Council, and *d* at Bushfield 8(?) Jan 1787, having had issue,

1 Mary WASHINGTON, *b* probably at Mount Vernon *ca* 1757; *d* probably at Bushfield *ca* 1762.

2 Jane WASHINGTON, *b* at Bushfield 20 June 1759, *m* 25 Sept 1777, as his 1st wife, her half 1st cousin Col William Augustine Washington, of Wakefield (*b* 25 Nov 1757; *d* 2 Oct 1810), and *d* at Sweet Springs, Virginia 16 Aug 1791, leaving issue (*see above, p* 48).

3 Bushrod WASHINGTON, LLD, of Mount Vernon, Assoc Justice, US Supreme Court 1798-1829, Pres American Colonization Soc which founded Liberia, *b* at Bushfield 5 June 1762, *m* at Rippon Lodge Oct 1785, Ann (*b* at Rippon Lodge *ca* 1768; *d* at Derby, Pennsylvania 28 Nov 1829), 2nd dau of Col Thomas Blackburn, of Rippon Lodge, Prince William County, Virginia, by his wife Christian Scott, and *dsp* at Philadelphia 26 Nov 1829.

4 Corbin WASHINGTON, of Walnut Farm, Westmoreland County, and later of Selby, Fairfax County, Virginia, *b* at Bushfield 1764, *m* at Chantilly, Westmoreland County, Virginia 10 May 1787, Hannah (*b* at Chantilly 1765; *d* at Alexandria, Virginia 23 Nov 1801), 2nd dau of Richard Henry Lee, by his 1st wife Anne Aylett (and sister of the 2nd Mrs William Augustine Washington—*see p* 50), and *d* at Bushfield 10 Dec 1799, leaving issue,

(1) Richard Henry Lee WASHINGTON, of Prospect Hill, Jefferson County, W Virginia, *b* at Walnut Farm 1788; *dunm* at Mount Vernon 17 Sept 1817.

(2) John Augustine WASHINGTON, of Blakeley, Jefferson County, W Virginia (which he built), and later also of Mount Vernon, *b* at Walnut Farm 6 Aug 1789, *m* at Rippon Lodge 14 Nov 1811, Jane Charlotte (*b* at Rippon Lodge 23 Aug 1786; *d* at Blakeley 6 Sept 1855), eldest dau and co-heiress of Major Richard Scott Blackburn, of Rippon Lodge, Prince William County, Virginia (brother of Mrs Bushrod Washington—*see above*), by his 1st wife Judith Ball, and *d* at Mount Vernon 13 June 1832, having had issue,

1*a* Anne Maria Thomasina Blackburn WASHINGTON, *b* at Blakeley 4 Nov 1816, *m* at Mount Vernon 15 May 1834, as his 1st wife, Dr William Fontaine Alexander (*b* at Mount Ida, nr Alexandria, Virginia 31 Oct 1811; *d* at Walnut Farm 7 Jan 1862), 2nd son of Charles Alexander,

of Mount Ida, by his wife Mary Bowles Armistead, and *d* at Blakeley 29 March 1850, having had issue, three sons and four daus.

2*a* George WASHINGTON, *b* at Blakeley 7 March 1818; *d ca* 1827.

3*a* Christian Scott WASHINGTON, *b* at Blakeley 5 Jan, *d* 18 May 1820.

4*a* John Augustine WASHINGTON, of Mount Vernon (which he sold 1858 to the Mount Vernon Ladies Association of the Union, which has since preserved and maintained it), and later of Waveland, Fauquier County, Virginia, Lt-Col CSA, ADC to Gen Robert E. Lee, *b* at Blakeley 3 May 1821, *m* at Exeter, Loudon County, Virginia 16 Feb 1843, Eleanor Love (*b* probably at Exeter 12 April 1824; *d* at Waveland 9 Oct 1860), only dau and heiress of Col Wilson Cary Selden, of Exeter, by his wife Louisa Elizabeth Fontaine Alexander (sister of Dr William Fontaine Alexander—*see above*), and was *k* in a skirmish at Cheat Mountain, Randolph County, W Virginia 13 Sept 1861, leaving issue,

1*b* Louisa Fontaine WASHINGTON, *b* at Mount Vernon 19 Feb 1844, *m* at Blakeley 15 Aug 1871, Col Roger Preston Chew, CSA, of Charles Town, Jefferson County, W Virginia (*b* in Loudon County, Virginia 9 April 1843; *d* at Charles Town 16 March 1921), son of Roger Chew, by his wife Sarah West Aldridge, and *d* at Charles Town 1 July 1927, having had issue, three sons and three daus (all of whom *dsp*).

2*b* Jane Charlotte WASHINGTON, *b* at Mount Vernon 26 May 1846, *m* at Blakeley 13 Jan 1869, Nathaniel Hite Willis, of Rock Hall, Jefferson County, W Virginia (*b* at Rock Hall 25 March 1842; *d* at Charles Town 26 Oct 1914), only surv son of Thomas Hite Willis, by his wife Elizabeth Ferguson Ryland, and *d* at Charles Town 7 Aug 1924, having had issue, three sons and five daus.

3*b* Eliza Selden WASHINGTON, *b* at Blakeley 17 July 1848, *m* 6 Oct 1895, as his 3rd wife, Major Robert Waterman Hunter, CSA, of Winchester, Frederick County, and of Alexandria, Virginia (*b* 12 July 1837; *d* 2 April 1916), and *dsp* at Charles Town 28 Aug 1909.

4*b* Anna Maria WASHINGTON, *b* at Mount Vernon 17 Nov 1851, *m* at Charles Town 22 July 1873, Rt Rev Beverley Dandridge Tucker, DD, Bishop of Southern Virginia (*b* at Richmond, Virginia 9 Nov 1846; *d* at Norfolk, Virginia 17 Jan 1930), son of Nathaniel Beverley Tucker, by his wife Jane Shelton Ellis, and *d* at Norfolk, Virginia 7 Jan 1927, leaving issue, nine sons and four daus.

5*b* Lawrence WASHINGTON, of Waveland, Fauquier County, Virginia, and later of Washington, DC, *b* at Mount Vernon 14 Jan 1854, *m* at Charles Town 14 June 1876, Fannie (*b* at Riverside, Jefferson County, W Virginia 17 May 1855; *d* at Washington, DC 26 March 1953), dau of Thomas Griggs Lackland, of Charles Town, by his wife Martha Ellen Willis (sister of Nathaniel Hite Willis—*see above*), and *d* at Washington, DC 28 Jan 1920, leaving issue,

1*c* John Augustine WASHINGTON, of Logan, Logan County, W Virginia, *b* at Waveland 20 Jan 1878, *m* 1st at Lawson Hall, Cabell County, W Virginia 8 Nov 1905, Eleanor Guye (*b* 20 Oct 1873; *d* at Logan 16 May 1949), dau of Simon Slade Altizer, by his wife Roxye Lawson, and had issue,

1*d* ● Eleanor Altizer WASHINGTON, *b* at Logan 20 Sept 1906, *m* there 8 Jan 1931, ● Clifford Douglas Lilly (*b* at Logan 3 March 1904) [*715 Southwest 27th Way, Boynton Beach, Florida 33435, USA*], son of William Riley Lilly, by his wife Martha Ellen McGinnis, and has two adopted children,

1*e* ● John Douglas LILLY, *b* 12 June 1944.

2*e* ● Linda Washington LILLY, *b* 31 Dec 1947, *m* at Boynton Beach, Florida 4 Nov 1972, ● Donald Wendell Kelly (*b* at Cincinnati 27 May 1931) [*37 Kings Highway, Huntingdon, West Virginia 25705, USA*], son of Donald Bartley Kelly, by his wife Elsie Yorke.

2*d* ● John Augustine WASHINGTON [*Holley Hotel, 1008 Quarrier Street, Charleston, West Virginia 25330, USA*], *b* at Logan 15 March

1913, *m* there 7 Sept 1950 (*m* diss by div), Virginia Dare (*née* Knighton) (*b* at Beckley, Raleigh County, W Virginia 20 May 1923), formerly wife of Max Welton Stell, and has issue,
●John Augustine WASHINGTON [*4341 Southwest 129th Place, Miami, Florida 33165, USA*], *b* at Miami, Florida 27 Dec 1952.
John Augustine WASHINGTON, of Logan *m* 2ndly at Jesup, Wayne County, Georgia 30 May 1952, ●Sybil Mildred (*b* at Logan 21 April 1919) [*Barnabus, Logan County, West Virginia 25609, USA*], formerly wife of Robson Roake Sage II, and dau of George Cleveland Steele, by his wife Ora Gustava Curry, and *d* at Logan 5 Nov 1962.
2*c* Lawrence WASHINGTON, *b* at Waveland 9 Aug 1879, *m* at Northfork, McDowell County, W Virginia 4 Feb 1913, Nell McKay (*b* at Falls Mills, Tazewell County, Virginia 13 May 1890; *d* at Bluefield, Mercer County, W Virginia 1 July 1931), dau of William Edward Dudley, by his wife Margaret Gillespie, and *d* at Northfork 20 Nov 1953, leaving issue,
●Frances Lackland WASHINGTON [*1120 Virginia Avenue, Bluefield, Virginia 24605, USA*], *b* at Northfork 4 July 1916.
3*c* Patty Willis WASHINGTON, *b* at Waveland 1 Oct 1880; *dunm* at Alexandria, Virginia 22 Feb 1971.
4*c* Anne Madison WASHINGTON, *b* at Waveland 27 May 1882; *dunm* at Arlington, Virginia 17 Oct 1966.
5*c* ●Louisa Fontaine WASHINGTON [*512 South George Street, Charles Town, Jefferson County, West Virginia 25414, USA*], *b* at Waveland 14 Nov 1883, *m* at Washington, DC 14 June 1921, Philip Dawson (*b* at Cameron, Fairfax County, Virginia 30 July 1880; *d* at Alexandria, Virginia 20 June 1963), son of Nicholas Dawson, by his wife Virginia Mason Cooper, and has issue,
1*d* ●Virginia Cooper DAWSON, *b* at Lynchburg, Campbell County, Virginia 2 April 1922, *m* at Alexandria, Virginia 4 Sept 1948, ●John Beebe (*b* at Washington, DC 10 Sept 1920) [*3570 Tupelo Place, Alexandria, Virginia 22304, USA*], son of Lawrence Laverne Beebe, by his wife Alma Pearl Lattin, and has issue,
1*e* ●Elizabeth Lattin BEEBE, *b* at Washington, DC 13 Dec 1952.
2*e* ●Louisa Fontaine BEEBE, *b* at Washington, DC 21 Nov 1953.
3*e* ●Virginia Cooper BEEBE, *b* at Washington, DC 30 June 1956.
4*e* ●John Washington BEEBE, *b* at Alexandria, Virginia 8 June 1963.
2*d* ●Louisa Fontaine Washington DAWSON, *b* at Lynchburg, Campbell County, Virginia 9 March 1925, *m* at Alexandria, Virginia 28 June 1958, ●Rev John Reed Smucker III (*b* at Kansas City, Missouri 20 April 1928) [*108 North Quaker Lane, Alexandria, Virginia 22304, USA*], son of John Reed Smucker, Jr, by his wife Dorothy Gorton, and has issue,
1*e* ●Anne Mason SMUCKER, *b* at Detroit, Michigan 19 July 1959.
2*e* ●Philip Gorton SMUCKER, *b* at Grosse Pointe, Michigan 31 Aug 1961.
6*c* Richard Blackburn WASHINGTON, *b* at Waveland 3 March 1885, *m* 1st at Alexandria, Virginia 27 March 1912, Agnes Harwood (*b* at Markham, Fauquier County, Virginia 1 Aug 1884; *d* at Arlington, Virginia April 1947), dau of Dr Jaquelin Ambler Marshall, by his wife Mary Douthat, and had issue,
1*d* ●Lawrence WASHINGTON [*127 Longview Drive, Alexandria, Virginia 22314, USA*], *b* at Alexandria, Virginia 29 Jan 1913, *m* 1st there 28 Feb 1934, Mary Katherine (*b* in Stafford County, Virginia 16 May 1915; *d* at Alexandria 29 Nov 1971), dau of Dwight Lee Armstrong, by his wife Lilla Payne, and has issue,
●Mary Katherine WASHINGTON, *b* at Alexandria, Virginia 19 July 1936, *m* there 16

June 1954, ●Edward Erwin Shaffner, Jr (*b* at Washington, DC 7 Oct 1932) [*1602 Revere Drive, Alexandria, Virginia 22308, USA*], son of Edward Erwin Shaffner, by his wife Frances Lincoln Stevens, and has issue,
1*f* ●Pamela Kay SHAFFNER, *b* at St Petersburg, Pinellas County, Florida 17 March 1955.
2*f* ●Patricia Kay SHAFFNER, *b* at St Petersburg, Pinellas County, Florida 17 March 1955 (twin with her sister Pamela Kay).
3*f* ●Elizabeth Darleen SHAFFNER, *b* at Washington, DC 16 Jan 1958.
4*f* ●Lawrence Washington SHAFFNER, *b* at Washington, DC 22 Aug 1960.
Lawrence Washington *m* 2ndly at Alexandria, Virginia 21 April 1973, ●Muriel Florence (*b* at Cambridge, Mass 25 Dec 1923), formerly wife of — Acton, and dau of Herbert Bradford Woodruff, by his wife Georgia Frances Wade.
2*d* ●Jaquelin Marshall WASHINGTON (Rev), Rector of St Paul's Church-on-the-Plains, Lubbock, Texas [*3009 Mesa Road, Lubbock, Texas 79403, USA*], *b* at Alexandria, Virginia 19 Dec 1914, *educ* Duke Univ, and Episcopal Theological Seminary, *m* 1st at Fairfax, Fairfax County, Virginia 17 Jan 1942, Frances Blanche (*b* at Manassas, Prince William County, Virginia 15 Oct 1915; *d* at Lubbock, Texas 29 Nov 1962), dau of Francis Norvell Larkin, by his wife Marie Herrell. He *m* 2ndly at Lubbock, Texas 14 July 1974, ●Louise (*née* Fagg) (*b* at Greeneville, Hunt County, Texas 16 Sept 1915), widow of Charles Maedgen, and dau of Cary Alvin Fagg.
3*d* ●Richard Blackburn WASHINGTON [*12044 East Archer Avenue, Aurora, Colorado 80012, USA*], *b* at Alexandria, Virginia 16 Jan 1917, *educ* Episcopal High Sch, *m* 1st at Alexandria 14 Jan 1941 (*m* diss by div), Dorothy Joan Catrow; and 2ndly at Key West, Florida 7 Jan 1944, ●Mildred Frances (*b* at Wellington, Alabama 12 Feb 1920), dau of Joseph Homer Smith, by his wife Huldah Frances Prickett, and by her has issue,
1*e* ●Richard Blackburn WASHINGTON, [*Scottsville, Virginia 24590, USA*], *b* at Fort Pierce, St Lucie County, Florida 2 Nov 1944.
2*e* ●Rilla WASHINGTON, *b* at Berlin, Coos County, New Hampshire 23 April 1946
4*d* ●Agnes Harwood WASHINGTON, *b* at Alexandria, Virginia 15 Dec 1919, *m* at Arlington, Virginia 3 Oct 1948, ●Walter Dean Hougas (*b* at Pembina, Pembina County, N Dakota 21 Oct 1924) [*4000 Rigby Road, Crystal Lake, Illinois 60014, USA*], son of Harley Jay Hougas, by his wife Maud Alberta Richardson, and has issue,
1*e* ●Anne Harwood HOUGAS, *b* at Madison, Wisconsin 8 Aug 1952.
2*e* ●Walter Dean HOUGAS, *b* at Madison, Wisconsin 26 June 1955.
3*e* ●Robert Hayer HOUGAS, *b* at Elgin, Illinois 25 Sept 1960.
5*d* ●John Augustine WASHINGTON, purchasing agent, Atomic Energy Commn [*19117 Bloomfield Road, Olney, Maryland 20832, USA*], *b* at Alexandria, Virginia 9 Dec 1921, *m* at Lynchburg, Virginia 24 Dec 1952, ●Geraldine Farrar (*b* at Brookneal, Halifax County, Virginia 15 Nov 1932), dau of Robert Lawrence Peake, by his wife Bernice Smith Puckett, and has issue,
●John Augustine WASHINGTON, *b* at Alexandria, Virginia 8 Jan 1959.
6*d* ●Fielding Lewis WASHINGTON, attorney [*623 North Erskine Street, Seguin, Texas 78155, USA*], *b* at Alexandria, Virginia 23 Jan 1924, *m* at Lubbock, Texas 23 May 1945, ●Jacqueline (*b* at Texico, Curry County, New Mexico 26 Oct 1923), dau of Clarence Vernon Young, by his wife Ola Mae Jackson, and has issue,

●Jacqueline Marshall WASHINGTON, *b* at Lubbock, Texas 10 Sept 1951, *m* at Seguin, Texas 15 June 1973, ●Stanley Martin Bode (*b* at Seguin Nov 1953), son of Henry R. Bode, by his wife Hulda Barth.

7*d*●Thomas Lackland WASHINGTON, USMC 1944-46, Dist Mgr Samuel Bingham Co, mfrs of print and litho materials [*1026 Revere Drive, Oconomowoc, Waukesha County, Wisconsin 53066, USA*], *b* at Alexandria, Virginia 8 Oct 1926, *educ* Purdue Univ (BSATE 1950), *m* at Alexandria 15 June 1948, ●Reva Fay, BSHE (Purdue) (*b* at Langhorne, Bucks County, Pennsylvania 30 Dec 1927), adopted dau of Dr Charles Everand Reeves, by his wife Frances Fugate, and has issue,

1*e*●Thomas Ryland WASHINGTON, *b* at Richmond, Virginia 4 June 1956, *educ* Univ of Wisconsin.

2*e*●Elaine Frances WASHINGTON, *b* at Richmond, Virginia 23 Jan 1958.

3*e*●Patricia Anne WASHINGTON, *b* at Baltimore, Maryland 26 March 1966.

Richard Blackburn Washington *m* 2ndly at Hagerstown, Washington County, Maryland 18 Sept 1948, ●Lillian Margaret (*b* at Needville, Fort Bend County, Texas 9 Dec 1905) [*2297 Forest Drive, Pittsburgh, Pennsylvania 15235, USA*], formerly wife of — Alexander, and dau of William Franklin Banker, by his wife Louise Cramer, and *d* at Dunn Loring, Fairfax County, Virginia 8 Dec

7*c* Willis Lackland WASHINGTON, *b* at Waveland 17 Jan 1887, *m* 13 March 1958, ●Mrs Mabel Miller (*b* 6 June 1895) [*Route 1, Box 146A, Foristell, Missouri 63348, USA*], dau of William Briggs Rogers, and *dsp* at Front Royal, Warren County, Virginia 21 June 1972.

8*c* Frances Jaquelin WASHINGTON, *b* at Waveland 14 June 1888, *m* at Washington, DC 25 April 1917, Owen Batchelder Lewis (*b* at Richmond, Virginia 22 Jan 1889; *d* at Germantown, Pennsylvania 17 April 1954), son of Louis Lewis, by his wife Jane Elizabeth Owen, and *d* at Charles Town, W Virginia July 1967, having had issue, one son (who *d* an inf) and leaving an adopted dau.

9*c* Wilson Selden WASHINGTON, mem Virginia House of Delegates, *b* at Waveland 13 Sept 1889, *m* at Washington, DC 14 April 1920, ●Irene Watkins (*b* at East Radford, Montgomery County, Virginia 18 March 1896) [*Goodwin House, 4800 Fillmore Avenue, Alexandria, Virginia 22311, USA*], dau of James Whitefield Tinsley, by his wife Nancy James, and *d* at Alexandria 21 July 1953, leaving issue,

1*d*●Nancy James WASHINGTON, *b* at Alexandria 16 June 1922, *m* there 21 July 1956, ●Kingston Chandler Ware McCoy (*b* at Marietta, Ohio 19 Aug 1906) [*804 Jacaranda Drive, Harbor Bluffs, Largo, Florida 33540, USA*], son of Asa Davis McCoy, by his wife Mary Rebecca Hancock, and has issue,

1*e*●John Washington McCOY, *b* at Washington, DC 29 June 1958.

2*e*●Chandler Ware McCOY, *b* at Washington, DC 25 Dec 1959.

2*d*●Wilson Selden WASHINGTON, Assist Dir Honolulu Acad of Arts from 1969 [*203 Aumoe Road, Kailua, Hawaii, 96734, USA*], *b* at Alexandria 11 June 1925, *educ* American Univ, Washington, DC, and Princeton, *m* at Washington, DC 8 Sept 1956, ●Barbara, dau of Charles Silas Baker, by his wife Elizabeth Lambert.

10*c* Preston Chew WASHINGTON, *b* at The Plains, Fauquier County, Virginia 30 Aug 1892, *m* at Huntington, W Virginia 24 April 1917, ●Lucille Hite (*b* at Chapmanville, Logan County, W Virginia 21 Nov 1897) [*505 Eleventh Avenue, Huntington, W Virginia 25701, USA*], dau of George Brammer, by his wife Roxie Anne Butcher, and *dsp* at Huntington 24 July 1968.

11*c* Julian Howard WASHINGTON, *b* at Alexandria 8 March 1894, *m* at Richmond, Virginia 23 Oct 1933, Mary Edna Eleanor (*b* at Washington, DC 31

Oct 1907; *d* at Baltimore, Maryland 1963), dau of John Warwick Daniel, Jr, by his wife Edna Bishop, and *dsp* at Benedict, Charles County, Maryland 12 Nov 1956.

12*c* ●Francis Ryland WASHINGTON [*103a Morgan Street, Winchester, Virginia 22601, USA*], *b* at Alexandria 18 Aug 1897, *m* at Annapolis, Maryland 30 Aug 1930, ●Rebecca Holmes (*b* 29 July 1903), dau of Rev Charles Noyes Tyndell, by his wife Rebecca Holmes Lewis, and has had issue, one child (who *d* an inf).

6*b* Eleanor Love Selden WASHINGTON, *b* at Mount Vernon 14 March 1856, *m* at Warsaw, Westmoreland County, Virginia 5 May 1880, Julian Smith Howard, of Richmond, Virginia (*b* 10 July 1853; *d* at Warsaw 17 May 1884), son of Charles Howard, by his wife Sarah Anne Smith, and *d* at Alexandria 7 Nov 1937, leaving issue, one dau.

7*b* George WASHINGTON, *b* at Mount Vernon 26 July 1858, *m* at Charles Town, W Virginia 16 Feb 1886, Emily Serena (*b* in Jefferson County, W Virginia 3 May 1863; *d* at Charles Town 10 Nov 1944), dau of Col George Alexander Porterfield, by his wife Emily Terrill, and *d* at Charles Town 31 Dec 1905, having had issue,

1*c* Richard Blackburn WASHINGTON (Rev), SJ, Pastor of the Shrine of the Sacred Heart, Hot Springs, Virginia, *b* at Charles Town 5 Feb 1887; *dunm* at Philadelphia 14 March 1962.

2*c* Louisa Fontaine WASHINGTON, *b* at Charles Town 15 Jan 1889; *d* there 8 Sept 1898.

5*a* Richard Scott Blackburn WASHINGTON, of Blakeley and Harewood, and later of Charles Town, W Virginia, *b* at Blakeley 12 Nov 1822, *m* at Philadelphia 20 Nov 1844, Christian Maria (*b* at Harewood 16 Dec 1826; *d* there 10 June 1895), 2nd dau of Dr Samuel Walter Washington (*see p 53*), and *d* at Charles Town 15 Oct 1910, having had issue,

1*b* Elizabeth Clemson WASHINGTON, *b* at Blakely 21 Aug 1845, *m* in Jefferson County, W Virginia 23 Jan 1868, as his 2nd wife, George Hite Flagg (*b* in Jefferson County 9 April 1832; *d* at Charles Town 25 March 1900), son of John R. Flagg, by his wife Susan Rutherford Hite, and *dsp* at Charles Town 3 Oct 1911.

2*b* John Augustine WASHINGTON, *b* at Blakeley 27 May 1847, *m* in Jefferson County, W Virginia 26 Nov 1890, Jane Keyes (*b* in Jefferson County 8 Feb 1862; *d* there 4 July 1891), eldest dau of Rev Charles Edward Ambler, by his 2nd wife Susan West Keyes, and *dsp* at Charles Town 14 Aug 1923.

3*b* Anna Maria Thomasina Blackburn WASHINGTON, *b* at Blakeley 1 Nov 1849; *d* 22 Sept 1852.

4*b* Louisa Clemson WASHINGTON, *b* at Blakeley 17 Nov 1851; *d* 22 Sept 1852.

5*b* Samuel Walter WASHINGTON, *b* at Blakeley 1 Nov 1853, *m* at Rock Hall, Jefferson County, W Virginia 11 Oct 1900, Elizabeth Ryland (*b* at Rock Hall 24 Jan 1870; *d* at Washington, DC 6 Feb 1960), eldest dau of Nathaniel Hite Willis, by his wife Jane Charlotte Washington (*see above, p 55*), and *d* at Charles Town 16 July 1923, leaving issue,

1*c*●Samuel Walter WASHINGTON, career diplomat 1926-53, Prof at Univs of Virginia and Puerto Rico 1954-69 [*2035 Guthrie Place, Las Cruces, New Mexico 88001, USA*], *b* at Charles Town 30 Sept 1901, *educ* Virginia Mil Inst, Lexington, and Hertford Coll Oxford (Rhodes Scholar), *m* 1st at Tokyo, Japan 29 Sept 1933 (*m* diss by div 1956), Simone Cecile (*b* at Paris, France 1 Sept 1905; *d* at Washington, DC 18 Dec 1973), widow of — Stecker, and dau of Benjamin Wilfred Fleisher, by his wife Blanche Blum, and has issue,

●John Augustine WASHINGTON II, Chief of Microbiology Section, Mayo Clinic [*1749 7th Street SW, Rochester, Minesota 55901, USA*], *b* at Istanbul, Turkey 29 May 1936, *educ* Univ of Virginia, and Johns Hopkins Univ (MD), *m* at Princeton, New Jersey 11 July 1959, ●Maaja (*b* at Tallin, Estonia 21 Jan 1938), dau of Eugen Härms, by his wife Gerda Elisabeth Pauming,

and has issue,
1e●Stephen Lawrence WASHINGTON, *b* at Bethesda, Maryland 28 March 1964.
2e●Richard Ryland WASHINGTON, *b* at Washington, DC 12 Feb 1967.
3e●Mikaela Ann WASHINGTON, *b* at Rochester, Minnesota 25 Sept 1970.
Samuel Walter Washington *m* 2ndly at New York 6 June 1958, ●Adriana Cornelia, MD (*b* at Amsterdam, Holland 27 Sept 1919), widow of —, and dau of Pieter Fenenga, by his wife Josephine Bource.
2d●John Augustine WASHINGTON, pediatrician [*Harewood, Charles Town, Jefferson County, West Virginia 25414, USA*], *b* at Charles Town 12 Oct 1903, *educ* Virginia Mil Inst, and Johns Hopkins Univ (MD), *m* at Georgetown, DC 24 Sept 1942, ●Margaret Hayes (*b* at Germantown, Pennsylvania 10 May 1908), elder dau of Henry Justice Kenderdine, by his wife Margaret McKinney, and has issue,
●Samuel Walter WASHINGTON, *b* at Washington, DC 1 April 1948, *educ* Carlton Coll, Northfield, Minnesota, and American Univ, Washington, DC.
6*b* Richard Scott Blackburn WASHINGTON, of Woodbury, New Jersey, *b* at Blakeley 21 March 1856, *m* at Louisville, Kentucky 19 Nov 1884, Nannie (*b* at Louisville 14 June 1859; *d* at Brant Beach, New Jersey 25 April 1947), only surv dau of Edward Tyler Sturgeon, by his wife Margaret Dye Fielder, and *d* at Woodbury, New Jersey 13 Oct 1922, having had issue,
1*c* Margaret Sturgeon WASHINGTON, *b* at Georgetown, Grant County, New Mexico 7 Sept 1885, *m* at Woodbury, New Jersey 2 March 1905, ●George Pepper Robins (*b* at Philadelphia 3 March 1882) [*Foulk Manor, 407 Foulk Road, Wilmington, Delaware 19803, USA*], son of William Bowdoin Robins, by his wife Ann Bronson Reed, and *d* at Wilmington, Delaware 27 Dec 1970, having had issue, three daus.
2*c* Richard Scott Blackburn WASHINGTON, of Germantown, Pennsylvania, *b* at Georgetown, Grant County, New Mexico 16 Sept 1887, *m* at Richmond, Virginia 9 May 1918, Eliza Mayo Atkinson (*b* at Charles Town, W Virginia 27 July 1897; *d* at Binghamton, New York 24 March 1965), only dau of Dr Van Lear Perry, by his wife Elizabeth Travers Green, and *d* at Binghamton, New York 29 Sept 1964, leaving issue,
1*d*●Bessie Van Lear WASHINGTON, *b* at Germantown, Pennsylvania 10 Feb 1919, *m* there 5 July 1941, ●Harry Berger Goodwin (*b* at Philadelphia 14 March 1916) [*1113 Colonial Avenue, Andalusia, Cornwells Heights, Pennsylvania 19020, USA*], son of Ralph Althouse Goodwin, by his wife Ida Berger, and has issue,
1*e*●Barbara Jean GOODWIN, *b* at Chestnut Hill, Pennsylvania 2 Jan 1943, *m* at Philadelphia 30 June 1962, ●Dr Mario Ceballos-Mejia (*b* at Antioquia, Colombia 13 Feb 1934) [*17 Oakbridge Drive, Binghamton, New York 13903, USA*], son of Dr Julio Ceballos, by his wife Matilde Mejia, and has issue,
1*f*●Daniel Harry CEBALLOS, *b* at Bogota, Colombia 23 April 1963.
2*f*●John Miguel CEBALLOS, *b* at Binghamton, New York 16 July 1966.
3*f*●David Scott CEBALLOS, *b* at Binghamton, New York 22 Dec 1971.
4*f*●Cristina Marie CEBALLOS, *b* at Binghamton, New York 6 Sept 1974.
2*e*●Harry Washington GOODWIN [*11711 Lanett Road, Philadelphia, Pennsylvania 19154, USA*], *b* at Chestnut Hill, Pennsylvania 21 Nov 1945, *m* at Philadelphia 27 Sept 1969, ●Constance Anne (*b* at Philadelphia 15 Dec 1948), dau of Robert Patrick Meehan, by his wife Anne Livingston, and has issue,

1*f*●Jennifer Anne GOODWIN, *b* at Philadelphia 25 Sept 1970.
2*f*●James Andrew GOODWIN, *b* at Philadelphia 10 Nov 1971.
2*d*●Nannie Sturgeon WASHINGTON, artist [*417 South Carlisle Street, Philadelphia, Pennsylvania 19146, USA*], *b* at Germantown 19 Feb 1920, *m* at Philadelphia 17 April 1943, Prof William Dall (formerly Dall Connor), Man Cons, Labor arbitrator (*b* at Brookline, Mass 5 May 1913; *d* at Philadelphia 6 May 1964), son of Charles Connor, by his wife Marian Dall.
3*d*●Richard Scott WASHINGTON [*11222 South Shore Drive, Reston, Virginia 22070, USA*], *b* at Germantown 26 May 1923, *m* at Philadelphia 27 April 1946, ●Lola Louise (*b* at Wilmington, Delaware 15 June 1917), widow of Maxwell Case, Jr, and dau of William Osborne Barnhill, by his wife Grace Elizabeth Pleasanton, and has issue,
1*e*●Lawrence Scott WASHINGTON [*Woodcrest Park Apartments, B-12, RD1, Tilton Road, Pleasantville, New Jersey 08232, USA*], *b* at Philadelphia 22 Sept 1948.
2*e*●Elizabeth WASHINGTON, *b* at Philadelphia 28 Feb 1951, *m* at Reston, Virginia 18 Sept 1971, ●John Joseph Keane, Jr (*b* at Washington, DC 11 June 1934) [*1854 Patten Terrace, McLean, Virginia 22101, USA*], son of John Joseph Keane, by his wife Irene Antoinette Buscher, and has issue,
●Katherine Irene KEANE, *b* at Arlington, Virginia 2 March 1973.
3*e*●Lola Louise WASHINGTON, *b* at Philadelphia 30 Dec 1952, *m* at Reston, Virginia 23 June 1973, ●Mark Patrick Monroe (*b* at Ridgecrest, California Jan 1949) [*2702 Paoli Pike, Apt 52, New Albany, Indiana 47150, USA*], son of Henry Lawrence Monroe, by his wife Cecilia Mary Lynch.
3*c* John Augustine WASHINGTON, of Clarksburg, W Virginia, and later of LeRoy, Genesee County, New York, *b* at Albuquerque, New Mexico 19 March 1891, *m* at Clarksburg, W Virginia 13 Nov 1917, Elise Sill (*b* at Columbus, Montana 3 Oct 1896; *m* 2ndly at Baltimore, Maryland 21 Sept 1933, Chesney Michael Carney, of Clarksburg, and *d* at Clarksburg 9 June 1955), 2nd dau of Francis Sprigg Gibson, by his 1st wife Sevilla Shaffner Friend, and *d* at LeRoy, New York 5 Oct 1928, leaving issue,
●John Augustine WASHINGTON, Man Washington, DC office of Alexander Brown & Sons, investment bankers [*4208 Rosemary Street, Chevy Chase, Maryland 20015, USA*], *b* at Clarksburg 4 May 1920, *educ* Hotchkiss Sch, and Harvard, *m* at Washington, DC 3 Sept 1960, ●Alice Claire (*b* at San Diego, California 3 Oct 1925), elder dau of Capt Henry Richard Lacey, USN (CEC), by his wife Edith Helen Johnson, and has issue,
1*e*●Edith Lacey WASHINGTON, *b* at Washington, DC 11 Dec 1961.
2*e*●John Augustine WASHINGTON, *b* at Washington, DC 15 July 1963.
4*c* Christian Maria WASHINGTON, *b* and *d* at Harewood 20 June 1893.
5*c* George Lafayette WASHINGTON, of Overbrook, Montgomery County, Pennsylvania, *b* at Harewood 20 June 1893 (twin with his sister Christian Maria), *m* at Winchester, Virginia 17 July 1913, ●Katherine Parke (*b* at Boston 26 Feb 1891) [*Bryn Mawr Terrace, Bryn Mawr, Pennsylvania 19010, USA*], dau of Joseph Blanchard Ames, by his wife Helen B., and *d* at Bryn Mawr, Pennsylvania 10 Feb 1968, leaving issue,
1*d*●Helen Ames WASHINGTON, *b* at Woodbury, New Jersey 22 Sept 1914, *m* 1st at Upper Darby, Delaware County, Pennsylvania 16 May 1935 (*m* diss by div 1946), as his 1st wife, Berthold John Heller, Jr, son of Berthold John

Heller, and has issue,

●Eugene Washington HELLER, *b* at Bryn Mawr, Pennsylvania 9 Dec 1935, *m* at Philadelphia 10 July 1965, ●Vivian (*b* at Fall River, Mass 10 Aug 1938), dau of Wilfred Joseph Vaudreuill, by his wife Aurore Levasseur, and has issue,

1*f*●Laura Eugenie HELLER, *b* at Philadelphia 27 July 1966.

2*f*●Eugenie Vivian HELLER, *b* at Philadelphia 24 Nov 1967.

Helen Ames Washington *m* 2ndly at Philadelphia 9 Jan 1971, ●Carlton Converse Day (*b* at Picture Rocks, Lycoming County, Pennsylvania 3 Jan 1912) [*Apt G411, 6150 Oxford Street, Philadelphia, Pennsylvania 19151, USA*], son of Howard Edgar Day, by his wife Anna May Converse.

2*d* Marie Blackburn WASHINGTON, *b* at Boston 23 Feb 1917, *m* at Philadelphia 25 Nov 1939 (*m* diss by div 1958), as his 1st wife, John Yocum Randolph Crawford (*b* 4 Aug 1915), and *d* at Philadelphia 17 July 1973, leaving issue, three daus.

7*b* Christine Maria WASHINGTON, *b* at Blakeley 13 June 1858; *dunm* at Charles Town 15 May 1937.

8*b* George Steptoe WASHINGTON, of Riverton, Burlington County, New Jersey, *b* at Blakeley 7 June 1860, *m* at Philadelphia 28 Oct 1886, May Tome (*b* at Lancaster, Pennsylvania 21 Aug 1865; *d* at Riverton 29 March 1959), dau of James King Alexander, by his wife Elizabeth Old Hopkins, and *d* at Riverton 17 June 1943, having had issue,

1*c* Richard Blackburn WASHINGTON, *b* at Philadelphia 29 Aug 1887; *d* at Riverton 15 April 1898.

2*c*●Elizabeth Alexander WASHINGTON [*408 Main Street, Riverton, New Jersey 08077, USA*], *b* at Philadelphia 31 Aug 1888, *m* at Riverton 10 Jan 1912, Rev William Hudson Cumpston (*b* at Leeds, Yorkshire, England 16 April 1878; *d* at Riverton 2 May 1960), son of Thomas Bowser Cumpston, by his wife Annie Martha Carter, and has issue,

1*d*●May Alexander CUMPSTON, *b* at Riverton 23 July 1913, *m* there 20 Sept 1947, ●Howland Dudley, Jr (*b* at Belmont, Mass 6 Feb 1910) [*Elephant Road, Dublin, Bucks County, Pennsylvania 18917, USA*], son of Howland Dudley, by his wife Helen Fuller, and has issue,

1*e*●Anne Carter DUDLEY, *b* at Glen Ridge, New Jersey 29 Dec 1948.

2*e*●Sarah Fuller DUDLEY, *b* at Glen Ridge, New Jersey 23 March 1951, *m* at Hilltown, Pennsylvania 14 Sept 1974, ●Michael Joseph Staub (*b* at Philadelphia 4 July 1952), son of Michael Joseph Staub, by his wife Elsie Lagler.

3*e*●Elizabeth Washington DUDLEY, *b* at Glen Ridge, New Jersey 16 Oct 1953.

4*e*●Laura Howland DUDLEY, *b* at Glen Ridge, New Jersey 30 Dec 1955.

2*d*●George Steptoe Washington CUMPSTON [*Allegro Apartments 16, 5656 East Orange Blossom Lane, Phoenix, Arizona 85018, USA*], *b* at Riverton 25 July 1918, *educ* St Andrew's Sch, Middletown, Delaware, *m* at Riverton 7 June 1952, ●Eileen Marie (*b* 4 Feb 1920), dau of Harry W. Bagnall, by his wife Mary, and has issue,

●William Hudson CUMPSTON, *b* at Lima, Peru 26 March 1957.

3*c* Christine Maria WASHINGTON, *b* at Riverton 31 July 1891, *m* there 7 Feb 1912, George Lincoln Ridley, of Riverton (*b* at Hyde Park, Mass 23 Nov 1888; *d* at Washington, DC 23 Nov 1963), son of George Lewis Ridley, by his wife Edith Horton Sears, and *d* at Riverton 15 May 1961, leaving issue, three daus.

4*c*●Howard Alexander WASHINGTON [*205 Bank Street, Riverton, New Jersey 08077, USA*], *b* at Riverton 17 July 1893, *m* 1st at Augusta, Georgia 11 April 1923, Lily Kate (*b* at Augusta 3 Feb 1896; *d* at

Avalon, New Jersey 3 Oct 1946), dau of Henry Balk, by his wife Florence McCarrell. He *m* 2ndly at Winter Haven, Florida 5 April 1948, ●Jane (*b* at Boston, Georgia 5 July 1905), formerly wife of — Bradshaw, and dau of John Hawkins McIntosh, by his wife Lawson Turner, and has adopted his stepson,

●William BRADSHAW.

5*c* George Steptoe WASHINGTON, *b* at Riverton 3 Nov 1900; *d* at Charles Town 15 Sept 1901.

6*c*●William de Hertburn WASHINGTON, Capt US Army (ret) [*408 Main Street, Riverton, New Jersey 08077, USA*], *b* at Riverton 21 Sept 1902, *educ* Shenandoah Valley Acad, and Lehigh Univ.

9*b* William de Hertburn WASHINGTON, of Douglas, Arizona, *b* in Jefferson County, W Virginia 14 Feb 1864, *m* at Pearce, Garland County, Arizona 1 Feb 1901, Alice Lee (*b* in Kimble County, Texas 5 March 1880; *d* at Douglas, Cochise County, Arizona 24 Dec 1960), dau of Paschal C. Lemons, by his wife Luella J. Tulk, and *d* at Douglas, Cochise County, Arizona 12 Feb 1937, leaving issue,

Richard Scott Blackburn WASHINGTON, of Douglas, Arizona, *b* at Pearce, Arizona 25 Oct 1901, *m* at Douglas 28 May 1929, ●Mabel Anne (*b* at Coeur d'Alène, Kootenai County, Idaho 20 July 1903) [*3621 Woodcrest Road, Sacramento, California 95821, USA*], dau of Jacob Hansen Wiks, by his wife Marie Louise Larsen, and *d* at Douglas 23 July 1966, leaving issue,

●Richard Scott WASHINGTON [*3405 Klamathwoods Place, Concord, California 94518, USA*], *b* at Douglas 15 Oct 1930, *m* there 9 Nov 1953, ●Patricia Anne (*b* at Douglas 15 Oct 1930, *m* there 9 Nov 1953, ●Patricia Anne (*b* there 27 July 1930), dau of Frank William Sharpe, Jr, by his wife Edith Jones, and has issue,

1*e*●Kathleen Lee WASHINGTON, *b* at Douglas 17 Jan 1956.

2*e*●Richard Scott WASHINGTON, *b* at Douglas 27 Dec 1956.

3*e*●Suzanne WASHINGTON, *b* at Douglas 23 July 1958.

4*e*●Mark Sharpe WASHINGTON, *b* at Douglas 24 Jan 1960.

5*e*●Timothy Edward WASHINGTON, *b* at Alamogordo, New Mexico 14 Sept 1961.

6*e*●Steven Patrick WASHINGTON, *b* at Mountain View, California 28 May 1965.

(3) Bushrod Corbin WASHINGTON, of Claymont, Jefferson County, (W) Virginia (which he built), mem Virginia House of Delegates, *b* at Walnut Farm 25 Dec 1790, *m* 1st at Rippon Lodge 1810, Anna Maria Thomasina (*b* at Rippon Lodge 30 Oct 1790; *d* at Washington, DC 24 Sept 1833), 2nd dau and co-heiress of Richard Scott Blackburn, of Rippon Lodge, Prince William County, Virginia, by his 1st wife Judith Ball (and sister of Mrs John Augustine Washington—*see above p 55*), and had issue,

1*a* Hannah Lee WASHINGTON, *b* at Rippon Lodge 19 May 1811, *m* June 1835 (*m* diss by div 1854), as his 2nd wife, William Pearson Alexander (*b* in King George County, Virginia *ca* 1803; *d* at Alexandria, Virginia *ca* 1862), son of Thomas Pearson Alexander, by his wife Sarah Mustin (and 1st cousin once removed of Dr William Fontaine Alexander—*see above p 55*), and *d* at Charles Town 12 Jan 1881, having had issue, five sons and three daus.

2*a* Thomas Blackburn WASHINGTON, of Claymont, *b* at Rippon Lodge 19 Aug 1812, *m* 28 Feb 1837, Rebecca Janet (*b* at Richlands, Frederick County, Maryland 13 Nov 1820; *m* 2ndly, Rev Edward William Syle, DD and *d* in London, England 23 Sept 1890), dau of James Cunningham, by his wife Catherine Campbell, and *d* at Alexandria, Virginia 3 Aug 1854, leaving issue,

Bushrod Corbin WASHINGTON, of Claymont, and later of Braddock, Jefferson County, W Virginia, and finally of Almira, Lincoln County, Washington, *b* at Claymont 14 May 1839, *m* 1st at Weehaw, Clarke County, Virginia 21 July 1864, his 2nd cousin once removed Catherine Thomas (*b* at Weehaw 25 Nov 1840; *d* at Braddock 15 Sept 1876), dau of Dr Richard

Scott Blackburn, by his wife Sarah Ann Eleanor Thomas, and had issue,

1c Bushrod Corbin WASHINGTON, *b* at Claymont 28 Dec 1865, *m* 1st 12 Oct 1887, Emma (*b* at Balclutha, Clarke County, Virginia 17 June 1864; *d* at Branford, New Haven County, Conn 27 Aug 1934), dau of William Temple Allen, by his wife Mary Elizabeth Bayly, and had issue,

1d●Katharine Cunningham WASHINGTON, *b* at Balclutha 13 Aug 1888, *m* 13 Dec 1912 (*m* diss by div), Matthew Smith Hopkins (*b* at White Hall, Howard County, Maryland 31 Dec 1879; *d* at Cotonsville, Maryland), son of Samuel Hopkins, by his wife Martha Tyson Smith, and has had issue,

1e Matthew Smith HOPKINS, Ensign US Merchant Marine, *b* at Washington, DC 31 Jan 1914; lost in the sinking of SS *Jacksonville* off the coast of Ireland 30 Aug 1944, *unm.*

2e●Bushrod Washington HOPKINS [*6761 Haviland Mill Road, Clarksville, Maryland 21029, USA*], *b* at Reading, Pennsylvania 31 July 1915, *m* at Washington, DC 26 Dec 1953, ●Mary Jozie (*b* at Burkburnett, Texas 7 July 1921), dau of Henry George Spence, by his wife Lola May Sides, and has two adopted children,

(a) ●Bushrod Washington HOPKINS, *b* 12 April 1955, *m* at Ellicott City, Maryland 17 Aug 1974, ●Donna Carol (*b* 1956), dau of Calvin Stanley Bassler, by his wife Diane.

(b) ●Glenn Spence HOPKINS, *b* 1 Oct 1957.

3e●Samuel Ellicott HOPKINS [*Route 3, Box 77, Centerville, Maryland 21617, USA*], *b* at Reading, Pennsylvania 7 May 1917, *m* at Centerville, Maryland 30 Aug 1951, ●Susan Green (*b* at Queenstown, Maryland 20 July 1915), dau of R. Carter Bryan, by his wife Mary Green, and has two adopted children,

(a) ●George Ellicott Tyson HOPKINS, *b* 14 Feb 1952.

(b) ●Betty Jean HOPKINS, *b* 12 Aug 1953.

4e Katharine Blackburn HOPKINS, *b* at Reading, Pennsylvania 4 April 1919, *m* 1st (*m* diss by div), Gilbert Ward Lewis, son of Charles Venable Lewis, by his wife — Motley, and had issue, one dau. She *m* 2ndly 12 Oct 1942, as his 2nd wife, James Knox Polk Mills (*b* at Princeton, Mercer County, W Virginia 1915; *d* July 1944), son of B. T. Mills, and had further issue, one dau. She *m* 3rdly at Santa Barbara, California 16 Sept 1945 (*m* diss by div 1958), as his 3rd wife, Andrew Jackson Linebarger (*b* at Santa Paula, California 23 Jan 1903), son of John George Linebarger, and had further issue, three sons and one dau. She *m* 4thly at Merced, California, ●Pedro Martinez, and *d* at Merced Oct 1963.

5e●Eleanor Blackburn HOPKINS, *b* at Reading, Pennsylvania 26 Jan 1921, *m* at Silver Spring, Maryland 18 Oct 1949, ●Leon Wesley Arnold Gray Sisson (*b* at Lynchburg, Virginia 18 July 1907) [*5925 Damascus Road, Gaithersburg, Maryland 20720, USA*], son of William Sisson, by his wife Roberta Odessa Gray, and has issue,

1f●Leon Gray SISSON, *b* at Queenstown, Maryland 5 Feb 1951.

2f●Odessa Gray SISSON, *b* at Sandy Spring, Maryland 25 Feb 1953.

3f●Sharon Gay SISSON, *b* at Sandy Spring, Maryland 6 Sept 1954.

4f●Byron Gray SISSON, *b* at Bethesda, Maryland 22 July 1956.

5f●Glenda Joy SISSON, *b* at Frederick, Maryland 17 Feb 1958.

6e●John Marsh Smith HOPKINS [*421 Indian Creek Drive, Cocoa Beach, Florida 32931, USA*], *b* at Washington, DC 17 May 1929, *m* 1st at Biloxi, Mississippi 17 June 1952 (*m* diss by div), Helen Krzwic-Ostoai; and 2ndly at Cocoa Beach, Florida 17 July 1966, ●Jean Ada

(*b* at Orlando, Florida 18 March 1931), formerly wife of — Risher, and dau of Arthur Ira Gould, by his wife Florence Ward, and by her has issue,

●Martha Ann HOPKINS, *b* at Cocoa Beach, Florida 6 Nov 1968.

2d●Emma Allen WASHINGTON [*541 South Lake Martha Drive, Winter Haven, Florida 33880, USA*], *b* at Balclutha 22 April 1890, *m* at Washington, DC 26 Sept 1917, Chester Carmen Baxter (*b* in Allen County, Ohio 1 June 1886; *d* at Winter Haven 2 Nov 1967), son of James Baxter, by his wife Clara MacBride, and has had issue,

1e Jane Blackburn BAXTER, *b* at Washington, 'DC 29 Jan 1919; *d* at Merchantville, New Jersey 20 Aug 1929.

2e●James BAXTER, metallurgical engr [*Balclutha, Druid Hills, Dickson, Tennessee 37055, USA*], *b* at Philadelphia 20 April 1920, *educ* Lafayette Coll, *m* at Columbia, Pennsylvania 23 April 1950, ●Beth Lane (*b* at Oak Hill, Fayette County, W Virginia 2 Feb 1928), dau of Kent Bailey Williams, by his wife Margaret Lucille Johnson, and has issue,

1f●James Chester BAXTER, *b* at São Paulo, Brazil 4 Aug 1951, *educ* Univ of Tennessee.

2f●Christopher Hale BAXTER, *b* at New Haven, Conn 31 July 1955.

3f●Stephen Allen BAXTER, *b* at New Haven, Conn 1 Jan 1959.

3e●William Temple Allen BAXTER [*921 Fairway Drive NE, Vienna, Virginia 22180, USA*], *b* at Philadelphia 19 Sept 1921, *m* at Wilmington, N Carolina 6 Oct 1943, ●Irene Blanche (*b* at Martins Creek, Pennsylvania 13 June 1924), dau of William Jennings Karabinus, by his wife Blanche Sinaly, and has issue,

1f●Jane Blackburn BAXTER, *b* at Camden, New Jersey 17 Dec 1946, *m* at Gainesville, Florida 17 March 1973, ●Paul Stephen Hughes (*b* 28 April 1949).

2f●William Temple Allen BAXTER, Jr, *b* at Melbourne, Florida 8 March 1955.

3d Bushrod Corbin WASHINGTON [*PO Box 8685, Sarasota, Florida 33578, USA*], *b* at Balclutha 25 Nov 1892, *m* at Washington, DC 5 April 1920, ●Edith (*b* at Washington, DC 1 Jan 1895), dau of Jesse E. Eastlack, by his wife Martha Featherer, and *d* 29 Sept 1974, leaving,

1e●Bushrod Corbin WASHINGTON [*2509 Popkins Lane, Alexandria, Virginia 22506, USA*], *b* at Washington, DC 1 Oct 1920, *m* there 15 June 1946, ●Lydia Elizabeth (*b* at Fayetteville, N Carolina 20 Aug 1925), dau of Lonnie Thomas Brown, by his wife Lena Burke, and has issue,

1f●Lydia Dianne WASHINGTON, *b* at Washington, DC 21 Jan 1951.

2f●Sharon Rose WASHINGTON, *b* at Washington, DC 27 July 1953.

3f●Bushrod Corbin WASHINGTON, *b* at Alexandria, Virginia 22 April 1956.

2e●Mary Martha WASHINGTON, *b* at Norristown, Pennsylvania 8 Dec 1927, *m* at Arcadia, California 2 Aug 1950, ●Bruce Enoch Sparling (*b* at Muscatine, Iowa 9 July 1927) [*3106 Pulaski Pike, Northwest, Huntsville, Alabama 35810, USA*], son of Enoch Albert Sparling, by his wife Lulu Mae, and has issue,

1f●Edith Mae SPARLING, *b* at Washington, DC 17 Jan 1952, *m* at Huntsville, Alabama 27 Sept 1974, ●Howard Ray Atchley (*b* at Atlanta, Georgia 12 Oct 1950), son of James Howard Atchley, by his wife Betty Wells.

2f●Bruce Edward SPARLING, *b* at Washington, DC 4 Oct 1956.

4d Eleanor Blackburn WASHINGTON, *b* at Balclutha 15 Dec 1896, *m* at Alexandria, Virginia

25 April 1919, as his 1st wife, Stuart Kaen Joice, son of John K. Joice, and *d* at Washington, DC 13 Aug 1920, having had issue, one son (who *d* an inf).

5*d*●Elizabeth Temple WASHINGTON, *b* at Washington, DC 8 Nov 1902, *m* 1st 9 Nov 1920 (*m* diss by div), as his 1st wife, Samuel Oliver Baldwin (*b* 22 Sept 1900). She *m* 2ndly at Washington, DC 6 Nov 1926, ●Charles William Phillips (*b* at Reading, Pennsylvania 20 Oct 1903) [*Apartado 1694, Ensenada, Baja California, Mexico*], son of Nathan Phillips, by his wife Emma Pauline Hettinger, and has issue,

●Charles Washington PHILLIPS [*165 Delta Lane, Arcadia, California 91006, USA*], *b* at Birmingham, Alabama 26 Oct 1927, *m* 1st at San Francisco 6 Oct 1950, Patricia June Ross (*b* at Baltimore, Maryland 18 June 1932; *d* 15 Feb 1956), and has issue,

1*f*●Charles Washington PHILLIPS, *b* at Fort Lewis, Washington 8 July 1951, *m* at Charleston, S Carolina 20 May 1973, ●Susan Louise Buckley (*b* 31 Oct 1951).

2*f*●Robert Ross PHILLIPS, *b* 24 Oct 1953.

Charles Washington Phillips *m* 2ndly at Arcadia, California 7 Aug 1968, ●Sharon Margaret Blecha (*b* at Glendale, California 14 May 1939), and has an adopted dau,

●Marla Dell PHILLIPS, *b* 17 June 1963.

Bushrod Corbin Washington *m* 2ndly 20 Oct 1934, Ruby (*née* McDonald) (*b* at White Post, Clarke County, Virginia 1 Jan 1884; *d* at Hendersonville, N Carolina 31 Dec 1945), widow of Taylor Stringer, and *d* at Oteen, N Carolina 15 June 1954.

2*c* Eleanor Blackburn WASHINGTON, *b* at Claymont 15 Aug 1867, *m* 26 Aug 1889, as his 1st wife, John Saunders Castleman (*b* in Clarke County, Virginia 12 Feb 1851; *d* at Leesburg, Virginia 27 March 1923), son of William Saunders Castleman, by his wife Mary Emily Sinclair, and *d* at Charles Town 25 Oct 1894, leaving issue, two sons.

3*c* Janet Fairleigh WASHINGTON, *b* at Claymont 28 Dec 1868; *dunm* at Ephrata, Grant County, Washington 4 Aug 1911.

4*c* Catherine Blackburn WASHINGTON, *b* at Claymont 5 Sept 1870, *m* 30 Oct 1902, Charles Henry Ward, Jr (*b* in Colorado 14 July 1873; *d* at Colorado Springs, Colorado 13 Dec 1927), son of Charles Henry Ward, by his wife Hannah Ogden, and *d* at Spokane, Washington 2 July 1940, having had issue, one son and two daus.

5*c* Hannah Lee WASHINGTON, *b* at Braddock, W Virginia 30 Dec 1871; *dunm* at Spokane, Washington 16 Jan 1917.

6*c* Richard Scott Blackburn WASHINGTON, *b* at Braddock, W Virginia 4 Sept 1873, *m* at Durango, Mexico 7 July 1915, Guadalupe (*b* at Durango 17 Feb 1891; *d* there 21 May 1916), dau of Juan I. Reyes, by his wife Jovita Natera, and *d* at Durango 1 June 1938, leaving issue,

●Guadalupe WASHINGTON [*Florida 1215, PTE, Durango, Durango, Mexico*], *b* at Durango 4 May 1916, *m* 8 Sept 1941, Ulpiano Arzac (*b* at Mazatlan, Sinalao, Mexico 7 Nov 1916; *d* at Durango 6 March 1969), son of Ulpiano Arzac, by his wife Adriana Rodreguez, and has issue,

1*e*●Ulpiano ARZAC, economist [*Florida 1213, PTE, Durango, Durango, Mexico*], *b* at Mazatlan, Sinalao, Mexico 4 Nov 1942.

2*e*●Ricardo ARZAC [*Olmos 207, Durango, Durango, Mexico*], *b* at Mexico, DF, Mexico 20 March 1944, *m* 8 July 1967, ●Elena Maria (*b* at Torreon, Coahuila, Mexico 3 Nov 1947), dau of Jesus Max Romo, by his wife Refugio Zozaya, and has issue,

●Ricardo ARZAC ROMO, *b* at Torreon, Coahuila, Mexico 1 Nov 1969.

3*e*●Ernesto ARZAC, lawyer [*Francisco de Ibarra 1125, Durango, Durango, Mexico*], *b* at Mexico, DF, Mexico 1 April 1945, *m* 19 April

1973, ●Virginia (*b* Chihuahua 1 Aug 1954), dau of Raul Lozoya and Mercedes Uribe, and has issue (●Ernesto, *b* 19 Sept 1974).

4*e*●Maria de Lourdes ARZAC, *b* at Mexico, DF, Mexico 31 March 1948, *m* 13 Sept 1969, ●Rodolfo Garza (*b* at San Pedro, Coahuila, Mexico 12 Sept 1935) [*Florida 1215b, PTE, Durango, Durango, Mexico*], son of Rodolfo Garza Martinez, by his wife Josefina Sada, and has issue,

1*f*●Rodolfo GARZA ARZAC, *b* 15 July 1970.

2*f*●Alfredo GARZA ARZAC, *b* 1 Jan 1973.

5*e*●Sergio ARZAC, *b* at Moclova, Coahuila, Mexico 19 Oct 1955, *educ* Instituto Tecnologico de Monterrey, Monterrey, Nuevo Leon, Mexico.

7*c* Thomas Campbell WASHINGTON, *b* at Braddock, W Virginia 9 Feb 1875, *m* at Mattapoisett, Plymouth County, Mass 7 Sept 1910, Elizabeth Harlow (*b* at Mattapoisett 28 May 1885; *d* at Annandale, Fairfax County, Virginia 13 April 1967), dau of Judge Lemuel LeBaron Holmes, by his wife Elizabeth Warren Harlow, and *d* at Washington, DC 3 Aug 1946, leaving issue,

1*d*●Thomas Campbell WASHINGTON, architect [*300 West Columbia Street, Falls Church, Virginia 22046, USA*], *b* at Washington, DC 24 Sept 1911, *m* there 27 April 1942, ●Marguerite (*b* at Oak Crest, Maryland 1 June 1917), dau of Eugene Lewis Culver, by his wife Florence Owna Bridges.

2*d*●Richard Blackburn WASHINGTON, Lt-Col US Army (ret), contracting offr USN [*21 Candlewood Springs, New Milford, Connecticut 06776, USA*], *b* at Washington, DC 14 Dec 1915, *educ* George Washington Univ, and Benjamin Franklin Univ, *m* at Washington, DC 5 June 1943, ●Joan Barbara (*b* at New York 13 July 1925), yr dau of Robert Lister Macneil, FSA, The Macneil of Barra, 45th Chief of Clan Niall and 25th of Barra (*see that family*, BURKE'S *LG*), by his wife Kathleen Gertrude Metcalf and has issue,

1*e*●Lyn Metcalf WASHINGTON, *b* at Washington, DC 27 Dec 1946, *m* at Marbledale, Conn 4 Oct 1969, ●Francis Joseph Keane (*b* at Cambridge, Mass 15 Sept 1945) [*24 Westminster Avenue, Watertown, Mass 02172, USA*], son of Francis Thomas Keane, by his wife Honora Kennelly, and has issue,

●Carlyn Corbin KEANE, *b* at Nuremberg, Germany 9 Sept 1973.

2*e*●Jan Blackburn WASHINGTON, *b* at Frankfurt, Germany 18 July 1948, *m* at Darmstadt, Germany 17 March 1971, ●Karsten Günther Stodte, architect (*b* at Köln, Germany 8 June 1937) [*Hornerstrasse 92, Bremen, Germany*], son of Dr Günther O. Stodte, by his wife Gertrud Richardson, and has issue,

●Maja STODTE, *b* at Darmstadt 14 Jan 1973.

3*e*●Richard Corbin WASHINGTON [*Apt 1100, 1433 Williams Street, Denver, Colorado 80218, USA*], *b* at Heidelberg, Germany 11 Aug 1949, *educ* Brown Univ, *m* at Alliance, Ohio 6 July 1974, ●Georgeta (*b* at Faragas, Roumania 20 Jan 1953), dau of George Blebea, by his wife Helen Livia Leancu.

3*d*●LeBaron Holmes WASHINGTON, instrumentation engr [*7044 Cindy Lane, Annandale, Virginia 22003, USA*], *b* at Washington, DC 9 April 1921, *educ* Univ of Maryland, and Cornell Univ, *m* there 26 Dec 1942, ●Dorothy Helen (*b* at Hickory Point, Tennessee 20 Dec 1924), dau of William Reid Tucker, by his wife Ruby R. Blackwell, and has issue,

1*e*●Carol Reid WASHINGTON, *b* at Arlington, Virginia 3 Jan 1946, *m* at Hyattsville, Maryland 14 Jan 1967, ●Robert Charles

Mongelli (*b* at Washington, DC 12 July 1940) [*5-J Eastway, Greenbelt, Maryland 20770, USA*], son of Charles Mongelli, by his wife Mary Ondus, and has issue,

1*f*●Brian Joseph MONGELLI, *b* at Silver Spring, Maryland 23 Dec 1968.

2*f*●Eric LeBaron MONGELLI, *b* at Washington, DC 26 Sept 1970.

2*e*●Faye Holmes WASHINGTON, *b* at Alexandria, Virginia 19 Aug 1953, *m* at Annandale, Virginia 1 June 1974, ●Robert Nelson Weyant, Jr (*b* at Windber, Pennsylvania 8 Sept 1947) [*Apt 201, 4522 Commons Drive, Annandale, Virginia 22003, USA*], son of Robert Nelson Weyant, by his wife Victoria Madeline Kieta.

3*e*●Bradley Tucker WASHINGTON, *b* at Alexandria, Virginia 19 Nov 1955.

8*c* Anne WASHINGTON, *b* at Braddock, W Virginia 1 Sept 1876, *m* at St Louis, Missouri 2 April 1901, John Taylor Hopkins, Jr (*b* at Hopkinsville, Christian County, Kentucky 23 Oct 1878; *d* at Madison, Florida 17 Jan 1947), son of John Taylor Hopkins, by his wife Elizabeth Edwards Hickman, and *d* at Washington, DC 4 March 1971, having had issue, one son and two daus.

Bushrod Corbin Washington *m* 2ndly at Charles Town 14 Nov 1878, Emma Edwards (*b* at Rock Hall, Jefferson County, (W) Virginia 12 Nov 1843; *d* at Ephrata, Washington 16 Oct 1930), 7th dau of Thomas Hite Willis, by his wife Elizabeth Ferguson Ryland (and sister of Nathaniel Hite Willis—*see above p 55*), and *d* at Almira, Lincoln County, Washington 24 Feb 1919, having by her had issue,

9*c* Nathaniel Willis WASHINGTON, *b* at Charles Town 6 April 1881, *m* at Bremerton, Kitsap County, Washington 13 Aug 1913, Gladys (*b* at Port Orchard, Kitsap County, Washington 29 Aug 1890; *m* 2ndly, as his 2nd wife, Corbin Washington Castleman, son of her 1st husband's half-sister Eleanor Blackburn Washington (*see p 61*), and *d* at Spokane, Washington 13 June 1969), dau of Francis Duane Fuller, and Nancy Jane Tate, and *d* in Douglas County, Washington 10 July 1926, having had issue,

1*d*●Nathaniel Willis WASHINGTON, Attorney-at-law, mem Washington State Senate [*42 C Street, Northwest, Ephrata, Grant County, Washington 98823, USA*], *b* at Coulee City, Washington 2 May 1914, *m* at Tucson, Arizona 24 April 1945, ●Wanda Florence WELLS (name legally changed from SOKOLSKA) (*b* at Brooklyn, New York 3 Jan 1918), dau of Andrew Sokolski, by his wife Mary Magdalene Kotik, and has issue,

1*e*●Nathaniel Willis WASHINGTON [*1619 Northeast 82nd Street, Seattle, Washington 98115, USA*], *b* at Spokane 3 May 1946, *m* at Seattle, Washington 19 Sept 1971, ●Lisa Gayle (*b* 8 Aug 1952), dau of Harold Chadwick, by his wife Geneva, and has issue,

●Sarah Elizabeth WASHINGTON, *b* at Portland, Oregon 2 July 1972.

2*e*●Thomas Fuller WASHINGTON [*4060 West Warwick Street, Chicago, Illinois 60641, USA*], *b* at Spokane 8 March 1949, *m* at Seattle, Washington 11 Aug 1973, ●Lois (*b* 27 April 1951), dau of Louie Mueller, by his wife Wilma.

2*d* Francis Duane WASHINGTON, *b* at Coulee City 25 Feb, *d* there 28 Feb 1916.

3*d*●Roberta Ryland WASHINGTON, *b* at Ephrata 21 Oct 1917, *m* at Spokane 21 Sept 1936, ●James Barclay Williams (*b* at Spokane 20 Jan 1912) [*Riddle, Douglas County, Oregon 97469*], son of Jay Carl Williams, by his wife Rose Butler, and has issue,

1*e*●James Donald WILLIAMS [*Riddle, Douglas County, Oregon 97469, USA*], *b* at Spokane 26 May 1937, *m* at Greenacres, Spokane County, Washington 31 July 1954, ●Sharon

Naomi (*b* at Tacoma, Pierce County, Washington 9 April 1937), dau of Roderick Peter Forrest, Jr, by his wife Minnie Grenville, and has issue,

1*f*●Rannah Louise WILLIAMS, *b* at Spokane 17 March 1955.

2*f*●David Allen WILLIAMS, *b* at Spokane 18 Nov 1957.

3*f*●Eugene Scott WILLIAMS, *b* at Oxnard, California 14 June 1960.

4*f* Frederick Russell WILLIAMS, *b* at Grants Pass, Oregon 19 July 1963.

2*e*●Glenora Susanne WILLIAMS, *b* at Spokane 29 July 1938, *m* at Greenacres 16 Nov 1956, ●Duane Donald Flick (*b* at Leavenworth, Washington 16 Oct 1934) [*Box 593, Cashmere, Chelan County, Washington 98115, USA*], son of Ezra Earl Flick, by his wife Jennie Dolores Latimer, and has issue,

1*f*●Robert Alan FLICK, *b* at Spokane 26 Sept 1957.

2*f*●Dale Duane FLICK, *b* at Spokane 4 Nov 1958.

3*e*●Nathaniel Robert WILLIAMS [*Apt 201, 6810 Walker Mill Road, District Heights, Maryland 20027, USA*], *b* at Spokane 3 April 1943, *m* 1st at Houston, Texas 19 Sept 1965 (*m* diss by div), Vermeda Louise Birmingham (*b* in Arkansas 1945). He *m* 2ndly at Weslaco, Texas 29 April 1967, ●Judith Ann (*b* at Weslaco 5 Feb 1947), dau of Glen Ernest Adams, by his wife Mary Jane Wilson, and by her has issue, one dau and also has an adopted son (*see* ADDENDUM).

4*e*●Carl Willis WILLIAMS [*1038 West Providence Avenue, Spokane, Washington 99205, USA*], *b* at Spokane 18 March 1944, *m* there 9 Feb 1968, ●Rita Lou (*b* there 10 April 1944), formerly wife of Joseph Occhipinti, and dau of John Andrew Hull, by his wife Margaret Alda McMillan, and has issue,

●Joy Tracy WILLIAMS, *b* at Spokane 27 Aug 1969.

5*e*●Roberta Ann WILLIAMS, *b* at Spokane 10 Dec 1945, *m* at Opportunity, Spokane County, Washington 27 Aug 1966, ●John Martin Bloom (*b* at Sedro Woolley, Skagit County, Washington 22 Sept 1946) [*6403 South Wapato Street, Tacoma, Washington 98409, USA*], son of John Frederick Bloom, by his wife Susie Marie Vander Laan.

6*e*●Patrick Orville WILLIAMS [*Apt 1, 715 Cherry Street, Suisun City, California 94585, USA*], *b* at Spokane 6 Sept 1950, *m* at Berkeley, California 14 Feb 1971, ●Bonnie Janine Billecci (name legally changed from ALBEN) (*b* 22 April 1953), dau of — Alben, by his wife — Willenberg, and step-dau of Andrew Billecci, and has issue,

●Paris Beckett WILLIAMS, *b* at Moscow, Idaho 12 July 1972.

7*e*●Hugh Jay WILLIAMS, *b* at Spokane 4 Feb 1954.

4*d*●Glenora Gertrude WASHINGTON, *b* at Ephrata 21 Oct 1917 (twin with her sister Roberta Ryland), *m* there 18 June 1941, ●Deming Bronson Brown, Prof of Russian Literature, Univ of Michigan (*b* at Seattle, Washington 26 Jan 1919) [*602 Oswego Street, Ann Arbor, Michigan 48104, USA*], son of Kirk Charles Brown, by his wife Lois Bronson, and has issue,

1*e*●Kate Deming BROWN, *b* at New York 9 May 1947.

2*e*●Sarah Fuller BROWN, *b* at Evanston, Illinois 30 Sept 1951.

10*c* James Cunningham WASHINGTON, *b* at Charles Town 9 March 1883; *dunm* in Douglas County, Washington 10 July 1926.

11*c* Peachey Ryland WASHINGTON, *b* at Charles Town 3 July 1884; *dunm* in Douglas County,

Washington 10 July 1926.

2*b* George WASHINGTON, *b* at Claymont 22 Feb 1842; *ka* nr Brownsburg, Rockbridge County, Virginia 30 June 1863, *unm.*

3*b* Catherine Campbell WASHINGTON, *b* at Claymont 28 Sept 1845; *d* there 20 Aug 1847.

4*b* James Cunningham WASHINGTON, *b* at Claymont 14 Sept 1847; *dunm* in military prison at Washington, DC 28 Feb 1865.

5*b* Thomas Blackburn WASHINGTON, *b* at Claymont 11 Jan 1851, *m* 5 Nov 1874, his 2nd cousin once removed Eleanor Thomas (*b* in Clarke County, Virginia 22 Oct 1844; *d* at Washington, DC 1 Sept 1921), dau of Dr Richard Scott Blackburn, by his wife Sarah Ann Eleanor Thomas, and *d* 9 Aug 1923, having had issue,

1*c* Rebecca Janet WASHINGTON, *b* at Knoxville, Maryland 3 Dec 1875; *dunm* at Washington, DC 8 March 1939.

2*c* Eleanor Thomas WASHINGTON, *b* at Braddock, W Virginia 30 April 1878, *m* 5 Jan 1904, Harris Lightfoot Forbes (*b* at Annapolis, Maryland 5 Feb 1877; *d post* 1953), son of Joseph Harris Forbes, by his wife Fanny Lightfoot, and *d* at Montrose, California 28 Oct 1953, leaving issue, one son.

3*c* John Sinclair WASHINGTON, *b* at Charles Town 12 Jan, *d* there 13 Jan 1880.

4*c* Sarah Watts WASHINGTON, *b* at Charles Town 3 Aug 1883, *m* at Washington, DC 3 Aug 1905, Walter Howell Lee (*b* at Washington, DC 3 Jan 1880; *d* there 8 July 1928), son of Mandeville Girard Lee, by his wife Frances Knapp, and *d* at Westmoreland Hills, Montgomery County, Maryland 11 Jan 1939, leaving issue, two sons and two daus.

6*b* Anne Maria Thomasina Blackburn WASHINGTON, *b* at Claymont 22 Oct 1854, *m* at Tokyo, Japan 14 May 1879, as his 1st wife, James Alfred Ewing, CB (later Sir Alfred Ewing, KCB) (*b* at Dundee, Scotland 27 March 1855; *d* at Cambridge, England 7 Jan 1935), 3rd son of Rev James Ewing, of Dundee, by his wife Marjory Ferguson, and *d* at Crockham Hill, nr Edenbridge, Kent, England 10 April 1909, leaving issue, one son and one dau.

Bushrod Corbin Washington *m* 2ndly at Leesburg, Virginia 29 Jan 1835, Maria Powell (*b* 27 July 1791; *d* 4 Nov 1847), dau of Matthew Harrison, and *d* at Albany, New York 27 July 1851.

(4) Jane Mildred WASHINGTON, *b* at Walnut Farm *ca* 1793; *d* at Mount Vernon Sept or Oct 1807.

(5) Mary Lee WASHINGTON, *b* at Walnut Farm *ca* 1796, *m* at Mount Vernon Nov 1813, Noblet Herbert (*b ca* 1784; *d* at Mount Vernon 15 Aug 1825), son of Thomas Herbert, by his wife Sarah, and *d* at Blakeley 16 Oct 1827, having had issue, four sons and one dau (all of whom *d* as infs or *unm*).

(6) Corbin Thomas WASHINGTON, *b* at Selby, Fairfax County, Virginia, *ca* 1798; *d ca* 1802.

5 William Augustine WASHINGTON, *b* at Bushfield *ca* 1767; *d ca* Feb 1784.

6 Mildred C. WASHINGTON, *b* at Bushfield *ca* 1769, *m* in Westmoreland County, Virginia 15 Oct 1788, as his 2nd wife, Thomas Lee, of Parke Gate, Prince William County, Virginia (*b* at Chantilly, Westmoreland County, Virginia 20 Oct 1758; *d* at Belmont, Loudoun County, Virginia 7 Sept 1805), eldest son of Richard Henry Lee, by his wife Anne Aylett (and brother of Mrs Corbin Washington and the 2nd Mrs William Augustine Washington), and *dsp* in Virginia *ca* 1797.

8 Charles WASHINGTON, of Mordington, Jefferson County, founder of Charles Town, W Virginia, Col Virginia Militia, *b* in Stafford County, Virginia 2 May 1738, *m* 1761, Mildred, dau of Col Francis Thornton, JP, of Fall Hill, by his wife Frances, dau and co-heiress of Roger Gregory, and *d* 16 Sept 1799, having had issue,

1 George Augustine WASHINGTON, Col US Army, *b* 1763, *m* 1785, Frances Bassett (*b* 1767), and *dvp* 1793, having had issue,

(1) George Fayette (or Frederick) WASHINGTON, *b* 1787; *d* an inf.

(2) Anna Maria WASHINGTON, *b* 1788, *m* 1810, Capt Reuben Thornton, and *d* 1814, leaving issue, two sons.

(3) George Fayette WASHINGTON, *b* 1790, *m* 1813, Frances (*d* 1860), dau of — Frame, of Charlestown, W Virginia, and *d* 1867, having had issue,

1*a* Charles Augustine WASHINGTON, *b* 1814; *dunm* 1861.

2*a* Francis Massey WASHINGTON, *b* 1816; *dunm.*

3*a* — WASHINGTON, *d* an inf.

4*a* George Fayette WASHINGTON, *b* 1823; *dunm* 1853.

5*a* Matthew Burwell WASHINGTON, *b* 1830, *m* 1862, Nannie Bird Dandridge, dau of — Buchanan, and *d* 1868, leaving issue,

Nannie Bird WASHINGTON, *b* 1864; *dunm* 1919.

(4) Charles Augustine WASHINGTON, *b* 1791; *d* an inf.

2 Frances WASHINGTON, *b* 1763, *m* 1st 1731, Col Burgess Ball (*b* 1749; *d* 1800), and had issue, four sons and four daus. She *m* 2ndly 1802, Dr Francis Peyton (*d* 1808), and *d* 1815, having had further issue, one dau.

3 Samuel WASHINGTON, of Fredericksburg, Virginia, later of Kanawha County (now W Virginia), Capt Virginia Militia, *b* 1765, *m* 1795, Dorothea, dau of — Thornton, of Fall Hill, Spottsylvania County, Virginia, and had issue,

(1) Samuel Thornton WASHINGTON, *b* 1796, *m* Wilhelmina Hudson (*d* 1853), and had issue,

Mary Martha WASHINGTON, *b* 1838, *m* 1858, Andrew J. Somerville (*b* 1827; *d* 1907), and *d* 1884, leaving issue, two daus.

(2) Augustine C. WASHINGTON, *b* 1798; *dunm.*

(3) George F. WASHINGTON, *b* 1800; *dunm.*

(4) Frances A. WASHINGTON, *b* 1805; *dunm.*

4 Mildred WASHINGTON, *b* 1777, *m* Col Thomas Hammond, and *dsp.*

9 Mildred WASHINGTON, *b* at Wakefield, Westmoreland County, Virginia 21 June 1739; *d* there 23 Oct 1740.

# Notes

1 Through the Kytson family the Washingtons can trace kinship with the Rt Hon Sir Winston Churchill (*see* APPENDIX D, SOME REMARKABLE KINSHIPS).

2 Through the Butler family a Royal Descent from King Edward I can be traced (*see* APPENDIX C, PRESIDENTS OF ROYAL DESCENT).

3 From Col John Washington's younger son, John Washington, of Mattox, Westmoreland County, and Hylton, Stafford County, Virginia (*ca* 1661-1698), descend Mr George Sydney Horace Lee Washington, MA, FSA, of 15 Clare Street, Cambridge, England (*see* BURKE'S *Distinguished Families of America* for full details of the descent) and his sister Helen Lawrence Lee Washington, who *m* 27 Jan 1940, Arthur Norris Kennard, Welsh Guards, only son of Sir Howard William Kennard, GCMG, CVO (*see* BURKE'S *Peerage*, KENNARD, Bt).

4 Through the Reade family several lines of Royal Descent can be traced (*see* APPENDIX C, PRESIDENTS OF ROYAL DESCENT) and also kinship with HM Queen Elizabeth II and with Gen Robert E. Lee (*see* APPENDIX D, SOME REMARKABLE KINSHIPS).

5 Through his mother George Washington was half first cousin to the maternal grandfather of the future President Madison, thus:—

Julia Romney (1) = Col Joseph Ball (*d* 1715) = (2) Mary Montague

Anne Ball
= Col Edwin Conway

Mary Ball
= Augustine Washington

Francis Conway

GEORGE WASHINGTON

Eleanor Rose Conway
James Madison

JAMES MADISON

6 The Dandridge family came from Oxfordshire, where Martha Dandridge's great-great-grandfather, Bartholomew Dandridge, farmed at Drayton St Leonard at the end of the sixteenth century. His grandson, John Dandridge, was Master of the Painter Stainers Company in London, and the father, by his second wife Ann, of Col John Dandridge, who emigrated to America and became the father of Martha (*see* "News of Martha Washington" by W. S. Bristowe in *The Genealogists' Magazine, Vol XV, p 608*, 1968).

7 Nicholas Lloyd Rogers married secondly Hortensia Hay, the grand-daughter of President Monroe (*see p 155*).

# John Adams

## 1735-1826

———

2nd President of the
United States of America
1797-1801

JOHN ADAMS, 2ND PRESIDENT

# John Adams

## 1735-1826

### 2nd President of the United States of America
### 1797-1801

IF THE ghost of John Adams returned to the United States in the present day he would probably think that some of his optimistic and some of his pessimistic predictions had been borne out. He would be proud to find that the United States was a populous and prosperous nation, still living under the Constitution of 1787. He might be depressed but not surprised to discover that while Washington and Jefferson had giant monuments in the nation's capital, John Adams remained uncommemorated—at least on that scale. Being a bookish man, he would no doubt explore the libraries and bookstores. If so, his jealousy would be aroused by the numbers of volumes devoted not only to Washington and Jefferson but to his maddeningly famous contemporary Benjamin Franklin. At least, though, he would be gratified to learn that the Massachusetts Historical Society housed the papers of the Adams family, and was publishing them in a magnificent many-volumed edition.

In short, John Adams was a prickly character who never quite felt that he was given his due; a fierce patriot; and a lover of New England generally, and his native state Massachusetts in particular. His services to the United States were in truth exceptional, and not always fairly assessed. An early member of the Continental Congress, he was one of the firebrands who impelled the colonies toward the final break with the mother country. He labored on innumerable Congressional committees. He served America as a diplomat, perhaps not as spectacularly as he liked to think but with considerable effect. He used his good lawyer's mind to explore constitutional history, for the benefit of Massachusetts and for the whole United States. As he saw the outcome, he was grudgingly rewarded, and undermined by enemies like Alexander Hamilton who reacted to him as a limb of Satan might to the presence of one of the heavenly host. Thanks to such machinations, he came an ignominious second-best to George Washington. When Washington received every possible electoral vote in 1789 and 1792, Adams as Vice-President fell far short of this universal acclaim. Presiding over the Senate, he felt superfluous and unpopular. "His Rotundity" and the "Duke of Braintree" were among the nicknames he writhed under. He could not help being insignificant in physique, or less magnetic than others among the Founding Fathers. Being John Adams, he scorned to ingratiate himself. He *knew* he was correct in debates, whether the theme was human nature, the structure of government, or what line to take with Britain and France. When his countrymen and his fellow Federalists attacked him for his policies as President he stuck to his guns. To his chagrin the electors denied him a second term. He did not stay in Washington for his successor Jefferson's inauguration, but set off to lick his wounds at home in Quincy, Massachusetts.

John Adams, however, was too resilient to brood for long. "I am of the cat kind", he once remarked to his admirable wife Abigail; no matter where people threw him, he always landed on his feet. He remained intellectually alert for another quarter of a century. Though he wore his rectitude like a ceremonial garment, not even his enemies claimed that he was dishonest or stupid. He and Jefferson were estranged for a number of years, and he had cause to believe that Jefferson had slandered him. But after Jefferson in turn had left the White House, the two old adversaries renewed their friendship through a wonderful series of letters. With the passing years death claimed one after another of the generation that had made the Revolution. The death of Abigail in 1818 was a bad blow. Yet Adams continued to find life amazingly interesting. For one thing he was the founder of a dynasty. He was able to watch the political progress of his eldest son, John Quincy Adams, and live long enough to see a second Adams generation installed in the White House.

John Adams will probably never have an imposing monument to himself in Washington, DC. The Adams family home, though open to the public, is no rival to Mount Vernon or Monticello. He was never a soldier or a duellist, or involved in romantic affairs or other spicy scandals. So he is unlikely to be chosen as the subject of some historical extravaganza. Witty and spirited though Abigail was, she remains too much the New England matron to be cast as a glamorous heroine. A notion lingers in the popular conception of the era that Adams was "a speller after places and offices", in the words of Tom Paine, who hankered after a hereditary monarchy for the United States. Or Adams is stuck with some such label as "conservative". Or merely thought to have been an intellectual, a poor judge of men, a bad loser.

There is a tincture of truth in all these verdicts. Adams believed that men and women would group themselves into classes—according to

ABIGAIL SMITH, MRS ADAMS

talent, looks, wealth, education—in any society. He doubted whether America ever could or should evolve into a fully fledged democracy. He could be explosively angry, and self-righteous. He resented being overshadowed. The hero of his inauguration in 1797 was, Adams confessed to Abigail, not himself but the outgoing president George Washington. "He seemed to enjoy a triumph over me. Methought I heard him say, 'Ay! I am fairly out and you fairly in! See which of us will be the happiest!'" At the end of his crisis-laden Administration the incoming Jefferson seemed to enjoy another easy triumph over him. Yet he is not finally to be judged in such severe ways. Only in physical stature was he a little man placed between two giants. He was as brave in his fashion as Washington, and probably more than Jefferson. He was as learned, as fluent and as inquisitive as Jefferson, and considerably more so than General Washington. In diplomacy, though less urbanely charming than Franklin, he worked harder and was conceivably a more zealous guardian of America's interests. As President he faced up to France, but also to the High Federalists who wanted to bring on a war. The cross-fire killed his political career: his honor was intact. As the bitterness of controversy receded into the past, old John Adams looked back with an understandable pride upon a half-century of world-shaking events in which he had played no mean part. He was confident that America would flourish, if only it remembered his precepts: make good laws, respect them, curb excessive power. Writing to Jefferson with cheerful tranquillity in 1816, he agreed he would be ready to live his life all over again. Theirs was a "sublime and beautiful" world, "and a very benevolent one, notwithstanding all our snarling, and a happy one, if it is not made otherwise by our own fault". A man who could speak thus was no mere misanthrope.

# Chronology

1735    Born at Braintree (now Quincy), Massachusetts 19/30 (*os*) Oct.

1741-49    Attended schools in Braintree.

1750-51    Tutored by Joseph Marsh.

1751    Entered Harvard Nov.

1755    Graduated from Harvard 16 July; became a school master at Worcester, Massachusetts Aug.

1756    Began studying law under James Putnam, of Worcester.

1758    Admitted to Massachusetts Bar at Boston 6 Nov.

1761    Elected Surveyor of Highways for Braintree.

1768    Moved to Boston Jan.

1770    Representative from Boston to Massachusetts General Court; joined Sons of Liberty.

1771    Moved back to Braintree April.

1774    Elected one of five Massachusetts Delegates to the first Continental Congress at Philadelphia June; attended opening session 5 Sept.

1775    Appointed Chief Justice of the Superior Court of Massachusetts.

1776    Appointed a member of the five man committee to draft the Declaration of Independence 11 June; Chairman of Board of War and Ordnance 12 June; signed Declaration of Independence 2 Aug; proposed Washington for General of Continental Army.

1777    Elected Commissioner to France Dec.

1778    Sailed for France 17 Feb; landed at Bordeaux 29 March; arrived in Paris 5 April and presented credentials to Comte de Vergennes, the French Foreign Minister; received by King Louis XVI at Versailles 8 May.

1779    Left France 18 June; arrived in Boston 2 Aug; elected Representative of Braintree to Massachusetts Constitutional Convention Aug; drafted state constitution; appointed Minister Plenipotentiary to negotiate treaties with Great Britain 27 Sept; sailed for France 14 Nov; landed at El Ferrol, Spain 8 Dec.

1780    Arrived in Paris 9 Feb; appointed Minister Plenipotentiary of Congress to the United Provinces of the Netherlands.

1781    Received commission as Minister to the Netherlands 25 Feb; suffered severe illness Aug-Oct.

1782    Presented credentials to Willem V, Prince of Orange at The Hague 19 April; negotiated Dutch loan of five million guilders July; signed treaty of amity and commerce with The Netherlands 7 Oct; arrived in Paris to enter into conversations with the British 26 Oct.

1783    With Benjamin Franklin signed preliminary armistice with Great Britain at Versailles 20 Jan; with Franklin and John Jay signed peace treaty with Great Britain at Paris 3 Sept; appointed with Franklin and Jay to negotiate commercial treaty with Great Britain; left for London 20 Oct; left for Amsterdam Dec; negotiated new loan with Dutch bankers.

1784    Appointed with Franklin and Jefferson to negotiate commercial treaties with all European powers; joined wife and daughter in London 7 Aug; left for Paris to confer with Franklin and Jefferson 8 Aug.

1785    Appointed by Congress first US Minister Plenipotentiary to the Court of St James's 24 Feb; returned to London 25 May; presented credentials to King George III 1 June.

1787    Bought a farm in Quincy from Leonard Vassall Borland Sept.

1788    Sailed for US 28 April; arrived in Boston 7 June; elected to Continental Congress as a Delegate from Massachusetts.

1789    Elected 1st Vice-President of the United States 4 Feb; officially declared elected after tabulation of electoral vote by Congress 6 April; inaugurated at New York 21 April.

1792    Re-elected Vice-President 5 Dec.

1793    Officially declared re-elected after tabulation of electoral vote by Congress 13 Feb.

1794    Bill to suspend all commercial relations with Great Britain defeated in Senate by his vote 17 April.

1796    Elected President as Federalist candidate by 71 electoral votes as opposed to 68 for Jefferson the Democratic-Republican candidate, who became Vice-President, and 137 divided among eleven other candidates.

1797    Electoral vote tabulated by Congress and Adams and Jefferson officially declared elected 8 Feb; inaugurated as 2nd President of the United States of America in the Chamber of the House of Representatives at Philadelphia 4 March; resisted pressure to declare war on France; delivered first State of the Union address to Congress 22 Nov.

1798    Signed Act establishing Mississippi Territory 7 April; signed Act establishing Navy Department 3 May; signed Alien and Sedition Acts; delivered second State of the Union address to Congress 8 Dec.

1799    Delivered third State of the Union address to Congress 3 Dec.

1800    Signed first Federal Bankruptcy Act 4 April; signed Act establishing Indiana Territory 7 May; took up residence in White House, Washington, DC 1 Nov; delivered fourth and last State of the Union address to Congress 22 Nov; defeated in Presidential election by Jefferson Dec.

1801    Signed Judiciary Act of 1801 13 Feb; retired from Presidency 4 March; returned to Quincy.

1811    Reconciled with Thomas Jefferson.

1820    Attended Massachusetts Constitutional Convention at Boston as Representative of Quincy Nov-Dec.

1821    Defended amendments to state constitution which were ultimately approved; reviewed US Military Academy Corps of Cadets at Quincy 14 Aug.

1826    Reluctantly declined invitation to participate in 50th anniversary celebration of Independence Day in Boston; died of debility at Quincy 4 July (the same day as Thomas Jefferson); buried under Quincy Congregational Church.

# The Writings of President John Adams

*A Dissertation on Canon and Feudal Law* (1765)

*Thoughts on Government* (1776)

*A Defence of the Constitutions of Government of the United States of America Against the Attacks of Mr Turgot*, 3 vols (1787-88)

*Discourses on Davila* (first printed in *United States Gazette* 1791; published in book form 1805)

*Correspondence of the late President Adams* (1810)

*Novanglus and Massachusettensis* (1819)

*Correspondence Between the Hon John Adams and the late William Cunningham, Esq* (1823)

Adams's *Works* were edited by his grandson Charles Francis Adams (1850-56). His *Papers*, together with those of other members of his family, are appearing in a comprehensive new edition (1961-   ) under the direction of Lyman H. Butterfield

# Lineage of President John Adams

JOHN ADAMS, of Barton David, Somerset, mentioned in the Muster Roll of 1539 among the billmen finding harness, was brother of Robert Adams, of Butleigh, Somerset, husbandman (will dated 8 April, *pr* 2 Aug 1557), and father of

HENRY ADAMS, of Barton David, husbandman, *b ca* 1531, *m*, and *d* 1596 (*admon* 12 Aug), leaving issue,

JOHN ADAMS, of Barton David, *b ca* 1555, *m ca* 1576, Agnes (*bur* 15 Jan 1616), probably dau of John Stone, and was *bur* 22 March 1604, leaving issue, with an elder son and two daus,

HENRY ADAMS, of Barton David, emigrated to America 1638[1] and settled at Braintree, Mass, *b ca* 1583, *m* 19 Oct 1609, Edith (*bapt* 29 May 1587; *m* 2ndly *ca* 1651, John Fussell, of Weymouth and Medfield, Mass; *d* 1673), dau of Henry Squire, of Charlton Mackrell, Somerset, and grand-dau of Rev William Squire, Rector of Charlton Mackrell 1545-67, and was *bur* at Braintree 8 Oct 1646, leaving issue, with seven other sons and one dau, a 7th son,

JOSEPH ADAMS, of Braintree, Mass, farmer and maltster, *b* at Kingweston, Somerset 1626, *m* 2 Nov 1650, Abigail (*b* Sept 1634; *d* 27 Aug 1692), dau of Gregory Baxter, by his wife Margaret Paddy, and *d* 6 Dec 1694, having had issue, with four other sons[2] and five daus, an eldest son,

JOSEPH ADAMS, of Braintree, Mass, *b* 24 Dec 1654, *m* 1st 1682, Mary (*b* 27 Aug 1662; *d* 14 June 1687), dau of Josiah Chapin, and had issue, two daus. He *m* 2ndly 1688, Hannah (*b* 22 June 1667; *d* 24 Oct 1705), dau of John Bass, by his wife Ruth, dau of John Alden, who sailed in the *Mayflower* 1620, and by her had issue, five sons and three daus. He *m* 3rdly *ca* 1708, Elizabeth (*dsps* 13 Feb 1739), dau of Caleb Hobart, and *d* 12 Feb 1737. His 2nd son (by his 2nd marriage),

JOHN ADAMS, of Braintree, Mass, cordwainer and farmer, *b* at Braintree 28 Jan/8 Feb 1691, *m* 31 Oct 1734, Susanna (*b* at Brookline, Mass 5 March 1699; *d* at Braintree 17 April 1797), dau of Peter Boylston, by his wife Ann, dau of Benjamin White, and *d* at Braintree 25 May 1761, leaving issue, with two yr sons (*see* BROTHERS OF PRESIDENT JOHN ADAMS, *p 85*),

JOHN ADAMS, **2nd President of the United States of America.**

# The Descendants of President John Adams

JOHN ADAMS *m* at Weymouth, Mass 25 Oct 1764, his 3rd cousin[3], Abigail (*b* at Weymouth 11/22 Nov 1744; *d* at Braintree (now Quincy) 28 Oct 1818, *bur* there), 2nd dau of Rev William Smith, Congregational Min of Weymouth, by his wife Elizabeth, dau of Col Hon John Quincy, of Mount Wollaston, Mass, and had issue,

1 Abigail ADAMS, *b* at Braintree, Mass 14 July 1765, *m* in London, England 12 June 1786, Col William Stephens Smith, mem House of Reps from New York in 13th Congress 1813-15 (*b* at Long Island, New York 8 Nov 1755; *d* at Lebanon, New York 10 June 1816), son of John Smith, by his wife Margaret Stephens, and *d* at Braintree 30 Aug 1813, having had issue,
 1 William Steuben SMITH, Sec to his uncle John Quincy Adams in St Petersburg, *b* in London, England 30 April 1787, *educ* Harvard, and Columbia Univ, New York, *m* 1813, Catherine Maria Frances (*d* 1869), 5th dau of Hon Joshua Johnson, by his wife Catherine Nuth, and sister of Mrs John Quincy Adams (*see p 169*), and *d* 12 May 1850, having had issue,
  Caroline Amelia SMITH, *b* in Russia 1814; *d* in New York *ca* 1 July 1815.
 2 John Adams SMITH, *b* at Long Island, New York 10 Nov 1788; *dunm* 1854.
 3 Thomas Hollins SMITH, *b* Sept 1790; *d* 1791.
 4 Caroline Amelia SMITH, *b* 27 Jan 1795, *m* 11 Sept 1814, John Peter de Windt (*b* 19 Oct 1786; *d* 18 Nov 1870), and was drowned in a steamboat disaster on the Hudson River 28 July 1852, having had issue,
  (1) Caroline Elizabeth DE WINDT, *b* 19 Oct 1815, *m* 1st 7 June 1838, Andrew Jackson Downing (*b* at Newburgh, New York 30 Oct 1815; drowned with his mother-in-law on the Hudson River 28 July 1852), son of Samuel Downing, by his wife Eunice Bridge. She *m* 2ndly 16 Feb 1860, Judge John James Monell (*d* 22 April 1885), and *dsp* 1896 (?).
  (2) Julia DE WINDT, *b* 24 Sept 1817, *m* 27 Sept 1842, William Alexander Van Wagenen (*b* 1816; *d* 5 June 1871), and *d* 22 Oct 1889, having had issue,
   1*a* Samuel Whittemore VAN WAGENEN, *b* 25 May 1843; *d* 24 Oct 1856.
   2*a* Julia Carmer VAN WAGENEN, *b* 15 Nov 1844; *dunm* 19 Jan 1895.
   3*a* Caroline Adams VAN WAGENEN, *b* at Beacon, New York 1847; *dunm* at Essex Falls, New Jersey 7 March 1939.
   4*a* Charles VAN WAGENEN, *m* Nettie Burke, and had issue,
    — VAN WAGENEN (a dau), *d* young.
   5*a* William Alexis VAN WAGENEN, *m* Flora Whitbeck (*b* 1853; *d* 25 April 1881), and had issue,
    1*b* Percy VAN WAGENEN, *d* 26 Oct 1882.
    2*b* Hazel VAN WAGENEN, *m* Henry Cleveland Wellman (*b* at Yonkers, New York 18 June 1872; *d* at Ossining, New York 3 May 1951), and *d* 30 Dec 1920, leaving issue,
     ●Henry Hamilton WELLMAN, *b* 7 Feb 1910, *m*
     ●Harriet Lambie, and has issue,

     1*d* ●William Hamilton WELLMAN, *b* 27 March 1941.
     2*d* ●Barbara Lambie WELLMAN, *b* 3 Feb 1944.
   6*a* Jessie VAN WAGENEN, *b* 20 July 1859, *m* June 1888, John Gorham Low (*b* 2 April 1840; *d* 26 Nov 1907), and *d* 20 Dec 1951, having had issue,
    1*b* Julia de Windt LOW, *b* 22 April 1890; *dunm*.
    2*b* ●Mary Langdon LOW, *b* 10 Aug 1892, *m* 14 Sept 1928, ●William Prichard Browne, and has issue,
     1*c* ●William Prichard BROWNE, *b* 2 July 1930, *m* 27 Nov 1954, ●Frances Ann Kiehn.
     2*c* ●Mary Langdon BROWNE, *b* 26 March 1934.
    3*b* John Gorham LOW, Jr, *b* 20 May 1894, *m* ●Frances Fiesenius, and *d* June 1953, leaving issue,
     1*c* ●John Gorham LOW III, *m* Sept 1952, ●Elizabeth.
     2*c* ●David Nicholson LOW, *m* 19 Feb 1955, ●Betty Bright Page.
    4*b* ●Rebecca Cordis LOW, *b* 2 Jan 1896.
    5*b* ●Caroline Van Wagenen LOW, *b* 10 Sept 1898, *m* 1st (*m* diss by div), Lawrence Manley, and has issue,
     1*c* ●Mary Louise MANLEY, *m* June 1951, ●Coley Rhodes, and has issue,
      ●Coley RHODES, Jr, *b* Feb 1954.
     2*c* ●Emma Hall MANLEY, *m* March 1951, ●Lee Hanner, and has issue,
      ●Dale Robert HANNER, *b* Oct 1953.
    Caroline Van Wagenen Low *m* 2ndly, ●John R. Burton.
    6*b* Alexander Van Wagenen LOW, *d* 1900.
  (3) Elizabeth DE WINDT, *b* 23 Sept 1819, *m* 10 Oct 1843, her 2nd cousin once removed Rev Christopher Pearse Cranch, Unitarian Minister, later an artist (*b* at Alexandria, Virginia 8 March 1813; *d* at Cambridge, Mass 20 Jan 1892), son of William Cranch (son of Judge Richard Cranch, by his wife Mary Smith, sister of Mrs John Adams), by his wife Anna Greenleaf, and had issue,
   1*a* George William CRANCH, *b* 11 March 1847; *d* 18 Sept 1867.
   2*a* Leonora CRANCH, *b* 4 June 1848, *m* 20 June 1872, Henry Bruce Scott (*b* 15 March 1840; *d* 22 Feb 1921), and *d* 8 July 1933, having had issue,
    1*b* George Cranch SCOTT, *b* 17 July 1873, *m* June 1905, Mary Kennard, and had issue,
     1*c* ●Mary Adams SCOTT, *m* ●Emerson Evans, and has issue,
      1*d* ●Robert Scott EVANS.
      2*d* ●Martha Pickering EVANS, *b* 17 Jan 1945.
     2*c* ●George Cranch SCOTT, Jr, *m* 18 Sept 1943, ●Emily Rice, and has issue,
      1*d* ●Emma SCOTT, *b* 19 Oct 1945.

2*d*●Henry Bruce SCOTT, *b* 23 Oct 1946.
3*d*●Mary Adams SCOTT, *b* 1948.
4*d*●George Gordon SCOTT, *b* 27 Jan 1950.
3*c*●Dr Oliver Kennard SCOTT [*Boston, USA; 940 East 3rd Street, Casper, Wyoming 82601, USA*], *m* 4 July 1942, ●Deborah Ann Hubbard, and has issue,
1*d*●Charles Kennard SCOTT, *b* 1945.
2*d*●Hustace Hubbard SCOTT, *b* 1947.
3*d*●George Cranch SCOTT III, *b* March 1950.
4*d*●Clifford Belcher SCOTT, *b* 12 April 1951.
2*b* Henry Russell SCOTT, *b* 19 Nov 1874, *m* 23 May 1910, Mary Derby Peabody, and *dsp* 23 March 1952.
3*b* Sarah Carlisle SCOTT, *b* 7 May 1877; *dunm* Oct 1954.
4*b* Richard Gordon SCOTT, *b* 25 July 1880, *m* 28 Feb 1908, Grace Cranch Eliot (*b* 13 Sept 1875), and had issue,
1*c*●Henry Eliot SCOTT, *b* 26 Feb 1909, *m* ●Florentia Metzger, and has issue,
1*d*●Louisa SCOTT.
2*d*●Elizabeth Anne SCOTT, *b* 14 Oct 1952.
2*c*●Richard Cranch SCOTT, *b* 1 June 1910, *m* June 1935, ●Madeleine Leonie Erhard, and has issue,
●Richard Cranch SCOTT, Jr, *b* 1939.
3*c*●Abigail Adams SCOTT, *b* 9 Feb 1912, *m* 1938, ●Henry Korson, and has issue,
●Thomas Eliot KORSON, *b* 1943.
4*c* Peter Chardon SCOTT, *b* 9 Sept 1917; *d* 12 May 1934.
5*b* Christopher Pearse SCOTT, *b* 19 Sept 1883, *m* 1st June 1910 (*m* diss by div), Julia Reichman, and had issue,
1*c*●Bruce Chardon SCOTT, *b* 7 March 1912.
2*c* Jean Elizabeth SCOTT, *b* 23 Sept 1913, *m* June 1936, ●Francis Coan, and *d* Dec 1939, having had issue,
— COAN, *d* an inf.
3*c* Josephine SCOTT, *b* 22 Nov 1914; *d* March 1925.
4*c*●Margaret SCOTT, *b* 4 Jan 1919, *m* ●Norman C. Jensen, and has issue,
1*d*●Norman Scott JENSEN, *b* 12 May 1946.
2*d*●Barbara Ellen JENSEN, *b* 15 April 1947.
3*d*●Elizabeth Ann JENSEN, *b* 5 Oct 1948.
5*c*●Ruth Carlisle SCOTT, *b* 15 Dec 1921, *m* Nov 1943, ●George Garvey, and has issue,
1*d*●Margaret GARVEY, *b* 3 Feb 1946.
2*d*●Deborah GARVEY, *b* 28 June 1947.
3*d*●Susan GARVEY, *b* 28 June 1947 (twin with Deborah).
4*d*●Richard Scott GARVEY, *b* 26 Nov 1951.
Christopher Pearse Scott *m* 2ndly, ●Margaret Scott, and *d* 4 July 1954.
6*b* Elizabeth Rose SCOTT, *b* 5 Feb 1886, *m* 9 Oct 1920 (*m* diss by div), Ernest Garfield (*b* 1 March 1884), and had issue,
1*c* Margaret Scott GARFIELD, *b* 18 Sept 1922, *m* 18 June 1949, ●Robert Allen Cunningham, and *dsp*.
2*c*●William Ernest GARFIELD, *b* 13 July 1924.
3*c*●Nancy GARFIELD, *b* 8 Aug 1926.
7*b* Margaret SCOTT, *b* 23 April 1889, *m* 11 Sept 1911, Edward Lewis Lincoln, and *d* 4 Jan 1919, leaving issue,
1*c*●Leonora Cranch LINCOLN, *m* Sept 1935, ●Richard F. Estes, and has issue,
1*d*●Richard F. ESTES, Jr.
2*d*●Margaret Lincoln ESTES.
3*d*● Jere ESTES.
2*c*●Elizabeth Scott LINCOLN, *m* Nov 1936, ●Byron Fairchild, and has issue,
1*d*●Martha Bond FAIRCHILD.
2*d*●Margaret Graham FAIRCHILD.
3*d*●Lincoln FAIRCHILD, *b* 12 Aug 1945.
3*a* Caroline Amelia CRANCH, artist, *b* 7 May 1853; *dunm* 30 June 1931.
4*a* Quincy Adams CRANCH, *b* Aug 1855; *d* 15 Nov 1875.
(4) Louisa W. DE WINDT, *b* 1 Sept 1821, *m* 1st 4 Aug 1840, Samuel Whittemore, and had issue,
1*a* John de Windt WHITTEMORE, *b* 15 Sept 1841, *m* 11 Oct 1869, Ella Carroll Hoyt (*d* 16 Oct 1890), sister of Mrs Frank Adams de Windt (*see below, p 78*), and *d* 10 June 1899, having had issue,

1*b* Louis Hoyt WHITTEMORE, *b* 13 Sept 1871, *m* 1st Sept 1903, Eliza Dietrich; and 2ndly 9 Sept 1931, Ethel Gardner, and *dsp*.
2*b* Grace Carroll WHITTEMORE, *b* March 1873, *m* 10 June 1899, DeLancey Verplanck Newlin, and had issue,
Grace DeLancey NEWLIN, *b* 1900; *dunm* 1930.
3*b* Samuel WHITTEMORE, Jr, *b* 24 Oct 1876; *d* 8 April 1893.
4*b* Mabel Thurston WHITTEMORE, *b* 9 Nov 1879, *m* Frederick Roth, and *dsp* 25 Aug 1929.
5*b* Harold WHITTEMORE, *b* 25 June 1885; *d* 16 March 1903.
2*a* Caroline Louisa WHITTEMORE, *b* ca 1843; *d* ca 1859.
Louisa W. De Windt *m* 2ndly 26 Oct 1852, Clarence Chatham Cook (*b* 1828; *d* 1900), and had further issue,
3*a* Clara COOK, *b* 4 Feb 1853; *d* 25 July 1854.
(5) Anna Maria DE WINDT, *b* 9 Dec 1823; *dunm* 15 June 1848.
(6) John Adams DE WINDT, *b* 4 Aug 1825, *m* 3 June 1854, Mary Elizabeth (*b* 1 May 1830; *d* 12 Nov 1912), and *d* 24 Sept 1874, leaving issue,
John Peter Heyliger DE WINDT, *b* 12 Nov 1855, *m* 1st (*m* diss by div), Millie Etta (*b* 1 Nov 1859; *d* 8 March 1945), dau of Forrest Berry, and had issue,
1*b* John Peter Heyliger DE WINDT, Jr, *b* at Andover, Mass 7 Aug 1883, *m* at Randolph, Mass 1902, Lucie Day (*b* at Suffield, Conn 21 Jan 1883; *d* at Bayside, New York 1970), dau of William H. Spencer, by his wife Mary L. Kellogg, and *d* at Bayside, New York 4 April 1948, having had issue,
1*c*●Florence Spencer DE WINDT, *b* at New York 29 Dec 1902, *m* at Jamaica, New York 12 March 1925, ●Philip Higbee Dowdell (*b* at Watsontown, Pennsylvania 15 Dec 1900) [*519 North Overlook Drive, Alexandria, Virginia 22305, USA*], son of Thomas Dowdell, by his wife Della Higbee Fulmer, and has issue,
1*d*●Florence Higbee DOWDELL, *b* at Danville, Pennsylvania 20 Jan 1926, *m* at Lewisburg, Pennsylvania 12 April 1948, ●Richard Warg Lins (*b* at Milton, Pennsylvania 15 Feb 1922), son of Charles R. Lins, by his wife Dorothy Warg, and has issue,
1*e*●Christine Deming LINS, *b* at Flushing, New York 25 June 1950.
2*e*●Douglas Warg LINS, *b* at Butler, Pennsylvania 24 March 1952.
3*e*●Adele Bradford LINS, *b* at Pittsburgh, Pennsylvania 31 Oct 1953.
4*e*●Katherine Ann LINS, *b* at Gary, Indiana 4 Nov 1960.
5*e*●Steven Gray LINS, *b* at Gary, Indiana 22 Oct 1962.
2*d*●Thomas de Windt DOWDELL, *b* at Danville, Pennsylvania 22 July 1930, *m* at Vineland, New Jersey 16 June 1951, ●Phyllis Ann (*b* at Vineland 1 April 1929), dau of Fred Davis Snyder, by his wife Alma, and has issue,
1*e*●Linda Jane DOWDELL, *b* at Vineland, New Jersey 14 Feb 1953, *m* at Saranac Lake, New York 14 July 1974, ●Edward Livingston Hoe (*b* at Poughkeepsie, New York 9 Aug 1952).
2*e*●Ann Phyllis DOWDELL, *b* at Philadelphia 6 Dec 1955.
3*e*●Thomas de Windt DOWDELL, Jr, *b* at Chestnut Hill, Pennsylvania 23 Oct 1959.
4*e*●Andrew Reeves DOWDELL, *b* at Chestnut Hill, Pennsylvania 26 June 1963.
2*c* John Peter Heyliger DE WINDT III, *b* at Suffield, Conn 3 July 1908, *m* 1st (*m* diss by div), Helene Poey. He *m* 2ndly 1939, ●Dorothy Kilbourne (*b* Aug 1912) [*Box 636, Fruitland, Maryland 21826, USA*], and *d* 30 Dec 1965, having by her had issue,
1*d*● John Peter Heyliger DE WINDT IV, *b* 15 July 1940.
2*d*●Spencer Worth DE WINDT, *b* 26 Jan 1947.
3*d*●David Adams DE WINDT, *b* 7 Aug 1953.
3*c* Adele Adams DE WINDT, *b* 14 May 1910, *m* 8 Jan 1935, ●William Harold Hayward, and *dsp* 30 July

1936.
4c●Mary Louise DE WINDT, *b* at New Haven, Conn 3 Jan 1913, *m* at Bayside, NY 1934, ●Harry Fitzmaurice Dunkerton (*b* at New York 18 Feb 1910) [*249 Hillside Avenue, Kentfield, California 94904, USA*], son of T. Henry Dunkerton, by his wife Elizabeth, and has issue,
  1d●Gail Spencer DUNKERTON, *b* at Flushing, NY 30 Oct 1936, *m* at Frankfurt, Germany 1 Oct 1966, ●Klaus Eckrich (*b* at Klein Auheim, Germany 5 Sept 1943), son of Rudolph Eckrich, and has issue,
    1e●Harry Rudolph ECKRICH, *b* at Frankfurt 13 Aug 1967.
    2e●Linda Gail ECKRICH, *b* at Frankfurt 30 Jan 1969.
  2d●Virginia Anne DUNKERTON, *b* at Flushing, NY 18 June 1939, *m* at Short Hills, New Jersey 25 May 1963, ●Clement Buckley Newbold, Jr (*b* at Jenkinstown, Pennsylvania 26 July 1934) [*Box 54, Norristown Road, Spring House, Pennsylvania 19477, USA*], son of Clement Buckley Newbold, by his wife Marianne Meade Morris, and has issue,
    1e●Pamela de Windt NEWBOLD, *b* at Jenkinstown 23 Oct 1964.
    2e●Marianne Meade NEWBOLD, *b* at Jenkinstown 30 Nov 1965.
    3e●Clement Buckley NEWBOLD III, *b* at Jenkinstown 30 Nov 1969.
  3d●Linda de Windt DUNKERTON, *b* at Mineota, NY 12 June 1945, *m* at Ross, California 23 July 1966, ●Jonathan Hubert Gates (*b* 26 June 1941), son of Lawrence Randall Gates, by his wife Charlotte Lafayette, and has issue,
    1e●Quintin Garner GATES, *b* at Mountain View, California 12 March 1967.
    2e●Andrea Lin GATES, *b* in Japan 14 Feb 1970.
    3e●Anthea Ora GATES, *b* in Japan 14 Feb 1970 (twin with her sister).
  4d●Kathy Elizabeth DUNKERTON, *b* at Summit, New Jersey 6 March 1946, *m* at Jackson, Missouri April 1972, ●Harry Remone Crimm, son of Harry R. Crimm, by his wife Susan, and has issue,
    ●Abigail Amanda CRIMM, *b* at Jackson, Missouri 31 May 1973.
5c Garrett Girard DE WINDT, *b* at Birmingham, Alabama 16 Aug 1915; *d* at Jamaica, New York 1918.
6c●Arthur Kellogg DE WINDT [*148 Laurel Hill Road, Mountain Lakes, New Jersey 07046, USA*], *b* 22 April 1920, *m* 1st (*m* diss by div), Angela de Menceni. He *m* 2ndly, ●Margaret Bonner (*b* 21 Feb 1922), and by her has issue,
  1d●Keith Adams DE WINDT, *b* 17 May 1951.
  2d●Bonnie Day DE WINDT, *b* 29 Nov 1954.
7c●Forrest Berry DE WINDT [*Jamaica, Long Island, New York, USA*], *b* 19 Dec 1923.
2b Mary Elizabeth DE WINDT, *b* 1887, *m* 11 April 1911, John Odell Hauser (*d* Feb 1941), and had issue,
  1c●John Henry HAUSER (Rev) [*626 Pomona Avenue, Colorado, California 92118, USA*], *b* 2 May 1912, *m* ●Ruth Arbenz, and has issue,
    1d●Virginia Arbenz HAUSER.
    2d●John Odell HAUSER II.
    3d●Millie Keith HAUSER.
  2c Peter de Windt HAUSER, *b* 8 Oct 1914, *m* ●Lydia Smith [*1835 Edgehill Road, Abington, Pennsylvania 19001, USA*] and had issue,
    1d●Jana Smith HAUSER.
    2d●Peter Keith HAUSER.
  3c●Doris HAUSER, *b* 21 Dec 1918, *m* ●Webster Fairbanks Williams, Jr, son of Webster Fairbanks Williams, by his wife Rachel Nichols, and has issue,
    1d●Elizabeth de Windt WILLIAMS.
    2d●Webster Fairbanks WILLIAMS III.
3b Carolyn Girard Adams DE WINDT, *b* at Hempstead, New York 3 Feb 1893, *m* Harlan B. Hays, and *d* 1919, leaving issue,

●Elizabeth de Windt HAYS, *b* 14 Nov 1914, *m* ●William A. Fisher (*b* 17 Dec 1905), and has issue,
  1d●Carolyn Hays FISHER, *b* 7 July 1940.
  2d●Robert Ward FISHER, *b* 22 Oct 1945.
John Peter Heyliger de Windt *m* 2ndly, Susan J. Anderson, and *d* 9 March 1936.
(7) William Stephens DE WINDT, *b* 30 Jan, *d* 23 Sept 1827.
(8) Isabella Adams DE WINDT, *b* 23 Sept 1828, *m* 25 June 1848, Gabriel Furman, and had issue,
  1a William Stephens FURMAN, *m*, and *dsp* 3 Jan 1925.
  2a Susan Booth FURMAN, *b* 14 Aug 1850, *m* 26 Aug 1875, as his 2nd wife, Charles Elliott Lord (*b* 8 Feb 1843; *d* 14 April 1883), and *d* 17 May 1916, having had issue,
    1b Susan Isabel LORD, *b* 16 July 1877, *m* 12 April 1898, Henry T. Alley (*b* 19 Sept 1866), and *d* 15 Feb 1927, leaving issue,
      Isabel E. ALLEY, *b* 18 Aug 1899, *m* 16 Nov 1920, Thornton Emmons, and *d* 15 Feb 1935, leaving issue,
        1d●Virginia EMMONS, *b* 23 Oct 1923, *m* ●William Harrison Kalthoof, Jr, son of William Harrison Kalthoof, and has issue,
          ●Craig Emmons KALTHOOF, *b* 27 Nov 1952.
        2d George T. EMMONS, *b* 6 March 1928; *d* 27 Aug 1939.
    2b Sarah LORD, *b* 9 March 1879, *m* 8 Feb 1911, Arthur Murphy (*b* 19 Dec 1876; *d* 25 Nov 1911), and had issue,
      ●Arthur Lord MURPHY, *b* 28 Dec 1911, *m* 24 Dec 1938, ●Eleanor Harlee (*b* 22 Nov 1910), and has issue,
        1d●Arthur Lord MURPHY, Jr, *b* 1952.
        2d●Gloria MURPHY, *b* 1954.
    3b Henry LORD, *b* 18 Nov 1880; *d* 12 Nov 1886.
  3a Amelia Seaman FURMAN, *dunm*.
(9) Emily Augusta DE WINDT, *b* 9 July 1830, *m* 30 May 1855, Frederick Clarke Withers (*b* 4 Feb 1828; *d* 7 Jan 1901), and *d* 1 July 1863, leaving issue,
  1a Frank WITHERS, *dsp*.
  2a Alice WITHERS, *m* J. Foster Jenkins and *dsp*.
(10) Arthur DE WINDT, *b* 28 July 1832, *m* 8 May 1855, Georgiana T. Rich (*b* 1836; *d* 7 May 1900), and *d* 30 Sept 1907, leaving issue,
  Heyliger Adams DE WINDT, *b* at Fishkill, New York 17 Feb 1858, *m* 1st at New Bedford, Mass 10 Sept 1889, Bertha Williams (*b* at New Bedford, Mass 8 Aug 1867; *d* at Winnetka, Illinois 27 July 1907), dau of Thomas Mandell, and had issue,
    1b Heyliger DE WINDT, *b* at Chicago 3 Aug 1890, *m* 10 Sept 1914, Clara Swigart (*b* 1892), and *dsp*.
    2b Delano DE WINDT, *b* at Chicago, Illinois 30 Oct 1892, *m* at Great Barrington, Mass 17 June 1916, ●Ruth, dau of John H. C. Church, by his wife Mary Loop, and *d* at Albany, NY 10 Nov 1953, leaving issue,
      1c●Ruth DE WINDT, *b* at New Bedford, Mass 24 April 1917, *m* at Great Barrington, Mass 16 Aug 1941, ●Archibald Robinson Hoxton, Jr (*b* at Alexandria, Virginia 20 April 1916) [*Episcopal High School, 1200 N Quaker Lane, Alexandria, Virginia 22302, USA*], son of Archibald Robinson Hoxton, by his wife Sara Purvis Taylor, and has issue,
        1d●Archibald Robinson HOXTON III, *b* at Washington DC 21 Oct 1943, *m* 25 July 1964, ●Constance Congdon, and has issue,
          1e●Archibald Robinson HOXTON IV, *b* at Erwin, Tennessee 22 Feb 1965.
          2e●Frederick Clayborne HOXTON, *b* at Erwin, Tennessee, 31 Oct 1966.
        2d●Ann HOXTON, *b* at Washington DC 13 Sept 1946, *m* at Sheperdstown, W Virginia 29 Aug 1970, ●Michael Frank Taylor, of Denver, Colorado.
      2c●Mary DE WINDT, *b* at New Bedford, Mass 14 Aug 1918, *m* at Great Barrington, Mass 1947 ●William Archer Speers, (*b* at New York 1918), son of William Speers, by his wife Olive Archer, and has issue,
        1d●Susan Archer SPEERS, *b* at New York 1948,

*m* Sept 1972, ●R. Leith Herrmann, son of Robert Henry Herrmann.

2*d*●Joan Adams SPEERS, *b* at New York 1950.

3*c*●Edward Mandell DE WINDT [*25299 Cedar Road, Lyndhurst, Ohio 44124, USA*], *b* at Great Barrington, Mass 31 March 1921, *m* at Englewood, New Jersey 21 June 1941, ●Elizabeth (Betsy) (*b* at Long Island, New York 1921), dau of Harold Bope, by his wife Elizabeth Baird, and has issue,

1*d*●William de Windt ALEXANDER, *b* at Battle Creek, Michigan 1942, *m* at Cleveland, Ohio 1964, ●Peter Charles Stick.

2*d*●Delano DE WINDT II, *b* at Battle Creek, Michigan 1944, *m* 3 March 1973, ●Adriane (*b* at Bloomfield Hills, Michigan), dau of Maynard Rudolph Andreae, by his wife Patricia.

3*d*●Dana DE WINDT, *b* at Cleveland, Ohio 1948, *m* there 19 June 1971, ●Kathy (*b* at Cleveland, Ohio 1949), dau of Victor Gelb, by his wife Joan Freeman.

4*d*●Elizabeth (Lisa) DE WINDT, *b* at Cleveland, Ohio 1953.

5*d*●Edward Mandell DE WINDT, Jr, *b* at Cleveland, Ohio.

4*c*●Ann DE WINDT, *b* at Great Barrington, Mass 7 April 1924, *m* there 1944, ●Frederick R. (Ted) Schroeder, the tennis player (*b* in New Jersey 1921), son of F. R. Schroeder, by his wife — Heath, and has issue,

1*d*●John SCHROEDER, *b* at Great Barrington, Mass 1945.

2*d*●Richard SCHROEDER, *b* at Glendale, California 1946.

3*d*●Robert SCHROEDER, *b* at Glendale, California 1956.

3*b*●Caroline DE WINDT, *b* 24 Aug 1900, *m* 10 June 1922 (*m* diss by div), Albert Sellner Gardner, and has issue,

1*c*●Carol GARDNER, *b* 21 April 1923, *m* 1st 15 June 1946 (*m* diss by div), James Edward Thompson, and has issue,

1*d*●Carol Ann THOMPSON.

She *m* 2ndly 16 July 1950, ●Orville E. Gower, and has further issue,

2*d*●April GOWER.

3*d*●Bretton Lee GOWER.

4*d*●Candice GOWER.

2*c*●William Alfred GARDNER, *b* 10 June 1925, *m* 20 Jan 1950, ●Joan Carolyn Arnold, and has issue,

1*d*●Deborah Ann GARDNER.

2*d*●William Alfred GARDNER, Jr, *b* 30 April 1955.

4*b*●Alice DE WINDT, has Bible (containing dates of de Windt family) which was originally given to Caroline Smith de Windt (*see p 75*) by her, grandfather Pres John Adams, *b* 27 Sept 1902, *m* 4 Oct 1924, ●Randolph Gibson Owsley, banker, late Lt-Cmdr USNR (*b* at Dallas, Texas 18 Sept 1900) [*16345 Redington Drive, Redington Beach, St Petersburg, Florida 33708, USA*], son of William Lucius Owsley, by his wife Virginia Marion (Maybird) Gibson, and a descendant of William Randolph, of Turkey Island, Virginia (ancestor of many famous Americans notably Peyton Randolph, Pres 1st Continental Congress (grandson); and Edmund Randolph, 1st Attorney-Gen of USA, Thomas Jefferson (*qv*), and Chief Justice John Marshall (all great-grandsons)), and has had issue,

1*c*●Alicia OWSLEY, *b* at Lake Forest, Illinois 21 Jan 1928, *m* ●William Cunningham, and *dsp* 1949.

2*c*●Randolph Gibson OWSLEY, Jr [*882 North Church Street, Lake Forest, Illinois, USA*], *b* at Lake Forest, Illinois 4 Sept 1929, *m* 22 Nov 1961, ●Barbara Ann Jones (*b* at Kansas City 15 Feb 1939), and has issue,

1*d*●Laura Alice OWSLEY, *b* at Chicago, Illinois 6 July 1962.

2*d*●Randolph Gibson OWSLEY III, *b* at Evanston, Illinois 25 June 1963.

3*d*●Barbara Adams OWSLEY, *b* at Kansas City 11 Jan 1966.

Heyliger Adams de Windt *m* 2ndly 16 March 1912, Alice Greene Arnold (*b* 20 June 1871; *d* 16 May 1944), and *d* 17 Nov 1941.

(11) Francis (Frank) Adams DE WINDT, *b* 9 June 1834, *m* 15 Jan 1857, Emily Adele Hoyt (*d* 16 Oct 1890), sister of Mrs John de Windt Whittemore (*see above, p 76*), and *d* 8 Aug 1866, leaving issue,

1*a* Francis Adams DE WINDT, Jr, *m* Eliza Counhoven (*b* 4 Jan 1849; *d* 8 May 1919), and *d* 1926, leaving issue,

1*b* Katherine Belden DE WINDT, *b* 11 Oct 1882, *m* William Brewster Werner (*b* 11 Nov 1881), and had issue,

●Edith Natalie WERNER, *b* 5 June 1905, *m* ●William Louis Alexander (*b* 13 July 1904), and has issue,

1*d*●William de Windt ALEXANDER, *b* 5 April 1923, *m* ●Elva Virginia De Voe (*b* 19 April 1920), and has issue,

●Nancy Virginia ALEXANDER, *b* 21 Sept 1944.

2*d*●Richard Bruenig ALEXANDER, *b* 20 Nov 1937.

2*b* Marjorie Counhoven DE WINDT, *b* 19 April 1884; *dunm*.

2*a* Cornelia (Nina) DE WINDT, *dunm*.

3*a* Elizabeth (Bessie) DE WINDT, *m* Forest Greenfield, and *dsp*.

4*a* Adele DE WINDT, *m* Van Vorhis, and *dsp*.

5*a* Garrett (Gary) Sprevit DE WINDT, *b* 25 Jan 1864, *m* 4 Feb 1931, Maude Hunter, and *dsp* 21 June 1937.

(12) Mary Catherine DE WINDT, *b* 5 Dec 1838, *m* 5 June 1861, George Allen Seaman, and *d* 26 March 1881, having had issue,

1*a* Caroline Amelia SEAMAN, *b* 22 March 1862; *d* 2 Aug 1863.

2*a* Emily de Windt SEAMAN, *b* 9 June 1865; *dunm* 21 July 1931.

3*a* George Williams SEAMAN, *b* 11 Nov 1868, *m* 1st 18 Nov 1896, Caroline Ward Halgin (*b* 14 June 1873; *d* 14 May 1899). He *m* 2ndly 9 June 1903, Irmingarde Van Horne Freeman (*b* 2 April 1878), and *d* at Beacon, New York 27 Feb 1942, having by her had issue,

1*b* Sarah Corvinus SEAMAN, *b* 9 May 1904, *m* 24 Dec 1940, ●A. P. Mullan (*b* 5 Sept 1892).

2*b* George Hurtin SEAMAN, *b* 5 Oct 1905; *d* 1 March 1907.

3*b* Ogden Van Horne SEAMAN, *b* 28 May 1908; *d* 12 Feb 1923.

4*b*●Margaret Osborne SEAMAN, *b* 20 July 1910, *m* 10 Nov 1939, ●Artimus Whitaker Jones (*b* 12 Nov 1905).

5*b*●Elizabeth Hurtin SEAMAN, *b* 23 Nov 1911, *m* 13 May 1938, ●Robert Campbell Barry (*b* 28 Dec 1912), and has issue,

1*c*●Michael Van Horne (Robert) BARRY, *b* 19 Oct 1940.

2*c*●Gail Stuart BARRY, *b* 15 Dec 1942.

3*c*●Christopher Quinn BARRY, *b* 15 March 1946.

4*c*●Paul Corbett BARRY, *b* 15 March 1946 (twin with Christopher Quinn).

6*b*●Anne Ogden SEAMAN, *b* 13 Feb 1914.

7*b*●Emily de Windt SEAMAN, *b* 21 Oct 1917, *m* 11 June 1942, ●Lawrence Henry Hadland (*b* 16 Nov 1919), and has issue,

1*c*●Janet Ruth HADLAND, *b* 4 May 1943.

2*c*●Richard Manning HADLAND, *b* 14 Aug 1944.

3*c*●Judy Anne HADLAND, *b* 13 July 1948.

4*c*●Kenneth Lawrence HADLAND, *b* 17 July 1949.

5*c*●Marie Patricia HADLAND, *b* 16 Sept 1951.

6*c*●George Robert HADLAND, *b* 16 Sept 1951 (twin with Marie Patricia).

8*b*●Mary Patricia SEAMAN, *b* 20 Sept 1920, *m* 5 June 1948, James Robinson Daniels (*b* at Wilson, N Carolina 13 March 1905; *d* at Sylva, N Carolina 18 June 1961).

4*a* Charles Henry SEAMAN, *b* 15 March 1870, *m* 22 Oct 1901, Grace Beulah Aldridge (*b* 14 Nov 1880; *d* 14 Aug 1926), and *d* 11 Oct 1949, leaving issue,

1*b*●Harriet Elizabeth SEAMAN, *b* 14 April 1903, *m* 1 April 1927, ●Joseph James Doyle, and has issue,

1*c*●Joseph James DOYLE, Jr, *b* 19 May 1928.

2c●Thomas Henry DOYLE, *b* 21 Oct 1930.
3c●Grace Pauline DOYLE, *b* 7 Dec 1932, *m*
●Edward George Greger (*b* 27 Oct 1929), and has
issue,
   1d●Pauline Elizabeth GREGER, *b* 16 July 1953.
   2d●Katherine Johanna GREGER, *b* 17 Sept
   1954.
4c●Harry DOYLE, *b* 1 July 1938.
2b●Mary Catherine SEAMAN, *b* 8 April 1904, *m* 17
July 1923, Dr Samuel Benajah Link (*b* 7 July 1900; *d*
at Stamford, Connecticut, 31 March 1961), and has
issue,
   1c●Patricia Ann LINK, *b* 31 Oct 1925, *m* 1st 1 May
   1944, Robert J. Cavanaugh (*d* Dec 1944). She *m*
   2ndly Nov 1947, ●Thomas Christopher Murphy,
   and has issue,
      1d●Thomas Christopher MURPHY, Jr, *b* 26 Aug
      1948.
      2d●Brian MURPHY, *b* 5 Jan 1950.
      3d●Sally Elizabeth MURPHY, *b* 31 Dec 1952.
   2c●Sally Elizabeth LINK, *b* 17 Jan 1927, *m* March
   1947, ●Robert Bilder, and has issue,
      ●Cynthia Curtis BILDER, *b* 9 Nov 1950.
   3c●Samuel Adams LINK, *b* 29 June 1932.
   4c●Walker Gordon LINK, *b* 11 Aug 1934, *m*
   ●Joyce Elliott (*b* 17 June 1934), and has issue,
      1d●Michael Elliott LINK, *b* 7 Feb 1952.
      2d●Catherine Ann LINK, *b* 16 July 1954.
3b●Charles Henry SEAMAN, Jr, *b* 2 June 1916, *m*
●Barbara Tunison (*b* 11 Sept 1914), and has issue,
   ●Gary Adams SEAMAN, *b* 25 Aug 1949.
5a Mary Groebe SEAMAN, *b* 1 July 1872, *m* 1 July 1903,
George Ketchum (*d* 1940), and *d* 7 Jan 1947, leaving
issue,
   1b●Mary Catherine Wolfe KETCHUM, *b* 29 Aug
   1904, *m* ●Ernest Cluett Walker (*b* 19 Feb 1905), and
   has issue,
      Richard Seaman WALKER, *b* 17 March 1931; *dunm*
      April 1953.
   2b●George Miller KETCHUM, *b* 4 Dec 1906, *m* 4 Dec
   1929, ●Grace Doughty (*b* 2 May 1908), and has issue,
      ●Jacqueline Joan KETCHUM, *b* 30 May 1932.
   3b●Morris KETCHUM, *b* 20 Nov 1909, *m* 1 Feb 1936
   (*m* diss by div), Jessie Nisbit (*b* 2 June 19—), and has
   issue,
      1c●Joy Anne KETCHUM, *b* 20 Nov 1936.
      2c●Morris George KETCHUM, *b* 24 May 1941.
6a Richard Heber SEAMAN, *b* 17 Jan, *d* 13 July 1881.
**2 JOHN QUINCY ADAMS, 6th President of the United
States of America** (*see p 159*).
3 Susanna ADAMS, *b* at Boston 28 Dec 1768; *d* there 4 Feb 1770.
4 Charles ADAMS, *b* at Boston 29 May 1770, *educ* Harvard. *m* 29
Aug 1795, Sarah (*b* 6 Nov 1769; *d* 8 Aug 1828), dau of John
Smith, by his wife Margaret Stephens (and sister of Col William
Stephens Smith — *see above, p 75*), and *d* at New York City 30
Nov 1800, leaving issue,
   1 Susan Boylston ADAMS, *b* at New York City 8 Aug 1796, *m*
   1st 3 Aug 1817, Lieut Charles Thomas Clark (*b* 1793; *d* 14
   April 1819), and had issue,
      Susanna Maria CLARK, *b* at Quincy, Massachusetts 2
      March 1818, *m* 13 May 1839, Adoniram Judson Crane, of
      Richmond, Virginia (*b* 2 Nov 1817; *d* 3 Jan 1867), and *d* at
      Philadelphia 27 Aug 1853, having had issue,
         1a Abigail Louisa CRANE, *b* 17 Feb 1840; *d* 8 Feb 1843.
         2a Charles Thomas CRANE, *b* 12 April 1842; *d* 1 Aug
         1843.
         3a Charles Thomas Clark CRANE, *b* 9 Jan 1844, *m* 1st 18
         Sept 1867, Annie Louise Levering (*b* 22 July 1845; *d* 12
         July 1906), and had issue,
            1b Charles Levering CRANE, *b* 1868; *dunm* 1902.
            2b Clinton CRANE, *b* 1870; *d* 1871.
            3b Elizabeth CRANE, *b* 1871; *d* 1872.
            4b Louis Woods KRANE, *b* 1873; *d* 1879.
            5b Churchill CRANE, *b* 1875; *d* 1876.
            6b Robert Treat CRANE, *b* at Baltimore, Maryland 9
            June 1880, *educ* Johns Hopkins Univ, *m* 20 June 1908,
            ●Maria Louise (*b* at St Louis, Missouri 6 Oct 1882) [*7
            Temple Street, Stonington, Connecticut, USA*], dau of
            George Washington Riggs, by his wife Kate
            Cheesman, and had issue,
               1c●Robert Treat CRANE, Jr [*1341 Monk Road,*

*Gladwyne, Pennsylvania, USA*], *b* at Montreal,
Canada 25 Aug 1909, *m* 31 Dec 1934, ●Virginia
Mary Ladd, and has had issue,
   1d Mary Truesdell CRANE, *b* 28 June 1938; *d* 9
   June 1940.
   2d●Robert Treat CRANE III, *b* 27 Dec 1939.
   3d●Sanford Ladd CRANE, *b* 28 July 1943.
   4d●Maria Louisa CRANE, *b* 27 Dec 1945.
2c●George Levering CRANE, *b* at Washington, DC
6 Oct 1911, *m* 1st (*m* diss by div), Ruth Carrington,
and had issue,
   1d●Elizabeth Louise CRANE, *b* 30 Dec 1939.
   2d●Ruth Carrington CRANE, *b* 30 Dec 1941.
George Levering Crane *m* 2ndly 2 Aug 1947, ●Lyle
Long, and by her has issue,
   3d●Marion Long CRANE, *b* 8 Jan 1949.
   4d●George Levering CRANE, Jr, *b* 18 June 1950.
   5d●Susan Adams CRANE, *b* 21 Dec 1953.
   6d●Thomas Francis CRANE, *b* 21 Dec 1953
   (twin with his sister Susan Adams Crane).
3c●Charles Thomas CRANE [*7 Temple Street,
Stonington, Connecticut, USA*], *b* at Ann Arbor,
Michigan 20 Dec 1913.
4c Laurason Riggs CRANE, *b* at Ann Arbor,
Michigan 20 Dec 1913 (twin with Charles Thomas
Crane); *d* 18 Oct 1922.
5c●Kate Cheesman CRANE [*7 Temple Street,
Stonington, Connecticut, USA*], *b* at Ann Arbor,
Michigan 26 Feb 1918.
6c●Matlack Cheesman CRANE, *b* at Ann Arbor,
Michigan 26 Feb 1918 (twin with Kate Cheesman),
*m*.
7b John Alden CRANE, Offr Field Art US Army, *b* at
St Georges, Maryland 2 Dec 1885, *educ* Johns
Hopkins Univ, *m* 21 Oct 1908, ●Mary Sterret, dau of
Sterrett McKim, of Baltimore, and had issue,
   1c●John Alden McKim CRANE, *b* at Fort
   McKinley, Philippine Islands 2 Aug 1909, *m* 28
   July 1950, ●Eva D. Rabbitt.
   2c●Mary McKim CRANE, *b* at Baltimore 6 Oct
   1917.
Charles Thomas Clark Crane *m* 2ndly 26 Oct 1907,
Gertrude Jackson, and *d* 23 March 1920.
4a Maria Louisa CRANE, *b* 15 Sept 1846, *m* Daniel C.
Woods, and *dsp*.
Susan Boylston Adams *m* 2ndly 1833, William R. H.
Treadway, of Richmond, Virginia (*b* 1795; *d* 1836), and *d* 21
Jan 1846.
2 Abigail Louisa Smith ADAMS, *b* 8 Sept 1798, *m* 14 Oct
1814, Alexander Bryan Johnson, of Utica, New York (*b* at
Gosport, Hants, England 29 May 1786; *d* 9 Sept 1867), and *d*
4 July 1838, having had issue,
   (1) John Adams JOHNSON, *b* 3 Oct 1815; *d* 29 Nov 1820.
   (2) Alexander Smith JOHNSON, Judge, *b* at Utica, New
   York 30 July 1817, *m* 8 Nov 1852, Catherine (*b* 19 April
   1833; *d* 5 Feb 1898), dau of — Crysler, of St Catherine,
   Ontario, Canada, and *d* at Nassau, Bahamas 26 Jan 1878,
   leaving issue,
      1a Catherine Maria Crysler JOHNSON, *b* 1 Aug 1853, *m*
      1st 2 June 1878, Harvey Doolittle Talcott (*b* 1844 (?)),
      and had issue,
         1b Margaret TALCOTT, *m* — Corbin, and had issue,
            ●Margaret CORBIN.
      Catherine Maria Crysler Johnson *m* 2ndly 14 June 1881,
      Judge George Edmund Otis, of Redlands, California (*b*
      1846; *d* 1906), and had further issue,
         2b●Elsie Gansevoort OTIS, *b* at San Francisco 13 July
         1882, *m* 30 Aug 1913, her 1st cousin, ●Horatio
         Seymour, Jr, and has issue (*see p 80*).
      2a Abigail Adams JOHNSON, *b* 23 Nov 1855, *m* 12 Oct
      1880, Horatio Seymour (*b* 8 Jan 1844; *d* 6 Jan 1907), son
      of John Forman Seymour, by his wife Frances Ancil
      Tappan, and nephew of Horatio Seymour, Democratic
      candidate for the Presidency 1868, and *d* 6 Jan 1915,
      leaving issue,
         1b Mary Ledyard SEYMOUR, *b* 30 Sept 1881, *m* 23 Oct
         1901, Henry St Arnauld (*b* 26 Jan 1846), and had
         issue,
            ●Marie Alice Gansevoort ST ARNAULD, *b* 23 Sept
            1902, *m* 26 Feb 1922, ●Lewis George Fowler,
            attorney [*131 Higby Road, Utica, New York,*

USA], and has issue,
1d●Jane Marie FOWLER, *b* 16 Feb 192–, *m* 7 Sept 1946, ●Russell F. Hoffman, and has issue,
  1e●Stephen Lewis HOFFMAN, US Army, *b* 7 Aug 1947.
  2e●Valerie Jane HOFFMAN, *b* 27 Oct 1953, *educ* Union Univ.
2d●George Ledyard FOWLER, *b* 16 Feb 192– (twin with Jane Marie), *m* 16 Oct 1948, ●Helen Frankl, and has issue,
  1e●Gail Marie FOWLER, *b* 9 Aug 1949, *m* ●Gary Bortnick.
  2e●George Ledyard FOWLER, Jr, *b* 11 July 1950.
2b●Horatio SEYMOUR, Jr, Capt US Army 1918-20, *b* at Marquette, Michigan 14 July 1883, *educ* Yale, *m* 30 Aug 1913, his 1st cousin, ●Elsie Gansevoort (*b* at San Francisco 13 July 1882), dau of Judge George Edmund Otis, by his wife Catherine Maria Crysler Johnson (*see p 79*), and has issue,
  1c●Horatio SEYMOUR III, *b* at Bronxville, New York 9 March 1915.
  2c●John Forman SEYMOUR, *b* at Bronxville, New York 13 June 1917.
3a A dau, *b* 23 Nov 1855 (twin with Abigail Adams); *d* an inf.
4a Alexander Bryan JOHNSON III, *b* 16 Sept 1860, *m* Louise Tilden White (*d* 1921), and *d* 1916, leaving issue,
  1b●Louise Alexandra Adams JOHNSON, *b* Dec 1908, *m* ●William R. Duryee [*3241 N Woodrow, Arlington 7, Virginia, USA*], and has issue,
    ●Sanford Huntington DURYEE, *b* Aug 1950, *m* at Oxon Hill, Maryland 15 April 1969, ●Janet L. Brown.
  2b ●Alexander Bryan JOHNSON V [*940 Park Avenue, New York, New York 10028, USA*], *b* July 1911, *m* ●Henrietta Louise Huntting, and has had issue,
    1c●Alexander Bryan JOHNSON VII, *b* May 1938.
    2c Thurston Huntting JOHNSON, *b* Jan, *d* May 1945.
    3c●John Adams JOHNSON, *b* 1948.
5a Alice Gansevoort JOHNSON, *b* 8 Jan 1867; *dunm* 1919.
(3) Bryan JOHNSON, *b* at Utica, New York 30 April 1819; *dunm* at New York 28 Oct 1837.
(4) John Adams JOHNSON, *b* at Utica, New York 28 Feb 1821; *d* there *unm* 12 Sept 1839.
(5) William Clarkson JOHNSON, *b* at Utica, New York 16 Aug 1823, *m* 1st 1 Nov 1847, Henrietta Maria, dau of — Douw, of Albany, New York, and had issue,
  1a Alexander Bryan JOHNSON, *b* 1848, *m* Mary Knight Brown, and *d* in a fire at Windsor Hotel, New York City 1899, *sp*.
William Clarkson Johnson *m* 2ndly 30 June 1853, his 2nd cousin, Mary Louisa (*b* 2 Dec 1828; *d* 16 July 1859), elder dau of John Adams II, by his wife Mary Catherine Hellen (*see p 169*), and by her had issue,
  2a Mary Adams JOHNSON, *b* 1854, *m* 1875, Charles A. Doolittle, of Utica, New York, and *d* 1920, having had issue,
    1b Julia Tyler Sherman Adams DOOLITTLE, *b* at Utica, New York 22 Nov 1876, *m* John Nelson Teeter, MD, and *dsp* 10 June 1903.
    2b William Clarkson Johnson DOOLITTLE, *b* at Utica, New York 16 April 1879, *m* there 1st 17 June 1902, Amelia Lowery (*b* at Utica 4 Aug 1879; *d* there 16 Oct 1922), and had issue,
      1c●William Clarkson Johnson DOOLITTLE, Jr, *b* at Utica, New York 24 July 1903, *m* 1st (*m* diss by div 1935), Gladys Louise Hamblin, and has issue,
        1d●William Clarkson Johnson DOOLITTLE III, *b* at Utica, New York 22 Sept 1930, *m* 1st 15 May 1951 (*m* diss by div), Frances Louise Council. He *m* 2ndly 1 June 1955 (*m* diss by div 1967), Elaine Nadine Moye, and by her has issue,
          1e●Gary Raymond DOOLITTLE, *b* at Reno, Nevada 22 April 1956.
          2e●William Joseph DOOLITTLE, *b* 20 Feb 1958.
          3e●Georgia Patricia DOOLITTLE, *b* 6 Jan 1959.

          4e●Julie Ann DOOLITTLE, *b* 31 Jan 1960.
          5e●Donald Patrick DOOLITTLE, *b* 20 Aug 1961.
          6e●Colleen Marie DOOLITTLE, *b* 6 Oct 1963.
      2d●Judith Adams DOOLITTLE, *b* at Los Angeles, California 23 Nov 1933, *m* 2 Feb 1954, ●Jerry Albert Plante, and has issue,
        1e●Michael Thomas PLANTE, *b* 11 Oct 1954, *m* 20 March 1972, ●Barbara Louise Clancy, and has issue,
          ●Dustin Michael PLANTE, *b* 20 Aug 1972.
        2e●Laurence William PLANTE, *b* 30 Oct 1955.
        3e●Erik Charles PLANTE, *b* 13 Oct 1956.
        4e●Anthony PLANTE, *b* 21 Sept 1967.
William Clarkson Johnson Doolittle, Jr *m* 2ndly 9 April 1947, ●Dorothea Justine Claessens.
2c●Julia Tyler Sherman DOOLITTLE, *b* at Utica, New York 25 Sept 1904, *m* 4 Oct 1924, Henry Bradley Ogden (*b* at New Hartford, New York 15 Aug 1896; *d* at Utica, New York 15 May 1951), and has issue,
  1d●Amelia Lowery OGDEN, *b* at Utica, New York 21 Aug 1925, *m* there 16 Aug 1947, ●Stanley Mason Babson (*b* at Orange, New Jersey 13 July 1925), and has issue,
    1e●Bradley Ogden BABSON, *b* at Orange, New Jersey 15 Feb 1950, *m* at Hingham, Mass 4 Aug 1972, ●Katharine Partridge Earle.
    2e●Mary Darby BABSON, *b* at Orange, New Jersey 6 May 1951.
    3e●James Gorham BABSON, *b* at Orange, New Jersey Jan 1957.
  2d●Elizabeth Clark OGDEN, *b* at Utica, New York 14 Nov 1927, *m* 25 Sept 1948 (*m* diss by div 1972), Richard Jarvis Brown (*b* 25 May 1925), and has issue,
    1e●Elizabeth Gale BROWN, *b* at Utica, New York 9 March 1950.
    2e●Cynthia Allen BROWN, *b* at Utica, New York 28 Nov 1951, *m* at New Hartford, New York 23 Sept 1972, ●Donald Major, and has issue,
      ●Tonia Kirstin MAJOR, *b* at New Hartford, New York 25 Dec 1972.
    3e●Philip Henry BROWN, *b* at Utica, New York 30 March 1954.
    4e●Allison Ogden BROWN, *b* at Utica, New York 25 Feb 1958.
3c Marklove Lowery DOOLITTLE, *b* at Utica, New York 1 Sept, *d* there 6 Nov 1906.
4c●Mary Adams DOOLITTLE, *b* at Utica, New York 12 Nov 1909, *m* at Valley Forge, Pennsylvania 3 July 1933, ●Aubrey Morgan Evans (*b* at Scranton, Pennsylvania 13 May 1902), and has issue,
  1d●James Stewart EVANS, *b* at St Louis, Missouri 14 Dec 1940.
  2d●Jenner Lowery EVANS, *b* at Utica, New York 30 Oct 1947.
Mr and Mrs Aubrey Evans also have two adopted children,
  1d●Daniel Adams EVANS, *b* at Boston, Mass 8 Oct 1935.
  2d●Bradley Beattie EVANS, *b* at Boston, Mass 18 Oct 1937, *m* at Nutley, New Jersey 3 Aug 1963, ●Beatrice Conde Blackwell (*b* 6 Dec 1941), and has issue,
    1e●Kimberly Ann EVANS, *b* at Nutley, New Jersey 26 March 1964.
    2e●John Blackwell EVANS, *b* at Nutley, New Jersey 18 March 1966.
5c●John Quincy Adams DOOLITTLE [*Menands Road, Menands, New York, USA*], at Utica, New York 8 March 1911, *m* at Albany, New York 20 June 1936, ●Mary Arthur (*b* at Albany, New York 7 Feb 1916), dau of Hiland Garfield Batcheller, by his wife Jessie Jackson, a great-niece of President Arthur (*qv*), and has issue,
  1d●John Quincy Adams DOOLITTLE, Jr, *b* at Albany, New York 24 Jan 1938, *m* at Montclair,

New Jersey 18 June 1966, ●June Kathleen Dallery (*b* 6 Oct 1940), and has issue,
  1*e*●John Quincy Adams DOOLITTLE III, *b* at Newport, Rhode Island 29 Nov 1967.
  2*e*●Andrew Carleton DOOLITTLE, *b* at Newport, Rhode Island 26 Oct 1969.
2*d*●Mary Arthur DOOLITTLE, *b* at Albany, New York 13 May 1940, *m* there 15 June 1963, ●John Wickersham Beebe (*b* at Albany, New York 29 March 1937), and has issue,
  1*e*●Jean Louise BEEBE, *b* at Albany, New York 28 Feb 1966.
  2*e*●Mary Arthur BEEBE, *b* at Albany, New York 7 April 1968.
3*d*●Hiland Garfield Batcheller DOOLITTLE, *b* at Albany, New York 25 June 1945, *m* there 2 Aug 1969, ●Judith Ruth Anderson (*b* at Waterford, New York 20 Feb 1946).
4*d*●Peter Lowery DOOLITTLE, *b* at Albany, New York 8 April 1949.
William Clarkson Johnson Doolittle, Sr *m* 2ndly at New York City 23 Oct 1923, Georgette (*b* at Kansas City, Missouri 8 Dec 1904; *m* 2ndly at Asherville, N Carolina Aug 1970, Edward K. Parmelee, and *d* July 1971), dau of George A. Leiter[4], and *d* at Utica, New York 26 Aug 1967, having by her had issue,
  6*c*●James Carrington Leiter DOOLITTLE, *b* at Utica, New York 13 Sept 1925, *m* 1st at Menlo Park, California 1948 (*m* diss by div), Lois Hawley, and has issue,
    1*d*●Graham DOOLITTLE (now Graham WILSON, having been legally adopted by his step-father James Wilson).
James Carrington Leiter Doolittle *m* 2ndly at Barneveld, New York 20 June 1953, ●Susan Rockwell Bray (*b* at Utica, New York 14 Aug 1933), and by her has issue,
  2*d*●William Johnson Hitchcock DOOLITTLE, *b* at Utica, New York 17 Nov 1953.
  3*d*●Edward Kimball Cowles DOOLITTLE, *b* at Utica, New York 3 April 1955.
  4*d*●Abigail Adams DOOLITTLE, *b* at Utica, New York 8 March 1956.
  5*d* Katharine Leiter DOOLITTLE, *b* at Utica, New York 7 Sept 1960.
  6*d*●James Carrington Leiter DOOLITTLE, Jr, *b* at New Hartford, New York 6 Oct 1964
  7*c*●George Leiter DOOLITTLE, *b* at Utica, New York 13 April 1934, *m* 1st 5 Feb 1956 (*m* diss by div), Susan Faulkner Johnson, and has issue,
    1*d*●Thomas Cary Johnson DOOLITTLE, *b* at Augusta, Georgia 9 Nov 1958.
    2*d*●Jane Leiter DOOLITTLE, *b* at Utica, New York 28 Nov 1962.
George Leiter Doolittle *m* 2ndly at Clinton, New York 4 March 1966, ●Alaric Marshall Bray Burke (*b* at Utica, New York 29 June 1938), and by her has issue,
    3*d*●George Andrew Leiter DOOLITTLE, *b* at New Hartford, New York 5 Nov 1967.
3*b* Charles Adams DOOLITTLE, Jr, *b* at Utica, New York 31 Dec 1881, *m* Eleanor Shotter (*d* 29 June 1965), and *d* at New York City 19 Oct 1935, having had issue,
  1*c* Peter DOOLITTLE, *d* an inf.
  2*c*●Eleanor DOOLITTLE, *m*●Waldo Johnson, and has issue.
4*b* John Quincy Adams DOOLITTLE, *b* at Utica, New York 7 Feb 1884; *k* when struck by lightning on golf course there 28 June 1900.
5*b* Ebener Brown Sherman DOOLITTLE, *b* at Utica, New York 24 Sept 1889, *m* Alice Watson Lowery (*b* at Utica, New York 20 July 1891; *d* at Boston, Mass 11 Feb 1961), and *d* at Washington, DC 9 April 1944, leaving issue,
  1*c*●Alice Parkinson DOOLITTLE, *b* 26 June 1925, *m* ●Henry Brooks, and has issue,
    1*d*●Alice Shearman BROOKS.
    2*d*●"Woody" BROOKS.
  2*c*●Lois Andrews DOOLITTLE, *b* at Boston, Mass 12 March 1928, *m* ●J. Carter Inches, and has issue,

    1*d*●David INCHES, *b* 27 Nov 1961.
    2*d*●Louisa Adams INCHES, *b* 7 Nov 1962.
3*a* Louisa Catherine Adams Johnson, *b* at Washington, DC 29 March 1856, *m* Erskine Clement, of Boston, and *d* 1948, having had issue,
  1*b* Mary Louisa Adams CLEMENT, *dunm* 23 Sept 1950.
  2*b* Clarence Erskine CLEMENT, *b* 1884, *m* Bianca, formerly wife of — Harrington, and dau of — Cogswell, and *d* 1927, leaving issue,
    ●Louisa Catherine Adams CLEMENT, *b* 1922, *m* 19 Aug 1943, ●Rear-Adm Harry Hull, Jr, USN (ret) (*b* at Athens, Georgia 18 Jan 1912) [*Uplands, Highland Avenue, Manchester, Massachusetts 01944, USA*], son of Harry Hull, by his wife Anne Spann Burnett, and has issue,
      1*d*●Harry HULL III, Lieut USN, *b* 4 March 1945, *m*.
      2*d*●Kimball Erskine Clement HULL, *b* 28 Nov 1947.
      3*d*●Louisa Catherine Adams HULL, *b* 10 Nov 1952.
4*a* John Quincy Adams JOHNSON, *b* at Washington, DC 12 Feb 1859, *m* 1st 1884. Caroline (*b* 1862; *d* 1932), dau of Curtiss, of Yonkers, New York, and had issue,
  1*b* William Curtiss JOHNSON, *b* 1884, *m* 1920, Jessie, dau of — Farrington, of Yonkers, New York, and *dsp* at Point Pleasant, New Jersey 17 April 1940.
  2*b* John Quincy Adams JOHNSON, Jr, *b* at Yonkers 1887, *m* 1913, Marian, dau of — Thomas, of Dayton, Ohio, and *d* at Yonkers 8 Dec 1953, leaving issue,
    1*c*●Winters Adams JOHNSON, *b* 1914, *m* 1948, ●Evelyn Walsh and has issue,
      ●Eric Winters JOHNSON, *b* 1951.
    2*c*●John Quincy Adams JOHNSON III, *b* 1917, *m* 1944, ●Helen Brady, and has issue,
      1*d*●Sherry Ann JOHNSON, *b* 1945.
      2*d*●John Quincy Adams JOHNSON IV, *b* 1949.
      3*d* ●Allen Curtiss JOHNSON, *b* 1951.
    3*c*●Marjorie Adams JOHNSON, *b* 1969.
  3*b*●Alexander Bryan JOHNSON IV, *b* 8 Aug 1890, *m* 1st 1915 (*m* diss by div 1934), Corinne, dau of — Carver, of Yonkers, New York, and had issue,
    1*c*●Nancy Corinne, JOHNSON, *b* 1916, *m* 1936, ●Frank Quirk, and has issue,
      1*d*●Dana QUIRK, *b* 1938.
      2*d*●Kathleen QUIRK, *b* 1945.
    2*c*●Alexander Bryan JOHNSON VI, *b* 1918, *m* 1st 1940 (*m* diss by div 1942), Flavia Ellen Bensing. He *m* 2ndly 1942 (*m* diss by div 1946), Eleanor Wagner, and by her has issue,
      1*d*●Alexander Bryan JOHNSON VIII, *b* 1944.
  Alexander Bryan Johnson VI *m* 3rdly 1951, ●Alese Psenicki, and by her has issue,
      2*d*●Wendy Alese JOHNSON, *b* 1952.
    3*c*●Audrey Curtiss JOHNSON, *b* 1922, *m* 1944, ●Robert Stolte Bailey, and has issue,
      1*d*●David BAILEY, *b* 1945.
      2*d*●Barbara BAILEY, *b* 1949.
Alexander Bryan Johnson IV *m* 2ndly 1934, ●Helen Moore Earle, and by her has issue,
  4*c*●Alexander Adams JOHNSON, *b* 1936.
  4*b* Caroline Curtiss JOHNSON, *b* 1893; *dunm* 1920.
  5*b*●Charles Adams JOHNSON, Jr, *b* 1896, *m* 1926, ●Katharyn, dau of — Starr, of Woodbury, New Jersey, and has had issue,
    1*c*●Charles Adams JOHNSON III, *b* 1927, *m* 1952, ●Lida Forsythe Wilson, and has issue,
      ●Cynthia Starr JOHNSON, *b* 1953.
    2*c* Lewis Starr JOHNSON, *b* 1929; *dunm* 1949.
  6*b*●Abigail Adams JOHNSON, *b* 1902, *m* 1944, ●Bradley Kelly.
  7*b*●Mary Louisa Adams JOHNSON, *b* 1903, *m* 1934, as his 2nd wife, her brother-in-law, ●Henry J. Dietrich (*see below*).
  8*b* Martha Johnson, *b* 1903 (twin with her sister Mary Louisa Adams Johnson), *m* 1927, as his 1st wife, ●Henry J. Dietrich, and *d* 1933, leaving issue,
    1*c*●Henry Curtiss DIETRICH, *b* 1928, *m* 1950, ●Betty Jane Anderson, and has issue,
      1*d*●Arthur Curtiss DIETRICH, *b* 1950.

2d●Jane Kirsten DIETRICH, b 1953
2c●Robert Gregory DIETRICH, b 1930, m 1952,
●Ann Rowling, and has issue,
1d●Martha Ann DIETRICH, b 1952.
2d●Melinda Adams DIETRICH, b May 1954.
John Quincy Adams Johnson m 2ndly 1933, Caroline (b 1859; d 1950), dau of — Sutherland, of Washington, DC, and d 9 April 1938.
William Clarkson Johnson m 3rdly 30 July 1860, Mary Cornelia Nicholson, and d at New York 28 Jan 1893, having by her had issue,
5a Abigail Adams JOHNSON, b at Newbury, Mass 1861, m there 1889, Milton Strong Thompson (b 1855; d 1933), and d at Newbury, Mass Feb 1947, having had issue,
1b Sarah Elizabeth THOMPSON, b at Newbury, Mass 1890; dunm in Connecticut 1973.
2b Gardiner THOMPSON, served in World War I, b at Newbury, Mass 1892; ka in France 1918.
3b Alexander Bryan THOMPSON, b at Newbury, Mass 1896; d there 1900.
4b●Milton Strong THOMPSON, Jr, b at Newbury, Mass 1901, m ●Elizabeth, widow of — May.
5b Abigail Adams THOMPSON, b at Newbury, Mass 1903, m there 1932, Joseph Whitmore Knapp (b 1887), and dsp 9 Nov 1951.
6a Elizabeth Lispenard JOHNSON, b at Newbury, Mass 1865, m 1st 1887, Walter Bell Phister, of Maysville, Kentucky (b 1858; d at Newbury, Mass 1912), son of Charles Phister, by his wife Margaret —, and had issue,
1b●Mary Cornelia PHISTER, b at Newbury, Mass 1888, m 1916, ●Dana Winslow Atchley, MD (b 1892) [180 Fort Washington Avenue, New York, New York 10032, USA], son of William A. Atchley, by his wife Florence Ames and has issue,
1c●Dana Winslow ATCHLEY, Jr [262 Oakwood Road, Englewood, New Jersey 07631, USA], b at New York City 1917, m 1st 1939 (m diss by div), Barbara Welch, and has issue,
1d●Dana Winslow ATCHLEY III, b 1941.
2d●Mary Babcock ATCHLEY, b 1942.
3d●Elizabeth Ross ATCHLEY, b 1946.
Dana Winslow Atchley, Jr m 2ndly, ●Barbara Payne, and by her has issue,
4d●Marion Woodward ATCHLEY, b 4 May 1955.
2c●John Adams ATCHLEY, MD [3 East 68th Street, New York, New York 10021, USA], b at Baltimore, Maryland 30 May 1920, m 27 Sept 1942, ●Martha Welch, and has issue,
1d●Susan ATCHLEY, b 1944.
2d●John Adams ATCHLEY, Jr, b 1947.
3d●Peter Ross ATCHLEY, b 1949.
3c●William Ames ATCHLEY, MD [1721 Mar West, Tiburon, California 94920, USA], b at New York City 1922, m 1st at Cleveland, Ohio 14 April 1945 (m diss by div 1955), Anstis Manton, dau of Russell Burwell, of Cleveland, Ohio, by his wife Aubrey, and has had issue,
1d●Mark Ames ATCHLEY, b at New York 14 Jan 1948.
2d Anthony Burwell ATCHLEY, b and d 1950.
Dr William Ames Atchley m 2ndly at Carmel, California 23 Oct 1955, ●Margaret Feiring, dau of Jesse Feiring Williams, by his wife Gertrude, and by her has issue,
3d●William Ames ATCHLEY, Jr, b at San Francisco, California 22 April 1958.
2b●Lispenard Bache PHISTER, b at Chicago, Illinois 1896.
Elizabeth Lispenard Johnson m 2ndly 1916, Spencer Gobel Lane, of Manila, Philippine Islands (b 1865; d 1922), and d at San Francisco, California 23 Aug 1948.
(6) Charles Adams JOHNSON, b 1825; dunm.
(7) Sarah Adams JOHNSON, b at Utica, New York 27 April 1827, m 28 April 1848, her 2nd cousin, James Stoughton Lynch, of Utica, New York (d at Utica 3 April 1889), and had issue,
1a Abigail Louisa Johnson LYNCH, b 31 March 1850; dunm 1932.
2a Johnson LYNCH, b 21 Nov 1852; d an inf.

3a Johnson Livingston LYNCH, b 1 April 1854; dunm 3 Oct 1883.
4a Sarah Leah LYNCH, b 7 June 1856, m 7 July 1878, Wilbur H. Booth, and dsp 15 Feb 1882.
5a Anne Margaret LYNCH, b 6 Feb 1858; dunm 1942.
6a Catherine Gertrude LYNCH, b 27 Jan 1861; dunm 1942.
7a Frances LYNCH, b 8 Aug 1863; d an inf.
8a James De Peyster LYNCH, b 17 May 1868, m 20 June 1898, Julia Henrietta Wright, and d April 1917, having had issue,
1b James De Peyster LYNCH, Jr, b 17 June 1899; d an inf.
2b Andrew Green LYNCH, in US Foreign Service, Amb to Somalia 1960-62, b at Utica, New York 3 Oct 1902, educ Harvard, m ●Jean Adele Bidwell, and dsp at Barneveld, New York 25 Jan 1966.
3b Leah LYNCH, b 4 March 1906; dunm 4 July 1924.
4b●Bryan Johnson LYNCH [Reading, Vermont, USA], b 24 Oct 1907, m 23 Feb 1935, ●Alicia Maria Calvo, and has issue,
●James Stoughton LYNCH, b 4 June 1938.
(8) Arthur Breese JOHNSON, b at Utica, New York 3 Dec 1829, m 12 May 1859, Eliza Stringham, dau of Justice Ward Hunt, and d 3 Nov 1883, leaving issue,
1a Ward Hunt JOHNSON, b at Utica, New York 9 May 1864; dunm.
2a Mary Savage JOHNSON, b at Utica, New York 28 June 1866; dunm at New Haven, Conn Aug 1952.
3a Laura Savage JOHNSON, b at Utica, New York 24 April 1870, m there 10 Oct 1901, Walter Hedden Morton (b at Springfield, Mass 12 June 1869; d at Cambridge, Mass 2 Feb 1945), son of James Hodges Morton, by his wife Elizabeth Hall Ashmun, and d 26 Jan 1933, leaving issue,
1b●George Ashmun MORTON, physicist [1122 Skycrest Drive, Apt 6, Walnut Creek, California 94595, USA], b at New Hartford, New York 24 March 1903, educ Mass Inst of Technology, m at Boston, Mass 15 Sept 1934, ●Lucy Mitchell (b at Massina, New York 29 Nov 1909), dau of Benjamin F. Groat, by his wife Harriet Grace Mitchell, and has issue,
1c●Walter Groat MORTON, b at Camden, New Jersey 21 June 1935.
2c●George Ashmun MORTON, Jr, b at Camden, New Jersey 21 July 1937, m ●Donna Lea, dau of Joseph Green, by his wife Clara June Funkhouser, and has issue,
●Heather Grace MORTON, b at San Pedro, California 13 March 1974.
3c●Grace Mitchell MORTON, b at Camden, New Jersey 1 July 1938.
4c●Lewis Hunt MORTON, b at Princeton, New Jersey 8 July 1944.
2b●Eliza Stringham MORTON, b at New Hartford, New York 15 March 1904, m at Cambridge, Mass 15 Oct 1932, ●James Post Borland (b at Oakland, New Jersey 22 Feb 1900) [8 Coolidge Hill Road, Cambridge, Mass, USA], son of Charles R. Borland, by his wife Elizabeth Post, and has issue,
1c●Elizabeth Morton BORLAND, b at Cambridge, Mass 5 Jan 1939, m there 17 June 1960, Gardner Murray Stultz (b at Boston, Mass 11 Oct 1937) [1504 Hampton Road, Charleston, West Virginia, USA], son of Irving W. Stultz, by his wife Marjorie MacEachern, and has issue,
1d●Laura Katherine STULTZ, b at Hartford, Conn 6 April 1964.
2d●Karen Elizabeth STULTZ, b at Hartford, Conn 29 Dec 1966.
3d●Janet Lynn STULTZ, b at Charleston, W Virginia 24 Jan 1972.
2c●Charles Randolph BORLAND, b 1 Nov 1940, m Dec 1963, ●Prudence Mahala Price, and has issue,
1d●Gillian Beecher BORLAND, b Oct 1966.
2d●Isabel Breese BORLAND, b 28 March 1969.
3d●Mahala Carlock BORLAND, b 5 Feb 1972.
3b●Montgomery Hunt MORTON [PO Box 433F, Marathon, Florida 33050, USA], b at New Hartford, New York 10 Dec 1905.
4a Montgomery Hunt JOHNSON, b 12 April 1872, m 3

Oct 1906, Frances Lillian Munger (*b* 15 Nov 1878), and *d* 7 Feb 1952, leaving issue,

  1*b*●Montgomery Hunt JOHNSON, Jr [*19002 East Dodge Avenue, Santa Ana, California 92705, USA*], *b* 21 Nov 1907, *m* 6 April 1946, ●Gwyneth Mary Johnson (*b* 13 Jan 1915), and has issue,

    1*c*●Sarah Langhorne JOHNSON, *b* 1 Jan 1947.

    2*c*●Gwyneth Mary JOHNSON, *b* 15 April 1948, *m* 26 Dec 1967 (*m* diss by div 1971), Costas Lymberis.

  2*b*●Francis Munger JOHNSON, *b* 28 Oct 1908, *m* 30 April 1931, ●Dorothy Elizabeth Ely.

  3*b*●Greig Adams JOHNSON, *b* 31 March 1911, *m* 1st (*m* diss by div), Marilyn Twite.

    1*c*●Greig Adams JOHNSON, Jr, *b* 7 Sept 1941, *m* 1965, ●Christine Gonsalves, and has issue,

      1*d*●Greig Adams JOHNSON III, *b* 25 Jan 1966.

      2*d*●Julie JOHNSON, *b* 21 Feb 1967.

      3*d*●Amy JOHNSON, *b* 6 Oct 1970.

Greig Adams Johnson, Sr *m* 2ndly 1 July 1950, ●Ann (*b* 4 Jan 1921), formerly wife of —, and dau of — Whitcomb, and by her has issue,

    2*c*●Mary Frances JOHNSON, *b* 21 Nov 1951.

Greig Adams Johnson, Sr has also adopted his stepson,

  ●William JOHNSON.

5*a* Louise Eliza JOHNSON, *b* 11 Nov 1873; *d* 8 June 1875.

6*a* Leon Arthur JOHNSON, *b* 11 Nov 1877; *dunm* 23 Aug 1909.

(9) Louisa Ann Smith JOHNSON, *b* at Utica, New York 24 Nov 1832, *m* 19 April 1852, George Bolton Alley (*b* 22 March 1831; *d* 1883), son of Saul Alley, and *d* 29 Nov 1929, leaving issue,

  1*a* Alexander Bryan ALLEY, *b* 1853, *m* Mary Gibb (*d* 1937), and *d* 8 Sept 1926, leaving issue,

  John Gibb ALLEY, *m* Dec 1928, Frances Ziegler, and *dsp*.

  2*a* William Shaw ALLEY, *m* Josephine Demarest, and *d* 1911, leaving issue,

    1*b* George Bolton ALLEY II, *m*, and has issue,

    ●William Shaw ALLEY, *m* 1956, ●Mary Argyle Kent.

    2*b*●William Shaw ALLEY, Jr.

  3*a* Harriet Douw ALLEY, *b* 9 Aug 1856, *m* 19 Dec 1877, Thomas Parmellee Wickes (*b* 17 April 1853), and *d* 27 May 1899, leaving issue,

    1*b* Henry Parmellee WICKES, *b* 7 Dec 1878, *m* 21 Nov 1896, Ethel Catlin Kinney, and had issue,

    ●Bradford WICKES, *b* 1 Sept 1897.

    2*b* Marie Louise WICKES, *b* 18 Dec 1881; *dunm*.

  4*a* Mary ALLEY, *m* William Robert Neal, and *d* 26 Nov 1942, having had issue,

    1*b* Dorothy NEAL.

    2*b* Herbert NEAL, *b* 1884, *m* Ann Peebles, and *d* 7 Oct 1951, leaving issue,

    ●Mary Ann NEAL, *b* 29 Oct 1942.

  5*a* Abigail Louise ALLEY, *b* 1860, *m* Edward Martin Talbot (*b* 1854; *d* 1927), and *d* Aug 1940, leaving issue,

    1*b* Abigail Adams TALBOT, *b* at New York 1884, *educ* Barnard, *m* 20 Feb 1905, Reuben Hallett (*b* 1883; *d* 1944), and *d* at Mattapoiset, Mass 12 May 1952, leaving issue,

      1*c*●Priscilla Alden HALLETT, *b* 20 Oct 1906, *m* 1930, ●Ira R. Hiller II (*b* 15 Nov 1905), and has issue,

        1*d*●Priscilla Alden HILLER, *b* 11 Feb 1933.

        2*d*●Charles Mathew HILLER, *b* 21 April 1937.

        3*d*●Ira R. HILLER III, *b* 23 Sept 1940.

      2*c*●Marion Marcus HALLETT, *b* 1909, *m* 1933, ●Edwin Lovejoy, and has issue,

        1*d*●Edwin Clinton LOVEJOY, *b* 12 Feb 1936.

        2*d*●Stephen Frederick LOVEJOY, *b* 23 April 1941.

      3*c* Reuben HALLETT, Jr, *b* 1912, *m* 26 Nov 1936, ●Berenice Regula and *d ante* 1952, leaving issue,

        1*d*●Noel HALLETT, *b* 8 Sept 1940.

        2*d*●Neil HALLETT, *b* 7 Jan 1942.

        3*d*●Ann Amory Jill HALLET, *b* 12 Sept 1946.

      4*c*●Abigail Adams HALLETT, *b* 1914, *m* 1934, ●Harold Warner, and has issue,

        1*d*●Alden Talbot WARNER, *b* 15 Jan 1935.

      2*d*●George Harold WARNER, *b* 27 Oct 1937.

      3*d*●Janet WARNER, *b* 18 Oct 1939.

      4*d*●Robert WARNER, *b* 13 Sept 1944.

      5*d*●Abigail Adams WARNER, *b* 25 Nov 1948.

      6*d*●Marianne WARNER, *b* 24 April 1950.

  2*b* Edwina Charlotte TALBOT, *b* 1888, *m* Reginald D. Taylor and had issue,

    1*c*●Edwina Charlotte TAYLOR, *b* 1912.

    2*c*●Katherine TAYLOR, *b* 1914, *m* ●J. Pearce Manning, Jr, son of J. Pearce Manning.

    3*c*●Reginald D. TAYLOR, Jr, *b* 1915, *m* ●Marion Reynolds, and has issue,

      1*d*●Marion TAYLOR, *b* 1938.

      2*d*●Sandra TAYLOR, *b* 1947.

    4*c*●Dorothy Quincy TAYLOR, *b* 1918, *m* 1941, ●James Kenny McMahon, and has issue,

      1*d*●Barbara Vernon McMAHON, *b* 1942

      2*d*●Martin William McMAHON, *b* 1943.

      3*d*●James Kenny McMAHON, Jr, *b* 1944.

      4*d*●Charles Reginald McMAHON, *b* 1946.

3*b* John Alden TALBOT, Mayor of Kinnelon, New Jersey, *b* 12 Aug 1890, *m* June 1919, Priscilla Peabody (*b* 29 Feb 1896; *d* Aug 1938), and *d* at Nassau, Bahamas 25 Dec 1962, leaving issue,

  ●John Alden TALBOT, Jr, *b* 30 March 1920, *m* 22 Feb 1952, ●Patricia, formerly wife of — Jessup, and dau of — Potter, and has issue,

    1*d*●John Alden TALBOT III, *b* 22 Jan 1953.

    2*d*●Henry Adams TALBOT, *b* 12 Jan 1954.

4*b*●Adrian Bancker TALBOT, *b* 25 Jan 1896, *m* 1st ●Jeanette Butler Strong (*b* 1905; *d* 1938), and has issue,

  1*c*●Virginia Wayne TALBOT, *b* 15 Dec 1930, *m* 15 Aug 1953, ●William Henry Harbaugh (*b* 1920).

  2*c*●Gail Adams TALBOT, *b* 16 Aug 1932, *m* 1956, ●Middleton Rose, Jr, son of Middleton Rose.

Adrian Bancker Talbot *m* 2ndly, ●Constance Burr (*b* 1915), and by her has issue,

  3*c*●Barbara TALBOT, *b* 16 March 1940.

  4*c*●Edward Richmond TALBOT, *b* 16 July 1943.

  5*c*●Deborah TALBOT, *b* 13 May 1945

6*a* Georgina ALLEY, *b* 27 Oct 1862, *m* Edwin Cameron Ffoulkes, and *dsp* 18 Jan 1954.

(10) Frances Elizabeth JOHNSON, *b* at Utica, New York 7 Nov 1835, *m* 10 Sept 1856, Charles Platt Williams, of Boonville, New York (*b* 27 Nov 1829; *d* 26 Dec 1901), and *d* 22 Nov 1902, leaving issue,

  1*a* Sarah Adams WILLIAMS, *b* at Forestport, New York 17 April 1859, *m* at Rouen, France 1 Aug 1885, James Edgar Bull (*b* in New Jersey Aug 1857; *d* at New York 2 Oct 1923), son of Richard Harrison Bull, by his wife Mary Ann Scouten, and *d* at New York 5 July 1955, having had issue,

    1*b* Marion Frances BULL, *b* 3 March 1888, *m* 16 Oct 1912, Butler Whiting (*b* at Larchmont, New York 6 Oct 1882; *d* at Deep River, Connecticut 7 Jan 1948), son of Eliot Butler Whiting, and *d* 29 Jan 1962, having had issue,

      1*c*●Florence Day WHITING, *b* at New York 27 April 1914, *m* 29 Jan 1938, ●John Joseph Hyland, Jr (*b* at Philadelphia 1 Sept 1912), son of John Joseph Hyland, and has issue,

        1*d*●John Joseph HYLAND III, Lt-Cmdr USN [*555 Uluhala Street, Kailua, Oahu, Hawaii 96734, USA*], *b* at San Diego, California 20 Aug 1939, *educ* Kent Sch, US Naval Acad, and Inst of Political Studies, Paris, France, *m* at Westover Air Force Base, Mass 1 Feb 1964, ●Sandra Ann (*b* at Bisbee, Arizona 29 Nov 1942), dau of Thomas Philip Coleman, by his wife Ann Marie Barnett, and has issue,

          1*e*●John Joseph HYLAND IV, *b* at New London, Conn 3 Oct 1965.

          2*e*●Thomas Philip HYLAND, *b* at Kittery, Maine 19 Oct 1966.

          3*e*●Ann-Marie HYLAND, *b* at Honolulu, Hawaii 22 Nov 1968.

        2*d*●Nancy HYLAND, *b* at Washington, DC 19 Aug 1944, *m* 1966, ●Thomas St John Arnold, Jr [*4404 North Willetta Drive, Richmond, Virginia 23221, USA*], son of Thomas St John Arnold,

and has issue,
●Robert Watson ARNOLD, *b* 1970.
3*d*●Pamela HYLAND, *b* 14 Feb 1947, *m* 1971, ●James Harvey Trenholme [*Apt 10-D, Escondido Village, Stanford, California 94305, USA*].
4*d*●Whiting Walker HYLAND [*4946 Kolohala Street, Honolulu, Hawaii 96816, USA*], *b* 28 April 1955.
2*c*●Sarah Adams WHITING, *b* 15 Aug 1915, *m* 10 June 1938, ●James Robert Baylis (*b* 13 July 1910) [*Box 667, Madison, Connecticut 06448, USA*], and has issue,
1*d*●Butler Whiting BAYLIS [*2240 Pacific Avenue, San Francisco, California 94115, USA*], *b* 27 Sept 1944, *m* 7 Aug 1971, ●Elizabeth Jenkins Mack (*b* at Baltimore, Maryland 22 Nov 1946).
2*d*●James Edgar BAYLIS [*129 Hamilton Road, Chappaqua, New York, USA*], *b* 17 Nov 1947, *m* 20 June 1969, ●Penelope Wakefield Crabb (*b* at New York 16 Oct 1946), and has issue,
●Kristen Wakefield BAYLIS, *b* 31 March 1974.
3*d*●Linda BAYLIS, *b* 2 March 1952.
3*c*●Edgar Bull WHITING, *b* 17 July 1917, *m* 22 Aug 1953, ●Gladys Dils (*b* 7 July 1911).
4*c*Butler WHITING, Jr, *b* 3 Aug 1921; *dunm* 23 Dec 1943.
2*b* Richard Harrison BULL, *b ca* 1891; *d* an inf.
3*b*●Priscilla Mullins BULL [*150 East 72nd Street, New York, New York 10021, USA*], *b* at New York 28 April 1894, *m* there 7 Nov 1914, Leonard Jarvis Wyeth IV (*b* at New York 4 Aug 1890; *d* there 17 March 1968), son of Leonard Jarvis Wyeth III, by his wife Louisa Alley Hopkins, and has issue,
1*c*●Priscilla Mullins WYETH, *b* at New York 1 Oct 1916, *m* there 8 Nov 1940, ●Arthur Zabriskie Gray (*b* at New York 30 May 1915) [*441 Bedford Road, Armonk, New York, USA*], son of Arthur Romeyn Gray, by his wife Laura Ferguson, and has issue,
1*d*●Priscilla Adams GRAY, *b* at New York 30 Aug 1941, *m* at Armonk, New York 2 April 1966, ●David Edward Baxter, son of C. David Baxter, by his wife Constance, and has issue,
1*e*●David Arthur BAXTER, *b* at Portland, Oregon 22 Feb 1967.
2*e*●Alexandra Wyeth BAXTER, *b* at Portland, Oregon 24 March 1969.
2*d*●Alexandra Romeyn GRAY, *b* at New York 19 Dec 1946, *m* at Armonk, New York 11 Nov 1967, ●Donald Price Hines (*b* at Dobbs Ferry, New York 20 Sept 1934) [*Kents Cliff, New York, USA*], son of Joseph B. Hines, by his wife Mary Price, and has issue,
1*e*●Dana Wyeth HINES, *b* at Mount Kisco,

New York 12 March 1971.
2*e*●Marni Alexandra HINES, *b* at Mount Kisco, New York 1973.
3*d*●Leonora Ferguson GRAY, *b* at White Plains, New York 2 Aug 1952, *m* at Homestead Air Force Base, Florida 26 May 1973, ●Michael Smith [*630 NE 55th Terrace, Miami, Florida 33137, USA*], son of Guy Smith, by his wife Ann.
2*c*●Leonard Jarvis WYETH V [*16 Pinnacle Mountain Road, Simsbury, Conn 06070, USA*], *b* at New York 9 Jan 1918, *m* at Buenos Aires, Argentina 18 Oct 1941, ●Pamela Isabel (*b* at Buenos Aires 26 Sept 1920), yr dau of Tyrrell Langley Evans, late Capt RHA, by his wife Elsie Canning (*see* BURKE'S *LG*, TYRRELL-EVANS *of Capel End*), and has issue,
1*d*●Pamela Isabel WYETH, *b* at Buenos Aires 9 July 1942, *m* 1st at Dayton, Ohio 6 July 1962 (*m* diss by div 1968), Dr Charles Klaus Beyer (*b* 4 June 1927), son of Hans Beyer, of Göttingen, W Germany, by his wife Charlotte. She *m* 2ndly at Boston, Mass 5 July 1969, ●Charles B. Margolis (*b* at Boston 18 March 1944) [*140 Swanson Terrace, Stroughton, Massachusetts 02072, USA*], son of Samuel O. Margolis, of Chelsea, Mass, by his wife Marion.
2*d*●Christina Langley WYETH, *b* at Dayton, Ohio 12 March 1950.
3*d*●Leonard Jarvis WYETH VI, *b* at Dayton, Ohio 24 March 1953.
2*a* Frances Elizabeth WILLIAMS, *b* at Forestport, New York *ca* 1862; *d* young.
3*a* Harriet Eaton WILLIAMS, *b* at Forestport, New York 2 March 1864, *m* 1st at Rouen, France 15 Jan 1889, James Ronald Watson (*b* at Rouen 13 May 1866; *d* in London, England 18 May 1899), and had issue,
Maud Emma WATSON, *b* in London 22 Oct 1889; *dunm* at Brighton, Sussex, England 25 June 1962.
Harriet Eaton Williams *m* 2ndly in London 22 Dec 1902, Peter Herbert Jones (*d* in London 23 Jan 1909).
5 Thomas Boylston ADAMS, Chief Justice of the Supreme Court of Mass, *b* at Penns Hill Farm, Braintree 15 Sept 1772, *educ* Harvard, *m* 1805, Ann Harrod (*b* 1774; *d* 1846), and *d* 13 March 1832, having had issue,
1 Abigail Smith ADAMS, *b* 1806, *m* 1831, John Angier, and *dsp* 1845.
2 Elizabeth Coombs ADAMS, *b* 1808; *dunm* 1903.
3 Thomas Boylston ADAMS, Jr, Lieut 2nd US Art, *b* 1809; *dunm* 1837.
4 Frances Foster ADAMS, *b* 1811; *d* 1812.
5 Isaac Hull ADAMS, *b* 1813; *dunm* 1900.
6 John Quincy ADAMS, *b* 1815; lost at sea from USS *Albany* 1854, *unm*.
7 Joseph Harrod ADAMS, *b* 1817; *d* on the Perry expdn on USS *Powhattan* 1853, *unm*.

# The Brothers of President John Adams

**1** Capt Peter Boylston ADAMS, of Braintree, *b* at Braintree 16 Oct 1738, *m* 1768, Mary Crosby, and *d* 1823, having had issue, one son and three daus. His issue is now *extinct*.

**2** Capt Elihu ADAMS, of Randolph, Mass, *b* at Braintree 29 May 1741, *m* 1765, Thankful White (*b* 1747), and *d* at Boston 18 March 1776, leaving issue, two sons and one dau, all of whom *m*, and had issue. The dau, Susanna Adams (1766-1826), *m* Aaron Hobart, and their yr son, Aaron Hobart (1787-1858), became a Judge and mem of Congress.

# Notes

[1] Henry Adams's emigration to America was probably brought about through his wife's connection with Aquila and Thomas Purchase, two of the leading parishioners and associates of Rev John White, Rector of Holy Trinity, Dorchester, organiser in 1623 of the "Dorchester Adventurers", and a great advocate for the colonization of New England. Aquila Purchase, Master of Trinity School, Dorchester, and himself an emigrant to New England, *m* 28 Jan 1614, Ann, sister of Edith Squire, who *m* Henry Adams.

[2] Joseph Adams's second son, John Adams, of Boston (1661-1702), was grandfather of Hon Samuel Adams (1722-1803), Governor of Mass 1794-97, Representative from Boston to Mass,General Court 1765-74, a vigorous opponent of the British Government, his being one of the two names excluded from the amnesty offered by Gen Gage in 1775, and who has been regarded as the chief moulder of public opinion in favour of revolution and separation.

[3] The relationship is as follows:—

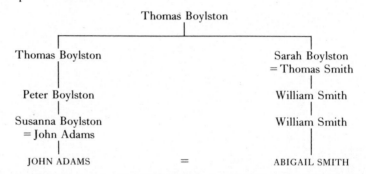

Thomas Boylston

Thomas Boylston — Sarah Boylston = Thomas Smith

Peter Boylston — William Smith

Susanna Boylston = John Adams — William Smith

JOHN ADAMS   =   ABIGAIL SMITH

[4] George A. Leiter was a first cousin of Levi Ziegler Leiter, of Washington, whose daughter Mary Victoria became the first wife of 1st Marquess Curzon of Kedleston, KG, PC, GCSI, GCIE, Viceroy of India (*see* BURKE'S *Peerage*, SCARSDALE, V, and RAVENSDALE, B).

# Thomas Jefferson
## 1743-1826

———

3rd President of the
United States of America
1801-1809

THOMAS JEFFERSON, 3RD PRESIDENT

# Thomas Jefferson

## 1743-1826

### 3rd President of the United States of America
### 1801-1809

TODAY THOMAS JEFFERSON is one of the most praised of American presidents. His features, together with those of George Washington, Abraham Lincoln and Theodore Roosevelt, gaze down from the colossal memorial carved in the rock of Mount Rushmore, South Dakota. A host of biographers pay tribute, much as President Kennedy did when he remarked at a dinner for Nobel prizewinners that it was "the most extraordinary collection of talent, of human knowledge, that has ever been gathered together at the White House, with the possible exception of when Thomas Jefferson dined alone". Jefferson is admired for his versatility. Perhaps only Benjamin Franklin rivalled him among contemporaries as a scholar, philosopher and inventor; and even Franklin could not match Jefferson in farming skills or in architectural taste. Jefferson is commended for his felicity as a phrasemaker, his geniality and informality, his lifelong concern for personal liberty and his intellectual flexibility. He seems to stand forth as one of the few Presidents who had no appetite for politics, and no driving ambition for high office. When he became Vice-President in 1797 he enjoyed the leisure that the position gave him, comparing his "honorable and easy" role with the "splendid misery" endured by President John Adams. The simple inscription on his tomb recorded the three acts by which he wished to be remembered. They did not include being President or Vice-President, or Governor of Virginia. He hoped posterity would recall him as author of the Declaration of Independence and of Virginia's statute for religious freedom, and as "Father of the University of Virginia". It would seem that if Jefferson loved the United States as an idea, his nearest and dearest affection was for what he continued to call "my country"—his own state, the hill-top home at Monticello he had designed for himself, and the nearby university at

Charlottesville whose construction he proudly supervised in his last years. Monticello as the visitor now sees it, a little miracle of grace and ingenuity, appears to epitomize the best of Jefferson. A near-perfect life, we feel—the fitting visual counterpart of the famous Jeffersonian affirmations: "all men are created equal . . ."; "I have sworn upon the altar of God, eternal hostility against every form of tyranny over the mind of man . . ."; "If there be any among us who would wish to dissolve the Union or to change its republican form, let them stand undisturbed as monuments of the safety with which error of opinion may be tolerated where reason is left free to combat it".

It is a shock to turn from this ideal view of Thomas Jefferson to the criticisms of his detractors. A common charge, voiced for instance by Theodore Roosevelt, is that Jefferson was a theorist, a fanatic, a person swayed by abstract notions—including the pernicious view that revolutions and blood-letting were now and then good for the health of the body politic. Roosevelt thought Jefferson's presidential policies, notably the embargo on trade with Europe, were absurd and cowardly. He concluded that intellectuals of the Jefferson stamp made very bad political leaders. A different accusation is that Jefferson was intellectually flighty, and that his actions were often at variance with his presumed beliefs. The unassuming democrat, it is pointed out, had an estate of over ten thousand acres, and at his death in 1826 owned 260 slaves. The pacifist sent American warships against the pirate kingdoms of North Africa. The advocate of freedom of speech, in office, convinced himself that some of his opponents were guilty of sedition and perhaps worse. Professors at his University of Virginia, he was sure, should be chosen for "correctness" of ideology. Jefferson pursued Aaron Burr, in the treason trial of 1807, with implacable hostility and scant regard for the evidence. The defender of local, decentralized Administration ("that government is best which governs least") was an adroit and sometimes ruthless manipulator of presidential authority. Largely on his own initiative, and with doubtful constitutional sanction, Jefferson almost doubled the size of the United States by purchaising the Louisiana Territory from Napoleon. He used political patronage to reward faithful supporters, and did not hesitate to punish the "wayward freaks" in Congress who resisted his programmes. He pushed the Embargo Acts through Congress with little or no debate and with—his enemies alleged—crippling results for national commerce.

It is impossible entirely to exonerate Thomas Jefferson. Or rather, the argument that he was invariably high-minded and consistent is not tenable. He was a complicated man, and his personality sometimes made him seem more devious than he was. By nature he was amiable and introspective. Correspondence and conversation were his favored styles. He was not at his best in public meetings, and he shrank from face-to-face quarrels. In consequence he let others bear the brunt of political battle;

MARTHA WAYLES SKELTON, MRS JEFFERSON

and as John Adams complained, he was apt to appear two-faced, saying one thing in public and another in private. He was at his worst in the Burr affair. The justification was that, during the 1790s and the years of his Administration, America was bitterly divided on matters of principle. In his more sanguine moments Jefferson trusted to the essential unity and good sense of the American people. At other moments, like his adversaries, he saw the division between Federalists and Republicans as dangerous and requiring extreme measures.

On the whole his conduct is more that of an intelligent pragmatist than of a zealot. Jefferson changed his mind because circumstances changed. Though he always considered farming to be the most useful and wholesome occupation, he came to realize that the United States also needed some manufactures. The Louisiana Purchase was an opportunity too alluring to miss. Jefferson was nevertheless uneasy at what he had done, and would have been glad to gain approval by means of a constitutional amendment. There was nothing unorthodox in his assumption that foreign policy was mainly the responsibility of the executive branch. In domestic affairs he was usually content to leave initiative with the states or with Congress. He was not a demagogue, nor power-mad. His Republican partisanship was certainly no more conspicuous than that of the extreme Federalists who derided and denounced him. The Jefferson of caricature and of panegyric dissolves on scrutiny into a fallible though gifted human being. The real Jefferson was a gentleman farmer caught up in the huge dramas of his day; sometimes wise, occasionally misguided; according to gossip a fairly merry widower, but also a family man, content to be spoiled by his adoring daughters. Like George Washington, he had more land than cash; he was close to bankruptcy in his final years. They were overshadowed too by increasing sectional antagonisms. Jefferson the Southerner rallied to the support of his region. Jefferson the democrat accepted that Negro slavery was a grave moral wrong. Jefferson the statesman could not discern a solution, other than the fanciful hope that black Americans could be shipped back to Africa. Jefferson the philosopher was well aware that the history of mankind was in large part a record of greed, violence, stupidity. But Jefferson the whole man even in old age kept alive his essential faith that America could inaugurate a new, far happier era in the world's chronicle.

# Chronology

1743    Born at Shadwell, Goochland (now Albemarle) County, Virginia 2/13 (*os*) April.

1757    Inherited Shadwell estate on the death of his father.

1760    Entered William and Mary College, Williamsburg 25 March.

1762    Left college without taking degree 25 April; entered law office of George Wythe, Williamsburg.

1764    Took over the management of his estate; appointed Justice of the Peace and Vestryman for Goochland County.

1766    Visited Philadelphia and New York May.

1767    Admitted to the Virginia Bar in Williamsburg 5 April; began planting at Monticello.

1769-75 Member of Virginia House of Burgesses.

1770    County Lieutenant of Albemarle County; house at Shadwell burnt down Feb; moved to Monticello 26 Nov.

1774    Elected to first Virginia Provincial Convention, but did not attend owing to illness.

1775    Elected Delegate to the Second Continental Congress 25 March; attended Congress at Philadelphia 21 June-31 July and 2 Oct-28 Dec; attended Virginia Convention March and Aug.

1776    Attended Continental Congress 15 May-2 Sept; appointed to Committee to draft Declaration of Independence 11 June; draft reported 28 June; debated 2-4 July; approved 4 July; Declaration signed 2 Aug; appointed Commissioner to France 11 Oct, but declined to serve; attended Virginia Assembly 11 Oct-14 Dec; appointed to Committee to Revise Virginia Laws 5 Nov.

1779    Elected Governor of Virginia Jan; took office 1 June; instrumental in removing State capital to Richmond; founded first professorship of Law in America at William and Mary College.

1780    Re-elected Governor.

1781    Forced to flee Richmond several times by near approach of the British; retired as Governor 1 June; investigation of his Administration ordered by Assembly 5 June; appointed Peace Commissioner by Continental Congress 14 June, but declined appointment 30 June; attended Virginia Assembly 5 Nov; Committee appointed to state charges against him 26 Nov; elected Delegate to Congress 30 Nov; voted thanks of Assembly 12 Dec.

1782    Appointed Peace Commissioner to Europe 12 Nov.

1783    Appointment as Peace Commissioner withdrawn 1 April; elected Delegate to Congress 6 June; took seat at Annapolis, Maryland Nov.

1784    Elected Chairman of Congress 12 March; appointed Commissioner to France 7 May; sailed from Boston 5 July; arrived in Paris 6 Aug.

1785    Appointed French Minister by Congress 10 March; notified of appointment 2 May; received at the French court 17 May.

1786    Visited England March-April; received by King George III at Windsor 22 March; his Act for Freedom of Religion passed by the Virginia Legislature; received LLD degree from Yale Oct.

1787    Visited Southern France and Northern Italy 3 March-10 June.

1788    Visited Amsterdam and Strasbourg 3 March-23 April; received LLD degree from Harvard June.

1789    Declined invitation to assist French Constitutional Committee July; nominated Sec of State 25 Sept (confirmed by Senate 26 Sept); left France 22 Oct; landed at Norfolk, Virginia 23 Nov.

1790    Accepted Secretaryship 14 Feb, becoming first US Secretary of State under the new Constitution; left for New York 1 March; arrived 21 March; took office 22 March.

1792    Wrote to President Washington stating his intention of resigning from the Cabinet 23 May.

1793    Re-considered resignation Jan; offered and declined French mission Feb; resigned as Secretary of State and retired to Monticello 31 Dec.

1794-95    Mainly engrossed in farming and improvements at Monticello.

1794    Offered and declined appointment as special envoy to Spain Sept.

1796    Democratic-Republican candidate for President; Presidential Electors cast their ballots 7 Dec.

1797    Electoral vote tabulated by Congress and Jefferson having received 68 votes was duly elected Vice-President 8 Feb; inaugurated as Vice-President at Philadelphia 4 March; elected President of American Philosophical Society.

1798    Drafted Kentucky Resolutions Oct; revised Madison's Virginia Resolutions Nov.

1800    Began to lay plans for the University of Virginia Jan; nominated for President by the Republican Caucus May; Presidential Electors cast their ballots 3 Dec.

1801    Electoral votes tabulated by Congress, Jefferson and Burr tying for first place with 73 votes each 11 Feb; House of Representatives balloted for President and Jefferson was elected on the 36th ballot, Burr becoming Vice-President, 17 Feb; delivered farewell address to the Senate 28 Feb; inaugurated as 3rd President of the United States of America in the Senate Chamber of the Capitol 4 March; moved into the White House 19 March; Tripoli declared war on US 14 May; reviewed the Marine Corps at the White House 4 July; sent first State of the Union message to Congress 8 Dec.

1802    Judiciary Act of 1801 repealed 8 March; signed Act establishing US Military Academy 16 March; Naturalization Act of 1798 repealed 14 April; signed Judiciary Act of 1802 29 April; signed first enabling Act authorizing the inhabitants of the eastern division of the Northwest Territory to hold a constitutional convention, the first step towards statehood for Ohio 30 April;

|      | Washington, DC incorporated as a city 3 May; sent second State of the Union message to Congress 15 Dec. |
|------|---|
| 1803 | Ohio admitted as the 17th State 1 March; Louisiana Territory purchased from France by treaty signed at Paris 2 May (ratified 20 Oct); sent third State of the Union message to Congress 17 Oct; Governor William C. C. Claiborne of Mississippi Territory took formal possession of Louisiana for US 20 Dec. |
| 1804 | Sent message to Congress on taking possession of Louisiana 18 Jan; nominated by Democratic-Republicans for second term 25 Feb; Vice-President Burr fatally wounded Alexander Hamilton in a duel 11 July; 12th Amendment to the Constitution ratified 25 Sept; sent fourth State of the Union message to Congress 8 Nov; election day 13 Nov; Presidential Electors cast their Ballots (162 for Jefferson and Clinton; 14 for Pinckney and King, the Federalist candidates) 5 Dec. |
| 1805 | Signed Act establishing Territory of Michigan 11 Jan (effective 1 July); electoral votes tabulated by Congress and Jefferson and Clinton officially declared elected 13 Feb; inaugurated for second term in the Senate Chamber of the Capitol 4 March; peace treaty with Tripoli signed 4 June; sent fifth State of the Union message to Congress 3 Dec. |
| 1806 | Issued proclamation warning persons not to conspire against Spain 26 Nov; sent sixth State of the Union message to Congress 2 Dec. |
| 1807 | Signed Judiciary Act increasing Supreme Court from six to seven members 24 Feb; signed Act banning the importation of slaves (as from 1 Jan 1808) 2 March; issued proclamation requiring all British warships to leave American waters 2 July; Aaron Burr acquitted of treason 1 Sept; sent seventh State of the Union message to Congress 27 Oct; signed Embargo Act prohibiting commerce with Great Britain and France 22 Dec. |
| 1808 | Signed second Embargo Act 9 Jan; Embargo Act of 1807 repealed 1 March; embargo modified 12 March; sent eighth and last State of the Union message to Congress 8 Nov. |
| 1809 | Signed Enforcement Act, supplementing Embargo Act and increasing the powers of collectors in making seizure of vessels 9 Jan; Territory of Illinois established 3 Feb; signed Non-Intercourse Act, repealing the embargo 1 March (effective from 15 March); retired from office and attended the inauguration of his successor President Madison 4 March; returned to Monticello 17 March. |
| 1814 | Resigned Presidency of the American Philosophical Society Nov. |
| 1815 | Congress passed Bill authorizing the purchase of his library, which was to form the basis of the Library of Congress 26 Jan. |
| 1817 | Drafted Bill for establishment of the University of Virginia. |
| 1819 | University of Virginia chartered; subsequently appointed Rector and supervised the construction of the university buildings to his own design at Charlottesville. |
| 1825 | Drafted Virginia Protest Dec. |
| 1826 | Made will 16 March; declined invitation to attend July Fourth Celebrations in Washington 24 June; died at Monticello 4 July (the same day as John Adams); buried there 5 July. |

# The Writings of President Jefferson

*A Summary View of the Rights of British America* (1774)

*Notes on the State of Virginia* (1785)

*Kentucky Resolutions* (1798)

*Manual of Parliamentary Practice* (1801)

*An Essay Towards Facilitating Instruction in the Anglo-Saxon and Modern Dialects of the English Language* (posthumously, 1851)

*Writings*, edited by P. L. Ford, 10 vols (1892-99); memorial edition, 20 vols (1903-04)

The *Jefferson Papers*, edited by Julian Boyd, are now in progress of publication and there have been several volumes of letters, etc, published from time to time.

# Lineage of President Jefferson[1]

SAMUEL JEAFFRESON, of Pettistree, nr Woodbridge, Suffolk, *m* Elizabeth — (will dated 23 Oct 1590), and *d ante* 23 Oct 1590, leaving issue,

JOHN JEAFFRESON, of Pettistree, *m*, and had issue, with two elder sons and two daus,

SAMUEL JEAFFRESON, who emigrated to the West Indies and acquired the Red House Plantation, St Kitt's, where he *d* 12 Dec 1649 (*bur* St Thomas's Church, Middle Island), leaving issue, with two elder sons,

SAMUEL JEAFFRESON, went to St Kitt's with his father and moved to Antigua *ca* 1669, *bapt* at Pettistree, Suffolk 11 Oct 1607, *m*, and *d post* 1685, leaving issue, with two other sons, a 2nd son,

THOMAS JEFFERSON, who settled in Virginia, where he was the owner of a plantation in Henrico County in 1677, *m* Martha, dau of William Branch, and grand-dau of Christopher Branch, of Kingsland, Chesterfield County, Virginia, and *d* 1697, leaving issue, with one dau,

CAPTAIN THOMAS JEFFERSON, of Osborne's, Chesterfield County, Justice of Chesterfield County Court 1706, High Sheriff 1718-19, *b* 1679 or 1680, *m* 1697 or 1698, Mary (*b* 1680; *d* 1715), elder dau of Major Peter Field, of Henrico and New Kent Counties, by his 2nd wife Judith, widow of Capt Henry Randolph, of Henrico County, and dau of Henry Soane, of James City County, Speaker of the House of Burgesses, and *d post* 1725 (probably 1731), having had issue, with two other sons and three daus, a yst son,

COLONEL PETER JEFFERSON, of Shadwell, Goochland (later Albemarle) County, Virginia, Justice of Goochland County Court 1735, High Sheriff 1737-39, JP (1744) Albemarle County, Lt-Col 1745, Col and County Lieut 1754, Burgess 1755, *b* probably at Osborne's, Chesterfield County 29 Feb 1707/8, *m* (bond dated 3 Oct) 1739, Jane (*bapt* at St Paul's Church, Shadwell, London 20 Feb 1720; *d* at Monticello 31 March 1776, *bur* there), eldest dau of Col Isham Randolph, of Dungeness[2]), by his wife Jane Rogers, and *d* at Shadwell 17 Aug 1757 (*bur* there), having had, with other issue (*see* BROTHERS AND SISTERS OF PRESIDENT JEFFERSON, *p 127*), an eldest son,

THOMAS JEFFERSON, **3rd President of the United States of America.**

# The Descendants of President Jefferson

THOMAS JEFFERSON *m* at her father's residence, The Forest, Charles City County, Virginia 1 Jan 1772, Martha (*b* in Charles City County 19/30 Oct 1748; *d* at Monticello 6 Sept 1782, *bur* there), widow of Bathurst Skelton (to whom she was *m* 20 Nov 1766 and who *d* 30 Sept 1768, having by her had issue an only son, John, *b* 7 Nov 1767; *d* 10 June 1771), and dau of John Wayles, of The Forest, Charles City County, Virginia (a native of Lancaster, England), by his 1st wife Martha Eppes, and had issue,

**1** Martha (Patsy) JEFFERSON, *b* at Monticello 27 Sept 1772, *m* there 23 Feb 1790, her 3rd cousin Thomas Mann Randolph, Jr, of Edgehill, Albemarle County, Virginia, Gov of Virginia 1819-22 (*b* at Tuckahoe, Goochland County, Virginia 17 May 1768; *d* at Monticello 20 June 1828, *bur* there), 2nd but eldest surv son of Col Thomas Mann Randolph, of Tuckahoe, by his 1st wife Anne, dau of Archibald Cary, and *d* at Edgehill 10 Oct 1836 (*bur* Monticello), having had issue,

1 Anne Cary RANDOLPH, *b* at Monticello 23 Jan 1791, *m* there 19 Sept 1808, Charles Lewis Bankhead (*b* 3 May 1788; *d* in Albemarle County, Virginia 1835), son of Dr John Randolph Bankhead, of Caroline County, Virginia, by his wife Mary Warner Lewis, and *d* at Monticello 11 Feb 1826 (*bur* there), leaving issue,

(1) John Warner BANKHEAD, of Missouri, *b* at Carlton, nr Monticello 2 Dec 1810, *m* 3 Nov 1832, Elizabeth Poindexter (*b* 9 March 1814; *d* at Prairieville, Missouri 23 Dec 1895), dau of Archibald Christian, by his wife Fanny Warren, and *d* 1896, having had issue,

1*a* Archer Christian BANKHEAD, *b* in Virginia 15 Sept 1833, *m* 10 June 1857, Mary Graves (*b* at St Louis, Missouri 10 April 1840; *d* in Pike County, Missouri 2 April 1906), dau of Col A. B. Chambers, and *d* 1911, leaving issue,

1*b* John Warren BANKHEAD, *b* in Pike County, Missouri 25 Feb 1859, *m* there 4 Nov 1886, Selma Presca (*b* at Ashburne, Missouri 12 May 1869; *d* at Hannibal, Missouri June 1956), dau of Charles William Purgahn, by his wife Pauline Waggoner, and *d* in Pike County, Missouri 19 Oct 1916, leaving issue,

1*c* ●Charles Archie BANKHEAD [*Higbee, Missouri 65257, USA*], *b* in Pike County, Missouri 28 April 1887, *m* at St Louis, Missouri 5 Jan 1909, Vera (*b* at New Hartford, Misssouri 17 Feb 1886; *d* at New London, Missouri 5 May 1924), dau of Eli Hugh Rees, by his wife Mary Elizabeth Johnson, and has issue,

1*d* ●Lowell Cary BANKHEAD [*Box 38, Higbee, Missouri 65257, USA*], *b* at Lyrene, Missouri 14 Oct 1909, *m* at Hannibal, Missouri 30 Jan 1937, ●Erma Lee (*b* at Hannibal, Missouri 4 Nov 1913), dau of Claude Green, by his wife Erma Lee Lillard, and has had issue,

1*e* Warren Lee BANKHEAD, *b* and *d* at Hannibal, Missouri 23 Feb 1943.

2*e* ●Lowell Cary BANKHEAD, Jr [*Box 38, Higbee, Missouri 65257, USA*], *b* at Hannibal, Missouri 14 Oct 1947, *m* at Higbee, Missouri 15 Sept 1968, ●Charla Marie (*b* 7 July 1950), dau of Charles J. Rockett, and has issue,

●Lowell Cary BANKHEAD III, *b* at Adana, Turkey 17 Sept 1972.

2*d* ●Audrey Louise BANKHEAD, *b* at Cyrene, Missouri 16 May 1913, *m* at Hannibal, Missouri 21 April 1935, ●Joseph Eugene Howard (*b* at Hannibal, Missouri 8 July 1912) [*2131 Flintridge Court, Riverside, California 92504, USA*], son of Orin William Howard, by his wife Nettie Rachel Rubison, and has issue,

1*e* ●Sharon Jo Ann HOWARD, *b* at Santa Barbara, California 31 Oct 1939, *m* at Riverside, California 14 July 1962, ●Steven George Stockwell (*b* 1939) [*438 Sycamore Road, Santa Monica, California, USA*], son of John F. Stockwell, by his wife Beatrice Gurlich, and has issue,

1*f* ●Todd Howard STOCKWELL, *b* at Los Angeles, California 1 Jan 1966.

2*f* ●Charlton Howard STOCKWELL, *b* at Los Angeles, California 29 May 1967.

2*e* ●Kristen Audell HOWARD, *b* at Santa Monica, California 4 July 1947, *m* there 4 April 1971, ●David Druker (*b* at St Paul, Minnesota) [*525 Midvale, Los Angeles, California 90024, USA*], son of Leonard Druker.

3*d* ●Iris Jean BANKHEAD, *b* at Cyrene, Missouri 5 May 1916, *m* at Macon, Missouri 14 March 1936, ●Wilford Cameron Caldwell (*b* at New London, Missouri 29 July 1914) [*777 North 15th Street, San Jose, California, USA*], son of Greenville Caldwell, by his wife Dollie Florence Smith, and has issue,

1*e* Stanley Terrill CALDWELL, *b* at Hannibal, Missouri 1 April 1942; *d* at San Jose, California 20 May 1958.

2*e* ●Randolph Cary CALDWELL [*1134 Rickenbacker Street, San Jose, California, USA*], *b* at Hannibal, Missouri 23 Aug 1945, *m* at San Jose, California, ●Roxanne (*b* at San Jose, California), dau of Wilbur Garlic, and has issue,

●Terrill Cameron CALDWELL, *b* at Mountain View, California 27 Sept 1973.

4*d* ●Selma Elizabeth BANKHEAD, *b* at Cyrene, Missouri 10 May 1918, *m* at Ventura, California 26 Nov 1938, ●Richard Philip West (*b* at Cicero, Illinois 14 Sept 1914) [*4280 Calle Real, Santa Barbara, California 93111, USA*], son of Maxwell Walter West, by his wife Gulborg Ruud, and has issue,

1*e* ●Stephen Matthew WEST, *b* at Santa Barbara, California 30 Oct 1939, *m* 1st at Montecito, California 1963 (*m* diss by div 1967), Lois Ione (*b* at Detroit, Michigan 1939), dau of Walter Harold Kleiber, Jr, by his

wife Augusta Adams, and had issue,
1f● Jeffrey Stephen WEST (adopted by his stepfather and now bears the surname of GROUDA), b at Detroit, Michigan May 1964.
Stephen Matthew West m 2ndly at Roseville, Michigan 1968, ● Linda (b at Springfield, Tennessee 1942), dau of George Gregory, by his wife Lena, and by her has issue,
2f● Richard Austin WEST, b at Alpena, Michigan 22 May 1971.
3f● Ruth Ann WEST, b at Santa Barbara, California 23 June 1972.
2e● Penny Jeanne WEST [6271 Guava Avenue, Goleta, California 93017, USA], b at Santa Barbara, California 11 March 1946, m 1st at Santa Barbara, California 1966 (m diss by div 1967), Duane Raymond La Moureaux (b at Corona, California), son of "Frenchie" LaMoureaux, by his wife Viola Stratton. She m 2ndly at Ventura, California 1968 (m diss by div 1972), Erich Kurt Hutzler (b at Boston, Mass 1944), son of Albert Hutzler, by his wife Ruth Harpel, and has issue,
● Megan Wayles HUTZLER, b at Santa Barbara, California 20 Nov 1969.
2c John Warren BANKHEAD, Jr, b at Cyrene, Missouri 1889, m ● Minnie Kirk, and d at Cyrene, Missouri 1918, leaving issue,
1d Robert Eugene BANKHEAD, b at Cyrene, Missouri 1913, m at Hannibal, Missouri, ● Evalina James (b at Hannibal, Missouri), and d at Hannibal, Missouri 1968, leaving issue,
● Deanna Marlene BANKHEAD, b at Hannibal, Missouri 1942, m there 11 Nov 1961, ● Kenneth Wayne Taylor.
2d● Pauline BANKHEAD, b at Cyrene, Missouri 1918, m at Hannibal, Missouri 1936, ● Paul Bramblett (b at Frankford, Missouri) [1845 Ninth Avenue, Yuma, Arizona, USA], and has issue,
● Sherrilee BRAMBLETT, b at Hannibal, Missouri 1940, m ● Del Berry of Detroit, Michigan, and has issue,
1f● Paul Edward BERRY, b at San Diego, California.
2f● Robert BERRY, b at Santa Monica, California.
3c Pauline BANKHEAD, b at Cyrene, Missouri 29 Aug 1893, m at Bowling Green, Missouri 8 Oct 1910, Ansel Sanderson (b at Edgewood, Missouri 31 Oct 1892; d at Jonesboro, Arkansas 7 June 1963), son of Samuel M. Sanderson, by his wife Cora Williams, and d at Cyrene, Missouri 24 Dec 1916, leaving issue,
1d● Genevie SANDERSON, b at Cyrene, Missouri 5 Jan 1913, m at Maywood, Missouri 9 Aug 1934, ● Lewis Olie Erickson (b at Bowling Green, Missouri 21 Nov 1911) [3636 North Olive, Kansas City, Missouri 64116, USA], son of Emil Erickson, by his wife Fannie Moore, and has issue,
1e● Charles Ansel ERICKSON [5436 North Lydia, Kansas City, Missouri 64116, USA], b at Maryville, Missouri 8 Jan 1939, m 1st at N Kansas City, Missouri 20 July 1960 (m diss by div), Barbara Jean O'Connor. He m 2ndly at N Kansas City, Missouri 26 Dec 1964, ● Kathryn M. (b at Valeo, California 19 Jan 1944), dau of Henry Joseph Hoon, by his wife Mary Sanders, and by her has issue,
1f● Kristina Marie ERICKSON, b at Kansas City, Missouri 2 Aug 1965.
2f● Karin Maria ERICKSON, b at Kansas City, Missouri 10 Nov 1966.
2e● John Lewis ERICKSON [120 East 69th Terrace, Kansas City, Missouri 64133, USA], b at Smithville, Missouri 8 Nov 1942, m at Liberty, Missouri 6 June 1970, ● Sarah Kathleen (b at Kansas City, Missouri 20 May 1945), dau of John P. Turner, by his wife

Marjorie Anstrand, and has issue,
● Thomas Jeffrey ERICKSON, b at Kansas City, Missouri 20 Sept 1973.
2d● Marjorie SANDERSON, b at Cyrene, Missouri 18 Jan 1916, m at Lawrence, Kansas 27 Oct 1945, ● Clifford A. Orcutt (b at Seminole, Oklahoma 24 Sept 1920) [1520 Kingston Road, Lincoln, Nebraska 68506, USA], son of Clifford O. Orcutt, by his wife Ina Charnick, and has issue,
● Pamela Sue ORCUTT, b at Lincoln, Nebraska 8 June 1952, m there 28 Dec 1973, ● Edward Lee Trehearn (b at Colorado Springs, Colorado 24 Jan 1952) [4610 Eden Circle, Lincoln, Nebraska 68506, USA], son of Art Trehearn, by his wife Edna.
4c Jay Houchins BANKHEAD, b in Pike County, Missouri 1898; dunm at Louisiana, Missouri 1925.
5c Mary Clara BANKHEAD, b in Pike County, Missouri 1901, m 1st at St Louis, Missouri, Samuel Owens; and 2ndly, Edwin Conrad, and dsp 1946.
2b Thomas Randolph BANKHEAD, b 1863, m 1891, Elizabeth Haynie, and d 1936, leaving issue,
1c● William Chambers BANKHEAD, b 1894, m 1914, ● Agnes Temple (b 1898), and has issue,
● Marie Elizabeth BANKHEAD, b 1923, m 1940, Lloyd Miller, and has issue,
● Warren Randolph MILLER, b 1947.
2c● Thomas Jefferson BANKHEAD [Bowling Green, Missouri 63334, USA], b 1897, m 1920, ● Blanche Kerr, and has had issue,
Robert Wayne BANKHEAD, b 1925; d at Louisiana, Missouri 1942.
3c● Katherine Bankhead BANKHEAD [604 West Centennial, Bowling Green, Missouri 63334, USA], b 1901, m 1920, ● Karl Emil Zuber, and has issue,
● Frieda Bell ZUBER, b 1925, m at Prairieville, Missouri 1950, ● Obed Hall, and has issue,
● Jeannine Bankhead HALL, b 1953.
3b Elizabeth Chambers BANKHEAD, b 1865, m 1886, William Everett Bell, and d 12 June 1958, leaving issue,
1c Mary Elizabeth BELL, b 3 Dec 1886, m Horace Leonard Hutchison (b at Bunceton, Missouri 1885; d at Pueblo, Colorado 2 April 1952), son of Edward Chilton Hutchison, by his wife Lacy Anderson Mann, and d 29 Nov 1969, leaving issue,
1d Lacy Elizabeth HUTCHISON, b 1912, m 1941, ● Frank Humbewtel [322 Crestone Avenue, Apt 9, Salida, Colorado 81201, USA].
2d● Horace Leonard HUTCHISON, Jr [2428 Eighteenth Street, Lake Charles, Louisiana 70601, USA], b at Bunston, Missouri 9 Feb 1915, m at Lake Charles, Louisiana 2 Nov 1946, ● Alice Elizabeth (b at Columbus, Mississippi 10 Oct 1923), dau of Ira Clinton Dimmick, Sr, by his wife Mary Ella Evans, and has issue,
1e● Janet Elizabeth HUTCHISON, b at Lake Charles, Louisiana 1 Jan 1949, m there 12 June 1971, ● Robert Carson Glenn, Jr (b at Charleston, South Carolina 22 Nov 1946) [1402 Oklahoma, Apt H, Harlingen, Texas 78550, USA], son of Robert Carson Glenn, by his wife Ethel Emeline McIver, and has issue,
● Roger Christopher GLENN, b at Harlingen, Texas 14 Feb 1974.
2e● Hal Thomas HUTCHISON, b at Orange, Texas 10 May 1950.
3e● Mary Lynn HUTCHISON, b at Lake Charles, Louisiana 12 March 1954.
4e● Susan Frances HUTCHISON, b at Lake Charles, Louisiana 19 Oct 1957.
3d● Everett Bell HUTCHISON [1503 Watts Place, Pueblo, Colorado 81008, USA], b at Cassville, Missouri 1918, m at Albuquerque, New Mexico 1950, ● Virginia (b at Joliet, Illinois 1924), dau of Earl C. Casey, by his wife Elizabeth, and has issue,
1e● Thomas Casey HUTCHISON [3601 Holly Brook, Pueblo, Colorado 81000, USA], b at Pueblo, Colorado 1952, m there 4 Oct 1972,

●Maribeth (*b* at Pueblo, Colorado 22 May 1954), dau of Merl Brooks, by his wife Annie.
2*e*●Holly Elizabeth HUTCHISON, *b* at Pueblo, Colorado 4 Jan 1956.
3*e*●Patricia Anne HUTCHISON, *b* at Pueblo, Colorado 24 Aug 1957, *m* there 11 Aug 1973, ●Neal C. Ramhorst.
4*e*●Kenneth Todd HUTCHISON, *b* at Pueblo, Colorado 25 Feb 1963.
2*c*●William Everett BELL III [*5037 Live Oak Street, Apt 2, Dallas, Texas 75206, USA*], *b* 1887, *m* Alma Arnoldy, and has issue,
●William Everett BELL IV, *b* 1927.
3*c* Emily Carr BELL, *b* 1889, *m* Frank F. Marr (*b* 1888; *d* 1948), and *d* 2 June 1972, leaving issue,
1*d*●William Bell MARR, *b* 1911, *m* ●Thelma Morrison, and has issue,
1*e*●Nancy Lee MARR, *b* 1933, *m* ●Richard Louis Urbina, and has issue,
1*f*●Laura Lee URBINA, *b* 1953.
2*f*●William Nicholas URBINA, *b* 11 Jan 1955.
2*e*●John Randolph MARR, *b* 1938.
2*d*●Helen Elizabeth MARR, *b* 1913, *m* ●A. A. Townsend [*225 East Plymouth, Long Beach, California 90805, USA*], and has issue,
●John David TOWNSEND, *b* 6 May 1955.
4*c*●Helen Catherine BELL [*4037 South West Sixth Street, Miami, Florida 33134, USA*], *b* at Nelson, Missouri 2 April 1893, *m* at Cassville, Missouri 14 May 1912, Earl Mitchell (*b* in Iowa 10 July 1891; *d* at St Louis, Missouri 1934), son of John Mitchell, and has issue,
1*d*●John William MITCHELL [*26920 South West 157th Avenue, Homestead, Florida, USA*], *b* at Cassville, Missouri 1 June 1914, *m* at Nashville, Tennessee 12 March 1943, ●Margaret (*b* at Quirigna, Guatemala 18 May 1967), dau of Earl Ames, by his wife Marjorie, and has issue,
1*e*●John William MITCHELL, Jr [*15885 S.W. 272 Street, Homestead, Florida, USA*], *b* at Miami Beach, Florida 30 May 1944, *m* at Homestead, Florida 22 March 1968, ●Alethea Sue (*b* at Homestead, Florida 20 Feb 1948), dau of Clinton James Bishop, by his wife Suzy Jane Leggett, and has issue,
●John William MITCHELL III, *b* at Coral Gables, Florida 27 June 1972.
2*e*●Robert Ames MITCHELL [*165 NW 16 Street, Homestead, Florida, USA*], *b* at Miami Beach, Florida 16 Dec 1948, *m* at Tallahassee, Florida 30 Sept 1972, ●Frances (*b* at Jamestown, New York 15 Sept 1950), dau of Dr John Lincoln, by his wife Martha.
2*d*●Leonard Bell MITCHELL [*1301 SW 94 Court, Miami, Florida 33100, USA*], *b* at Cassville, Missouri 30 Sept 1916, *m* ●Louise, dau of W. G. Quisenberry, and has issue,
1*e*●Leonard Bell MITCHELL, Jr, *b* at Shelbyville 5 Sept 1945.
2*e*●Earl Spencer MITCHELL, *b* at Miami Beach, Florida 15 Oct 1946.
3*d*●Betty Jane MITCHELL, *b* at St Louis, Missouri 10 Feb 1928, *m* at Coral Gables, Florida 23 Nov 1949, ●George Solberg (*b* at Coral Gables 31 Aug 1928) [*8125 South West 64th Street, Miami, Florida 33143, USA*], son of Harry Solberg, by his wife Bernice, and has issue,
1*e*●Robert M. SOLBERG, *b* at Miami, Florida 26 April 1951, *m* at Fayetteville, North Carolina 22 Dec 1972, ●Marion Patrice (*b* in Virginia 11 May 1951), dau of Marion Walker, by his wife Patricia.
2*e*●Janet SOLBERG, *b* at Coral Gables, Florida 3 March 1954.
5*c*●Robert Griffith BELL [*1012 North Ocean Boulevard, Pampano Beach, Florida 33062, USA*], *b* at Nelson, Missouri 8 March 1902, *m* 1st at St Louis, Missouri 1931, Hortense (*b* at St Louis, Missouri 1906; *d* there Nov 1950), dau of Theo

Lucks, by his wife Anna, and has issue,
1*d*●Robert Griffith BELL, Jr [*140E Reading Way, Winter Park, Florida 32789, USA*], *b* at St Louis, Missouri 26 May 1936, *m* 1st at St Louis, Missouri 7 May 1960 (*m* diss by div), Donna Dorothy (*b* at St Louis, Missouri May 1932), dau of William DeWitt, by his wife Margaret, and has issue,
1*e*●William BELL, *b* 1961.
2*e*●Robert BELL, *b* 1964.
Robert Griffith Bell, Jr *m* 2ndly ●Peggy Conway, and by her had issue,
3*e*●Michael BELL, *b* 1970.
4*e*●Matthew BELL, *b* 1972.
2*d*●Randolph Bankhead BELL [*PO Box 195, Conway, Massachusetts 01341, USA*], *b* at St Louis, Missouri 26 April 1945.
Robert Griffith Bell, Sr *m* 2ndly 21 May 1952, ●Kathleen (*b* at Marion, Kansas 10 April 1910), widow of — Bair, and dau of Albert H. Wheeler, by his wife Naomi Malone.
6*c*●Kenneth Cary BELL [*5716 Berget Street, Amarillo, Texas 79106, USA*], *b* 1904, *m* ●Martha Jane Brown, and has issue,
●Kenneth Cary BELL, Jr [*4214 Emil Street, Amarillo, Texas 79106, USA*], *b* 1942, *m* 6 June 1969, ●Bette Jon Fitzpatrick.
4*b* Benjamin Chambers BANKHEAD, *b* 1867, *m* Kate Smith (*b* 1865; *d* 1951), and *dsp* 1928.
5*b* Archie Cary BANKHEAD, *b* 1874, *m* 1901, Grace Major, and *d* 1921, leaving issue,
1*c*●Mary Clio BANKHEAD, *b* 1901.
2*c*●Benjamin Nelson BANKHEAD, *b* 1907, *m* ●Betty Varweek, and has had issue,
1*d* Judith Ann BANKHEAD, *b* 1937; *d* 1942.
2*d*●Mary Elizabeth BANKHEAD, *b* 1940.
3*d*●Thomas Randolph BANKHEAD, *b* 1942.
4*d*●Jeanne BANKHEAD, *b* 1945.
2*a* Cary Randolph BANKHEAD, MD, *b* 1835, *m* 1860, Amanda Ellen Errett (*b* 1839; *d* 1895), and *d* 1911, having had issue,
1*b* Elizabeth BANKHEAD, *b* 1860; *d* 1864.
2*b* Martha BANKHEAD, *b* 1862; *dunm* 1930.
3*b* Joseph Errett BANKHEAD, MD, *b* 1864, *m* 1st, Laura Hughes (*d* 1900). He *m* 2ndly, Elizabeth Cake, and *d* 1942, having by her had issue,
●Ellen Cary BANKHEAD, *b* 1905, *m* 1st, Robert Benton Mackey, and has issue,
1*d*●Joseph Benton MACKEY, *b* 1928, *m* 1949, ●Jean Smith, and has issue,
●Joellen MACKEY, *b* 20 June 1952.
2*d*●Betsy Cake MACKEY, *b* 1934.
Ellen Cary Bankhead *m* 2ndly, ●William B. Weakley.
4*b* Mary Archer BANKHEAD, *b* 1867, *m* 1887, Mark Miller Gillum (*d* 1950), and *d* 17 July 1944, having had issue,
1*c* Cary Randolph Bankhead GILLUM, *b* 1889, *m* Ruth Stark, and *d* 1953, having had issue,
1*d*●Mildred GILLUM, *b* 1913, *m* ●Ross Elgin.
2*d* Rachel Errett GILLUM, *b* 1917; *d* an inf.
2*c* Rachel Errett GILLUM, *b* 1891, *m* Clinton Talbert Yates, and *d* 1917, leaving issue,
●Mark Milton YATES, *b* 1913.
5*b* Charles Lewis BANKHEAD, MD, *b* 1868, *m* 1915, Margaret Cheatwood (*d* 1954), and *d* 29 Nov 1949, leaving issue,
●Charles Lewis BANKHEAD III, *b* 1925, *m* 1946, ●Marion Omohundro, and has had issue,
1*d*●Michael BANKHEAD, *b* 1947.
2*d*●Margaret Elaine BANKHEAD, *b* 1949.
3*d* — BANKHEAD, *b* 1954; *d* an inf.
6*b* Ellen Cary BANKHEAD, *b* 1871, *m* 1892, Clemence Smith, MD, and had issue,
1*c*●Kathryn SMITH, *b* 1893, *m* 1916, ●Willard Moyer, and has issue,
1*d*●William Bankhead MOYER, *b* 1919, *m* 1944, ●Atha Bell Peacock.
2*d*●Anne Cary MOYER, *b* 1926, *m* 1944, ●Billie Waers, and has issue,
1*e*●Anne Randolph WAERS, *b* 27 Oct 1946.

2e●David Moyer WAERS, *b* 12 May 1951.
3d●Jane Randolph MOYER, *b* 30 April 1931, *m* 14 Jan 1952, ●William Emmett Banks IV, son of William Emmett Banks III.
2c Ellen Clemence SMITH, *b* 1895, *m* Paul Edgar Hamilton, MD, and *d* 6 April 1946, leaving issue,
  1d●Richard Edgar HAMILTON, *b* 1923, *m*, and has issue,
    ●Gary Paul HAMILTON, *b* 1952.
  2d●Ann HAMILTON, *b* 16 Dec 1929, *m* 1947, ●Thomas Beauchamp, and has issue,
    1e●Lynne BEAUCHAMP, *b* 1949.
    2e●Thomas Laurence BEAUCHAMP, *b* 27 March 1951.
3c●Mary Emily SMITH, *b* 1901, *m* 1925, Frank W. Minor.
7b Henry Russell BANKHEAD, of Bowling Green, Missouri, *b* 1873, *m* Edith Kemble and *d* 1946 (?), leaving issue,
  1c●Martha Lou BANKHEAD, *b* 1906, *m* ●Charles Staufer, and has issue,
    ●Martha Jane STAUFER, *b* 1926.
  2c●Charles Kemble BANKHEAD, *b* 1909, *m* ●Billie Brandshaw.
8b Fannie Warren BANKHEAD, *b* 1876; *d* 1879.
9b Cary Randolph BANKHEAD, Jr, MD, *b* 1878, *m* 1905, Mary Lucilla Miller (*d* 1935), and *d* 1935, having had issue,
  1c●Henry Miller BANKHEAD, *b* 1906, *m* 1942, ●Annette Gosser, and has issue,
    1d●Barbara BANKHEAD.
    2d●Malvern Miller BANKHEAD.
    3d●Polly BANKHEAD.
    4d●Betty BANKHEAD.
  2c●Cary Randolph BANKHEAD III, *b* 1910, *m* ●Kay —.
  3c Marion Swain BANKHEAD, *b* 1912; *d* 1915.
  4c●Joseph Russell BANKHEAD, *b* 1917, *m* ●Katharyn Jones, and has issue,
    1d●Joseph Russell BANKHEAD, Jr.
    2d●James BANKHEAD.
10b Katie Clyde BANKHEAD, *b* 1880; *dunm* 28 July 1960.
11b Bessie Guy BANKHEAD, *b* 1883; *dunm*.
3a Martha Jefferson BANKHEAD, *b* 1837, *m* 1858, Kinsey Howard Norris, and *d* 1891, leaving issue,
1b Elizabeth NORRIS, *b* 1858, *m* Peter Norton, and *d* 1898, leaving issue,
  Natalia NORTON, *m* 1st, Eugene Schmierle; and 2ndly, William Dallet.
2b Mollie NORRIS, *b* 1860, *m* 1st, Eugene Wells, and had issue,
  1c Howard Custis WELLS, *b* 1881, *m* Meta Fragstein, and *dsp* 1950.
  2c Dixie Annette WELLS, *m* Alfred Lund, and *dsp*.
Mollie Norris *m* 2ndly, James Augustus Sublette.
3b Ellen NORRIS, *b* 1862, *m* Emanuel Daniels, and *dsp*.
4b Charles Bankhead NORRIS, *b* 1866, *m* Harriet Amos, and *dsp* 1921.
5b John Bankhead NORRIS, *b* 1868; *dunm* 1901.
4a Thomas Jefferson BANKHEAD, *b* 1839; *k* in the Civil War 1863, *unm*.
(2) Thomas Mann Randolph BANKHEAD, of Arkansas, *b* at 30 Dec 1811, *m* Elizabeth Pryor, and *dsp* in Arkansas 1880.
(3) Ellen Wayles Randolph BANKHEAD, *b* 5 Sept 1813, *m* John Coles Carter, eldest son of Robert Hill Carter, by his wife Polly Coles, and had issue,
1a Anne CARTER, *b* 1833, *m* 1852, Henry Preston and *d* 1915, having had issue,
1b Mary Coles PRESTON, *b* 1854; *dunm* 1914.
2b Margaret B. PRESTON, *b* 1855; *dunm* 1926.
3b Ellen PRESTON, *b* 1857, *m* Otway Giles Bailey, and *d* 1923, having had issue,
  1c Preston H. BAILEY, *b* 25 May 1891, *m* 19 June 1917, Elizabeth Marie Leftwich, and *d* 11 Oct 1918, leaving issue,
    ●Margaret Preston BAILEY, *b* 1918, *m* 1941, ●Robert Jacobson, and has issue,
      ●Betty Rae JACOBSON, *b* 1942.

  2c●Otway Giles BAILEY, Jr, *b* 1895, *m* 1923, ●Ellen Verena De Ford, and has issue,
    1d●Otway Giles BAILEY III, *b* 1924, *m* 1948, ●Elsie Watson, and has issue,
      1e●Anne Lynne BAILEY, *b* 1950.
      2e●Barbara Leigh BAILEY, *b* 1955.
    2d●Ellen Olivia BAILEY, *b* 1926, *m* 1950, ●Curtis Geannini, and has issue,
      1e●David Curtis GEANNINI.
      2e●Stephen Philip GEANNINI.
      3e●Giles Anderson GEANNINI.
    3d●Jeanne BAILEY, *b* 1920, *m* 1952, ●Robert Pierce Whitman, and has issue,
      ●Robert Pierce WHITMAN, *b* 1953.
4b Elizabeth PRESTON, *b* 1858, *m* 1900, James White Cummings, MD, and *dsp* 1906.
5b Henry PRESTON, Jr, *b* 1861, *m* 1890, Mary Helen (Nellie) Carson, and *d* 1921, leaving issue,
  1c Sidney PRESTON, *b* 1891; *dunm* 1938.
  2c●Henley PRESTON, *b* 1891 (twin with Sidney).
  3c●Anne Carter PRESTON, *b* 1893.
  4c●Henry PRESTON III, *b* 1895, *m* 1930, ●Leta P. Wilson, and has issue,
    ●Henry Donald PRESTON, *b* 1933, *m* 1952, ●Nancy Neal.
  5c Robert Carson PRESTON, *b* 1902; *dunm* 1941.
6b Anne Cary PRESTON, *b* 1863, *m* Albert Pendelton Killinger, and *dsp* 1931.
7b Jane PRESTON, *b* 1863; *dunm* 1907.
8b Isetta R. PRESTON, *b* 1865; *dunm* 1916.
9b Eugenia F. PRESTON, *b* 1868, *m* 1889, Charles Cummings Gibson, and *dsp* 1913.
10b Percy Thomas PRESTON, *b* 1875, *m* 1905, Corinne Roane Wills, and *d* 1941, leaving issue,
  1c●Virginia Wills PRESTON, *b* 1906, *m* 1928, ●Albert Basil Wilson, Jr, son of Albert Basil Wilson, and has issue,
    1d●Elizabeth Ann WILSON, *b* 23 June 1931, *m* 27 Aug 1951, ●Dwight Eugene Bogle, and has issue,
      1e●Keith Eugene BOGLE, *b* 9 Aug 1952.
      2e●Barbara Ann BOGLE, *b* 10 Oct 1953.
      3e●Jerry Wayne BOGLE, *b* 11 Dec 1954.
    2d●Albert Percy WILSON, *b* 5 July 1933, *m* 8 July 1956, ●Betty Lou Umbarger.
    3d●Charlotte Louise WILSON, *b* 13 Dec 1937.
  2c●Percy Thomas PRESTON, Jr, *b* 1909, *m* 1933, ●Mary Marguerite Carter.
  3c●Elizabeth Madison PRESTON, *b* 1913, *m* 1940, ●Kyle Roosevelt Ferris.
2a Robert Hill CARTER, *dunm*.
3a John Coles CARTER, Jr, *m* Sarah E. Calvert, and had issue,
1b Anne C. P. CARTER, *m* Edward Clark, and had issue,
  Carter B. CLARK.
2b Mary Randolph CARTER, *dunm*.
(4) William Stuart BANKHEAD, of Albemarle, nr Courtland, Alabama, *b* at Monticello 30 Jan 1826, *m* 1st 1850, Martha Jane Watkins (*d* 1851), and had issue,
1a — BANKHEAD, *d* an inf.
William Stuart Bankhead *m* 2ndly 1854, Barbara Elizabeth Garth (*d* 1867), and by her had issue,
2a Anne Cary (Nannie) Randolph BANKHEAD, *b* 1856, *m* 1873, J. Harvey Gilchrist, and *d* 1900, leaving issue,
Katie Frank GILCHRIST, *b* 19 Oct 1876, *m* 29 Sept 1896, Lawson Sykes, and *d* 10 Feb 1968, having had issue,
  1c — SYKES (dau), *d* an inf.
  2c●Leila Scaife SYKES, *b* 7 Oct 1905, *m* 1934, ●David L. Martin, and has issue,
    ●Lawson Sykes MARTIN [ *View Celeste, Courtland, Alabama 35618, USA*], *b* 18 July 1936, *m* 24 Nov 1962, ●Donie De Bardeleben Neal, and has issue,
      1e●Virginia Larkin MARTIN, *b* 2 Sept 1963.
      2e●Anne Randolph MARTIN, *b* 19 Jan 1965.
      3e●Ellen Pratt MARTIN, *b* 19 Jan 1965 (twin with her sister Anne Randolph Martin).
      4e●Donie Neal MARTIN.
3a William Stuart BANKHEAD, Jr, *d* an inf.

4a — BANKHEAD (dau), d an inf ca 1860.
5a Elizabeth Garth BANKHEAD, b28 Aug 1865, m1886,
William Edgar Hotchkiss (b1855; d1932), and d9 April
1942, leaving issue,
  1b Cary Randolph HOTCHKISS, b 18 May 1887;
  dunm.
  2b Anna Frances HOTCHKISS, b 18 Nov 1889, m 5
  Sept 1911, Campbell Houston Gillespie, of Sherman,
  Texas, and d 26 Nov 1943, leaving issue,
    1c● Campbell Houston GILLESPIE, Jr [*1313 East
    Richards Street, Sherman, Texas 75090, USA*], b7
    Aug 1913, m 1937, ●Mary Ruffin (b14 Oct 1913),
    yst dau of Robert Montagu McMurdo, by his wife
    Caryanne Randolph Ruffin (*see p107*), and has issue,
      1d●Campbell Houston GILLESPIE III [*1710
      Shields Drive, Sherman, Texas 75090, USA*], b
      21 Aug 1938, m1 Sept 1962, ●Mary Bert Patillo,
      and has issue,
        1e●Maryanna Keeval GILLESPIE, b 1 May
        1968.
        2e●Cary Ruffin GILLESPIE, b14 April 1970.
      2d●Roberto McMurdo GILLESPIE [*1313 East
      Richards Street, Sherman, Texas 75090, USA*], b
      29 July 1945.
    2c●Stuart Edgar GILLESPIE, b 13 Sept 1919, m
    ●Layle Church, and has issue,
      1d●Clark Patton GILLESPIE, b 13 April 1944.
      2d●Layle Christine GILLESPIE, b 7 Feb 1946.
      3d●William Stuart GILLESPIE, b18 April 1948.
  3b Elizabeth Bankhead HOTCHKISS, b 29 July 1891,
  m 1924, Virgil James, and d 27 Feb 1944.
  4b David Stuart HOTCHKISS (Rev), b 28 June 1894,
  m 22 Dec 1919, Martha Maddox Smith, and d23 Aug
  1935, leaving issue,
    1c●David Stuart HOTCHKISS, Jr, b 5 Oct 1920.
    2c●Martha Jane HOTCHKISS, b28 May 1924, m19
    Dec 1942, ●Robert Tweedy McWhorter (b20 July
    1918), and has issue,
      1d●Robert Tweedy McWHORTER, Jr, b28 Sept
      1943.
      2d●Roger Barton McWHORTER, b9 Sept 1945.
      3d●Martha Stuart McWHORTER, b 25 June
      1947.
    3c●William Edgar HOTCHKISS III (Rev), b at
    Dunedin, Florida 24 Aug 1926, m 8 Sept 1951,
    ●Jean Downer Hinson, and has issue,
      1d●Jean Randolph HOTCHKISS, b Sept 1952.
      2d●William David HOTCHKISS, b Dec 1953.
      3d●Odus Hinson HOTCHKISS, b 12 Nov 1955.
      4d●William Edgar HOTCHKISS IV, b 20 Nov
      1958.
      5d●Stuart Andrew HOTCHKISS, b12 Feb 1961.
      6d●Mae Stone HOTCHKISS, b 1 May 1963.
  5b William Edgar HOTCHKISS, Jr, b 1899, m 1921,
  ●Mary, widow of — Walker, and dau of — Beard,
  and d 4 July 1959, leaving issue,
    1c●William Bankhead HOTCHKISS, bDec 1923, m
    31 Aug 1947, ●Jo Vaughn Paulus, and has issue,
      1d●Nancy Vaughn HOTCHKISS, b 1949.
      2d●Charles William HOTCHKISS, b 1951.
    2c●Cary Randolph HOTCHKISS [*Kelona Farms,
    Box 4, Route 1, Courtland, Alabama 35618, USA*], b
    23 Aug 1931, m 26 Feb 1953, ●Charlotte Taylor
    Shackelford, and has issue,
      1d●Ellen Garth HOTCHKISS, b 29 Sept 1954.
      2d●Michael Cary HOTCHKISS, b 22 July 1957.
      3d●Elizabeth Bankhead HOTCHKISS, b 27 Feb
      1963.
  6b Charles Wilcox HOTCHKISS, b 22 July 1903, m 3
  July 1929, ●Gene Marie Fennel, and d14 Dec 1952,
  leaving issue,
    1c●Gene Bankhead HOTCHKISS, b 7 Oct 1930, m
    19 May 1953, ●Wilbur Craft (b 1928), and has
    issue,
      ●Rebecca Lecky CRAFT, b 30 July 1954.
    2c●John Fennel HOTCHKISS, b 20 March 1938.
William Stuart Bankhead m3rdly 1868, Catharine, widow
of — Garth, and dau of — Gilchrist, and d Nov 1898,
having by her had issue,
  6a Stuart Gibbons BANKHEAD, b 1869; d an inf.
2 Thomas Jefferson RANDOLPH, of Edgehill, financier, mem

Virginia legislature, Rector of the Univ of Virginia, Pres
Democratic Nat Convention, Baltimore 1872, Col Virginia
Militia, b at Monticello 12 Sept 1792, *educ* Univ of
Pennsylvania, m at her father's residence Mount Warren,
Albemarle County 7 March 1815, Jane Hollins (b 16 Jan
1798; d at Edgehill 18 Jan 1871, *bur* Monticello), dau of
Wilson Cary Nicholas, sometime Gov of Virginia by his wife
Margaret Smith, and d at Edgehill 8 Oct 1875 (*bur*
Monticello), having had issue,
(1) Margaret Smith RANDOLPH, b at the Governor's
House, Richmond, Virginia 7 March 1816, m2 Sept 1839,
her 2nd cousin, William Mann Randolph, Judge of the
Probate Court (d at Pass Christian, Mississippi 1850),
eldest son of Dr John Randolph, of Middle Quarter, by his
wife Judith Lewis, and d 20 Dec 1842, leaving issue,
  1a Jane Margaret RANDOLPH, b7 May 1840, m8 Nov
  1860, Edward Clifford Anderson, Jr, of Savannah,
  Georgia, Col 7th Georgia Cav CSA (b17 Jan 1839; d 27
  Sept 1876), son of George Wayne Anderson, by his wife
  Eliza Clifford Stites, and d 27 June 1914, having had
  issue,
    1b Jefferson Randolph ANDERSON, hon DCL Univ of
    the South (1931), of Savannah, Georgia, lawyer, mem
    Georgia House of Reps 1905-06 and 1909-12, mem
    Georgia State Senate 1913-14 (Pres), mem Democra-
    tic Nat Convention 1912, Pres Monticello Assoc
    1933-35 and Historian 1937-38, b at Savannah 4 Sept
    1861, *educ* Chatham Acad, Virginia, Univ of Virginia
    (BL 1885), and Univ of Göttingen, m 27 Nov 1895,
    Anne Page (b 15 April 1873), dau of Joseph John
    Wilder, of Savannah, by his wife Georgia Page King,
    and d at Savannah 17 July 1950 (*bur* there), having
    had issue,
      1c● Page Randolph ANDERSON, bat Oakton, Cobb
      County, Georgia 27 Aug 1899, m 2 April 1921,
      ●Henry Norris Platt [*6 Norman Lane, Chestnut
      Hill, Philadelphia, Pennsylvania 19118, USA*], son
      of Charless Platt, of Philadelphia, by his wife
      Elizabeth Norris, and has issue,
        1d●Henry Norris PLATT, Jr, b at Philadelphia
        23 March 1922, m 26 June 1953, ●Lenore Guest
        MacLeish, and has issue,
          1e●Henry Norris PLATT III, b12 June 1954.
          2e●Lenore McCall PLATT, b 17 May 1956.
          3e●Martha Hillard PLATT, b 29 April 1959.
          4e●Caroline Anderson PLATT, b 23 Nov
          1961.
        2d●Ann Page PLATT, b at Philadelphia 22 Nov
        1924, m1 July 1950, ●Thomas Elliott Allen, and
        has issue,
          1e●Page Randolph ALLEN, b6 Sept 1951, m
          19 June 1970, ●William Scott Morris.
          2e●James Elliot ALLEN, b 26 July 1953.
          3e●Samuel Wilder ALLEN, b9 Nov 1956.
          4e●Abigail Brewster ALLEN, b 14 Feb 1960.
          5e●Mary Davis ALLEN, b 11 April 1963.
        3d●Jefferson Randolph PLATT, b at Philadel-
        phia 13 May 1929, m 22 Aug 1971, ●Veronica
        Chisholm.
      2c Jefferson Randolph ANDERSON, Jr, b 3 Sept
      1902; d 29 Nov 1903.
      3c●Joseph Randolph ANDERSON, b at Savannah
      22 April 1905, m 15 Nov 1930, ●Edith O'Driscoll
      Hunter, of Savannah, and has issue,
        ●Page O'Driscoll ANDERSON, b 7 Nov 1932, m
        26 April 1953, ●James Eggleston Hungerpillar
        [*12730 Rockwell Avenue, Savannah, Georgia
        31406, USA*], and has issue,
          1e●Susan Page HUNGERPILLAR, b 23 Feb
          1954.
          2e●James Randolph HUNGERPILLAR, b 25
          Nov 1956.
          3e●John Colin HUNGERPILLAR, b18 March
          1959.
  2b George Wayne ANDERSON, of Richmond,
  Virginia, City Attorney of Richmond 1921, Col 1st
  Virginia Regt, Historian Monticello Assoc 1916-18, b
  at Edgehill 10 July 1863, *educ* Hanover Acad,
  Virginia, and Univ of Virginia (BL 1888), m at
  Charlottesville 21 Dec 1889, Estelle Marguerite, dau
  of Frederick George Burthe, of New Orleans, by his

wife Mary, dau of Senator Robert Carter Nicholas and grand-dau of Gov Wilson Cary Nicholas, and *d* at Richmond 30 Dec 1922, having had issue,

1*c*●Edward Clifford ANDERSON, served in World War I as Lieut 5th Field Art 1st Div AEF, awarded Croix de Guerre with silver star [*1234 Rothesay Road, Richmond, Virginia, USA*], *b* at Richmond 26 Nov 1893, *educ* Univ of Virginia, *m* 12 Jan 1922, ●Isabel, dau of — Scott, of Richmond, and has issue,

  1*d*●George Wayne ANDERSON [*1315 Loch Lomond Lane, Richmond, Virginia, USA*], *b* 1 May 1927, *m* 4 Oct 1952, ●Virginia Lee Richardson, and has issue,

    1*e*●Cary Randolph ANDERSON, *b* 30 June 1953.

    2*e*●Edward Clifford ANDERSON, *b* 2 Dec 1958.

  2*d*●Elizabeth Strother ANDERSON, *b* 11 April 1929, *m* 6 Dec 1952, ●Jonathan Bryan III, son of Jonathan Bryan, Jr, and has issue,

    1*e*●Robert Carter BRYAN, *b* 31 Jan 1954.

    2*e*●Isabel Scott BRYAN, *b* 5 April 1955.

    3*e*●John Randolph BRYAN, *b* 8 March 1959.

  3*d*●Isabel Scott ANDERSON, *b* 27 Sept 1932, *m* 1st 29 Dec 1962, James Turner Sloan, Jr (*d* 18 April 1965), son of James Turner Sloan, and has issue,

    1*e*●Louise Williams SLOAN, *b* 24 June 1963.

    2*e*●Edward Anderson SLOAN, *b* 16 July 1965.

  Isabel Scott Anderson *m* 2ndly 24 May 1968, ●Harry Wilkinson Fitzgerald [*Severn Forest, Annapolis, Maryland 21401, USA*], and has further issue,

    3*e*●Isabel Scott FITZGERALD, *b* 28 June 1969.

    4*e*●Caroline Harris FITZGERALD, *b* 1970.

2*c* George Wayne ANDERSON, Jr, Capt 313th Field Art 80th Div AEF, served in World War I, *b* at Richmond 20 June 1896, *educ* Univ of Virginia, *ka* at Le Grand Carre Farm in the Meuse-Argonne, France 1 Nov 1918, *unm.*

3*c*●Cary Nicholas ANDERSON, *b* at Richmond 4 Feb 1903, *m* 10 April 1926, Manfred Keller (*b* at Zurich, Switzerland 1904; *d* at Wilmington, Delaware 19 June 1959), and has issue,

  1*d*●Estelle Wayne KELLER, *b* 7 June 1927.

  2*d*●Ursula Sophie KELLER, *b* 26 Sept 1928, *m* 8 Sept 1951, ●Irénée DuPont May, and has issue,

    1*e*●Sophie Christine MAY, *b* 2 Aug 1953, *m* 16 June 1973, ●Peter Charles Rupert Gerard (*b* 27 Sept 1951), yr son of Major Rupert Charles Frederick Gerard, MBE, late Gren Guards, film actor (*see* BURKE'S *Peerage*, GERARD, B).

    2*e*●Irénée DuPont MAY, *b* 21 April 1965.

3*b* Eliza Clifford ANDERSON, *b* 24 Oct 1864; *d* 11 Sept 1876.

4*b* Margaret Randolph ANDERSON, *b* at Savannah 21 Aug 1866, *m* 1st 22 Nov 1893, Abbott Lawrence Rotch, of Boston, Mass, meteorologist (*b* at Boston 6 Jan 1861; *d* 7 April 1912), son of Benjamin Smith Rotch, by his wife Annie Bigelow Lawrence, and had issue,

1*c* Elizabeth ROTCH, *d* 29 June 1895.

2*c* Margaret Randolph ROTCH, *b* at Boston 15 June 1896, *m* 1 June 1916, James Jackson Storrow, Jr, son of James Jackson Storrow, and *d* 19 March 1945, leaving issue,

  ●James Jackson STORROW, *b* 7 May 1917, *m* ●Patricia Blake (*b* 13 April 1917), and has issue,

    1*e*●Gerald Blake STORROW, *b* 15 July 1944.

    2*e*●Peter STORROW, *b* 26 Sept 1946.

    3*e*●Arthur Rotch STORROW, *b* 7 June 1948.

    4*e*●Margaret Randolph STORROW, *b* 4 Jan 1955.

3*c* Arthur ROTCH, *b* at Boston 1 Feb 1899, *m* at Dedham, Mass 30 April 1935, Alice Gedney (*b* at Milton, Mass 21 Nov 1900; *d* there 19 Sept 1971), dau of Edward Cabot Storrow, by his wife Caroline and *d* at Boston Feb 1972, leaving issue,

  1*d*●Ann Storrow ROTCH, *b* at Boston 28 Jan

1937, *m* at Milton, Mass 16 July 1960, ●Henry G. Magendantz (*b* 20 Aug 1936) [*15 Birch Road, Branford, Conn 06405, USA*], son of Heinz Magendantz, by his wife Marianna.

  2*d*●Abbott Lawrence ROTCH [*1636 Canton Avenue, Milton, Massachusetts 02186, USA*], *b* at Boston 8 March 1939, *m* at N Edgecomb, Maine 31 Aug 1963, ●Emily Beaumelle (*b* at Berkeley, California 1943), dau of Robert Roe, by his wife Mary Elizabeth, and has issue,

    1*e*●Elizabeth Ann ROTCH, *b* at Boston 23 Oct 1964.

    2*e*●Arthur Randolph ROTCH, *b* at Boston 11 Aug 1966.

    3*e*●Andrew Lawrence ROTCH, *b* at Boston 6 Feb 1970.

  3*d*●Edward Cabot ROTCH, *b* at Boston 9 July 1941.

4*c*●Katherine Lawrence ROTCH, *b* at Boston 26 May 1906, *m* 17 June 1925, Malcolm Whelan Greenough (*b* Jan 1904; *d* 7 Feb 1948), son of Malcolm Scollay Greenough, by his wife Violet Whelan, and has had issue,

  1*d*●Malcolm Whelan GREENOUGH, Jr [*93 Pinckney Street, Boston, Massachusetts, USA*], *b* 11 June 1926, *m* 7 Feb 1948, ●Sarah Eden Browne, and has issue,

    1*e*●Katherine Lawrence GREENOUGH, *b* 16 Nov 1949.

    2*e*●Sarah Eden GREENOUGH, *b* 25 May 1951.

    3*e*●Margaret Randolph GREENOUGH, *b* 19 July 1954.

    4*e*●Malcolm Whelan GREENOUGH III, *b* Sept 1957.

  2*d* Lawrence Rotch GREENOUGH, *b* 16 Dec 1930, *m* 14 April 1956, ●Pamela Antoinette Marguerite Seddon, and *d* 17 April 1964, leaving issue,

    1*e*●Elizabeth Tiffany GREENOUGH, *b* 31 May 1957.

    2*e*●Lawrence Rotch GREENOUGH, Jr, *b* 2 June 1959.

Margaret Randolph Anderson *m* 2ndly 1 Nov 1919, Henry Parkman, Jr, and *d* at Milton, Mass 3 May 1941.

5*b* Sarah Randolph ANDERSON, *b* 21 May 1872; *dunm* 17 Jan 1960.

2*a* William Lewis RANDOLPH, of Dunlora, Ordnance Offr Armistead's Bde, Pickett's Div CSA, *b* 20 Dec 1841, *m* 1st 1866, Agnes (*b* 23 Jan 1846; *d* 8 May 1880, *bur* Monticello), dau of Michael Dillon, of Savannah, formerly of Ireland, by his wife Margaret Riley, and had issue,

1*b* Margaret Gibson RANDOLPH, *b* 19 Nov 1866; *d* 13 Sept 1872 (*bur* Monticello).

2*b* Thomas Jefferson RANDOLPH IV, *b* 21 July 1868, *m* 1st 14 Nov 1895, Laura Lester, and had issue,

  1*c* Laura Lester RANDOLPH, *b* 9 Feb 1899, *m* 18 Dec 1920, ●Alfred Wright Thompson [*1723 South Edgewood Avenue, Jacksonville 5, Florida, USA*], and *d* 19 March 1969, leaving issue,

    ●Randolph Hines THOMPSON, *b* 13 July 1924, *m* 30 June 1951, ●Sarah Beauvois L'Engle (*b* 6 Sept 1929), and has issue,

      ●Michael L'Engle THOMPSON, *b* 26 June 1955.

  2*c* Martha Jefferson RANDOLPH, *m* 9 June 1920, John Porter Stevens, of Savannah (*d* 10 May 1969), and *d* 23 Aug 1969, having had issue,

    1*d* Martha Randolph STEVENS, *b* 23 July 1921; *d* 29 July 1935.

    2*d*●Laura Randolph STEVENS, *b* 23 Nov 1931, *m* 1st 14 Oct 1950 (*m* diss by div), Frank Kohler Peeples, and has issue,

      1*e*●Martha Stevens DEVENDORF (formerly PEEPLES), *b* 10 Dec 1951.

      2*e*●Daryn Stewart DEVENDORF (formerly PEEPLES), *b* 15 April 1954.

    She *m* 2ndly 2 Aug 1961, ●Donald Allan Devendorf, and has further issue,

3e●Meredith Randolph DEVENDORF, *b* 11 Oct 1970.

Thomas Jefferson Randolph IV *m* 2ndly Nancy Clifton de Marclay, and *d* 18 Feb 1926 (*bur* Monticello).

3*b* William Mann RANDOLPH, *b* in Albemarle County 14 Jan 1870, *educ* Virginia Univ (MD 1900), *m* 20 Oct 1894, his 1st cousin once removed, Mary Walker (*b* in Albemarle County 14 June 1866; *d* at Wild Acres, Charlottesville 9 Dec 1957, *bur* Monticello), yst dau of Thomas Jefferson Randolph, Jr (*see p 110*), and *d* 25 Jan 1944 (*bur* Monticello), having had issue,

1*c* Carolina Ramsey RANDOLPH, author of *School Health Services* (1941) and other works, Sec-Treas Monticello Assoc 1951-56, *b* at Charlottesville 24 Sept 1895, *educ* Agnes Scott Coll, Atlanta, and Johns Hopkins Univ (MS), *dunm* at Wild Acres, Charlottesville 1 March 1958 (*bur* Monticello).

2*c*● Sarah Nicholas RANDOLPH [*1600 South Eads Street, Apt 9215, Arlington, Virginia 22202, USA*], *b* 8 Dec 1896, *m* 29 March 1919, Gen Lucian King Truscott, Jr, US Army (*b* at Chatfield, Texas 9 Jan 1895; *d* at Washington, DC 12 Sept 1965), son of Lucian King Truscott, by his wife Maria Temple Tully, and has issue,

1*d*●Mary Randolph TRUSCOTT, *b* 3 May 1920, *m* 1st 28 April 1942 (*m* diss by div), Robert Wilbourn; and 2ndly 14 Dec 1957, ●Graeme Grant Bruce [*4 Chepstow Villas, London W11, England*].

2*d*●Lucian King TRUSCOTT III, Col US Army [*8120 Northridge Avenue, NE, Albuquerque, New Mexico 87110, USA*], *b* in Hawaii 17 Sept 1921, *m* 16 April 1946, ●Anne Harloe, and has issue,

1*e*●Lucian King TRUSCOTT IV, *b* 12 April 1947.

2*e*●Francis (Frank) Meriwether TRUSCOTT [*1332 Mass Street, Lawrence, Kansas 66044, USA*], *b* 28 Jan 1949, *m* 3 Jan 1970, ●Deborah Newell Jackson.

3*e*●Susan Harloe TRUSCOTT, *b* 19 Jan 1953, *m* 5 June 1971, ●Allan Moskowitz [*814 Thirteenth Street, NW, Albuquerque, New Mexico 87102, USA*], and has issue,

1*f*●Rachel MOSKOWITZ.

2*f*●Sara MOSKOWITZ, *b* 25 June 1972.

4*e*●Mary Randolph TRUSCOTT, *b* 7 Aug 1959.

5*e*●Virginia Anne TRUSCOTT, *b* 12 May 1961.

3*d*●James Joseph TRUSCOTT, Lt-Col US Army, *b* 26 Dec 1930, *m* 31 Aug 1957, ●Helen Kelly Haydock, and has issue,

1*e*●James Joseph TRUSCOTT, *b* 1 Aug 1958.

2*e*●Thomas Haydock TRUSCOTT, *b* 30 Nov 1959.

3*e*●Patrick Moore TRUSCOTT, *b* 16 July 1962.

4*e*●Sarah Randolph TRUSCOTT.

3*c*●Agnes Dillon RANDOLPH, *b* 13 April 1898, *m* 1st 25 May 1925, George Marvin; and 2ndly 28 Dec 1934, Edward Buffam Hill (*b* at Brooklyn, New York 1879; *d* at Woodside, California 14 Oct 1957).

4*c* William Lewis RANDOLPH, *b* 10 July 1899; *d* 7 Jan 1906.

5*c*●Thomas Jefferson RANDOLPH V, Col US Army, Pres Monticello Assoc 1953-55 [*Box 881, Charlottesville, Virginia 22901, USA*], *b* at Charlottesville 7 Oct 1900, *m* 24 April 1930, ●Augusta Luell Blue, and has issue,

1*d*●Virginia Hyland RANDOLPH, *b* 10 May 1931, *m* 28 Dec 1957, ●Landry Thomas Slade [*Department of Chemistry, American University of Beirut, Beirut, Lebanon*], and has issue,

1*e*●Lyell Landry SLADE, *b* 19 Sept 1959.

2*e*●Lawrence Randolph SLADE, *b* 9 Aug 1964.

3*e*●William Learned SLADE, *b* 10 Feb 1967.

2*d*●William Mann RANDOLPH, Lt-Col US Army [*HQ 54th Engineer Battalion, APO, New York 09026, USA*], *b* 20 April 1933, *m* 28 Jan

1956, ●Maria Teresa Osma, and has had issue,

1*e*●Helen Augusta RANDOLPH, *b* 14 March 1958.

2*e*●Elizabeth Virginia RANDOLPH, *b* 15 Sept 1959.

3*e* Peter Jefferson RANDOLPH, *b* 6 March, *d* 9 March 1961.

4*e*●Susan Carolina RANDOLPH, *b* 5 Feb 1964.

5*e*●Thomas Joseph RANDOLPH, *b* 30 July 1965.

6*c*●Mary Walker RANDOLPH, Pres Monticello Assoc 1948-49 [*1623 Bruce Avenue, Charlottesville, Virginia 22903, USA*], *b* 30 April 1903.

7*c*●Hollins Nicholas RANDOLPH, Jr [*RD2, Charles Town, West Virginia 25414, USA*], *b* at Charlottesville 14 June 1904, *m* 22 Aug 1933, ●Mary Virginia (*b* at Wheeling 1908), dau of William Hoge, by his wife Virginia Blue, and has issue,

1*d*●Hollins Nicholas RANDOLPH III [*Rt 1, Box 263-513, Charles Town, West Virginia 25414, USA*], *m* 25 May 1957, ●Nancy Lee (*b* at Winchester, Virginia 26 July 1939), dau of Sewell Walter Wilson, by his wife Hilda Walford, and has issue,

1*e*●Bonnie Sue RANDOLPH, *b* at Oklahoma City 8 Jan 1958.

2*e*●Martha Christine RANDOLPH, *b* at Winchester, Virginia 31 Dec 1959.

3*e*●Hollins Nicholas RANDOLPH IV, *b* at Winchester, Virginia 28 Sept 1961.

4*e*●Angela Marie RANDOLPH, *b* at Winchester, Virginia 16 March 1971.

2*d*●Thomas Jefferson RANDOLPH VI [*Route 1, Box 38, Winchester, Virginia 22601, USA*], *b* 8 Oct 1936, *m* 20 Dec 1958, ●Marie Spitler, and has issue,

1*e*●Thomas Jefferson RANDOLPH VII, *b* 11 Feb 1960.

2*e*●William Franklin RANDOLPH, *b* 8 July 1963.

3*e*●John Michael RANDOLPH, *b* 23 April 1972.

8*c*●Francis Meriwether RANDOLPH, *b* 22 April 1906, *m* 21 Dec 1935, ●Leonne Gouaux, and has issue,

1*d*●Thomas Mann RANDOLPH, *b* 24 Sept 1936, *m* Nov 1960, ●Evelyn Adele Morash, and has issue,

1*e*●Margaret Elizabeth RANDOLPH, *b* 26 Aug 1961.

2*e*●Hugh Jefferson RANDOLPH, *b* Nov 1962.

3*e*●Ailine RANDOLPH, *b* 17 March 1964.

2*d*●William Lewis RANDOLPH, *b* 28 Sept 1940, *m* Dec 1961, ●Brenda Theresa Cherami, and has issue,

1*e*●Katherine RANDOLPH, *b* Dec 1962.

2*e*●Joseph Adam RANDOLPH, *b* 26 Nov 1963.

3*d*●Michael Joseph RANDOLPH, *b* 19 Dec 1942.

4*b* Hollins Nicholas RANDOLPH, of Atlanta, Georgia, attorney, Pres Monticello Assoc 1926-29, *b* at Dunlora 25 Feb 1872, *educ* Virginia Univ (BL 1895), *m* 17 Oct 1899, Caroline Tison (*b* 1875; *d* 1960), dau of George Walter, of Savannah, and *dsp* at Washington, DC 29 April 1938 (*bur* Monticello),

5*b* Arthur Dillon RANDOLPH, *b* 9 Feb, *d* 6 Nov 1874 (*bur* Monticello).

6*b* Agnes Dillon RANDOLPH, *b* 12 July 1875; *dunm* 3 Dec 1930 (*bur* Monticello).

William Lewis Randolph *m* 2ndly 9 Nov 1887, his 1st cousin, Margaret Randolph (*b* 14 Nov 1843; *d* 12 Feb 1898, *bur* Monticello), 3rd dau of John Charles Randolph Taylor, of Lego (*see p 106*), and *d* 7 June 1892 (*bur* Monticello).

(2) Martha (Patsy) Jefferson RANDOLPH, *b* at Mount Warren 20 July 1817, *m* at Edgehill 22 Dec 1834, John Charles Randolph Taylor, of Elmington, Clarke County, Virginia (*b* at Elmington 30 May 1812; *d* at Lego, Albemarle County, Virginia 6 Jan 1875, *bur* Monticello), son of Bennett Taylor, by his wife Susan Beverley, dau of

Edmund Randolph, Gov of Virginia, and *d* at Midway, Albemarle County, Virginia 16 July 1857 (*bur* Monticello), having had issue,

1*a* Bennett TAYLOR, Lt-Col 19th Virginia Regt CSA, *b* at Edgehill 15 Aug 1836, *m* in Albemarle County 1866, Lucy (*b* 9 March 1842; *d* at Page, W Virginia 4 March 1928), dau of Edward Colston, by his wife Sarah Jane Brockenbrough, and *d* at Badford, Virginia 9 April 1898 (*bur* Monticello), leaving issue,

1*b* Patsy Jefferson TAYLOR, *b* 24 March 1867; *dunm* at Ansted, W Virginia 20 Nov 1903 (*bur* Monticello).

2*b* Raleigh Colston TAYLOR, of Lego and Charlottesville, Pres Monticello Assoc 1929-31, *b* in Albemarle County, Virginia 22 June 1869, *m* 1907, Mary Tayloe (*b* 1875; *d* at Charlottesville, Virginia 1949, *bur* Monticello), and *d* at Charlottesville 11 April 1952 (*bur* Monticello), leaving issue,

Raleigh Colston TAYLOR, Jr, *b* at Ansted, W Virginia 13 Feb 1909, *m* at Richmond, Virginia 1940, ●Margaret (*b* 22 July 1904) [*1011 Dacian Avenue, Durham, North Carolina 27701, USA*], dau of Paul Howard Lamb, by his wife Margaret, and *d* at Tuscaloosa, Alabama 19 April 1959 (*bur* Monticello), leaving issue,

●Jane Colston TAYLOR, MD, *b* at Washington, DC 8 July 1941, *m* at Winston-Salem, N Carolina 12 Feb 1966, ●William Hanks Gaede (*b* at Pittsburgh, Pennsylvania 6 Feb 1922) [*PO Box 747, Hillsborough, North Carolina 27278, USA*], son of William Adolf Gaede, by his wife Lucy Lucas.

3*b* Lewis Randolph TAYLOR, *b* 22 Sept 1871, *m* 10 Sept 1901, Natalie Dorsey Sefton (*d* at Martinsburg, W Virginia 5 July 1969), and *d* at Martinsburg, W Virginia 12 April 1945 (*bur* Monticello), leaving issue,

1*c* ●Bennett TAYLOR III [*1304 West King Street, Martinsburg, West Virginia 25401, USA*], *b* 14 May 1904, *m* 8 June 1935, ●Anne Spottswood Harris.

2*c* ●Lewis Randolph TAYLOR, Jr [*3459 Sea Grape Drive, Sarasota, Florida 33581, USA*], *b* at Roanoke, Virginia 11 March 1909, *m* at Bluefield W Virginia 7 June 1941, ●Carolyn, dau of Harry Douthat, by his wife Anna, and has issue,

●Susan Randolph TAYLOR, *b* at New York City 3 Aug 1949, *educ* Duke Univ, Durham, N Carolina.

3*c* ●Walter Dorsey TAYLOR [*1004 Abingdon Road, Virginia Beach, Virginia 23451, USA*], *b* 5 Dec 1916, *m* at Norfolk, Virginia, ●Emily Rawlings, and has issue,

1*d* ●Emily Hume TAYLOR, *b* at Norfolk, Virginia 6 July 1942, *m* 16 April 1966, ●Bradford Willis Gile [*RDF, 2 Webster Lake, West Franklin, New Hampshire 03235, USA*].

2*d* ●Walter Dorsey TAYLOR, Jr [*Box 60, Rt 7, Roanoke, Virginia 24018, USA*], *b* at Norfolk, Virginia 23 Dec 1946, *m* 8 June 1968, ●Linda Sue Bohon, and has issue,

●Linda Bohon TAYLOR, *b* 2 Aug 1971.

4*b* John Charles Randolph TAYLOR, Jr, *b* at Lego, Albemarle County, Virginia 21 Aug 1874, *m* at Halifax, Virginia 18 June 1907, Mary Grammer (*b* at Leigholm, Virginia 7 Sept 1881; *d* at Halifax, Virginia 1 Aug 1959), dau of Thomas Watkins Leigh, by his wife Mary Elizabeth Faulkner, and *d* at Salem Virginia 27 Jan 1962, leaving issue,

1*c* ●Martha Jefferson TAYLOR, worked as a research biologist 1931-71, author of scientific papers on leukemia in mice, resistance to anthrax in rats, bacterial genetics, etc, Sec Monticello Assoc from 1973, *b* at Page, W Virginia 10 Dec 1910, *m* at Edinburgh, Scotland 8 Sept 1964, ●Edgar Stedman, DSc, PhD, FRS (*b* at Guildford, Surrey, England 12 July 1890) [*13 Kline Boulevard, Frederick, Maryland 21701, USA*], son of Albert Stedman, by his wife Ellen Eagle.

2*c* ●John Charles Randolph TAYLOR III [*1336 Westover Avenue, Norfolk, Virginia 23507, USA*], *b* at Page, W Virginia 22 Sept 1914, *m* at Norfolk, Virginia 9 Dec 1944, ●Mary Farant (*b* at Norfolk, Virginia 7 Nov 1922), dau of George E. Ferebee, by his wife Mary Farant, and has issue,

1*d* ●John Charles Randolph TAYLOR IV, *b* at Norfolk, Virginia 26 March 1946.

2*d* ●Emory Randolph TAYLOR, *b* at Norfolk, Virginia 1 Oct 1947.

3*c* ●William Leigh TAYLOR, [*310 Townes Street, Danville, Virginia 24541, USA*], *b* at Page, W Virginia 7 May 1919, *m* at Norfolk, Virginia 24 Jan 1942, ●Norma (*b* at Hamilton, Ontario, Canada 8 Oct 1918), dau of Stanley C. Pamplin, by his 1st wife Mae Roberts, and has issue,

1*d* ●Mary Leigh TAYLOR, *b* at Savannah, Georgia 9 Dec 1942, *m* at Danville, Virginia 10 July 1965, ●Phillip Wilson Shepard (*b* at Haverhill, Mass 20 Oct 1938) [*3609 Whispering Lane, Falls Church, Virginia 22041, USA*], son of Paul W. Shepard, by his wife Helen Carey, and has issue,

1*e* ●Jennifer Leigh SHEPARD, *b* at Washington, DC 29 April 1969.

2*e* ●Douglas Carey SHEPARD, *b* at Washington, DC 16 May 1972.

2*d* ●William Leigh TAYLOR, Jr, *b* at Norfolk, Virginia 26 Feb 1947.

3*d* ●Charles MacLellan TAYLOR, *b* at Staunton, Virginia 2 Sept 1949.

4*d* ●Martha Jefferson TAYLOR, *b* at Danville, Virginia 9 Jan 1954.

4*c* ●Mary Leigh TAYLOR, *b* at Page, W Virginia 1 Aug 1922, *m* at Halifax, Virginia 13 Jan 1951, ●Martin Nisbet Shaw, Jr (*b* at Leaksville, N Carolina 17 April 1925) [*33 Woodvale Avenue, Asheville, North Carolina 28804, USA*], son of Martin Shaw, by his wife Jane Nelson Marr, and has issue,

1*d* ●Christopher Gordon SHAW, *b* at Elizabeth City, N Carolina 28 Feb 1953.

2*d* ●Margaret Hope SHAW, *b* at Asheville, N Carolina 19 Jan 1956.

5*b* Edward Colston TAYLOR, Sr, *b* 22 Feb 1877, *m* Jessie Alwine (*d* at Charleston, W Virginia 6 Dec 1973, *bur* Monticello), and *d* at Charleston, W Virginia 23 June 1940 (*bur* Monticello), leaving issue,

●Edward Colston TAYLOR, Jr, Vice-Pres Monticello Assoc 1953-55, Pres 1955-57 [*1656 Franklin Avenue, Charleston, West Virginia 25414 USA*], *b* 21 March 1911, *m* 9 Sept 1972, ●Alys, widow of — Cremer, and dau of — Shanks.

6*b* Jane Brockenbrough TAYLOR, *b* 29 Jan 1881; *dunm* 11 Nov 1955 (*bur* Monticello).

2*a* Jane Randolph TAYLOR, *b* at Avonwood 2 April 1838; *dunm* at Lego 12 Jan 1917 (*bur* Monticello).

3*a* Susan Beverley TAYLOR, *b* at Avonwood 8 Feb 1840; *m* John Sinclair Blackburn, of Alexandria (*d* at Lego), and *d* at Alexandria, Virginia 22 Sept 1900, having had issue,

1*b* Richard Scott BLACKBURN, MD, of Orange Grove, Fresno County, California, *b* 29 April 1875, *m* Ruth Darwin (*b* 1884; *d* 1948, *bur* Monticello), and *d* 11 April 1946 (*bur* Monticello), having had issue,

1*c* John Sinclair BLACKBURN, *b* 31 March 1916; *d* 27 May 1935 (*bur* Monticello).

2*c* ●Gertrude BLACKBURN, *b* 10 June 1918, *m* ●George F. Fowler.

3*c* ●Ruth BLACKBURN, *b* 17 May 1920, *m* ●Walter Thomas Nobles, and has issue,

●Charlotte Ruth NOBLES, *b* 3 Nov 1949.

2*b* Charlotte Moncure BLACKBURN, *b* 1881, *m* 23 Dec 1909, Thomas Shepherd and *d* 27 July 1917, leaving issue,

1*c* ●John Blackburn SHEPHERD, *m*, and has issue,

●James SHEPHERD.

2*c* ●Arnold Page SHEPHERD, *m*, and has issue,

●Richard SHEPHERD.

3*c* ●Blackburn Edward WILLIAMS (formerly SHEPHERD; adopted by Mr and Mrs Eustace Williams after his mother's death), *b* 22 July 1917.

4*c* Moncure SHEPHERD, *b* 22 July (twin with Blackburn Edward), *d* 9 Sept 1917.

3*b* John Sinclair BLACKBURN, Jr, *d* an inf.

4*a* Jefferson Randolph TAYLOR (Rev), *b* 27 Dec 1841, *m* at Accomac, Virginia, Mary Hubard (*b* 20 Nov 1857; *d*

18 Feb 1909, *bur* Monticello), dau of Edward C. Bruce, by his wife Eliza Thompson Hubard, and *d* 15 April 1919 (*bur* Monticello), leaving issue,

1*b* Martha Randolph TAYLOR, *b* 31 May 1892, *m* 6 April 1935, as his 2nd wife, her brother-in-law, George Hyndman Esser, Sr (*b* 5 May 1880; *d* at Norton, Virginia 28 March 1956, *bur* Monticello), son of John Alfred Esser, by his wife Esther Hyndman, and *dsp* 11 Jan 1968.

2*b* Mary Cary TAYLOR, *b* 10 Aug 1894, *m* 4 Sept 1920, as his 1st wife, George Hyndman Esser, Sr (*b* 5 May 1880; *d* at Norton, Virginia 28 March 1956, *bur* Monticello), son of John Alfred Esser, by his wife Esther Hyndman, and *d* 2 Jan 1923 (*bur* Monticello), leaving issue,

1*c* ● George Hyndman ESSER, Jr, Recording Sec Monticello Assoc 1950-54, Vice-Pres 1959-61, Pres 1961-63 [*1041 Oakdale NE, Atlanta, Georgia 30307, USA*], *b* 6 Aug 1921, *m* 20 June 1953, ● Mary Parker, and has issue,

1*d* ● Mary Cary ESSER, *b* 16 Sept 1955.

2*d* ● John Parker ESSER, *b* 1 Nov 1957.

3*d* ● George Randolph ESSER, *b* 8 Sept 1960.

2*c* ● Jefferson Randolph Cary ESSER [*29 Black Horse Drive, Acton, Massachusetts 01720, USA*], *b* at Norton, Virginia 28 Dec 1922, *m* at Waukegan, Illinois 18 July 1953, ● Kathryn (*b* at Waukegan 27 Aug 1927), dau of B. C. Swanson, by his wife Jessie A., and has issue,

1*d* ● Jefferson Randolph ESSER, *b* at Hinsdale, Illinois 26 April 1954.

2*d* ● Karyn Ann ESSER, *b* at Milwaukee, Wisconsin 16 April 1957.

3*d* ● Douglas Swanson ESSER, *b* at Hinsdale, Illinois 1 April 1963.

5*a* Margaret Randolph TAYLOR, *b* at Avonwood 14 Nov 1843, *m* 9 Nov 1887, as his 2nd wife, her 1st cousin, William Lewis Randolph, of Dunlora (*b* 20 Dec 1841; *d* 7 June 1892), son of Judge William Mann Randolph, by his 1st wife Margaret Smith, eldest dau of Thomas Jefferson Randolph (*see p 102*), and *dsp* at Lego 12 Feb 1898 (*bur* Monticello).

6*a* Charlotte TAYLOR, *b* 17 Dec 1845; *d* 17 May 1846.

7*a* Stevens Mason TAYLOR, *b* at Avonwood 6 July 1847, *m* at Staunton, Virginia 14 Feb 1882, Mary Mann (*b* at Locust Grove 24 Feb 1852; *d* at Lochlyn, Virginia 3 March 1954, *bur* Monticello), dau of Edwin Randolph Page, by his wife Olivia Alexander, and *d* at Lego, Virginia 10 Jan 1917 (*bur* Monticello), having had issue,

1*b* ● Page TAYLOR [*Lochlyn, RFD8, Charlottesville, Virginia 22901, USA*], *b* at Ansted, W Virginia 25 Jan 1885, *m* at Lego 26 June 1913, Edwin Kirk (*b* at Richland, S Dakota 6 Dec 1884; *d* at Washington, DC 17 Nov 1955, *bur* Monticello), son of Nathan Allen Kirk, by his wife Caroline Freeman, and has issue,

1*c* ● Mary Mann Page KIRK, *b* at Washington, DC 9 Sept 1915, *m* there 6 June 1942, ● James Charles Moyer (*b* at Guelph, Ontario, Canada 24 Feb 1914) [*141 White Springs Road, Geneva, New York 14456, USA*], son of Joseph B. Moyer, by his wife Emma Keleher, and has issue,

1*d* ● Margaret Randolph MOYER, *b* at Geneva, New York 16 Sept 1944.

2*d* ● Stevens Mason MOYER, *b* at Geneva, New York 6 June 1947.

3*d* ● Elizabeth Duncan MOYER, *b* at Geneva, New York 23 Oct 1952.

2*c* ● Edwin Roger KIRK [*4156 Jamesway Drive, Toledo, Ohio 43606, USA*], *b* at Washington, DC 27 June 1917, *m* at Toledo, Ohio 21 Sept 1946, ● Charlotte Louise Homrighaus, and has issue,

1*d* ● Charlotte Louise KIRK, *b* at Raleigh, N Carolina 26 July 1949.

2*d* ● Elizabeth Page KIRK, *b* at Toledo, Ohio 24 July 1953.

2*b* Mary Randolph TAYLOR, *b ca* 1886; *d ca* 1887.

3*b* ● Margaret Randolph TAYLOR [*Lochlyn, RFD8, Charlottesville, Virginia 22901, USA*], *b* at Ansted, W Virginia 9 June 1888.

4*b* ● Olivia Alexander TAYLOR, Sec-Treas Monticello Assoc 1941-51, Historian 1953-64, Pres 1971-73

[*Lochlyn, RDF8, Charlottesville, Virginia 22901, USA*], *b* at Lexington, Virginia 31 Oct 1890.

8*a* Cornelia Jefferson TAYLOR, a founder of the Monticello Assoc, Vice-Pres 1913-37, *b* at Avonwood, Jefferson County, Virginia 29 March 1849; *dunm* at Washington, DC 3 March 1937 (*bur* Monticello).

9*a* Moncure Robinson TAYLOR, *b* at Avonwood 23 Feb 1851, *m* at Gordonsville, Virginia 1901, Lucie Madison (*b* in Orange County, Virginia 29 Sept 1871; *d* at New York City 11 Aug 1944, *bur* Monticello), dau of John Willis, by his wife Mary Elizabeth Lupton (*see* MADISON, *p 139*), and *d* at Gordonsville 7 Dec 1915 (*bur* Charlottesville), leaving issue,

● John Byrd TAYLOR, Recording Sec Monticello Assoc 1938-41, Vice-Pres 1949-51, Pres 1951-53 [*16 North Lancaster Avenue, Margate City, New Jersey 08402, USA*], *b* at Lego 4 March 1903, *m* at Northport, Long Island, New York 4 Oct 1930, ● Mildred Powell (*b* at Norfolk, Virginia 9 July 1906), dau of Minor Bronaugh, by his wife Mildred Lee Drewry, and has issue,

1*c* ● Moncure Robinson TAYLOR, Jr [*1221 Sidcup Road, Maitland, Florida 32805, USA*], *b* at Lynchburg, Virginia 8 Nov 1932, *m* at Pasadena, Texas 22 March 1957, ● Patsy Harline (*b* at Abilene, Texas 30 Oct 1933), dau of Harper Williams, by his wife Pauline Evans, and has issue,

1*d* ● Moncure Robinson TAYLOR III, *b* at Wareham, Mass 6 Nov 1957.

2*d* ● John Harper TAYLOR, *b* at Raleigh, N Carolina 7 Nov 1959.

3*d* ● Minor Bronaugh TAYLOR, *b* at Winter Park, Florida 4 June 1960.

4*d* ● Lawrence Colston TAYLOR, *b* at Winter Park, Florida 27 May 1969.

2*c* ● Mildred Lee Drewry TAYLOR, *b* at Lynchburg, Virginia 17 July 1936, *m* at Margate, New Jersey 7 Sept 1963, ● Claude Crisp Farmer, Jr (*b* at Richmond, Virginia 10 Dec 1937) [*6003 Morningside Drive, Richmond, Virginia 24541, USA*], son of Claude Crisp Farmer, by his wife Eliza Ragland, and has had issue,

1*d* Claude Crisp FARMER III, *b* at Carlisle, Pennsylvania 28 March, *d* 1 April 1965.

2*d* ● Taylor Bronaugh FARMER, *b* at Richmond, Virginia 3 Jan 1968.

3*d* ● Paul Crisp FARMER, *b* at Richmond, Virginia 3 June 1971.

3*c* ● Lucie Bronaugh TAYLOR, *b* at Lynchburg, Virginia 14 Dec 1938, *m* at Middlesex, New Jersey 21 Sept 1958, ● Louis John Carnesale (*b* at Pleasantville, New Jersey 15 June 1934) [*955 North Fairview Avenue, Goleta, California 93017, USA*], son of Peter L. Carnesale, by his wife Mary Saviano, and has issue,

1*d* ● Louis Vincent CARNESALE, *b* at Santa Barbara, California 16 Jan 1963.

2*d* ● John Lawrence CARNESALE, *b* at Santa Barbara, California 16 Jan 1963 (twin with Louis Vincent).

3*d* ● Carrie Lee CARNESALE, *b* at Santa Barbara, California 28 April 1969.

10*a* Edmund Randolph TAYLOR, Sr, *b* at Avonwood, Virginia 12 July 1853, *m* 7 July 1892, Julia Paca Kennedy, and *d* 16 June 1919, leaving issue,

1*b* ● Juliana Paca TAYLOR [*318 East First Avenue, Charles Town, West Virginia 25414, USA*], *b* 31 Jan 1894.

2*b* ● Elizabeth Gray TAYLOR [*318 East First Avenue, Charles Town, West Virginia 25414, USA*], *b* 10 June 1895.

3*b* ● Edmund Randolph TAYLOR, Jr [*318 East First Avenue, Charles Town, West Virginia 25414, USA*], *b* 5 Oct 1898, *m* 26 Dec 1924, ● Alice Hunt, and has issue,

● Edmund Randolph TAYLOR III [*108 Lake Road, North Tarrytown, New York 10591, USA*], *b* 21 Oct 1925, *m* 29 May 1954, ● Patricia Ann Kilmartin, and has issue,

● Patricia TAYLOR, *b* 1 Aug 1959.

4*b* ● Margaret Beverley TAYLOR [*318 East First*

*Avenue, Charles Town, West Virginia 25414, USA*], *b* 1 Sept 1904.

11*a* Sidney Wayles TAYLOR, *b* at Midway, Charlottesville, Virginia 27 Nov 1854; *d* there 4 Aug 1856 (*bur* Monticello).

12*a* John Charles Randolph TAYLOR, *b* at Midway, Charlottesville, Virginia 8 May 1857; *d* at Edgehill 8 June 1863 (*bur* Monticello).

(3) Mary Buchanan RANDOLPH, *b* at N Milton 23 Nov 1818; *d* 20 Oct 1920.

(4) Caryanne Nicholas RANDOLPH, *b* at Tufton 22 April 1820, *m* at Edgehill 28 Dec 1840, Francis (Frank) Gildart Ruffin, of Valley Farm, Chesterfield County, Virginia, Lt-Col CSA (*b* 1816; *d* 1892), son of William Ruffin, by his wife Frances Gildart, and *d* 28 July 1857 (*bur* Monticello), having had issue,

1*a* Spencer Roane RUFFIN, *b* 1841, *d* an inf.

2*a* Jefferson Randolph RUFFIN, *b* 16 Nov 1842; *dunm* Feb 1908 (*bur* Monticello).

3*a* William Roane RUFFIN, *b* at Valley Farm, Chesterfield County, Virginia 3 July 1845, *m* at Petersburg, Virginia 7 April 1870, Sally Walthall (*b* at Petersburg 30 Aug 1851; *d* there 12 Feb 1932), dau of James McIlwaine, of Petersburg, by his wife Fannie Susan Dunn, and *d* at Valley Farm, Chesterfield County, Virginia 27 May 1899, having had issue,

1*b* James McIlwaine RUFFIN, of Petersburg, *b* at Charles City 22 Feb 1871, *m* at Petersburg, Virginia 31 Oct 1901, Anne Lillian (*b* at Petersburg, Virginia 17 Jan 1878; *d* at Hilton Village, Virginia 21 Feb 1941), dau of William Robert Nichols, by his wife Nora Preot, and *d* at Chesterfield County, Virginia 21 Nov 1936, leaving issue,

1*c* James McIlwaine RUFFIN, *b* at Petersburg, Virginia 3 Aug 1902, *m* at Cincinnati, Ohio 27 July 1929, ●Jean Fairfax (*b* at Portsmouth, Ohio 18 March 1908), dau of F. H. Dickey, by his wife Charlotte Lewis, and *d* at Atlanta, Georgia 8 Aug 1961, leaving issue,

1*d*●Page Dickey RUFFIN, *b* at Cincinnati, Ohio 27 July 1930, *m* 1st there 14 Oct 1950, Richard Anthony Meyers (*b* at Cincinnati, Ohio 15 Oct 1928; *d* 1963), son of Charles H. Meyers, by his wife Lucy Campbell. She *m* 2ndly at Belvedere, S Carolina 16 July 1964, ●Dean Hale Case (*b* at Estherville, Iowa 26 Oct 1932) [*Route 1, Box A69, Keg Creek Drive, Appling, Georgia, USA*], son of Charles Edward Case, by his wife Lola Hale, and has issue,

1*e*●Michael Dean CASE, *b* at Augusta, Georgia 2 Aug 1966.

2*e*●Toni Page CASE, *b* at Augusta, Georgia 16 May 1968.

2*d*●Jean Fairfax RUFFIN, *b* at Richmond, Indiana 26 Jan 1946, *m* at Augusta, Georgia 6 March 1971, ●Louis Ruben Wegner (*b* at Elgin, N Dakota 2 Feb 1941) [*509 Cumberland Avenue, North Augusta, South Carolina, USA*], son of Ruben Samuel Wegner, by his wife Phyllis Hunkle.

3*d*●Jane McIlwaine RUFFIN, *b* at Richmond, Indiana 26 Jan 1946 (twin with her sister Jean Fairfax Ruffin), *m* 1st at N Augusta, S Carolina 16 April 1966 (*m* diss by div 1971), James R. Knapp (*b* at Toronto, Canada 31 May 1946), son of Frank I. Knapp, by his wife Erna. She *m* 2ndly at N Augusta, S Carolina 14 June 1973, ●Clayton Hartzell (*b* at Augusta, Georgia 24 Aug 1946) [*917 Yardley Drive, North Augusta, South Carolina, USA*], son of William McKinley Hartzell, by his wife Myrtice Lee Kirkendohl.

2*c*●William Nichols RUFFIN [*1699 Wilton Road, Petersburg, Virginia 23803, USA*], *b* at Petersburg, Virginia 9 Oct 1905, *m* at Las Vegas, Nevada 10 Aug 1936, ●Naomi (*b* at Petersburg, Virginia 22 April 1912), dau of James Fulford, by his wife Alice Walker, and has issue,

1*d*●William Nichols RUFFIN, Jr [*Gowrie House, Mobjack, Virginia 23118, USA*], *b* at Los Angeles, California 9 March 1938, *m* at Petersburg, Virginia 10 Sept 1960, ●Dorothy

Leonard (*b* at Petersburg, Virginia 10 Sept 1938), dau of Marvin Winfree Gill, Jr, by his wife Dorothy Feild Leonard, and has issue,

1*e*●Anne Sutherland RUFFIN, *b* at Petersburg, Virginia 22 Sept 1962.

2*e*●Robert Nichols RUFFIN, *b* at Shelby, N Carolina 21 May 1964.

2*d*●Thomas Randolph RUFFIN [*62 Eleventh Street, Shalimar, Florida 32579, USA*], *b* at Los Angeles, California 22 July 1947, *m* at Petersburg, Virginia 10 Aug 1969, ●Bonnie Susan (*b* at Petersburg, Virginia 25 June 1947), dau of Clyde L. Bowman, by his wife Martha Worsham, and has issue,

●Susan Randolph RUFFIN, *b* at Petersburg, Virginia 5 April 1970.

2*b* Francis Gildart RUFFIN, *b* at Valley Farm, Chesterfield County, Virginia 21 Aug 1874; *dunm* there 12 Feb 1898.

3*b* Caryanne Randolph RUFFIN, Custodian of the Monticello Graveyard 1922-38, *b* at Valley Farm, Chesterfield County, Virginia 31 May 1876, *m* at Petersburg, Virginia 3 Dec 1901, Robert Montagu McMurdo (*b* at Roorkee, NW Provinces, India 8 May 1867; *d* at Richmond, Virginia 1 Jan 1952), son of Charles Edward McMurdo, by his wife Madeline Susan Baxter, and *d* at Petersburg, Virginia 5 Nov 1945 (*bur* Monticello), leaving issue,

1*c*●Sally Roane MCMURDO, *b* at Petersburg, Virginia 5 Dec 1904, *m* at Edgehill Chapel, Albemarle County 8 June 1929, ●William Wardlaw Williston (*b* at Northampton, Mass 9 Oct 1904) [*163 California Avenue, Oak Ridge, Tennessee 37830, USA*], son of Robert Lyman Williston, by his wife Margaret Randolph Bryan, and has issue,

1*d*●Anne Cary WILLISTON, *b* at Northampton, Mass 24 April 1934, *m* there 16 June 1956, ●Charles Henry Nowlin (*b* at Wilmington, Delaware 1 Feb 1932) [*117 Malvern Road, Oak Ridge, Tennessee 37830, USA*], son of Charles Mackey Nowlin, by his wife Gertrude Agnes Craig, and has had issue,

1*e* Elizabeth Anne NOWLIN, *b* at Oak Ridge, Tennessee 15 May, *d* there 16 June 1963.

2*e*●William Charles NOWLIN, *b* at Oak Ridge, Tennessee 1 Oct 1964.

3*e*●Margaret Anne NOWLIN, *b* at Oak Ridge, Tennessee 4 Nov 1966.

2*d*●Margaret Randolph WILLISTON, *b* at Northampton, Mass 10 Sept 1937, *m* there 14 Sept 1957, ●Ernest John Laidlaw, Jr (*b* at Toronto, Ontario, Canada 28 July 1927) [*99 Glencairn Avenue, Toronto 310, Ontario, Canada*], son of Ernest John Laidlaw, by his wife Hilda Clara Brown.

2*c*●Madeline Montagu MCMURDO, Historian The Monticello Assoc, *b* at Charlottesville, Virginia 8 Sept 1906, *m* at Charlottesville, Virginia 3 Sept 1932, ●Herbert Bruce Whitmore (*b* at Brooklyn, NY 3 Jan 1906) [*Colthurst Farm, Cavalier Drive, Charlottesville, Virginia 22901, USA*], son of Walter Gray Whitmore, by his wife Kathryn Marcellus Buttrick, and has issue,

1*d*●Caryanne Randolph WHITMORE [*15 Short Street, Apt 2, Brookline, Massachusetts 02146, USA*], *b* at East Orange, New Jersey 24 May 1937.

2*d*●Bruce Gray WHITMORE [*6100 Canterbury Drive, 209, Culver City, California 90230, USA*], *b* at Glencore, NY 7 May 1944, *m* at New York City 18 Nov 1972, ●Carol Elizabeth (*b* at Pittsburgh, Pennsylvania 7 Aug 1949), dau of Daniel M. Rugg, Jr, by his wife Carol Van Zandt.

3*c*●Robert Montagu MCMURDO, Jr [*1901 Brook Drive, Camden, South Carolina 29020, USA*], *b* at Charlottesville, Virginia 31 Oct 1911, *m* at Petersburg, Virginia 6 June 1942, ●Betty W. (*b* at Petersburg, Virginia 14 Dec 1911), dau of Robert Hamilton Seabury, by his wife Janie McIlwaine Vaughan, and has issue,

1*d* Jane Vaughan MCMURDO, *b* at Washington,

DC 31 Oct 1944, *m* at Camden, S Carolina 22 July 1967, ●William Demord Bagwell (*b* at Savannah, Georgia 10 Aug 1940) [*942 Linwood Road, Birmingham 35222, Alabama, USA*], son of Jesse Greenbury Bagwell, by his wife Thealia Salyer, and has issue,
 ●Keith Montagu BAGWELL, *b* at Birmingham, Alabama 19 May 1972.
2*d*●Martha Seabury McMURDO [*8a Town House Apartments, Chapel Hill, North Carolina 27514, USA*], *b* at Petersburg, Virginia 4 Feb 1948.
3*d*●Sally Ruffin McMURDO [*1901 Brook Drive, Camden, South Carolina 29020, USA*], *b* at Camden, S Carolina 4 Sept 1951.
4*c*●Mary Ruffin McMURDO, *b* at Petersburg, Virginia 14 Oct 1913, *m* at Charlottesville, Virginia 1937, ●Campbell Houston Gillespie, Jr (*b* 7 Aug 1913), and has issue (*see p 102*).
4*b* William Roane RUFFIN, *b* at Valley Farm, Chesterfield County, Virginia 8 March 1878, *m* in Amelia County, Virginia 1919, Martha Cocke (*b* in Amelia County, Virginia; *d* there), dau of Harvey Taylor, and *dsp* 26 June 1943.
5*b* John Francis Walthall RUFFIN, *b* in Chesterfield County, Virginia 17 May 1880, *m* at Gordonsville 19 Oct 1910, Sara McElroy (*b* at Pittsburgh, Pennsylvania 19 April 1882; *d* at Pottstown, Philadelphia 31 July 1971), dau of John M. Osborne, by his wife Virginia McElroy, and *d* at Pottstown, Pennsylvania 22 May 1952, leaving issue,
1*c*●John Francis Walthall RUFFIN [*429 Linden Avenue, Wilmette, Illinois 60091, USA*], *b* at Gordonsville, Virginia 2 Sept 1911, *m* at Pottstown, Pennsylvania 6 May 1937, ●Jane (*b* at Perkasie, Pennsylvania 1913), dau of St Clair Barnes, by his wife Edith Morgan, and has issue,
1*d*●Sara Jane RUFFIN, *b* at Pottstown, Pennsylvania 5 June 1939, *m* at Christ Church, Winnetka, Illinois 1 Feb 1964, ●Michael Kennerley (*b* at St Germain-en-laye, Paris, France 2 Nov 1934) [*68 Anderson Avenue, Toronto, Ontario, Canada*], son of John Kennerley, by his wife Jane Atkinson, and has issue,
1*e*●Elizabeth Anne KENNERLEY, *b* at Toronto, Ontario, Canada 29 Nov 1970.
2*e*●Michael Andrew Ruffin KENNERLEY, *b* at Toronto, Ontario, Canada 26 April 1972.
2*d*●Elizabeth Anne RUFFIN, *b* at Pottstown, Pennsylvania 12 June 1941, *m* at Christ Church, Winnetka, Illinois 30 June 1962, ●Ivor Lee Balyeat (*b* at Mansfield, Ohio 1938) [*2754 Ewing Avenue, Evanston, Illinois, USA*], son of Ivor A. Balyeat, by his wife Hildegarde Weinert, and has issue,
 ●Jonathan Lee BALYEAT, *b* at Chicago, Illinois 13 April 1970.
2*c*●William Roane RUFFIN III [*1215 Sylvan Avenue, Latrobe, Pennsylvania 15650, USA*], *b* at Gordonsville, Virginia 13 Nov 1912, *m* at Harrisburg, Pennsylvania 30 June 1945, ●Jane (*b* at Ligonier, Pennsylvania 18 Nov 1919), dau of W. Boyd Evans, by his wife Elizabeth Fillion, and has issue,
1*d*●William Roane RUFFIN IV, *b* at Latrobe, Pennsylvania 6 Feb 1948.
2*d*●Elizabeth Evans RUFFIN, *b* at Latrobe, Pennsylvania 5 April 1953.
3*c*●Sidney Mathews RUFFIN, Vice-Pres Monticello Assoc 1963-64 [*150 North Drive, Pittsburgh, Pennsylvania 15238, USA*], *b* at Gordonsville, Virginia 5 June 1915, *m* at Roxborough, Pennsylvania, ●Harriet (*b* at Ogontz, Pennsylvania 30 May 1920), dau of Sydney E. Martin, by his wife Margaret Fox, and has issue,
1*d*●Nicholas Cary RUFFIN, *b* at Philadelphia, Pennsylvania 20 Aug 1944.
2*d*●Martha Martin RUFFIN, *b* at Pittsburgh, Pennsylvania 11 March 1947, *m* there 8 April 1972, ●Bruce Lawrence Ackerman (*b* at

Philadelphia 30 Nov 1945) [*501 N Eighth Street, Millville, New Jersey, USA*], son of Samuel Ackerman, by his wife Wilma.
3*d*●Caryanne Randolph RUFFIN, *b* at Pittsburgh, Pennsylvania 9 Aug 1951.
4*d*●Harriet Fox RUFFIN, *b* at Pittsburgh, Pennsylvania 12 July 1954.
4*c*●Virginius Osborne RUFFIN [*Skipbackpike, Worcester, Pennsylvania, USA*], *b* at Gordonsville, Virginia 12 March 1918, *m* at Pottstown, Pennsylvania 16 June 1951, ●Nancy (*b* at Pottstown, Pennsylvania 18 May 1921), dau of Harry J. Diefenbeck, by his wife Frances Healy.
6*b* Mary McIlwaine RUFFIN, *b* at Valley Farm, Chesterfield County, Virginia 17 Dec 1883; *dunm* at , Petersburg, Virginia 5 May 1951.
7*b* Sally Walthall RUFFIN, *b* at Valley Farm, Chesterfield County, Virginia 17 Feb 1886; *dunm* at Petersburg, Virginia 21 Jan 1966.
8*b* Wilson Cary Nicholas RUFFIN, *b* at Valley Farm, Chesterfield County, Virginia 5 July 1888; *d* there 17 Dec 1892.
4*a* Wilson Nicholas RUFFIN, of Danville, Virginia, *b* at 19 March 1848, *m* 20 April 1875, Mary Winston (*d* 6 Jan 1939), dau of John Harvie, by his wife Mary Blair, and *d* 22 Feb 1919, having had issue,
1*b* John Harvie RUFFIN, of Louisville, exec with British American Tobacco Co, Pres Monticello Assoc 1946-48, *b* at Richmond, Virginia 15 Jan 1876, *m* 17 April 1907, Laura Virginia (*d* April 1958), dau of — Walters, of Washington, DC, and *d* at Charlottesville 3 May 1961, leaving issue,
 ●Nelson Randolph RUFFIN, of Charlottesville, Virginia, USA, *b* 13 April 1910.
2*b* Ellen Harvie RUFFIN, *b* 24 Sept 1877, *m* 27 June 1906, James M. Featherston, and had issue,
Ellen Ruffin FEATHERSTON, *b* 26 May 1907, *m* 7 July 1932, ●Rev William Franklin Taylor (*b* at Johnson City, Tennessee 17 July 1906), son of William Franklin Taylor, by his wife Ada Lee Wood, and *d* 10 July 1941, leaving issue,
1*d*●Ellen Ruffin TAYLOR, *b* 24 Dec 1933, *m* 23 Nov 1954, ●John Rodney Stevens [*8509 Fairburn Drive, Springfield, Virginia 22150, USA*], and has issue,
1*e*●Laura Lynn STEVENS, *b* 3 Aug 1957.
2*e*●Ellen Elizabeth STEVENS, *b* 5 May 1959.
3*e*●John Rodney STEVENS, Jr, *b* 16 Dec 1961.
2*d*●Ada Lee TAYLOR, *b* 30 April 1940, *m* 18 Nov 1972, ●Richard J. Thomas [*136 College Street, South Hedley, Massachusetts, USA*].
3*b* Wilson Nicholas RUFFIN, *b* 15 Sept 1879, *m* 18 Aug 1910, Martha Pearl Woods, and *d* 2 June 1951.
4*b* Francis Gildart RUFFIN, *b* 1881; *d* 1883.
5*b* Lewis Rutherford RUFFIN, *b* 29 Oct 1884; *dunm* 18 Aug 1907.
6*b* Cary Randolph RUFFIN, *b* 22 Dec 1886; *dunm* 24 April 1915.
7*b* William Pickett RUFFIN, *b* 19 April 1889; *dunm* 24 April 1915.
8*b* Mary Blair Harvie RUFFIN, *b* 13 June 1892; *dunm*.
5*a* George Randolph RUFFIN, of Texas, *b* 1849, *m* 1883, Amarilla Gholson (*b* 1861; *d* 1888), dau of William Bell, by his wife Mary, and *d* 1915, having had issue,
1*b* William Ragsdale RUFFIN, *b* 1884; *d* an inf.
2*b* Mary Helen RUFFIN, *b* at Hope, Arkansas, 9 April 1886, *m* at Marshall, Texas 5 March 1913, Fred Marshall (*b* at Terry, Mississippi 1880; *d* at Texarkana, Arkansas 1940), son of Bishop McKendre Marshall, by his wife Caroline Barnes, and *d* at Urbana, Illinois 22 Sept 1972, having had issue,
1*c*●Mary Bell MARSHALL, *b* 26 March 1914, *m* Sept 1942, ●Robert D. Sard [*401 West Nevada Street, Urbana, Illinois, USA*], and has issue,
1*d*●David Paul SARD [*434 West 120th Street, New York, USA*], *b* 10 Nov 1943, *m* ●Sarah Dooley, and has issue,
 ●Kristen Anna SARD, *b* 2 April 1966.
2*d*●Frederick Marshall SARD, *b* 27 Feb 1946.
3*d*●Hannah Belloch SARD, *b* 31 May 1951.

2c George Randolph Ruffin MARSHALL, b 7 July 1915, m 21 Aug 1954, ●Olga di Nicola [*70 Brookside Place, New Rochelle, New York, USA*], and d 20 March 1964, leaving issue,
  1d●Mary Helen Ruffin MARSHALL, b 24 Dec 1955.
  2d●George Ruffin MARSHALL, b 25 March 1957.
  3d●Clara Ann MARSHALL, b 13 Jan 1959.
3c●Caroline Margaret MARSHALL, b at Texarkana, Arkansas 24 April 1927, m at Hope, Arkansas 14 July 1950, ●Armand William Kitto, Jr (b at New Orleans, Louisiana 15 April 1929) [*2221 E Mulberry Street, Evansville, Indiana 47714, USA*], son of Armand William Kitto, by his wife Cornelia Bridger, and has issue,
  1d●Katherine Babette KITTO, b at New Orleans, Louisiana 31 July 1951, m at Detroit, Michigan 28 Sept 1973, ●Joseph Kott III (b at Detroit 15 July 1947) [*11649 Mitchell, Hamtramck, Michigan 48212, USA*], son of Joseph Kott II.
  2d●Laurence Bridger KITTO, b at New Orleans, Louisiana 7 Sept 1953.
  3d●Robert Marshall KITTO, b at New Orleans, Louisiana 31 Jan 1955.
  4d●Jonathan Bell KITTO, b at St Louis, Missouri 23 Aug 1958.
6a Francis (Frank) Gildart RUFFIN, Jr, of Mobile, Alabama, b 6 Jan 1852, m 1887, Margaret Ellen, authoress (b 26 Aug 1861), dau of Thomas Henry, and d 12 Jan 1902, leaving issue,
  1b Frances RUFFIN, b 27 Feb 1889, m 8 Jan 1914, Joseph Francis Durham, and d 23 June 1972, leaving issue,
    ●Mary Frances DURHAM, b 4 Nov 1914, m 1st 3 Sept 1938, Paul de Vendal Chaudron, Jr, son of Paul de Vendal Chaudron, and has issue,
      1d●Lucia Marie CHAUDRON, b 24 June 1939, m 21 March 1963, ●Heino Kristall.
    Mary Frances Durham m 2ndly, ●Samuel P. Militano, and has further issue,
      2d●Michael Francis MILITANO, b 29 Sept 1944, m 29 Sept 1965, ●Nancy Helen Hiler, and has issue,
        ●Angela Marie MILITANO, b 16 Dec 1966.
2b●Mary Henry RUFFIN (a Sister of Charity as Sister Miriam), b 5 May 1890.
3b●Ellen Randolph RUFFIN (a Sister of Charity as Sister Rita), b 10 July 1892.
4b●Thomas Henry RUFFIN, b 31 Oct 1894, m 1924, Anna Cecilia Kelly, and has issue,
  ●Joseph Henry RUFFIN.
5b●Thomas Jefferson RUFFIN, b 31 Oct 1894 (twin with Thomas Henry).
6b Caroline Randolph RUFFIN, b 27 April 1897; dunm Oct 1919.
7b Elizabeth de l'Esprit RUFFIN, b June 1901; d March 1903.
7a Benjamin Randolph RUFFIN, d an inf.
8a Eliza McDonald RUFFIN, b 26 July 1853; dunm 20 April 1904 (bur Monticello).
9a Cary Randolph RUFFIN (later Cary Ruffin RANDOLPH), inherited Edgehill, b 9 July 1857, m Ethel Patterson (d 1910), and dsp 27 Aug 1910 (bur Monticello).
(5) Mary Buchanan RANDOLPH, Prin of Edgehill Sch for Girls, b at Tufton 17 Dec 1821; dunm 23 June 1884 (bur Monticello).
(6) Eleanor (Ellen) Wayles RANDOLPH, b at Tufton 1 Dec 1823, m at Edgehill 1 May 1859, as his 2nd wife, William Byrd Harrison, of Upper Brandon, Virginia (b at Brandon 1800; d at Ampthill, Cumberland County 22 Sept 1870), and d 15 Aug 1896 (bur Monticello), having had issue,
  1a Evelyn Byrd HARRISON, b at Upper Brandon 14 March, d 16 March 1860.
  2a Jane Nicholas Randolph HARRISON, b at Ampthill 26 June 1862, m 31 Dec 1892, Alexander Burton Randall, of Annapolis, Maryland (b 1856; d 23 March 1938), son of Col Burton Randall, by his wife Virginia Taylor, and d at

Waterbury, Connecticut 16 Aug 1926 (bur Monticello), leaving issue,
  Burton Harrison Randolph RANDALL, served in World War I as Lieut FA, AEF, Pres Monticello Assoc 1949-51, b 13 Oct 1893, m 1st 25 Aug 1919, Louise Florentine (Florence) Monganaste (b 1896), and had issue,
    1c●Edith Richards RANDALL, b 3 Aug 1920, m 3 March 1946, ●John J. Kotz [*116 Laurel Drive, Broomall, Pennsylvania 19008, USA*], and has issue,
      1d●Randall Michael KOTZ, b 15 Nov 1952.
      2d●Nancy Margaret KOTZ, b 10 Dec 1958.
    2c A son, stillborn June 1924 (bur Monticello).
  Burton Harrison Randolph Randall m 2ndly 31 Aug 1935, ●Anne Holloway (b 17 Aug 1902) [*Four Chimneys, RD, Melja, Virginia, USA*], and d 1971.
3a Jefferson Randolph HARRISON, b at Ampthill 9 Dec 1863; dunm 11 May 1931 (bur Monticello).
(7) Maria Jefferson Carr RANDOLPH, b at Tufton 2 Feb 1826, m 1848, Charles Mason, of King George County, and d 12 July 1902, having had issue,
  1a Jefferson Randolph MASON, of Texas, b 12 July 1850; dunm 1888.
  2a Lucy Wiley MASON, m 26 April 1881, Edward Jacquelin Smith, and d 18 July 1922, leaving issue,
    1b Charles Mason SMITH, MD, b 29 July 1882, m 10 Nov 1914, Emma Copeland Lawless, and d 2 Jan 1933, leaving issue,
      1c●Jacquelin Randolph SMITH, b 21 Oct 1915, m 10 Nov 1939, ●Angus Slater Lamond [*7509 Fort Hunt Road, Alexandria, Virginia 22307, USA*], and has issue,
        1d●Cary Randolph LAMOND, b 1 Aug 1940, m 10 Nov 1962, ●Francis Patrick Dillon [*32-14 214th Place, Bayside, New York 11361, USA*].
        2d●Jacquelin Ambler LAMOND, b 22 Sept 1942, m 18 April 1970, ●Peter Mueller Schluter [*3305 Dent Place, NW, Washington DC 20007, USA*], and has issue,
          ●Jane Randolph SCHLUTER, b 25 March 1972.
        3d●Angus Slater LAMOND [*210½ South Eastern Street, Grenville, North Carolina 27834, USA*], b 17 April 1946, m 6 Nov 1970, ●Sandra Delayne Taylor.
        4d●Lucy Mason LAMOND [*1021G South Sunset Drive, Winston-Salem, North Carolina 27103, USA*], b 28 July 1947.
      2c●Cary Ambler SMITH, b 28 July 1917, m 15 Aug 1935, ●Addison Gordon Billingsley, Jr [*PO Box 287, Whitestone, Virginia 22578, USA*], and has a dau,
        ●Cary Copeland BILLINGSLEY, b 27 Sept 1948.
  2b William Taylor SMITH, b 24 Aug 1885, m 10 Sept 1914, Ellen Dickinson Wallace (b 1884), and had issue,
    ●Lucy Randolph Smith, b 6 Nov 1915, m 1st 1934, Stiles Morrow Decker, Jr, son of Stiles Morrow Decker, and has issue,
      1d●Randolph Morrow DECKER, b 28 Feb 1935.
      2d●Joel Porter DECKER, b 5 April 1936.
      3d●Diane Lewis DECKER, b 17 March 1943.
      4d●Christine Cary DECKER, b 17 March 1951.
    Lucy Randolph Smith m 2ndly, ●Douglas Hammond.
3a John Enoch MASON, b 11 July 1854, m 1885, Kate Kearney Henry (b 20 Feb 1932), and d 5 Dec 1910, having had issue,
  1b Flora Randolph MASON, b 1888, m 1st 2 April 1917, George B. Nicholson; and 2ndly 24 Oct 1931, Joseph Parkes Crockett (b 1901), and dsp.
  2b Charles T. MASON, b 1893; d 1896.
  3b Thomas Jefferson MASON, b 1896; dunm 1916.
  4a Wilson Cary Nicholas MASON, b 1856; d 1866.
(8) Carolina Ramsay RANDOLPH, b at Edgehill 15 Jan 1828; d there unm 28 June 1902.
(9) Thomas Jefferson RANDOLPH, Jr, b at Edgehill 29 Aug 1929, m 1st July 1853, Mary Walker Meriwether (b 29 April 1833; d 4 Oct 1863), and has issue,

1*a* Francis (Frank) Meriwether RANDOLPH, *b* 22 Oct 1854, *m* 1883, his 1st cousin, Charlotte Nelson (*d* 24 May 1935), dau of George W. Macon, by his wife Mildred Nelson Meriwether, and *d* in Albemarle County, Virginia 8 Sept 1922, having had issue,

  1*b* Margaret Douglas RANDOLPH, Vice-Pres Monticello Assoc 1937-45, *b* at Cloverfields, Albermarle County, Virginia 17 March 1884; *d* there *unm* 15 Feb 1955 (*bur* Grace Episcopal Church, Cismont).

  2*b* Mildred Nelson RANDOLPH, *b* 27 Oct 1885; *d* 16 Jan 1886.

  3*b* Carolina Ramsay RANDOLPH, *b* 28 Oct 1886, *m* 1 Aug 1906, Edward H. Joslin, and *dsp* 16 Aug 1971.

  4*b*●Charlotte Nelson RANDOLPH [*Cloverfields, Keswick, Virginia 22947, USA*], *b* 5 May 1888, *m* Gilbert T. Rafferty, Jr (*d* 12 Aug 1929), son of Gilbert T. Rafferty, and has issue,

    1*c*●Caroline Randolph RAFFERTY, *b* 23 July 1919, *m* ●Richard White Hall [*Keswick, Virginia 22947, USA*].

    2*c*●Anne RAFFERTY, *b* 19 Sept 1920, *m* 9 June 1947, ●Silas W. Barnes [*Crozet, Virginia 22932, USA*], and has issue,

      1*d*●Charlotte Randolph BARNES, *b* 13 Nov 1949, *m* 2 Sept 1972, ●Ralph Kellogg Dammann.

      2*d*●Sara Lee BARNES, *b* 4 Aug 1952.

    3*c*●Frances Douglas RAFFERTY, *b* 13 April 1922.

    4*c*●Doris RAFFERTY, *b* 9 June 1925, *m* 27 March 1951, ●Robert Coles, Jr, son of Robert Coles, and has issue,

      1*d*●Robert COLES III, *b* 7 May 1952.

      2*d*●John COLES, *b* 26 Nov 1953.

      3*d*●Margaret Douglas COLES, *b* 19 April 1955.

      4*d*●Caroline COLES, *b* 15 June 1959.

2*a* Thomas Jefferson RANDOLPH III, *b* 23 Oct 1855; *d* 30 Sept 1884.

3*a* Margaret Douglas RANDOLPH, *b* 6 Aug 1857; *dunm* 17 Dec 1880.

4*a* Francis Nelson RANDOLPH, *b* 4 Oct 1858; *dunm* 15 Dec 1880.

5*a* Jane Hollins RANDOLPH, *b* 1 Aug 1861; *d* 30 Nov 1862.

6*a* George Geiger RANDOLPH, *b* 15 Aug 1863; *dunm* 23 Dec 1893.

Thomas Jefferson Randolph *m* 2ndly 1865, Charlotte Nelson Meriwether (*d* 1876), and *d* nr Hawk's Nest, W Virginia 8 Aug 1872, having by her had issue,

7*a* Mary Walker RANDOLPH, *b* in Albemarle County, Virginia 14 June 1866, *m* 20 Oct 1894, her 1st cousin once removed, William Mann Randolph, MD (*b* in Albemarle County 14 Jan 1870; *d* 25 Jan 1844), 2nd son of William Lewis Randolph, of Dunlora, by his 1st wife Agnes Dillon, and *d* at Charlottesville 9 Dec 1957, leaving issue (*see p 104*).

8*a* Charlotte Nelson RANDOLPH, *b* 28 Dec 1868; *d* 1 Nov 1870.

(10) Jane Nicholas RANDOLPH, *b* at Edgehill 11 Oct 1831, *m* 24 May 1854, as his 1st wife, Robert Garlick Hill Kean, of Lynchburg (*b* 1828; *d* 1898), son of John Vaughan Kean, by his wife Caroline Hill, and *d* 26 Aug 1868, leaving issue,

  1*a* Lancelot Minor KEAN, of New Orleans, *b* at Edgehill 11 Jan 1856, *educ* Virginia Univ (BL 1877), *m* 1st at Lynchburg, Virginia 11 May 1880, Elizabeth Tucker (*b* at Magnolia Plantation, Washington, Louisiana 5 June 1854; *d* at Washington, Louisiana 17 Jan 1902), dau of William Marshall Prescott, of Washington, St Landry Parish, Louisiana, by his wife Evalina Moore, and had issue,

    1*b* Jane Randolph KEAN, *b* at Lynchburg 19 May 1881, *m* at Alexandria, Louisiana 21 Dec 1903, John Samuel Butler, Jr (*b* at Opelousas, Louisiana 1861; *d* at Baton Rouge, Louisiana 6 Oct 1916), son of John Samuel Butler, and *d* 18 Oct 1948, leaving issue,

      1*c*●John Samuel BUTLER III, *b* at Chenneyville, Louisiana 26 Jan 1905, *m* at Abbeville, Louisiana 9 June 1934, ●Miriam Elizabeth (*b* at Abbeville, Louisiana 12 May 1907), dau of Francis Marie Legeune, by his wife Maybelle Thompson, and has issue,

●Miriam Elizabeth BUTLER, *b* at Abbeville, Louisiana 21 May 1938, *m* at New Orleans, Louisiana 19 March 1960, ●Lt-Cmdr Richard Joseph Moore, USN (*b* at Denver, Colorado 6 Oct 1936) [*29 W Myrtle Street, Alexandria, Louisiana 22301, USA*], son of Edward William Moore, by his wife Frances Isabel Nolan, and has issue,

        1*e*●Richard Joseph MOORE, Jr, *b* at New Orleans, Louisiana 21 Aug 1961.

        2*e*●Sean Butler MOORE, *b* at New Orleans, Louisiana 9 Sept 1962.

        3*e*●Patrick Edward MOORE, *b* at Charleston, S Carolina 16 Aug 1964.

        4*e*●Jefferson Kean MOORE, *b* at Charleston, S Carolina 16 Aug 1964 (twin with his brother Patrick Edward Moore).

    2*c* Lancelot Kean BUTLER, *b* 16 July 1906, *m* 25 Dec 1939, ●Eddy Louise Hood, and *dsp* 23 May 1957.

    3*c* Jane Randolph BUTLER, *b* 26 Oct 1908, *m* 15 March 1941, ●Wesley C. Lancaster, and *d* 28 Jan 1963, having had issue,

      1*d* Wesley Cary LANCASTER, *b* 19 March, *d* 20 March 1943.

      2*d*●Susan Jane LANCASTER, *b* 15 June 1944.

      3*d*●William Joseph LANCASTER, *b* 29 Oct 1945.

    4*c*●Joseph Edmund BUTLER, *b* 29 Jan 1912, *m* 25 April 1937, ●Boyd Evelyn Phillips.

  2*b* Lancelot Minor KEAN, *d* an inf.

  3*b* A son, *d* an inf.

  4*b* A son, *d* an inf.

  5*b*●Evalina Prescott KEAN, *b* at Sioux City, Iowa 30 July 1891, *m* at Washington, DC 15 Jan 1927, ●Constant Southworth (*b* at Duluth, Minnesota 12 Aug 1894) [*Apt 733B, 4000 Cathedral Avenue, NW, Washington, DC 20016, USA*], son of D. D. Franklin Chester Southworth, by his wife Alice Berry.

  6*b* Elizabeth Carolina Hill KEAN, *b* at Sioux City, Iowa 12 Jan 1896, *m* 3 June 1920, Raymond H. Campbell (*d* at New Orleans, Louisiana 21 Oct 1969), and *d* at New Orleans 25 April 1969, leaving issue,

    1*c*●Elizabeth Eva CAMPBELL [*1340 Cherry Street, Apt 4, San Carlos, California 94070, USA*], *b* 6 Jan 1921.

    2*c*●Althée Marion CAMPBELL, *b* 21 Sept 1922, *m* 25 March 1942, ●Francis Thomas Moore [*4609 Alexander Drive, Metaire, Louisiana 70003, USA*], and has issue,

      1*d*●Francis Thomas MOORE, Jr, *b* 15 March 1947.

      2*d*●Roy Victor MOORE, *b* 26 May 1948.

      3*d*●Terry Carol MOORE, *b* 7 Nov 1952, *m* 24 Jan 1973, ●Chris Joseph Bode.

      4*d*●Patricia Ellen MOORE, *b* 22 Nov 1955.

      5*d*●Renee Ersel MOORE, *b* 23 Aug 1961.

    3*c*●Raymond Henry CAMPBELL, Jr, *b* 27 May 1924, *m* 18 June 1948, ●Betty Cantelli, and has issue,

      1*d*●Kristen Marie CAMPBELL, *b* 13 July 1949.

      2*d*●Michael Raymond CAMPBELL, *b* 14 Jan 1955.

    4*c*●Ruth Virginia CAMPBELL, *b* 7 July 1925, *m* 30 June 1960, ●Claude Benoit Walker [*2900 Winston Street, New Orleans, Louisiana 70114, USA*], and has issue,

      1*d*●Jacques Doak WALTER, *b* 18 March 1962.

      2*d*●Dantin Kean WALKER, *b* 11 Nov 1963.

    5*c*●Martin Bradburn CAMPBELL, *b* 26 Oct 1928.

Lancelot Minor Kean *m* 2ndly 3 Oct 1911, Martha Foster (*b* at Jeanerette, Louisiana 10 June 1879), dau of James Crow Murphy, of St Mary Parish, Louisiana, and *d* 8 Jan 1931, having by her had issue,

  7*b*●James Louis Randolph KEAN, *b* at New Orleans 17 May 1913, *m* 16 Nov 1940, ●Mary Louise McCarter (*b* 8 Dec 1914), and has issue,

    1*c*●James Louis Randolph KEAN, *b* 18 June 1942.

    2*c*●Susan Foster KEAN, *b* 1 Oct 1949.

    3*c*●John Michael KEAN, *b* 28 Jan 1952.

    4*c*●Thomas Jefferson KEAN, *b* 8 Jan 1954.

2*a* Martha (Pattie) Cary KEAN, *b* at Lynchburg 11 April

1858, *m* there 27 April 1882, John Speed Morris (*b* at Lynchburg 1 April 1855; *d* 24 Oct 1928), yst son of Dr William Sylvanus Morris, by his wife Laura Page Waller, and *d* at Annapolis, Maryland 5 March 1939 (*bur* Monticello), leaving issue,

　1*b* Robert Kean MORRIS, *b* at Lynchburg 12 April 1883, *m* 1st 1906, Meta, dau of Frank B. Thomas, of Flaribault, Minnesota, and had issue,

　　1*c* ● Dorothy Elaine MORRIS, *b* 14 July 1907, *m* 1st 30 Nov 1930, Janvier L. Lamar, and has issue,

　　　1*d* ● Dorothy Elaine LAMAR, *b* 20 Aug 1932.

　　Dorothy Elaine Morris *m* 2ndly, Daniel Smith, and has further issue,

　　　2*d* ● Bonnycastle SMITH.

　　　3*d* ● Daniel SMITH.

　　Dorothy Elaine Morris *m* 3rdly ● Raymon Price.

　　2*c* ● Robert Kean MORRIS, Jr [*3831 Goldfinch Street, San Diego, California 92103, USA*], *b* 24 Dec 1915, *m* ● Muriel Ellen Walker, and has issue,

　　　1*d* ● — MORRIS, *b* 12 Dec 1946.

　　　2*d* ● Cynthia Anne MORRIS, *b* 13 June 1949.

　Robert Kean Morris, Sr *m* 2ndly 18 April 1925, ● Louise R., formerly wife of — Baughman, and *d* 14 Dec 1961 (*bur* Monticello).

　2*b* Mary Randolph MORRIS, *b* at Lynchburg 5 Feb 1885, *m* at Washington, DC 12 May 1909, Lieut Allen M. Sumner, US Marine Corps (*b* at Boston 4 Oct 1883; *ka* in France 19 July 1918), and *d* 2 Aug 1955, leaving issue,

　　● Margaret Page SUMNER, *b* 21 Feb 1910, *m* 24 Sept 1932, ● Burton Francis Miller, and has issue,

　　　1*d* ● Margaret Page MILLER, *b* 13 Sept 1933, *m* 12 Nov 1955, ● Robert Sander Hinton, Jr, son of Robert Sander Hinton.

　　　2*d* ● Adelaide Randolph MILLER, *b* 4 Feb 1935, *m* 31 March 1956, ● Gordon Conrad Coiner.

　3*b* Page Waller MORRIS, *b* at Edgehill 1 July 1886, *m* 20 June 1910, Frederick Campbell Stuart Hunter (*d* 1930), and *d* 19 Sept 1956 (*bur* Monticello), leaving issue,

　　1*c* ● Frederick Cambell Stuart HUNTER, Jr, *b* 14 March 1911, *m* 1 Jan 1939 (*m* diss by div), Dorothy Dulany, and has issue,

　　　● Grace Page HUNTER, *b* 15 Jan 1941.

　　2*c* ● John Morris HUNTER, *b* 17 Jan 1916, *m* 23 Jan 1943, ● Juliet King Lehman (*b* 1911).

　4*b* William Sylvanus MORRIS, *b* in Campbell County, Virginia 5 May 1888, *m* 2 Aug 1923, Pearl Lenore Oberg, and *d* at Duluth, Minnesota 6 Sept 1947, leaving issue,

　　Mary Elizabeth MORRIS, *b* 28 March 1924; *dunm* 14 April 1962.

　5*b* ● Pattie Nicholas MORRIS [*c/o Ermisch, 1801 East 12th Street, Cleveland, Ohio 44114, USA*], *b* in Indian Territory 9 April 1893, *m* at Washington, DC 28 April 1920, Horace King Hutchens (*b* at Pulaski, New York; *d* at Euclid, Ohio 1972, *bur* Monticello), son of James Lovell Hutchens, by his wife Katherine Douglas King, and has issue,

　　● Katharine King HUTCHENS, *b* at New York City 25 Feb 1921, *m* 1st at New Rochelle, New York 6 June 1942, George William Wiley (*b* at Oak Park, Illinois 13 July 1913; *d* at Cleveland, Ohio 1 April 1970, *bur* Monticello), son of William Joseph Wiley, by his wife Helen Gettle, and has issue,

　　　● John Hutchens WILEY [*377 N Main Street, Apt 201, Monroe Falls, Ohio 44262, USA*], *b* at New York City 30 Nov 1948.

　　Katharine King Hutchens *m* 2ndly at Cleveland, Ohio 12 Oct 1973, ● William Joseph Ermisch [*1801 East 12th Street, Cleveland, Ohio 44114, USA*].

　6*b* Adelaide Prescott MORRIS, *b* in Indian Territory 28 April 1896, *m* at Washington DC 21 April 1919, Vice-Adm Thomas Ross Cooley, US Navy (*b* at Grass Valley, California 26 June 1893; *d* at Quantico, Virginia 28 Nov 1959, *bur* Monticello), son of Thomas Ross Cooley, by his wife Mary Adelaide Cota, and *d* 23 Nov 1958 (*bur* Monticello), having had issue,

　　1*c* ● Adelaide Morris COOLEY, *b* 6 March 1920, *m* 1st 8 May 1943, Hal Waugh Smith, MD, and has issue,

　　　1*d* ● Ross Emerson SMITH (name changed to GADEBERG), *b* 10 May 1949.

　　　2*d* ● Margaret Waugh SMITH (name changed to GADEBERG), *b* 3 June 1950, *m* ● Michael Anthony Morrow, and has issue,

　　　　● Adelaide Lee MORROW, *b* 24 May 1969.

　　　3*d* ● Adelaide Leigh SMITH (name changed to GADEBERG), *b* 15 Feb 1952, *m* 30 June 1972, ● William James Cleese.

　　Adelaide Morris Cooley *m* 2ndly 31 March 1955, ● Burnett Laurance Gadeberg [*3367 Lubich Drive, Mount View, California 94040, USA*].

　　2*c* ● Mary Lawrence COOLEY, *b* 21 May 1930, *m* 8 Jan 1951, ● Hugh Somerville Aitken [*3216 South Seventh Street, Arlington, Virginia 22204, USA*], and has issue,

　　　1*d* ● Mary Lawrence AITKEN, *b* 28 Oct 1951.

　　　2*d* ● Elizabeth Sommerville AITKEN, *b* 11 Nov 1952, *m* 28 April 1971, ● Frank Peter Cruickshank, and has issue,

　　　　● Elizabeth Marie CRUICKSHANK, *b* Aug 1972.

　　　3*d* ● Hugh Wylie AITKEN, *b* 26 June 1955.

　　　4*d* ● William Ormond AITKEN, *b* 25 April 1961.

　　　5*d* ● Thomas Ross Cooley AITKEN, *b* 28 Oct 1964.

　　　6*d* ● Margaret Randolph AITKEN, *b* 18 Jan 1966.

　　3*c* Margaret Ross COOLEY, *b* 14 Dec 1931; *d* 24 Aug 1940 (*bur* Monticello).

3*a* Jefferson Randolph KEAN, MD, Gen US Army Med Corps (ret 1924), commn'd 1884, served on W Frontier against Sioux 1890-91, and in Spanish War with 7th Army, Corps Area Ch Surg and Supt Dept Chantres Cuba 1898-1902, Advr Dept of Sanitation Provisional Govt of Cuba 1906-09, i/c Sanitary Div Office of Surg Gen of US Army and noted sanitary reformer, served in World War I, Dir-Gen American Red Cross 1916-17, Ch US Ambulance Service and Dep Ch Surg AEF in France 1917-19, mem Commns for Nat Expansion Memorial, St Louis 1934 and Thomas Jefferson Memorial, Washington, DC 1938, Pres Assocn Mil Surgs 1914-15, Sec (and Editor of Journal) 1924-34, has DSM, Legion d' Honneur (France), Gd Cross Order of Merit, Carlos J. Finley (Cuba), and Gorgas Medal of Assocn Mil Surgs (1942), *b* at Lynchburg 27 June 1860, *educ* Virginia Univ, *m* 1st at St Augustine, Florida 10 Oct 1894, Louise Hurlbut (*b* 1 Sept 1877; *d* at Fort Leavenworth, Kansas 5 Dec 1915, *bur* Monticello), dau of Mason Young, of New York, by his wife Louisa M. Hurlbut, and had issue,

　1*b* ● Martha Jefferson KEAN [*2927 Patrick Henry Drive, Falls Church, Virginia 22044, USA*], *b* at Key West, Florida 7 Aug 1895, *m* at Washington, DC 5 Dec 1917 (*m* diss by div 1932), William Chason, and has issue,

　　1*c* ● William Randolph CHASON, *b* 8 April 1919.

　　2*c* ● Louise Young CHASON [*2927 Patrick Henry Drive, Falls Church, Virginia 22044, USA*], *b* at Hopewell, Virginia 11 Sept 1921.

　　3*c* ● Robert Leonard CHASON, Col US Air Force (ret) [*Greenwood, South Carolina, USA*], *b* at Hopewell, Virginia 30 Oct 1923, *m* 7 March 1945, ● Shirley Lucille Flynn, and has issue,

　　　1*d* ● Patricia Lucille CHASON, *b* 11 Aug 1955.

　　　2*d* ● Carol Randolph CHASON, *b* 18 Jan 1962.

　　4*c* ● Helen Borodell CHASON, *b* at Miami, Florida 16 July 1928, *m* at Alexandria, Virginia 21 Nov 1945, ● John Wesley Crump (*b* at Philadelphia, Pennsylvania 24 Aug 1923) [*4838 Broad Brook Drive, Bethesda, Maryland 20014, USA*], son of James E. Crump, by his wife Hazel Everett and has issue,

　　　● Sheila Kean CRUMP, *b* Alexandria, Virginia 14 Sept 1946.

　2*b* ● Robert Hill KEAN, Emeritus AIChem Engrs (1972), a chemical engr, noted for his work on compounds of phosphorous and plant design, Research Assoc Univ of Virginia 1956-62, Trustee Virginia Inst for Scientific Research 1949-68, Chm Virginia Section of Chemical Soc 1945-46, and Chemistry Section of Virginia Acad of Science 1946-47 [*4800 Fillmore Avenue, Apt 704, Alexandria,*

*Virginia 22311, USA*], *b* at Morristown, New Jersey 5 July 1900, *educ* Univ of Virginia (PhD), and Mass Inst of Technology (BS, MS), *m* at New Orleans 26 Dec 1927, ●Sarah Rice (*b* in Albemarle County, Virginia 19 June 1905), dau of John Barnwell Elliott, by his wife Noel Forsyth, and has issue,

1*c*●Jefferson Randolph KEAN [*1733 South Quincy Street, Arlington, Virginia 22204, USA*], *b* at New Orleans, Louisiana 18 Feb 1930, *m* 1st at Evanston, Illinois 13 July 1957 (*m* diss by div 1968), Barbara (*b* 4 May 1932), adopted dau of Lewis Miller, and his wife Helen Mathews, and has issue,
  ●Evelina Southworth KEAN, *b* at Washington, DC 5 Nov 1964.
Mr & Mrs Jefferson R. Kean also adopted a son,
  ●Robert Hill KEAN, *b* in Prince George's County, Maryland 5 July 1961.
Jefferson Randolph Kean *m* 2ndly at Alexandria, Virginia 24 April 1971, ●Leah (*b* at West Point, New York 30 June 1943), dau of Brig-Gen John DuVal Stevens, by his wife Frances Cramer.
3*c*●Margaret Young KEAN, *b* at Charlottesville, Virginia 24 Sept 1938, *m* there 17 June 1961, ●Edward Alexander Rubel [*80 Le Baron Drive, East Greenwich, Rhode Island 02818, USA*], son of Adrian Rubel, by his wife Elizabeth Smith, and has issue,
  1*d*●Daniel Martin RUBEL, *b* at Providence, Rhode Island 16 March 1965.
  2*d*●Stephen Elliott RUBEL, *b* at Providence, Rhode Island 12 Dec 1966.
  3*d*●Sarah Rice RUBEL, *b* at Providence, Rhode Island 13 Sept 1968.
Gen Jefferson Randolph Kean *m* 2ndly at Tours, France 24 March 1919, Cornelia Butler (*b* 1 March 1875; *d* at Washington, DC April 1954), dau of Col Thomas T. Knox, US Army, and *d* at Washington, DC 4 Sept 1950 (*bur* Monticello).
4*a* Robert Garlick Hill KEAN, Jr, *b* 26 Dec 1862; *dunm* 1883.
5*a* George Randolph KEAN, *b* 6 April 1866; *d* 27 Aug 1869 (*bur* Monticello).
(11) Wilson Cary Nicholas RANDOLPH, MD, of Charlottesville, Col CSA Med Corps, Rector of Univ of Virginia 1889-1904, *b* at Edgehill 26 Oct 1834, *m* 1st 11 Nov 1858 Anne Elizabeth (Nannie) (*b* at Sunning Hill, Louisa County, Virginia 19 July 1839; *d* at Charlottesville 9 Oct 1888), dau of John Zachary Holladay, of Louisa County, lawyer, mem Virginia House of Delegs 1841-42, by his wife Julia Ann Minor, and had issue,
1*a* Virginia Minor RANDOLPH, *b* at Underhill, Albemarle County 28 Nov 1859, *m* at Charlottesville 1 July 1884, George Scott Shackelford, of Orange, Virginia, Judge of 9th Virginia Judicial Circuit, mem Virginia House of Delegs 1889-92, State Senate 1901-06, and Bd of Visitors of Univ of Virginia (*b* at Warrenton, Virginia 12 Dec 1856; *d* at Orange 29 Dec 1918), son of Benjamin Howard Shackelford, by his wife Rebecca Beverley Green, and *d* at Orange 28 Jan 1937 (*bur* Graham Cemetery, Orange), leaving issue,
1*b* Virginius Randolph SHACKELFORD, of Orange, Virginia, lawyer, Pres Virginia State Bar Assoc 1931-32, Pres Orange County Chamber of Commerce, Dir Nat Bank of Orange and Kentucky Flooring Corpn of Virginia, mem Virginia House of Delegs 1918, Sec-Treas Monticello Assoc 1913-20, Treas 1920-23 and Pres 1937-39, *b* at Orange, Virginia 15 April 1885, *educ* Woodberry Forest Sch and Univ of Virginia (BA, LLB 1907), *m* at Orange 10 Nov 1910, ●Peachy Gascoigne (*b* at Fairview, Orange County, Virginia 16 July 1887) [*Willow Grove, RD1, Box 6, Orange, Virginia 22960, USA*], dau of William Henry Lyne, of Richmond, mem 3rd Richmond Howitzers CSA, by his wife Cassandra Oliver Moncure, and *d* at Willow Grove, Orange County 19 Jan 1949 (*bur* Graham Cemetery, Orange), having had issue,
1*c* Randolph SHACKELFORD, *b* at Orange 24 Aug 1911; *d* 25 July 1912.
2*c*●Lyne Moncure SHACKELFORD, banker, served in World War II as Major US Army [*Box 65,*

*Orange, Virginia 22960, USA*], *b* at Orange 22 May 1914, *educ* Woodberry Forest Sch, and Univ of Virginia (BA) *m* at Orange 2 Oct 1948, ●Elizabeth (*b* in Greenbriar County, W Virginia 25 Oct 1911), dau of John Devereux Burrow, by his wife Jeraldine Dixon, and has issue,
  ●Lyne Moncure SHACKELFORD, Jr, *b* at Charlottesville 17 Nov 1950, *educ* Blue Ridge Sch, and St Andrew's Presbyterian Coll (BA 1971).
3*c*●Virginius Randolph SHACKELFORD, Jr, served in World War II as Major US Army, lawyer, Pres Virginia State Bar Assoc 1964-65, mem Bd of Visitors Med Coll of Virginia, Pres Monticello Assoc 1957-59 [*Brampton, Orange, Virginia 22960, USA*], *b* at Orange 14 Jan 1916, *educ* Woodberry Forest Sch, and Univ of Virginia (BA, LLB 1937), *m* at Kansas City, Missouri 7 Aug 1943, ●Carroll (*b* at Newcastle, Wyoming 31 Oct 1920), dau of Senator James Preston Kem, of Missouri, by his wife Mary Elizabeth Carroll, and has issue,
  1*d*●Virginius Randolph SHACKELFORD III, lawyer [*Brampton, Orange, Virginia 22960, USA*], *b* at Charlottesville 27 July 1946, *educ* Woodberry Forest Sch, Princeton (AB 1968), and Univ of Virginia (JD 1974).
  2*d*●Carroll Preston SHACKELFORD, lawyer [*St Helena, California, USA*], *b* at Charlottesville 30 Jan 1948, *educ* Chatham Hall, Smith Coll, State Univ of New York at Old Westbury (BA 1970), and Univ of California at Berkeley (JD 1973).
  3*d*●Mary Gascoigne Lyne SHACKELFORD, *b* at Charlottesville 19 May 1953, *educ* Chatham Hall, Woodberry Forest Sch, and Univ of Colorado.
  4*d*●Kem Moncure SHACKELFORD, *b* at Charlottesville 22 Oct 1954, *educ* Chatham Hall, and Univ of Virginia.
4*c*●George Green SHACKELFORD, Prof of History, Virginia Polytechnic Inst and State Univ, served in World War II as Lieut USNR, mem Bd of Advrs Nat Trust for Historic Preservation, Pres Monticello Assoc 1969-71 [*Casa Leona, Box 219, Blacksburg, Virginia 24060, USA*], *b* at Orange 17 Dec 1920, *educ* Woodberry Forest Sch, Univ of Virginia (BA 1943, MA 1948, PhD 1955), and Columbia Univ, *m* at Blacksburg 9 June 1962, ●Grace Howard (*b* at Marion, Virginia 3 Dec 1925), dau of Earle Lambert McConnell, by his wife Ruby Winston Dickinson.
2*b* Nannie Holladay SHACKELFORD, *b* at Orange, Virginia 23 Feb 1887, *m* 1 Oct 1913, Rt Rev Karl Morgan Block, DD, Episcopal Bishop of California (*b* at Washington, DC 27 Sept 1886; *d* at San Francisco 20 Sept 1958), son of Sigismund Joseph Block, by his wife Joanna Christine Linden, and *d* at San Francisco 15 Feb 1945, leaving issue,
1*c*●Virginia Randolph BLOCK, *b* 5 May 1915, *m* 3 Jan 1941, ●Wayne Horton Snowden [*970 Santa Barbara Road, Berkley, California 94704, USA*], and has issue,
  1*d*●Wayne Scott SNOWDEN, *b* 6 April 1946, *m* 17 Oct 1969, ●Nancy Helen Jones.
  2*d*●Randolph Fort SNOWDEN, *b* 12 Sept 1949, *m* 19 Sept 1970, ●Janet Fake.
2*c*●Karl Morgan BLOCK, Jr [*22 Dromara Road, Ladue 24, Missouri, USA*], *b* 16 Jan 1921, *m* 2 June 1945, ●Marion Lambert Niedringhaus, and has issue,
  1*d*●Karl Morgan BLOCK III, *b* 6 April 1946.
  2*d*●Lambert Stafford BLOCK, *b* 26 Jan 1948.
  3*d*●Nancy Holladay BLOCK, *b* 17 Oct 1949.
  4*d*●Florence Parker BLOCK, *b* 25 April 1951.
  5*d*●Warne Niedringhaus BLOCK, *b* 8 June 1955.
  6*d*●Anne Randolph BLOCK, *b* 11 Feb 1959.
  7*d*●Marion Lambert BLOCK, *b* 11 Feb 1959 (twin with her sister Anne Randolph Block).
  8*d*●Amy Carter BLOCK, *b* 25 April 1963.
3*b* George Scott SHACKELFORD, Jr, *b* at Orange, Virginia 22 Jan 1897, *m* at Roanoke, Virginia 26 Feb 1927, ●Mary Evelyn (*b* at Roanoke, Virginia 6 March 1898) [*2725 Longview Avenue, Roanoke, Virginia*

*24014, USA*], dau of Junius Blair Fishburn, by his wife Grace Parker, and *d* at Roanoke, Virginia 31 July 1965, leaving issue,

1*c*●Mary Parker SHACKELFORD, *b* at Roanoke, Virginia 19 Jan 1929, *m* there 1951, John Crosland, Jr (*b* at Charlotte, N Carolina 20 Sept 1928) [*2240 Lemon Tree Lane, Charlotte, North Carolina 28211, USA*], son of John Crosland, by his wife Lillian Mason Floyd, and has issue,

  1*d*●Mary Parker CROSLAND, *b* at Roanoke, Virginia 4 Jan 1954.

  2*d*●John CROSLAND III, *b* at Charlotte, N Carolina 30 Jan 1957.

2*c*●George Scott SHACKELFORD III [*2919 Wycliffe Avenue, Roanoke, Virginia 24014, USA*], *b* at Roanoke, Virginia 20 Sept 1933, *m* there 10 Sept 1960, ●Virginia Ria (*b* at El Paso, Texas 4 Jan 1940), dau of William Stephenson Thomas, by his wife Armistead Hardy, and has issue,

  1*d*●William Scott SHACKELFORD, *b* at Roanoke, Virginia 12 May 1962.

  2*d*●George Randolph SHACKELFORD, *b* at Roanoke, Virginia 7 Nov 1964.

  3*d*●Virginia Travis SHACKELFORD, *b* at Roanoke, Virginia 17 March 1967.

4*b* Margaret Wilson SHACKELFORD, *b* at Orange, Virginia 28 Oct 1898, *m* at St Thomas's Church, Orange, Virginia 5 Dec 1923, Frank Stringfellow Walker (*b* at Woodberry Forest, Virginia 1 Feb 1883; *d* at Gordonsville, Virginia 10 June 1971), son of Robert Stringfellow Walker, by his wife Anne Goss, and *d* at Charlottesville, Virginia 13 July 1963, leaving issue,

1*c*●Anne Carter WALKER, *b* at Charlottesville, Virginia 4 April 1925, *m* at St Thomas's Church, Orange, Virginia 18 Oct 1948, ●Atwell Wilson Somerville (*b* at Hillsville, Virginia 1921) [*Box 629, Orange, Virginia 22960, USA*], son of Walter Gray Somerville, by his wife Hattie Nottingham, and has issue,

  1*d*●Atwell Wilson SOMERVILLE, Jr, *b* at Charlottesville, Virginia 24 Nov 1949.

  2*d*●Frank Walker SOMERVILLE, *b* at Charlottesville, Virginia 21 Feb 1952.

  3*d*●Anne Carter SOMERVILLE, *b* at Charlottesville, Virginia 3 Jan 1954.

2*c*●Virginia Randolph WALKER, *b* in Madison County, Virginia 23 April 1927, *m* at St Thomas's Church, Orange, Virginia 19 Sept 1949, ●Andrew Henry Christian (*b* at Richmond, Virginia 26 Jan 1921) [*3318 Devon Road, Durham, North Carolina 27707, USA*], son of Andrew Christian, by his wife Eleanor Rennolds, and has issue,

  1*d*●Andrew Henry CHRISTIAN, Jr, *b* at Richmond, Virginia 19 Sept 1950.

  2*d*●Scott Shackelford CHRISTIAN, *b* at Richmond, Virginia 3 Sept 1953.

  3*d*●Virginia Randolph CHRISTIAN, *b* at Richmond, Virginia 19 May 1957.

3*c*●Margot Shackelford WALKER, *b* in Madison County, Virginia 8 Aug 1931, *m* at St Thomas's Church, Orange, Virginia 18 Dec 1954, ●Cary Hill Humphries (*b* at Culpeper, Virginia 17 Oct 1929) [*4512 Mooreland Avenue, Edina, Minnesota 55424*], son of — Humphries, by his wife Anne Green, and has issue,

  1*d*●Raleigh Green HUMPHRIES, *b* at Baltimore, Maryland 6 Feb 1956.

  2*d*●Cary Hill HUMPHRIES, Jr, *b* at Bryn Mawr, Pennsylvania 6 Feb 1958.

  3*d*●Robert Walker HUMPHRIES, *b* at Memphis, Tennessee 30 July 1960.

4*c*●Frank Stringfellow WALKER, Jr [*Rosni, Orange, Virginia 22960, USA*], *b* in Madison County, Virginia 11 Oct 1935, *m* at St Paul's Church, Richmond, Virginia 3 Dec 1960, ●Bernice, dau of Stamo Spathey (by his wife *née* Wilson), and has issue,

  1*d*●Susan Stringfellow WALKER, *b* at Charlottesville, Virginia 22 Jan 1964.

  2*d*●Margaret Austin WALKER, *b* at Charlottes-

ville, Virginia 27 Feb 1967.

2*a* Wilson Cary Nicholas RANDOLPH, Jr, of Lynchburg, Virginia, *b* 1 Aug 1861, *m* 2 Jan 1890, Margaret Henderson Hager (*b* 27 Dec 1861; *d* 29 March 1946), and *d* 1 March 1923, leaving issue,

●John Hager RANDOLPH [*3816 Hawthorne Avenue, Richmond, Virginia 23222, USA*], *b* 16 July 1893, *m* 15 Aug 1917, ●Grace Lee (*b* 15 April 1892), and has issue,

  1*c*●Margaret Lee RANDOLPH, *b* 15 Sept 1919, *m* 2 Jan 1946, ●William Moreau Platt (*b* 2 March 1912) [*3816 Hawthorne Avenue, Richmond, Virginia 23222, USA*], and has issue,

    ●William Moreau PLATT, Jr, *b* 4 Jan 1955.

  2*c*●John Hager RANDOLPH, Jr [*6327 Ridgeway Road, Richmond, Virginia 23226, USA*], *b* at Fredericksburg, Virginia 27 July 1921, *m* 7 Sept 1946, ●Rebecca Holmes Mem (*b* 15 March 1920), and has issue,

    1*d*●Beverley Langhorne RANDOLPH, *b* 25 April 1948.

    2*d*●Rebecca Hutter RANDOLPH *b* 22 July 1949.

  3*c*●Cary Ann RANDOLPH, *b* 12 April 1925, *m* 23 April 1949, ●Carroll Marcus Cooper (*b* 4 July 1926) [*1210 Mallicotte Lane, Newport News, Virginia 23606, USA*], and has issue,

    1*d*●Carroll Marcus COOPER, Jr, *b* 17 July 1950.

    2*d*●Margaret Lee COOPER, *b* 24 Feb 1953.

3*a* Mary Buchanan RANDOLPH, *b* 1865; *dunm* 1900.

4*a* Julia Minor RANDOLPH, *b* 19 Feb 1866, *m* 26 Sept 1891, William Porterfield, and *d* 10 July 1946, having had issue,

1*b* Mary Elizabeth PORTERFIELD, *b* 17 July 1893; *dunm* at Staunton, Virginia 8 May 1965.

2*b* Virginia Randolph PORTERFIELD, *b* 23 Aug 1897; *d* 22 July 1898.

3*b* John PORTERFIELD, *b* 7 March 1900; *d* at Orange, Virginia 5 July 1916.

4*b*●Wilson Randolph PORTERFIELD [*973 North Main Street, Conyers, Georgia 30207, USA*], *b* 17 Feb 1903, *m* 30 July 1931, ●Mary Hamilton Cook.

Dr Wilson Cary Nicholas Randolph *m* 2ndly 10 June 1891, Mary, dau of — McIntire, of Charlottesville, and *d* at Charlottesville 26 April 1907 (*bur* Maplewood Cemetery, Charlottesville), having by her had issue,

5*a* Elizabeth McIntire RANDOLPH, *b* 9 Jan 1893, *m* 19 Aug 1917, Gen Thomas Jeffries Betts, US Army [*650 Independence Avenue, SE, Washington, DC 20003, USA*], and *d* 28 Feb 1966, leaving issue,

1*b*●Mary McIntire BETTS, artist, *b* at Richmond, Virginia 29 May 1920, *educ* George Washington Univ (BA), Corcoran Sch of Art, Art Inst, and Art League Workshop, *m* at Washington, DC 30 Sept 1944, ●Walter Stratton Anderson, Jr, BS (Harvard), US Foreign Service Offr 1937-62, Vice-Pres GTE Internat (*b* at New York 1912) [*5310 Albemarle Street, Washington, DC 20016, USA*], son of Walter Stratton Anderson, by his wife Virginia Miller Ewing, and has issue,

  1*c*●Virginia Randolph ANDERSON, *b* in London, England 20 Dec 1947.

  2*c*●Thomas Stratton ANDERSON, *b* at Washington, DC 27 July 1951.

2*b*●Elizabeth Hill BETTS [*650 Independence Avenue, SE, Washington, DC 20003, USA*], *b* 29 March 1923.

(12) Meriwether Lewis RANDOLPH, Capt CSA, *b* at Edgehill 17 July 1837, *m* 1869, Anna David (*b* 1851; *d* July 1873, *bur* Monticello), and *d* at Aiken, S Carolina 1 Feb 1871 (*bur* Monticello), leaving issue,

Meriwether Lewis RANDOLPH, Jr, *b* 1870; *d* March 1877 (*bur* Monticello).

(13) Sarah Nicholas RANDOLPH, Prin of Patapsco Inst, Ellicott City, Maryland, and of Miss Randolph's Sch for Girls, Eutaw Place, Baltimore, author of *The Domestic Life of Thomas Jefferson* (1871), *b* at Edgehill 10 Oct 1839; *dunm* at Baltimore 25 April 1892 (*bur* Monticello).

3 Ellen Wayles RANDOLPH, *b* at Monticello 30 Aug 1794; *d* there 26 July 1795 (*bur* there).

4 Ellen Wayles RANDOLPH, *b* at Monticello 13 Oct 1796, *m* there 27 May 1825, Joseph Coolidge, Jr, of Boston, Mass (*b* at Boston Oct 1798; *d* there 15 Dec 1879), son of Joseph

Coolidge, Sr *(see* BURKE'S *Distinguished Families of America)*, by his wife Elizabeth Bulfinch, and *d* at Boston 21 April 1876, having had issue,

(1) Ellen Randolph COOLIDGE, *b* at Boston 30 March 1826, *m* 24 Jan 1855, Edmund Dwight (*b* 30 Sept 1824; *d* 6 June 1900), and *dsp* 9 May 1894.

(2) Elizabeth Bulfinch COOLIDGE, *b* at Boston 1827; *d* there 9 June 1932.

(3) Joseph Randolph COOLIDGE, *b* at Boston 29 Jan 1828, *m* there 18 Dec 1860, Julia (*b* at Boston 4 Aug 1841; *d* there 6 Jan 1921, *bur* Mount Auburn Cemetery, Cambridge, Mass), dau of John Lowell Gardner, of Boston, by his wife Catherine Elizabeth, dau of Capt Joseph Peabody, of Salem, and *d* at Boston 9 Feb 1925 (*bur* Mount Auburn Cemetery), having had issue,

1*a* Joseph Randolph COOLIDGE, Jr, of Center Harbor, New Hampshire, architect, *b* at Boston 17 May 1862, *educ* Harvard (AB 1883, AM 1884), Dresden Polytechnic, Berlin Univ, Mass Inst of Technology, and Ecole des Beaux Arts, Paris, *m* at King's Chapel, Boston 28 Oct 1886, Mary Hamilton (*b* at Boston 16 Oct 1862; *d* at Groton 6 Oct 1952), dau of Hamilton Alonzo Hill, of Boston, by his wife Mary Eliza Robbins, and *d* at Center Sandwich, New Hampshire 8 Aug 1928, having had issue,

1*b* Joseph Randolph COOLIDGE III, served in World War I as 1st Lieut and Capt Engrs US Army in France, *b* at Boston 13 Dec 1887, *educ* Harvard, *m* at Emmanuel Church, Boston 30 July 1913, ●Anna Lyman (*b* at Cambridge, Mass 17 Nov 1888) [*Far Pastures, Center Sandwich 27, New Hampshire, USA*], dau of William Brooks Cabot, by his wife Elizabeth Lyman Parker, and *d* at Sandwich, New Hampshire 22 Sept 1936, leaving issue,

1*c* ●Julia Gardner COOLIDGE, *b* at Brookline, Mass 8 March 1914.

2*c* ●Joseph Randolph COOLIDGE IV [*c/o Mrs Joseph Randolph Coolidge III, Far Pastures, Center Sandwich 27, New Hampshire, USA*], *b* at Brookline, Mass 17 Feb 1916, *m* at Lindsay Memorial Chapel, Emmanuel Church, Boston 8 Nov 1952, ●Peggy (*b* at Swampscott, Mass 19 July 1913), dau of Willoughby H. Stuart, by his wife Claire Ingalls.

2*b* Julia Gardner COOLIDGE, *b* at Brookline, Mass 6 Sept 1889, *m* at King's Chapel, Boston 21 June 1910, Henry Howe Richards (*b* at Boston 23 Feb 1876; *d* at Groton, Mass 16 Nov 1968), son of Henry Richards, by his wife Laura Elizabeth Howe, and *d* at Center Harbor, New Hampshire 22 June 1961, leaving issue,

1*c* ●Henry Howe RICHARDS, Jr [*Center Sandwich, New Hampshire, USA*], *b* at Groton, Mass 15 March 1911, *m* at St John's Chapel, Groton 21 June 1952, Mary Pauline (*b* at Lawrence, Mass 17 July 1918; *d*), dau of Charles Henry Choate, by his wife Mary Pauline Culver.

2*c* ●Hamilton RICHARDS [*83 High Rock Lane, Westwood, Massachusetts, USA*], *b* at Groton 15 Sept 1913, *m* at First Parish Church, Brookline, Mass 8 Oct 1937, ●Edith (*b* at Cohasset, Mass 22 April 1917), dau of Geoffrey Whitney Lewis, by his wife Edith Louise Lincoln, and has issue,

1*d* ●Hamilton RICHARDS, Jr, *b* at Boston 14 Feb 1939.

2*d* ●James Lincoln RICHARDS, *b* at Glen Cove, New York 22 Oct 1942, *m* 12 June 1965, ●Deborah Ann Davis.

3*d* ●Anne Hallowell RICHARDS [*640 Homer, Palo Alto, California, USA*], *b* 7 Nov 1946.

3*c* ●Tudor RICHARDS [*Hopkinton Village, RD1, Concord, New Hampshire, USA*], *b* at Groton 15 Feb 1915, *m* at Wolverton Parish Church, Oxford, England 10 Aug 1949, ●Barbara (*b* at Oxford, England 1 Jan 1929), dau of William Robert Day, by his wife Ida Levick, and has issue,

1*d* ●Francis Tudor RICHARDS, *b* at Ann Arbor, Michigan 15 Feb 1952.

2*d* ●Victoria Day RICHARDS, *b* at Keene, New Hampshire 18 Nov 1956.

3*d* ●Robert Gardner RICHARDS, *b* at Keene, New Hampshire 7 Nov 1960.

4*c* ●Anne Hallowell RICHARDS, *b* at Groton 13 Sept 1917, *m* 3 April 1966, ●John Robert Knowlton Preedy, MD, Prof of Med, Emory Univ, Atlanta [*904 Clifton Road NE, Atlanta, Georgia 30307, USA*].

5*c* ●John RICHARDS II [*Phillips Andover Academy, Andover, Massachusetts, USA*], *b* at Groton 15 March 1932, *m* at Old Lyme Congregational Church, Connecticut 14 June 1955, ●Carol Meredith (*b* at New York City 10 Oct 1936), dau of David Pierre Guyot Cameron, by his wife Carol Moore Dunbar, and has issue,

1*d* ●Laura Elizabeth RICHARDS, *b* at Harlingen, Texas 2 Nov 1956.

2*d* ●Pamela Moore RICHARDS, *b* at Methuen, Massachusetts 3 June 1958.

3*d* ●Christopher Cameron RICHARDS, *b* 4 May 1963.

4*d* ●John Timothy RICHARDS, *b* 4 May 1963 (twin with his brother Christopher Cameron Richards).

5*d* ●Catherine Coolidge RICHARDS, *b* 11 June 1964.

3*b* Mary Eliza COOLIDGE, *b* at Paris, France 10 Dec 1890; *dunm* at Brookline, Mass 21 Aug 1935.

4*b* Hamilton COOLIDGE, Capt Air Service US Army, had French Croix de Guerre and DSC, *b* at Brookline, Mass 1 Sept 1895, *educ* Harvard, *ka* in World War I at Chevières, nr Grand Pré, France 27 Oct 1918, *unm*.

5*b* ●John Gardner COOLIDGE II [*640 Harland Street, Milton, Massachusetts 02186, USA*], *b* at Boston 12 Dec 1897, *educ* Harvard, *m* at Emmanuel Church, Boston 12 June 1918, ●Mary Louise (*b* at Boston 1 May 1899), dau of Arthur Dehon Hill, by his wife Henriette McLean, and has had issue,

1*c* Natalie McLean COOLIDGE, *b* at Boston 30 April 1919, *m* at Emmanuel Church, Boston 23 Nov 1941, ●John Wilbur Keller (*b* at Newton, Mass 9 Sept 1919), son of Capt Harold Russell Keller, USN, by his wife Edith B. Wilbur, and *d* 24 March 1965, leaving issue,

1*d* ●Jeremy KELLER, *b* at Boston 23 Aug 1942, *m*.

2*d* ●Natalie Russell KELLER, *b* at Boston 17 July 1945.

3*d* ●Peter Gardner KELLER, *b* at Laconia, New Hampshire 17 July 1949.

4*d* ●Mary Hill KELLER, *b* at Laconia, New Hampshire 30 Aug 1955.

2*c* ●Mary Hamilton COOLIDGE, *b* at Boston 8 July 1921, *m* 1st at Boston 4 June 1942 (*m* diss by div), Albert Lamb Lincoln, Jr (*b* at Boston 27 Oct 1920), son of Albert Lamb Lincoln, by his wife North Winnett, and has issue,

1*d* ●Albert Lamb LINCOLN III, *b* at Lake City, Florida 16 March 1945, *m* 23 March 1968, ●Joan Miller.

2*d* ●Christine LINCOLN, *b* at Laconia, New Hampshire 16 Sept 1947.

3*d* ●Matthew Dehon LINCOLN, *b* at Boston 30 Nov 1948.

Mary Hamilton Coolidge *m* 2ndly 18 Feb 1968, ●George Nichols, Jr, MD, son of George Nichols.

3*c* ●Olivia Hill COOLIDGE, *b* at Brookline, Mass 8 April 1923, *m* at Rye, New York 17 June 1950, ●Harry William Dworkin (*b* at New York City 13 June 1919) [*150 Gordonhurst Avenue, Upper Montclair, New Jersey, USA*], son of Isidore Dworkin, by his wife Molly Gotthelf, and has issue,

1*d* ●Michael Hill DWORKIN, *b* at Philadelphia 28 May 1953.

2*d* ●Victoria Gail DWORKIN, *b* at Philadelphia 29 April 1955.

3*d* ●Thomas Adam DWORKIN, *b* at Harrisburg, Pennsylvania 11 June 1959.

4*c* ●Hamilton COOLIDGE II [*235 Goddard Avenue, Brookline, Massachusetts 02146, USA*], *b* at Boston 11 Nov 1924, *m* at New York City 16 Oct 1948, ●Barbara Fiske (*b* at Springfield, Mass 27 Aug 1927), dau of Chester Bowles, by his wife Julia Mayo Fiske, and has issue,

1*d*●John Hamilton COOLIDGE, *b* at Boston 21 Feb 1950.
2*d*●Linda Bowles COOLIDGE, *b* at Boston 7 March 1952.
3*d*●Hope McLean COOLIDGE, *b* at Boston 20 Aug 1953.
4*d*●Malcolm Hill COOLIDGE, *b* at Boston 20 April 1956.
6*b*●Eleonora Randolph COOLIDGE, *b* at Boston 31 Jan 1899, *m* at King's Chapel, Boston 20 June 1921, ●Charles Enoch Works (*b* at Rockford, Illinois 18 Jan 1897) [*127 Lafayette Street, Denver, Colorado 80218, USA*], son of Charles Augustus Works, by his wife Eva Panthea Enoch, and has issue,
1*c*●Charles Chandler WORKS, *b* at Denver, Colorado 25 March 1923.
2*c*●John Hamilton WORKS [*4500 West 54th Terrace, Rocland Park, Kansas 66205, USA*], *b* at Denver 29 March 1925, *m* at Emmanuel Baptist Church, Ridgewood, New Jersey 27 Aug 1950, ●Ellen Linnaea (*b* at Melcher, Iowa 20 July 1924), dau of Edwin Nikolas Johnson, by his wife Lillian Olson, and has issue,
1*d*●Linnaea Coolidge WORKS, *b* at Philadelphia 17 Aug 1952.
2*d*●John Hamilton WORKS, Jr, *b* at Kansas City, Missouri 13 July 1954.
3*d*●David Aaron WORKS, *b* at Kansas City, Missouri 3 Sept 1956.
3*c*●Josephine Randolph WORKS, *b* at Denver 28 April 1929, *m* at St Martin's Chapel, St John's Episcopal Cathedral, Denver 20 Dec 1949, ●Willis Lloyd Turner (*b* at Loveland, Colorado 9 Sept 1927), son of Gerald Simpson Turner, by his wife Edith Christina Johnson, and has two adopted children,
  (a) ●Michael Gerald TURNER, *b* 25 Sept 1958.
  (b) ●Erika Edith TURNER, *b* 9 Aug 1960.
7*b*●Oliver Hill COOLIDGE [*Center Sandwich, New Hampshire 03227, USA*], *b* at Manchester, Mass 5 Aug 1900, *educ* Harvard, *m* at St Peter's Church, Cazenovia, New York 31 Aug 1925, ●Elizabeth Ten Eyck (*b* at Boston 2 Nov 1903), dau of John Arthur Brooks, by his wife Mary Ten Eyck Oakley, and has had issue,
1*c*●Oliver Hill COOLIDGE, Jr [*711 Warren Avenue, Thornwood, New York, USA*], *b* at New York City 13 March 1927, *m* at Shadwell, Bedford Hills, New York 29 Dec 1956, ●Lee (Leonarda) (*b* at Cleveland, Ohio 21 June 1924), dau of James P. McGrath, by his wife Sylvia Slovak, and has issue,
1*d*●Peter Brian COOLIDGE, *b* at New York City 3 Oct 1957.
2*d*●Liza Hill COOLIDGE, *b* at New York City 27 May 1959.
2*c*●Peter Jefferson COOLIDGE, *b* at New York City 24 Aug 1928; *d* at Bedford Hills, New York 14 Feb 1934.
3*c*●Henry Ten Eyck COOLIDGE [*7 Irene Street, Burlington, Massachusetts 01803, USA*], *b* at Mount Kisco, New York 14 May 1935, *m* at Guly Port, Mississippi 9 Jan 1959, ●Camilla Starnes (*b* at Birmingham, Alabama 28 Dec 1935), dau of Vincent H. Tedford, by his wife Camilla Johnson, and has issue,
1*d*●Henry Ten Eyck COOLIDGE, Jr, *b* at Guly Port, Mississippi 4 Oct 1959.
2*d*●John Vincent COOLIDGE, *b* at Camden, New Jersey 20 Feb 1962.
8*b*●Roger Sherman COOLIDGE [*Bunchrew House, Bedford, New York 10506, USA*], *b* at Brookline, Mass 30 Sept 1904, *educ* Groton Sch, and Harvard (BA 1927), *m* at Cantitoe Farm, Katonah, New York 1 July 1950, ●Barbara V. (*b* at Greenwich, Connecticut 10 Aug 1910), formerly wife of Warren Milne, and dau of Bayard S. Litchfield, by his wife Marguerite V. Berg, and has issue,
●Bayard Randolph COOLIDGE [*Box 385, Bedford, New York 10506, USA*], *b* at New York 16 Aug 1951, *educ* Brooks Sch, and Univ of Miami (BSEE 1974).

2*a* John Gardner COOLIDGE, of Boston, diplomat, *b* at Boston 4 July 1863, *educ* Harvard (AB 1884), *m* at Stevens Estate, North Andover 29 April 1909, Helen Granger (*b* at North Andover 3 April 1876; *d* at Boston 19 April 1962), dau of Henry James Stevens, by his wife Helen Granger, and *dsp* at Boston 28 Feb 1936.
3*a* Archibald Cary COOLIDGE, Prof of History at Harvard, Harvard Exchange Prof to France 1906-07 and Berlin 1913-14, Dir Harvard Univ Library 1913-28, Pres Monticello Assoc 1921-23, author of *The United States as a World Power* (1908), *Origins of the Triple Alliance* (1917) and *Ten Years of War and Peace* (1927), *b* at Boston 6 March 1866, *educ* Harvard (AB 1887, LLD 1916), Berlin Univ and Freiburg Univ (PhD 1892), *dunm* at Boston 14 Jan 1928.
4*a* Charles Apthorp COOLIDGE, *b* at Boston 10 Jan; *d* 11 Jan 1868.
5*a* Harold Jefferson COOLIDGE, of Boston, lawyer, Dir Nat Shawmut Bank of Boston, Pres Monticello Assoc 1931-32, author of *The Life and Letters of Archibald Cary Coolidge* (with Robert Howard Lord) and *Thoughts on Thomas Jefferson or What Thomas Jefferson Was not* (1936), *b* at Nice, France 22 Jan 1870, *educ* Hopkinson's Sch, Boston, and Harvard (AB 1892, LLB 1896), *m* at the Church of Our Savior, Longwood, Brookline 19 Feb 1903, Edith (*b* at Boston 10 Nov 1879; *m* 2ndly at Boston 30 June 1936 (*m* diss by div 1953), James Amory Sullivan; and 3rdly at Beverley, Mass 28 May 1954, Gen Sherman Miles; and *d* 7 Oct 1966), dau of Amory Appleton Lawrence, of Boston, by his wife Emily Fairfax Silsbee, and *d* at Squam Lake, New Hampshire 31 July 1934 (*bur* Mount Auburn Cemetery), leaving issue,
1*b*●Harold Jefferson COOLIDGE, Jr [*38 Standley Street, Beverly, Massachusetts 01915, USA*], *b* at Boston 15 Jan 1904, *educ* Arizona Univ, Harvard, and Camb Univ, *m* 1st at Westminster Presbyterian Church, Scranton, Pennsylvania 25 Jan 1931 (*m* diss by div 1972), Helen Carpenter (*b* at Scranton 5 Nov 1907), dau of Albert George Isaacs, by his wife Anne Carpenter Richards, and has issue,
1*c*●Nicholas Jefferson COOLIDGE [*200 East End Avenue, New York, NY 10028, USA*], · *b* at Brookline, Mass 12 Feb 1932, *m* at St John's Church, Fisher's Island, New York 11 July 1959, ●Sarah Flanagan (*b* at New York City 6 Nov 1939), dau of Albert Hamilton Gordon, by his wife Mary Rousmaniere, and has issue,
1*d*●Nicole Rousmaniere COOLIDGE, *b* at New York City 29 May 1961.
2*d*●Peter Jefferson COOLIDGE, *b* at New York 17 April 1963.
2*c*●Thomas Richards COOLIDGE [*520 East 86th Street, New York, NY 10028, USA*], *b* at Boston 29 Jan 1934, *m* at Greenwich, Connecticut 8 May 1965, ●Susan Lane (*b* 6 Nov 1940), dau of Albert Freiberg, by his wife Harriet Hall, and has issue,
1*d*●Laura Jefferson COOLIDGE, *b* at New York 27 June 1967.
2*d*●Anne Richards COOLIDGE, *b* at New York 10 Feb 1969.
3*d*●Thomas Lawrence COOLIDGE, *b* at New York 6 July 1973.
3*c*●Isabella Gardner COOLIDGE, *b* at Boston 1 June 1939.
Harold Jefferson Coolidge, Jr *m* 2ndly at West Medford, Mass 26 May 1972, ●Martha Thayer (*b* at Cambridge, Massachusetts 26 Jan 1925), dau of Robert Graham Henderson, by his wife Lucy Gregory.
2*b* Lawrence COOLIDGE, *b* at Boston 17 Jan 1905, *educ* Groton Sch, Arizona Univ, and Harvard (AB 1927, LLB 1931), *m* at Bethlehem Chapel, Washington Cathedral 16 Jan 1932, ●Victoria Stuart (*b* at Tyringham, Massachusetts 23 Oct 1909; *m* 2ndly at Hamilton, Mass 1952, Gilbert L. Steward [*Windy River, Topsfield, Massachusetts, USA*]), dau of Robb De Peyster Tytus, by his wife Grace S. Henop, and *d* at Beverly, Massachusetts 3 Jan 1950 (*bur* Hamilton Cemetery), leaving issue,
1*c*●Robert Tytus COOLIDGE [*27 Rosemount*

*Avenue, Westmount 217, Quebec, Canada*], *b* at Boston 30 March 1933, *m* at the Church of the Resurrection, New York City 10 Sept 1960, ●Ellen Leonard (*b* at New York 8 Dec 1936), dau of Edmund Burke Osborne, by his wife Anne Louise Loeb, and has issue,

   1*d*●Christopher Randolph COOLIDGE, *b* at Oxford, England 4 April 1962.
   2*d*●Miles Cary COOLIDGE, *b* at Montreal, Canada 22 Dec 1963.
   3*d*●Matthew Perkins COOLIDGE, *b* at Montreal, Canada 31 Dec 1966.
2*c*●Lawrence COOLIDGE, Jr [*85 Mount Vernon Street, Boston, Massachusetts, USA*], *b* at Boston 2 March 1936, *m* at Lexington, Mass 22 June 1963, ●Nancy Winslow Rich, and has issue,
   1*d*●David Steward COOLIDGE, *b* at Boston 7 Aug 1964.
   2*d*●Edward Winslow COOLIDGE, *b* at Boston 30 June 1967.
   3*d*●Elizabeth Appleton COOLIDGE, *b* at Boston 12 Oct 1969.
3*c*●Nathaniel Silsbee COOLIDGE [*Still Pond, Topsfield Road, Boxford, Massachusetts 01921, USA*], *b* at Boston 24 Jan 1939, *m* at St John's Chapel, Groton 14 June 1961, ●Camilla (*b* at Boston 17 June 1940), dau of Robert Bradley Cutler, by his wife Marion Lawrence, and has issue,
   1*d*●Richard Lawrence COOLIDGE, *b* at Boston 6 April 1965.
   2*d*●Hilary COOLIDGE, *b* at Boston 9 Sept 1966.
   3*d*●Joanna COOLIDGE, *b* at Boston 19 April 1970.
3*b*●Emily Fairfax COOLIDGE [*860 United Nations Plaza, Apt 25D, New York, USA*], *b* at Boston 13 Oct 1907, *m* 1st at the Chapel of the Isabella Stewart Gardner Museum, Boston 23 Oct 1927, Harry Adsit Woodruff (*b* at Fort Wright, Washington 29 Jan 1903; *d* at Brooklyn, New York 12 Jan 1952), son of Harry Adsit Woodruff, by his wife Regina Dravo, and has had issue,
   1*c*●Edith Lawrence WOODRUFF, *b* at Paris, France 25 April 1932, *m* at St Matthew's Church, Bedford Village, New York 2 July 1952 (*m* diss by div 1970), Kenneth Bradish Kunhardt (*b* at New York City 6 Jan 1930), son of Philip Kunhardt, by his wife Dorothy Meserve, and has issue,
      1*d*●Kenneth Bradish KUNHARDT, Jr, *b* at New York City 1 March 1954.
      2*d*●Linda Lawrence KUNHARDT, *b* at New York City 27 Dec 1955.
      3*d*●Christopher Calve KUNHARDT, *b* at New York City 1 July 1959.
      4*d*●Timothy Woodruff KUNHARDT, *b* 2 Oct 1964.
   2*c* John WOODRUFF, *b* at New York City 9 Nov 1935; *d* there 22 June 1947.
Emily Fairfax Coolidge *m* 2ndly 17 Nov 1962, Thomas Archibald Stone, Canadian Foreign Service (*b* at Chatham, Ontario, Canada 1901; *d* at Fontainebleau, France 26 July 1965), son of Spencer Stone.
6*a* Julian Lowell COOLIDGE, Prof of Mathematics at Harvard Univ and Master of Lowell House 1930-40, author of important mathematical works, *b* at Brookline, Mass 8 Sept 1873, *educ* Harvard (AB 1895, LLD 1940), Balliol Coll Oxford (BSc 1897), and Bonn Univ (PhD 1904), *m* at St Paul's Church, Boston 17 Jan 1901, Theresa (*b* at Nahant, Mass 26 Sept 1874; *d* at Cambridge, Mass 16 Jan 1972), dau of John Phillips Reynolds, of Boston, by his wife Jane Minot Revere, a great-grand-dau of Paul Revere, the engraver and celebrated patriot (and sister of Mrs Nicholas Philip Trist Burke—*see below p 120*), and *d* at Cambridge, Massachusetts 5 March 1954, having had issue,
   1*b*●Jane Revere COOLIDGE, *b* at Lynn, Mass 17 July 1902, *educ* Vassar (AB 1923), and Radcliffe (AM 1926), *m* at Cambridge, Mass 5 June 1930, ●Walter Muir Whitehill, PhD(Lond), FSA, Dir and Librarian, Boston Athenaeum 1946-73, Pres Thomas Jefferson Memorial Foundation (*b* at Cambridge,

Mass 28 Sept 1905) [*44 Andover Street, North Andover, Massachusetts 01845, USA*], son of Rev Walter Muir Whitehill, by his wife Florence Marion Williams, and has issue,
   1*c*●Jane Coolidge WHITEHILL, *b* at Barcelona, Spain 2 Dec 1931, *educ* Radcliffe (AB 1953, AM 1957), *m* at Boston 20 Dec 1952, ●William Rotch (*b* at Cambridge, Mass 19 Nov 1929) [*Route du Pavement 5, 1018 Lausanne, Switzerland*), son of Charles Morgan Rotch, by his wife Helen Bradley, and has issue,
      1*d*●Jane Revere ROTCH, *b* at Charlottesville, Virginia 31 Oct 1959.
      2*d*●William ROTCH, Jr, *b* at Charlottesville, Virginia 2 May 1962.
      3*d*●Sarah Aldis ROTCH, *b* at Charlottesville, Virginia 20 Dec 1965.
   2*c*●Diana WHITEHILL, *b* at 7 Cheltenham Terrace, London SW3 1 Aug 1934, *educ* Bryn Mawr, *m* at the Memorial Church, Harvard Univ 30 Oct 1954, ●Charles Christopher Laing, a naturalized US citizen (*b* at Bronant, Nurawa Eliya, Ceylon 10 Feb 1930) [*2 Albert Gate Court, 124 Knightsbridge, London SW7*], son of Charles Arthur John Laing, by his wife Jessie Anderson, and has issue,
      1*d*●Diana Randolph LAING, *b* at Chelsea, Mass 3 Aug 1957.
      2*d*●Julia Gardner LAING, *b* at Cambridge, Mass 4 Oct 1958.
      3*d*●Christopher Stephens LAING, *b* at Cambridge, Mass 8 March 1961.
2*b* Julian Gardner COOLIDGE, *b* at Turin, Italy 30 Sept 1903; *d* at Cambridge, Mass 18 Feb 1907.
3*b*●Archibald Cary COOLIDGE II [*RD3, Cambridge, Maryland 21613, USA*], *b* at Cambridge, Mass 10 Dec 1905, *educ* Harvard, Balliol Coll Oxford, and Trin Coll Dublin, *m* 1st at the Chapel of the Holy Cross, Holderness, New Hampshire 27 June 1927 (*m* diss by div 1946), Susan Thistle (*b* at Brooklyn, New York 22 Feb 1905), dau of John Edward Jennings, by his wife Florence Isabel Thistle, and has had issue,
   1*c*●Archibald Cary COOLIDGE, Jr, Prof of English in Univ of Iowa [*624 Grant Street, Iowa City, Iowa 52240, USA*], *b* at Oxford, England 9 June 1928, *m* at All Souls' Unitarian Church, Washington, DC 29 June 1951, ●Lillian Dobbel (*b* at Washington, DC 26 Aug 1929), dau of Charles White Merrill, by his wife Lillian May Dobbel, and has issue,
      1*d*●Lillian Merrill COOLIDGE, *b* at Providence, Rhode Island 21 May 1953.
      2*d*●Emily White COOLIDGE, *b* at Providence, Rhode Island 5 Aug 1955.
      3*d*●Sarah Revere COOLIDGE, *b* at Iowa City 16 April 1957.
      4*d*●Archibald Cary COOLIDGE III, *b* at Iowa City 4 Nov 1959.
      5*d*●Anne Edwards COOLIDGE, *b* at Iowa City 14 March 1963.
      6*d*●John Jennings COOLIDGE, *b* at Iowa City 24 June 1967.
      7*d*●Alexander Reynolds COOLIDGE, *b* at Iowa City 3 Aug 1969.
   2*c* Joel COOLIDGE, *b* and *d* at Brooklyn, New York 21 Nov 1929.
   3*c*●Susan Thistle COOLIDGE, *b* at Sharon, Connecticut 3 April 1931, *m* at Trinity Church, Westport, Connecticut 8 May 1954, ●Henry Hammond Barnes (*b* at Pittsfield, Mass 15 Jan 1929) [*10102 Daphne Avenue, Palm Beach Gardens, Florida 33404, USA*], son of Hammond Barnes, by his wife Gladys Wright, and has issue,
      1*d*●Henry Hammond BARNES, Jr, *b* at Providence, Rhode Island 11 March 1955.
      2*d*●Nancy Susan BARNES, *b* at Providence, Rhode Island 27 Aug 1957.
      3*d*●Deborah Coolidge BARNES, *b* at Berwyn, Pennsylvania 12 June 1961.
   4*c*●Julian Lowell COOLIDGE II, *b* at Sharon, Connecticut 1 Sept 1933, *educ* US Naval Acad, *m* at City Court, Yonkers, New York 13 Sept 1958,

●Gail (*b* at Honolulu, Hawaii 30 Dec 1937), dau of Albert Lilly Becker, by his wife Marjorie Emily Tarr, and has issue,

1*d*●Margaret Olivia COOLIDGE, *b* at New London, Connecticut 9 May 1959.

2*d*●David Andrew COOLIDGE, *b* at New London, Connecticut 30 Aug 1961.

5*c*●Elizabeth Crane COOLIDGE, *b* at Sharon, Connecticut 29 Nov 1939, *m* at St Matthew's Church, Wilton, Connecticut 17 June 1960, ●Lewis Holmes Miller, Jr (*b* at New York City 24 Sept 1937), son of Lewis Holmes Miller, by his wife Alice Levy, and has issue,

1*d*●Susan Thistle MILLER, *b* at Ithaca, New York, 12 July 1962.

2*d*●Lewis Holmes MILLER III, *b* 10 Nov 1964.

Archibald Cary Coolidge *m* 2ndly at the house of Mrs Emerson B. Quaile, Lakeville, Connecticut 14 June 1946, ●Margaret Olivia (*b* in London, England 16 Oct 1908), dau of Sir Robert Charles Kirkwood Ensor, by his wife Helen Fisher.

4*b*●Margaret Wendell COOLIDGE, *b* at Cambridge, Mass 17 Oct 1907, *m* at the Memorial Church, Harvard Univ 10 Dec 1938, ●Charles Stacy French (*b* at Lowell, Mass 3 Oct 1907) [*11927 Rhus Rige Road, Los Altos Hills, California 94022, USA*], son of Charles Ephraim French, by his wife Helena Stacy, and has issue,

●Helena Stacy FRENCH, *b* at Minneapolis, Minnesota 16 Nov 1941, *m* at Hidden Ranch Villa, Los Altos Hills, California 23 Sept 1962, Bertrand Israel Halperin (*b* at New York City 6 Dec 1941) [*66 Mountain Avenue, Summit, New Jersey 07901, USA*], son of Morris Halperin, by his wife Eva Teplitsky, and has issue,

1*d*●Jeffery Arnold HALPERIN, *b* at Berkeley, California 5 May 1963.

2*d*●Julia Stacy HALPERIN, *b* at Summit, New Jersey 17 March 1967.

Mr and Mrs Charles Stacy French also have an adopted son,

●Charles Ephraim FRENCH, *b* 30 Oct 1943.

5*b*●Elizabeth Peabody COOLIDGE [*5 Concord Avenue, Cambridge, Massachusetts 02138, USA*], *b* at Vinal Haven, Maine 30 Aug 1909, *m* at Paris, France 27 Feb 1933, Charles Joseph Moizeau (*b* at Noirmoutiers, Vendée, France 31 Dec 1901; *dec*), son of Charles Moizeau, by his wife Aline Victorine Gautier, and has issue,

1*c*●Charles Julian MOIZEAU [*33 Old Forge Road, Millington, New Jersey 07946, USA*], *b* at Paris, France 7 Feb 1934, *m* at Western Presbyterian Church, Elmira, New York 27 Aug 1960, ●Gail Stark (*b* at Rochester, New York 19 Jan 1936), dau of Edward William Fisher, by his wife Sidonia Ender, and has issue,

1*d*●Catherine Elizabeth MOIZEAU, *b* at New York City 22 Nov 1961.

2*d*●Margaret MOIZEAU, *b* 1966.

2*c*●Elizabeth Peabody MOIZEAU, *b* at St Cloud, Seine, France 14 Sept 1937, *m* 1st at Berkeley, California 9 July 1957 (*m* diss by div), Sylvain Merenlender (*b* at Paris, France 1932), son of Z. Merenlender, and has issue,

●Havzalet MERENLENDER, *b* Dec 1957.

Elizabeth Peabody Moizeau *m* 2ndly 22 Oct 1972, ●Frederick Shima.

6*b*●Rachel Revere COOLIDGE, *b* at Cambridge, Mass 21 Feb 1911, *m* there 3 Oct 1936, ●Frederick Milton Kimball (*b* at Lawrence, Mass 15 Feb 1911) [*66 Bartlet Street, Andover, Massachusetts 01810, USA*], son of Walter Milton Kimball, by his wife Jessie Fifield, and has issue,

1*c*●Rachel Revere KIMBALL, *b* at New York City 20 Oct 1938.

2*c*●Carolyn Coolidge KIMBALL, *b* at New York City 7 Sept 1940, *m* at Christ Church, Andover, Mass 15 Sept 1962, ●Bryant Franklin Tolles, Jr (*b* at Hartford, Connecticut 14 March 1939), son of Bryant Franklin Tolles, by his wife Grace Frances Ludden, and has issue,

1*d*●Thayer Coolidge TOLLES, *b* 7 Aug 1965.

2*d*●Bryant Franklin TOLLES III, *b* 11 July 1968.

3*c*●Margaret Revelle KIMBALL, *b* at New York City 2 Sept 1945.

4*c*●Cynthia Fifield KIMBALL, *b* at New York City 2 Sept 1945 (twin with her sister Margaret Revelle Kimball), *m* at Andover, Mass 26 Aug 1972, ●Richard L. Merriam [*21 Summer Street, Bedford, Massachusetts, USA*].

7*b*●John Phillips COOLIDGE [*24 Gray Gardens West, Cambridge, Massachusetts 02138, USA*], *b* at Cambridge, Mass 16 Nov 1913, *educ* Harvard, and New York Univ, *m* at 50 Holyoake Street, Cambridge, Mass 25 May 1935, ●Mary Elizabeth (*b* at Boston 14 Jan 1912), dau of Ralph Waldo Welch, by his wife Elizabeth Bruce, and has issue,

Mary Elizabeth COOLIDGE [*520 East 86th Street, New York, USA*], *b* at New York City 19 March 1936, *m* at St James's Protestant Episcopal Church, Florence, Italy 6 Aug 1955 (*m* diss by div), William Bradford Warren (*b* at Boston 25 July 1934), son of Minton Machado Warren, by his wife Sarah Ripley Robbins, and has issue,

1*d*●John Coolidge WARREN, *b* at Boston 16 May 1956.

2*d*●Sarah Robbins WARREN, *b* at Boston 4 Jan 1958.

8*b*●Theresa Reynolds COOLIDGE [*52 East 72nd Street, New York, NY 10021, USA*], *b* at Cambridge, Mass 21 May 1915, *m* at New York 2 Dec 1967 (*m* diss by div), as his 3rd wife, William Tracy Ceruti.

(4) Philip Sidney COOLIDGE, Major US Army, *b* at Boston 22 Aug 1830; *k* at the Battle of Chattanooga 19 Sept 1863, *unm*.

(5) Algernon Sidney COOLIDGE, surg, *b* at Boston 22 Aug 1830 (twin with Philip Sidney), *educ* Harvard (MD 1853), *m* 15 July 1856, Mary Lowell (*b* 1833; *d* 1915), and *d* 4 Jan 1912, leaving issue,

1*a* Algernon COOLIDGE, of Boston, Prof of Laryngology at Harvard, *b* at Boston 24 Jan 1860, *educ* Harvard (AB 1881, MD 1886), *m* 15 Dec 1896, Amy Peabody, dau of Thornton Kirkland Lothrop, and *d* 16 Aug 1939, having had issue,

1*b*●Anne COOLIDGE, *b* at Boston 4 Nov 1897, *educ* Bryn Mawr, *b* 1946, ●Edward W. Moore.

2*b* Algernon Lothrop COOLIDGE, *b* at Boston 24 May 1900; *dunm* 16 Nov 1927.

3*b*●Thornton Kirkland COOLIDGE, *b* at Boston 11 Oct 1906.

2*a* Francis Lowell COOLIDGE, *b* at Boston 20 Nov 1861, *m* 19 Nov 1901, Alice Brackett White (*b* 2 April 1864; *d* 22 Dec 1927), and *dsp* at Milton, Mass 2 Sept 1942.

3*a* Sidney COOLIDGE, *b* at Boston 8 March 1864, *educ* Harvard (AB 1911 as of 1886), *m* 13 Aug 1890, Mary Laura (*b* at St Joseph, Missouri 17 Dec 1866), dau of B. F. Colt, of St Joseph, and *d* 6 June 1939, having had issue,

1*b* Mary Lowell COOLIDGE, *b* at La Grange, Illinois 9 Dec 1891; *dunm* at Wellesley, Mass 8 Oct 1958.

2*b* Sidney COOLIDGE, *b* at La Grange, Illinois 9 Nov 1894, *educ* Harvard (SB 1915), *m* 19 Aug 1917, Lucy Kent Richardson, and *d* 17 Feb 1958, leaving issue,

1*c* Sidney COOLIDGE, *b* 20 May 1919, *m* 22 May 1954, ●Adele Chevillat.

2*c*●Mary Elizabeth COOLIDGE, *b* 16 April 1923, *m* 1948, ●Raymond L. Barnett, and has issue,

1*d*●Patricia Elizabeth BURNETT, *b* 15 Aug 1949.

2*d*●Sidney Louis BURNETT, *b* 19 Aug 1952.

3*b*●Edmund Jefferson COOLIDGE, served in World War I, DSC and Croix de Guerre, *b* at Concord, Mass 13 April 1899, *educ* Harvard (AB 1921), *m* 1940, ●Elizabeth Francesca Bender, and has issue,

1*c*●Edmund Dwight COOLIDGE, *b* 22 Jan 1943.

2*c*●Katherine Tenbrinck COOLIDGE, *b* 7 Sept 1946.

3*c*●Marta Elizabeth COOLIDGE, *b* 29 Oct 1948.

4*b*●Thomas Buckingham COOLIDGE, *b* at Concord, Mass 2 July 1901, *m* 1st 24 June 1924 (*m* diss by div), Eleanor Whitney Watson, and has issue,

1c●Thomas Buckingham COOLIDGE, Jr, b 20 Feb 1926.
2c●John Lowell COOLIDGE, b 24 July 1927.
3c●Richard Warren COOLIDGE, b 11 Aug 1930.
Thomas Buckingham Coolidge m 2ndly 15 Feb 1944, ●Helen Knight, and by her has issue,
4c●Algernon Knight COOLIDGE, b 30 Sept 1945.
5c●Robert Buckingham COOLIDGE, b 6 April 1947.
5b John Lowell COOLIDGE, b 19 Dec 1902; d 11 Dec 1918.
6b●Helen COOLIDGE, b at Concord, Mass 24 May 1904, m ●Arthur Maxwell Stevens, and has issue, ●Amy STEVENS.
7b●Francis Lowell COOLIDGE, b at Concord, Mass 4 Dec 1906, m 17 May 1940, ●Helen Read Curtis, and has issue,
1c●Mary COOLIDGE, b 21 May 1942, m 26 June 1965, ●Thomas Benham Hillais.
2c●Georgina Lowell COOLIDGE, b 5 Oct 1943.
3c●Francis Lowell COOLIDGE, b 4 Aug 1945.
4c●Ellen Randolph COOLIDGE, b 4 Aug 1945 (twin with her brother Francis Lowell Coolidge), m 13 June 1970, ●Stephen Bradner Burbank.
8b Philip COOLIDGE, b at Concord, Mass 25 Aug 1908; dunm at Los Angeles, California 23 May 1967.
4a Ellen Wayles COOLIDGE, b 24 Jan 1866; dunm 29 April 1953.
5a Mary Lowell COOLIDGE, b 14 Aug 1868, m 14 June 1898, Frederick Otis Barton (d 14 Feb 1904), and d 3 Nov 1957, having had issue,
1b●Otis BARTON, b 5 Jan 1899.
2b Ellen Randolph BARTON, b 21 Aug 1900; dunm 5 Feb 1922.
3b●Mary Lowell BARTON, b 5 Dec 1901, m 7 July 1927, ●Edward Delos Churchill, MD (b at Chenoa, Illinois 25 Dec 1895) [*269 Prospect Street, Belmont 78, Massachusetts, USA*], son of Ebenezer Delos Churchill, by his wife Marion A. Farnsworth, and has issue,
1c●Mary Lowell CHURCHILL, b 15 Oct 1930, m 1st 25 June 1955 (m diss by div), John Herd Hart. She m 2ndly 11 March 1960, ●Robert Lynn Fischelis [*43 Livingston Street, New Haven, Connecticut, USA*], and has issue,
1d●Peter Conway FISCHELIS, b 20 April 1962.
2d●William Churchill FISCHELIS, b 21 April 1964.
3d●Mary Lowell FISCHELIS, b 29 May 1968.
2c●Frederic Barton CHURCHILL, b 14 Dec 1932.
3c●Edward Delos CHURCHILL, b 5 May 1934, m 18 June 1971, ●Ellen Buntzie Ellis.
4c●Algernon Coolidge CHURCHILL, b 15 Aug 1937, m 31 Oct 1959, ●Ann Marshall Chapman, and has issue,
1d●Susan Lowell CHURCHILL, b 22 May 1960.
2d●David Lawrence CHURCHILL, b Nov 1962.
4b●Francis Lowell BARTON, b 4 June 1903, m 24 Feb 1930, ●Elizabeth Harris, and has issue,
1c●James Harris BARTON [*128 Appleton Street, Cambridge, Massachusetts 02138, USA*], b at 10 April 1934, m 12 June 1957, ●Alberta Vaughan Castellanos, and has issue,
1d●Matthew Vaughan BARTON, b 16 May 1961.
2d●Patrick Lowell BARTON, b 19 Feb 1964.
2c●Elizabeth Lowell BARTON, b 13 May 1937, m 1 Sept 1962, ●Garrett Gregory Gillespie.
(6) Thomas Jefferson COOLIDGE, US Min to France 1892-96, b at Boston 26 Aug 1831, educ Harvard, m 4 Nov 1852, Mehitabel (Hetty) Sullivan, dau of William Appleton, of Boston, and d at Boston 17 Nov 1920, having had issue,
1a Marian Appleton COOLIDGE, b 7 Sept 1853, m 16 Nov 1876, Lucius Manlius Sargent (b 5 July 1848; d 14 Nov 1893), and d 15 Feb 1924, having had issue,
Hetty Appleton SARGENT, b 28 Oct 1877, m 7 June 1905, Francis Lee Higginson, Jr (b at Boston 29 Nov 1877), son of Francis Lee Higginson, by his wife Julia Borland, and d 27 June 1921, leaving issue,
1c●Francis Lee HIGGINSON III [*Box 198, Rye Beach, New Hampshire 03781, USA*], b 5 June

1906, m 1st 10 Oct 1927 (m diss by div), Dorothy Lucas. He m 2ndly 1935 (m diss by div), Harriet Beecher Scoville, and by her has issue,
1d●Francis Lee HIGGINSON IV [*823 Main Street, Amherst, Massachusetts 01002, USA*], b 12 Aug 1937, m 22 July 1961, ●Cornelia Parker Wilson, and has issue,
1e●Francis Lee HIGGINSON V, b 3 May 1962.
2e●James Samuel HIGGINSON, b 26 Sept 1965.
2d●John HIGGINSON [*Nobel and Greenough School, 507 Bridge Street, Dedham, Massachusetts 02026, USA*], b 2 May 1939, m 8 July 1967, ●Lida Windover Reismeyer, and has issue, ●Hadley Scoville HIGGINSON, b 16 March 1969.
Francis Lee Higginson III m 3rdly 30 Jan 1959, ●Katherine Duies Hobson.
2c●Joan HIGGINSON, b in London, England 7 March 1908, m 1st at Boston, Mass 16 June 1928 (m diss by div 1948), Alexander Mackay-Smith (b at New York 31 Jan 1903), son of Clarence Bishop Smith, by his wife Catharine Cook, and has had issue,
1d●Alexander MACKAY-SMITH, Jr [*One High Street, Ipswich, Massachusetts 01938, USA*], b at New York 31 March 1929, m at Deming, New Mexico 1949, ●Virginia Leigh (b at White Post, Virginia 29 Jan 1930), dau of Arthur Le Baron Ribble, by his wife Helen Mae Simpson, and has issue,
1e●Mark Sargent MACKAY-SMITH, b at Miami, Florida 5 Dec 1949.
2e●Francis Higginson MACKAY-SMITH, b at Alexandria, Louisiana 7 Oct 1951, m at Ipswich, Mass 23 Jan 1971, ●Janet Leslie (b at Salem, Mass 15 Feb 1951), dau of Lester I. Hills, by his wife Phyllis Guerette.
3e●Catharine Cook MACKAY-SMITH, b at Wiesbaden, Germany 15 July 1954.
4e●Virginia Leigh MACKAY-SMITH, b at Charlottesville, Virginia 14 April 1956.
5e●Anne Carter MACKAY-SMITH, b at Charlottesville, Virginia 19 Oct 1957.
6e●Mary Alexandra MACKAY-SMITH, b at Cincinnati, Ohio 10 Sept 1960.
7e●Helen Susanne MACKAY-SMITH, b at Ipswich, Mass 17 Nov 1962.
8e●Barbara Joan MACKAY-SMITH, b at Ipswich, Mass 9 Oct 1964.
2d●Mehibatel MACKAY-SMITH, b 22 Aug 1931, m 29 Sept 1961, ●Charles C. Abeles [*4531 Dexter Street, NW, Washington, DC 20007, USA*] and has issue,
1e●Nathaniel Calvert ABELES, b 26 June 1962.
2e●Damaris Mackay-Smith ABELES, b 28 March 1964.
3e●Jessica Appleton Kay ABELES, b 17 May 1969.
3d●Matthew Page MACKAY-SMITH, DVM, MSciMed [*RD4, Box 548, Coatesville, Pennsylvania 19320, USA*], b at Washington, DC 15 Sept 1932, m at Annapolis, Maryland 16 June 1958, ●Wingate (b at Annapolis 1939), dau of Rear-Adm Ian Crawford Eddy, by his wife Emily Austin, and has issue,
1e●Wingate Joan MACKAY-SMITH, b at West Chester, Pennsylvania 10 March 1960.
2e●Juliet Higginson MACKAY-SMITH, b at Philadelphia 15 March 1962.
3e●Emily Austin MACKAY-SMITH, b at Philadelphia 19 Feb 1968.
4d Frances Lee MACKAY-SMITH, b 23 Sept 1934; d 15 April 1935.
5d●Amanda Joan MACKAY-SMITH, b 25 Jan 1940, m 1st 19 Aug 1961, Jacobus E. DeVries; and m 2ndly 25 Nov 1972, ●James David Barber [*Alban Towers, 3700 Massachusetts Avenue, Washington, DC, USA*].
6d●Justin MACKAY-SMITH [*28 County Street,*

*Ipswich, Massachusetts 01938, USA*], *b* at Washington, DC 24 Sept 1945, *m* at Malden, Mass 23 Nov 1964, ●Meridith (*b* at New York 1947), dau of Frederick M. Stone, by his wife Jane, and has issue,

1*e*●Joshua Dabney MACKAY-SMITH, *b* at Wilmington, Delaware 6 Feb 1969.

2*e*●Seth Wentworth MACKAY-SMITH, *b* at Cambridge, Mass 15 Aug 1972.

Joan Higginson *m* 2ndly 19 Sept 1971, ●Sigourney Bond Romaine.

3*c*●Griselda HIGGINSON, *b* 6 Jan 1915, *m* 1st 16 Jan 1935 (*m* diss by div), Abram Stevens Hewitt (*b* at Hampstead, Long Island 27 Jan 1902), son of Edward Ringwood Hewitt, by his wife Mary E. Ashley, and has issue,

●Camilla C. HEWITT [*305 Lexington Avenue, Apt 4B, New York, NY 10016, USA*], *b* 26 March 1936.

Griselda Higginson *m* 2ndly Dec 1954, ●Robert N. Cunningham [*Montana Hall, White Post, Virginia 22663, USA*].

2*a* Eleonora Randolph COOLIDGE, *b* 21 Sept 1856, *m* 18 June 1879, Frederick Richard Sears, Jr (*b* 1 March 1855; *d* 31 Dec 1939), son of Frederick Richard Sears, by his wife Marian Shaw, and *d* 19 Dec 1912, leaving issue,

1*b* Frederick Richard SEARS III, *b* at Boston 30 March 1881, *m* 1925, Norma Fontaine, and *dsp* at New York City Jan 1948.

2*b* Eleonora Randolph SEARS, *b* at Boston 28 Sept 1882; *dunm* at Palm Beach, Florida 26 March 1968.

3*a* Sarah Lawrence COOLIDGE, *b* at Boston 2 Jan 1858, *m* there 2 June 1880, Thomas Newbold (*b* at New York 19 May 1849; *d* there 21 Nov 1929), son of Thomas Haines Newbold, by his wife Mary Elizabeth Rhinelander, and *d* at New York 27 Dec 1922, leaving issue,

1*b* Mary Edith NEWBOLD, *b* at New York 19 Feb 1883, *m* at Hyde Park, New York 3 June 1916, Gerald Morgan (*b* at New York 1879; *d* there), son of William Mare Morgan, by his wife Angelica, and *d* at Hyde Park, New York 28 Oct 1969, leaving issue,

1*c*●Gerald MORGAN, Jr, Sec-Treas Monticello Assoc 1956-61, Vice-Pres 1961-63, Pres 1963-64 [*2608 Melbourne Drive, Richmond, Virginia 23225, USA*], *b* at New York 2 June 1923, *m* at Rochester, New York 19 Sept 1953, ●Mary Emily Dalton, and has issue,

1*d*●David Gerald MORGAN, *b* 7 Oct 1956.

2*d*●John Dalton MORGAN, *b* 11 March 1959.

3*d*●Nancy MORGAN, *b* 15 Aug 1961.

2*c*●Thomas Newbold MORGAN [*14 East 93rd Street, New York, New York 10028, USA*], *b* at New York 6 May 1928.

2*b* Thomas Jefferson NEWBOLD, *b* at New York City 26 March 1886, *m* 21 Jan 1914, Katherine Hubbard, and *d* nr Saranac Lake, New York 4 July 1939, leaving issue,

1*c* Thomas Jefferson NEWBOLD, *b* 2 Nov 1914, *m* 29 Aug 1942, ●Mary Dell Mathis, and *d* 3 March 1960, having had issue,

1*d*●Thomas Jefferson NEWBOLD, *b* 7 Oct 1943.

2*d* Peter Mathis NEWBOLD, *b* 29 April 1948; *d* 4 July 1953.

2*c*●Thomas NEWBOLD, *b* 4 Jan 1916, *m* 19 Oct 1945, ●Mary Noreen Maxwell, and has issue,

1*d*●Thomas NEWBOLD, *b* 7 June 1947.

2*d*●John Cunningham NEWBOLD, *b* 1 June 1950.

3*d*●Peter Jefferson NEWBOLD, *b* 1 June 1950 (twin with his brother John Cunningham Newbold).

4*d*●Alexander Maxwell NEWBOLD, *b* 1 Aug 1954.

5*d*●Richard Coolidge NEWBOLD, *b* 1 Aug 1954 (twin with his brother Alexander Maxwell Newbold).

6*d*●Robert Hubbard NEWBOLD, *b* 24 Aug 1960.

3*c*●Katherine NEWBOLD, *b* 6 March 1918, *m* 12 March 1955, ●George Hale Lowe III, son of George Hale Lowe, Jr, and has issue,

●Jonathan Newbold LOWE, *b* 4 Jan 1960.

4*c* Sarah Hubbard NEWBOLD, *b* 23 March 1922, *m* 27 April 1957, ●Charles Alan Krahmer, and *d* 6 Oct 1962, leaving issue,

●Frances Penelope KRAHMER, *b* 19 Feb 1960.

5*c*●Herman LeRoy NEWBOLD [*625 Lowell Road, Concord, Massachusetts 01742, USA*], *b* 8 July 1924, *m* 12 June 1948, ●Mary Cheney Crocker, and has issue,

1*d*●Beth Weyman NEWBOLD, *b* 16 Jan 1955.

2*d*●David LeRoy NEWBOLD, *b* 22 Aug 1956.

3*d*●Stephen Randolph NEWBOLD, *b* 15 Feb 1959.

4*d*●Susan Crocker NEWBOLD, *b* 8 April 1961.

5*d*●Wendy Jefferson NEWBOLD, *b* 8 April 1961 (twin with her sister Susan Crocker Newbold).

3*b* Julia Appleton NEWBOLD, *b* at New York 1 Nov 1891, *m* there 19 April 1913, William Redmond Cross, of New York City (*b* at Orange, New Jersey 8 June 1874; *d* at Princeton, New Jersey 16 Nov 1940), son of Richard James Cross, by his wife Matilda Redmond, and *d* at New York 10 May 1972, leaving issue,

1*c*●Emily Redmond CROSS, *b* at New York 10 Feb 1914, *m* there 13 March 1940, ●Rt Hon Sir John Kenyon Vaughan-Morgan, Baron Reigate (Life Peerage), 1st Bt, PC, formerly MP and sometime UK Min of State Bd of Trade (*b* in London 2 Feb 1905) [*36 Eaton Square, London SW1*], yr son of late Sir Kenyon Pascoe Vaughan-Morgan, OBE, DL (*see* BURKE'S *Peerage*), by his wife Muriel Marie Collett, and has issue,

1*d*●Hon Julia Redmond VAUGHAN-MORGAN, *b* in London 14 Jan 1943, *educ* Lond Univ (BA 1965), *m* at St Margaret's, Westminster 3 April 1962, ●Henry Walter Wiggin, MA, Solicitor (*b* at Worcester 12 Aug 1939) [*The Brainge, Putley, Ledbury, Herefordshire; 33 Ladbroke Gardens, London W11*], yr son of late Col Sir William Henry Wiggin, KCB, DSO, TD, DL, JP (*see* BURKE'S *Peerage*, WIGGIN, Bt), by his wife Elizabeth Ethelston Power, and has issue,

1*e*●Lucy Redmond WIGGIN, *b* in London 25 Aug 1965.

2*e*●Caroline Julia WIGGIN, *b* in London 25 Nov 1970.

2*d*●Hon Deborah Mary VAUGHAN-MORGAN, *b* at Paignton, Devon 1 Sept 1944, *m* at St Margaret's, Westminster 3 May 1966, ●Michael Whitfeld (*b* in London 3 March 1939) [*8 Scarsdale Villas, London W8*], yr son of Lt-Col Ernest Hamilton Whitfeld, MC, of St Anne's, Mere, Wilts, by his wife Iris Esme Scully, and has issue,

1*e*●Nicholas John WHITFELD, *b* in London 31 Jan 1968.

2*e*●Mark David WHITFELD, *b* in London 27 Aug 1971.

2*c*●Richard James CROSS, MD [*210 Elm Road, Princeton, New Jersey 08540, USA*], *b* at New York 31 March 1915, *m* at Rosemont, Pennsylvania 28 June 1939, ●Margaret Whittemore (*b* at Bryn Mawr, Pennsylvania 14 Jan 1916), dau of John Kidd Lee, by his wife Margaret Whittemore, and has issue,

1*d*●Richard James CROSS, Jr [*120 Forrest Hill Road, North Haven, Connecticut 06473, USA*], *b* at New York 28 June 1940, *m* at Newport, Rhode Island 11 Oct 1969, ●Ann Marie, dau of John D. Dyman, by his wife Catherine, and has issue,

●Donna Louise CROSS, *b* at New Haven, Connecticut 16 Dec 1971.

2*d*●Margaret Lee CROSS [*1110 South Carolina Avenue, SE, Washington, DC 20003, USA*], *b* at New York 8 March 1942.

3*d*●Alan Whittemore CROSS [*114 Elmerston Road, Rochester, New York 14620, USA*], *b* at New York 11 July 1944, *m* at Stamford, Connecticut 31 Aug 1968, ●Marion Morgan, dau of Bernhard Johnson, and has issue,

●Julia Marion CROSS, *b* at Columbus, Georgia 4 April 1972.

4d● Anne Redmond CROSS [*Central Bureau of Statistics, Box 30266, Nairobi, Kenya*], *b* at New York 10 March 1948.

5d● Jane Randolph CROSS, *b* at New York 18 Feb 1953.

3c● William Redmond CROSS, Jr, banker, Exec Vice-Pres Morgan Guaranty Trust Co, New York City from 1973 [*RD2, Box 299, South Bedford Road, Mount Kisco, New York 10549, USA; Yale, Racquet and Tennis, Sky (New York City), and Bedford Golf and Tennis Clubs*], *b* at New York 26 April 1917, *educ* Groton Sch, and Yale (BS 1941), *m* at New York 14 June 1958, ● Sally Curtiss (*b* at New York 21 Feb 1929), dau of F. Harold Smith, by his wife Pauline Curtiss, and has issue,

1d● William Redmond CROSS III, *b* at New York 21 July 1959.

2d● Pauline Curtiss CROSS, *b* at New York 19 Oct 1960.

3d● Frederic Newbold CROSS, *b* at New York 3 Dec 1962.

4c● Thomas Newbold CROSS, MD [*310 Corrie Road, Ann Arbor, Michigan 48105, USA*], *b* at New York 19 Feb 1920, *m* there 22 March 1946, ● Patricia Geer (*b* at New York 21 May 1920), dau of Harold Townsend, by his wife Grace Carpenter, and has issue,

● Peter Redmond CROSS, *b* at Ann Arbor, Michigan 19 Aug 1955.

Dr and Mrs Thomas Newbold Cross also have two adopted children,

(a) ● John Townsend CROSS, *b* at Evanston, Illinois 28 May 1951.

(b) ● Katherine Newbold CROSS, *b* at Evanston, Illinois 23 Sept 1954.

5c● Mary Newbold CROSS, *b* at Manchester, Mass 5 Aug 1925, *m* at Bernardsville, New Jersey 2 June 1951, ● Donald Pond Spence (*b* at New York 8 Feb 1926) [*9 Haslet Avenue, Princeton, New Jersey 085407, USA*], son of Ralph Beckett Spence, by his wife Rita Pond, and has issue,

1d● Alan Keith SPENCE, *b* at New York 10 June 1952.

2d● Sarah Coolidge SPENCE, *b* at New York 14 Aug 1954.

3d● Laura Newbold SPENCE, *b* at New York 5 Oct 1959.

4d● Katherine Beckett SPENCE, *b* at New York 22 Aug 1961.

4a Thomas Jefferson COOLIDGE, Jr, banker, *b* at Boston 16 March 1863, *m* 30 Sept 1891, Clara, dau of Charles W. Amory, of Boston, and *d* at Manchester, Mass 14 April 1912, leaving issue,

1b Thomas Jefferson COOLIDGE III, of Brookline, Mass, Vice-Pres First Nat Bank, Boston, Chm Old Colony Trust Co, Pres Boston Museum of Fine Art 1917-19, Pres Monticello Assoc 1943-46, author of *Why Centralized Government?* (1941), *b* at Manchester, Mass 17 Sept 1893, *educ* St Mark's Sch, and Harvard (AB 1915), *m* 20 Aug 1927, ● Catherine Hill, dau of William Spear Kuhn, of Pittsburgh, Pennsylvania, and *d* at Beverly, Mass 6 Aug 1959, having had issue,

1c A son, *b* 1 Sept, *d* 4 Sept 1928.

2c● Catherine COOLIDGE, MD, *b* 26 Sept 1930, *m* 29 May 1965, ● John Winthrop Sears [*Box 1443, Manchester, Massachusetts 01944, USA*].

3c● Thomas Jefferson COOLIDGE IV [*Ninth Floor, 100 Charles River Plaza, Boston, Massachusetts 02114, USA*], *b* 6 Oct 1932.

4c● John Linzee COOLIDGE [*73 Tremont Street — Room 1018, Boston, Massachusetts 02108, USA*], *b* 10 Dec 1937, *m* 5 Jan 1973, ● Elizabeth, formerly wife of — O'Donahoe, and dau of — Graham.

2b Amory COOLIDGE, *b* at Boston 23 March 1895, *educ* Harvard, *dunm* 2 April 1952.

3b● William Appleton COOLIDGE [*70 Memorial Drive, Cambridge, Massachusetts 02142, USA*], *b* at Boston 22 Oct 1901.

4b John Linzee COOLIDGE, *b* 21 March 1905; *d* 22 May 1917.

5 Cornelia Jefferson RANDOLPH, assisted her grandfather Thomas Jefferson in drawing up the plans for Univ of Virginia, *b* at Edgehill 26 July 1799; *dunm* at Alexandria, Virginia 24 Feb 1871 (*bur* Monticello).

6 Virginia Jefferson RANDOLPH, *b* at Monticello 22 Aug 1801, *m* at Monticello 11 Sept 1824, Nicholas Philip Trist, Chief Clerk of US State Dept, who effected the Treaty of Guadalupe Hidalgo 1848 (*b* at Charlottesville 2 June 1800; *d* at Alexandria 11 Feb 1874, *bur* there), eldest son of Hore Browse Trist, Port Collector for the Lower Mississippi River, by his wife Mary Louise Brown (later Mrs Philip Livingston Jones), and *d* at Alexandria 26 April 1882 (*bur* there), leaving issue,

(1) Martha Jefferson TRIST, *b* at Monticello 8 May 1826, *m* 12 Oct 1858, as his 2nd wife, John Woolfolk Burke, of Ivy Mount, Caroline County, Virginia, mem of the firm of Burke and Herbert, bankers, of Alexandria (*b* at Ivy Mount 21 Jan 1824; *d* at Alexandria 1907), son of John Muse Burke, by his wife Sophia F. Woolfolk, and *d* at Alexandria 8 Aug 1915, having had issue,

1a Nicholas Philip Trist BURKE, *b* at Philadelphia 16 July 1859, *m* at Boston 18 Jan 1901, Jane Revere (*b* at Boston 3 June 1871; *d* at Bryn Mawr, Pennsylvania 24 April 1965), dau of John Phillips Reynolds, by his wife Jane Minot Revere, a great-grand-dau of Paul Revere (and sister of Mrs Julian Lowell Coolidge—*see above, p 116*), and *d* at Alexandria 12 Feb 1907, leaving issue,

1b Jane Revere BURKE, *b* at Alexandria 14 Nov 1902; *d* at Milton, Mass 15 April 1920.

2b● John Randolph BURKE [*816 Youngsford Road, Gladwyne, Pennsylvania 19035, USA*], *b* at Alexandria 19 April 1906, *m* at New York 22 March 1941, ● Phyllis (*b* at New York 4 April 1914), dau of Robert S. Brewster, by his wife Mabel Tremaine, and has issue,

● Nicholas Randolph BURKE [*27 West 44th Street, Box 300, New York, New York 10036, USA*], *b* at New York 6 Oct 1942.

2a Frances (Fanny) Maury BURKE, *b* at Alexandria 25 March 1861; *dunm* there 18 Jan 1903.

3a John Woolfolk BURKE, *b* 9 Feb 1863; *d* there 1 Aug 1865.

4a Harry Randolph BURKE, *b* at Alexandria 14 Oct 1864, *m* at New Orleans 19 April 1898, Rosella Gordon (*b* at New Orleans 26 May 1869; *d* at Alexandria 3 March 1945), dau of Nicholas Browse Trist, of New Orleans, by his wife Augustine Gordon, and *d* at Alexandria 21 Nov 1947, having had issue,

1b Nicholas Browse Trist BURKE, *b* at Alexandria 28 Feb 1899, *m* 1 Sept 1928, ● Mary Weeden (*b* at Matunck, Rhode Island), dau of Nathanael Smith, and *dspvp* 28 Jan 1930.

2b● Ellen Coolidge BURKE [*5100 Fillmore Avenue, Alexandria, Virginia 22311, USA*], *b* at Alexandria 10 May 1901.

3b● Rosella Trist BURKE, *b* at Fairfax County 30 Nov 1903, *m* at Alexandria 3 Nov 1924, ● Robert Edwin Graham (*b* 24 July 1899) [*210 69th Street, Virginia Beach, Virginia 23451, USA*], son of Robert Montrose Graham, by his wife Alice Henderson, and has issue,

1c● Robert Montrose GRAHAM II [*7701 Greenview Terrace, Baltimore, Maryland 27204, USA*], *b* 6 Feb 1926, *m* 1st at Charlottesville, Virginia 27 Nov 1950 (*m* diss by div), Hazel Delmer, and has issue,

● Martina Trist GRAHAM, *b* 9 May 1958.

Robert Montrose Graham *m* 2ndly 6 Oct 1969, ● Patricia, dau of Dr Laurence Shemonek, by his wife Bernice Weldon.

2c● Rosella Trist GRAHAM, *b* at Alexandria 13 Jan 1930, *m* 1st there 3 Feb 1915 (*m* diss by div), Richard Charles Lamb, and has issue,

1d● John Graham LAMB, *b* at Cleveland, Ohio 23 Nov 1951.

2d● Elizabeth Randolph LAMB, *b* at Cleveland, Ohio 7 Dec 1953.

Rosella Trist Graham *m* 2ndly 1 Aug 1963, ● Walter Gerald Schendel, Jr, son of Walter Gerald Schendel, and has further issue,

3d● Walter Gerald SCHENDEL III, *b* 24 May 1964.

4*b* Gordon Trist BURKE, *b* at Alexandria 6 Jan 1906, *m* at Omaha 19 April 1926, ●Cornelia Lee (*b* 21 Dec 1904), dau of Daniel Baum, by his wife Harriet H. Hackett, and *d* 7 Nov 1964, leaving issue,

●Nicholas Gordon Trist BURKE [*6240 Factor Avenue, Las Vegas, Nevada 89107, USA*], *b* at Omaha 20 Oct 1930, *m* at Omaha 19 April 1954, ●Betty Ann Clayton, and has issue,

●Jane Randolph BURKE, *b* 15 May 1963.

Mr and Mrs Gordon Trist Burke also had an adopted dau,

●Harriet Holland Hackett BURKE, *b* 26 March 1940.

5*a* Virginia Randolph BURKE, *b* at Alexandria 20 Oct 1866; *dunm* there 29 Dec 1953.

6*a* Ellen Coolidge BURKE, *b* at Alexandria 11 Oct 1868, *m* at Alexandria 7 June 1902, Charles Brown Eddy, of West Hartford, Connecticut, lawyer (*b* at New Britain, Connecticut 29 Nov 1872; *d* at Hartford, Connecticut 9 Jan 1951), son of James Henry Eddy, by his wife Maria Nancy Brown, and *d* at Plainfield, New Jersey 30 Sept 1941, having had issue,

1*b* Martha Jefferson EDDY, *b* at Plainfield, New Jersey 28 June 1903; *d* an inf.

2*b* James Henry EDDY, *b* at Plainfield, New Jersey 28 Jan 1907, *m* at Wallingford, Conn 28 Oct 1939, ●Phyllis Audrey (*b* at Port Chester, New York 9 Dec 1916) [*210 Southport Woods Drive, Southport, Connecticut 06490, USA*], dau of Philip Ambrose Merian, by his wife Bessie Strobridge, and *d* at Port Chester, New York 29 March 1971, leaving two adopted children,

(a) ●Phyllis Merian EDDY, *b* at Chicago 13 Dec 1944.

(b) ●James Henry EDDY, *b* at Chicago 14 Sept 1946.

3*b* ●Charles Brown EDDY, Jr [*238 Old Short Hills Road, Short Hills, New Jersey 07078, USA*], *b* at Plainfield, New Jersey 19 Oct 1908, *m* at New York 23 Nov 1946, ●Mary Elizabeth (*b* at Peapack, New Jersey 1923), dau of Charles Hillard, by his wife Rose Boyer, and has issue,

1*c* ●Ellen Hillard EDDY, *b* at Morristown, New Jersey 8 Sept 1947, *m* at Scarborough, Maine 13 July 1974, ●Alan Thorndike (*b* at New York 14 March 1946), son of Joseph Thorndike, by his wife Virginia Lemont.

2*c* ●Charles Brown EDDY III, *b* at Morristown, New Jersey 1 June 1950.

4*b* ●John Burke EDDY [*5840 King's Road, Los Angeles, California 90056, USA*], *b* 15 Nov 1910, *m* 6 Jan 1945, ●Elizabeth Westcott, and has issue,

1*c* ●Stephen Burke EDDY [*667 Midvale Avenue, Apt 3, Los Angeles, California 90024, USA*], *b* 28 Oct 1945, *m* 29 Aug 1970, ●Susan Lorraine Osborn.

2*c* ●Susan Westcott EDDY, *b* 30 Aug 1948, *m* 27 Aug 1971, ●Thomas Richard Fuller.

7*a* Edmund Jefferson BURKE, *b* at Alexandria 10 Dec 1870, *m* 13 April 1903, Gertrude Lucy Storey, and *d* 14 Nov 1942, having had issue,

1*b* John Woolfolk BURKE, *b* 20 May 1904; *d* 29 March 1905.

2*b* Martin Jefferson BURKE, *b* 18 March 1907; *dunm* 14 Oct 1957.

(2) Thomas Jefferson TRIST, a deaf mute, *b* 1828, *m* 1st, Ellen Dorothea, formerly wife of — Lyman, and dau of — Strong; and 2ndly, Sophia Knabe, and *dsp*.

(3) Hore Browse TRIST, *b* 20 Feb 1832, *m* 1961, Anna Mary, dau of — Waring, of Savannah, Georgia, and *d* 1896, having had issue,

1*a* Nicholas Browse TRIST, *b* 1 April 1862, *m* 1st, Delia Porter. He *m* 2ndly, Alice Cook, and by her had issue,

●Mary Cook TRIST, *m* 1st 23 Sept 1908, Albert R. Kenny, and has had issue,

1*c* Katherine Mary KENNY, *b* 2 June 1909, *m* 23 Aug 1934, ●John William Fulton, and *d* 2 Oct 1966, leaving issue,

●John William FULTON, Jr, *b* 15 May 1936.

2*c* Virginia Jefferson KENNY, *b* 11 Feb 1911, *m* 8 June 1935, ●Seward Davis, Jr, and *d* 30 May 1960,

leaving issue,

1*d* ●Virginia Jefferson DAVIS, *b* 17 May 1936, *m* 29 April 1966, ●Richard Duckworth Irwin.

2*d* ●Katherine Roy DAVIS, *b* 3 July 1939, *m* 13 Oct 1962, ●James William Flynn, Jr, son of James William Flynn, and has issue,

●Virginia Kenny FLYNN, *b* 16 Oct 1964.

Mary Cook Trist *m* 2ndly Oct 1949, ●Edward Joseph Rude.

Nicholas Browse Trist *m* 3rdly 19 June 1920, Kathleen B. Watts, and *d* 1928.

2*a* George Waring TRIST, *b* 16 Nov 1863; *d* 1884.

3*a* Hore Browse TRIST, *b* 12 Sept 1865; *d* an inf.

4*a* Mary Helen TRIST, *b* 12 Sept 1872; *dunm* 6 March 1959.

7 Mary Jefferson RANDOLPH, *b* at Edgehill 2 Nov 1803; *dunm* at Alexandria 29 March 1876.

8 James Madison RANDOLPH, *b* at the White House, Washington (the first child to be born there) 17 Jan 1806; *dunm* at Tufton 23 Jan 1834 (*bur* Monticello).

9 Benjamin Franklin RANDOLPH, MD, of Round Top, nr Carter's Bridge, Albemarle County, *b* at Edgehill 14 July 1808, *educ* Virginia Univ, *m* at Redlands 13 Nov 1834, Sarah Champe (*b* 1810; *d* at Round Top 20 May 1896), dau of Robert Hill Carter, of Redlands, by his wife Polly Coles, and *d* at Round Top 18 Feb 1871 (*bur* Christ Church, Glendower, nr Keene, Albemarle County), leaving issue,

(1) Isaetta Carter RANDOLPH, *b* at Round Top 24 March 1836, *m* there 13 Nov 1860, James Lenaeus Hubard (*b* 1835; *d* 1913), son of Robert Thruston Hubard, of Chellow, Buckingham County, Virginia, by his wife Susan Pocahontas Bolling, and *d* 9 Dec 1888, having had issue,

1*a* Benjamin Randolph HUBARD, *b* 1861.

2*a* Susan Bolling HUBARD, *b* 5 Oct 1863, *m* 1888, John Slaughter, and *d* 20 Feb 1894, leaving issue,

1*b* ●Charles Hubard SLAUGHTER [*607 Jefferson Tower Building, Dallas, Texas 75208, USA*], *b* 16 April 1889, *m* 8 Sept 1914, ●Evelyn Morman Meech.

2*b* Isaetta Randolph SLAUGHTER, *b* 12 Oct 1892, *m* 15 April 1912, Harry Benjamin Mundy, and had issue,

1*c* ●Harry Benjamin MUNDY, *b* 1 Feb 1913, *m* ●Pauline Vaughn.

2*c* ●Mary Frances MUNDY, *b* 23 Jan 1930, *m* 25 Oct 1952, ●Robert Lawrence Warwick.

3*a* James Thruston HUBARD, *b* 17 April 1865; *d* 17 June 1882.

4*a* Robert Thruston HUBARD, *b* 31 Oct 1866, *m* 1st 1897, Leila C. Moss, and had issue,

1*b* Robert Thruston HUBARD, Jr, *b* 1898; *dec*.

2*b* Martha Randolph HUBARD, *b* 29 April 1900, *m* 6 Jan 1920, Louis Elsinger, and had issue,

●James Hubard ELSINGER, *b* 1 May 1924, *m* 6 Aug 1949, ●Jo Ann Fossett, and has issue,

●Patricia Ann ELSINGER, *b* 2 July 1953.

Robert Thruston Hubard *m* 2ndly, Mary Brennan Swift, and *d* 3 Jan 1923, having by her had issue,

3*b* Stephen Swift HUBARD, *b* 14 April 1914; *dunm* 6 March 1956.

5*a* Sarah Champe HUBARD, *b* 18 Aug 1868; *dunm* 1 Jan 1903.

6*a* Mary Randolph HUBARD, *b* 7 May 1870, *m* 28 Oct 1895, Edward Miles Mathewes (*b* 8 Oct 1868; *d* Dec 1952), and *d* 25 Aug 1930, having had issue,

1*b* Eliza Peronneau MATHEWES, *b* 15 Sept 1897; *d* 15 April 1898.

2*b* Edward Miles MATHEWES, *b* 19 Dec 1898; *d* 4 March 1906.

3*b* ●Mary Randolph Hubard MATHEWES, *b* 16 Aug 1902; *dunm* 12 March 1943.

4*b* Celia Peronneau MATHEWES, *b* 2 Aug 1906, *m* 23 Sept 1933, ●Thomas Richard Waring (*b* at Charleston, S Carolina 10 May 1907) [*10 Atlantic Street, Charleston, South Carolina 29401, USA*], son of Thomas Richard Waring, by his wife Laura Campbell Witte, and *d* at Charleston, S Carolina 3 July 1967, leaving issue,

1*c* ●Mary Randolph WARING, *b* 20 March 1939, *m* 1st 15 March 1958, Kenneth J. Elder, and has issue,

1*d* ●Thomas Waring ELDER BERRETTA, *b* 9 Dec 1960.

Mary Randolph Waring *m* 2ndly 22 Sept 1962, ●Robert Eugene Berretta [*2523 Falcon Courts North, McGuire Air Force Base, New Jersey 08641, USA*], and has further issue,
  2*d*●Mary Randolph BERRETTA, *b* 7 Dec 1964.
2*c*●Thomas WARING [*10 Atlantic Street, Charleston, South Carolina 29401, USA*], *b* 5 March 1944.
5*b*●James Hubard MATHEWES [*1029 Glendalyn Circle, Spartanburg, South Carolina 29302, USA*], *b* 16 June 1908, *m* 25 Nov 1939, ●Elizabeth Gaillard Lowndes.
7*a* Isaetta Carter HUBARD, *b* 18 April 1872, *m* 28 Jan 1916, Beverley Landon Ambler *d* 23 Oct 1940), and *dsp* 3 March 1952.
8*a* Bernard Markham HUBARD.
9*a* Ellen Wayles HUBARD, *m* — Robinson, and *dsp*.
10*a* Jefferson Randolph HUBARD, *b* 14 March 1877, *m* 18 Nov 1908, Louise Moore, and *d* 1925, having had issue,
  Agnes Moore HUBARD, *b* 2 Aug 1909; *d* 10 Oct 1910.
11*a* Archibald Blair HUBARD, *b* in Nelson County, Virginia 21 July 1879, *m* 28 Oct 1905, Carlotta D. (*b* 2 May 1885; *d* at Doylestown, Pennsylvania 4 Jan 1954), dau of Charles D. Barney, by his wife Laura E. Cooke, and *d* at Doylestown, Pennsylvania 26 May 1952, leaving issue,
  ●Randolph Bolling HUBARD, Lt-Col US Army [*North Run, Caves Road, Owings Mills, Maryland 21117, USA*], *b* 15 Jan 1906, *m* 2 May 1936, ●Ina Cochran (*b* 22 Sept 1910), and has issue,
    1*c*●John Bolling HUBARD, Col US Army [*267 Clearview Drive, Lexington, Kentucky 40533, USA*], *b* 20 April 1937, *m* 29 May 1970, ●Margaret Bate Cobb, and has issue,
      ●Randolph Bolling HUBARD III, *b* 3 Oct 1971.
    2*c*●Cynthia Ann HUBARD, *b* 17 March 1942, *m* 1st 14 March 1964, Samuel Barton Strong III, son of Samuel Barton Strong, Jr, and has issue,
      ●Samuel Barton STRONG IV, *b* 22 Sept 1964.
    Cynthia Ann Hubard *m* 2ndly, ●James Ziegler.
(2) Lewis Carter RANDOLPH, *b* 13 June 1838, *m* 29 Jan 1867, Louisa, only dau of Robert Thruston Hubard, of Chellowe, Buckingham County, by his wife Susan Pocahontas Bolling (*see p 121*), and *d* 29 May 1887, leaving issue,
  1*a* Robert Hubard RANDOLPH, *b* 11 Dec 1867, *m* 31 Oct 1906, Letitia Lawrence, and *dsp* 9 July 1939.
  2*a* Louise Hubard RANDOLPH, *b* 22 May 1869; *dunm* 23 Aug 1951.
  3*a* Sarah Champe RANDOLPH, *b* 1 July 1871, *m* 24 June 1908, Randolph Warren Hammerslough, and *dsp* 1 Jan 1959.
  4*a* Susan Bolling RANDOLPH, *b* 28 Aug 1974; *dunm* 19 April 1929.
  5*a* Benjamin Franklin RANDOLPH, *b* 9 Sept 1876; *dunm* 31 March 1951.
  6*a* Lewis Carter RANDOLPH, *b* 28 July 1877, *m* 6 Sept 1906, Dorothy Atkins, and *d* 19 Aug 1934, leaving issue,
    ●John RANDOLPH, *b* 23 April 1915.
  7*a* Eugene Jefferson RANDOLPH, *b* 19 March 1880, *m* 1901, Anne E. Carrier, and *d* 6 Oct 1950, having had issue,
    1*b* Hubard C. RANDOLPH, *b* 21 Dec 1902; *dunm* 28 Oct 1929.
    2*b*●Catherine RANDOLPH, *b* 22 July 1904, *m* 3 Oct 1931, ●E. Reid Russell (*b* 1898) [*30 White Oak Road, Biltmore Forest, Asheville, North Carolina 28803, USA*], and has issue,
      ●Catherine Randolph RUSSELL [*30 White Oak Road, Biltmore Forest, Asheville, North Carolina 28803, USA*], *b* 25 June 1933, *m* 27 June 1957 (*m* diss by div 1962), James Leake Little and has issue,
        ●Catherine Randolph LITTLE, *b* 17 May 1958.
    3*b*●Elizabeth RANDOLPH, *b* 10 Nov 1905, *m* 1st 28 Oct 1928 (*m* diss by div), Joseph D. Rivers (*b* 1900), and has issue,
      ●William Lord RIVERS [*Box 1136, Fort Myers, Florida, USA*], *b* 10 Aug 1933, *m* 11 July 1959, ●Gayle Musick, and has issue,
        ●Laura RIVERS, *b* 15 Feb 1961.
    Elizabeth Randolph *m* 2ndly, ●Monroe Stanley

Bobst.
  8*a* Janet Thruston RANDOLPH, *b* 27 Jan 1884; *dunm* 19 April 1951.
  (3) Robert Mann RANDOLPH, *b* 15 April 1851, *m* 1885, Margaret Calhoun Harris *d* 1927), and *dsp*.
10 Meriwether Lewis RANDOLPH, Sec of the Territory of Arkansas 1835-36, *b* at Monticello 31 Jan 1810, *educ* Virginia Univ, *m* at Clifton, nr Nashville, Tennessee 9 April 1835, Elizabeth (who *m* 2ndly 1841, as his 2nd wife, her 1st cousin once removed Andrew Jackson Donelson, nephew of Mrs Andrew Jackson (*see p 183*)), dau of James Glasgow Martin, of Clifton, nr Nashville, Tennessee, by his wife *née* Donelson, niece of Mrs Andrew Jackson, and *d* at Terre Noire, Arkansas 24 Sept 1837 (*bur* there), leaving issue,
  Lewis Jackson RANDOLPH, *b* at Nashville March 1836; *d* there 1840.
11 Septimia Anne RANDOLPH, *b* at Monticello 3 Jan 1814, *m* at Havana, Cuba 13 Aug 1838, Dr David Scott Meikleham (*b* at Glasgow, Scotland 6 Jan 1804; *d* at New York City 20 Nov 1849), son of William Meikleham, LLD, Prof of Natural Philosophy Glasgow Univ, and *d* at Washington, DC 14 Sept 1887 (*bur* New York), having had issue,
  (1) William Morland MEIKLEHAM, Vice-Pres New York Life Ins and Trust Co 1878-89, *b* at Havana 11 Dec 1839, *educ* Columbia Univ (AB 1868), *m* 1st 25 April 1865, Fannie Cassidy (*b* 9 Oct 1845; *d* 1 Jan 1885), and had issue,
    1*a* William Arabin MEIKLEHAM, *b* 1 March 1866, *m* 28 Jan 1903, Margaret Breckenridge *d* 31 July 1950), and *dsp* at Short Hills, New Jersey 12 Nov 1942.
    2*a* (Thomas Mann) Randolph MEIKLEHAM, of Edgartown, Massachusetts, engr, *b* at Fordham, NY 14 Feb 1869, *educ* Columbia Univ (CE 1890), *m* 7 Oct 1896, Agnes (*b* at New York City 31 Oct 1868), dau of Bowie Dash, of New York, and *d* 10 April 1854, having had issue,
      1*b*●Frances Louise MEIKLEHAM [*Edgartown, Martha's Vineyard, Massachusetts 02539, USA*], *b* at New York City 4 Aug 1902.
      2*b* Martha Randolph MEIKLEHAM, *b* 8 May 1905; *d* 15 Sept 1919.
    3*a* Frank Sydney MEIKLEHAM, *b* in Westchester County, New York 28 May, *d* 14 Sept 1872.
    4*a* Henry Parish MEIKLEHAM, *b* in Westchester County, New York 28 May 1872 (twin with Frank Sydney), *m* 1st 9 June 1897 (*m* diss by div 1912), Virginia Grafton; and *m* 2ndly 16 Jan 1926, Juliet Howell widow of — Graves, and dau of — Howell, and *dsp* 23 July 1937.
  William Morland Meikleham *m* 2ndly 8 June 1887, Isabella Parlby Cuthbert, and *d* 27 July 1889.
  (2) Thomas Mann Randolph MEIKLEHAM, *b* at Havana 30 Dec 1840; *dunm* 7 April 1922.
  (3) Esther Alice MEIKLEHAM, *b* at Havana 12 Nov 1842; *d* at Glasgow, Scotland 4 Sept 1843.
  (4) Esther Alice MEIKLEHAM, *b* at Glasgow, Scotland 28 Dec 1843; *dunm* 6 Feb 1927.
  (5) Ellen Wayles MEIKLEHAM, *b* at New York City 29 Aug 1846; *dunm* 22 Feb 1913.
12 George Wythe RANDOLPH, served in the Navy, mem Virginia Secession Convention, joined Confederate Army 1861 and became Brig-Gen, Confederate Sec of War 1862-64, *b* at Monticello 10 March 1818, *educ* Univ of Virginia (LLB 1840), *m* at New Orleans 20 April 1852, Mary Elizabeth (*b* 1830; *d* Edgehill 1871), widow of — Pope, and dau of — Adams, of Richmond, and *dsp* at Edgehill 3 April 1867 (*bur* Monticello).
2 Jane Randolph JEFFERSON, *b* at Monticello 3 April 1774; *d* there Sept 1775.
3 A son, *b* at Monticello 28 May, *d* there 14 June 1777.
4 Mary (Maria) JEFFERSON, *b* at Monticello 1 Aug 1778, *m* there 13 Oct 1797, as his 1st wife, her half 1st cousin, John Wayles Eppes, Senator and Congressman (*b* at City Point, Virginia 7 April 1773; *d* at Millbrook, Buckingham County 5 Sept 1823, having *m* 2ndly 1809, Martha Burke Jones, of Halifax, N Carolina, by whom he had further issue), eldest son of Francis Eppes, of Eppington, Chesterfield County, Virginia, by his 1st wife Elizabeth Wayles (half-sister of Mrs Thomas Jefferson), and *d* at Monticello 17 April 1804 (*bur* there), having had issue,
  1 A child, *b* and *d* 1800.
  2 Francis Wayles EPPES, *b* at Monticello 20 Sept 1801, *m* 1st

at Ashton, Albemarle County 28 Nov 1822, his 4th cousin, Mary Elizabeth Cleland (*b* 16 Jan 1801; *d* at L'Eau Noir April 1835), eldest dau of Thomas Eston Randolph, of Ashton, by his wife Jane Cary Randolph (sister of Thomas Mann Randolph, Jr—*see above, p* 98), and had issue,
(1) Jane Cary EPPES, *b* at Ashton, Virginia 9 Nov 1823; *dunm* 12 Feb 1893.
(2) John Wayles EPPES, MD, *b* in Bedford County, Virginia 4 July 1825, *m* 10 Nov 1854, Josephine H. Bellamy, and *d* 1908, having had issue,
  1*a* Francis EPPES, *d* an inf.
  2*a* Eliza Wayles EPPES, *b* 1857, *m* 1878, Alexander Kennedy and *d* 1898, leaving issue,
    1*b* Margaret KENNEDY, *b* 1878, *m* 1915, Alberto Hernandez Blanc, son of — Hernandez, by his wife — Blanc, and *dsp* 1918.
    2*b* Josephine Bellamy KENNEDY, *b* 6 May 1879, *m* 1908, Marion Howard Bradley (*b* 1871; *d* 21 Feb 1920), and *d* 7 May 1961, having had issue,
      1*c* Annie Ward BRADLEY, *b* and *d* 1911.
      2*c*●Marion Howard BRADLEY, Jr [*2006 Azalea Circle, Decatur, Georgia 30033, USA*], *b* 11 Dec 1914, *m* 30 Dec 1941, ●Joyce Patricia Clark (*b* 23 March 1919), and has issue,
        1*d*●Ann Randolph BRADLEY, *b* 29 Jan 1944, *m* 1 Dec 1962, ●Robert Bradford Burnette [*2216 Brighton Place, Valdosta, Georgia 31601, USA*], and has issue,
          ●Catherine Randolph BURNETTE, *b* 20 April 1966.
        2*d*●Josephine Eppes BRADLEY, *b* 10 Sept 1947.
        3*d*●Marion Howard BRADLEY III, *b* 18 Sept 1951.
    3*b* Agnes KENNEDY, *b* 1882, *m* 1917, James Washington Herbert, and had issue,
      1*c*●Eliza Eppes HERBERT, *b* 23 March 1921, *m* 24 April 1943, ●Joseph Byron Davis (*b* 10 March 1914), and has issue,
        1*d*●Joseph Byron DAVIS, Jr, *b* 10 March 1944.
        2*d*●Ann Lynwood DAVIS, *b* 7 Aug 1945.
        3*d*●James Kennedy DAVIS, *b* 18 Sept 1947.
        4*d*●William Lewis DAVIS, *b* 1 Feb 1950.
      2*c*●Julia Francis HERBERT, *b* 15 June 1922, *m* Sept 1943, ●Robert Edward Lee Hall Forbes, and has issue,
        1*d*●Julia Lee FORBES, *b* 25 June 1945.
        2*d*●Florence Patty Kennedy FORBES, *b* 8 Oct 1946.
        3*d*●Robert Edward Lee Hall FORBES, Jr, *b* 29 Sept 1948.
        4*d*●George Joseph FORBES, *b* 7 May 1951.
        5*d*●Clarence Aloysius Hall FORBES, *b* 18 July 1952.
      3*c* Agnes Kennedy HERBERT, *d* an inf.
    3*b* Alexander KENNEDY, Jr, *b* 1885; *d* 1903.
    4*b* John Wayles KENNEDY, *b* 14 June 1889, *m* 19 Nov 1921, Laura Cecilia Hebb, and *d* 4 July 1932, leaving issue,
      1*c*●John Wayles KENNEDY, Jr, *b* 24 Feb 1923, *m* 1 June 1949, ●Dina Morelli, and has issue,
        ●Lisa Morelli KENNEDY, *b* 21 Feb 1952.
      2*c*●Margaret Combs KENNEDY, *b* 29 Sept 1924, *m* 14 Aug 1954, ●Eugene Hall Johnstone [*St Marys County, Mechanicsville, Maryland 20659, USA*], and has issue,
        1*d*●Eugene Hall JOHNSTONE, Jr, *b* 19 July 1955.
        2*d*●Laura Hebb JOHNSTONE, *b* 19 Dec 1956.
        3*d*●Virginia Coad JOHNSTONE, *b* Dec 1958.
        4*d*●Margaret Kennedy JOHNSTONE.
        5*d*●Jane Randolph JOHNSTONE.
        6*d*●Ann Katherine JOHNSTONE.
        7*d*●Rebecca Chisholm JOHNSTONE.
      3*c*●Alexander KENNEDY, *b* 15 April 1926, *m* 25 March 1957, ●Mary Collette Barrett, and has issue,
        1*d*●Mary Grace KENNEDY, *b* 23 Dec 1957.
        2*d*●John Wayles KENNEDY, *b* 24 Aug 1959.
      ·4*c*●Patricia Hebb KENNEDY, *b* 28 June 1928, *m* 22 Oct 1955, ●Samuel Robert Garrabrant, and has issue,

        1*d*●Laura Wayles GARRABRANT, *b* 31 Aug 1956.
        2*d*●Robert Bayard GARRABRANT, *b* 24 Feb 1957.
      5*c*●Anne Katherine KENNEDY, *b* 4 Nov 1929, *m* 20 Jan 1953, ●Owen William Hendon, and has issue,
        1*d*●Nicole HENDON, *b* 8 Nov 1955.
        2*d*●McKim Kennedy HENDON, *b* 18 March 1957.
        3*d*●Robert Derek HENDON, *b* 23 Aug 1959.
      5*b*●Florence Patti KENNEDY [*3526 Whitehaven Parkway, NW, Washington, DC 20007, USA*], *b* 1891.
(3) Thomas Jefferson EPPES, *b* 29 June 1827, *m* 28 April 1859, Theodosia Burr Bellamy, and *d* 1869, having had issue,
  1*a* Thomas Jefferson EPPES, Jr, *b* 22 Feb 1861, *m* 1st, Kate Edna Shaler, and had issue,
    1*b* Thomas Jefferson EPPES III, *b* 6 Sept 1884, *m* Katherine Davis, and *dsp* 1 Feb 1944.
Thomas Jefferson Eppes, Jr *m* 2ndly, Mamie Jeanette (*b* 18 Oct 1868; *d* 21 April 1923), widow of — Gones, and dau of — Shoemaker, and *d* 2 Nov 1910, having by her had issue,
    2*b*●Edna Bellamy EPPES [*28 Thackery Place, Savannah, Georgia 31405, USA*], *b* 12 Dec 1892, *m* 1 Sept 1915, Dr Ralston Lattimore (*b* 1871; *d* 1938), and has issue,
      1*c*●Edna Eppes LATTIMORE, *b* 9 Sept 1916, *m* 12 July 1941, ●Jack Stacey Clancy, and has issue,
        1*d*●Helen Lattimore CLANCY, *b* 6 March 1943.
        2*d*●Jack Stacey CLANCY, *b* 14 June 1947.
        3*d*●Carol CLANCY, *b* 2 July 1949.
      2*c*●William LATTIMORE [*1005 Ashley Road, Savannah, Georgia 31404, USA*], *b* 8 June 1918, *m* 20 Dec 1943, ●Helen M. Clancy, and has issue,
        1*d*●Anne Eppes LATTIMORE, *b* 19 Feb 1947, *m* 1966, ●Henry M. Eason, Jr, son of Henry M. Eason, and has issue,
          ●Sterling Fennel EASON, *b* 20 March 1968.
        2*d*●Elizabeth Bellamy LATTIMORE, *b* 24 Nov 1949, *m* June 1971, ●William Earl Sparks.
        3*d*●William LATTIMORE, Jr, *b* 25 May 1954.
      3*c*●Harry Lays LATTIMORE, *b* 18 March 1924.
  2*a* Victoria EPPES, *b* 1862, *m* 1st, Carlton M. Marshall; and 2ndly, Arthur B. Harrison, and *dsp*.
  3*a* Mary EPPES, *b* 1863, *m* George Morrison, and had issue,
    Theodosia Bellamy MORRISON, *m* 1st 29 Dec 1909, Dudley Shepard Shine, Jr (*b* 19 Dec 1885; *d* June 1933), son of David Shepard Shine, by his wife Caroline Matilda Eppes, and had issue (*see below, p* 126). She *m* 2ndly, Cyril Norman Boland.
  4*a* Frances EPPES, *b* 1865, *m* 1892, Alberta R. Wharton, and had issue,
    1*b*●Francis EPPES, *b* 1894, *m*, and has issue,
      1*c*●Alberta EPPES, *b* 1923.
      2*c*●Francis EPPES, *b* 1925.
    2*b*●Mary EPPES, *b* 1896.
  5*a* Paul EPPES, *b* 1866; *d* 1868.
  6*a* Randolph EPPES, *b* 21 Oct 1868, *m* 15 Dec 1898, Sarah Josephine Mays, and *d* 5 Dec 1941, leaving issue,
    1*b*●Edith Bellamy EPPES, *b* 26 Dec 1899, *m* 16 Nov 1920, ●Haskell Harris Bass (*b* 18 Sept 1893), and has issue,
      1*c*●Edith Eppes BASS, *b* 19 Dec 1921, *m* 18 Nov 1944, ●William Ellison Thompson, Jr (*b* 3 Dec 1923), son of William Ellison Thompson, and has issue,
        1*d*●William Ellison THOMPSON III, *b* 29 Aug 1945.
        2*d*●David Craig THOMPSON, *b* 22 March 1947.
        3*d*●Mark Randolph THOMPSON, *b* 29 March 1952.
        4*d*●Sarah Ann THOMPSON, *b* 6 Nov 1953.
      2*c*●Eleanor Mays BASS, *b* 23 Jan 1924, *m* 19 Oct 1946, ●Dr Joseph Brannen Ganey (*b* 28 May 1921) [*Bradenton, Florida, USA*], and has issue,
        1*d*●Joseph Brannen GANEY, Jr, *b* 25 July 1949.
        2*d*●James Nowell GANEY, *b* 16 July 1950.

3*d*●Thomas Harris GANEY, *b* 15 Nov 1954.
3*c*●Dr Haskell Harris BASS, Jr [*Bradenton, Florida, USA*], *b* 6 June 1930.
2*b*●Martha Simkins EPPES, *b* 30 June 1903, *m* 1st 1923, Edward Baldwin Young, and has issue,
 1*c*●Meta Baldwin YOUNG, *b* 6 Nov 1924, *m* 12 April 1947, ●William Dyer Shackelford [*Box 190, Clanton, Alabama 35045, USA*], and has issue,
  1*d*●Martha Eppes SHACKELFORD, *b* 9 June 1954.
  2*d*●Theresa Dyer SHACKELFORD, *b* 8 May 1956.
  3*d*●Meta Baldwin SHACKELFORD, *b* 22 Feb 1961.
  4*d*●Maria Eppes SHACKELFORD, *b* 29 March 1962.
Martha Simpkins Eppes *m* 2ndly 26 April 1934, ●Francis Putney Wetherbee [*1102 North Harding, Albany, Georgia 31705, USA*], and has further issue,
 2*c*●Francis Putney WETHERBEE, Jr [*1102 North Harding, Albany, Georgia 31705, USA*], *b* 3 April 1935, *m* 17 March 1959, ●Nancy Elizabeth Butts.
 3*c*●James Roland WETHERBEE, *b* 4 Jan 1940.
 4*c*●Sarah Eppes WETHERBEE, *b* 23 Jan 1943.
(4) William Eston EPPES (Rev), *b* at L'Eau Noir, Tallahassee 5 July 1830, *m* 1st Aug 1854, Emily Bancroft (*d* 1873), and had issue,
1*a* Matilda Bancroft EPPES, *b* 1855; *dunm* 26 Jan 1929.
2*a* Elizabeth Cleland EPPES, *b* 1857; *dunm* 1881.
3*a* Francis EPPES, *b* 1859, *m* 1881, his 1st cousin Mary Margaret Bancroft (*b* 1861; *d* 27 March 1950), and *d* 1921, having had issue,
 1*b* Fred EPPES, *b* 1882.
 2*b* William Eston EPPES, *b* 10 June 1885; *dunm* 1918.
 3*b*●James Bancroft EPPES [*Route 5, Box 286, Annapolis, Maryland, USA*], *b* 1888, *m* 1st 1908, Elizabeth Williford (*b* 1890; *d* 1944), and has had issue,
  1*c* Elizabeth EPPES, *b* 1910.
  2*c*●Caroline Frances EPPES, *b* 1911, *m* 1st 1929, Stanford Ivan Hoff, and has had issue,
   1*d* Stanford Ivan HOFF, Jr, *b* 1930; *d* on active service in Korea 4 Nov 1950.
  Caroline Frances Eppes *m* 2ndly 1934, ●William Bernard Loving [*5315 South Street, Arlington, Virginia, USA*], and has had further issue,
   2*d*●William Bernard LOVING, Jr [*5315 South 12th Street, Arlington, Virginia, USA*], *b* 1936, *m* 7 Jan 1959, ●Myrna Joyce Bruner.
   3*d*●Claire Bancroft LOVING, *b* 1938, *m* 1st 2 March 1959 (*m* diss by div), Dr Merrill Eugene Speelman. She *m* 2ndly 23 Nov 1964, ●Dr Albert Dworkin (*b* 1926) [*1102 Brantin Road, Chatham, Wilmington, Delaware, 19803, USA*], and has issue,
    1*e*●Carol Elizabeth DWORKIN, *b* 15 July 1966.
    2*e*●Kathryn DWORKIN, *b* 18 Nov 1969.
    3*e*●Paul Joseph DWORKIN, *b* 8 Feb 1972.
  3*c*●James Bancroft EPPES, Jr [*5413 Williamsburg Road, Arlington, Virginia 22207, USA*], *b* 1913, *m* 18 May 1940, ●Elizabeth Claude Fuller (*b* 1919), and has issue,
   1*d*●John Williford EPPES [*Box 22684, Emery University, Atlanta, Georgia 30322, USA*], *b* 21 June 1941.
   2*d*●James Bancroft EPPES III [*2055 North Glebe Road, Arlington, Virginia 22207, USA*], *b* 1 Nov 1942.
   3*d*●Thomas Jefferson EPPES, *b* 21 May 1946.
   4*d*●Lucy Elizabeth EPPES, *b* 16 June 1956.
 4*c* Emily EPPES, *b* 1914; *d* 1921.
 5*c*●Mary EPPES, *b* 1921, *m* 1943, ●Remus Strother Turner, MD (*b* 1921) [*111 Battle Road, Greensboro, North Carolina 27410, USA*], and has issue,
  1*d*●Remus Strother TURNER, Jr, *b* 4 Feb 1945, *m* 16 June 1968, ●Diane Elizabeth Morris.
  2*d*●Janet Elizabeth TURNER, *b* 6 April 1947, *m* 21 Dec 1968, ●William Carroll Chewning.
  3*d*●Joseph Eppes TURNER [*111 Battle Road,*

*Greensboro, North Carolina 27410, USA*], *b* 11 June 1950.
  4*d*●Paul Allan TURNER, *b* 26 April 1954.
 6*c*●Williford EPPES, MD [*19 Bridle Bridge Road, Covered Bridge Farm, Newark, Delaware, USA*], *b* 1923, *m* 9 Oct 1948, ●Emily Mulligan, and has issue,
  1*d*●Emily Elizabeth EPPES, *b* 27 July 1949.
  2*d*●Douglas Williford EPPES, *b* 26 June 1950.
  3*d*●Thomas Wayne EPPES, *b* 24 Sept 1952.
  4*d*●Barbara Caroline EPPES, *b* 30 July 1955.
  5*d*●David Charles EPPES, *b* 6 June 1957.
James Bancroft Eppes *m* 2ndly 1945, ●Carrie Frances Williford (*b* 1893).
4*b* Lillie Jeannerette EPPES, *b* 1890; *d* 1892.
5*b* John Wayles EPPES, *b* 1892, *m* 1915, Mary Lou Lemon, and *d* 6 Nov 1961, leaving issue,
 ●John Francis EPPES, *b* 4 April 1921, *m* 27 Aug 1944, ●Margaret Temple, and has issue,
  ●Constance Bancroft EPPES, *b* 27 Nov 1953.
4*a* James Bancroft EPPES, *b* 1860; *d* 1861.
5*a* Lucy Randolph EPPES, *b* 1861, *m* 1881, her 1st cousin Edward Bancroft, and *d* 1896, having had issue,
 1*b* Lucy Eppes BANCROFT, *b* 1882; *d* at 1883.
 2*b* Irene Scott BANCROFT, *b* 1883; *dunm.*
 3*b* Dr Edward BANCROFT, Jr, *b* 1886; *dunm* 1924.
 4*b* Emily Cleland BANCROFT, *b* 1888; *dunm* 22 June 1956.
 5*b* Matilda Eppes BANCROFT, *b* 10 Oct 1893, *m* 27 Sept 1929, Thomas Wetzell Richards, and had issue,
  ●Thomas Edward RICHARDS, *b* 26 Feb 1932, *m* 6 Sept 1953, ●Carlene Jeanette Ruark, and has issue,
   1*d*●Keith Randolph RICHARDS, *b* 26 Jan 1955.
   2*d*●Thomas Jeffrey RICHARDS, *b* 18 Oct 1958.
6*a* Jane Cary EPPES, *b* 1863; *d* an inf.
7*a* William Eston EPPES, Jr, *b* 1864, *m* 1889, Irene Ada Bancroft, and had issue,
 1*b* Adele Evelyn EPPES, *b* 6 June 1890, *m* 13 April 1913, James William Lockett, and *d* 17 April 1966, having had issue,
  1*c*●Martha Anne LOCKETT, *b* 26 April 1914, *m* 1st 1935, William Ewell Lewis; and *m* 2ndly 30 Aug 1957, ●Emory McNeil [*110 Holcomb Street, Isle of Hope, Savannah, Georgia 31406, USA*].
  2*c* Evelyn Eppes LOCKETT, *b* 1916; *d* an inf.
  3*c*●Frances Hunter LOCKETT, *b* 25 Dec 1917, *m* 1938, ●Alton A. Rogers, and has issue,
   1*d*●Jane Elizabeth ROGERS, *b* 1939, *m* 23 Aug 1958, ●William Carl Quante, and has issue,
    1*e*●William Carl QUANTE, Jr, *b* 17 May 1959.
    2*e*●Timothy Alton QUANTE, *b* 26 April 1961.
    3*e*●Albert John QUANTE, *b* 16 Feb 1963.
   2*d*●Joyce Hunter ROGERS, *b* 1940, *m* 10 Aug 1963, ●David Roy Tyler, and has issue,
    1*e*●David Roy TYLER, Jr, *b* 19 Sept 1964.
    2*e*●Michael Edward TYLER, *b* 14 Jan 1967.
  4*c*●James William LOCKET, Jr, *b* 20 Nov 1920, *m* 1941, ●Madie Sapp, and has issue,
   1*d*●Evelyn Mae LOCKETT, *b* 1943, *m* ●Marion Russell Pierce, and has issue,
    1*e*●Gary Russell PIERCE, *b* 18 March 1965.
    2*e*●Deborah Lynn PIERCE, *b* 21 May 1966.
   2*d*●Patricia Fay LOCKETT, *b* 1945, *m* 24 Nov 1965, ●Terry James Woods, and has issue,
    1*e*●Alicia Faye WOODS, *b* 3 Sept 1966.
    2*e*●Terry James WOODS, *b* 18 Feb 1973.
   3*d*●Martha Anne LOCKETT, *b* 1950, *m* 16 Aug 1969, ●Richard Allen Stoops, and has issue,
    ●Richard Allen STOOPS, Jr, *b* 30 July 1970.
   4*d*●James William LOCKETT III, *b* 24 June 1956.
  5*c*●Randolph Eppes LOCKETT, *b* 11 May 1922, *m* 1st 1942, Catherine Roberts. He *m* 2ndly 4 Sept 1951, ●Betty Ruth Reynolds, and by her has issue,
    ●Randolph Eppes LOCKETT, Jr, *b* 3 Jan 1956.
  6*c*●Frederick Buckner LOCKETT, *b* 1930, *m* ●Josephine Rodewolt, and had issue,
   1*d*●Cynthia Diane LOCKETT, *b* June 1952.
   2*d*●Frederick Buckner LOCKETT, Jr, *b* 18 Jan 1955.
   3*d*●David Michael LOCKETT, *b* 29 Jan 1964.

4d● Allen John LOCKETT, *b* 10 Aug 1965.
2*b* William Randolph EPPES, *b* 20 Aug 1892, *m* 2 Jan 1918, Marion Grey McCorkle, and *d* 13 Jan 1919, leaving issue,
  Randolph Marion EPPES, *b* (posthumously) and *d* June 1919.
3*b* Arthur Beverley EPPES, *b* 22 Oct 1893, *m* 1st 1921, Nora Nedra Reddick. He *m* 2ndly 9 June 1927, ● Klara Elizabeth Schmitt, and *d* 8 Aug 1959, having by her had issue,
  ● Clara Elizabeth EPPES, *b* 20 May 1928, *m* 21 Aug 1948, ● James Patrick Evans [*1537 Forsyth Road, Savannah, Georgia 31406, USA*], and has issue,
    1*d* ● Lynn Carol EVANS, *b* 12 Dec 1952.
    2*d* ● James Randolph EVANS, *b* 13 Feb 1955.
    3*d* ● David Arthur EVANS, *b* 12 July 1957.
    4*d* ● Nancy Elizabeth EVANS, *b* 12 July 1957 (twin with her brother David Arthur Evans).
4*b* ● Irene Ada EPPES, *b* 23 Oct 1895, *m* 10 July 1939, ● Thomas Maloney Hallam.
5*b* ● Catherine EPPES, *b* 21 May 1897, *m* 1st 20 May 1895, Joseph Forrester Buckner, and has had issue,
  1*c* ● Emily Bancroft BUCKNER, *b* 16 April 1926, *m* May 1948, ● Arthur Cody, Jr, and has issue,
    1*d* ● Craig Stephen CODY, *b* 29 July 1949.
    2*d* ● Donald Alan CODY, *b* 23 Aug 1951.
    3*d* ● Arthur Gary CODY, *b* 6 Dec 1954.
  2*c* Joseph Forrester BUCKNER, Jr, *b* 16 April 1928; *d* 30 May 1941.
Catherine Eppes *m* 2ndly Dec 1952, ● William E. Ratcliffe [*409 East 49th Street, Savannah, Georgia, USA*].
6*b* Thomas Jefferson EPPES, *b* at Athens, Georgia 7 Feb 1899, *m* 1st at Augusta, Georgia 11 Oct 1919, Lilla Camille (*b* at Thompson, Georgia 15 Sept 1899; *d* at Atlanta, Georgia Oct 1962), dau of Thomas Bowdre Hamilton, by his wife Lilla Lee Hunt, and has had issue,
  ● Gloria Camille EPPES, *b* at Orlando, Florida 13 Nov 1926, *m* 1st at Valdosta, Georgia 20 July 1947 (*m* diss by div), Francis Xavier Mulherrin, Jr (*b* at Augusta, Georgia 13 March 1913), son of Francis Xavier Mulherrin, by his wife Eulalia, and has issue,
    1*d* ● Linda Anne MULHERRIN (name legally changed to MCDAVID 1966), *b* at Augusta, Georgia 21 April 1948, *m* at Athens, Georgia 30 Dec 1967, ● Arthur Eugene Sturgill, Jr (*b* at El Paso, Texas 6 Jan 1947), son of Arthur Eugene Sturgill, by his wife Curtis Strain, and has issue,
      Christine Camille STURGILL, *b* at Athens, Georgia 14 May 1969.
Gloria Camille Eppes *m* 2ndly at Athens, Georgia 16 Sept 1949, ● Joseph Terrell McDavid (*b* at Lowell, Mass 12 Oct 1926) [*10219 Scout Drive, Fairfax, Virginia, USA*], son of Hubert H. McDavid, by his wife Laura Henderson, and has further issue,
    2*d* ● Gloria Elizabeth MCDAVID, *b* at Memphis, Tennessee 15 Aug 1953, *m* at Dallas, Texas 23 Sept 1973, ● Gene Craig Stephens (*b* at Dallas 6 Jan 1950), son of David H. Stephens, by his wife Alice.
    3*d* ● Carole Hamilton MCDAVID, *b* at Memphis, Tennessee 5 Nov 1954.
Thomas Jefferson Eppes *m* 2ndly, Eunice, formerly wife of — Burrell, and dau of — Treadwell, and *d* 29 Sept 1961.
7*b* William Eston EPPES III, *b* 3 Oct 1901; *d* 11 Jan 1919.
8*b* ● Marion Theresa EPPES, *b* 29 Oct 1904, *m* 16 May 1928, ● William Byrd Moss [*6603 Vernon Street, La Grange, Georgia 30240, USA*], and has issue,
  1*c* ● William Lee MOSS, *b* 14 Feb 1929, *m* 24 Dec 1950, ● Betty Ann Reiber, and has issue,
    1*d* ● Michael MOSS, *b* 6 Oct 1951.
    2*d* ● Theresa Anne MOSS, *b* 25 April 1954.
    3*d* ● William Scott MOSS, *b* 5 Nov 1959.
    4*d* ● Judith Marie MOSS, *b* 25 Jan 1963.
  2*c* ● Mary Catherine MOSS, *b* 3 June 1931, *m* 26 Feb 1949, ● Thomas James Woods, and has issue,

1*d* ● James Anthony WOODS, *b* 14 Dec 1949, *m* 9 June 1969, ● Cynthia Margaret Johnson, and has issue,
      ● Stephen Lance WOODS, *b* 12 Jan 1970.
    2*d* ● David William WOODS, *b* 19 Nov 1954.
    3*d* ● Richard Lee WOODS, *b* 4 Dec 1955.
  3*c* ● John Hill MOSS [*3112 Quimby Road, Virginia Beach, Virginia, USA*], *b* 17 July 1937, *m* 13 June 1959, ● Joy Louise Pickler, and has issue,
    1*d* ● Daniel Lee MOSS, *b* 1 Sept 1960.
    2*d* ● John Eric MOSS, *b* 21 Jan 1961.
    3*d* ● Steven Patrick MOSS, *b* 1 July 1964.
    4*d* ● Julia MOSS, *b* 12 July 1969.
9*b* ● Benjamin Scott EPPES, *b* 15 Aug 1906, *m* 28 June 1932, ● Frances Crane, and has issue,
  1*c* ● Frances Crane EPPES, *b* 21 Dec 1933, *m* 4 June 1954, ● Albert Whitman Brame.
  2*c* ● Amalia Scott EPPES, *b* 29 Jan 1937, *m* 17 Aug 1960, ● Howard Griffin Rogers.
  3*c* ● Benjamin Scott EPPES, *b* 17 April 1943.
8*a* John Wayles EPPES, *b* 1866; *d* 1874.
9*a* Emily Bancroft EPPES, *b* at Clarksville, Georgia 1868; *d* 1876.
10*a* Edward Bancroft EPPES, *b* at Clarksville, Georgia 1868 (twin with Emily Bancroft), *m* at Spartanburg, S Carolina 1 July 1908, Jennie (*b* at Eufaula, Alabama 10 Feb 1886; *d* there 27 Sept 1965), dau of John Marshall Kendall, by his wife Sally Jennings, and *d* at Augusta, Georgia 1918, leaving issue,
  Dr John Kendall EPPES, *b* at Augusta, Georgia 13 Sept 1916, *m* at Salt Lake City, Utah 16 July 1943, ● Nell Richardson (*b* at Baton Rouge, Louisiana 1919) [*210 East Broad Street, Box 557, Eufaula, Alabama 36027, USA*], dau of Edward Carroll Reilly, by his wife Hilda Richardson, and *d* at Birmingham, Alabama 7 May 1974 (*bur* Eufaula), leaving issue,
    ● John Kendall EPPES, Jr [*3388 Kings Canyon Drive, Baton Rouge, Louisiana 70814, USA*], *b* at Eufaula, Alabama 9 Dec 1944, *m* at Abbeville, Alabama 26 Jan 1965, ● Carol (*b* at Fort Wayne, Indiana 4 Oct 1944), dau of Donald I. Reaves, by his wife Joanne Gunter, and has issue,
      1*d* ● John Kendall EPPES III, *b* at Opelika, Alabama 6 Dec 1966.
      2*d* ● David Marshall EPPES, *b* at Baton Rouge, Louisiana 29 July 1969.
11*a* Maria Jefferson EPPES, *b* 1871; *dunm* 1916.
Rev William Eston Eppes *m* 2ndly 1877, Augusta Jones Kollock (*d* 1896), and *d* 1896.
(5) Mary Elizabeth Cleland EPPES, *b* at L'Eau Noir 5 July 1832; *dunm* 1903.
(6) Francis EPPES, *b* L'Eau Noir April 1835; *d* an inf.
Francis Wayles Eppes *m* 2ndly 15 March 1837, Susan Margaret, widow of — Crouch, and dau of Senator Nicholas Ware, and *d* 30 May 1881, having by her had issue,
(7) Susan Frances EPPES, *b* 15 March 1839, *m* 25 April 1861, John Armstrong Craig, and *d* 21 Jan 1908, leaving issue,
  1*a* John Armstrong CRAIG, Jr, *b* 8 Dec 1862; *dunm* Sept 1927.
  2*a* Frances Maude CRAIG, *b* 28 Jan 1870, *m* 27 Oct 1906, Albert George Goodbody, and had issue,
    ● Amy GOODBODY, *b* 14 Dec 1907, *m* 30 Sept 1947, ● Dr George Lester Patterson [*1126 Maple Drive, Tallahassee, Florida, USA*].
  3*a* Francis Eppes CRAIG, *b* 25 Feb 1872, *m* 7 Sept 1921, his 1st cousin Mary Armstrong, widow of Forbes, and dau of — Craig, and *dsp*.
  4*a* Thomas Eppes CRAIG, *dunm* 22 Aug 1927.
(8) Maria Jefferson EPPES, *b* 1840, *m* 1868, Dr William Francis Shine, and *d* 1897, leaving issue,
  Dr Francis Eppes SHINE, *b* at St Augustine, Florida 13 Jan 1871, *m* 2 Aug 1904, Ann Barker (*b* at Toronto, Canada 1874; *d* at Los Angeles, California 29 April 1955, *bur* Monticello), and *d* at Paris, France 8 Sept 1922 (*bur* Monticello), leaving issue,
    1*b* ● Francis Eppes SHINE, Jr [*425 Scott Place, Pasadena, California 91103, USA*], *b* 13 May 1906, *m* ● Elinor Goodrich, and has issue,
      ● Francis Eppes SHINE III [*626 Bellefontaine Street, Pasadena, California 91105, USA*], *b* 16 Jan

1933, *m* 26 July 1958, ●Alice C. Miller, and has issue,
  1*d*●Christine Eppes SHINE, *b* 2 Oct 1960.
  2*d*●Anne Wayles SHINE, *b* 27 March 1962.
  3*d*●John Randolph SHINE.
2*b*●Randolph Eppes SHINE, *b* 9 July 1907, *m* 29 April 1950, ●Bernice Johnson Reed.
3*b*●Elizabeth SHINE [*942 Valencia Mesa Drive, Fullerton, California 92632, USA*], *b* 7 Nov 1912, *m* (*m* diss by div 1938), Adolf Semler, and has issue, ●Anne Leys SEMLER, *b* 29 Sept 1935.
(9) Nicholas Ware EPPES, *b* 1 Nov 1843, *m* 1 Nov 1866, Susan Branch (*b* 3 March 1846; *d* 2 July 1942), dau of Dr Edward Bradford, by his wife Martha Lewis Henry, and *d* 3 Sept 1904, having had issue,
  1*a* Edward Bradford EPPES, *b* 15 March 1868; *dunm* 25 Jan 1934.
  2*a* Susan Ware EPPES, *b* 8 May 1871; *dunm* 30 Dec 1965.
  3*a* Frances EPPES, *b* 25 March 1874; *d* 28 July 1875.
  4*a* Martha Branch EPPES, *b* 18 Aug 1876, *m* 24 June 1903, Richard H. Bradford, and *dsp.*
  5*a* Elizabeth Cleland EPPES, *b* 15 Feb 1882; *dunm* 20 Feb 1950.
  6*a* Alice Bradford EPPES, *b* 24 Jan 1886; *dunm* 13 Oct 1962.
(10) Mary EPPES, *b* 1845; *d* an inf.
(11) Martha Virginia EPPES, *b* 1847, *m* 1st 1867, Thomas J. Shine, and had issue,
  1*a* Lillias Eleanor SHINE, *b* 5 May 1869, *m* 14 April 1914, Frank B. Stoneman (*b* at Indianapolis, Indiana 26 June 1857; *d* at Miami, Florida 1 Feb 1941), son of Dr Mark D. Stoneman, by his wife Aletha White, and *dsp* 6 March 1956.
  2*a* Francis Wayles SHINE, MD, *b* 25 June 1874, *m* 14 May 1938, Efna, widow of — Bedell, and dau of — Wood, and *dsp* 23 Sept 1941 (*bur* Monticello).
  3*a* Richard Alexander SHINE, *b* 28 May 1876, *m* 1907, Rose Boyd, and had issue,
    1*b*●Richard Alexander SHINE, Jr, *b* 29 July 1910.
    2*b*●Virginia Elizabeth SHINE, *b* 18 April 1913.
    3*b*●William Boyd SHINE, *b* 30 Sept 1924.
  4*a* Thomas Jefferson SHINE, *b* 1881; *d* 1884.
  5*a* William Eston SHINE, *b* 18 May 1885, *m* 19 April 1911, Florence Dunn Howard, and *dsp* 8 Jan 1913.
Martha Virginia Eppes *m* 2ndly 1891, Henry W. Greatham, and *d* 9 Sept 1920.
(12) Robert Francis EPPES, *b* 1851, *m* 1881, Martha Rebecca Whitehead, and *d* 1894, having had issue,
  1*a* Amos Whitehead EPPES, *b* 1883; *d* 1890.
  2*a* Susan Margaret EPPES, *b* 12 Jan 1886, *m* 22 May 1907, Hugh Moultrie Griffin (*b* 8 July 1880; *d* 14 May 1958), and *d* 21 Dec 1971, having had issue,
    1*b*●Susan Ola GRIFFIN, *b* at Tallahassee, Florida 24 June 1908, *m* 24 May 1935, ●Thomas H. McRorie (*b* 8 Dec 1913) [*620 South East Fourth Avenue, Gainesville, Florida 32601, USA*], son of Thomas Henry McRorie, by his wife Emma, and has issue,
      1*c*●Thomas Henry MCRORIE [*9642 Bay Meadow Drive, Huntington Beach, California 92646, USA*], *b* at Raleigh, N Carolina 28 Oct 1936, *m* at Gainesville, Florida 30 Jan 1958, ●Joyce, dau of Harold Monck, by his wife Eleanor, and has issue,
        1*d*●Thomas Hugh MCRORIE, *b* at Gainesville, Florida 7 Sept 1962.
        2*d*●James Michael MCRORIE, *b* at Gainesville, Florida 6 Oct 1964.
        3*d*●Devon Lynn MCRORIE, *b* in Scotland 27 Nov 1967.
      2*c*●Hugh Larry MCRORIE [*Route 1, Box 1026, Mulberry, Florida 33860, USA*], *b* at Jacksonville 19 Dec 1938, *m* at Lakeland, Florida 19 July 1972, ●Camie McClelland.
    2*b* Hugh Moultrie GRIFFIN, Jr, *b* at Waldo, Florida 18 Sept 1911; *dunm* at Gainesville 3 June 1951.
    3*b*●Helen Martha GRIFFIN [*Box 297, Waldo, Florida 32694, USA*], *b* at Waldo, Florida 21 May 1914, *m* 1st, Marcus Daughtry; and 2ndly 16 July 1945 (*m* diss by div 1973), Horace L. Mock.
    4*b*●Richard Eppes GRIFFIN [*Box 151, Waldo, Florida 32694, USA*], *b* at Waldo 2 June 1921, *m* at Clayton, Georgia 30 March 1946, ●Eva Ruth (*b* at

Abbeville, S Carolina 16 March 1925), dau of Bennett G. Campbell, by his wife Essie, and has issue,
  1*c*●Margaret Jeanette GRIFFIN [*620 SE Fourth Avenue, Gainesville, Florida 32601, USA*], *b* at Gainesville 12 March 1947, *m* at Waldo 2 Sept 1967 (*m* diss by div 1973), ●Martin Fryer.
  2*c*●Evely Ann GRIFFIN, *b* at Jacksonville 21 Jan 1949, *m* at Waldo 22 Jan 1970, ●Sammy Walden (*b* in N Carolina 20 Jan 1948) [*1404 E Lemon Street, Goldsboro, North Carolina, USA*].
  3*c*●Sherry Lee GRIFFIN, *b* at Gainesville 16 Aug 1950, *m* 28 Jan 1972, ●David A. Edwards, and has issue,
    ●Ranee Lynn EDWARDS, *b* at Goldsboro, N Carolina 5 Jan 1974.
  5*b*●Cladie Ruth GRIFFIN, *b* at Waldo, Florida 5 June 1923, *m* there 13 Feb 1943, ●William Clyde Dees (*b* in Florida 21 Sept 1923) [*4716 SW 56th Terrace, Gainesville, Florida 32608, USA*], son of Marvin C. Dees, by his wife Minnie, and has issue,
    1*c*●Margaret Elizabeth DEES, *b* at Jacksonville, Florida 25 Nov 1943, *m* 1st 2 June 1962 (*m* diss by div 1972), Clayton Averitte Jones, and has issue,
      1*d*●Clayton Averitte JONES, Jr, *b* 31 Jan 1963.
      2*d*●James Edward JONES, *b* 1 Jan 1964.
    Margaret Elizabeth Dees *m* 2ndly 1972, ●Horace De Wayne Bruce (*b* 11 June 1941) [*5024 SW 66th Street, Gainesville, Florida 32608, USA*].
    2*c*●William Clyde DEES, *b* at Gainesville 27 Feb 1947, *m* 1st Dec 1966 (*m* diss by div 1968), Sharon Ann Kennedy, and has issue,
      1*d*●Louie Ann DEES, *b* 12 July 1967.
    William Clyde Dees *m* 2ndly, ●Carolyn J. Beazlie, and by her has issue,
      2*d*●Brenda Renée DEES, *b* 8 Sept 1969.
3*a* Francis EPPES, *b* 1887; *dunm*.
4*a* Thomas Jefferson EPPES, *b* 1890, *m* 29 March 1914, Nannie Edrie Bowen, and had issue,
  1*b*●Thomas Jefferson EPPES, Jr [*Tampo, Florida, USA*], *b* 24 Aug 1916, *m* 1944, ●Kathleen Newton, and has issue,
    1*c*●Rosemary Edrie EPPES.
    2*c*●Rebecca Diane EPPES.
  2*b*●Francis Edward (Jack) EPPES (Rev), of Jacksonville, Florida, *b* 17 Oct 1917.
  3*b*●Richard Llewellyn EPPES, *b* 27 Jan 1919, *m* 15 July 1944, ●Estelle Brewer, and has issue, ●Wanda EPPES, *b* 11 Oct 1945.
  4*b*●James Alfred EPPES, *b* 24 Jan 1921, *m* ●Martha Ann Stelts (*b* 1927), and has issue,
    1*c*●Marguerite EPPES, *b* 9 Sept 1945.
    2*c*●Susan Bradford EPPES, *b* 23 Feb 1947.
    3*c*●Martha Lucille EPPES, *b* 18 Jan 1950.
  5*b*●Nicholas Ware EPPES, *b* 4 Nov 1923, *m* 4 Oct 1952, ●Bette Fletcher.
5*a*●Sarah Ruth EPPES [*111 South Boulevard Street, Tallahassee, Florida 32301, USA*], *b* 1894.
(13) Caroline Matilda EPPES, *b* 1857, *m* 30 Oct 1882, David Shepard Shine, and *d* 20 Jan 1940, having had issue,
  1*a* Dudley Shepard SHINE, *b* 19 Dec 1885, *m* 29 Dec 1909, Theodosia Bellamy (who *m* 2ndly, Cyril Norman Boland), only dau of George Morrison, by his wife Mary Eppes (*see above, p 123*), and *d* June 1933, leaving issue,
    1*b*●Dudley Shepard SHINE, Jr, *b* 17 July 1914, *m* 4 March 1936, ●Margaret Pinkham, and has issue,
      1*c*●Dudley Shepard SHINE III, *b* 22 Feb 1938.
      2*c*●Randolph SHINE, *b* 3 April 1942.
    2*b*●Theodosia Morrison SHINE, *b* 5 June 1916, *m* ●Dean Rader, and has issue,
      ●Randolph RADER, *b* 22 Oct 1945.
  2*a* Wharton Hume SHINE, *b* 1887; *d* 1888.
  3*a* Dr Cecil Eppes SHINE, *b* 28 Sept 1888, *m* 13 Dec 1917, Alice Munnerlyn (*b* 21 July 1889; *d* 29 June 1953), and *d* 7 Dec 1963, leaving issue,
    1*b*●Cecil Eppes SHINE, Jr, *b* 11 June 1919, *m* ●Jessie Jones, and has issue,
      1*c*●Elizabeth Eppes SHINE, *b* 27 Oct 1946.
      2*c*●Cecil Eppes SHINE III, *b* 11 Nov 1948.
      3*c*●Marilyn SHINE, *b* 23 July 1951.
    2*b*●Sarah Coachman SHINE, *b* 13 Jan 1931, *m* 7 Sept

1946, ●Jesse Miller, and had issue,
  1c●Daniel Wayne MILLER, b 22 Aug 1947.
  2c●Jane MILLER, b 27 Oct 1950.
  3c●David Wendell MILLER, b 18 Aug 1954.
  3b●Caroline Eppes SHINE, b 9 Feb 1926, m 6 May 1950, ●Judson Marshall, and has issue,
  ●Sarah Alice MARSHALL, b 11 July 1955.
  4b●James Munnerlyn SHINE, b 14 Jan 1928, m 12 March 1955, ●Mary Julia Tonnisen, and has issue,
  1c●James Munnerlyn SHINE, Jr, b 8 April 1958.
  2c●Wallace Tonnisen SHINE, b 28 Dec 1959.
  3a●Margaret Virginia SHINE, b 15 Jan 1890, m 15 July

1917, Harold M. Wilson (d 1955), and has had issue,
  1b Margaret Shine WILSON, b and d 10 Feb 1920.
  2b●Margaret Virginia WILSON, b 17 Sept 1921, m Guy Bailey, and has issue,
  ●Susan Ware BAILEY, b 1953.
  5a Lillias Eleanor SHINE, b and d 1895.
3 Maria Jefferson EPPES, b at Edgehill 15 Feb 1804; d July 1807.
5 Lucy Elizabeth JEFFERSON, b at Monticello 3 Nov 1780; d there 15 April 1781.
6 Lucy Elizabeth JEFFERSON, b at Monticello 8 May 1782; d of whooping cough at Eppington ca 13 Oct 1784.

# The Brothers and Sisters of President Jefferson

1 Jane JEFFERSON, b at Shadwell 27 June 1740; dunm 1 Oct 1765.

2 Mary JEFFERSON, b at Shadwell 1 Oct 1741, m 24 June 1760, Col John Bolling, of Chestnut Grove, Chesterfield County, Virginia (a descendant of Pocahontas), and d 1817, leaving issue, one son.

3 Elizabeth JEFFERSON, b at Shadwell 4 Nov 1744; dunm 1 Jan 1773.

4 Martha JEFFERSON, b at Tuckahoe 29 May 1746, m 20 July 1765, Dabney Carr (b 26 Oct 1743; d at Charlottesville 16 May 1773; bur Monticello), son of John Carr, of Louisa County, Virginia, by his wife Barbara, and d 3 Sept 1811 (bur Monticello), having had issue, three sons and three daus. Her yst son Dabney Carr (1773-1837) became a Judge of the Virginia Court of Appeals, and his yst dau Jane Cary Carr (1809-1858) m Rev Peyton Randolph Harrison, of Clifton, Cumberland County, Virginia, son of Randolph Harrison, a 1st cousin of President William Henry Harrison (qv).

5 Peter Field JEFFERSON, b at Tuckahoe 16 Oct, d there 29 Nov 1748.

6 A boy, b and d at Tuckahoe 9 March 1750.

7 Lucy JEFFERSON, b at Tuckahoe 10 Oct 1752, m 12 Sept 1769, her 1st cousin Col Charles Lilburn Lewis, Jr, of Buck Island, Virginia, son of Charles Lilburn Lewis, by his wife Mary Randolph, and had issue, one son and five daus.

8 Anna Scott JEFFERSON, b at Shadwell 1 Oct 1755, m Oct 1788, Hastings Marks (d ca 1813), son of Peter Marks, and d 1828.

9 Randolph JEFFERSON, of Snowden, Buckingham County, Virginia, b at Shadwell 1 Oct 1755 (twin with Anna Scott), m 1st 30 July 1781, his 1st cousin Anna, dau of Charles Lilburn Lewis, by his wife Mary Randolph, and had issue, three sons and one dau (Anna Scott Jefferson, who m Col Zachariah Nevil (d 1830), mem of the House of Reps from Nelson County, and had issue). Randolph Jefferson m 2ndly Mitchie B. Pryor, sister of Nicholas B. Pryor, and d at Snowden 7 March 1815, having by her had issue, one son.

# Notes

[1] The lineage is based largely on *The Ancestry of Thomas Jefferson,* by Olivia Taylor, published in *Collected Papers to Commemorate Fifty Years of the Monticello Association of the Descendants of Thomas Jefferson* (1965). Jefferson himself believed his family to be of Welsh descent and to have come from the Snowdon area, and it was in this belief that his brother Randolph (*see p 127*) named his property Snowden (*sic*).

[2] Through the Randolph family President Jefferson derived a Royal descent from David I, King of Scots (*see* APPENDIX C, PRESIDENTS OF ROYAL DESCENT) and also a relationship to John Marshall, the first Chief Justice of the US Supreme Court (*see* APPENDIX D, SOME REMARKABLE KINSHIPS). The intermarriages between the Jeffersons and Randolphs were many and complex.

# James Madison
## 1751-1836

———

4th President of the
United States of America
1809-1817

JAMES MADISON, 4TH PRESIDENT

# James Madison

## 1751-1836

### 4th President of the United States of America
### 1809-1817

MADISON HAS two quite distinct reputations. The first in the history books praises him as perhaps the most acute political theorist the United States has ever produced. When he arrived in Philadelphia in 1787 as a Virginia delegate to the Constitutional Convention, Madison had spent most of the past seven years in reading and thinking about government. He had also experienced government at first hand, as a member of the Continental Congress and the Virginia legislature. He was convinced that the United States faced disaster under the Articles of Confederation. He had analyzed the weakness of other confederacies, ancient and modern.

Other delegates shared Madison's view that the United States must create a stronger instrument of government; that there should be two houses of Congress, instead of the existing single chamber, and a separate executive branch; that the large states (including Virginia) must have a bigger say (under the Articles each state had only one vote); and that whatever new Constitution was devised, it must be ratified by the people, not by legislatures. But no one had pondered these problems as thoroughly as Madison. "Every Person", said one of Madison's Philadelphia associates, "seems to acknowledge his greatness. He blends together the profound politician, with the Scholar. In the management of every great question he evidently took the lead in the Convention, and tho' he cannot be called an Orator, he is a most agreeable, eloquent, and convincing Speaker. . . . The affairs of the United States, he perhaps, has the most correct knowledge of, of any Man in the Union".

Madison's fame as a well-grounded theorist rests with posterity still more upon the brilliantly cool and cogent essays he wrote pseudonymously, in company with Alexander Hamilton and John Jay, as *The Federalist*. These papers, produced in a hurry to encourage ratification in New York, are usually regarded as a classic, indeed *the* classic American contribution to the world's literature on the art and science of government; and the best were Madison's pieces, such as his celebrated *Federalist No. 10*, which explained that various economic groups must inevitably collide, so that the task of government was to mediate between them. In the next decade, the 1790s, Madison once more became involved in practical politics. No longer an exponent of federal supremacy, he was one of the architects of America's first system of constitutional opposition, in the shape of Jeffersonian Republicanism. In fact the cardinal principles of Jeffersonianism, and its political strategies, might well have been called Madisonianism. From his seat in the House of Representatives Madison defined a following for Jefferson, and persuaded his friend into leadership. He became Jefferson's Secretary of State in 1801, and the President signified in 1808 that Madison ought to succeed him.

Somewhere during these years the first Madison reputation shades into the second. In the second portrait he ceases to appear as the shrewd, omniscient "grey eminence". Instead he is characterized as the "withered little apple-John" of Washington Irving's much-quoted phrase: literally and figuratively insignificant, lost in the crush of White House receptions while the guests thronged round his ebullient wife Dolley, harassed and blundering in his conduct of affairs. Along with Jefferson he had been held responsible for the strains of neutrality during the Napoleonic Wars. Both were pilloried for the failure of their Embargo policy. Historians still debate that between the main combatants Britain was a worse enemy than France. Madison, who eventually recommended a declaration of war in June 1812, probably could not have withstood Congressional pressure even if he had wanted to. But, except for some naval victories, the war went badly for the United States. The peace of Ghent, signed between Britain and America in December 1814, covered none of the points for which the war was supposed to have been fought. The British held most of Maine, dominated the Atlantic seaboard, and had driven the President out of Washington in a humiliating incursion. Federalist orators poured derision on "Mr Madison's War". New Englanders threatened secession. In October 1814, an eyewitness noted, Madison was looking "shattered and woe-begone . . . heart-broken". If the British Army under Lord Pakenham had defeated Andrew Jackson at New Orleans, as seemed likely, the Union might have collapsed. Madison would certainly have passed into the record as among the most disastrous of Presidents. In view of Jackson's sensational victory (two weeks after the peace was signed), Madison should perhaps be seen as among the luckiest of all the Presidents. The return of peace, and the rejoicings over Jackson's triumph, effaced the grim prospects of the previous months. Madison, hitherto the scapegoat for an apparently rash, mismanaged conflict, was able to leave office in 1817, if not exactly trailing clouds of glory, at any rate with reasonable credit. No one, however, has claimed he was a great

DOLLEY PAYNE TODD, MRS MADISON

President. On the whole he is judged as a courageous little man, no warrior by temperament, who as he afterward explained "knew the unprepared state of the country, but he esteemed it necessary to throw forward the flag of the country, sure that the people would press forward and defend it". Not all of them did, yet enough to save the day.

James Madison lived on at his Virginia home Montpelier (originally spelled Montpellier) until 1836, childless but solaced by the cheerful company of his wife, who was seventeen years his junior. Pensionless, he had to sell part of his land. He took part in occasional public service, including attendance at the Virginia Constitutional Convention of 1829. He sorted out his papers. Among these were the confidential notes he had kept of the Philadelphia debates of 1787—our best source today for what went on behind those closed doors. The English writer Harriet Martineau, visiting Montpelier in 1835, found him physically enfeebled but still mentally alert, and full of "inexhaustible faith . . . that a well-founded commonwealth may . . . be immortal". Having never been easy in his mind about owning Negro slaves, he hoped that the American commonwealth would somehow cease to be based upon this "calamity". Otherwise the old Founding Father, reviewing the past sixty years, could conclude that providence must have been guiding the new nation—aided by some timely interventions by James Madison.

# Chronology

1751    Born at Port Conway, King George County, Virginia 16 March (5 March 1750/1 *os*).

1762-67 Attended Donald Robertson's school at Innes Plantation, King and Queen County, Virginia.

1767-69 Tutored at home by Rev Thomas Martin.

1769    Entered College of New Jersey (now Princeton Univ), Princeton, New Jersey Aug.

1771    Graduated with baccalaureate degree 29 Sept.

1772    Left College April and returned home to Montpelier, Orange County, Virginia.

1774    Travelled to Pennsylvania and New York May-June; elected to Orange County Committee of Safety (of which his father was Chairman) 2 Dec.

1775    Address to Capt Patrick Henry and the Gentlemen Independents of Hanover (probably written by Madison) 9 May; commissioned Col of Orange County Militia 2 Oct.

1776    Elected Orange County Delegate to Virginia Convention at Williamsburg 25 April; Convention met 6 May; served on committee to draft State Constitution; Constitution adopted 29 June; Constitution adjourned 5 July; elected to first House of Delegates, Lower House of State Assembly 7 Oct.

1777    Defeated for re-election to House of Delegates 24 April; elected by General Assembly to Virginia Council of State 15 Nov.

1778    Took seat in Council of State 14 Jan and served under Governors Patrick Henry and Thomas Jefferson; election to House of Delegates rejected because he was serving on Council of State 27 May.

1779    Declined election by General Assembly as Delegate to Continental Congress 16 June; elected a Virginia Delegate to second Continental Congress 14 Dec.

1780    Took seat in Continental Congress (being its youngest member) 20 March.

1783    Term as Delegate to Continental Congress ended 25 Oct.

1784    Re-elected to House of Delegates and served until 1786.

1786    Attended Annapolis Convention 11 Sept; re-elected to second Continental Congress.

1787    Took seat in Continental Congress, New York City Feb; arrived in Philadelphia for Convention 3 May; Constitutional Convention opened 25 May; played a prominent part in the debates earning himself the name of "Father of the Constitution"; signed the Constitution 17 Sept.

| | |
|---|---|
| 1788 | Elected to Virginia Convention to consider ratification of the Constitution March; Convention met 2 June; Constitution ratified 26 June; defeated for election to Senate Oct. |
| 1789 | Elected to House of Representatives 2 Feb; took seat 6 April; served in 1st, 2nd, 3rd and 4th Congresses. |
| 1798 | Drafted Virginia Resolutions (adopted by Virginia legislature 24 Dec). |
| 1799 | Re-elected to House of Delegates 24 April. |
| 1801 | Appointed Secretary of State by President Jefferson 5 March; took office 2 May. |
| 1808 | Nominated for President by a congressional caucus of Democratic-Republicans 23 Jan; elected President by 122 electoral votes as opposed to 47 for Charles Cotesworth Pinckney, the Federalist candidate and 6 for George Clinton (vice-presidential candidate with Madison) 7 Dec. |
| 1809 | Electoral votes tabulated by Congress and Madison officially declared elected 8 Feb; resigned as Secretary of State 3 March; inaugurated as 4th President of the United States of America in the chamber of the House of Representatives in the Capitol, Washington 4 March; issued proclamation terminating Non-Intercourse Act, renewing trade with Great Britain 19 April; issued proclamation legalizing trade with Great Britain 28 June; renewed Non-Intercourse Act 9 Aug; sent first State of the Union message to Congress 29 Nov. |
| 1810 | Signed Act banning British and French armed vessels from US waters 1 May; issued proclamation on taking possession of West Florida from Mississippi to Perdido Rivers as part of the Louisiana Purchase 27 Oct; sent second State of the Union message to Congress 5 Dec. |
| 1811 | Authorized by Congress in secret session to take possession of East Florida if local authorities consented or a foreign power attempted to occupy 15 Jan; vetoed Bill to incorporate Alexandria, Virginia church 21 Feb; vetoed Mississippi Church Land Grant Bill 28 Feb; sent third State of the Union message to Congress 5 Nov. |
| 1812 | Purchased papers purporting to show disaffection of New England States from John Henry, a political adventurer, for \$50,000 10 Feb; laid papers before Congress 9 March; vetoed Bill regulating trials in district courts 3 April; authorized to call on States and Territories for respective quotas of 100,000 militia for six months' service 10 April; Louisiana admitted as 18th State 30 April; re-nominated for Presidency by Democratic-Republicans 18 May; sent war message to Congress 1 June; issued proclamation of declaration of war against Great Britain 19 June; sent fourth State of the Union message to Congress 4 Nov; refused to sign Naturalization Bill; re-elected President by 128 electoral votes as opposed to 89 for De Witt Clinton, candidate of an anti-Administration faction of the Democratic-Republican party. |
| 1813 | Electoral votes tabulated by Congress and Madison officially declared elected 10 Feb; inaugurated for second term in the Chamber of the House of Representatives 4 March; sent Albert Gallatin and James A. Bayard to St Petersburg as Peace Commissioners to discuss offer to mediate by Emperor Alexander I of Russia; British declined offer of mediation 5 July (before Commissioners arrived in St Petersburg); British offered to negotiate for peace directly with US 4 Nov; sent fifth State of the Union message to Congress 7 Dec; signed Embargo Act 17 Dec. |

1814      British offer received at Washington 3 Jan; signed Act repealing Embargo and Non-Importation Acts 14 April; American and British peace commissions met at Ghent, Belgium 8 Aug; White House, Capitol, and all government buildings except Patent Office burnt by the British 24-25 Aug in retaliation for burning of York (now Toronto), Ontario, Canada by US forces on 27 April 1813; Madison and cabinet fled to Virginia; returned to Washington 27 Aug; sent sixth State of the Union message to Congress 20 Sept; peace treaty with Great Britain signed at Ghent 24 Dec.

1815      Battle of New Orleans 8 Jan; vetoed Bill to incorporate Bank of US 30 Jan; peace treaty unanimously ratified by Senate 15 Feb; issued proclamation ending War of 1812 17 Feb; treaty signed with Dey of Algiers 30 June (concluded 3 July); sent seventh State of the Union message to Congress 5 Dec.

1816      Sent eighth and last State of the Union message to Congress 3 Dec.

1817      Signed Act establishing Alabama Territory 3 March; vetoed Internal Improvements Bill for federally subsidized highway and canal system 3 March; attended inauguration of his successor President Monroe 4 March; left Washington for his estate at Montpelier, Virginia April.

1818      Addressed Agricultural Society of Albemarle (of which he was President) 12 May.

1824      Visited by Lafayette Nov.

1826      Succeeded Jefferson as member of board of rectors of University of Virginia.

1834      Served as Delegate to Virginia Constitutional Convention.

1836      Died of debility at Montpelier, Orange County, Virginia 28 June; buried there.

# The Writings of President Madison

*Writings*, edited by Gaillard Hunt, 9 vols (1900-10)

# Lineage of President Madison

JOHN MADISON, a ship's carpenter from Gloucester, received grants of land in Virginia from 1653, and *d ante* 16 April 1683, leaving issue,

JOHN MADISON, Sheriff of King and Queen County, Virginia 1714, *m* Isabella Minor Todd, and had, with other issue,

AMBROSE MADISON, *m* 29 Aug 1721, Frances (*b* 1700; *d* 25 Nov 1761), dau of James Taylor, of Hare Forest, Orange County, Virginia, by his wife Martha Thompson[1], and *d* 1732 (will dated 31 July 1732, *pr* 6 Feb 1732/3), leaving, with other issue,

JAMES MADISON, of Orange County, Virginia, planter and farmer, Lieut of Orange County, *b* probably in Orange County 27 March 1723, *m* 15 Sept 1749, Eleanor (Nelly) Rose (*b* in Caroline County, Virginia 9 Jan 1731; *d* at Montpelier, Orange County, Virginia 11 Feb 1829), dau of Francis Conway[2], by his wife Rebecca Catlett, and *d* at Montpelier, Orange County, Virginia 27 Feb 1801, leaving, with other issue (*see* BROTHERS AND SISTERS OF PRESIDENT MADISON, *p 139*), an eldest son,

JAMES MADISON, **4th President of the United States of America.**

# President Madison's Wife and Stepchildren

JAMES MADISON *m* at the house of her sister Lucy (Mrs George Steptoe Washington—*see p 53*), Harewood, nr Charles Town, Jefferson County, Virginia 15 Sept 1794, Dolley (*b* in Guilford County, N Carolina 20 May 1768; *d* at Washington, DC 12 July 1849, *bur* first at the Congressional Cemetery, Washington, later removed to Montpelier, Orange County, Virginia), widow of John Todd, Jr, and eldest dau of John Payne, of Scotchtown, Hanover County, Virginia, by his wife Mary, dau of William Coles, of Coles Hill, Hanover County, Virginia.

There were no children of the marriage and thus there are *no descendants* in the direct line from President Madison. Mrs Madison, however, had *m* 1st at Philadelphia 7 Jan 1790, John Todd, Jr (*d* 24 Oct 1793), and had issue (President Madison's step-children),

1 John Payne TODD, *b* at Philadelphia 29 Feb 1792; *dunm.*
2 A son, *b* Oct 1793; *d* two weeks after his father Nov 1793.

# The Brothers and Sisters of President Madison

**1** Francis MADISON, *b* 1753, *m* 1772, Susanna Bell, and *d* 1800, having had issue, three sons (or five according to a family tree drawn up by President Madison and now in the Library of Congress) and five daus.

**2** Ambrose MADISON, Capt 3rd Virginia Regt, *b* 1755, *m ca* 1780, Mary Willis Lee (*d* 1798), and *d* 1793, leaving issue (with one other dau according to the family tree mentioned above), Nelly Conway MADISON, *m* John Willis, MD (*d* 1812), and *d* 1865, leaving issue,

　(1) John WILLIS, *m* 1838, his 2nd cousin Lucy Taliaferro (*b* 1820; *d* 1868), eldest dau of Major Ambrose Madison, of Woodbury Forest, Virginia, by his wife Jane Bankhead Willis (*see below, p 141*), and *d* 1885, leaving issue,

　　1*a* Mary Lee WILLIS, *b* 1840; *dunm* 1908.

　　2*a* Jane Champe WILLIS, *m* Major John D. Richardson, and had issue,

　　　1*b* Maria Jane RICHARDSON, *b* 1877, *m* 1907, George Lauman Pollock, of Chicago, and had issue,

　　　　1*c* Janie Willis POLLOCK, *b* 1909; *d* 1912.

　　　　2*c* ● Margaret Lee POLLOCK, *b* 1914.

　　　2*b* Lucy Lee RICHARDSON, *b* 1878, *m* 1918, her 1st cousin Lewis Byrd Willis (*b* 1884), only son of William Byrd Willis, by his wife Nelly Conway Willis (*see below, p 141*).

　　　3*b* Ambrose Madison RICHARDSON, *b* 1880, *m* 1912, Louise McDonald, and had issue,

　　　　1*c* ● Irving RICHARDSON, *b* 1914.

　　　　2*c* ● Ambrose Madison RICHARDSON, *b* 1916.

　　　　3*c* ● Louise RICHARDSON, *b* 1919.

　　　4*b* Alice Balmaine RICHARDSON, *b* 1882, *m* 1909, Philip Brown Shillito, and had issue,

　　　　● Jane Champe SHILLITO, *b* 1917.

　　3*a* John Willis, *m* 1st 1866, Lucie Robinson, and had issue,

　　　1*b* James Shephard WILLIS, *b* 1867, *m* 1891, Evelyn McDonald, and *d* 1908, leaving issue,

　　　　George WILLIS.

　　John Willis *m* 2ndly 1870, Mary Elizabeth Lupton, and by her had issue,

　　　2*b* Lucie Madison WILLIS, *b* 1871, *m* 1901, Moncure Robinson Taylor (*b* 23 Feb 1851; *d* 7 Dec 1915), son of John Charles Randolph Taylor, by his wife Martha Jefferson Randolph, and had issue (*see* DESCENDANTS OF PRESIDENT JEFFERSON, *p 106*).

　　　3*b* Bessie Milton WILLIS, *b* 1873; *dunm* 1926.

　　　4*b* Nellie Ross WILLIS, *b* 1875; *d* 1892.

　　　5*b* John Byrd WILLIS, *b* 1877, *m* 1908, Verna Gabbert, and had issue,

　　　　● Mary Francis WILLIS, *b* 1909, *m* ● Frederick K. Keisker.

　　　6*b* Annie Scott WILLIS, *b* 1879.

　　　7*b* William Taylor WILLIS (Rev), Rector of St Luke's Church, Norfolk, Virginia, *b* 1885, *m* 1917, Gertrude Scott Hendrix, and had issue,

　　　　● William Taylor WILLIS, *b* 1920.

　　4*a* Claudia Marshall WILLIS, *m* 1869, William Wallace Scott, and had issue,

　　　1*b* Philip Henshaw SCOTT, *m* Martha M. Leitch, and had issue,

　　　　1*c* Philip Henshaw SCOTT, Jr, *d* aged 11.

　　　　2*c* Martha M. SCOTT, *m* William S. Belfield.

　　　　3*c* William Wallace SCOTT, *dunm* aged 25.

　　　　4*c* Meredith SCOTT.

　　　　5*c* John SCOTT.

　　　2*b* Claudia Dennis SCOTT, *m* 1st, Dr Robert Sylvester Blakeman; and 2ndly, Thomas Edwin Grimsley.

　　　3*b* Robert Lewis Madison SCOTT, *dunm* 1918.

　　　4*b* Ellen Ritchie SCOTT, *m* 1901, Rev James Jeffries Chapman, and had issue,

　　　　1*c* ● Claudia Marshall Willis CHAPMAN, *m* ● Hugh Wood Roger, and has issue,

　　　　　1*d* ● Edwin Dennis ROGER.

　　　　　2*d* ● Robin D. ROGER.

　　　　2*c* ● Dennis Scott CHAPMAN.

　　　　3*c* ● James Jeffries CHAPMAN, Jr.

　　　　4*c* ● Ellen Ritchie CHAPMAN, *m* 1933, ● John I. Woodriff.

　　　　5*c* ● Marijane Stewart CHAPMAN.

　　　　6*c* ● Josephine J. CHAPMAN.

　　　　7*c* ● William Wallace Scott CHAPMAN.

　　　5*b* Garrett Willis SCOTT, *m* Alice S. Shields, and *d* 1927, leaving issue,

　　　　1*c* ● Wyklif SCOTT.

　　　　2*c* ● Willis Shields SCOTT.

　　　　3*c* ● Garrett SCOTT.

　　　　4*c* ● Harriet S. SCOTT.

　　　6*b* Wyklif SCOTT, *dunm* 1906.

　　　7*b* Caroline Barbour SCOTT, *m* Joseph Hayward Stratton, and *d* 1918, leaving issue,

　　　　1*c* ● Caroline Barbour STRATTON.

　　　　2*c* ● Joseph Hayward STRATTON, Jr.

　　　8*b* John SCOTT, *dunm* 1933.

　　5*a* Nelly Conway WILLIS, *m* 1877, William Byrd Willis, and had issue,

　　　1*b* Jane Bailey WILLIS, *b* 1879, *m* 1906, Norbert Edward Mulick, and had issue,

　　　　1*c* ● Norbert Edward MULICK, Jr, *b* 1907.

　　　　2*c* ● Margaret Lee MULICK, *b* 1909.

　　　　3*c* ● Dorothy Madison MULICK, *b* 1909 (twin with her sister Margaret Lee Mulick), *m* 1930, Nicholas K. Lyons, and has issue,

　　　　　● Florence Lee LYONS, *b* 1931.

　　　2*b* Lewis Byrd WILLIS, *b* 1884, *m* 1918, his 1st cousin Lucy Lee (*b* 1879), 2nd dau of Major John D. Richardson, by his wife Jane Champe Willis (*see above*), and *dsp*.

　　　3*b* Mary Lee WILLIS, *b* 1886, *m* 1911, John William Browning.

　　6*a* Lucy Cornelia WILLIS, *b* 1851, *m* 1880, Charles Norris (*d* 1910), and *dsp*.

　　7*a* Ambrose Madison WILLIS, *m* Maude Bagley, and had issue,

　　　David Madison WILLIS, *m* Clothoe Newcomb, and had issue,

　　　　1*c* ● Newcomb WILLIS, *b* 1914.

　　　　2*c* ● David Madison WILLIS, Jr, Major US Army.

　　　　3*c* ● Barbara WILLIS.

8a Andrew Johnson WILLIS (Rev), *m* 1st, Margaret Mitchell, and had issue,
　1b John Mitchell WILLIS, *m* Anne Gibson, and had issue,
　　●John Mitchell WILLIS, Jr, *b* 1916.
　2b Andrew Hunter WILLIS, *m* Elizabeth Sheldon, and had issue,
　　1c●Andrew Hunter WILLIS, Jr, *b* 1916.
　　2c●Mary Elizabeth WILLIS, *b* 1919.
　　3c●Edward WILLIS, *b* 1921.
　3b Margaret WILLIS, *m* Floyd Bliven, and had issue,
　　1c●Floyd BLIVEN, Jr, *b* 1921.
　　2c●Andrew BLIVEN.
　　3c●Margaret BLIVEN.
Rev Andrew Johnson Willis *m* 2ndly, Georgette Strider.
(2) Mary Lee WILLIS, *m* Col John Hancock Lee, of Orange, Virginia, and had issue,
　1a Nelly LEE, *dunm.*
　2a Lucy LEE, *dunm.*
　3a Letitia Ramolino LEE, *m* Robert Madison, MD, and had issue,
　　1b Mary MADISON.
　　2b Letitia MADISON.
**3** Catlett MADISON, *b* and *d* 1758.
**4** Nelly Conway MADISON, *b* 1760, *m* 1783, Major Isaac Hite, Jr, of Belle Grove, Virginia (*b* 1758; *d* 1836), son of Isaac Hite, and *d* 1802, having had issue,
　1 James Madison HITE, *b* 1788; *d* 1791.
　2 Nelly Conway HITE, *b* 1789, *m* 1809, Cornelius Baldwin, MD (*b* 1791; *d* 1849), and had issue,
　　(1) Eleanor Conway BALDWIN, *m* 1835, Edward Jaquelin Davison (*b* 1805), and had issue,
　　　1a Eleanor Cornelia DAVISON, *b* 1836, *m* 1855, John H. Pedigo (*b* 1823), and had issue,
　　　　1b Eleanor Conway PEDIGO, *b* 1857, *m* 1880, John Warren Edwards (*b* 1842), and had issue,
　　　　　1c Ann Eleanor EDWARDS, *b* 1881, *m* 1898, Herbert Martin Grandon, and had issue,
　　　　　　1d●Herbert Martin GRANDON, *b* 1899.
　　　　　　2d●Eleanor Katherine GRANDON, *b* 1901.
　　　　　2c Mabel Pedigo EDWARDS, *b* 1885; *d* 1893.
　　　　　3c John Cummins EDWARDS, *b* 1892.
　　　　　4c Maury EDWARDS, *b* 1896.
　　　　2b Lallie Louis PEDIGO, *b* 1859.
　　　　3b Jenny Grey PEDIGO, *b* 1861.
　　　　4b Robert Edward PEDIGO, *b* 1863.
　　　　5b Norborne Elijah PEDIGO, *b* 1865.
　　　　6b Mack Henry PEDIGO, *b* 1867.
　　　　7b Mary Louisa PEDIGO, *b* 1870.
　　　　8b John Hardin PEDIGO, *b* 1871.
　　　　9b Ann Maury PEDIGO, *b* 1878.
　　　　10b Jessie Davison PEDIGO, *b* 1880.
　　　2a Mary Baldwin DAVISON, *b* 1837; *d* 1846.
　　　3a Edward Jaquelin DAVISON, Jr, *b* 1842; *d* 1844.
　　　4a Judge William Smith DAVISON, *b* 1845, *m* 1876, Anna Maria Davison (*b* 1848), and *d* 1904, having had issue,
　　　　1b Edmonia Louisa DAVISON, *b* 1881.
　　　　2b Cecil Armstrong DAVISON, *b* 1883; *d* 1888.
　　　　3b Fontaine Hite DAVISON, *b* 1884.
　　　　4b Joseph William DAVISON, *b* 1888.
　　　　5b Anna DAVISON, *b* and *d* 1894.
　　　5a Edmonia Louise DAVISON, *b* 1848; *d* 1856.
　　(2) Mary Briscoe BALDWIN, missionary of the Protestant Episcopal Church, *b* 1811; *dunm* 1877.
　　(3) Isaac Hite BALDWIN, MD, Assist Surg US Army, *b* 1813, *m*, and *dsp* 1882.
　　(4) Ann Maury BALDWIN, *b* 1817, *m* 1844, Isaac Hite Hay, lawyer, US Consul at Jaffa, and had issue,
　　　John Baldwin HAY, US Consul-Gen in Constantinople, *b* 1845, *m* Cornelia Badger (*d* 1879), and had issue, with three other children,
　　　　1b Alice HAY, *m* John Leeds.
　　　　2b Errol HAY.
　　(5) James Madison BALDWIN, *m*, and had issue,
　　　1a Hite BALDWIN.
　　　2a Mary BALDWIN.
　　　3a Briscoe BALDWIN.
　　　4a Ann BALDWIN.
　　　5a Eleanor BALDWIN.
　　(6) Robert Stuart BALDWIN, MD, Surg CSA, *b* 1824, *m*

Letitia Jane Speck (*b* 1824), and had issue,
　　　1a Cornelius Hite BALDWIN, *b* 1846; *d* 1864.
　　　2a Robert Stuart BALDWIN, Jr, lawyer, *b* 1848.
　　　3a Frederica Briscoe BALDWIN, *b* 1850; *dunm* 1883.
　　　4a Augusta Madison BALDWIN, *b* 1852, *m* 1875, Thomas L. Watts, and had issue,
　　　　Mary Baldwin WATTS, *b* 1879.
　　　5a William Daniel BALDWIN, *b* 1856; *d* young.
　　　6a Martha Daniel BALDWIN, *b* 1865; *dunm* 1883.
**3** James Madison HITE, *b* 1793, *m* 1815, Matilda Irvine, and *d* 1860, leaving issue,
　(1) Caroline Matilda HITE, *m* Alexander Baker, and had issue, with six other children,
　　1a Alexander BAKER.
　　2a Lillian BAKER.
　(2) Isaac Irvine HITE, *b* 1820, *m* 1st 1838, Susan Meade, and had issue, with two other children,
　　1a William Meade HITE.
　　2a Isaac Irvine HITE, Jr.
　　3a Susan HITE, *m* — Baker.
　　4a Mary Meade HITE, *m* — Baker.
　Isaac Irvine Hite *m* 2ndly, Ann Maria, widow of — Cutler, and dau of — Hopkins.
　(3) James Madison HITE, Jr, *m* 1849, Harriet Green Meade, and had issue,
　　1a Drayton Meade HITE.
　　2a Mattie HITE, *d* 1886.
　(4) Ann Eliza HITE, *b* 1831, *m* 1848, Thomas Julian Skinker, and had issue,
　　1a Thomas Julian SKINKER, Jr, *b* 1849, *m* 1872, Nannie Brown Rose.
　　2a Hampson SKINKER, *m* 1st, Maria Carr; and 2ndly, Annie Mai Kennerley, and had issue,
　　　1b Mary Clothilde SKINKER.
　　　2b Dorothy Ann SKINKER.
　　3a Cornelius Hite SKINKER, *m* 1888, Minnie Lee Gravey, and had issue,
　　　1b Howard SKINKER.
　　　2b Cornelius Hite SKINKER, Jr.
　　　3b Lois Evelyn SKINKER.
　　4a Hugh Garland SKINKER, *m* Annie Lee Rucker, and had issue,
　　　1b Hugh Garland SKINKER, Jr.
　　　2b Julian Hampson SKINKER.
　　　3b Susan Hite SKINKER.
**4** Frances Madison HITE, *m* James Lackland Ransom, and had issue,
　Georgianna Hite RANSOM, *b* in Jefferson County, Virginia, *ca* 1822, *m* at Charlestown, Virginia 22 Oct 1845, Benjamin Franklin Washington (*b* at Cedar Lawn, Jefferson County, Virginia 7 April 1820; *d* at San Francisco 22 Jan 1872), 3rd son of John Thornton Augustine Washington, by his wife Elizabeth Conrad Bedinger, and *d* at San Francisco 3 Dec 1860, having had issue (*see p 51*).
**5** William MADISON, of Woodbury Forest, Virginia, Gen US Army, served in the War of Independence as Lieut of Artillery, *b* 1762, *m* 1783, Frances Throckmorton (*b* 1765; *d* 1832), and *d* 1843, having had issue,
　1 Rebecca Conway MADISON, *b* 1795, *m* 1803, Reynolds Chapman, of Berry Hill, Orange County, Virginia (*b* 1778; *d* 1844), and *d* 1860, leaving issue,
　　(1) William Madison CHAPMAN, *dunm.*
　　(2) Judge John Madison CHAPMAN, *b* 1810, *m* 1842, Susan Digges Cole, of Effingham, Prince William County, Virginia, and *d* 1879, leaving issue,
　　　1a Mary Ella CHAPMAN, *m* Dr Nathaniel Chapman, of Charles County, Maryland, Lieut CSA, and had issue,
　　　　1b Ridgely CHAPMAN.
　　　　2b Mary Sigismunda CHAPMAN.
　　　　3b Emma Boykin CHAPMAN, *m* Mitchell Smoot.
　　　　4b John Madison CHAPMAN.
　　　　5b Nathaniel CHAPMAN.
　　　　6b Cora CHAPMAN.
　　　　7b Helen CHAPMAN.
　　　　8b Minnie Thomas CHAPMAN.
　　　　9b John Webb CHAPMAN.
　　　2a Emma CHAPMAN, *m* 1st, Capt Robert V. Boykin, Hampton Legion, CSA, and had issue,
　　　　1b Virginia Young BOYKIN, *m* — Grant, of Norfolk, Virginia.

2*b* Mary Madison BOYKIN, *m* — Powers, of Washington, DC.

3*b* Robert V. BOYKIN, Jr, of Glymont, Charles County, Maryland.

Emma Chapman *m* 2ndly, Samuel Culver.

3*a* Constance CHAPMAN (twin with Emma), *d* an inf.

4*a* Susie Ashton CHAPMAN, *m* 1878, Calvin Perkins, of Memphis, Tennessee, lawyer, and had issue,

  1*b* Blakeney PERKINS, *b* 1880.

  2*b* Belle Moncure PERKINS, *b* 1881.

  3*b* Ashton Chapman PERKINS, *b* 1883.

  4*b* Mary Anderson PERKINS, *b* 1884.

  5*b* Louis Allen PERKINS, *b* 1885.

  6*b* William Alexander PERKINS, *b* 1886.

5*a* Sallie Foote Alexander CHAPMAN.

6*a* Belle CHAPMAN, *b* 1858, *m* 1878, William Moncure, of Richmond, Virginia (*b* 1851), and had issue,

  1*b* William MONCURE, MD, *b* 1880.

  2*b* Belle Perkins MONCURE, *b* 1882.

  3*b* Vivienne Daniel MONCURE, *b* 1885.

7*a* Ashton Alexander CHAPMAN, *b* 1867, *m* 1895, Nannie Eaton Gregory, of Oxford, N Carolina.

(3) Jane CHAPMAN, *m* Thomas Towles Slaughter, MD (*b* 1804; *d* 1890), and had issue,

1*a* Thomas Towles SLAUGHTER, Jr, *d* young.

2*a* Larkin SLAUGHTER, *d* Young.

3*a* A son, *d* an inf.

4*a* Reynolds Chapman SLAUGHTER, Capt of Engrs CSA, *m* Louis Lake, of Vicksburg, Mississippi.

5*a* Philip Peyton SLAUGHTER, Lt-Col CSA, *m* Emma Thompson, and had issue,

  Elizabeth Pendleton SLAUGHTER, *m* Lucien Smith, and had issue,

    Katherine Mercer SMITH.

6*a* Thomas Towles SLAUGHTER, CSA, *k* in the Seven Days Battle.

7*a* Alfred Edwin SLAUGHTER, MD, Surg 17th Virginia Regt CSA (Stonewall Bde), *b* 1839, *m* 1869, Eugenia Taylor (*b* 1842), and *d* 1893, leaving issue,

  1*b* Robert Carroll SLAUGHTER, *m* Lucy Lawrence Lyne, and had issue,

    1*c*● Lucy Lawrence SLAUGHTER, *b* 1923.

    2*c*● Jane Madison SLAUGHTER, *b* 1924.

    3*c*● Robert Carroll SLAUGHTER, Jr, *b* 1925.

  2*b* Jane Chapman SLAUGHTER, *m* Charles Forest Moore, and had issue,

    Donna MOORE, *m* John Matthews.

  3*b* Sadie Patton SLAUGHTER, *m* 1905, William Bane Snidow (*b* 1877), and had issue,

    1*c*● William Bane SNIDOW, Jr, *b* 1906.

    2*c*● Eugenia Tilghman SNIDOW, *b* 1907.

    3*c*● John Temple SNIDOW, *b* 1909.

    4*c*● Carroll SNIDOW, *b* 1916.

  4*b* Alfred Edwin SLAUGHTER, Jr.

8*a* Mercer SLAUGHTER, Lieut Fry's Battery CSA (Stonewall Bde), *b* 1844, *m* Mary Shepherd Bull, and *d* 1897, having had issue,

  1*b* Mary SLAUGHTER, *d* an inf.

  2*b* Vivian SLAUGHTER, Lieut 23rd Lond Regt (Queen's Regt), served in World War I, *b* 1880; *ka* in Flanders 1918.

9*a* James Shepherd SLAUGHTER, 17th Virginia Regt (Montpelier Guards) CSA (Stonewall Bde), *d* of yellow fever in Mississippi.

10*a* Richard Chapman SLAUGHTER, Midshipman CSN, *dunm*.

(4) James Alfred CHAPMAN, *b* 1813, *m* 1837, Mary Edmonds Kinney (*b* 1817; *d* 1886), and *d* 1876, leaving issue,

  Anna Madison CHAPMAN, *b* 1844, *m* 1866, Joseph D. McGuire (*b* 1842; *d* 1914), and *d* 1904, leaving issue,

    1*b* Major James Clark McGUIRE, of New York City, *b* 1867.

    2*b* Mary Madison McGUIRE.

(5) Ella CHAPMAN, *m* — Meyers, of Richmond, Virginia.

(6) Richard Conway CHAPMAN, *dunm*.

2 John MADISON, *b* 1787; *dunm* 16 Sept 1819.

3 William MADISON, *b* 1789; *dunm* 1812.

4 Alfred MADISON, *b* 1791; *dunm* 1811.

5 Robert Lewis MADISON, *b* 1794; *dunm* 1828.

6 Major Ambrose MADISON, of Woodbury Forest, Virginia,

*b* 1796, *m* Jane Bankhead Willis (*b* 1803; *d* 1862), sister of Lewis Willis (*see below*), and had issue,

(1) Lucy Taliaferro MADISON, *b* 1820, *m* 1838, her 2nd cousin Col John Willis (*d* 1885), son of John Willis, MD, by his wife Nelly Conway Madison, and *d* 1868, leaving issue (*see above, p 139*).

(2) Mary Frances MADISON, *b* 1823, *m* Col Robert B. Marye, of Fredericksburg, Virginia, and had issue,

  1*a* Alfred J. MARYE, *m* Nancy C. Anderson, and had issue,

    1*b* Robert B. MARYE.

    2*b* Ambrose Madison MARYE.

    3*b* Janey Colquhoun MARYE.

    4*b* William Gordon MARYE.

  2*a* Ambrose MARYE.

(3) William Willis MADISON, *b* 1826, *m* Roberta Willis Taliaferro, sister of Col Thomas Dorsey Taliaferro (*see below*), and *d* 1888, leaving issue, one child (who *dunm*).

(4) James Ambrose MADISON, *b* 1828, *m* 1850, Lucy Hiden, and had issue,

  1*a* Ambrose Gilmer MADISON, *b* 1851, *m* Margaret McGary, and had issue,

    1*b* Margaret MADISON.

    2*b* Kate MADISON.

    3*b* William MADISON.

    4*b* Ambrose MADISON.

    5*b* Annie MADISON.

  2*a* Fanny Throckmorton MADISON, *m* Rev J. A. French.

  3*a* Susan Daniel MADISON.

  4*a* James MADISON.

  5*a* Edward Cooper MADISON, *b* 1857, *m* 1886, Elizabeth Fox Stagg (*b* 1864), and had issue,

    1*b* Ida Renshaw MADISON, *b* 1887, *m* Thomas Patrick.

    2*b* Susan Daniel MADISON, *b* 1891, *m* Dr C. C. Richards.

    3*b* Lucy Hiden MADISON, *b* 1893, *m* Chesley A. Haden.

    4*b* James Gordon MADISON, of Tuscaloosa, Alabama, lawyer, *b* 1900, *m* 1924, Mabel Curtis Campbell (*b* 1903), and had issue,

      1*c*● James Gordon MADISON, Jr, *b* 1926.

      2*c*● Richard Fleetwood MADISON, *b* 1930.

  6*a* Alfred MADISON, *dunm*.

  7*a* Joseph Hiden MADISON, *b* 1868.

(5) Eliza Lewis MADISON, *b* 1834, *m* 1854, Col Thomas Dorsey Taliaferro, CSA, brother of Roberta Willis Taliaferro (*see above*), and had issue, with three other children,

  1*a* Fanny Lewis TALIAFERRO.

  2*a* Jane TALIAFERRO, *m*, and had issue, two children.

  3*a* Edmonia TALIAFERRO.

(6) Leila Bankhead MADISON, *b* 1837, *m* Judge William Pope Dabney, of Powhatan County, Virginia, and had issue,

  1*a* Robert Kelso DABNEY, *b* 1858, *m*.

  2*a* Leila DABNEY, *m* Marshall Taylor, of Richmond, Virginia.

  3*a* Julia Byrd DABNEY.

  4*a* Percy DABNEY, *m* Ethel Crane.

  5*a* Champe DABNEY.

  6*a* James Madison DABNEY.

  7*a* Ruby Bailey DABNEY.

7 James Edwin MADISON, *b* 1798; *dunm* 1821.

8 Lucy Frances MADISON, *b* 1800; *d* 28 Dec 1813.

9 Elizabeth MADISON, *b* 1802, *m* Lewis Willis, brother of Jane Bankhead Willis (*see above*), and had issue,

  Frances WILLIS, *m* Col John Hancock Lee, of Litchfield, Orange County, Virginia, and had issue,

    1*a* Mary Willis LEE, *b* 1845; *d* young.

    2*a* Lizzie Madison LEE, *b* 1848, *m* 1872, William A. Bragg (*b* 1840; *d* 1901), and *d* 1907, leaving issue,

      1*b* Hancock Lee BRAGG, *b* 1874.

      2*b* Elise Calvin BRAGG, *b* 1876, *m* 1904, Granville Gray Valentine, of Richmond, Virginia, and had issue,

        1*c*● Elizabeth Lee VALENTINE, *b* 1907, *m* 1931, ● Wilfred Lacy Goodwin, Jr, son of Wilfred Lacy Goodwyn.

2c●Maria Gray VALENTINE, *b* 1914.
3c●Granville Gray VALENTINE, *b* 1920.
3*b* Frances Madison BRAGG, *b* 1878, *m* 1901, George Small, of York, Pennsylvania, and had issue,
  1c●Elizabeth Lee SMALL, *b* 1902, *m* 1926, ●Rev Richard Henry Baker, DD, and has issue,
    ●Frances Lee BAKER, *b* 1928.
  2c●Katharine Moore SMALL, *b* 1904, *m* 1929, ●Laurence Talbot.
  3c●Anna Maria SMALL, *b* 1907.
  4c●Frances Madison SMALL, *b* 1919.
3*a* Lewis Herman LEE, *b* 1849, *m* 1876, Georgia G. Hansbrough, and *d* 1878, leaving issue,
  Mary Madison LEE.
10 Letitia MADISON, *b* 1804, *m* Daniel French SLAUGHTER, and had issue,
(1) James Edwin SLAUGHTER, Brig-Gen CSA.
(2) Philip Madison SLAUGHTER, Major CSA, *m* Clementine Luzenburg, and had issue,
  1*a* Edward Luzenburg SLAUGHTER, *m* Lucy Williams.
  2*a* Mary Clementine SLAUGHTER, *m* Hugh Mercer Hamilton, and had issue,
    1*b* Cornelia Long HAMILTON.
    2*b* Edwin Slaughter HAMILTON.
    3*b* Kathryn HAMILTON.
    4*b* Philip HAMILTON.
**6** Sarah Catlett MADISON, *b* 1764, *m* 1790, Thomas Macon (*b* 1765; *d* 1838), and *d* 1843, having had issue, with seven sons (the yst *b* 1808) and one other dau (*b* 1803; *d* 1805),
  Lucie H. MACON, *b* 1794, *m* Reuben Conway (*b* 1788; *d* 1838), and *d* 1871.
**7** A boy, *b* and *d* the same day 1766.
**8** Elizabeth MADISON, *b* 1768; *d* of dysentery 17 May 1775.
**9** A stillborn child 1770.
**10** Reuben MADISON, *b* 19 Sept 1771; *d* of dysentery 5 June 1775.
**11** Frances Taylor MADISON, *b* 1774, *m* 1800, Robert Henry Rose, MD (*d* 1833), eldest son of Col Hugh Rose, of Amherst County, Virginia, by his wife Caroline Matilda Jordan, and *d* 1823, having had issue,
1 Hugh Francis ROSE, MD, of Tennessee, *b* 1801, *m* Emma Taliaferro Newman, and *d* 1856, having had issue,
(1) Ellen Conway ROSE, *m* R. J. Jones.
(2) Frances Madison ROSE.
(3) Eliza Camilla ROSE, *m* H. A. Rogers.
(4) Octavia ROSE.
(5) Emma Newman ROSE, *m* T. A. Moore.
(6) Robert ROSE.
(7) Samuel Patrick ROSE, *m* 1st, Celeste Coombs; and 2ndly, Mildred L. Cage, and by her had issue,

1*a* Harriet Howard ROSE.
2*a* Telisflora ROSE.
3*a* Hugh Francis ROSE.
(8) Anne Fitzhugh ROSE, *m* W. L. Bell, MD.
(9) Hugh Francis ROSE.
2 Ambrose James ROSE, *b* 1802, *m* — Kelly, of Mississippi, and had issue,
(1) Jennie ROSE, *dunm.*
(2) Frances ROSE, *m* William Winston.
3 James Madison ROSE, *d* an inf.
4 Henry ROSE, *b* 1804, *m* Sarah Smith, of Rushville, Illinois, and had issue,
(1) Robert Henry ROSE, *m* Maggie M. Fisher, and had issue,
  1*a* Nellie Madison ROSE.
  2*a* Belle ROSE.
  3*a* Hugh Francis ROSE.
  4*a* Sadie Madison ROSE.
(2) Samuel Jordan ROSE, of Macon, Tennessee.
(3) Margaret Ellen ROSE, *m* Hugh Francis ROSE.
(4) Nannie T. ROSE, *m* 1st, Dr Belle; and 2ndly, — McCarty.
5 Samuel Jordan ROSE, of Randolph County, Tennessee, *b* 1805, *m* 1st, Prudence W. Jones, and had issue, five children who all *d* young. He *m* 2ndly, Dorothy W. Jones, and *d* 1868, having by her had issue,
(1) Maria Jones ROSE.
(2) Polly Ward ROSE, *m* John G. Hall.
(3) Bronson Baylis ROSE, of Texas, *m* Mrs Alice T. Lytle.
6 Erasmus Taylor ROSE, MD, of Tennessee, *b* 1806, *m* Mary Louise Rose, of Macon, Georgia, and *d* 1874, leaving issue,
(1) Mary Ella ROSE.
(2) Hugh James ROSE.
(3) John Nicholas ROSE.
(4) Robert ROSE, *m* Mrs Matilda W. Christian.
7 Ann Fitzhugh ROSE, *d* young.
8 Nelly Conway ROSE, *m* Capt John Francis Newman, and had issue,
(1) Ellen Rose NEWMAN, *m* Rev John Ambrose Wheelock (*d* 1866), and *d* 1869, leaving issue,
  Elizabeth Josephine WHEELOCK..
(2) Mary Frances NEWMAN, *m* James Rose, and had issue,
  1*a* William Arthur ROSE, *m* Ella Baggett.
  2*a* Dr Francis Newman ROSE, *m* Mary E. Clements.
  3*a* Nelly Conway ROSE, *m* William T. Baggett, of California, lawyer, and had issue,
    Nelly Rose BAGGETT.
9 Frances ROSE, *d* young.
10 Mary ROSE, *d* young.
11 Robert H. ROSE, of Illinois, *m*, and had issue.

# Notes

[1] Through his paternal grandmother President Madison was a second cousin of the future President Zachary Taylor (*qv*)—

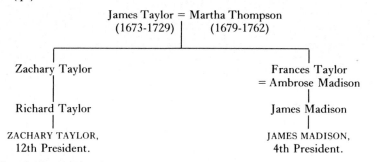

James Taylor = Martha Thompson
(1673-1729)    (1679-1762)

Zachary Taylor

Richard Taylor

ZACHARY TAYLOR,
12th President.

Frances Taylor
= Ambrose Madison

James Madison

JAMES MADISON,
4th President.

[2] Through the Conway family President Madison was a first cousin twice removed of George Washington, 1st President (*see p 64*).

# James Monroe
## 1758-1831

———

5th President of the
United States of America
1817-1825

JAMES MONROE, 5TH PRESIDENT

# James Monroe

## 1758-1831

### 5th President of the United States of America
### 1817-1825

THE TOURIST who makes a pilgrimage to James Monroe's two Virginia homes, Ash Lawn in Charlottesville and Oak Hill in Leesburg, carries away a sense of serenity, dignity and decent accomplishment. In the nation's folklore Monroe figures as one of the Virginia Dynasty, the fourth of five Presidents to come from the Old Dominion. He is associated with the Monroe Doctrine. His eight years in the White House are recalled as the "era of good feelings"—a period almost free from political strife. According to legend Monroe would have received a unanimous electoral vote when he was re-elected in 1820, except that a single elector who plumped for John Quincy Adams did so merely in order to reserve the unique distinction of unanimity for George Washington.

In actuality Monroe's career was much less comfortable. As a diplomat in Europe he offended both President Washington and President Jefferson. He irritated Madison by offering himself as a rival candidate for the Presidency in 1808. Though he made a good enough record in Madison's Administration as Secretary of State, later also managing to carry out the duties of Secretary of War, he was not the universal favorite among the Republicans for the presidential nomination in 1816. Stiff in manner and old-fashioned in dress, he was a less attractive than the big, handsome William H. Crawford of Georgia. Some politicos grumbled that it was time to look outside Virginia. Nor was his wife, the daughter of an officer in the British Army, a match for Dolley Madison in natural vivacity. The Monroes went to considerable expense to redecorate the White House—badly needed after the British raid of 1814. They entertained ambitiously. But Elizabeth Kortright Monroe suffered increasingly from migraines and depression. There was plenty in the Washington scene to give headaches to the White House. Gossip soon dismissed Monroe as a dull, mediocre person, nowhere near as politically successful as Jefferson and less intellectually gifted than Madison. With an eye to their own presidential chances, his Secretary of State (J. Q. Adams) and his Secretary of the Treasury (Crawford) began to provoke one another. Monroe could assert himself neither with his cabinet nor with Congress. The Administration, Adams sourly noted in his journal, "is at war with itself, both in the Executive, and between the Executive and the Legislature". Much of the initiative for the Monroe Doctrine (a section of the President's annual message to Congress in 1823) came from Adams. Monroe was almost a cipher in his second term. In the words of the powerful Congressman Henry Clay, "there was nothing further to be expected by him or from him".

Worse still for Monroe, his re-election coincided with an economic depression. There was little he could do to remedy matters. But his apparent indifference to business failures and out-of-work operatives made him seem still more impotent, unlikeable and irrelevant. His own salary of $25,000 a year (a sum fixed in 1789, and to remain fixed until it was doubled in 1873) looked opulent in comparison with the Vice-President's $5,000 or the niggardly $3,500 paid to heads of executive departments. His expenses however were heavy, and nineteenth-century Presidents did not receive a pension. When he retired from office in 1825, with six years still to live, Monroe's finances were in disastrous shape. Like Jefferson and Madison before him, he was on the brink of ruin when he died. Indeed, Mount Vernon, Monticello, Montpelier and Ash Lawn are all in better condition today, thanks to careful restoration, than when their owners were laid to rest.

This sounds like a gloomy verdict on Monroe—in colors as dark as the formal clothes he wore. If it is true, why was he nevertheless selected in 1816, and again in 1820? One of the axioms of presidential politics is that a depression kills the chances of re-election. Van Buren was to be punished in this way in 1840, and Herbert Hoover in 1932. Another general rule is that those who follow in the wake of strong Presidents usually face a counter-attack from Congress. And from a twentieth-century perspective, one would not expect the nation to accept a sequence of Presidents from the same state.

The main explanation is that the political circumstances of Monroe's era were different from ours, and still seeking firm definition. It looked as though the route to the Presidency would run from the Vice-Presidency or the Secretaryship of State. Monroe had strong claims to the White House. He had served his country or his state almost continuously ever since his enlistment in the Continental Army at the age of eighteen. He had been a member of the Continental Congress, a leader of the US Senate, and twice Governor of Virginia. He was an experienced if not a dazzlingly successful diplomat. Perhaps most important of all, he had been closely connected

ELIZABETH KORTRIGHT, MRS MONROE

with Jefferson ever since 1780. A cynic might have said that Monroe was a veteran professional patriot. A fairer comment is that he was a thoroughly deserving public figure, untouched by scandal, who was given his due reward—the ultimate, highest office in the land.

In a sense he was lucky to be nominated in 1816, and again in 1820. He was chosen because he was *there*, the most obvious person for the Republican caucus to pick, and because the rival Federalist party was in collapse. He was renominated and re-elected not out of positive enthusiasm but in the absence of any viable alternative. (Incidentally, the New Hampshire elector who cast a solitary vote for Adams did so simply because he preferred Adams: he had no idea he was the only dissenter.)

Monroe was unlucky, though, in other respects. It was not his fault that the Presidency had fallen into partial eclipse, overshadowed by Congress. Much of the political bad feeling that in fact marred the supposed era of good feeling was a consequence of the temporary blurring of party lines. Americans had not yet come to regard a two-party system as a desirable arrangement. According to the conventional wisdom of the period, which Monroe shared, "party" was a sign of corruption and crisis. He and his contemporaries were baffled by the rancorous mood in Washington, when the United States as a whole was clearly prospering. Monroe's situation, rather than any personal deficiencies, is the reason why his leadership was so indecisive. Deprived of a political organization, including the reinforcement of patronage, he was a general without an army. He had the trappings of authority but not its weaponry. As President he did what he could—doggedly, decently, a little dismally. The last of the Jeffersonians, at least he contrived to die on the same day as his great mentor, July 4, five years after Jefferson, as if to remind his countrymen that he too belonged in the Revolutionary pantheon.

# Chronology

1758    Born at Monroe's Creek, Westmoreland County, Virginia 28 April.

1770-74    Attended the Rev Archibald Campbell's private School in Westmoreland County.

1774    Entered William and Mary College 20 June.

1776    Left William and Mary College; Cadet in 3rd Virginia Regt under Col Hugh Mercer; commissioned Lieut and ordered to main Army under Gen Washington; fought in Battles of Harlem Heights (16 Sept) and White Plains (28 Oct); retreated with Army through New Jersey; wounded at Battle of Trenton (26 Dec) and promoted Capt for his service there.

1777    ADC to C-in-C William Alexander (styled Earl of Stirling) July; fought in Battles of Brandywine (11 Sept) and Germantown (4 Oct); promoted Major 20 Nov.

1778    Served with Washington and Alexander at Valley Forge; fought in Battle of Monmouth 28 June; returned to Virginia and on Washington's recommendation was apptd Lt-Col of a command to be raised in Virginia, but the exhausted finances of the state prevented this; re-entered William and Mary College.

1780-83    Studied law under Thomas Jefferson at Williamsburg.

1780    Visited Southern Army as Military Commissioner (with rank of Lt-Col) from Virginia.

1782    Elected to House of Delegates from King George County and appointed member of Executive Council by Virginia Assembly.

1783    Elected delegate from Virginia to Continental Congress 6 June for three-year term beginning 3 Nov; ratification of peace treaty with Great Britain at Annapolis 13 Dec.

1784    Toured NW frontier to investigate what type of government Congress should establish for frontier lands June; attended Congress at Trenton Nov.

1786    Member of Virginia Assembly; admitted to Virginia bar Oct; attended Annapolis Convention Nov.

1787    Re-elected to Virginia Assembly.

1788    Apptd to the Virginia Convention to ratify the Federal Constitution 2 June; published *Observations Upon the Proposed Plan of Federal Government*, but withheld it from circulation later; defeated by Madison for the House of Representatives in the 1st Congress under the new Constitution.

1789    Returned to law practice.

1790   Elected United States Senator from Virginia to fill vacancy caused by death of William Grayson 9 Nov; took seat in Senate at Philadelphia 6 Dec.

1791   Re-elected Senator 3 March; member of Commission for revising laws of Virginia.

1792   Member of Senatorial Committee to investigate Alexander Hamilton's handling of public funds.

1794   Retired from Senate 27 May on appointment as US Minister Plenipotentiary to the French Republic; arrived in Paris and was received by the National Convention Aug; effected release of Thomas Paine (the author of the celebrated *Declaration of the Rights of Man*, published three years previously) from Luxembourg Prison, Paris 4 Nov.

1796   Recalled 22 Aug (received letter of recall Nov); took leave of French Government 30 Dec.

1797   Arrived in Philadelphia June.

1798   Moved to Ash Lawn, Charlottesville, Virginia.

1799   Elected Governor of Virginia 6 Dec.

1802   Retired as Governor.

1803   Appointed Envoy Extraordinary and Minister Plenipotentiary to France to arrange terms of Louisiana Purchase 11 Jan; arrived in Paris 12 April; appointed Minister Plenipotentiary to Great Britain 18 April; Louisiana Purchase concluded 30 April; left France for England July.

1803-07  Minister Plenipotentiary to Great Britain and Envoy Extraordinary to Spain.

1806   Appointed Commissioner (jointly with William Pinkney) for settlement of differences between US and Great Britain 12 May; signed (with Pinkney) Treaty of Amity, Commerce, and Navigation with Great Britain 31 Dec.

1807   Jefferson refused to send Treaty of Amity to Senate for Consideration March; left London 29 Oct and arrived in US Dec.

1808   Unsuccessful candidate for the Presidency.

1810-11  Member of Virginia Assembly.

1811   Governor of Virginia Jan-March.

1811-14  Secretary of State under President Madison.

1811   Took office 6 April; gave tacit approval to Gen George Mathews's plans to invade Florida.

1812   Withdrew support from Mathews.

1813   Secretary of War *ad interim* 1 Jan-5 Feb.

1814   Secretary of War *ad interim* 3-27 Sept; Secretary of War 27 Sept; retired as Secretary of State 30 Sept but continued as Secretary *ad interim* till 28 Feb 1815.

1815   Re-appointed Secretary of State 28 Feb; retired from Secretaryship 2 March.

1816   Nominated for President by Democratic-Republicans 4 March; elected President with 183 electoral votes as opposed to 34 for Rufus King, the Federalist candidate, 4 Dec.

1817   Inaugurated as 5th President of the United States on the east portico of the Capitol 4 March; Rush-Bagot Agreement with Great Britain signed 29 April; first Seminole War began 20 Nov.

| | |
|---|---|
| 1818 | Signed Flag Act 4 April (establishing flag as having 13 horizontal red and white stripes and a white star for each state on blue field); 1st Seminole War ended 24 May. |
| 1819 | Signed treaty with Spain whereby US received Florida 22 Feb. |
| 1820 | Signed Missouri Compromise Bill 3 March; re-elected President without opposition 6 Dec. |
| 1821 | Inaugurated for second term as President in Hall of Representatives of the Capitol 5 March (the 4th, the actual anniversary, fell on a Sunday). |
| 1823 | Drew up the celebrated Monroe Doctrine (against foreign colonization or intervention in the New World) with aid of Secretary of State John Quincy Adams and enunciated the same 2 Dec. |
| 1825 | Retired from office; attended inauguration of his successor John Quincy Adams 4 March; moved to Oak Hill, Loudoun County, Virginia. |
| 1826 | Voted $30,000 by Congress in settlement of claims against the Government for reimbursement of expenses in public service. |
| 1828-31 | Member of Board of Visitors of University of Virginia. |
| 1829 | President of Virginia Constitutional Convention. |
| 1831 | Sold Oak Hill and moved to New York City; died of debility in New York City 4 July; buried in Marble Cemetery, New York City. |
| 1858 | Re-interred at Hollywood Cemetery, Richmond, Virginia. |

# The Writings of President Monroe

*Observations Upon the Proposed Plan of Federal Government* (1788)

*A View of the Conduct of the Executive in the Foreign Affairs of the United States* (1797)

*The Writings of James Monroe,* 7 vols (1898-1903)

*Papers of James Monroe* (1904)

Some of President Monroe's letters have been published in *Proceedings of the Massachussetts Historical Society,* Vol XLII (1909) and in *Bulletin of the New York Public Library* (1900, 1901 and 1902)

Diplomatic correspondence has been published in *American State Papers, Foreign Relations, Vol III* (1832)

*The Autobiography of James Monroe,* edited by Stuart Gerry Brown with assistance of Donald G. Baker (1959)

# Lineage of President Monroe

The Monroes are cadets of the great Scottish baronial house of MUNRO *of Foulis* (*see* BURKE'S *Peerage*, MUNRO *of Foulis-Obsdale*, Bt for a full account of the family).

GEORGE MUNRO (*or* MONROE) of Katewell; 5th son of Robert Munro of Foulis (*see* BURKE'S *Peerage*, MUNRO *of Foulis-Obsdale*, Bt), by his wife Margaret, dau of Sir Alexander Dunbar of Westfield, Sheriff of Moray; *k* at the Battle of Pinkie (with his father) 10 Sept 1547, leaving issue,

GEORGE MONROE, 2nd of Katewell, *m* 1st, Katherine, dau of Hector Mackenzie, 4th of Fairburn. He *m* 2ndly, Euphemia, dau of John Monroe of Pittonachy, and by her had issue. He *m* 3rdly, Agnes, only dau of Hugh Monroe of Coul and Balconie. His son by his 2nd marriage,

DAVID MONROE, *m* Agnes, dau of Rev Alexander Munro, of Durness, by his wife Janet, dau of James Cumming[1], and had with other issue, a 3rd son,

ANDREW MONROE, went to St Mary's County, Maryland *ca* 1641, and was assessed there July 1642 in a tax of fifty pounds of tobacco to sustain the war against the Susquehanna Indians, apptd to sit (or to send his proxy) on the Assembly 22 Aug 1642, and on joining Col Claiborne in 1644-45, he with several others (including Nathaniel Pope, an ancestor of George Washington) supported the claims of one Richard Ingle, who claimed to represent Parliament, and raised an insurrection against the Dep Gov, but had their property confiscated and fled across the Potomac into Virginia, believed to have returned to Scotland 1648 and to have fought under Gen Sir George Monroe at the Battle of Preston 17 Aug 1648, been taken prisoner and banished to Virginia, but escaped and settled in Northumberland County, where he received several grants of land 8 June 1650, later patented other and more extensive lands in Westmoreland County, *m* 1652, Elizabeth (who *m* 2ndly *ante* 30 July 1679, George Horner; and 3rdly *ante* 23 Feb 1686, Edward Mountjoy), believed to have been the dau of John Alexander, and *d* 1668 (*bur* nr Doctors Point, Westmoreland County, Virginia), leaving issue, with one other son,

WILLIAM MONROE, of Westmoreland County, Virginia, *b* 1666, *m* 1689, Margaret, dau of Thomas Bowcock, and *d* 1737 (will dated 13 March), having had, with other issue (*see* BURKE'S *Distinguished Families of America*), a yr son,

ANDREW MONROE, Sheriff of Westmoreland County in 1731, *m* Christian Tyler, widow of his cousin Spence Monroe, and *dvp* 1735, leaving issue,

SPENCE MONROE, of Westmoreland County, Virginia, farmer and circuit judge, a signer of Westmoreland County, Virginia Resolutions forbidding the enforcement of the Stamp Act in that County, *m* 1752, Elizabeth (*b* probably in King George County, Virginia), dau of James Jones, architect, by his wife Hester, and sister of Judge Joseph Jones (1727-1805), and *d* 1774 (will dated 14 Feb), leaving, with other issue (*see* BROTHERS AND SISTER OF PRESIDENT MONROE, *p* 157), an eldest son,

JAMES MONROE, **5th President of the United States of America.**

# The Descendants of President Monroe

JAMES MONROE *m* at Trinity Episcopal Church, New York 16 Feb 1786, Elizabeth (*b* in New York City 30 June 1768; *d* at Oak Hill, Loudoun County, Virginia 23 Sept 1830, *bur* first at Oak Hill, reinterred beside her husband at Hollywood, Richmond, Virginia 1903), eldest dau of Laurence Kortright, of New York, merchant, one of the founders of the New York Chamber of Commerce (descended from a family of Flemish origin), by his wife Hannah Aspinwall[2], and had issue,

**1** Eliza Kortright MONROE, known in France as "La Belle Americaine", *b* at Fredericksburg, Virginia 5 Dec 1787, *educ* in France, *m* 1808, as his 2nd wife, Judge George Hay, of Richmond, Virginia, who as US District Attorney conducted the prosecution for treason of Vice-Pres Aaron Burr 1806-07 (*b* at Williamsburg, Virginia 15 Dec 1765; *d* at Richmond, Virginia 21 Sept 1830), son of Anthony Hay, by his wife Elizabeth Davenport, and *d* in Paris, France (*bur* Père La Chaise Cemetery), leaving issue,

Hortensia (Hortense)[3] Monroe HAY, *m* as his 2nd wife, Nicholas Lloyd Rogers[4] of Druid Hill, Baltimore, Maryland (*ca* 1787, *d* at Baltimore 12 Nov 1860), son of Nicholas Rogers, by his wife Eleanor Buchanan, and had issue,

  (1) Harriet ROGERS, *m* Charles Wilmer, and *dsp*.

  (2) Mary Custis ROGERS, *m* Richard Hardesty (*d* 1871), and *d* 1869, leaving issue,

    1*a* Hortense Hay HARDESTY, *b* 1866, *m* William Watson McIntire, mem House of Reps (*d* 1912), and *d* 1933, having had issue,

      1*b* Mary Custis McINTIRE, *b* 1889; *d* 1897.

      2*b* Hortense Rogers McINTIRE, *b* at Baltimore 3 Jan 1889, *m* there 23 Jan 1907, John William Stork, of Roland Park, Maryland (*b* at Baltimore 26 Jan 1871; *d* there 13 Nov 1958), son of William L. Stork, by his wife Clintonia, and *d* 1923, leaving issue,

        1*c* Anne Monroe STORK, *b* at Baltimore 20 June 1909; *dunm* 8 Oct 1936.

        2*c* Lloyd Rogers STORK, *b* at Baltimore 5 Aug 1911; *d* there 29 Jan 1929.

        3*c* ● Jean Monroe STORK, *b* at Baltimore 24 Dec 1913, *m* there 17 June 1938, ● Bernard S. Kamtman (*b* at Baltimore 16 March 1907) [*14 St Martin's Road, Baltimore, Maryland 21218, USA*], son of George Kamtman, by his wife Helen Kaufman, and has issue,

          ● Sandra Monroe KAMTMAN, *b* at Baltimore 8 Jan 1943, *m* there Sept 1966, ● Robert Urie Patterson, Jr (*b* at Washington, DC) [*5605 Enderly Road, Baltimore, Maryland 21212, USA*], son of Robert Urie Patterson, by his wife Eleanor Reeve, and has issue,

            1*e* ● Robert Baden PATTERSON, *b* at Baltimore 20 Dec 1968.

            2*e* ● Lloyd Reeve PATTERSON, *b* at Baltimore 11 April 1970.

    2*a* Elizabeth Kortright HARDESTY, *b* 1867, *m* John S. Richardson, of Bel Air, Maryland (*b* 1864; *d* 1927), and *d* 26 May 1955, having had issue,

      1*b* John Monroe RICHARDSON, *b* 1890, *m* 1st,

Evelyn Davis; and 2ndly, Marguerite McIntire, and *dsp* 1954.

      2*b* ● Lloyd Nicholas RICHARDSON, *b* 1891, *m* ● Mary Geneva Dean.

      3*b* Elizabeth Hardesty RICHARDSON, *b* 1893; *d* aged 8 months.

      4*b* ● Richard Hardesty RICHARDSON, *b* 1894, *m* ● Margaret Hoffman, and has issue,

        1*c* ● Richard Hardesty RICHARDSON, Jr, *b* 1941.

        2*c* ● Nancy RICHARDSON, *b* 1947.

      5*b* ● Eleanor Agnes RICHARDSON, *b* 1896, *m* 1923, ● Dr Charles B. Canton, and has issue,

        1*c* ● Eleanor Agnes CANTON, *b* 1927, *m* 1952, ● John Zink.

        2*c* ● Geraldine CANTON, *b* 1928.

      6*b* ● James Jerome RICHARDSON, *b* 1901, *m* 1927, ● Martha Evans, and has issue,

        ● James Jerome RICHARDSON, Jr, *b* 1931, *m* 1953, ● Sally Brown Thomas, and has issue,

          ● John David RICHARDSON, *b* April 1955.

      7*b* ● Frances Kortright Monroe RICHARDSON [*610 North Carolina Avenue, S.E., Washington, DC 20003, USA*], *b* 1904, *m* 1935, Dr Aloysius William Valentine (*b* 1875; *d* 1951).

  (3) Hortense ROGERS, *dunm*.

**2** A son[5], *b* May 1799; *d* 28 Sept 1800.

**3** Maria Hester MONROE, *b* in Paris, France 1803, *m* at the White House, Washington, DC[6] 9 March 1820, her 1st cousin, Samuel Laurence Gouverneur, of New York, mem New York State Legislature, priv sec to his father-in-law Pres Monroe, Postmaster of New York City 1828-36 (*b* 1799; *d* 1867), son of Nicholas Gouverneur, of New York, by his wife Hester, dau of Laurence Kortright (and sister of Mrs James Monroe—*see above*), and *d* at Oak Hill, Loudoun County, Virginia 1850, leaving issue,

  **1** James Monroe GOUVERNEUR, *dunm*.

  **2** Elizabeth GOUVERNEUR, *b* at Washington, DC, *m* 1st there 9 June 1842, Henry Lee Heiskell, MD, Major and Surg US Army (*b* at Winchester, Virginia 1799; *d* at Meechwood 12 Aug 1855, *bur* Washington, DC), son of John Heiskell, by his wife Ann Sowers, and had issue,

    (1) James Monroe HEISKELL, lawyer, one of "Mosby's men" in the CSA, candidate for the mayoralty of Baltimore, *b* at Washington, DC 5 June 1844, *m* 1st at Leesburg, Virginia 26 Feb 1867, Esther Fairfax (*b* 1847; *d* at Baltimore, Maryland 18 July 1873), dau of Col John West Minor, by his wife Louisa Fairfax, and had issue,

      1*a* Minor Fairfax Heiskell GOUVERNEUR (assumed the surname of Gouverneur in lieu of that of his patronymic

Heiskell), of Baltimore, inventor and banker, *b* at Baltimore 15 Dec 1869, *m* at Wilmington, N Carolina 2 Dec 1896, his 3rd cousin Mary Fairfax (*b* at Wilmington 30 Sept 1874; *d* at Alexandria, Virginia 27 May 1956), elder dau of George Davis, Attorney-Gen of the Confederacy, by his wife Monimia, 3rd dau of Dr Orlando Fairfax, of Alexandria and Richmond, Virginia, by his wife Mary Randolph, 2nd dau of Wilson Jefferson Cary, of Carysbrook, great-nephew of Pres Jefferson, and *d* at Baltimore 8 June 1933, leaving issue,

1*b* Fairfax Heiskell GOUVERNEUR, OBE, served in World War I and World War II as US Army Air Corps Offr, investment banker, *b* at Wilmington 5 Sept 1898, *educ* Philips Exeter Acad, *m* at Rochester, New York 6 June 1922, ●Caroline Erickson, dau of Thornton Jeffress, by his wife Caroline Erickson Perkins, and *d* at Clearwater Beach, Florida 16 April 1967, having had issue,

1*c*●Minor Fairfax Heiskell GOUVERNEUR II, engr, designer and mfr of tools [*PO Box 105, Goshen, Connecticut, USA*], *b* at Rochester, New York 9 Sept 1923, *educ* Rensselaer Polytechnic Inst, Troy, New York, *m* at Maplewood, New Jersey 21 May 1949, ●Carolyn Marie, dau of Reynier Jacob Wortendyke, Jr, and has issue,

1*d*●Elizabeth Rogers GOUVERNEUR, *b* 17 May 1950.
2*d*●Sallie Thornton GOUVERNEUR, *b* 3 Nov 1951.
3*d*●Jeffress GOUVERNEUR, *b* 30 Oct 1955.
4*d*●Abigail Josephine GOUVERNEUR, *b* 29 Dec 1960.
5*d*●Jacob Reynier GOUVERNEUR, *b* 3 Feb 1968.
2*c* Sallie Thornton GOUVERNEUR, *d* an inf.
3*c*●Caroline Erickson GOUVERNEUR [*165 Mallorca Way, San Francisco, California, USA*], *b* at Rochester, New York 23 March 1927.
4*c*●Jane Fairfax GOUVERNEUR, *b* at Rochester, New York 29 April 1931, *m* there 21 Dec 1954, ●Benjamin Lansing Boyd Ten Eyck IV, son of Benjamin Lansing Boyd Ten Eyck III, and has issue,

1*d*●Benjamin Boyd TEN EYCK, *b* at Rochester, New York 8 April 1956.
2*d*●Thomas Jeffress TEN EYCK, *b* at Rochester, New York 18 Sept 1959.
3*d*●Peter Fairfax TEN EYCK, *b* at Rochester, New York 7 Nov 1960.
2*b*●Esther GOUVERNEUR, *b* at Wilmington, N Carolina 21 Feb 1905, *m* at Bastia, Corsica 22 Dec 1944, ●Harris Elliott Kirk, Jr (*b* at Nashville, Tennessee 4 May 1898) [*Pine Knoll Townes 22, Morehead City, North Carolina 28557, USA*], son of Rev Harris Elliott Kirk, of Baltimore, Moderator of Gen Assembly of the Presbyterian Church in US 1928, by his wife Helen McCormick, and has issue,

●Mary Fairfax KIRK, *b* at Baltimore 16 Feb 1950, *educ* Roanoke Coll (AB 1972), *m* at Alexandria, Virginia 30 Sept 1972, ●Robert Webb Wright (*b* at Richmond, Virginia 5 May 1950) [*808 Arendell Street, Morehead City, North Carolina 28557, USA*].
2*a* Marian Gouverneur HEISKELL, *b* at Baltimore 1886, *m* 1st there, Richard Emory (*b* at Inverness, Baltimore County, Maryland 1870; *d* at San Jose, California 1906), son of Thomas Lane Emory, by his wife Griselda Holmes, and had issue,

●Elizabeth Kortright Monroe EMORY, *b* at Baltimore Feb 1907, *m* there 1929, ●G. Gordon Gatchell (*b* at Baltimore 1898) [*1 Harvest Road, Baltimore, Maryland 21200, USA*], son of Skipwith Gordon Gatchell, by his wife Gertrude Gantz, and has issue,

1*c*●G. Gordon GATCHELL, Jr [*Bedford Road, Lincoln, Massachusetts 01773, USA*], *b* at Baltimore 1930, *educ* Babson Inst, *m* at Philadelphia 1953, ●Esther Allen (*b* at Philadelphia 23 Jan 1932), dau of Donald MacLea, by his wife Catharine Miskey, and has issue,

1*d*●Catharine Allen GATCHELL, *b* at Bryn Mawr, Pennsylvania 1954.
2*d*●Elizabeth Emory GATCHELL, *b* at Concord, Mass 1956.
3*d*●William Hugh GATCHELL, *b* at Concord, Mass 1962.
2*c*● Richard Emory GATCHELL, real estate broker, partner in firm of Hill and Co, Trustee of Peale Museum, mem Bd of Soc for Preservation of Maryland Antiquities, Baltimore Heritage, and Soc for the Preservation of Fells Point and Federal Hill [*Box 505B, West Joppa Road, Lutherville, Maryland 21093, USA*], *b* at Baltimore 20 March 1933, *educ* Calvert Sch, Gilman Sch for Boys, and Johns Hopkins Univ, *m* at the Church of the Redeemer, Baltimore 1960, ●Margaret Brian (*b* at Pittsburgh, Pennsylvania 2 Sept 1935), dau of Thomas Brian Parsons, by his wife Fanny Glenn Whitman, and has issue,

1*d*●Margaret Parsons GATCHELL, *b* at Baltimore 7 July 1963.
2*d*●Richard Emory GATCHELL, Jr, *b* at Baltimore 8 March 1965.
3*c*●Monroe Tyler GATCHELL [*1402 Ruxton Road, Baltimore, Maryland 21204, USA*], *b* at Baltimore 1940, *educ* Gilman Sch, and Johns Hopkins Univ, *m* at Baltimore 1965, ●Susan Miller (*b* at Baltimore 1942), dau of Joseph Eugene Rowe, Jr, by his wife Gene Claire Miller.
Marian Heiskell *m* 2ndly at Baltimore 1915, E. Griswold Thelin (*b* at Baltimore 1872; *d* there 1924), son of William T. Thelin, by his wife Elizabeth Griswold, and *d* at Baltimore 1931.
James Monroe Heiskell *m* 2ndly at Philadelphia, Mary (who *m* 2ndly, J. Herman Ireland, and *d* at Baltimore 1941), dau of Bronaugh Deringer, by his wife Estalena Woodland.
(2) Henry Lee HEISKELL, in mercantile business in St Louis and Yazoo City, Mississippi 1869-76, Pte and then Sgt US Signal Corps 1876 until that service was trans to Agric Dept as US Weather Bureau 1888, Prof of Meteorology, US Weather Bureau 1913, *b* at Washington, DC 17 Oct 1850, *educ* Rock Hill Coll, Ellicott City, Maryland, and US Naval Acad, *m* 1st 16 Oct 1878, Emma Leona Heiskell (*d* 1890), and had issue,
1*a* Esther Hill HEISKELL, *b* 1879, *m* 1900, Edward Sefton, lawyer, and *d* 2 July 1943, leaving issue,
●Elizabeth Monroe SEFTON, *b* 1901, *m* ●Charles Wayne Kerwood (*b* 1 Aug 1897), and has issue,
●Wayne Sefton KERWOOD, *b* 20 Feb 1929.
2*a*●Elizabeth Kortright Gouverneur HEISKELL [*2264 Cathedral Avenue, Washington, DC 20008, USA*], *b* 1884, *m* 1905, Harry Freeman Clark, of Washington, DC, Sec and Treas of Washington Steel and Ordnance Co (*b* 23 Sept 1871; *d* 11 Dec 1944), and has issue,
1*b* James Monroe CLARK, *b* and *d* 2 July 1912.
2*b*●James Monroe CLARK, *b* 1913, *m* 1936, ●Sarah Williams.
3*b*●Henry Lee CLARK [*3806 Leland Road, Chevy Chase, Maryland, USA*], *b* 22 Aug 1915, *m* 27 June 1942, ●Ann Lewis (*b* 8 July 1920), and has issue,
1*c*●Elise CLARK, *b* 21 Oct 1942, *m* ●Philip P. Heald [*771 Sandalwood Drive, El Centro, California 92243, USA*].
2*c*●Ann Lewis CLARK, *b* 18 July 1944.
3*c*●Susan Hill CLARK, *b* 15 Oct 1946.
4*c*●Henry Lee CLARK, Jr, *b* 20 Oct 1947.
5*c*●Mary F. CLARK.
Henry Lee Heiskell *m* 2ndly 12 Oct 1892, Henrietta Brent, and *d* 28 Jan 1914, having by her had issue,
3*a* John Carroll Brent HEISKELL, *d* 1893.
4*a* John Carroll Brent HEISKELL, *b* 1896; *d* 1908.
(3) Sydney Otho HEISKELL, MD, *b* 1853, *m* 1st 1882, Abbie (*d* 1884), dau of — Townsend, of Baltimore; and 2ndly, Doralyn, dau of — Miller, of Philadelphia, and *dsp* 1906.
Elizabeth Gouverneur *m* 2ndly, Gouverneur Bibby. She *m* 3rdly, Dr Grafton D. Spurrier, and had further issue,
(4) Grafton D. SPURRIER, Jr, *dunm* 1930.
3 Samuel Laurence GOUVERNEUR, Jr, served in Mexican War as 2nd Lieut 4th US Arty, brevetted 1st Lieut for

gallantry at Contreras and Cherubusco, first US Consul at Foo Chow, China under Pres Buchanan, Delegate from Maryland to Convention of Liberal Republicans which nominated Greeley for President 1872, proprietor of *Maryland Herald*, *b* 182ϭ, *m* 5 March 1855, Marian, author of *As I Remember—Recollections of American Society During the 19th Century* (1911) (*b* at Jamaica, Long Island, New York 1821; *d* at Washington, DC 12 March 1914), dau of Judge James Campbell, by his wife Mary Ann Hazard, and *d* at Washington, DC 1880, leaving issue,

(1) Maud Campbell GOUVERNEUR, *b* at Washington, DC; *dunm* there.

(2) Ruth Monroe GOUVERNEUR, *b* at Washington, DC 27 Nov 1858, *m* there 6 Dec 1882, Dr William Crawford Johnson (*b* at Frederick, Maryland 17 July 1856; *d* there 28 Dec 1943), son of George Johnson, by his wife Emily Ann Crawford, and *d* at Frederick, Maryland 28 Feb 1949, leaving issue,

1*a* Marian Campbell JOHNSON, *b* 19 June 1885, *m* at Washington, DC 1913, Brig-Gen Green Clay Goodloe, Paymaster USMC (*b* at Lexington, Kentucky 1845; *d* at Washington, DC 1917), son of — Goodloe, by his wife Sally Ann Smith, and *d* at Washington, DC, leaving issue,

Green Clay GOODLOE, Jr, Lt-Cmdr USN, served in World War II, *b* 1914, *educ* US Mil Acad Annapolis, *dunm* 1945.

2*a* ●Emily Crawford JOHNSON [*112 North Bentz Street, Frederick, Maryland 21701, USA*], *b* at Frederick, Maryland 1 Aug 1887.

3*a* ●William Monroe JOHNSON, attorney (ret), sometime Sgt 127th Inf AEF, mem Soc of the Cincinnati, author of numerous historical articles [*PO Box 66, Woodston, Kansas 67675, USA*], *b* at Frederick, Maryland 19 Feb 1895, *educ* George Washington Univ (LLB), *m* at Downs, Kansas 25 Dec 1921, ●Lillian Elizabeth (*b* at Whitehall, Illinois 14 Aug 1897), dau of

Thomas Bryant Smith, by his wife Eva Lonella Bentley, and has issue,

1*b* ●Elizabeth Gouverneur JOHNSON, *b* at Washington, DC 1 Sept 1923.

2*b* ●Monroe JOHNSON, Major USAFR, personnel adminr, historian [*3221 Bristolhall Drive, Bridgeton, Missouri 63044, USA*], *b* at Savannah, Georgia 7 July 1930, *educ* Washburn Univ, *m* at Joplin, Missouri 6 Oct 1956, ●June Edith (*b* at Joplin 12 July 1935), dau of Elmer Franklin Mitchell, by his wife Edith Laura Snyder, and has issue,

1*c* ●Bradley Monroe JOHNSON, *b* at Wichita, Kansas 25 Sept 1958.

2*c* ●Elizabeth June JOHNSON, at Wichita, Kansas 3 May 1961.

(3) Rose de Chine GOUVERNEUR, *b* at Foo Chow, China 1860, *m* at Washington, DC 5 Dec 1888, Rev Roswell Randall Hoes, Capt and Chaplain USN (*b* 1850; *d* 1921), and *d* at Washington, DC 26 May 1933, having had issue,

1*a* Gouverneur HOES, Capt US Army, *b* 1889, *m* ●Gourley Edward [*2204 Q Street, N.W., Washington, DC, USA*], and *dsp*.

2*a* Roswell Randall HOES.

3*a* ●Laurence Gouverneur HOES, investment banker, lectr, historian and writer, owner and founder of James Monroe Nat Shrine, Fredericksburg, Virginia, mem Sons of the Revolution [*1 Berlin 19, Skirenweg 2, Germany*], *b* 8 Jan 1900, *educ* St Alban's Sch, Washington, DC, *m* 1st 24 Nov 1928 (*m* diss by div), Ingrid, dau of Dr Joseph Per Ludwig Westesson, of Philadelphia; and 2ndly, —. He has issue by his 1st marriage,

●Monroe Randall HOES, [*c/o James Monroe Memorial Library, 908 Charles Street, Fredericksburg, Virginia 22401, USA*], *b* 26 Sept 1931, *m*, and has issue, two children.

# The Brothers and Sister of President Monroe

**1** Elizabeth MONROE, *b* 1754, *m* William Buckner, of Mill Hill (*b* 1753), and had issue, three sons and four daus. Two of her sons *d* young; the 3rd only had one son (who *dsp*). The daus all *m*, but only the eldest, Elizabeth Bankhead Buckner, left issue by her marriage to Norborne Taliaferro. Col Thomas Dorsey Taliaferro, CSA (grandson of the last), *m* 1854 Eliza Lewis Madison, a great-niece of President Madison, and his sister Roberta Willis Taliaferro *m* William Willis Madison (1826-1888), Eliza Lewis's brother (*see p 141*).

**2** Spence MONROE, *b* 1759 (?).

**3** Andrew MONROE, *m* 1789, Ann Bell, and *d* 1836, leaving issue, two sons, of whom the yr, Col James Monroe (1799-1870) was a mem House of Reps. By his marriage to Elizabeth Mary Douglas he had one son (who *d* an inf) and one dau, Fannie Monroe (1826-1906), whose only son, by her marriage to Douglas Robinson, of New York, also Douglas Robinson (1855-1918), *m* Corinne Roosevelt, sister of President Theodore Roosevelt (*qv*).

**4** Joseph Jones MONROE, Commonwealth Attorney, Albemarle County, Virginia, priv sec to his brother Pres Monroe, Clerk of Dist and Circuit Courts, Northumberland County, Virginia, *b* 1764, *m* 1st 1790, Elizabeth Kerr, and had issue, one dau, who *m*, and had issue. He *m* 2ndly 1801, Sarah Gordon; and 3rdly 1808, Elizabeth Glasscock, by neither of whom he had issue, and *d* 1824.

# Notes

[1] Through James Cumming President Monroe had several Royal descents (*see* APPENDIX C, PRESIDENTS OF ROYAL DESCENT).

[2] Through the Aspinwalls Mrs Monroe was related to the future President Franklin D. Roosevelt (*qv*).

[3] She was named after her mother's friend Hortense, Queen of Holland, the step-daughter and sister-in-law of Napoleon.

[4] His first wife was Eliza Parke Custis Law, a great-grand-daughter of Martha˙Washington (*see* PRESIDENT WASHINGTON'S WIFE AND STEPCHILDREN, *p 40*).

[5] His name is unrecorded, but his gravestone bears the initials "J. S. M.", probably for James Spence Monroe.

[6] She was the first daughter of a President to be married in the White House.

# John Quincy Adams
## 1767-1848

———

6th President of the
United States of America
1825-1829

JOHN QUINCY ADAMS, 6TH PRESIDENT

# John Quincy Adams

## 1767-1848

### 6th President of the United States of America
### 1825-1829

ON PAPER, no man could have been better qualified than John Quincy Adams to become President. His father had already held the office. Through this family connection, young John Quincy had from his early teens been involved in American official business, as a secretary in diplomatic missions. He knew Europe intimately and struck some remarkably good bargains on behalf of the United States as Monroe's Secretary of State. He had served in the Massachusetts Senate and in the US Senate. He had practiced as a lawyer, written some doughty political pieces, and even briefly been a professor at Harvard. He was a man of formidable intelligence and integrity. He had made an appropriate marriage to Louisa Catherine Johnson, whose father had been American consul in London. With her he was to enjoy fifty years of domestic happiness.

His presidential term, though, did not bring bliss. He did not exactly think that he had a hereditary right to the office. But he did feel his claims were undeniable, and stronger than those of the other contenders in 1824—the war-hero Andrew Jackson, Treasury Secretary William H. Crawford, Secretary of War John C. Calhoun, or Kentucky's Henry Clay, the darling of the House of Representatives. The 1824 election was a humiliation for Adams. In the electoral vote he trailed Jackson by 84 to 99. Crawford, who came third with 41 votes, suffered a stroke and dropped out of the running. Clay was fourth with 37 votes. Since no candidate received a majority, the election went to the House of Representatives, where each state had one vote. Crawford was eliminated by illness and Clay by the rule that only the leading three candidates could be considered by the House. Clay was therefore in effect the president-maker. He swung his support to Adams. There were good enough reasons for doing so. Clay preferred Adams as a man. He and Adams also broadly agreed on what became known as Clay's "American System"—the idea that the Federal Government should play a decisive part in developing the nation's roads and canals and its intellectual potential. But Adams appointed Clay his Secretary of State—the cabinet position that seemed to make him heir-apparent according to the convention of the day. Jackson genuinely felt he had been cheated, having received more popular as well as electoral votes than Adams. His supporters raised the cry that he had also been cheated by a "corrupt bargain" between Adams and Clay: the Secretaryship of State in exchange for Clay's backing in the House election.

Once in the White House, Adams could never recover from this bad start. He was a Puritan gentleman, and the combination did not sit quite easily upon him. He rose at dawn, swam before breakfast in the Potomac, and worked hard at his job. But much of his job entailed being accessible to endless callers, and a round of evening entertainments. Though he loved knowledgeable dinner-table conversation, Adams like his father was not naturally gregarious. Washington small talk wearied and exasperated him, especially since the undercurrents were treacherous, as is the way of capital cities. Thus, the Adamses' cosmopolitan tastes fed malicious rumors that they had spent too long abroad. The most ludicrous story was that as Minister at St Petersburg he had procured a pretty American girl for Tsar Alexander. An absurd fuss was made over the discovery that Adams had installed a billiard-table in the White House, as if this were the height of aristocratic extravagance. In popular report, Adams was a social and intellectual snob. Opponents harped on the contrast between "Jackson who can fight, and Adams who can write".

In common with his father, John Quincy had always refused to toe a party line. Following Madison and Monroe, he assumed that national parties were the main source of faction. Adams therefore tried to pick for his cabinet the best men, without regard for political coloration. He saddled himself with a group of ambitious and quarrelsome *prima donnas*, whom he could not persuade to agree with him on the policy recommendations in his annual messages to Congress. Congress almost contemptuously brushed aside his cherished vision of using the revenue from the sale of public lands to create a better America. Whatever retirement would be like, the embittered Adams confided to his diary in 1827, it could not be "worse than this perpetual motion and crazing cares. The weight grows heavier from day to day". Meanwhile, the Jacksonians were building a national party around a few simple, effective, reiterated notions. Jackson was the rightful President. It was time for a President from the West. Jackson would be the people's President, a gallant old democrat, who would purge Washington of its false Europeanized conceptions of government and society.

LOUISA CATHERINE JOHNSON, MRS ADAMS

If Adams had been politically more cunning, and perhaps more affable in manner, he might have beaten the Jacksonians at their own game. Instead, he went down to defeat in 1828, convinced that in repudiating him the United States had wrecked its chances for the future, and so bruised in spirit that he would not attend Jackson's inauguration—just as his father had declined to wait for the incoming Jefferson. Like his father he went back to Massachusetts with his tail between his legs. But the Adamses were of too tough a breed to admit permanent defeat. In 1831 John Quincy, at the age of 64, started a new career as a member of the House of Representatives. "Old Man Eloquent" was still a member when he died seventeen years later. He had endured some hard domestic blows. Two of his three sons died before him—the eldest, George Washington Adams, by falling overboard from a boat when probably drunk. He was never quite free from money cares, though at least his remaining son Charles Francis solved the problem for the third generation by marrying an heiress. But Adams was a public man, equating family prestige with that of the whole nation. In Congress, whether on the floor of the House or in committee, no one was allowed to forget that the Adamses were still watchdogs for the United States, above all for the old ideals of excellence and integrity. As an anti-slavery New Englander, Adams fought to prevent a predominantly complaisant Congress from ignoring anti-slavery petitions. He hammered away at the need for federal support of research and education. Near the end of his long, hard, contumacious, valuable existence Adams gained one of his points. The big Smithsonian benefaction, bequeathed to the United States by an English millionaire, was to be used for purposes Adams approved—including the astronomical observatory he had unsuccessfully suggested back in 1829. One of the Adams' weaknesses was also a strength: the unshakeable conviction that they were right, even if everyone else was out of step.

# Chronology

1767    Born at Braintree (now Quincy), Massachusetts 11 July.

1775    Witnessed Battle of Bunker Hill with his mother from the top of Penn's Hill 17 June.

1778    Went to Paris with his father; entered school at Passy.

1779    Returned to Braintree Aug; again sailed for Europe with brother Charles; landed in Spain 8 Dec.

1780    Arrived in Paris Feb; resumed schooling; travelled with father and brother to the Netherlands July; attended school in Amsterdam.

1781    Entered Leyden University Jan; travelled to St Petersburg as secretary and interpreter to Francis Dana 7 July-27 Aug.

1783    Arrived at The Hague after travels through Finland, Sweden, Denmark and Germany April; returned to Paris with his father Aug; travelled to London with his father Sept-Oct.

1784    Accompanied his father to The Hague Jan; met mother and sister in London July; family settled at Auteuil, nr Paris Aug.

1785    Sailed for US May; arrived July.

1786    Entered Harvard March.

1787    Graduated from Harvard 18 July; began law studies with Theophilus Parsons in Newburyport, Massachusetts Sept.

1790    Admitted to the Massachusetts Bar 15 July; opened law office in Boston Aug.

1791    Published series of articles in the *Columbian Centinel* under the pseudonym of "Publicola", attacking Thomas Paine's theories in *Declaration of the Rights of Man* June-July.

1792-93  Published sundry political and critical articles under pseudonyms of "Menander", "Marcellus" and "Columbus".

1794    Appointed Minister Resident to the Netherlands by President Washington 29 May (confirmed by Senate 30 May); sailed from Boston 17 Sept; arrived in London 15 Oct and at The Hague 31 Oct.

1795    Went to London to exchange ratifications of Jay's Treaty with Great Britain Oct.

1796    Returned to The Hague 31 May; appointed Minister Plenipotentiary to Portugal, but never proceeded to Lisbon.

1797    Left Holland for England June; appointed Minister Plenipotentiary to Prussia by his father; presented credentials in Berlin Nov.

1799    Negotiated treaty of amity and commerce with Prussia.

| | |
|---|---|
| 1800 | Travelled through Germany and Silesia July-Oct. |
| 1801 | Decided to resign diplomatic post Feb; sailed from Hamburg 8 July; arrived at Philadelphia 4 Sept; arrived in Quincy 24 Nov; resumed law practice in Boston. |
| 1802 | Elected as a Federalist to the Massachusetts State Senate April; defeated in election for House of Representatives from Boston Nov. |
| 1803 | Appointed US Senator from Massachusetts to fill an unexpired term until 1808; took seat in Senate 17 Oct. |
| 1805 | Appointed Boylston Professor of Rhetoric and Oratory at Harvard. |
| 1806 | Received honorary degree of LLD from the College of New Jersey. |
| 1807 | The only Federalist to support Jefferson's Embargo Act Dec. |
| 1808 | Attended Republican caucus on the Presidential nomination Jan; denied Federalist renomination to the Senate; resigned from Senate 8 June; resumed law practice in Boston. |
| 1809 | Appointed Minister Plenipotentiary to Russia by President Madison 6 March; commissioned June; sailed for Russia 5 Aug; arrived in St Petersburg 23 Oct. |
| 1811 | Appointed Associate Justice of the Supreme Court by President Madison 21 Feb (confirmed by Senate 22 Feb); declined to serve 5 April. |
| 1812 | Received offer from Emperor Alexander I of Russia to mediate between US and Great Britain 21 Sept. |
| 1813 | Great Britain declined to negotiate with the peace commissioners. |
| 1814 | Appointed one of five commissioners to negotiate peace with Great Britain Jan; peace talks began at Ghent 8 Aug; Treaty of Ghent signed 24 Dec. |
| 1815 | Left Ghent 26 Jan; arrived in Paris 4 Feb; commissioned Envoy Extraordinary and Minister Plenipotentiary to Great Britain 28 Feb; arrived in London 26 May; one of three US signatories of new commercial treaty with Great Britain 13 July; took up residence at Little Ealing 1 Aug. |
| 1817 | Appointed Secretary of State by President Monroe 5 March; Left London 10 June; arrived in New York 6 Aug and in Washington 20 Sept; took office 22 Sept. |
| 1818 | Concluded the Convention of 1818 on fisheries, boundaries and transatlantic commerce with Great Britain. |
| 1819 | Signed Adams-Onís Treaty with Spain by which US acquired Florida 22 Feb. |
| 1820 | Took up residence in Washington; received only electoral vote not cast for Monroe in Presidential Election 6 Dec. |
| 1821 | Transcontinental Treaty with Spain ratified by the Senate 22 Feb. |
| 1823 | Played an important part in the formulation of the Monroe Doctrine against foreign intervention in the New World. |
| 1824 | With wife gave ball for Andrew Jackson on ninth anniversary of the Battle of New Orleans 8 Jan; nominated for President by western faction of the Republicans 15 Feb; concluded a Convention with Russia fixing boundary of the American sphere of influence and ensuring the later incorporation of Oregon as a US Territory April; National Election 9 Nov; Presidential Electors cast their ballots 1 Dec. |
| 1825 | Elected 6th President of the United States of America by the House of Representatives in accordance with the 12th Amendment to the Constitution, no |

candidate in the election having received a majority of the electoral votes 9 Feb; inaugurated in the Hall of Representatives in the Capitol 4 March; sent first State of the Union message to Congress 6 Dec.

1826    Sent second State of the Union message to Congress 5 Dec.

1827    Signed Act raising salary of Postmaster General to level of executive department heads 2 March; sent third State of the Union Message to Congress 4 Dec.

1828    Treaty with Mexico fixing boundary line as designated in the Adams-Onís Treaty 12 Jan (not effective until 5 April 1832); signed Tariff Act 19 May; broke ground for Chesapeake and Ohio Canal 4 July; defeated for re-election as President by Andrew Jackson Nov; sent fourth and last State of the Union message to Congress 2 Dec.

1829    Retired from office 4 March; travelled from Washington to Quincy June; returned to Washington Dec.

1830    Elected to Board of Overseers of Harvard College; elected to House of Representatives as member from Plymouth District 1 Nov.

1831    Took seat in House of Representatives 5 Dec.

1832    Member of special committee to inquire into affairs of the Bank of the United States at Philadelphia 22 March-17 April.

1833    Defeated as Anti-Masonic candidate for Governor of Massachusetts.

1834    Delivered national eulogy on Lafayette 31 Dec.

1836    Voted against House of Representatives resolution on slavery 26 May; defeated as candidate for the Senate.

1836-43  Vigorously opposed annexation and admission of Texas.

1841-43  Chairman of House Committee on Foreign Affairs.

1841    Successfully argued case of the Africans of the *Amistad* before the Supreme Court 24 Feb and 1 March.

1842    Presented petition to Congress from citizens of Haverhill requesting dissolution of the Union because of Southern slavery, thereby incurring a resolution of censure 25 Jan; House voted to refuse to receive the petition 7 Feb.

1843    Delivered speech at cornerstone-laying ceremony of Cincinnati Astronomical Observatory 23 Nov; received formal thanks of Mexican Government for upholding the Mexican cause in the Texas Question Dec.

1844    Succeeded in repealing all gag rules 3 Dec.

1845    Efforts to prevent annexation of Texas finally defeated Feb.

1846    Voted against declaration of war with Mexico 11 May; instrumental in getting a favorable vote from Congress for the establishment of the Smithsonian Institution Aug; suffered first stroke in Boston 20 Nov.

1847    Returned to House of Representatives Feb.

1848    Collapsed with second stroke in his seat in the House of Representatives 21 Feb; died in the Speaker's Room at the Capitol 23 Feb; buried at Quincy 11 March (re-buried with his wife in the crypt of the Stone Temple, Quincy, beside his parents 16 Dec 1852).

# The Writings of President John Quincy Adams

*A Journal by John Quincy Adams 1779-1845* (irregular until 1795)

*Letters from Silesia* (1804)

*Lectures on Rhetoric and Oratory,* 2 vols (1810)

*A Letter to the Hon Harrison Gray Otis* (1808)

*Report on Weights and Measures* (1821)

*The Duplicate Letters, the Fisheries and the Mississippi* (1822)

*Eulogy on James Monroe* (1831)

*Dermot Macmorrogh, or The Conquest of Ireland* (an epic poem) (1832)

*Oration on Lafayette* (1835)

*Eulogy on James Madison* (1836)

*Speech of John Quincy Adams, of Massachusetts, upon the Right of the People, Men and Women, to Petition; on the Freedom of Speech and of Debate in the House of Representatives* (1838)

*Poems of Religion and Society* (1848)

A seven volume edition of the *Writings of John Quincy Adams*, edited by W. C. Ford, was published in 1913, and an earlier collection of *Memoirs*, edited by Charles Francis Adams, 12 vols (1874-77). A new edition of *Adams Papers*, supervised by Lyman H. Butterfield, is in preparation.

# Lineage of President John Quincy Adams

JOHN QUINCY ADAMS was the eldest son of JOHN ADAMS, **2nd President of the United States of America** (*qv*), by his wife Abigail Smith[1] (*see p 79*).

# The Descendants of President John Quincy Adams

(**NB** *All the descendants of President John Quincy Adams are, of course*, also *descendants of his father President John Adams—see p 75*)

JOHN QUINCY ADAMS *m* at All Hallows, Barking-by-the-Tower, London 26 July 1797, Louisa Catherine (*b* in London 12 Feb 1775; *d* at Washington, DC 15 May 1852, *bur* first in the Congressional Cemetery, Washington, later removed to Quincy with her husband), 2nd dau of Hon Joshua Johnson, of Baltimore, Maryland, American Consul-Gen in London 1785-99 (and yr brother of Thomas Johnson, first Gov of Maryland), by his wife Catherine Nuth, and had issue,

**1** George Washington ADAMS, Capt US Army, mem Mass legislature, *b* in Berlin 12 April 1801; drowned in Long Island Sound (either an act of suicide or an accident) 30 April 1829, *unm*.

**2** John ADAMS II, priv sec to his father as Pres, *b* at Washington, DC 4 July 1803, *m* at the White House[2] 25 Feb 1828, his 1st cousin Mary Catherine (*b ca* 1806; *d* 1870), dau of Walter Hellen, by his 1st wife Nancy (or Ann), eldest dau of Hon Joshua Johnson, and *dvp* at Washington, DC 23 Oct 1834, leaving issue,

   **1** Mary Louisa ADAMS, *b* at the White House, Washington, DC 2 Dec 1828, *m* 30 June 1853, as his 2nd wife, her 2nd cousin[3] William Clarkson Johnson (*b* at Utica, New York 16 Aug 1823; *d* at New York 28 Jan 1893), 4th son of Alexander Bryan Johnson, of Utica, New York, by his wife Abigail Louisa Smith Adams, and *d* at Far Rocksway, Long Island, New York 16 July 1859, leaving issue (*see p 80*).

   **2** Georgeanna Frances (Fanny) ADAMS, *b* at Quincy, Mass 1830; *d* there (in the same room and same bed in which she was born) 2 Oct 1839.

**3** Charles Francis ADAMS, mem Congress, US Min to England 1861-68, *b* at Boston 18 Aug 1807, *educ* Harvard (AB 1825), *m* at Medford, Mass 3 Sept 1829, Abigail Brown (*b* at Medford, Mass 25 April 1808; *d* 6 June 1889), 3rd and yst dau of Peter Chardon Brooks, by his wife Ann Gorham, and *d* at Boston 21 Nov 1886, having had issue,

   **1** Louisa Catherine ADAMS, *b* at Boston 13 Aug 1831, *m* 1854, Charles Kuhn, of Philadelphia (*b* 1821; *d* 1899), and *dsp* at Bagni di Lucca, Italy 13 July 1870.

   **2** John Quincy ADAMS II, of Mount Wollaston Farm, Mass, served in the Civil War as Col on the Staff of Gov Andrew, *b* at Boston 22 Sept 1833, *educ* Harvard (AB 1853), *m* 29 April 1861, Fanny Cadwallader (*b* 15 Oct 1839; *d* 16 May 1911), dau of George Caspar Crowninshield, by his wife Harriet Sears, and *d* at Quincy 14 Aug 1894, having had issue,

     (1) John Quincy ADAMS III, *b* at Boston 23 Feb 1862; *d* 12 April 1876.

     (2) George Caspar ADAMS, *b* at Boston 24 April 1863, *educ* Harvard (AB 1886), *dunm* at Quincy 13 July 1900.

     (3) Charles Francis ADAMS III, of Boston, Treas of

Harvard Univ, Mayor of Quincy, Sec of the Navy 1929-33, *b* at Quincy 2 Aug 1866, *educ* Harvard (AB 1888), *m* 3 April 1899, Frances, dau of Hon William Croade Lovering, of Taunton, Mass, mem Congress for Mass 1897-1910, and *d* at Boston 10 June 1954, leaving issue,

1*a*●Catherine ADAMS, *b* 13 Jan 1902, *m* 26 June 1923, ●Henry Sturgis Morgan (*b* in London, England 24 Oct 1900) [*120 East End Avenue, New York, NY, USA*], yr son of John Pierpont Morgan, of Wall Hall, Watford, Herts, England, and Matinicock Point, Glen Cove, Long Island (*see* BURKE'S *Distinguished Families of America*), by his wife Jane Norton Grew, and has issue,

1*b*●Henry Sturgis MORGAN, Jr, Rear-Adm USN [*Brookvale, Stonington, Conn, USA*], *b* 10 Aug 1924, *educ* Harvard, *m* 28 March 1945, ●Fanny Gray (*b* 30 Sept 1925), dau of Leon M. Little, and has issue,

1*c*●Catherine Adams MORGAN, *b* 2 Oct 1946, *m* Aug 1967, ●Alec Mitchell Peltier, and has issue,
●Patricia Gray PELTIER, *b* 6 May 1972.

2*c*●Henry MORGAN, *b* 20 Oct 1948.

3*c*●Polly MORGAN, *b* 11 July 1951.

4*c*●Joan MORGAN, *b* 4 Dec 1953, *m* at Northport, Long Island, New York 22 Sept 1973, ●Peter Lincoln Folsom.

2*b*●Charles Francis MORGAN, *b* 16 April 1926, *m* Feb 1960, ●Sarah Baldwin Lambert (*b* 17 July 1934), and has issue,

1*c*●Charles Francis MORGAN, Jr, *b* 4 March 1961.

2*c*●Maria Baldwin MORGAN, *b* 7 June 1963.

3*c*●Samuel Lambert MORGAN, *b* 15 March 1965.

3*b*●Miles MORGAN [*Via della Penitenza, Rome, Italy*], *b* 1 Nov 1928.

4*b*●John Adams MORGAN, *b* 17 Sept 1930, *m* 1st 6 June 1953 (*m* diss by div), Elizabeth Robbins Choare (*b* 13 Dec 1933), and has issue,

1*c*●John Adams MORGAN, Jr, *b* 13 Aug 1954.

John Adams Morgan *m* 2ndly Feb 1961, ●Tania Goss (*b* 17 Nov 1935), and by her has issue,

2*c*●Chauncey Goss MORGAN, *b* 19 April 1963.

5*b*●Peter Angus MORGAN [*15 Lafayette Road, Schenectady, New York, USA*], *b* 23 Oct 1938.

2*a*●Charles Francis ADAMS IV, hon DBA Suffolk Univ 1953, and Northeastern Univ 1959, LLD Bates Coll 1960, Chm Raytheon Co, Waltham, Mass from 1964, served in World War II with USNR [*Dedham Street, Dover, Massachusetts 02030, USA; Somerset, Brook, Eastern Yacht, New York Yacht, and Cruising of America Clubs*], *b* at Boston 2 May 1910, *educ* St Mark's Sch, Southboro, Mass, and Harvard (AB 1932), *m* 16 June 1934, Margaret (*b* 22 April 1915; *d* 11 July 1972), dau of Philip Stockton, of Boston, and has issue,

1*b*●Abigail ADAMS, *b* 29 April 1935, *m* 11 June 1955, ●James Craven Manny [*530 East 86th Street, New York, New York, USA*], and has issue,

1*c*●Alison Adams MANNY, *b* 16 March 1956.

2*c*●Walter R. MANNY II, *b* 11 June 1957.

3*c*●Alix MANNY, *b* 12 Nov 1960.

4*c*●Timothy MANNY, *b* 5 Nov 1970.

2*b*●Alison ADAMS, *b* 18 March 1937, *m* (*m* diss by div), Beverley Robinson, and has issue,

1*c*●S. Philippse ROBINSON II.

2*c*●John ROBINSON.

3*c*●Stephen ROBINSON.

3*b*●Timothy ADAMS, *b* 7 Oct 1947.

(4) Fanny Crowninshield ADAMS, *b* at Quincy 19 Aug 1873; *d* there 11 April 1876.

(5) Arthur G. ADAMS, of Dover, Mass, sometime Vice-Pres Adams Trust Co, City Trust Co, etc, served in World War I as Lieut USN, *b* at Quincy 20 May 1877, *educ* Harvard (AB 1899), *m* 5 Oct 1921, ●Margery (*b* at Brookline, Mass 2 May 1893), widow of Francis Williams Sargent, and dau of George Lee, by his wife Eva Ballerina, and *d* 19 May 1943, leaving issue,

1*a*●John Quincy ADAMS V, insurance co exec [*200 Berkeley Street, Boston, Massachusetts 02116, USA*], *b* at Dover, Mass 24 Dec 1922, *educ* St Paul's Sch, and Harvard (AB 1945), *m* 1 Feb 1947, ●Nancy Motley (*b* 4 April 1926), and has issue,

1*b*●Nancy Barton ADAMS, *b* 1 Oct 1948.

2*b*●John Quincy ADAMS VI [*Wilsondale Road, Dover, Massachusetts 02023, USA*], *b* 2 Nov 1950.

3*b*●Margery Lee ADAMS, *b* 13 April 1954.

4*b*●Benjamin Crowninshield ADAMS, *b* 13 Dec 1964.

2*a*●Arthur ADAMS, Jr [*Dover, Massachusetts 02023, USA*], *b* 5 Nov 1926.

(6) Abigail ADAMS, *b* at Quincy 6 Sept 1879, *m* there 10 June 1907, Robert Homans, of Boston (*b* there 3 Oct 1873; *d* there 23 April 1934), son of John Homans, by his wife Helen Amory Perkins, and *d* at Boston 4 Feb 1974, having had issue,

1*a*●George Caspar HOMANS, Prof of Sociology at Harvard from 1953, Ford Foundation Visiting Prof to Graduate Sch of Business Admin 1961, Simon Visiting Prof to Manchester Univ, England 1953, Prof of Social Theory, Camb 1955-56, Visiting Prof of Kent Univ, England 1967, served in World War II with USNR 1941-45 (Lt-Cmdr), mem American Acad of Arts and Sciences, American Sociological Assoc (Pres 1963-64), and American Philosophical Soc [*11 Francis Avenue, Cambridge, Massachusetts 02138, USA*], *b* at Boston 11 Aug 1910, *educ* St Paul's Sch, Concord, Harvard (AB 1932), and Camb Univ (MA 1955), *m* at Hyde Park, New York 27 June 1941, ●Nancy Parshall (*b* at Keokula 28 Nov 1913), dau of Dexter Cooper, by his wife Gertrude Sturgis, and has issue,

1*b*●Elizabeth Cooper HOMANS, *b* at Boston 6 Oct 1942.

2*b*●Susan Welles HOMANS, *b* at Boston 11 July 1944.

3*b*●Peter Charndon Brooks HOMANS, *b* at Boston 6 Aug 1955.

2*a*●Fanny Crowninshield HOMANS, *b* at Boston 21 Aug 1911, *educ* Radcliffe, *m* 1st, Howland Shaw Warren (*b* 2 Feb 1910); and 2ndly 15 Aug 1939, ●Henry Lowell Mason, Jr (*b* 17 Feb 1910), and has issue,

1*b*●Henry Lowell MASON III, *b* 10 Feb 1941, *m* June 1969, ●Elaine Brobcowicz.

2*b*●Abigail Adams MASON, *b* 17 Dec 1943, *m* 19 Aug 1967, ●Alfred L. Browne, Jr (*b* 7 July 1937), and has issue,

1*c*●Alfred L. BROWNE III, *b* 18 Oct 1968.

2*c*●Priscilla Crowninshield BROWNE, *b* 5 Aug 1970.

3*b*●John Homans MASON, *b* 24 Oct 1945.

3*a*●Helen Amory HOMANS, *b* at Boston 29 Oct 1913, *educ* Radcliffe, *m* 27 June 1936, ●Carl Joyce Gilbert (*b* at Bloomfield, New Jersey 3 April 1906), son of Seymour Parker Gilbert by his wife Carrie Jennings Cooper, and has issue,

●Thomas Tibbots GILBERT, *b* 8 Jan 1947, *m* 28 June 1968, ●Margaret Helen Bay (*b* 28 Nov 1946).

4*a* Robert HOMANS, Jr, *b* at Boston 25 Oct 1918, *educ* Harvard, *m* 12 Jan 1946, ●Mary Aldrich (*b* 25 Jan 1921), and *d* at Hillsboro, New Hampshire 18 Dec 1964, leaving issue,

1*b*●Robert HOMANS III, *b* 12 Oct 1946.

2*b*●Lucy Aldrich HOMANS, *b* 18 Feb 1948.

3*b*●Abigail HOMANS, *b* 25 Oct 1955.

3 Charles Francis ADAMS, Jr, LittD, LLD, Pres of Mass Historical Soc 1895-1915, Lt-Col of Cav in the Civil War 1861-65, Brevet Brig-Gen of Vols, Pres Union Pacific Railroad, *b* at Boston 27 May 1835, *educ* Harvard (AB 1856), *m* at Newport, Rhode Island 8 Nov 1865, Mary Hone (*b* at New York City 23 Feb 1843; *d* at Concord, Mass 23 March 1935), dau of Edward Ogden, of New York City and Newport, by his wife Caroline Hone Callender, and *d* at Washington, DC 20 March 1915, leaving issue,

(1) Mary Ogden ADAMS, *b* at Quincy, Mass (the last mem of the family to be born in house of Pres and Mrs John Adams) 27 July 1867, *m* 30 Sept 1890, Grafton St Loe Abbott, of Concord, Mass (*b* at Lowell, Mass 14 Nov 1856; *d* at Concord, Mass 27 Feb 1915), son of Hon Josiah Gardiner Abbott, mem of Congress from Mass, by his wife Caroline Livermore, and *d* at Concord, Mass 21 Aug 1933, leaving issue,

1*a*●Henry Livermore ABBOTT, Capt USN, served in World Wars I and II, cmd'd US Sub *LI* 1916-18, Snr Naval Mem Jt and combined Intell Staff of Jt Chiefs of Staff 1943-46, had Naval Cross (1918) and Green Commendation Ribbon (1946), *b* at Lewiston, Maine 12 April 1892, *educ* Concord Public Schs, Groton Sch, and US Naval Acad, *m* 1st at Washington DC 24 April 1920, Elizabeth Lee, poetess (*dec*), dau of William Morton

Grinnell, by his wife Elizabeth Lee Ernst, and had issue,
1b●Mary Lee ABBOTT, artist, b 27 July 1921, m 1st 2 March 1943 (m diss by div), R. Lewis Teague; and 2ndly 17 May 1950 (m diss by div), Thomas Hill Clyde.
2b●William Henry Grafton ABBOTT, b 19 March 1923.
Capt Henry L. Abbott m 2ndly at Eaglewood, New Jersey 2 Jan 1932, ●Marie Farnsworth (b 18 Oct 1900), dau of Orlando Blodget Willcox, by his wife Jessie Cook, and d at Washington, DC 2 April 1969, having by her had issue,
1b●Elizabeth Marsden ABBOTT, Soc Service, b 14 Sept 1942.
2a●Mary Ogden ABBOTT, painter and sculptress [*Sudbury Road, Concord, Mass 01742, USA*], b at Concord, Mass 12 Oct 1894, *educ* Sch of Boston Mus of Fine Arts.
3a●John Adams ABBOTT, mem Mass Gen Hosp Consultation Bd, and Snr Cons Staff of McLean Hosp, USA Amb Extraord to Republic of Niger from 1970 [*Beaver Pond Road, Lincoln, Massachusetts 01773, USA*], b at Concord, Mass 7 July 1902, *educ* Concord Public Schs, Groton Sch, Harvard Coll (BA 1925), and Harvard Med Sch (MD 1931), m at Concord, Mass 9 Aug 1945, ●Diana Asken, BS, MA, MPH, Chm of Dept and Assoc Prof of Nutrition Simmons Coll Boston (b at Calcutta, India 4 Aug 1913), dau of Herbert Ballin, by his wife Esther Raleigh Michael, and has issue,
1b●Peter Michael ABBOTT, b at Burlington, Vermont 9 Oct 1952, *educ* Lincoln Public Schs, Cardigan Mountain Sch and Hoosac Sch.
2b●Rosemarie Livermore ABBOTT, b at Patras, Greece 22 Oct 1953, *educ* Lincoln Public Schs, House in the Pines, and Cambridge Sch.
(2) Louisa Catherine ADAMS, b 28 Dec 1871, m 6 June 1900, Thomas Nelson Perkins, of Westwood, Mass, lawyer (b at Milton, Mass 6 May 1870; d 7 Oct 1937), son of Edward Cranch Perkins, by his wife Jane Sedgwick Watson, and had issue,
1a●Elliott PERKINS, Prof of History at Harvard and former Master of Lowell House, Harvard Univ [*18 Hawthorn Street, Cambridge, Mass 02138, USA*], b at Westwood, Mass 17 March 1901, *educ* Harvard, m 1 April 1937, ●Mary Frances (b 19 Aug 1904), 2nd dau of late Sir Philip Wilbraham Baker Wilbraham, 6th Bt, KBE (*see* BURKE'S *Peerage*).
2a●James Handasyd PERKINS, b at Westwood, Mass 7 Nov 1903, m 28 June 1930, ●Marion H. Gibbs (b 17 May 1904), and has issue,
1b●Louisa Catherine PERKINS, b 14 April 1934, m 10 July 1961, ●Henry H Porter (b 13 Nov 1934), and has issue,
· 1c●Mary K. PORTER, b 2 June 1963.
2c●Louisa Catherine PORTER, b 16 Oct 1966.
2b●James Handasyd PERKINS, Jr, b 29 Jan 1936, m Dec 1966, ●Judith O'Connel (b 25 March 1939), and has issue,
1c●Elliot K. PERKINS, b 30 Oct 1968.
2c●Edith PERKINS, b 1 Nov 1970.
3b●Rufus Gibbs PERKINS, b 14 Oct 1939.
3a Thomas Nelson PERKINS, Jr, b at Westwood, Mass 30 April 1907, m 2 June 1938, ●Anne Bissell Houghton (b 4 Nov 1910), and d 3 May 1965, leaving issue,
1b●Mary PERKINS, b 21 May 1940, m 12 Sept 1964, ●John H. Baughan (b 22 Jan 1932), and has issue,
1c●Hobart Perkins BAUGHAN, b 20 Aug 1965.
2c●John H. BAUGHAN, b 26 Dec 1966.
3c●Anne Laughlin BAUGHAN, b 5 Sept 1969.
2b●Anne PERKINS, b 15 July 1941, m 3 June 1967, ●William McDowell (b 7 Nov 1936), and has issue,
1c●Stewart Laughlin McDOWELL, b 17 Sept 1969.
2c●Susan Houghton McDOWELL, b 16 Jan 1972.
3b●Thomas Nelson PERKINS III, b 2 Aug 1944, m 3 June 1968, ●Laura Kerrin (b 23 Sept 1945), and has issue,
1c●Thomas Nelson PERKINS IV, b 27 Oct 1968.
2c●Samuel Houghton PERKINS, b March 1971.
(3) Elizabeth Ogden ADAMS, b 3 Dec 1873; *dunm.*
(4) John ADAMS III, of Lincoln, Mass, b at Quincy 17 July

1875, *educ* Harvard (AB 1898), m 3 Oct 1905, Marian (b at Topeka, Kansas 9 March 1878; d 25 June 1959), dau of Charles F. Morse, by his wife Ellen Holdredge, and d at Concord, Mass 30 Aug 1964, leaving issue,
1a Mary Ogden ADAMS, b 13 Aug 1906, m 14 June 1941, ●James Barr Ames (b 20 April 1911), and d 23 July 1967, leaving issue,
1b Elizabeth Bigelow AMES, b 1 May 1942, m 24 Aug 1968, Michael Joseph Wollan (d 28 Aug 1968), and *dsp* 30 Aug 1968.
2b●Richard AMES, b 23 April 1944, m 26 April 1967, ●Heather Ann Woods (b 13 July 1945), and has issue,
●Michael Wollan AMES, b 24 Oct 1970.
3b●Charles Cabell AMES, b 3 April 1947, m 30 June 1968, ●Kathleen Lawrence Fisk (b 19 April 1947), and has issue,
●Brooks Averill AMES, b 20 Jan 1971.
2a●John Quincy ADAMS IV, b 15 July 1907, m 12 Oct 1937, ●Lucy Dodge Rice (b 21 Dec 1907), and has issue,
1b●Benjamin Dodge ADAMS, b 23 June 1938, m ●Serita Babson (b 26 Feb 1937), and has issue,
●Benjamin Dodge ADAMS, Jr, b 29 April 1959.
2b●Elizabeth Ogden ADAMS, b 27 Aug 1939, m ●Samuel D. Weaver (b 31 May 1939), and has issue,
1c●Marian Adams WEAVER, b 1 June 1962.
2c●Samuel D. WEAVER, Jr, b 16 July 1963.
3c●Timothy WEAVER, b 2 Dec 1968.
3b●Susanna Boylston ADAMS, b 1 May 1944, *educ* Colorado Univ, m 1 Nov 1969, ●Nicholas Whittemore, son of John Howard Whittemore.
4b●Lydia Staniford ADAMS, b 5 June 1951.
3a●Thomas Boylston ADAMS, served in World War II as Capt USAF, b 25 July 1910, *educ* Harvard, m 5 Jan 1940, ●Ramelle Frost Cocharne (b 14 Aug 1916), and has issue,
1b●John ADAMS, b 13 April 1941, m 3 June 1967, ●Patricia Jones (b 17 March 1943), and has issue,
●Samuel ADAMS, b 25 Aug 1972.
2b●Peter Boylston ADAMS, b 27 Aug 1942, m 16 Feb 1969, ●Sharon Kaye Pruett (b 19 May 1948).
3b●Francis Douglas ADAMS, b 12 Feb 1945, m 17 Aug 1968, ●Patricia Ingersoll (b 2 Nov 1944).
4b●Henry Bigelow ADAMS, b 12 May 1949, *educ* Harvard, m 12 June 1971, ●Ann Louise Jensen (b 3 July 1949).
5b●Ramelle Frost ADAMS, b 16 Feb 1953.
4a●Frederick Ogden ADAMS [*Old Concord Road, Lincoln, Mass 01773, USA*], b 13 Sept 1912.
5a●Abigail ADAMS, b 3 June 1915, m 14 June 1940, ●Gilbert W. King (b 13 Jan 1914), and has issue,
1b●Helen Elizabeth KING, b 29 May 1942, m 12 March 1971, ●Theodore Coronges.
2b●James Anthony KING, b 3 April 1947, m 21 June 1970, ●Dione Read Christensen (b 5 July 1948).
(5) Henry ADAMS, of Lincoln, Mass, served in World War I with Red Cross in France and Russia, b at Quincy 17 July 1875, *educ* Harvard (AB 1898), *dunm* 26 April 1951.
4 Henry (Brooks) ADAMS, Prof of History at Harvard, author of *History of the United States under the Administrations of Jefferson and Madison*, and many other historical works, b at Boston 16 Feb 1838, *educ* Harvard (AB 1858), m 27 June 1872, Marian (b at Boston 13 Sept 1843; d at Washington, DC 6 Dec 1885, *bur* Rock Creek Cemetery, Washington), dau of Dr Robert William Hooper, by his wife Ellen Sturgis, and *dsp* at Washington, DC 27 March 1918.
5 Arthur ADAMS, b at Boston 23 July 1841; d 9 Feb 1846.
6 Mary ADAMS, b at Boston 19 Feb 1846, m 20 June 1877, Henry Parker Quincy, MD, and d 1928, leaving issue,
(1) ●Dorothy Adams QUINCY, b at Dedham, Mass 14 Dec 1885, m 7 Feb 1906, Frederic Russell Nourse (b 24 May 1877; d 3 April 1952), and has had issue,
1a●Dorothy Quincy NOURSE, b 6 July 1907, m 1st 20 Oct 1928 (m diss by div), Edwin Lawrence Beckwith (b 25 July 1905; d April 1968), and has issue,
1b●Dorothy Quincy BECKWITH, b 2 Jan 1930, m 23 June 1956, ●Warren G. Nelson (b 7 Oct 1931), and has issue,
1c●George Adams NELSON, b 8 Jan 1957.
2c●Dorothy Quincy NELSON, b 18 Feb 1959.
3c●Brooks Endicott NELSON, b 13 April 1962.

4c●Abigail Thorndike NELSON, *b* 17 Aug 1968.
2b●Harry Lawrence BECKWITH, *b* 10 May 1933, *m* 2 Oct 1964, ●Kristina Adelle Landall (*b* 14 Aug 1942), and has issue,

1c●Daniele Bastean BECKWITH, *b* 6 Dec 1965.
2c●Stephanie Adams BECKWITH, *b* 24 July 1967.
3c●David Lincoln BECKWITH, *b* 3 Feb 1970.
3b●Richard Adams BECKWITH, *b* 6 May 1936, *m* 28 Dec 1957, ●Virginia Churchill Dangelmayer, and has issue,

1c●Jacqueline Churchill BECKWITH, *b* 14 May 1961.
2c●Scott Adams BECKWITH, *b* 14 April 1964.
3c●Russell Lawrence BECKWITH, *b* 4 April 1968.
Dorothy Quincy Nourse *m* 2ndly 2 Jan 1944, ●Henry V. Pope (*b* Sept 1907).
2a Frederic Russell NOURSE, Jr, *b* 5 Feb 1910, *m* 26 Jan 1935, ●Margaret Dunn (*b* 21 Aug 1916), and *d* 5 June 1943, leaving issue,

1b●Frederic Russell NOURSE III, *b* 9 Feb 1936, *m* ●Jane Buxton, and has issue,
●Frederic Russell NOURSE IV, *b* 22 March 1958.
2b●George Dunn NOURSE, *b* 16 June 1938.
3b●Martha Elsie NOURSE, *b* 23 July 1941, *m* 24 April 1971, ●Martha Elsie NOURSE, *b* 23 July 1941, *m* 24 April 1971, ●Stephen Dalrymple Reynolds, Jr.
(2) ●Eleanor Adams QUINCY, *b* at Dedham, Mass 11 March 1888, *m* Oct 1920, Claude Simpson.
7 Brooks ADAMS, of Boston, Mass, Counsellor-at-law, lectr Boston Univ Law Sch 1904-11, author of numerous papers and articles on political and economic subjects, *b* at Quincy 24 June 1848, *educ* Harvard (AB 1870), *m* 7 Sept 1889, Evelyn (*b* at Cambridge, Mass 4 Jan 1853; *d* 14 Dec 1926), dau of Rear-Adm Charles Henry Davis, by his wife Harriette Blake Mills, and *dsp* at Boston 13 Feb 1927.
4 Louisa Catherine ADAMS, *b* at St Petersburg, Russia 12 Aug 1811; *d* there 15 Sept 1812.

# The Brothers and Sisters of President John Quincy Adams

These are given under DESCENDANTS OF PRESIDENT JOHN ADAMS (*see pp 75-84*).

# Notes

[1] Through his mother John Quincy Adams had several Royal descents from King Edward I (*see* APPENDIX C, PRESIDENTS OF ROYAL DESCENT).

[2] John Adams was the only son of a President to be married in the White House.

[3] This is the first instance of an intermarriage between the descendants of two Presidents. Both bride and bridegroom were descended from John Adams (but only the bride from John Quincy Adams).

# Andrew Jackson
## 1767-1845

———

7th President of the
United States of America
1829-1837

ANDREW JACKSON, 7TH PRESIDENT

# Andrew Jackson

## 1767-1845

### 7th President of the United States of America
### 1829-1837

AN ORATOR at a Washington centennial occasion in 1889 said: "We have exchanged the Washingtonian dignity for the Jeffersonian simplicity, which in due time came to be only another name for the Jacksonian vulgarity". For the twentieth-century reader this is a surprising remark. We understand and probably accept the praise accorded to Washington and Jefferson: but why the jab at Andrew Jackson? Most present-day scholars put Jackson among the great Presidents. Yet the speaker in question, Bishop Henry Codman Potter, was neither an eccentric nor a nonentity. He thought Jackson had been a bad influence on American political life, and his opinions were quite typical of the second half of the nineteenth century.

The accusation of men like Potter was that Jackson divided instead of uniting the nation, and that his followers—with his sanction—brought graft into politics. Jackson, they thought, governed by vendetta, rewarding his friends and hunting down his enemies. They instanced his lack of education, and claimed his best known statements such as the Bank Veto of 1832 were written for him. In their view Jackson was a product of frontier violence, a Tennessee brawler. He got men to vote for him by denouncing the rich. He was not even consistent; having proposed that Presidents should be restricted to a single term, Jackson made sure of a second term for himself and then bullied the Democratic party into nominating his pet candidate Martin Van Buren. Having declared his support for state's rights, he suddenly became a defender of federal supremacy over South Carolina's threat to "nullify" unjust federal laws. This too, when he had shown contempt for Chief Justice John Marshall and the rest of the Supreme Court. In his eight years in office he managed to alienate many of his supporters, including Davy Crockett.

It is easy to point to weaknesses in this bill of charges. For one thing, the people who first voted for him in 1828 may have visualized him as a war hero. But they saw him as a veteran, dignified and white-haired, not as a wild frontiersman. In the election campaign Jackson's opponents were at least as scurrilous as his own side. Jackson was called a murderer, a duellist, a gambler, an adulterer. His mother, in one flagrant bit of gutter journalism, was described as "a COMMON PROSTITUTE, brought to this country by the British soldiers! She afterwards married a MULATTO MAN, with whom she had several children, of which number GENERAL JACKSON IS ONE!!" Equally vicious things were said of Jackson's blameless wife Rachel Donelson. She had married Andrew Jackson under the mistaken impression that she had already got a divorce from a previous husband, Lewis Robards. The error was innocent, though Jackson was assailed as an adulterer and Rachel as a bigamist. When the divorce was made final the Jacksons went through a second marriage ceremony. True, Jackson was a slaveholder, but so were Washington and Jefferson. Nor did he invent the "spoils system". The idea of rotation in office went back to the Revolution; that of appointing loyal adherents to federal posts had already commended itself to Jefferson. In the main Andrew Jackson stuck to Jeffersonian principles as he understood them: equality of opportunity, decentralization, modest and minimal government (for a brief period in the latter half of Jackson's Presidency the United States was entirely free from a national debt).

Why then the charge of vulgarity? Though Jackson was not of an elegant family (there were also stories of his mother smoking a clay pipe), he had acquitted himself well enough as a judge, a planter, a general, a member of Congress and of the Senate. So the problem lies less in the man than in what he seemed to characterize or to advocate. Jackson symbolized Jacksonianism. Jacksonianism was symbolized by the familiar anecdotes of the inauguration in 1829: the huge crowds converging on the capital, the throng rushing into the White House for the public reception they had been collectively offered. Reactions to this hectic inaugural day differed. Those who opposed Jackson were puzzled and disapproving. Social and political democracy were not his invention, after all, or even his particular passion. Yet, Daniel Webster noted, people had "come five hundred miles to see General Jackson, *and they really seem to think that the country is rescued from some dreadful danger*". At the White House, said another shocked observer, the mob "broke in, in thousands . . . in one uninterrupted stream of mud and filth". Supporters of Jackson however emphasized enthusiasm rather than disorder, the "people" rather than the "mob". As Jackson appeared on the east portico of the Capitol, for the inaugural ceremony, an ecstatic witness recorded, "all hats were off at once, and the dark tint which usually pervades a mixed map of men was turned . . . into the bright hue of ten thousand upturned . . . faces, radiant

RACHEL DONELSON ROBARDS, MRS JACKSON

with sudden joy".

Since Presidents are not dictators, none could actually impose his will upon America as a Napoleon could change the shape of France. Andrew Jackson affected the United States, for good or ill, less than admirers or detractors claimed. Being a passionate, colorful individual, he was always in the news. The big controversies of his day were dramatized as personal encounters: Jackson *versus* Nicholas Biddle and the Bank of the United States, Jackson *versus* Henry Clay, Jackson *versus* John C. Calhoun. He thus served to bring excitement into politics, and to revive the alignment of the nation into two major parties when party-affiliations had seemed about to disappear. In the decades after his death in 1845 he was blamed for having lowered the tone of American public life. The Easterners who still dominated the national scene tended to regard the West as a region beyond the pale of civilization. From the 1890s, however, "West" and "frontier" became increasingly identified with the best instead of the worst features of America. Jackson, a Westerner, was again taken on the valuation of the enthusiasts of his own day. He was seen, and on the whole continues to be seen, as not a vulgar but a popular President, who by instinct responded to fresh currents.

We may agree that he was not a tyrant or a demagogue. Whoever had been President in the 1830s, there was a national appetite for bold, simple issues boldly and simply presented. This was, in short, the era of the common man, paradoxically demanding recognizable yet uncommon qualities in his leaders. Andrew Jackson, "Old Hickory", was splendidly suitable for such an electorate. He was the first President to stress that he and he alone in the American system represented the entire nation. Those who admired him had good reason to insist that the development was wholesome. Those who disliked him were guilty of some exaggeration. But they too had a potential point. If the President alone was the interpreter of the national welfare, what of Congress and the courts? Mercifully, Jackson embodied another fairly characteristic American paradox. He was a strong President who did not believe in a strong, busy executive branch. His duty he perceived as essentially Washingtonian or Jeffersonian: to keep the United States on the right road, but not himself to prescribe the route or compel Americans to march in his steps.

# Chronology

1767  Born (posthumously) probably in the log cabin of his mother's brother-in-law George McCamie (or McKemey) at Waxhaws, S Carolina 15 March.

1780  Joined the Revolutionary Army as a mounted orderly or messenger July; present at the Battle of Hanging Rock 6 Aug.

1781  Taken prisoner by the British with his brother Robert 10 April; wounded in the head and hand in an incident with his captors; released 25 April.

1784  Began Law studies in the office of Spruce Macay in Salisbury, N Carolina.

1786-87  Studied Law under Col John Stokes in Salisbury.

1787  Admitted to the N Carolina Bar Nov; began law practice in Johnsonville, N Carolina.

1788  Fought a duel (in which both contestants shot into the air deliberately) with Col Waightsill Avery; moved to Nashville (then in N Carolina; now in Tennessee) 26 Oct; appointed Prosecuting Attorney for western district of N Carolina Nov.

1796  Delegate from Davidson County to Knoxville Convention to draft constitution for State of Tennessee Jan-Feb; elected unopposed as first member for Tennessee to the House of Representatives; took seat therein at Philadelphia 5 Dec.

1797  Voted against White House Furniture Appropriation Bill; term as member of the House of Representatives ended 3 March; declined to seek re-election; elected to the Senate in place of Senator William Blount, who had been expelled; took seat in Senate 20 Nov.

1798  Resigned from Senate April; appointed Judge of Tennessee Superior Court Oct.

1802  Elected Major-General of Militia.

1803  Pursued quarrel with John Sevier, ex-Governor of Tennessee.

1804  Resigned as Judge of the Superior Court 24 July; moved to The Hermitage, nr Nashville (a property he had purchased in 1795) Aug or Sept.

1805  Entertained Aaron Burr at The Hermitage.

1806  Fought a duel with Charles Dickinson (who had disparaged Mrs Jackson) nr Harrison's Mills, Kentucky, in which Dickinson was killed and Jackson wounded 30 May; involved in Aaron Burr's schemes to conquer Texas.

1807  Summoned as witness in Burr's trial for treason at Richmond, but not called upon to give evidence.

1812  Offered services of his 2,500 men militia division after declaration of war on Great Britain June; appointed Major-General of US Volunteers by Governor William Blount of Tennessee.

| | |
|---|---|
| 1813 | Left for Natchez, Mississippi with 2,000 Volunteers 7 Jan; ordered to demobilize on arrival by General James Wilkinson, but refused to do so and marched his men back to Tennessee, earning his famous nickname of "Old Hickory"; shot at the City Hotel, Nashville by Jesse Benton (with whose brother Thomas Hart Benton he had quarrelled) and severely wounded in left arm and shoulder 4 Sept; informed Governor Blount of offer to lead volunteers against the Creek Indians who had massacred 250 people at Fort Mims, Mississippi Territory (now Alabama) 24 Sept; took command of Volunteers at Fayetteville, Tennessee 7 Oct; defeated Creeks at Talladega 9 Nov. |
| 1814 | Tennessee Volunteers defeated in three battles with the Creeks 22, 24 and 27 Jan; Creeks and Cherokees defeated in decisive battle at Horseshoe Bend 27 March; offered rank of Brigadier-General in US Army 22 May; accepted commission 8 June; accepted further promotion to Major-General 20 June; given command of Seventh Military District, including Tennessee, Louisiana and Mississippi Territory; Left Pierce's Stockade on Alabama River to march on Pensacola with 3,000 men 2 Nov; captured Pensacola from the British 7 Nov; left Mobile for New Orleans 22 Nov; arrived 1 Dec; declared martial law in New Orleans 15 Dec; fought night engagement with the British outside New Orleans 23 Dec. |
| 1815 | Artillery attack on British 1 Jan; won decisive victory in Battle of New Orleans 8 Jan; celebrated day of thanksgiving in New Orleans 23 Jan; fined $1,000 for contempt of court 31 March. |
| 1817 | Refused appointment as Secretary of War by President Monroe 5 March; assumed command of expedition sent after hostile Indians in Spanish Florida. |
| 1818 | Wrote to Monroe urging that possession of the Floridas by US would be desirable 6 Jan; captured Spanish post at St Marks 7 April; captured Pensacola 24 May, bringing end to first Seminole War; Senate committee appointed to investigate Jackson's actions in Florida 18 Dec. |
| 1821 | Appointed Military Governor of Florida by President Monroe 5 April; resigned 5 Oct; capital of Mississippi named "Jackson" in his honour 28 Nov. |
| 1822 | Nominated for President by Tennessee Legislature 20 July. |
| 1823 | Appointed Minister Plenipotentiary to Mexico by President Monroe 5 Jan; refused appointment 19 Feb; again elected to the Senate by Tennessee legislature 1 Oct; took seat 5 Dec. |
| 1824 | Election day 2 Nov; Presidential Electors cast their ballots 1 Dec. |
| 1825 | Defeated as candidate for President in House of Representatives 9 Feb; resigned from Senate 12 Oct, following re-nomination for President by Tennessee legislature. |
| 1828 | Election day 4 Nov; Presidential Electors cast their ballots 3 Dec. |
| 1829 | Electoral votes tabulated by Congress 11 Feb and Jackson and Calhoun officially declared elected; inaugurated as 7th President of the United States on the east portico of the Capitol 4 March; sent message to Creek Indians 23 March; instructed Secretary of State Van Buren to renew boundary change proposals with Mexico 13-15 Aug; sent first State of the Union message to Congress 8 Dec. |
| 1830 | Vetoed Maysville Road Internal Improvements Bill 27 May; vetoed Washington Road Internal Improvements Bill 31 May; signed Extension of Cumberland Road Act 31 May; issued proclamation that trade with British West Indies was open to American vessels; sent second State of the Union message to Congress |

6 Dec; vetoed Lighthouse and Beacons and Canal Stock Internal Improvements Bills 7 Dec.

1831     Signed Harbor Improvement Act 2 March; sent third State of the Union message to Congress 6 Dec.

1832     Sent special message to Congress recommending speedy migration of Indians beyond the Mississippi River 15 Feb; Black Hawk War began 6 April; re-nominated for President at Democratic National Convention, Baltimore 21 May; vetoed Extension of Charter of Second Bank of US Bill 10 July; signed Tariff Act 14 July; Black Hawk War ended 27 Aug; ordered Charleston, S Carolina harbor forts to be placed on alert by Secretary of War; election day 6 Nov; instructed collector at Charleston to seize vessels entering port and hold until duties paid 6 Nov; sent fourth State of the Union message to Congress 4 Dec; Presidential Electors cast their ballots 5 Dec; vetoed Interest on State Claims and Rivers and Harbors Bills 6 Dec; issued proclamation to people of S Carolina 10 Dec.

1833     Sent special message to Congress asking for power to enforce collection of tariff by use of military if necessary 16 Jan; electoral vote tabulated by Congress 13 Feb and Jackson and Van Buren officially declared elected; signed Compromise Tariff Act 2 March; inaugurated for second term in the Hall of Representatives in the Capitol 4 March; toured eastern States June-July; submitted Kendall report on availability of state banks to cabinet 10 Sept; read Taney draft of reasons for removal of funds to cabinet 18 Sept; requested resignation of William J. Duane as Secretary of the Treasury 22 Sept; appointed Roger B. Taney as recess Secretary of the Treasury 23 Sept; sent fifth State of the Union message to Congress 3 Dec; vetoed Proceeds of Land Sales Bill 4 Dec; refused to produce Taney report to the Senate 11 Dec; resolution of censure introduced in Senate by Henry Clay 26 Dec.

1834     Senate adopted resolution of censure stating that Jackson had assumed authority unconstitutionally in ordering the removal of public funds 28 March; entered formal protest against resolution 15 April; Senate refused to make protest part of official record 7 May; Senate rejected appointment of Taney as Secretary of the Treasury 23 June; signed Act establishing Department of Indian Affairs 30 June; vetoed Wabash River Internal Improvements Bill 1 Dec; sent sixth State of the Union message to Congress (announcing elimination of the national debt) 1 Dec.

1835     Fired at by Richard Lawrence (who missed and was later committed to an asylum) on leaving the chamber of the House of Representatives 29 Jan; vetoed Compromising Claims against the Two Sicilies Bill 3 March; sent seventh State of the Union message to Congress 7 Dec.

1836     Sent special message to Congress reviewing relations with France 18 Jan; vetoed Regulations of Congressional Sessions Bill 9 June; Arkansas admitted as 25th State 15 June; signed Surplus Revenue Act 23 June; signed Act reorganizing Post Office Department 2 July; issued Specie Circular 11 July; election day 8 Nov; sent eighth and last State of the Union message to Congress 5 Dec.

1837     Resolution of censure expunged from the Senate record 16 Jan; Michigan admitted as 26th State 26 Jan; submitted list of 46 claims (dating from 1816) against Mexico to Congress, recommending reprisals; recognized Republic of Texas 3 March; signed Judiciary Act, increasing membership of Supreme Court from seven to nine Judges 3 March; vetoed Funds Receivable as US Revenue Bill

3 March; retired from office and attended inauguration of his successor Martin Van Buren 4 March; left Washington for The Hermitage 6 March.

1838    Joined the Presbyterian Church July.

1840    Took part in 25th Anniversary celebrations of the Battle of New Orleans 8 Jan; campaigned for Van Buren Sept-Oct.

1844    Received repayment of fine with interest (on orders of Congress) levied in 1815 (*see above*); actively supported annexation of Texas.

1845    Died of consumption and dropsy at Nashville, Tennessee 8 June; buried in the grounds of The Hermitage.

# The Writings of President Jackson

President Jackson wrote no major work, but his letters have been published in seven volumes, edited by J. S. Bassett (1926-35).

# Lineage of President Jackson

The Jacksons were of Scottish-Irish descent.

HUGH JACKSON, of Carrickfergus, co Antrim, weaver and merchant, *m*, and *d ca* 1782, having had issue, with three other sons,

ANDREW JACKSON, emigrated from Ireland to S Carolina 1765 and farmed at Waxhaws settlement there, *b* in Ireland *ca* 1730, *m* Elizabeth Hutchinson (*b* in Ireland; *d* at Charleston, S Carolina of yellow fever Nov 1781), and *d* at Waxhaws *ca* 1 March 1767 (*bur* Waxhaws Churchyard), leaving issue, with two other sons (*see* BROTHERS OF PRESIDENT JACKSON, *p 185*), a yst (and posthumous) son,

ANDREW JACKSON, **7th President of the United States of America.**

# President Jackson's Wife and Adopted Son

ANDREW JACKSON *m* at Natchez, Mississippi Aug 1791, and again at Nashville, Tennessee 17 Jan 1794, Rachel (*b* in Pittsylvania County, Virginia June 1767; *d* at The Hermitage, nr Nashville 22 Dec 1828, *bur* in The Hermitage garden), formerly wife of Lewis Robards (to whom she was *m* at Harrodsburg, Kentucky 1785, and who obtained a divorce from her Sept 1793, although she had mistakenly supposed he had done so Dec 1790), and 4th dau of Col John Donelson, mem House of Burgesses of Virginia, by his wife Rachel Stockley.

There were no children of the marriage and thus there are *no descendants* of President Jackson. However, Mr and Mrs Jackson legally adopted her nephew (the son of her brother Severn Donelson, by his wife Elizabeth Rucker) who became Andrew Jackson, Jr (*see below*).

Andrew JACKSON, Jr, of The Hermitage, Nashville, Tennessee, *b* nr Nashville 22 Dec 1809; legally adopted by his aunt and uncle Rachel (*née* Donelson) and Andrew Jackson Jan 1810; *educ* Nashville Univ, *m* at Philadelphia 24 Nov 1831, Sarah (*b* at Philadelphia July 1805; *d* at The Hermitage 23 Aug 1887), dau of Peter Yorke, of Philadelphia, and was accidentally *k* 17 April 1865, having had issue,

   1 Rachel JACKSON, *b* at The Hermitage 1 Nov 1832, *m* 25 Jan 1853, Dr John Marshall Lawrence (*b* 6 Sept 1823; *d* 30 Nov 1882), and *d* 3 Feb 1923, having had issue,

     (1) Sarah Yorke LAWRENCE, *b* at The Hermitage 15 March 1854, *m* 18 May 1880, Dr Charles W. Winn, and *d* in Maury County, Tennessee 6 May 1882, leaving issue,

Charles Lawrence WINN, *b* 17 March 1882, *m* 1st 31 Oct 1907, Minnie Henderson (*b* 8 June 1882; *d* 3 July 1951), and had issue,

   ●Marian Henderson WINN, *b* 9 July 1912, *m* 6 Oct 1932, ●Charles G. Fuller, Jr, son of Charles G. Fuller, and has issue,

   ●Jean Winn FULLER, *b* 25 Dec 1934, *m* 2 Sept 1955, ●Charles Brandon Guy, and has issue,

     1*d*●Karen GUY, *b* 1957.

     2*d*●Charles Brandon GUY, Jr, *b* 1958.

     3*d*●Judith Fuller GUY, *b* 1960.

Charles Lawrence Winn *m* 2ndly, ●Grace M. McKibbon, and *d* 1967.

(2) Annie Laurie LAWRENCE, *b* 3 April 1855, *m* Joshua Wright Smith, and *d* 4 Feb 1937, leaving issue,
  1*a* ●Walton Lawrence SMITH (Rev) [*311 Kingwood Drive Murfreesboro, Tennessee 37130, USA*], *b* at Nashville 1 July 1891, *m* 18 Oct 1921, Lucinda Mayfield Alexander (*d* 1970), and has had issue,
    Martha Ann SMITH, *dec.*
  2*a* ●Rachel Jackson SMITH [*3335 Harrison Street, Kansas City, Missouri 64109, USA*], *b* 1893, *m* Leonard H. Donelson.
(3) Andrew Jackson LAWRENCE, MD, *b* 9 July 1857, *m* 1st, Emma H. George (*b* 16 Oct 1867; *d* 3 March 1894), and had issue,
  1*a* Andrew Jackson LAWRENCE, Jr, MD, *b* 26 Sept 1888, *m* ●Sarah Foster Schell (*b* 18 Oct 1889), and *d* 1971, leaving issue,
    ●Andrew Jackson LAWRENCE III, *b* 22 May 1923, *m* ●Mary L. Humphrey (*b* 16 Oct 1924), and has issue,
      1*c* ●Sara Louise LAWRENCE, *b* 23 Sept 1948.
      2*c* ●Deborah Anne LAWRENCE, *b* 30 July 1950.
      3*c* ●Rachel Jackson LAWRENCE, *b* 21 Sept 1955.
      4*c* ●Andrew Jackson LAWRENCE IV.
  2*a* ●Marie Guerrant LAWRENCE [*300 McNaughton Lane, Fort Worth, Texas 76114, USA*], *b* 19 Sept 1891.
Dr Andrew Jackson Lawrence *m* 2ndly, Julia Millican (*b* 30 June 1878; *d* 11 June 1938), and *d* 24 June 1935, having by her had issue,
  3*a* ●Mary Louise LAWRENCE, *b* 26 Aug 1903, *m* ●Cecil H. Graham (*b* 23 Oct 1896), and has issue,
    1*b* ●Mary Lu GRAHAM, *b* 30 July 1926, *m* ●James Hay Page (*b* 17 April 1924), and has issue,
      1*c* ●Ellen Marie PAGE, *b* 31 March 1949.
      2*c* ●Lucille PAGE, *b* 25 June 1951.
      3*c* ●Jane Louise PAGE, *b* 28 Feb 1955.
    2*b* ●Julia Ann GRAHAM, *b* 16 June 1932, *m* ●Richard Dwight Kanakanui (*b* 6 July 1929), and has issue,
      ●Karen Ann KANAKANUI, *b* 8 Aug 1955.
  4*a* ●James Walton LAWRENCE, MD, *b* 1 Aug 1907, *m* Lillie Mae Dinkins (*b* 26 Aug 1911; *d* 1971), and has issue,
    1*b* ●Barbara Josephine LAWRENCE, *b* 29 Aug 1932.
    2*b* ●James Walton LAWRENCE, Jr, *b* 29 June 1938.
    3*b* ●Pamela Ann LAWRENCE, *b* 16 May 1946.
  5*a* ●Edward Montgomery LAWRENCE, *b* 1 Aug 1914, *m* ●Barbara Decker (*b* 8 July 1916), and has issue,
    ●Linda Marie LAWRENCE, *b* 21 Feb 1939.
Mr and Mrs Edward M. Lawrence also have an adopted son,
    ●Robert Decker LAWRENCE.
(4) John Marshall LAWRENCE, Jr, *b* 5 July 1859; *dunm* 26 June 1926.
(5) Carrie Minerva LAWRENCE, *b* 29 April 1861, *m* Rev Dr William D. Bradfield, and had issue,
  1*a* Florence BRADFIELD, *b* 16 June 1893; *d* young.
  2*a* ●William Landon BRADFIELD, *b* 23 June 1895, *m* ●Nell E. Walling (*b* 12 Sept 1895), and has issue,
    1*b* ●Thomas Walling BRADFIELD, *b* 12 Oct 1921, *m* ●Mary Ann Latham (*b* 13 Sept 1926), and has issue,
      1*c* ●Rebecca Ruth BRADFIELD, *b* 5 Dec 1952.
      2*c* ●Melinda Nell BRADFIELD, *b* 18 July 1954.
    2*b* ●Elizabeth Ann BRADFIELD, *b* 12 May 1929, *m* ●Donald Hugh Cummins (*b* 9 Oct 1928), and has issue,
      1*c* ●William Bradfield CUMMINS, *b* 1 Oct 1952.
      2*c* ●Thomas Walling CUMMINS, *b* 7 June 1955.
  3*a* James Lee BRADFIELD, *d* young.
  4*a* ●John Lawrence BRADFIELD, MD [*506 Medical Arts Building, Dallas, Texas 75201, USA*], *b* 8 Dec 1901, *educ* Baylor Univ, *m* 1969.
(6) Samuel Jackson LAWRENCE, MD, *b* 22 June 1863, *m* Maude V. Johnson (*b* 18 Sept 1866; *d* 8 Oct 1937), and *d* 1 March 1935, having had issue,
  1*a* Samuel Jackson LAWRENCE, *d* young.
  2*a* ●John Marshall LAWRENCE III, *b* 5 Nov 1895, *m* ●Helen G. Barton (*b* 3 Dec 1900), and has issue,
    1*b* ●Helen Virginia LAWRENCE, *b* 20 July 1923, *m* ●Henry C. Trussel (*b* 17 May 1923).
    2*b* ●Dorothy Ann LAWRENCE, *b* 15 Nov 1925, *m* ●Collins Mason (*b* 5 March 1924), and has issue,
      1*c* ●Lawrence Collins MASON, *b* 19 Jan 1948.

2*c* ●Dorothy Ann MASON, *b* 13 Jan 1949.
3*c* ●Robert Ralph MASON, *b* 10 June 1953.
2*c* ●— MASON, *b* 1955 (?).
  3*a* ●Maude Wanda LAWRENCE, *b* 4 May 1897, *m* ●William Horace Barse, Jr, son of William Horace Barse.
  4*a* ●Clifton Hyde LAWRENCE, MD, *b* 9 Nov 1900, *m* ●Kathleen Goodman (*b* 3 May 1907), and has issue,
    1*b* ●Thomas N. LAWRENCE, *b* 7 May 1934.
    2*b* ●Kay LAWRENCE, *b* 2 March 1936.
    3*b* ●Samuel Jackson LAWRENCE II, *b* 12 May 1941.
(7) William Walton LAWRENCE, *b* 1866 (?), *m* Mary Fisher, and *d* 1924, leaving issue,
  ●Edith Eudora LAWRENCE, *m* 2 June 1920, ●Charles Murphey Candler, Jr (*b* at Decatur, Georgia 5 Feb 1898), son of Charles Murphey Candler, by his wife Mary Hannah Scott, and has issue,
    ●Edith Lawrence CANDLER, *m* 1st, Philip Shaw, and has issue,
      1*c* ●Murphey Candler SHAW.
      2*c* ●Pattie SHAW.
    Edith L. Candler *m* 2ndly, ●Lon C. Thomas, and has further issue,
      3*c* ●Lon C. THOMAS, Jr.
(8) Marion Yorke LAWRENCE, *b* 15 Nov 1869, *m* John Cleves Symmes (*b* 27 Jan 1868; *d* 1918), a great-nephew of Mrs William Henry Harrison (*see p 216*), and *d* at Philadelphia 1 Feb 1971 (aged 101), having had issue,
  1*a* ●John Cleves SYMMES, *b* 15 Jan 1891, *m* ●Catherine Crichton, and had issue,
    ●John Cleves SYMMES III, *m* 1st (*m* diss by div), Gwendolyn Jefferson, and has issue,
      1*c* ●Carol SYMMES, *b* 12 Nov 1944, *m* 15 March 1967, ●Louis J. Mitchell (*b* 24 Nov 1944), and has issue,
        ●John P. MITCHELL, *b* 14 Jan 1969.
      2*c* ●Holly Sue SYMMES, *b* 4 April 1947, *m* 5 Dec 1970, ●Ernest Montford.
    John Cleves Symmes III *m* 2ndly 1956, ●Jane H. Campbell, and by her has issue,
      3*c* ●Jeanne Campbell SYMMES, *b* 9 Nov 1959.
      4*c* ●Anne Cleves SYMMES, *b* 15 Jan 1962.
  2*a* ●Sue Rae SYMMES, *b* 12 Aug 1893, *m* 13 Oct 1920, ●James J. McCutcheon, (*b* 17 Nov 1891), son of James J. McCutcheon, and has had issue,
    ●Sue Symmes MCCUTCHEON, *b* 3 Oct 1924, *m* ●William Nice Wilmerton Pass, Jr (*b* Sept 1930) [*6375 Sherman Street, Philadelphia, Pennsylvania 19144, USA*], son of William Nice Wilmerton Pass, and has issue,
      1*c* ●Suzanne Lee PASS, *b* 25 Dec 1946, *m* 26 Dec 1970, ●Gordon Lash.
      2*c* ●William Nice Wilmerton PASS III, *b* 26 July 1948.
      3*c* ●(John) Mark PASS, *b* 3 Sept 1950.
      4*c* ●Barbara Jean PASS, *b* 26 April 1952.
    2*b* Essy MCCUTCHEON, *b* 29 July 1926; *d* 9 July 1935.
    3*b* ●Sarah Yorke MCCUTCHEON, *b* 7 April 1928, *m* 1st 1949 (*m* diss by div), James Adams, and has issue,
      1*c* ●James Edward ADAMS, *b* 22 Nov 1950.
      2*c* ●Dorothy Lee ADAMS, *b* 22 Jan 1952.
      3*c* ●Robert Benjamin ADAMS, *b* 22 Oct 1953.
    Sarah Yorke McCutcheon *m* 2ndly 1962, ●James O. Stevenson (*b* 17 Oct 1930), and has further issue,
      4*c* ●David Andrew STEVENSON, *b* 30 April 1965.
      5*c* ●Linda Sue STEVENSON, *b* 20 July 1966.
    4*b* ●James S. J. MCCUTCHEON [*7836 Old North Court, Charlotte, North Carolina, USA*], *b* 20 April 1934, *m* 20 Dec 1958, ●Linda Weis, and has two adopted children,
      (a) ●Kelly Elizabeth MCCUTCHEON, *b* 25 March 1963.
      (b) ●James Christopher MCCUTCHEON, *b* 5 March 1967.
  3*a* ●Marion Yorke SYMMES, *b* 8 Aug 1895, *m* 1916, ●Milton Anthony Candler (*b* at Decatur, Georgia 19 Nov 1892), son of Charles Murphey Candler, of Atlanta, Georgia, by his wife Mary Hannah Scott (and brother of Charles Murphey Candler, Jr — *see above*), and has issue,

●Marion Lawrence CANDLER, *b* 26 Oct 1920, *m*
●William Gordon Emrey, and has issue,
  1c●William Gordon EMREY, Jr.
  2c●Milton Candler EMREY.
(9) Thomas Donelson LAWRENCE, *b* 1870 (?); *dunm ante* 1953.
2 Andrew JACKSON III, of The Hermitage, Nashville, Col CSA, *b* at The Hermitage 4 April 1834, *educ* West Point, *m* 15 Oct 1877, Amy A. Rich (*b* in Ohio 31 Aug 1851; *d* 9 Jan 1921), and *d* 17 Dec 1906, leaving issue,
(1) Andrew JACKSON IV, of The Hermitage, Nashville, High Sch Teacher and later an actor, *b* at The Hermitage 1887, *educ* S California, and Paris, *m* 4 Jan 1913 (*m* diss by div), Marion Caulkins, and *d* at Los Angeles, California 23 May 1953, leaving issue,
  1a●Amy Lee JACKSON.
  2a●Andrew JACKSON V, *m* 1st (*m* diss by div), Lola Kapps; and 2ndly 1955, ●Carolyn —.
  3a●Edith JACKSON, *m* ●West Moreland, and has issue,
    1b●Sharon MORELAND.
    2b●Diane MORELAND.
    3b●Robin MORELAND.
  4a●Douglas JACKSON, *b* 1923, *m* ●Violet Lower (*b* 1925), and has issue,
    1b●Barbara JACKSON, *b* 1947.
    2b●Cynthia JACKSON, *b* 1950.
    3b●Douglas William JACKSON, *b* 1953.
(2) Albert Marble JACKSON, *m*, and disappeared 1919, *sp*.
3 Thomas Jefferson JACKSON, *b* 1836; *d* 1840.
4 Samuel JACKSON, Capt CSA, wounded at the Battle of Chickamauga, *b* at The Hermitage 9 June 1837; *dunm* 27 Sept 1863.
5 Robert Armstrong JACKSON, *b* 18 June, *d* 11 Nov 1843.

# The Brothers of President Jackson

**1** Hugh JACKSON, a volunteer in Col William R. Davie's Regt in the Revolutionary War, *b* in Ireland 1762 or 1763; *k* at the Battle of Stono Ferry 20 June 1779, *unm*.

**2** Robert JACKSON, *b* in Ireland 1764 or 1765; *d* of smallpox 27 April 1781, *unm*.

# Martin Van Buren
## 1782-1862

---

8th President of the
United States of America
1837-1841

MARTIN VAN BUREN, 8TH PRESIDENT

# Martin Van Buren

## 1782-1862

## *8th President of the United States of America*
## 1837-1841

MARTIN VAN BUREN faced four insuperable difficulties in his national
political career. The first was that he came immediately after Andrew
Jackson, whom he had served as Secretary of State and as Vice-President.
Ardent Jacksonians, some with their own presidential ambitions, tended
to regard Van Buren as an anticlimax. He himself in his inaugural address
confessed he could not claim to share in the achievements of the
Revolution, to which his predecessors had contributed so much. "I feel",
he said, "that I belong to a later age and that I may not expect my
countrymen to weigh my actions with the same kind and partial hand". He
was no Founding Father. Nor, unlike Jackson, was he a war-hero. He was
"Little Matty", five foot-six inches high. Whig opponents, reacting
against what they denounced as the dictatorial style of Jackson, meant to
show no mercy to the man they portrayed as Jackson's puppet.

Van Buren's second misfortune was that his single term coincided with
a severe economic depression. Having approved of Jackson's policies, and
sometimes actually formulated them, he could be held responsible for the
crash. Congress blocked his efforts to remedy the situation. Political
enemies caricatured him as incompetent and hard hearted. In such an
atmosphere the Democrats could not present themselves very
convincingly to the electorate in 1840, when Van Buren stood for
re-election.

His third disadvantage was that, in contrast to his predecessors, he was
a professional politician. So of course were most of the Presidents who
came after him. But in the 1830s the public was still hesitant to accept the
idea that a man could be both honest and a politician. In truth Van Buren's
career, both in New York state and then in Washington, had been
reasonably consistent and honorable. But his reputation was that of an

operator behind the scenes, the "Sly Fox of Kinderhook". He was alleged
to be too cunning, and too devoid of fixed principles, ever to commit
himself to any definite position. According to Davy Crockett, "he could
take a piece of meat on one side of his mouth, a piece of bread on the other,
and cabbage in the middle, and chew and swallow each severally while
never mixing them together". The Whig opposition was quick to imitate
some of the political techniques, including oversimplification and
personal insult, which the Democrats had developed. Thus, John Quincy
Adams had been attacked a decade earlier as an aristocratic President with
expensive tastes. Now it was Van Buren's turn to be misrepresented.
Because he dressed neatly he was declared to be a dandy. Because he liked
food and wine he was depicted as "King Matty", ensconced in his
"palace", eating off gold dinner plates and swigging champagne. His
debonair son John, one of four borne to him by his wife Hannah, was
nicknamed "Prince John". The suggestion was that the Democrats had
monarchical pretensions and that their dynasties intended to monopolize
the White House. At least he was free from sexual scandal. Van Buren's
wife died in 1819 and he never remarried, though late in life he made an
unsuccessful proposal to the daughter of his old employer and tutor in
Law.

Van Buren's fourth dilemma involved the problem of slavery. Along
with other level-headed political leaders of his time, he strove to prevent
sectional antagonism from becoming acute. He believed that national
political parties were not simply devices to attract votes and distribute
patronage. As nationalizing agencies, they were forces for good. Van
Buren therefore tried to hold together the Northern and Southern wings
of his party. He hoped the Democrats would choose him again as their
presidential candidate in 1844. But the slavery issue would not lie quiet.
Van Buren was pressed to explain his views on the annexation of Texas,
which in 1836 had broken away from Mexico as an independent republic.
If Texas joined the Union it would enter as a large slave state, and at the
price of almost certain war with Mexico. Van Buren pleased Northern
supporters by announcing he did not favor annexation. But he alienated
Southern Democrats; and the nomination went instead to James K. Polk
of Tennessee. As a New Yorker, Van Buren was impelled during the next
few years into an anti-slavery position, though he was never an abolitionist
and sought to keep faith with the badly split Democrats in the 1850s.

Politically speaking, Martin Van Buren was a victim of circumstance.
He rose to the top by means of shrewd work as a party organizer, and
by making himself Jackson's indispensable lieutenant. He lost the
Presidency, and never quite regained his former status, because the dice
rolled against him. Van Buren was no crusader. But neither was he the
ingratiating opportunist of Whig legend. He sought power for the good
reason that he was ambitious. He enjoyed the game of politics. He also

HANNAH HOES, MRS VAN BUREN

wanted power, however, as a genuine believer in the basic Jacksonian notions, which included the devolution of power, who wanted to be in a position to further them. Now and then he was annoyed by the behavior of people with whom he had dealings. His response was never an explosion of wrath on the Jackson pattern. Nor did he display petulance or self-pity. He was a person of almost unfailing good humor. There was a good deal of the gentleman in his manner—indeed that of the "perfect gentleman". Van Buren was courteous, hospitable, intelligent, a good conversationalist, excellent company at the dinner table. Jackson called him "a *true man* with no guile". Van Buren was perhaps hardly guileless. But he was not devious; Jackson's judgement was essentially correct.

A quality Jackson had particular reason to respect was Van Buren's cool good judgement. In spite of what his critics said he was not a mere manipulator. But like all skilful politicians he knew he had to move within the bounds of what was possible. He was one of the best analysts in his era of the structure of politics. When most other men were still declaring their antipathy to party politics, Van Buren saw that national parties were necessary in America. He also understood the nature of the appeal a man like Jackson held for the ordinary citizen. People, he reflected, would readily forgive a President for mistakes, even bad ones, if at bottom they trusted him. They were ready to love a person who was vivid and fierce. Not least of Van Buren's virtues was his cheerful acceptance of the lesson that he was himself not built on the Jackson scale. He could hope to be respected by Americans, but not to be adored by them. If Jackson was "Old Hickory", he knew it was his own fate to be dismissed as the "Mistletoe Politician"—a parasite clinging to the Jackson tree. But he had some harder decisions to make than Jackson. Beyond a certain point, for instance, he would not compromise with the slaveholders. Old Van Buren despised the men in his party, including Presidents Pierce and Buchanan, who in his view confused cowardice with calmness.

# Chronology

1782      Born at Kinderhook, Columbia County, New York 5 Dec[1].

1796      Began law studies in office of Francis Silvester at Kinderhook.

1801      Completed law studies under William Peter Van Ness, of New York City.

1803      Admitted to the New York Bar Nov; began law practice in Kinderhook.

1808      Moved from Kinderhook to Hudson, New York; appointed Surrogate of Columbia County, New York March.

1812      Elected to New York State Senate May.

1813      Resigned as Surrogate; took seat in New York State Senate.

1815      Appointed Attorney-General for the State of New York Feb.

1816      Re-elected to State Senate.

1819      Retired from office of State Attorney-General July.

1820      Retired from State Senate.

1821      Elected to the Senate by legislature 6 Feb; chosen member of State Constitutional Convention; took seat in Senate 3 Dec.

1824      Supported William H. Crawford for President.

1827      Re-elected to the Senate.

1828      Supported Jackson for President; elected Governor of New York; resigned seat in Senate 20 Dec.

1829      Inaugurated as Governor of New York 1 Jan; appointed Secretary of State by President Jackson 6 March; resigned as Governor 12 March; took oath as Secretary of State 28 March.

1831      Resigned as Secretary of State 11 April (effective from 23 May); appointed Minister to Great Britain 25 June; sailed for England 16 Aug; nomination as Minister sent to Senate 7 Dec.

1832      Rejected as Minister by the Senate 25 Jan; notified of rejection 15 Feb; received by King William IV at Windsor Castle 5 March; travelled through France, Germany and The Netherlands April-June; nominated for Vice-President 21 May; arrived in New York City 5 July; elected Vice-President 6 Nov.

1833      Inaugurated as Vice-President 4 March.

1836      Election day 8 Nov; Presidential Electors cast their ballots 7 Dec.

1837      Electoral vote tabulated by Congress and Van Buren and Richard Mentor Johnson officially declared elected 8 Feb; inaugurated as 8th President of the United States on the east portico of the Capitol 4 March; panic of 1837 began 10

May following fall of cotton prices and suspension of specie payments by the banks; called special session of Congress 15 May; sent special message to Congress recommending specie currency and criticizing State banks 5 Sept; fourth installment of treasury surplus to States suspended 2 Oct; sent first State of the Union message to Congress 5 Dec.

1838    Issued proclamation of neutrality regarding insurgent rising in Canada 5 Jan; signed Act establishing Territory of Iowa 12 June; issued second proclamation of neutrality regarding Canada 21 Nov; sent second State of the Union message to Congress 3 Dec.

1839    Authorized to send troops to Maine in connection with boundary dispute between New Brunswick, Canada and Maine (the Aroostook War—a bloodless conflict) 3 March; pocket vetoed joint resolution providing for distribution in part of the Madison papers; sent third State of the Union message to Congress 2 Dec.

1840    Issued executive order establishing ten hour day for Government employees without reduction of pay 31 March; signed Independent Treasury Act 4 July; election day 10 Nov; Presidential Electors cast their ballots 2 Dec; sent fourth and last State of the Union message to Congress 5 Dec.

1841    Electoral vote tabulated by Congress 10 Feb and Van Buren officially declared defeated by Harrison; retired from office and attended President Harrison's inauguration 4 March; returned to Kinderhook (where he had purchased a farm which he renamed Lindenwald) May.

1842    Made a six month trip along Atlantic seaboard.

1844    Issued letter opposing annexation of Texas 20 April; unsuccessful as candidate for President at Democratic National Convention, Baltimore 27-30 May.

1845    Declined appointment as Minister to Great Britain.

1848    Nominated for President by the Barnburners faction (anti-Administration Democrats), Utica, New York 22 June; and by Free-Soil Party, Buffalo, New York 9 Aug; received 291,263 popular votes but no electoral votes in ensuing Presidential Election.

1850    Returned to Democratic Party.

1852    Supported Franklin Pierce for President.

1853-55 Toured Europe, visiting England, France, Switzerland, Belgium, Holland and Italy and being received by Queen Victoria and Pope Pius IX.

1856    Supported James Buchanan for President.

1860    Supported Stephen Arnold Douglas for President.

1862    Died of asthma spasms at Lindenwald 24 July; buried at Kinderhook.

# The Writings of President Van Buren

President Van Buren was the author of one book, *Inquiry into the Origin and Course of Political Parties in the United States,* begun in 1852, edited by his sons and published posthumously in 1867. His *Autobiography,* edited by John C. Fitzpatrick, was published in 1920.

# Lineage of President Van Buren

CORNELIS MAESSEN (VAN BUREN), came to America from Buurmalsen, Gelderland 1631, and settled at Papsknee, nr Greenbush, New York, *m* Catalyntje Martense (*d* 1648), and *d* 1648, leaving issue, with three other sons (one of whose descendants adopted the surname of BLOEMENDAAL) and one dau,

MARTEN CORNELISZ (VAN BUREN), of Albany, New York, Capt of a mil company in Col Pieter Schuyler's Regt 1700, *b* at Houten, Netherlands *ca* 1638/9, *m* 1st, Marritje Quackenbush (*b* probably at Oestgeest, nr Leiden, Netherlands *ca* 1646), dau or sister of Pieter Quackenbush, and had issue. He *m* 2ndly 7 May 1693, Tanneke Adams, widow of Pieter Pieterson Winne, and *d* 13 Nov 1703. His son by his 1st marriage,

PIETER MARTENSE (VAN BUREN), of Albany, *b* 1670, *m* 15 Jan 1693, Adriaantje, dau of Barent Meynders, of Albany, shoemaker, by his wife Eytie, and *d ca* 1755, leaving, with other issue,

MARTIN VAN BUREN, of Albany, *bapt* at Albany 28 Sept 1701, *m* 7 Nov 1729, Dirkje (*bapt* 30 April 1710), dau of Abraham Janse Van Alstyne, of Kinderhook, New York, by his wife Marritje, dau of Teuwis (Matheeus, or Matthew) Abrahamse Van Deusen, and had with other issue,

ABRAHAM VAN BUREN, of Kinderhook, New York, farmer and tavern keeper, *bapt* at Albany 27 Feb 1737, *m* 1776, Maria (*b* at Claverack, New York 16 Jan 1747/8; *d* at Kinderhook 16 Feb 1817), widow of Johannes Van Alen (*bapt* 21 Oct 1744; *d ca* 1773) (to whom she was *m* at Linlithgo, New York 31 Dec 1767 and had issue—*see* BROTHERS AND SISTERS OF PRESIDENT VAN BUREN, *p 199*), and dau of Johannes Dircksen Hoes, by his wife Jannetje Laurense Van Schaick[2], and *d* at Kinderhook 8 April 1817, leaving with other issue (*see* BROTHERS AND SISTERS OF PRESIDENT VAN BUREN, *p 199*), an eldest son,

MARTIN VAN BUREN, **8th President of the United States of America.**

# The Descendants of President Van Buren

MARTIN VAN BUREN *m* at the Haxtun House (owned by her brother-in-law Judge Moses Cantine), Catskill, New York 21 Feb 1807, his 1st cousin once removed Hannah (*b* at Kinderhook, New York 8 March 1783; *d* at Albany, New York 5 Feb 1819, *bur* first in the cemetery of the Second Presbyterian Church, Albany, later (1855) removed to Kinderhook), dau of his 1st cousin John Dircksen Hoes, by his wife Maria Quackenboss, and had issue,

**1** Abraham VAN BUREN, priv sec to his father 1837, served in the Mexican War, *b* at Kinderhook 27 Nov 1807, *educ* West Point, *m* Nov 1838, Angelica, who acted as White House hostess for her father-in-law 1838-41 (*b* at Sumpter Dist, S Carolina 1816; *d* 29 Dec 1878), dau of Richard Singleton, by his wife a dau of John Coles, of Albemarle County, Virginia (and cousin of Mrs James Madison—*see p 138*), and *d* 1873, leaving issue,
  1 Singleton VAN BUREN, *b* 1840, *educ* Columbia Law Sch, *dunm* 1879.
  2 Travis VAN BUREN, *dunm*.
  3 Martin VAN BUREN, *dunm*.
**2** John VAN BUREN, admitted to New York Bar 1830, attaché of US Legation to the Court of St James's 1831, Attorney-Gen of New York State 1845, *b* at Hudson, Columbia County, New York 10 Feb 1810, *educ* Yale, *m* 22 June 1841, Elizabeth Vanderpoel (*d* 1844), on board ship *Scotia* on way to New York 13 Oct 1866 (*bur* Albany), leaving issue,
  Anna Vanderpoel VAN BUREN, *b* 1842, *m* 1870, Edward Alexander Duer (*b* 1840; *d* 1906), son of William Denning Duer, by his wife Caroline King, and had issue,
    (1) Edward Alexander DUER, of Camden, New Jersey, *b* at New York 28 June 1871, *educ* Columbia (AB 1893), *m* 29 April 1916, Dorothea (*b* at N Wales, Pennsylvania 6 April 1886), dau of Edward Harrison King, by his wife Elizabeth Whitall Atkinson, and *dsp ca* 1940.
    (2) Elizabeth Vanderpoel DUER, *b* at Poultney, Vermont 21 Aug 1874, *m* at Hoboken, New Jersey 5 Oct 1898, Daniel Carroll Harvey (*b* 25 Sept 1867; *d* at Merrick, New York 6 May 1939), son of Samuel Dawes Harvey, MD, by his wife Mary Beatty, and had issue,
    Alexander Duer HARVEY, *b* at Hoboken, New Jersey 5 Sept 1889, *educ* Mass Inst of Technology, *m* at Black Point, Connecticut 8 Sept 1928, ●Anna Maricka (*b* at Staten Island 19 June 1900) [*139E 66th Street, New York, New York 10021, USA*], dau of Pierce Jay, by his wife Louisa Barlow, and *d* at New York Jan 1968, leaving issue,
      1*b*●Dereke Jay HARVEY [*139 E 66th Street, New York, New York 10021, USA*], *b* at Norwalk, Connecticut 3 Aug 1929.
      2*b*●Phoebe Duer HARVEY, *b* at Norwalk, Connecticut 27 Dec 1932, *m* 1st at New York 19 June 1952, Bertrand F. Bell III (*b* at Mount Kisco, New York 15 April 1931), son of Bertrand F. Bell, Jr, by his wife Helen Runkle, and has issue,
        1*c*●Daphne Jay BELL, *b* at Philadelphia 20 Jan 1953.
        2*c*●Alexandra Duer BELL, *b* at Bryn Mawr, Pennsylvania 29 Jan 1956.
        3*c*●Frederick Talmadge BELL, *b* at Chestnut Hill, Pennsylvania 2 April 1958.

Phoebe Duer Harvey *m* 2ndly at New York 27 Dec 1963, ●Robert J. Frackman (*b* at New York 25 Sept 1926) [*Baptist Church Road, Yorktown Heights, New York 105987, USA*], son of H. David Frackman, by his wife Ruth Warren, and has further issue,
    4*c*●David Alexander FRACKMAN, *b* at New York 2 Aug 1970.
  (3) Sarah Gracie DUER, *b* at Poultney, Vermont 1876; *dunm* at New York Sept 1950.
  (4) Angelica Singleton DUER, *b* 1878, *m* 1st 1901, Lucius Tuckerman Gibbs (*d* 1909), and had issue,
    1*a*●Oliver Wolcott GIBBS, *b* 1902, *m* 1929, Ada Elizabeth Crawford (*d* 1930).
    2*a*●Angelica Singleton GIBBS, *b* 1908, *m* 1932, ●Robert Canfield.
  Angelica Singleton Duer *m* 2ndly, Ewing Speed.
  (5) Denning DUER, *b* at Weehawken, New Jersey 1880; *d* there.
  (6) John Van Buren DUER, of Altoona, Pennsylvania, *b* at Poultney, Vermont 9 April 1882, *educ* Stevens Inst of Technology (ME 1903), *m* 7 Sept 1911, Mary Aline Sabine (*d* at Essex, Conn Dec 1967), dau of Charles Davis Haines, by his wife Mary Taunton Sabine, and had issue,
    ●Rufus King DUER [*18 Parker Terrace, Essex, Connecticut 06426, USA*], *b* at New York 30 June 1912, *educ* Yale, *m* ●Rosella Barry, and has issue, two daus.
  (7) James Gore King DUER, *b* at Poultney, Vermont 5 May 1885; *dunm* at West Chester, Pennsylvania Jan 1961.
  (8) William Alexander DUER, *b* 1886; *dunm* at Weehawken, New Jersey *ca* 1900.
**3** Martin VAN BUREN, Jr, *b* at Hudson 20 Dec 1812; *dunm* at Paris, France 19 March 1855.
**4** Smith Thompson VAN BUREN, *b* at Hudson 16 Jan 1817, *m* 1st 1842, Ellen King (*b* 1813; *d* 1849), dau of William James, by his wife Catharine Barber, and had issue,
  1 Ellen James VAN BUREN, *b* at Albany, New York 10 June 1844, *m* at St Mark's Church, New York 10 Dec 1868, Stuyvesant Fish Morris, MD, of New York (*b* at New York 3 Aug 1843; *d* there 10 May 1928), yst son of Dr Richard Lewis Morris, by his wife Elizabeth Sarah Stuyvesant Fish, and *d* 1929, having had issue,
    (1) Elizabeth Marshall MORRIS, *b* at New York 1869, *m* B. Woolsey Rogers, and *dsp* 10 Jan 1919.
    (2) Ellen Van Buren MORRIS, *b* at New York 10 June 1873, *m* there 9 Oct 1899, Francis Livingston Pell, of New York, architect (*b* at New York 23 Sept 1873; *d* there 1945), 2nd son of Walden Pell, by his wife Melissa Augusta Hyatt, and *d* 1954, leaving issue,
      1*a*●Walden PELL II (Rev), sometime Headmaster of St Andrew's Sch, Middletown, Delaware [*Perfect End, RD2, Elkton, Maryland, USA*], *b* at Quogue, Long

Island 3 July 1902, *educ* St Mark's, Princeton, and Ch Ch Oxford, *m* at Lenox, Mass 1928, Edith Minturn (*b* at Newport, Rhode Island 1902; *d* 20 Dec 1973), dau of W. Roscoe Bonsal, by his wife Mary Minturn Potter, and has issue,

1*b*●Melissa PELL, *b* at Lenox, Mass 29 Dec 1929, *m* at Middletown, Delaware 1948, ●John Schuyler Thomson (*b* 1926) [*Rose Hill, Rostherne, Knutsford, Cheshire, England*], son of Alexander Thomson, and has issue,

  1*c*●Ellen Van Buren THOMSON, *b* at New Haven, Connecticut.

  2*c*●Abbie Hotchkiss THOMSON, *b* at New Haven, Connecticut 1953, *m* Oct 1972, ●Ian Christian Spires.

  3*c*●Melissa Pell THOMSON, *b* at New Haven, Connecticut 1957.

2*b*●Stuyvesant Bonsal PELL, insurance broker with Chubb & Son, New York City [*697 Rosedale Road, Princeton, New Jersey, USA*], *b* at Lenox, Mass 1931, *educ* Princeton, *m* at Wilmington, Delaware 1956, ●Patricia C., dau of Ira Doom, by his wife Marion, and has issue,

  1*c*●Alison Chancellor PELL, *b* at Bronxville, New York 1960.

  2*c*●Sarah Bonsal PELL, *b* 1964.

3*b*●Mary Leigh PELL, *b* at Middletown, Delaware 29 April 1934, *m* there 1957, ●Robert Foster Whitmer III (*b* at New York) [*95 Evergreen Hill Road, Fairfield, Connecticut 06430, USA*], son of Robert Foster Whitmer, Jr, by his wife Laura Taylor, and has issue,

  1*c*●Robert Foster WHITMER IV, *b* at Hartford, Connecticut 1961.

  2*c*●Walden Pell WHITMER, *b* at Hartford, Connecticut 1963.

  3*c*●John Love WHITMER, *b* at Hartford, Connecticut 1965.

2*a*●Stuyvesant Morris PELL, *b* at New York 12 March 1905.

3*a*●Francis Livingston PELL, Jr [*301 Stenton Avenue, Plymouth Meeting, Pennsylvania, USA*], *b* at New York 26 Nov 1906, *m* 1932, ●Clarissa Wardwell, and has issue,

  1*b*●Robert L. PELL [*3419 Dent Place, Washington, DC, USA*].

  2*b*●Edward W. PELL [*167 Carroll Place, Staten Island, New York, USA*].

(3) Richard Lewis MORRIS, of New York, investment banker, *b* at New York 26 Nov 1875, *educ* St Mark's Sch, and Columbia (AB 1896), *m* 9 June 1908, Carolyn Whitney (*b* at New York 24 April 1882), dau of Cornelius Fellowes, of New York, and had issue,

1*a*●Cornelia Fellowes MORRIS, *b* at Wave Crest, Long Island 24 June 1909, *m* 1933, ●Malcolm Graham Field [*82 Eagle Valley Road, Sloatsburg, New York, USA*].

2*a* Eileen James MORRIS, *b* 22 Aug 1913; *d* 19 April 1916.

3*a* Richard Lewis MORRIS, Jr, *b* at New York 22 Aug 1917; *dunm.*

(4) Stuyvesant Fish MORRIS, Jr, *b* at New York 22 May 1877, *educ* Columbia (AB 1898), *m* 27 Dec 1900, Elizabeth Hilles, dau of Dr Gerardus Hilles Wynkoop, by his wife Ann Eliza Woodbury, and *d* 1925, leaving issue,

1*a*●Stuyvesant Fish MORRIS III, *b* 19 Feb 1902, *m* 29 April 1925, ●Madeleine Marie White, and has issue,

  1*b*●Stuyvesant Fish MORRIS IV, *b* 1926.

  2*b*●Livingston Van Buren MORRIS, *b* 1930.

  3*b*●Peter McKinney MORRIS, *b* 1931.

2*a*●Martin Van Buren MORRIS [*3845 La Playa Boulevard, Miami, Florida, USA*], *b* 23 Sept 1904, *m* ●Helen de Russy Sloan, and has issue,

  1*b*●Helen de Russy MORRIS [*4131 Park Avenue, Coconut Grove, Florida 33133, USA*].

  2*b*●Martin Van Buren MORRIS, Jr [*1021 Matanzas Avenue, Coral Gables, Florida 33134, USA*], *m* Sara E. Layman.

3*a*●Hilles MORRIS, *b* at Quogue, Long Island, New York 28 June 1907, *m* 1st at Grace Church, New York

City 1 Nov 1926, Louis Gordon Hamersley (*b* at Newport, Rhode Island 20 July 1892; *d* at Southampton, New York 2 June 1942), only son of James Hooker Hamersley, by his wife Margaret Willing Chisholm, and has issue,

1*b*●Louis Gordon HAMERSLEY, Jr [*Box 302, Poughkeepsie, New York 12602, USA*], *b* at New York 14 Jan 1928, *educ* Harvard, *m* at Poughkeepsie, New York 27 Aug 1949, ●Elsey de Riemer (*b* at Poughkeepsie 18 June 1929), dau of Baltus Barentsen Van Kleeck, by his wife Ethelyn Hinkley, and has issue,

  1*c*●Louis Gordon HAMERSLEY III [*267 Allston Street, Cambridge, Mass 02138, USA*], *b* at Boston 23 Feb 1951, *educ* Boston Univ.

  2*c*●Andrew Carré HAMERSLEY [*267 Allston Street, Cambridge, Mass 02138, USA*], *b* at New York 8 Oct 1954, *educ* Boston Univ.

  3*c*●Nicholas Bayard HAMERSLEY, *b* at New York 15 May 1959.

  4*c*●Katherine Van Kleek HAMERSLEY, *b* at New York 4 June 1962.

2*b*●Stuyvesant Morris HAMERSLEY [*Box 147, Sorrento, British Columbia, Canada*], *b* at New York 11 June 1932, *m* at Tuxedo, New York 9 Jan 1960, ●Irmy (*b* at Hamadan, Iran Oct 1930), dau of Eduard Borowski, by his wife Elinor Kuhn, and has issue,

  1*c*●Linda Hilles HAMERSLEY, *b* at New York 17 Feb 1961.

  2*c*●Leslie Carrée HAMERSLEY, *b* at New York 13 Jan 1963.

3*b*●Hilles Elizabeth HAMERSLEY [*47 Station Road, Irvington, New York 10533, USA*], *b* at New York 7 April 1935, *m* at Southampton, New York 6 Oct 1956, Terence Michael Martin (*d* 29 Jan 1970), and has issue,

  1*c*●Terrence Michael MARTIN, *b* at New York 25 Sept 1957.

  2*c*●Tracy Hamersley MARTIN, *b* at New York 24 Nov 1958.

  3*c*●Elizabeth Hilles MARTIN, *b* at Ridgewood, New Jersey 8 Feb 1963.

4*b*●James Hooker HAMERSLEY [*112 East 91st Street, New York, New York 10028, USA*], *b* at New York 16 Nov 1937, *educ* Washington and Lee.

Hilles Morris *m* 2ndly at Quogue, Long Island 17 June 1947 (*m* diss by div 1965), George Leslie Bartlett (*b* at New York 22 Nov 1908), son of Horace Edward Bartlett, by his wife Camille Harriet Levieux. She *m* 3rdly at Tuxedo, New York 15 Jan 1966, as his 3rd wife, ●Robert Clermont Livingston Timpson, late Major US Army Air Corps, banker (*b* in Hampshire, England 14 May 1908) [*Maizeland, 12 Insala Road, Kloof, Natal 3600, South Africa: Box 1241, Southampton, Long Island, New York 11968, USA*], 2nd son of late Lawrence Timpson, of Appleton Manor, Berks, mem New York Bar, by his wife Katharine Livingston (*see* BURKE'S *LG, TIMPSON formerly of Appleton Manor*).

2 Hannah VAN BUREN, *d* an inf.

3 Edward Singleton VAN BUREN, *b* 1848; *dunm* 1873.

4 Katherine Barber VAN BUREN, *b* 1849, *m* 1st, Peyton F. Miller; and 2ndly, — Wilson, and *dsp.*

Smith Thompson Van Buren *m* 2ndly 1855, Henrietta Irving (*d* 1921), and *d* 1876, having by her had issue,

5 Martin VAN BUREN.

6 Eliza Eckford VAN BUREN, *b* 1858; *dunm.*

7 Marion Irving VAN BUREN, *b* 1860, *m* Hamilton Emmons, and *d* 1927, leaving issue,

(1) Robert Van Buren EMMONS, *b* 1919, *m* 1st, Sally Robinson (*d* 1926). He *m* 2ndly 1928, ●Anita Mazzini, and had issue,

  1*a*●Giulietta Elizabeth EMMONS, *b* 1929.

  2*a*●Hamilton EMMONS, *b* 1931.

(2) ●Marion Van Buren EMMONS, *m* Richard Sears Humphrey, and has issue,

  1*a*●Joan Van Buren HUMPHREY, *b* 1924.

  2*a*●Richard Sears HUMPHREY, Jr [*450 Essex Street, Beverly, Mass, USA*], *b* 1925, *m* Linda D. Stern.

  3*a*●Marion Irving HUMPHREY, *b* 1927.

# The Brothers and Sisters of President Van Buren

**A:** HALF-BROTHERS AND HALF-SISTER (*being the issue of his mother's first marriage to Johannes Van Alen—see above*, LINEAGE OF PRESIDENT VAN BUREN, *p 196*)

**1** Marytje VAN ALEN, *bapt* at Kinderhook 20 Aug 1768, *m ca* 1787, John Goes (*bapt* at Kinderhook 25 May 1766; *d* 23 Dec 1838), son of Laurens Goes (Hoes), by his wife Maria Van Alstyne, and *d* at Adolphustown, Upper Canada 1 Sept 1829 (*bur* with her husband at Kinderhook), leaving issue, two daus.

**2** Johannes VAN ALEN, *bapt* at Kinderhook 15 July 1770; *dunm* 13 April 1805 (*bur* Kinderhook).

**3** Jacobus VAN ALEN, Town Clerk of Kinderhook 1797-1801, JP 1801-04, Surrogate of Columbia County 1804-08 and 1815-22, mem New York State Assembly 1804, mem House of Reps (Federalist) 1807-09, *bapt* at Kinderhook 1 Jan 1773; *dunm* 18 May 1822 (*bur* there).

**B:** FULL BROTHERS AND SISTERS

**4** Derike VAN BUREN, *b* 1777, *m* 1806, Barent Hoes, and *d* 1865, leaving issue, four sons and four daus.

**5** Hannah VAN BUREN, *b* 1780; *dunm*.

**6** Lawrence VAN BUREN, *b* 1786, *m* Harriet Vosburgh, and *d* 1868, leaving issue, two sons and three daus.

**7** Abraham VAN BUREN, *b* 1788, *m* 1816, Catherine Hogeboom, and *dsp* 1836.

# Notes

[1] Martin Van Buren was the first President to be born a citizen of the United States; all preceding Presidents had been born British Subjects. He was in fact the first of only five Presidents who were not of British descent (the others being the two Roosevelts, Hoover and Eisenhower—*qv*).

[2] Through his mother President Van Buren was doubly related to the future President Theodore Roosevelt—

(a) as third cousin twice removed—

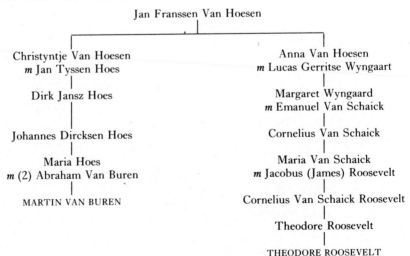

Claas Gerritse Van Schaick

Laurens Van Schaick

Jannetje Laurense Van Schaick
*m* Johannes Dircksen Hoes

Maria Hoes
*m* (2) Abraham Van Buren

MARTIN VAN BUREN

Emanuel Van Schaick

Cornelius Van Schaick

Maria Van Schaick
*m* Jacobus (James) Roosevelt

Cornelius Van Schaick Roosevelt

Theodore Roosevelt

THEODORE ROOSEVELT

(b) as fourth cousin twice removed—

Jan Franssen Van Hoesen

Christyntje Van Hoesen
*m* Jan Tyssen Hoes

Dirk Jansz Hoes

Johannes Dircksen Hoes

Maria Hoes
*m* (2) Abraham Van Buren

MARTIN VAN BUREN

Anna Van Hoesen
*m* Lucas Gerritse Wyngaart

Margaret Wyngaard
*m* Emanuel Van Schaick

Cornelius Van Schaick

Maria Van Schaick
*m* Jacobus (James) Roosevelt

Cornelius Van Schaick Roosevelt

Theodore Roosevelt

THEODORE ROOSEVELT

# William Henry Harrison
## 1773-1841

———

### 9th President of the
### United States of America
### 1841

WILLIAM HENRY HARRISON, 9TH PRESIDENT

# William Henry Harrison

## 1773-1841

### 9th President of the United States of America
### 1841

WILLIAM HENRY HARRISON was inaugurated as President on 4 March 1841 and died exactly one month later—before his wife Anna Symmes Harrison, who was unwell, had even been able to join him in Washington. He is commemorated, somewhat negatively, for having established a number of presidential records. Aged sixty-eight, he is the oldest man to have been installed in the office; and his has been the shortest Administration. Harrison's inaugural address, which took an hour and three-quarters to deliver, still holds the record for length. Perhaps his successors took the achievement as a cautionary tale. He wore neither hat nor coat, despite the rigor of the Washington winter, while he read his speech. After this unwise ordeal he attended three inaugural balls. He ended the day with a cold; the cold developed into a chill, the chill into pneumonia. The lesson would seem to be that for Presidents on such occasions longevity and longwindedness may be incompatible.

Harrison is also remembered in popular accounts as the principal figure in the famous "Log Cabin and Hard Cider" election of 1840. In the familiar story, Harrison's Whig party decided to take a leaf out of the book of the rival Democratic party. The Democrats had capitalized upon their claim to be the party of the people and had conducted themselves accordingly, with a good deal of demagogic flamboyance. The Whigs, though more conservative in style, adapted their appeal to the electorate. Denouncing the Democratic candidate, President Van Buren, as an aristocrat, they presented Harrison as a plain, unaffected, Western pioneer and an old Indian fighter who had beaten the Shawnees at Tippecanoe in 1811 and later killed the warrior Tecumseh. This portrait was, to say the least, incomplete. "Old Tip" was the son of Benjamin Harrison and Elizabeth Bassett, representatives of two distinguished

Virginia families. His father was a "signer" of the Declaration of Independence. His wife was the daughter of Judge John Cleves Symmes, who had been a member of the Continental Congress and who had secured title to a land grant of several hundred thousand acres in the Ohio country. William Henry Harrison had attended Hampden-Sidney College in Virginia, and as a professional Army officer had risen to the rank of Major-General. His home at North Bend, near Cincinnati, was considerably less primitive than the simple log cabin of electioneering legend, although it did incorporate a five-room structure he had raised at the time of his marriage in 1795.

Garbled or not, the Whig propaganda was effective. The Democrats protested in vain that "Granny" Harrison was an elderly nonentity. They said he had blundered in all of his various careers, including his campaigns against the Indians and the British. There was some justification for such criticism. Harrison had been a brave enough soldier but he had never won a victory as dazzling as New Orleans. His service in Congress had been unremarkable. Despite his and his father-in-law's early prominence in the Northwest Territory, he had not become wealthy as a landowner or a farmer. He could be caricatured as "General Mum," a pseudo-Jackson who kept quiet on political issues because he had nothing to say about them and because the Whig leaders cynically chose him as a mere figure-head. No matter: in contrast with "Matt" Van Buren he was an appealingly average figure in the Whig election songs of 1840:

> Old Tip he wears a homespun coat,
> He has no ruffled shirt-wirt-wirt.
> But Matt he has the golden plate,
> And he's a little squirt-wirt-wirt.

The actual William H. Harrison was a decent, dignified person. He was less combative than Andrew Jackson, and less canny than Van Buren. He was unwise enough, for example, to be affable to too many of the men who besieged him for federal appointments. Some convinced themselves he had promised them jobs. Their pestering when he was tired and ill may have contributed to his collapse and death. If he had survived his term he would probably not have sought re-election. He would not have attempted any very bold new policies, because he did not believe that the executive branch ought to do much more than preside, on the model of a committee chairman, over the nation's affairs. In the nature of the situation, he could not have joined the list of "strong" or "great" Presidents. But he might well have retained the respect of the nation, and have gained a certain popularity.

Instead, there was the fatigued old man, bareheaded in the icy blast of a Washington winter, reading aloud his blameless sentiments to an increasingly restive audience:

ANNA TUTHILL SYMMES, MRS HARRISON

> It is the part of wisdom for a republic to limit the service of that officer . . . to whom she has intrusted the management of her foreign relations, the execution of her laws, and the command of her armies and navies to a period so short as to prevent his forgetting that he is the accountable agent not the principal; the servant, not the master.

In the 1970s such comments would again sound striking and relevant. In Harrison's day they were commonplaces, though neither he nor his listeners anticipated that his period in office would be limited to thirty-one days. His illness and death came so swiftly that his Vice-President, John Tyler, was away at his home in Williamsburg, Virginia, and did not even know the President was ailing. Harrison's final, negative claim to uniqueness, in the history of the Presidency, is that as the first man to die in office, he raised a constitutional issue the nation had not yet had to face: did the Vice-President automatically become President?

# Chronology

1773    Born at Berkeley, Charles City County, Virginia 9 Feb.

1786    Entered Hampden-Sidney College, Virginia.

1787-89 Attended academy in Southampton County, Virginia, after leaving Hampden-Sidney College without graduating.

1790-91 Studied medicine under Dr Benjamin Rush in Philadelphia.

1791    Commissioned Ensign in 1st Infantry Regt US Army 16 Aug; joined regiment at Fort Washington (now Cincinnati), Ohio, Nov.

1792    Promoted Lieut June; appointed ADC to Gen Anthony Wayne; took part in expedition which erected Fort Recovery on the Wabash River and was thanked in general orders Dec.

1794    Took part in the Battle of Fallen Timbers against Little Turtle's force of 800 Indians on the Maumee River, south of present Toledo, Ohio, 20 Aug.

1795    Promoted Capt May.

1798    Resigned commission 1 June; appointed Secretary of Northwest Territory by President John Adams 28 June.

1799    Elected Territorial Delegate to Congress Sept; took seat at Philadelphia 2 Dec.

1800    Appointed Governor of new Indiana Territory by President John Adams 12 May.

1801    Took office as Governor at Vincennes, Indiana, Jan.

1803    Built a house which he named Grouseland in Vincennes.

1804    Served for a brief period as Governor of Louisiana Territory.

1806    One of the founders of Vincennes University Junior College 6 Dec.

1809    Concluded treaty with several Indian tribes, buying three million acres of land on the Wabash and White Rivers, 30 Sept.

1810    Invited Tecumseh, Chief of the Shawnees, and his brother Elskwatawa (the Prophet) to confer with him in Vincennes July; unsuccessful discussions took place 12-14 Aug.

1811    Second unsuccessful conference with Tecumseh 27 July; left Vincennes with about 900 men to establish military post at junction of the Wabash and Tippecanoe Rivers 26 Sept; defeated Indian confederation at the Battle of Tippecanoe 7 Nov; congratulated by President Madison.

1812    Retired as Governor of Indiana Territory; commissioned Major-General of Kentucky Militia 25 Aug; commissioned Brig-Gen US Army 2 Sept.

1813    Promoted Major-General 2 March; took part in invasion of Canada; defeated British and Indians at the Battle of the Thames 5 Oct.

1814    Resigned from the Army May.

1816    Elected to the House of Representatives to fill Ohio vacancy.

1818    Received gold medal for his victory at the Battle of the Thames 24 March.

1819    Declined to stand for re-election to Congress; elected member of Ohio State Senate.

1820    Served as Presidential Elector for Ohio, voting for Monroe.

1821    Retired from Ohio State Senate.

1822    Unsuccessful candidate for the House of Representatives.

1824    Served as Presidential Elector for Ohio, voting for Henry Clay; elected to the Senate.

1825    Took seat in the Senate.

1828    Resigned from the Senate on appointment as first US Minister to Colombia by President John Quincy Adams 19 May; sailed for Colombia 11 Nov.

1829    Arrived in Bogota 5 Feb; recalled by President Jackson 8 March.

1830    Sailed for US 9 Jan; retired to his farm at North Bend, Ohio.

1835    Nominated for President in several States.

1836    Unsuccessful Whig candidate for President Nov.

1839    Nominated for President by Whig Party National Convention at Harrisburg, Pennsylvania, 4 Dec.

1840    Election day (in most States) 10 Nov; elected President by 294 electoral votes as opposed to 60 for Van Buren.

1841    Inaugurated as 9th President of the United States of America on the east portico of the Capitol 4 March; took to his bed with a severe chill 27 March; died of pneumonia at the White House 4 April (the first President to die in office, after the shortest presidential term of 31 days); buried in the Harrison Tomb, opposite Congress Green Cemetery, North Bend, Ohio.

# The Writings of President William Henry Harrison

*Messages and Letters*, edited by Logan Esarey, 2 vols (1922)

William Henry Harrison left no other major writings apart from a few public addresses, of which the most important is *A Discourse on the Aborigines of the Ohio*. His surviving correspondence is also very scanty, but some selections have been printed in the Historical and Philosophical Society of Ohio's *Quarterly Publications*, Vols II and III.

# Lineage of President William Henry Harrison

The place of origin of this family in England has not been discovered. A very full account of the Virginia Harrisons is to be found in *The Virginia Magazine of History and Biography*, Vols XXX-XLI (1922-33).

BENJAMIN HARRISON, came to Virginia *ante* 15 March 1633/4, when he signed a document as Clerk of the Council, received grants of land on the James River, mem Virginia House of Burgesses 1642, *m* Mary — (who *m* 2ndly, Benjamin Sidway, of Surry County, Virginia, and *d* 1688 (will dated 1 March 1687/8, *pr* 29 May 1688), leaving further issue), and *d* between 1643 (or 1645) and 1649 (? *bur* Jamestown), leaving issue, with a yr son (who probably *dsp*),

BENJAMIN HARRISON, of Wakefield, Surry County, Virginia, Justice of Surry 1671, Sheriff 1679, mem Virginia House of Burgesses for Surry 1680, 1682, 1692, 1696 and 1698, mem Council 1698-1713, *b* 20 Sept 1645, *m* Hannah — (*b* 13 Feb 1651/2; *d* 16 Feb 1698/9), and *d* 30 Jan 1712/13 (*bur* Cabin Point), having had issue, with two other sons and three daus, an eldest son,

BENJAMIN HARRISON, of Berkeley, Charles City County, Virginia, Clerk of Charles City 1702, mem Virginia House of Burgesses 1704 and 1705 (Speaker), Treas of the Colony 1705-10, *b* 1673, *m* Elizabeth (*d* 30 Dec 1734), 2nd dau of Col Lewis Burwell, Jr, of Carter's Creek, Gloucester County, and King's Creek, York County, Virginia, a member of the Council, by his 1st wife Abigail, dau of Anthony Smith, of Colchester, Virginia[1], and *d* 10 April 1710 (*bur* Westover Churchyard), leaving issue, with one dau,

COLONEL BENJAMIN HARRISON, of Berkeley, mem Virginia House of Burgesses for Charles City County 1736, 1738, 1740, 1742 and 1744, *educ* William and Mary Coll, *m* 1722, Anne (*d* between 17 Oct 1743 (date of husband's will) and Aug 1745), dau of Col Robert Carter, of Corotoman, President of the Council, by his wife Sarah, dau of Gabriel Ludlow[2], and was *k* (with his two yst daus) when his house was struck by lightning 12 July 1745, having had issue, with five other sons and four daus, a 2nd (but eldest surv) son,

BENJAMIN HARRISON, of Berkeley, known as "The Signer", member Virginia House of Burgesses for Charles City County 1749-75, represented Charles City County in Revolutionary Conventions 1775, mem Congress 1774-78, mem House of Delegates for Charles City County 1776-81 (Speaker 1778-81), Gov of Virginia 1781-84, signed Declaration of Independence 4 July 1776, *b* at Berkeley *ca* April 1726, *m* 1748, Elizabeth (*b* at Eltham, New Kent County, Virginia 13 Dec 1730; *d* at Berkeley 1792), dau of Col William Bassett, Jr, of Eltham, by his wife Elizabeth, dau of William Churchill, and *d* at Berkeley 24 April 1791, leaving, with other issue (*see* BROTHERS AND SISTERS OF PRESIDENT WILLIAM HENRY HARRISON, *p 215*), a yst son,

WILLIAM HENRY HARRISON, **9th President of the United States of America.**

# The Descendants of President William Henry Harrison

WILLIAM HENRY HARRISON *m* at her father's house in North Bend, Ohio 22 Nov 1795, Anna Tuthill (*b* at Flatbrook, Sussex County, New Jersey 25 July 1775; *d* at North Bend 25 Feb 1864, *bur* with her husband), yr dau of Col John Cleves Symmes, sometime Chief Justice of the New Jersey Supreme Court, by his 1st wife[3] Anna, dau of Henry Tuthill, of Southhold, Long Island, New York, and had issue,

**1** Elizabeth Bassett HARRISON, *b* at North Bend, Ohio 29 Sept 1796, *m* Judge John Cleves Short, and *dsp* 1846.
**2** John Cleves Symmes HARRISON, *b* at North Bend, Ohio 28 Oct 1798, *m* Clarissa, dau of Gen Zebulon Montgomery Pike, and *dvp* 1830, leaving issue,
  1 Rebecca Pike HARRISON, *b* 1821, *m* John Hunt, and *d* 1849, leaving issue,
    (1) Symmes Harrison HUNT, *m* Josephine Albertine Cheek, and had issue,
      Zebuline Adelaide Pike Harrison HUNT, *m* 1889, Paul Joseph Schafer, and had issue,
        1*b* Josephine Symmes SCHAFER.
        2*b* Paul Joseph SCHAFER, Jr.
    (2) Clara Pike HUNT, *m* James Vaughn, and *dsp*.
    (3) Mary Susan HUNT, *m* 1st, George Souter, and had issue,
      1*a* Clara Hunt SOUTER, *m* William H. Whiteman, and had issue,
        1*b* William John WHITEMAN.
        2*b* Lee WHITEMAN.
        3*b* Nellie WHITEMAN.
      2*a* Brenhilda Harrison SOUTER, *dunm*.
      3*a* Nellie Pike SOUTER, *dunm*.
    Mary Susan Hunt *m* 2ndly, William J. McGee.
  2 Anna Maria Symmes HARRISON, *b* 1822, *m* James Madison Roberts, and *d* 1849, leaving issue,
    (1) Gabriella ROBERTS, *d* young.
    (2) James Montgomery ROBERTS, *m* Elizabeth Allen, and had issue,
      Anna Maria ROBERTS, *dunm*.
  3 Clarissa Louisa HARRISON, *b* 1824, *m* 1st, Tomlin Miller Banks, MD, and had issue,
    (1) Symmes Harrison BANKS, *d* young.
    (2) Mary Florer BANKS, *d* young.
    (3) Tomlin Pike BANKS, *d* young.
  Clarissa Louisa Harrison *m* 2ndly, Oliver Perry Morgan, and *d* 1883, having had further issue,
    (4) William Henry Harrison MORGAN, *d* young.
    (5) Oliver Perry MORGAN, Jr, *dunm*.
    (6) Montgomery Pike MORGAN, *d* young.
  4 William Henry HARRISON, *b* 1828, *m* 1st, Elvira Rogers (*d* 1875), and had issue,
    (1) Montgomery Pike HARRISON, *m* — Scott, and had issue,
      1*a* William Scott HARRISON.
      2*a* Elvira Willis HARRISON, *dunm*.
      3*a* Oliver Pike HARRISON.
      4*a* Clarence Willis HARRISON.
    (2) William Taylor HARRISON, *d* young.
    (3) John Scott HARRISON, *dunm*.

    (4) Clara Elvira HARRISON, *dunm*.
    (5) Henry Lewis HARRISON, *dunm*.
  William Henry Harrison *m* 2ndly Mary Anne McIntyre.
  5 Montgomery Pike HARRISON, *dunm*.
  6 John Cleves Symmes HARRISON, *dunm*.
**3** Lucy Singleton HARRISON, *b* at Richmond, Virginia 5 Sept 1800, *m* David K. Estes, Judge of the Superior Court of Ohio, and *d* 1826, leaving issue,
  1 William Harrison ESTES, *d* young.
  2 Lucy Anne Harrison ESTES, *b* 1822, *m* Joseph F. Reynolds (*b* 1815; *d* 1895), and *d* 1868, leaving issue,
    (1) Anna Harrison REYNOLDS, *b* 1844, *m* John Law Crawford, and *d* 1875, leaving issue,
      1*a* Lucy Estes CRAWFORD, *m* George C. Woodruff, and *dsp*.
      2*a* Alexander Grisbrooke CRAWFORD, *d* young.
    (2) John Estes REYNOLDS, *b* 1846, *m* Lydia Presstman, and *d* 1888, leaving issue,
      1*a* Joseph Graeme REYNOLDS.
      2*a* Minna REYNOLDS, *dunm*.
      3*a* Isaac Trimble REYNOLDS.
      4*a* Lydia Presstman REYNOLDS, *dunm*.
    (3) David Estes REYNOLDS, *b* 1849, *m* Mary Stuart Davidson, and *d* 1887, leaving issue,
      Henrietta Davidson REYNOLDS, *dunm*.
    (4) Joseph REYNOLDS, *b* 1854, *m* 1894, Louise Moller Smith (*b* 1870), and had issue,
      1*a* ● Louise Harrison REYNOLDS, *b* 1895.
      2*a* ● Dorothea Estes REYNOLDS, *b* 1896.
    (5) Lucy Singleton REYNOLDS, *b* 1858; *dunm* 1912.
    (6) William Henry Harrison REYNOLDS, *b* 1861; *dunm* 1904.
    (7) Mary REYNOLDS, *b* 1864; *dunm* 1917.
  3 William Henry Harrison ESTES, *d* young.
  4 David ESTES, *d* young.
**4** William Henry HARRISON, of Cincinnati, Ohio, lawyer, *b* at Vincennes, Indiana 3 Sept 1802, *m* 1824, Jane Findlay (*b* 1804; *d* 1846), dau of Archibald Irwin, by his wife Mary Ramsey (and sister of the second Mrs John Scott Harrison—*see below, p 211*), and *d* 6 Feb 1838, leaving issue,
  1 James Findlay HARRISON, admitted to Indiana Bar, served as Lieut in the Mexican War and as Col of an Ohio Regt in the Civil War, *b* at Cincinnati, Ohio 9 March 1825, *educ* West Point, *m* 1st, 1848, Caroline M. (*d* 1863), dau of — Alston, of S Carolina, and had issue,
    (1) James Findlay HARRISON, Jr, *b* 1848; *dunm vp* 1870.
    (2) William Alston HARRISON, *b* 1850; *d* 1851.
    (3) William Henry HARRISON, *b* 1852; *d* 1861.
  Col James Findlay Harrison, Sr *m* 2ndly 24 Dec 1864, Alice Merriam (*b* at Natchez, Mississippi 28 Oct 1842; *d* at Kansas

City, Missouri 6 June 1911), dau of John Kennedy, formerly of Belfast, Ireland, and *d* at Mound City, Kansas 14 Feb 1907, having by her had issue,

(4) Jane Alice HARRISON, *d* young.

(5) John Scott HARRISON, of Helena, Montana, civil engr, US dist cadastral engr, *b* at Mound City, Kansas 30 April 1867, *educ* in Kansas, *m* at Helena, Montana 24 March 1903, Mary Sophie (*b* at Sun River, Montana 10 Jan 1875; *d* at Helena, Montana May 1938), dau of Joseph Hill, by his wife Augusta Ford, and *d* at Calico Rock, Arkansas 29 April 19—, having had issue,

1*a* James Findlay Hill HARRISON, *b* at Helena, Montana 1905; *d* aged 1 week.

2*a*●William Henry HARRISON, Dir Fruitlands Museum, Harvard, Mass from 1949, lectr [*Prospect Hill, Harvard, Massachusetts 01451, USA*], *b* 4 Aug 1906, *educ* George Washington Univ, *m* 1st at Washington, DC 1935 (*m* diss by div 1958), Margaret Ann Linforth Willgoose. He *m* 2ndly in London, England 1958, ●Eleni Clio Marie, formerly wife of — Apostolides, and dau of Rev Charles James Hamilton Dobson, MC, by his wife Eleni Georgoulopoulos, and by her has issue,

●Anthea Io HARRISON, *b* 25 Feb 1961.

3*a* Scott Hill HARRISON, engr with Arabian American Oil Co, *b* at Helena, Montana 30 Sept 1907, *educ* Montana State Univ, *m* at Boulder, Montana Sept 1931, ●Elizabeth (*b* at Helena, Montana 14 Dec 1910) [*1611 Jerome Street, Helena, Montana 59601, USA*], dau of Hiram Bower, by his wife Rose Runyan, and *d* at Minneapolis, Minnesota 19 Aug 1971, leaving issue,

1*b*●Sylvia Hill HARRISON, *b* at Helena, Montana 12 Nov 1933, *m* at Portland, Oregon 29 Dec 1953, ●John Palmer Egan (*b* at Portland, Oregon 5 Sept 1930) [*Arabian American Oil Co, Box 1815, Dhahran, Saudi Arabia*], son of John Egan, by his wife Beatrice Palmer, and has issue,

1*c*●John Harrison EGAN, *b* at Dhahran, Saudi Arabia 4 Sept 1956, *educ* Oregon Episcopal Schs, Portland, Oregon.

2*c*●Scott Edward EGAN, *b* at Portland, Oregon 6 Sept 1958.

3*c*●Michael Patrick EGAN, *b* at Portland, Oregon 24 Nov 1963.

2*b*●Sheila Elizabeth HARRISON, *b* at Helena, Montana 25 March 1938, *m* at Portland, Oregon 20 March 1965, ●David M. Dougherty (*b* in Mass 8 Dec 1930) [*6720 SW King Boulevard, Beaverton, Oregon, USA*], son of David Dougherty.

3*b*●John Scott HARRISON [*American Arabian Oil Co, Box 1958, Dhahran, Saudi Arabia*], *b* at Helena, Montana 17 May 1941, *educ* Montana Univ, *m* at Long Island, New York 11 Aug 1971, ●Maria Alma (*b* at New York 20 March 1944), dau of Albin Cibeu, by his wife Antoinette Marinig, and has issue,

●Erika Nicole HARRISON, *b* at Dhahran, Saudi Arabia 21 Oct 1972.

(6) William Henry HARRISON, of Kansas City, Missouri, partner in real estate firm of Harrison & Harrison with his double 1st cousin John Scott Harrison (brother of President Benjamin Harrison), *b* at La Cygne, Kansas 27 March 1869, *m* 1st at Mound City, Kansas 6 Nov 1893, Lura Myrtle (*b* at Detroit, Michigan 28 Sept 1869; *d* at Kansas City, Missouri 9 Feb 1922), dau of Charles Newton Adams, by his wife Amelia Dawes, and had issue,

1*a*●Alice Amelia HARRISON, *b* at Kansas City, Missouri 19 Oct 1896, *m* 1st at Kansas City, Missouri Sept 1915, Reuben Nathan Fredlund (*b* 1893; *d* at Iola, Kansas 5 Aug 1916); and 2ndly at Glendale, California 16 March 1921, Joseph Lawrence Green (*d* at Glendale, California 1948), and *dsp* Feb 1946.

2*a*●Virginia HARRISON [*7548 Wandotte Street, Kansas City, Missouri 64114, USA*], *b* at Kansas City, Missouri 31 Dec 1899, *m* there 23 Sept 1922, Albert Randolph Ware (*b* at Chicago, Illinois 2 Nov 1897; *d* at Oakland, California 1969), son of Albert R. Ware, by his wife Marcia, and has had issue,

1*b*●Virginia Louise WARE, *b* at Kansas City, Missouri 22 Aug 1923, *m* at Hemet, California 13 Nov 1943, ●Charles W. Dreyer (*b* at Kansas City, Missouri 10 Dec 1921) [*3808 Van Demen Drive, Fort Worth, Texas 76116, USA*], son of Albert F. Dreyer,

by his wife Laura, and has issue,

1*c*●Constance Louise DREYER, *b* at Dayton, Ohio 6 July 1949, *m* at Prairie Village, Kansas 12 Aug 1970, ●Dale Edward Bell [*1252 North 78th East Avenue, Tulsa, Oklahoma 74115, USA*], son of L. M. Bell, by his wife Mary.

2*c*●Lawrence Harrison DREYER, US Army, *b* at Minneapolis, Minnesota 15 Oct 1954.

3*c*●Lori Diane DREYER, *b* at Minneapolis, Minnesota 28 March 1962.

2*b* William Randolph WARE, *b* at Kansas City, Missouri 9 March 1927; *d* at Independence, Missouri 23 Feb 1938.

William Henry Harrison *m* 2ndly at Edwardsville, Kansas 1 March 1923, Ethel Etzenhouser (*b* 1889; *d* at Independence, Missouri 2 May 1970), and *d* at Independence, Missouri 15 April 1945.

(7) Mary Randolph HARRISON, *b* at Mound City, Kansas 28 Oct 1871, *m* at Kansas City, Missouri 16 Jan 1896, John Walter Farrar (*b* at Chicago, Illinois 1872; *d* at Kansas City, Missouri 3 Feb 1960), son of Samuel Henry Farrar, by his wife Winnie Scott Harrison, and *d* at Kansas City, Missouri 1938, leaving issue,

1*a*●James Harrison FARRAR, rancher and cattleman [*Haines, Oregon 97833, USA*], *b* at Kansas City, Missouri 7 Sept 1907, *m* at Yuma, Arizona 5 June 1935, ●Dorothy (*b* at Santa Barbara, California 22 July 1898), dau of Carl Stoddard, by his wife Linda Romero.

2*a*●Alice Elizabeth FARRAR, *b* at Kansas City, Missouri 8 Oct 1908, *m* there 14 June 1947, ●Norman Stanley Quay (*b* at Fort Lauderdale, Florida 1914) [*7609 Conser, Overland Park, Kansas 66204, USA*], and has issue,

●Mary Katherine QUAY, *b* at Kansas City, Missouri 5 May 1948, *m* at Chillicothi, Missouri 1970, ●Richard M. Wray (*b* at Kansas City, Missouri Aug 1949) [*7609 Conser, Overland Park, Kansas 66204, USA*], and has issue,

●Robert Harrison WRAY, *b* at Kansas City 4 April 1971.

3*a*●Agnes Winifred FARRAR [*673 Orchard Avenue, Santa Barbara, California 93108, USA*], *b* at Kansas City, Missouri 23 Nov 1911, *m* at Olatha, Kansas 8 Jan 1938, Rex Clifford Black (*b* at Hurley, S Dakota 9 Aug 1905; *d* at Denver, Colorado 26 Dec 1946).

(8) James Findlay HARRISON, of Dell, Montana, served in Spanish-American War with 3rd Missouri Regt, *b* at La Cygne, Kansas 28 Dec 1876; *dunm* at Calico Rock, Arkansas 25 Feb 1958.

(9) Archibald Irwin HARRISON, served in World War I as Sgt 3rd US Engrs, *b* 7 April 1881; *dunm* 7 March 1920.

2 William Henry HARRISON, *dunm* 1849.

**5** John Scott HARRISON, of North Bend, Ohio, mem House of Reps 1853-57, *b* at Vincennes, Indiana 4 Oct 1804, *m* 1st 1824, Lucretia Knapp (*b* in Boone County, Kentucky 16 Sept 1804; *d* 6 Feb 1830), and had issue,

1 Elizabeth Short HARRISON, *b* 1825, *m* George Coleman Eaton, MD (*d* 1866), and *d* 1904, having had issue,

(1) Scott Harrison EATON, *dunm*.

(2) Mary Goodrich EATON, *dunm*.

(3) George Coleman EATON, *b* 1853, *m* 1880, Lillian Antoinette Storch (*b* 1854; *d* 1932), and *d* 1889, leaving issue,

1*a* Robert Brown EATON, *d* young.

2*a* Scott Harrison EATON, *b* 1883; *dunm*.

3*a* George Coleman EATON, *d* young.

(4) Anna Harrison EATON, *d* young.

(5) Archibald Irwin EATON, *d* young.

2 William Henry Harrison, *b* 1827; *d* young.

3 Sarah Lucretia HARRISON, *b* 1829, *m* Thomas Jefferson Devin, and had issue,

(1) Anna Harrison DEVIN, *dunm*.

(2) Scott Harrison DEVIN, *m* Lucretia Griffith, and had issue,

Scott Harrison DEVIN.

John Scott Harrison *m* 2ndly, 12 Aug 1831, Elizabeth Ramsey (*b* at Mercersburg, Pennsylvania 18 July 1810; *d* at North Bend, Ohio 15 Aug 1850), dau of Archibald Irwin, by his wife Mary Ramsey (and sister of Mrs William Henry Harrison—*see above, p 210*), and *d* at Point Farm, nr North Bend, Ohio 25 May 1878 (*bur* Harrison Tomb), having by her had issue.

4 Archibald Irwin HARRISON, Lt-Col US Vols, *b* at North

Bend, Ohio 1832, *m* Elizabeth L. Sheets, and *d* 1870, leaving issue,
  (1) Mary Randolph HARRISON, *m* Frank Campbell Nickels, and had issue,
    Harrison Campbell NICKELS, *dunm.*
  (2) William Sheets HARRISON, *dunm* 1890.
  (3) Elizabeth Irwin HARRISON, *m* her 2nd cousin, Thornton Lewis, eldest son of John Calvin Lewis, by his wife Alice Fitzhugh Thornton, and had issue (*see below, p 213*).
  (4) Jean Carter HARRISON, *dunm.*
5 BENJAMIN HARRISON, **23rd President of the United States of America** (*qv*).
6 Mary Jane HARRISON, *b* 1835, *m* 1859, as his 1st wife Samuel Vance Morris, and *d* 1867, having had issue,
  (1) Scott Harrison MORRIS, *b* 1860, *m* Laura Pease, and *d* 1913, having had issue,
    1*a* Mabel May MORRIS, *m* George Duffield Slaymaker, and had issue,
      Clara Morris SLAYMAKER, *d* young.
    2*a* Jane Elizabeth MORRIS, *m* Russell McDaniel, and *dsp.*
    3*a* Louis Parker MORRIS, *d* young.
    4*a* Anna Harrison MORRIS, *m* Marcus Walker, and had issue,
      1*b* ● Scott Harrison Morris WALKER.
      2*b* ● Nancy Annette WALKER.
  (2) Frank MORRIS, *d* 1863.
  (3) Elizabeth Irwin MORRIS, *b* 1863, *m* 1903, Edmund Gordon Reel, and *dsp.*
7 Anna Symmes HARRISON, *b* 1837; *d* 1838.
8 John Irwin HARRISON, *b* and *d* 1839.
9 Carter Bassett HARRISON, of Tennessee, *b* 1840, *m* 1863, Sophia Ridgely, widow of William Lytle, and dau of — Dashiell, and had issue,
  (1) John Scott HARRISON, *b* 25 Feb 1864, *m* 19 Aug 1886, Margaret Willis, and had issue,
    1*a* Alyn HARRISON, *b* 18 Dec 1887, *m* 21 July 1921, Mary Matheny, and had issue,
      ● Alyn HARRISON, *b* 3 April 1922.
    2*a* Margaret HARRISON, *b* 31 July 1889, *m* 3 Oct 1909, Samuel Harvey Kinney, and *dsp.*
  (2) Carter Bassett HARRISON, *b* 1868; *dunm* 1892.
  (3) Elizabeth Irwin HARRISON, *b* 1874, *m* 1893, William Thornton Taliaferro Buckner, and had issue,
    1*a* ● Sophia Harrison BUCKNER, *b* 1894, *m* 1927,
    ● William Proctor Bell, and has issue,
    ● Elizabeth Buckner BELL, *b* 1928.
    2*a* ● Elizabeth Harrison BUCKNER, *b* 1902, *m* 1921,
    ● Daniel W. McCarthy [*200 West Galbreth Road, Cincinnati, Ohio, USA*].
10 Anna Symmes HARRISON, *b* 1842, *m* 1869, as his 2nd wife, her brother-in-law, Samuel Vance Morris, and *d* 1926, having had issue,
  (1) Samuel Vance MORRIS, Jr, *b* 1870, *m* 1897, Nellie Prouse, and *d* 1928, leaving issue,
    ● Margaret MORRIS, *b* 1898.
  (2) Margaret Vance MORRIS, *b* 1872, *m* 1891, William H. Curtiss, and had issue,
    Ray Harrison CURTISS, *b* 1893, *m* Janet Hood, and had issue,
    1*b* ● Jean Eleanor CURTISS, *b* 1919, *m* ●— Curt.
    2*b* ● Nancy Harrison CURTISS, *b* 1922.
  (3) Allen Harrison MORRIS, *b* 1874; *dunm* 1913.
  (4) Clara Vaughn MORRIS, *b* 1877; *d* 1889.
  (5) Anna Thornton MORRIS, *b* at Indianapolis, Indiana 1879, *m* at Minneapolis, Minnesota 1903, Charles Thompson Stevenson (*b* at Edinburgh, Scotland 1877; *d* at Minneapolis 1958), son of William Stevenson, by his wife Mary Ann Hare, and *d* at Minneapolis 1968, leaving issue,
    1*a* ● Mary STEVENSON, *b* at Minneapolis 1905, *m* there 1928, ● George F. Williamson [*1715 Logan Avenue S, Minneapolis, Minnesota 55403, USA*], son of James F. Williamson, by his wife Emma Elmore, and has issue,
    ● Ann WILLIAMSON, *b* at Minneapolis 1930, *m* there 1952, ● Lane McGovern (*b* at Boston 1924) [*12 Dartmouth, Winchester, Massachusetts, USA*], son of James F. McGovern, by his wife Marion Stritzinger, and has issue,
      1*c* ● Susan McGOVERN, *b* at Boston 1954.
      2*c* ● Sara McGOVERN, *b* at Boston 1956.

      3*c* ● Lisa McGOVERN, *b* at Boston 1959.
      4*c* ● Laura McGOVERN, *b* at Boston 1962.
    2*a* ● Nancy Morris STEVENSON [*Rabbit Hill, 4625 Highland Road, Minnetonka, Minnesota 55343, USA*], *b* at Minneapolis 1907, *m* there 1933, James Sargent Lane (*b* at Minneapolis 1902; *d* 1947), son of Mark M. Lane, by his wife Corabelle Gould, and has issue,
    1*b* ● James Sargent LANE III, *b* 1939, *m* at Minneapolis 1961, ● Joan Lee, and has issue,
      1*c* ● Anne Stevenson LANE, *b* in Hawaii 1962.
      2*c* ● Joan Harrison LANE, *b* at Minneapolis 1964.
      3*c* ● Jacqueline Lee LANE, *b* in Virginia 1968.
      4*c* ● Linda Wells LANE, *b* at Minneapolis 1970.
    2*b* ● Charles Stevenson LANE [*Green Bay, Wisconsin, USA*], *b* 1942.
  (6) Eleanor MORRIS, *b* 1882, *m* 1908, Albert Lewis Butler, and had issue,
    ● Vance BUTLER, *b* 1912.
11 John Scott HARRISON, of Kansas City, Missouri, *b* 12 Nov 1844, *m* 7 Oct 1872, Marie Sophie Elizabeth Lytle, and *d* 9 Jan 1926, having had issue,
  (1) Archibald Irwin HARRISON, *b* at Kansas City, Missouri 27 Nov 1874, *m* at Portland, Oregon 6 Oct 1902, Louise Irene Mount, and *dvp* 19 Oct 1912, having had issue,
    1*a* Archibald Irwin HARRISON, *b* at Fort Snelling, Minnesota 9 July, *d* 18 July 1903.
    2*a* ● Katherine Louise HARRISON [*4600 J.C. Nichols Parkway, Kansas City, Missouri 64112, USA*], *b* at San Francisco, California 1904, *m* at Kansas City, Missouri 6 Oct 1927, David Pollard Caldwell (*b* at Union City, Tennessee 1888; *d* at Kansas City, Missouri 25 Sept 1942), son of David Caldwell, by his wife Maude Bostar, and has issue,
      1*b* ● Katherine Louise CALDWELL, *b* at Topeka, Kansas 22 July 1936, *m* at Kansas City, Missouri 21 Aug 1965, ● James Hannon Conely, Jr, USAF (*b* at New Smyrna Beach, Florida 9 July 1938) [*33c Cedar Street, Maxwell Air Force Base, Alabama 36113, USA*], son of James Hannon Conely, by his wife Euda, and has issue,
        1*c* ● Karen Louise CONELY, *b* at New York 15 May 1966.
        2*c* ● David Hannon CONELY, *b* at Colorado Springs, Colorado 27 Nov 1968.
        3*c* ● Anne Katherine CONELY, *b* at Colorado Springs, Colorado 27 Nov 1968 (twin with David Hannon).
      2*b* ● David Pollard CALDWELL, Jr, *b* at Chattanooga, Tennessee 27 Feb 1940, *m* at Kansas City, Missouri 8 Jan 1972, ● Sue Etrick.
  (2) Lytle HARRISON, of Los Angeles, California, apptd Paymr USN by Pres McKinley during Spanish-American War, rancher and developer, *b* at Kansas City, Missouri 22 Feb 1876, *m* there 4 Feb 1904, Esther Allen (*b* at Kansas City, Missouri 10 Oct 1878; *d* at San Bernardino, California 28 March 1952), dau of Steven Davis Thatcher, by his wife Esther Allen, and *d* at Los Angeles 23 March 1956, leaving issue,
    ● Lytle HARRISON, Jr, served in World War II with US Army, Armd Cmd, exec and adminr [*11970 Montana Avenue, Los Angeles, California 90049, USA*], *b* at Mercedes, Texas 29 Sept 1908, *m* at Los Angeles 25 Aug 1926, ● Antoinette (*b* at Los Angeles 29 Sept 1905), dau of John Munro, by his wife Ella Mae Heinzeman, and has issue,
    ● William Lytle HARRISON, USN (ret), served in World War II, Korea and Vietnam, logistics engr [*Belle Vue/Cascade Box 353, Mahe, Seychelles Islands, Indian Ocean, East Africa*], *b* at Cameron, Texas 20 May 1927, *m* at Auckland, NZ 29 May 1945, ● Edith Elizabeth (*b* at Dunedin, NZ 29 June 1926), dau of Alexander Bell, by his wife Jesse Bethune Duncan, and has issue,
    ● Loretta Elizabeth HARRISON, *b* at San Francisco, California 14 Jan 1947, *educ* Anokia Sch, and St Mary's Acad, *m* at Reno, Nevada 7 July 1968, ● Leonard Laverne ' Nunes (*b* at Chico, California 23 July 1947) [*46 Huggins Drive, Orland, California 95963, USA*], son of William Robert

Nunes, by his wife Velma Louise Landingham, and has issue,

1d●Ainsley Marie NUNES, *b* at Paradise, California 12 April 1969.

2d●Marcia Louise NUNES, *b* at Paradise, California 12 Aug 1971.

(3) James Ridgeley HARRISON, *b* 1880; *d* young.

(4) John Scott HARRISON, of Kansas City, Missouri, *b* 22 April 1882, *m* 5 Feb 1910, Norma Freschley, and had issue,

1a●Edward Webb HARRISON.

2a●John Scott HARRISON.

3a● Carter Ridgeley HARRISON [*428 West 57th Terrace, Kansas City, Missouri 64113, USA*].

(5) Margaretta HARRISON, *b* 9 Dec 1884, *m* 1st 4 June 1905, Simpson Robinson; and 2ndly 1927, William F. Saeger, and *dsp*.

(6) Benjamin HARRISON, of Kansas City, Missouri, *b* 1892, *m* Julia Sandres, and had issue,

1a●Julia Margaretta HARRISON, *b* 1920.

2a●Benjamin HARRISON, *b* 1922.

12 James Findlay HARRISON, *b* 1847; *d* 1848.

13 James Irwin HARRISON, *b* 1849; *d* 1850.

**6** Benjamin HARRISON, MD, *b* at Vincennes, Indiana 5 May 1806, *m* 1st, Louise Bonner, and had issue,

1 John Cleves Short HARRISON, *m* 1st Mary Frances Harrison, and had issue,

(1) Frank Hanson HARRISON, MD, *m* Adella Elvira Young, and had issue,

1a●Ella HARRISON.

2a●Margaret HARRISON.

(2) Benjamin Harrison.

(3) George Washington HARRISON, *m* Julia Talbott, and *dsp*.

(4) Julia Callus HARRISON.

John Cleves Short Harrison *m* 2ndly, Margaret Ruth McCarty, and had issue,

(5) Nicholas McCarty HARRISON.

(6) Cleves HARRISON.

Dr Benjamin Harrison *m* 2ndly, Mary Raney, and *d* 1840, having by her had issue,

2 Benjamin HARRISON, *dunm*.

3 William Henry HARRISON, *dunm*.

**7** Mary Symmes HARRISON, *b* at Vincennes, Indiana 22 Jan 1809, *m* 1829, John Henry Fitzhugh Thornton, MD, and *d* 1842, having had issue,

1 William Henry Harrison THORNTON, *dunm*.

2 Charles THORNTON, MD, *dunm*.

3 Anna Harrison THORNTON, *b* 1835, *m* 1863, Lee Mason Fitzhugh (*b* 1838), and *d* 1883, having had issue,

(1) Thornton FITZHUGH, *b* 1864, *m* 1888, Anne Harrison McClung (*see below*), and had issue,

James McClung FITZHUGH, *dunm*.

(2) George Lee FITZHUGH, *b* 1866, *m* 1891, Mary Phipps, and *dsp*.

(3) Charles Harrison FITZHUGH, *b* 1868; *d* 1869.

(4) Anna Thornton FITZHUGH, *b* 1873; *dunm*.

(5) Lee Mason FITZHUGH, *b* 1876; *dunm*.

4 Alice Fitzhugh THORNTON, *b* 1838, *m* John Calvin Lewis, and had issue,

(1) Thornton LEWIS, *m* his 2nd cousin Elizabeth Irwin, 2nd dau of Lt-Col Archibald Irwin Harrison, by his wife Elizabeth L. Sheets (*see above, p 212*), and had issue,

William Sheets Harrison LEWIS, *dunm*.

(2) Joseph Dixon LEWIS, *m* — Melcher, and *dsp*(?).

(3) Charles Rea LEWIS, *dunm*.

(4) Mary Wakefield LEWIS, *dunm*.

(5) Frank Edwin LEWIS, *dunm*.

(6) Harry LEWIS, *d* young.

5 Lucy Harrison THORNTON, *d* young.

6 John Fitzhugh THORNTON, *b* 1842, *m* Leila Morgan West, and had issue,

Charles West THORNTON, *d* young.

**8** Carter Bassett HARRISON, *b* 26 Oct 1811, *m* Mary Anne Sutherland, and *d* 1839, leaving issue,

Anna Carter HARRISON, *b* 1837, *m* David W. McClung, and had issue,

Anne Harrison MCCLUNG, *m* 1888, her 2nd cousin Thornton Fitzhugh (*b* 1864), eldest son of Lee Mason Fitzhugh, by his wife Anna Harrison Thornton, and had issue (*see above*).

**9** Anna Tuthill HARRISON, *b* 28 Oct 1813, *m* 1836, her 1st cousin once removed William Henry Harrison Taylor (*b* 1813; *d* 1894), eldest son of Thomas Taylor, by his wife Lucy Harrison, dau of Capt Anthony Singleton, by his wife Lucy, sister of Pres William Henry Harrison (*see p 215*), and *d* 5 July 1865, having had issue,

1 William Henry Harrison TAYLOR, *b* 1837, *m* 1st, Mary King, and had issue,

(1) William Rennick TAYLOR.

(2) Harry Serrill TAYLOR.

(3) Myra TAYLOR.

William Henry Harrison Taylor *m* 2ndly, Clara Jenkins, and *d* 1906, having by her had issue,

(4) Mattie Fullerton TAYLOR.

(5) John Thomas TAYLOR, *d* 1906.

2 Lucy Singleton TAYLOR, *b* 1839, *m* Harrison Scott Howell (*d* 1907), and *d* 1906, having had issue,

(1) Harrison Taylor HOWELL, *d* young.

(2) Jean Lyall HOWELL, *d* young.

(3) Scott Singleton HOWELL, *d* young.

(4) Bessie HOWELL, *d* young.

(5) Cleves Harrison HOWELL, *b* 13 Aug 1880, *m* Sara May Hill, and had issue,

●Cleves Harrison HOWELL, Jr, *b* 25 July 1911, *m* ●Edith Shallenberger, and has issue,

●Cleves Harrison HOWELL III.

3 Anna Harrison TAYLOR, *b* 7 April, *d* 7 Nov 1840.

4 John Thomas TAYLOR, *b* 1841, *m* 1st, Agnes Kennedy, and had issue,

(1) Alice Kennedy TAYLOR, *d* young.

(2) Anna Harrison TAYLOR, *d* young.

John Thomas Taylor *m* 2ndly, Amelia Martha Wilson.

5 Mary Thornton TAYLOR, *b* 1843, *m* 1870, George Albert Plummer (*d* 1914), and *d* 1905, leaving issue,

(1) Virginia Berkeley PLUMMER, *b* 1872, *m* 1st 1893, Silas Decker (*d* 1894). She *m* 2ndly 1900, William A. Badger (*d* 1909), and *d* 1929, leaving issue,

●Virginia Berkeley BADGER, *b* 1903, *m* 1934, ●Corwin Gibson (*b* 1890), and has issue,

1b●Mary Virginia GIBSON, *b* 1935.

2b●Corwin Henry GIBSON, *b* 1941.

(2) Scott Howell PLUMMER, *b* 1874, *m* 1904, Lucy Towler (*b* 1878), and *d* 1927, leaving issue,

1a●William Howell PLUMMER, *b* 1905, *m* 1931, ●Margaret Gale Merrick, and has issue,

1b●William Howell PLUMMER, Jr, *b* 1932.

2b●Joanne PLUMMER, *b* 1935.

2a●Robert Kinsman PLUMMER, *b* 1910.

(3) Harriett Putman PLUMMER, *b* 1878, *m* 1902, Arthur L. Helliwell, of Chelan, Washington, DC (*b* 1870; *d* 1941), and *d* 1946, leaving issue,

1a●George Albert Plummer HELLIWELL (Rev), *b* 1903, *m* ●Eleanor McAfree, and has issue,

1b●Thomas HELLIWELL, *b* 1936.

2b●Sally Sue HELLIWELL, *b* 1936.

2a●Elizabeth HELLIWELL, *b* 1906, *m* 1934, ●George Sylling (*b* 1904), and has issue,

1b●Patricia SYLLING, *b* 1936.

2b●David SYLLING, *b* 1942.

(4) Bess Taylor PLUMMER, *b* 1881; *dunm*.

6 Anna Cleves TAYLOR, *b* 1844, *m* at Keokuk, Iowa 1873, George Henry Comstock (*b* at Lee, Mass 1838; *d* at Minneapolis, Minnesota 1903), son of William H. Comstock, by his wife Phebe Bassett Spellman, and *d* at Minneapolis 1937, leaving issue,

(1) Anna Harrison COMSTOCK, *b* at Keokuk, Iowa 3 June 1874, *m* at St Paul, Minnesota 15 Oct 1895, Charles Mann (*b* at New Albany, New York 9 July 1870; *d* at Minneapolis 1952), son of Walter Mann, by his wife Elizabeth Butler, and *d* at Minneapolis 25 June 1946, having had issue,

1a Charles Edward MANN, Jr, *b* at St Paul, Minnesota 15 Feb 1898; *d* there 2 Feb 1902.

2a●Stewart Harrison MANN, radio announcer and sports writer [*1335 Edgewood Avenue N, Minneapolis, Minnesota 55427, USA*], *b* at St Paul, Minnesota 26 Dec 1903, *educ* Parsons Coll., *m* 1st at Minneapolis 27 July 1934 (*m* diss by div), Alice M., dau of Marcus Gilbertson, by his wife Mattie. He *m* 2ndly at Minneapolis 12 Sept 1947 (*m* diss by div), Vivian Leona, exec sec (*b* at Truman, Minnesota 16 May 1918), dau of Hans Albert Hansen, by his wife Anna Marie Nielsen, and by her has issue,

●Gina Laurin MANN, *b* at Minneapolis, Minnesota 11 Feb 1949, *educ* Minnesota Univ (BSc 1971), *m* at Minneapolis 17 July 1971, ●Raymond Lea Salisbury, science and mathematics teacher (*b* at Buffalo, New York 28 June 1949) [*1916 Story Street, Boone, Iowa 50036, USA*], son of Donald Leroy Salisbury, by his wife Joan Edna Barber, and has issue,

●Emily Anna-Marie SALISBURY, *b* at Boone, Iowa 7 Feb 1973.

Stewart Harrison Mann *m* 3rdly, ●Mrs Delores Dutton, and has adopted her two children,

(a) ●Marcia MANN (formerly Dutton).

(b) ●Bruce MANN (formerly Dutton).

3*a*●George Comstock MANN, proprietor of women's shoe store [*2031 Charleen Circle, Carlsbad, California 92008, USA*], *b* at Minneapolis 31 Aug 1906, *m* at Stillwell, Oklahoma 8 Aug 1929, ●Erma Edna Toney (*b* 17 Nov 1910), and has issue,

1*b*●Erma Dean MANN, *b* at Minneapolis 22 Oct 1934, *m* at Chandler, Arizona 2 July 1952, ●Dale Allen Yeager [*250 West Tulsa, Chandler, Arizona, USA*], and has issue,

1*c*●Dana Allen YEAGER, *b* 3 Jan 1956.

2*c*●Karen Ann YEAGER, *b* 27 Oct 1960.

2*b*●Charles Eugene MANN, air pilot, *b* at Shreveport, Louisiana 8 Aug 1939, *m* 15 Sept 1959 (*m* diss by div), Mary Diann Stapley, and has issue,

1*c*●Carrie Diann MANN, *b* 19 Jan 1961.

2*c*●Kelli MANN, *b* 20 Nov 1963.

4*a*●Anna Elizabeth MANN, *b* at Minneapolis 23 Nov 1910, *m* there 10 Aug 1940, ●Richard Warren Stein (*b* at Cass Lake, Minnesota 1904) [*5004 Chicago Avenue, Minneapolis, Minnesota 55417, USA*], son of George Stein, by his wife Minnie McMullen.

(2) Lucy Bassett COMSTOCK, *m* George McKay, and *dsp.*

7 Bessie Short TAYLOR, *b* 1846, *m* John Ogden, and *dsp* 1940.

8 Fanny Gault TAYLOR, *b* 1848, *m* 1876, Charles Fitch Hendryx (*b* 1847; *d* 1935), and *d* 1932, leaving issue,

(1) James Beardsley HENDRYX, *b* 1880, *m* 1915, Hermione Flagler (*b* 1888), and had issue,

1*a*●Hermione Flagler HENDRYX, *b* 1918, *m* 2 Sept 1942, ●Dr Fred George Swartz, Jr [*1137 Balfour Road, Grosse Pointe, Michigan 48230, USA*], son of Fred G. Swartz, and has issue,

1*b*●Fred George SWARTZ III, *b* 10 Aug 1943.

2*b*●Mary Anne SWARTZ, *b* 5 June 1946.

3*b*●Edith Myra SWARTZ, *b* 5 Sept 1952.

2*a*●James Beardsley HENDRYX, Jr [*350 Madison Avenue, Cresskill, New Jersey 07626, USA*], *b* 1919, ●Terry Lang, and has issue,

1*b*●Patricia HENDRYX, *b* 1945.

2*b*●Susan Harrison HENDRYX, *b* 1948.

3*a*●Betty Harrison HENDRYX, *b* at Cincinnati, Ohio 4 May 1921, *m* at Annapolis, Maryland 9 June 1943, ●Capt Robert James Loomis, USN(ret) [*4303 Argonne Drive, Fairfax, Virginia 22030, USA*], and has issue,

1*b*●Robert James LOOMIS, Jr, *b* at Portland, Maine 23 Aug 1946, *m* at Detroit, Michigan 29 Nov 1969, ●Elaine Marie Babiarz.

2*b*●Stephen Hendryx LOOMIS, *b* at Norfolk, Virginia 23 Feb 1949, *m* at Arlington, Virginia 22 Jan 1972, ●Ruth Staley.

3*b*●Barbara Anne LOOMIS, *b* at Bethesda, Maryland 19 Sept 1950, *m* at Fairfax, Virginia 4 Dec 1971, ●James Michael Altis.

4*b*●Betty Jo LOOMIS, *b* at Bethesda, Maryland 19 Sept 1950 (twin with her sister Barbara Anne Loomis), *m* at Fairfax, Virginia 2 Oct 1971, ●Reginald Saunders Early, and has issue,

1*c*●Ryan Saunders EARLY, *b* at Arlington, Virginia 21 March 1972.

2*c*●Carrie Tae EARLY, *b* at Arlington, Virginia 25 Feb 1973.

5*b*●Timothy Glenn LOOMIS, *b* at Traverse City, Michigan 19 Oct 1954.

6*b*●Cynthia Sue LOOMIS, *b* at Newport, Rhode Island 19 Feb 1958.

(2) Anna Harrison HENDRYX, *b* 1883, *m* 1st 1914, William Sinclair Bacot (*b* 1860; *d* 1917). She *m* 2ndly 1919, Rev Frederick Lincoln Flinchbaugh (*b* 1874), and *d* 1930, leaving issue,

●Anne Harrison FLINCHBAUGH, *m* ●Job Taylor.

(3) Myra Bingham HENDRYX, *b* 1885, *m* 1912, John C. Oakes, and *dsp* 1947.

9 Virginia Berkeley TAYLOR, *b* 1851, *m* Frank W. Stratton, and *dsp* 1928.

10 Jane Harrison TAYLOR, *b* 1852, *m* 1875, Edward Jason Davenport (*b* 1852; *d* 1930), and *d* 1939, having had issue,

(1) Lee Butler DAVENPORT, *b* 1876, *m* 1904, Evita Clara Rait, and had issue,

1*a*●Donald Murray DAVENPORT, *b* 1910, *m* 1933, ●Helga Clarkson Andenberg, and has issue,

1*b*●Donald McKinnon DAVENPORT, *b* 1940.

2*b*●Anne Melissa DAVENPORT, *b* 1943.

3*b*●Bret Carstairs DAVENPORT, *b* 1947.

2*a*●Lee Butler DAVENPORT, Jr, *b* 1915.

(2) Cleves Harrison DAVENPORT, *b* and *d* 1881.

(3) Murray Taylor DAVENPORT, Capt US Army, *b* 1882, *m* 1920, Ethel Margaret (*b* 1898; *d* 1952), widow of — Wilson, and dau of — Douglas, and *dsp.*

11 Nellie Bassett TAYLOR, *b* 1853; *d* 5 Jan 1864.

12 Edward Everett TAYLOR, *b* 1856, *m* 1st, Belle Bradley; and 2ndly, Mrs Harriet Chapman, and *dsp.*

**10** James Findlay HARRISON, *b* 15 May 1814.

# The Brothers and Sisters of President William Henry Harrison

**1** Elizabeth HARRISON, *b* 1751, *m* 1st, William Rickman, MD, Dir-Gen Continental Hosp at Richmond, Virginia during the Revolution. She *m* 2ndly, — Edmonson, and *dsp*.

**2** Anne HARRISON, *b* at Berkeley 21 May 1753, *m* there 9 March 1775, as his 2nd wife, David Coupland, of Springfield, Buckingham County, Virginia, Justice of Cumberland County (*b* in Nansemond County, Virginia 3 Aug 1749; *d* 1821), 2nd son of William Coupland, by his wife Alice Apsley, dau of David O'Sheals, of Nansemond County, and *d* 1821, having had issue, four sons and six daus.

**3** Benjamin HARRISON, of Berkeley, *b* 1755, *m* 1st 1785, Anna (*b* 9 Sept 1760; *d* 28 Aug 1787), dau of Judge James Mercer, of the Court of Appeals of Virginia, and had issue, one son, whose issue is still *extant*. He *m* 2ndly *ante* 16 Nov 1787, Susan, dau of Richard Randolph, Jr, of Curles Neck, and *d* 1799.

**4** Lucy HARRISON, *m* 1st, Major Peyton Randolph, of Wilton, Henrico County, Virginia, ADC to Marquis de Lafayette, and had issue, three sons and one dau. She *m* 2ndly (licence 8 Oct 1788), Anthony Singleton, of Williamsburg and Richmond, Capt of Artillery in the Revolution (*d* 1795), and *d* 1809, having had further issue, two sons and one dau (Lucy Harrison Singleton (1789-1855), who *m* Thomas Taylor (1767-1832), and had, with other issue, William Henry Harrison Taylor, who *m* Anna Tuthill, yst dau of Pres William Henry Harrison—*see p 213*).

**5** Carter Bassett HARRISON, member of the House of Delegates from Surry 1784-85 and 1785-86, and from Prince George 1805-06, 1806-07 and 1807-08, member of Congress 1793-99, *educ* William and Mary Coll, *m* 1st, Mary Howell, dau of William Allen, of Claremont, Surry County, Virginia, and had issue, two sons and one dau. He *m* 2ndly, Jane Byrd, by whom he had no issue,

**6** Sarah HARRISON, *b* 1770, *m* John Minge, of Weyanoke, Charles City County, Virginia, and *d* 1812, leaving issue, seven sons and two daus.

# Notes

[1] Through Abigail Smith the Harrisons descend from James Bacon, Alderman of London, a brother of Sir Nicholas Bacon, Lord Keeper of the Great Seal of England, and uncle of the celebrated writer Francis Bacon, 1st and last Viscount St Albans, Lord Keeper of the Great Seal, and Lord High Chancellor of England (*see* BURKE'S *Peerage*, BACON, Bt). The descent is as follows—

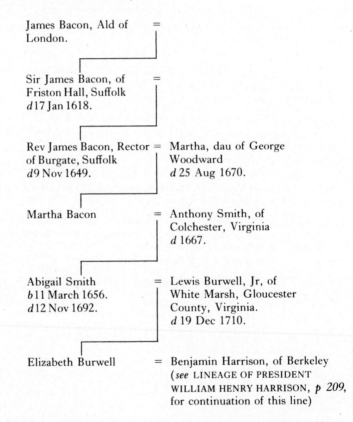

James Bacon, Ald of London. =

Sir James Bacon, of Friston Hall, Suffolk *d* 17 Jan 1618. =

Rev James Bacon, Rector of Burgate, Suffolk *d* 9 Nov 1649. = Martha, dau of George Woodward *d* 25 Aug 1670.

Martha Bacon = Anthony Smith, of Colchester, Virginia *d* 1667.

Abigail Smith *b* 11 March 1656. *d* 12 Nov 1692. = Lewis Burwell, Jr, of White Marsh, Gloucester County, Virginia. *d* 19 Dec 1710.

Elizabeth Burwell = Benjamin Harrison, of Berkeley (*see* LINEAGE OF PRESIDENT WILLIAM HENRY HARRISON, *p 209*, for continuation of this line)

[2] Through the Carter family the Harrisons have a Royal descent from King Henry III (*see* APPENDIX C, PRESIDENTS OF ROYAL DESCENT).

[3] The second wife of John Cleves Symmes was Susan, dau of William Livingston, sometime Governor of New Jersey. A great-nephew of Mrs William Henry Harrison, John Cleves Symmes (1868-1918) *m* Marion Yorke Lawrence, a grand-dau of Andrew Jackson, Jr, the adopted son of President Andrew Jackson (*see p 184*).

# John Tyler
## 1790-1862

―――

10th President of the
United States of America
1841-1845

JOHN TYLER, 10TH PRESIDENT

# John Tyler

## 1790-1862

### 10th President of the United States of America
### 1841-1845

"TIPPECANOE AND Tyler Too" was the Whig campaign slogan in the election of 1840. A disgruntled Whig later remarked that "there was rhyme, but no reason in it". John Tyler had been picked as William H. Harrison's running mate mainly to balance the ticket: a Southern state (Virginia) to balance Harrison's Northern one (Ohio). Tyler, the son of a planter-lawyer, had been Governor of Virginia and a member of the Federal Senate. He had been brought up in a tradition of public service. He had developed a strong dislike of Andrew Jackson. Otherwise he was an unlikely figure to set beside Whig leaders like Henry Clay and Daniel Webster. They believed in the promotion of national economic programs, such as a protective tariff to help American industry. Tyler, on the other hand, was an unabashed defender of states rights, convinced that the Federal Government had no authority to interfere with the individual states in their domestic concerns.

The expectation was that Vice-President Tyler would be consigned to the usual ceremonial impotence associated with his office. Clay, the Whig leader in the Senate, looked forward to dominating policy-making during Harrison's term, and then to the Whig presidential nomination in 1844 which he took as his rightful due. Suddenly, however, Harrison was dead and John Tyler was hurrying back to Washington to assume control. But on what terms? The succession clause of the Constitution said:

> In case of the Removal of the President from Office, or of his Death, Resignation, or Inability to discharge the Powers and Duties of the said Office, the same shall devolve on the Vice President. . . .

Former President John Quincy Adams was among those who felt that at most Tyler—never contemplated as an actual President—was entitled to be merely acting President. In this interpretation only the "Powers and Duties" and not the office itself devolved upon the Vice-President.

Tyler however made clear that he regarded himself as Harrison's automatic constitutional successor. In this he was backed by Harrison's cabinet, especially by Secretary of State Daniel Webster, and by a majority in Congress. Gradually the objectors fell silent, and both Houses voted that Tyler was henceforward "President" Tyler. But the difficulties were not over. Tyler refused to be bound by the Harrison method by which the President and each member of the cabinet had one vote, and executive policy was decided round the table. He also soon began to veto important Bills passed by the Whig Congress, to the fury of Henry Clay. Within a few months Tyler's entire cabinet except for Webster had resigned in protest, and he was formally expelled from the Whig party. He was told that he ought to quit, that he would be impeached, that he could not have a modest sum he sought for necessary repairs to the increasingly dingy White House. By 1843, when Webster also resigned, "Old Veto" stood apparently alone, a stubborn Southerner without a political following.

There is no doubt that John Tyler was exceptionally tenacious and resilient. This showed in his private life. He held up manfully under the death of his wife Letitia Christian, who had borne him eight children. Two years later, in 1844, he married a New Yorker, Julia Gardiner, who at 24 was thirty years his junior. She was to bear him seven children. The first of his fifteen offspring was born in 1815, the last in 1860. And though he was at odds with most of the Whig and Democrat leaders, he remained personally courteous and cheerful. He behaved like a Virginia gentleman, sure that his principles were correct but refraining from belligerent self-righteousness. After all, he had never disguised his opinions, and he found nothing in the Constitution that obliged him to conform to a party program.

Some historians have treated Tyler as a freakish exception to the general story of the Presidency, or as an illustration of the element of accident in history. It is true that Clay—a far more gifted candidate than Harrison—might well have secured the Whig nomination in 1840; in which case Tyler's name would today be unknown except to the scholar. It is also intriguing to reflect on the might-have-beens of February 1844; Tyler was aboard a warship when there was an explosion that killed Secretary of State Abel Upshur, the Navy Secretary, and Julia Gardiner's father. Tyler himself was within a few feet of death. If he had died in the catastrophe the succession would have passed to the President *pro tempore* of the Senate, and the John Quincy Adamses would have been even more uneasy about the legitimacy of such an attenuated line.

But Tyler did not die; it was not his fault he had been catapulted into the Presidency; and once he was in the White House he showed an

LETITIA CHRISTIAN, MRS TYLER

JULIA GARDINER, MRS TYLER

impressive capacity to get things done as well as to stop them from being done. He had an orderly mind and a clear sense of priorities. Tyler encouraged or accepted a surprising amount of useful legislation and administrative reform, including reform of the Navy. The project closest to his heart, perhaps, was a treaty of annexation with Texas. He played his cards shrewdly. When Senate approval with the necessary two-thirds majority was not feasible, he had the satisfaction—three days before his term expired—of seeing the same end accomplished by means of a joint resolution of Congress. He was able to retire to his Virginia plantation, "Sherwood Forest", with the handsome and affluent Julia Tyler, and begin to raise his second family. His home life was delightful. The nation's circumstances perturbed him—and the allegations that he had heightened sectional tension by bringing Texas into the Union. He was tempted to return to political life—perhaps even as a presidential candidate. He would probably have done no worse than the incumbents of the 1850s. John Tyler was an old-fashioned Southerner who would like to have been a statesman rather than a politician. He was proud to recall that his father had been a good friend of Thomas Jefferson. He himself was a would-be Jeffersonian, and in his way a patriot. He believed that as President he had acted in the best interests of the whole nation, and in obedience to his own conscience. He hoped that because of his record "future Vice-Presidents who may succeed to the Presidency may feel some slight encouragement to pursue an independent course". There is a nice edge of understatement in that demure sentence.

# Chronology

| | |
|---|---|
| 1790 | Born at Greenway, Charles City County, Virginia 29 March. |
| 1806 | Attended William and Mary College. |
| 1807-09 | Studied Law under his father until 1808, then under Edmund Jennings Randolph, a former Secretary of State. |
| 1809 | Admitted to the Virginia Bar. |
| 1811 | Elected member of the House of Delegates from Charles City County; took seat Dec. |
| 1812 | Introduced resolution calling for censure of the two Virginia Senators, Richard Brent and William B. Giles, for voting contrary to the instructions of the State legislature 14 Jan. |

1813    Appointed Capt of a company of Militia formed to assist in the defence of Richmond April.

1815    Resigned from the House of Delegates on election to the State Council.

1816    Elected member of the House of Representatives to fill unexpired term of John Clopton Nov; took seat 17 Dec.

1817    Re-elected to the House of Representatives.

1819    Re-elected unopposed.

1821    Declined to seek re-election on the grounds of failing health Jan; retired to private life 3 March.

1823    Again elected member of the House of Delegates.

1824    Nominated to fill vacancy in the Senate; opposed attempted removal of William and Mary College from Williamsburg to Richmond.

1825    Elected Governor of Virginia 10 Dec.

1826    Delivered oration at the funeral of Thomas Jefferson 11 July; unanimously re-elected Governor 10 Dec.

1827    Elected Senator 13 Jan; resigned as Governor 4 March; took seat in the Senate 3 Dec.

1829-30  Member of Virginia Convention for revising the State Constitution.

1833    Re-elected Senator 15 Feb; only Senator to vote against the Jackson Bill to enforce the revenue laws by military force, if necessary 20 Feb.

1835    Nominated for Vice-President by the Whigs.

1836    Resigned from the Senate 29 Feb after refusing to vote in accordance with the instructions of the Virginia Legislature to expunge the vote of censure on President Jackson; received 47 electoral votes as unsuccessful candidate for Vice-President 1 Nov.

1838    Elected President of American Colonization Society 10 Jan; again elected to Virginia House of Delegates and Speaker of the House.

1839    Nominated for the Senate 15 Feb; election postponed after indecisive ballots; nominated for Vice-President at Whig National Convention in Harrisburg, Pennsylvania 4 Dec.

1840    "Tippecanoe and Tyler Too" campaign; elected Vice-President 3 Nov.

1841    Inaugurated Vice-President 4 March; succeeded as 10th President of the United States of America on the death of William Henry Harrison 4 April; took the oath of office at the Indian Queen Hotel, Washington, DC 6 April; signed Act granting pension of $25,000 to Mrs William Henry Harrison 30 June; vetoed Bill to incorporate Fiscal Bank 16 Aug; signed second Federal Bankruptcy Act 19 Aug (repealed 1846); signed Distribution-pre-emption Act, authorising purchase of surveyed public lands by settlers, 4 Sept; vetoed second Fiscal Bank Incorporation Bill 9 Sept; issued proclamation warning against participation in proposed armed invasion of Canada 25 Sept; sent first State of the Union message to Congress 7 Dec.

1842    Vetoed "Little tariff" Bill 29 June; vetoed Second Tariff Bill 9 Aug; Webster-Ashburton Treaty, fixing Maine-Canadian border, ratified 20 Aug; signed Tariff Act of 1842; sent second State of the Union message to Congress 6 Dec; vetoed proceeds of public land sales and testimony in contested Election

Bills 14 Dec; vetoed payment of Cherokee Certificates Bill 18 Dec; sent special message to Congress on recognition of the independence of the Hawaiian Islands 31 Dec.

1843    Resolution for impeachment (for gross usurpation and abuse of power) rejected 10 Jan; attended dedication of Bunker Hill Monument in Boston 17 June; sent third State of the Union message to Congress 5 Dec.

1844    Escaped injury when a gun exploded on the USS *Princeton,* killing eight men (including Cdre Beverley Kennon—*see p 43*), 28 Feb; submitted Texas Annexation Treaty to the Senate urging ratification 22 April (rejected by Senate 8 June); nominated for re-election as President by Tyler Democrats at Baltimore 27 May; vetoed Rivers and Harbors Bill 11 June; withdrew as candidate for re-election 22 Aug; sent fourth and last State of the Union message to Congress 3 Dec.

1845    Signed Act establishing date for future Presidential elections 23 Jan; vetoed Revenue Cutters and Steamers for Defence Bill 20 Feb; signed joint resolution for the annexation of Texas 1 March; Florida admitted as the 27th State 3 March; veto of 20 Feb over-ridden 3 March; retired from office and attended the inauguration of his successor James Knox Polk 4 March; retired to his plantation at Sherwood Forest, Virginia.

1859    Appointed Chancellor of William and Mary College.

1861    Elected Chairman of Peace Convention at Washington, DC 4 Feb; recommended secession of Virginia 28 Feb; took seat in Virginia Convention on Policy 1 March; elected member of Provisional Congress of Confederation at Richmond 5 May; elected to the Confederate Congress at Richmond autumn.

1862    Died of bilious fever at Richmond, Virginia 18 Jan; buried at Richmond.

# The Writings of President Tyler

See *Letters and Times of the Tylers,* 3 vols (1884-96), by Lyon G. Tyler

# Lineage of President Tyler

HENRY TYLER, emigrated from Shropshire, England and settled at Middle Plantation, nr Williamsburg, Virginia, *b ca* 1604, *m* 1st, Mary —; and 2ndly, Ann, widow of John Orchard, and *d* at Middle Plantation 13 April 1672, having by her had issue, with two other sons,

HENRY TYLER, of Bruton Parish, Justice, Coroner and High Sheriff of York County, Virginia, *b* 1661, *m* Elizabeth, dau of Walter Chiles (son of Col Walter Chiles, a mem Council of State 1652), by his wife Elizabeth, dau of Col John Page (who came from England to Virginia 1650), and *d* 1729, having had issue, with two other sons and one dau, a 2nd son,

JOHN TYLER, Justice of James City, *b* 1686, *educ* William and Mary Coll, *m* Elizabeth, dau of John Garrett, and *dvp* 1727, leaving issue, with two other sons,

JOHN TYLER, Marshal to the Vice-Admiralty Court of Virginia, *b ca* 1710, *m* Anne, dau of Dr Louis Contesse (a Huguenot who came from France to Williamsburg, Virginia *ca* 1715), by his wife Mary Morris, and *d* Aug 1773, leaving, with other issue,

JOHN TYLER, of Greenway, Charles City County, Virginia, member (and sometime Speaker), of the Virginia House of Burgesses, Judge of the Admiralty Court, Vice-President of Virginia Constitutional Convention 1788, Judge Gen Court 1788-1808, Gov of Virginia 1808-11, Judge US Dist Court of Virginia 1811, *b* at Yarmouth, Virginia 28 Feb 1747, *m* 1776, Mary Marot (*b* probably in York County, Virginia 1761; *d* at Greenway, Charles City County 5 April 1797), dau of Robert Booth Armistead (descended from William Armistead, who came from England to Virginia 1635 and was a patentee in Elizabeth City County 1636), by his wife Anne, dau of James Shields, and *d* at Greenway, Charles City County 6 Jan 1813, having had, with other issue (*see* BROTHERS AND SISTERS OF PRESIDENT TYLER, *p 233*), a 2nd son,

JOHN TYLER, **10th President of the United States of America.**

# The Descendants of President Tyler[1]

JOHN TYLER m 1st at Cedar Grove, New Kent County, Virginia 29 March 1813, Letitia (b at Cedar Grove 12 Nov 1790; d at the White House 10 Sept 1842), 3rd dau of Robert Christian, of Cedar Grove, by his wife Mary Brown, and had issue,

**1** Mary TYLER, b 15 April 1815, m Dec 1835, Henry Lightfoot Jones, of Woodham, Virginia, and d 17 June 1848, leaving issue,
  1 John JONES, dunm.
  2 Henry JONES, dunm.
  3 Robert Tyler JONES, m Sally Breedon Gresham, and dsp.
**2** Robert TYLER, served in Mexican War as Col Vol Regt, priv sec to his father Pres Tyler, Registrar Confederate States Treas, Editor *Montgomery Mail and Advertiser*, Alabama, b in Charles City County, Virginia 9 Sept 1816, m at St James's Episcopal Church, Bristol, Pennsylvania 12 Sept 1839, (Elizabeth) Priscilla (b at New York 14 June 1816; d at Montgomery, Alabama 29 Dec 1889), 2nd dau of Thomas Abthorpe Cooper, a well-known actor, by his 2nd wife Mary Fairlie, and d at Montgomery, Alabama 3 Dec 1877, having had issue,
  1 Mary Fairlie TYLER, b Dec 1840; d at Philadelphia June 1845.
  2 Letitia Christian TYLER, b at the White House 1842; dunm at Montgomery, Alabama 1927.
  3 John TYLER IV, b July 1844; d at Philadelphia July 1846.
  4 Grace Rae TYLER, b at Philadelphia May 1845, m at Mount Meigs, Alabama Nov 1863, John Baytop Scott (b at Lowndesboro, Alabama 16 Oct 1831; d at Scotia, Montgomery, Alabama 1894), grandson of John Baytop Scott, a founder of the city of Montgomery and one of the first Presidential Electors for Alabama, and d at Montgomery, Alabama 1919, leaving issue,
    (1) James Marks SCOTT, b 17 May 1866, m 8 Oct 1888, Adelaide Bauerlein (b 29 March 1869; d 5 May 1957), and d 13 Oct 1932, having had issue,
      1a Grace Fairlie SCOTT, b at Montgomery, Alabama 1891; d 1894.
      2a●John Baytop SCOTT, b at Montgomery, Alabama 23 March 1906, m ●Ellie Dreyspring, and has issue,
        1b●John Baytop SCOTT, Jr, b at Montgomery, Alabama 21 July 1934, m 23 Nov 1956, ●Elizabeth Bowers Hill (b 23 April 1934), and has issue,
          1c●Elliott Dreyspring SCOTT, b at Montgomery, Alabama 22 Sept 1957.
          2c●Laura Hill SCOTT, b at Montgomery, Alabama 5 June 1960.
          3c●Amelie Katherine SCOTT, b at Montgomery, Alabama 17 July 1964.
        2b●James Marks SCOTT, b at Montgomery, Alabama 23 July 1936, m 31 May 1960, ●Vivian McLean Butler (b at Montgomery, Alabama 13 May 1937), and has issue,
          1c●Anderson Butler SCOTT, b at Montgomery, Alabama 26 Sept 1961.
          2c●Virginia Fairlie SCOTT, b at Montgomery, Alabama 31 Dec 1969.
      3a Louise Stewart SCOTT, b at Montgomery, Alabama 19 Jan 1908, m ●Clifton Fonville, and dsp 20 Nov 1945.
      4a●Mary Virginia SCOTT, b at Montgomery, Alabama 1 Jan 1910, m 19 June 1937, ●Emory Malcolm Martin (b 22 Sept 1910), and has issue,
        1b●Louise Scott MARTIN, b at Montgomery,

Alabama 7 June 1939, m ●John Calvin Hunt (b 16 Sept 1936), and has issue,
          ●John Emory HUNT, b 11 May 1964.
        2b●Mary Virginia MARTIN, b at Montgomery, Alabama 7 Aug 1940.
        3b●William Kelly MARTIN, b at Montgomery, Alabama 27 Jan 1946, m 28 Sept 1973, ●Dorothy Molly Dunn.
    (2) Mary Virginia SCOTT, b 1868, m Charles A. Coleman, and d having had issue,
      ●Elizabeth COLEMAN [*34 Guild's Wood, Tuscaloosa, Alabama 35401, USA*].
    (3) Robert Tyler SCOTT.
    (4) Julia Campbell SCOTT, b at Mount Meigs, Alabama 3 June 1876, m 6 Sept 1899, William Adams Gunter II, Mayor of Montgomery, Alabama (b at Rembert Hills, Marengo County, Alabama 9 Oct 1872; d at Montgomery, Alabama 4 Dec 1940), son of William Adams Gunter, by his wife Ellen Poellnitz, and d at Montgomery, Alabama 23 Oct 1955, leaving issue,
      1a Grace Scott GUNTER, b at Montgomery, Alabama 13 April 1901, m 1 July 1925, Colquitt Hill Lane (b at Auburn, Lee County, Alabama 22 Sept 1899; d at Montgomery 1 Nov 1957), and has issue,
        1b●Virginia Fairlie LANE, b at Montgomery 24 Jan 1933, m 28 July 1951, ●Oliver Lynn Haynes II (b at Montgomery 11 June 1927), and has issue,
          1c●Fairlie Gunter HAYNES, b at Montgomery 26 Oct 1954.
          2c●Oliver Lynn HAYNES III, b at Montgomery 22 May 1959.
          3c●William Sidney HAYNES, b at Montgomery 11 Jan 1962.
        2b●Elizabeth Tyler LANE, b at Montgomery 18 Aug 1935, m 24 Aug 1960, ●Paul Geoffrey Fischer (b at Douglaston, Nassau County, Long Island 13 Feb 1937), and has issue,
          ●Jason Chase FISCHER, b at Santa Monica, California 13 March 1974.
      2a●William Adams GUNTER III, Fell American Coll of Surgs, practised gen surg in Montgomery, Alabama 1930-63, served in World War II as Col USAF Med Corps 1942-46 [*66 Haardt Drive, Montgomery, Alabama, USA*], b at Montgomery 3 Nov 1902, educ Alabama Univ (BS 1922), Johns Hopkins Sch of Med (MD 1926), and New York Hosp, m 14 Oct 1946, ●Annie Laurie (b at Tarheel, Bladen County, N Carolina 23 June 1919), dau of — Cain, of Lake Wales, Florida, and has issue,
        ●William Adams GUNTER IV, b at Montgomery 23 Nov 1952.
      3a●Ellen Von Poellnitz GUNTER, b at Montgomery 7 Feb 1904, m 29 Sept 1925, Charles Platt Rogers (b at Madison, Morris County, New Jersey 18 July 1898; d at Montgomery 8 Nov 1970), and has issue,
        ●Ellen Von Poellnitz ROGERS, b at Montgomery 14 April 1933, m 1st 18 Dec 1951 (m diss by div), Frank

Randolph (*b* at Montgomery 11 March 1931), and has issue,

1*c*●Frank Gunter RANDOLPH (now TROTMAN), *b* at Montgomery 18 Sept 1952.

Ellen Von Poellnitz Rogers *m* 2ndly 14 Oct 1955, ●John McNeill Trotman (*b* at Troy, Pike County, Alabama 12 March 1927), and has further issue,

2*c*●John McNeill TROTMAN II, *b* at Montgomery 5 Aug 1956.

3*c*●Charles Rogers TROTMAN, *b* at Montgomery 15 March 1958.

4*c*●Robert Tyler TROTMAN, *b* at Montgomery 10 Feb 1962.

4*a*●Mary Virginia GUNTER [*1656 Gilmer Avenue, Montgomery, Alabama 36104, USA*], *b* at Montgomery 2 Aug 1906, *m* 1st 7 Sept 1927 (*m* diss by div), Robert Henry Haas (*b* at Pittsburgh, Pennsylvania 17 Dec 1905; *d* there 14 Sept 1972), and has issue,

●Henry Paul HAAS, *b* at Montgomery 14 Sept 1928, *m* 11 April 1953, ●Dora Pratt Smith (*b* at Montgomery 6 Jan 1930), and has issue,

1*c*●Robert Gunter HAAS, *b* at Montgomery 13 April 1963.

2*c*●Josephine Pratt HAAS, *b* at Montgomery 3 Oct 1968.

Mary Virginia Gunter *m* 2ndly, Homer Waitstill Orvis (*b* at S Orange, New Jersey 23 Aug 1890; *d* at Montgomery 17 June 1972).

5*a* Rose Darrington GUNTER, *b* at Montgomery 22 Feb 1908, *m* 30 Nov 1932, ●Thomas Seay Lawson, Justice of Alabama Supreme Court (*b* at Greensboro, Alabama 3 May 1907), and *d* 23 March 1963, leaving issue,

1*b*●Thomas Seay LAWSON, Jr [*1262 Glen Grattan Avenue, Montgomery, Alabama, USA*], *b* at Montgomery 10 Oct 1935, *m* 27 May 1961, ●Sarah Hunter Clayton (*b* at Clayton, Alabama 23 July 1937), and has issue,

1*c*●Rose Gunter LAWSON, *b* at Montgomery 23 Nov 1963.

2*c*●Gladys Robinson LAWSON, *b* at Montgomery 22 Oct 1966.

3*c*●Thomas Seay LAWSON III, *b* at Montgomery 9 Nov 1971.

2*b*●Jule Gunter LAWSON, *b* at Montgomery 15 Dec 1939, *m* 6 Dec 1963, ●Clifford Anderson Lanier, Jr (*b* at Montgomery 22 Jan 1936), son of Clifford Anderson Lanier, and has issue,

1*c*●Jule Gunter LANIER, *b* at Montgomery 13 Dec 1964.

2*c*●Clifford Anderson LANIER III, *b* at Montgomery 8 April 1968.

6*a*●Julia Fairlie GUNTER, *b* at Montgomery 11 April 1914, *m* 28 Nov 1934, ●Ethelbert Henry Evans (*b* at Montgomery 5 March 1910), and has issue,

●Florence Phillips EVANS, *b* at Montgomery 11 Oct 1939, *m* 27 April 1962, ●George Edmund Jordan (*b* at Montgomery 28 Jan 1933), and has issue,

1*c*●Julia Fairlie JORDAN, *b* at Montgomery 1 Feb 1963.

2*c*●George Edmund JORDAN, Jr, *b* at Montgomery 16 May 1965.

3*c*●Ethelbert Evans JORDAN, *b* at Montgomery 25 June 1970.

7*a*●Elizabeth Tyler GUNTER, *b* at Montgomery 29 Aug 1916, *m* 1 Aug 1942, ●Bruce Johnson Downey, Jr (*b* at Nashville, N Carolina 23 Feb 1918), son of Bruce Johnson Downey, and has issue,

1*b*●Bruce Johnson DOWNEY III, *b* at Montgomery 10 Oct 1943, *m* 13 June 1970, ●Victoria Ann Stewart (*b* at Great Lakes, Illinois 22 April 1947), and has issue,

●Victoria Tyler DOWNEY, *b* at Montgomery 13 May 1974.

2*b*●Elizabeth Tyler Gunter DOWNEY, *b* at Montgomery 23 May 1947, *m* 24 Aug 1968, ●Mat Constantine Raymond, Jr (*b* at Durham, N Carolina 2 April 1945), son of Mat Constantine Raymond, and has issue,

●Mat Constantine RAYMOND III, *b* at Jacksonville, N Carolina 18 June 1972.

(5) Thomas Baytop SCOTT, *m* Kitty Swain, and had issue,

1*a*●Kathleen Mozelle SCOTT, *m* ●Charles Pointer.

2*a*●Grace SCOTT, *b* 1912, *m* ●Benjamin Watkins Lacy III, and has issue,

1*b*●Benjamin Watkins LACY IV, *b ca* 1941.

2*b*●Thomas Scott LACY.

3*b*●Kathleen LACY.

3*a*●Mary Helen SCOTT, *m* ●George Hails Foster, and has issue,

1*b*●Mary Fairlie FOSTER.

2*b*●Scott FOSTER.

3*b*●Kathleen FOSTER.

4*a*●Robert SCOTT, *m* ●Margaret Scott, and has issue, ●Susan SCOTT.

5*a*●Anne SCOTT, *m* ●Milton L. Wood [*Rt 1, Box 26, Sandersville, Georgia 31082, USA*], and has issue,

1*b*●Elizabeth Leigh WOOD.

2*b*●Kathleen Anne WOOD.

6*a*●Priscilla SCOTT, *m* ●Quentin Crommelin, and has issue,

●Quentin CROMMELIN, Jr.

(6) Priscilla Cooper SCOTT, *b* at Mount Meigs, Alabama 1 Nov 1883, *m* at Savannah, Georgia 3 July 1903, Charles Lewis Marks, MD (*b* at Montgomery 31 March 1882; *d* there 30 April 1943), and *d* at Perdido Beach, Baldwin County, Alabama 29 June 1957, leaving issue,

1*a*●Catherine Crain MARKS, *b* at Montgomery 17 Feb 1904, *m* 7 Sept 1923, ●Zachary Taylor Trawick (*b* at Opelika, Lee County, Alabama 27 Sept 1901), and has issue,

1*b*●Zachary Taylor TRAWICK, Jr, MD, *b* at Montgomery 9 Feb 1926, *m* 1st 3 June 1951 (*m* diss by div), Jeanne Carolyn Rogers (*b* at Montgomery 20 Nov 1925), and has issue,

1*c*●Zachary Taylor TRAWICK III, *b* 19 Nov 1952.

2*c*●James Rogers TRAWICK, *b* 3 June 1954.

3*c*●Charles Leonard TRAWICK, *b* 30 Dec 1956.

4*c*●Michael Kelley TRAWICK, *b* 7 May 1959.

5*c*●Robert Scott TRAWICK, *b* 3 Sept 1961.

Dr Zachary T. Trawick, Jr *m* 2ndly, ●Patricia Brannon Little (*b* at Hendersonville, Henderson County, N Carolina 29 June 1931).

2*b*●Katherine Marks TRAWICK, *b* at Montgomery 5 Nov 1933, *m* 1st 5 Sept 1953 (*m* diss by div), Hugh Browning Thornton (*b* 19 Nov 1928), and has issue,

1*c*●Hugh Browning THORNTON, Jr, *b* 16 Aug 1954.

2*c*●Katherine Trawick THORNTON, *b* 30 July 1957.

Katherine M. Trawick *m* 2ndly, ●Allyn Mabson Thames (*b* at Montgomery 8 May 1920).

2*a*●John Scott MARKS (Rev), LLB, BD, a priest of the Protestant Episcopal Church [*Baldwin County, Alabama, USA*], *b* at Montgomery 2 Sept 1905, *m* 1st, Ellen Norwood Allison (*b* at Montgomery 14 Oct 1904; *d* at Mobile, Alabama 26 Dec 1957), and has issue,

1*b*●John Scott MARKS, Jr, MD, neurosurg [*Indianapolis, Indiana, USA*], *b* at Montgomery 7 March 1931, *m* 1st (*m* diss by div), Jan McDonald, of Knoxville, Tennessee, and has issue,

1*c*●John Scott MARKS III.

2*c*●Ellen Allison MARKS.

Dr John S. Marks, Jr *m* 2ndly, ●Julia McLain Rhinehart (*b* at Louisville, Kentucky 20 Sept 1942), and by her has issue,

3*c*●Ellen Caroline MARKS, *b* 10 Dec 1964.

4*c*●Anna Meriwether MARKS, *b* 29 May 1968.

5*c*●Juliet Scott MARKS, *b* 23 July 1970.

2*b*●William Allison MARKS, PhD, biophysicist [*c/o Johns Hopkins University, Baltimore, Maryland, USA*], *b* at Montgomery 28 July 1933, *m* ●Anne Pattillo Foerster (*b* at San Antonio, Texas 4 Dec 1933), and has issue,

1*c*●Matthew Pattillo MARKS, *b* 12 May 1959.

2*c*●Michael Meriwether MARKS, *b* 2 March 1961.

3*c*●Laura Underhill MARKS, *b* 14 Sept 1963.

3*b*●Charles Lewis MARKS III, *b* at Montgomery 2 Sept 1935.

Rev John S. Marks *m* 2ndly, ●Lillian Davis.

3*a*●Samuel Blackburn MARKS, *b* at Montgomery 9 Dec 1907, *m* 10 June 1939, ●Regna Worthington (*b* at Petrey, Crenshaw County, Alabama 6 Dec 1914), and has had issue,

1*b* Samuel Blackburn MARKS, Jr, *b* 26 July 1945; *d* 15 Nov 1948.
2*b*●Scott Chesser MARKS, *b* 27 Jan 1951, *m* ●Donna Jean Donaldson (*b* 25 Feb 1950), and has issue,
   ●Megan Gwynneth MARKS, *b* at Houston, Texas 21 Oct 1969.
4*a*●Charles Lewis MARKS, Jr, *b* at Montgomery 27 Aug 1912, *m* 16 Nov 1938, ●Mary Jeanne Saunders (*b* at Montgomery 14 July 1919), and has issue,
   1*b*●Fairlie MARKS, *b* at Montgomery 29 July 1939, *m* 6 Oct 1960, ●Charles Homer Odell, and has issue,
      1*c*●Kevin Scott ODELL, *b* at Atlanta, Georgia 31 July 1961.
      2*c*●Charles Marks ODELL, *b* 1 July 1963.
   2*b*●Jeanne Saunders MARKS, *b* at Montgomery 5 July 1946, *m* 22 July 1967, ●Steven Huddart Swingenstein, and has issue,
      ●Allison SWINGENSTEIN, *b* 14 Oct 1971.
5*a*●Priscilla Fairlie MARKS, has resumed the surname of Thornton [*3610 Thomas Avenue, Montgomery, Alabama 36111, USA*], *b* at Montgomery 13 May 1916, *m* 1st 13 Sept 1942, Jonathan Mills Thornton, Jr (*b* at Montgomery 10 April 1915; *d* at Rochester, Minnesota 21 Aug 1960), son of Jonathan Mills Thornton, by his wife Katherine Hailes, and has had issue,
   1*b*●Jonathan Mills THORNTON III, PhD, Assist Prof of History, Univ Of Michigan, *b* at Montgomery 27 Oct 1943.
   2*b*●Priscilla Fairlie THORNTON, *b* at Montgomery 8 May 1946, *m* 15 July 1967, ●Capt John Ledbetter Condon, Jr, US Army (*b* at Birmingham, Alabama 29 Aug 1940), son of John Ledbetter Condon, and has issue,
      ●Priscilla Tyler CONDON, *b* at Montgomery 24 July 1970.
   3*b* Charles Marks THORNTON, *b* at Montgomery 21 Jan 1959; *d* there 2 May 1961.
Priscilla F. Marks *m* 2ndly (*m* diss by div), Thomas Seay Lawson (*b* at Greensboro, Hale County, Alabama 3 May 1907).
6*a*●Henry Churchill MARKS, *b* at Montgomery 4 Oct 1920, *m* 30 July 1943, ●Frances Evelyn Keyton (*b* at Montgomery 25 Aug 1921), and has issue,
   1*b*●Emily Keyton MARKS, *b* at Montgomery 6 Nov 1948, *m* 22 Sept 1973, ●Peter William Curtis (*b* at Woking, Surrey, England 29 Aug 1945).
   2*b*●Catherine Churchill MARKS, *b* at Montgomery 17 May 1955.
   3*b*●Lucille Watkins MARKS, *b* at Montgomery 16 June 1959.
5 Thomas Cooper TYLER, *b* 1848; *d* July 1849.
6 Elizabeth (Lizzie) TYLER, *b* at Philadelphia Jan 1852, *m* at Montgomery, Alabama April 1871, Thomas Gardner Foster (*b* at Elberton, Georgia 1845; *d* at Montgomery, Alabama 1915), son of Thomas Flournoy Foster, by his wife Elizabeth Gardner, and at Montgomery 1915, leaving issue,
   (1) James Henry FOSTER, *b* at Montgomery 1871, *m* there 1913, Alice Borgfeldt (*b* at Montgomery 1880), dau of James Lahey, by his wife Lucy Winter, and *d* 1938, leaving issue,
      1*a* Lyra Nickerson FOSTER, *b* 1915, *m* ●George Ware Smith (*b* 1909), and *d* May 1968, leaving issue,
         ●Alice Lahey SMITH, *b* at Montgomery 1940, *m* there 1971, ●Robert Nyberg [*201 Huntley Drive, Montgomery, Alabama, USA*], and has issue,
            ●Robert Kel NYBERG, *b* at Montgomery 1973.
      2*a*●Elizabeth Gindrat FOSTER, *b* 1919, *m* ●Davis Fouville Stakeley, Jr (*b* at Montgomery 1917) [*2353 College Street, Montgomery, Alabama 36106, USA*], son of Davis Fouville Stakeley, by his wife LeGrand Smith.
   (2) Priscilla Tyler FOSTER, *b* at Montgomery 1873, *m* there 1899, Forney Caldwell Stevenson, MD (*b* at Jacksonville, Alabama 1873; *d* at Montgomery 1951), son of Horace Lee Stevenson, by his wife Mary Abernathy, and *d* at Montgomery 1951, leaving issue,
      1*a* Elizabeth Tyler STEVENSON, *b* at Montgomery 1900, *m* there 1926, ●Sparta Fritz, Jr (*b* at Philadelphia 1902) [*1902 Graham Street, Montgomery, Alabama 36016, USA*], son of Sparta Fritz, by his wife Emily Weiss, and *d* at Philadelphia 1955, leaving issue,
         1*b*●Susan Dunlop FRITZ, *b* at Philadelphia 1928, *m*

there 1958, ●John H. Blye III (*b* at Philadelphia 1926) [*8130 E Cloud Road, Tuscon, Arizona, USA*], son of John H. Blye, Jr, by his wife Eleanore Trenchard Wurts, and has issue,
            1*c*●Eleanore Wurts BLYE, *b* at Andrews Air Force Base, Maryland 1961.
            2*c*●John H. BLYE IV, *b* at Andrews Air Force Base 1962.
         2*b*●Priscilla Tyler FRITZ, *b* at Philadelphia 1932, *m* at Indian Head, Maryland 1962, ●John E. Henderson (*b* at Waco, Texas 1922) [*1703 Belle Haven Road, Alexandria, Virginia, USA*], and has issue,
            ●Elizabeth Tyler HENDERSON, *b* at Alexandria, Virginia 1968.
      2*a*● Frances Abernathy STEVENSON, *b* at Montgomery 1905, *m* at Philadelphia 1938, ●Francis Nott Pruyn (*b* at New York 1902) [*30 Eldridge Place, Dobbs Ferry, New York, USA*], son of Francis N. Pruyn, by his wife Adelaide Mills, and has an adopted dau,
         ●Priscilla Thusber PRUYN, *b* 1944.
   (3) Thomas Gardner FOSTER, MD, Lt-Cmdr USN Med Corps, *b* at Montgomery 1875, *educ* Virginia Univ, *m* at New York 1945, Evelyn Stitchell (*b* at Cortland, New York), and *dsp* at Buenos Aires 1964.
7 Priscilla Cooper TYLER, *b* at Bristol, Pennsylvania 15 Oct 1848, *m* at St John's Episcopal Church, Montgomery, Alabama 22 Dec 1869, Albert Taylor Goodwyn (*b* at Robinson Springs, Alabama 17 Dec 1842; *d* at Birmingham, Alabama 1 July 1931), son of Dr Albert Gallatin Goodwyn, by his wife Harriet Bibb, and *d* at Birmingham, Alabama 24 Feb 1936, leaving issue,
   (1) Robert Tyler GOODWYN, attorney, *b* at Montgomery, Alabama 4 Nov 1870, *m* at Wetumpha, Alabama 21 Nov 1895, Jessie Dora (*b* at Wetumpha 27 July 1875; *d* at Robinson Springs 16 Sept 1941), 2nd dau of Judge John Lancaster, by his wife Aldora Lett, and *d* at Montgomery 10 May 1949, leaving issue,
      1*a*●Elizabeth Aldora GOODWYN [*Apt 3B, 1018 Glen Grattan Avenue, Montgomery, Alabama 36111, USA*], *b* at Wetumpha 22 Oct 1896, *m* at Montgomery 22 Jan 1921, James Francis Hegenwald (*b* at Albany (now Decatur), Alabama 13 Feb 1896; *d* at Montgomery 6 April 1966), 4th son of John George Hegenwald, by his wife Belle Roberts, and has issue,
         1*b*●James Francis HEGENWALD, Jr, aircraft design mgr with N America, Rockwell, Englewood, California [*225 South Rio Vista, Apt 54, Anaheim, California 92806, USA*], *b* at Albany, Georgia 6 Feb 1922, *educ* Alabama Univ, *m* at Los Angeles 16 Feb 1945, ●Rebecca Elizabeth (*b* 13 April 1924), dau of Russell Porter Coleman, by his wife Frances Deason, and has issue,
            1*c*●Elizabeth Rebecca HEGENWALD, *b* at Los Angeles 12 Dec 1951, *educ* Univ of California at Riverside.
            2*c*●James Francis HEGENWALD III, *b* at Los Angeles 25 April 1954, *educ* Univ of California at Los Angeles.
         2*b*●Tyler Goodwyn HEGENWALD, stockbroker, account exec with Hutton [*445 Pennsylvania Avenue, Shreveport, Louisiana 71105, USA*], *b* at Albany, Georgia 24 Jan 1924, *educ* Alabama Univ, *m* at Conshetta, Louisiana 1 Nov 1952, ●Shirley Ann (*b* at Conshetta 4 Sept 1927), dau of Henry Bethard, by his wife Shirley Edgerton, and has issue,
            1*c*●Ann HEGENWALD, *b* at Shreveport, Louisiana 21 Sept 1954, *educ* Louisiana State Univ.
            2*c*●Janet HEGENWALD, *b* at Shreveport, Louisiana 8 April 1956.
      2*a*●Priscilla Cooper GOODWYN, *b* at Wetumpha, Alabama 15 Jan 1898, *m* at Montgomery Jan 1923, ●James Thomas Fowler, Jr (*b* 21 Dec 1897) [*2533 Montevallo Drive, Birmingham, Alabama 35223, USA*], son of Dr James Thomas Fowler, and has issue,
         1*b*●James Thomas FOWLER III [*2068 Lakewood Drive, Birmingham, Alabama 35216, USA*], *b* 10 Sept 1923, *m* ●Lila Jean Hodges (*b* 26 Jan 1927), and has issue,
            1*c*●James Thomas FOWLER IV, *b* 9 May 1948.
            2*c*●Jean Hodges FOWLER, *b* 1955, *educ* Alabama Univ.

2*b*●William Goodwyn FOWLER, attorney, *b* 4 Dec 1925, *educ* Alabama Univ, *m* 1st at Birmingham, Alabama (*m* diss by div) Jane Steele Darnall (*b* 17 Dec 1927), and has issue,
  1*c*●William Goodwyn FOWLER, Jr, *b* at Birmingham, Alabama 19 Jan 1951.
  2*c*●Gertrude Browning FOWLER, *b* at Birmingham, Alabama 26 March 1952.
  3*c*●John Darnall FOWLER, *b* at Birmingham, Alabama 1954.
William Goodwyn Fowler *m* 2ndly at Birmingham, Alabama, ●Dawn —, and by her has issue,
  4*c*●Priscilla Goodwyn FOWLER, *b* at Birmingham, Alabama 1971.
3*a* Robert Tyler GOODWYN, Jr, attorney, Clerk of the Alabama House of Reps, *b* at Wetumpha, Alabama 10 Aug 1900, *educ* Alabama Univ, *m* at Montgomery, Alabama 9 July 1932, ●Alice McGehee (*b* 18 May 1909), dau of George A. Thomas, by his wife Mildred Spencer McGehee, and *d* at Montgomery, Alabama 13 April 1957, leaving issue,
  1*b*●Robert Tyler GOODWYN III, Col USAF [*4202 Pickering Place, Alexandria, Virginia, USA*], *b* at Montgomery, Alabama 18 July 1933, *educ* West Point, *m* at Leonia, New Jersey, ●Judith (*b* 2 Jan 1935), dau of Edward Millar, by his wife Erma, and has issue,
    1*c*●Leslie GOODWYN, *b* at Columbus, Georgia 1957.
    2*c*●Robert Tyler GOODWYN IV, *b* at Wurtzburg, Germany 3 March 1960.
    3*c*●Reid Millar GOODWYN, *b* at Wurtzburg, Germany 25 July 1962.
  2*b*●George Thomas GOODWYN, US Army Engr in Germany, civil engr in Montgomery, Alabama [*1719 Pine Needle Road, Montgomery, Alabama 36106, USA*], *b* at Montgomery 8 March 1937, *educ* Alabama Univ, and ROTC, *m* at Teesheeger, Alabama, ●Winifred Hutchison (*b* at Teesheeger 17 June 1940), dau of Phillip Lightfoot, by his wife Winifred Hutchison, and has issue,
    1*c*●George Thomas GOODWYN, Jr, *b* at Bad Hersfeld, Germany 18 July 1960.
    2*c*●Phillip McGowan GOODWYN, *b* at Bad Hersfeld, Germany 18 Dec 1961.
    3*c*●Winifred Lightfoot GOODWYN, *b* at Montgomery, Alabama 14 July 1967.
4*a* William Bibb GOODWYN, served in World War II as Lt-Cmdr Civil Engr Corps USN, bridge constructor, *b* at Wetumpha, Alabama 4 Feb 1902, *educ* Auburn Univ (BS) *m* at Brundidge, Alabama 4 Oct 1928, ●Foy Glen (*b* at Brundidge 8 Oct 1905) [*1302 Augusta Avenue, Montgomery, Alabama 36111, USA*], dau of Willis Glen Gilmore, by his wife Julia Wilkerson, and *d* at Montgomery 20 Sept 1973, leaving issue,
  ●William Bibb GOODWYN, Jr, bridge constructor [*3119 Pinehurst Drive, Montgomery, Alabama 36106, USA*], *b* at Montgomery 13 Aug 1930, *educ* Auburn Univ, *m* at Montgomery 8 May 1954, ●Jean Elizabeth, dau of Harris Aubrey Fleming, by his wife Elizabeth McKibben, and has issue,
    1*c*●Elizabeth McKibben GOODWYN, *b* at Montgomery 25 April 1955, *educ* Auburn Univ.
    2*c*●William Bibb GOODWYN III, *b* at Montgomery 10 April 1957.
    3*c*●Foy Gilmore GOODWYN, *b* at Montgomery 12 May 1962.
5*a* John Lancaster GOODWYN, attorney, Mayor of Montgomery, Justice of Alabama Supreme Court, *b* at Montgomery 13 Oct 1903, *educ* Alabama Univ, *m* at Montgomery 16 April 1931, ●Elizabeth Hudson (*b* 22 Jan 1905) [*1567 Gilmer Avenue, Montgomery, Alabama 36104, USA*], dau of Dr R. S. Hill, by his wife Elizabeth Hudson, and *d* at Montgomery April 1968, leaving issue,
  1*b*●Warren Hudson GOODWYN, *b* 1934.
  2*b*●Elizabeth Lancaster GOODWYN, *b* 1946.
6*a*●Louise Tyson GOODWYN [*1600 Forrest Lake Drive, Tuscaloosa, Alabama 35401, USA*], *b* at Montgomery, Alabama 13 June 1906, *m* 1st at Robinson Springs, Alabama 21 Aug 1935, James William Mustin, Jr (*d* at Tuscaloosa, Alabama 16 May 1954), son of James William Mustin, by his wife Lucile Noble, and has issue,

1*b*●Priscilla Goodwyn MUSTIN, *b* 9 Feb 1938, *m* (*m* diss by div) James Mason Pledge, and has issue,
  1*c*●Marcus Shaw PLEDGE, *b* 1 Oct 1959.
  2*c*●Grace PLEDGE, *b* 8 Sept 1961.
2*b*●James William MUSTIN III, *b* 25 May 1941, *m* ●Peggy Grant.
3*b*●Lucile Noble MUSTIN, *b* 18 Jan 1958, *m* (*m* diss by div) William Walden Boothe, and has issue,
  ●Louise Tyson BOOTHE.
Louise Tyson Goodwyn *m* 2ndly at Tuscaloosa, Alabama, James M. Faircloth (*dec*).
7*a* Albert Taylor GOODWYN, Jr, Lt-Col US Army Engrs, *b* 19 June 1911, *educ* Alabama Univ, *m* at Miami, Florida Dec 1944 (*m* diss by div 1972), Mary Spears (*b* 18 April 1914), and *d* at Montgomery, Alabama 8 April 1973, leaving issue,
  ●Albert Taylor GOODWYN III [*Albuquerque, New Mexico, USA*], *b* 28 Dec 1945.
(2) Adele GOODWYN, *b* 6 Nov 1873, *m* John Davidson McNeel (*b* 13 Oct 1872; *d* 8 March 1940), and *d* 28 April 1939, leaving issue,
  1*a*●Letitia Tyler McNEEL, *b* 7 Nov 1898, *m* ●William Douglas Arant (*b* 19 May 1897) [*2815 Argyle Road, Birmingham, Alabama 35213, USA*], and has issue,
    1*b*●Adele Goodwyn ARANT, *b* 26 June 1931, *m* Sept 1951, ●Richard James Stockham.
    2*b*●Letitia Christian ARANT, *b* 14 March 1935.
    3*b*●Frances Fairlie ARANT, *b* 25 Sept 1936.
  2*a*●Hulda McNEEL, *b* 5 Nov 1906, *m* ●Peyton Dandridge Bibb (*b* 3 Oct 1904), and has issue,
    1*b*●Adele Goodwyn BIBB, *b* 23 Aug 1940.
    2*b*●Peyton Dandridge BIBB, Jr, *b* 15 Nov 1941.
(3) Albert Gallatin GOODWYN, Col US Army, *b* at Robinson Springs, Alabama 1 Oct 1875, *m* at Nashville, Tennessee 30 Aug 1902, Charlie (*b* at Huntsville, Alabama 9 Jan 1878; *d* at Summerville, S Carolina 29 Jan 1955), dau of Hector Davis Lane, by his wife Margaret Mason, and *d* at Summerville, S Carolina 28 Jan 1956, leaving issue,
  1*a*●Marion Ely GOODWYN, *b* at Guimeras, Philippine Islands 25 June 1903, *m* 1929, ●Milton Cogswell Shattuck (*b* at Manila, Philippine Islands 23 March 1901) [*Gray Craig, Paradise Avenue, Middleton, Rhode Island 02840, USA*], son of Amos Blanchard Shattuck, by his wife Susan, and has issue,
    1*b*●Margaret Lane SHATTUCK, *b* at Washington, DC 12 Dec 1929, *m* at Fort Benning, Georgia 27 July 1954, ●John Charles Rahmann (*b* at Tarentum, Pennsylvania 11 Aug 1927) [*599 Greenleaf Avenue, Glencoe, Illinois 60022, USA*], son of Carl Antone Rahmann, by his wife Dorothy Lucille, and has issue,
      1*c*●John Charles RAHMANN, Jr, *b* at Fort Benning, Georgia 17 Oct 1955.
      2*c*●Pamela Lane RAHMANN, *b* at Natrona Heights, Pennsylvania 28 Sept 1957.
      3*c*●Susan Marion RAHMANN, *b* at Syracuse, New York 8 May 1962.
    2*b*●(Marion) Pamela SHATTUCK, *b* at Honolulu, Hawaii 17 Sept 1931, *m* at St James's Episcopal Church, Augusta, Maine 7 July 1951, ●John Medlicott Burleigh (*b* at Springfield, Mass 25 Jan 1928) [*43 Oak Ridge Lane, West Hartford, Connecticut 06107, USA*], son of Lewis Albert Burleigh, by his wife Harriet Medlicott, and has issue,
      ●Christopher Medlicott BURLEIGH, *b* at Hartford, Connecticut 10 Aug 1955.
Mr and Mrs John M. Burleigh also have an adopted child,
      ●Lane Shattuck BURLEIGH, *b* at Boston, Mass 15 May 1958.
    3*b*●Milton Cogswell SHATTUCK, Lt-Col US Army [*Box 132, Fort Gulick, Panama Canal Zone*], *m* ●Susan Shattuck.
    4*b*●Susan Lane SHATTUCK, *b* at Missoula, Montana 12 April 1939, *m* at Newport, Rhode Island 6 Sept 1968, ●William M. Benson [*618 Constitution Avenue NE, Washington, DC 20002, USA*].
  2*a*●Margaret Lane GOODWYN, *b* at Fort Douglas, Utah 17 Oct 1904, *m* at Deland, Florida 13 Feb 1926, ●Julius Blake Middleton (*b* at Charleston 9 Nov 1900) [*42 Society Street, Charleston, South Carolina, USA*], son of William Dehon Middleton, by his wife Julia

Blake, and has issue,
1b●Julius Blake MIDDLETON, Jr [*19745 Lakeview Avenue, Excelsior, Minnesota 55331, USA*], *b* at Cleveland, Ohio 15 Aug 1932, *educ* Williams Coll, Mass, *m* at Milwaukee, Wisconsin 15 Sept 1954 ●Nancy (*b* at Milwaukee), dau of Harold Daniels, by his wife Grace King, and has issue,
  1c●Julius Blake MIDDLETON III, *b* at Milwaukee 12 Feb 1959.
  2c●Marke Tyler MIDDLETON, *b* at Milwaukee 15 Sept 1960.
  3c●Gardner King MIDDLETON, *b* at Milwaukee 10 May 1962.
  4c●Lane Goodwyn MIDDLETON, *b* at Milwaukee 16 Sept 1964.
2b●Charlie Lane MIDDLETON, *b* at Toledo, Ohio 9 May 1938, *educ* Heathfield Sch, Ascot, England, and the Sorbonne, Paris, *m* at the Grosvenor Chapel, S Audley Street, London 7 Aug 1959, ●Francis John Morland Kinsman (*b* in London 28 Aug 1934) [*The Mossings, Great Maplestead, Halstead, Essex, England*], son of Harold John Alfred Kinsman, by his wife Barbara Moncaster, and has issue,
  1c●Blake Middleton KINSMAN, *b* in London 10 Dec 1960.
  2c●Emmeline Hilbery KINSMAN, *b* in London 28 March 1962.
  3c●Francis John KINSMAN, *b* at Dacca, Pakistan (now in Bangladesh) 29 Sept 1964.
(4) Gardner F. GOODWYN, *b* 1877, *m* Lora Williams, and had issue,
1a●Gardner F. GOODWYN, Jr (Judge) [*3 Meadow Lane, Lakewood, Bessemer, Alabama 35020, USA*].
2a●Marvin William GOODWYN, Col USAF (ret 1964), served in World War II (20 decorations) [*2220 Park Newport, Newport Beach, California 92660, USA*], *b* at Bessemer, Alabama 29 March 1917, *educ* Alabama Univ (LLD 1940), *m* at Montgomery, Alabama 22 Jan 1954 (*m* diss by div), Lilla Davenport (*b* at Birmingham, Alabama 1923), dau of Charles Frederick Anderson, by his wife Lilla Davenport, and has issue,
  ●Marvin William GOODWYN, Jr, *b* at Macon, Georgia 7 Feb 1955, *educ* Vanderbilt Univ, Nashville, Tennessee.
(5) Priscilla Cooper GOODWYN, *b* 25 Feb 1887, *m* 1 April 1913, Frank Hastings Griffin (*b* 16 July 1886), and *d* 3 July 1965, leaving issue,
1a●Adele Goodwyn GRIFFIN, *b* at Swarthmore, Pennsylvania 25 June 1920, *m* 1st 1941, William Logan McCoy, Jr (*b* April 1920; *d* 19 June 1943), son of William Logan McCoy, and has issue,
  1b●Marguerite Logan McCOY, *b* 5 Oct 1943, *m* ●James Pinckney Borden, Jr, son of James Pinckney Borden, and has issue,
    1c●Elizabeth Evans BORDEN, *b* 23 May 1969.
    2c●William McCoy BORDEN, *b* 29 April 1971.
Adele Goodwyn Griffin *m* 2ndly 18 Jan 1947, ●James. A. Sands [*Sunnyside, Wawa, Pennsylvania, USA*], and has further issue,
  2b●Priscilla Goodwyn SANDS, *b* 10 Oct 1947, *m* ●Robert E. Watson III, son of Robert E. Watson, Jr, and has issue,
    1c●Adele Griffin WATSON, *b* 29 July 1970.
    2c●Robert Sands WATSON, *b* 15 March 1972.
  3b●James A. SANDS, Jr, *b* 12 Sept 1949.
  4b●William Franklin SANDS III, *b* 25 July 1951.
  5b●Elizabeth Keating SANDS, *b* 6 April 1953.
  6b●Adele Griffin SANDS, *b* 21 April 1961.
  7b●Geoffrey Keating SANDS, *b* 14 Aug 1962.
2a●Frank Hastings GRIFFIN, Jr [*Old Orchard, Wawa, Pennsylvania, USA*], *b* at Swarthmore, Pennsylvania 26 Aug 1921, *m* 10 June 1943, ●Mary Dorcum Mifflin (*b* 25 Feb 1925), and has issue,
  1b●Frank Hastings GRIFFIN III [*1000 Conestoga Road, Rosemont, Pennsylvania, USA*], *b* 31 May 1946, *m* 16 Nov 1968, ●Jeffory Anne Horning (*b* at Jacksonville, Florida 27 May 1947).
  2b●Elizabeth Dorcum GRIFFIN, *b* 21 July 1948, *m* 10 Aug 1968, ●Charles Davis Belcher, Jr (*b* 27 Jan 1947), son of Charles Davis Belcher.
  3b●Mary Lloyd GRIFFIN, *b* 27 Feb 1951.

  4b●Samuel Wright Mifflin GRIFFIN, *b* 28 May 1953.
3a●John Tyler GRIFFIN [*32 South Fairfield Drive, Devon, Pennsylvania 19333, USA*], *b* at Wawa, Pennsylvania 30 Aug 1923, *m* 21 Sept 1944, ●Sophronia Marguerite Worrell (*b* 18 Nov 1925), and has issue,
  1b●Marguerite Worrell GRIFFIN, *b* 17 Nov 1945, *m* 18 Oct 1969, ●Larry Wayne Chartier.
  2b●John Tyler GRIFFIN, Jr, *b* 24 Sept 1949, *m* 18 May 1974, ●Mary C. Barili.
  3b●Priscilla Goodwyn GRIFFIN, *b* 4 Oct 1952, *m* 28 Aug 1971, ●Erik Tank-Nielsen.
4a●Priscilla Tyler GRIFFIN, *b* at Wawa, Pennsylvania 6 Dec 1927, *m* 15 March 1952, ●Herman Albert Schaefer (*b* 14 March 1921), and has issue,
  1b●Nancy Griffin SCHAEFER, *b* 14 July 1953.
  2b●Priscilla Goodwyn SCHAEFER, *b* 25 Jan 1956.
  3b●Herman Albert SCHAEFER, Jr, *b* 18 July 1958.
8 Julia Campbell TYLER, *b* at Philadelphia 6 Dec 1854, *m* at Montgomery, Alabama 15 April 1874, Henry Hewlings Tyson (*b* 5 Dec 1845; *d* 7 Sept 1887), and *d* 5 July 1884, leaving issue,
  (1) Marie Louise TYSON, *b* 26 Jan 1875; *dunm* at Upperville, Virginia *ca* 1950.
  (2) Grace TYSON, *b* 20 June 1878, *m* 5 Dec 1901, Eugene Cameron Gatewood (*b* 27 Aug 1877; *d* 30 Nov 1926), and *d* at Upperville, Virginia 1962, leaving issue,
    Julia Campbell GATEWOOD, *b* at Rectortown, Virginia 19 Sept 1903; *dunm* 1966.     •
  (3) Alan Campbell TYSON, *b* 14 Aug 1877, *m* 1st (*m* diss by div), Gabriella Smythe, and had issue, one child (who *d* at birth). He *m* 2ndly, Sophie von Riesner; and 3rdly, Cora Barnhart.
9 Robert TYLER, *b* at Philadelphia Dec 1857; *dunm* at Montgomery, Alabama 1937.
3 John TYLER, Assist Sec of War of the Confederacy, *b* 27 April 1819, *m* 25 Oct 1838, Martha Rochelle (*b* 23 Jan 1820; *d* 11 Jan 1867), and *d* 1896, leaving issue,
1 James Rochelle TYLER, *b* 9 Sept 1839; *dunm*.
2 Letitia Christian TYLER, *b* 27 April 1844, *m* 13 Sept 1860, Gen William Briggs Shands (*b* 7 Feb 1820; *d* 1906), and *d* 23 Jan 1863, leaving issue,
  William SHANDS, State Senator, *b* 6 Sept 1861, *m* 1st, Nancy Pretlow. He *m* 2ndly 5 Nov 1895, Annie Byrum Ridley (*b* 27 Feb 1877), and by her had issue,
    1a●William Ridley SHANDS, *b* 17 Aug 1896, *m* June 1922, ●Josephine Winston, and has issue,
      1b●Martha Jane SHANDS, *b* 20 Feb 1924, *m* ●John W. Albus.
      2b●William Ridley SHANDS, Jr, *b* 23 Nov 1932.
    2a●Letitia Christian SHANDS, *b* 19 Aug 1898.
    3a●Bessie Thomas SHANDS, *b* 20 June 1900.
3 Mattie Rochelle TYLER, *b* 1 March 1844; *dunm* Jan 1928.
4 Letitia TYLER, acted as hostess at White House 1844, *b* 11 May 1821, *m* Feb 1839, James A. Semple, and *dsp* at Baltimore 28 Dec 1907.
5 Elizabeth (Lizzie) TYLER, *b* 11 July 1823, *m* at the White House 31 Jan 1842, as his 1st wife, William Nevison Waller, of Williamsburg, Virginia, son of William Waller, of Williamsburg, by his wife Mary Berkely Griffin, and *d* 1 June 1850, leaving issue,
1 William Griffin WALLER, CSA, Assist Editor *Savannah News*, Man Editor *Richmond Times*, *m* 1st at the Confederate White House, Richmond Nov 1863, Jenny Kent, dau of William Burr Howell, of The Briers, Natchez, Mississippi, by his wife Margaret Louisa Kempe (and sister of the second Mrs Jefferson Davis—*see* APPENDIX A), and had issue,
  (1) Elizabeth Tyler WALLER, *dunm*.
  (2) William Griffin WALLER, *dunm*.
  (3) Maggie Howell WALLER, *d* an inf.
William Griffin Waller *m* 2ndly, Elizabeth Hale Austin, and by her had issue,
  (4) Mary Austin WALLER, *b* 1879, *m* 1908, John De Saussure (*d* 1945), and had issue,
    1a●Elizabeth Waller DE SAUSSURE, *b* 1909, *m* ●R. H. Knapp, and has issue,
      1b●Dana M. KNAPP.
      2b●R. H. KNAPP, Jr.
    2a●Mary C. DE SAUSSURE, *b* 1916, *m* ●C. G. Mortenson, and has issue,
      1b●Karel MORTENSON.
      2b●Ellen MORTENSON.

(5) John Tyler WALLER, *b* 1881, *m* Lucy Bacon, and *dsp*.
(6) Clara WALLER, *d* an inf.
2 John WALLER, one of Mosby's men in CSA, *ka, unm*.
3 Letitia WALLER, *d* an inf.
4 Mary Stuart WALLER, *m* 1867, Gen Louis G. Young, of Savannah, Georgia, and *dsp*.
5 Robert WALLER, *m* Emily Johnstone, and had issue,
Robert Tyler WALLER, *b* 1879; *dunm* 1943.
**6** Ann Contesse TYLER, *b* 5 April 1825; *d* an inf.
**7** Alice TYLER, *b* 23 March 1827, *m* at Sherwood Forest, Charles City County, Virginia 11 July 1850, Rev Henry Mandeville Denison, Rector of Bruton Parish, Williamsburg, of St Paul's, Louisville, and of St Peter's, Charleston (*b* at Wyoming, Pennsylvania 1822; *d* 1858), and *d* 8 June 1854, leaving issue,
Elizabeth Russell DENISON, *b* 1852, *m* 1st, William Gaston Allen, US Consular Service (*b* 1849; *d* 1891), and had issue,
(1) Alice Denison ALLEN, *b* 1887, *m* 1st 1910, William Bachofen, and had issue,

William Henry BACHOFEN, *b* 1913; *d* 1915.
Alice Denison Allen *m* 2ndly 1919, Raymond Pierson Nicholson (*b* 1892).
(2) William Gaston ALLEN, *b* 1890, *m* 1st 1914, Edna Knowles, and had issue,
1*a* ● Louise ALLEN, *b* 1915.
2*a* ● Elizabeth Denison ALLEN, *b* 1917.
3*a* ● Edna ALLEN, *b* 1921.
William Gaston Allen *m* 2ndly 1926, Megan Jones (*d* 1928), and by her had issue,
4*a* ● Megan ALLEN, *b* 1928.
William Gaston Allen *m* 3rdly 1929, ● Nanie Jones.
Elizabeth Russell Denison *m* 2ndly, Rev Williamson, and *d* 1928.
**8** Tazewell TYLER, MD, Surg CSA, *b* 6 Dec 1830, *m* 1857 (*m* diss by div 1873), Nannie Bridges, and *d* in California 8 Jan 1874, leaving issue,
1 James TYLER, *m* May —, and *dsp*.
2 Martha TYLER, *dunm* 1943.

**JOHN TYLER** *m* 2ndly at the Church of the Ascension, New York 26 June 1844, Julia (*b* at Gardiner's Island, New York 4 May 1820; *d* at Richmond, Virginia 10 July 1889, *bur* with her husband at Hollywood Cemetery, Virginia), dau of Senator David Gardiner (descended from Lion Gardiner, who emigrated from Holland to Boston 1635 and settled at Saybrook, Connecticut), by his wife Juliana, dau of Michael McLachlan, and by her had issue,

**9** (David) Gardiner ("Gardie") TYLER, of Sherwood Forest, Charles City County, Virginia, served in CSA 1863-65, mem Virginia Senate 1891-92 and 1900-04, mem 53rd and 54th Congresses 1893-97, Judge of the 14th Judicial Circuit of Virginia 1904, *b* at E Hampton, New York 12 July 1846, *educ* Washington Coll (now Washington and Lee Univ), *m* at Richmond, Virginia 6 June 1894, Mary Morris (*b* at Richmond, Virginia 1 June 1865; *d* at Sherwood Forest 30 Aug 1931), dau of James Alfred Jones, of Richmond, Virginia, by his wife Mary Henry Lyon, and *d* at Sherwood Forest 1 Sept 1927, having had issue,
1 ● Mary Lyon TYLER, *b* at Washington, DC 31 March 1895, *m* at Sherwood Forest, Charles City County, Virginia 25 Sept 1926, ● George Peterkin Gamble (*b* at Richmond, Virginia 20 Sept 1899) [*1821 Viking Way, La Jolla, California 92037, USA*], son of Cary Gamble, by his wife Elizabeth Hanson Peterkin, and has issue,
● Mary Morris GAMBLE, *b* at Richmond, Virginia 31 Dec 1927, *m* at Kirkwood, Missouri 29 Dec 1951, ● (Augustus) Lea Booth (*b* at Danville, Virginia 28 Sept 1918) [*3809 Peakland Place, Lynchburg, Virginia 24503, USA*], son of Augustus Arsell Booth, by his wife Emma Lea, and has issue,
1*a* ● Mary Lyon BOOTH, *b* at Lynchburg, Virginia 23 June 1954.
2*a* ● George Lea BOOTH, *b* at Lynchburg, Victoria 8 Oct 1957.
3*a* ● Cary Gamble BOOTH, *b* at Lynchburg, Virginia 8 Oct 1957 (twin with his brother George Lea Booth).
2 ● Margaret Gardiner TYLER, *b* at Washington, DC 3 Feb 1897, *m* at Sherwood Forest, Virginia 2 July 1919, ● Stephen Fowler Chadwick (*b* at Colfax, Washington 14 Aug 1894) [*1121 41st Avenue East, Seattle, Washington 98102, USA*], son of Stephen James Chadwick, by his wife Emma Plummer, and has issue,
(1) ● Mary Tyler CHADWICK, *b* at Seattle, Washington 5 May 1921, *m* at Webster Groves, Missouri 11 May 1949, ● William Chave McCracken (*b* at New York 21 June 1920) [*3071 North Park Boulevard, Cleveland Heights, Ohio 44118, USA*], son of Frederick Beekman McCracken, by his wife Mildred Chave, and has issue,
1*a* ● Adelaide Tyler MCCRACKEN [*Box 109, Bridgewater Corners, Vermont 05035, USA*], *b* at Oberlin, Ohio 13 May 1950.
2*a* ● Margaret Chadwick MCCRACKEN, *b* at Oberlin, Ohio 17 Nov 1952.
3*a* ● Sara Chave MCCRACKEN, *b* at Oberlin, Ohio 4 Oct 1954.
(2) ● Stephen Fowler CHADWICK, Jr [*Route 8, Box 8205,*

*Bainbridge Island, Washington 98140, USA*], *b* at Seattle, Washington 20 Oct 1924, *m* 1953, ● Diane Halsey.
3 ● David Gardiner TYLER, Jr [*Creek Plantation, Charles City, Virginia 23030, USA*], *b* at Sherwood Forest, Virginia April 1899, *educ* William and Mary Coll, *m* ● Anne Shelton, and has issue,
(1) ● David Gardiner TYLER III, *m* ● Dolores —, and has issue,
1*a* ● David TYLER.
2*a* ● William TYLER.
(2) ● Ann Shelton TYLER.
(3) ● George Keesee TYLER.
4 James Alfred Jones TYLER, of Sherwood Forest, Charles City County, Virginia, Commonwealth's Attorney for Charles City County, Virginia 1927-51 and 1955-63, *b* at Sherwood Forest 16 Aug 1902, *educ* Virginia Univ, *m* at Richmond, Virginia 1938, Katherine Thomason (*b* at Richmond 1909; *d* 1967), and *d* at Richmond, Virginia 27 July 1972, leaving issue,
(1) ● Emily Thomason TYLER [*539 Woodland Drive, Greensboro, North Carolina 27408, USA*], *b* 1941.
(2) ● Mary Gardiner TYLER, *b* 1943, *m* 1968, ● Garnett Edward Stover, Jr, son of Garnett Edward Stover, and has issue,
● — STOVER.
(3) ● James Alfred Jones TYLER, Jr, Stockbroker with Scott & Stringfellow in Richmond, Virginia [*Sherwood Forest, Charles City County, Virginia 23030, USA*], *b* at Richmond 9 June 1945, *educ* Washington and Lee Univ, *m* at Greenville, S Carolina 1966, ● Alice (*b* at Greenville 25 June 1947), dau of W. E. Watt by his wife Alice Sharp, and has issue,
1*a* ● James Alfred Jones TYLER III, *b* at Staunton, Virginia 3 March 1967.
2*a* ● Benjamin Alexander TYLER, *b* at Richmond, Virginia 24 March 1970.
5 John TYLER VI, *d* an inf.
**10** (John) Alexander TYLER, served in CSA 1864-65, mining engr, fought in Franco-Prussian War 1870-71, US Surveyor for Dept of Interior in New Mexico 1879-83, *b* at Sherwood Forest, Virginia 7 April 1848, *m* at E Hampton 5 Aug 1875, Sarah Griswold, dau of Samuel Buell Gardiner, New York State Assemblyman, and *d* at Santa Fe 1 Sept 1883, having had issue,
1 A child, *d* at birth June 1876.
2 Samuel Gardiner TYLER, *b* Jan 1878; *d* March 1892.
3 Lilian Horsford TYLER, *b* 1879, *m* Aug 1910, Alben N. Margraf, German Naval Offr, and *d* May 1918, leaving issue,
● Margaret MARGRAF, *b* March 1912.
**11** Julia Gardiner TYLER, *b* at Sherwood Forest, Virginia 25

Dec 1849, *educ* Sacred Heart Convent, Halifax, *m* at the Church of the Ascension, New York 26 June 1869, William H. Spencer, and *d* 8 May 1871, leaving issue,
  Julia Tyler SPENCER, *b* May 1871, *m* 1st, George Fleurot, and had issue,
    Fanny FLEUROT, *b* 1893; *dunm* 1921.
  She *m* 2ndly, W. Durant Cheever.
**12** Lachlan TYLER, MD, practiced med in Washington and Elkhorn, W Virginia, *b* at Sherwood Forest, Virginia 2 Dec 1851, *m* 1876, Georgia Powell, and *dsp* 1902.
**13** Lyon (formerly Lion) Gardiner ("Lonie") TYLER, LLD (Trinity 1895, Pittsburgh Univ 1911, Brown Univ 1914, William and Mary Coll 1919), Pres William and Mary Coll 1888-1919, Pres Emeritus from 1919, proprietor and Editor of *William and Mary College Quarterly Historical Magazine*, *b* at Sherwood Forest, Virginia 24 Aug 1853, *educ* Univ of Virginia (AB 1874, AM 1875), *m* 1st 14 Nov 1878, Annie Baker (*b* at Charlottesville 8 April 1855; *d* at Richmond 2 Nov 1921), dau of Lt-Col St George Tucker, CSA, of Ashland, Virginia, by his wife Elizabeth Anderson Gilmer, and had issue,
  1 Julia Gardiner TYLER, *b* at Memphis, Tennessee 7 Dec 1881, *m* at Bruton Church, Williamsburg, Virginia 17 April 1911, James Southall Wilson, PhD, Poe Prof of Literature Virginia Univ (*b* at Bacon's Castle, Surry County, Virginia 12 Nov 1880; *d* at Charlottesville 26 June 1963), son of John S. Wilson, by his wife Mary Eliza Jordan, and *d* at Charlottesville 29 Nov 1965, leaving issue,
    (1) ●Nancy Tucker WILSON, *b* at Williamsburg 24 Feb 1912, *m* 1st (*m* diss by div), John Metcalf Drewry, and has issue,
      1*a*●Patricia Metcalf DREWRY, *b* 20 Sept 1940, *m* 1966, ●Cmdr Kenneth Tisdale Sanger, USN [*800 Duke of Suffolk, Virginia Beach, Virginia, USA*], and has issue,
        1*b*●Kenneth Scott SANGER, *b* 20 Oct 1967.
        2*b*●Derek John SANGER, *b* 10 Dec 1973.
      2*a*●John Tyler DREWRY [*120 Borges Avenue, Silver Spring, Maryland, USA*], *b* 3 July 1942, *m* at Baltimore 2 July 1965, ●Diane Patricia Robinson, and has issue,
        1*b*●Laura Katherine DREWRY, *b* 15 Aug 1969.
        2*b*●Alison Tucker DREWRY, *b* 10 May 1971.
      3*a*●James Southall Wilson DREWRY, *b* 9 April 1944.
    Nancy Tucker Wilson *m* 2ndly at Norfolk, Virginia 2 May 1970, ●James Mann, Jr (*b* 2 Dec 1911) [*1404 Crystal Parkway, Virginia Beach, Virginia 23451, USA*], son of James Mann.
    (2) ●Alida WILSON, *b* at Williamsburg 27 Nov 1913, *m* at Charlottesville 10 Sept 1938, ●Charles Marshall Davison, Jr, Prof of Law Virginia Univ (*b* at Richmond 19 June 1914) [*1856 Edgewood Lane, Charlottesville, Virginia 22903, USA*], son of Charles Marshall Davison, by his wife Katherine Stonestreet, and has had issue,
      1*a*●Katherine Stonestreet DAVISON, Headmistress Tuckahoe Montessori Sch [*4618 Leonard Parkway, Richmond, Virginia 23226, USA*], *b* at Charlottesville 9 May 1942.
      2*a* Julia Tyler DAVISON, *b* 16 April, *d* 18 April 1945.
  2 ●Elizabeth Gilmer TYLER [*9 Raleigh Court Apartments, University Circle, Charlottesville, Virginia 22903, USA*], *b* at Richmond, Virginia 13 March 1885, *m* at Bruton Church, Williamsburg 16 Oct 1907, Capt Alfred Hart Miles, USN, author of the nautical song *Anchors Aweigh* (*b* at Norfolk, Virginia 2 Nov 1883; *d* there 6 Oct 1956), son of Lieut Charles Richard Miles, USN, by his wife Evelyn Wayne Wilson, and has had issue,
    Lion Tyler MILES, Lieut USN, *b* at Williamsburg, Virginia 4 March 1910, *educ* US Naval Academy, *m* at Yuma, Arizona 23 June 1932, ●Elizabeth Innes (*b* at Minneapolis 19 June 1914), dau of John Holwill Lighthipe, by his wife Alice Innes Graves, and *d* in action at sea off Java 2 March 1942, leaving issue,
      ●Lion Gardiner MILES, Capt American Airlines [*110 East 36th Street, Apt 11a, New York, New York 10016, USA*], *b* at Pensacola, Florida 17 March 1934, *educ* Yale, William and Mary (AB 1961), and Columbia Univ (AM 1964), *m* 1st at Williamsburg, Virginia 1 Dec 1956 (*m* diss by div), Patricia Lee (*b* at Pittsburgh, Pennsylvania 5 Nov 1933), dau of Edward Hubert Rouen, by his wife Helene Violette Affolter, and has issue,
        1*b*●Julia Gardiner MILES, *b* at Naha, Okinawa 26 Nov 1958.
        2*b*●Margaret Rouen MILES, *b* at New York 22 June

1963.
        3*b*●Elizabeth Tyler MILES, *b* at N Tarrytown, New York 28 May 1966.
    Capt Lion Gardiner Miles *m* 2ndly at New York 22 May 1971, ●Susanna (*b* at Pittsburgh, Pennsylvania 6 Nov 1939), dau of Edwin Wilhard Laatu, by his wife Charlotte Irwin Caum.
  3 John TYLER, Assoc Prof, US Naval Acad, *b* at Richmond, Virginia 1 Feb 1887, *educ* William and Mary Coll, Mass Inst of Technology, and Ohio State Univ, *m* at Virginia Beach, Virginia 18 Sept 1916, ●Elizabeth (*b* at Virginia Beach, Virginia 1894), dau of William George Parker, of Portsmouth, Virginia, by his wife May Isabel Godwin, and *d* at Annapolis, Maryland 14 June 1969, leaving issue,
    (1) ●Elizabeth Parker TYLER [*3 Southgate Avenue, Annapolis, Maryland, USA*], *b* at Annapolis, Maryland 3 ʿFeb 1918.
    (2) ●Anne Gardiner TYLER, *b* at Annapolis, Maryland 29 Oct 1920, *m* at Honolulu, Hawaii 12 June 1941, ●Capt Clay Hayes Raney, USN (ret) (*b* at Newark, Arkansas 1915) [*5300 Edgewood Road, Little Rock, Arkansas, USA*], son of Thomas Jefferson Raney, by his wife Inez Brannan, and has issue,
      1*a*●John Tyler RANEY, *b* at Norfolk, Virginia 22 Oct 1942, *educ* St Louis Univ, Missouri, *m* at St Louis, Missouri 1963, ●Catherine Frances (*b* Nov 1942), dau of Firmin Desloge Fusz, by his wife Catherine Cowey, and has issue,
        1*b*●Ann Desloge RANEY, *b* 18 Feb 1964.
        2*b*●Catherine Hayes RANEY, *b* 18 March 1965.
        3*b*●Julia Fusz RANEY, *b* 3 July 1970.
      2*a*●Mary Brannan RANEY, *b* at Bremerton, Washington 16 Feb 1946, *m* at Little Rock, Arkansas Aug 1969, ●Francis Stephen Hiegel (*b* 3 Aug 1946), son of Theodore Joseph Hiegel, by his wife Frances Enderlin, and has issue,
        1*b*●Francis Stephen HIEGEL, Jr, *b* at Little Rock 25 Oct 1970.
        2*b*●Theodore Joseph HIEGEL II, *b* at Little Rock 27 Dec 1972.
      3*a*●Teresa Gardiner RANEY, *b* at Annapolis, Maryland 7 June 1949, *m* 29 June 1973, ●Earl Ray Ball (*b* 4 May 1945), son of Charles Ball, by his wife Edna.
      4*a*●Anne St George Tucker RANEY, *b* at Charleston, S Carolina 26 March 1952.
      5*a*●Elizabeth Gilmer RANEY, *b* at Annapolis, Maryland 5 June 1958.
  Dr Lonie Tyler *m* 2ndly 12 Sept 1923, Sue (*b* in Charles City County, Virginia 5 May 1889; *d* 2 May 1953), dau of John Ruffin, of Charles City County, by his wife Jane Cary Harrison, and *d* 12 Feb 1935, having by her had issue,
  4 ●Lyon Gardiner TYLER, Jr, Commonwealth's Attorney of Charles City County, Virginia 1951-55, Assoc Prof of History, Virginia Mil Inst and Citadel [*PO Box 474, Charleston, South Carolina, USA*], *b* at Richmond, Virginia 3 Jan 1925, *educ* William and Mary Coll (PhD), *m* 18 Jan 1958, ●Lucy Jane (*b* 10 April 1924), dau of Barton Pope, and has issue,
    ●Susan Selina Pope TYLER, *b* 27 March 1964.
  5 ●Harrison Ruffin TYLER, Pres Chemical Treatment Co [*401 North Allen Avenue, Richmond, Virginia 23220, USA*], *b* at Lions Den, Charles City, Virginia 9 Nov 1928, *educ* William and Mary Coll, *m* at Mulberry Hill Plantation, Johnston, S Carolina, ●Frances Payne (*b* at Mulberry Hill 11 March 1933), dau of William Miller Bouknight, by his wife Frances Payne Turner, and has issue,
    (1) ●Julia Gardiner TYLER, *b* 30 Dec 1958.
    (2) ●Harrison Ruffin TYLER, Jr, *b* 16 Sept 1960.
    (3) ●William Bouknight TYLER, *b* 3 Jan 1962.
  6 Henry TYLER, *b* at Richmond, Virginia 18 Jan, *d* 26 Jan 1931.
**14** Robert FitzWalter TYLER, farmer in Hanover County, Virginia, *b* at Sherwood Forest, Virginia 12 March 1856, *educ* Georgetown Coll, *m* Fannie Glinn, and *dsp* 1927.
**15** Pearl TYLER, *b* at Sherwood Forest, Virginia 13 June 1860, *m* 1894, Major William Mumford Ellis (*b* 1846; *d* 1921), and *d* 1947, leaving issue,
  1 Pearl Tyler ELLIS, *b* 1885; *dunm*.
  2 John Tyler ELLIS, *b* 1887, *m* Helen R. Watson, and *dsp*.
  3 Leila MacLachlan ELLIS, *b* 1888, *m* 1920, Ambrose Madison Marye (*b* 1887) and had issue,

●Madison Ellis MARYE, *b* 1925, *m* 1950, ●Charlotte Urbas, and has issue,
   1*a*●Charlotte Madison MARYE, *b* 1951.
   2*a*●Juliana Madison MARYE, *b* 1953.
4 Cornelia Horsford ELLIS, *m* 1916, Yelverton E. Booker, and *dsp*.
5 Gardiner Tyler ELLIS, *b* 1893; *dunm*.

6 Mumford ELLIS, *b* 1895, *m* Ruth Woods.
7 ●Julia Fleurot ELLIS, *b* 1898, *m* 1924, ●William Robinson, and has issue,
   (1) ●Pearl Tyler ROBINSON, *b* 1927.
   (2) ●Elizabeth B. ROBINSON, *b* 1930.
8 Lyon Alexander ELLIS, *b* 1900, *m* Margaret Northcross, and *dsp* 1954.

# The Brothers and Sisters of President Tyler

**1** Anne Contesse TYLER, *b* 1778, *m* 1795, James Semple, Judge Gen Court of Virginia and Prof of Law William and Mary Coll (*b* 1768; *d* 1834), and *d* 1803, leaving issue, two sons and three daus.

**2** Elizabeth Armistead TYLER, *b* 1780, *m* 1798, John Clayton Pryor (*b* 1780; *d* 1846), and *d* 1824, having had issue, two sons (who both *d* young) and five daus.

**3** Martha Jefferson TYLER, *b* 1782, *m* 1805, Thomas Ennalls Waggaman (*b* 1782; *d* 1832), and *d* 1855, having had issue, three sons and five daus.

**4** Maria Henry TYLER, *b* 1784, *m* 1800, John Boswell Seawell, of Gloucester, Virginia (*b* 1780), and *d* 1843, leaving issue, six sons and one dau.

**5** Wat Henry TYLER, MD, *b* 1788, *m* 1st, Elizabeth Warren Walker, and had issue, three sons and one dau. He *m* 2ndly, Margaret Govan, and *d* 1862, having by her had issue, one son and one dau.

**6** William TYLER, mem Virginia House of Delegates, *b* 179-, *m* Susan Harrison Walker, and *d* 1856, leaving issue, five sons and three daus.

**7** Christiana Booth TYLER, *b* 1795, *m* 1813, Henry Curtis, MD (*b* 1793; *d* 1862), and *d* 1842, having had issue, six sons and three daus.

# Note

President Tyler, with five sons and three daughters by his first marriage and five sons and two daughters by his second marriage, had more children than any other President.

# James Knox Polk

## 1795-1849

———

## 11th President of the
## United States of America

### 1845-1849

JAMES KNOX POLK, 11TH PRESIDENT

# James Knox Polk

## 1795-1849

### *11th President of the United States of America*
### 1845-1849

"WHO IS James K. Polk?" was the Whig taunt in the presidential campaign of 1844. Their own candidate was the great Kentuckian Henry Clay. Clay had been prominent in Washington ever since the War of 1812. He had held cabinet rank, he was a Senator, he had been Speaker of the House of Representatives and a serious presidential contender for twenty years. By contrast Polk was a far less glamorous figure, and less of a hero within his own party. At the Democratic convention he emerged as a "dark horse" candidate, the first in the history of the Presidency. He was not even nominated until the eighth ballot. In other words, in 1844 Polk was a candidate whom few would place at the head of their lists, but on whom they could agree to avoid a deadlock. The Whigs made the most of the notion that Polk was a second-best and therefore a second-rate choice.

In fact he was not as obscure as they pretended. He had been Governor of Tennessee, and before that a diligent Congressman who had actually risen—like Clay—to the important position of Speaker of the House. Except for military service Polk's career had paralleled that of his mentor Andrew Jackson. Both were born in the Carolinas, both were Scotch-Irish Presbyterians, both moved to Tennessee, both were trained in law, both established a political base in their home state and then launched themselves upon Washington. Both were fiercely partisan Democrats. Their party tried to make political capital of the comparison. Jackson's nickname was "Old Hickory": Polk was passed off as "Young Hickory".

He had two great advantages in the 1844 campaign. One was the support and advice of Jackson. The other was that, unlike Clay, he was not publicly committed to delicate and controversial issues. Jackson sagely recommended Polk to ignore the most vexed issue of all, that of slavery, and to base his campaign upon American expansion westward toward the

Pacific. The Whigs were critical of expansionism, and Clay allowed himself to be trapped into positions on slavery that cost him votes in the North. After Tyler's Presidency the Whigs were in any case in disarray in 1844. The outcome was a narrow victory for Polk; a few thousand votes in New York would have tipped the balance and put Clay in the White House.

A Whig orator had dismissed Polk as "a blighted burr that has fallen from the mane of the warhorse of the Hermitage"—the "Hermitage" being Jackson's home in Tennessee. But Polk in office soon proved himself to be a formidable force. He meant to have only one term as President, and in that time to carry out a definite and ambitious program. Part of it had to do with tariff reform. Polk's main effort, however, was directed to planting the American flag up in the Oregon territory, and in some of Mexico's great Southwestern domains. The present states of Oregon and Washington were secured through a sensible diplomatic compromise with Britain, after a good deal of sabre-rattling. At the price of a war with Mexico, over the situation of Texas, Polk gained for the United States an even bigger area than the Louisiana Purchase. He gave Mexico about the same sum ($15 million) that Jefferson had paid for Louisiana. Included in Polk's bargain were Texas, the present states of California and New Mexico, and portions of the present states of Utah, Nevada, Colorado and Arizona.

It is commonly said that Polk paid a terrible personal price. He died three months after leaving office, at the age of fifty-four, having apparently worked himself to death. The explanation may be a little more complicated. Presidents, like other busy men, often experience a kind of psychic collapse when the sustaining pressures are removed. Possibly it is not the harness but the removal of the harness that kills them. Whatever the reason in Polk's case, he applied himself with almost alarming zeal. During his four-year term he was away from Washington for a total of only six weeks. Others, including Secretary of War William L. Marcy, sought relief elsewhere from the sticky heat of a Washington summer. Polk remained at his desk, also absorbing most of Marcy's responsibilities. He met his cabinet twice a week. A typical day stretched on for ten or twelve hours. Polk was especially irked by the incessant stream of callers—some impelled by idle curiosity, many by the hope he would find a job for them or their friends and relations. He did not enjoy the obligatory White House entertainments, at which on principle he and his wife Sarah Childress Polk would not allow alcohol, dancing or card-playing. Mrs Polk was a sensible and loyal companion, but she could not persuade her husband to relax. She told a friend that she had arranged for the President to come out for a drive one day; "the carriage waited and waited. . . . It would have been obliged to wait all day, for somebody was always in the office, and Mr Polk would not, or could not, come". In the evenings he

SARAH CHILDRESS, MRS POLK

wrote copiously in a private diary. "I prefer to supervise the whole operations of the Government myself", he noted, "and this makes my duties very great".

Probably he occupied himself too much with details of expenditure or patronage or military logistics that should have been left to subordinates. In his handling of the Mexican War he was obsessively anxious to claim credit for the Democrats, and to prevent the Whig Generals Zachary Taylor and Winfield Scott from acquiring glory. Latter-day critics have questioned whether there was any need to have got into war with Mexico—a conflict that Polk was eager to promote. He was a narrow, humorless man who could be vindictive and prejudiced. It was not possible to love Young Hickory as Old Hickory was loved by the Democratic following. But he was unquestionably the "strongest" President in the generation between Jackson and Lincoln. Polk galvanized Washington. Underlings knew they could not conceal slackness from him. Polk's was the all-seeing eye, like the Masonic symbol on the nation's Great Seal. Executive heads had to obey his dictates: for instance, that they could not remain in his cabinet if they intended to be presidential candidates in 1849. Polk was master in his own sphere. The atmosphere in Polk's Washington was grim, sometimes sour, but usually purposeful. He drove toward victory, grumbling in his diary at the incompetence or treachery of those around him. The Presidency, he sighed, was "no bed of roses". But then, nor was life itself for a dour, dedicated Presbyterian in the mould of James K. Polk. "Who is James K. Polk?" By 1849 everyone in America was well aware of the answer.

# Chronology

1795  Born in Mecklenburg County, N Carolina 2 Nov.

1806  Family moved to Duck River valley (now Maury County), Tennessee.

1816  Entered N Carolina University, Chapel Hill Jan.

1818  Graduated from University with AB degree 4 June.

1819  Studied Law in office of Felix Grundy at Nashville, Tennessee; appointed Clerk of Tennessee Senate 20 Sept.

1820  Admitted to the Tennessee Bar 5 June.

1823  Elected member of Tennessee House of Representatives.

1825  Elected member of the House of Representatives Aug; took seat 5 Dec.

1827  Appointed member of Foreign Affairs Committee 3 Dec.

1832  Appointed member of Ways and Means Committee Dec.

1833  Elected Chairman of Ways and Means Committee.

1835  Elected Speaker of the House of Representatives 7 Dec.

1837  Re-elected Speaker 4 Sept.

1838  Candidate for Governor of Tennessee.

1839  Resigned from the House of Representatives 3 March; began campaign for Governor 11 April; elected Governor 1 Aug; inaugurated 14 Oct.

1840  Nominated for Vice-President by Tennessee Legislature.

1841  Received one electoral vote as Vice-Presidential candidate 19 Feb; defeated for re-election as Governor 5 Aug.

1843  Again unsuccessful candidate for Governor.

1844  Declared in favour of annexation of Texas 22 April; nominated for President at Democratic National Convention, Baltimore 29 May; election day 12 Nov; Presidential Electors cast their ballots 4 Dec and Polk received 170 of the 275 electoral votes.

1845  Electoral vote tabulated by Congress 12 Feb and Polk and George Mifflin Dallas officially declared elected; inaugurated as 11th President of the United States of America 4 March; Mexico broke off diplomatic relations with US 28 March; ordered General Zachary Taylor to occupy point "on or near the Rio Grande" and to limit action to the defence of Texas unless war be declared by Mexico 15 June; instructed Secretary of State Buchanan to withdraw Oregon offer to the British 30 Aug; appointed John Slidell as secret agent to negotiate with Mexico 16 Sept; sent first State of the Union message to Congress 2 Dec; sent special message to Congress announcing that Texas had accepted terms of admission 9 Dec; received request from Great Britain to renew offer of 49th parallel as boundary of Oregon but rejected it 27 Dec; Texas admitted as 28th State 29 Dec.

1846   Through Secretary of War ordered Gen Taylor to occupy positions on or near left bank of the Rio Grande 13 Jan; informed cabinet of intention to recommend Congress to adopt stern measures against Mexico 21 April; first Mexican-US military skirmish 25 April; signed joint resolution authorizing him to give notice to Great Britain of termination of joint occupation of Oregon 27 April; Battles of Palo Alto and Resaca de la Palma in which Mexicans were defeated 8-9 May; sent message to Congress declaring that a state of war existed by virtue of Mexico's invasion of American soil; war declared on Mexico 13 May; served notice of termination of joint occupation of Oregon on Great Britain 21 May; new treaty with Great Britain for settlement of Oregon boundary ratified 15 June; signed Act re-assigning 36 square miles of District of Columbia to Virginia 9 July; signed Tariff Act of 1846 30 July; vetoed Rivers and Harbors Bill 3 Aug; vetoed French Spoliation Claims Bill 8 Aug; Monterey surrendered 25 Sept; sent second State of the Union message to Congress 8 Dec; Iowa admitted as 29th State 28 Dec.

1847   Gen Zachary Taylor's victory at Buena Vista ended war in northern Mexico 23 Feb; Veracruz occupied 29 March; toured eastern States June-July; Mexico City captured 14 Sept; sent third State of the Union message to Congress 7 Dec; vetoed Wisconsin Territory Internal Improvements Bill 15 Dec.

1848   Treaty of Guadalupe Hidalgo ended Mexican War 2 Feb; sent special message to Congress urging immediate action on Oregon 29 May; Wisconsin admitted as 30th State 29 May; Treaty of Guadalupe Hidalgo proclaimed effective 4 July; attended laying of cornerstone of Washington Monument 4 July; signed Act establishing Territory of Oregon 14 Aug; sent fourth and last State of the Union message to Congress, including confirmation of the discovery of gold in California, 5 Dec.

1849   Signed Act establishing Territory of Minnesota and act creating Department of the Interior 3 March; retired from office 4 March and attended inauguration of his successor Zachary Taylor 5 March; left Washington 4 May for his new home Polk Place, Nashville, Tennessee; taken ill on journey; died at Nashville of an intestinal disorder 15 June; buried at Nashville.

# The Writings of President Polk

*The Diary of James K. Polk*, edited by Milo M. Quaife, 4 vols (1910)

A new edition of *The Papers of President Polk* is now appearing.

# Lineage of President Polk

The first three generations of this lineage are in fact unproven, but appear highly probable.

SIR JOHN POLLOK, of Renfrewshire, Scotland, *m* Janet Mure, and was *k* at the Battle of Lecherbie 1593, leaving issue,

ROBERT POLLOK, who received a grant of lands in Coleraine, co Derry, Ireland 1605/8, *m*, and had issue,

ROBERT POLLOK, of Coleraine, a Covenanter, *b ca* 1595/8, *m*, and *d ca* 1640, leaving issue,

ROBERT POLLOK (*or* POLKE), served as a Capt in Col Porter's Regt against King Charles I, later emigrated to Maryland and was granted land known as "Polke's Lott" and "Polke's Folly" by Lord Baltimore 7 March 1687, *m* Magdalen (will dated 7 April 1726), widow of — Porter, and dau of — Tasker, of Moneen, nr Strabane, co Tyrone, Ireland, and *d* in Somerset County, Maryland (will *pr* 5 June 1704), leaving, with other issue,

WILLIAM POLK, of White Hall, Maryland, *b* probably in co Donegal *ca* 1664, *m* 1st, Nancy, widow of — Owen, and dau of — Knox; and 2ndly, — Gray, widow, and *d* (will *pr* 24 Feb 1739), leaving issue,

WILLIAM POLK, Jr, settled first in Hopewell Township, Cumberland County, Pennsylvania, then "west of the Yadkin River" in N Carolina, *b* at White Hall *ca* 1700, *m ca* 1730, Margaret Taylor (who survived him), and *d* in N Carolina *ca* 1753, leaving with other issue[1],

COLONEL EZEKIEL POLK, served in the Revolutionary War, later acquired large tracts of land in Tennessee Territory, N Carolina, *b* in Cumberland County, Pennsylvania 7 Dec 1747, *m* 1st *ca* 1769, Mary (*d* 1791, *bur* Polk Cemetery, nr Pineville, N Carolina), dau of Samuel Wilson, of Mecklenburg County, N Carolina, by his wife Mary Winslow, and had issue. He *m* 2ndly in N Carolina *ca* 1792, Bessie Davis; and 3rdly in Maury County, Tennessee *ca* 1812, Sophia, widow of — Leonard, and dau of — Neely, and *d* at Bolivar, Tennessee 31 Aug 1824. His son by his 1st marriage,

SAMUEL POLK, settled in Maury County, Tennessee 1806, served as a Major in the War of 1812, *b* probably in Tryon County, N Carolina 5 July 1772, *m* at Hopewell Church, Mecklenburg County, N Carolina 25 Dec 1794, Jane (*b* probably in Iredell County, N Carolina 13 Nov 1776; *d* at Columbia, Maury County, Tennessee 11 Jan 1852, *bur* Greenwood Cemetery, Columbia), dau of Capt James Knox, of Iredell County, N Carolina (who served in the Revolutionary War), by his wife Lydia Gillispie, and *d* at Columbia, Maury County, Tennessee 5 Nov 1827 (*bur* Greenwood Cemetery), leaving, with other issue (*see* BROTHERS AND SISTERS OF PRESIDENT POLK, *p 244*), an eldest son,

JAMES KNOX POLK, **11th President of the United States of America.**

# President Polk's Wife

JAMES KNOX POLK *m* at Murfreesboro, Rutherford County, Tennessee 1 Jan 1824, Sarah (*b* nr Murfreesboro 4 Sept 1803; *d* at Nashville, Tennessee 14 Aug 1891, *bur* at Nashville with her husband), dau of Joel Childress, merchant and farmer, by his wife Elizabeth Whitsitt. There were no children of the marriage and thus there are *no descendants* of President Polk.

# The Brothers and Sisters of President Polk

**1** Jane Maria POLK, *b* in Mecklenburg County, N Carolina 14 Jan 1798, *m* in Maury County, Tennessee 24 Feb 1813, James Walker (descended from James Walker, of Wigtown, Scotland, who emigrated to America 1726), and *d* at Columbia, Tennessee 11 Oct 1876, having had issue, six sons (of whom the 3rd, James Knox Walker (1818-1863), was priv sec to his uncle Pres Polk 1845-49) and five daus.
**2** Lydia Eliza POLK, *b* in Mecklenburg County, N Carolina 17 Feb 1800, *m* 1st in Maury County, Tennessee 5 Aug 1817, Silas William Caldwell, and had issue, two sons. She *m* 2ndly, Edward Richmond, by whom she had no issue, and *d* in Haywood County, Tennessee 29 May 1864.
**3** Franklin Ezekiel POLK, *b* in Mecklenburg County, N Carolina 23 Aug 1802; *dunm* at Columbia, Tennessee 21 Jan 1831.
**4** Marshall Tate POLK, *b* in Mecklenburg County, N Carolina 17 Jan 1805, *m* at Charlotte, N Carolina 25 Oct 1827, Laura Teresa, dau of Judge Joseph Wilson, by his wife Mary Wood, and *d* at Charlotte 12 April 1831, leaving issue,
    **1** Roxana (Eunice Ophelia) POLK, *b* 1828; *d* 1842.
    **2** Marshall Tate POLK, Jr, brought up by his uncle and aunt President and Mrs Polk, Capt of Arty, CSA, wounded and captured at the Battle of Shiloh, released and paroled through the intervention of Mrs James Knox Polk, widow of the President, later Treas State of Tennessee, *b* at Charlotte 15 May 1831, *educ* Georgetown Univ, and US Mil Acad, *m* at Bolivar 10 Jan 1856, Evelina McNeal, dau of Major John Houston Bills, by his wife Prudence Tate McNeal, and *d* at Nashville 29 Feb 1884 (*bur* Polk Cemetery, Bolivar), having had issue,
        (1) Edward McNeal POLK, *b* at Bolivar, Tennessee 18 Nov 1856; *d* 19 Sept 1858.
        (2) James Knox POLK, Capt 1st Tennessee Vol Inf, served in Spanish-American War, *b* at Bolivar 26 Jan 1859, *m* at Bolivar 27 Jan 1880, Mary Frances (*d* 26 Oct 1932), dau of Robert Hibbler, by his wife Ann Kelsey, and had issue,
           1*a* James Knox POLK, Jr, of Nashville, served in Spanish-American War with 1st Tennessee Vol Inf, *b* at Nashville 3 March 1881, *m* there 27 Jan 1915, ●Virginia Galtney [*Macon Plantation, Inverness, Mississippi 38753, USA*], dau of W. G. Prichard, by his wife Mary Gibson, and *d* 7 Nov 1960, leaving issue,
           1*b*●Mary POLK, *b* at Nashville 26 Oct 1915, *m* 1942, ●John Selden Kirby-Smith, and has had issue,
               1*c*●Marshall Selden KIRBY-SMITH, *b* 5 Nov 1945.
               2*c*●Laurance Polk KIRBY-SMITH, *b* 5 Aug 1951, *m* at Washington, DC 1973, ●Thomas Gibson.
               3*c* John Selden KIRBY-SMITH, Jr, *b* 1 Feb 1953; *d* in Switzerland 10 July 1968.
           2*b*●Virginia Knox POLK, *b* at Nashville 31 May 1918, *m* 22 March 1947, ●Thomas K. Van Zandt, and has issue,
               1*c*●Mary Gibson VAN ZANDT, *b* at Nashville 31 May 1949.
               2*c*●Effie Morgan VAN ZANDT, *b* at Nashville 29 March 1951, *m* 10 June 1972, ●Walter Merrill.
               3*c*●James Knox Polk VAN ZANDT, *b* at Greenville, Mississippi 29 Nov 1952.
        2*a* Kelsey Hibbler POLK, of Nashville, *b* at Nashville 30 Dec 1884, *m* at Mount Pleasant, Tennessee 18 Oct 1910, Eleanor Frances, dau of Edward Gregory, and had issue, one dau.
        3*a* Albert McNeal POLK, served in World War I with 50th Inf US Army, *d* 12 Aug 1888.
        4*a* Edward Marshall POLK, *b* at Chattanooga, Tennessee 1 June 1891, *m* at Nashville 8 Dec 1912, Olivia Winston, dau of Charles F. Sharpe, by his wife Olivia Winston Scott, and had issue, one dau.
        5*a* Lawrence Norton POLK, served in World War I as Lieut 25th Aero Sqdn in France, *b* at Nashville 17 Feb 1896.
        (3) Mary Wilson POLK, *b* at Bolivar 24 Aug 1861, *m* at Nashville 26 Nov 1884, Alexander Humphreys Kortrecht, of Memphis, Tennessee, son of Judge Charles Kortrecht,

by his wife Augusta Betts, and had issue,

1*a*●Charles Murray KORTRECHT, *b* at Memphis Aug 1886.

2*a*●Humphreys KORTRECHT, *b* at Memphis 15 May 1888.

3*a*●Evelyn Marshall KORTRECHT, *b* at Memphis 30 Jan 1890, *m* at Nashville 6 June 1918, Edgar Morrison Richardson, son of Edgar Morrison Richardson, by his wife Anna B. Price, and had issue, one dau.

4*a*●Eunice Polk KORTRECHT, *b* at Memphis 13 Jan 1892.

5*a*●Augustus KORTRECHT, *b* at Memphis 30 Jan 1897.

(4) Laura Prudence POLK, *b* at Bolivar 4 Feb 1865.

(5) Eunice Ophelia POLK, *b* at Bolivar 2 Aug 1867, *m* at Nashville 15 Nov 1894, Jesse Rowland Norton, of Nashville, Tennessee, and had issue,

1*a*●Evelyn Polk NORTON, *b* at Chicago 25 Aug 1895.

2*a*●Frederick Rowland NORTON, *b* at Chicago 6 Aug 1897.

3*a*●Jesse Rowland NORTON, *b* at Nashville 29 Oct 1900.

(6) Clara Allison POLK, *b* at Bolivar 16 Nov 1870; *d* 21 March 1872.

(7) Marshall Tate POLK III, of Nashville, Tennessee, *b* at Bolivar 8 March 1873, *m* at Nashville 19 April 1902, Annie Sperry, dau of Robert Hill, by his wife Ann Patterson, and had issue,

1*a*●Robert Hill POLK, *b* at Nashville 27 April 1903.

2*a*●Marshall Tate POLK IV, *b* at Nashville 1 Nov 1904.

3*a*●Prudence McNeal POLK, *b* at Nashville 5 Sept 1906.

4*a*●Thomas Wilson POLK, *b* at Nashville 13 Dec 1908.

5*a*●Anne Patterson POLK, *b* at Nashville 5 April 1911.

6*a*●John Houston POLK, *b* at Nashville 14 June 1913.

7*a*●Evelina McNeal POLK, *b* at Nashville 15 April 1916.

(8) Evelyn McNeal POLK, *b* at Bolivar 9 Dec 1875, *m* at Nashville 12 Jan 1904, Dique Orson Eldred, of Princeton, Kentucky, son of Orson P. Eldred, by his wife Susan Delia Harpending, and *d* at Princeton, Kentucky 28 Jan 1963 (*bur* Cedar Hill Cemetery, Princeton), leaving issue,

1*a*●George Orson ELDRED, lawyer [*Princeton, Kentucky, USA*], *b* at Princeton 14 Sept 1904, *educ* Vanderbilt Univ, and Coll of Law, Kentucky Univ, *m* at Washington, DC 9 Oct 1943, ●Olive Seaton, and has issue,

1*b*●John Shelley ELDRED, *b* at Paducah, Kentucky 21 Jan 1945, *m* at Owensboro, Kentucky 30 Sept 1969, ●Ann Stanton Macdonald.

2*b*●George Orson ELDRED, Jr, *b* at Princeton, Kentucky 13 Jan 1954, *educ* Univ of The South Sewanee, Tennessee.

2*a*●Marshall Polk ELDRED, lawyer [*Louisville, Kentucky, USA*], *b* at Princeton 14 Sept 1904 (twin with

George Orson), *educ* Vanderbilt Univ, and Coll of Law, Kentucky Univ, *m* at Princeton 10 July 1935, ●Laura Hale, and has issue,

●Marshall Polk ELDRED, Jr, lawyer [*Louisville, Kentucky, USA*], *b* at Princeton 28 Nov 1938, *educ* Vanderbilt Univ, and Coll of Law, Kentucky Univ, *m* at Louisville 15 June 1962, ●Penelope Harrison, and has issue,

1*c*●Marshall Polk ELDRED III, *b* 15 June 1965.

2*c*●Katherine Owen ELDRED, *b* 15 March 1967.

3*a*●Mary Wilson ELDRED, regnl librarian [*719 West Main Street, Princeton, Kentucky 42445, USA*], *b* at Princeton 7 Aug 1907, *educ* Mary Baldwin Coll, Ohio Univ, and Sch of Library Sc, Kentucky Univ.

(9) Leonidas POLK, of Toledo, Ohio, served in Spanish-American War with 1st Tennessee Vol Inf, *b* at Nashville 27 March 1878, *m* at Toledo, Ohio 28 March 1908, Rachel Marie Scott, and had issue,

1*a*●Elmer Scott POLK, *b* at Toledo, Ohio 24 May 1909.

2*a*●Dora Marie POLK, *b* at Toledo, Ohio 12 Jan 1911.

3*a*●Leonidas POLK, Jr, *b* at Toledo, Ohio 3 July 1912.

4*a*●William McNeal POLK, *b* at Toledo, Ohio 1 Aug 1915.

5*a*●Eva Bills POLK, *b* at Toledo, Ohio Oct 1916.

(10) Thomas Allison POLK, *b* at Nashville 13 June 1879; *d* there 14 Sept 1884.

**5** John Lee POLK, *b* in Maury County, Tennessee 23 March 1807; *dunm* at Columbia, Tennessee 28 Sept 1831.

**6** Naomi Tate POLK, *b* in Maury County, Tennessee 2 July 1809, *m* at Columbia, Tennessee 18 Aug 1825, Adlai O. Harris, and *d* at Memphis 6 Aug 1836, leaving issue, four daus.

**7** Ophelia Clarissa POLK, *b* in Maury County, Tennessee 6 Sept 1812, *m* at Columbia, Tennessee 24 Sept 1829, John B. Hays, and *d* at Columbia 18 April 1851, leaving issue, two daus.

**8** William Hawkins POLK, mem Tennessee legislature, US Chargé d'Affaires in Kingdom of the Two Sicilies, Major 3rd Tennessee Dragoons, mem House of Reps, *b* in Maury County, Tennessee 24 May 1815, *m* 1st, Belinda G. Dickinson. He *m* 2ndly 1847, Mary L. Corse, and by her had issue,

1 James Knox POLK, *b* 1849, *m* 1885, Louise von Isenberg, and *dsp* 1912.

Major William Hawkins Polk, *m* 3rdly 1854, Lucy Eugenia Williams, and *d* 1862, having by her had issue,

2 William Hawkins POLK, *b* 1856, *m* 1885, Adelaide Marabel, and *dsp* 1886.

3 Tasker POLK, lawyer, Mayor of Warrenton, North Carolina, mem N Carolina Senate, Lieut 3rd N Carolina Inf, *b* 1861, *m* 1895, Eliza Tannahill Jones, and had issue,

(1)●William Tannahill POLK, *b* 1896.

(2)●Mary Tasker POLK, *b* 1898.

(3)●Lucy Fairfax POLK, *b* 1901.

(4)●James Knox POLK, *b* 1904.

**9** Samuel Wilson POLK, *b* in Maury County, Tennessee 17 Oct 1817; *dunm* at Columbia, Tennessee 24 Feb 1839.

# Note

[1] Another son of William Polk was Thomas Polk, a delegate to the Continental Congress, who *d* 1794. His son William Polk (1758-1834) was father of Rt Rev Leonidas Polk, Bishop of Louisiana in 1841, who became a Lt-Gen in the Confederate Army and was shot while reconnoitring on Pine Mountain, Georgia 14 June 1864.

# Zachary Taylor
## 1784-1850

———

12th President of the
United States of America
1849-1850

ZACHARY TAYLOR, 12TH PRESIDENT

# Zachary Taylor

## 1784-1850

### 12th President of the United States of America
### 1849-1850

THE MEXICAN War made Zachary Taylor a presidential candidate. In 1845 he was a grizzled old soldier, a veteran of nearly forty years of mainly obscure service in the small, fragmented regular Army of the United States. Apart from a period in Florida, hunting down Seminole Indians, he had spent most of his time in humdrum frontier duties. By 1848, however, when the Whigs nominated him, Taylor had been metamorphosed into "Old Rough and Ready", the hero of Palo Alto, Monterrey, Buena Vista and other battles fought by the Army of the Rio Grande.

It is tempting to poke fun at Taylor, and at bleary old Lewis Cass of the sagging face and grotesque red wig, his Democratic rival in 1848. Washington, Jackson and William H. Harrison before him had all owed their presidential appeal to military renown. But they were also politically experienced. Taylor was a soldier and nothing else. He had never voted in a presidential election; and though he was presumed to be a Whig he was without any party affiliation. Other senior officers such as Winfield Scott and Edmund Gaines were well known to the public, having made themselves conspicuous in one way or another. In comparison, Zachary Taylor was obscure—and possibly, as was said of Louis Napoleon, a "sphinx without a secret". Even within his profession he lacked éclat. He had been commissioned directly into the Army without passing through the military academy at West Point. Reared on a remote Kentucky plantation, he had no formal schooling. His spelling was casual and his style unpolished. It was said that he was ignorant of military science and that his battle tactics were rudimentary. He was small, bow-legged, rumpled and ungainly. Wherever possible he wore civilian clothes, including a battered straw hat.

The supposition, then, is that the Whigs picked him simply because his name was in the papers. They counted on him as a vote-getter, with the added cynical consideration that his political opinions, being hitherto non-existent, could be "taylored" to suit the immediate needs of 1848. They were unlikely to win with any other candidate; the aging Henry Clay was too entangled in political defeat and controversy, and General Scott's brilliant victories in Mexico were offset by a reputation for prickliness and pomposity. "Old Rough and Ready" sounded like a better candidate than "Old Fuss and Feathers" (Scott's nickname) for a party that was suspected by ordinary Americans of being a vehicle for rich businessmen. Taylor could be presented as a Southerner, born in Virginia (the son of a Revolutionary War colonel), raised in Kentucky, with a home at Baton Rouge in Louisiana and a plantation upriver in Mississippi. By virtue of his Army service in Wisconsin, Iowa, Arkansas and other areas he could stand as a Westerner. This regional appeal was balanced on the party ticket by selecting Millard Fillmore of New York as Taylor's vice-presidential partner. And, to reiterate, Taylor was an authentic, up-to-the-minute war hero. The Whigs indeed could only hope to win with some such candidate, and by electioneering with all their might and main. As it was, the whole campaign turned on the votes of Philadelphia, which drew Pennsylvania's 26 electoral votes into the Taylor-Fillmore column.

Taylor in fact possessed more positive advantages. Though he was rough he was no simpleton. He was sophisticated enough, for example, to send his son Richard (later a General in the Confederate army) to Harvard and Yale. His own parents were of respectable Virginia stock. His wife Margaret Mackall Smith came from a prominent Maryland family. His three daughters all married army officers. One, who was claimed by the promising young West Pointer Jefferson Davis, died soon after of malarial fever. Another, Mrs William Bliss, provided Taylor with a highly literate son-in-law who became invaluable as his confidential aide. And beneath his breezy, artless manner Taylor soon showed that he understood political nuances. This was not altogether surprising. Army officers, after all, depended upon contacts with politicians for success in their careers, and most of them were skilled in the art of pulling strings. Now and then Taylor blundered during the election campaign, and the Democrats tried to ridicule him as an ignoramus or denounce him as a slaveholder. But on the whole he conducted himself cannily. March 1849 found him installed in the White House.

Sixteen months later he was dead, from a coronary thrombosis following an acute attack of gastro-enteritis. Attending a July Fourth ceremony in Washington, Taylor found the heat disagreeable and consumed some raw food, cold water and iced milk that may have been tainted. He died five days afterwards. He had already demonstrated that

MARGARET MACKALL SMITH, MRS TAYLOR

he intended to be a firm President, and that his basic instincts were sound. But he was discovering that making and keeping peace was harder than making war. His cabinet appointments were not well received, and a financial scandal involved three of his department chiefs. Anti-slavery sentiment was growing in the North, stimulated by the creation of the new Free Soil party in 1848. Pro-slavery passions were correspondingly inflamed in the South. As a Southern moderate Taylor offended opinion in both sections. Every attempt to work out an acceptable division of the territories acquired from Mexico heightened sectional strife. Taylor passed from the scene before the great Compromise of 1850 was hammered out in Congress. If he had lived he would probably have felt inclined to characterize the Presidency in language similar to that of James Buchanan, who wrote in 1853 that it was "a distinction far more glorious than the crown of any hereditary monarch in Christendom; but yet it is a crown of thorns".

Zachary Taylor, though, never lacked courage. He liked to think that he resembled George Washington—warrior turned statesman, applying to whatever task confronted him a fundamental, uncomplicated common sense, directness and briskness. The comparison flattered him, perhaps. But he did not disgrace his high office; and it must be said that while the America of 1850 dwarfed that of Washington's day in size, wealth and power, so did the perplexities engendered by antagonism between the free North and the slave South. Taylor was the last President to own slaves, and the last nationally minded Southerner until Woodrow Wilson to occupy the White House. One wonders whether he ever regretted having been an agent in a war which, by enlarging the United States so dramatically, increased the risk of shattering the Union.

# Chronology

1784    Born at Montebello, Orange County, Virginia 24 Nov.

1785    Family moved to Beargrass Creek, nr Louisville, Kentucky.

1808    Commissioned 1st Lieut in Seventh Infantry Regt US Army 3 May.

1809    Assumed temporary command of Fort Pickering (now Memphis), Tennessee May.

1810    Promoted Capt Nov.

1811    Re-organized garrison at Fort Knox, Vincennes, Indian Territory 1 July.

1812    War of 1812 began 18 June; repulsed Indian attack on Fort Harrison, above Vincennes 4 Sept; promoted Brevet Major 31 Oct.

1812-15 Took part in frontier campaigns against British and Indians from Indiana to Missouri.

1815    Notified of promotion (dated 5 May 1814) to Major Jan; resigned commission and returned to Kentucky 17 May.

1816    Re-commissioned as Major in US Army 17 May.

1816-18 Stationed at Fort Howard, Green Bay, Michigan Territory (now Wisconsin).

1818-19 Supervisor of recruiting service at Louisville, Kentucky.

1819    Promoted Lt-Col 20 April.

1820    Moved to Bayou Sara, Louisiana Feb.

1821    Established Fort Selden, Louisiana, Nov.

1822    Established Cantonment Jesup (later Fort Jesup), Louisiana March; appointed Commander of Cantonment Robertson, nr Baton Rouge, Louisiana Nov.

1823    Bought 300 acre plantation in Feliciana Parish, Louisiana 27 Jan.

1826    Appointed member of a board of officers convened to study future operations of the militia in Washington Oct.

1827    Returned to duty in Louisiana Feb.

1828    Appointed Commander of Fort Snelling, Northwest Territory (now Minnesota) 1 May.

1829    Transferred to Fort Crawford, Prairie du Chien, Michigan Territory (now Wisconsin), June.

1831    Bought 137 acres of land in Wilkinson County, Mississippi, 6 March.

1832    Promoted Col 5 April; served in Black Hawk War May-Aug; assumed command of Fort Crawford 5 Aug.

1836    Assumed command of Jefferson Barracks, Missouri Nov.

1837    Re-assigned to Fort Crawford to combat Indian scares May-June; transferred to Florida during Second Seminole War Nov; defeated the Seminoles near Lake Okeechobee, Florida 25 Dec.

1838    Promoted Brevet Brig-Gen; appointed commanding officer of all Florida forces 15 May; bought 163 acres of land in West Feliciana Parish, Louisiana, Nov.

1840    Resigned Florida command 6 May; toured Eastern US May-Nov.

1841    Assumed command of second department of western division of the Army at Fort Smith, Arkansas; sold Mississippi and Louisiana properties Dec.

1842    Bought Cypress Grove plantation in Jefferson County, Louisiana 21 April.

1844    Assumed command of first department of Western Division of the Army at Fort Jesup, Louisiana 17 June.

1845    Arrived at Corpus Christi, Texas, following orders received from President Polk 31 July.

1846    Defeated Mexicans in Battles of Palo Alto and Resaca de la Pama 8-9 May; war declared on Mexico 13 May; occupied Matamoros 18 May; promoted Major-Gen 29 June; Battle of Monterey 21-24 Sept; Mexicans surrendered conditionally 25 Sept.

1847    Battle of Buena Vista 23 Feb; commanded US forces in northern Mexico March-Nov; left Monterey 8 Nov; arrived in New Orleans 30 Nov; hailed as a national hero 3 Dec; retired to Baton Rouge 5 Dec.

1848    Nominated for President at the Whig National Convention in Philadelphia 7 June; election day 7 Nov; Presidential Electors cast their ballots 6 Dec and Taylor received 163 of the 290 electoral votes against 127 for Lewis Cass, the Democratic candidate.

1849    Electoral vote tabulated by Congress and Taylor and Fillmore officially declared elected; inaugurated 5 March; issued proclamation warning citizens against participating in armed expeditions against Cuba 11 Aug; sent his only State of the Union message to Congress 4 Dec.

1850    Clayton-Bulwer Treaty with Great Britain ratified 19 April; second Lopez expedition against Cuba failed 19 May; died of a coronary thrombosis at the White House 9 July (the second President to die in office); buried at Louisville, Kentucky.

# The Writings of President Taylor

*Letters of Zachary Taylor from the Battlefields of the Mexican War* (1908)

# Lineage of President Taylor

JAMES TAYLOR, emigrated from Carlisle, England *ca* 1635 and settled in Tidewater County (later called Caroline County), Virginia, where he acquired large estates on the Mattaponi River, *m* 1st, Frances —, and had issue. He *m* 2ndly 1682, Mary Gregory, and *d* 1698, having by her had issue (*see* BURKE'S *Distinguished Families of America*). His son by his 1st marriage,

COLONEL JAMES TAYLOR, of Caroline, King and Queen and Orange Counties, Virginia, Col of Militia, mem Virginia House of Burgesses, Surveyor-Gen of the Colony, *b* 14 March 1674, *m* 23 Feb 1699, Martha (*b* 1679; *d* 1762), dau of Col William Thompson, and grand-dau of Sir Roger Thompson, of Yorkshire, England, and *d* 23 June 1729, leaving issue, with three other sons and five daus[1], a 2nd son,

ZACHARY TAYLOR, *b* 1707, *m* Elizabeth, dau of Hancock Lee, by his wife Sarah, dau of Isaac Allerton, and *d* 1768, leaving issue,

RICHARD TAYLOR, fought in the Revolutionary War, later Collr of Internal Revenues at Louisville, Kentucky, *b* in Orange County, Virginia 3 April 1744, *m* 20 Aug 1779, Sarah Dabney (*b* probably in Orange County, Virginia 14 Dec 1760; *d* 13 Dec 1822), dau of William Strother, and *d* nr Lexington, Kentucky 19 Jan 1829, having had, with other issue (*see* BROTHERS AND SISTERS OF PRESIDENT TAYLOR, *p 258*), a 3rd son,

ZACHARY TAYLOR, **12th President of the United States of America.**

# The Descendants of President Taylor

ZACHARY TAYLOR m in Jefferson County, Kentucky 21 June 1810, Margaret Mackall (b in Calvert County, Maryland 21 Sept 1788; d at East Pascagoula, Mississippi 14 Aug 1852, bur with her husband in the Zachary Taylor National Cemetery, Jefferson County, Kentucky), dau of Walter Smith, a wealthy planter who served in the Revolutionary War (descended from Richard Smith, Attorney-Gen of Maryland), by his wife Ann Mackall, and had issue,

**1** Ann Mackall TAYLOR, b 9 April 1811, m at Fort Crawford, Prairie du Chien, Michigan Territory (now Wisconsin) 1829, Robert Crooke Wood, MD, Actg Surg-Gen of the Union Army during the Civil War (b 1801; d 1869), and d 1875, leaving issue,
  **1** John Taylor WOOD, served in USN and CSN, Lieut on the *Merrimac* during the engagement with *Monitor*, cmd'd CSS *Tallahassee*, Col on the Staff of his uncle by marriage Pres Jefferson Davis, b 1830, m 1856, Lola (b 1834; d 1909), dau of — Mackubin, of Annapolis, Maryland, and d 1904, having had issue,
    (1) Anne Mackall WOOD, b 1858; d an inf.
    (2) Zachary Taylor WOOD, CMG (1913), of Dawson City, Yukon, Canada, joined RNW Mtd Police, served in NW Frontier Rebellion 1885, Insp 1885, Lt-Col and Assist Commr 1892, went to Yukon 1897, mem Council of Yukon Territory 1900, b 27 Nov 1860, educ RMC Kingston, Ontario, m 9 April 1888, Frances Augusta, dau of Joseph Daly, of Kingston, Ontario, and d 15 Jan 1915, leaving issue,
      1a Stuart Taylor WOOD, of Vancouver, BC, Canada, Major R Canadian Mtd Police, b 1889, m 1918, ●Gertrude Peterson, and had issue,
        1b●Donald Taylor WOOD, b 1918.
        2b●Herschel Theodore WOOD, b 1924.
        3b●John Taylor WOOD, b 1931.
      2a John Taylor WOOD, b 1901; dunm 1930.
    (3) Elizabeth Simms WOOD, b 1862; d an inf.
    (4) Lola Mackubin WOOD, b 1864; dunm.
    (5) Robert Crooke WOOD, b 1867; d 1884.
    (6) Eleanor Mackubin WOOD, b 1869, m 1894, Duncan Campbell, of Montreal, Canada (b 1856; d 1920), and had issue,
      1a Duncan J. M. CAMPBELL, served in World War I with Canadian Expdny Force, b 1895; ka in Belgium 1916, unm.
      2a●Archibald Bruce CAMPBELL, served in World War I with RCAF, b 1899, m 1930, ●Miriam, dau of — Harrop, of Regina, Saskatchewan, Canada, and has issue,
        1b●Duncan CAMPBELL, b 1931.
        2b●Bruce CAMPBELL, b 1932.
      3a●Charles Carroll Wood CAMPBELL, b 1903.
      4a●Lola Henrietta CAMPBELL, b 1908.
    (7) John Taylor WOOD, b 1871; dunm.
    (8) George Mackubin WOOD, b 1872, m 1923, Mary, dau of — Buss, of Victoria, BC, Canada, and dsp 1927.
    (9) Nina Wood, b 1873; dunm.
    (10) Mary Catherine WOOD, b 1875; dunm 1898.
    (11) Charles Carroll WOOD, served in S African War with Loyal N Lancs Regt, b 1876; ka in S Africa 1899, unm.
  **2** Robert Crooke WOOD, Col CSA, b 1832, m Mary Wilhelmine Trist, and d 1900, having had issue,

    (1) John Burke Trist WOOD, of New Orleans, dunm.
    (2) Mary Wilhelmine Trist WOOD, dunm.
    (3) Richard Taylor WOOD (twin with his sister Mary Wilhelmine Trist Wood), d young.
    (4) Nina Sarah WOOD, d young.
    (5) Marie R. WOOD, m William E. Brickell, and had issue,
      William E. BRICKELL.
    (6) Robert Crooke WOOD, d young.
    (7) Zachary Taylor WOOD, Lieut US Army, m 1st, Helen McGloin, and had issue,
      Helen WOOD.
    Zachary Taylor Wood m 2ndly, Beatrice Thomas.
  **3** Blandina Dudley WOOD, b 1834, m 1st, Major Edward Boyce, US Army; and 2ndly, Baron Guido von Grabow, and d 1892, leaving issue,
    (1) Baron VON GRABOW, dunm.
    (2) Baron VON GRABOW, dunm.
  **4** Sarah Knox WOOD, dunm 1906.
**2** Sarah Knox TAYLOR, b at Vincennes, Indiana 6 March 1814, m at Louisville, Kentucky 17 June 1835, as his 1st wife, Jefferson Davis, later President of the Confederate States of America (see APPENDIX A) (b at Fairview, Kentucky 3 June 1808; d at New Orleans 6 Dec 1889), son of Samuel Emory Davis, by his wife Jane Cook, and dsp of malarial fever at Locust Grove, Louisiana 15 Sept 1835.
**3** Octavia Pannill TAYLOR, b 16 Aug 1816; d of fever at Bayou Sara, Louisiana 8 July 1820.
**4** Margaret Smith TAYLOR, b 27 July 1819; d of fever at Bayou Sara, Louisiana 22 Oct 1820.
**5** Mary Elizabeth TAYLOR, b 20 April 1824, m 1st 1848, Lt-Col William Smith Bliss, Adjt-Gen to his father-in-law Pres Taylor. She m 2ndly, as his 2nd wife, Philip Pendleton Dandridge, 2nd son of Adam Stephen Dandridge, of The Bower, Jefferson County, Virginia, by his wife Sarah Pendleton, and dsp 1909.
**6** Richard TAYLOR, Lt-Gen CSA, b 27 Jan 1826, educ Harvard, and Yale, m Louise Marie Myrthé (b at Hermitage Plantation, St James Parish, Louisiana), dau of Michel Doradon Bringier, by his wife Aglaé du Bourg de St Colombe, and d 1879, having had issue,
  **1** Louise Margaret TAYLOR, b 1852; dunm 1901.
  **2** Betty TAYLOR, b 1854, m 1881, Walter Robinson Stauffer, son of Isaac Hull Stauffer, by his wife Marie Céleste Bonford, and brother of Isaac Hull Stauffer, Jr (see p 257), and had issue,
    (1) Myrthé STAUFFER, m Albert Schwartz, and had issue,
      1a●Wilhelmina SCHWARTZ [*2111 St Charles Avenue, New Orleans, Louisiana, USA*].
      2a Marie Louise SCHWARTZ, m Bernard J. McCloskey, and had issue,
        1b●Patrick MCCLOSKEY [*509 Mesa Road, Santa Monica, California, USA*].
        2b●Walter S. MCCLOSKEY [*170 Centre Street,*

Milton, Massachusetts, USA], *m* ●Josephine Grace, and has issue,
    ●Walter R. McCLOSKEY.
3*a*●Harry P. SCHWARTZ [*730 Esplanade Avenue, New Orleans, Louisiana 70116, USA*], *m* ●Eugenie Chavanne, and has issue,
    ●Eugenie Chavanne SCHWARTZ.
(2) Alice STAUFFER, *m* Lewis Hardie, and had issue,
  1*a*●Walter S. HARDIE [*1521 Eighth Street, New Orleans, Louisiana 70115, USA*], *m* ●Betty Thomas, and has had issue,
    1*b* Walter S. HARDIE, Jr.
    2*b*●Alice HARDIE.
  2*a*●Betty HARDIE, *b* at New Orleans 1909, *m* there 1937, ●Marchese Benedetto Capomazza di Campolattaro (*b* at Naples 1903), son of Marchese Carlo Emilio Capomazza di Campolattaro, and has issue,
    1*b*●Simonetta CAPOMAZZA DI CAMPOLATTARO, *b* at Copenhagen, Denmark 1942, *m* at Rome, Italy 1968, ●Gino Corigliano [*Via Bocca del Leone 60, Rome, Italy*], and has issue,
      ●Piero CORIGLIANO, *b* at Rome, Italy.
    2*b*●Carlo CAPOMAZZA DI CAMPOLATTARO, Steamship exec [*1614 State Street, New Orleans, Louisiana, USA*], *b* at Stockholm, Sweden 1943, *m* at New Orleans 1970, ●Rosemonde (*b* at New Orleans 1942), dau of Emile N. Kuntz, by his wife Julia Hardin, and has issue,
      ●Carlo Luigi CAPOMAZZA DI CAMPOLATTARO, *b* at New Orleans 22 Feb 1972.
(3) Anita STAUFFER, *m* John A. McIlhenny, and had issue,
  1*a*●John A. McILHENNY, Jr [*8337 Jefferson Highway, Baton Rouge, Louisiana 70809, USA*].
  2*a*●Walter Stauffer McILHENNY [*Avery Island, Louisiana 70513, USA*].
(4) Walter J. STAUFFER, *m* Elizabeth White, and *dsp*.
(5) Richard STAUFFER, *dunm*.
(6) Celeste STAUFFER, *m* Harry Burnett, and had issue,
  ●Peter BURNETT, Col US Army [*25 Juniper Lane, Framingham Centre, Massachusetts 01701, USA*], *m* ●Norma —, and has issue,
    1*b*●Medora BURNETT.
    2*b*●Celeste BURNETT.
(7) William STAUFFER, *dunm*.
3 Zachary TAYLOR, *b* 1857; *d* young.
4 Richard TAYLOR, *b* 1860; *d* young.
5 Myrthé Bianca TAYLOR, *b* at Nachitoches, Louisiana Nov 1864, *m* at New Orleans 1884, Isaac Hull Stauffer, Jr (*b* at New Orleans 1861; *d* at Haverford, Pennsylvania 1897), son of Isaac Hull Stauffer, by his wife Marie Céleste Bonford, and brother of Walter Robinson Stauffer (*see p 256*), and *d* at New Orleans 1942, leaving issue,
(1) Isaac Hull STAUFFER III, *b* at New Orleans 30 March 1885, *m* there 1 June 1910, Hélène (*b* at Paris, France 8 May 1887; *d* at New Orleans May 1957), dau of James Henry Maury, by his wife Helen Deas Ross, and *d* at New Orleans 9 May 1967, having had issue,
  1*a* Marie Myrthé STAUFFER, *b* at New Orleans 19 April 1911, *m* there 12 May 1937, ●Eugene Truax, and *dsp* 9

Jan 1946.
  2*a* Marie Hélène Alice STAUFFER, *b* at New Orleans, Louisiana 22 May 1913, *m* there 28 March 1936, ●Alvin Anthony Hero (*b* at New Orleans 8 Oct 1908) [*1213 Third Street, New Orleans, Louisiana 70130, USA*], son of George Alfred Hero, by his wife Anna Olivier, and *d* at New Orleans April 1965, leaving issue,
    1*b*●Hélène Claire HERO, *b* at New Orleans 30 Sept 1938, *m* there 21 Dec 1960, ●Dr Alfred Jackson Rufty, Jr (*b* at Atlanta, Georgia 8 Feb 1936) [*639 Arbor Road, Winston-Salem, North Carolina 27104, USA*], son of Alfred Jackson Rufty, by his wife Anne Graham, and has issue,
      1*c*●Hélène Stauffer RUFTY, *b* at New Orleans 10 May 1962.
      2*c*●Alfred Jackson RUFTY III, *b* at New Orleans 22 June 1963.
    2*b*●Myrthé Taylor HERO, *b* at New Orleans 1 Feb 1940, *m* there 2 April 1963, ●John Young Le Bourgeois (*b* at New Orleans 25 April 1938) [*205 Brookwood Drive, Clemson, South Carolina 29631, USA*], son of Joseph C. Le Bourgeois, by his wife Astrid Johannessen, and has issue,
      1*c*●Marie Louise Stauffer LE BOURGEOIS, *b* at New Orleans 13 Jan 1964.
      2*c*●Anne Charless LE BOURGEOIS, *b* at New Orleans 13 April 1965.
    3*b*●Céleste Bringier HERO, *b* at New Orleans 12 June 1942, *m* there 20 April 1968, ●Richard Warren Martin (*b* in Ireland 1930) [*18773 45th Court NE, Seattle, Washington 98155, USA*].
    4*b*●Ann Olivier HERO, *b* at New Orleans 14 Nov 1947, *m* there 1 Feb 1969, ●Dr Irving J. Johnson [*5726 Shepherd Canyon Road, Oakland, California 94611, USA*], son of Lee Johnson, by his wife Eulalie McKay.
    5*b*●Caroline Gray HERO, *b* at New Orleans 29 June 1952, *m* there 29 June 1974, ●Charles Lamont Ephraim, son of Herbert Charles Ephraim, by his wife Marguerite Lamont.
  3*a*●Marie Louise STAUFFER, *b* at New Orleans 14 May 1916, *m* there 26 May 1939, ●Warren Gabriel Posey (*b* at New Orleans 24 Jan 1910) [*7008 Chestnut Street, New Orleans, Louisiana 70118, USA*], son of John Francis Posey, by his wife Lillian Songy, and has issue,
    ●Warren Maury POSEY, in Internat Finance Dept of Anthony Cork Co, Lancaster, Pennsylvania [*540 North President Avenue, Lancaster, Pennsylvania 17603, USA*], *b* at New Orleans 16 Sept 1940, *educ* California Univ (BA), and Wharton Sch of Finance, Pennsylvania Univ (MBA), *m* at Shenandoah, Pennsylvania 18 Sept 1965, ●Alexandra Jane, dau of Edward Peter Wowak, by his wife Mary Dorothy Nadzon, and has issue,
      1*c*●Melissa Fontaine POSEY, *b* at Alexandria, Virginia 21 April 1968.
      2*c*●Matthew Tyler POSEY, *b* at Lancaster, Pennsylvania 1 Feb 1974.
(2) Marie Louise STAUFFER, *b* at New Orleans 27 Sept 1886; *d* there *unm* June 1964.

# The Brothers and Sisters of
# President Taylor

**1** Hancock TAYLOR, of Springfield, nr Louisville, Kentucky, *b* 1781, *m* 1st 1806, Sophia Elizabeth Hoard, and had issue, one son (who *m*, and had issue). He *m* 2ndly 1814, Annah Hornsby Lewis (*b* 1796; *d* 1882), and *d* 1841, having by her had issue, six other sons and four daus (of whom several *m*, and had issue).

**2** William Dabney Strother TAYLOR, Surg US Army, *b* 1782.

**3** Strother (or Richard) TAYLOR, *d* an inf.

**4** George TAYLOR, *b* 1790; *d* young.

**5** Elizabeth Lee TAYLOR, *b* 1792, *m* 1812, John Gibson Taylor (*b* 1786; *d* 1828), and *d* 1845, leaving issue, two sons (who both *dunm*) and seven daus (five of whom *m*, and had issue).

**6** Joseph Pannill TAYLOR, Brig-Gen and Commissary Gen of Subsistence, US Army, served in Indian, Mexican and Civil Wars, *b* 1796, *m* Evelyn McLean (*d* 1887), and *d* 1864, having had issue, five sons and four daus (several of whom *m*, and had issue).

**7** Sarah Bailey TAYLOR, *b* 1799, *m* French Strother Grey, and *dsp*.

**8** Emily Richard TAYLOR, *b* 1801, *m* John S. Allison, and had issue, two sons and two daus (who both *d* as infs.).

# Note

[1] Col James Taylor's eldest daughter Frances became the grandmother of President Madison (*see p 143*).

# Millard Fillmore
## 1800-1874

———

13th President of the
United States of America
1850-1853

MILLARD FILLMORE, 13TH PRESIDENT

# Millard Fillmore

## 1800-1874

### 13th President of the United States of America
### 1850-1853

THE NAME of Millard Fillmore arouses few emotions in the average person. He does not figure in lists either of exceptionally good Presidents or of exceptionally bad ones. One reason is that he was among the "accidental Presidents", having reached the White House through the death of President Zachary Taylor. He was picked as Taylor's running mate because his home state New York complemented Taylor's Louisiana and because he was in no way linked with slavery or cotton. A second reason is that Fillmore, succeeding Taylor in July 1850, had only a couple of years in which to make his mark before the country became engrossed in the presidential campaign of 1852. Since a series of political factors combined to deny him the Whig nomination in 1852, he was a "lame-duck" president for his last few months in office. A third reason is that he was not particularly memorable, in background or in temperament. He did not come from a distinguished family, but from respectably obscure New England parents who had migrated to northern New York two years before he was born, in 1798. He rose from comparative poverty to a successful career in law and politics, by his own efforts. But though he was in this sense a self-made man he did not strike the voters as a rough diamond on the Zachary Taylor pattern. On the contrary, Fillmore was well dressed, affable and personable. He was much admired in his home city, Buffalo; he had a good record as a member of Congress. But as such he was simply a capable politician among a number of others. He did not stand out as flamboyant, reckless, a colorful phrasemaker. Though he was not ordinary, neither was he extraordinary. So Millard Fillmore is for casual students of American history one of the forgettable Presidents.

Given the chances open to him, however, Fillmore performed his presidential duties with a fair degree of skill and independence. Having as Vice-President chaired meetings of the Senate, he was closely familiar with the issues of the day, especially those concerning compromises over slavery. He took a more conciliatory line than Taylor's on the territorial provisions for slavery and the idea of a fugitive-slave law. He did so not out of weakness but from a genuine conviction that realistic concessions were the best way, indeed the only way of holding the Union together. His hope was that the 1850 Compromise would, by reassuring the South, put an end to sectional strife. The hope was soon to prove illusory. But within the context of 1850 he honestly believed he was doing the right thing—a view he shared with most of the nation's sagest political leaders, including Daniel Webster. Together with Webster, he made himself extremely unpopular with abolitionist groups. In 1852, he and Webster were both leading contenders at the Whig nominating convention. They had the chagrin of watching the nomination go instead to the grandiloquent General Winfield Scott, who had already been passed over on previous occasions and who now went down to defeat against the Democratic candidate Franklin Pierce.

Fillmore looked back on his Administration with a certain amount of pardonable pride. For one innovation his wife was responsible. Abigail Powers Fillmore, a former schoolteacher with a strong appetite for the printed word, was horrified to discover that there were no books in the White House—not even a Bible, it was said. At her prompting, a small library was established with an initial modest appropriation of $250 from Congress. Official Washington saw little of Mrs Fillmore. She was an invalid, whose functions as hostess were taken over by her only daughter, Mary Abigail Fillmore. Mrs Fillmore was like President Harrison a victim of the harsh weather common at inaugural ceremonies; she caught a chill at Pierce's inauguration in March 1853 and died a month later. Mary Abigail died a year later, aged only 32, leaving Millard Fillmore with only one other child, a son. He endured a few lonely years before he married again in 1858. His second wife Caroline Carmichael McIntosh was a widow of Albany.

Fillmore lived on until 1874, active and dignified but with an inevitable aura of anticlimax. He made some unfortunate though understandable decisions. After 1852 the Whig party, hopelessly divided over slavery, began to disintegrate. Some Whigs, including ex-Congressman Abraham Lincoln, went over to the new Republican party. Fillmore, not wishing to align himself with a frankly sectional group, became associated with another new party, the American or Know-Nothing movement which chose him as presidential candidate in 1856. The Know-Nothings sought national unity by means of a dubious appeal to the patriotism (and ethnic prejudice) of native-born Americans. It was thus a party with only one idea, and that an ungenerous one.

ABIGAIL POWERS, MRS FILLMORE

CAROLINE CARMICHAEL McINTOSH,
MRS FILLMORE

Fillmore ran third to the Democratic and Republican candidates and was never again a serious presidential possibility. Thereafter he seemed out of step on national issues. He was sharply critical of Lincoln's wartime Administration, and supported General George B. McClellan—Lincoln's Democratic rival—in the election of 1864. Subsequently he sympathized with President Andrew Johnson, when many other Americans assailed this unhappy incumbent.

If Fillmore seemed to pick the wrong side, his dilemmas were in fact those of thousands of honest citizens who felt that civil war spelt the end of the American experiment in federal, republican democracy. He was on firmer ground in local affairs. Here he was accepted as Buffalo's first citizen, Chancellor of the University of Buffalo, a moving spirit in a dozen civic and philanthropic schemes. He was a good citizen; and men respected him for an inner, decent modesty which, for example, led him to refuse the offer of an honorary degree from Oxford in 1855 on the score that he did not possess the requisite amount of literary or scientific eminence. There may have been a tinge of political calculation in the refusal. Yet Millard Fillmore, while he was a professional politician, was not merely a political animal. The biographer must wish that this worthy person had left more evidences of singularity, vividness, even outrageousness. Lacking these, one is left with a somewhat misleading impression of a man without color or bulk.

# Chronology

1800    Born in a log cabin at Locke (now Summerhill), Cayuga County, New York 7 Jan.

1814    Apprenticed as wool carder and cloth dresser June; finished first term as apprentice and walked one hundred miles home Dec.

1815    Re-apprenticed as wool carder and cloth dresser June.

1818    Schoolmaster at Scott, New York.

1819-21    Studied Law at Montville and Moravia, New York.

1821    Moved to Aurora (now East Aurora), Erie County, New York.

1822    Studied Law at Buffalo, New York.

1823    Admitted to the New York Bar at Court of Common Pleas of Erie County; began law practice in Aurora.

1827      Admitted as Attorney of New York Supreme Court.

1828      Elected to New York State Assembly as representative for Erie County Nov.

1830      Moved to Buffalo, New York.

1831      Drafted Bill (with John C. Spencer) to abolish prison terms for debt which was passed and signed by the Governor of New York 26 April.

1832      Elected member of the House of Representatives Nov.

1833      Took seat in Congress 2 Dec.

1834      Joined the Whig Party.

1835      Retired from active politics and resumed law practice.

1836      Again elected to House of Representatives (re-elected 1838 and 1840)'.

1841-43   Chairman of Way and Means Committee.

1842      Declined to stand for re-election.

1844      Unsuccessful candidate for Vice-President at Whig National Convention, Baltimore, May; nominated for Governor of New York by Whigs Sept; defeated by Silas Wright Nov.

1846      Appointed Chancellor Buffalo University.

1847      Elected Comptroller of New York State.

1848      Took office as Comptroller 1 Jan; nominated for Vice-President by Whig National Convention, Philadelphia 9 June; elected Vice-President 7 Nov.

1849      Announced resignation as State Comptroller (effective from 20 Feb) 1 Jan; inaugurated as Vice-President of the United States of America 5 March.

1850      Succeeded as 13th President of the United States of America on the death of Zachary Taylor 9 July; took the oath of office in the Hall of Representatives in the Capitol 10 July; California admitted as 31st State 9 Sept; signed Acts establishing Territories of New Mexico and Utah 9 Sept; signed Fugitive Slave Act 18 Sept; signed Act abolishing slave trade in the District of Columbia 20 Sept; appointed Brigham Young, the Mormon leader, Governor of Utah Territory 28 Sept; sent first State of the Union message to Congress 2 Dec.

1851      Issued proclamation calling on officers and citizens to recapture Shadrach, a fugitive slave (who managed to escape to Canada); issued proclamation warning against participation in expeditions against Cuba 25 April; laid cornerstone of extension of the Capitol 4 July; issued proclamation warning against participation in expeditions against Mexico; sent second State of the Union message to Congress 2 Dec.

1852      Signed Act appropriating $72,500 for repairs to the Library of Congress (damaged by fire 24 Dec 1851), 19 March; failed to obtain renomination for President at Whig National Convention in Baltimore 17-20 June; sent third and last State of the Union message to Congress 6 Dec.

1853      Signed Coinage Act, reducing silver content of all coins below the value of one dollar and providing for the minting of three dollar gold pieces, 21 Feb; signed Act establishing Territory of Washington 2 March; signed Act raising salary of Vice-President from $5,000 to $8,000 3 March; retired from office and attended the inauguration of his successor Franklin Pierce 4 March; returned to Buffalo April.

1854      Toured Southern States March-May, and Midwest May-June.

1855    Sailed for Europe 17 May; visited England, France and Italy; received in audience by Pope Pius IX.

1856    Nominated for President by the American (or Know-Nothing) National Convention at Philadelphia 22 Feb; wrote from Paris accepting nomination 21 May; returned to New York 22 June; nomination endorsed by the Whig National Convention at Baltimore 17 Sept; received eight electoral votes (all from Maryland) 4 Nov.

1858-59    Visited Europe again.

1862    Elected Chairman of Buffalo Committee for Public Defense; elected President of Buffalo Historical Society 20 May (served until 1867).

1865    Escorted Lincoln's body from Batavia to Buffalo April.

1867    Elected first President of Buffalo Club.

1869    Presided at a commercial convention in Louisville, Kentucky 13 Oct.

1870    Elected President of Buffalo General Hospital.

1873    Delivered his last public address at the Third International Exhibition, Buffalo 1 Oct.

1874    Died at Buffalo 8 March; buried there.

# The Writings of President Fillmore

The only work published during his lifetime was a sixteen page pamphlet, *Is it Right to Require any Religious Test as a Qualification to be a Witness in a Court of Justice?*, published at Buffalo 1832

In 1870 and 1871 he prepared a short autobiography which was published posthumously with other documents and letters as the *Millard Fillmore Papers* by the Buffalo Historical Society under the editorship of Frank H. Severance in two volumes 1907. The Buffalo Historical Society also possess 44 volumes of unpublished letters and papers which were discovered in 1908

# Lineage of President Fillmore

The first known ancestor of this family in America was—

JOHN FILLMORE (*or* PHILLMORE), of Ipswich, Mass, mariner, who bought an estate at Beverly, Mass 1704, *m* Abigail Tilton, and had issue,

JOHN FILLMORE, *m* Dorcas Day, and had issue,

NATHANIEL FILLMORE, fought in the Revolutionary War, *m* Hepzibah, dau of Ebenezer Wood, by his wife Philippa, dau of Stephen Storey, and had issue,

NATHANIEL FILLMORE, farmer, moved from Bennington, Vermont to Locke (now Summerhill), Cayuga County, New York *ca* 1798, *b* at Bennington 19 April 1771, *m* 1st *ca* 1795, Phoebe (*b* at Pittsfield, Mass 1778; *d* at Locke 2 May 1831), dau of Abiather Millard, by his wife Hannah Eddy, and had, with other issue (*see* BROTHERS AND SISTERS OF PRESIDENT FILLMORE, *p 268*), an eldest son,

    MILLARD FILLMORE, **13th President of the United States of America.**

Nathaniel Fillmore *m* 2ndly 1834, Eunice Love, and *d* 28 March 1863.

# The Descendants of President Fillmore

MILLARD FILLMORE *m* 1st at Moravia, New York 5 Feb 1826, Abigail (*b* at Stillwater, Saratoga County, New York 17 March 1798; *d* at the Willard Hotel, Washington, DC (having caught cold at the inauguration of Pres Pierce and developed pneumonia) 30 March 1853, *bur* Forest Lawn Cemetery, Buffalo), yr dau of Rev Lemuel Powers, a Baptist Minister, by his wife Abigail Newland, and had issue,

> **1** Millard Powers FILLMORE, lawyer, *b* at East Aurora, New York 25 April 1828; *dunm* 15 Nov 1889.
> **2** Mary Abigail FILLMORE, *b* at Buffalo 27 March 1832; *dunm* at Aurora, New York 26 July 1854, *bur* Forest Lawn Cemetery, Buffalo.

MILLARD FILLMORE *m* 2ndly at Albany, New York 10 Feb 1858, Caroline (*b* at Morristown, New Jersey 21 Oct 1813; *d* at Buffalo 11 Aug 1881, *bur* Forest Lawn Cemetery, Buffalo), widow of Ezekiel C. McIntosh, of Albany, New York, and dau of Charles Carmichael, merchant, by his wife Temperance Blachley.

# The Brothers and Sisters of President Fillmore

**1** Olive Armstrong FILLMORE, *b* 1797, *m* 1816, Henry S. Johnson, and had issue, five sons and one dau.

**2** Cyrus FILLMORE, *b* 1801, *m* 1825, Laura Morey, and had issue, three sons and three daus.

**3** Almon Hopkins FILLMORE, *b* 1806; *dunm* 1830.

**4** Calvin Turner FILLMORE, *b* 1810, *m* 1830, Miranda Waldo.

**5** Julia FILLMORE, *b* 1812, *m* 1840, A. C. Harris.

**6** Darius Ingraham FILLMORE, *b* 1814; *dunm* 1837.

**7** Charles De Witt FILLMORE, *b* 1817, *m* 1840, Julia Etta Green, and *d* 1854.

**8** Phoebe Maria FILLMORE, *b* 1819; *dunm* 1843.

# Franklin Pierce
## 1804-1869

———

14th President of the
United States of America
1853-1857

FRANKLIN PIERCE, 14TH PRESIDENT

# Franklin Pierce

## 1804-1869

## *14th President of the United States of America*
## 1853-1857

MOST HISTORIANS dismiss Franklin Pierce as one of the most ineffectual of all the Presidents. "Woefully inept" is a typical comment. A visitor to the Pierces' White House remarked that "everything in that mansion seems cold and cheerless. I have seen hundreds of log cabins which seemed to contain more happiness". The sources of this gloom were partly public and in part domestic. Yet in previous years Franklin Pierce appeared to be an unusually fortunate person. His father Benjamin Pierce was a General in the Revolutionary War and then a leader in New Hampshire politics, where he served as Governor. The path lay open for young Franklin to follow. He was a popular undergraduate at Bowdoin College, and eventually married the daughter of Bowdoin's president, Jane Means Appleton. Well-connected, handsome and likeable, he always looked the most youthful figure in any gathering. Indeed he often was—Speaker of the New Hampshire state legislature at 26, a member of Congress at 29 and of the US Senate at 33. He was only 47 when the Democrats nominated him as their presidential candidate at their Baltimore convention in 1852. He took pains to be well liked and usually succeeded. The crowd at his inauguration, for example, appreciated his having memorized his address. Pierce's predecessors had read aloud from a prepared text: he spoke directly to the audience with no recourse to a wad of manuscript. His Bowdoin classmate, the novelist Nathaniel Hawthorne, wrote in a campaign biography that Pierce "has in him many of the chief elements of a great ruler. His talents are administrative, he has a subtle faculty of making affairs roll onward according to his will, and of influencing their course without showing any trace of his action. . . . He is deep, deep, deep".

Pierce's Whig opponents naturally alleged that, on the contrary, he was shallow, shallow, shallow. Some of their criticism was mere party malevolence. Democrats and Whigs alike were in chaos; as a result they focussed upon personalities and marginal issues. For instance, the Whigs falsely accused Pierce of being anti-Catholic and anti-immigrant. They also, inconsistently, claimed the Democrats were trying to pass Pierce off as being of Irish descent, when in fact the family was of English stock. They came nearer to a genuine point in taunting Pierce as a pale imitation of his father, whose career had been nurtured in General Pierce's New Hampshire hothouse. The Whigs likewise derided him as a spurious military hero. In the Mexican War Pierce had enlisted as a private, but had quickly been promoted by Polk to the rank of Brigadier-General, largely because he was a Democrat. He had served with Winfield Scott in the advance on Mexico City, but having hurt himself by a fall from his horse at an early stage, had played little part in the major encounters with the enemy. The Whigs hinted, none too delicately, that General Pierce was a fraud and a coward. And they spread the rumor that he was an alcoholic. For good measure, Whig propaganda noted that Pierce's name did not emerge at the Baltimore convention until the 35th ballot, and that he did not win until the 49th wearisome vote-count. In the first two days he was very much a dark horse possibility, far overshadowed by the Democrats' chief contenders—Lewis Cass, James Buchanan, William L. Marcy, William O. Butler, Sam Houston and the brilliant young Stephen Douglas. Only when these had stalemated one another did Pierce's managers begin to press his claims as an "available" man. Viewed as a piece of political computing, they were correct. Pierce was not completely unknown, yet he was not prominent enough to have alienated influential politicos. He was young enough to please delegates who were tired of "Old Fogies" such as Cass and Marcy. He was acceptable to the South as a Northerner who had never condemned slavery, and who was perfectly willing to take William King of Alabama as his Vice-President.

The election was heated and the victory a close one. According to the custom of the time, Pierce himself did not campaign actively. Once he had won, however, everything began to go wrong. Family problems were at the centre of Pierce's unhappiness. His wife had never liked Washington, perhaps because the social life of legislators encouraged Franklin to drink too much. At any rate he had resigned his Senate seat back in 1842 and returned to the primmer atmosphere of New Hampshire. Mrs Pierce was a sickly woman, introspective and nervously dependent upon the consolations of religion. One son had died three days after his birth. A second had succumbed to typhus at the age of four. Their third remaining child, Bennie, was her chief solace in this world, and his father's pride. But in January 1853, when the family was travelling by train in New Hampshire, their carriage rolled over in an accident. The parents escaped injury: Bennie was killed. His mother was too stunned to attend the

JANE MEANS APPLETON, MRS PIERCE

inauguration in March. Throughout their Administration she wore mourning and remained in seclusion. An aunt, Mrs Abby Kent Means, had to replace her as official hostess.

The President's personal griefs had their counterpart in his administrative troubles. Attempting like others before and since to distract attention from the nation's internal divisions, he sought to develop a swaggeringly bold foreign policy, but at the end had little to show for his initiative. He appointed a cabinet balanced between North and South, and retained it intact—the first President to have done so. He did his best to bring together all factions of the Democratic party, and to seek out expedients that were both firm and moderate in dealing with what was becoming almost a civil war in Kansas. The task was impossible, even for a leader of superhuman capacities. Pierce was conscientious and sometimes resourceful. But he left the impression of alternating between obstinacy and indecision.

He retreated to New Hampshire in 1857 a weary, disillusioned man. His popularity was gone in New England, and before his death in 1869 his stock had sunk even lower on account of his opposition to Lincoln's conduct of the Civil War. When he attended the funeral of his old friend Hawthorne, in 1864, he was snubbed by the rest of the gathering. Haunted by a sense of failure and condemnation, Pierce had tasted the bitterness that is frequently inseparable from fame. He was a lightweight who had fought to the best of his ability. Accustomed to trust and admiration, he was deeply, mortally wounded when instead he was met with scowls and mockery. He loved life, only to find that life had apparently not loved him.

# Chronology

1804    Born at Hillsborough (now Hillsboro), New Hampshire 23 Nov.

1818-20  Attended Hancock Academy and Francestown Academy.

1820    Entered Bowdoin College, Brunswick, Maine 4 Oct.

1824    Graduated from Bowdoin College with AB degree 1 Sept; began reading Law with John Burnham in Hillsborough Oct.

1825    Studied Law under Senator Levi Woodbury in Portsmouth, New Hampshire April-Nov.

1827    Admitted to the New Hampshire Bar 5 Sept; began law practice in Hillsborough.

1829    Elected to represent Hillsborough in the State legislature (re-elected 1830, 1831 and 1832); appointed Justice of the Peace for Hillsborough May.

1833    Elected member of the House of Representatives; took seat 2 Dec.

1835    Re-elected to the House of Representatives.

1836    Elected to the Senate

1837    Took seat in the Senate 4 March.

1838    Moved to Concord, New Hampshire Aug.

1842    Resigned from the Senate 16 Feb (effective 28 Feb); returned to Concord and resumed law practice March.

1844    Appointed US District Attorney for New Hampshire by President Polk.

1845    Declined appointment to the Senate and Democratic nomination for Governor of New Hampshire.

1846    Enlisted as a private soldier in Concord Volunteers on hearing that war had been declared on Mexico May; offered cabinet post as Attorney-General by President Polk but declined Sept.

1847    Commissioned as Col of Infantry in US Army 15 Feb; promoted Brig-Gen 3 March; sailed from Newport, Rhode Island for Mexico 27 May; arrived at Veracruz 27 June; joined Gen Scott at Puebla de Zaragoza 6 Aug; took part in Battles of Contreras 19 Aug and Churubusco 20 Aug; served on Armistice Commission 22-23 Aug; entered Mexico City 14 Sept; left for US 28 Dec.

1848    Received hero's welcome in Concord 5 Jan; resumed law practice; again declined Democratic nomination for Governor.

1850    Elected President of State Constitutional Convention; supported Compromise of 1850.

1852    Nominated for President by Democratic National Convention at Baltimore 4 June; election day 2 Nov; Presidential Electors cast their ballots 1 Dec.

1853     Electoral vote tabulated by Congress and Pierce and King officially declared elected President and Vice-President; inaugurated as 14th President of the United States of America 4 March; opened Crystal Palace Exhibition of Industry of All Nations in New York 14 July; sent first State of the Union message to Congress 5 Dec.

1854     Issued proclamation warning against participation in expeditions against Mexico 18 Jan; vetoed Land Grants for Indigent Insane Bill 3 May; signed Kansas-Nebraska Act 30 May; issued proclamation warning against participation in expeditions against Cuba 31 May; vetoed Internal Improvements Bill 4 Aug; directed the Ministers to Great Britain, France and Spain to meet and form a policy regarding Cuba 16 Aug; sent second State of the Union message to Congress 4 Dec.

1855     Signed Act securing rights of citizenship for children born abroad 10 Feb; vetoed French Spoliation Claims Bill 17 Feb; signed Act creating first US Court of Claims 24 Feb; vetoed subsidy for Ocean Mails Bill 3 March; sent third State of the Union message to Congress 3 Dec; issued proclamation warning against participation in expedition against Nicaragua 8 Dec.

1856     Sent special message to Congress recognising the pro-slavery legislature of the Territory of Kansas 24 Jan; issued proclamation warning against unlawful combinations opposing constitutional authorities of Kansas 11 Feb; vetoed Mississippi River and St Clair Flats, Michigan Internal Improvements Bill 19 May; vetoed St Mary's River, Michigan, Internal Improvements Bill 22 May; failed to obtain renomination for Presidency by Democratic National Convention at Cincinnati 2-6 June; vetoed Des Moines Rapids, Michigan Internal Improvements Bill 11 Aug; vetoed Patapsco River, Maryland Internal Improvements Bill 14 Aug (all these last five vetoes were over-ridden); called special session of Congress in unsuccessful attempt to settle Kansas question 19 Aug; sent fourth and last State of the Union message to Congress 2 Dec.

1857     Signed Act declaring foreign coins no longer legal tender in US 21 Feb; signed Tariff Act of 1857 3 March; retired from office and attended the inauguration of his successor James Buchanan 4 March.

1858-59  Toured Europe.

1860-61  Spent winter in Nassau, Bahamas.

1861     Suggested meeting (which never materialized) of five former Presidents in an attempt to avert the Civil War April; although in general opposed to Lincoln's Civil War policies addressed mass meeting in Concord urging people to sustain the Government against the Confederacy 21 April.

1865     Joined the Protestant Episcopal Church.

1868     Suffered severe illness; made last speech at annual meeting of the Society of the Cincinnati in Baltimore.

1869     Died at Concord of inflammation of the stomach 8 Oct; buried there.

# Lineage of President Pierce

THOMAS PIERCE, emigrated from England to Charlestown, Mass 1634-35, *m* Elizabeth Cole, and had issue,

STEPHEN PIERCE, *m* Tabitha, dau of Jacob Parker, by his wife Sarah, and had issue,

STEPHEN PIERCE, *m* Esther, dau of William Fletcher, by his wife Sarah, dau of Josiah Richardson, and had with other issue,

BENJAMIN PIERCE, *m* Elizabeth Merrill, and *d* 1764, leaving issue, with nine other children,

GENERAL BENJAMIN PIERCE, served in the Revolutionary War, mem New Hampshire legislature 1789-1801, Gov New Hampshire 1827-30, Vice-Pres Mass Soc of the Cincinnati, *b* at Chelmsford, Mass 25 Dec 1757, *m* 1st 24 May 1787, Elizabeth Andrews (*b* probably at Hillsborough (now Hillsboro), New Hampshire 1768; *d* 13 Aug 1788), and had issue, one dau (*see* BROTHERS AND SISTERS OF PRESIDENT PIERCE, *p 278*). He *m* 2ndly 1 Feb 1790, Anna (*b* probably at Amherst, New Hampshire 1768; *d* probably at Hillsborough (now Hillsboro), New Hampshire 10 Dec 1838), dau of Benjamin Kendrick, and *d* at Hillsborough (now Hillsboro), New Hampshire 1 April 1839, having by her had, with other issue (*see* BROTHERS AND SISTERS OF PRESIDENT PIERCE, *p 278*), a 4th son,

FRANKLIN PIERCE, **14th President of the United States of America.**

# The Descendants of President Pierce

FRANKLIN PIERCE *m* at Amherst, New Hampshire 19 Nov 1834, Jane Means (*b* at Hampton, New Hampshire 12 March 1806; *d* at Andover, Mass 2 Dec 1863, *bur* at Concord, New Hampshire), dau of Rev Jesse Appleton, a Congregational Min and Pres of Bowdoin Coll, by his wife Elizabeth, dau of Robert Means, and had issue,

> **1** Franklin PIERCE, *b* 2, *d* 5 Feb 1836.
> **2** Frank Robert PIERCE, *b* at Concord, New Hampshire 27 Aug 1839; *d* there of typhus 14 Nov 1843.
> **3** Benjamin PIERCE, *b* at Concord, New Hampshire 13 April 1841; *k* in a train accident nr Andover, Mass 6 Jan 1853.

# The Brothers and Sisters of President Pierce

**A**: HALF-SISTER(*issue of his father's 1st marriage—see p 275*)

1 Elizabeth PIERCE, *b* 13 Aug 1788, *m* 1811, Brig-Gen John McNeil, US Army and *d* 1855, having had issue, two sons (who both *dunm*) and two daus.

**B**: FULL BROTHERS AND SISTERS

2 Benjamin Kendrick PIERCE, Lt-Col 1st US Arty, Col Creek Mounted Vols, *b* 29 Aug 1790, *m* 1st, Josephine La Framboise (*d* 1820), and had issue,
  1 Langdon PIERCE.
  2 Harriet Josephine PIERCE, *b* 1817, *m* 1840, Major-Gen James Brewerton Ricketts, US Army (*b* 1817; *d* 1887), and *d* 1850, leaving issue, one dau (who *m*, and left descendants).
Col Benjamin Kendrick Pierce *m* 2ndly, —; and 3rdly, — Reed, of Newcastle, Delaware, and *d* 1850.
3 Nancy PIERCE, *b* 2 Nov 1792, *m* 1815, Gen Solomon McNeil, and *d* 1837, leaving issue, two sons and one dau.
4 John Sullivan PIERCE, *b* 5 Nov 1796, *m* 1818, Marietta O. (*b* 1802; *d* at Detroit, Michigan 1829), dau of — Putthoff, of Detroit, Michigan, and *d* 1824, leaving issue,
  1 Mary O. PIERCE, *b* 1820, *m* A. B. Warbaugh.
  2 Anne Kendrick PIERCE, *b* 1824, *m* Dr C. E. Parker, of Springfield, Illinois.
5 Harriet B. PIERCE, *b* 1800, *m* 1822, Hugh Jameson.
6 Charles Grandison PIERCE, *b* 1803; *dunm* 1828.
7 Charlotte PIERCE, *d* an inf.
8 Henry Dearborn PIERCE, *b* 19 Sept 1812, *m* 1841, Susan Tuttle (*b* 1815; *d* 1874), and *d* 1880, leaving issue,
  1 Kirk Dearborn PIERCE, *b* 1846, *m* 1879, Mary Ann Collins (*b* 1845), and had issue,
    (1) Susan H. PIERCE, *dunm*.
    (2) Mary Kirk PIERCE, *dunm*.
  2 Frank H. PIERCE, *b* 1848; *dunm*.

# James Buchanan
## 1791-1868

———

15th President of the
United States of America
1857-1861

JAMES BUCHANAN, 15TH PRESIDENT

# James Buchanan

## 1791-1868

### 15th President of the United States of America
### 1857-1861

JAMES BUCHANAN as President was a competent, reasonable man trapped in a crisis which neither his training nor his temperament enabled him to master. By nineteenth-century standards he was extremely well qualified for the office. He was, in common with Andrew Jackson and many other American political leaders, of Scotch–Irish origins—a genetic inheritance that seemed to produce ambition, energy, skill in argument, and a fierce attachment to American democratic nationalism (with, often, a corresponding belief that Great Britain was a corrupt and dangerous hostile power). Again like many American politicians, Buchanan gained his start in life as a lawyer. He was a very successful one, soon earning a substantial income. Since he lived frugally he was able to save money; and through shrewd investment he provided himself with a financial cushion.

His political fortunes were associated with his native state of Pennsylvania. It was one of the most important states of the Union, occupying a key position between North and South. Buchanan thus emerged as a spokesman for domestic harmony, especially over the issue of slavery. In the 1820s he involved himself with Jackson's Democratic party. He rose steadily through the ranks, rarely putting a foot wrong, as member of Congress, in the Senate, and as James K. Polk's Secretary of State. By the 1840s he was a seasoned and respected party chieftain, one of the half-dozen men who were regarded by Democrats as potential Presidents.

Buchanan's claims were strengthened by his interest in foreign policy. He had served as American Minister to Russia, which gave him a chance of foreign travel and some insight into diplomatic protocol. As Secretary of State, and later as Minister to Britain, he followed a consistently expansionist line. His motives in seeking to secure territory in the Pacific Northwest, and south-westward at the expense of Mexico, were genuine enough. Buchanan was a patriot, a "manifest destiny" man anxious to acquire Cuba from Spain. He was convinced that all other governments were inferior to his own. He was suspicious of British activity in Honduras and other parts of Central America. He was also aware, however, that a vigorous foreign policy was politically expedient. "Twisting the lion's tail" went down well with a large section of the American electorate. National pride was stirred by the Oregon settlement with England in 1846, and by the acquisition of a great deal of land, including California, as a result of the war with Mexico. Sectional antagonism over slavery was the main threat to American unity. Buchanan hoped that expansionism would remind Americans, North and South, of their common advantages. And, of course, it would be particularly consoling to the South, since most of the opportunities lay in slaveholding latitudes.

Buchanan's dreams of the White House were frustrated more than once. But he concealed his disappointment with good humor and a display of party loyalty. He had few enemies and a large number of friendly acquaintances, more and more of whom came to owe him political debts. Though he was a bachelor and never renowned for conviviality, he was lucky in having as his hostess an orphaned niece, Harriet Lane, who was ideally equipped. Her charms did much to ensure his social popularity—in London as well as in Washington. By 1856 his party was ready to nominate him. He was sixty-five years old and hardly an exciting choice. Yet that was his appeal. Buchanan was known as a Northerner who regretted the existence of slavery but insisted that it was constitutionally guaranteed. He was judicious. He deplored extravagant or violent language and behaviour, such as that of Northern abolitionists. He would be oil upon troubled waters.

Buchanan honestly tried to be a President for the entire nation, according to his lights. He was on easy terms with such prominent Southerners as Senator Jefferson Davis. He kept the "sacred balance" by giving half his cabinet appointments to Davis and other men from slaveholding states. To judge from the gossip columns, Washington under his Administration was a sparkling city. Miss Lane was only one of several talented hostesses. The visit of the Prince of Wales in 1860 was a universal subject of conversation. With age the President had mellowed into a kind of dignified geniality. His attitudes were well-known, and straight-forward. Secession, he kept on saying, was wrong; but the Union could be held together only if Southern rights were acknowledged. Salvation lay in compromise. In Buchanan's view there was not very much that the national Government, or the President, could or should do to direct events. He believed the powers of the executive branch were limited; and he announced in his inaugural address that Presidents should restrict themselves to one term in office.

The results of these well-meaning, compromising tenets were disastrous. Buchanan's benevolent impartiality failed to appease the South, and appeared to more and more Northerners as cowardice or pro-Southern bias. He was attacked as a "doughface"—a Northern man with Southern principles. The country seemed almost paralyzed in the fatal months between November 1860, when Abraham Lincoln was elected President, and March 1861 when Lincoln was inaugurated. The Deep South seceded, led by South Carolina. Still hoping for peace and reconciliation, Buchanan agonized—and understandably failed to exert an authority he had already insisted he did not possess. The war came. Buchanan supported the Union, and toiled over a book to justify his conduct.

His last years, until his death in 1868, were ignominious; and history has treated him harshly. In truth he was no Jackson or Lincoln. He was something better than a party hack, yet essentially a product of a half-century of American political tradition. He was lucid and worthy, but there was no fire in him. Biographers have suggested that his inner coldness and deadness were revealed by the situation in his early life that impelled his fiancée to break off their engagement; or that there is something significant in the fact that he was nearsighted in one eye and farsighted in the other—and did not realize this until he was in middle age. He could have acted more decisively in the secession crisis if he had been a younger and stronger man. But it is unfair to imply that he or anyone else could have averted secession or war, on terms acceptable to the whole United States. Buchanan was inadequate because the principles on which he had been nurtured were also inadequate as guides to an unprecedented, possibly insoluble, set of problems.

# Chronology

| | |
|---|---|
| 1791 | Born in a log cabin at Stony Batter, nr Mercersburg, Pennsylvania 23 April. |
| 1796 | Family moved into Mercersburg. |
| 1796-1806 | Attended local schools, including Old Stone Academy, Mercersburg. |
| 1807 | Entered Dickinson College, Carlisle, Pennsylvania Sept. |
| 1808 | Expelled from College for disorderly conduct, but later reinstated on the promise of good behavior. |
| 1809 | Graduated with the degree of Bachelor of Arts 27 Sept; studied Law under James Hopkins in Lancaster, Pennsylvania. |
| 1812 | Moved to Elizabethtown, Kentucky, but later returned to Lancaster; admitted to the Pennsylvania Bar in Lancaster 17 Nov. |
| 1813 | Appointed Assistant Prosecutor of Lebanon County, Pennsylvania 20 March. |
| 1814 | Nominated for the State Assembly as a Federalist 24 Aug; joined an unofficial body, Shippen's Company, which marched to Baltimore to offer its services to Major Charles Sterret Ridgely, 3rd Cavalry, following the burning of Washington by the British; elected to the State Assembly Nov. |
| 1815 | Re-elected to State Assembly Oct. |
| 1816 | Retired from State Assembly and resumed law practice in Lancaster in partnership with Molton C. Rogers. |
| 1817 | Degree of Master Mason conferred by Lodge No 43, Lancaster. |
| 1819 | Became engaged to Ann Caroline Coleman, dau of Robert Coleman, a millionaire, but the engagement was broken Dec; Miss Coleman died suddenly (rumored by suicide) in Philadelphia 9 Dec. |
| 1820 | Nominated for the House of Representatives by the Federalists 25 Aug; elected Oct. |
| 1821 | Took seat in the House of Representatives 3 Dec (re-elected four times). |
| 1831 | Appointed US Minister to Russia by President Jackson. |
| 1832 | Sailed for Russia 8 April; arrived in St Petersburg June; treaty of commerce with Russia signed 18 Dec. |
| 1833 | Left Russia 8 Aug; visited Paris and London; arrived in US Nov. |
| 1834 | Elected to the Senate by Pennsylvania Legislature 6 Dec; took seat 15 Dec. |
| 1836 | Re-elected to the Senate Nov. |
| 1837 | Elected Chairman of Senate Foreign Affairs Committee. |

| 1839 | Declined offer of appointment as Attorney-General made by President Van Buren. |
|------|---|
| 1843 | Re-elected to the Senate Jan. |
| 1844 | Declined offer of appointment as Associate Justice made by President Tyler April; defeated in bid for Presidential nomination at Democratic National Convention in Baltimore May. |
| 1845 | Appointed Secretary of State by President Polk; took office 10 March. |
| 1846 | Negotiated Oregon Treaty with Great Britain. |
| 1848 | Defeated in bid for Presidential nomination at Democratic National Convention in Baltimore May. |
| 1849 | Retired to Wheatland, Lancaster, Pennsylvania. |
| 1852 | Again defeated in bid for Presidential nomination at Democratic National Convention in Baltimore June. |
| 1853 | Appointed first President of the Board of Trustees of Franklin and Marshall College, Lancaster; appointed US Minister to Great Britain by President Pierce 11 April; arrived in London 17 Aug. |
| 1854 | Conferred with the Ministers to Spain and France at Ostend, Belgium and framed the Ostend Manifesto, recommending the purchase or annexation of Cuba 9 Oct. |
| 1856 | Returned to US April; nominated for President at the Democratic National Convention in Cincinnati 5 June; election day 4 Nov; Presidential Electors cast their ballots 3 Dec. |
| 1857 | Electoral vote tabulated by Congress and James Buchanan and John Cabell Breckinridge officially declared elected; inaugurated as 15th President of the United States of America 4 March; Panic of 1857 began 24 Aug following failure of the New York branch of the Ohio Life Insurance and Trust Company of Cincinnati; sent first State of the Union message to Congress 8 Dec. |
| 1858 | Issued proclamation declaring Mormon government of Utah in rebellion 6 April; signed English Act 4 May; Minnesota admitted as 32nd State 11 May; exchanged greetings with Queen Victoria by Atlantic cable 16 Aug; sent second State of the Union message to Congress 6 Dec. |
| 1859 | Vetoed Overland Mails Bill 7 Jan; Oregon admitted as 33rd State 14 Feb; vetoed Land Grants for Agricultural Colleges Bill 24 Feb; sent third State of the Union message to Congress 19 Dec. |
| 1860 | Vetoed St Clair Flats, Michigan Internal Improvements Bill 1 Feb; vetoed Mississippi River Internal Improvements Bill 6 Feb; House of Representatives adopted resolution for committee to be set up to investigate the President's conduct 5 March; vetoed relief of A. Edwards and Company Bill 17 April; vetoed Homestead Bill 22 June; sent fourth and last State of the Union message to Congress 3 Dec. |
| 1861 | Vetoed Relief of Hockaday and Legget Bill 25 Jan; Kansas admitted as 34th State 29 Jan; signed Act establishing Territories of Dakota and Nevada 2 March; retired from office and attended the inauguration of his successor Abraham Lincoln 4 March; returned to his home at Wheatland, Lancaster, Pennsylvania 9 March. |

1868    Died at Wheatland of rheumatic gout 1 June; buried at Lancaster, Pennsylvania. He was unmarried (the only bachelor President) and there are thus *no descendants* of President Buchanan.

# The Writings of President Buchanan

*Mr Buchanan's Administration on the Eve of the Rebellion* (1866)

*Works of James Buchanan,* edited by John Bassett Moore, 12 vols (1908-1911)

# Lineage of President Buchanan

This family is a branch of the Scottish Baronial House of BUCHANAN *of that Ilk.*

SIR WALTER BUCHANAN of that Ilk, *m* Isabella, only dau of Murdoch Stewart, Duke of Albany (*d* 1425), and great-grand-dau of Robert II, King of Scots (*see* BURKE'S *Guide to the Royal Family*), and had issue,

THOMAS BUCHANAN, *m*, and had issue,

JOHN BUCHANAN, of Gartincaber, Perthshire, *b* 1545, *m*, and had issue,

GEORGE BUCHANAN, of Gartincaber, *m* Elizabeth Leckie, and had issue,

JOHN BUCHANAN, of Blairlusk, *m*, and had issue,

GEORGE BUCHANAN, went to co Tyrone, Ireland, *b* 1648, *m* Elizabeth Mayne, and had issue,

JOHN BUCHANAN, of co Tyrone, *b* 1676, *m* 1703, Catherine Black, and had issue,

THOMAS BUCHANAN, *m*, and had issue,

JOHN BUCHANAN, of Ramelton, co Donegal, *m* Jane, dau of Samuel Russell, and had issue,

JAMES BUCHANAN, who went to Pennsylvania 1783, *b* at Ramelton, co Donegal, Ireland 1761 or 1762, *m* 16 April 1788, Elizabeth (*b* in Lancaster County, Pennsylvania 1767; *d* at Greensburg, Pennsylvania 14 May 1833), dau of James Speer, by his wife Mary Patterson, and *d* at Mercersburg, Pennsylvania 11 June 1821, having had, with other issue (*see* BROTHERS AND SISTERS OF PRESIDENT BUCHANAN, *p 288*), an eldest son,

JAMES BUCHANAN, **15th President of the United States of America.**

# The Brothers and Sisters of President Buchanan

**1** Mary BUCHANAN, *b* 1789; *d* 1791.

**2** Jane BUCHANAN, *b* 1793, *m* at Mercersburg 1813, Elliott Tole Lane (*b* 1784; *d* 1840), and *d* 1839, having had issue,

  1 James Buchanan LANE, of Lancaster, Pennsylvania, *b* 1814, *m* 1845, Martha Armor (*b* 1820), dau of William Jenkins, by his wife — Hubley, and *d* 1863, having had issue, five sons (three of whom *d* young) and four daus (who all *d* young).

  2 Thomas Newton LANE, *b* 1817; *d* 1835.

  3 Joseph Stark LANE, *b* 1820; *d* 1822.

  4 Elliott Eskridge LANE, of Lancaster, *b* 1823; *dunm* at Washington, DC April 1857.

  5 Mary Elizabeth Speer LANE, *b* 1826, *m* 1848, George Washington Baker, and *dsp* 1855.

  6 Harriet Rebecca LANE, hostess at the White House for her uncle Pres Buchanan 1857-61, founded the Choir Sch of the Cathedral of SS Peter and Paul, Washington, DC, and the Harriet Lane Home for Invalid Children, Johns Hopkins Hosp, Baltimore, Maryland, *b* 1830, *m* at Wheatland, Lancaster, Pennsylvania Jan 1866, Henry Elliott Johnston, of Baltimore, Maryland, banker, and *d* 1906, having had issue, two sons (who both *d* young).

  7 William Edward LANE, *b* 1833; *d* 1834.

**3** Maria BUCHANAN, *b* 1795, *m* 1st, Jesse Magaw, MD, and had issue, one dau. She *m* 2ndly, Thomas Samuel Johnson; and 3rdly, Charles M. Yates, MD, and *d* 1849, leaving further issue, three sons and two daus.

**4** Sarah BUCHANAN, *b* 1798, *m* James J. Huston, and *d* 1825, leaving issue, one dau.

**5** Elizabeth BUCHANAN, *b* 1800; *d* 1801.

**6** Harriet BUCHANAN, *b* at Mercersburg 5 Aug 1802, *m* there 21 May 1832, Rev Robert Henry, Min of Greensburg Presbyterian Church, Greensburg, Pennsylvania (*b* in Allegheny County, Pennsylvania 9 June 1801; *d* at Greensburg Nov 1838), son of John Henry, of Allegheny County, Pennsylvania (*see* BURKE'S *Distinguished Families of America*), by his wife Margaret McMillan, and *d* at Greensburg 23 Jan 1840, having had issue,

  1 James Buchanan HENRY, priv sec to his uncle Pres Buchanan, later Assist US Attorney for S Dist of New York, *b* at Greensburg 1 March 1833, *m* 1st 1859, Mary Hagner (*b* 1837; *d* 1863), dau of Joseph H. Nicholson, of Annapolis, Maryland, and had issue,

    (1) Buchanan HENRY, *b* 1860; *d* 1862.

    (2) Joseph Nicholson HENRY, MD, Major and Surg US Vols, *b* 1862, *m* 1890, Alice, widow of — Truehart, and dau of Rev Thomas A. Hoyt, DD, of Philadelphia, and *dsp* 1904.

James Buchanan Henry *m* 2ndly 18 Dec 1872, Louisa (*b* 3 June 1848; *d* 10 March 1886), dau of Dr William Astley Cooper Anderson, of Staten Island, New York, by his wife Louisa Morgan, and by her had issue,

    (3) William Cooper Anderson HENRY, railroad engr, Gen Supt of motive power, Pennsylvania System SW Regn, *b* at Staten Island, New York 1873, *m* at Atlanta, Georgia 16 Oct 1906, Mary Lamar (*b* at Woodville Plantation, Milledgeville, Georgia 1881; *d* at Atlanta, Georgia 19 Feb 1972), dau of Fleming Grantland du Bignon, of Savannah, Georgia, by his wife Caro Nicoll Lamar, and *d* at Tryon, N Carolina 8 Dec 1943, leaving issue,

     1*a* ● William Anderson HENRY, with du Pont Co [*3213 Fordham Road, Wilmington 19807, Delaware, USA*], *b* at Columbus, Ohio 17 April 1908, *m* 24 Sept 1937, ● Bessie Agens (*b* at Louviers, Colorado 9 June 1910), dau of Edward Washburn Maynard, by his wife Harriet Ledair Harrington, and has issue,

      1*b* ● Mary du Bignon HENRY, *b* at Wilmington, Delaware 7 Nov 1938, *m* there 20 Sept 1959, ● Stephen Richard Lyne (*b* at Fall River, Mass 20 May 1935), and has issue,

       1*c* ● Deborah Elizabeth LYNE, *b* at Alexandria, Virginia 13 Sept 1961.

       2*c* ● Richard James LYNE, *b* at Bangkok, Thailand 20 Aug 1963.

      2*b* ● Elizabeth Maynard HENRY, *b* at Wilmington, Delaware 6 Feb 1940, *m* there 20 Aug 1966, ● David Zachariah Walley, Jr (*b* at Chattanooga, Tennessee 24 May 1938), and has issue,

       1*c* ● David Zachariah WALLEY III, *b* at Chattanooga, Tennessee 15 Sept 1969.

       2*c* ● Edward Harrington WALLEY, *b* at Chattanooga, Tennessee 1 March 1971.

     2*a* ● Caro du Bignon HENRY, *b* at Columbus, Ohio 8 Nov 1909, *m* at Atlanta, Georgia 23 Oct 1930, ● Albert Howell, architect (*b* at Atlanta, Georgia 27 Sept 1904) [*601 Peachtree Battle Road NW, Atlanta, Georgia, USA*], son of Clark Howell, by his wife Annie Comer, and has issue,

      ● Henry Lamar HOWELL, banker [*2492 Habersham Road, Atlanta, Georgia 30305, USA*], *b* at Atlanta 11 Feb 1938, *m* at New Haven, Connecticut 29 June 1963, ● Stephanie Southgate (*b* at New Haven 2 March 1939), dau of William Huse Dunham, by his wife Helen Garrison, and has issue,

       1*c* ● Helen Garrison HOWELL, *b* at Atlanta, Georgia 9 Nov 1966.

       2*c* ● Catherine Caro HOWELL, *b* at Atlanta 24 July 1970.

    (4) James Buchanan HENRY, Jr, of Tucson, Arizona, Ensign USN, Lt-Col 12th US Cav, *b* 1875, *m* 1904, Mary Catherine, dau of Major R. W. McClaughry, of Leavenworth, Kansas, and *d* 1948, leaving issue,

     1*a* ● Elizabeth McClaughry HENRY, *b* 1905, *m* 1st 1939, Paul Gad; and 2ndly 1956, ● Henry H. Bruhn, mining engr [*Tucson, Arizona, USA*].

     2*a* ● James Buchanan HENRY III, lawyer, served as Capt and Adjt 93rd Engrs in World War II [*86 Prospect Avenue, Montclair, New Jersey 07042, USA*], *b* 1919, *m* 1945, ● Eleanor McNeill (*née* Nixon), and has issue,

      1*b* ● James Buchanan HENRY IV, *b* 1949.

      2*b* ● Mary Catherine HENRY, *b* 1949 (twin with her brother James Buchanan Henry IV).

      3*b* ● Elizabeth Eleanor HENRY, *b* 1952.

    (5) Robert Edward HENRY, of Sentinel Pines, Hague, Lake George, New York, Pres Assoc Industrials Corpn, partner in Hallowell & Henry, New York City, *b* at

Stapleton, Staten Island, New York 12 June 1877, *m* at Fort Hamilton, Brooklyn, New York 26 Oct 1904, Virginia Bell (*b* at St John's Place, Brooklyn, New York 17 Aug 1877; *d* at Sentinel Pines 8 July 1956), dau of John R. Tolar, of Fayetteville, N Carolina, by his wife Ella Bell, and *d* 22 Feb 1943, leaving issue,

1*a* Robert Edward HENRY, Jr, securities analyst with Foster & Adams, New York City, *b* 28 Feb 1906, *educ* Yale (AB), and Harvard Business Sch (MBA), *m* at Lake George, New York 25 June 1930, ●Hester Makepeace (*b* at Santa Ana, California 21 July 1911), dau of Sidney Homer, by his wife Louise Beatty, and *d* 1973, leaving issue,

1*b* ●Virginia Tolar HENRY, *b* at New York City 11 Jan 1932, *m* 1st 1957, Jon Van Winkle, son of John R. Van Winkle, by his wife Margaret, and has issue,

1*c* ●Geoffrey VAN WINKLE, *b* at Schenectady, New York 4 Nov 1958.

Virginia Tolar Henry *m* 2ndly 1960, ●John Aldrich Achey (*b* at Santa Ana, California 21 July 1928), son of Arthur C. Achey, by his wife Linda Cox, and has further issue,

2*c* ●John Stephen ACHEY, *b* at Berkeley, California 9 Nov 1960.

3*c* ●Linda Katherine ACHEY, *b* at Flushing, New York City 15 Jan 1963.

4*c* ●James Sidney ACHEY, *b* at Princeton, New Jersey 29 Feb 1964.

2*b* ●Louise Homer HENRY, *b* at New York City 27 April 1934, *m* at Ticonderoga, New York 7 Dec 1958, ●John Sherman Beekley, Jr (*b* at Charleston, W Virginia 31 Aug 1931) [*c/o Wilmington Trust Co, Wilmington, Delaware 19899, USA*], son of John Sherman Beekley, by his wife Louise Tatnall, and has issue,

1*c* ●Louise Homer BEEKLEY, *b* at Wilmington, Delaware 27 Sept 1959.

2*c* ●John Sherman BEEKLEY III, *b* at Hagerstown, Maryland 10 March 1961.

3*c* ●Robert Edward Henry BEEKLEY, *b* at Hagerstown, Maryland 27 July 1963.

3*b* ●Hester Makepeace HENRY, *b* at New York City 26 April 1938.

4*b* ●Julia Morgan HENRY, *b* at New York City 9 Jan 1948, *m* at Hague, New York 28 June 1969, ●Kenneth Joseph McPartlin (*b* at Joliet, Illinois 21 May 1947), son of Arthur Robert McPartlin, by his wife Helen Jean Garrett.

2*a* ●John Tolar HENRY, Vice-Pres and Gen Man of Tolar Hart & Holt Mills, Fayetteville, N Carolina, Analyst CIA, Washington, DC [*Viewpoint, Hague, Lake George, New York, USA; 5013 Browner Street, McLean, Virginia 22101, USA*], *b* at New York City 6 Oct 1913, *educ* Virginia Univ, *m* 1st at Rye, New York 29 June 1937, Priscilla Abele, dau of Henry C. Speers, by his wife Lillian Palmer. He *m* 2ndly at Ticonderoga, New York 30 June 1945, ●Dorothy Jane, dau of Ernest Wilbur Byer, by his wife Mary Elizabeth Dickson, and by her has issue,

1*b* ●John Robert HENRY, USN, *b* at Ticonderoga 4 Dec 1947, *m* 1st at Detroit, Michigan 27 Oct 1967 (*m* diss by div), Geraldine McCabe (*b* 2 Nov 1946), and has issue,

1*c* ●Lisa Jane HENRY, *b* at Port Deposit, Maryland 10 Sept 1968.

2*c* ●Jennifer Lynn HENRY, *b* at Ceba, Puerto Rico 2 Oct 1971.

John Robert Henry *m* 2ndly at Ceba, Puerto Rico 17 March 1974, ●Nellita Tomàs (*b* at Luquillo, Puerto Rico 19 March 1947).

2*b* ●Mary Virginia HENRY, *b* at Ticonderoga 6 Feb 1949.

3*b* ●Edward Anderson HENRY, *b* at Arlington, Virginia 13 June 1952.

(6) Sidney Morgan HENRY, of New York City, Capt Construction Corps USN, Vice-Pres Balto Dry Docks and Ship Building Co, Vice-Pres US Shipping Bd EFC, Vice-Pres Munson SS Line, *b* at Staten Island, New York 2 Dec 1878, *educ* Georgetown Univ, US Naval Acad, Annapolis, and Mass Inst of Technology, *m* at Mare Island, California 11 Sept 1907, Julia Barnett (*b* at Opelika,

Alabama 15 March 1888; *d* at Lake George, New York 24 Sept 1933), dau of Cmdre Remus Charles Persons, Med Dir USN, by his wife Susan Barnett, and *d* at Tucson, Arizona 16 March 1959, having had issue,

1*a* ●Sidney Morgan HENRY, Jr, with American-Hawaiian SS Co, New York 1935-41, Assist to Financial Vice-Pres 1935-41, served in USN 1941-45 (Lt.-Cmdr), Assist Treas, Treas, and Assist Sec of American-Hawaiian SS Co 1945-55, Assist Treas and Assist Sec of Transport, Trading and Terminal Corpn 1945-55, Dir 1954-55, Investment Management at Brown Bros, Harriman and Co, New York 1955-61, partner in Farley Assocs, New York from 1960, Vice-Pres and Dir E. I. Farley and Co, New York from 1960, mem Maritime Assocs (Pres 1939-41), mem Church Club Bd, mem and Treas Windham Children's Service 1950-55 [*520 East 86th Street, New York, New York, USA*], *b* at San Francisco 13 Aug 1908, *educ* St Albans Sch, Yale (BA 1930), and Harvard (MBA 1932), *m* at New York 19 June 1948, ●Mrs Olivia Ames Pool (*b* at Milton, Mass 26 Nov 1917), dau of R. Dudley Peters, by his wife Ruth Sumner Draper, and has issue,

1*b* ●Olivia Peters HENRY, *b* at New York 29 June 1950.

2*b* ●Sidney Morgan HENRY III, *b* at New York 30 Jan 1953.

2*a* Julia Persons HENRY, *b* 24 Nov 1909, *d* 26 June 1911.

(7) Reginald Buchanan HENRY, MD, of Norfolk, Virginia, Capt MC USN, compiler of *Genealogies of the Families of the Presidents* (1935), *b* at Long Island, New York 1881, *m* at Norfolk, Virginia 1918, ●Jane Byrd [*616 Redgate Avenue, Norfolk, Virginia 23507, USA*], dau of Edmund Sumter Ruffin, of Norfolk, Virginia, by his wife Cordelia Byrd, and *d* 1969, leaving issue,

1*a* ●Evelyn Byrd HENRY, *b* 1919, *m* 1946, ●George Harris Sargeant, Jr [*52 Post Street, Newport News, Virginia, USA*], son of George Harris Sargeant, and has issue,

1*b* ●Evelyn Byrd SARGEANT, *b* 1948, *m* 1973, ●Lt-Col Paul Churchill Hutton, Jr, US Army.

2*b* ●Jane Byrd SARGEANT, *b* 1949, *m* 1973, ●Ian Arrison McCurdy [*Cold Spring Harbor, Long Island, New York, USA*], and has issue,

●Peter Johnston McCURDY, *b* 1974.

3*b* ●Louisa Morgan SARGEANT, *b* 1954.

2*a* ●Reginald Buchanan HENRY, Jr, MD, Lt-Cmdr MC USNR [*1350 W Princess Anne Road, Norfolk, Virginia 23507, USA*], *b* 1926, *m* 1st 1945, Ruth McAfee, of Cincinnati, Ohio (*d* 1966), and has issue,

1*b* ●Reginald Buchanan HENRY III, *b* 1956.

2*b* ●Elizabeth Davidson HENRY, *b* 1958.

Dr Reginald B. Henry *m* 2ndly, ●Barbara Anne Dix (*b* 1932), and by her has issue,

3*b* ●Edmund Ruffin HENRY, *b* 1969.

4*b* ●Thomas Dix HENRY, *b* 1971.

(8) Frank Anderson HENRY, US Consul at Valparaiso, Chile, Nassau, Bahamas, Melbourne, Australia, Malta, and Port Elizabeth, S Africa, *b* at Garden City, Long Island, New York 1883, *m* at Tenerife, Canary Islands 1921, Gladys (*b* at Cork, Ireland 1882; *d* at Nutley, Sussex, England 1959), widow of Richard Martin, and dau of Robert Allen, of Jersey, Channel Islands, by his wife Alica Townsend, and *d* at Nutley, Sussex, England 1967, leaving issue,

●Pamela Joan HENRY [*The Laurels, Nutley, Uckfield, Sussex, England*], *b* at Barcelona, Spain June 1923.

James Buchanan Henry *m* 3rdly 1904, Margaret Grote, dau of Henry B. Elliman, of New York City, and *d* at Cocoanut Grove, Florida 17 Feb 1915.

2 Jane Elliott HENRY, *b* and *d* 1836.

**7** John BUCHANAN, *b* and *d* 1804.

**8** William Speer BUCHANAN, *b* 1805; *dunm* 1826.

**9** George Washington BUCHANAN, US Attorney for W Dist of Pennsylvania at age of 22, *b* 1808; *dunm* 1832.

**10** Edward Young BUCHANAN (Rev), DD, Rector of Trin (Episcopal) Church, Oxford, Philadelphia, *b* 1811, *m* 1833, Ann Eliza Foster, sister of Stephen C. Foster, the poet and composer, and *d* 1895, having had issue,

1 James BUCHANAN, priv sec to his uncle Pres Buchanan, *b* 1834, *m* 1868, Florence Myers, and *dsp* 1871.

2 Charlotte Foster BUCHANAN, *b* 1836; *d* 1850.

3 Ann Elizabeth Speer BUCHANAN, *b* 1838; *dunm* 1927.
4 Harriet BUCHANAN, *b* 1841; *dunm* 1912.
5 Edward Young BUCHANAN, Jr, of San Francisco, civil engr, *b* 1843, *m* 1870, Agnes Scott, and *d* 1927, leaving issue,
　(1) James BUCHANAN, *dunm*.
　(2) Agnes Foster BUCHANAN, *m* 1908, Daniel Crosby, MD, and *dsp* 1924.
　(3) Henrietta Jane BUCHANAN, *dunm* 1894.
6 Henrietta Jane BUCHANAN, *b* 1844; *dunm* 1906.
7 Maria Lois BUCHANAN, *b* 1847, *m* Alexander Johnston Cassatt, Pres of Pennsylvania Railroad Co (*b* 1839; *d* 1906), and *d* 1920, having had issue,
　(1) Edward Buchanan CASSATT, Capt 13th US Cav, Lt-Col US Army, sometime US Mil Attaché in London, *b* 1869, *m* 1st, Emily Louise Phillips, and had issue,
　　1*a*●Lois Buchanan CASSATT, *m* 1917, ●John Borland Thayer III [*103 Airdale Road, Rosemont, Pennsylvania, USA*], son of John Borland Thayer, Jr, and has had issue,
　　　1*b*●John Borland THAYER IV, *b* 1918, *m* 1942, ●Charlotte Rush Toland and has issue,
　　　　1*c*●Lois Cassatt THAYER, *b* 1943.
　　　　2*c*●John Borland THAYER V, *b* 1946.
　　　　3*c*●Emily B. THAYER, *b* 1953.
　　　　4*c*●Edward Dale THAYER, *b* 1955.
　　　2*b* Alexander Johnson Cassatt THAYER, *b* and *d* 1919.
　　　3*b* Edward Cassatt THAYER, Lieut USAF, served in World War II, *b* 1920; lost in action over the Pacific 1943.
　　　4*b*●Lois THAYER, *b* 1923, *m* 1945, ●William West Frazier, Jr, son of William West Frazier, and has issue,
　　　　1*c*●Lois FRAZIER, *b* 1946.
　　　　2*c*●William West FRAZIER III, *b* 1949.
　　　5*b*●Julie THAYER, *b* 1928, *m* 1953, ●C. Oliver Iselin III [*Fiddler's Green, Middlebury, Virginia, USA*], son of C. Oliver Iselin, Jr, and has issue,
　　　　●Julie ISELIN, *b* 1958.
　　　6*b*●Pauline THAYER, *b* 1930, *m* 1954, ●James Robert Maguire, lawyer, and has issue,
　　　　1*c*●James Robert MAGUIRE, *b* 1955.
　　　　2*c*●Pauline Thayer MAGUIRE, *b* 1956.
　　　　3*c*●George E. B. MAGUIRE, *b* 1958.
　Col Edward Buchanan Cassatt *m* 2ndly, Eleanor Blackford Smith, of Virginia, and *d* 1922, having by her had issue,
　　2*a* Edward Buchanan CASSATT, *b* 1910, and *d* 1911.
　(2) Katherine Kelso Johnston CASSATT, *b* 1871, *m* 1903, James Pemberton Hutchinson, MD, of Philadelphia, and *dsp* 1905.
　(3) Robert Kelso CASSATT, banker, partner in Cassatt & Co, Philadelphia, *b* 1873, *m* 1900, Minnie Drexel Fell (*d* 1955), dau and *d* 1944, having had issue,
　　1*a* Sarah D. CASSATT, *d* an inf.
　　2*a*●Alexander Johnston CASSATT [*304 Windsor Avenue, Wayne, Pennsylvania, USA*], *b* 1904, *m* 1st 1928, Cassandra Morris, dau of — Stewart, of Baltimore, Maryland, and has issue,
　　　1*b*●Robert Kelso CASSATT [*Brooksville, Maine, USA*], *b* 1929, *m* 1954, ●Sheila Simpson, and has issue,
　　　　1*c*●Lydia S. CASSATT.
　　　　2*c*●Sheila S. CASSATT.
　　　2*b*●Alexander Johnston CASSATT, *b* 1933.
　　　3*b*●Cassandra CASSATT, *b* 1939.
　　Alexander Johnston Cassatt *m* 2ndly, ●Leona E. Burns.
　　3*a*●Anthony Drexel CASSATT [ *c/o Guaranty Trading Co, 14 Place Vendôme, Paris, France*], *m* 1930, ●Madeleine, widow of — Randolph, and dau of — Cochrane, and has issue,
　　　●Minnie Fell CASSATT, *b* 1931, *m* 1953, ●Daniel Willis James.
　(4) Eliza Foster CASSATT, *b* 1875, *m* 1902, William Plunket Stewart, of Baltimore, Maryland, and *d* 1931, having had issue,
　　1*a* Alexander Johnston Cassatt STEWART, *b* 1903; *d* 1912.
　　2*a*●Katherine Kelso STEWART, *b* at Bar Harbor, Maine

13 July 1905, *m* 1932, Vicomte Eric Antoine Ghislain Joseph de Spoelberch (*b* at Brussels, Belgium 15 Feb 1903; *d* at Nivelles, Belgium 27 Jan 1939), yr son of Vicomte Guillaume de Spoelberch, by his wife Colienne de Neufforge, and has issue,
　　　1*b*●Vicomte Guillaume DE SPOELBERCH, *b* at Brussels 28 March 1933.
　　　2*b*●Vicomte Jacques DE SPOELBERCH, *b* at Brussels 8 June 1936.
　　3*a*●Doris Lurman STEWART, *b* 1910, *m* 1931, ●William Potter Wear [*Enterprise, Cecilton, Maryland, USA*], and has had issue,
　　　1*b*●Elsie Cassatt WEAR, *b* 1933, *m* 1952, ●James Stockwell.
　　　2*b*●Joseph WEAR, *b* 1935.
　　　3*b*●Nancy Holliday WEAR, *b* 1937, *m* 1960, ●Frank Lyon Polk, Jr.
　　　4*b* A son, *b* and *d* 1939.
　　　5*b*●Priscilla Stewart WEAR, *b* 1940.
　　　6*b*●Adeline Potter WEAR [*1720 Pine Street, Philadelphia, Pennsylvania, USA*], *b* 1942.
　　4*a*●Elsie Cassatt STEWART, *b* 1915, *m* 1944, ●Thomas F. Simmons.
8 William Foster BUCHANAN, *b* 1849; *dunm* 1875.
9 Ridley BUCHANAN, *b* and *d* 1851.
10 Alice Conyngham BUCHANAN, *b* 1853, *m* 1876, Maskell Ewing, of Philadelphia (*b* 1847; *d* 1931), and *d* 1931, having had issue,
　(1) Cornelia Lansdale EWING, *b* 1877, *m* 1898, Robert E. Brooke, of Brooke Manor, Birdsboro, Pennsylvania (*d* 1942), and had issue,
　　1*a*●Robert Clymer BROOKE [*6 Wakefield Drive, St Louis, Missouri, USA*], *b* 1898, *m* 1st 1925, Virginia Lafayette, dau of — Blair, of Washington, DC, and has issue,
　　　1*b*●Virginia Blair BROOKE, *b* 1927, *m* 1949, ●Nathaniel Ramsay Pennypacker [*915 Sorrel Lane, Bryn Mawr, Pennsylvania, USA*], and has issue,
　　　　●D. Ramsay PENNYPACKER.
　　　2*b*●Robert Clymer BROOKE, Jr, *b* 1929, *m* ●Ellen —, and has issue.
　　Robert Clymer Brooke *m* 2ndly, ●Miriam Clymer.
　　2*a*●Maskell Ewing BROOKE, *b* 1903.
　　3*a*●John Louis Barde BROOKE [*Ludlow Cottage, Lenox, Mass, USA*], *b* 1906, *m* 1946, ●Louisa Geary Ludlow, and has issue,
　　　1*b*●Louisa G. BROOKE [*235 West 76th Street, New York, New York, USA*].
　　　2*b*●Cornelia E. BROOKE [*71 Old Niskayuna Road, Loudonville, New York, USA*].
　　　3*b*●John L. BROOKE, *educ* Cornell.
　　　4*b*●James B. BROOKE, *educ* St Paul's Sch.
　　4*a*●Cornelia Lansdale BROOKE, *b* 1912, *m* 1940, ●Charles Donnell Marshall, Jr [*Laurel Locks Farm, Pottstown, Pennsylvania, USA*], son of Charles Donnell Marshall, and has issue,
　　　1*b*●Charles Noble MARSHALL, *b* 1942.
　　　2*b*●Alice Brooke MARSHALL, *b* 1944.
　　　3*b*●Eliza Phipps MARSHALL [*500 East 86th Street, New York, New York, USA*].
　(2) Alice Buchanan EWING, artist, *b* 1879; *dunm*.
　(3) Anne Foster EWING, *b* 1880; *dunm* 1909.
　(4) Lois Buchanan EWING, *b* and *d* 1884.
　(5) Maskell EWING, Jr, of Philadelphia, lawyer, served in World War I as Lieut US Army, *b* 1885; *dunm* 1938.
　(6) Buchanan EWING, civil engr, *b* 1887, *m* 1915, Belinda Meeks, and *d* 1930, leaving issue,
　　1*a*●Helen EWING, *b* 1916, *m* 1938, ●Richard Rundle Pleasants, and has issue,
　　　1*b*●Belinda PLEASANTS, *b* 1941.
　　　2*b*●Elizabeth PLEASANTS.
　　2*a*●Buchanan EWING, Jr, *b* 1917, *m* 1941, ●Gretchen Winifred Wunder, and has had issue,
　　　1*b*●Buchanan EWING III, *b* 1942.
　　　2*b* Timothy Wunder EWING, *d* an inf.
　　3*a*●James Hunter EWING, *b* 1920.
　　4*a*●Edward Buchanan EWING, *b* 1921.

# Abraham Lincoln
## 1809-1865

---

16th President of the
United States of America
1861-1865

ABRAHAM LINCOLN, 16TH PRESIDENT

# Abraham Lincoln

## 1809-1865

### 16th President of the United States of America
### 1861-1865

THERE IS general agreement that Lincoln is among the greatest of America's Presidents. Some would put him at the top of the list, perhaps in company with George Washington. Yet when he was elected in 1860 Abraham Lincoln had not emerged as a leader of national quality. He had served one unspectacular term in Congress. Unlike several of the other contenders for a presidential nomination in 1860, he had never been in the Senate or won election as Governor of a state. In his own Republican party, William H. Seward of New York seemed to many (including Seward) a better candidate. Lincoln was a sectional President; not a single vote came to him from the Southern States that were to form the Confederacy. He was a minority President, having won only 40% of the national popular vote. And he was seen as a failure or a villain by large numbers of people, North and South, during his entire span of office. Cartoonists and journalists derided him as vulgar, ungainly, facetious—a sallow wrinkled man, ill-proportioned and much too tall to match his plump, pretentious little wife. As late as 1864 James Gordon Bennett of the New York *Herald* wrote: "President Lincoln is a joke incarnated. . . . The idea that such a man as he should be the President of such a country as this is a very ridiculous joke. . . . His début in Washington society was a joke; for he introduced himself and Mrs Lincoln as 'the long and short of the Presidency'. . . . His conversation is full of jokes. . . . His title of 'Honest' is a satirical joke". His famous Gettysburg Address was criticized at the time as being perfunctorily brief. Radicals in his own party grumbled that Lincoln was feeble and indecisive—and possibly even pro-Southern, for after all he had been born in Kentucky, and several members of his wife's family had sided with the Confederacy. Others complained that, out of ignorance or conceit, he had vastly exceeded the powers given him by the Constitution. There was a move to deny him renomination in 1864. Though he was re-elected (with 55% of the popular vote), Lincoln himself had gloomy forebodings that he might be beaten.

Why then does his reputation stand so high? Part of the answer, no doubt, is the pathos of his death in the moment of victory. Assassination made him a martyr (on Good Friday, 1865). The Union's triumph over the South suggested that "Honest Abe" must have been a much more effective statesman than his detractors realized. If Booth's pistol had misfired, Lincoln might well have run into serious trouble, as his successor Andrew Johnson did, over post-war Reconstruction policies. Instead he was suddenly removed; and his brutal murder assumed the stature of a classical tragedy. Some commentators passed overnight from mockery to reverence. The London *Punch*, which had caricatured Lincoln as heartless and moronic, confessed its error in a memorial poem. Their imaginary lout was metamorphosed into a "prince".

Was the prince also imaginary? Certainly Lincoln was no plaster saint. He was a poor boy who had come up the hard way, in the tussling, jocular world of Illinois politics and county courts. The thrust of his own will propelled him; or as his law partner William Herndon put it, Lincoln's ambition was "a little engine that knew no rest". Nor was he a crusading abolitionist. Historians have argued that he was anti-slavery because he wanted the West to be a land of opportunity for the white man, and so hoped to exclude the Negro—slave or free. In 1862 he told a visiting delegation that the best solution would be to return the blacks to Africa. He showed a good deal of hesitation, especially in his first year as President. If what the United States needed was a figure of Napoleonic assurance, as was often said, then Abe Lincoln was hardly the man. "I claim not to have controlled events", he told a correspondent in 1864, "but confess plainly that events have controlled me".

These reservations, however, overlook the appalling difficulties he faced, and the peculiar genius of what the novelist Nathaniel Hawthorne called "this . . . grave, quaint man". In the four months between his election and his inauguration the Deep South seceded and the states of the upper South hung in the balance. If he used force against the infant Confederacy he would drive Virginia and other key states out of the Union. If he allowed the Confederacy to "depart in peace" he would display fatal weakness. But if he brought on a war, how could it be fought? Union military capacity was feeble. Lincoln himself had no experience of war, except for a few weeks of semi-farcical militia mustering against the Indians in 1832. At the outset there was no definite war-aim on which the Union could agree, other than the preservation of the Union. The abolition of slavery was as yet a divisive, not a unifying proposal. And even if Lincoln had possessed a dictatorial temperament, the nation was not accustomed to the idea of a forceful, overriding federal authority. The

MARY TODD, MRS LINCOLN

Whig party in which he grew up had insisted that the Presidency ought not to be entrusted with such power.

So a man of apparently middling ability was thrust into a nightmare for which no amount of previous American training could have adequately prepared him. Perhaps this is the essential clue to understanding Lincoln. He was in the dark, but in company with everyone else. Having few rules to go upon, he was obliged to make them up as he went along. The situation put a premium on common sense, and on a feel for the basic American values. These Lincoln in fact embodied with supreme instinctual skill, decency and wry humor. His background stood him in extraordinarily good stead. He knew how to spot the differences between effective men or policies and foolish ones. He developed his talents, under the fearful stress of the war years—encouraging the timid, deflating the arrogant, compromising where necessary, or standing firm, according to circumstance. Perceptive Americans gradually realized how much of themselves he embodied, and yet transcended. He was shrewd but not devious. Profoundly civilian, he displayed a better grasp of the principles of war than several of his commanders. Kind to the verge of softness—for example in pardoning deserters—Lincoln could be a tough taskmaster for generals reluctant to fight. He never pretended that he had all the answers; but he had a rare gift for discerning what were the important questions, and for phrasing them in some homely, succinct metaphor. More than that: as in the Gettysburg Address or in his Second Inaugural speech, Lincoln revealed a felicity of language that any writer might envy and that no President has surpassed. He was, in all these respects, the plain man transfigured, the American democrat raised to glory.

# Chronology

1809    Born in a log cabin at Sinking Spring Farm, near Hodgenville, Hardin County (now Larne County), Kentucky 12 Feb.

1811    Family moved to Knob Creek, Kentucky.

1816    Family moved to Indiana.

1826    Worked on James Taylor's ferry on the Anderson River.

1828    Built a boat and took a cargo of produce to New Orleans, where he sold it and the boat and returned home by steamboat.

1830    Family moved to Illinois.

1831    Made second trip to New Orleans; moved to New Salem Sept.

1832    Decided to run for State legislature March; volunteered for military service in Black Hawk War 21 April; sworn into service 9 May; mustered out 10 July; defeated as candidate for State legislature 6 Aug; bought a half interest in a general store at New Salem.

1833    Partnership in general store dissolved March; appointed Postmaster of New Salem 7 May; began work as deputy to the County Surveyor autumn.

1834    Elected to the State legislature 4 Aug; began study of Law; took seat in legislature at Vandalia, then capital of Illinois Dec.

1836    Appointment as Postmaster terminated on removal of the Post Office to Petersburg 30 May; re-elected to State legislature 1 Aug; licensed to practice law 9 Sept; served as Whig floor leader in Tenth General Assembly, Vandalia 5 Dec.

1837    Moved from New Salem to Springfield 15 April; went into law partnership with John T. Stuart.

1838    Re-elected to State legislature 5 Aug; legislature met for last time at Vandalia Dec.

1839    Springfield became new capital of Illinois 4 July.

1840    Re-elected for fourth term to State legislature.

1841    Dissolved law partnership with John T. Stuart and entered into partnership with Stephen L. Long.

1843    Failed to obtain Whig nomination as candidate for the House of Representatives May.

1844    Dissolved law partnership with Stephen L. Long and entered into partnership with William H. Herndon, which remained in effect until his death.

1846    Nominated for the House of Representatives by the Whig State Convention at Petersburg 1 May; elected 3 Aug.

| | |
|---|---|
| 1847 | Took seat in House of Representatives 6 Dec. |
| 1848 | Attended Whig National Convention at Philadelphia 7-9 June and supported Zachary Taylor; campaigned for Taylor Aug-Nov. |
| 1849 | Applied for and received a patent for "an improved method of lifting vessels over shoals" by means of "adjustable buoyant chambers"; retired from the House of Representatives and resumed law practice in Springfield April; declined appointments as Secretary and Governor of Oregon Territory. |
| 1854 | Re-entered politics; elected to fifth term in State legislature 7 Nov. |
| 1855 | Defeated as candidate for the Senate 8 Feb. |
| 1855-56 | Resumed law practice in Springfield. |
| 1856 | Failed to obtain nomination for Vice-President at first Republican National Convention in Philadelphia June. |
| 1858 | Unanimously nominated for the Senate by Republican State Convention at Springfield 16 June; debated with Senator Stephen Arnold Douglas 21 Aug-15 Oct. |
| 1859 | Defeated as candidate for the Senate by Douglas 5 Jan; toured Midwest Aug and Kansas Nov-Dec. |
| 1860 | Toured New England March-April; nominated for President by Republican National Convention at Chicago 18 May; election day 6 Nov; Presidential Electors cast their ballots 5 Dec. |
| 1861 | Electoral vote tabulated by Congress and Lincoln and Hannibal Hamlin officially declared elected President and Vice-President 13 Feb; inaugurated as 16th President of the United States of America 4 March; Fort Sumter attacked 12 April and surrendered 13 April; issued proclamation declaring that a state of insurrection existed and calling on the States to supply 75,000 militia 15 April; issued proclamation ordering blockade of all ports of seceded States 19 April (extended by further proclamation to ports of North Carolina and Virginia 27 April); called for 42,000 volunteers to increase Army and Navy 3 May; declared martial law and suspension of writ of *habeas corpus* on Key West, Tortugas and Santa Rosa islands 10 May; presided at Council of War 29 June; sent war message to Congress 4 July; Confederates won first Battle of Bull Run 21 July; authorized to call out militia to suppress rebellion 29 July; signed Income Tax Act 5 Aug; signed Confiscation Act 6 Aug; issued proclamation forbidding commerce with the seceded States 16 Aug; sent first State of the Union message to Congress 3 Dec. |
| 1862 | Issued War Order No 1 27 Jan; authorized to take possession of railroads and telegraph lines when public safety involved 31 Jan; signed Legal Tender Act 25 Feb; sent special message to Congress recommending compensation for emancipation of slaves in States adopting gradual abolition 6 March (adopted by joint resolution 10 April); Union won Battle of Shiloh 6-7 April; signed Act abolishing slavery in the District of Columbia 16 April; Department of Agriculture established 15 May; signed Homestead Act 20 May; authorized to appoint diplomatic representatives to Negro republics of Haiti and Liberia 5 June; signed Act prohibiting slavery in US Territories 19 June; vetoed bank notes in District of Columbia bill 23 June; signed Act providing for railroad and telegraph lines from Missouri River to the Pacific Coast and Act establishing office of Commissioner of Internal Revenue 1 July; issued proclamation calling for 300,000 volunteers for three-year service 2 July; vetoed Medical Offices in |

Army Bill 2 July; signed Morrill Act 2 July; authorized to call up militia between ages of 18 and 45, admit Negroes to military service, appoint Judge-Advocate Gen, and organize Army corps at his discretion 17 July; issued call for 300,000 militia for nine-month service 4 Aug; Confederates won Battle of Cedar Mountain 9 Aug; Union troops forced to retreat to Washington after second Battle of Bull Run 29-30 Aug; Confederates captured Harper's Ferry, W Virginia 15 Sept; Battle of Antietam 17 Sept; issued preliminary Emancipation Proclamation 22 Sept; issued proclamation suspending writ of *habeas corpus* for persons in rebellion and arrested insurgents and declaring them subject to trial by court-martial or military commission 24 Sept; sent second State of the Union message to Congress 1 Dec; signed Act to admit W Virginia as State (on 20 June 1863) 31 Dec.

1863     Issued Emancipation Proclamation 1 Jan; Territory of Arizona established 24 Feb; signed national banking system act 25 Feb; Territory of Idaho established 3 March; signed first Conscription Act 3 March; authorized to suspend writ of *habeas corpus* wherever necessary 3 March; signed Judiciary Act of 1863 3 March; vetoed amended Navy Bill 3 March; issued proclamation regarding desertions 10 March; Confederates won Battle of Chancellorsville 2-4 May; issued proclamation calling for 100,000 militia for six-month service 15 June; W Virginia admitted as 35th State 20 June; Union victory at Gettysburg 1-3 July; Vicksburg surrendered 4 July; issued proclamation for protection of Negro soldiers from retaliation by the Confederates 30 July; issued proclamation declaring general suspension of writ of *habeas corpus* when necessary 15 Sept; Confederates won Battle of Chickamauga 19-20 Sept; issued call for 300,000 volunteers for three-year service or duration of war 17 Oct; delivered the Gettysburg Address 19 Nov; Union armies won Battle of Chattanooga 23-25 Nov; sent third State of the Union message to Congress 8 Dec; issued proclamation granting amnesty to all Confederates who would take oath of allegiance to the Union 8 Dec.

1864     Issued call for 500,000 volunteers for three-year service or duration of war; Confederates won Battle of Olustee (or Ocean Pond) 20 Feb; authorized to call for such numbers of men for military service as needed, provision being made for draft if the quota assigned be not filled by volunteers 24 Feb; issued second amnesty proclamation 26 March; first Battle of the Wilderness 5-7 May; indecisive second and third Battles of the Wilderness 8-12 May; Territory of Montana established 26 May; Battle of Cold Harbor 1-3 June; nominated for re-election by National Union Convention at Baltimore 7 June; Battle of Petersburg 15-18 June; Fugitive Slave Act of 1850 repealed 28 June; signed Internal Revenue Act 30 June; signed Act prohibiting coastal slave trade 2 July; vetoed Wade-Davis Reconstruction Bill 4 July; issued proclamation suspending writ of *habeas corpus* and declaring martial law in Kentucky 5 July; issued proclamation explaining refusal to sign Wade-Davis Reconstruction Bill 8 July; issued call for 500,000 men for one-, two- or three-year service 18 July; sent Horace Greeley to confer with Southern Peace Commissioners at Niagara Falls, Ontario, Canada 18 July; Atlanta occupied 2 Sept; Nevada admitted as 36th State 31 Oct; election day 8 Nov; issued proclamation declaring ports of Norfolk, Virginia, and Fernandina and Pensacola, Florida, open to commerce 19 Nov; sent fourth and last State of the Union message to Congress 6 Dec; Presidential Electors cast their ballots 7 Dec; Savannah captured 22 Dec.

1865     13th Amendment to the Constitution submitted to the States for ratification 1 Feb; unsuccessful meeting with Southern Peace Commissioners 3 Feb; electoral votes tabulated by Congress 8 Feb and Lincoln and Andrew Johnson officially declared elected; Columbia and Charleston captured 17-18 Feb; vetoed repeal of section of Reconstruction Act and joint resolution concerning certain railroads 3 March; inaugurated for second term 4 March; issued proclamation ordering all absentees from the Army and Navy to return to duty within 60 day or forfeit rights as citizens 11 March; Battle of Five Forks, Virginia 1 April; Union troops occupied Petersburg and Richmond 3 April; visited Richmond 4 April; Confederates surrendered at Appomattox Courthouse 9 April; issued proclamation closing all Southern ports 11 April; shot in the head by John Wilkes Booth while attending a performance at Ford's Theater, Washington, DC 14 April; died without regaining consciousness at the William Petersen House, Washington, DC 15 April; buried at Springfield, Illinois. He was the first President to be assassinated and the third to die in office.

# The Writings of President Lincoln

*Collected Works of Abraham Lincoln,* edited by Roy P. Basler, 8 vols (1953-55)

# Lineage of President Lincoln

This family was long established in Norfolk, England, and Sir Thomas Lincoln is mentioned as a benefactor of the church in Norwich as early as 1298.

ROBERT LINCOLN, of Hingham, Norfolk, *m* Johanna Bawdiven, and *d* 1543 (will dated 18 April 1540), leaving issue,

ROBERT LINCOLN, of Hingham, *m* Margaret Abell, and *d* 1556 (will dated 14 Jan 1556), leaving issue, with an elder son John, whose descendants also emigrated to America (*see* BURKE'S *Distinguished Families of America*),

RICHARD LINCOLN, of Hingham, had issue,

SAMUEL LINCOLN, mariner, went to Salem, Mass 1635, settled at Hingham, Mass 1637, proprietor there 1649, *b* at Hingham, Norfolk *ca* 1619, *m* Martha Lewis (*d* 10 April 1693), and *d* 26 May 1690, leaving, with other issue (*see* BURKE'S *Distinguished Families of America*),

MORDECAI LINCOLN, *b* 14 June 1657, *m* Sarah, dau of Abraham Jones, of Hull, Mass[1], by his wife Sarah, dau of Deacon John Whitman, of Weymouth, Mass, and had issue,

MORDECAI LINCOLN, *m* 1st, Hannah, dau of Richard Salter, of Scituate, Mass, by his wife Sarah, dau of Major John Browne, and had issue,

JOHN LINCOLN, settled in Rockingham County, Virginia *ca* 1750, *m* Rebecca, dau of Enoch Flowers, by his wife Rebecca, and had issue,

CAPTAIN ABRAHAM LINCOLN, of Kentucky, *m* 1st, Mary Shipley; and 2ndly, Bathsheba, dau of Leonard Herring, and was *k* by Indians, having by her had issue,

THOMAS LINCOLN, farmer and carpenter, of Kentucky, Indiana and Illinois, *b* in Rockingham County, Virginia 6 Jan 1778, *m* 1st 12 June 1806, Nancy (*b* probably in Campbell County, Virginia 5 Feb 1784; *d* in Spencer County, Indiana 5 Oct 1818), dau of Joseph Hanks[2], by his wife Nancy, dau of Robert Shipley, of Fayette County, Kentucky, and had, with other issue (*see* BROTHER AND SISTER OF PRESIDENT LINCOLN, *p 303*),

ABRAHAM LINCOLN, **16th President of the United States of America.**

Thomas Lincoln *m* 2ndly 2 Dec 1819, Sarah (*b* probably in Hardin County, Kentucky 12 Dec 1788; *d* probably at Charleston, Illinois 10 April 1869), widow of Daniel Johnston (by whom she had issue[3]), and dau of — Bush, and *d* in Coles County, Illinois 17 Jan 1851.

# The Descendants of President Lincoln

ABRAHAM LINCOLN *m* at Springfield, Illinois 4 Nov 1842, Mary Ann (*b* at Lexington, Kentucky 13 Dec 1818; *d* at Springfield, Illinois 16 July 1882, *bur* there), dau of Robert Smith Todd, banker, by his wife Ann Eliza Parker, and had issue,

**1** Robert Todd LINCOLN, Capt on the staff of Gen Ulysses S. Grant, Sec of War under Pres Garfield and Pres Arthur 1881-85, Min to GB 1889-93, Pres The Pullman Co, *b* at Springfield, Illinois 1 Aug 1843, *m* 1868, Mary (*b* 1846), dau of James Harlan, of Iowa, Sec of the Interior 1865-66, and *d* 26 July 1926, having had issue,

    1 Mary LINCOLN, *b* 1869, *m* 1891, Charles Isham (*b* 1853; *d* 1919), and had issue,

        Lincoln ISHAM, *m* Leahalma Correa, and *dsp*.

    2 Abraham LINCOLN, *b* 1873; *d* 1890.

    3 Jessie Harlan LINCOLN, *b* 1875, *m* 1st Warren Beckwith, and had issue,

        (1) ●Mary Lincoln BECKWITH.

        (2) ●Robert Todd Lincoln BECKWITH.

    Jessie Harlan Lincoln *m* 2ndly, Robert J. Randolph, and *d* at Bennington, Vermont 5 Jan 1948.

**2** Edward Baker LINCOLN, *b* at Springfield, Illinois 10 March 1846; *d* there 1 Feb 1850.

**3** William Wallace LINCOLN, *b* at Springfield, Illinois 21 Dec 1850; *d* at the White House, Washington, DC 20 Feb 1862.

**4** Thomas (Tad) LINCOLN, *b* at Springfield, Illinois 4 April 1853; *d* 1871.

# The Brother and Sister of President Lincoln

1 Sarah LINCOLN, *b* in Hardin County, Kentucky 1807; *d* in Spencer County, Indiana 20 Jan 1828.

2 Thomas (?) LINCOLN, *b* at Knob Creek, Kentucky 1811 or 1812; *d* an inf.

# Notes

¹ Through the Jones Family Abraham Lincoln was a fourth cousin once removed of his Secretary of the Treasury Salmon Portland Chase (*see* APPENDIX D, SOME REMARKABLE KINSHIPS).

² Through the Hanks family President Lincoln was descended from the sister of the great Welsh hero Owen Glendower and from King Edward I of England (*see* APPENDIX C, PRESIDENTS OF ROYAL DESCENT).

³ President Lincoln had two step-sisters and one step-brother: Elizabeth Johnston, *b* 1807; Matilda Johnston, *b* 1811; and John D. Johnston, *b* 1814.

# Andrew Johnson
## 1808-1875

———

17th President of the
United States of America
1865-1869

ANDREW JOHNSON, 17TH PRESIDENT

# Andrew Johnson

## 1808-1875

### 17th President of the United States of America
### 1865-1869

IN 1864, when President Lincoln sought renomination, he was by no means certain that he would get it, or that he could win the election. The Civil War was still dragging on. Lincoln was denounced, inside and outside his own party, for many supposed sins of omission or commission. In an effort to stress patriotic harmony, the Republicans took on the label of the National Union party. Having been renominated, Lincoln decided he must find a more appealing figure as running mate than his 1860 choice: Hannibal Hamlin of Maine was an orthodox Republican from a state of only minor political significance. In place of Hamlin, Lincoln fastened upon the civil Governor of Tennessee, Andrew Johnson.

The choice seemed to be characteristically shrewd. Johnson was valuable as a War Democrat, a Southerner who had resisted secession and striven manfully to hold Tennessee in the Union. He had other, personal qualities that probably attracted Lincoln—above all, blunt courage in the face of odds. Andrew Johnson had as humble an origin as Lincoln, and even less formal training. He was born in Raleigh, North Carolina. His father died when Andrew was three years old. At thirteen, devoid of schooling, he was apprenticed to a tailor. In 1826, four years later, he moved with his mother and stepfather to Tennessee, and settled in Greeneville. There he met Eliza McCardle, a shoemaker's daughter. They were married when he was eighteen and she only sixteen—a happy partnership unbroken until his death in 1875, nearly half a century later. He could hardly read: Eliza taught him to write. But he already had a passion to educate and to better himself, and to improve the lot of other poor people in America. His intensity commended itself to the inhabitants of Eastern Tennessee, a region of small farms in which slave plantations were unfamiliar and sometimes resented. After serving effectively in the state legislature, in 1843 he began a ten-year spell as member of the House of Representatives, followed by two terms as Governor of Tennessee and then election to the US Senate. In later terminology Andrew Johnson might be described as a Populist. He disliked slavery because it threatened the livelihood of the poor whites. He favored money for educating the underprivileged, and a Homestead Bill to give men without capital the chance to acquire a farm. There is a story that when he heard he had been nominated on the ticket with the rail-splitter Lincoln, he said "What will the aristocrats do?"

In the war years he had the nightmarish task of administering a state half-Southern and half-Unionist in sympathy, fought over by Union and Confederate armies. He was vilified and in constant danger of assassination. When Lincoln was assassinated, in April 1865, Johnson faced an unenviable task. The war was practically over; the Union had been preserved. But there was a fundamental division of opinion over what should be done next. Johnson's inclination, and his apparent duty, was to continue with Lincoln's policy of moderate Reconstruction, bringing the ex-Confederate states back into the Union with the minimum of delay or punishment. President Johnson was challenged however by a phalanx of Republican leaders formidable in power though various in motive. Their impulses embraced a sincere belief that the Southern "slaveocracy" was evil and must be exterminated; a related wish to break up the plantation system to provide farms for emancipated slaves; a determination to enfranchize the Negro, at any rate in the South; resentment at the extension of presidential power under Lincoln; a desire to curb these "encroachments" and to reassert the authority of Congress; and a partisan ambition to consolidate Republican control at the expense of the discredited Democrats.

Johnson made some mistakes in trying to resist this powerful and vehement opposition. His belligerent temperament drew him into slanging matches. Unlike Lincoln, he was incapable of using humor as a political weapon. Having unluckily taken too much brandy—a rare occurrence—on the occasion of the inaugural ceremony in March 1865, he opened himself to the malign legend that he was a drunkard as well as an ignorant brute. Inheriting Lincoln's cabinet, he erred in retaining Secretary of War Edwin Stanton, a dangerous man who was aligned with the Radical Republicans.

His basic difficulties, though, were insuperable. He was a Democrat nominally at the head of the Republican party, and thereafter isolated and suspect. He was a Southerner attempting to deal with men like Thaddeus Stevens of Pennsylvania and Benjamin F. Wade of Ohio, for whom Southerners were anathema. In foreign policy, where his Administration ended French intervention in Mexico and purchased Alaska, he had a fairly free hand. At home, however, he and Congress were on a collision

ELIZA McCARDLE, MRS JOHNSON

course. His Reconstruction measures were cast aside. His vetoes were overridden. Congress passed Bills such as the Tenure of Office Act which struck at seemingly well-established presidential prerogative. Some of these were subsequently seen to be clearly unconstitutional.

As early as 1866 moves were in train to impeach him. They reached a climax in February 1868, with a large House vote in favor of impeachment. The trial began in the Senate in March. Eleven articles accused Andrew Johnson of a variety of violations of the Constitution and of misconduct in relation to Congress. Gideon Welles, one of his loyal cabinet supporters, remarked that the "mountain of words" contained "not even a mouse of impeachment material". Johnson's lawyers, during his reluctant absence, pounced upon the many weaknesses in the case against him. But the Senate vote, at the end of May, hung upon the decision of one man, Ross of Kansas. In opting for acquittal Ross saved Johnson; some would say he saved the Presidency itself, though events of the 1970s have caused some second thoughts on that opinion. In the light of the evidence, however, Johnson did not deserve to be convicted. He reacted to the crisis with typical pugnacity, and even had some hope of being chosen as presidential candidate again in 1868—this time by the Democrats. Even his harshest critics admitted that he was no weakling. As the passions of the impeachment episode died down, Johnson enjoyed one sweet moment, four months before he died. In March 1875 he returned from retirement in Tennessee to claim his seat as newly elected Senator. When he entered the Senate chamber (primed with brandy as once before), the galleries began to applaud; the Senate joined in; and at his desk he was greeted with a garland of flowers.

# Chronology

1808    Born at Casso's Inn, Fayetteville Street, Raleigh, N Carolina 29 Dec.

1822    Apprenticed to James J. Selby, a tailor in Raleigh.

1824    Ran away from his apprenticeship and worked as a journeyman tailor in Laurens, S Carolina.

1826    Returned to Raleigh May; moved to Greeneville, Tennessee with his mother and stepfather; set up shop as a tailor in Greeneville.

1828    Elected Alderman of Greeneville (re-elected 1829 and 1830).

1830    Elected Mayor of Greeneville.

1831    Purchased a shop and house in Greeneville.

1833    Retired from office of Mayor.

1835    Elected representative for Greene and Washington Counties to the State legislature.

1837    Defeated for re-election to State legislature on opposing internal improvements.

1839    Re-elected to State legislature.

1840    Campaigned for Van Buren.

1841    Elected to the State Senate as representative for Greene and Hawkins Counties.

1843    Elected to the House of Representatives; took seat 4 Dec.

1851    Purchased house on Main Street, Greeneville; had degree of Master Mason conferred by Greeneville Lodge No 119.

1853    Elected Governor of Tennessee.

1855    Re-elected Governor.

1857    Elected to the Senate; took seat 7 Dec.

1858    Made speech in favor of Homestead bill 20 May.

1860    Supported John C. Breckinridge, the southern Democratic candidate for the Presidency; proposed amendment to the Constitution 13 Dec; denounced secession in Senate speech 18-19 Dec.

1861    Made vigorous anti-secession speech 2 March; Tennessee seceded from the Union 8 June, became the only Southerner remaining in the Senate.

1862    Appointed Military Governor of Tennessee by President Lincoln and commissioned as Brig-Gen US Volunteers 4 March; resigned from Senate and returned to Nashville 12 March to organize provisional government; issued proclamation calling upon Tennesseans to return to their allegiance and accept an amnesty 18 March; issued a proclamation ordering congressional elections 8 Dec; levied assessment on rich Confederate sympathizers 15 Dec.

1863    Issued proclamation ordering business agents to retain funds of Southern firms 20 Feb.

1864    Nominated for Vice-President by National Union Convention at Baltimore 7 June; elected 8 Nov.

1865    Resigned commission in US Volunteers 3 March; took oath as Vice-President at Washington, DC 4 March; succeeded as 17th President of the United States of America on the assassination of President Lincoln and took oath of office in his suite at the Kirkwood Hotel, Washington, DC 15 April; issued executive order discontinuing most of Southern commercial restrictions 29 April; issued executive order for trial by military commission of alleged assassins of President Lincoln 1 May; issued executive order for the arrest of Jefferson Davis 2 May; issued executive order re-establishing US authority in Virginia and recognizing Francis Pierpont as Governor 9 May; issued proclamation announcing the end of military hostilities 10 May; issued executive order removing commercial restrictions on Southern ports 22 May; attended review of the Armies of Potomac, Tennessee and Georgia in Washington 22-23 May; issued first amnesty proclamation 29 May; issued proclamation removing restrictions on trade east of Mississippi River 13 June; issued proclamation rescinding blockade as to foreign commerce 23 June; issued proclamation removing restrictions on trade west of Mississippi River 24 June; issued proclamation lifting all restrictions on Southern ports 29 Aug; issued proclamation ending martial law in Kentucky 12 Oct; issued proclamation revoking suspension of writ of *habeas corpus* in Northern states 1 Dec; sent first State of the Union message to Congress 4 Dec; sent special message on insurgent states, with Grant report, to Congress 18 Dec; signed special Act for relief of Mrs Abraham Lincoln 21 Dec.

1866    Vetoed Freedmen's Bureau Bill 19 Feb; denounced Congressional Committee on Reconstruction 22 Feb; vetoed Civil Rights Bill 27 March; issued proclamation declaring insurrection and Civil War at an end everywhere except Texas 2 April; vetoed Admission of Colorado Bill 15 May; issued proclamation warning against participation in Fenian invasion of Canada and ordering strict enforcement of neutrality laws 6 June; vetoed Montana Iron Company Public Lands Bill 15 June; sent special message to Congress opposing submission of 14th Amendment to the Constitution to the States 22 June; vetoed continuation of Freedmen's Bureau Bill 15 July; Tennessee re-admitted to the Union 24 July; vetoed survey of Territory of Montana Bill 28 July; received Queen Emma of Hawaii 14 August; issued proclamation declaring insurrection and Civil War at an end everywhere, including Texas 20 Aug; left on political tour 28 Aug; laid cornerstone of monument to Stephen A. Douglas in Chicago 6 Sept; sent second State of the Union message to Congress 3 Dec.

1867    Vetoed suffrage in District of Columbia Bill 5 Jan; charges of usurpation of power and corrupt practices made against him referred to House judiciary committee 7 Jan; vetoed Bills to admit Colorado and Nebraska as States 29 Jan; Act to admit Nebraska passed over his veto 9 Feb; Nebraska admitted as 37th State 1 March; vetoed Tenure of Office Bill and first Reconstruction Bill (both passed over his veto) 2 March; signed Act declaring valid all presidential proclamations from 4 March 1861 to 1 July 1866 regarding martial law and military trials 2 March; vetoed second Reconstruction Bill (passed over his veto) 23 March; issued proclamation calling special session of Senate 30 March; Alaska purchase treaty with Russia signed 30 March (ratified by Senate 9 April); vetoed third Reconstruction Bill and Reconstruction joint resolution (both passed over his vetoes) 19 July; issued executive order suspending Secretary of War Edwin McMasters Stanton, who had refused to resign on request, 12 Aug; issued proclamation granting general amnesty 7 Sept; judicial committee report recommended his impeachment "for high crimes and misdemeanors" 25 Nov; sent third State of the Union message to Congress 3 Dec; impeachment resolution defeated in the House of Representatives 7 Dec.

1868    Senate refused to concur in suspension of Secretary of War Stanton 13 June; motion to impeach presented by Representative John Covode of Pennsylvania and referred to the Committee on Reconstruction 21 Feb; Committee report recommended resolution for impeachment 22 Feb; House voted to impeach (by 126 to 47) 24 Feb; impeachment reported at bar of Senate 25 Feb; nine articles of impeachment agreed upon in House 2 March; two additional articles agreed upon 3 March; Senate convened as court of impeachment 5 March and Johnson summoned to appear and answer charges; Court re-opened and again adjourned 13 March; Johnson's answer to charges read by counsel 23 March; vetoed amended Judiciary Bill (passed over his veto) 25 March; trial began 30 March; acquitted on 11th article of impeachment 16 May; acquitted on 2nd and 3rd articles and court adjourned *sine die* (by a vote of 34 to 16) 26 May; received Chinese diplomatic mission at the White House 5 June; vetoed Admission of Arkansas Bill (passed over his veto) 20 June; signed Act providing eight-hour workday for laborers and workmen in Government employ 25 June; vetoed Southern States Admission to Congress Bill (passed over his veto) 25 June; issued proclamation of amnesty pardoning all not under presentment or indictment 4 July; failed to obtain renomination by Democratic National Convention in New York City 4-9 July; vetoed Exclusion of Electoral Votes on Unreconstructed States Bill (passed over his veto) 20 July; vetoed Discontinuance of Freedmen's Bureau Bill (passed over his veto) 25 July; sent fourth and last State of the Union message to Congress 9 Dec; issued proclamation of unconditional pardon and amnesty to all concerned in insurrection 25 Dec.

1869    Vetoed Trustees of Negro Schools in District of Columbia Bill 13 Feb; vetoed Tariff on Copper Bill (passed over his veto) 22 Feb; 15th Amendment to the Constitution submitted to the States for ratification 26 Feb; retired from office 4 March; returned to Greeneville April.

1871    Unsuccessful candidate for the Senate.

1872    Unsuccessful candidate for the House of Representatives.

1875    Elected to the Senate Jan; took seat 5 March; returned to Greeneville at end of session 24 March; suffered a stroke while visiting his daughter at Carter's Station, Tennessee and died there 31 July; buried at the Andrew Johnson Cemetery, Greeneville.

# Lineage of President Andrew Johnson

The ancestry of President Andrew Johnson has not been established earlier than his father,

JACOB JOHNSON, of Raleigh, N Carolina, ostler, janitor and constable, *b* 5 April 1778, *m* 9 Sept 1801, Mary (Polly) McDonough (*b* 17 July 1783; *m* 2ndly, Turner Daugherty, of Raleigh, N Carolina, and *d* 13 Feb 1856), and *d* at Raleigh, N Carolina 4 Jan 1812, having had, with other issue (*see* BROTHER AND SISTER OF PRESIDENT ANDREW JOHNSON, *p 315*),

ANDREW JOHNSON, **17th President of the United States of America.**

# The Descendants of President Andrew Johnson

ANDREW JOHNSON *m* at Warrensburg, Tennessee 17 May 1827, Eliza (*b* at Greenville, Tennessee 4 Oct 1810; *d* at the farm of her daughter Mrs Brown, Carter's Station, Tennessee 15 Jan 1876, *bur* with her husband in the Andrew Johnson National Cemetery, Greeneville), dau of John McCardle (McCardell, or McArdle), of Warrensburg, shoemaker and subsequently an innkeeper, by his wife Sara(h) Phillips, and had issue,

**1** Martha JOHNSON, hostess at the White House for her father Pres Andrew Johnson 1865-69, *b* at Greeneville, Tennessee 25 Oct 1828, *m* there 13 Dec 1856, David Trotter Patterson, Judge of the Circuit Court of Tennessee and US Senator (*b* at Cedar Creek, Tennessee 28 Feb 1818; *d* at Afton, Tennessee 3 Nov 1891, *bur* Andrew Johnson National Cemetery, Greenville), son of Andrew Patterson, by his wife Susanna Trotter, and *d* at Greeneville 10 July 1901 (*bur* Andrew Johnson National Cemetery, Greeneville), having had issue,

  **1** Mary Belle PATTERSON, *b* at Greeneville 11 Nov 1859, *m* there 17 Feb 1886, John Landstreet, of Loudoun County, Virginia (*b* in Loudoun County 25 April 1853; *d* at Richmond, Virginia 1 Aug 1927), son of Rev John Landstreet, by his wife Mary, and *d* at Auburn, California 9 July 1891 (*bur* Andrew Johnson National Cemetery, Greeneville), leaving issue,

    Martha Belle Patterson LANDSTREET, *b* at Port Richmond, Staten Island, New York 6 Aug 1887, *m* at Richmond, Virginia 1907, Robert Josiah Willingham, Jr, of Richmond, Virginia (*b* at Athens, Georgia 27 June 1875; *d* at Washington, DC 10 Oct 1953), son of Robert Josiah Willingham, by his wife Corneille Bacon, and *d* at Richmond, Virginia 26 Dec 1969, having had issue,

      *1a* ● Martha Belle WILLINGHAM [*21 South Park Street, Hanover, New Hampshire, USA*], *b* at Richmond, Virginia 20 Dec 1908, *m* there 1933 (*m* diss by div 1951), Thomas Clyde Colt, Jr (*b* at East Orange, New Jersey 20 Feb 1905), son of Thomas Clyde Colt, by his wife Florence Clery, and has issue,

        *1b* ● Thomas Clyde COLT III, writer and journalist [*440 Westview Place, Fort Lee, New Jersey 07024, USA*], *b* at Richmond, Virginia 1 March 1935, *educ* Oregon Univ, Eugene (BS 1959).

        *2b* ● Jon Landstreet COLT, municipal planning consultant [*1109 Marion Street, Denver, Colorado, USA*], *b* at Richmond, Virginia 21 July 1938, *educ* Dartmouth Coll, Hanover, New Hampshire (BA 1959).

        *3b* ● Corinne Patterson COLT [*2122 Vista del Mar, Hollywood, California, USA*], *b* at Richmond, Virginia 28 Oct 1946, *educ* George Washington Univ, Washington, DC.

      *2a* Elizabeth Landstreet WILLINGHAM, *b* at Richmond, Virginia 19 Nov 1910, *m* there, ● James Taylor Ellyson Crump (*b* at Richmond, Virginia), son of Frank T. Crump, by his wife Nancy Ellyson, and *d* 1968,

leaving issue,
●Taylor Nicholas CRUMP [*3020 Scarsborough Drive, Richmond, Virginia 23235, USA*], *b* at Richmond, Virginia 16 Sept 1935, *m* there 1957, ●Katherine Morris, and has issue,
1*c*●Kevin L. CRUMP, *b* at Richmond, Virginia 30 April 1958.
2*c*●Taylor Nicholas CRUMP, Jr, *b* at Richmond, Virginia 17 Aug 1959.
2 Andrew Johnson PATTERSON, *b* at Greeneville, Tennessee 25 Feb 1857, *m* at Limestone, Tennessee 19 Dec 1889, Martha Ellen (*b* in Washington County, Tennessee 28 May 1864; *d* at Greeneville 13 March 1948), dau of John Henry Barkley, by his wife Margaret Susanna Nelson, and *d* at Greeneville 25 June 1932, leaving issue,
●Margaret Johnson PATTERSON [*107 West McKee Street, Greeneville, Tennessee, USA*], *b* at Greeneville 29 Sept 1903, *m* there 15 June 1949, William Thaw Bartlett, of Maryville, Tennessee (*b* 20 Sept 1876; *d* 27 Nov 1954), son of Peter Mason Bartlett, by his wife Florence Alden.
2 Charles JOHNSON, *b* at Greeneville, Tennessee 8 Feb 1830; *dunm* at Nashville, Tennessee 4 April 1863 (*bur* Andrew Johnson National Cemetery, Greeneville).
3 Mary JOHNSON, *b* at Greeneville, Tennessee 8 May 1832, *m* 1st at Greeneville 27 April 1852, Col Daniel Stover, of Carter County, Tennessee (*b* in Carter County 14 Nov 1826; *d* at Nashville 18 Dec 1864), son of William Stover, by his wife Sarah Murray Drake, and had issue,
1 Lily STOVER, *b* in Carter County, Tennessee 11 May 1855, *m* at Greeneville 14 Oct 1874, Thomas Fleming Maloney (*b* at Warrensburg, Tennessee 6 Dec 1846; *d* at Ogden, Utah 17 March 1904), son of William Conway Maloney, by his wife

Louisa Cureton, and *dsp* at Knoxville, Tennessee 5 Nov 1892 (*bur* Andrew Johnson National Cemetery, Greeneville).
2 Sarah Drake STOVER, *b* in Carter County, Tennessee 27 June 1857, *m* at Bluff City, Tennessee 7 June 1881, as his 1st wife, William Bruce Bachman (*b* at Kingsport, Tennessee 24 Nov 1852; *d* at Bluff City 9 Sept 1922), son of Samuel Bachman, by his wife Sarah Kitzmiller, and *d* at Bluff City 22 March 1886 (*bur* Andrew Johnson National Cemetery, Greeneville), leaving issue,
(1) Andrew Johnson BACHMAN, *b* at Bluff City 13 June 1882, *m* at Nashville 8 Sept 1920, ●Ethel Crockett (*b* 15 Aug 1892), dau of James Irwin, by his wife Emma Johnson, and *dsp* (*bur* Andrew Johnson National Cemetery, Greeneville).
(2) Samuel Bernard BACHMAN, *b* in Carter County, Tennessee 13 May 1884; *dunm* at Bluff City 3 April 1914 (*bur* Morning View Cemetery, Bluff City).
3 Andrew Johnson STOVER, *b* in Carter County, Tennessee 6 March 1860; *dunm* there 25 Jan 1923 (*bur* Andrew Johnson National Cemetery, Greeneville).
Mary Johnson *m* 2ndly 1869, as his 2nd wife, William Ramsay Brown[1], and *d* at Bluff City, Tennessee 19 April 1883.
4 Robert JOHNSON, Col 1st Tennessee Cav in Civil War, *b* at Greeneville, Tennessee 22 Feb 1834; *dunm* there 22 April 1869 (*bur* Andrew Johnson National Cemetery, Greeneville).
5 Andrew (Frank) JOHNSON, Jr, *b* at Greeneville, Tennessee 5 Aug 1852, *m* at Rutland, Hot Springs, N Carlonia 25 Nov 1875, Kate May (Bessie), dau of James H. Rumbough, by his wife Caroline Powell, and *dsp* at Elizabethtown, Tennessee 12 March 1879 (*bur* Andrew Johnson National Cemetery, Greeneville).

# The Brother and Sister of
# President Andrew Johnson

1 William JOHNSON, *b* 1803.
2 A girl, *d* an inf.

# Note

[1] William Ramsay Brown's first wife was Mary Sophia Lincoln (1833-1867), a second cousin of President Lincoln (*qv*). The relationship is shown in the table below—

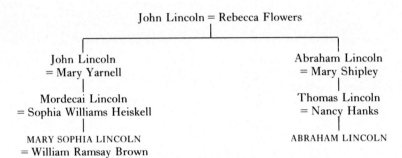

John Lincoln = Rebecca Flowers

John Lincoln
= Mary Yarnell

Mordecai Lincoln
= Sophia Williams Heiskell

MARY SOPHIA LINCOLN
= William Ramsay Brown

Abraham Lincoln
= Mary Shipley

Thomas Lincoln
= Nancy Hanks

ABRAHAM LINCOLN

# Ulysses S. Grant
## 1822-1885

———

18th President of the
United States of America
1869-1877

ULYSSES S. GRANT, 18TH PRESIDENT

# Ulysses S. Grant

## 1822-1885

### 18th President of the United States of America
### 1869-1877

WHEN THE Civil War broke out Ulysses S. Grant was nearly forty years old and by the usual reckoning a failure. Born in 1822, the son of a tanner and a farmer's daughter, he had grown up in Ohio. His father, an amateur politician and a Whig supporter, managed to secure a nomination to West Point for Ulysses through his Congressman. Such nominations were prized because cadets who stayed the course received a free four-year college training and an officer's commission. They also carried an obligation to serve in the Army for a few years. Father Grant, eager to provide his children with the educational opportunities he himself had been deprived of, was more enthusiastic about West Point than Ulysses was. "A military life", he later recalled, "had no charms for me, and I had not the faintest idea of staying in the Army even if I should be graduated, which I did not expect".

"Uncle Sam", as fellow-cadets nicknamed him, did survive, and graduate in 1843. The Academy brought him one personal benefit: a meeting with his room-mate's sister, Julia Dent, whose father was a judge and a planter in Missouri. The couple were married in 1848 and were to live contentedly together for nearly 37 years. They were survived by their four children, three sons and a daughter. The daughter, Nellie, was to marry an Englishman, Algernon Sartoris, at a lavish ceremony in the White House in 1874. In 1848 Grant emerged from the Mexican War as a Lieutenant and Brevet Captain, having acquitted himself well. But he still did not like soldiering. Post-war existence was tedious, pay scanty and promotion a remote prospect. Captain Grant began to drink too much (a habit to which, perhaps unfairly, he is said to have reverted now and then in his later career). Disgusted and at odds with his brother officers, he resigned his commission in 1854. His next few years were drab. He tried his hand at a variety of jobs, at last working as a clerk in a leather store run by two brothers in Galena, Illinois.

The Civil War rescued him. Trained officers were in short supply. Within a few weeks, to his astonishment, he was a Colonel of Volunteers and soon afterward a Brigadier-General. His first great moment came in February 1862 with the capture of Forts Henry and Donelson and 14,000 Confederate prisoners. The Union had hitherto enjoyed very little success. The news of Grant's victory made him a hero overnight, and gained him instant promotion to a major-generalcy. His demand to the Confederate General for "unconditional surrender" pleased the public's fancy. "U.S." Grant was now "Unconditional Surrender" Grant. Newspaper reports that he had calmly smoked a cigar during the fight for Fort Donelson brought him innumerable "boxes of the choicest brands". By his own account this unlooked-for bounty made him addicted to smoking; and cartoonists usually drew him with a cigar in his mouth.

The war destroyed many a military reputation. Grant drew criticism as a slogger, indeed as a "butcher", willing to incur heavy casualties. But unlike several other Union generals he was tenacious and he got results. In March 1864 Lincoln summoned him to Washington and promoted him to Lieutenant-General, with full command of the Union armies. In little over a year Grant was pursuing Lee's army to its surrender at Appomattox. The nation adored him. Congress made him a full General—a rank that had lain in abeyance since George Washington last held it in 1799. In a confused disagreement between Grant and President Johnson over the post of Secretary of War, popular opinion sided with Grant.

In 1868 he was by all odds the favorite choice to follow Johnson in the Presidency. Grant's own political views were obscure, and certainly not tied to the Republicans; he had voted for Buchanan in 1856 and he disclaimed presidential ambitions. But he was easily wooed into acquiescence, nominated with acclaim, and comfortably victorious in November 1868. His personal standing was so great that he was renominated and re-elected in 1872; and his supporters assured him that he could win a further, unprecedented third term nomination in 1880. In face of such evident prestige one must note that his Administrations were weak to the point of near disaster. The decisive warrior-organizer turned out to be vague and naïve. Enemies joked that unconditional surrender now meant handing over presidential authority to the Republicans' lordly bosses in the Senate. Grant made bad appointments. There was corruption in his Administration and his Secretary of War was impeached on a charge of accepting a bribe.

Why then was Grant re-elected in 1872? One editor described him as "an ignorant soldier, coarse in his taste and blunt in his perceptions, fond of money and material enjoyment and of low company". There is a degree

JULIA BOGGS DENT, MRS GRANT

of truth in this hostile verdict. Having been hard up for most of his life, he was probably overimpressed by wealth and luxury. Snobbish Americans sneered at the casual atmosphere in the White House, where his garrulous old father was an occasional guest, and his father-in-law—another visitor—was apt to confide to journalists that the President was actually a Democrat. On the other hand there was no suggestion that Grant himself was corrupt. He was known to be short of money when his second term ended, and at end of his life, dying of cancer, he had to force himself with stoical courage to write his memoirs in order to leave his family in comfort. This was perhaps his only successful financial venture. Grant's autobiography, written in longhand and completed four days before he died, was to bring in about half a million dollars in royalties. He remained enormously popular, abroad as well as at home. The world tour he undertook after leaving the Presidency was a prolonged triumphal tribute from nation after nation. But his prestige was gradually eroded. He won in 1872 because disaffected Republicans combined with the Democrats to select a catastrophically maladroit candidate, Horace Greeley, who obligingly ensured his own defeat. The third term trial balloon in 1880 was quickly punctured. The public still worshipped the inelegant little man with the cigar and the scraggly beard. But those in the know in Washington had ceased to be impressed. He would always be the Hero of Appomattox, and the essential honest plainness of his character would be movingly recalled by the direct soldier's prose of his memoirs. But a large number of his countrymen would have agreed with the comment of the New York *Tribune*, on Grant's death, that "the greatest mistake of his life was the acceptance of the Presidency".

# Chronology

1822    Born at Point Pleasant, Clermont County, Ohio 27 April, and named Hiram Ulysses[1].

1823    Family moved to Georgetown, Brown County, Ohio.

1836-37  Attended Maysville Seminary, Maysville, Kentucky.

1838-39  Attended Presbyterian Academy, Ripley, Ohio.

1839    Appointed to United States Military Academy, West Point, NY 22 March; arrived at West Point 29 May.

1843    Graduated from West Point and was commissioned Brevet 2nd Lieut 4th Infantry, June; reported for duty at Jefferson Barracks, nr St Louis, Missouri 30 Sept.

1844    Reported at Camp Salubrity, nr Natchitoches, Louisiana 3 June.

1845    Regiment sailed from New Orleans to Corpus Christi, Texas, Aug; promoted 2nd Lieut 30 Sept.

1846-48  Served in Mexican War.

1847    Promoted 1st Lieut 16 Sept; Brevet rank as 1st Lieut and Capt dated from 8 Sept and 13 Sept for gallantry at the Battle of Molino del Rey and the storming of Chapultepec.

1848    War ended by Treaty of Guadalupe Hidalgo 30 May; Grant landed at Pascagoula, Mississippi 23 July; reported at Detroit and was reassigned to duty at Madison Barracks, Sackets Harbor, NY 17 Nov.

1849    Reported at Detroit after transfer from Sackets Harbor 18 April.

1851    Transferred back to Sackets Harbor 12 June.

1852    Regiment ordered to California; Grant left New York 5 July; arrived at Columbia Barracks (later Fort Vancouver), Oregon (later Washington) Territory 20 Sept.

1853    Promoted Capt 5 Aug.

1854    Reported for duty at Fort Humboldt, California 5 Jan; resigned commission 11 April; rejoined family at White Haven, nr St Louis, Missouri.

1855    Moved from White Haven to Wish-ton-wish.

1856    Moved from Wish-ton-wish to Hardscrabble.

1858    Entered real estate business in St Louis in partnership with his wife's cousin Harry Boggs.

1860    Left real estate business; moved to Galena, Illinois, and began work in his father's hardware and leather goods store at salary of $800 a year.

1861    Fort Sumter attacked 12 April; Grant rejoined US Army as Volunteer at Springfield, Illinois 23 April; promoted Col commanding 21st Illinois Regt 17 June; given command of SE Dist of Missouri 29 July; promoted Brig-Gen 7 Aug (antedated to 17 May); District Commander at Cairo, Illinois 4 Sept; occupied Paducah, Kentucky 6 Sept; captured Belmont, Missouri 7 Nov, but later withdrew.

1862    Captured Fort Henry, Tennessee 6 Feb; captured Fort Donelson, Tennessee and was promoted Major-Gen of Volunteers 16 Feb; with Major-Gen Buell defeated Johnston and Beauregard at the Battle of Shiloh 6-7 April; appointed second-in-command to Henry Wager Halleck, the Union C-in-C 11 April; appointed to command Armies of the Tennessee and the Mississippi 11 July; defeated Van Dorn at Corinth, Mississippi 4-4 Oct; appointed to command Dept of the Tennessee 16 Oct; had advanced base at Holly Springs, Mississippi destroyed by Van Dorn 20 Dec.

1863    Assumed command of operations against Vicksburg, Mississippi 30 Jan; crossed Mississippi below Vicksburg 30 April; occupied Fort Gibson, Mississippi 1 May; defeated J. E. Johnston at Jackson, Mississippi 14 May; defeated Pemberton at Champion's Hill 16 May; unsuccessfully attacked Vicksburg 19 and 22 May; received surrender of Vicksburg from Pemberton and was promoted Major-Gen in Regular Army 4 July; appointed C-in-C in Western theater 16 Oct; defeated Bragg at Battle of Chattanooga, Tennessee 24-25 Nov.

1864    Summoned to Washington by President Lincoln to command all Union land forces 3 March; promoted Lt-Gen US Army 9 March; established HQ at Culpeper Court House 26 March; crossed Rapidan to outflank Lee 4 May; fought indecisive Wilderness battle with Lee 4-6 May; repulsed by Lee at Spottsylvania 9-19 May, on the North Anna 23-26 May, and at Cold Harbor 1-3 June; President Lincoln visited HQ at City Point 21 June; captured Fort Harrison on James River 29 Sept.

1865    Opened final offensive at Petersburg 29 March; received surrender of Lee at Appomattox Court House 9 April; toured Northern US and Canada June-Aug; citizens of Galena presented house to the Grants 18 Aug.

1866    Promoted Gen (retired list) July.

1867    Appointed Secretary of War in the cabinet of President Andrew Johnson 12 Aug.

1868    Unanimously nominated for President at Republican National Convention, Chicago 21 May; elected President with 214 electoral votes as opposed to 80 for Horatio Seymour, the Democratic candidate 3 Nov.

1869    Inaugurated as 18th President of the United States 4 March; signed Public Credit Act 18 March; signed amended Tenure of Office Act 5 April; sent special message to Congress concerning claims against Great Britain 7 April; signed Act amending Judiciary Act 10 April; vetoed Relief of Blanton Duncan Bill 10 April; sent first State of the Union message to Congress 6 Dec.

1870    Received HRH Prince Arthur (later Duke of Connaught), 3rd son of Queen Victoria 24 Jan; signed Act re-admitting Virginia to representation in Congress 26 Jan; signed Act re-admitting Mississippi to representation in Congress 23 Feb; 15th Amendment to Constitution ratified 30 March; signed Act re-admitting Texas to representation in Congress 30 March; issued proclamation warning against participation in Fenian raids into Canada 24 May; signed first Enforcement Act 31 May; sent special message to Congress announcing strict neutrality regarding Cuban revolution 13 June; signed Act organizing

Department of Justice 22 June; Senate rejected Treaty to annex Dominican Republic 30 June; signed Act providing annual pension of $3,000 for Mrs Abraham Lincoln 14 July; vetoed Southern Union troops bill 14 July; signed Act re-admitting Georgia to representation in Congress and Act reducing Army to peace-time footing 15 July; issued proclamation of neutrality in Franco-Prussian War 22 Aug; issued proclamation forbidding military expeditions against nations at peace with US 12 Oct; sent second State of the Union message to Congress 5 Dec.

1871    Signed Act providing territorial government for District of Columbia 21 Feb; signed Act establishing first Civil Service Commission and Indian Appropriation Act 3 March; issued proclamation against unlawful combinations in S Carolina 24 March; sent special message to Congress recommending the annexation of San Domingo 5 April; signed second Enforcement Act 20 April; Treaty of Washington concluded with Great Britain 8 May; issued proclamation ordering Ku Klux Klan in S Carolina to disperse and surrender arms 12 Oct; sent third State of the Union message to Congress 4 Dec.

1872    Re-elected with 286 electoral votes as opposed to 66 for Horace Greeley, the Democratic and Liberal Republican candidate 5 Nov.

1873    Inaugurated for second term as President 4 March; financial panic following failure of Jay Cooke & Co (Sept) caused withdrawal of foreign capital from US.

1875    The Resumption Act (providing for resumption of specie payment, suspended in 1861, from 1 Jan 1879) passed by Congress 14 Jan.

1876    Impeachment of Secretary of War William W. Belknap on charges of financial impropriety; charges of dishonesty made against Grant's private secretary Orville Babcock.

1877    Retired from office 4 March; attended inauguration of his successor Rutherford Hayes 5 March.

1877-79  Made world tour.

1880    Sought nomination for a third term but was beaten in the convention June.

1881    Moved from Galena to New York City.

1884    Unsuccessful with business ventures; failure of brokerage firm of Grant & Ward May.

1885    Nominated General on retired list with full pay by President Arthur 3 March; completed memoirs 19 July; died of cancer of the throat at Mount McGregor, New York 23 July; buried in magnificent mausoleum (Grant's Tomb) in Riverside Park on the Hudson.

# The Writings of President Grant

*Personal Memoirs of U. S. Grant*, 2 vols (1885-86)

*Battles and Leaders of the Civil War*, 4 vols (1887)

*General Grant's Letters to a Friend, 1861-1880*, edited by James Grant Wilson (New York 1897)

*Letters of Ulysses S. Grant to his Father and his Youngest Sister, 1857-78*, edited by Jesse Grant Cramer (New York and London 1912)

*The Papers of Ulysses S. Grant, Volume I: 1837-1861*, edited by John Y. Simon (1967)

# Lineage of President Grant

WILLIAM GRANT, *m* Jane, dau of William Burton, of Ingmanthorpe, Yorks, and had issue,

JOHN GRANT, of Roxby, in the parish of Pickhill, Yorks, *m* Jane, dau and co-heiress of Edward Belford, of Exelby, Yorks, and had issue, with three other sons and one dau, a 2nd son,

GEORGE GRANT, *m* 7 Nov 1570, Julian, dau of Marmaduke Claryonette, and had issue, with three other sons, a 2nd son,

JOHN GRANT, *b* May 1573, *m* 7 July 1600, Alice, dau of Matthew Turberville, of Woolbridge, Dorset, and had issue,

MATTHEW GRANT, emigrated from Plymouth, Devon, sailing in the *Mary and John*, and landed at Nantasket 30 May 1630, settled first at Dorchester, Mass (Freeman there 18 May 1631), moved to Windsor, Conn 1635, Town Clerk of Windsor 1652-77, *b* 27 Oct 1601, *m* 1st 16 Nov 1625, Priscilla (*b* 1602; *d* 27 April 1644), dau of Rev Anthony Grey, Rector of Burbage, Leics, and had issue, five sons and one dau. He *m* 2ndly 29 May 1645, Susanna (*b* 5 April 1602; *d* 14 Nov 1666), widow of William Rockwell, and dau of Bernard Capen, and *d* at Windsor, Conn 16 Dec 1681. His 2nd son by his 1st marriage,

SAMUEL GRANT, *b* 12 Nov 1631, *m* 27 May 1658, Mary (*b* 1638), dau of John Porter[2], by his wife Anna White, and *d* 10 Sept 1718, having had issue, with four yr sons and three daus,

SAMUEL GRANT, *b* 20 April 1659, *m* 1st 6 Dec 1683, Anna Filley (*b* 1644; *d* 1686), and had issue, one dau. He *m* 2ndly 11 April 1688, Grace (*b* 1670; *d* 1753), dau of Capt John Minor[3], by his wife Elizabeth Booth, and *dvp* 1710, having by her had issue, with four other sons and three other daus, a 2nd son,

NOAH GRANT, *b* 16 Dec 1692, *m* 12 June 1717, Martha (*b* 9 Dec 1696), dau of John Huntington, by his wife Abigail Lothrop, and *d* 1727, leaving issue, with two yr sons and one dau,

CAPTAIN NOAH GRANT, of Grant's Hill, Conn, Lieut Capt Rodger's Scouts at Lake George Nov 1755, Capt 7th Co 2nd Conn Regt 1756, *b* at Tolland, Conn 12 July 1718, *m* there 5 Nov 1746, Susanna (*b* Tolland 23 June 1724; *m* 2ndly, Capt Buell), 5th and yst dau of Jonathan Delano II[4], by his wife Amey Hatch, and was *k* in the French and Indian War 20 Sept 1756, leaving issue, with a yr son,

CAPTAIN NOAH GRANT, Revolutionary Army, *b* 20 June 1748, *m* 1st, Anna (*d ca* 1787), widow of — Richardson, and dau of — Buell, and had issue, two sons. He *m* 2ndly at Greensburg, Westmoreland County, Pennsylvania 4 March 1792, Rachel Kelly (*d* at Deerfield, Ohio 10 April 1805), and *d* at Maysville, Kentucky 14 Feb 1819, having by her had issue, with three yr sons and three daus,

JESSE ROOT GRANT, of Georgetown, Brown County, Ohio, tanner and farmer, *b* at Deerfield, Ohio 23 Jan 1794, *m* at Point Pleasant, Ohio 24 June 1821, Hannah (*b* in Montgomery County, Pennsylvania 23 Nov 1798; *d* at Jersey City, New Jersey 11 May 1883), dau of John Simpson, and *d* at Covington, Kentucky 29 June 1873, having had issue, with two yr sons and three daus (*see* BROTHERS AND SISTERS OF PRESIDENT GRANT, *p 331*),

ULYSSES S. GRANT, **18th President of the United States of America.**

# The Descendants of President Grant

ULYSSES S. GRANT *m* at St Louis, Missouri 22 Aug 1848, Julia Boggs (*b* at White Haven, St Louis, Missouri 16 Feb 1826; *d* at Washington, DC 14 Dec 1902, *bur* with her husband), eldest dau of Col Frederick Dent (descended from Thomas Dent, an Englishman who settled in Maryland in 17th cent), by his wife Ellen Bray Wrenshall, and had issue,

**1** Frederick Dent GRANT, Major-Gen US Army, US Min to Austria-Hungary 1889-93, *b* at St Louis, Missouri 30 May 1850, *m* at Chicago, Illinois 20 Oct 1874, Ida Marie (*b* at Louisville, Kentucky 1854; *d* at Washington, DC 1930), dau of Henry Hamilton Honoré, of Chicago, by his wife Elizabeth Carr, and *d* at New York 11 April 1912 (*bur* West Point), leaving issue,
  **1** ●Julia GRANT [*2126 Connecticut Avenue, Washington, DC, USA*], *b* at the White House 7 June 1876, *m* at Newport, Rhode Island 25 Sept 1899 (*m* diss by div 1934), Major-Gen Prince Michael Cantacuzene, Count Speransky, sometime Chief of Staff to HIH Grand Duke Nicholas of Russia, C-in-C of the Russian Armies (*b* at Odessa, Russia 29 April (*os*) 1875; *d* at Sarasota, Florida 25 March 1955), eldest son of Prince Michael Cantacuzene, Count Speransky, by his wife Elisabeth Sicard, and has had issue,
    (1) Prince Michael CANTACUZENE, Count Speransky, *b* at St Petersburg, Russia 21 July 1900, *m* at Nahant, Mass 26 June 1921 (*m* diss by div 1935), Clarissa (*b* at Boston, Mass 27 Nov 1899; *d* at New York 30 Aug 1939), dau of Thomas Pelham Curtis, by his wife Frances Kellogg Small, and *d* at Lake Forest, Illinois 25 Dec 1972, leaving issue,
      1*a*●(Princess) Irina CANTACUZENE, *b* at Chicago, Illinois 30 Dec 1925, *m* at Wadsworth, Illinois 5 Oct 1945, ●Douglas Erickson (*b* at Swampscott, Mass 24 July 1915) [*3952 Douglas Road, Coconut Grove, Miami, Florida 33133, USA*], son of A. Wentworth Erickson, by his wife Cecile Macy, and has issue,
        1*b*●Douglas Mihael ERICKSON [*40 Morningside Drive, Miami, Florida 33133, USA*], *b* at Santa Barbara, California 29 June 1946, *m* at Montreal, Canada 14 June 1969, ●Pauline Janet (*b* at Grandmere, Quebec, Canada 17 Dec 1948), dau of James Stephen Oppé, by his wife Isabel Morgan, and has issue,
          1*c*●Irina ERICKSON, *b* at Miami, Florida 17 Nov 1971.
          2*c*●Douglas Oppé ERICKSON, *b* at Miami, Florida 14 March 1974.
        2*b*●Irina ERICKSON, *b* at Nassau, Bahamas 30 Oct 1948, *m* at Coconut Grove, Florida 26 June 1971, ●Baron Alexander von Korff (*b* at Madrid, Spain 16 Nov 1946), son of Baron Arnt von Korff, by his wife Baroness Irina von Korff, and has issue,
          ●Baron Alexei VON KORFF, *b* at Vienna, Austria 25 Dec 1973.
        3*b*●Michael Stråle ERICKSON, *b* at Nassau, Bahamas 3 Feb 1952.
      2*a*●(Prince) Rodion CANTACUZENE, Capt USN [*Aldie, Virginia 22001, USA*], *b* at Chicago, Illinois 22 Oct 1928, *m* at Ellicott City, Maryland, 24 Sept 1960, ●Melissa (*b* at New York 1 Feb 1939), dau of Merrill Macneille, by his wife Adelaide Close, and has issue,

      1*b*●Michael CANTACUZENE, *b* at Washington, DC 12 July 1961.
      2*b*●Rodion CANTACUZENE, *b* at Washington, DC 7 Aug 1963.
      3*b*●Clarissa CANTACUZENE, *b* at Washington, DC 6 Dec 1965.
    (2) ●Princess Barbara CANTACUZENE [*2707 Riedling Drive, Apt 2, Louisville, Kentucky 40206, USA*], *b* at St Petersburg, Russia 27 March 1904, *m* 1st at Washington, DC 10 Oct 1926 (*m* diss by div 1933), Bruce Smith (*b* at Louisville, Kentucky 3 March 1901; *d* there 4 Oct 1942), and has issue,
    ●Bruce Michael SMITH, 1st Lieut USAF 1954-56, Sales Man Louisville Paper Co 1956-69, Pres 1969-72 and Pres and Chief Exec Offr from 1972 [*620 Lucas Lane, Louisville, Kentucky 40213, USA*], *b* at Louisville, Kentucky 7 Feb 1932, *educ* Yale (BS 1953), and Harvard Sch of Business, *m* at Rockford, Illinois 18 June 1953, ●Dorothy Diane (*b* at Geneva, Illinois 22 Dec 1932), dau of Robert Decker Frick, by his wife Dorothy May McConnell, and has issue,
      1*b*●Julia Elise SMITH, *b* at Dayton, Ohio 11 May 1955.
      2*b*●Mary Bruce SMITH, *b* at Louisville, Kentucky 25 May 1957.
      3*b*●Barbara Grant SMITH, *b* at Louisville, Kentucky 7 Jan 1959.
      4*b*●Bruce Michael SMITH, *b* at Louisville, Kentucky 26 Aug 1961.
Princess Barbara *m* 2ndly at New Albany, Indiana 11 Nov 1934, William Durrell Siebern (*b* at Cincinnati, Ohio 28 Nov 1894; *d* at Louisville, Kentucky 6 Jan 1973), son of John Siebern, by his wife Orietta Durrell.
    (3) ●Princess Zenaida CANTACUZENE [*The Glebe House, Clonmellon, via Navan, co Westmeath, Ireland*], *b* at St Petersburg, Russia 17 Nov 1908, *m* at Washington, DC 1 Nov 1928, Sir John Coldbrook Hanbury-Williams, CVO, sometime High Sheriff of London, Chm of Courtaulds Ltd, Gentleman Usher to TM King George V, King Edward VIII, King George VI and Queen Elizabeth II (*b* at Henley-on-Thames, Oxon, England 28 May 1892; *d* at the London Clinic 10 Aug 1965), yr son of late Major-Gen Sir John Hanbury-Williams, GCVO, KCB, CMG, Marshal of Diplomatic Corps (*see* BURKE'S *LG,* HANBURY-WILLIAMS *formerly of Nant Oer and Coldbrook Park*), and has issue,
      1*a*●Barbara HANBURY-WILLIAMS, *b* at 14 West Halkin Street, London 6 Dec 1929, *m* 1st at St Paul's Church, Knightsbridge, London 26 Jan 1950 (*m* diss by div 1963), her 1st cousin once removed Prince Michael Cantacuzene, Count Speransky (*b* at Poltava, Russia 12 Oct 1913), only son of Prince Serge Cantacuzene, Count Speransky (yst brother of Major-Gen Prince Michael

Cantacuzene—*see above*), by his wife Marie Okolisc-zanyi, and has issue,

1*b*●Prince Serge Michael CANTACUZENE, Count Speransky, *b* at the American Hosp, Paris 13 May 1952, *educ* Harrow.

2*b*●Princess Alexandra Elizabeth CANTACUZENE, *b* at Princess Beatrice Hosp, London 16 June 1956.

Barbara Hanbury-Williams *m* 2ndly in London 31 July 1965, ●James Valentine Edwards, Headmaster of Heatherdown Sch (*b* at Bryn Arthur, St Asaph, Flintshire, N Wales 4 Feb 1925) [*Heatherdown, Ascot, Berks*], yst son of late Capt Alfred Harold Edwards, OBE, of Bryn Polyn, St Asaph, Flintshire, N Wales, by his wife Eleanor Hayes, and has further issue,

3*b*●Caroline Antonia EDWARDS, *b* at Heatherdown, Ascot 1 June 1966.

4*b*●Charlotte Eleanor Marina EDWARDS, *b* at Windsor 12 Sept 1968.

2*a*●Elizabeth Frances HANBURY-WILLIAMS, *b* at 14 West Halkin Street, London 6 Dec 1929 (twin with her sister Barbara Hanbury-Williams, *m* 1st at St James's (Roman Catholic) Church, Spanish Place, London 24 July 1951 (*m* diss by div 1968), Brian Patrick Morgan Keeling (*b* in London 10 July 1927), 3rd and yst son of Sir John Henry Keeling, of Hurst House, Sedlescombe, Sussex, by his wife Dorothy May Finucane, and has issue,

1*b*●Sara Elizabeth KEELING [*Flat 6, 5 Elm Park Gardens, London, SW10*], *b* at 10 Astell Street, London 6 July 1954.

2*b*●Patrick James KEELING [*Flat 6, 5 Elm Park Gardens, London SW19*], *b* at 10 Astell Street, London 31 May 1956.

Elizabeth Frances Hanbury-Williams *m* 2ndly in London 6 June 1972, ●John Grinnell Wetmore Husted (*b* 22 June 1926) [*Willow Brook, Bedford, NY, USA*], elder son of John Grinnell Wetmore Husted, of David's Brook, Bedford, New York (*see* BURKE'S *Distinguished Families of America*).

3*a*●John Michael Anthony HANBURY-WILLIAMS, late 2nd Lieut Green Howards, T/Capt Oxf and Bucks LI [*Huxley Lane Farm, nr Chester, Cheshire*], *b* at 14 West Halkin Street, London 7 July 1933, *educ* Eton, *m* at St Paul's Church, Knightsbridge, London 4 April 1956, ●Diane (*b* in London 28 Aug 1936), dau of Lister Hartley, of 60 Prince's Gate, London SW7, by his wife Lucila D'Alkaine, and has issue,

1*b*●Nicholas John HANBURY-WILLIAMS, *b* in London 1 Jan 1957, *educ* Eton.

2*b*●Charles Lister HANBURY-WILLIAMS, *b* in London 18 Nov 1958, *educ* Eton.

3*b*●Michael Anthony HANBURY-WILLIAMS, *b* in London 28 June 1961.

4*b*●Victoria Mary HANBURY-WILLIAMS, *b* at Tarporley, Cheshire 27 Oct 1967.

2 Ulysses S. GRANT III, of Clinton, New York, commn'd US Army 1903, Col Corps of Engrs 1934, Col NA 1917-20, T/Major-Gen 1943, had DSM and Legion of Merit (USA) and decorations of six foreign countries, *b* nr Chicago, Illinois 4 July 1881, *educ* Theresianum, Vienna, Cutler Sch, New York City, Columbia Univ, and West Point, *m* at Washington, DC 27 Nov 1907, Edith (*b* at New York City 1 Dec 1878; *d* at Clinton, New York 23 May 1962), only dau of Hon Elihu Root, Sec of State under Pres Theodore Roosevelt, by his wife Clara Frances Wales, and *d* at Clinton, New York 29 Aug 1968, leaving issue,

(1)●Edith GRANT [*3016 N Pollard Street, Arlington, Virginia 22207, USA*], *b* at Clinton, New York 9 Sept 1908, *educ* Bryn Mawr (AB, MA), *m* at Governors Island, New York 21 Nov 1936, as his 2nd wife, Col David Wood Griffiths, US Army (*b* at Austin, Illinois 5 Nov 1896; *d* at Arlington, Virginia 14 Feb 1967), and has issue,

1*a*●John Grant GRIFFITHS, with US Dept of Agric, Beltsville, Maryland [*3016 N Pollard Street, Arlington, Virginia 22207, USA*], *b* at Little Rock, Arkansas 15 July 1938, *educ* Univ of Iowa.

2*a*●Frances Elizabeth GRIFFITHS [*220 East 87th Street, New York 10028, USA*], *b* at Galveston, Texas 29 April 1941, *educ* Smith Coll (AB).

3*a*●Nancy Root GRIFFITHS, *b* at Galveston, Texas 5 Dec 1946, *educ* Beloit Coll (AB), *m* at Clinton, New

York 6 Sept 1969, ●Brian H. Price (*b* 19 Feb 1947) [*No 5, 3801 Milan Drive, Alexandria, Virginia 22305, USA*].

(2)●Clara Frances GRANT, *b* at Clinton, New York 4 Sept 1912, *educ* Bryn Mawr (AB), *m* at Belmore, New York 18 May 1935, ●Major-Gen Paul Ernest Ruestow, USAF (ret) (*b* at Rockville Center, New York 29 Dec 1908), son of Ernest W. Ruestow, by his wife Louella Kiermaier, and has issue,

1*a*●George Frederick RUESTOW, in US Civil Service [*313 Rigby Road, Fairborn, Ohio, USA*], *b* at San Antonio, Texas 14 Jan 1936, *educ* Univ of Dayton (AB), and Auburn Univ (MA), *m* at Dayton, Ohio 12 June 1965, ●Juanita Marie (*b* at Minster, Ohio Oct 1943), dau of Norbert Meyer, by his wife Wilma, and has issue,

1*b*●Tanya René RUESTOW, *b* at Alexandria, Virginia 25 April 1966.

2*b*●Kristin Marie RUESTOW, *b* at Dayton, Ohio 9 Dec 1967.

3*b*●Kendra Frances RUESTOW, *b* at Dayton, Ohio 23 June 1969.

2*a*●Edward Grant RUESTOW, Assist Prof of History, Univ of Colorado [*320 S 40th Street, Boulder, Colorado, USA*], *b* at Honolulu, Hawaii 30 Sept 1937, *educ* Pennsylvania Univ (AB, MA), George Washington Univ (MA), and Indiana Univ (PhD), *m* at Boulder, Colorado 25 June 1973, ●Carmen Gutierrez (*b* at Avila, Spain).

3*a*●Claire RUESTOW, *b* at Utica, New York 19 April 1945, *educ* Vassar (AB), *m* at Clinton, New York 2 May 1970, ●George J. Telecki (*b* in Yugoslavia 26 May 1933) [*377 N Broadway, Yonkers, New York, USA*], son of Joseph Telecki, by his wife Meta von Riesenfelder, and has issue,

●Nicole TELECKI, *b* at New York 23 June 1971.

(3)●Julia GRANT, *b* at New York 20 Jan 1916, *m* at Clinton, New York 18 Aug 1945, ●John Sanderson Dietz [*402 Sedgwick Drive, Syracuse, New York 13203, USA*], son of Robert E. Dietz, by his wife Barbara, and has had issue,

1*a*●John Edwin DIETZ [*509 N Columbia Street, Chapel Hill, North Carolina, USA*], *b* at Syracuse, New York 4 Jan 1948, *educ* Univ of N Carolina (AB), *m* at Chapel Hill, N Carolina 29 June 1974, ●Julia McMillan.

2*a*●Edith Root DIETZ, *b* at Syracuse, New York 25 Dec 1951, *educ* Stanford Univ, *d* at New York 20 Oct 1971.

3*a*●Ulysses Grant DIETZ, *b* at Syracuse, New York 22 July 1955, *educ* Yale.

4*a* Edward Johnson DIETZ, *b* at Syracuse, New York 7 Aug 1956; *d* 17 June 1969.

2 Ulysses S. GRANT, Jr, of San Diego, California, admitted to Bar 1876, candidate for US Senate 1899, delegate-at-large Republican Nat Conventions 1896 and 1900, Presidential Elector-at-large 1904 and 1908, *b* at Bethel, Clermont County, Ohio 22 July 1852, *educ* Harvard (AB 1874), and Columbia Univs (LLB 1876), *m* 1st at New York 1 Nov 1880, (Fannie) Josephine (*b* at Adrian, Michigan 16 Jan 1857; *d* 1909), yr dau of Jerome Bunty Chaffee, US Senator for Colorado, by his wife Miriam Barnard Comstock, and had issue,

1 Miriam GRANT, *b* at New York 26 Sept 1881, *m* 1st there 17 Oct 1904, Adm Ulysses Samuel Macy, USN, and had issue,

(1)●Fannie Chaffee Grant MACY, *b* at Salem Center, New York 18 Oct 1905, *m* ●Edward C. Hasset.

(2) Grant MACY, *d* an inf.

Miriam Grant *m* 2ndly, John Rice.

2 Chaffee GRANT, *b* at New York 28 Sept 1883, *m* 1st at Washington, Pennsylvania 5 June 1907 (*m* diss by div), Helen Dent (Nellie) Wrenshall (who *m* 2ndly, Isaac Hart Purdy, formerly husband of her sister-in-law Fannie Grant—*see* p 330), and had issue,

(1)●Jane GRANT, *b* 22 March 1908, *m* 1st 1930, Martin Smith, and has issue,

1*a*●Peter Martin SMITH.

Jane Grant *m* 2ndly 1943, ●Cormac de McCarty, and has further issue,

2*a*●Grant MCCARTY.

3*a*●Dent L. MCCARTY.

(2) Jerome Chaffee GRANT, *b* Aug 1913, *m* 1943, ●Elizabeth Wurster, and *dsp* at Salem Center, New York 1949.

Chaffee Grant *m* 2ndly, Mrs Marion Potter (*née*

Farnsworth).
3 Julia Dent GRANT, *b* at New York 15 April 1885, *m* 8 Oct
1910, Edmund Cathcart King, and had issue,
(1) ●Fannie Chaffee KING, *b* 23 July 1912, *m* 1 Jan 1948,
●Henry Castleton, and has issue,
●Julia Dent CASTLETON.
(2) ●Grant KING, *b* 15 Nov 1913, *m* ●Mary Lee, and has
issue,
1*a*●Jessica Mary KING.
2*a*●Julia Eunice KING.
(3) ●Julia Dent KING, *b* 7 Oct 1917, *m* Aug 1945,
●William Watson, and has issue,
1*a*●Kirk WATSON.
2*a*●Steven WATSON.
3*a*●Fannie Grant WATSON.
4 Fannie GRANT, *b* at Salem Center, New York 11 Aug 1889,
*m* 1911 (*m* diss by div), Isaac Hart Purdy (who *m* 2ndly,
Helen Dent Wrenshall, formerly wife of his brother-in-law
Chaffee Grant—*see p 329*), and had issue,
●Isaac Grant PURDY, *b* 1914.
5 Ulysses S. GRANT IV, Prof of Geology, Univ of Los
Angeles, *b* at Salem Center, New York 23 May 1893, *m* 1st
1917, Matilda Bartikofsky; and 2ndly, Frances Dean.
Ulysses S. Grant, Jr *m* 2ndly 1913, Mrs America Will (*née*
Workman), and *d* in California 26 Sept 1929.
3 Ellen (Nellie) Wrenshall GRANT, *b* at Wish-ton-wish 4 July
1855, *m* 1st at the White House, Washington, DC 21 May 1874,
Algernon Charles Frederick Sartoris, JP Carmarthenshire, of
Warsash House, Titchfield, Hants, England (*b* in London,
England 1 Aug 1851; *d* on the Isle of Capri, Italy 3 Feb 1893),
yr son of Edward John Sartoris, JP, of Warnford Park, Bishop's
Waltham, Hants, England (*see* BURKE'S *LG*, 1937 *Edn*,
SARTORIS *late of Rushden*), by his wife Adelaide Kemble, and
had issue,
1 Grant Greville Edward SARTORIS, *b* at Elberon, New
Jersey 11 July 1875; *d* at Titchfield, Hants, England 21 May
1876.
2 Algernon Edward Urban SARTORIS, Capt US Vols in
Spanish-American War, *b* at Washington, DC 17 March
1877, *m* at Paris, France 1904, Cécile Noufflard, and *d* 17 Jan
1928, leaving issue,
●Herbert Charles Urban Grant SARTORIS, *b* at Paris,
France 17 Aug 1906, *m* 6 April 1929, ●Alix Jeuffrain, and
has had issue,
1*a*●Oliver Algernon SARTORIS, *b* 24 March 1930.
2*a*●Francois Charles Henry SARTORIS, *b* 19 Nov 1931.
3*a* Guy SARTORIS, *b* 3 Dec 1932; *d* 3 April 1933.

4*a*●Claude SARTORIS, *b* 7 Sept 1934.
5*a*●Jean SARTORIS.
6*a*●Antoine SARTORIS.
7*a*●Anne SARTORIS.
3 Vivien May SARTORIS, *b* in London, England 7 April
1879, *m* 1903, Frederick Roosevelt Scovel, of New York (*d*
27 July 1930), and *dsp* Dec 1933.
4 Rosemary Alice SARTORIS, *b* in London, England 30 Nov
1880, *m* 29 Oct 1906, George Henry Woolston, of Florida (*d*
27 Jan 1930), and *d* 28 Aug 1914, leaving issue,
●Rosemary WOOLSTON, *b* 17 Jan 1909.
Nellie Wrenshall Grant *m* 2ndly 4 July 1912, Frank Hatch
Jones, of Chicago, first Assist Postmaster-Gen under President
Cleveland, and *d* at Chicago 30 Aug 1922.
4 Jesse Root GRANT, of Sausalito, California, author of *In the
Days of My Father General Grant* (1925), *b* at Hardscrabble 6
Feb 1858, *educ* Cornell, and Columbia Law Sch, *m* 1st at San
Francisco 30 Sept 1880 (*m* diss by div), Elizabeth (*b* at
Minneapolis, Minnesota 10 Jan 1858), dau of William Smith
Chapman, by his wife Sarah Armstrong, and had issue,
1 Nellie GRANT, *b* at Elberon, New Jersey 5 Aug 1881, *m*
1913, Capt William Piggott Cronan, USN (*b* 9 Feb 1879),
and *d* at La Jolla, California June 1972, leaving issue,
(1) ●Elizabeth Grant CRONAN, *b* 8 May 1915, *m* April
1943 (*m* diss by div), Don Waller, and has issue,
1*a*●Marie WALLER.
2*a*●Carolyn WALLER.
(2) ●Nellie Grant CRONAN, *b* 24 Feb 1917, *m* ●Col
Franklin D. Rothwell, US Army, and has issue,
●Theresa Lauren ROTHWELL.
2 Chapman GRANT, Major US Army, *b* at Salem Center,
New York 22 March 1887, *educ* Williams Coll (AB 1910), *m*
1917, ●Mabel Ward (*b* 11 Feb 1892), and had issue,
(1) ●Mabel Chapman GRANT, *b* 24 Aug 1918, *m* ●Bruce
Hazard (*b* Nov 1917), and has issue,
1*a*●Terry HAZARD.
2*a*●Polly HAZARD.
3*a*●Thomas HAZARD.
(2) ●Ulysses S. GRANT V, *b* 1920, *m* 1944, ●Dorothy
Jean Nichols, and has issue,
1*a*●Chapman, F. GRANT.
2*a*●Millard W. GRANT.
3*a*●Bonnie J. GRANT.
Jesse Root Grant *m* 2ndly 26 Aug 1918, Lillian (*b* 1864; *d* 1 July
1924), widow of John Anthony Wilkins, and only dau of Capt
Owen Burns, USN, of Burnsville, N Carolina, by his wife
Martha Ann Armstrong, and *d* 1934.

# The Brothers and Sisters of President Grant

**1** Samuel Simpson GRANT, of Galena, Illinois, merchant, *b* at Georgetown, Ohio 23 Sept 1825; *dunm* at St Paul, Minnesota 13 Sept 1861.

**2** Clara Rachel GRANT, *b* at Georgetown 11 Dec 1828; *dunm* at Covington, Kentucky 6 March 1865.

**3** Virginia Paine GRANT, *b* at Georgetown 20 Feb 1832, *m* at Covington, Kentucky 13 May 1869, as his 2nd wife Hon Abel Rathbone Corbin, of New York (*b* at Otsego, New York 24 March 1808; *d* 1881), son of Eliakim Lyon Corbin, by his wife Lodama, and had issue, one dau (who *d* an inf).

**4** Orvil Lynch GRANT, *b* at Georgetown 15 May 1835, *m* at Bethel, Ohio April 1857, Mary (*b* 1835; *d* 10 April 1894), dau of Asher Medary, by his wife Elizabeth Thornton, and *d* at Elizabeth, New Jersey 4 Aug 1881, leaving issue, three sons and one dau.

**5** Mary Frances GRANT, *b* at Georgetown 28 July 1839, *m* at Covington, Kentucky 27 Oct 1863, Rev Michael John Cramer, DD, US Min to Denmark 1871-81, Res US Min and Consul-Gen at Berne 1881-85 (*b* at Schaffhausen, Switzerland 6 Feb 1835; *d* at Carlisle, Pennsylvania 23 Jan 1898), son of John Jacob Cramer, by his wife Magdalene Bowman, and had issue, one son and one dau.

# Notes

[1] Although christened Hiram Ulysses, Grant was always known by the second name. When nominated for West Point by his father's friend Congressman Thomas L. Hamer his name was entered in error as "U. S. Grant" (the "S" probably being taken from his mother's maiden name of Simpson). He had already reversed his first two names and usually signed himself as "Ulysses H. Grant" or "U.H. Grant". On graduation he finally adopted the name of Ulysses S. Grant, but never expanded the middle initial.

[2] Through the Porter family President Grant was a sixth cousin once removed to the future President Cleveland. The relationship is set out in the following table:

John Porter = Anna White
(1594-1648) | (1600-1647)

| Mary Porter | Samuel Porter |
|---|---|
| (1638-    ) | (d 1689) |
| = Samuel Grant | = Hannah Stanley |
| (1631-1718) | (d 1708) |
| | |
| Samuel Grant | Samuel Porter |
| (1659-1710) | (1660-1712) |
| = Grace Minor | = Joanna Cook |
| (1670-1753) | (1665-1713) |
| | |
| Noah Grant | Aaron Porter |
| (1692-1727) | (1689-1722) |
| = Martha Huntington | = Susannah Sewall |
| (1696-    ) | (1691-1747) |
| | |
| Capt Noah Grant | Susannah Porter |
| (1718-1756) | (1716-1788) |
| = Susanna Delano | = Aaron Cleveland |
| (1724-    ) | (1715-1757) |
| | |
| Capt Noah Grant | Aaron Cleveland |
| (1748-1819) | (1744-1815) |
| = Rachel Kelly | = Abiah Hyde |
| (d 1805) | (1749-1788) |
| | |
| Jesse Root Grant | William Cleveland |
| (1794-1873) | (1770-1837) |
| = Hannah Simpson | = Margaret Falley |
| (1798-1883) | (1776-    ) |
| | |
| ULYSSES S. GRANT | Richard Falley Cleveland |
| | (1804-1853) |
| | = Anne Neal |
| | (1806-1882) |
| | |
| | GROVER CLEVELAND |

[3] Through Grace Minor the Grants derive a Royal descent from David I, King of Scots (*see* APPENDIX C, PRESIDENTS OF ROYAL DESCENT). It was also through Grace Minor that President Grant was connected with Richard Henry Dana, author of *Two Years Before the Mast* (*see* APPENDIX D, SOME REMARKABLE KINSHIPS).

[4] Through the Delano family President Grant was a fourth cousin once removed to the future President Franklin Delano Roosevelt, who was born three years before Grant's death. The relationship is set out in the following table:

```
              Lieut Jonathan Delano = Mercy Warren, grand-dau of Richard
              (1647-1720)           | Warren, who sailed in the Mayflower.
                    ┌───────────────────────────────────┐
          Jonathan Delano II                      Thomas Delano
             (1680-1752)                            (b 1704)
            = Amey Hatch                          = Jean Peckham

          Susanna Delano                      Capt Ephraim Delano
             (b 1724)                             (1733-1815)
          = (1) Noah Grant                     = Elizabeth Cushman

            Noah Grant                         Capt Warren Delano
            (1748-1819)                           (1779-1866)
          = (2) Rachel Kelly                    = (1) Deborah Church

          Jesse Root Grant                       Warren Delano
            (1794-1873)                           (1809-1898)
          = Hannah Simpson                  = Catherine Robbins Lyman

          ULYSSES S. GRANT                       Sarah Delano
                                                 (1854-1941)
                                               = James Roosevelt

                                         FRANKLIN DELANO ROOSEVELT
```

[5] The Princes Cantacuzene claim descent from the Byzantine family of that name, from which sprang the Emperor John VI (1347-1354). In the seventeenth and eighteenth centuries several members of the family served as reigning Princes of Moldavia and Wallachia under the Turkish Sultans. The branch to which Prince Michael Cantacuzene belonged were granted recognition as Princes of the Russian Empire by the Emperor Alexander II in 1865 and created Counts Speransky by the same in 1872 as heirs of the legislator Michael Speransky (1772-1839).

# Rutherford Birchard Hayes

## 1822-1893

———

19th President of the
United States of America
1877-1881

RUTHERFORD BIRCHARD HAYES, 19TH PRESIDENT

# Rutherford Birchard Hayes

## 1822-1893

### 19th President of the United States of America
### 1877-1881

IN SOME ways the career of Rutherford B. Hayes sounds typical of a whole generation of Republican candidates. New England parents, emigrating to Ohio and having a hard time of it; a father dying of fever in 1822, before young Rutherford was born; three other children dying in infancy, so that the boy was left with only a mother and an elder sister—these form the first chapter of what could be a composite biography. Next in sequence came education, with financial help from his uncle Sardis Birchard: a degree from Kenyon College, further study at Harvard Law School. Next, law practice in Lower Sandusky (now Fremont), Ohio, and in Cincinnati. There was marriage in 1852 to Lucy Ware Webb of Chillicothe, Ohio, who was a student when Hayes met her at Wesleyan Female College in Cincinnati and who was to bear him a daughter and seven sons—such a quantity that Hayes described himself and Lucy as being in "the boy business". Next the Civil War, a terrible shock for Americans and yet a golden opportunity for the ambitious. Hayes, beginning as a Major of Ohio volunteer infantry, saw a great deal of action, was five times wounded, and ended with a brevet major-generalcy and a lasting, nostalgic fondness for regimental reunions. War service was immediately followed by a term in Congress. In 1876 he was for the second time Governor of Ohio, and a faithful Republican. In sum, he was presidential timber—though Henry Adams (the grandson of John Quincy Adams and a rather lofty observer of contemporary politics) dismissed Hayes as "a third rate nonentity, whose only recommendation is that he was obnoxious to no one".

It is true that there were several others of similar background, as the rise of James Abram Garfield was to show. It is also true that Hayes was not particularly impressive in manner or appearance. People who eyed him with some curiosity, for example on his visit to the Philadelphia Centennial Exposition in 1876, saw a figure of medium build, the lower half of his face obscured with a beard of Civil War vintage, in slightly dingy clothing. But of course like other "available" candidates he was already pre-selected, not merely through having done the right things but through having done them with conspicuous competence. If Hayes had hailed from Kansas or Kentucky instead of Ohio, a key state, things would not have gone so smoothly for him. But he was not an average man. We can only speculate on what inner features distinguish a person's history. There are unusual elements in Hayes, intriguing for the psychoanalytic biographer. One of these is his extraordinarily close attachment to his sister, who addressed him almost as if he were a lover. When she married he declined to attend the wedding. Though she begged him to set up in law practice in the thriving city of Columbus, where she and her husband lived, Rutherford thought it more prudent to install himself in Fremont, where litigation was less interesting and less profitable. He may unconsciously have been drawn to Lucy Webb because she resembled Fanny. When his sister died from childbirth in 1856, Hayes told his wife: "You are Sister Fanny to me now". It seems possible that in transferring his whole affection to his wife Hayes gained not only a marriage of rare harmony but a new access of wholeness and strength. Another possibility is that the comparatively unfruitful years in Fremont redoubled his determination to succeed, so as to make up for lost time. He was nearly forty years old when he became a soldier—nine years older than Garfield. Nor can Lucy's own qualities be left out of the reckoning. She was a handsome, good-natured woman, better educated than most Presidents' wives had been. She was laughed at in Washington by sophisticates as "Lemonade Lucy" because she was a total abstainer who would not serve alcohol in the White House. She had principles and she stuck to them. Yet Lucy Hayes was no joyless bigot but a strong, cheerful companion for a sometimes sorely perplexed President.

Since he was attacked even before inauguration as "Rutherfraud" Hayes, he needed all the moral support he could get. 1876 was the most tortuous and least satisfactory presidential election in the nation's history. The first count gave a definite superiority both in popular and in electoral votes to the Democratic candidate, Samuel J. Tilden of New York. Widespread cheating was however suspected, with the Democrats somewhat more culpable than the Republicans. The result hinged on the situation in Florida, South Carolina and Louisiana, three states in the South which were still not fully "reconstructed". In other words, they were still occupied by Union troops and still to some extent manipulable by the Republican party machine. Not until the eve of the inauguration, after four months of furious controversy and seemingly hopeless confusion, did the special electoral commission gain grudging assent to its

LUCY WARE WEBB, MRS HAYES

decision that Hayes was the winner. Concessions, including the final end of Reconstruction, were necessary to appease the South and the Democrats.

Hayes took office under the worst auspices. Moreover, he had already announced that he would not seek a second term. He looked like a "lame duck" President from the start. Republican chieftains of the "Stalwart" persuasion assumed that he would be as malleable as Grant had been, in leaving them to run their own networks of patronage and graft. But Hayes wrote in his diary: "I shall show a *grit* that will astonish those who predict weakness". He ignored the spoilsmen in picking a cabinet of much higher caliber than Grant's. He challenged the very heart of the spoils system, the New York Custom House, by dismissing its two principals, Chester A. Arthur and Alonzo Cornell, because they persisted in using Federal appointments for political purposes. At issue was the whole question of presidential versus legislative and local power. Hayes won a battle on behalf of his office in what was to be a long struggle. He showed good sense in conciliating the South, and courage in vetoing a California-inspired bill to exclude the Chinese.

Hayes's witty Secretary of State William Evarts remarked that at White House receptions "the water flowed like wine". The domestic atmosphere, if dowdy, was homely in the good sense. It was Mrs Hayes who introduced the custom of Easter egg-rolling—a more innocent pastime than others in Washington. The Hayeses were genuinely esteemed when they retired from the capital. Hayes kept himself modestly and worthily active, though badly hit by Lucy's death in 1889. Shortly before his death in January 1893 he wrote that he wanted to be resting quietly beside her. And so it was to be.

# Chronology

1822      Born (posthumously) at Delaware, Ohio 4 Oct.

1828-36  Attended school in Delaware and Norwalk Academy, Ohio.

1837      Attended Isaac Webb's School, Middletown, Connecticut.

1838      Entered Kenyon College, Gambier, Ohio, Nov.

1842      Graduated BA 3 Aug; began Law studies with Sparrow and Matthews, Gambier, Ohio.

1843      Entered Harvard Law School Aug.

1845      Admitted to Ohio Bar 10 March; graduated from Harvard Law School with LLB degree 27 Aug; received MA degree from Kenyon College.

1846      Began law practice in partnership with Ralph P. Buckland at Lower Sandusky (now Fremont), Ohio, April.

1848-49  Wintered in Texas for health reasons.

1850      Opened law office in Cincinnati, Ohio.

1854      Moved into own house Sept.

1855      Joined Republican Party; Delegate to State Republican Convention.

1856      Declined Republican nomination for Common Pleas Judge, Cincinnati.

1858      Appointed City Solicitor by Cincinnati City Council.

1861      Commissioned Major in 23rd Regt Ohio Volunteer Infantry under Col William S. Rosecrans 27 June; regiment posted to W Virginia July; appointed Judge Advocate of Department of Ohio 19 Sept; promoted Lt-Col 24 Oct.

1862      Led charge in Battle of South Mountain, Maryland, and was wounded in the left arm 14 Sept; promoted Col 24 Oct.

1863-64  Commanded Gen George Crooke's 1st Infantry Brigade.

1864      Took part in Battle of Winchester, Virginia 23-24 July nominated for House of Representatives at Republican District Convention, Cincinnati Aug; took part in Battle of Cedar Creek, Virginia, and promoted Brevet Brig-Gen 19 Oct.

1865      Promoted Brevet Major-Gen 13 March; resigned from Army 8 June; took seat in House of Representatives 4 Dec.

1866      Re-elected to House of Representatives.

1867      Nominated for Governor of Ohio at Republican State Convention 20 June; elected Oct.

1868      Inaugurated as Governor of Ohio Jan.

1869    Re-elected Governor.

1871    Declined to seek re-election for third term as Governor.

1872    Retired as Governor of Ohio, and declined offer of a seat in the Senate Jan; nominated for House of Representatives July; defeated in election Oct.

1873    Retired to Fremont, Ohio.

1874    Inherited the estate of his maternal uncle Sardis Birchard in Fremont.

1875    Again nominated for Governor of Ohio at Republican State Convention; elected Oct.

1876    Inaugurated as Governor of Ohio Jan; nominated "favorite son" candidate for President at Republican State Convention 29 March; nominated for President at Republican National Convention in Cincinnati 16 June; election day 7 Nov; Presidential Electors cast their ballots 6 Dec.

1877    Electoral Commission established 29 Jan; met in the Hall of the House of Representatives 1 Feb; electoral vote tabulated by Congress 2 March and Hayes and William Almon Wheeler officially declared elected; inaugurated on the steps of the east portico of the Capitol (having taken the oath privately at the White House 3 March) 5 March; issued executive order prohibiting electioneering by Government officers 22 June; issued proclamations against domestic violence in W Virginia 18 July, Maryland 21 July, and Pennsylvania 23 July; sent first State of the Union message to Congress 3 Dec.

1878    Vetoed Bland-Allison Silver Bill (passed over his veto) 28 Feb; vetoed special Term of Courts in Mississippi Bill 6 March; signed Greenback Act 31 May; signed District of Columbia Government Act 11 June; suspended Chester A. Arthur as Collector of the Port of New York 11 July; received members of first resident Chinese embassy at the White House 4 Oct; issued proclamation against domestic violence in New Mexico 7 Oct; sent second State of the Union message to Congress 2 Dec.

1879    Resumption of specie payments (suspended since 1861) begun 1 Jan; signed Act allowing women to practice before the Supreme Court 15 Feb; vetoed Chinese Immigration Restriction Bill 1 March; pocket vetoed Relief of Certain Settlers on Public Lands Bill 3 March; issued proclamation ordering removal of squatters from Indian Territory 26 April; vetoed Army Appropriation Bill 29 April; vetoed legislative Executive and Judicial Appropriations Bill 29 May; signed second Army Appropriations Act 23 June; vetoed Payment of Marshals Bill 23 June; sent special message to Congress regarding Marshals' payments 30 June; sent third State of the Union message to Congress 1 Dec.

1880    Sent special message to Congress regarding Ponca Indians 1 Feb; issued second proclamation against squatters in Indian Territory 12 Feb; sent special message to Congress regarding inter-oceanic canal 8 March; vetoed Payment of Marshals Bill 15 June; visited San Francisco 8 Sept; Chinese exclusion treaty signed at Peking 17 Nov; sent fourth and last State of the Union message to Congress.

1881    Issued executive order banning sale of intoxicating liquor at military installations 22 Feb; vetoed Refunding of National Debt Bill 3 March; retired from office and attended the inauguration of his successor President Garfield 4 March; retired to Fremont.

1883-93  President of the National Prison Association.

1893    Suffered a heart attack while on a train returning to Fremont from a business trip 14 Jan; died at Fremont 17 Jan; buried there.

# The Writings of President Hayes

*Diary and Letters* edited by Charles R. Williams, 5 vols (1922-26)

# Lineage of President Hayes

GEORGE HAYES, emigrated from Scotland 1680 and settled at Windsor, Connecticut, *m* Abigail Dibble, and had issue,

DANIEL HAYES, *m* Sarah, dau of John Lee, and had issue,

EZEKIEL HAYES, *m* Rebecca, dau of John Russell, by his wife Sarah Trowbridge, and had issue,

RUTHERFORD HAYES, *m* Chloe Smith, and had issue,

RUTHERFORD HAYES, farmer and storekeeper, *b* at Brattleboro, Vermont 4 Jan 1787, *m* 13 Sept 1813, Sophia (*b* at Wilmington, Vermont 15 April 1792; *d* at Columbus, Ohio 30 Oct 1866), dau of Roger Birchard, by his wife Druscilla, dau of Daniel Austin, and *d* at Delaware, Ohio 20 July 1822, having had with other issue (*see* BROTHERS AND SISTERS OF PRESIDENT HAYES, *p 346*), a yst son (born posthumously),

RUTHERFORD BIRCHARD HAYES, **19th President of the United States of America.**


# The Descendants of President Hayes

RUTHERFORD BIRCHARD HAYES *m* at Cincinnati, Ohio 30 Dec 1852, Lucy Ware (*b* at Chillicothe, Ohio 28 Aug 1831; *d* at Fremont, Ohio 25 June 1889, *bur* first at Oakwood Cemetery, Fremont, later transferred to Spiegel Grove), only dau of Dr James Webb, by his wife Maria, dau of Judge Isaac Cook, of Ross County, Ohio, and had issue,

**1** Sardis Birchard (later called Birchard Austin) HAYES, *b* at Cincinnati 4 Nov 1853, *educ* Cornell Univ, *m* 30 Dec 1886, Mary Nancy (*b* at Erie County, Ohio 15 May 1859; *d* at Toledo, Ohio 22 June 1924), dau of Nathan Isould Sherman, by his wife Elizabeth Otis, and *d* at Toledo 24 Jan 1926, having had issue,

  **1** Rutherford Birchard HAYES, *b* at Toledo, Ohio 2 Oct 1887; *d* there 27 Nov 1888.

  **2** Sherman Otis HAYES, served in World War I as Lieut 14th US Inf, *b* at Toledo 11 Oct 1888, *m* 14 Feb 1912, Beatrice Henrietta (*d* 1939), dau of Royal F. Baker, and *d* at Boston 27 Feb 1949, leaving issue,

    ● Lucy Webb HAYES, *b* at Portland, Oregon 8 Jan 1915, *m* 17 April 1950, ● Col Lloyd Webster Hough, US Army, and has issue,

      1*a* ● Lucy Webb Hayes HOUGH, *b* in Indiana 30 Sept 1952.

      2*a* ● Lloyd Webster Hayes HOUGH, *b* 7 Feb 1954.

  **3** Webb Cook HAYES II, of Spiegel Grove, Fremont, Ohio, hon LLD Bowling Green State Univ, Rear-Adm USN (promoted 1954), commn'd Ensign 1911, served in World War I, *b* at Toledo, Ohio 25 Sept 1890, *educ* US Naval Acad (BS 1911), *m* 29 April 1919, ● Martha (*b* at Toledo 23 Dec 1896), dau of Arthur Earnest Baker, and *d* at Fremont, 10 July 1957, leaving issue,

    (1) ● Webb Cook HAYES III, lawyer in Washington, DC [*8510 Longfellow Place, Chevy Chase, Maryland, USA*], *b* at Toledo 25 Sept 1920, *educ* Yale, *m* 14 May 1945, ● Betty (*b* 28 Aug 1923), dau of Norman B. Frost, and has issue,

      1*a* ● Webb Cook HAYES IV, *b* at Washington, DC 18 Aug 1948, *educ* Maryland Univ.

      2*a* ● Norman Burke Frost HAYES, *b* at Washington, DC 2 Jan 1951.

      3*a* ● Stephen Austin HAYES, *b* at Washington, DC 2 Jan 1953, *educ* Laurenceville.

      4*a* ● Jeffrey Kent HAYES, *b* at Washington, DC 7 Dec 1955, *educ* Mercersburg Acad.

    (2) ● Arthur Baker HAYES, *b* at Toledo, Ohio 4 June 1924, *m* 20 Dec 1947, ● June, dau of Charles A. Feltman, and has

issue,
  1*a*●Leslie June HAYES, *b* at Cleveland, Ohio 24 Dec 1950.
  2*a*●Arthur Baker HAYES, Jr [*3214 Leyland Street, Chevy Chase, Maryland, USA*], *b* at Bay Village 29 March 1954.
(3) ●Scott Birchard HAYES, *b* at Washington, DC 2 April 1926, *m* 27 Oct 1951, ●Dorothy Deborah (*b* at Worcester, Mass 2 June 1931), dau of Harold John Walter, and has issue,
  1*a*●Scott Birchard HAYES, Jr, *b* at Cleveland, Ohio 19 Jan 1953.
  2*a*●James Walker HAYES, *b* at Virginia, Minnesota 11 Feb 1955.
  3*a*●Timothy Wheelock HAYES, *b* at Royal Oak, Michigan 17 Jan 1958.
  4*a*●Michael Sherman HAYES, *b* at Cleveland, Ohio 10 Dec 1960.
4 ●Walter Sherman HAYES, served in World War I as Ensign USN in USS *Utah, b* at Toledo, Ohio 27 July 1893, *m* 19 Oct 1935, Rachel (*b* at Toledo 18 April 1908), dau of William Clifton Carr, by his wife Cora Elizabeth Crim, and has issue,
  (1) ●Walter Sherman HAYES, Jr, *b* at Toledo, Ohio 26 Feb 1938, *educ* Wooster Coll, *m* 12 Sept 1964, ●Jean, dau of John Brand, of Wilmington, Delaware, by his wife Dorothy, and has issue,
  ●Elizabeth HAYES, *b* 21 April 1968.
  (2) ●Mary Elizabeth HAYES, *b* at Toledo, Ohio 30 March 1940, *m* 24 Aug 1963, ●Gregg Wiley Parks.
5 Scott Russell HAYES, served in World War I with Field Arty, *b* 23 Sept 1895, *m* 20 Oct 1934, Muriel (*b* at Leonia, New Jersey 2 Dec 1909), dau of William O. Gantz, and *d* at Los Angeles 18 Nov 1968, leaving issue,
  (1) ●Nancy Sherman HAYES, *b* at Los Angeles 23 June 1938, *m* 18 June 1961, ●Keith Leavitt (*b* 4 Feb 1937), son of R. C. Leavitt, Jr, of Gorham, and has issue,
  ●Scott Alan LEAVITT, *b* 29 June 1964.
  (2) ●Martha Jean HAYES, *b* at Los Angeles 7 Dec 1940, *m* 18 June 1961, ●Carl Edward Lusk (*b* 23 Sept 1937), son of Edward Lusk, of Los Angeles, and has issue,
  1*a*●Karen Marie LUSK, *b* 7 Dec 1963.
  2*a*●Robert Edward LUSK, *b* 8 April 1966.
  (3) ●Margaret Frances HAYES, *b* at Los Angeles 19 Dec 1942, *m* 29 Dec 1964, ●James Clark (*b* 11 Nov 1942), and has issue,
  ●Dorothy CLARK, *b* 21 Jan 1966.
5 Scott Russell HAYES, 1st Lieut Field Arty, US Army, *b* at Toledo 23 Sept 1895, *m*, and *d* at Los Angeles 18 Nov 1968, leaving issue.
2 James Webb (later called Webb Cook) HAYES, Lt-Col USV, awarded Congressional Medal of Honor for services in the Philippines, served with British and French bdes on Italian front in World War I, built the Hayes Memorial Library and Museum jtly with the State of Ohio, *b* at Cincinnati, Ohio 20 March 1856, *educ* Cornell Univ, *m* 30 Sept 1912, Mary Otis (*b* at Fremont, Ohio 11 April 1856; *d* at Phoenix, Arizona 3 March 1935), widow of — Brinkerhoff, and dau of Anson H. Miller, by his wife Nancy Otis, and *dsp* 26 July 1935.
3 Rutherford Platt HAYES, *b* at Cincinnati, Ohio 24 June 1858, *educ* Cornell Univ, *m* 24 Oct 1894, Lucy Hayes (*b* at Columbus, Ohio 14 Sept 1868; *d* at Clearwater, Florida 4 Dec 1939), dau of William Augustus Platt, by his wife Sarah Follet, and *d* at Tampa, Florida 31 July 1927, having had issue,
1 Rutherford Birchard HAYES, *b* at Columbus, Ohio Jan 1896; *d* at Asheville, N Carolina 2 Feb 1902.
2 ●William Platt HAYES, served in World War I, *b* at Columbus, Ohio 9 Dec 1897, *m* 1st 28 June 1924, Sarah Taylor (*b* at Waynesville, N Carolina 23 Oct 1895), dau of Howard Taylor Rogers, by his wife Mary Ann Bavenson, and has issue,
(1) ●Lucy Rogers HAYES, *b* at Tampa, Florida 18 Oct 1926, *m* 25 Sept 1948, ●Edward Scott Lawhorne (*b* at Philadelphia 10 Oct 1925), son of William B. Lawhorne, by his wife Emily B., and has issue,
  1*a*●William Scott LAWHORNE, *b* 27 July 1949.

  2*a*●Sarah Hayes LAWHORNE, *b* 6 Aug 1951.
  3*a*●Katherine Rogers LAWHORNE, *b* 10 Sept 1954.
(2) ●Rutherford Platt HAYES II, *b* at Tampa, Florida 27 Dec 1928, *m* 24 June 1950, ●Inge Christine (*b* at Vienna, Austria 12 Aug 1930), dau of Paul Peter Haas, by his wife Claire Marie Horry, and has issue,
  1*a*●Scott Taylor HAYES, *b* 19 Jan 1952.
  2*a*●Rutherford Platt HAYES III, *b* 29 Jan 1955.
(3) ●William Taylor HAYES, *b* at Philadelphia 15 Aug 1934, *m* 22 Dec 1956, ●Sue (*b* at Tulsa, Oklahoma 14 Oct 1933), dau of Paul Ward Cooper, by his wife Velna Iva Strout, and has three adopted children,
  1*a*●Katherine Renée HAYES.
  2*a*●Kristin Ann HAYES.
  3*a*●William Dean HAYES.
William Platt Hayes *m* 2ndly 9 Oct 1947, ●Lillian (*b* at Saginaw, Michigan 24 Feb 1899), widow of — Kirk, and dau of Augustus Burns Chalmers, by his wife Lillian Knight.
3 Birchard Platt HAYES, *b* at Asheville, N Carolina 4 July 1902, *m* 24 June 1927, ●Dorothy Ruth (*b* 24 Oct 1905), dau of Harry H. Toohey, and *d* nr Bamberg, S Carolina 3 Jan 1958, leaving issue,
  ●Margaret Lucy HAYES, *b* at Lakeland, Florida 17 July 1928, *m* 18 Aug 1951, ●Malcolm Alexander Taylor (*b* 23 Jan 1922), son of Alexander J. Taylor, and has had issue,
  1*a*●Lucy Hayes TAYLOR, *b* at Ponghkeepsie, New York 21 Sept 1953.
  2*a* Rutherford Van Wyck TAYLOR, *b* 25 Sept 1955; accidentally *k* at New Paltz, New York 29 June 1958.
  3*a*●Birchard Malcolm TAYLOR, *b* at Ponghkeepsie 6 April 1957.
  4*a*●Scott Alexander TAYLOR, *b* at Kingston, New York 9 March 1960.
Mr and Mrs Birchard P. Hayes also had five adopted children,
  (a) ●Jonathan Bradbury HAYES.
  (b) ●Carolyn Bradbury HAYES.
  (c) ●Richard Platt HAYES.
  (d) ●Libby Lu HAYES.
  (e) ●James Birchard HAYES.
4 Joseph Thompson HAYES, *b* at Cincinnati, Ohio 21 Dec 1861; *d* nr Charleston, W Virginia 24 June 1863.
5 George Crook HAYES, *b* at Chillicothe, Ohio 29 Sept 1864; *d* there 24 May 1866.
6 Frances (Fanny) HAYES, resumed her maiden name of Hayes, *b* at Cincinnati, Ohio 2 Sept 1867, *m* 1 Sept 1897, Harry Eaton Smith (*b* at Fremont, Ohio 28 Dec 1869; *d* 1931), and *d* at Lewiston, Maine 18 March 1950, having had issue,
Dalton HAYES (formerly Dalton Hayes SMITH), served in World War I with 165th Inf, 42nd Div, AEF (wounded), *b* 22 June 1898, *m* 17 April 1926, ●Corinne (*b* at Columbus, Ohio 1 Jan 1906), dau of Nicholas Daubeney Monsarrat, by his wife Jean Andrews, dau of Major-Gen John Grant Mitchell, USV, by his wife Laura, dau of William Augustus Platt, by his wife Fanny Arabella, sister of Pres Hayes (*see* BROTHERS AND SISTERS OF PRESIDENT HAYES, *p* 346), and *d* at Pompano Beach, Florida 13 Jan 1950, leaving issue,
(1) ●Chloë HAYES, *b* at Cape Town, S Africa 24 Jan 1927, *m* 13 Dec 1952, ●Harold Martin Schroeder, and has issue,
  1*a*●Maude SCHROEDER, *b* at Berkeley, California 10 Dec 1953.
  2*a*●Jean SCHROEDER, *b* at Hightstown, New Jersey 16 March 1955.
(2) ●Jean HAYES, *b* at Cape Town, S Africa 26 April 1928, *m* ●Edward Sylvester Rogers II (*b* 2 May 1923) [*570 Park Avenue, New York, NY, USA*], and has issue,
  ●Corinne ROGERS, *b* at Albuquerque, New Mexico 29 Dec 1954.
7 Scott Russell HAYES, *b* at Columbus, Ohio 8 Feb 1871, *m* Sept 1912, Maude Anderson (*b* 7 July 1873; *d* at San Francisco 19 Nov 1966), and *dsp* at Croton-on-Hudson, New York 6 May 1923.
8 Manning Force HAYES, *b* at Fremont, Ohio 1 Aug 1873; *d* there 28 Aug 1874.

# The Brothers and Sisters of President Hayes

**1** A boy, *b* 1814; *d* an inf.

**2** Lorenzo HAYES, *b* 1815; *d* 1825.

**3** Sarah Sophia HAYES, *b* 1817; *d* 1821.

**4** Fanny Arabella HAYES, *b* 1820, *m* 1839, William Augustus Platt (*b* 1809; *d* 1882), and *d* in childbirth 1856, having had issue, two sons and four daus. Their dau, Laura became the grandmother of Corinne, Mrs Dalton Hayes (*see* DESCENDANTS OF PRESIDENT HAYES, *p 345*).

# James Abram Garfield
## 1831-1881

———

20th President of the
United States of America
1881

JAMES ABRAM GARFIELD, 20TH PRESIDENT

# James Abram Garfield

## 1831-1881

### 20th President of the United States of America
### 1881

WHEN JAMES GARFIELD received the Republican presidential nomination in 1880, President Hayes set down in his diary an outline of the candidate's selling points which ought to be stressed in the campaign. There was, he noted, "a great deal of strength in Garfield's life and struggles as a self made man. Let it be thoroughly presented. . . . How from poverty and obscurity . . . he became a great scholar, a Statesman, a Major General, a Senator, a Presidential Candidate. Give the amplest details—a school teacher—a laborer on the [Ohio] canal—the name of his boat. . .". Hayes concluded that Garfield was "the ideal candidate because he is the ideal self made man".

Garfield's career was indeed almost improbably perfect for campaign purposes. He was like the hero of a Horatio Alger "luck-and-pluck" novelette. In fact the maxims by Garfield included in the Republicans' campaign handbook for 1880 could well have come from the pages of Alger. He was credited with the observation that "a pound of pluck is worth a ton of luck", and with a more extended truism: "Poverty is uncomfortable, as I can testify; but nine times out of ten the best thing that can happen to a young man is to be tossed overboard and compelled to sink or swim for himself. In all my acquaintance I never knew a man to be drowned who was worth the saving". His New England parents had come out to Ohio, "hungry for the horizon", where James Garfield was born in a log cabin, "so politically perfect a mansion", in 1831. His mother was widowed when James was two. The boy had to turn his hand to every variety of work, from chopping wood to steering a canal boat, to help support the family and to pay for an education. By the age of thirty, in the early stages of the Civil War, Garfield was Colonel of a regiment of Ohio volunteers. In the meantime he had managed to work his way through

Williams College and to become a teacher and then head of a small college in Hiram, Ohio. He had married a childhood playmate and former pupil, Lucretia Rudolph. He was a lay preacher in the Disciples of Christ. He had joined the Republicans and been elected to the Ohio state senate. He was big, broad-shouldered, earnest and intense. He was also remarkably quick to absorb and master information. He taught himself the elements of soldiering, and applied them so efficiently that when he left the Army at the end of 1863 he was a Major-General. Having compressed a whole military career into two and a half years, he was ready to concentrate his energies on politics as a newly elected member of the House of Representatives.

Garfield remained in Congress until 1880. This was his *annus mirabilis,* beginning with an election to the US Senate which he was never to take up, and culminating with victory in the presidential election. The story of that ultimate success also had an Algerish ring to it. Garfield went to the Republican convention in June to press the cause of his fellow Ohioan, Senator John Sherman, on whose behalf he made a much admired nominating speech. Gradually, as ballot followed ballot in the stifling, hectic convention hall, it emerged that of the three main contenders, Grant, Sherman and James G. Blaine, none could carry the requisite support. On the 34th ballot Wisconsin suddenly shifted to Garfield. Two ballots later, with a swiftness that struck many observers as providential, Garfield had the necessary majority of votes.

Professional politicians believe in giving providence an assist. Garfield was the beneficiary of masterly promotion behind the scenes by men who realized that the party was badly split between rival factions, especially the "Stalwarts" and the "Half-Breeds". They differed over patronage rather than principles but these disagreements were bitter and irreconcilable. Garfield, whose own part in the maneuver was perfectly honorable, was an excellent choice for a compromise candidate. Though the outcome of the presidential election depended upon frenzied and not always scrupulous stratagems by local groups, Garfield was also more impressive than the Democratic candidate, the West Point regular officer General Winfield Scott Hancock.

We can only conjecture how good a President Garfield might have been. Four months after his inauguration, when he was about to set out from the Washington railroad station for a visit to his old college, Garfield was shot in the back by Charles J. Guiteau, a lawyer who is variously described as a "madman" and a species of that special American nineteenth-century breed, a "disappointed office-seeker". The President lay in bed for two and a half months, first at the White House and then at a summer resort in New Jersey, where he died. He need not have died, and with modern surgery could have made a perfect recovery, since the bullet was lodged in a muscle and had not done any vital damage. The fatal

LUCRETIA RUDOLPH, MRS GARFIELD

damage was produced by the doctors' probing in a vain effort to find and extract the bullet. As a result the wound became infected and Garfield died of blood poisoning. Guiteau was subsequently tried, convicted and hanged for murder.

The men who had watched Garfield closely did not expect that he would be a powerful President. Rutherford B. Hayes, while praising his good qualities, added that Garfield was "not executive in his talents, not original, not firm,—not a moral force". This is an oddly lukewarm assessment and perhaps inconsistent, since no one desired a Caesar in the White House. Hayes probably measured Garfield by his own performance. In other words, he did not expect Garfield to show much courage in resisting the spoilsmen. In fact the President had considerable pluck, though far less luck, during his brief tenure. He refused to knuckle under to the arrogant "Stalwarts" of New York and got the better of their two leaders in the Senate, Roscoe Conkling and Thomas Platt. And he encouraged his Attorney-General to persist in an investigation of frauds in Post Office contracts that was sure to harm certain Republicans. Guiteau may or may not have been unhinged. The politics of the era stimulated corruption, fraud, hysteria, and violence. Garfield was thus a victim of the very system that raised him high. He had once calmed a shrieking mob at the time of Lincoln's assassination by calling out: "Fellow citizens: God reigns, and the Government at Washington still lives!" This could have been his own epitaph, though a nobler one than the poisonous Washington of 1881 perhaps deserved.

# Chronology

1831      Born in a log cabin at Orange, Ohio 19 Nov.

1841-47  Worked as a farm hand, attending a local school during the winters.

1848      Visited Cleveland, Ohio.

1848-49  Worked on Ohio canal boats.

1849-50  Attended Geauga Seminary, Chester, Ohio.

1850      Joined the Disciples of Christ Church.

1851      Entered Hiram Eclectic Institute (now Hiram College), Hiram, Ohio.

1854      Entered Williams College, Williamstown, Massachusetts Sept.

1856      Graduated from Williams College with BA degree 30 July.

1856-57   Taught Latin and Greek at Hiram Eclectic Institute.

1857-60   President of Hiram Eclectic Institute.

1858      Studied Law in Hiram.

1859      Elected to represent Portage and Summit Counties in the State Senate.

1860      Admitted to the Ohio Bar in Hiram.

1861      Commissioned Lt-Col 42 Regt Ohio Volunteers 21 Aug; promoted Col 27 Nov; given command of 18th Brigade, Army of Ohio 17 Dec.

1862      Took part in Battle of Middle Creek, Kentucky, and promoted Brig-Gen 10 Jan; took part in second day's fighting at Battle of Shiloh 7 April; supervised rebuilding of Memphis and Charleston railroad bridges June; returned to Hiram 30 July; ill for two months with camp fever; elected to the House of Representatives Sept; reported to Washington and assigned to court-martial duty 25 Sept.

1863      Appointed Chief of Staff by Gen William S. Rosecrans Jan; promoted Major-Gen for gallantry during Battle of Chickamauga 19 Sept; resigned commission to take seat in House of Representatives 5 Dec.

1865      Appointed to Ways and Means Committee.

1867      Chairman of Committee on Military Affairs.

1869      Chairman of first Committee on Banking and Currency.

1871      Chairman of Committee on Appropriations.

1875      Member of Ways and Means Committee.

1876      Bought a farm (which he renamed Lawnfield) at Mentor, Ohio; sent by Grant to witness counting of Louisiana vote.

1877      Member of Electoral Commission.

1880      Elected to the Senate by the Ohio legislature 13 Jan (for term to commence 4 March 1881); nominated for President at Republican National Convention, Chicago 8 June; election day 2 Nov; resigned from the House of Representatives 8 Nov; Presidential Electors cast their ballots 1 Dec; declined seat in Senate 23 Dec.

1881      Electoral votes tabulated by Congress and Garfield and Arthur officially declared elected 9 Feb; inaugurated as 20th President of the United States of America 4 March; shot in the back by Charles J. Guiteau at Baltimore and Potomac Railroad Station, Washington, DC 2 July; removed from the White House to Francklyn Cottage, Elberon, New Jersey 6 Sept; died there of his injuries 19 Sept; buried at Cleveland, Ohio. He was the second President to be assassinated and the fourth to die in office.

# Lineage of President Garfield

EDWARD GARFIELD, whose place of origin in England is unknown[1], emigrated to New England *ca* 1630 and was one of the first settlers of Watertown, Mass, receiving grants of land there in 1636 and 1637, a selectman 1638, 1655 and 1662, constable (or tax-collector) 1661, *b* in England *ca* 1575, appears to have *m* 1st, and had issue, at least one son (Samuel). He *m* probably 2ndly, Rebecca — (*b ca* 1606; *d* at Watertown 16 April 1661), and by her had issue[2]. He *m* probably 3rdly, 1 Sept 1661, Johanah, widow of Thomas Buckmaster (*or* Buckminster), of Brookline, Mass, and *d* at Watertown 14 June 1672, aged about 97 (will dated 30 Dec 1668, *pr* 11 July 1672). His yst son (by his 2nd marriage),

BENJAMIN GARFIELD, of Watertown, Capt of Militia, admitted Freeman 18 April 1690, nine times Rep to Gen Court, Selectman for twenty years, and Town Clerk of Watertown, *b ca* 1643, *m* 1st 1673, Mehitabel Hawkins (*d* 9 Dec 1675), and had issue, two sons. He *m* 2ndly 17 Jan 1677/8, Elizabeth (*b* at Cambridge, Mass 17 Aug 1659; *m* 2ndly 25 Oct 1720, Daniel Harrington), yst dau of Matthew Bridge, of Lexington, Mass, by his wife Anne, dau of Nicholas Danforth, and *d* 28 Nov 1717, having by her had issue, with one other son and five daus, a 3rd son,

THOMAS GARFIELD, of Lincoln, Mass, Lieut Lincoln Militia, *b* 12 Dec 1680, *m* 2 Jan 1706/7, Mercy (*b* 1686; *d* 28 Feb 1744/5), dau of Joshua Bigelow[3], by his wife Elizabeth Flagg, and *d* at Weston, Mass 4 Feb 1752, leaving issue, with five other sons and six daus, an eldest son,

THOMAS GARFIELD, of Lincoln, Mass, Lieut Lincoln Militia, *b* 28 Feb 1713, *m* 21 Oct 1742, Rebecca (*b* 2 Nov 1719; *d* 3 Feb 1763), dau of Deacon Samuel Johnson, of Lunenburgh, by his wife Rebecca, and *d* at Lincoln 3 Jan 1774, leaving issue, with a yr son and three daus,

SOLOMON GARFIELD, of Westminster, and later of Cherry Valley, Otsego County, New York, served in the Revolutionary War with Noah Miles's Co and Whitcomb's Regt, fought at Concord 19 April 1775, *b* at Lincoln, Mass 18 July 1743, *m* 27 Aug 1769, Sarah, widow of James Stimson, of Sudbury, and dau of Abraham Briant, of Sudbury, Mass, by his wife Sarah Frinks, and *d* as the result of a fall at Worcester, New York 1807, having had issue, with a yr son and three daus,

THOMAS GARFIELD, of Worcester, New York, *b* at Westminster 19 March 1773, *m* 1794, Asenath Hill, of Schoharie County, New York (*b* 1778; *d* at Newberg, Cuyahoga County, Ohio 5 Feb 1851), and *dvp* at Worcester, New York 1801, leaving issue, with a yr son and two daus,

ABRAHAM (called ABRAM) GARFIELD, of Orange, Ohio, farmer and canal construction supervisor, *b* at Worcester, New York 28 Dec 1799, *m* 3 Feb 1820, Eliza (*b* at Richmond, New Hampshire 21 Sept 1801; *d* at Mentor, Ohio 21 Jan 1888), dau of James Ballou, of Richmond, New Hampshire, farmer[4], by his wife Mehitabel, dau of Henry Ingalls, and *d* in Otsego County, New York 3 May 1833, having had with other issue (*see* BROTHERS AND SISTERS OF PRESIDENT GARFIELD, *p 357*), a yst son,

JAMES ABRAM GARFIELD, **20th President of the United States of America.**

# The Descendants of President Garfield

JAMES ABRAM GARFIELD *m* at her home in Hiram, Portage County, Ohio 11 Nov 1853, Lucretia (*b* at Garrettsville, Portage County, Ohio 19 April 1832; *d* at South Pasadena, California 13 March 1918, *bur* in the Garfield Memorial, Lake View Cemetery, Cleveland, Ohio), dau of Zebulon Rudolph, of Hiram, Ohio, farmer and carpenter (a native of Virginia), by his wife Arabella, dau of Elijah Mason, of Lebanon, Connecticut, and had issue,

**1** Eliza Arabella GARFIELD, *b* 3 July 1860; *d* 3 Dec 1863.
**2** Harry Augustus GARFIELD, of Washington, DC, and Williamstown, Mass, hon LLD Princeton and Dartmouth (1908), Amherst and Wesleyan (1909), William and Mary (1921), Harvard (1928), and Toronto (1933), LHD Whitman (1919), admitted to the Bar 1888, Prof of Contracts, Western Reserve Univ 1891-97, Prof of Politics, Princeton Univ 1903-08, Pres of Williams Coll 1908-34, US Fuel Adminr 1917, *b* at Hiram, Ohio 11 Oct 1863, *educ* Williams Coll (AB 1885, LLD 1934), and Columbia Univ Law Sch, *m* at Cleveland, Ohio 14 June 1888, Belle Hartford (*b* at Cleveland, Ohio 7 July 1864), dau of James Mason, of Cleveland, Ohio, and *d* 12 Dec 1942, leaving issue,
  **1** ●James GARFIELD [*987 Memorial Drive, Cambridge, Massachusetts 02138, USA*], *b* at Cleveland, Ohio 28 Oct 1889, *m* 20 Jan 1923, ●Edith (*b* 17 Jan 1899), dau of Frederick De Peyster Townsend, of Mystic, Connecticut, by his wife Katherine Jermain Savage, and has issue,
    (1) ●John Robinson GARFIELD, *b* 11 May 1924.
    (2) ●Elizabeth Ann GARFIELD, *b* 29 July 1926.
    (3) ●Harry Augustus GARFIELD, *b* 4 Aug 1934.
    (4) ●Edith Townsend GARFIELD, *b* 3 Nov 1935.
  **2** ●Mason GARFIELD, *b* at Cleveland, Ohio 5 Oct 1892, *educ* Williams Coll (BA 1914), and Harvard (AM 1915), *m* 19 Feb 1916, ●Harriet Winchester (*b* at Salem, Mass 29 Oct 1894), dau of Gen William Alden Pew, of Salem, by his wife Alice Huntington, and has issue,
    (1) ●Alicia Rudolph GARFIELD, *b* 22 July 1917.
    (2) ●Louisa Huntington GARFIELD, *b* 16 Feb 1919.
  **3** Lucretia GARFIELD, *b* at Cleveland, Ohio 18 Jan 1894, *m* 22 Dec 1925, ●John Preston Comer (*b* 1888) [*Charlottesville, Virginia, USA*], son of Samuel Allen Comer, of Williamstown, Mass, by his wife Amanda Belle Haskins, and *d* at Charlottesville, Virginia Jan 1968, having had issue,
    (1) John Preston COMER, Jr, mathematical statistician, *b* at Boston, Mass 23 Oct 1926, *educ* Mass Inst of Technology (BS, MS), and Columbia Univ (PhD), *m* at New York 6 July 1963, ●Lucette [*1836 Metzerott Road, Adelphi, Maryland 21783, USA*], dau of Ray Landis Bowers, by his wife Ella Smith, and *dsp* at Cincinnati, Ohio 13 Oct 1969.
    (2) Mary Laura COMER, *b* at Pinsfield, Mass 1928; *d* in Northern Italy 1931.
    (3) Elizabeth COMER, *m* at Williamstown, Mass, ●Neil Russell Marks, and *d* at Charlottesville, Virginia 26 Dec 1969, leaving issue,
      ●Russell Preston MARKS.
  **4** ●Stanton GARFIELD, MD, *b* at Willoughby, Ohio 3 Aug 1895, *m* 9 Sept 1922, ●Lucy Shaler (*b* 17 Feb 1900), dau of George Seymour Hedges, of Baltimore, Maryland, by his wife Harriette Martha Goodwillie, and has issue,

    (1) ●Mary Barrett GARFIELD, *b* 9 May 1924.
    (2) ●Stanton GARFIELD, Jr, MD [*Snowbound, Georges Mills, New Hampshire, USA*], *b* 22 Oct 1925.
    (3) ●George Hedges GARFIELD, *b* 17 March 1928.
    (4) ●John Mason GARFIELD, *b* 9 Aug 1934.
**3** James Rudolph GARFIELD, of Cleveland, Ohio, hon LLD Howard Univ (1908) and Pittsburgh (1909), lawyer, admitted to the Bar 1888, mem Ohio State Senate 1896-1900, mem US Civil Service Commn 1902-03, Commr of Corpn, US Dept of Commerce and Labor 1903-07, Sec of the Interior 1907-09, *b* at Hiram, Ohio 17 Oct 1865, *educ* St Paul's Sch, Concord, New Hampshire, Williams Coll (AB 1885), and Columbia Law Sch, *m* 30 Dec 1890, Helen Newell (*b* at Cleveland, Ohio 12 Feb 1866; *d* 26 Aug 1930), dau of John Hills, of West Newbury, Mass by his wife Judith Poore, and *d* at Cleveland, Ohio 24 March 1950, having had issue,
  **1** John Newell GARFIELD, served in World War I as Capt 34th Field Arty US Army, *b* at Chicago 3 Feb 1892, *educ* Williams Coll, *m* at Cleveland, Ohio 27 June 1916, Janet Sutherland (*b* at Cleveland, Ohio 6 Sept 1889; *d* at Troy, New York 6 March 1959), dau of Samuel D. Dodge, by his wife Jeannette M. Groff, and *dvp* at Mentor, Ohio 23 May 1931, leaving issue,
    (1) ●Janet Dodge GARFIELD, *b* at Cleveland, Ohio 24 Sept 1917, *m* there 2 Jan 1939, ●Alexander Cushing Brown, Jr (*b* at Cleveland, Ohio 1 Dec 1913) [*30 Abbotsford Court, Providence 6, Rhode Island 02906, USA*], son of Alexander Cushing Brown, by his wife Mary Bristol Dana, and has issue,
      1*a* ●Alexander Cushing BROWN III [*Tingley Drive, RD2, Cumberland, Rhode Island, USA*], *b* at Cleveland, Ohio 8 Sept 1941, *educ* Union Coll, *m* at Hartford, Conn 27 June 1964, ●Jean F., dau of Dr John G. Martin, by his wife Elisabeth Parsons, and has issue,
        1*b* ●Elisabeth BROWN, *b* 24 Feb 1967.
        2*b* ●Samantha BROWN, *b* 15 Jan 1969.
      2*a* ●Cornelia BROWN, *b* at Cleveland, Ohio 10 Feb 1944, *m* at Short Hills, New Jersey 14 Dec 1968, ●Robert Lawton Elmore, Jr, son of Robert Lawton Elmore, by his wife Dorothy Woodbridge, and has issue,
        ●Alexander Garfield ELMORE, *b* 6 Jan 1972.
    (2) ●James Rudolph GARFIELD, *b* at Cleveland, Ohio 12 Jan 1920.
    (3) ●Frances GARFIELD, *b* at Cleveland, Ohio 19 Sept 1921, *m* ●Charles M. Tillinghurst [*8754 Booth Road, Mentor, Ohio, USA*].
    (4) ●John Newell GARFIELD, Jr, real estate broker in Chicago [*19E Scott Street, Chicago, Illinois, USA*], *b* at Cleveland, Ohio 5 Oct 1923, *educ* S Kent, *m* 1st 9 March 1946 (*m* diss by div 1966), Christine (*b* 13 Sept 1927), dau

of Horace Fuller Henriques, by his wife Christine Corlett, and has issue,

1a● John Newell GARFIELD III, *b* at Youngstown, Ohio 11 April 1947.

2a● Thames Corlett GARFIELD, *b* at Youngstown, Ohio 20 Oct 1948.

3a● Christine GARFIELD, *b* at Lake Forest, Illinois 9 Dec 1950.

4a● Horace Fuller GARFIELD, *b* at Sewickley, Pennsylvania 3 July 1953.

John Newell Garfield, Jr *m* 2ndly at Lake Forest, Illinois 1967, ●Lynn (*b* at Madison, Wisconsin 1934), dau of Albert Hanson.

(5) ●Douglas Dodge GARFIELD, *b* 20 May 1927.

2 James Abram GARFIELD, served in World War I as Major 322nd Field Arty US Army, *b* 13 April 1894, *m* 31 Dec 1917, ●Edwina Forbes (*b* 1895) [*PO Box 945, West Palm Beach, Florida 33401, USA*], dau of Major-Gen Edwin Forbes Glenn, of Chillicothe, Ohio, and had issue,

(1) ●Helen Louise GARFIELD [*PO Box 945, West Palm Beach, Florida 33401, USA*], *b* 23 Nov 1918.

(2) ●Elizabeth GARFIELD [*PO Box 945, West Palm Beach, Florida 33401, USA*], *b* 15 Feb 1921.

3 ● Newell GARFIELD, served in World War I as Capt 322nd Field Arty US Army [*47 Lexington Road, Concord, Massachusetts 01742, USA*], *b* at Chicago 1 Aug 1895, *m* 7 Oct 1922, ●Mary Louise Wyatt (*b* 1899), and has issue,

(1) ●Newell GARFIELD, Jr [*180 East End Avenue, New York, New York 10028, USA*], *b* at Rochester, New York 8 July 1923, *m* 1st 1946 (*m* diss by div), Jane O. Day, and has issue,

1a● William Wyatt GARFIELD, *b* 12 July 1948.

2a● Susan GARFIELD, *b* 8 July 1949, *m* May 1971, ●John Wilson, and has issue,

●Cristian WILSON, *b* March 1972.

3a● Newell GARFIELD III, *b* 19 April 1951.

4a● Stephen K. GARFIELD, *b* 25 Feb 1954.

Newell Garfield, Jr *m* 2ndly at New York 16 Nov 1961, ●Jane Harrison (*b* at New York 3 Nov 1929), only dau of James Blaine Walker, Jr, of New York, by his wife Elizabeth, yst dau of Benjamin Harrison, 23rd President of the United States (*qv*), and by her has issue,

5a● Elizabeth Newell GARFIELD, *b* at New York 23 Nov 1962.

(2) ●Wyatt GARFIELD [*Myrick Road, Princeton, Massachusetts 01541, USA*], *b* 8 Oct 1924, *m* ●Katherine D. Barney, and has issue,

1a● Sarah B. GARFIELD.

2a● Louise R. GARFIELD.

3a● Wyatt GARFIELD, Jr.

4a● Seth GARFIELD.

5a● Angus GARFIELD.

6a● Benjamin GARFIELD.

(3) ●Sarah Winslow GARFIELD, *b* at Hartford, Connecticut 19 April 1929, *m* at Concord, Mass 14 Dec 1957, ●Peter Huntington Smith (*b* at St Louis, Missouri 30 Nov 1913) [*University Lane, Manchester, Massachusetts 01744, USA*], son of Huntington Smith, by his wife Caroline Lackland, and has issue,

1a● Sarah Wyatt SMITH, *b* at Guatemala City 9 May 1959.

2a● Elise Griswold SMITH, *b* at New Bedford, Mass 20 Aug 1960.

3a● Peter Huntington SMITH, Jr, *b* at Boston, Mass 29 July 1963.

4 Rudolph Hills GARFIELD, served in World War I with USN, *b* at Mentor, Ohio 13 Sept 1899, *m* 26 Oct 1925, ●Eleanor Borton (*b* 1899) [*Mentor, Ohio 44060, USA*], and had issue,

(1) Molly Ann GARFIELD, *b* 20 Sept 1926; *d* 23 Sept 1926.

(2) ●Rudolph Hills GARFIELD, Jr, *b* 16 July 1928.

(3) ●Borton GARFIELD, *b* 5 April 1931.

4 Mary GARFIELD, *b* at Washington, DC 16 Jan 1867, *m* at Mentor, Ohio 14 June 1888, Joseph Stanley Brown, of Washington, DC (*b* at Washington, DC 19 Aug 1858; *d* at Pasadena, California 2 Nov 1941), son of John Leopold Brown, by his wife Elizabeth Frances Marr, and *d* at Pasadena, California 1947, having had issue,

1 Rudolph STANLEY-BROWN, *b* at Mentor, Ohio 9 April 1889, *educ* Sheffield Scientific Sch, Columbia Sch of Architecture, and Beaux Arts, Paris, *m* at East Orange, New Jersey 6 June 1922, Katharine Schermerhorn (*b* at Philadelphia 30 April 1892; *d* at Boston, Mass 15 April 1972), dau of Charles A. Oliver, of East Orange, New Jersey, by his wife Mary Schermerhorn Henry, and *d* at Augusta, Georgia 8 Feb 1944, leaving issue,

(1) ●Edward Garfield STANLEY-BROWN, MD [*860 Roslyn Road, Ridgewood, New Jersey 07450, USA*], *b* at Cleveland, Ohio 11 Nov 1923, *educ* S Kent Sch, Connecticut, Virginia Univ, and Pennsylvania Univ Med Sch, *m* at Ridgewood, New Jersey 1 Nov 1952, ●Jeanne (*b* at Ridgewood, New Jersey 12 July 1927), dau of Walter Olson, by his wife Claire Drake, and has issue,

1a● Jeanne Drake STANLEY-BROWN, *b* at New York 5 Sept 1954.

2a● David Garfield STANLEY-BROWN, *b* at New York 12 April 1956.

3a● Elizabeth Powell STANLEY-BROWN, *b* at New York 21 April 1958.

(2) ●Katharine Oliver STANLEY-BROWN, *b* at Cleveland, Ohio 2 March 1928, *m* at Boston, Mass 27 May 1955, ●Gordon Abbott, Jr (*b* at Boston 2 May 1927) [*2 Eagle Head Road, Manchester, Mass 01944, USA*], son of Gordon Abbott, by his wife Esthei Lowell Cunningham, and has issue

1a● Christopher Cunningham ABBOTT, *b* at Boston 22 Oct 1956.

2a● Katrina Schermerhorn ABBOTT, *b* at Boston 29 April 1958.

3a● Victoria McLane ABBOTT, *b* at Boston 31 Jan 1961.

4a● Alexandra Garfield ABBOTT, *b* at Boston 4 May 1967.

2 ●Ruth STANLEY-BROWN [*1161 Willa Vista Trail, Maitland, Florida 32751, USA*], *b* at Mentor, Ohio 3 Aug 1892, *educ* Vassar, *m* at Mentor 25 March 1922, Herbert Feis, Prof of Economics, Kansas State Univ (*b* at New York City 1893; *d* 2 March 1972), son of Louis J. Feis, by his wife Louise.

3 Margaret STANLEY-BROWN, *b* at Washington, DC 2 Oct 1895, *educ* Vassar, and Coll of Physicians & Surgs, New York (MD 1923), *m ca* 1949, Max Sellers, and *dsp* at New Milford, Connecticut 12 June 1958.

5 Irvin McDowell GARFIELD, of Boston, Mass, lawyer, *b* at Hiram, Ohio 3 Aug 1870, *educ* Williams Coll, and Harvard Law Sch, *m* at Boston 16 Oct 1906, Susan (*b* at Boston 1878), dau of Nathaniel Henry Emmons, of Boston, by his wife Eleanor Gassett Bacon, and *d* at Boston 19 July 1951, leaving issue,

1 ●Eleanor GARFIELD, *b* 27 June 1908.

2 ●Jane GARFIELD, *b* 10 May 1910, *m* ●Charles E. Cheever [*Farm Street, Dover, Massachusetts, USA*].

3 ●Irvin McDowell (Mike) GARFIELD, Jr [*84 Main Street, Southboro, Massachusetts, USA*], *b* 19 Jan 1913.

6 Abram GARFIELD, of Cleveland, Ohio, architect, *b* at Washington, DC 21 Nov 1872, *educ* Williams Coll (AB 1893), and Mass Inst of Technology (BS 1896), *m* 1st at Cleveland 14 Oct 1897, Sarah Granger (*d* at Cleveland, Ohio 3 Feb 1945), dau of Edward Porter Williams, of Cleveland, Ohio, by his wife Mary Louise Mason, and had issue,

1 ●Edward Williams GARFIELD, *b* at Cleveland, Ohio 17 May 1899, *m* 1928 ●Hope Dillingham (*b* 1905), and has issue,

(1) ●Louise Dillingham GARFIELD, *b* 1929.

(2) ●Edward Williams GARFIELD, Jr [*3378 Washington Avenue, Cleveland, Ohio, USA*], *b* 1930.

(3) ●Dorothy Hope GARFIELD, *b* 1932.

2 ●Mary Louise GARFIELD, *b* at Cleveland, Ohio 5 July 1903, *m* 1931, ●William Richard Hallaran, MD (*b* 1904) [*12564 Cedar Road, Cleveland, Ohio, USA*], and has issue (●Sarah Newton; ●William Garfield; and ●Michael Terence—*see* ADDENDUM).

Abram Garfield *m* 2ndly at Shaker Heights, Ohio April 1947, ●Helen Matthews (*b* 1902), and *d* at Cleveland, Ohio 16 Oct 1958.

7 Edward GARFIELD, *b* at Hiram, Ohio 25 Dec 1874; *d* at Washington, DC 25 Oct 1876.

# The Brothers and Sisters of
# President Garfield

**1** Mehitabel GARFIELD, *b* in Ohio 28 Jan 1821, *m* 1837, Stephen D. Trowbridge, of Solon, Ohio, and had issue, three daus.

**2** Thomas GARFIELD, of Jamestown, Michigan, *b* in Ohio 16 Oct 1822, *m* Jane Harper, and had issue, one son and one dau.

**3** Mary GARFIELD, *b* in Ohio 19 Oct 1824, *m* Marenus G. Larabee, of Solon, Ohio, and *d* 4 Nov 1884, leaving issue, one son and three daus.

**4** James Ballou GARFIELD, *b* in Ohio 31 Oct 1826; *d* 28 Jan 1829.

# Notes

[1] A family tradition held that the American Garfields came from Wales, or the neighbourhood of Chester. There were also Garfield families in Warwickshire and Northamptonshire in the sixteenth century. Ralph Garfield, a native of Kilsby in the latter county, was a substantial London merchant and the owner of two vessels *The Falcon* and *The Rose*, and it has been surmised that Edward Garfield was perhaps a kinsman and emigrated on one of them.

[2] Edward Garfield's daughter Rebecca was the great-great-great-grandmother of the celebrated Mormon leader Brigham Young, who was thus a fifth cousin once removed of President Garfield (*see* APPENDIX D, SOME REMARKABLE KINSHIPS).

[3] Through the Bigelow family President Garfield derived a Royal descent from Henri I, King of France (*see* APPENDIX C, PRESIDENTS OF ROYAL DESCENT).

[4] Through the Ballous a further Royal descent is derived from Rhys ap Tewdwr, King of Deheubarth (*see* APPENDIX C, PRESIDENTS OF ROYAL DESCENT).

# Chester Alan Arthur
## 1830-1886

———

21st President of the
United States of America
1881-1885

CHESTER ALAN ARTHUR, 21ST PRESIDENT

# Chester Alan Arthur

## 1830-1886

### 21st President of the United States of America
### 1881-1885

THE MAN who shot James Garfield in July 1881 cried out, "I am a Stalwart and now Arthur is President!" In other words he identified Chester Arthur with a rival faction of the Republican party antipathetic to the "Half-Breeds" with whom Garfield was associated. There was plenty of evidence to suggest that he was correct. In popular estimation Arthur was a spoilsman. Originally appointed as Collector of Customs in New York, in 1871, Chester Arthur was a prominent figure in the political apparatus run by Senator Roscoe Conkling. Conkling believed, no doubt sincerely, that the thousands of federal offices around the nation, most of them connected with the Post Office or with the Customs Service, should actually be in the gift of men such as himself. The White House should make appointments at that level in merely a nominal sense: "senatorial courtesy" should be the actual rule. As head of the New York Custom House, Arthur controlled over a thousand employees. Owing their appointment and continuance to the Republicans, they were naturally expected to contribute time and cash to party activities. In general, it must be said, they did not object. After all, if the Democrats won there would be a complete turnover of personnel; to the victors belonged the spoils. Orthodox politicians felt there was no other way of establishing party cohesion at the local level.

Their views collided with the more highminded advocates of civil service reform—"snivel service" to Conkling—who wanted to make entry into federal service conditional upon merit, this to be established by competitive examination, and to guarantee tenure for the successful. Eyeing the British system, the reformers claimed that the result would be to create a much more honest, stable and efficient civil service. Reform ideas appealed to Presidents Hayes and Garfield, in part because they were anxious to escape from the aura of collusion that had humiliatingly enveloped the Grant régime.

Chester Arthur, ousted from his post by President Hayes, was a conspicuous early casualty of the clash between the reformers and the Stalwarts. "The Gentleman Boss", tall, elegant and portly, attended the Republican convention in 1880 along with Conkling and others. They were hoping with a fair amount of confidence that Grant would be nominated for a third term—in which case they expected their troubles would be over.

Instead, to Conkling's fury, the nomination went to James Garfield. Well aware that discontented Stalwarts could make life wretched for him, Garfield risked the disapproval of the reformers and Half-Breeds by deciding to offer the vice-presidential place to a Stalwart. His appeasing gesture was spurned by the first man he approached. Garfield's second choice was Chester Arthur: New York to balance Ohio on the ticket, and a candidate who had proved himself a good organizer, in the Custom House and before that as the state's Quartermaster-General during the Civil War. Arthur dutifully passed on word of the offer to Conkling, who told him to "drop it as you would a red-hot shoe from the forge"; Garfield was a "trickster" who would be beaten in November. But Arthur persisted, telling the indignant Conkling with a certain wistfulness: "The office of Vice-President is a greater honor than I ever dreamed of attaining".

He probably also never dreamed of succeeding Garfield. This was the only comfort that anti-Stalwart Republicans could derive. *The Nation* said of Arthur: "There is no place in which his powers of mischief will be so small as in the Vice-Presidency, and it will remove him during a great part of the year from his own field of activity. It is true that General Garfield, if elected, may die during his term of office, but this is too unlikely a contingency to be worth making extraordinary provision for". To all appearances Arthur remained in sympathy with the Conkling group. After the inauguration, when President Garfield named an enemy of Conkling to the New York collectorship, Arthur sided with Conkling in the subsequent furore. The Vice-President even journeyed to Albany to lobby for the Conkling faction—an intervention condemned as unseemly, if not disgraceful. In the summer of 1881, as Garfield lay incapacitated, Arthur shied away from any discussion of the possibility that he ought to assume executive responsibility. When Garfield at last died, an acquaintance exclaimed: "Chet Arthur, President of the United States! Good God!"

His actual record was surprisingly good. Though he tended to lean toward the Stalwart wing, Arthur avoided gross partisanship. Indeed he broke with Conkling—a gesture which a cartoonist compared with the repudiation of Falstaff by Prince Hal in the Shakespeare play. He carried out various obligations inherited from President Garfield, such as

ELLEN LEWIS HERNDON, MRS ARTHUR

prosecutions for Post Office frauds. To the astonishment of former critics he committed himself to civil service reform. His Administration witnessed the passage of the Pendleton Act (1883), which established the Civil Service Commission. He vetoed some undesirable Bills. The newspapers began to applaud instead of caricaturing him. Columnists admired his stylish competence. Arthur was, they noted, one of the best fishermen in the country; he had refurnished the White House in modern taste, and his entertainments were pleasingly convivial. His private life was impeccable. Arthur's Virginia-born wife, Ellen Lewis Herndon, was the daughter of a naval officer. Since she died in 1880, leaving two children not yet grown up, the duties of mistress of the White House were performed by the President's sister, Mrs John McElroy.

All in all, Arthur effaced his previous image. He himself hoped to be nominated in his own right in 1884. But the Republican party was too full of intrigue. His abortive candidacy collapsed, though he had the wry satisfaction of seeing the party's choice, James G. Blaine, beaten in November 1884. Arthur died only two years later. He is often characterized as a person of doubtful honor ennobled by sudden elevation to the Presidency. Something of the sort does seem to have happened. But it would be unwise to assume that the rule is universally applicable. In his case, we should note that while he sometimes kept bad company, there is no evidence that Chester Arthur was corrupt. He was accustomed to regard politics as a business: he did not behave as though it were a crooked business.

# Chronology

| | |
|---|---|
| 1830 | Born at Fairfield, Vermont[1] 5 Oct. |
| 1845 | Entered Union College, Schenectady, New York 5 Sept. |
| 1848 | Graduated with BA degree 26 July; schoolmaster at N Pownal, Vermont. |
| 1849 | Appointed Principal of North Pownal Academy. |
| 1851 | Awarded MA degree by Union College. |
| 1853 | Joined law firm of Culver and Parker in New York City as clerk. |
| 1854 | Admitted to the New York Bar 4 May. |
| 1856 | Formed law firm with Henry D. Gardiner in New York City. |

1861    Appointed State Engineer-in-Chief (with rank of Brig-Gen) on Governor Edwin
        D. Morgan's staff 1 Jan; appointed Assist Quartermaster Gen 15 April.

1862    Appointed Inspector-Gen 14 April; acted as secretary at conference of
        Governors of Loyal States in New York City 28 June; appointed Quartermaster
        Gen 27 July; resigned commission 31 Dec.

1863    Resumed law practice in New York.

1867    Appointed member of Republican City Executive Committee (Chm 1868).

1869-70 Counsel to New York City Tax Commission.

1871    Appointed Collector of the Port of New York by President Grant 20 Nov
        (confirmed by Senate 12 Dec and commissioned for four years 16 Dec).

1875    Re-appointed Collector by President Grant 17 Dec.

1876    Attended Republican National Convention at Cincinnati 14-16 June; Chairman
        Republican State Convention, Saratoga, New York 23 Aug.

1877    Declined request to resign as Collector by Secretary of Treasury Sherman 7
        Sept; replied to Jay Commission charges regarding his management of the
        Custom house 23 Nov.

1878    Suspended as Collector of the Port of New York by President Hayes 11 June;
        resumed law practice.

1880    Delegate to Republican National Convention at Chicago 2-8 June; nominated
        Republican candidate for Vice-President 8 June; accepted nomination 5 July;
        elected Vice-President 2 Nov.

1881    Took the oath as Vice-President in the Senate Chamber 4 March; succeeded as
        21st President of the United States of America on the death of President Garfield
        19 Sept; took the oath of office at his home, 123 Lexington Avenue, New York
        City 20 Sept (repeated in a private ceremony in the Capitol 22 Sept); issued
        proclamation declaring 22 Dec a day of mourning for President Garfield 26 Sept;
        took part in dedication of Revolutionary War Monument at Yorktown, Virginia
        19 Oct; sent first State of the Union message to Congress 6 Dec.

1882    Signed amended Anti-Polygamy Act 22 March; signed Widows of Presidents
        Pension Act 31 March; vetoed Chinese Immigration Bill 4 April; sent special
        message to Congress asking for system of supplemental levees on Mississippi
        River 17 April; sent special message to Congress concerning proposed
        Pan-American Peace Congress 18 April; issued proclamation against violence of
        Arizona cowboys 3 May; signed Chinese Exclusion Act 6 May; signed Tariff
        Commission Act 15 May; Commercial Treaty with Korea signed 22 May; vetoed
        Rivers and Harbors Bill (passed over his veto) 1 Aug; postponed proposed
        Pan-American Peace Congress indefinitely 9 Aug; removed postal and
        Government printing officials for involvement in Star Route frauds 25 Nov; sent
        second State of the Union message to Congress 4 Dec.

1883    Signed Civil Service Reform Act 16 Jan; reciprocal Commercial Treaty with
        Mexico signed 20 Jan; signed Repeal of Stamp Taxes Act 3 March; received
        envoys of Queen Ranavalona II of Madagascar 7 March; published new Civil
        Service Regulations 8 May; attended opening of Brooklyn Bridge 24 May; issued
        executive order reducing internal revenue districts 25 June; attended opening of
        Southern Exposition in Louisville, Kentucky 1 Aug; received Korean diplomats
        in New York City 18 Sept; sent telegraph message to Emperor Pedro II of Brazil
        opening the telegraphic communication between US and Brazil 21 Sept;
        attended unveiling of monument to Gen Ambrose E. Burnside at Bristol, Rhode

Island 25 Sept; attended unveiling of statue of Washington on the steps of the Sub-Treasury Building in New York City 26 Nov; sent third state of the Union message to Congress 4 Dec.

1884    Sent special message to Congress recommending system for permanent improvement of Mississippi River navigation 8 Jan; sent special message to Congress asking for appropriations to reconstruct the Navy and establish Army and Navy gun factories 26 March; sent special message to Congress recommending annual appropriation of $1,500,000 for armament of fortifications 11 April; defeated for renomination at Republican National Convention in Chicago 3-6 June; signed Act creating Bureau of Labor in Department of the Interior 27 June; issued proclamation warning squatters against settling in Oklahoma 1 July; vetoed Relief of Fitz-John Porter Bill 2 July; signed Act creating Bureau of Navigation in the Treasury Department 5 July; signed Act creating Central and South American Commission 7 July; pocket vetoed six private relief and military appointments Bills 7 July; attended laying of cornerstone for pedestal of Statue of Liberty in New York 5 Aug; sent fourth and last State of the Union message to Congress 1 Dec; opened World's Industrial and Cotton Centennial Exposition in New Orleans by telegraph 16 Dec.

1885    Announced expiration (as from 1 July) of Treaty of Washington with Great Britain 31 Jan; sent special message to Congress recommending passage of Bill creating office of General of the Army on the retired list 3 Feb; signed Act preventing and providing penalties for illegal enclosures of public lands 25 Feb; signed Act prohibiting entrance of contract laborers into US 26 Feb; signed Act appointing one General of the Army on the retired list with rank and full pay, amended Postal Appropriation Act, and Act appropriating $1,895,000 for four new naval vessels 3 March; pocket vetoed two private Bills 3 March; retired from office and attended the inauguration of his successor President Cleveland 4 March; resumed law practice; appointed President of New York Arcade Railway Company.

1886    Retired from business on medical advice Feb; died in New York City from cerebral haemorrhage and Bright's disease 18 Nov; buried at Albany, New York.

# Lineage of President Arthur

GAVIN ARTHUR, of The Draen ("The Place of Thorns"), nr Ballymena, co Antrim, Ireland, *b* 1735, *m* Jane Campbell, and had issue,

ALAN ARTHUR, of The Draen, *b* 1776, *m* Eliza MacHarg, and had issue,

THE REVEREND WILLIAM ARTHUR, MA, DD, Baptist Min, went to America 1815, a noted antiquary, author of *The Antiquarian* and *The Derivation of Family Names, b* at The Draen 5 Dec 1796, *m* 12 April 1821, Malvina (*b* nr Berkshire, Vermont 24 April 1802; *d* at Newtonville, New York 16 Jan 1869), dau of George Washington Stone (4th in descent from Hugh Stone, of Andover, Mass), and *d* at Newtonville, New York 27 Oct 1875, leaving, with other issue (*see* BROTHERS AND SISTERS OF PRESIDENT ARTHUR, *p 368*), an eldest son,

CHESTER ALAN ARTHUR, **21st President of the United States of America.**

# The Descendants of President Arthur

CHESTER ALAN ARTHUR *m* at Calvary Church, New York 25 Oct 1859, Ellen Lewis (*b* at Culpeper, Virginia 30 Aug 1837; *d* at New York 12 Jan 1880, *bur* Rural Cemetery, Albany, New York), only child of Cdre William Lewis Herndon, the explorer of the Amazon, by his wife Frances Elizabeth, dau of Col Joseph Hansbrough, of Culpeper, Virginia, and had issue,

**1** William Lewis Herndon ARTHUR, *b* at New York 10 Dec 1860; *d* there 7 July 1863.

**2** Chester Alan ARTHUR, Jr, of Hobgoblin Hall, Colorado Springs, Colorado, *b* at New York 25 July 1864, *educ* Princeton (AB 1885), *m* 1st 8 May 1900, Myra Townsend (*b* at New York 1 Jan 1870), widow of — Andrews, and dau of Joel A. Fithian, of Bridgeton, New Jersey, by his wife Fannie Barrett Conolly, and had issue,

    Chester Alan ARTHUR III, of Moy Mell, Oceano, California, and 346 East 51st Street, New York, *b* at Colorado Springs, Colorado 21 March 1901, *m* 1st in London, England 29 June 1922 (*m* diss by div), Charlotte (*b* 16 Aug 1897), dau of Charles S. Wilson, of Los Angeles, California. He *m* 2ndly 20 April 1935 (*m* diss by div 1961), Esther Knesborough (*d* in Paris, France Jan 1963), formerly wife of Evelyn John St Loe Strachey, MP, author and journalist (later Rt Hon John Strachey, Min of Food 1946-50, and Sec of State for War 1950-51) (*see* BURKE'S *Peerage*, STRACHIE, B), and only dau of Patrick Francis Murphy, of New York, and *dsp.*

Chester Alan Arthur, Jr *m* 2ndly 3 Nov 1934, Rowena, widow of — Graves, and dau of Richard Edward Dashwood, and *d* 18 July 1937.

**3** Ellen (Nell) Herndon ARTHUR, *b* at New York 21 Nov 1871, *m* 1907, as his 1st wife, Charles Pinkerton, of Mount Kisco, New York[2] (*b* at West Chester, Pennsylvania 2 July 1871; *d* at Mount Kisco 31 Jan 1974, aged 102, *bur* Rock Spring Cemetery, Rock Spring, Maryland), and *dsp* 1915.

# The Brothers and Sisters of President Arthur

**1** Regina ARTHUR, *b* 1822 or 1823.
**2** Jane ARTHUR, *b* 14 March 1824.
**3** Almeda ARTHUR.
**4** Ann Eliza ARTHUR.
**5** Malvina ARTHUR.
**6** William ARTHUR, Major US Army, *m*, and had issue, two daus.
**7** George ARTHUR, *b* 24 May 1836.
**8** Mary ARTHUR, acted as White House hostess for her brother Pres Arthur, *m* John Edward McElroy, of Albany, New York (*d* 1915), and *d* 1916, having had issue,
   1 May MCELROY, *m* Charles H. Jackson, and had issue,
      (1) ●Charles H. JACKSON, Jr [*PO Box 390, Santa Barbara, California 93102, USA*], *m* ●Ann Gavit, and has issue,
         1*a*●Flora B. JACKSON, *m* 1st (*m* diss by div), David Basham, and has issue, six children. She *m* 2ndly, ●Dr Douglas Elliott Ramsey [*50 Moncada Way, San Rafael, California 94901, USA*].
         2*a*●Palmer Gavit JACKSON, *m* ●Joan —, and has issue, ●Palmer Charles JACKSON.
         3*a*●Peter JACKSON, *m*, and has issue.
      (2) ●Jessie JACKSON, *m* ●Hiland Garfield Batcheller, and has had issue,
         1*a*●Mary Arthur BATCHELLER, *b* at Albany, New York 7 Feb 1916, *m* there 20 June 1936, ●John Quincy Adams Doolittle (*b* at Utica, New York 8 March 1911) [*Menands Road, Menands, New York, USA*], son of William Clarkson Johnson Doolittle, by his 1st wife Amelia Lowery, and has issue (*see* DESCENDANTS OF PRESIDENT JOHN ADAMS, *p* 80).
         2*a*●Elizabeth BATCHELLER, *m* ●Woods McCahill [*Menands Road, Menands, New York, USA*].
         3*a* Hiland Garfield BATCHELLER, Jr, *ka* in World War II.
         4*a*●Jessie Jackson BATCHELLER, *b* 1929, *m* 1953, ●Arnold Cogswell, Jr [*Niskauyuna Road, Loudonville, New York, USA*], son of Arnold Cogswell, and has issue,
            1*b*●Arnold COGSWELL III.
            2*b*●Jessie COGSWELL.
            3*b*●Elizabeth COGSWELL.
   2 William MCELROY, *d* 1892.
   3 Jessie MCELROY, *dunm*.
   4 Charles Edward MCELROY, *m* 1901, Harriet Langdon, dau

of Amasa J. Parker, by his wife Cornelia Kane Strong, and had issue,
      (1) Charles Edward MCELROY, Jr, *b* 1904; *d* 1915.
      (2) Cornelia Kane MCELROY, *b* 4 Sept 1905, *m* 22 Jan 1926, as his 1st wife, ●Schuyler Merritt II (*b* 9 April 1899) [*Briarwood Crossing, Cedarhurst, Long Island, New York, USA*], son of Henry C. Merritt, by his wife Camilla von Bach, and *d* 10 Aug 1971, leaving issue,
         1*a*●Cornelia Kane MERRITT, *b* 29 Dec 1927, *m* 20 Oct 1951, ●Norcross Sheldon Tilney (*b* 29 Dec 1913) [*Tanglewood Crossing, Lawrence, Long Island, New York, USA*], son of I. Sheldon Tilney, by his wife Augusta Munn, and has issue,
            1*b*●Victoria Merritt TILNEY, *b* at New York 6 Oct 1953.
            2*b*●Schuyler Merritt TILNEY, *b* at New York 27 Sept 1955.
            3*b*●Cornelia Kane TILNEY, *b* at New York 10 Feb 1959.
            4*b*●Augusta Munn TILNEY, *b* at New York 6 Dec 1962.
         2*a*●Harriet Parker MERRITT, *b* 3 Nov 1929, *m* 19 May 1951, ●Lawrence Howland Dixon (*b* 3 Dec 1923) [*105 Ocean Avenue, Lawrence, Long Island, New York 11559, USA*], son of Courtlandt Palmer Dixon, by his wife Hortense H. Howland, and has issue,
            1*b*●Wendy Merritt DIXON, *b* at Locust Valley, New York 7 May 1953.
            2*b*●Meredith Howland DIXON, *b* at Locust Valley, New York.
         3*a*●Camilla MERRITT, *b* 5 July 1934, *m* 21 May 1955, ●Robert Milligan McLane (*b* 2 Feb 1929) [*Piping Rock Road, Locust Valley, Long Island, New York 11560, USA*], son of Allan McLane, by his wife Edith Pratt Maxwell, and has issue,
            1*b*●Cornelia Gibb MCLANE, *b* at Locust Valley, New York 19 Jan 1957.
            2*b*●Robert Milligan MCLANE, Jr, *b* at Locust Valley, New York 9 Jan 1959.
      (3) ●John Ewell MCELROY [*2616 Treasure Lane, Naples, Florida 33940, USA*], *educ* Taft Sch, and Yale, *m* ●Cornelia Ransome, and has issue,
         1*a*●Cornelia Ransome MCELROY, *m*.
         2*a*●Louise Parker MCELROY, *m*.

# Notes

[1] Although his birthplace was officially given as Fairfield, Vermont, Chester Alan Arthur was probably born in Canada. Since his parents were US citizens, his eligibility for the Presidency was never challenged.

[2] Charles Pinkerton *m* 2ndly 1917, his 2nd cousin, Sarah Harrison, a relation of the Harrison Presidents, and by her had issue, two sons: Charles Pinkerton, Jr; and Peyton R. H. Pinkerton.

# (Stephen) Grover Cleveland
## 1837-1908

———

22nd *and* 24th President of the
United States of America
1885-1889 and 1893-1897

(STEPHEN) GROVER CLEVELAND, 22ND AND 24TH PRESIDENT

# (Stephen) Grover Cleveland

## 1837-1908

### 22nd and 24th President of the
### United States of America
### 1885-1889 and 1893-1897

SEVERAL FEATURES of Grover Cleveland's political career are unusual, and at first sight would appear as serious disadvantages, or oddities that call for explanation. To begin with, he was a Democrat—the only Democrat to break a Republican run that otherwise stretched from Lincoln to Theodore Roosevelt. Next, he had never been a soldier, whereas all the Republican Presidents of the post-war generation had won distinction of some sort in the Union Army: Grant, Hayes and Garfield before him, Benjamin Harrison and William McKinley after him. Even Chester A. Arthur had served as a Quartermaster. Cleveland, however, did not join the Union Army but hired a substitute. In the third place, he had never been a member of the House of Representatives or the Senate. His political exploits were confined to New York State, and in particular Erie County and the city of Buffalo. District attorney, sheriff, mayor: these did not sound like exalted positions, though it is true that Cleveland was installed in 1883 as Governor of New York. A fourth, scandalous impediment was the news that Cleveland had once fathered an illegitimate child. How then did he reach the White House in 1885 and, having been defeated in 1888, stage a successful comeback in 1892?

The first explanation is the Democrats were a very strong party. They recovered rapidly from the supposed stigma of Civil War disloyalty. Most of the presidential election contests of the Gilded Era were very close; and by the natural process of two-party politics, a long sequence in power made the Republicans slack and increasingly unappealing. Cleveland benefited from the nation's disenchantment. Nor were the Republicans able to taunt him with cowardice in the Civil War, since their own candidate James G. Blaine had himself not donned uniform. His remoteness from the Washington scene did him little harm at a time when legislators were, with some justification, regarded as corrupt. Cleveland's connection with New York was a powerful asset; with 36 electoral votes it was the most significant state in the Union. And his record, whether as a local official or as Governor, defined him as a fearless opponent of wrongdoing—embodying the same code as the sheriff in a cowboy story. While he was the law officer of Erie County, Cleveland dramatized his role by superintending the hanging of a couple of convicted criminals. As reform mayor he faced down and outwitted the "Buffalo Ring". Guarding the city treasury, tackling the sewage problem—these activities enhanced Cleveland's reputation for toughness and energy. As Governor in Albany, breaking with machine politics and vetoing a mass of questionable money Bills, he was equally effective. Cleveland exemplified integrity. His opponent Blaine was by contrast implicated in at least one seamy transaction. The disclosure of Cleveland's liaison with a Buffalo widow was damaging and would have cost him the Democratic nomination if it had come out before the convention met. But he answered it promptly and candidly, showing that he had made ample provision for the mother and the child. The indiscretion dated back to 1874. American voters were prepared to forgive and perhaps secretly to admire an error that was at least manly. In the words of a witty comment by a contemporary reformer: "We are told that Mr Blaine has been delinquent in office but blameless in private life, while Mr Cleveland has been a model of official integrity, but culpable in his personal relations. We should therefore elect Mr Cleveland to the public office which he is so well qualified to fill, and remand Mr Blaine to the private station he is admirably fitted to adorn". And so the electorate decided, in 1884, though by only a tiny margin.

In his 1885 inaugural address President Cleveland called for "reform in the administration of the government, and the application of business principles to public affairs". He carried out his promises, choosing a strong cabinet and doing his best to curb the abuses of political patronage. He vetoed hundreds of private pension Bills, suspecting that most of them were on behalf of undeserving ex-soldiers. He tackled the intricate and politically delicate issue of tariff schedules. Cleveland the bachelor of 49 provided endless material for gossip columnists by marrying Frances Folsom, a girl of 21 who was the daughter of his former law partner.

"We love him most for the enemies he has made": such was a tribute paid to Cleveland in 1884. But his enemies in New York state, with headquarters in Tammany Hall, helped to defeat him four years later. The Democratic machine resented the imputation that they were corrupt. More austere Democrats criticized Cleveland for not having done more to purge the civil service of political patronage. Others disliked his tariff policy. The Republican majority in the Senate, angered by his vetoes, insinuated that the "butcher of Buffalo" was indifferent to the plight of starving veterans. His Administration's record actually compared well

FRANCES FOLSOM, MRS CLEVELAND

with those of Republican Presidents. The popular vote for Cleveland in 1888 topped that of Benjamin Harrison, the Republican candidate, by 100,000; but in losing New York by 13,000 votes he lost the election.

"We are coming back just four years from today", Mrs Cleveland is said to have told the White House servants when she departed in March 1889. Sure enough, the Clevelands returned in March 1893, bringing with them a baby daughter. A second daughter was to be born in the White House, and a third at their Massachusetts summer home, during Cleveland's renewed term. Two sons were born later. Grover Cleveland had in his absence built up a lucrative law practice in New York. But critics complained that this experience had made the "Stuffed Prophet" more complacently conservative; his firmness, they asserted, had hardened into extreme insensitivity. Most of the unpopularity he now encountered arose from economic circumstance; in 1893 America was hit by a severe depression. Cleveland was not to blame. But his insistence that the Federal Government bore no responsibility for the poor and unemployed, and his impatience with strikers and free-silverites, made him appear obtusely negative. He was accused of being a Republican in disguise. In the South and West aggrieved citizens by the thousand deserted the Democrats in favor of the People's or Populist party. Cleveland never lost his courage, but he seemed badly out of touch with a divided and angry nation. He retired from office amid ridicule and hate. With another eleven years of life left him, however, he mellowed into elder statesmanship. As the radical fervors of the 1890s died down, Cleveland's good qualities—above all his inner strength of character—were once more appreciated. After all, he had not claimed to be a crusader, but simply a law enforcer.

# Chronology

1837    Born at Caldwell, New Jersey 18 March.

1841    Family moved to Fayetteville, New York.

1851    Family moved to Clinton, New York.

1853    Family moved to Holland Patent, New York.

1853-54  Worked as clerk and assistant teacher with New York Institute for the Blind in New York City.

1855    Worked as assistant to his uncle Lewis F. Allen, founder and editor of the *American Shorthorn Handbook* in Black Rock (now part of Buffalo), New York; began studying Law with Rogers, Bowen & Rogers of Buffalo.

1859    Admitted to the New York Bar in Buffalo; became managing clerk for Rogers, Bowen & Rogers.

1863    Appointed Assistant District Attorney of Erie County 1 Jan.

1865    Unsuccessful Democratic candidate for District Attorney; formed law firm in partnership with Isaac K. Vanderpoel.

1870    Elected Sheriff of Erie County.

1871    Took office as Sheriff 1 Jan.

1874    Returned to law practice on expiration of term of office as Sheriff.

1881    Elected Mayor of Buffalo.

1882    Took office as Mayor 1 Jan; nominated for Governor of New York by Democratic State Convention at Syracuse 22 Sept; elected Governor 7 Nov.

1883    Took office as Governor of New York 1 Jan.

1884    Nominated for President by Democratic National Convention at Chicago 11 July; formally accepted nomination 18 Aug; election day 4 Nov; Presidential Electors cast their ballots 3 Dec.

1885    Resigned as Governor of New York 6 Jan; electoral vote tabulated by Congress and Cleveland and Thomas Andrews Hendricks officially declared elected 11 Feb; inaugurated as 22nd President of the United States of America 4 March; issued proclamation warning against attempts to settle on Oklahoma lands 13 March; issued proclamation nullifying Arthur executive order 17 April; issued proclamation ordering cattlemen to vacate Indian lands of Cheyenne and Arapaho reservations 23 July; issued proclamation ordering land office agents to destroy illegal enclosures of public lands 7 Aug; attended the funeral of Ulysses S. Grant in New York City 8 Aug; issued proclamation ordering all insurgents and unlawful assemblages in Washington Territory to disperse 7 Nov; sent first State of the Union message to Congress 8 Dec.

1886        Signed Act providing order of Presidential succession 19 Jan; sent special message to the Senate asserting that the power of removal of federal officers belonged to the President 1 March; sent special message to Congress recommending indemnity for anti-Chinese riots of 1885 2 March; vetoed Relief of J. H. McBlair Bill (one of many private pension Bills) 10 March; sent special message to Congress suggesting commission of labor for settlement of disputes 22 April; signed Act legalizing incorporation of national trade unions 29 June; signed Act restoring Fitz-John Porter to the Army 1 July; vetoed Right of Way to Railroads in N Montana Bill 7 July; vetoed Public Building in Dayton, Ohio Bill 9 July; issued executive order warning office holders and subordinates against use of official positions to influence political movements 14 July; pocket vetoed ten Bills 5 Aug; toured West and South Oct; dedicated Statue of Liberty in New York City 28 Oct; sent second State of the Union message to Congress 6 Dec.

1887        Signed Mexican War Pension Act 29 Jan; signed Electoral Count Act 3 Feb; signed Interstate Commerce Commission Act 4 Feb; signed Indian Severalty Act 8 Feb; vetoed Dependent Pension Bill 11 Feb; vetoed Texas Seed Bill 16 Feb; signed Act prohibiting importation of opium from China 23 Feb; authorized to adopt retaliatory measures in fishery dispute with Canada 2 March; signed Hatch Act 2 March; Tenure of Office Act repealed 3 March; pocket vetoed 47 bills 3 March; appointed first Interstate Commerce Commission 22 March; revoked War Department order to return captured Union and Confederate flags to States 16 June; sent third State of the Union message to Congress 6 Dec.

1888        Authorized to appoint a General of the Army 1 June; renominated for President by Acclamation at Democratic National Convention in St Louis, Missouri 6 June; signed Act establishing Department of Labor 13 June; vetoed Right-of-Way for Railroad through Indian Lands Bill 26 July; sent special message to Congress outlining plan of retaliation regarding fishery dispute with Canada 23 Aug; accepted Democratic re-nomination 8 Sept; vetoed Sale of Military Reservation in Kansas Bill 24 Sept; pocket vetoed 22 Bills 20 Oct; election day 6 Nov; sent fourth State of the Union message to Congress 3 Dec.

1889        Presidential Electors cast their ballots 14 Jan; signed Act establishing Department of Agriculture as executive department 9 Feb; electoral vote tabulated by Congress and Harrison and Morton officially declared elected 13 Feb; vetoed Bill to refund direct tax levied by Act of 5 Aug 1861 to States and Territories 2 March; pocket vetoed 31 Bills 3 March; retired from office and attended the inauguration of his successor President Benjamin Harrison 4 March; resumed law practice in New York City; attended celebration of centennial of Washington's inauguration in Washington, DC 30 April.

1892        Nominated for President by Democratic National Convention in Chicago 23 June; accepted nomination 26 Sept; election day 8 Nov.

1893        Presidential Electors cast their ballots 9 Jan; electoral vote tabulated by Congress and Cleveland and Adlai Ewing Stevenson officially declared elected 8 Feb; inaugurated as 24th President of the United States of America (the only President to serve for two non-consecutive terms) 4 March; withdrew Hawaiian annexation treaty from the Senate 9 March; received Crown Princess Kaiulani of Hawaii at the White House 13 March; informed that Great Britain and France had elevated representatives in US to rank of Ambassador 24 March; attended International Columbian Naval Review in New York City 27 April; formally opened World's Columbian Exposition in Chicago 1 May; Panic of 1893 began 27 June; had secret operations for cancer of the jaw 1 and 17 July; sent special message to Congress urging repeal of Sherman Silver Purchase Act 8 Aug; issued proclamation opening Cherokee Strip, Oklahoma, to settlement 23 Aug; addressed Pan-American Medical Congress in Washington, DC 5 Sept; signed Act repealing Sherman Silver Purchase Act 1 Nov; signed amended Chinese Exclusion Act 3 Nov; sent fifth (first of second term) State of the Union message to Congress 4 Dec; sent special message to Congress defining his position on Hawaii 18 Dec.

1894    Vetoed Relief of Timber and Stone Lands Purchasers Bill 17 Jan; vetoed Hudson River Bridge Bill 20 Jan; vetoed Coinage of Silver Bullion Bill 29 March; signed Act to carry out terms of the Bering Sea decision 6 April; signed Labor Day Act 28 June; ordered US troops to Chicago to enforce federal injunction against Pullman strike 3 July; signed Act to admit Utah as a State 17 July; recognized the new Republic of Hawaii 8 Aug; signed Act authorizing one million acre grants to public land States 18 Aug; Tariff Act of 1894 became law without his signature 27 Aug; pocket vetoed six bills 28 Aug; issued proclamation granting amnesty to persons convicted of polygamy under Edmunds Act 27 Sept; issued proclamation setting apart Ashland Forest Reserve in Oregon 28 Sept; sent sixth (second of second term) State of the Union message to Congress 3 Dec; issued proclamation of new Chinese Treaty 8 Dec; issued proclamation of Japanese Treaty 9 Dec; issued executive order placing internal revenue workers in classified civil service 12 Dec.

1895    Vetoed Railroad Right-of-Way through San Carlos Indian Reservation, Arizona Bill 1 Feb; decided boundary dispute between Brazil and Argentine Republic 6 Feb; called J. Pierpont Morgan to the White House for gold crisis conference 7 Feb; sent special message to Congress regarding Morgan-Belmont Loan 8 Feb; pocket vetoed 57 Bills 4 March; issued proclamation warning against participation in Cuban filibustering expeditions 12 June; sent seventh (third of second term) State of the Union message to Congress 2 Dec; laid diplomatic correspondence regarding Venezuelan boundary dispute before Congress 17 Dec.

1896    Appointed Venezuela Boundary Commission 1 Jan; Utah admitted as 45th State 4 Jan; Cuban Resolution passed in the House of Representatives 28 Feb, and in the Senate 6 April; vetoed Rivers and Harbors Bill (passed over his veto) 3 June; pocket vetoed 16 Bills 11 June; issued second proclamation against Cuban filibusters 30 July; sent eighth (fourth of second term) and last State of the Union message to Congress 7 Dec.

1897    Reduced number of pension agencies 6 Feb; vetoed new Division of Eastern Judicial District of Texas Bill (passed over his veto) 8 Feb; issued proclamation setting apart forest reserves in six western States 22 Feb; received report of Venezuela Boundary Commission 27 Feb; vetoed amended Immigration Bill 2 March; vetoed two pensions Bills (both passed over his veto) 3 March; pocket vetoed 49 Bills 4 March; retired from office and attended the inauguration of his successor President McKinley 4 March; moved to new home Westland, Princeton, New Jersey 18 March.

1899    Appointed Henry Stafford Little Lecturer in Public Affairs at Princeton University.

1901    Appointed member of board of trustees of Princeton University.

1906    Re-organized the Equitable Life Assurance Society of US in New York City.

1907    President of Association of Presidents of Life Insurance Companies.

1908    Died of a heart attack at Princeton, New Jersey 24 June; buried there.

# The Writings of President Cleveland

*Presidential Problems* (1904)
*Fishing and Shooting Sketches* (1906)
*Good Citizenship* (1908)

# Lineage of President Cleveland

WILLIAM CLEVELAND, Sheriff of York 1456, great-grandfather of

THE REVEREND THOMAS CLEVELAND, Vicar of Hinckley, Leicestershire, *m*, and had issue,

MOSES CLEVELAND, who went with his brother Aaron from Ipswich, Suffolk to Plymouth, Mass 1635, *m* Anne Winn, and had with other issue,

AARON CLEVELAND, *b* 1654, *m* Dorcas Wilson (*b* 1657; *d* 1714), and *d* 1716, leaving issue,

AARON CLEVELAND, *m* Abigail Waters, and had issue,

AARON CLEVELAND, *b* 1715, *m* Susannah (*b* 1716; *d* 1788), dau of Aaron Porter[1], by his wife Susannah Sewall, and *d* 1757, leaving issue,

THE REVEREND AARON CLEVELAND, *b* 1744, *m* Abiah (*b* 1749; *d* 1788), dau of James Hyde, by his wife Sarah, dau of Abiel Marshall, and *d* 1815, leaving issue,

WILLIAM CLEVELAND, *b* 1770, *m* Margaret (*b* 1776), dau of Richard Falley, by his wife Margaret, dau of Samuel Hitchcock, and *d* 1837, leaving issue,

THE REVEREND RICHARD FALLEY CLEVELAND, Presbyterian Min, *b* at Norwich, Connecticut 19 June 1804, *m* 10 Sept 1829, Anne (*b* at Baltimore, Maryland 4 Feb 1806; *d* at Holland Patent, New York 19 July 1882), dau of Abney Neal, of Baltimore, by his wife Barbara Reel, and *d* at Holland Patent, New York 1 Oct 1853, leaving, with other issue (*see* BROTHERS AND SISTERS OF PRESIDENT CLEVELAND, *p 383*), a 3rd son,

(STEPHEN) GROVER CLEVELAND, **22nd and 24th President of the United States of America.**

# The Descendants of President Cleveland

(STEPHEN) GROVER CLEVELAND *m* at The White House, Washington, DC (the only President to be married there) 2 June 1886, Frances (*b* at Buffalo, New York 21 July 1864; *m* 2ndly 10 Feb 1913, Thomas Jex Preston, Jr, Prof of Archaeology Princeton Univ; *d* at Baltimore, Maryland 29 Oct 1947, *bur* Princeton, New Jersey), dau of Oscar Folsom, attorney, by his wife Emma Cornelia, dau of Elisha Harmon, and had issue,

1 Ruth CLEVELAND, *b* at New York City 3 Oct 1891; *d* at Princeton, New Jersey 7 Jan 1904.

2 ● Esther CLEVELAND [*The Meadow House, Tamworth, New Hampshire, USA*], *b* at the White House, Washington, DC (the only dau of a President to be born there) 9 Sept 1893, *m* at Westminster Abbey 14 March 1918, Capt William Sidney Bence Bosanquet, DSO, Coldstream Guards (*b* 1893; *d* 5 March 1966), yst son of late Sir Frederick Albert Bosanquet, KC, of 12 Grenville Place, London SW, and Cobbe Place, Lewes, Sussex, England, Common Serjeant of City of Lond (*see* BURKE'S LG, BOSANQUET *of Dingestow*), by his 2nd wife Philippa Frances, yst dau of William Bence-Jones, JP, Barrister-at-law, author, of Lisselane, co Cork, Ireland, and 34 Elvaston Place, London SW (*see* BURKE'S *Irish Family Records*), and has issue,

   1 ● Marion Frances BOSANQUET, *b* in Lincs, England 28 Aug 1919, *educ* Univ Coll Lond (BA 1950), *m* at Westminster Register Office, London 13 Dec 1973, ● Prof Peter Maxwell Daniel, MA, MB, BCh, DM, DSc, FRCP, FRCS, FCPath, FInstBiol, Prof of Neuropathology Lond Univ (*b* at 1a Wimpole Street, London W1 14 Nov 1910) [*5 Seaforth Place, Buckingham Gate, London SW1*], son of Peter Daniel, FRCS, surg to Charing Cross Hosp, London, by his wife Beatrice Laetitia Herskind.

   2 ● Philippa Ruth BOSANQUET, Lectr in Philosophy Somerville Coll Oxford 1946-49, Fell and Tutor in Philosophy and Univ Lectr 1949-69, Vice-Prin Somerville 1967-69, Snr Research Fell from 1969, Visiting Prof at Cornell Univ, Mass Inst of Technology and Berkeley Univ, Snr Visiting Prof Soc for Humanities at Cornell, Snr Old Dominion Fell Soc for Humanities at Princeton Univ, Prof in Residence California Univ (Los Angeles) [*c/o Somerville College, Oxford, England*], *b* at Owston Ferry, Lincs, England 3 Oct 1921, *educ* Somerville Coll Oxford (BA 1942, MA 1948), *m*-in London 21 June 1945 (*m* diss by div 1960), Michael Richard Daniell Foot (now Prof of Modern History Manchester Univ, England), historian and biographer of Gladstone (*b* in London 14 Dec 1919), son of late Brig Richard Cunningham Foot, OBE, MC, TD, by his wife Nina Raymond.

3 ● Marion CLEVELAND, *b* 7 July 1895, *m* 1st 1917 (*m* diss by div), Stanley Dell (*b* 1894), and had issue,

   1 ● Frances Folsom DELL, *b* 1920, *m* 1st, — Alley; and 2ndly, ● David M. Payne [*Christopher Road, Bedford, New York, USA*].

Marion Cleveland *m* 2ndly 1926, ● John Harlan Amen, US Attorney [*404 East 66th Street, New York, New York 10021, USA*], and has further issue,

   2 ● Grover Cleveland AMEN, *b* 1932.

4 Richard Folsom CLEVELAND, of Baltimore, attorney, served

in World War I with US Marine Corps, *b* at Princeton, New Jersey 28 Oct 1897, *educ* Princeton Univ, and Harvard Law Sch, *m* 1st 1923 (*m* diss by div 1940), Ellen Douglas (*b* 1897) [*121 Woodlawn Road, Baltimore, Maryland 21210, USA*], dau of — Gailor, of Memphis, Tennessee, and had issue,

   1 ● Ann Mary CLEVELAND, *b* at Baltimore 1925, *m* there 30 April 1949, ● T. Bolling Robertson (*b* in Virginia 1924) [*4410 Atwick Road, Baltimore, Maryland, USA*], son of Rolfe Robertson, and has issue,

      (1) ● T. Bolling ROBERTSON, Jr, *b* 1950.
      (2) ● Elizabeth A. ROBERTSON, *b* 1952.
      (3) ● Ruth ROBERTSON, *b* 1955.

   2 ● Thomas Grover CLEVELAND, teacher at Milton Acad, Mass [*94 Centre Street, Milton, Mass, USA*], *b* at Baltimore 1927, *educ* Princeton Univ, and Virginia Theological Seminary, *m* at Groton, Mass 1950, ● Charlotte (*b* 1927), dau of John Crocker, by his wife Mary Hallowell, and has issue,

      (1) ● Thomas Grover CLEVELAND, Jr, *b* 1952.
      (2) ● John C. CLEVELAND, *b* 1953.
      (3) ● Sarah G. CLEVELAND, *b* 1955.
      (4) ● Ellen D. CLEVELAND, *b* 1957.

   3 ● Charlotte Gailor CLEVELAND, *b* at Baltimore 1930, *m* there 3 May 1958, ● David Look (*b* in New Jersey 1929) [*Far Hills, New Jersey, USA*], son of Edward Look, by his wife Carol, and has issue,

      (1) ● Lucy LOOK, *b* 1955.
      (2) ● Ellen LOOK, *b* 1959.
      (3) ● Carol LOOK, *b* 1961.
      (4) ● Charlotte LOOK, *b* 1963.

Richard Folsom Cleveland *m* 2ndly 12 June 1943, ● Jessie Maxwell (*b* at Baltimore 1 March 1919) [*121 Woodlawn Road, Baltimore, Maryland 21210, USA*], dau of George C. Black, by his wife Jessie Maxwell, and *d* at Baltimore 10 Jan 1974, having by her had issue,

   4 ● Frances Black CLEVELAND, *b* at Baltimore 1946, *m* at Tamworth, New Hampshire 3 May 1969, ● Frederick Corcoran [*Rowley, Mass, USA*], and has issue,

      (1) ● Richard Cleveland CORCORAN, *b* at Wellesley, Mass 24 June 1971.
      (2) ● Marion Maxwell CORCORAN, *b* at Wellesley, Mass 3 June 1972.

   5 ● George Maxwell CLEVELAND, *b* at Baltimore 1952, *educ* Lenox Sch, Mass.

   6 ● Margaret Folsom CLEVELAND, *b* at Baltimore 1956, *educ* Skidmore Coll.

5 ● Francis Grover CLEVELAND, *b* at Princeton, New Jersey 18 July 1903, *m* 1925, ● Alice (*b* 1904), dau of — Erdman, of Princeton, New Jersey, and has issue,

   ● Marion CLEVELAND, *b* 1926.

# The Brothers and Sisters of President Cleveland -

**1** Anna Neal CLEVELAND, *b* 1830, *m* 1853, Rev Eurotas Parmalee Hastings, DD, Pres of Jaffna Coll, Manepay, Ceylon (*b* 1821; *d* 1890), and *d* 1909, having had issue, three sons and four daus.

**2** Rev William Neal CLEVELAND, *b* 1832, *m* 1860, Mrs Anita Marie Scholl (*née* Thomas) (*b* 1835; *d* 1898), and *d* 1906, having had issue, two sons and one dau.

**3** Mary Allen CLEVELAND, *b* 1833, *m* 1853, William Edward Hoyt (*b* 1829; *d* 1901), and *d* 1914, having had issue, two sons and one dau.

**4** Richard Cecil CLEVELAND, *b* 1635; lost in the burning of the steamer *Missouri* off the Bahamas 1872, *unm.*

**5** Margaret Louise Falley CLEVELAND, *b* 1838, *m* 1873, Norval Baldwin Bacon, architect, of East Hamilton, New York (*b* 1837; *d* 1913), son of Norval Comins Bacon (*see* BURKE'S *Distinguished Families of America*), by his wife Janette Terry, and *d* 1932, leaving issue, one son and one dau.

**6** Lewis Frederick CLEVELAND, *b* 1841; lost with his brother Richard in the burning of the *Missouri* 1872, *unm.*

**7** Susan Sophia CLEVELAND, *b* 1843, *m* 1867, Lucien Theron Yeomans, mem New York State legislature (*b* 1840; *d* 1906), and had issue, two sons and three daus.

**8** Rose Elizabeth CLEVELAND, authoress, *b* 1846; *dunm* 1918.

# Note

[1]  Through the Porter family President Cleveland was a sixth cousin once removed of President Grant (*see p 332*).

# Benjamin Harrison
## 1833-1901

———

23rd President of the
United States of America
1889-1893

BENJAMIN HARRISON, 23RD PRESIDENT

# Benjamin Harrison

## 1833-1901

### 23rd President of the United States of America
### 1889-1893

AS THE presidential election of 1888 loomed ahead the Republicans concentrated on finding a candidate with a good prospect of pushing Grover Cleveland out of the White House. James G. Blaine, the "Plumed Knight" of Maine, still had a powerful attraction for many of the party faithful. But he was a loser with a slightly shopsoiled reputation, who wisely decided to withdraw from the race. There were half a dozen other candidates, none of outstanding superiority. The choice would obviously rest on a combination of factors. With the two major parties almost balanced in voter strength, the psephologists of the day (expert assessors of trends, tickets and tribunes, though the name for their profession had not yet been invented) reckoned that the vote in a handful of states would be crucial. Among these "swing states" were Indiana and New York. A favorite son from a swing state would have an advantage. So of course would a Republican judged to be moderate, loyal, free from scandal, experienced in politics, reasonably well known to the public, and the possessor of some military prowess demonstrated during the Civil War. With so large a field of contenders, a successful candidate would also need the support of skilful managers to promote his interests in the smoke-filled rooms were political bargains were negotiated.

On all counts Governor Benjamin Harrison was a most satisfactory figure. He was from one of the significant states—and later was to strengthen the ticket by picking Levi Morton of New York as running mate. His name was a useful asset, since he was the son of a former Congressman and the grandson of "Old Tippecanoe", President William Henry Harrison. He was well educated; an excellent lawyer with an unusually remunerative practice in Indianapolis; a keen early member of the Republican party; a devout Presbyterian who taught a men's Bible class and superintended a Sunday school; and he was suitably married, to Caroline Lavinia Scott, whom he had met in college and by whom he had two children. Benjamin Harrison had served a term in the US Senate. And his Civil War record was impeccable; he ended three years in uniform with a promotion to Brigadier-General "for ability and manifest energy and gallantry". He had already been mentioned as a dark horse candidate in 1880 and 1884. By 1888 his supporters were in a position to nominate him on the first ballot at the party's Chicago convention, and to have him acclaimed on the eighth ballot.

When Harrison was inaugurated in March 1889 he began promisingly, at least in foreign affairs. In James G. Blaine he chose a very shrewd Secretary of State; and the appointment was politically helpful. Harrison was keenly interested in America's external development. Under his Administration the nation began to build a modern navy to replace the "ruins and curiosities" of the old dispensation. But executive authority had dwindled since Lincoln's day. Initiative lay with the "millionaires' club" of the Senate. Harrison was typical of the Presidents of the post-Civil War generation in accepting this state of affairs, which in fact he could do little to combat. "The President", he was grandly informed by Senator Sherman, "should touch elbows with Congress. He should have no policy distinct from that of his party; and this is better represented in Congress than in the Executive".

No one questioned Harrison's intelligence or honesty. He became however a somewhat helpless figure, surrounded by spoilsmen and importunate office-seekers. He made himself vulnerable by giving minor posts to his brother, his father-in-law and various other deserving relations. His Administration, bolstered yet embarrassed by a large treasury surplus, handed out so much money for pensions and public works that the Fifty-first Congress was dubbed the "Billion Dollar Congress". Much of the blame for lax and lavish spending stuck unfairly to Harrison. Men in Washington were apt to denigrate him because they found him devoid of warmth. He was charming among his family and friends, and a remarkably persuasive platform speaker. But with acquaintances or strangers, as had been said of him earlier, he was "as cold as an iceberg". Indiana Democrats nicknamed him "Kid-glove" Harrison. In the opinion of someone who had studied him, "Harrison can make a speech to ten thousand men, and every man of them will go away his friend. Let him meet the same ten thousand men in private, and every one will go away his enemy". The unfortunate effect of presidential remoteness was intensified when Caroline Scott Harrison was confined to her room with a lingering illness from which she died in October 1892.

Benjamin Harrison might have been more relaxed if the situation had permitted. In common with other Presidents he was continually irked by the "circus atmosphere", the lack of privacy, of White House life. Always

CAROLINE LAVINIA SCOTT,
MRS HARRISON

MARY SCOTT LORD DIMMICK,
MRS HARRISON

stiff in posture—he was likened to a pouter pigeon—Harrison held himself even more erectly aloof on his daily walk around Lafayette Square, as if to ward off intrusion. "There is my jail", he was heard to say more than once, indicating the nearby White House.

Also in common with some other Presidents, he found new sources of happiness after his release from executive bondage. He had not been eager to run again for office in 1892. Defeated by Cleveland, he returned cheerfully home to Indianapolis, safe from the senators and the bosses, the importunings and the Democratic scurrilities. He was in demand as lawyer, orator and author. He wrote an attractively unpretentious set of articles about the Federal Government for the *Ladies' Home Journal*, subsequently published and widely praised as a book, *This Country of Ours*. It still offers some revealing glimpses, for example on the uncertainty of the American public as to how the President should be styled: "Sometimes he is addressed by letter writers as plain 'Mister', sometimes as 'His Majesty', or 'His Lordship', and very often as 'His Excellency'". That was in the 1890s. One wonders whether the uncertainty persists.

When Caroline Scott Harrison became an invalid, her widowed niece Mary Scott Dimmick was brought to the White House as official hostess. She and Benjamin Harrison were married in New York in 1896. Mrs Dimmick was 37, the groom 62. A year later, and four years before Harrison's death, a daughter was born to them. They created a wonderful tangle of family relationships; their child, for instance, was younger than Harrison's four grandchildren. Harrison himself gave every indication in his closing years of being happy, alert and productive.

# Chronology

1833    Born at North Bend, Ohio 20 Aug.

1836-47 Attended local school and was also tutored at home.

1848    Entered Farmer's College, nr Cincinnati, Ohio.

1850    Entered Miami University, Oxford, Ohio Sept.

1852    Graduated from Miami University with BA degree 24 June; began reading Law with Bellamy Storer, senior partner of Storer & Gwynne, Cincinnati.

1854    Admitted to the Bar in Cincinnati.

1855    Formed law partnership with William Wallace in Indianapolis, Indiana.

1856    Joined the Republican Party.

1857    Elected City Attorney of Indianapolis 5 May.

1858    Declined to run for State Legislature; appointed Secretary of Republican State Central Committee.

1860    Nominated for Reporter of Indiana Supreme Court 5 Feb; elected 9 Oct.

1861    Took office as Reporter 13 Jan; member of Indianapolis committee which greeted Lincoln *en route* to Washington 11 Feb; formed law partnership with William Pinkney-Fishback (William Wallace having been elected County Clerk) 11 Dec.

1862    Commissioned 2nd Lieut 70th Indiana Infantry 14 July; promoted Capt 22 July; promoted Col 7 Aug; led regiment to join Union army at Louisville, Kentucky 13 Aug.

1862-63 On active service in Kentucky and Tennessee.

1864    Assigned command of First Brigade, First Division, XI Army Corps 9 Jan; again nominated for Reporter of Indiana Supreme Court 23 Feb (accepted nomination conditionally on his release from the Army 27 April); Brigade left for Georgia 24 Feb; took part in Battle of Resaca, Georgia 14-15 May; took part in Battle of New Hope Church 25-27 May; took part in action at Golgotha, nr Kenesaw Mountain, Georgia 16 June; assigned command of First Brigade, Third Division, XX Army Corps 29 June; took part in Battle of Peach Tree Creek 20 July and was recommended for promotion to Brig-Gen by Gen Joseph Hooker, CO of the XX Corps; entered Atlanta 2 Sept; reported for special duty to Governor Oliver P. Morton of Indiana at Indianapolis 20 Sept; made series of speeches supporting State and National Republican candidates Sept-Oct; elected Reporter of Indiana Supreme Court 11 Oct; left Indianapolis to rejoin XX Army Corps 9 Nov; took part in Battle of Nashville 15-16 Dec.

1865    Relieved of duty and given furlough 16 Jan; breveted Brig-Gen of Volunteers 23 Jan; taken ill with scarlet fever at Narrowsburg, New York 30 Jan; left New York City to rejoin XX Army Corps 26 Feb; arrived in Savannah, Georgia 2 March; rejoined XX Army Corps at Goldsboro, N Carolina 19 April; witnessed surrender of Gen Johnston to Gen Sherman at Durham's Station, N Carolina 26 April; received commission as Brig-Gen at Richmond, Virginia 9 May; discharged from Army 8 June; returned to Indianapolis 16 June; resumed law practice.

1871    Served as Defence Attorney in the Milligan case May.

1872    Defeated for nomination as Governor at Republican State Convention 22 Feb.

1876    Nominated for Governor by State Central Committee 4 Aug; accepted nomination 7 Aug; defeated in election by James D. Williams 10 Oct.

1879    Appointed to Mississippi River Commission by President Hayes 28 June; accepted 5 Aug.

1880    Chairman of Indiana Delegation to Republican National Convention in Chicago 2-8 June; campaigned for Garfield and Arthur.

1881    Elected to the Senate 18 Jan; resigned commissionership 3 March; took seat in Senate 4 March.

1884    Attended Republican National Convention in Chicago as Delegate-at-large 3 June.

1887    Defeated for re-election to Senate 5 Feb; opened campaign for the Presidency in Detroit, Michigan 22 Feb; nominated for President at Republican National Convention in Chicago 25 June; election day 6 Nov.

1889    Presidential Electors cast their ballots 14 Jan; electoral vote tabulated by Congress and Harrison and Morton officially declared elected 13 Feb; inaugurated as 23rd President of the United States of America 4 March; issued proclamation warning against entering Bering Sea for unlawful hunting of furbearing animals 21 March; attended celebration of Centennial of Washington's Inauguration in Washington, DC 30 April; N Dakota and S Dakota admitted as 39th and 40th States 2 Nov; Montana admitted as 41st State 8 Nov; Washington admitted as 42nd State 11 Nov; sent first State of the Union message to Congress 3 Dec.

1890    Gave state dinner for the Vice-President and Cabinet at the White House 7 Jan; issued proclamation announcing ratification of Samoan Treaty 4 Feb; issued proclamation opening part of Sioux Reservation for settlement 10 Feb; issued proclamation against use of the Cherokee Strip for grazing under private contracts with Indians 17 Feb; issued second proclamation against entering Bering Sea 15 March; signed Act establishing Territory of Oklahoma 2 May; appointed national commission for World's Columbian Exposition 27 June; signed Sherman Anti-Trust Act 2 July; Idaho admitted as 43rd State 3 July; Wyoming admitted as 44th State 10 July; signed Act authorizing building of bridge across the Hudson River between New York and New Jersey 11 July; signed Sherman Silver Purchase Act 14 July; sent special message to Congress recommending legislation to close mails and express lines of US to lottery companies 29 July; signed Act authorizing inspection of certain imports and exports by the Department of Agriculture 30 Aug; signed Rivers and Harbors Act 19 Sept; signed Act establishing Sequoia and Yosemite National Parks 25 Sept; signed Act establishing Weather Bureau of the Department of Agriculture 1 Oct; pocket vetoed 11 Bills 1 Oct; signed McKinley Tariff Act 6 Oct; sent second State of the Union message to Congress 1 Dec; issued proclamation announcing World's Columbian Exposition to take place in Chicago 24 Dec.

1891     Signed Reapportionment of House of Representatives Act 7 Feb; signed Circuit Court of Appeals Act, International Copyright Act, and Forest Reserve Act 3 March; pocket vetoed ten bills 4 March; opened Patent Centennial in Washington, DC 8 April; toured South and West 14 April-15 May; issued proclamation announcing temporary agreement with Great Britain over Bering Sea dispute 15 June; ordered the Cherokee Strip closed 13 Aug; issued proclamation setting apart forest reserve adjoining Yellowstone National Park, Wyoming 10 Sept; issued proclamation opening 900,000 acres of Indian land in Oklahoma to settlement 18 Sept; sent third State of the Union message to Congress 9 Dec.

1892     Issued proclamation setting apart forest reserve in New Mexico 11 Jan; sent special message to Congress regarding Chile 27 Jan; issued proclamation setting apart Pike's Peak forest reserve in Colorado 11 Feb; issued proclamation opening greater part of Lake Travesse Indian Reservation, N Dakota, for settlement 11 April; issued proclamation opening Cheyenne and Arapaho Indian lands in Oklahoma for settlement 12 April; signed Chinese Exclusion Act 5 May; renominated for President at the Republican National Convention in Minneapolis 10 June; sent special message to Congress recommending retaliation against Canada for discrimination against US vessels 20 June; signed Rivers and Harbors Act 13 July; sent 2,000 troops to Idaho to suppress miners' strike 14 July; vetoed Circuit Courts of Appeals Bill 19 July; signed Act authorizing tolls on St Mary's Falls Canal, Michigan 26 July; signed Indian Wars Pension Act 27 July; vetoed Bill providing for bringing suits against the Government 3 Aug; issued proclamation setting tolls on St Mary's Falls Canal 20 Aug; ordered twenty day quarantine for all immigrant vessels from cholera ports 1 Sept; issued proclamation opening Crow Reservation, Montana for settlement 15 Oct; election day 8 Nov; sent fourth and last State of the Union message to Congress 6 Dec; issued proclamation setting apart South Platte Forest Reserve in California 9 Dec; issued proclamation setting apart Battlement Forest Reserve, Colorado, and Afognak Forest and Fish Culture Reserve, Alaska 20 Dec.

1893     Issued proclamation of Mormon amnesty 4 Jan; Presidential Electors cast ballots 9 Jan; electoral votes tabulated by Congress with Harrison being officially declared defeated by Cleveland 8 Feb; issued proclamation setting apart Sierra Forest Reserve, California, 14 Feb; submitted Hawaiian Treaty of Annexation to the Senate 15 Feb; signed National Cholera Quarantine Act 15 Feb; issued proclamation setting apart Pacific Coast Reserve, Washington, and Grand Canyon Forest Reserve, Arizona 20 Feb; suspended part of St Mary's Falls tolls proclamation 21 Feb; issued proclamation setting apart Trabuco Canon Forest Reserve, California 25 Feb; signed Diplomatic Appropriation Act 1 March; signed Interstate Railway Safety Act 2 March; pocket vetoed three Bills 4 March; retired from office and attended the inauguration of his successor President Cleveland 4 March; returned to Indianapolis.

1894     Gave series of lectures on Constitutional Law at Stanford University, Palo Alto, California.

1896     Declined to seek Republican nomination for President 4 Feb.

1897     Appointed Chief Counsel to represent Venezuela in boundary dispute with Great Britain.

1898   Visited Yellowstone National Park.

1899   Argued Venezuelan case before arbitration tribunal in Paris; toured France, Belgium, Germany and England; returned to US Nov.

1900   Presided at Ecumenical Conference of Foreign Missions in New York April; appointed to Permanent Court of Arbitration by President McKinley 24 Nov.

1901   Died of pneumonia at Indianapolis, Indiana 13 March; buried in Indianapolis.

# The Writings of President Benjamin Harrison

*This Country of Ours* (1897) [originally published as a series of articles in *Ladies' Home Journal*; and published in England as *The Constitution and Administration of the United States of America*]

*Views of An Ex-President*, a collection of addresses and writings made after his term of office compiled by his widow (1901)

# Lineage of President Benjamin Harrison

BENJAMIN HARRISON, **23rd President of the United States of America**, was the grandson of PRESIDENT WILLIAM HENRY HARRISON, 9th President (*see* DESCENDANTS OF PRESIDENT WILLIAM HENRY HARRISON, *p 212*).

# The Descendants of President Benjamin Harrison

(**NB** *All the descendants of President Benjamin Harrison are, of course,* also *descendants of President William Henry Harrison—qv*)

BENJAMIN HARRISON *m* 1st at Oxford, Ohio 20 Oct 1853, Caroline Lavinia[1] (*b* at Oxford, Ohio 1 Oct 1832; *d* at the White House 25 Oct 1892, *bur* Crown Hill Cemetery, Indianapolis, Indiana), 3rd dau of Rev Dr John Witherspoon Scott, Presbyterian Min and Prof of Mathematics and Natural Sciences, Miami Univ, by his wife Mary Potts, dau of John Neal, and had issue,

**1** Russell Benjamin HARRISON, Lt-Col US Vols, served in Spanish-American War, *b* at Oxford, Ohio 12 Aug 1854, *m* at Omaha, Nebraska 9 Jan 1884, Mary Angeline Saunders, and had issue,
  **1** Marthena HARRISON, *m* Harry A. Williams, Jr, of Norfolk, Virginia, son of Harry A. Williams, and had issue,
    (1) ●Sally Ann WILLIAMS.
    (2) ●Mary Virginia WILLIAMS, *m* ● — Devine [*1200 Corbin Court, McLean, Virginia 22101, USA*].
  **2** ●William Henry HARRISON (Hon), admitted to Indiana Bar 1925, Wyoming Bar 1937, mem Indiana House of Reps 1927, and of Wyoming House of Reps 1945, 1947 and 1949, mem-at-large for Wyoming, mem 82nd-83rd, 87th-88th and 90th Congresses, mem Renegotiations Bd 1968, County Chm Wyoming Republican Cttee 1948-50, State Committeeman 1946-48 [*Box 6046, Sheridan, Wyoming 82801, USA*], *b* at Terre Haute, Indiana 10 Aug 1896, *educ* Friends' Sch, Washington, and Nebraska Univ (LL D Vincennes Univ), *m*

19 Oct 1920, ●Mary Elizabeth Newton, and has issue,
    (1) ●Mary Elizabeth HARRISON.
    (2) ●William Henry HARRISON, Jr [*4651 Massachusetts Avenue, Washington, DC 20016, USA*].
**2** Mary Scott HARRISON, *b* at Indianapolis, Indiana 3 April 1858, *m* there 5 Nov 1884, James Robert McKee (*b* at Madison, Indiana 9 Dec 1857; *d* at Greenwich, Connecticut 21 Oct 1942), son of Robert S. McKee, by his wife Celine E., and *d* at Greenwich, Connecticut 28 Oct 1930, leaving issue,
  **1** Benjamin Harrison MCKEE, *b* at Indianapolis, Indiana 15 March 1887, *m* 1st at Wimbledon, Surrey, England 5 April 1917, Constance Elizabeth Magnett (*d* at Palm Beach, Florida 23 Jan 1954), and had issue,
    Patricia MCKEE, *b* in Paris, France 30 March 1921, *m* 1st 1944 (*m* diss by div), Gerald Rohmer (*b* in New York City 27 March 1918), son of Gerald Rohmer, by his wife Beebe Bentley, and has issue,
      1*a* ●Carole ROHMER, *b* at Greenwich, Connecticut 5

Dec 1944, *m* at Milwaukee, Wisconsin 19 Dec 1964, ●Harold Holbrook, Jr (*b* at Statesville, N Carolina 1944), son of Harold Holbrook, by his wife Jane Brooks, and has issue,
   ●Gerald McKee HOLBROOK, *b* at Milwaukee, Wisconsin 13 Feb 1967.
Patricia McKee *m* 2ndly at Milwaukee, Wisconsin 14 Nov 1953, ●Richard E. Monahan (*b* at Monticello, Iowa 13 June 1915) [*Mequon, Wisconsin, USA*], son of Michael Monahan, by his wife Eleanor Peil, and *d* at Milwaukee 17 July 1956, leaving further issue,
  2*a*●Michael MONAHAN, *b* at Milwaukee 30 July 1955.
Benjamin Harrison McKee *m* 2ndly at Nice, France 24 Sept 1954, Marcelle Claudon (*d* 1973), and *d* at Nice, France 1 April 1958.
2 Mary Lodge MCKEE, *b* at Indianapolis 11 July 1888, *m* at New York 15 Nov 1913 (*m* diss by div 1922), Curt Hugo Reisinger (*b* at New York 27 Oct 1891; *d* there 17 Dec 1964), son of Hugo Reisinger, by his wife Edmée Busch, and *d* at New York 2 March 1967, leaving issue,
  (1) ●Edmée Roberta REISINGER, *b* at New York 18 June 1915, *m* at Greenwich, Connecticut 16 Feb 1937, ●Joseph Jenry Morsman, Jr (*b* at Chicago 1 July 1912) [*40 Bridle Trail, Darien Connecticut, USA*], son of Joseph Jenry Morsman, by his wife Helen Elizabeth Kimball, and has issue,
    1*a*●Joseph Jenry MORSMAN III, *b* at New York 11 Oct 1937, *educ* Yale, and Mass Univs (MA), *m* at Kenilworth, Illinois 26 Aug 1967, ●Laura Cornell (*b* at Chicago 26 Aug 1947), dau of Herbert Cornell De Young, by his wife Virginia Winston, and has issue,
      1*b*●Laura Winston MORSMAN, *b* at Greenfield, Mass 18 Feb 1969.
      2*b*●Joseph Jenry MORSMAN IV, *b* at Greenfield, Mass 5 July 1970.
      3*b*●Virginia Harrison MORSMAN, *b* at Greenfield, Mass 2 March 1972.
    2*a*●Edmée Roberta MORSMAN, *b* at New York 21 March 1943, *m* at Darien, Connecticut 9 June 1962, ●David Robertson Geis (*b* at New York 30 March 1939), son of Philip Geis, by his wife Edythe Robertson, and has issue,
      1*b*●Edmée Elizabeth GEIS, *b* at Stamford, Connec-

ticut 8 March 1964.
      2*b*●David Robertson GEIS, Jr, *b* at Stamford, Connecticut 10 Feb 1970.
      3*b*●Alexandra Lynne GEIS, *b* at Concord, Massachusetts 13 Aug 1971.
  3*a*●Kimball Harrison MORSMAN, *b* at New York 14 Dec 1946, *educ* Yale and Harvard (MBA), *m* at Darien, Connecticut 28 Dec 1968, ●Ingrid Anne (*b* at Cambridge, Massachusetts 15 Nov 1947), dau of Thomas Selmer Thompson, by his wife Nathalie Brown, and has issue,
    1*b*●Kristin Kjaer MORSMAN, *b* at Landstuhl, Germany 9 April 1971.
    2*b*●Whitney Harrison MORSMAN, *b* at Wellesley, Massachusetts 27 March 1974.
  (2) ●Mary Harrison REISINGER, *b* at New York 3 Dec 1919, *m* 1st at New York (*m* diss by div), Albert Oelschlager, son of Albert E. Oelschlager. She *m* 2ndly at New York 31 May 1945 (*m* diss by div), Bradford Lorin Tobey (*b* at Evanston, Illinois 9 May 1913), son of William Hayward Tobey, by his wife Myra E. Bates, and has issue,
    1*a*●Curt Reisinger TOBEY, financial analyst with New England Merchants Nat Bank, Boston [*50 Commonwealth Avenue, Apt 201, Boston, Massachusetts 02116, USA*], *b* at Evanston, Illinois 10 June 1946, *educ* Choate, Vermont Univ, and NW Univ Graduate Sch of Business Admin, *m* at Winnetka, Illinois 14 June 1969, ●Barbara Warner (*b* at Lake Forest, Illinois), dau of Morris R. Eddy, by his wife Barbara McNair.
    2*a*●Mary Harrison TOBEY, *b* at Evanston, Illinois 25 Dec 1948, *m* at Winnetka, Illinois 31 Jan 1970, ●Lieut Rodney Wendell Cook (*b* at Springfield, Vermont 26 Nov 1946), son of Wendell W. Cook, by his wife Lillian Casey, and has issue,
      ●Kelly Harrison COOK, *b* at Greensboro, N Carolina 20 Dec 1973.
Mary Harrison Reisinger *m* 3rdly at New York 6 Jan 1962, ●Charles Joseph Stevens (*b* at Erie, Pennsylvania 6 Oct 1906) [*1616 Sheridan Road, Apt 7E, Wilmette, Illinois 60091, USA*], son of George W. Stevens, by his wife Gertrude Zinck.
**3** A dau, *d* at birth 1861.

BENJAMIN HARRISON *m* 2ndly at St Thomas's Protestant Episcopal Church, New York 6 April 1896, his 1st wife's niece, Mary Scott[2] (*b* at Honesdale, Pennsylvania 30 April 1858; *d* at New York 5 Jan 1948, *bur* Crown Hill Cemetery, Indianapolis), widow of Walter Erskine Dimmick (to whom she was *m* Oct 1881, and who *d* Jan 1882), and dau of Russell Farnham Lord, Chief Engineer and General Manager of Delaware and Hudson Canal Co, by his wife Elizabeth Mayhew Scott (sister of the first Mrs Benjamin Harrison—*see p 395*), and by her had issue,

**4** Elizabeth HARRISON, admitted to the Indiana and New York Bars, Sec Cttee for Economic Development, *b* at Indianapolis 21 Feb 1897, *educ* Westover Sch, and New York Univ (LLB 1919, BS 1920), *m* at New York 6 April 1921, ●James Blaine Walker, Jr, investment banker (*b* at Helena, Montana 20 Jan 1889) [*135 East 74th Street, New York, New York 10028, USA*], son of James Blaine Walker, by his wife Mary Gertrude Scannell, and *d* in New York 25 Dec 1955, leaving issue,
  1 ●Benjamin Harrison WALKER, mem of New York Bar, Assist Gen Counsel, The Equitable Life Assurance Soc of US, served in reserve of Army and Air Force 1942-57 (active service 1943-46 and 1951-52) [*108 East 82nd Street, New York, New York 10028, USA*], *b* at New York 27 Dec 1921, *educ* St Mark's Sch, Princeton Univ (AB 1943), and Harvard Law Sch (LLB 1949), *m* at New York 14 Jan 1956, ●Elizabeth (*b* at Rumson, New Jersey 31 Aug 1916), dau of

late Henry Sillcocks, by his wife Ada Jackson, and has issue,
    (1) ●James Harrison WALKER, *b* at New York 24 Feb 1957, *educ* Tabor Acad, Marion, Mass.
    (2) ●Benjamin Harrison WALKER, Jr, *b* at New York 8 Aug 1958, *educ* St Mark's Sch, Southborough, Mass.
2 ●Jane Harrison WALKER (formerly Mary Jane Walker), chest specialist, *b* at New York 3 Nov 1929, *educ* Chapin, Westover, Bryn Mawr Coll (AB 1951), and Cornell Med Sch (MD 1955), *m* at New York 16 Nov 1961, as his 2nd wife ●Newell Garfield, Jr (*b* at Rochester, New York 8 July 1923) [*180 East End Avenue, New York, New York 10028, USA*], son of Newell Garfield, of Concord, Mass, by his wife Mary Louise Wyatt, and great-grandson of President Garfield (*see p 356*), and has issue,
    ●Elizabeth Newell GARFIELD, *b* at New York 23 Nov 1962.

# The Brothers and Sisters of
# President Benjamin Harrison

These are given under the DESCENDANTS OF PRESIDENT WILLIAM HENRY HARRISON(*see pp 211-213*).

# Notes

[1] She was the first President-General of the Daughters of the American Revolution, organized in Washington, DC in 1890, and presided at the first Continental Congress of that Society in Washington 22 Feb 1892.

[2] She had acted as secretary to her aunt the first Mrs Harrison.

# William McKinley
## 1843-1901

———

### 25th President of the
### United States of America
#### 1897-1901

WILLIAM McKINLEY, 25TH PRESIDENT

# William McKinley

## 1843-1901

### 25th President of the United States of America
### 1897-1901

WILLIAM McKINLEY'S career ran along behind that of Rutherford B.
Hayes, with a time interval of a couple of decades (Hayes was born in
1822, McKinley in 1843). Both were born in Ohio, of unprosperous
parents. Both were delicate and bookish children. Both were reared as
Methodists: indeed McKinley's mother envisaged her son as a Methodist
minister. Both joined the 23rd Ohio Volunteer Infantry in June 1861,
Hayes as a Major and McKinley as a private. McKinley won a commission
after the battle of Antietam, when he was still only nineteen years old. He
ended the war as a youthful Brevet Major, described by his commanding
officer Hayes as "one of the bravest and finest officers of the army". Both
turned to the law, and identified themselves with the Republican party.
Both delayed marriage until they were well established, and chose
attractive Ohio girls for whom they formed model husbands.

In this particular instance McKinley was less fortunate than his
mentor. The Hayeses produced a large family, as if to compensate for
Rutherford's somewhat isolated boyhood. McKinley was the seventh of
nine brothers and sisters, but both of his own two daughters died very
young. The shock of this deprivation, combined with the death of her
mother, severely impaired Ida Saxton McKinley. She began to suffer
from phlebitis and also developed epilepsy. For the rest of their marriage
Mrs McKinley was on the edge of invalidism. The vivacious, pretty young
woman became garrulous, nervous and sometimes querulous. With
exemplary devotion McKinley ministered to her needs and whims. Since
she usually accompanied him at his innumerable social functions, he had
to learn to watch for the signs of an impending epileptic seizure. One of
these occurred during the second inaugural ball.

Otherwise McKinley seemed a favorite of the gods. He was elected to

Congress in 1876, where he remained with one short break until 1891. President Hayes paid him marked attention. Representative McKinley chose the tariff as his special field of interest. Convinced that protective tariffs were essential to foster American business and agriculture, he helped to establish protection as a dogma of the Republican party. The McKinley Tariff Act of 1890 fixed his name in the public mind; he was identified with sound economic practices, and with expert legislative activity. Republican talent scouts brought him into their presidential calculations.

McKinley does not look charming in photographs. We see him as a thickset person, staring fixedly and unsmilingly at the camera. But it is clear that he possessed an exceptional charm, different from and superior to that of the falsely jovial public figure. He was likeable because he was genuinely concerned for the well-being of others; his unceasing regard for his wife suggested as much. Mark Hanna, a wealthy Republican from Cleveland, Ohio, was impressed by McKinley's political assets, befriended him, and promoted him tirelessly. Hanna did much to ensure McKinley's election to the governorship of Ohio for two successive terms; to organize sufficient support to gain McKinley his party's presidential nomination at the very first ballot in 1896; and, as chairman of the Republican National Committee, to provide campaign resources (including money) in an abundance the Democrats could not match. Trainloads of Republicans were delivered to Canton, Ohio at excursion rates to greet McKinley on his front porch, while the relatively impoverished Democratic candidate, William Jennings Bryan, had to catch trains and go in search of voters. To those who admired him McKinley symbolized respectability, prosperity, tariff protection, the gold standard. To his opponents, who linked him with Hanna the capitalist, McKinley represented selfish conservatism, the Eastern banker and mortgage-holder, indifference to the plight of the poor. They construed McKinley's hostility to the unlimited coinage of silver as subservience to business interests. McKinley was certainly no radical. Perhaps his views were limited. But the relationship between himself and Hanna was far more than a compact between politician and promoter. "I love McKinley!" Hanna confessed. "He is the best man I ever knew". Hanna backed him as a winner because he found McKinley irresistibly winning. The history of the Presidency reveals several such pairings—none more harmonious or effective than the bond between McKinley and Hanna. When McKinley moved to Washington to enter the White House, Hanna too came to the capital as a newly elected senator. They remained bosom friends, though with McKinley always as the finer being in Hanna's eyes.

McKinley's Administration was compelled within a year to turn from tariff schedules and other domestic niceties to a growing crisis with Spain

IDA SAXTON, MRS McKINLEY

over Cuba. He was no warmonger. Public opinion impelled him, however, to recommend a declaration of war, in April 1898. Within a few months sensational victories sensationally reported in the "yellow press" brought the Spanish-American War to a triumphant close. Cuba was declared independent. The United States—also annexing Hawaii in the same year—acquired Puerto Rico, Guam and the Philippines, McKinley was a hero, who was duly renominated by the Republicans in 1900 and duly repeated his 1896 success in again defeating Bryan by a comfortable margin. But the strain upon the President was immense. His small and somnolent War Department, saddled with a woebegone Secretary who had to be replaced, was overwhelmed by the sudden pressure to raise, train, supply and transport an Army. When the excitement of Manila Bay had died down, McKinley had to decide what to do about the Philippines; and having decided to take them from Spain he found himself not only with an overseas empire to administer but with a guerilla war waged by Filipino nationalists. He was challenged by prominent citizens, including Mark Twain, and by a sizeable Senate bloc who argued that the United States was behaving like any other greedy great power.

McKinley did not see matters in that light. Although his actions extended both American power and that of the executive branch, he entered his second term with his usual air of amiable aplomb. He had a strong cabinet, and an ebullient new Vice-President, Theodore Roosevelt. He was 58 years old and in good health. Republicans could boast that they had supplied the nation's working men with the "full dinner pail" they had promised. But an out-of-work factory hand and self-styled anarchist named Leon Czolgosz felt differently. Czolgosz was living in Buffalo when the President arrived there in September 1901 to visit the Pan-American Exposition. He shot McKinley with a revolver wrapped in a handkerchief. The President died a week later. His assassin tried to explain: "I didn't believe one man should have so much service, and another man should have none". Czolgosz gave an alias to the police: Fred Nieman, or Fred Nobody. When Nobody sought revenge for years of obscure failure, the nation's most successful Somebody was holding out a hand to shake that of Czolgosz. As McKinley collapsed, and bystanders seized and began to pummel his assailant, he murmured: "Don't let them hurt him". A little later, he whispered to his secretary: "My wife—be careful, Cortelyou, how you tell her—oh, be careful".

# Chronology

| | |
|---|---|
| 1843 | Born at Niles, Ohio 29 Jan. |
| 1849-52 | Attended school in Niles. |
| 1852 | Family moved to Poland, Ohio. |
| 1852-59 | Attended Union Seminary, Poland. |
| 1859 | Entered Allegheny College, Meadville, Pennsylvania. |
| 1860 | Left college owing to illness; worked as a schoolmaster in Poland. |
| 1861 | Worked as a clerk in Poland Post Office; enlisted as a Private in Company E, 23rd Ohio Volunteer Infantry 11 June ; took part in first action in Carnifex Ferry, W Virginia 10 Sept. |
| 1862 | Promoted Commissary Sergeant 15 April; took part in Battle of Antietam 16 Sept; commissioned 2nd Lieut 23 Sept. |
| 1863 | Promoted 1st Lieut 7 Feb. |
| 1864 | Took part in Battle of Winchester, Virginia 23-24 July; promoted Capt 25 July; took part in Battle of Opequon (Virginia) 19 Sept; took part in Battle of Cedar Creek (Virginia) 22 Sept; took part in Battle of Fishers Hill (Virginia) 19 Oct. |
| 1864-65 | Served on Staffs of Gen George Crook and Gen Winfield S. Hancock. |
| 1865 | Promoted Brevet Major 14 March; degree of Master Mason confirmed by Hiram Lodge No 21, Winchester, Virginia, 3 May; mustered out of Army 26 July; studied Law with Judge Charles E. Glidden and David M. Wilson in Youngstown, Ohio. |
| 1866 | Attended Albany Law School, Albany, New York. |
| 1867 | Admitted to the Bar at Warren, Ohio 5 March; began law practice in Canton, Ohio. |
| 1869 | Elected Prosecuting Attorney of Stark County, Ohio. |
| 1871 | Failed to obtain re-election as Prosecuting Attorney. |
| 1876 | Elected to the House of Representatives 5 Oct. |
| 1877 | Took seat in House of Representatives 4 March. |
| 1880 | Chairman of Republican State Convention; attended Republican National Convention in Chicago 2-8 June; campaigned for James A. Garfield June-Nov; appointed member of House Ways and Means Committee Dec. |
| 1881 | Chairman of Committee for Garfield Memorial Services in the House. |
| 1884 | Chairman of Republican State Convention; attended Republican National Convention in Chicago 3-6 June; campaigned for James G. Blaine. |

1886   Delivered memorial address at presentation of Garfield statue to Congress 19 Jan.

1888   Presented minority report of Ways and Means Committee on Mills Tariff Bill to Congress 2 April; made tariff speech in Congress 18 May; attended Republican National Convention in Chicago 19-25 June.

1889   Introduced Tariff Bill 17 Dec.

1890   Chairman of Ways and Means Committee; introduced McKinley Tariff Bill 16 April; spoke in Congress in favour of sustaining Civil Service Law 24 April; defeated for re-election to the House Oct.

1891   Nominated for Governor of Ohio June; elected Oct.

1892   Inaugurated as Governor of Ohio 11 Jan; permanent Chairman of Republican National Convention in Chicago 7-10 June; campaigned for Harrison June-Nov.

1893   Re-elected Governor of Ohio Oct.

1894   Made national speaking tour Sept-Nov.

1896   Retired as Governor 13 Jan; nominated for President at the Republican National Convention in St Louis, Missouri 17 June; election day 3 Nov.

1897   Presidential Electors cast their ballots 11 Jan; electoral vote tabulated by Congress and McKinley and Hobart officially declared elected; inaugurated as 25th President of the United States of America 4 March; sent special message to Congress urging tariff revision 15 March; spoke at dedication of Grant's Tomb 27 April; ordered Secretary of the Navy to dispatch cruiser to Honduras to protect American interests 9 May; signed Act creating commission to examine all possible canal routes across Nicaragua 4 June; issued proclamation setting apart land reserve at Nogales, Arizona 25 June; revoked Cleveland's executive order reducing the number of pension agencies 14 July; signed Dingley Tariff Act 24 July; sent first State of the Union message to Congress 6 Dec; signed Act prohibiting killing of seals in N Pacific 29 Dec.

1898   Issued proclamation setting apart Pine Mountain and Zack Lake Forest Reserves in California 2 March; signed Act appropriating $50,000,000 for national Defence 9 March; instructed Minister to Spain to communicate American desires and intentions 27 March; sent special message to Congress with report on the destruction of USS *Maine* 28 March; notified that Spain had granted armistice in Cuba 10 April; sent war message to Congress asking for "forcible intervention" to establish peace in Cuba 20 April; Spain severed diplomatic relations 21 April; ordered blockheads of Cuban ports 22 April; called for 125,000 volunteers 23 April; Spain declared war on US 24 April; US declared war on Spain 25 April; Battle of Manila Bay in which Spanish were heavily defeated 1 May; issued proclamation setting apart Prescott Forest Reserve in Arizona 10 May; called for 75,000 volunteers 25 May; issued proclamation setting apart Pecos River Forest Reserve in New Mexico 27 May; Spanish fleet blockaded at Santiago de Cuba 29 May; signed War Revenue Act 13 June; Guam occupied 20 June; Battle of Las Guasimas 24 June; signed Federal Bankruptcy Act 1 July; Battles of El Canez and San Juan 1 July; Spanish fleet destroyed 3 July; Wake Island captured 4 July; signed joint resolution adopting Treaty of Annexation of Hawaii 7 July; Santiago surrendered 17 July; Nipe occupied 21 July; Puerto Rico occupied 25 July; Spanish Government asked for peace terms 26 July; peace terms formally accepted by Spain 9 Aug; issued proclamation announcing suspension of hostilities 12 Aug; Manila surrendered 13 Aug; issued proclamation setting apart San Francisco Mountains Forest Reserve in Arizona

17 Aug; appointed Peace Commission to conclude treaty with Spain 9 Sept; issued proclamation setting apart Black Hills Forest Reserve in S Dakota and Wyoming 19 Sept; sent second State of the Union message to Congress 5 Dec; Treaty of Paris (by which Spain relinquished all claim to Cuba and ceded Guam, Puerto Rico and the Philippine Islands to US) signed 10 Dec; sent instructions to Secretary of War regarding temporary government of the Philippines 21 Dec.

1899    Issued proclamation setting apart forest reserves in Montana and Utah 10 Feb; signed Act creating rank of Admiral of the Navy 2 March; issued proclamation authorizing Mount Rainier National Park, Washington, and setting apart a forest reserve in New Mexico 2 March; issued executive order modifying Civil Service Rules 29 May; called for ten regiments to put down Philippine insurrection 7 July; sent third State of the Union message to Congress 5 Dec.

1900    Signed Gold Standard Act 14 March; appointed second Philippine Commission 7 April; issued proclamation opening part of Colville Indian Reservation, Washington, for settlement 10 April; signed Act providing for establishment of civil government in Puerto Rico 12 April; signed Act granting territorial status to Hawaii (effective from 14 June) 30 April; pocket vetoed two Bills 7 June; renominated for President at Republican National Convention in Philadelphia 20 June; election day 6 Nov; sent fourth and last State of the Union message to Congress 3 Dec.

1901    Presidential Electors cast their ballots 14 Jan; electoral vote tabulated by Congress and McKinley and Roosevelt officially declared elected 13 Feb; signed amended Army Appropriation Act 2 March; signed Act establishing National Bureau of Standards 3 March; pocket vetoed 29 bills 3 March; inaugurated for second term as President 4 March; issued proclamation establishing San Isabel Forest Reserve in Colorado 11 April; issued proclamation setting apart Wichita Forest Reserve in Oklahoma 4 July; issued proclamation establishing free trade between Puerto Rico and US 25 July; issued proclamation establishing Payson Forest Reserve in Utah 3 Aug; spoke at Pan-American Exposition in Buffalo, New York 5 Sept; shot in the chest and stomach in the Temple of Music at the Pan-American Exposition by Leon F. Czolgosz (an anarchist, who was tried and executed 29 Oct 1901) 6 Sept; died of his wounds in the house of John G. Milburn at Buffalo New York 14 Sept; buried at Canton, Ohio. He was the third President to be assassinated and the fifth to die in office.

# The Writings of President McKinley

*The Tariff in the Days of Henry Clay and Since* (1896)

# Lineage of President McKinley

This family is of Scottish-Irish origin and emigrated to the American colonies at the end of the 17th century.

DAVID McKINLEY, *m* Esther —, and had issue,

JOHN McKINLEY, *m* Margaret —, and had issue,

DAVID McKINLEY, who fought in the Revolutionary War, *m* Hannah Rose, and had issue,

JAMES McKINLEY, *m* Mary, dau of Andrew Rose, and had issue,

WILLIAM McKINLEY, of Ohio, *b* in Mercer County, Pennsylvania 15 Nov 1807, *m* 6 Jan 1829, Nancy Campbell (*b* at New Lisbon (now Lisbon), Ohio 22 April 1809; *d* at Canton, Ohio 12 Dec 1897), dau of Abner Allison, by his wife Ann Campbell, and *d* at Canton, Ohio 24 Nov 1892, having had, with other issue (*see* BROTHERS AND SISTERS OF PRESIDENT McKINLEY, *p 409*), a 3rd son,

WILLIAM McKINLEY, **25th President of the United States of America.**

# The Descendants of President McKinley

WILLIAM McKINLEY *m* at the First Presbyterian Church, Canton, Ohio 25 Jan 1871, Ida (*b* at Canton, Ohio 8 June 1847; *d* there 26 May 1907, *bur* there with her husband), elder dau of James Asbury Saxton, banker, of Canton, Ohio, by his wife Kate, dau of George Dewalt, proprietor of the Eagle Hotel, Canton, and had issue,

**1** Katherine (Katie) McKINLEY, *b* at Canton, Ohio 25 Dec 1871; *d* there of typhoid fever 25 June 1876.
**2** Ida McKINLEY, *b* at Canton, Ohio 1 April, *d* there 22 Aug 1873.

# The Brothers and Sisters of
# President McKinley

**1** David Allison MCKINLEY, sometime US Consul in Honolulu and Hawaiian Consul Gen in San Francisco, *b* 1829; *dunm* 1892.

**2** Anna MCKINLEY, *b* 1832; *dunm* 1890.

**3** James MCKINLEY, *dunm* 1889.

**4** Mary MCKINLEY, *m* Daniel May, and *dsp*.

**5** Helen MCKINLEY, *dunm*.

**6** Sarah Elizabeth MCKINLEY, *b* 1841, *m* 1867, Andrew J. Duncan (*b* 1836), and had issue, two sons and two daus.

**7** Abbie Celia MCKINLEY, *d* an inf.

**8** Abner MCKINLEY, lawyer, *b* 1849, *m* 1876, Anna Endsley, of Johnstown, Pennsylvania, and *d* 1904, leaving issue,
    Mabel MCKINLEY, *m* Dr Hermanus Baer, of Reading, Pennsylvania.

# Theodore Roosevelt
## 1858-1919

———

26th President of the
United States of America

1901-1909

THEODORE ROOSEVELT, 26TH PRESIDENT

# Theodore Roosevelt

## 1858-1919

## *26th President of the United States of America*

### 1901-1909

"WHEN THEODORE attends a wedding he wants to be the bride, and when he attends a funeral he wants to be the corpse". "He wanted to put an end to all evil in the world between sunrise and sunset". "He killed mosquitoes as if they were lions". "A mixture of St Paul and St Vitus". These comments on Theodore Roosevelt are typical of the reactions he aroused. He threw himself into each of his manifold activities with a consuming enthusiasm. Whether he actually worked harder than any of his predecessors in the White House is impossible to say. Beyond question, however, his labors were more conspicuous, and he enjoyed them more. Owen Wister, a Harvard class-mate, novelist and friend, testified that when Roosevelt entered a room his electric vitality was at once communicated to everyone else. The English writer Rudyard Kipling paid a similar tribute to Roosevelt's conversational brilliance. A third novelist, Ellen Glasgow of Virginia, met him on a ship crossing the Atlantic at the end of his Presidency. She had expected to find him preposterous. To her gratified astonishment Roosevelt not only paid her compliments but showed that he knew and understood her work. Friends joked affectionately that there was something of the eternal boy about him. "You must always remember", said an admiring English diplomat, "that the President is about six". Roosevelt's critics said the same thing without affection: they described him as an overgrown schoolboy.

His origins would not have prepared one for such a phenomenon. The Roosevelts were wealthy New York businessmen of high social standing. Theodore's mother Martha Bulloch was the half-sister of James D. Bulloch of Georgia, who directed Confederate naval purchases in England during the Civil War. As a child Theodore was puny and suffered chronically from asthma. He turned to gymnastics and boxing in an effort to build up his physique. By the time he reached Harvard he was wiry and extrovert in manner. He was intensely interested in natural science and in American history, and already busy with research that was to lead to his first book, *The Naval War of 1812.* But he also mingled in Boston society, and in his graduating year married Alice Hathaway Lee. The young couple settled in New York. The probabilities were that Theodore would live in gentlemanly affluence, or occupy himself as a man of letters. From time to time, indeed, he did produce books and articles, and speak of himself as if literature was his destined career. He did not in any way resemble an aspiring politician. The American upper class of the day held aloof from political infighting; and in any case, the voters were suspicious of a "dude" such as Roosevelt with his squeaky voice, his Harvard accent and his rimless pince-nez.

But he confounded expectation by gaining a seat in the New York State Assembly. He was shattered by the death on the same day in 1884 of his mother (of typhoid fever) and of his wife (in giving birth to a daughter, Alice) and took himself off to the West for an interlude of ranching in the Dakotas. Thereafter he made his name not as a legislator but as a historian, journalist, and flamboyantly reformist public official. He had married a second time. Edith Kermit Carow Roosevelt was to bear him five children. Quentin, the youngest, was to die in battle in 1918. Theodore, Jr, the eldest, was to meet the same fate, also in France, in 1944.

Roosevelt's chance for military glory came with the Spanish-American War in 1898. Resigning his post as Assistant Secretary of the Navy, he became Lieutenant-Colonel of a regiment of volunteer cavalry, the "Rough Riders", which he recruited, took to Cuba and brought back again in triumph. Roosevelt's new-found celebrity brought him the governorship of New York. Soon afterward New York's Republican bosses, regarding him as a dangerous troublemaker, steered him into the Vice-Presidency. Mark Hanna was appalled: "Don't any of you realize there's only one life between this madman and the White House?"

In September 1901 Hanna's worst fears came true. As McKinley lay dying in Buffalo, Roosevelt was hastily summoned from an Adirondack hunting trip. "Now look", exclaimed Hanna, "that damned cowboy is President of the United States". Roosevelt began circumspectly. Shrewd Republicans soon realized that by accident they had acquired an extraordinarily successful Chief Executive. The voters wanted a vigorous foreign policy consonant with America's new imperial strength. Roosevelt was their man: navalist, expansionist, treaty-maker, mediator, instigator of the Panama Canal. The "Roosevelt corollary" to the Monroe Doctrine announced that the United States was henceforward policeman for the American hemisphere, entitled to intervene as it saw fit in order to restore law and order in Latin America. The voters also wanted an active Federal

ALICE HATHAWAY LEE,
MRS ROOSEVELT

EDITH KERMIT CAROW,
MRS ROOSEVELT

Government, to challenge big business monopolies and promote social justice. Roosevelt was again the man of the hour, with his dramatic intervention in the 1902 coal strike and his denunciations of greed and corruption. On the other hand, since he wholeheartedly approved of business as such, and believed that organized labor was potentially as great a menace as business monopoly, he did not attempt any drastic transformation. What he did above all was to convince the nation that its affairs were in excellent hands. In the process he made everything that went on in the White House wonderfully entertaining: his guest-lists, his recreations, his conferences, the antics of his children. Editors and cartoonists were never short of copy when "T.R." was President. He easily won his party's nomination for a term in his own right—the first Vice-President to do so. In the second term Roosevelt kept up the pace. Having announced that he would not run again, he picked William Howard Taft to succeed him, and in 1909 set out on a world tour. Lecturing, hunting and sightseeing kept him content for a while.

However, he began to fidget on his return. His own inclinations, along with those of a sizeable proportion of the population, were swinging toward more comprehensive social reform. He was impatient with the more cautious Taft—"no more backbone than a chocolate éclair!"—and gradually became convinced that the nation needed a Roosevelt at the helm once more. In 1912, when the Republican convention decided to stay with Taft, he took control of the recently formed Progressive party. The Progressives nominated him at their Chicago convention, in an atmosphere resembling that of a religious revival. Wags proclaimed that such and such an hour T.R. would walk upon the waters of Lake Michigan. The ensuing split between conservative and reform Republicans gave the election to the Democrats. Roosevelt was suddenly a leader without a major following, regarded as a traitor by many of his former associates. His "Bull Moose" Progressivism, though, was genuine enough. The Progressive party would probably have produced the same effect with some other candidate, such as Senator Robert M. LaFollette. Roosevelt did not create the gulf between reformism and "standpattism".

Nevertheless his last years were an anticlimax. He was estranged from Taft, once his closest companion. He chafed under the Woodrow Wilson Administrations, feeling first that the Democrats had stolen his Progressive thunder, and then that Wilson was a weak creature who would never dare to punish German malefactions. When Wilson did take the country into war, Roosevelt pestered the Administration to be given command of a division, or even a regiment, to take into action on the Western front. Back came the humiliating answer that Roosevelt was too old, and too "intolerant of discipline". He died of a coronary attack two months after the Armistice, like some superannuated old warhorse.

This was not a fitting final scene for Theodore Roosevelt: America's first "modern" President, the youngest to be inaugurated (at 42), the first to travel by motor-car and by aeroplane, the heartiest and most talkative and in many respects most endearing. He was a one-man orchestra. "If he was a freak", said the Kansas journalist William Allen White, "God and the times needed one".

# Chronology

1858   Born at 33 (later re-numbered 28) East Twentieth Street, New York 27 Oct.

1869-70 Visited Europe with family.

1872-73 Again visited Europe and also Egypt and the Holy Land.

1873   Family moved to 6 West 57th Street, New York July.

1876   Entered Harvard.

1880   Graduated from Harvard with AB degree 30 June; went on camping and hunting trips.

1880-82 Studied Law at Columbia Law School.

1881   Toured Europe with wife May-Sept; elected to New York State Assembly 9 Nov.

1882-85 Member of New York State Assembly.

1884   Member of Republican Delegation of New York in National Political Convention which nominated Blaine for the Presidency; gained seat in New York State Assembly; went on ranching trip to the West following deaths of mother and first wife.

1885   Appointed Deputy Sheriff of Billings County, Dakota Territory.

1886   Unsuccessful candidate for mayoralty of New York.

1889-94 US Civil Service Commissioner.

1895   President New York City Police Board.

1897-98 Assistant Secretary of US Navy.

1898   Raised cavalry regiment known as "Roosevelt's Rough Riders" and was appointed Lt-Col; served with distinction in Spanish-American War, taking part in Battle of Santiago de Cuba; elected Gov of New York State 5 Nov.

1899   Received LLD degree from Columbia University.

1899-1900 Governor of State of New York.

1900   Nominated for Vice-President by Republican National Convention at Philadelphia 21 June; elected 6 Nov.

1901    Took oath of office as Vice-President 4 March; degree of Master Mason conferred by Matinecock Lodge No 806, Oyster Bay, New York 24 April; succeeded as 26th President of the United States on the assassination of President McKinley and took the oath of office at the residence of Ansley Wilcox at Buffalo, New York 14 Sept; issued executive order revoking McKinley Civil Service modification order of 29 May 1899 19 Nov; authorized application of Civil Service rules to Indian agencies 27 Nov; sent first State of the Union message to Congress 3 Dec; Hay-Pauncefore Treaty with Great Britain ratified 16 Dec; received LLD degrees from Hope College and Yale.

1902    Signed Permanent Census Bureau Act 6 March; vetoed Removal of Charge of Desertion from Naval Record of John Glass Bill 11 March; issued proclamation setting apart Santa Rita Forest Reserve in Arizona 11 April; issued proclamation establishing Niobrasa Forest Reserve in Nebraska 16 April; issued proclamation setting apart Fort Hall Forest Reserve in Idaho 7 May; issued proclamations setting apart Medicine Bow, Yellowstone and Teton Forest Reserves in Wyoming 22 May; signed Conservation Act 17 July; issued proclamation setting apart Chiricahua Forest Reserve in Arizona 30 July; issued proclamation setting apart Little Belt Mountains and Madison Forest Reserves in Montana 16 Aug; issued proclamation setting apart Alexander Archipelago Forest Reserve in Alaska 20 Aug; sent second State of the Union message to Congress 2 Dec; received LLD degree from Harvard.

1903    Signed Act increasing Supreme Court salaries 12 Feb; signed Act establishing Department of Commerce and Labor 14 Feb; pocket vetoed six Bills 3 March; sent first message on Pacific cable to the Philippines 4 July; recognized independence of Panama 6 Nov; sent third State of the Union message to Congress 7 Dec.

1904    Re-elected President over Alton B. Parker, the Democratic candidate, by 336 votes as opposed to 140 8 Nov; enunciated the Roosevelt Corollary of the Monroe Doctrine, in which he stated that chronic wrong-doing by western powers might compel the US to exercise an international police power as the only means of forestalling European intervention 2 Dec.

1905    Inaugurated as President for second term 4 March; offered services as mediator between Russia and Japan; peace conference opened at Portsmouth, New Hampshire 9 Aug.

1906    Instrumental in bringing about Algeciras Conference 16 Jan; intervened to relieve strained relations with Japan caused by segregation of Japanese children in San Francisco schools Oct; awarded Nobel Peace Prize.

1909    Retired from office and attended the inauguration of his successor President Taft 4 March; went on big game expedition to East Africa.

1910    Made speech in Cairo defending English policy in Egypt; entertained by Kaiser Wilhelm II in Berlin; attended funeral of King Edward VII in London 20 May.

1912    Announced acceptance of Republican nomination as President 24 Feb; carried preferential primaries over Taft in six states and was successful in four state conventions but was eventually defeated by party machine and Taft gained nomination 22 June; nominated as candidate by the Progressive Party 7 Aug; shot at and wounded.

1919    Died of coronary embolism at his residence Sagamore Hill, Oyster Bay, Long Island, New York 6 Jan; buried at Oyster Bay.

# The Writings of President Theodore Roosevelt

*The Naval War of 1812* (1882)

*Hunting Trips of a Ranchman* (1885)

*Personal Experiences of Life on a Cattle Ranch* (1885)

*Life of Thomas Hart Benton* (1887)

*Gouverneur Morris* (1888)

*Ranching Life and Hunting Trail* (1888)

*The Winning of the West 1769-1807* (1889-96)

*New York* (1891)

*The Wilderness Hunter: An Account of the Big Game of the United States* (1893)

*Hero Tales from American History* (1895)

*Rough Riders* (1899)

*The Strenuous Life* (1900)

*Addresses* (1904)

*Outdoor Pastimes of an American Hunter* (1905)

*African Game Trails* (1910)

*The New Nationalism* (1910)

*History as Literature, and Other Essays* (1913)

*Theodore Roosevelt, an Autobiography* (1913)

*Through the Brazilian Wilderness* (1914)

*Life Histories of African Game Animals* (1914)

*America and the World War* (1915)

*Fear God and Take Your Own Part* (1916)

*The Foes of Our Own Household* (1917)

*National Strength and International Duty* (1917)

*Theodore Roosevelt: An Autobiography,* published posthumously (1920)

*The Letters of Theodore Roosevelt,* edited by Elting E. Morison with John M. Blum, 8 vols (1951-54)

# Lineage of President
# Theodore Roosevelt

CLAES MAERTENSZEN VAN ROSENVELT, emigrated to New Netherlands *ante* 1648, *m* 6 Aug 1655 Jannetje Samuels Thomas (*d* 1660), and *d ca* 1659, having had issue, with one other son (who *d* an inf) and four daus, a yr son,

NICHOLAS ROOSEVELT, Ald of New York 1698-1701, *bapt* 2 Oct 1658, *m* 26 Dec 1682, Heyltje, dau of Jans Bartensen Kunst, by his wife Jakemyntje Cornelis and *d* 30 July 1742, having had issue, with six other children,

   **1** Nicholas.

   **2** JOHANNES, *of whom presently.*

   **3** JACOBUS, ancestor of FRANKLIN DELANO ROOSEVELT, **32nd President of the United States of America** (*see p 503*).

The 2nd son,

JOHANNES ROOSEVELT, *bapt* at Esopus, New York 27 Feb 1689, *m* 25 Feb 1708 Heyltje, dau of Olfert Sjoerts, by his wife Margaret Clopper, and had issue, with ten other children,

JACOBUS ROOSEVELT, served with New York Colonial Troops, *bapt* 9 Aug 1724, *m* Annatje (*bapt* 1728; *d ante* 1774), dau of John Bogart, by his wife Hannah Peck, and had issue, with one yr son,

JACOBUS (JAMES) ROOSEVELT, Commissary in New York Troops during the Revolutionary War, *bapt* 26 Oct 1759, *m* Mary Helen (*b* 23 Dec 1773; *d* 3 Feb 1845), dau of Cornelius Van Schaack, by his wife Angeltje Yates and *d* 13 Aug 1840, leaving issue, with one yr son,

CORNELIUS VAN SHAACK ROOSEVELT, *b* 30 Jan 1794, *m* 1821, Margaret (*b* 13 Dec 1799; *d* 23 July 1861), dau of Robert Barnhill, by his wife Elizabeth, dau of Thomas Potts, mem of the New Jersey Prov Congress, and *d* 17 July 1871, leaving, with other issue, a 6th and yst son,

THEODORE ROOSEVELT, Collector of the Port of New York, *b* at New York 22 Sept 1831, *m* at Roswell, Cobb County, Georgia 22 Dec 1853, Martha (*b* at Hartford, Connecticut 8 July 1834; *d* at New York 14 Feb 1884), dau of Major James Stephens Bulloch[1], by his 2nd wife Martha, dau of Gen Daniel Stewart, and *d* at New York 9 Feb 1878, leaving, with other issue (*see* BROTHERS AND SISTERS OF PRESIDENT THEODORE ROOSEVELT, *p 423*),

THEODORE ROOSEVELT, **26th President of the United States of America.**

# The Descendants of President Theodore Roosevelt

THEODORE ROOSEVELT *m* 1st at the First Parish Church (Unitarian), Brookline, Mass 27 Oct 1880, Alice Hathaway (*b* at Chestnut Hill, Boston, Mass 29 July 1861; *d* at 6 West 57th Street, New York 14 Feb 1884, *bur* Greenwood Cemetery, Brookline), 2nd dau of George Cabot Lee, banker, of Boston, by his wife Caroline Watts Haskell, and had issue,

> 1 ●Alice Lee ROOSEVELT [*2009 Massachusetts Avenue, Washington, DC 20008, USA*], *b* at 6 West 57th Street, New York 12 Feb 1884, *m* at the White House, Washington, DC 17 Feb 1906, Hon Nicholas Longworth, Speaker of the House of Reps 1925-31 (*b* at Cincinnati, Ohio 5 Nov 1869; *d* 9 April 1931), elder son of Nicholas Longworth, Justice of the Supreme Court of Ohio, by his wife Susan, dau of Judge Timothy Walker, and has had issue,
>> Paulina LONGWORTH, *b* at Chicago 14 Feb 1925, *m* 26 Aug 1944, Alexander McCormick Sturm (*b* 1923; *d* at Norwalk, Connecticut 13 Nov 1951), elder son of Justin Sturm, the author, sculptor and playwright, of Westport, Connecticut, by his wife Katherine McCormick, and was accidentally *k* at Washington, DC 27 Jan 1957, leaving issue,
>>> ● Joanna STURM [*2009 Massachusetts Avenue, Washington, DC 20008, USA*], *b* 1946.

THEODORE ROOSEVELT *m* 2ndly at St George's Church, Hanover Square, London 2 Dec 1886, Edith Kermit (*b* at Norwich, Conn 6 Aug 1861; *d* at Sagamore Hill, Oyster Bay, Long Island, New York 30 Sept 1948, *bur* Youngs Memorial Cemetery, Oyster Bay), dau of Charles Carow[2], by his wife Gertrude Elizabeth, dau of Daniel Tyler, and by her had issue,

2 Theodore ROOSEVELT, Jr, DSC, DSM, mem New York State Assembly 1919-20, Assist Sec of the Navy 4 March 1921-5 Oct 1924 (resigned), Republican candidate for Governorship of New York State 1924, Gov Puerto Rico 1929-32, Gov-Gen Philippine Islands 1932-33, served in World War I as Lt-Col 26th Inf US Army in France (wounded twice), awarded Purple Heart, Silver Star with Oak Leaf Cluster, Legion of Honour and Croix de Guerre with three palms (France), Grand Cordon of Prince Danilo I and War Cross (Montenegro), Grand Cross of Order of the Crown and Croix de Guerre with palms (Belgium), and Grand Blue Cordon of Order of the Jade (China), *b* at Oyster Bay, Long Island, New York 13 Sept 1887, *educ* Harvard (BA 1908, hon MA 1919), *m* at Fifth Avenue Presbyterian Church, New York 20 June 1910, Eleanor Butler (*b* at New York 1889; *d* at Oyster Bay 29 May 1960), dau of Henry Addison Alexander, by his wife Grace Green, and *d* in Normandy, France 12 July 1944 (*bur* American Military Cemetery, St Laurent, France), leaving issue,
> 1 ●Grace Green ROOSEVELT, *m* 1934, ●William McMillan [*Box 483B, Lutherville, Maryland, USA*].
> 2 ●Theodore ROOSEVELT III, investment exec (*Silver Spring Farm, Paoli, Pennsylvania 19301, USA; Gulph Mills Golf Club*), *b* at New York 14 June 1914, *educ* Groton Sch, and Harvard (AB 1936), *m* 1940, ●Anne M. Babcock, and has issue,
>> ●Theodore ROOSEVELT IV [*37 Sydney Place, Brooklyn, New York, USA*], *b* 27 Nov 1942, *m* 7 Aug 1970, ●Constance Lane Rogers (*b* 5 July 1944) [*see*

ADDENDUM].
3 ●Cornelius Van Schaack ROOSEVELT mining engr, herpotologist and archaeologist, served in World War II with USN, Pres and Dir William Hunt & Co Fed Inc (Hongkong and Taiwan) 1949-50, and of Internat Industries Inc in Far East 1949-50, Vice-Pres Far East Security Banknote Co Inc, Philadelphia 1949-55, Pres and Dir Linderman Engrg Co Inc (Washington, DC) 1954-68, Offr and Dir Columbia Research Co Inc (Washington, DC) from 1968 [*2500 Que Street, NSW, Washington, DC, USA*], *b* at New York 23 Oct 1915, *educ* Groton Sch, Deutsch Segelflugschule, Harvard, and Mass Inst of Technology (BS 1938).
4 Quentin ROOSEVELT, *b* 1920; *k* in a flying accident nr Hong Kong 21 Dec 1948.
3 Kermit ROOSEVELT, Major US Army, served in World War I, explorer, Pres Roosevelt Steamship Co, Vice-Pres Internat Mercantile Marine Co, *b* at Oyster Bay 10 Oct 1889, *educ* Harvard, *m* at Madrid, Spain 10 June 1914, Belle Wyatt (*b* at Baltimore, Maryland 1 July 1892; *d* at Manhattan, New York 30 March 1968), dau of Joseph Edward Willard, of Fairfax, Virginia, sometimes US Amb to Spain, by his wife Belle Layton Wyatt, and *d* in Alaska 4 June 1943, leaving issue,
> 1 ●Kermit ROOSEVELT, Jr, teacher of history at Harvard 1937-39 and at California Inst of Technology 1939-41, Cons in Middle Eastern and Communist Affairs to Sec of State 1947-57, Dir Govtal relations with Gulf Oil Corpn 1958-60, Vice-Pres Kermit Roosevelt & Assocs Inc 1960-64, Pres 1964, Snr Vice-Pres Downs & Roosevelt Inc, Dir Near East

Foundation, American Friends of Middle East, Chm African Wild Life Leadership Fund, Councilman Harvard Foundation, served with OSS 1941-46, author of *Arabs, Oil and History* (1949) and *A Sentimental Safari* (1963) [*4727 Berkeley Terrace NW, Washington, DC 20007, USA*], *b* at Buenos Aires, Argentina 13 Feb 1916, *educ* Harvard (AB 1938), *m* 28 June 1937, ●Mary Lowe Gaddis, and has issue,
  (1) ●Kermit ROOSEVELT III [*5501 Hawthorne Place NW, Washington, DC, USA*], *m*, and has issue (*see* ADDENDUM).
  (2) ●Jonathan ROOSEVELT, Secondary Sch Teacher at Moshi, Tanganyika 1962-63, in US Foreign Service Dept of State 1966-73, served at Kinshasa, Zaire 1969-71, and Accra, Ghana 1971-73, Vice-Pres Kermit Roosevelt & Assocs Inc from 1973 [*4731 Berkeley Terrace NW, Washington, DC, USA*], *b* at Pasadena, California 30 Jan 1940, *educ* Groton Sch, Harvard (BA 1962), and Harvard Law Sch (JD 1966), *m* at Washington, DC 14 June 1961, ●Jae McKown (*b* 5 May 1941), dau of Joel Barlow, by his wife Eleanor Livingston Poe, and has issue,
    1*a*●Ashley Barlow ROOSEVELT, *b* at Washington, DC 2 Nov 1966.
    2*a*●Jonathan ROOSEVELT, Jr, *b* at Washington, DC 31 Aug 1968.
    3*a*●Katherine ROOSEVELT, *b* at Washington, DC 31 Aug 1968 (twin with her brother Jonathan Roosevelt).
  (3) ●Anne Cooper ROOSEVELT.
  (4) ●Mark ROOSEVELT, *educ* Harvard.
2 ●Joseph Willard ROOSEVELT [*138 West 13th Street, New York 10011, USA*], *b* at Madrid, Spain 14 Jan 1917, *m* twice and has had issue by his 1st wife,
  Simon Willard ROOSEVELT, *m*, and was *k* accidentally 1 May 1967, leaving issue,
    ●— ROOSEVELT (son), *b* June 1964.
3 ●Belle Wyatt ROOSEVELT, *b* at New York 10 Nov 1919.
4 Dirck ROOSEVELT, *b* 1925; *dunm* at New York City 6 Jan 1953.
4 ●Ethel Carow ROOSEVELT [*Oyster Bay, Long Island, New York 11771, USA*], *b* 13 Aug 1891, *m* at Christ Protestant Episcopal Church, Oyster Bay 4 April 1913, Richard Derby, MD (*b* at New York 7 April 1881; *d* 21 July 1963), eldest son of Dr Richard Henry Derby, by his wife Sarah Coleman Alden, and has had issue,
  1 Richard DERBY, Jr, *b* at New York 7 March 1914; *d* 2 Oct 1922.
  2 ●Edith Roosevelt DERBY, *b* at New York 17 June 1917, *m* Andrew M. Williams, Jr [*Mileta Farm, Burton, Washington, USA*], son of Andrew M. Williams, and has issue,
    (1) ●Sarah G. WILLIAMS.
    (2) ●Andrew M. WILLIAMS III [*901 W 30th Street, Anchorage, Alaska, USA*].
  3 ●Sarah Alden DERBY, *b* at New York City 11 Dec 1920, *m* ●Robert T. Gannett [*RD2, W Brattleboro, Vermont, USA*], and has issue,

  (1) ●Robert T. GANNETT, Jr, *educ* Harvard.
  (2) ●William B. GANNETT, *educ* Groton Sch.
  4 Judith Quentin DERBY, *b* 1923, *m* ●Dr Adelbert Ames III [*51 Nashoba Road, Concord, Mass, USA*], son of Adelbert Ames, Jr, and *d* at Concord, Mass 26 Sept 1973, leaving issue,
    (1) ●Judith Quentin AMES.
    (2) ●Mark A. AMES.
    (3) ●David H. AMES.
5 ●Archibald Bulloch ROOSEVELT, financier, served in World War I as Capt American Expdny Force [*Hope Sound, Florida, USA*], *b* at Washington, DC 9 April 1894, *educ* Harvard (AB 1917), *m* at Emmanuel Church, Boston, Massachusetts 14 April 1917, Grace Stackpole (*d* at Cold Spring Harbor, New York June 1971), only dau of Thomas St John Lockwood, of 111 Bay State Road, Boston, by his wife Emmeline Dabney Stackpole, and has issue,
  1 ●Archibald Bulloch ROOSEVELT, Jr, in US Foreign Service [*3122 N Street, NW, Washington, DC 20007, USA; Boone and Crockett (New York), City Tavern (Washington), and Garrick (London) Clubs*], *b* at Boston 18 Feb 1918, *educ* Groton Sch, and Harvard (AB 1939), *m* 1st at the Little Church Around the Corner, New York 18 May 1940 (*m* diss by div 1950), Katharine Winthrop (*b* at New York 16 Jan 1920), 2nd dau of Harrison Tweed, lawyer, of New York, by his wife Eleanor, dau of William Roelker, of Greene Farm, East Greenwich, Rhode Island, and has issue,
    ●Tweed ROOSEVELT, with Human Resources Admin [*29 Middagh Street, Brooklyn Heights, New York 11201, USA*], *b* at Berkeley, California 28 Feb 1942, *educ* Millbrook Sch and Harvard.
  Archibald Bulloch Roosevelt, Jr *m* 2ndly at New York 1 Sept 1950, ●Selwa (*b* at Kingsport, Tennessee 13 Jan 1929), dau of Salim Showker, by his wife Najla Choucaire.
  2 ●Theodora ROOSEVELT, novelist, *b* at New York 30 June 1919, *m* 1st (*m* diss by div), Thomas Keogh. She *m* 2ndly, ●Thomas O'Toole [*c/o A. A. Rauschfuss, PO Box 25, Patterson, North Carolina, USA*].
  3 ●Nancy Dabney ROOSEVELT, *b* at New York 26 July 1923, *m* ●William E. Jackson [*530 E 87th Street, New York, NY, USA*], son of Robert Jackson, and has issue,
    (1) ●Miranda D. JACKSON.
    (2) ●Melissa C. JACKSON.
    (3) ●Melanie E. JACKSON.
    (4) ●Melinda R. JACKSON.
    (5) ●Marina Q. JACKSON.
  4 ●Edith ROOSEVELT, *b* at New York Dec 1928, *m* there 1949, ●Alexander Barmine (*b* in Russia) [*1661 Crescent Place, Washington, DC, USA*], and has issue,
    ●Margot Roosevelt BARMINE, *b* 13 Aug 1950.
6 Quentin ROOSEVELT, served in World War I as Offr Aviation Corps, American Expdny Force, *b* 19 Nov 1897, *educ* Harvard, *ka* at Cambrai, France 14 July 1918, *unm*.

# The Brothers and Sisters of President Theodore Roosevelt

1 Anna ROOSEVELT, *b* at New York City 18 Jan 1855, *m* in London, England 25 Nov 1895, Rear-Adm William Sheffield Cowles, USN (*b* at Farmington, Connecticut 1 Aug 1846; *d* 1 May 1923), son of Thomas Cowles, by his wife Elizabeth Sheffield, and had issue,
  ●William Sheffield COWLES [*148 Main Street, Farmington, Connecticut, USA*], *b* 1898, *educ* Yale (BA 1921), *m* 1921, ●Margaret A. Krech, and has issue,
    ●William Sheffield COWLES III [*Shelburne Orchard, Shelburne, Vermont, USA*], *b* 1925, *educ* Yale (BA 1945), and Mass Inst of Technology, *m* ●Virginia F. L. Smith, and has issue,

    1*a*●Victoria L. S. COWLES, *educ* Bennington.
    2*a*●Thomas S. COWLES, *educ* Lake Forest Coll.
    3*a*●William R. COWLES.
    4*a*●Evan R. COWLES, *educ* Groton Sch.
    5*a*●Nicholas Z. COWLES, *educ* Stowe.
2 Elliott ROOSEVELT, *b* 28 Feb 1860, *m* 1883, Anna Rebecca (*b* 1863; *d* 1892), dau of Valentine Hall (by his wife née Ludlow), and *d* 1894, having had issue,
  1 (Anna) Eleanor ROOSEVELT, First Lady of USA 1933-45, *b* at New York City 11 Oct 1884, *m* there 17 March 1905, her 5th cousin once removed, Franklin Delano Roosevelt, 32nd President of the United States of America (*qv*), and *d* at New

York City 7 Nov 1962, having had issue (*see p 504*).
2 Elliott ROOSEVELT, *b* 1889; *d* 1893.
3 Gracie Hall ROOSEVELT, of Detroit, Michigan, electrical engr, served in World War I as Pte and 2nd Lieut Aviation Section, Signal Corps, and 1st Lieut ASORC, *b* at Neuilly, France 28 June 1891, *educ* Harvard (AB 1913, MEE 1914), *m* 17 June 1912, Margaret (*b* at Boston 29 May 1892; *dec*), dau of Prof Maurice Howe Richardson, MD, by his wife Margaret White Peirson, and *d* 1941, leaving issue,

  (1) ●Henry Parish ROOSEVELT, *b* at Dawson City, Alaska 11 April 1915.
  (2) ●Daniel Stewart ROOSEVELT, *b* in Warren County, New York 26 July 1917.
  (3) ●Eleanor ROOSEVELT, *b* at Schenectady, New York 14 Nov 1919.

3 Corinne ROOSEVELT, authoress and poetess, mem Adv Cttee of President Coolidge and President Hoover, mem Exec Council of Republican Nat Cttee, founded first Red Cross War Chapter Oct 1914, *b* at New York City 27 Sept 1861, *m* 29 April 1882, Douglas Robinson, of New York (*b* 3 Jan 1855; *d* 12 Sept 1918), son of Douglas Robinson (*see* BURKE'S *LG*, 1952 *Edn*, ROBERTSON *of Orchardton*), by his wife Fannie, dau of Col James Monroe, a nephew of James Monroe, 5th President of the United States of America (*see p 157*), and *d* 17 Feb 1933, having had issue,

1 Theodore Douglas ROBINSON, mem New York Assembly, mem New York Senate, Assist Sec of the Navy, *b* 28 April 1883, *m* 1904, his 6th cousin, Helen Rebecca (*b* 1881), only dau of James Roosevelt Roosevelt (*see p 506*), by his 1st wife Helen Schermerhorn Astor, and *d* April 1934, leaving issue,
  (1) ●Helen Douglas ROBINSON, *m* ●John Arthur Hinckley, and has issue,
    ●John Arthur HINCKLEY, Jr.
  (2) Elizabeth Mary Douglas ROBINSON, *m* as his 1st wife, ●Jacques Blaise de Sibour [*200 Ocean Lane Drive, Key Biscoyne, Florida, USA*], and had issue,
    1*a* ●Betsy Mary DE SIBOUR.
    2*a* ●Jacques Blaise DE SIBOUR [*9005 Old Dominion Drive, McLean, Virginia, USA*], *educ* Princeton (BA 1954), *m* ●Diane L. Tate, and has issue,
      ●Stephanie D. DE SIBOUR.
  (3) ●Douglas ROBINSON, *m* 1933, ●Louise Miller.
  (4) ●Alida Douglas ROBINSON, *m* 1933, ●Kenneth Stewart Walker.
2 Corinne Douglas ROBINSON, mem Connecticut legislature, *b* at Orange, New Jersey 2 July 1886, *m* there 4 Nov 1909, Joseph Wright Alsop, of Woodford Farm, Avon, Connecticut (*b* at Middletown, Conn 2 April 1876; *d* at Charleston, S. Carolina 17 March 1953), son of Joseph Wright Alsop, by his wife Elizabeth Winthrop Beach, and *d* at Avon, Conn 23 June 1971, leaving issue,
  (1) ●Joseph Wright ALSOP, the newspaper columnist

[*2720 Dumbarton Avenue, Washington, DC, USA*], *b* 10 Nov 1910, *educ* Groton Sch, and Harvard, *m* ●Mrs Susan M. Patten (*née* Jay).
  (2) ●Corinne Roosevelt ALSOP, *b* 14 March 1912, *m* 28 May 1932, ●Percy Chubb II [*Chester, New Jersey, USA*], and has issue,
    1*a* ●Hendon CHUBB, *b* 1933.
    2*a* ●Joseph A. CHUBB [*110 Riverside Drive, New York, NY, USA*].
    3*a* ●James A. CHUBB [*1750 Star Hill Road, Woodside, California, USA*].
    4*a* ●Caldecot CHUBB.
    5*a* ●Percy CHUBB III [*Claremont Road, Bernardsville, New Jersey, USA*], *m* ●Sally G. Gilady, and has issue,
      1*b* ●Sarah C. CHUBB.
      2*b* ●Percy L. CHUBB.
  (3) Stewart Johonnot Oliver ALSOP, the political columnist, contributor to *Saturday Evening Post* and *Newsweek*, author of *The Centre*, and *Stay of Execution*, an account of his struggle against leukaemia (1973), served in World War II as Lieut KRRC in British Army, *b* 17 May 1914, *educ* Groton Sch, and Harvard, *m* 20 June 1944, ●Patricia Barnard (*b* 17 March 1926) [*3520 Springland Lane NW, Washington 8 DC, USA*], only dau of Arthur Barnard Hankey, of 60 Pont Street, London SW1 (*see* BURKE'S *LG*, BARNARD-HANKEY *formerly of Fetcham Park*), by his wife Cecilia Mosley, and *d* at Washington, DC 26 May 1974, leaving issue, six children.
  (4) ●John de Koven ALSOP, Pres Covenant Gp, Republican Nat Committeeman, served in World War II, Capt with OSS in occupied France and occupied China [*95 Woodland Street, Hartford, Connecticut 06101, USA*], *b* at Avon, Connecticut 4 Aug 1915, *educ* Groton Sch, and Yale, *m* at Hartford, Connecticut 19 June 1947, ●Augusta (*b* at Hartford, Connecticut 24 Dec 1924), dau of Lucius Robinson, of Hartford, Connecticut, by his wife Augusta McLane, and has issue,
    1*a* ●Mary Oliver ALSOP [*74 Nod Road, Avon, Connecticut, USA*], *b* at Hartford, Connecticut 2 April 1948.
    2*a* ●Augusta McLane ALSOP [*18 Lancaster Street, Cambridge, Mass, USA*], *b* at Hartford, Connecticut, 22 Aug 1950.
    3*a* ●John de Koven ALSOP, Jr [*c/o Postmaster, Palermo, Maine, USA*], *b* at Hartford, Connecticut 20 Nov 1951.
3 Monroe Douglas ROBINSON, served in World War I as Capt US Army, *b* 19 Dec 1887, *m* 1915 (*m* diss by div), Dorothy, dau of — Jordan, of Boston, Mass, and *d* 7 Dec 1947, leaving issue,
  ●Dorothy ROBINSON.
4 Stewart Douglas ROBINSON, *b* 19 March 1889, *educ* Harvard, *d* there 22 Feb 1909.

# Notes

[1]  Through his mother President Theodore Roosevelt was 17th in descent from Robert III, King of Scots (*see* APPENDIX C, PRESIDENTS OF ROYAL DESCENT).

[2]  The Carow family is of Huguenot descent. Elias Quereau left France after the Revocation of the Edict of Nantes in 1685. His son Joshua settled in New York 1721, and the latter's son Isaac was the first to adopt the form of Carow.

# William Howard Taft
## 1857-1930

———

27th President of the
United States of America
1909-1913

WILLIAM HOWARD TAFT, 27TH PRESIDENT

# William Howard Taft

## 1857-1930

### 27th President of the United States of America
### 1909-1913

IN MOST presidential biographies the years in the White House are the high point. What comes before is an ascent toward the ultimate reward; what comes after is anticlimax. In the case of William Howard Taft his single term as President was in many ways the low point in his life. By training and temperament he was a lawyer-administrator rather than a politician. His dearest wish was to become a Supreme Court justice. "I love judges", he once said, "and I love courts. They are my ideals, that typify on earth what we shall meet hereafter in heaven under a just God". The greatest moment in his career for Taft was therefore in 1921, when President Warren G. Harding named him Chief Justice of the Supreme Court. In comparison with his years as Chief Executive, Taft's final exquisitely gratifying decade at the Court was port after stormy seas.

Various elements had combined to commit him to that fatal term of servitude. One of these was being the son of Alphonso Taft, the product of a New England legal family who on graduation from Yale came out to Cincinnati in the shrewd belief that as the city grew, so would he. Alphonso prospered, became a civic dignitary and a Republican, and was brought to Washington to serve as Secretary of War and Attorney-General under President Grant. He expected his children to excel, and indeed created a Taft dynasty. William Howard Taft's half-brother Charles Phelps Taft, a leading figure in Cincinnati, urged William to set his sights high; and William's son Robert Alphonso Taft was to come very close to the Presidency in the next generation. The corpulent William responded to urging a little more sluggishly than his family or his ambitious wife Helen Herron Taft would have liked. By the exacting standards of the family he was inclined to torpor and procrastination—especially where difficult decisions confronted him.

To the outside world, however, Taft was a man of outstanding ability. In the 1890s he was Solicitor-General under President Harrison, and a circuit court judge and law school dean in Ohio. From 1900 to 1904 he made a great success as a firm, fairminded civil Governor of the Philippines. President Roosevelt, his friend since the Harrison era, saw Taft as a splendid exemplar of leadership in America's new great-power role—a judicious, conscientious, selfless bearer of the white man's burden. The President's admiration and affection deepened when Taft joined the cabinet as Secretary of War. The two men were a perfect foil for one another: Taft's genial, loyal willingness to follow met Roosevelt's need to lead and to get results. He sent Taft to Panama, to Cuba and back on a visit to the Philippines as the President's trusty "troubleshooter".

One night as the Tafts sat with Roosevelt in the White House library he pretended to be a clairvoyant. Screwing his eyes shut, the President said in a sepulchral voice: "I see a man weighing three hundred and fifty pounds. There is something hanging over his head. I cannot make out what it is. . . . At one time it looks like the presidency, then again it looks like the chief justiceship". "Make it the presidency", Nellie Taft responded. "Make it the chief justiceship", Taft said. In both cases the reaction was genuine. But the Chief Justiceship was not vacant and the Presidency would be in 1908. There was the snag that the Presidency was an elective office. Taft, who did not truly want to occupy the White House, had first to secure the Republican nomination and then to win the election. Roosevelt applied his formidable energies to the elimination of these two difficulties. He persuaded the party's leaders that, next to himself, Taft was the ideal candidate. In the election, which Taft won comfortably over William Jennings Bryan, the intimacy of Taft and Roosevelt was stressed. A campaign button showed them beaming at one another with clasped hands, under the slogan "U-N-I-TED" ("You and I Ted").

Taft well knew that he lacked the dynamic flair of his friend. Psychologically he was an excellent junior partner. He had graduated second in his high school, second again in his class at Yale; and it was now assumed that he would act as a sort of stand-in, carrying out policies already formulated by Roosevelt. His actual record as President was creditable. He tackled tariff problems that Roosevelt had preferred to shelve. Less clamant than his predecessor, he in fact instituted twice as many anti-trust suits under the Sherman Act. He was not unduly disturbed by cartoons in which Roosevelt was portrayed as a human dynamo and himself as an inert mass of flesh. What hurt was the discovery that Roosevelt too was beginning to criticize and disagree. Along with others Roosevelt found the Taft Administration unimaginative. Taft for example disliked talking with newspapermen, where Roosevelt had welcomed the press corps into the White House. More seriously, Taft's

HELEN HERRON, MRS TAFT

innate conservatism led him into rapport with old guard Republicanism, while Roosevelt was increasingly sympathetic to reform programs. The gap between the two wings would have widened in any case. But as the two former friends came to symbolize different, opposing groups, the personal aspect made the disagreement painful and rancorous. "Roosevelt was my closest friend", Taft mournfully confessed to a reporter when he at length publicly answered the Roosevelt challenge. Then he burst into tears.

The 1912 Republican nomination brought little joy to Taft. Deserted by Roosevelt's "Bull Moose" supporters, he ran far behind both the Democrats and the Progressives—an inglorious end. Taft's consolation lay in a return to his law career, first as a Yale professor. He believed that the Roosevelt conception of the Presidency was dangerously aggressive, and wrote a book entitled *Our Chief Magistrate* to say so. By 1921, when Taft at length was installed as Chief Justice, American public opinion probably agreed with him. He was not an innovator in his years with the Supreme Court. Most of his decisions were cautiously conservative. Again, he was in step with the majority of his colleagues and with the nation. He relished the ceremony of the silk-robed bench, the deliberate pace, the insulation from Washington's political clamor. Administering the oath of office to Calvin Coolidge in 1925 and to Herbert Hoover in 1929, the Chief Justice looked Olympianly benign. Roosevelt, Wilson and Harding, casualties of political warfare, were all dead. William Howard Taft may well have felt that he was like the lone survivor of some terrible affray, spared by the gods and permitted by them to ripen into an almost godlike sagacity.

# Chronology

1857  Born at 2038 Auburn Avenue, Cincinnati, Ohio 15 Sept.

1874  Graduated from Woodward High School, Cincinnati.

1874  Graduated from Woodward High School, Cincinnati.

1878  Graduated from Yale with BA degree 27 June; entered Cincinnati Law School.

1879-80  Reported court cases for *Cincinnati Commercial.*

1880  Graduated from Cincinnati Law School with LLB degree; admitted to the Bar at Columbus, Ohio 5 May.

1881  Appointed Assistant Prosecutor of Hamilton County, Ohio 3 Jan.

1882  Appointed Collector of Internal Revenue by President Arthur March.

1883-84  Practiced law in partnership with Harlan Page Lloyd in Cincinnati.

1885  Appointed Assistant County Solicitor of Hamilton County 1 Jan.

1887  Appointed Judge of Cincinnati Superior Court March.

1890  Appointed Solicitor-General of the United States by President Benjamin Harrison 14 Feb.

1892  Appointed US Circuit Judge by President Benjamin Harrison 21 March.

1893  Succeeded as senior US Circuit Judge of the Sixth Circuit March.

1896-1900  Professor of Law and Real Property and Dean of Cincinnati Law School.

1900  Appointed Chairman of Commission to establish civil government in the Philippines by President McKinley 6 Feb; appointed President of second Philippine Commission 13 March; arrived in Manila 4 June.

1901  Appointed first civil Governor-General of the Philippine Islands 4 July.

1902  Returned to Washington, DC Jan; received by Pope Leo XIII in Rome 5 June; returned to Manila 22 Aug; declined appointment to the Supreme Court 27 Oct.

1903  Again declined appointment to the Supreme Court 7 Jan; left Manila 23 Dec.

1904  Received by the Emperor of Japan in Tokyo 6 Jan; took office as Secretary of War in the Cabinet of President Theodore Roosevelt 1 Feb; travelled to Panama Nov-Dec.

1905  Escorted Congressional Delegation to the Philippines July-Sept; conferred with Count Taro Katsura, the Japanese Prime Minister, in Tokyo 27-29 July; served as acting Secretary of State during the illness of John Hay.

1906  Again declined appointment to the Supreme Court Jan; Provisional Governor of Cuba 29 Sept-13 Oct.

1907    Made world tour Sept-Dec.

1908    Travelled to Panama April-May; nominated for President at the Republican National Convention in Chicago 18 June; resigned as Secretary of War 30 June; election day 3 Nov.

1909    Presidential Electors cast their ballots (321 for Taft; 162 for William Jennings Bryan, the Democratic candidate) 11 Jan; visited Panama 29 Jan-7 Feb; electoral vote tabulated by Congress and Taft and Sherman officially declared elected 10 Feb; made a Mason "at sight" by Grand Lodge of Ohio 18 Feb; inaugurated as 27th President of the United States of America 4 March; sent special message to Congress urging "prompt revision" of the tariff 16 March; issued executive order restoring Marine Corps to the Navy under the same conditions as prevailed prior to the Roosevelt order 26 March; issued executive order establishing central committee to purchase all Government supplies 13 May; issued executive orders opening 700,000 acres of Government land for settlement in Idaho, Montana and Washington 22 May; abolished Council of Fine Arts created by Roosevelt 25 May; opened Alaska-Yukon-Pacific Exposition in Seattle, Washington by pressing a gold telegraph key in the White House 1 June; sent special message to Congress recommending imposition of 2% tax on net incomes of corporations; 16th Amendment to the Constitution submitted to the States for ratification 12 July; signed Payne-Aldrich Tariff Act 5 Aug; issued executive order reducing the Army by ten per cent 21 Aug; appointed first Tariff Commission 11 Sept; began tour of the States 15 Sept; returned to Washington 10 Nov; sent first State of the Union message to Congress 7 Dec.

1910    Issued proclamations extending minimum rates of tariff to all nations 31 March; issued executive order placing Assistant Postmasters of first and second class Post Offices in classified service list 1 April; signed Railroad Act 20 June; signed Arizona and New Mexico Statehood Act 21 June; signed Postal Savings System Act and Rivers and Harbors Act and pocket vetoed three Bills 25 June; made inspection tour of Panama Canal 10-11 Nov; ordered tax returns of corporations to be made public 25 Nov; sent second State of the Union message to Congress 6 Dec.

1911    Sent special message to Congress asking for appropriation of $5,000,000 to begin fortification of Panama Canal 12 Jan; pocket vetoed two Bills 4 March; celebrated his silver wedding anniversary at the White House 19 June; signed Canadian Reciprocity Act 26 July; vetoed resolution to Admit Arizona and New Mexico as States 15 Aug; vetoed Wool Bill 17 Aug; signed joint resolution for admission of Arizona and New Mexico 21 Aug; vetoed Cotton Bill 22 Aug; made cross-country speaking tour 15 Sept-12 Nov; sent third State of the Union message to Congress 7 Dec.

1912    Signed proclamation admitting New Mexico as the 47th State 6 Jan; sent special message to Congress recommending appointment of international commission to study world prices 2 Feb; signed proclamation admitting Arizona as the 48th State 14 Feb; issued proclamation warning American citizens to observe neutrality laws and abstain from participation in Mexican disturbances 2 March; issued executive order prohibiting exportation of war materials to Mexico 14 March; 17th Amendment to the Constitution submitted to the States for ratification 13 May; renominated for President at the Republican National Convention in Chicago 22 June; accepted nomination 1 Aug; vetoed compromise Wool Tariff Schedule Bill 9 Aug; vetoed Steel and Iron Schedule Bill 14 Aug; vetoed Legislative, Executive and Judicial Appropriation Bill 15 Aug; signed Panama Canal Act 24 Aug; pocket vetoed two Bills 26 Aug; created

National Oil Reserve No 1 at Elks Hill, California 2 Sept; reviewed fleet of 123 warships in the Hudson River at New York 14 Oct; election day 5 Nov; signed proclamation fixing Panama Canal toll rates; sent fourth and last State of the Union message to Congress 3 Dec; issued executive order declaring land and waters within Panama Canal Zone a military reservation; left Washington for short trip to the Canal Zone 19 Dec.

1913   Presidential Electors cast their ballots 13 Jan; electoral votes tabulated by Congress and Taft officially declared defeated 12 Feb; vetoed Immigration Bill containing literacy test for immigrants 14 Feb; gave farewell dinner for Washington news correspondents at the White House 23 Feb; 16th Amendment to the Constitution ratified 25 Feb; vetoed Webb-Kenyon Bill 28 Feb (passed over his veto 1 March); attended farewell function at the National Press Club in Washington 1 March; signed Act establishing Department of Labor, pocket vetoed two bills, retired from office and attended the inauguration of his successor President Wilson 4 March; Kent Professor of Law in Yale University April; elected President of American Bar Association 4 Sept.

1918   Appointed Joint Chairman (with Frank P. Walsh) of the National War Labor Board by President Wilson 8 April.

1921   Appointed Chief Justice of the Supreme Court of the United States by President Harding 30 June.

1922   Presided at first annual Conference of Senior Circuit Court Judges 27 Dec.

1925   Administered the oath of office to President Coolidge 4 March.

1929   Administered the oath of office to President Hoover 4 March.

1930   Resigned from the Supreme Court owing to illness 3 Feb; died at Washington, DC 8 March; buried at Arlington National Cemetery, Arlington, Virginia.

# The Writings of President Taft

*Four Aspects of Civic Duty* (1906)

*The Presidency: Its Duties, Its Powers, Its Opportunities and Its Limitations* (1915)

*Our Chief Magistrate and His Powers*, an expanded version of the above (1915)

# Lineage of President Taft

ROBERT TAFT (TAFFE), emigrated from England *ca* 1678 and settled at Braintree, Mass, later becoming an original settler at Mendon when it was set off from Braintree, mem first Bd of Selectmen 1680, *b ca* 1640, *m* Sarah — (*d* 1725), and had with other issue[1],

JOSEPH TAFT, Capt Militia at Uxbridge, Mass, *b* 1680, *m* Elizabeth (*b* 1687; *d* 1760), dau of James Emerson, by his wife Sarah, and *d* 1747, leaving issue,

PETER TAFT, minute man at Bunker Hill, *b* 1715, *m* Elizabeth (*b* 1707), dau of Josiah Cheney, by his wife Hannah, and had issue,

AARON TAFT, minute man at Bunker Hill, *b* 1743, *m* Rhoda (*b* 1749; *d* 1827), dau of Abner Rawson[2] (descended from Edward Rawson, who came from England *ca* 1632 and was Sec of the Colony of Massachusetts Bay 1650-81), by his wife Mary Allen, and *d* 1808, leaving issue,

PETER RAWSON TAFT, of Windham County, Vermont, settled in Cincinnati, Ohio 1841, Judge of the Superior Court, *b* 1785, *m* 1810, Sylvia, dau of Levi Howard, by his wife Bethiah Chapin, and *d* 1867, leaving issue,

ALPHONSO TAFT, of Cincinnati, Ohio, Judge of the Cincinnati Superior Court 1865-72, unsuccessful candidate for the Republican nomination as Gov of Ohio 1875 and 1879, Sec of War March-May 1876, Attorney-Gen 1876-77, US Min to Austria-Hungary 1882-84 and to Russia 1884-85, *b* nr Townshend, Vermont 5 Nov 1810, *educ* Yale (AB 1833), *m* 1st 29 Aug 1841, Fanny (*b* at Townshend, Vermont 28 March 1823; *d* at Cincinnati, Ohio 2 June 1852), dau of Judge Charles Phelps, of Vermont, and had issue (*see* BROTHERS AND SISTERS OF PRESIDENT TAFT, *p 436*). He *m* 2ndly 26 Dec 1853, his 4th cousin once removed[1] Louisa Maria (*b* at Boston, Mass 11 Sept 1827; *d* at Milbury, Mass 7 Dec 1907), dau of Samuel Davenport Torrey[3], by his wife Susan Holman, dau of Asa Waters, and *d* at San Diego, California 21 May 1891, having by her had with other issue (*see* BROTHERS AND SISTERS OF PRESIDENT TAFT, *p 436*), a 6th son,

WILLIAM HOWARD TAFT, **27th President of the United States of America.**

# The Descendants of President Taft

WILLIAM HOWARD TAFT *m* at Cincinnati, Ohio 19 June 1886, Helen (Nellie), author of *Recollections of Full Years* (1914) (*b* at Cincinnati 2 June 1861; *d* at Washington, DC 22 May 1943, *bur* with her husband in Arlington National Cemetery), 3rd dau of Judge John Williamson Herron, of Cincinnati, by his wife Harriet Anne, dau of Ela Collins, and had issue,

**1** Robert Alphonso TAFT, Speaker of Ohio House of Reps, mem Ohio Senate, *b* at Cincinnati 8 Sept 1889, *educ* Yale (BA 1910, MA 1936), and Harvard (LLB 1913), *m* at Washington, DC 17 Oct 1914, Martha Wheaton (*b* in Minnesota 17 Dec 1891; *d* at Cincinnati Oct 1958), dau of Lloyd Wheaton Bowers, US Solicitor-Gen, by his wife Louise Bennett Wilson, and *d* at New York City 31 July 1953, leaving issue,

  **1** ● William Howard TAFT III, hon LLD Dublin (1959), Instr in English Univ of Maryland 1940-41, Haverford Coll 1941-42, and Yale 1945-46, Special Assist to Chief of Mission, Economic Cooperation Assoc in Ireland 1948-51, with Central Intell Agency 1952-53, US Amb to Ireland 1953-57, mem Dept of Policy Planning staff 1957-60, Consul Gen at Lourenọ Marques, Mozambique 1960-62, assigned Dept of State 1962, Office of Internat Scientific Affairs 1963, civilian mem special branch of US Army Intell 1942-45 [*3101 35th Street NW, Washington, DC 20016, USA*], *b* at Bar Harbor, Maine 7 Aug 1915, *educ* The Taft Sch, Watertown, Yale (AB 1937), and Princeton Univ (PhD 1942), *m* at Grand Rapids, Michigan 27 June 1942, ● Barbara Hoult, PhD, MA (*b* at Grand Rapids 1917), dau of Thomas Bradfield, by his wife Irene Hoult, and has issue,

    (1) ● Maria Herron TAFT, *b* at Washington, DC 1943, *m* at Paris, France 1 Dec 1971, ● John Clemon (*b* in London, England 17 March 1921) [*Eithin-y-gaer, Churchstoke, Montgomeryshire, Wales*], son of Albert Clemon, by his wife Helen Edwards.

    (2) ● William Howard TAFT IV [*3215½ Cathedral Avenue, Washington, DC*], *b* at Washington, DC 1945, *educ* St Paul's, Yale (AB 1966), and Harvard (JD 1969), *m* at Washington, DC 4 May 1974, ● Julia (*b* at New York 1942), dau of Antony Vadala, by his wife Shirley.

    (3) ● Martha Bowers TAFT, *b* at New Haven, Conn 25 Dec 1946, *m* at St Andrews, Scotland 1971, ● Michael Golden (*b* at Greenock, Scotland 1946) [*92 Maynard Place, London E17*], son of Michael Golden, by his wife Margaret.

    (4) ● John Thomas TAFT, *b* at Dublin, Ireland 9 July 1950, *educ* St Paul's, Yale (AB 1972), and Univ Coll Oxford (BA 1974).

  **2** ● Robert TAFT, mem Ohio Bar, partner in firm of Taft, Stettinius & Hollister, Cincinnati 1946-67, mem Ohio House of Reps 1955-62 (majority floor leader 1961-62), mem 88th Congress at-large from Ohio, mem 90th and 91st Congresses from 1st Dist of Ohio, Senator from Ohio from 1971, served in World War II with USNR 1942-46 [*4300 Drake Road, Cincinnati, Ohio 45243, USA; Carmargo, Racquet, Literary, and Queen City (Cincinnati) Clubs*], *b* at Cincinnati 26 Feb 1917, *m* 1st 27 June 1939, Blanca Duncan Noel, and has issue,

    (1) ● Robert Alphonso TAFT II, in Africa with the Peace Corps, *b* 1942, *educ* Yale, *m* 17 June 1967, ● Janet Hope, dau of Matthew H. Rothart, of Camden, Arkansas.

    (2) ● Sarah Butler TAFT, *b* 1943, *educ* Radcliffe, *m* 1963

    ● Winfield Payne Jones II [*1 East End Avenue, New York, NY, USA*], and has issue,

      1*a* ● Eloise Dickey JONES, *b* 29 March 1967.

      2*a* ● Natalie Duncan JONES, *b* 22 April 1969.

    (3) ● Deborah TAFT.

    (4) ● Jonathan D. TAFT.

Senator Robert Taft *m* 2ndly at Indian Hill, Ohio July 1969, ● Katharine W. Perry.

  **3** ● Lloyd Bowers TAFT, investment banker [*320 East 72nd Street, New York, NY, USA*], *b* 1923, *educ* Yale (BA 1944), *m* 1947, ● Virginia Ann Stone, and has issue,

    (1) ● (Ann) Louise TAFT, *b* 1949, *educ* Mount Holyoke, *m* 19 Dec 1970, ● Carleton Perry Cooke III, son of Carleton Perry Cooke, Jr, of Buffalo.

    (2) ● Virginia S. TAFT, *b* 1950.

    (3) ● Lloyd Bowers TAFT, Jr, *b* 1954, *educ* The Taft Sch.

    (4) ● Julia Wilson TAFT, *b* 1958.

  **4** ● Horace Dwight TAFT, Prof of Physics at Yale from 1964, Master of Davenport Coll 1966-71, Dean from 1971, Trustee of The Taft Sch, Watertown, Connecticut from 1966, served in World War II with US Army 1943-46 [*55 Hillhouse Avenue, New Haven, Connecticut 06511, USA*], *b* at Cincinnati 2 April 1925, *educ* Yale (BA 1950), and Chicago Univ (MS 1953, PhD 1955), *m* 9 Sept 1952, ● Mary Jane Badger, and has issue,

    (1) ● John Godfrey TAFT, *b* 1954.

    (2) ● Hugh Bancroft TAFT, *b* 1957.

    (3) ● Horace Dutton TAFT, *b* 1962.

**2** ● Helen Herron TAFT, Dean of Bryn Mawr Coll, and actg Pres 1919-20 [*Featherbed Lane, Haverford, Pennsylvania 19041, USA*], *b* at Cincinnati 1 Aug 1891, *educ* Bryn Mawr Coll (BA 1915), and Yale (MA 1917), *m* 15 July 1920, Frederick Johnson Manning, and has issue,

  **1** ● Helen Taft MANNING, *b* 1921, *m* 31 Jan 1946, ● Holland Hunter [*Featherbed Lane, Haverford, Pennsylvania 19041, USA*], and has issue,

    (1) ● Ann Herron HUNTER, *b* 1947.

    (2) ● Barbara Walrath HUNTER, *b* 1949, *educ* Swarthmore.

    (3) ● Christine Manning HUNTER, *b* 1952.

    (4) ● Timothy White HUNTER, *b* 1955.

  **2** ● Caroline MANNING, *b* 1925.

**3** ● Charles Phelps TAFT, hon LLD Rochester, Miami, Ohio Wesleyon and Yale (1952) Univs, DCL Union Coll and DHL Hebrew Union Coll, mem Ohio Bar 1922, partner in firm of Taft, Stettinius & Hollister, mem Cincinnati City Council 1938-42, 1948-51 and from 1955, Cincinnati, Mayor of Cincinnati 1955-57, served in World War I as 1st Lieut FA, US Army in France [*1071 Celestial Street, Cincinnati, Ohio 45202, USA*], *b* at Cincinnati 20 Sept 1897, *educ* The Taft Sch, Watertown, Yale (BA 1918, LLB 1921), and Toledo Univ (LLD 1934), *m* at Waterbury, Conn 6 Oct 1917, Eleanor Kellogg (*b* at Waterbury, Conn 9 Oct 1891; *d* at Cincinnati 28 Aug 1961), 2nd dau of Irving Hall Chase, of Rose Hill,

Waterbury, Connecticut, by his wife Elizabeth Hosmer, dau of Gen Stephen Wright Kellogg, and has had issue,

1 ●Eleanor Kellogg TAFT, *b* at Waterbury, Connecticut 16 Sept 1918, *m* at Cincinnati 1941, ●Donald T. Hall [*3655 Hunts Point Road, Bellevue, Seattle, Washington 98004, USA*], son of Dr David C. Hall, by his wife Katharine, and has issue,

(1) ●Rosalyn HALL, *m* ●— Barbieri [*177 Bolivar Lane, Portola Valley, California 94025, USA*].
(2) ●David C. HALL III [*1111 E Columbia, Seattle, Washington 98122, USA*], *m*, and has issue, one child.
(3) ●Katharine HALL, *m* ●— Mann [*16 Newport Drive, Plainview, New York 11803, USA*], and has issue, two children.
(4) ●Deborah HALL [*3655 Hunts Point Road, Bellevue, Seattle, Washington 98004, USA*].

2 ●Sylvia Howard TAFT [*514 Wellesly Road, Philadelphia, Pennsylvania 19119, USA*], *b* at Narragansett Pier, Rhode Island, New York 7 Aug 1920, *m* at Cincinnati 1942, William Lotspeich, son of Claude Lotspeich, by his wife Helen, and has issue,

(1) ●Sylvia LOTSPEICH [*3311 Baring Street, Philadelphia, Pennsylvania 19104, USA*].
(2) ●Charles LOTSPEICH [*Stockbridge School, West Stockbridge, Mass 01266, USA*], *m*, and has issue, two children.
(3) ●Stephen LOTSPEICH.

3 ●Seth Chase TAFT, Lieut JG USN, attorney with business law firm of Jones, Day, Cockley & Reavis, Cleveland, Ohio from 1948, Commr of Cuyahoga County, Ohio from 1971 [*6 Pepper Ridge Road, Cleveland, Ohio 44124, USA*], *b* at

Cincinnati 31 Dec 1922, *educ* Taft Sch, Yale Coll (AB 1942), and Yale Law Sch (LLB 1948), *m* at New Haven, Conn 19 July 1943, ●Frances Bradley (*b* at New Haven, Conn 12 Dec 1921), dau of William E. Prindle, of New Haven, and has issue,

(1) ●Frederick Irving TAFT [*2384 Euclid Heights Boulevard, Cleveland, Ohio 44106, USA*], *b* at New Haven, Connecticut 26 June 1945, *m* at Cleveland, Ohio 28 July 1973, ●Susan Scott (*b* at Cleveland 3 April 1945), dau of Kenneth Hoefflinger, by his wife June Reynolds.
(2) ●Thomas Pringle TAFT [*421 Dana Street, Providence, Rhode Island 02906, USA*], *b* at Cleveland, Ohio 19 July 1948, *m*, and has issue, one child.
(3) ●Cynthia Bradley TAFT, *b* at Cleveland, Ohio 24 May 1950.
(4) ●Seth Tucker TAFT, *b* at Cleveland, Ohio 4 March 1953.

4 Lucia Chase TAFT, *b* at Waterbury, Connecticut 9 June 1924; *dunm* at Cincinnati Oct 1955.

5 ●Cynthia Herron TAFT, *b* at Cincinnati 28 April 1928, *m* there, ●Donald R. Morris [*3030 Arizona Avenue, Washington, DC 20016, USA*], and has issue,

(1) ●David MORRIS, *b* 14 March 1961.
(2) ●Michele MORRIS, *b* Nov 1967.

6 Rosalyn Rawson TAFT, *b* at Cincinnati 6 June 1930; *d* at Narragansett, Rhode Island Sept 1941.

7 ●Peter Rawson TAFT, law clerk for Chief Justice Earl Warren 1962-63, mem firm of Munger, Tolles, Hills & Rickershauser [*2700 Neilson Way, Santa Monica, California 90405, USA*], *b* at Cincinnati 3 March 1936, *educ* The Taft Sch, and Yale (AB 1958, LLB 1961).

# The Brothers and Sisters of President Taft

*President Taft had nine siblings. His father married twice (see* LINEAGE OF PRESIDENT TAFT, *p 434 for full details) and by his first marriage had issue, four sons and one dau (who were thus half-siblings to the President); and by his second marriage, four sons (including the President) and one dau.*

## A: HALF-BROTHERS AND HALF-SISTER OF PRESIDENT TAFT

1
2 } Two half-brothers and one half-sister: all *d* as infs.
3

4 Charles Phelps TAFT, hon LLD Cincinnati Univ and Lincoln Memorial Univ (1922), lawyer, editor and publisher of *Cincinnati Times-Star* from 1879, mem House of Reps 1895-97, Pres Bd of Sinking Fund Trustees, Cincinnati, *b* at Cincinnati 21 Dec 1843, *educ* Yale (BA 1864, MA 1867), and Heidelberg Univ (JUD 1868), *m* 4 Dec 1873, Anne, only dau of David Sinton, iron mfr, of Cincinnati, and *d* 1929, having had issue,

1 Jane Ellison TAFT, *b* 1874, *m* Albert Stimson Ingalls, and had issue,

(1) ●David Sinton INGALLS, mem Ohio House of Reps, Assist Sec of the Navy for Aeronautics, Dir Public Health and Welfare, Cleveland, Ohio [*Stonybrook Farm, Chagrin Falls, Ohio, USA*], *b* 1899, *m* 1922, ●Louise, dau of — Harkness, of New York City, and has issue,

1*a* ●Edith INGALLS, *m* ●Paul J. Vignos [*Appletree Farm, River Road, Chagrin Falls, Ohio, USA*], and has issue,

1*b* ●Kathleen VIGNOS.
2*b* ●Paul VIGNOS.
2*a* Jane INGALLS.
3*a* Louise H. INGALLS, *m* ●Willard W. Brown [*Fairmount Road, Chagrin Falls, Ohio, USA*], and had issue,

1*b* ●Alice BROWN.
2*b* ●Barbara BROWN.
3*b* ●Willard W. BROWN, Jr.
4*b* ●David Ingalls BROWN.
4*a* ●Ann INGALLS.
5*a* ●David Sinton INGALLS, Jr [*Oak Hill Farm, Chagrin Falls, Ohio, USA*], *m* ●Cynthia Robinson.
(2) ●Albert Stimson INGALLS, Jr, *m* 1928, ●Eileen Brodie, and has issue,

●Albert Stimson INGALLS III.
(3) ●Anne Taft INGALLS, *m* 1928, ●Rupert E. L. Warburton [*70 Fircrest Lane, Cleveland, Ohio, USA*], and has issue,

1*a* ●Wanda WARBURTON.

2a●Jane WARBURTON.
3a●Evelyn A. WARBURTON.
2 David Sinton TAFT, *b* 1876; *d* 1891.
3 Anne Louise TAFT, *b* 1879, *m* Walter T. Semple, and had issue,
    Charles T. SEMPLE, *b* 1918; *d* 1927.
4 Charles Howard TAFT, *b* 1882; *dunm* 1931.
5 Peter Rawson TAFT, *m* Annie Matilda Hulbert, and *d* 1889, leaving issue,

**B**: FULL BROTHERS AND SISTER OF PRESIDENT TAFT

6 Samuel Davenport TAFT, *b* 1855; *d* an inf.
7 Henry Waters TAFT, of New York, partner in law firm of Cadwalader, Wickersham & Taft, *b* at Cincinnati 27 May 1859, *educ* Yale (BA 1880, hon MA 1905), *m* 28 March 1883, Julia Walbridge, dau of — Smith, of Troy, New York, and had issue,
    1 Walbridge Smith TAFT, of New York, partner in law firm of Cadwalader, Wickersham & Taft, *b* 1884, *m* 1923, Elizabeth, dau of — Clark, of Detroit, Michigan, and had issue,
        (1)●Lucie Clark TAFT, *b* 1924.
        (2)●Henry Waters TAFT II, *b* 1926.
        (3)●Elizabeth TAFT, *b* 1933.
    2 William Howard TAFT, of New York, *m* Marguerite T.,

Hulbert TAFT, *m* Nellie Leaman, and had issue,
    (1)●Katherine TAFT, *m* ●James P. Benedict [*439 Lafayette Avenue, Cincinnati, Ohio, USA*].
    (2)●Hulbert TAFT, Jr [*8420 Shawnee Run Road, Cincinnati, Ohio, USA*], *m* ●Eleanor L. Gholson.
    (3)●Margo TAFT, *m* ●John Tytus III [*8605 Indian Hill Road, Cincinnati, Ohio, USA*], son of John Tytus, Jr.
    (4) David Sinton TAFT, *dec.*

dau of — O'Neill, of Pittsburgh, Pennsylvania, and *dsp*.
3 Louise Walbridge TAFT, *m* George H. Snowdon, and had issue,
    (1)●Charles Taft SNOWDON, *b* 1911.
    (2)●Henry Taft SNOWDON, *b* 1912.
    (3)●Marion Louise SNOWDON, *b* 1916.
8 Horace Dutton TAFT, admitted to the Bar 1885, founded The Taft Sch 1890, *b* at Cincinnati 28 Dec 1861, *educ* Yale (BA 1883, MA 1893), *m* 29 June 1892, Winifred S. (*d* Dec 1909), dau of — Thompson, of Niagara Falls, New York, and *dsp* 1943.
9 Frances Louise TAFT, *b* at Cincinnati 1865, *m* William A. Edwards, MD (*d* 1933), and *dsp*.

# Notes

[1] A yr son of Robert Taft was Israel Taft, who *m* Mercy, dau of Jacob Aldrich, and had issue, Huldah Taft, who *m* David Daniel, and had issue, Chloe Daniel, who *m* Seth Davenport, and had issue, Anna Davenport, who *m* William Torrey, and had issue, Samuel Davenport Torrey, father of the 2nd Mrs Alphonso Taft.

[2] Through the Rawson family President Taft was 24th in descent from David I, King of Scots (*see* APPENDIX C, PRESIDENTS OF ROYAL DESCENT).

[3] Through his mother's family President Taft was a 7th cousin twice removed of Richard Milhous Nixon, 37th President (*qv*). The relationship is as follows:

Ralph Hemingway = Elizabeth Hewes

Elizabeth Hemingway
= John Holbrook

Joshua Hemingway
(1643-1716)
= Joanna Evans (*d* 1678)

Daniel Holbrook
= Abigail Crafts

Joshua Hemingway
(*b* 1668)
= Rebecca Stanhope

Rebecca Holbrook
= Samuel Davenport

Joshua Hemingway
(1697-1754)
= Abigail Morse (*d* 1739)

Seth Davenport
= Chloe Daniel

Isaac Hemingway
(1730-1778)
= Elizabeth Haven

Anna Davenport
= William Torrey

James Hemingway
(1760-1822)
= Elizabeth Armstrong
(1760-1837)

Samuel Davenport Torrey
= Susan Holman Waters

James Hemingway
(1801-1893)
= Hope Malmsbury
(1804-1865)

Louisa Maria Torrey
= Alphonso Taft

Jane Hemingway
(1824-1890)
= Oliver Burdg (1821-1908)

WILLIAM HOWARD TAFT

Almira Park Burdg
(1849-1943)
= Franklin Milhous
(1848-1919)

Hannah Milhous
(1885-1967)
= Francis Anthony Nixon
(1878-1956)

RICHARD MILHOUS NIXON

# (Thomas) Woodrow Wilson

## 1856-1924

————

28th President of the
United States of America
1913-1921

(THOMAS) WOODROW WILSON, 28TH PRESIDENT

# (Thomas) Woodrow Wilson

## 1856-1924

### 28th President of the United States of America
#### 1913-1921

THOMAS WOODROW WILSON—he dropped the "Tommy" as Stephen Grover Cleveland discarded his first name, in a search for something more sonorous and distinctive—has been much praised and much condemned. That is the fate of every exceptional President. His critics have tended to portray him as a sanctimonious Calvinist because he was the son of a Presbyterian minister, or as an intellectual snob because he was the first President to earn a PhD. They dislike Wilson's austere, bony face, and the high moral tone he often took. William Bullitt, an American diplomat, even collaborated with Sigmund Freud in a book that sought to prove psychoanalytically how Wilson's inner tensions were responsible for the Treaty of Versailles.

Wilson was no doubt a man of unusual temperament. There was a tightly coiled spring inside him. As a child in Virginia he had seen the Confederacy go down to defeat. He grew up in genteel poverty. His father and his English-born mother would have liked him to enter the church. But such pressures were not unique in the America of his time. Several Presidents had been children of the manse; and religiosity was almost a stock-in-trade of politicians aspiring to be statesmen. Several Presidents had likewise begun their careers as teachers: Garfield is one example. Wilson differed from his predecessors in qualifying at a higher level. He was a successful scholar who went on to become president of Princeton University. But he was never a scholarly recluse. As a young professor he coached football teams, and bubbled with collegiate enthusiasm. All of his books, including his Johns Hopkins PhD (published as *Congressional Government*), were brightly written. His ambitions were not permanently directed toward academic life. Wilson wanted either to be an author or a leader in some important public sphere.

Like other famous men, he was both strengthened and undermined by his idiosyncrasies. Wilson loved to have his own way. So long as he could persuade people to follow, he was dazzingly impressive: quick, intuitive, clear, high-spirited. This was the Wilson who transformed Princeton in his first years there; who as Governor of New Jersey outwitted the machine politicians; and who began his first presidential Administration at a pace calculated to raise the hackles, and the jealousy, of his arch-enemy Theodore Roosevelt. This was the Wilson who, far from being a dreary pedagogue, could enthrall an audience with his oratory. His speeches in the presidential campaign of 1912, for example, read quite as well as those of Roosevelt. This, too, was the Wilson who was liked by women and who liked them in return. There was no lack of romantic ardor in the letters he wrote to his fiancée Ellen Louise Paxson (whose father was also a Presbyterian minister). Their marriage was extremely congenial. By all accounts Ellen Wilson doted on her husband, as did their three daughters. When Mrs Wilson died in 1914, the President remarried in less than two years. His second wife, Edith Bolling Galt, was a widow of 43. Wilson was then 58, but he continued to display a gallantry toward her that would have done credit to a younger man.

The reverse side of the coin was a tendency to be irritable, self-righteous and obstinate when he could not get his way. This was evident in the later stages of his reign at Princeton, which terminated sourly. It has become the stuff of legend in relation to his second presidential term, when Wilson the Democrat alienated powerful Republican leaders such as Roosevelt's friend Senator Henry Cabot Lodge, tried to appeal beyond them to the American people, exhausted himself on a speaking tour, suffered a paralytic stroke from which he never fully recovered, and failed to secure ratification of the Treaty of Versailles with which he had so passionately identified himself. The doubleness of Woodrow Wilson's nature is exemplified in his remarkable friendship with Colonel Edward House. House was a Texan who devoted himself to Wilson in an almost worshipping way. Wilson reciprocated with the utmost warmth and trust. House was his confidential emissary on wartime missions to Europe, and his eyes and ears in the preliminary period of peacemaking before Wilson himself set sail for France—the first President to cross the Atlantic while in office. As soon as House showed signs of disagreeing with him, however, Wilson abruptly and completely severed the relationship.

Woodrow Wilson was fundamentally conservative. As a young scholar he admired the British system of government, and argued that the Speaker of the House of Representatives, being analogous to the Prime Minister, was a more significant figure than the President. He changed his mind when the Administrations of McKinley and Roosevelt created a new conception of executive authority. Perhaps indeed he and Roosevelt had a

ELLEN LOUISE AXSON, MRS WILSON

EDITH BOLLING GALT, MRS WILSON

good deal in common. They had more energy and self-confidence than most men; and though they were strongwilled they yearned for popular approval. They detested muddle, cowardice, sloth, dishonesty. To this extent they were reformers, determined to drive the seven deadly sins out of America. But they were not radicals. Wilson was an excellent President, like Roosevelt, within the limits of what he considered desirable.

He faced a problem of awesome difficulty when Europe went to war in 1914. Rightly sceptical of European motives, and horrified by the bloodbath of the Western front, Wilson campaigned as the Democratic candidate in 1916 on a basis of maintaining American neutrality. He was perfectly sincere; yet within a few months the United States was at war with Germany. Like most Americans, Wilson was "neutral in deed" but not in sentiment. American emotions, economic ties, strategic considerations: all pushed Wilson toward a war he loathed. The feeling that he personally had sent tens of thousands of young Americans to their death made him view the peacemaking with peculiar commitment. The war would, he thought, have been totally, criminally, tragically pointless unless it led to a just and lasting peace. The League of Nations would be Wilson's cenotaph for the war dead.

No doubt he made mistakes. The other negotiators in Paris —Clemenceau, Lloyd George, Orlando—felt that Wilson was too idealistic. He was foolish not to invite one or two Senate Republicans to accompany him to Paris. He should not perhaps have so vehemently refused to bargain with opponents. A version of the Treaty, amended but not ruined, could have secured Senate ratification. For Wilson it was all or nothing. The United States did not adhere to the Treaty and therefore did not join the League of Nations. The Nobel peace prize, presented to him in 1920, was a poor consolation for one who had aimed so high. In Wilson's last year, when he was too incapacitated to attend to executive business, there was much truth in the gibe that Mrs Wilson was actually President.

Was Wilson naïve, moralistic, dictatorial? Had he brought his troubles down upon himself? Did it make any real difference whether the United States was a member of the League or not in the 1920s and 1930s? Was he a great man thwarted in a noble vision by cynical European diplomats and jealously partisan Republicans? He was certainly not a monster of arrogance. As we have seen, Woodrow Wilson's essential attitudes were those of American democratic nationalism. If he was somewhat less flexible than other American leaders, he was also somewhat more imaginatively bold. The irony is that in aspiring more loftily than they, he may have achieved less than they might have done. But he could not know that. In retrospect, Wilson's vision of a world made safe for democracy, whatever its defects of detail, was more wholesome than the cautious opportunism of his opponents.

# Chronology

1856    Born at the Presbyterian Manse, N Coalter Street, Staunton, Virginia 28 Dec.

1857    Family moved to Augusta, Georgia Nov.

1870    Family moved to Columbia, S Carolina.

1873    Entered Davidson College, Davidson, N Carolina.

1874    Left College owing to ill health and returned to Columbia June; family moved to Wilmington, N Carolina Oct.

1875    Entered College of New Jersey (now Princeton University), Princeton, New Jersey Sept.

1879    Graduated from College with BA degree 18 June; entered University of Virginia Law School Sept.

1880    Left Law School owing to ill health and returned to Wilmington.

1882    Moved to Atlanta, Georgia June; admitted to the Georgia Bar in Atlanta 19 Oct; formed law practice with Edward Ireland Renick.

1883    Gave up law practice; enrolled as graduate student at Johns Hopkins University, Baltimore Sept.

1885    Appointed Associate Professor of History at Bryn Mawr College, Bryn Mawr, Pennsylvania.

1886    Received PhD degree in political science from Johns Hopkins University.

1887    Gave series of lectures at Johns Hopkins University.

1888    Appointed Professor of History at Wesleyan University, Middletown, Connecticut.

1890    Appointed Professor of Jurisprudence and Political Economy in the College of New Jersey (now Princeton).

1902    Elected President of Princeton 9 June; took office 25 Oct.

1909    Elected President of Short Ballot Association Oct.

1910    Agreed to run for Governor of New Jersey 15 July; nominated for Governor by Democratic State Convention at Trenton 15 Sept; resigned as President of Princeton 20 Oct; elected Governor 8 Nov.

1911    Inaugurated as Governor of New Jersey 17 Jan.

1912    Nominated for President by the Democratic National Convention at Baltimore 2 July; election day 5 Nov.

1913    Presidential Electors cast their ballots (435 for Wilson; 88 for Roosevelt; 8 for Taft) 13 Jan; electoral vote tabulated by Congress and Wilson and Marshall officially declared elected 12 Feb; inaugurated as 28th President of the United States of America on the east portico of the White House 4 March; appeared in person before joint session of Congress to deliver special tariff message 8 April; formerly recognized Republic of China 2 May; issued proclamation of adoption of the 17th Amendment 31 May; sent special message to Congress asking for legislation to decentralize banking system 23 June; signed Newlands Act 15 July; addressed joint session of Congress on Mexican policy 27 Aug; signed Underwood Tariff Act 3 Oct; vetoed private bill to reinstate dismissed West Point cadet 1 Dec; delivered first State of the Union message to Congress in person 2 Dec; signed Owen-Glass Federal Reserve Act 23 Dec.

1914   Delivered special message to Congress recommending legislation to strengthen Sherman Anti-Trust Act 20 Jan; issued executive order establishing permanent civil government in Panama Canal Zone (effective 1 April) 27 Jan; issued proclamation lifting embargo on exportation of arms to Mexico 3 Feb; delivered special message to Congress recommending repeal of tolls exemption clause of Panama Canal Act of 1912 5 March; signed Act authorizing construction of railways in Alaska 12 March; signed amended Copyright Act 28 March; Tampico incident 9 April; delivered special message to Congress regarding Mexican situation 20 April; ordered seizure of customs house at Veracruz, Mexico 21 April; Mexico severed diplomatic relations with US 22 April; signed amended Panama Canal Act 15 June; mediation plan with Mexico put forward by Argentina, Brazil and Chile accepted by US 24 June; issued proclamations of neutrality at commencement of World War I 4, 5 and 7 Aug; Panama Canal opened to traffic 15 Aug; signed Ship Registry Act 18 Aug; issued further proclamations of neutrality 18, 24 and 27 Aug; addressed joint session of Congress requesting legislation to assure additional revenue of $100,000,000; issued executive order providing for Government operation of all wireless stations 5 Sept; signed Federal Trade Commission Act 26 Sept; signed Clayton Anti-Trust Act 15 Oct; signed War Revenue Act 22 Oct; issued proclamation of neutrality of Panama Canal Zone 13 Nov; delivered second State of the Union message to Congress 8 Dec.

1915   Signed Act establishing Rocky Mountain National Park in Colorado 26 Jan; vetoed Immigration Bill 28 Jan; signed amended Federal Reserve Bank Act 3 March; signed Act creating Naval Oil Reserve No 3, nr Casper, Wyoming 30 April; *Lusitania* sunk off Irish coast by German submarine 7 May; sent protest note to Germany 13 May; reviewed Atlantic fleet of US Navy in New York City Harbor 17 May; sent second *Lusitania* note to Germany 9 June; signed Act reorganizing Department of Agriculture 1 July; sent third *Lusitania* note to Germany 21 July; ordered military occupation of Haiti 28 July; attended World Series in Philadelphia 9 Oct; recognized Carrauza Government in Mexico 19 Oct; delivered third State of the Union message to Congress 7 Dec; signed extension of 1914 Emergency War Tax Act 17 Dec.

1916   Toured Middle West 29 Jan-4 Feb; ordered expedition against Pancho Villa 10 March; sent ultimatum to Germany following further submarine warfare involving American subjects 18 April; received German apology for sinking of the *Sussex* 9 May; signed executive order adopting official Presidential Flag 29 May; signed Army Reorganization Act 3 June; renominated for President by Democratic National Convention at St Louis, Missouri 15 June; signed Good Roads Act 11 July; signed Federal Farm Loan Act 17 July; sent treaty for purchase of Danish West Indies to the Senate 8 Aug; vetoed Army Appropriations Bill 18 Aug; signed Naval Appropriations Act and Philippine Islands Organic Act 29 Aug; signed Child Labor Act 1 Sept; signed Adamson

Eight-Hour Act 3 Sept; signed Shipping Act 7 Sept; signed Revenue Act 8 Sept; pocket vetoed Appropriation for Arming and Equipping Militia of Georgia Bill 8 Sept; election day 7 Nov; delivered fourth State of the Union message to Congress 5 Dec.

1917 Presidential Electors cast their ballots (277 for Wilson; 254 for Charles Evans Hughes, the Republican Candidate) 8 Jan; vetoed Immigration Bill (which included literacy test) 29 Jan; severed diplomatic relations with Germany 3 Feb; Immigration Act passed over his veto 5 Feb; electoral vote tabulated by Congress and Wilson and Marshall officially declared elected 14 Feb; signed Vocational Education Act 23 Feb; asked joint session of Congress for emergency powers to authorize the arming of American merchant ships 26 Feb; signed Act establishing Puerto Rico as a US Territory 2 March; inaugurated for second term as President on the east portico of the Capitol 5 March; issued proclamation suspending eight-hour day for Government workers and providing for overtime pay 24 March; issued executive order calling up National Guard of eastern States 25 March; issued executive order establishing General Munitions Board 31 March; delivered message to Congress asking for a declaration of war against Germany 2 April; signed joint resolution of declaration of war and issued proclamation announcing state of war with Germany 6 April; issued executive order establishing committee on public information 14 April; signed Liberty Loan Act 24 April; authorized strengthening of Army to 223,000 men; issued executive order establishing Air Production Board 16 May; signed Selective Service Act 18 May; issued proclamation of neutrality of the Panama Canal 23 May; signed Espionage Act 15 June; issued executive order calling all National Guard for military service 3 July; issued proclamation placing export of foods and other products under Government control 9 July; issued executive order drafting 678,000 men into military service 13 July; issued executive order imposing censorship on transatlantic cables 18 July; signed Food and Fuel Control Act 10 Aug; issued proclamation prohibiting export of currency or bullion 7 Sept; issued executive order establishing labor mediation commission 19 Sept; signed new War Revenue Act 3 Oct; signed Trading With Enemy Act 6 Oct; issued proclamation licensing production of bakery items 7 Nov; issued proclamation requiring registration of enemy aliens 16 Nov; issued executive order conveying price-fixing powers to Food Administration 27 Nov; delivered fifth State of the Union message to Congress 4 Dec; issued proclamation announcing state of war with Austria-Hungary 11 Dec; signed joint resolution submitting the 18th Amendment to the Constitution to the States 18 Dec; issued proclamation placing railroads under government control 26 Dec.

1918 Addressed Congress listing 14 points for peace 8 Jan; issued proclamation establishing one meatless, two wheatless and two porkless days per week 26 Jan; issued executive order providing for control of enemy property 2 Feb; authorized Distinguished Service Medal for US Army 7 March; signed Act establishing daylight saving time throughout US 19 March; issued proclamation confiscating 40 Dutch vessels 20 March; signed Railroad Control Act 21 March; issued proclamation establishing War Finance Corporation 8 April; signed Export Trade Associations Act 10 April; issued proclamation assuming control of four principal Atlantic coastline steamship companies 11 April; signed Sedition Act 16 May; issued executive order reorganizing Signal Corps and signed Act authorizing reorganization of Executive Department 20 May; issued executive order establishing War Labor Policies Board 8 June; signed Act authorizing Government control of American shipping for duration of the war 18 July; issued proclamation placing telephone and telegraph systems under Government control 22 July; armistice requested by Prince Max of Baden, the German Imperial Chancellor 5 Oct; agreed to submit German proposals to the Allies 23 Oct; Armistice signed 11 Nov; delivered sixth State of the Union message to Congress 2 Dec; sailed from Hoboken, New Jersey, to attend Peace Conference in Paris 4 Dec; arrived at Brest 13 Dec; accepted honorary citizenship of Paris 16 Dec; visited England 26-31 Dec.

1919   Visited Italy 2-6 Jan; returned to Paris 7 Jan; addressed opening session of Peace Conference 18 Jan; League of Nations included in peace settlement 25 Jan; 18th ("Prohibition") Amendment to the Constitution ratified 29 Jan (effective from 16 Jan 1920); submitted draft covenant of the League of Nations to plenary session 14 Feb; sailed for US 15 Feb; arrived in Boston 24 Feb; sailed for France 5 March; arrived in Paris 14 March; visited Belgium 18-19 June; returned to Paris 20 June; Treaty of Versailles signed 28 June; sailed for US 29 June; arrived in New York 8 July; submitted covenant of League of Nations and Treaty of Versailles to the Senate for ratification 10 July; issued proclamation prohibiting exportation of arms to Mexico and vetoed Agricultural Appropriations Bill 12 July; issued proclamation placing embargo on arms and ammunition to Mexico 25 July; vetoed Repeal of Daylight Saving time Bill 15 Aug (passed over his veto 20 Aug); began speaking tour in support of the League of Nations 4 Sept; steel strike began 22 Sept; taken ill in Pueblo, Colorado and forced to cancel remainder of tour 26 Sept; suffered a stroke in Washington, DC 2 Oct; vetoed Volstead Prohibition Enforcement Bill 27 Oct (passed over his veto 28 Oct); issued executive order restoring coal price and distribution powers to Fuel Administration 30 Oct; issued proclamation re-establishing functions of Food Administration under Attorney General 21 Nov; delivered seventh State of the Union message to Congress 5 Dec; issued proclamation returning railroads and express companies to private operation (as from 1 March 1920) 24 Dec.

1920   Issued executive order returning commercial radio to private ownership 13 Feb; issued executive order abolishing price-fixing of coal (as from 1 April) 23 March; vetoed joint resolution declaring war with Germany at an end 27 May; vetoed Budget Bill on constitutional grounds 4 June; depression began June; issued proclamation announcing ratification of the 19th Amendment 26 Aug; sent eighth (and last) State of the Union message to Congress 7 Dec; awarded Nobel Peace Prize 10 Dec.

1921   Vetoed joint resolution to reinstitute War Finance Corporation 3 Jan (passed over his veto 4 Jan); vetoed Army Enlistment Bill 5 Feb (passed over his veto 7 Feb); vetoed amendment to 1914 Act to provide drainage of Indian allotments of Five Civilized Tribes 24 Feb (passed over his veto 2 March); pocket vetoed Immigration and Army Appropriation Bills, retired from office and rode to the Capitol with his successor President Harding, but did not attend the inauguration 4 March; admitted to the Bar in Washington, DC and New York City June.

1922   Accepted the Polish Order of the White Eagle.

1923   Attended the funeral of President Harding 5 Aug; made only speech by radio 10 Nov; made last public speech 11 Nov.

1924   Taken ill with digestive trouble Jan; died of a stroke at Washington, DC 3 Feb; buried at Washington.

# The Writings of President Wilson

*Congressional Government; A Study in American Politics* (1885)

*The State; Elements of Historical and Practical Politics* (1889; revised 1898)

*Division and Reunion 1829-1889* (1893)

*An Old Master, and Other Political Essays* (1893)

*More Literature, and Other Essays* (1896)

*George Washington* (1896)

*When a Man Comes to Himself* (1901)

*A History of the American People*, 5 Vols (1902)

*Constitutional Government in the United States* (1908)

*President Wilson's Case for the League of Nations* (1923)

# Lineage of President Wilson

JAMES WILSON, emigrated from Scotland 1807, *b* 1786 (or 1787), *m* Mary Adams, of Philadelphia, and had issue, with six other sons (two of whom were Generals in the Union Army during the Civil War),

THE REV JOSEPH RUGGLES WILSON, DD, Prof of Theology, Moderator of the Presbyterian General Assembly 1879, *b* at Steubenville, Ohio 28 Feb 1822, *educ* Jefferson Coll, Pennsylvania (AB 1844), and Princeton (BD 1846), *m* 7 June 1849, Janet (called Jessie) (*b* at Carlisle, Cumberland, England 20 Dec 1826; *d* at Clarksville, Tennessee 15 April 1888), dau of Rev Thomas Woodrow, Presbyterian Minister (who emigrated from England 1836), by his wife Marion Williamson, and *d* at Princeton, New Jersey 21 Jan 1903, leaving with other issue (*see* BROTHER AND SISTERS OF PRESIDENT WILSON, *p 452*), an elder son,

(THOMAS) WOODROW WILSON, **28th President of the United States of America.**

# The Descendants of President Wilson

(THOMAS) WOODROW WILSON *m* 1st at Savannah, Georgia 24 June 1885 (the officiating ministers being the bride's grandfather, Rev Isaac Stockton Keith Axson, and the bridegroom's father), Ellen Louise (*b* at Savannah 15 May 1860; *d* at the White House, Washington, DC 6 Aug 1914, *bur* Myrtle Hill Cemetery, Rome, Georgia), eldest dau of Rev Samuel Edward Axson, Presbyterian Minister, by his wife Margaret Jane, dau of Rev Nathan Hoyt, of Athens, Georgia, and had issue,

**1** Margaret Woodrow WILSON, *b* 16 April 1886; *dunm.*

**2** Jessie Woodrow WILSON, *b* at Gainesville, Georgia 28 Aug 1887, *m* at the White House, Washington, DC 25 Nov 1913, Francis Bowes Sayre, Professor of Law, Harvard Law School, sometime Assist Sec of State (*b* at South Bethlehem, Pennsylvania 30 April 1885; *d* 1973), 2nd son of Robert Heysham Sayre, Gen Man of Bethlehem Steel Works, by his wife Martha Finley Nevin, and *d* at Washington, DC Dec 1946, leaving issue,

  1 ●Francis Bowes SAYRE (Very Rev), ordained 1940, Chaplain USNR 1942-46, Rector of St Paul's, E Cleveland, Ohio 1947-51, Dean of Washington (Protestant Episcopal) Cathedral from 1951, Chm Woodrow Wilson Memorial Commn 1962-68 [*The Deanery, Mount St Alban, Washington, DC 20016, USA*], *b* at the White House 17 Jan 1915, *educ* Williams Coll (AB 1937, (hon)DD 1963), and Episcopal Theological Sch, Cambridge, Mass (BD 1940), hon LHD Wooster Coll (1956), hon DD Virginia Theological Sch (1957), Wesleyan Univ, Conn (1958), and Hobart Coll (1966), STD Queen's Univ Belfast (1966), *m* 8 June 1946, ●Harriet Taft Hart, and has issue,

    (1) ●Jessie Wilson SAYRE, *b* 1949.
    (2) ●Thomas Hart SAYRE, *b* 1950.
    (3) ●Harriet Brownson SAYRE.
    (4) ●Francis Nevin SAYRE.

2 ●Eleanor Axson SAYRE [*33 Sibley Court, Cambridge, Mass, USA*], *b* at Philadelphia 26 March 1916.

3 ●Woodrow Wilson SAYRE, Professor of Philosophy at Tufts Univ 1957-64, and at Springfield Coll, Mass from 1965, led first American expdn to N face of Mount Everest 1962 [*17 Loring Road, Springfield, Massachusetts 01105, USA*], *b* at Philadelphia 22 Feb 1919, *educ* Williams Coll (BA 1940), and Harvard (MA 1942, PhD 1957), *m* 16 May 1942, ●Edith Warren Chase, and has two daus,

    (a) ●Jennifer Pomeroy SAYRE.
    (b) ●Martha Nevin SAYRE.

**3** Eleanor Randolph WILSON, *b* at Middletown, Connecticut 5 Oct 1889, *m* 1st at the White House, Washington, DC 7 May 1914 (*m* diss by div 1934), as his 2nd wife Senator William Gibbs McAdoo, Sec of the Treasury 1913-18 (*b* nr Marietta, Georgia 31 Oct 1863; *d* 1 Feb 1941), son of Judge William Gibbs McAdoo, by his wife Mary Faith Floyd, and had issue,

  1 ●Ellen Wilson MCADOO, *m* 1934 (*m* diss by div), Rafael Lopez de Oñate, and has issue,

    ●Richard F. MCADOO (formerly LOPEZ) [*PO Box 39483, Los Angeles, California 90039, USA*].

  2 ●Mary Faith MCADOO.

Eleanor Randolph Wilson *m* 2ndly, ●William A. Hinshaw [*18026 Burbank Boulevard, Apt 2, Encino, California 91316, USA*], and *d* at Montecito, California April 1967.

WOODROW WILSON *m* 2ndly at Washington, DC 18 Dec 1915, Edith (*b* at Wytheville, Virginia 15 Oct 1872; *d* at Washington, DC 28 Dec 1961, *bur* Washington, DC), widow of Norman Galt, of Washington, DC (who *d* 1908), and only dau of Judge William Holcombe Bolling, of Wytheville, Virginia (a direct descendant of the Indian Princess Pocahontas), by his wife Sally White. There was *no issue* of this marriage.

# The Brother and Sisters of
# President Wilson

**1** Marion Williamson WILSON, *b* 20 Oct 1851; *dunm.*

**2** Annie Josephson WILSON, *b* 8 Sept 1853, *m* 1874, George Howe, MD (*b* 1848; *d* 1895), and *d* 1916, having had issue,
  1 Joseph Wilson HOWE, *b* 1874, *m* Virginia Peyton Knight.
  2 George HOWE, *b* 1876, *m* 1903, Margaret Smyth Flinn (*b* 1878).
  3 Jessie Woodrow HOWE, *b* 1878; *d* 1884.
  4 Annie Josephson HOWE, *b* 1891, *m* Frank E. Compton.

**3** Joseph Ruggles WILSON, *b* at Augusta, Georgia 20 July 1867; *dunm.*

# Warren Gamaliel Harding

## 1865-1923

---

29th President of the
United States of America

1921-1923

WARREN GAMALIEL HARDING, 29TH PRESIDENT AND
FLORENCE MABEL KLING DE WOLFE, MRS HARDING

# Warren Gamaliel Harding

## 1865-1923

### 29th President of the United States of America
### 1921-1923

WHEN THE Republican nominating convention met in Chicago in June 1920 there was a plethora of candidates. Among the front runners, however, none stood out. Several ballots went by inconclusively. An Ohio political hack named Harry Micajah Daugherty had already prophesied the outcome, several weeks earlier. After days of frustration, he said, at about two o'clock in the morning, "some fifteen men, bleary-eyed with loss of sleep and perspiring profusely with the excessive heat, will sit down in seclusion around a big table. I will be with them and will present the name of Senator Harding to them, and before we get through they will put him over". That was more or less what happened. The inner conclave, which included half a dozen Senators, decided by process of elimination that Harding was their best bet. They summoned him to the "smoke-filled room" in the Blackstone Hotel and asked him to pledge that there was nothing in his past to embarrass the party. Harding declared his innocence and on the same day, at the tenth ballot, he was duly nominated.

If he had been entirely candid, which was perhaps too much to expect, Harding would have confessed to a liaison with a married lady in his home town of Marion, Ohio, and to keeping a mistress in New York, Nan Britton, by whom he had had a daughter less than a year previously. He might also have mentioned to the caucus the rumors maliciously spread in Marion that the Hardings were part Negro. Possibly, though, his interrogators were mainly concerned with financial scandal, in which Harding had never been implicated. According to his own lights, and those of his many friends at home and in Washington, Warren Harding was simply a good red-blooded American, a hornplayer in the town band, a golfer, fond of a glass of whisky and a hand of poker. The Republican bosses were under no illusion that he was a saint or a genius, even if party propaganda began to boost him as a worthy successor to Abe Lincoln and Teddy Roosevelt. At the beginning of the campaign Senator Boies Penrose of Pennsylvania, who had inspected Harding in 1919, offered some concise strategic advice: "Keep Warren at home. Don't let him make any speeches. If he goes out on a tour somebody's sure to ask him questions, and Warren's just the sort of damned fool that will try to answer them". Harding himself doubted whether he was "a big enough man for the race". He knew his limitations. He had been the editor of an insignificant local newspaper. A marriage of covenience to Florence Kling De Wolfe changed his circumstances. She was a divorcee with a son, five years older than Warren and distinctly unglamorous. Her father, though, was a magnate by Marion standards, and she was a far stronger character than her handsome, amiable husband. Her money and her drive ensured the modest success of Harding's paper. Good looks, bonhomie and blameless opinions took him into politics, where Harry Daugherty discovered him and managed his election to the US Senate. Along the way Harding developed a certain talent for public speaking. In the Senate he voted with complete Republican orthodoxy.

Why then was Harding nominated? Partly because he was "available". Partly because he could be relied on to leave most of the initiative to Congress; there was a revulsion from presidential aggrandisement as practised by Roosevelt and Wilson. Also the Democrats were in disarray; it was assumed, correctly, that any presentable Republican was certain to win in 1920. Finally, Harding looked and sounded perfect for the part. Wilson thought Harding appallingly banal: "a bungalow mind" was his phrase. No matter. Harding's rhetoric, which reminded H. L. Mencken of "stale bean soup, of college yells, of dogs barking idiotically through endless nights", was perfectly attuned to the millions of voters who wanted a retreat from high taxes, war, foreign entanglements, and grandiose schemes of reform. Harding promised "normalcy": a huge Republican majority responded to him.

He was still very popular among the general public when he died in August 1923, less than two-and-a-half years after being inaugurated. He chose Charles Evans Hughes (Republican candidate in 1916) as Secretary of State, Herbert Hoover as Secretary of Commerce, and Andrew Mellon as Treasury Secretary—three sound appointments. Hughes, while keeping America well clear of the suspect League of Nations, won applause for inducing the great powers to agree to naval disarmament. Harding's public appearances were usually a success; Mrs Harding blossomed into a reasonably competent hostess. But there was trouble beneath the outwardly smooth surface. Some of Harding's other appointments were disastrous. Daugherty, rewarded with the post of Attorney-General, turned a blind eye to increasing evidence of graft in federal bureaux. Albert B. Fall, Secretary of the Interior, was implicated in the corrupt transfer of Government oil reserves, at Teapot Dome, Wyoming and in California, to private companies. The "Ohio gang" dragged Harding's Administration into the mire. He seems not to have suspected the extent of the mess until it was too late. In his last weeks, touring in the West, he was ailing and sick with worry. The storm broke after his death in a San Francisco hotel. Fall was sent to prison; Daugherty narrowly escaped a jail sentence.

Most historians rate Harding as among the worst of all the Presidents. The usual verdict is that he was a genial, mediocre man hopelessly out of his depth. "I knew this job would be too much for me", he plaintively remarked to a White House visitor. In recent years some attempts have been made to rehabilitate Harding. A scholarly biographer has pointed out that he worked extremely hard, despite the legends of heavy drinking and late-night poker sessions with Ohio cronies. His sexual peccadilloes were of no great importance, perhaps; he and his wife were apparently not close. He was genuinely good-natured. Though his opinions could be called right-wing, he released the Socialist leader Eugene V. Debs from the penitentiary to which the Wilson Administration had vindictively confined him. Harding, in this defense, was the President that the country desired: a more aggressively active Chief Executive would have got nowhere. Probably he has been excessively condemned. The fairest judgement may be that in Warren G. Harding the United States was given the President that it deserved. He and his time were a match.

# Chronology

1865    Born at Blooming Grove, Ohio 2 Nov.

1873    Family moved to Caledonia, Ohio.

1880    Entered Ohio Central College, Iberia, Ohio (formerly Iberia College).

1882    Graduated with BSc degree; family moved to Marion Ohio; taught at the White Schoolhouse, nr Marion.

1883    Worked for the Marion *Mirror*.

1884    Purchased the Marion *Star* with two partners.

1886    Became sole proprietor of the *Star*; appointed member of Republican County Committee 2 Nov.

1892    Defeated for County Auditor.

1900-04    Member of Ohio State Senate.

1904-06    Lieutenant-Governor of Ohio.

1910    Defeated as Republican nominee for Governor of Ohio.

1915-20    Member of US Senate from Ohio.

1920    Nominated for President by Republican National Convention in Chicago 12 June; degree of Master Mason conferred by Marion Lodge No 70 27 Aug; election day 2 Nov.

1921    Presidential Electors cast their ballots (404 for Harding; 127 for James Middleton Cox, the Democratic candidate) 10 Jan; electoral vote tabulated by Congress and Harding and Coolidge officially declared elected 9 Feb; inaugurated as 29th President of the United States of America 4 March; held first press conference 22 March; appointed commission to investigate conditions in the Philippines 23 March; opened telephone line between US and Cuba 11 April; issued executive order transferring management of naval oil reserves from the Navy to interior departments 10 May; signed first Immigration Quota Act 19 May; signed Emergency Tariff Act 27 May; signed Budget and Accounting Act 10 June; signed Packers and Stockyards Act 15 Aug; signed Grain Futures Trading Act 24 Aug; peace treaty with Austria signed at Vienna 24 Aug; peace treaty with Germany signed at Berlin 25 Aug; peace treaty with Hungary signed at Budapest 29 Aug; issued proclamation ordering marching miners of W Virginia to return home 30 Aug; issued proclamation establishing Armistice Day (11 Nov) as a legal holiday 5 Nov; attended burial of the Unknown Soldier at Arlington National Cemetery 11 Nov; issued proclamation of termination of war with Germany (as from 2 July) 14 Nov; delivered first State of the Union message to Congress 6 Dec; Four-Power Pacific Treaty signed at Washington 13 Dec.

1922    Five-Power and Nine-Power Treaties signed at Washington 6 Feb; signed
        Co-operative Marketing Act 18 Feb; issued proclamation prohibiting export of
        arms and munitions to China 4 March; issued executive order to withdraw all
        American troops from Germany 20 March; issued executive order reorganizing
        Bureau of Engraving and Printing 31 March; signed Act establishing Federal
        Narcotics Control Board 26 May; dedicated Francis Scott Key Memorial at
        Baltimore 14 June; issued executive order concerning German dye and drug
        plants 1 July; vetoed Soldiers' Bonus Bill 19 Sept; signed Fordney–McCumber
        Tariff Act 21 Sept; vetoed amendment to Department of Agriculture
        Appropriations Act 22 Sept; issued executive order directing prohibition agents
        not to act outside three-mile limit 26 Oct; delivered second State of the Union
        message to Congress 8 Dec.

1923    Vetoed Pension Bill 3 Jan; issued executive order ending American Army
        occupation of the Rhine 10 Jan; ordered troops to Mexican border 15 Feb; sent
        special message to Congress urging consent to US membership of World Court
        24 Feb; issued executive order setting apart 35,000 square miles in Alaska as
        naval oil reserve 27 Feb; issued executive order instructing tariff commission to
        investigate high price of sugar 27 March; began nationwide speaking tour 20
        June; visited Canada July; arrived in San Francisco 29 July; died suddenly at the
        Palace Hotel, San Francisco 2 Aug; buried at Marion, Ohio. He was the sixth
        President to die in office.

# The Writings of President Harding

*Rededicating America* (1920)
*Our Common Country* (1921)

# Lineage of President Harding

RICHARD HARDING, "a mariner engaged in fishing", emigrated from England to Braintree, Mass 1623 and settled at Wessagusett, nr Braintree, *b* 1587, *m* Elizabeth Adams, and *d* 1657, leaving issue,

STEPHEN HARDING, of Providence, Rhode Island, blacksmith, admitted Freeman 1669, *b* 1623, *m* Bridget Estance, and *d* 1698, having had issue,

ABRAHAM HARDING, *b* 1656, *m* Deborah —, and *dvp* 1694, leaving, with other issue,

STEPHEN HARDING, worked first as a tanner and currier in Providence, later a ship-builder and sea captain, bought a farm in New London County, Conn and moved there with his brother Israel, *b* 1681, *m*, and *d* 1750, leaving with other issue, a 2nd son,

ABRAHAM HARDING, moved to Orange County, New York 1761, highway master and fence viewer there, served as 2nd Lieut in the Continental Army during the Revolutionary War and later as 2nd Major in the State Militia, *b* 1720, *m* Anna Dolson, and *d* 1806, leaving issue, with five other sons, an eldest son,

ABRAHAM HARDING, moved to Wyoming Valley, Pennsylvania 1772 and left there in the "Big Runaway" 1778, *b* 1744, *m* 1762, Huldah Tryon, of New London, Conn (*b* 1743; *d* 1812), and *d* 1815, having had, with other issue, an eldest son,

AMOS HARDING, moved to Luzerne County 1800 and to the present Morrow County, Ohio 1820, *b* 1764, *m* 1784, Phoebe, dau of Isaac Tripp, by his wife Catherine La France, and *d* 1832, having had issue with sixteen other children an eldest son,

GEORGE TRYON HARDING, settled in Blooming Grove, Ohio 1820, *b* 1791, *m* 1st, Anna Roberts; and 2ndly 1816, Elizabeth (*b* 1799), dau of William Madison, by his wife Mary Hooper, and *d* 1860, having by her had with other issue,

CHARLES ALEXANDER HARDING, of Blooming Grove, Ohio, *b* 1820, *m* 1840, Mary Anne, dau of Joshua Crawford, and *d* 1878, having had issue with nine other children, an only surv son,

GEORGE TRYON HARDING, of Blooming Grove, Ohio, physician, purchased the *Caledonia Argus* 1875, *b* at Blooming Grove 12 June 1844, *educ* Iberia Coll, Iberia, Ohio (BA 1860), Ontario Academy, and Western Coll of Homeopathy, Cleveland, Ohio (MD 1873), *m* 1st at Galion, Ohio 7 May 1864, Phoebe (or Phebe) Elizabeth (*b* nr Blooming Grove, Ohio 21 Dec 1843; *d* 20 May 1910), dau of Isaac Haines Dickerson, of Blooming Grove, by his wife Charity Malvina, dau of William Van Kirk, and had with other issue (*see* BROTHERS AND SISTERS OF PRESIDENT HARDING, *p 462*) an eldest son,

WARREN GAMALIEL HARDING[1], **29th President of the United States of America.**

Dr George Tryon Harding *m* 2ndly at Anderson, Indiana 23 Nov 1911 (*m* diss by div 1916), Mrs Eudora Kelley Luvisi, a widow (*b* nr Bartonia, Indiana 25 Sept 1868; *d* at Union City, Indiana 24 July 1955). He *m* 3rdly at Monroe, Michigan 12 Aug 1921, Mary Alice Severns (*b* at Marion, Ohio 13 Nov 1869; *d* there 27 Nov 1964), and *d* at Santa Ana, California 19 Nov 1928.

# President Harding's Wife and Stepson

WARREN GAMALIEL HARDING *m* at his own house in Mount Vernon Avenue, Marion, Ohio 8 July 1891, Florence Mabel (called "Duchess" by Harding) (*b* at Marion, Ohio 15 Aug 1860; *d* there 21 Nov 1924, *bur* with her husband), formerly wife of Henry (Pete) De Wolfe (whom she *m* March 1880 and div May 1886, resuming her maiden name, and who *d* 1894), and only dau of Amos H. Kling, of Marion, banker and merchant, by his 1st wife Louisa M., dau of Harvey Bouton. There were no children of this marriage and thus President Harding has *no descendants*. However, he had a stepson through his wife's 1st marriage,

> Eugene Marshall (Pete) DE WOLFE, *b* at Prospect, Ohio 22 Sept 1880, *m* Esther Naomi (*b* 1890; *m* 2ndly 1916, Roscoe Mezger), dau of — Neely, of Marion, Ohio, and *d* in Colorado 1 Jan 1914, leaving issue,
>> 1 ●Eugenia (Jeanne) DE WOLFE, *b* 1911, *m* 1st, — Weil, and has issue,
>>> ●George D. WEIL [*San Juan, Puerto Rico*].
>> Eugenia De Wolfe *m* 2ndly —; and 3rdly, —.
>> 2 George Warren DE WOLFE, *b* 30 Sept 1913, *m* —, and *d* leaving issue,
>>> (1) ●David DE WOLFE [*Euclid, Ohio, USA*].
>>> (2) ●— DE WOLFE (son).

# The Brothers and Sisters of President Harding

**1** Charity Malvina HARDING, *b* at Blooming Grove, Ohio 1 March 1867, *m* 23 June 1886, Elton Elsworth Remsberg, and had issue,

  1 Nelle Marie REMSBERG.

  2 Edgar Harding REMSBERG.

  3 Helen Lucile REMSBERG.

  4 Katherine Elizabeth REMSBERG.

**2** Mary Clarissa HARDING, *b* at Blooming Grove, Ohio 26 April 1868; *dunm* 28 Oct 1913.

**3** Eleanor Persilla HARDING, *b* at Blooming Grove, Ohio 11 Nov 1872; *d* at Caledonia, Ohio 9 Nov 1878.

**4** Charles Alexander HARDING, *b* at Caledonia, Ohio April 1874; *d* there 9 Nov 1878.

**5** Abigail Victoria (Daisy) HARDING, *b* at Caledonia, Ohio 1876, *m* 1924, as his 1st wife, Ralph Tobias Lewis (who *m* 2ndly, 1938, Mrs Hazel Kling Longshore, a niece of Mrs Warren G. Harding, and *d* in Florida 27 March 1967), and *dsp* March 1935.

**6** George Tryon HARDING, Jr, of Worthington, Ohio, *b* at Caledonia, Ohio 11 March 1878, *educ* Battle Creek Coll, Michigan, and Univ of Michigan (MD 1900), *m* 21 July 1903, Elsie (*b* 23 June 1881), dau of Jacob Charles Weaver, and *d* 18 Jan 1934, leaving issue,

  1 ●George Tryon HARDING III, psychiatrist [*430 East Granville Road, Worthington, Ohio, USA; Torch, Kit Kat, University, and Rotary (Columbus) Clubs*)], *b* at Columbus, Ohio 27 May 1904, *educ* Columbia Union Coll (AB 1923), and Loma Linda Univ, California (MD 1928), *m* 2 June 1927, ●Mary Virginia Woolley, and has issue,

    (1) ●George Tryon HARDING IV [*650 Andover Road, Worthington, Ohio, USA*].

    (2) ●Herndon P. HARDING [*6487 Northland, Worthington, Ohio, USA*].

    (3) ●Ann Elizabeth HARDING.

    (4) ●Warren Gamaliel HARDING III, orthopedic surg, Lt-Cmdr Med Corps USNR [*6505 Vista Del Mar, La Jolla, California 92037, USA*], *b* at Columbus, Ohio 21 April 1941, *educ* Loma Linda Univ (BA 1963, MD 1967), and Univ of California, Los Angeles.

    (5) ●Richard Kent HARDING.

  2 ●Warren Gamaliel HARDING II, MD, *b* at Columbus, Ohio 2 Nov 1905.

  3 ●Ruth Virginia HARDING, *b* at Columbus, Ohio 5 April 1910.

  4 ●Charles Weaver HARDING [*970 High Street, Worthington, Ohio, USA*], *b* at Columbus, Ohio 22 Nov 1915.

  5 ●Mary Elizabeth HARDING, *b* at Columbus, Ohio 17 May 1919.

**7** Phoebe Caroline (Carolyn) HARDING, *b* 1879, *m* 4 Aug 1903, Heber Herbert Votaw, of Toledo, Ohio, and *dsp*.

# Note

[1] He was named after the Rev Warren Gamaliel Bancroft, of Wisconsin, a Methodist Minister and the husband of his maternal aunt Malvina Dickerson.

# (John) Calvin Coolidge
## 1872-1933

———

### 30th President of the
### United States of America
#### 1923-1929

(JOHN) CALVIN COOLIDGE, 30TH PRESIDENT

# (John) Calvin Coolidge

## 1872-1933

### 30th President of the United States of America

### 1923-1929

FOR HUMORISTS of the 1920s Coolidge was easy meat. As the story of the decade became fixed, Harding represented one side of the national character and Coolidge the other. Harding was folksy, banal, venial. Coolidge was reserved, taciturn, parsimonious—a Yankee of the Yankees or, in the phrase of a biographer, *A Puritan in Babylon.* His life seemed to be built on negations. Self-respect, he remarked in one of the dry, flat Coolidge aphorisms that delighted the satirists, depended on spending "less than you make". He did not marry until he was able to afford the extra expense, at the age of 33—though he was deeply in love with his fiancée Grace Anna Goodhue. His habits were frugal and he did not like to stay up late. Seeing him in the audience at a theater, the comedian Groucho Marx called out, "Isn't it past your bedtime, Calvin?" He was more famous for his silences than for his speeches. His legislative creed was summed up in advice to his father, who also had a modest political career: "It is much more important to kill bad bills than to pass good ones". He distrusted displays of temperament: "what we need in politics is more of the office desk and less of the show window". When he himself was lured into posing for the camera, especially for the newsreels of the day, he looked ludicrously ill at ease. Tongue-in-cheek, the journalist Wolcott Gibbs suggested that Coolidge was actually a comic genius on a par with Charlie Chaplin and Harry Langdon. "There was a great pathos about him as he went awkwardly and unhappily though the gaudy antics which were so hilariously at variance with his appearance". These included being rigged out in a feathered Indian headdress.

A complementary explanation was that Coolidge's rise to the White House was a fluke. His career as Massachusetts lawyer-Republican led him by unremarkable stages to a narrow victory in the 1918 gubernatorial election. He happened to be Governor during the Boston police strike of 1919. Belatedly intervening on the side of law and order (that is, against the police unionizers), he won acclaim throughout a nervous nation for his assertion that "there is no right to strike against the public safety by anybody, anywhere, any time". Re-elected by a large majority, Coolidge was enough of a celebrity to be considered along with Harding and others as a presidential possibility in 1920. The Republican leadership rejected him as small fry. However, resentful delegates at the convention, feeling that they were being stampeded, refused to accept the platform's vice-presidential nominee and plumped instead for Coolidge. In the next three years he seemed to agree with others in Washington that as Vice-President he had reached his ceiling. When President Harding died suddenly in August 1923, Coolidge was vacationing at his birthplace, the little township of Plymouth, Vermont. The oath of office was administered to him by his father, a Justice of the Peace, by the light of two kerosene lamps. It was as if the new, accidental President belonged to an earlier era.

In office, according to the caustic H. L. Mencken, "Coolidge's chief feat was to sleep more than any other President. . . . The itch to run things did not afflict him; he was content to let them run themselves". One cannot deny that Coolidge maintained what would nowadays be called a low profile. The foreign policy achievements of his Administration, which included the Kellogg–Briand pact and some constructive activity in Latin America, were mainly the work of subordinates. He did not mention foreign affairs in his autobiography, published in 1929. In domestic matters Coolidge was as always a conservative. His instincts were much more those of a businessman than a farmer, despite his semi-rural Vermont background. He believed in *laissez-faire*. Again the negations: the boat should *not* be rocked, the nation's ailing agriculture should *not* be propped up by price-support, government should *not* interfere with the automatic operation of the laws of supply and demand. And he himself should *not* remain at the helm, though he had a fairly good chance of securing the Republican nomination for a second time in his own right. On the fourth anniversary of his succession, in August 1927, he issued the terse announcement: "I do not choose to run for President in 1928".

It is easy to see why he was nominated in 1924. The scandals of the Harding cabinet were beginning to break. Coolidge's dour, thrifty style was an enormous relief for his embarrassed party. Theodore Roosevelt's outspoken daughter Alice Longworth had been horrified by the brassy vulgarity of the Harding régime. She found the White House distinctly improved under the influence of "Cautious Cal" and his unpretentiously attractive, intelligent wife. "The atmosphere", she said, "was as different as a New England front parlor is from a back room in a speakeasy". For the public too, it was as if a bowl of field flowers had replaced an ashtray full of

GRACE ANNA GOODHUE, MRS COOLIDGE

cigar ends. Coolidge stood for traditional virtues: prudence, probity, common sense, understatement. The American people could not exactly love Coolidge, as they worshipped Charles A. Lindbergh for his solo flight over the Atlantic in 1927. But they drew the same lesson in both cases. The true American hero was Everyman—plucky, stubborn, laconic, self-reliant, sublime in his ordinariness.

If this seems too extravagant an estimate of Calvin Coolidge, we must note that he was not so null as the humorists made him out to be. Within his limits he was a thorough, clear-witted person, well respected by associates in Massachusetts. Without pushing himself, he gained the wholehearted admiration of a circle of Boston Republicans who distributed his speeches and sang his praises throughout the party. His economy of utterance, in part the result of shyness, was shrewdly turned into an asset—a distinctive Coolidge trademark. He knew perfectly well what he was doing. Nor was he devoid of wit. Paying tribute to Grace Coolidge, at that time a teacher at a school for the deaf, he observed of their marriage that "having taught the deaf to hear, Miss Goodhue might perhaps cause the mute to speak". In fact he was a fairly effective speaker, and quick to grasp the political advantages of broadcasting. "I am very fortunate", he told an eloquent Senator, "that I came in with the radio. I can't make an engaging, rousing . . . speech to a crowd as you can, . . . but I have a good radio voice, and now I can get my messages across . . . without acquainting them with my lack of oratorical ability". While he capitalized upon his remoteness, Coolidge also held frequent press conferences and never refused to be photographed in the interests of publicity. He had not been endowed with a great deal of stamina. He joked about his apparent indolence, claiming that he kept fit as President by avoiding the big problems. But he was gradually worn down by the strain of office. The death of his son Calvin from blood poisoning desolated him. He sensed that the United States was economically unstable, and he knew he was not equipped to deal with major troubles. There was an irrefutable logic in his performance as Chief Executive. Other politicians tried to bluff the electorate, passing themselves off as wizards and supermen. Coolidge merely impersonated himself. There was no deception. If the American people chose to vote for him, that was their concern.

# Chronology

1872    Born at Plymouth, Vermont 4 July.

1890    Graduated from Black River Academy, Ludlow, Vermont; failed entrance examination to Amherst College owing to illness; entered St Johnsbury Academy, Vermont.

1891    Entered Amherst College, Amherst, Mass.

1895    Graduated from College with BA degree 26 June; began reading Law in office of Hammond and Field, Northampton, Mass, Sept.

1896    Won Sons of American Revolution essay contest with essay on the principles of the Revolution.

1897    Admitted to the Massachusetts Bar.

1898    Elected to the Common Council of Northampton; elected Vice-President of Northampton Savings Bank.

1899-
1902    City Solicitor of Northampton.

1904    Chairman of Republican County Committee of Hampshire County.

1905    Defeated as candidate for Northampton Board of Education.

1906    Elected to Massachusetts House of Representatives (served two terms 1907-08).

1909    Resumed law practice in Northampton.

1910-11    Mayor of Northampton.

1911    Elected to Massachusetts Senate (served four terms 1912-15).

1914-15    President of the Massachusetts Senate.

1915    Elected Lieutenant-Governor Massachusetts.

1918    Elected Gov Governor nf Massachusetts Nov.

1919    Took office as Governor 1 Jan; welcomed President Wilson in Boston on his return from the Paris Peace Conference 24 Feb; refused to intervene in Boston Police crisis 8 Sept; Police strike began 9 Sept; called out State Guard 11 Sept; made celebrated reply to Samuel Gompers, Pres of the American Federation of Labor 12 Sept; re-elected Governor Nov; received honorary degree of LLD from Amherst College.

1920    Took office as Governor for second term 1 Jan; nominated for Vice-President by Republican National Convention in Chicago 12 June; elected Vice-President 2 Nov.

1921    Inaugurated as Vice-President of the United States 4 March.

1923    Succeeded as 30th President of the United States of America on the death in office of President Harding 2 Aug; took oath of office at his own house in Plymouth Notch, Vermont 3 Aug (the oath being administered by his father, as a Justice of the Peace); appointed commission to investigate imminent coal strike 24 Aug; recognized Obregon Government in Mexico 31 Aug (diplomatic relations 3 Sept); coal strike began in Pennsylvania 1 Sept; ended 8 Sept; received Rt Hon David Lloyd George, wartime Prime Minister of Britain, at the White House 5 Nov; delivered first State of the Union message to Congress 6 Dec; accepted invitation for US to participate in Reparations Conference 11 Dec.

1924    Issued proclamation prohibiting sale of munitions to Mexican rebels 7 Jan; signed joint resolution charging former Secretary of the Interior Fall and Secretary of the Navy Denby with fraud and corruption in the execution of 1922 oil leases 8 Feb; sent special message to Congress urging adherence to Permanent Court of International Justice 24 Feb; issued proclamation raising tariff rates on wheat and wheat products 7 March; issued proclamation prohibiting export of arms and munitions to Cuban rebels 2 May; vetoed Pension Increase for Civil War and Spanish-American War Veterans Bill 3 May; vetoed Soldiers' Bonus Bill 15 May (passed over his veto 19 May); signed Act authorizing Secretary of the Interior to issue certificates of citizenship to Indians and act reducing income taxes by 25% 2 June; issued executive order providing regulations for reformed Foreign Service and vetoed Postal Salaries Bill 7 June; nominated for re-election by the Republican National Convention at Cleveland, Ohio 7 July; election day 4 Nov; appointed Commission to investigate agricultural conditions 7 Nov; delivered second State of the Union message to Congress 3 Dec.

1925    Presidential Electors cast their ballots (382 for Coolidge; 136 for John William Davis, the Democratic candidate; 13 for Robert Marion La Follette, the Progressive candidate) 12 Jan; exchanged greetings with King Alfonso XIII of Spain on the new cable between US and Spain 19 Jan; signed Air Mail Act 2 Feb; electoral vote tabulated by Congress and Coolidge and Dawes officially declared elected 11 Feb; signed Postal Pay and Rate Increase Act 25 Feb; Supreme Court decision in Grossman case held that the President had power of pardon regarding persons who had been found guilty of contempt of court 2 March; signed Executive and Legislative Salaries Act and pocket vetoed four Bills 4 March; inaugurated on the east portico of the Capitol (the oath of office being administered by ex-President Chief Justice William Howard Taft) 4 March; issued executive order transferring Patent Office from the Department of the Interior to the Department of Commerce 19 March; issued executive order transferring Bureau of Mines from the Department of the Interior to the Department of Commerce 4 June; issued executive order remitting last of Boxer indemnity to China 16 July; appointed National Air Board 12 Sept; delivered third State of the Union message to Congress 7 Dec; sent special message to Congress recommending adherence to World Court 21 Dec.

1926    Signed Revenue Act 26 Feb; appointed commission to investigate economic and political conditions in the Philippines 2 April; issued executive order authorizing employment of state and local officers as prohibition agents 8 May; signed Air Commerce Act 20 May; signed Public Buildings Act 25 May; signed Act creating Army Air Corps 2 July; signed Pension Act and pocket vetoed five Bills 3 July; issued proclamation prohibiting illegal shipment of arms and munitions to Nicaragua 15 Sept; delivered fourth State of the Union message to Congress 7 Dec.

1927    Sent special message to Congress defending intervention in Nicaragua 10 Jan; signed Radio Control Act 23 Feb; signed National Bank Consolidation Act and Act granting US citizenship to certain inhabitants of the Virgin Islands and vetoed McNary–Haugen Farm Relief Bill 25 Feb; signed Naval Appropriation Act 2 March; signed amended Organic Act of Puerto Rico and pocket vetoed two Bills 4 March; issued executive order returning naval oil reserves to the Navy Department 2 April; vetoed Act of legislature of the Philippines 6 April; Geneva Naval Conference 20 June-4 Aug; delivered fifth State of the Union message to Congress 5 Dec.

1928    Delivered opening address at Pan-American Conference in Havana, Cuba 16 Jan; dedicated National Press Club Building in Washington, DC 4 Feb; signed amended Antitrust Act 9 March; signed Settlement of War Claims Act 10 March; vetoed revised McNary–Haugen farm relief Bill and signed Flood Control Act 15 May; signed Merchant Marine Act 22 March; signed Revenue Act reducing income tax and pocket vetoed three Bills 29 May; sent sixth (and last) State of the Union message to Congress 4 Dec; signed Boulder Dam Act 21 Dec.

1929    Signed Naval Appropriation Act 13 Feb; made last public address as President at George Washington University, Washington, DC 22 Feb; signed amended Prohibition Enforcement Act 2 March; pocket vetoed 16 Bills, retired from office and attended the inauguration of his successor President Hoover 4 March; retired to Northampton, Mass; attended ceremony at the White House for proclamation of the Kellog–Briand Peace Pact by President Hoover 24 July.

1930-31    Contributed a daily column "Thinking Things Over with Calvin Coolidge" to the New York *Herald Tribune* and other papers.

1933    Died of coronary thrombosis at Northampton, Mass 5 Jan; buried at Plymouth, Vermont.

# The Writings of President Coolidge

*Have Faith in Massachusetts!* (1919)

*The Price of Freedom; Speeches and Addresses* (1924)

*Foundations of the Republic; Speeches and Addresses* (1926)

*The Autobiography of Calvin Coolidge* (1929)

# Lineage of President Coolidge

SIMON COOLEDGE, of Cottenham, Cambridgeshire, England, *m* Agnes Kingston, and *d* (will dated 1591) leaving with other issue,

WILLIAM COOLEDGE, of Cottenham, Churchwarden in 1612, *m* Margaret — (*bur* 1620), and *d* (will dated 1618) leaving with other issue,

JOHN COOLIDGE, emigrated to Watertown, Mass *ca* 1630, Freeman 25 May 1636, Selectman many times between 1639 and 1677, Deputy to the General Court 1658, *bapt* at Cottenham 16 Sept 1604, *m* Mary Maddock, née Wellington, and *d* at Watertown 22 Aug 1691, leaving with other issue[1],

SIMON COOLIDGE, *b* 1632, *m* 1st, Hannah Barron (*d* 14 July 1680), and had issue. He *m* 2ndly 19 Jan 1681/2, Priscilla (*d* 1694), dau of John Rogers, by his wife Priscilla, and *d* 1693. His son,

OBADIAH COOLIDGE, *b* 1663 (or 1664), *m* 28 Feb 1686/7, Elizabeth Rouse, of Hartford, Conn (who *m* 2ndly 16 Feb 1714, John Cunningham, and *d ante* 6 Nov 1732), and *d* (will dated 18 Feb, *pr* 19 June) 1706, leaving with other issue,

OBADIAH COOLIDGE, of Watertown, and later of Marlboro, Mass, cordwainer, *b* at Watertown 27 Aug 1694, *m* 24 July 1717, Rachel Goddard, of Watertown, and *d* 1741, leaving with other issue,

JOSIAH COOLIDGE, *b* 17 July 1718, *m* Mary —, and *d* 1780, leaving issue,

JOHN COOLIDGE, *b* 1752, *m* 1779, Hannah, dau of James Priest, by his wife Hannah, and *d* 1822, leaving issue,

CALVIN COOLIDGE, *b* 1780, *m* 1814, Sarah Thompson, and *d* 1853, leaving issue,

CALVIN GELUSHA COOLIDGE, *b* 1815, *m* 1844, Sarah Almeda, dau of Israel Putnam Brewer, by his wife Sarah, dau of Israel Putnam Brown[2], and *d* 1878, leaving issue,

COLONEL JOHN CALVIN COOLIDGE, of Plymouth, Vermont, JP, politician, farmer and storekeeper, *b* at Plymouth, Vermont 31 March 1845, *m* 1st 6 May 1868, Victoria Josephine (*b* at Pinney Hollow, Vermont 14 March 1846; *d* at Plymouth, Vermont 14 March 1885), dau of Hiram Dunlop Moor, by his wife Abigail, dau of Luther Franklin, and had with other issue (*see* SISTER OF PRESIDENT COOLIDGE, *p 473*), an only son,

(JOHN) CALVIN COOLIDGE, **30th President of the United States of America.**

Col John Calvin Coolidge *m* 2ndly 9 Sept 1891, Caroline Brown (*b* probably at Plymouth, Vermont 22 Jan 1857; *d* at Plymouth, Vermont 19 May 1920), and *d* at Plymouth, Vermont 18 March 1926.

# The Descendants of President Coolidge

(JOHN) CALVIN COOLIDGE *m* at Burlington, Vermont 4 Oct 1905, Grace Anna (*b* at Burlington, Vermont 3 Jan 1879; *d* at Northampton, Mass 8 July 1957, *bur* at Plymouth, Vermont), dau of Andrew I. Goodhue, steamboat inspector, by his wife Lemira Barrett, and had issue,

**1** ● John COOLIDGE, retired corpn executive, dir and trustee of various corpns and insts. [*48 Garden Street, Farmington, Connecticut 06032, USA*], *b* at Northampton, Mass 7 Sept 1906, *educ* Amherst (BA), *m* at Plainville, Conn 23 Sept 1929, ● Florence (*b* at Plainville 30 Nov 1904), dau of Gov John H. Trumbull, of Plainville, Conn, by his wife Maude Usher, and has issue,

    **1** ● Cynthia COOLIDGE, *b* at New Haven, Conn 28 Oct 1933, *m* at Farmington, Conn 26 Sept 1964, ● S. Edward Jeter (*b* at Hartford, Conn 1 Sept 1937) [*221 Deer Cliff Road, Avon, Connecticut, USA*], son of Sherwood F. Jeter, Jr, by his wife Edwina Pabst, and has issue,

        ● Christopher Coolidge JETER, *b* at Hartford, Conn 3 Jan 1967.

    **2** ● Lydia COOLIDGE, *b* at New Haven, Conn 14 Aug 1939, *m* at Farmington, Conn 17 June 1966, ● Jeremy Whitman Sayles (*b* at Schenectady, New York 9 June 1937) [*30 Hillandale Road, Ashburnham, Mass, USA*], son of Phil Whitman Sayles, by his wife Mildred Jones, and has issue,

        ● Jennifer Coolidge SAYLES, *b* at Boston, Mass 27 July 1970.

**2** Calvin COOLIDGE, *b* at Northampton, Mass 13 April 1908; *d* at Washington, DC 7 July 1924.

# The Sister of President Coolidge

Abigail Gratia COOLIDGE, *b* 1875; *d* 1890.

# Notes

1 John Coolidge's youngest son Jonathan Coolidge (1647-1724) was the father of John Coolidge, of Boston, the father of Joseph Coolidge (*d* 1771), the father of Joseph Coolidge (1747-1820), the father of Joseph Coolidge (1773-1840), the father of Joseph Coolidge who married Eleanora Wayles Randolph, granddaughter of President Jefferson (*see* DESCENDANTS OF PRESIDENT JEFFERSON, *p 113*).

2 Through the Brown family President Coolidge derived kinship with General Israel Putnam (1718-1790), who shared the command at Bunker Hill and was defeated by General Howe at Brooklyn Heights (*see* APPENDIX D, SOME REMARKABLE KINSHIPS).

# Herbert Clark Hoover
## 1874-1964

———

### 31st President of the United States of America
1929-1933

HERBERT CLARK HOOVER, 31ST PRESIDENT

# Herbert Clark Hoover

## 1874-1964

### *31st President of the United States of America*

### 1929-1933

AT SOME periods in American history the best men seem not to have been picked for President. In the nineteenth century, how could candidates as impressive as Henry Clay and Daniel Webster have been rejected in favour of lesser men? In 1928, however, the Republican nomination went to a person of quite exceptional ability who had proved his talents in several fields. Herbert Hoover, orphaned in Iowa at the age of eight, was reared by Quaker grandparents. He graduated from Leland Stanford Jr University in California, where he met his wife Lou Henry, the daughter of a local banker. He made his career and a substantial fortune as a mining engineer, from the bottom up. His profession took him all over the world; Hoover was easily the most travelled of American Presidents. For some years before World War I he was living in London, where his two sons were born. Later, his presidential eligibility was to be challenged on the inaccurate ground that as a British ratepayer he had voted in a foreign (municipal) election.

On the outbreak of the war Hoover took charge of a giant philanthropic program, the Commission for Relief in Belgium. When the United States entered the conflict in 1917 he returned to Washington to act as food administrator. At the end of the war he went back to Europe, this time to organize relief for the continent's starving millions. He was in Paris for the peace conference. Here and in all his previous enterprises Hoover won nothing but praise. Others were talkers: Hoover was a doer of brilliant effectiveness. A perceptive English observer, disgusted by the dishonesty and stupidity of the swarm of diplomats, said that Hoover was the only man who emerged from the Paris conference "with an enhanced reputation". Franklin Roosevelt, who became acquainted with him in wartime Washington, remarked: "He is certainly a wonder, and I wish we could make him President of the United States".

As Roosevelt's comment indicates, Hoover's renown had nothing to do with party politics. Perhaps misguidedly, Hoover allowed himself to be drawn into Republicanism, and to calculate his chances of reaching the White House. He added to his already formidable reputation by accepting a cabinet post under Harding and Coolidge as Secretary of Commerce. The office was of secondary importance until Hoover's driving energy converted the Department of Commerce into a model of governmental efficiency.

By 1920 or thereabouts Herbert Hoover had developed a personal philosophy from which he never budged. His own rise from poverty to riches through hard work had convinced him of the soundness of the old American creed of rugged individualism––the theme of a book he published in 1922. There was a God of justice and mercy; but God helped those who helped themselves. Hoover's experience of the rest of the world taught him that American private-enterprise democracy was the only worthwhile system. Other nations were morally and economically inferior, and deserved to be. If these were conventional sentiments, Hoover held to them with exceptional intensity. They were not simply things he had been told: they were precepts he had confirmed by first-hand observation. Harding and Coolidge accepted more or less the same doctrine, as their fathers and fathers' fathers had done. Hoover expounded such truths with an intellectual force based on deep emotion.

In 1928 the Republican party responded enthusiastically. They recognized in their candidate the highest product of go-getting American idealism: a pioneer from out of the West who was also versed in modern technology. By contrast the Democratic candidate Al Smith was a city boy, a professional vote-catcher, and a Roman Catholic. Hoover's victory was spectacular. If the conditions of the previous half-century had continued he would no doubt have become a hero in the Republican pantheon to place beside Lincoln and Theodore Roosevelt. Instead there came the stock market crash of October 1929, followed by a steady worsening of the whole world's economic situation. Clearly Hoover was not a brutal or a stupid man. But given his philosophy there was little he could or should do to put matters right. He did not believe the Federal Government should compete with private enterprise. The most he could countenance, by means of the Reconstruction Finance Corporation (RFC), was a program to lend money to worthy businessmen. He did not believe in dole for the unemployed: it would sap their initiative in going out to look for work—as he had done as a young man in the mining camps. Mistrustful of Europe, he thought the Depression was a result of foreign error. Instead of seeking international agreement on monetary and trade policies, he sanctioned economic nationalism—the raising of tariff barriers which only worsened Europe's economic plight. He resisted

LOU HENRY, MRS HOOVER

giving diplomatic recognition to Soviet Russia, which some Americans recommended in the hope of winning a new export market. He followed party orthodoxy in continuing to support Prohibition, which he called "an experiment noble in motive", though the experiment had ruined the brewery industry and only enriched the racketeers. He had no words of comfort for the angry "bonus marchers" who descended on Washington in 1932. His only apparent panacea was the repetition of ancient reassurances: all would be well if the nation recovered its business confidence.

Herbert Hoover, beaten by Franklin Roosevelt in 1932 as calamitously as he had beaten Al Smith, left office under a cloud. His name was linked with every evil feature of the Depression. The tarpaper shacks of the unemployed were "Hoovervilles." An empty pocket turned inside out was a "Hoover flag". Of course not every American despised him. Republicans felt he had been victimized; and indeed inside most of his countrymen, including Roosevelt, there resided a secret assent that the traditional creed was still worthy of respect: it only needed modification in the light of the crisis of the Depression. Such flexibility eluded Hoover. Nevertheless more than thirty years of life were left to him. As prosperity returned, so by degrees did his standing. Scholars respected him for endowing the Hoover Institute of War and Peace at Stanford, and for books that included a sympathetic analysis of Woodrow Wilson and the Paris conference. Two later Presidents, Harry Truman and Dwight D. Eisenhower, acknowledged his administrative talents by appointing him to head commissions on the structure of the Federal Government. When he died in 1964 he was not quite a national hero; yet he had long ceased to be a national bogeyman.

# Chronology

1874     Born at Downey Street, West Branch, Iowa 10 Aug.

1884     Went to live with his uncle Dr Henry John Minthorn at Newberg, Oregon.

1885     Moved with the Minthorns to Salem, Oregon.

1895     Graduated from Leland Stanford Jr University, Palo Alto, California with AB degree 29 May.

1895-96  Worked as a miner in California.

1897-
1901     Worked as mining engineer in Western Australia and China.

1901-14  Employed as mining engineer in Australia, China, France, India, England, Hawaii, New Zealand, South Africa, Canada, Germany, Malaya, Russia and US.

1914     Organized American Relief Committee in London to aid US citizens stranded in Europe at the outbreak of World War I.

1917     Appointed to US Food Administration by President Wilson 19 May.

1918     Appointed Director-General of Relief and Reconstruction of Europe by President Wilson 9 Nov.

1919     Served as member and alternate Chairman of Supreme Economic Council; member of committee of economic advisers to American delegation to Paris Peace Conference; founded Hoover Institution on War, Revolution and Peace at Stanford University.

1921     Appointed Secretary of Commerce by President Harding 5 March.

1923     Appointment as Secretary of Commerce retained by President Coolidge 3 Aug.

1928     Nominated for President by the Republican National Convention at Kansas City, Missouri 14 June; election day 6 Nov; made goodwill tour of Central and South America Nov-Dec.

1929     Presidential Electors cast their ballots (444 for Hoover; 87 for Alfred Emanuel Smith, the Democratic candidate) 14 Jan; electoral vote tabulated by Congress and Hoover and Curtis officially declared elected 13 Feb; inaugurated as 31st President of the United States of America on the east portico of the Capitol 4 March; issued executive order regarding income tax funds 14 March; sent special message to Congress on farm relief and tariff revision 16 April; appointed commission to investigate law enforcement 20 May; signed Agricultural Marketing Act 15 June; signed Census and Reapportionment Act 18 June; issued proclamation announcing agreement of six states regarding Boulder

Canyon project 25 June; gave state dinner at the White House for Ramsay MacDonald, the British Prime Minister 7 Oct; stock market broke 24 Oct; crashed 29 Oct; sent first State of the Union message to Congress 2 Dec; sent budget message to Congress 4 Dec; signed joint resolution reducing income tax revenue 16 Dec; fire destroyed executive offices of the White House 24 Dec.

1930    Sent special message to Congress outlining six specific recommendations for immediate legislation to strengthen prohibition enforcement 13 Jan; issued executive order banning import of parrots 24 Jan; vetoed Bill to authorize coinage of 50 cents silver pieces to commemorate 75th anniversary of Gadsden Purchase 22 April; sent London Naval Treaty (signed by US, Great Britain, France, Italy and Japan 22 April) to the Senate for ratification 1 May; reviewed Navy off Virginia coast 20 May; vetoed Soldiers, Sailors and Nurses Pensions Bill 28 May (passed over his veto 2 June); delivered Memorial Day address at Gettysburg, Pennsylvania 30 May; vetoed World War I Veterans' Pension Bill 26 June; pocket vetoed three Bills 3 July; signed Rivers and Harbors Act 4 July; Senate ratified London Naval Treaty 21 July; pushed button lighting Lindbergh Beacon at Chicago from the White House 27 Aug; issued executive order prohibiting shipping of arms and munitions to Brazilian revolutionaries 22 Oct; sent second State of the Union message to Congress 2 Dec; signed Emergency Construction to Aid Unemployed Act and Drought Relief Act 20 Dec; signed Farm Board Appropriation Act 22 Dec.

1931    Sent special message to Congress announcing his opposition to the repeal of the 18th ("Prohibition") Amendment 20 Jan; vetoed Veterans' Bonus Bill 26 Feb (passed over his veto 27 Feb); vetoed joint resolution to create a corporation to operate Government properties at Muscle Shoals, Alabama 3 March; visited Puerto Rico 23 March; visited Virgin Islands 25 March; entertained King Prajadhipok and Queen Rambhai Barni of Siam at the White House 29 April; again delivered Memorial Day address at Gettysburg 30 May; spoke at the dedication of President Harding's tomb at Marion, Ohio 16 June; dedicated Memorial to War Dead at Washington, DC 11 Nov; sent third State of the Union message to Congress 8 Dec; signed moratorium of war reparations and war debts 23 Dec.

1932    Signed Reconstruction Finance Corporation Act 22 Jan; signed Land Banks Expansion Act 23 Jan; addressed joint session of Congress on bi-centenary of Washington's birth 22 Feb; signed Credit Expansion Act 27 Feb; 20th Amendment to the Constitution submitted to the States 3 March; signed Anti-Injunction Act 23 March; sent special message to Congress proposing joint executive department-congressional commission to study governmental economics and recommend legislation 4 April; vetoed Omnibus Pension Bill 27 April; sent special message to Congress regarding delay in balancing budget 5 May; vetoed Amendment to Tariff Act of 1930 Bill 11 May; Supreme Court decided that President could sign Bills after final adjournment of Congress 31 May; signed Tax Act 6 June; renominated for President by Republican National Convention at Chicago 16 June; vetoed Unemployment Relief Bill 11 July; voluntarily cut his own salary by 20% 15 July; signed Relief and Construction Act and amended Veterans Administration Act 21 July; signed Federal Home Loan Bank Act 22 July; laid cornerstone of new Post Office Department Building in Washington, DC (using same trowel with which Washington had laid the cornerstone of the Capitol in 1793) 26 Sept; laid cornerstone of new Supreme Court Building in Washington, DC 13 Oct; election day 8 Nov; sent fourth (and last) State of the Union message to Congress 6 Dec.

1933    Attended funeral of his predecessor former President Coolidge at Northampton, Mass 7 Jan; Presidential Electors cast their ballots 9 Jan; vetoed Philippine Independence Bill (passed over his veto) 13 Jan; vetoed Deficiency Bill 24 Jan; electoral votes tabulated by Congress and Hoover officially declared defeated for re-election 8 Feb; 21st Amendment to the Constitution sent to the States for ratification 20 Feb; signed amended Banking Act 25 Feb; pocket vetoed seven Bills, retired from office and attended the inauguration of his successor President Franklin D. Roosevelt 4 March; retired to his home at Palo Alto, California.

1936    Appointed Chairman of Boys Club of America.

1938    Toured Europe.

1939    Appointed Chairman of Polish Relief Commission and Finnish Relief Fund.

1940    Appointed Chairman of Committee on Food for Small Democracies.

1942    Appointed Chairman of Belgian Relief Fund.

1946    Appointed co-ordinator of Food Supply for World Famine by President Truman.

1947    Asked by President Truman to make a study of food and economic conditions in Germany and central Europe; submitted report 27 Feb; Boulder Dam officially renamed Hoover Dam in his honor; first Hoover Commission on Organization of the Executive Branch of the Government established by Act of Congress 7 July.

1949    Final report of Hoover Commission submitted 1 April; declined appointment to the Senate.

1952    Addressed Republican National Convention (at Chicago) for the last time 7 July.

1953    Appointed member of 12 man Commission on Government Operations (second Hoover Commission) by President Eisenhower 24 July; Chairman 10 Aug (until 30 June 1955).

1962    Herbert Hoover Presidential Library and Museum opened at West Branch, Iowa.

1964    Celebrated his 90th birthday 10 Aug; died of internal haemorrhage at New York 20 Oct 1964; buried at West Branch, Iowa.

# The Writings of President Hoover

*Principles of Mining* (1909)

Translation of Georgius Agricola's *De Re Metallica* (1912)

*American Individualism* (1922)

*The State Papers and Other Public Writings of Herbert Hoover*, edited by William Star Myers, 2 vols (1934)

*Addresses Upon the American Road, 1933-1938* (1938)

*Further Addresses Upon the American Road, 1938-1940* (1940)

*The Problems of Lasting Peace* (1942)

*America's First Crusade* (1943)

*Addresses Upon the American Road; World War II, 1941-1945* (1946)

*Addresses Upon the American Road, 1945-1948* (1949)

*Addresses Upon the American Road, 1948-1950* (1951)

*Memoirs* (3 vols): *Years of Adventure, 1874-1920; The Cabinet and the Presidency, 1920-1933;* and *The Great Depression, 1929-1941* (1951-52)

*Addresses Upon the American Road, 1950-1955* (1955)

*The Ordeal of Woodrow Wilson* (1958)

*An American Epic*, 3 vols (1959-61)

*Addresses Upon the American Road, 1955-1960* (1961)

# Lineage of President Hoover

This family originated in Switzerland and migrated to the Palatinate about the middle of the seventeenth century.

JOHANN HEINRICH HUBER, of Oberkulm, in the County of Lenzburg, Canton of Aargau, Switzerland, was the father of—

JONAS HUBER, of Ellerstadt, nr Dürkheim, Palatinate, *b* Aug 1668, *m* Maria —, and *d* at Ellerstadt 13 April 1741, leaving issue,

ANDREAS HUBER, emigrated to America 1738 and settled on Pipe Creek, Maryland, where he built a mill and farmed land acquired from the Government in 1746 and 1748, moved to Randolph County, N Carolina 1762, anglicized his name as Andrew Hoover *ca* 1763, *bapt* at Ellerstadt 29 Jan 1723, *m ca* 1745, Margaret Fouts, and *d* 1794, leaving issue, with seven other sons and five daus,

JOHN HOOVER, millwright, settled at West Milton, Miami County, Ohio 1802, *b ca* 1760, *m* in N Carolina *ca* 1785, Sarah Burket, and had issue,

JESSE HOOVER, of Hubbard, Iowa, where he settled in 1854, *b* in N Carolina *ca* 1799, *m* 1819, Rebecca, dau of John Yount, by his wife Mary, and *d* at Hubbard Nov 1856, leaving issue,

ELI HOOVER, *b* at West Milton, Ohio 6 Oct 1820, *m* 1st, Mary Davis (*d* in Ohio 3 March 1852), and had issue. He *m* 2ndly in Iowa 17 Aug 1854, Hannah Leonard (*b* in Ireland 14 Feb 1832), and *d* 24 July 1892. His son by his 1st marriage,

JESSE CLARK HOOVER, of West Branch, Iowa, blacksmith and farm equipment salesman, *b* at West Milton, Ohio 2 Sept 1847, *m* in Iowa 12 March 1870, Hulda Randall (*b* at Burgersville, Ontario, Canada 4 May 1848; *d* at West Branch, Iowa 22 Feb 1883), dau of Theodore Minthorn[1], by his wife Mary Wasley, and *d* at West Branch, Iowa 13 Dec 1880, leaving with other issue (*see* BROTHER AND SISTER OF PRESIDENT HOOVER, *p* 486), a yr son,

HERBERT CLARK HOOVER, **31st President of the United States of America.**

# The Descendants of President Hoover

HERBERT CLARK HOOVER *m* at Monterey, California 10 Feb 1899, Lou (*b* at Waterloo, Iowa 29 March 1874; *d* at Waldorf Astoria Towers, New York 7 Jan 1944, *bur* Hoover Cemetery, West Branch, Iowa), elder dau of Charles Delano Henry, banker, by his wife Florence Weed, and had issue,

**1** Herbert Charles HOOVER, Under Sec of State 1954-57, geophysicist, *b* in London, England 4 Aug 1903, *educ* Stanford Univ (AB), and Harvard (MBA), *m* at Stanford 25 June 1925, ●Margaret E. Watson (*b* at San Francisco, California 1904), and *d* at Pasadena, California 9 July 1969, leaving issue,
  **1** ●Margaret Ann HOOVER, *b* at Boston, Mass 17 March 1926, *m* at Pasadena, California July 1949, ●Richard Tatem Brigham (*b* at Boston, Mass 1925) [*1120 Meeting House Road, West Chester, Pennsylvania, USA*], and has issue,
    (1) ●Katherine Storrs BRIGHAM, *b* at Boston 8 June 1950.
    (2) ●Ann Dyer BRIGHAM, *b* at Boston 13 Feb 1952.
    (3) ●Robert Hoover BRIGHAM [*1107½ 24th Street, Parkersburg, West Virginia 26101, USA*], *b* at Boston 2 July 1953.
    (4) ●Deborah Miles BRIGHAM, *b* at Wilmington, Delaware 6 Feb 1959.
    (5) ●Douglas Ward BRIGHAM, *b* at Wilmington, Delaware 15 Feb 1960.
  **2** ●Herbert HOOVER [*1520 Circle Drive, San Marino, California, USA*], *b* at Boston, Mass 5 Nov 1927, *m* at Virginia City, Nevada 1949, ●Meredith McGilvray, and has issue,
    (1) ●Stephen HOOVER, *b* at Palo Alto, California 29 Aug 1949.
    (2) ●Michael HOOVER, *b* at Tucson, Arizona 13 March 1951.
    (3) ●Leslie HOOVER, *b* at Palo Alto, California 17 Jan 1956.
  **3** ●Joan Leslie HOOVER, *b* at Los Angeles, California 12 April 1930, *m* 29 June 1951, ●William Leland Vowles (*b* 9 Feb 1926) [*1461 Newfoundland Drive, Sunnyvale, California, USA*], and has issue,
    (1) ●Mark Leland VOWLES, *b* at San Jose, California 21 Feb 1954.
    (2) ●Aaron Clay VOWLES, *b* at San Jose, California 2 Nov 1955.
    (3) ●Brian Arthur VOWLES, *b* at San Jose, California 24 Sept 1958.
**2** ●Allan Henry HOOVER [*181 Claproad Ridge Road, Greenwich, Connecticut, USA*], *b* in London, England 17 July 1907, *educ* Stanford Univ (AB), *m* at Los Angeles, California 17 March 1937, ●Margaret, dau of William Baylor Coberly, by his wife Winifred Wheeler, and has issue,
  **1** ●Allan Henry HOOVER, Jr [*290 Via Lerida, Greenbrae, California, USA*], *b* at Palo Alto, California 15 Nov 1938, *m* ●Marion Cutler.
  **2** ●Andrew HOOVER, *b* at Palo Alto, California 9 Nov 1940.
  **3** ●Lou Henry HOOVER, *b* at Palo Alto, California 9 Jan 1943.

# The Brother and Sister of President Hoover

**1** Theodore Jesse HOOVER, mining engineer, Dean of Sch of Engineering at Stanford Univ, *b* at West Branch, Iowa 28 Jan 1871, *educ* Stanford Univ (AB 1901), *m* at San Francisco, California 6 June 1899, Mildred Crew (*b* at West Liberty, Iowa 14 Feb 1872; *d* at Palo Alto, California 3 Sept 1940), dau of Thomas Snowden Brooke, of Maryland, by his wife Mildred Stanley, and *d* at Santa Cruz, California 5 Feb 1955, leaving issue,
  **1** ●Mildred Brooke HOOVER, *b* at Palo Alto 13 May 1901, *educ* Stanford Univ, *m* at Santa Cruz, California 27 Aug 1922, ●Cornelius Grinnell Willis (*b* at Washington, DC 26 Jan 1879) [*1 Carter Avenue, Sierra Madre, California 91024, USA; Rancho Del Oso, Davenport, California 95017, USA*], son of Dr Bailey Willis, by his wife Margaret Baker, and has issue,
    (1) ●Theodore Hoover WILLIS, oil company executive [*Rancho Del Oso, Davenport, California 95017, USA*], *b* at Palo Alto 4 June 1925, *educ* Stanford Univ (BSEng 1948, MBA 1950), *m* at Stanford 30 Sept 1944 (*m* diss by div 1968), Jessie Beryl (*b* at Elko, Nevada 9 Sept 1925), dau of

Stanley William Rigsby, by his wife Jessie Tanner, and has issue,

1*a*●Theodore Hoover WILLIS, *b* at Palo Alto 13 Nov 1947, *m* at Costa Mesa, California 3 Dec 1973, ●Ruth Ann Murray, and has issue,

●Irina Angela WILLIS, *b* at Costa Mesa, California 16 May 1974.

2*a*●Teryl Bailey WILLIS, *b* at Palo Alto 25 Sept 1949, *educ* Occidental Coll (BA 1973), *m* at Tecate, California 21 Oct 1973, ●Jeffrey Kanner.

3*a*●Tracy Jane WILLIS, *b* at Pasadena 29 Sept 1951.

(2) ●David Grinnell WILLIS, scientist [*98 Reservoir Road, Atherton, California 94025, USA*], *b* at Palo Alto 7 Nov 1926, *educ* Stanford Univ (BSEng 1947, MS 1953, PhD 1954), and Harvard (MBA 1951), *m* at Omaha, Nebraska 4 April 1953, ●Jean Lee (*b* at Omaha, Nebraska 8 April 1932), dau of James Allan, by his wife Gretchen Langdon, and has issue,

1*a*●James Allan WILLIS, *b* at Houston, Texas 15 Oct 1956, *educ* Yale.

2*a*●Cornelius Grinnel WILLIS, *b* at Redwood City, California 21 March 1961.

3*a*●Nathaniel Parker WILLIS, *b* at Redwood City, California 9 May 1965.

(3) ●Mildred Ann WILLIS, *b* at Los Angeles 9 Aug 1932, *educ* Stanford Univ, *m* 1st at Sierra Madre, California 15 Nov 1952 (*m* diss by div), John Richmond Hugens (*b* 29 Sept 1931), son of Earle Hugens (originally Huggins), by his wife Mary Jacobs, and has issue,

1*a*●John Richmond HUGENS, Jr, *b* at Pittsburgh, Pennsylvania 22 Oct 1955.

2*a*●Daniel Willis HUGENS, *b* at Pasadena, California 4 Sept 1957.

3*a*●Paul Brooke HUGENS, *b* at Pasadena, California 9 March 1961.

Mildred Ann Willis *m* 2ndly at Santa Cruz 7 June 1973, ●Robert Owen Briggs (*b* at Evansville, Illinois 7 Feb 1925) [*c/o Rancho del Oso, Davenport, California 95017, USA*], son of George Briggs, by his wife Evelyn Rist.

2 ●Hulda Brooke HOOVER, *b* at Palo Alto 19 Aug 1906, *m* at Yuba City, California 5 Dec 1925, ●Charles Alexander McLean, Jr (*b* at Spokane, Washington 13 April 1906) [*Rancho del Oso, Davenport, California 95017, USA*], son of Charles Alexander McLean, by his wife Lilian Robertson, and has issue,

(1) ●Charles Alexander McLEAN III, mining engineer [*Coast Road, Davenport, California 95017, USA*], *b* at Palo Alto 19 Sept 1931, *educ* Stanford Univ (AB, MBA, MBS), *m* at Kuala Lumpur, Malaya 28 April 1962, ●Mary Georgina (*b* in Somerset, England 15 Nov 1939), yr dau of Rear-Adm George Arthur Thring, CB, DSO and bar, DL, of Alford House, Castle Cary, Somerset, by his wife Betty Mary Blacker, JP (*see* BURKE'S *LG*, THRING *of Alford House*, and BURKE'S *Irish Family Records*, BLACKER).

(2) ●Allan Hoover McLEAN, Human Factors Engineer with Lockheed [*830 Mission Street, Santa Cruz, California, USA*], *b* at Palo Alto 10 Oct 1935, *educ* Univ of California

(MS), *m* at Reno, Nevada 9 Oct 1954, ●Hazel Bassett, and has issue,

1*a*●John David McLEAN, *b* at Santa Cruz 4 Nov 1955.

2*a*●Cheryl Anne McLEAN, *b* at Santa Cruz 20 Nov 1957.

3*a*●Skyelar Robertson McLEAN, *b* at Santa Cruz 11 June 1959.

4*a*●Theodore Kirkland McLEAN, *b* at Santa Cruz 27 March 1961.

5*a*●Allison Brooke McLEAN, *b* at Santa Cruz 26 Sept 1963.

6*a*●Robanne Canna McLEAN, *b* at Marietta, Georgia 22 March 1967.

(3) ●Robertson Brooke McLEAN [*619 San Juan Avenue, Santa Cruz, California, USA*], *b* at Palo Alto 10 July 1939, *m* at Santa Cruz 27 Feb 1960, ●Rosanna Jean Branstetter, and has issue,

1*a*●William Stuart McLEAN, *b* at Santa Cruz 16 Dec 1963.

2*a*●Judith Ann McLEAN, *b* at Santa Cruz 12 Nov 1965.

3 ●Louise Brooke HOOVER [*1801 Alameda Street, Alameda, California 94501, USA*], *b* in London, England 29 March 1908, *m* 1st at Stanford 21 June 1925 (*m* diss by div), Ernest Albert Dunbar, and has issue,

(1) ●Della Lou DUNBAR, *b* at Palo Alto 1 Aug 1926, *m* 1950, ●Wayne Swan, and has had issue,

1*a*●Jane Beatrice SWAN, *b* at Palo Alto 10 Dec 1953.

2*a*●Thomas Peter SWAN, *b* at Shelbyville, Tennessee 7 June 1955.

3*a*●Rachel Merlyn SWAN, *b* in Alaska 6 Nov 1957.

4*a* A dau, *d* an inf March 1961.

5*a*●Ernest SWAN, *b* at Palo Alto 6 March 1964.

(2) ●Judith Dawn DUNBAR, *b* at Palo Alto 27 May 1928, *m* 1950, ●Louis Centofanti [*860 Geneva Avenue, San Francisco, California, USA*].

Louise Brooke Hoover *m* 2ndly 1938 (*m* diss by div), Harold Fouts; 3rdly 1942 (*m* diss by div), Kenneth Stevenson; and 4thly 1947 (*m* diss by div), William Hawsell.

2 Mary (May) HOOVER, *b* at West Branch, Iowa 1 Sept 1876, *m* at Newbury, Oregon 1899, Cornelius Van Ness Leavitt (*b* 1 March 1874; *d* at Santa Monica, California 7 April 1962), and had issue,

●Van Ness Hoover LEAVITT [*1617 Franklin Street, Santa Monica, California, USA*], *b* at San Francisco 1 July 1908, *m* 1st at Santa Monica 30 Jan 1928 (*m* diss by div), Dorothy Juanita Berry. He *m* 2ndly at Santa Monica, ●Patricia Agnes Rheinschild (*b* 9 Nov 1914), and by her has issue,

(1) ●Michael Van Ness LEAVITT, *b* at Santa Monica 13 March 1946, *educ* UCLA (BA), *m* 1970, ●Joanne —, and has issue,

1*a*●Thomas Van Ness LEAVITT, *b* at Santa Monica 21 Jan 1972.

2*a*●Gregory Charles LEAVITT, *b* at Santa Monica 4 Feb 1974.

(2) ●David LEAVITT, *b* at Santa Monica 5 June 1951, *m* there 1973, ●Bridgit —.

# Note

[1] Through his mother President Hoover was an eighth cousin once removed of Richard Milhous Nixon, 37th President (*qv*). The relationship is as follows:

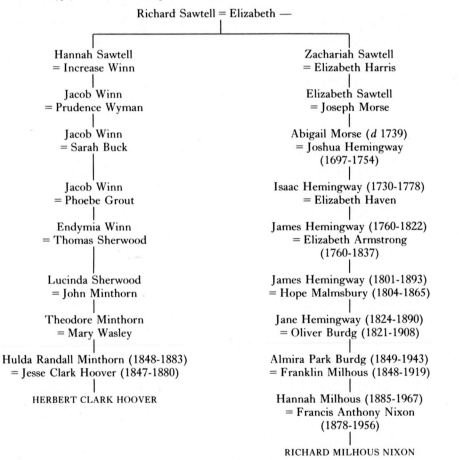

Richard Sawtell = Elizabeth —

Hannah Sawtell
= Increase Winn

Jacob Winn
= Prudence Wyman

Jacob Winn
= Sarah Buck

Jacob Winn
= Phoebe Grout

Endymia Winn
= Thomas Sherwood

Lucinda Sherwood
= John Minthorn

Theodore Minthorn
= Mary Wasley

Hulda Randall Minthorn (1848-1883)
= Jesse Clark Hoover (1847-1880)

HERBERT CLARK HOOVER

Zachariah Sawtell
= Elizabeth Harris

Elizabeth Sawtell
= Joseph Morse

Abigail Morse (*d* 1739)
= Joshua Hemingway
(1697-1754)

Isaac Hemingway (1730-1778)
= Elizabeth Haven

James Hemingway (1760-1822)
= Elizabeth Armstrong
(1760-1837)

James Hemingway (1801-1893)
= Hope Malmsbury (1804-1865)

Jane Hemingway (1824-1890)
= Oliver Burdg (1821-1908)

Almira Park Burdg (1849-1943)
= Franklin Milhous (1848-1919)

Hannah Milhous (1885-1967)
= Francis Anthony Nixon
(1878-1956)

RICHARD MILHOUS NIXON

# Franklin Delano Roosevelt

## 1882-1945

———

32nd President of the
United States of America

1933-1945

FRANKLIN DELANO ROOSEVELT, 32ND PRESIDENT

# Franklin Delano Roosevelt

## 1882-1945

### 32nd President of the United States of America

### 1933-1945

WHEN FRANKLIN ROOSEVELT received the Democratic nomination in 1932 he was not universally viewed as an outstanding contender. The advantage of a distinguished name was cancelled out by the fact that he was of the opposite political persuasion from his distant relative Theodore Roosevelt. For some people of his patrician circle, not to mention prosperous Republicans, he was suspect in having deserted what they took to be the only proper allegiance. How could a man educated at Groton and Harvard, a wealthy landed proprietor, hobnob with uncouth Democrats such as Al Smith? Many observers considered him a political lightweight. He had entered politics in a dilettante spirit. He had followed Theodore in becoming Assistant Secretary of the Navy and a vice-presidential nominee, but with the difference that he ran in 1920 and suffered a crashing defeat. Thereafter, disabled by a severe attack of poliomyelitis, he disappeared from politics for a while, and for the rest of his life could only walk a few steps with the aid of leg-braces. He made a good impression in a nominating speech for Al Smith, which described the candidate as "the happy warrior". Governor Smith, however, had accompanied the invitation to Roosevelt with a copy of the prepared text of the address. When Smith lost the election to Hoover in 1928 he still regarded Roosevelt as a second-rater, with slightly disagreeable upper-class mannerisms. Smith was mortified when Roosevelt, stepping into his shoes as Governor of New York, began to sound and act like a leader. At Albany he launched a vigorous welfare program to cope with the already grim effects of the Depression. Roosevelt's star rose as Smith's declined. Yet the columnist Walter Lippman typified the reaction of many when he wrote in 1932 that, so far as one could gather, Roosevelt was simply a young man who would very much like to be President.

Roosevelt did very much like being President. Perhaps at bottom he always remained a little superficial. He was no expert in economics. He had been brought up to think that economy and budget-balancing were the only remedies for hard times. Deficit financing on the Keynes model was a mystery to him. Beyond putting the American economy on its feet, he had no intention—despite the accusations of his enemies—of revolutionizing the social and economic order. He probably had less instinctive compassion for the plight of the poor than the warm-hearted Eleanor Roosevelt, the cousin he married, whose sterling qualities he benefited from but sometimes failed to appreciate. Exasperated associates complained that Roosevelt was not a good administrator. Washington in the 1930s was a chaos of overlapping bureaucracies. Their activities were not firmly co-ordinated. Roosevelt, temperamentally unable to rebuke or get rid of subordinates he thought incompetent, often appeared devious or even dishonest. He would jovially evade discussion of subjects he was disinclined to tackle. He made some bad mistakes. One of the worst miscalculations was Roosevelt's "court-packing" scheme of 1937-38, when he threatened to alter the composition of the Supreme Court and alienated men whose backing he needed.

Such defects were outweighed by F.D.R.'s strengths. He never succeeded in wiping out unemployment. There were still several million men out of work in 1940; it took the boom years of World War II to restore prosperity. What Roosevelt did accomplish, with magnificent aplomb, was the restoration of the nation's courage. When he took office in 1933, Hitler was coming to power in Germany. It was widely felt that some equally drastic fate awaited the United States. Roosevelt lived up to his inaugural reassurance that "the only thing we have to fear is fear itself". Paternal, genial, confident, resolute, he projected his confidence by means of superbly effective "fireside chats" upon the radio. He developed a consummate skill in dealing with the press. No President before or since has been on such good terms with America's fourth estate.

Words alone would not have carried far. Roosevelt backed them up with an immediate torrent of legislation designed to provide relief and jobs for the unemployed, and to start the wheels turning again. New agencies—NRA, CCC, WPA, the "alphabet soup" of the New Deal—mushroomed overnight. Some were ruled unconstitutional and killed by the Court. Some were ill-conceived. Some were wasteful. Nevertheless, when taken together they had a noticeably beneficial effect upon the unemployment figures, and a more important psychological effect. They demonstrated that the Depression was being tackled by an Administration that made up in enthusiastic dedication whatever it lacked in business efficiency.

The result was a substantial victory for Roosevelt when he ran again for office in 1936. During his second term the approach of war in Europe

(ANNA) ELEANOR ROOSEVELT, MRS ROOSEVELT

became an additional source of worry. Here again F.D.R. was not well equipped by previous training. He was interested in naval questions, but otherwise not versed in diplomacy or strategy. His basic assets as hitherto were confidence and readiness to act. For Roosevelt the worst sin of an executive was to do nothing; errors could be rectified, but a power-vacuum was disastrous. He did not deliberately engineer American involvement in World War II, as some conspiracy-minded historians have alleged. Nevertheless, he did stretch presidential prerogative to the limit in committing the nation to large-scale support of the Allies; and in a sense he welcomed the Japanese attack on Pearl Harbor at the end of 1941. The situation was now clear; the United States was no longer equivocally placed between neutrality and intervention. Moreover, war with the Axis powers silenced those who had criticized him for accepting a further nomination in 1940. If a third presidential term was unprecedented, then so was America's situation.

Controversy surrounds Roosevelt's role as wartime leader. Outwardly he was as ebullient, charming and persuasive as ever. In 1944 the nation paid him the extraordinary honor of nomination for a fourth term. By then the war was clearly in its last phase, and the nation's war effort had in general been organized with great effect. The Allies were dominant in the air, at sea and on land. Germany and Japan were reeling under the weight of combined assaults. The charge against Roosevelt is first that he was an exhausted man behind the façade of robustness, who should not have clung to office in 1944; and second that, apart from being fatigued, he was no match in summitry for Churchill or Stalin. Such charges have of course the advantages of hindsight. Roosevelt did not know that he had only a few months to live. He would have been amused to discover that he was to be accused both of giving way too easily at Casablanca, Yalta and Teheran, and of plotting an anti-Communist American imperium. The truth may be that, being human, he did not exactly know what he was aiming at, beyond ending the war. Being an American, he assumed that his nation had a moral obligation to shape the peace. Being Roosevelt, and more truly the "happy warrior" than Al Smith, he was ready to believe that things would come out right in the end.

# Chronology

1882    Born at Springwood, Hyde Park, Dutchess County, New York 30 Jan.

1896    Entered Groton School, Groton, Mass.

1899    Left Groton.

1900    Entered Harvard University Sept.

1903    Graduated from Harvard with AB degree 24 June.

1904    Entered Columbia Law School, New York City.

1905    Toured Europe on honeymoon trip.

1907    Admitted to the New York Bar; employed as junior clerk in law firm of Carter, Ledyard and Milburn, of New York.

1910    Elected to New York State Senate 8 Nov.

1911    Took seat in New York State Senate Jan; degree of Master Mason conferred by Holland Lodge No 8, New York City, 28 Nov.

1912    Re-elected to State Senate 5 Nov.

1913    Appointed Assistant Secretary of the Navy by President Wilson April.

1914    Defeated in Democratic primary for the Senate.

1918    Toured European naval bases July-Sept.

1919    Travelled to Europe to supervise dismantling of naval establishment Jan-Feb.

1920    Nominated for Vice-President by Democratic National Convention at San Francisco 6 July; resigned as Assistant Secretary of the Navy 6 Aug; returned to law practice; defeated in election for Vice-President 2 Nov.

1921    Suffered attack of poliomyelitis at Campobello, New Brunswick, Canada Aug.

1928    Nominated for Governor of New York by Democratic State Convention at Rochester 25 Sept; elected 6 Nov.

1929    Took office as Governor of New York 1 Jan.

1930    Re-elected Governor 4 Nov.

1932    Nominated for President by Democratic National Convention at Chicago 1 July; election day 8 Nov.

1933    Presidential Electors cast their ballots (472 for Roosevelt; 59 for Hoover) 9 Jan; electoral vote tabulated by Congress and Roosevelt and Garner officially declared elected 8 Feb; shot at in assassination attempt by Giuseppe Zangara at Miami, Florida 15 Feb; inaugurated as 32nd President of the United States of America on the east portico of the Capitol 4 March; signed Emergency Banking Relief Act

9 March; signed Economy Act 20 March; signed Beer-Wine Revenue Act 22 March; issued executive order abolishing Federal Farm Board 27 March; signed Civilian Conservation Corps Reconstruction Relief Act 31 March; gold standard abandoned 19 April; signed Federal Emergency Relief Act 12 May; signed Agricultural Adjustment Act 13 May; signed Tennessee Valley Authority Act 18 May; signed Tennessee Valley Authority Act 18 May; signed Federal Securities Act 27 May; signed Home Owners Refinancing Act 13 June; signed National Industrial Recovery Act, Banking Act of 1933, Farm Credit Act and Emergency Railroad Transportation Act and pocket vetoed amendment to Federal Farm Loan Act 16 June; issued executive order to federal contractors to conform to National Recovery Administration codes or face cancellation 10 Aug; issued executive order modifying embargo on newly-mined gold to allow restricted sale and export at world price 29 Aug; issued executive order organizing Commodity Credit Corporation 18 Oct; issued executive order revising retail code 23 Oct; recognized USSR 16 Nov; 21st Amendment (repealing 18th ("Prohibition") Amendment) declared ratified 5 Dec; issued executive order providing for purchase of newly-mined US silver 21 Dec; restored civil rights to 1,500 people who had served prison terms for violations of Selective Service Act during World War I 24 Dec; issued proclamation relinquishing federal control of state banks not members of the federal reserve system 30 Dec.

1934    Delivered first State of the Union message to Congress 3 Jan; sent budget message to Congress 4 Jan; signed Liquor Tax Act 11 Jan; sent special message to Congress requesting additional gold legislation 15 Jan; signed Gold Reserve Act 30 Jan; issued proclamation fixing price of gold and value of dollar and signed Farm Mortgage Refinancing Act 31 Jan; issued executive order establishing export-import bank for trade with USSR 2 Feb; signed Civil Works Emergency Relief Act 15 Feb; signed Crop Loan Act 23 Feb; issued executive order establishing National Recovery Administration board of review 27 Feb; vetoed Relief Bill 1 March; issued executive order excluding from future Government contracts all companies and individuals not certifying compliance with National Recovery Administration codes 5 March; signed Philippine Independence Act 31 March; signed Jones-Connally Act 7 April; signed Cotton Control Act 21 April; signed Home Owners Loan Act 28 April; signed Jones-Costigan Act 9 May; signed six Crime Control Acts 18 May; signed Municipal Bankruptcy Act 24 May; issued proclamation prohibiting sale of arms and munitions to Bolivia and Paraguay 28 May; delivered Memorial Day address at Gettysburg 30 May; reviewed fleet outside New York harbour 31 May; signed Federal Securities Exchange Act 6 June; signed Corporate Bankruptcy Act 7 June; signed Airmail Act, Reciprocal Tariff Act and Farm Mortgage Foreclosure Act 12 June; signed National Guard Act 15 June; signed Free Zone Act 18 June; Silver Purchase Act and Labour disputes joint resolution 19 June; received honorary LLD degree from Yale University 20 June; signed Tobacco Control Act, Federal Farm Bankruptcy Act and National Housing Act 28 June; issued executive order prohibiting shipment of arms and military equipment to cuba except under State Department licence 29 June; issued executive order abolishing National Recovery Administration board of review 30 June; went on cruise to Hawaii July; issued executive order recalling all silver to mints within 90 days 9 Aug; issued proclamation authorizing waiving of import duties on hay and other forage 10 Aug; issued proclamation announcing reciprocal tariff treaty with Cuba 24 Aug; dedicated monument to pioneers at Harrodsburg, Kentucky 16 Nov.

1935    Delivered second State of the Union message to Congress; sent special message to Congress asking for US adherence to World Court 16 Jan; issued executive order withdrawing all remaining public lands from use 8 Feb; signed Emergency Relief Appropriation Act 8 April; signed Soil Conservation Act 27 April; issued executive order establishing Resettlement Administration 1 May; issued executive order establishing Rural Electrification Administration 11 May; vetoed soldiers' bonus 22 May; Supreme Court declared National Industrial Recovery Act of 1933 unconstitutional 27 May; issued executive order establishing National Resources Committee 7 June; sent special tax message to Congress 19 June; issued executive order establishing National Youth Administration 26 June; signed Labor Relations Act 5 July; signed War Pension Act 13 Aug; signed Social Security Act 14 Aug; signed Banking Act of 1935 23 Aug; signed Public Utility Holding Company Act 28 Aug; signed joint resolution for mandatory ban on arms shipments to belligerents 31 Aug; issued proclamation through State Department imposing embargo on arms and minitions to both Italy and Ethiopia 5 Oct; issued proclamation warning US citizens that travel on Italian or Ethiopian ships was undertaken at their own risk 6 Oct.

1936    Delivered third State of the Union message to Congress 3 Jan; issued executive order placing Kure Island under control of the Navy Department 21 Feb; signed amended neutrality resolution and Soil Conservation and Domestic Allotment Act 29 Feb; Supreme Court invalidated Municipal Bankruptcy Act of 1934 25 May; signed Federal Anti-Price-Discrimination Act 20 June; signed Revenue Act of 1936 22 June; signed Revenue Act of 1936 22 June; signed Merchant Marine Act 26 June; renominated for President by Democratic National Convention at Philadelphia 26 June; pushed button to open Great Lakes Exposition in Cleveland, Ohio 27 June; signed Government Contracts Act 30 June; issued executive order placing all first, second and third class postmasters under Civil Service 20 July; conferred with Canadian leaders at Quebec, Canada 31 July; election day 3 Nov; issued executive order regarding export of military aircraft 10 Nov; pushed button to open San Francisco-Oakland Bridge 12 Nov; visited Brazil, Argentina and Uruguay Nov-Dec; Presidential Electors cast their ballots (523 for Roosevelt; 8 for Alfred Mossman Landon, the Republican candidate) 14 Dec.

1937    Delivered fourth State of the Union message to Congress 6 Jan; electoral votes tabulated by Congress and Roosevelt and Garner officially declared elected 6 Jan; signed joint resolution placing embargo on shipments of arms and munitions to Spain 8 Jan; sent special message to Congress asking for legislation to reorganize executive branch 12 Jan; inaugurated for second term as President on the east portico of the Capitol 20 Jan; sent special message to Congress recommending reorganization of the judiciary 5 Feb; signed Reciprocal Trade Agreements Act and Supreme Court Retirement Act 1 March; signed Neutrality Act of 1937 1 May; sent special message to Congress asking for end to oil-depletion clause of income tax law 1 June; signed National Housing Act 1 Sept; issued executive order prohibiting transport of war materials to China and Japan in Government-owned merchant ships 14 Sept; made western tour Sept; sent special message to Congress recommending legislation for governmental reorganization, wages and hours regulation, tax relief for small businesses, agricultural aid and conservation, and development of natural resources 15 Nov.

1938    Delivered fifth State of the Union message to Congress 3 Jan; sent special defence armaments message to Congress 28 Jan; signed amended Federal Housing Act 4 Feb; signed Agricultural Adjustment Act of 1938 16 Feb; sent special message to Congress with recommendations to combat recession 14 April; sent special message on federal and state tax exemptions 25 April; signed

Naval Expansion Act of 1938 17 May; signed Emergency Relief Appropriation Act 21 June; signed Civil Aeronautics Act 23 June; signed Food, Drug and Cosmetic Act 24 June; signed Fair Labor Standards Act 25 June; reviewed fleet at San Francisco 14 July; visited Panama and Panama Canal Zone 4-5 Aug; visited Canada and received honorary degree of DCL from Queen's University, Kingston, Ontario Aug; appealed to European leaders to continue negotiations regarding Czechoslovakia 26 and 27 Sept; Munich Agreement 30 Sept; announced that German refugees in US on visitors' permits would not be forced to return 18 Nov.

1939    Delivered sixth State of the Union message to Congress 4 Jan; signed Deficiency Relief Act 7 Feb; sent special message to Congress urging federal aid to combat water pollution 16 Feb; opened Golden Gate Exposition in San Francisco by radio from Key West, Florida 18 Feb; attended fleet maneuvers 19 Feb-3 March; issued proclamation ending embargo on sales of arms and munitions to Spain 1 April; signed Administrative Reorganization Act of 1939 3 April; signed War Department Appropriation Act and sent special message to Congress asking for immediate construction of additional naval bases in the Pacific, Alaska, Puerto Rico, and continental US 26 April; opened New York World's Fair in New York City 30 April; welcomed King George VI and Queen Elizabeth of Great Britain at the White House 8 June; signed Emergency Relief Appropriation Act of 1939 and Agricultural Appropriation Act 30 June; sent special message to Congress asking for revision of neutrality laws 14 July; signed Hatch Act 2 Aug; broadcast to nation on outbreak of war in Europe 3 Sept; issued proclamation of neutrality and proclamation prohibiting export of arms and munitions to the belligerents 5 Sept; issued proclamation of limited national emergency 8 Sept; issued proclamation restricting use of US territorial waters by foreign submarines 18 Oct; signed Neutrality Act of 1939 4 Nov; laid cornerstone of Jefferson Memorial at Washington, DC 15 Nov; condemned Russian invasion of Finland 1 Dec; issued executive order extending ten million dollars credit to Finland for the purchase of supplies in US 10 Dec.

1940    Delivered seventh State of the Union message to Congress 3 Jan; sent special message to Congress urging immediate appropriation of fifteen million dollars for strategic war materials 13 Feb; inspected Panama Canal 27 Feb; vetoed Bill requiring deportation of alien drug addicts 6 April; issued executive order prohibiting transactions in Norwegian and Danish credits and assets in US following German invasion of Norway and Denmark 10 April; condemned invasion of Norway and Denmark 13 April; issued proclamation of neutrality in war between Germany and The Netherlands, Belgium and Luxembourg and issued executive order prohibiting transactions in Dutch, Belgian and Luxembourg credits and assets in US 11 May; asked Congress for $1,182,000,000 in additional appropriations for national defense 16 May; sent special message to Congress asking for additional $1,277,741,170 for national defense and authority to call up National Guard and reserves 31 May; received appeal for military supplies from the British Prime Minister, Winston Churchill 3 June; issued proclamation of neutrality in war between Italy and France and Great Britain and condemned Italian invasion of France 10 June; sent special message to Congress asking for additional fifty million dollars for the relief of refugees and signed Navy Department Appropriation Act 11 June; signed War Department Appropriation Act 13 June; signed Revenue Act of 1940 25 June; signed Emergency Relief Appropriation Act of 1940 26 June; signed Alien Registration Act 29 June; issued proclamation prohibiting export of war materials and strategic raw products except by State Department licence 2 July;

outlined Four Freedoms during press conference 5 July; sent special message to Congress asking for additional $4,848,171,957 for national defense 10 July; renominated for President by Democratic National Convention at Chicago 18 July; sent special message to Congress again asking that National Guard be ordered into active service 29 July; signed Act authorizing induction of National Guard into federal service 27 Aug; sent special message to inform Congress of acquisition of naval and air bases from Great Britain in exchange for 50 destroyers 3 Sept; signed Selective Training and Service Act 16 Sept; issued proclamation banning export of scrap iron and steel to any nation outside western hemisphere except Great Britain 26 Sept; signed Excess Profits Tax-amortization Tax 8 Oct; signed ratification of Treaty of Havana 10 Oct; issued proclamation of neutrality in war between Italy and Greece 15 Nov; signed Act amending Sedition Act of 1918 to make sabotage a federal offence in peacetime as well as wartime 2 Dec; Presidential Electors cast their ballots (449 for Roosevelt; 82 for Wendell Lewis Wilkie, the Republican candidate) 16 Dec; established Office of Production Management 20 Dec.

1941      Electoral votes tabulated by Congress and Roosevelt and Wallace officially declared elected 6 Jan; delivered eighth State of the Union message to Congress 6 Jan; inaugurated for third term as President (the first and only President to serve a third term) 20 Jan; signed Lend-Lease Act 11 March; sent special message to Congress requesting seven thousand million dollars to finance lend-lease program 12 March; dedicated National Gallery of Art at Washington, DC 17 March; issued executive order establishing National Defense Mediation Board 19 March; signed Defense Aid Supplemental Appropriation Act 27 March; issued executive order forming United Service Organizations for National Defense 7 April; announced agreement with Denmark providing for US military bases in Greenland 10 April; issued executive order for increased production of heavy bomber aircraft 5 May; sent special message to Congress asking for additional $22,500,000 to train defense workers 14 May; declared Vichy Government's collaboration with Germany a menace to the western hemisphere 15 May; sent special message to Congress requesting legislation to build a pipeline from Texas to Middle Atlantic refineries 20 May; signed Crop Loan Act 26 May; issued proclamation of unlimited national emergency 27 May; signed Act permitting requisition of idle foreign vessels in US waters 6 June; issued executive order of seizure by the Army of North American Aviation Company plant at Inglewood, California following a wildcat strike 9 June; issued executive order prohibiting transactions in US credits and assets by Germany, Italy and other European countries 14 June; issued executive order to State Department to close German and Italian Consulates in US 16 June; sent special message to Congress announcing the sinking of US merchant ship *Robin Moor* in the S Atlantic by a German submarine 20 June; promised US aid to USSR following German invasion 24 June; informed Congress of landing of US troops in Iceland, Trinidad and British Guiana 7 July; sent his personal representative, Harry L. Hopkins, to confer with Winston Churchill in London 13 July; issued proclamation black listing 1,800 Latin American firms and individuals for aiding Germany and Italy 17 July; sent special message to Congress urging extension of one-year military training by selectees; issued executive order nationalizing Philippine armed forces for the duration of the emergency and executive order prohibiting transactions in US credits and assets by Japan and China 26 July; sent special message to Congress requesting price control legislation to avert inflation, signed Act authorizing construction of oil pipelines, and issued executive orders establishing Economic Defence Board conferred with British

Prime Minister Winston Churchill on board USS *Augusta* and HMS *Prince of Wales*, nr Argentia, Newfoundland and Canada 9-12 Aug; announced Atlantic Charter 14 Aug; signed Service Extension Act 18 Aug; signed Tax Act 20 Sept; sent special message to Congress requesting authorization to arm merchant ships and revision of the Neutrality Act of 1939 9 Oct; signed Act authorizing requisition of inventories of vital materials for national defence 16 Oct; issued executive order establishing Office of Facts and Figures 24 Oct; issued executive order establishing Lend-Lease Administration 28 Oct; sent special message to Congress again requesting revision of Neutrality Act of 1939 13 Nov; Pearl Harbor attacked by the Japanese 7 Dec; addressed joint session of Congress asking for a declaration of war against Japan 8 Dec; war declared with only one dissenting vote; Germany and Italy declared war on the US 11 Dec; issued executive order appointing commission to investigate Pearl Harbor attack and executive order establishing Office of Defence Transportation 18 Dec; issued executive order establishing Office of Censorship 19 Dec; signed amended Selected Service Act 22 Dec; conferred with Winston Churchill at the White House 22-23 Dec; issued proclamation pledging support to the Philippines 28 Dec.

1942     Signed joint declaration of United Nations pledging co-operation for victory 1 Jan; delivered ninth State of the Union message to Congress 6 Jan; issued executive order establishing National War Labor Board 12 Jan; sent special message to Congress recommending legislation to handle private claims against the Federal Government 14 Jan; issued executive order establishing War Production Board 16 Jan; Battle of Macassar Strait inflicted severe damage on a Japanese invasion convoy 24-27 Jan; signed Emergency Price Control Act of 1942 30 Jan; issued executive order establishing War Shipping Administration 7 Feb; vetoed Bill to provide for registration of certain foreign propaganda agencies 9 Feb; issued executive order establishing National Housing Agency 24 Feb; Battles of Java Sea and Sunda Strait 27-28 Feb; issued executive order reorganizing War Department 28 Feb; issued executive order establishing Office of Alien Property Custodian 11 March; issued executive order reorganizing Navy Department 12 March; issued executive order establishing War Relocation Authority 18 March; received message of surrender of Bataan to the Japanese 10 April; issued executive order establishing War Manpower Commission 18 April; sent special message to Congress outlining seven-point economic stabilization program 27 April; Corregidor surrendered 6 May; Battle of Coral Sea halted Japanese advance 7-8 May; signed Act establishing Women's Army Auxiliary Corps 14 May; sent special message to Congress requesting additional $600 million for war housing 27 May; conferred with the Soviet Foreign Minister Vyacheslav M. Molotov at the White House 29 May-1 June; Japanese Navy defeated in Battle of Midway 3-6 June; signed joint resolution of state of war between US and Hungary, Rumania and Bulgaria 5 June; received King George II of the Hellenes at the White House 10 June; issued executive order establishing Office of War Information and military order establishing Office of Strategic Services 13 June; conferred with Winston Churchill at Hyde Park, New York and the White House 20-25 June; received King Peter II of Yugoslavia at the White House 24 June; issued military order establishing military commission to try eight captured German saboteurs 2 July; signed Act establishing Women Appointed for Voluntary Emergency Service (WAVES), the women's branch of the Navy, 30 July; Battle of Savo Island 8-9 Aug; sent special message to Congress reiterating seven-point anti-inflation program 7 Sept; issued executive order providing for co-ordination of rubber program 17 Sept, made inspection tour of war plants and Army, Navy and Air Force training camps 17 Sept-1 Oct; signed Stabilization Act of 1942 2 Oct; sent special message to Congress asking for re-establishment of Veterans' Rehabilitation Service 9 Oct; signed Act repealing clause of Neutrality Act of 1939 which required US citizens living abroad to return every two years to retain citizenship 10 Oct; signed Act to increase income tax revenue 21 Oct; sent special message to Congress urging integration of war production with Canada 2 Nov; naval Battle of Guadalcanal ending in victory over the Japanese 12-15 Nov; signed Act lowering the draft age to 18 13 Nov; issued executive order establishing Petroleum Administration for War 2 Dec; issued executive order centralizing war food policies under the Department of Agriculture 5 Dec; signed joint resolution increasing pay of over one and a quarter million Government workers 24 Dec.

1943    Delivered tenth State of the Union message to Congress 7 Jan; flew to Trinidad 11 Jan; flew from Trinidad to Brazil 12 Jan; flew from Brazil to Gambia 13 Jan; flew from Gambia to Casablanca, French Morocco 14 Jan; conferred with Winston Churchill at Casablanca 14-21 Jan; reviewed American troops at Rabat and Port Lyautey, Morocco 21 Jan; flew from Marrakesh to Gambia 25 Jan; visited Liberia 27 Jan; flew to Brazil 27 Jan; conferred with President Getulio Vargas of Brazil 28-29 Jan; flew to Trinidad 29 Jan; flew to Miami 30 Jan; returned by train to Washington 31 Jan; issued executive order establishing interdepartmental committee within the Department of Justice to consider cases of subversive activities by federal employees 5 Feb; issued executive order establishing 48 hour minimum work week in war plants 9 Feb; Japanese fleet destroyed in Battle of Bismarck Sea 2-3 March; made inspection tour of training camps 13-18 April; issued executive order establishing Solid Fuels Administration for War 19 April; visited Mexico 20-21 April; continued inspection tour of training camps 22-28 April; returned to Washington 29 April; issued executive order to Secretary of the Interior to seize coal mines 1 May; conferred with Winston Churchill at the White House (Trident Conference) 12-25 May; issued executive order establishing Office of War Mobilization 27 May; signed final amendment to Lanham Act 7 July; allied invasion of Sicily began 10 July; issued executive order establishing Office of Economic Warfare 15 July; conferred with Winston Churchill at Quebec, Canada (Quadrant Conference) 17-24 Aug; allied invasion of Italy began 3 Sept; Italy surrendered unconditionally 8 Sept; issued executive order establishing Foreign Economic Administration 25 Sept; sent special message to Congress recommending self-government for Puerto Rico 28 Sept; sent special message to Congress requesting authority to proclaim freedom of the Philippines 6 Oct; again ordered Secretary of the Interior to seize coal mines 1 Nov; signed Act extending terms of President Manuel Quegon and Vice-President Sergio Osmena of the Philippines until the Japanese had been expelled 13 Nov; arrived at Oran, Algeria 20 Nov; flew to Tunis 21 Nov; conferred with Churchill and Generalissimo Chiang Kai-shek in Cairo 22-26 Nov; flew to Teheran 27 Nov; conferred with Churchill and Stalin in Teheran 28 Nov-1 Dec; flew from Teheran to Cairo 2 Dec; conferred with Churchill and President Inönü of Turkey in Cairo 4-6 Dec; flew to Tunis 7 Dec; flew to Malta with Gen Eisenhower 8 Dec; flew to Sicily 9 Dec; sailed from Italy 10 Dec; arrived in Washington 17 Dec; signed Act repealing Chinese expulsion laws 17 Dec; issued executive order to US Army to seize railroads 27 Dec.

1944    Sent 11th State of the Union message to Congress 11 Jan; issued executive order establishing War Refugee Board 22 Jan; US forces invaded Marshall Islands 31 Jan; US forces invaded Admiralty Islands 29 Feb; spent holiday at Hobcaw

Barony, nr Georgetown, S Carolina 8 April-7 May; signed Lend-lease Extension Act 17 May; allied invasion of France (D Day) 6 June; US forces invaded Mariana Islands 15 June; Battle of Philippine Seas 19-20 June; signed Public Health Service Act of 1944 1 July; US forces captured St Lô 18 July; renominated for President by Democratic National Convention at Chicago 20 July; visited Pearl Harbor, Hawaii 26 July; visited Alaska 3 Aug; Dumbarton Oaks Conference 21 Aug; conferred with Churchill at Quebec, Canada 11-16 Sept; US forces entered Germany 12 Sept; US forces invaded Palan Islands 14 Sept; issued executive order expanding Office of War Mobilization to Office of War Mobilization and Reconversion 3 Oct; US forces invaded the Philippines 20 Oct; Aachen captured 21 Oct; decisive defeat of the Japanese at Battle of Leyte Gulf 23-26 Oct; election day 7 Nov; Battle of the Bulge 16-26 Dec; Presidential Electors cast their ballots (432 for Roosevelt; 99 for Thomas Edmund Dewey, the Republican candidate) 18 Dec.

1945 Electoral vote tabulated by Congress and Roosevelt and Truman officially declared elected 5 Jan; delivered twelfth (and last) State of the Union message to Congress 6 Jan; inaugurated for fourth term as President (the first and only President to serve a fourth term) 20 Jan; left Washington for Yalta Conference 22 Jan; arrived in Malta 2 Feb; flew from Malta to Yalta, Crimea 3 Feb; conferred with Churchill and Stalin 3-11 Feb; flew to Egypt 12 Feb; sailed through Suez Canal to Alexandria 14 Feb; sailed from Alexandria to Algiers 17 Feb; arrived back in Washington 28 Feb; addressed Congress on the Yalta Conference 1 March; sent special message to Congress urging strengthening of Trade Agreements Act 26 March; held last press conference at the Little White House, Warm Springs, Georgia 5 April; died suddenly of cerebral haemorrhage at the Little White House 12 April; buried at Hyde Park, New York 15 April. He was the seventh President to die in office, having served longer than any other President.

# The Writings of President Franklin Delano Roosevelt

*The Happy Warrior, Alfred E. Smith* (1928)

# Lineage of President
# Franklin Delano Roosevelt

JACOBUS ROOSEVELT, yst surv son of Nicholas Roosevelt, Alderman of New York (*see* LINEAGE OF PRESIDENT THEODORE ROOSEVELT, *p 421*), *b* 1692, *m* 31 Jan 1713, Catharina (*bapt* 25 Feb 1694; *d* 1761), eldest dau of Johannes Hardenbroeck (a native of Amsterdam), by his wife Sara Van Laer, and *d* 1776, leaving with other issue a 6th son,

ISAAC ROOSEVELT, of New York, sugar refiner, mem New York Constitutional Convention and New York Senate, a founder of New York Hospital, *bapt* 18 Dec 1726, *m* in Dutchess County, New York 1752, Cornelia (*b* 1734; *d* 13 Nov 1789), dau of Martinus Hoffman, of Dutchess County (of Finnish-Swedish descent), and *d* 1794, having had with other issue,

JAMES ROOSEVELT, of Hyde Park, New York, and Mount Hope, Dutchess County, New York, *b* 1760, *educ* Princeton, *m* 1st 1786, Mary Eliza Walton (*b* 1769; *d* 1810), and had issue, ten children. He *m* 2ndly 1812, Catherine Eliza Barclay (*d* 1816), and by her had issue, two children. He *m* 3rdly 1821, Harriet Howland, and *d* 1847. His son (by his 1st marriage),

ISAAC ROOSEVELT, MD, of Mount Hope, Dutchess County, *b* 1790, *educ* Princeton, and Columbia Univ, *m* 1827, Mary Rebecca (*b* 1809; *d* 1886), dau of John Aspinwall, Jr, of New York[1], by his wife Susan Howland (sister of Harriet Howland—*see above*), and *d* 1863, leaving with other issue,

JAMES ROOSEVELT, of Mount Hope (burnt down 1865), and later of Springwood, Hyde Park, New York, railway executive, *b* at Mount Hope 16 July 1828, *educ* Dr Hyde's Academy, Lee, Mass, New York Univ, Union Coll, Schenectady (AB 1847), and Harvard, *m* 1st 1853, his 2nd cousin Rebecca Brien (*b* 15 Jan 1831; *d* 21 Aug 1876), dau of Gardiner Greene Howland, and had issue (*see* HALF-BROTHER OF PRESIDENT FRANKLIN DELANO ROOSEVELT, *p 506*). He *m* 2ndly at Algonac, nr Newburgh, New York 7 Oct 1880, Sara (*b* at Algonac 21 Sept 1854; *d* at Springwood, Hyde Park 7 Sept 1941), 5th and yst dau of Warren Delano[2], by his wife Catherine Robbins, dau of Joseph Lyman[3], and *d* at Springwood, Hyde Park 8 Dec 1900, having by her had issue,

FRANKLIN DELANO ROOSEVELT, **32nd President of the United States of America.**

# The Descendants of President Franklin Delano Roosevelt

FRANKLIN DELANO ROOSEVELT *m* at 6-8 East Seventy-sixth Street, New York 17 March 1905, his 5th cousin once removed (Anna) Eleanor (*b* at New York City 12 Oct 1884; *d* there 7 Nov 1962, *bur* with her husband at Hyde Park, New York), only dau of Elliott Roosevelt (brother of President Theodore Roosevelt—*see* BROTHERS AND SISTERS OF PRESIDENT THEODORE ROOSEVELT, *p 423*), by his wife Anna Rebecca Hall, and had issue,

1 ●Anna Eleanor ROOSEVELT, *b* at New York City 3 May 1906, *m* 1st 1926 (*m* diss by div), Curtis B. Dall, of New York, and has issue,
  1 ●Anna DALL BOETTIGER (adopted by her stepfather), *b* 25 March 1927, *m* at Phoenix, Arizona July 1948, ●Van H. Seagraves [*1813 Sheppard Street NW, Washington, DC 20011, USA*], and has issue,
    (1) ●Nicholas Delano SEAGRAVES [*1813 Sheppard Street NW, Washington, DC 20011, USA*], *b* at Portland, Oregon Aug 1949.
    (2) ●David SEAGRAVES.
    (3) ●Anna Eleanor SEAGRAVES, *b* 16 Aug 1955.
  2 ●Curtis Roosevelt DALL BOETTIGER (adopted by his stepfather), later assumed the name of Curtis ROOSEVELT, advertising executive, later chief of non-governmental liaison section, Public Information Dept UN [*41 Morton Street, New York, New York 10014, USA*], *b* 19 April 1930, *educ* Southwestern Military and Naval Head, Lake Geneva, Wisconsin, *m* 1st at Santa Monica, California 23 May 1950 (*m* diss by div 1954), Robin H. Edwards, and has issue,
    ●Juliana ROOSEVELT, *b* 1952.
  Curtis Roosevelt *m* 2ndly March 1955 (*m* diss by div), Ruth W. Sublette. He *m* 3rdly 2 May 1961, ●Jeanette Schlottman.
Anna Eleanor Roosevelt *m* 2ndly at New York Jan 1935 (*m* diss by div 1949), John Boettiger, newspaper correspondent (*b* 1900; *d* at Manhattan, New York 31 Oct 1950), and has further issue,
  3 ●John Roosevelt BOETTIGER, Associate Prof in Human Development, Hampshire Coll [*143 Woodbridge Street, South Hadley, Massachusetts 01075, USA*], *b* at Seattle 30 March 1939, *m* at De Witt, New York Aug 1960, ●Deborah Ann Bentley (*b* 1938), and has issue,
    (1) ●Adam BOETTIGER.
    (2) ●Sara BOETTIGER.
    (3) ●Joshua BOETTIGER.
Anna Eleanor Roosevelt *m* 3rdly at Malibu, California 11 Nov 1952, ●James A. Halsted, MD [*RFD2, Hillsdale, New York 12529, USA*].
2 ●James ROOSEVELT, mem of the House of Representatives, 84th-89th Congresses, Col US Marine Corps, US Rep to UN Economic and Social Council, Dir Investors Overseas Service, financial consultant, teacher at Univ of California [*27 Point Loma Road, Corona Del Mar, California 92625, USA; 321 South Beverly Drive, Beverly Hills, California 90212, USA*], *b* at New York City 23 Dec 1907, *educ* Groton Sch, and Harvard, *m* 1st at Brookline, Mass 1930 (*m* diss by div 1940), Betsey, dau of Dr Harvey Cushing, of Boston, and has issue,
  1 ●Sara Delano ROOSEVELT, *b* at Boston 13 March 1932, *m* 1st at New York 12 June 1953 (*m* diss by div 1972), Anthony di Bonaventura, son of Fred di Bonaventura, and has issue,

    (1) ●Anthony Peter Christopher DI BONAVENTURA [*1120 Fifth Avenue, New York, New York 10028, USA*], *b* at Washington, DC 10 June 1954.
    (2) ●Andrea Isabelle DI BONAVENTURA [*1120 Fifth Avenue, New York, New York 10028, USA*].
    (3) ●Betsey Maria DI BONAVENTURA.
    (4) ●Peter John DI BONAVENTURA.
    (5) ●Sarina Rosario DI BONAVENTURA.
Sara Delano Roosevelt *m* 2ndly Jan 1973, ●Ronald A. Wilford [*1120 Fifth Avenue, New York, New York 10028, USA*].
  2 ●Kate ROOSEVELT, *b* at New York 16 Feb 1936, *m* there 17 Oct 1959, ●William Haddad (*b* at Charlotte, N Carolina 25 July 1928) [*88 Central Park West, New York, New York, USA*], and has issue,
    (1) ●Andrea Whitney HADDAD.
    (2) ●Camilla Cushing HADDAD.
    (3) ●Laura Whitney HADDAD.
Col James Roosevelt *m* 2ndly at Beverly Hills, California April 1941 (*m* diss by div 1955), Romelle Schneider (*b* 1916), and by her has issue,
  3 ●James ROOSEVELT, Jr [*4120 Suitland Road 402, Suitland, Maryland 20034, USA*], *b* at Hollywood, California 9 Nov 1945, *educ* Harvard (AB 1968), *m* at Cambridge, Mass 15 June 1968, ●Ann Martha, dau of Walter N. Conlon.
  4 ●Michael Anthony ROOSEVELT, lawyer [*1945 Broadway 401, San Francisco, California 94109, USA*], *b* at Los Angeles 7 Dec 1946, *educ* Harvard, and Columbia Law Sch, *m* at Schenectady, New York 21 Aug 1972, ●Deborah Wilson, dau of F. Hubbard Horn.
  5 ●Anna Eleanor ROOSEVELT, *b* at Santa Monica, California 10 Jan 1948, *educ* Stanford Univ, *m* ●Robert K. Johnston [*Box 6068 College Station, Durham, N. Carolina 27708, USA*].
Col James Roosevelt *m* 3rdly at Los Angeles, California 2 July 1956 (*m* diss by div 1969), Mrs Gladys Irene Owens (*b* 1917), and with her adopted a son,
  ●Hall Delano ROOSEVELT, *b* June 1957.
Col James Roosevelt *m* 4thly at Hyde Park, New York 3 Oct 1969, ●Mary Lena (*b* at Birkenhead, Cheshire, England 5 June 1939), dau of — Winskill, of Bromborough, Cheshire, England, and by her has issue,
  6 ●Rebecca Mary ROOSEVELT, *b* 1971.
3 Franklin Delano ROOSEVELT, *b* at New York City 18 March 1909; *d* there 8 Nov 1909.
4 ●Elliott ROOSEVELT, rancher in Colorado, elected Mayor of Miami Beach 1965 [*Quirita Dos Cedros, Pombois, Odivelas, Portugal*], *b* at New York City 23 Sept 1910, *educ* Groton Sch, *m* 1st Jan 1932 (*m* diss by div 1933), Elizabeth Browning, dau of William Henry Donnor, steel manufacturer, and has issue,

1 ●William Donnor ROOSEVELT, investment banker [*Wilson Point, South Norwalk, Connecticut 06854, USA*], b at New York 17 Nov 1932, *educ* Harvard, *m* at Denver, Colorado 14 June 1957, ●Karyl Kyle, and has issue,
   (1) ●Christopher Kyle ROOSEVELT, *b* at Meeker, Colorado 2 Aug 1959, *educ* Malcolm Gordon Sch, Garrison, New York.
   (2) ●Dana Donnor ROOSEVELT, *educ* St George's Sch, Newport, Rhode Island.
   (3) ●— ROOSEVELT (son).
Elliott Roosevelt *m* 2ndly at Burlington, Iowa 22 July 1933 (*m* diss by div 1944), Ruth Josephine Googins, of Fort Worth, Texas, and by her has issue,
2 ●Ruth Chandler ROOSEVELT, *b* at Fort Worth, Texas 9 May 1934, *m* there April 1956, ●Henry D. Lindsley III [*4209 Arcady, Dallas, Texas 75205, USA*], son of Henry D. Lindsley, Jr, and has issue,
   (1) ●Chandler LINDSLEY.
   (2) ●Henry Hays LINDSLEY.
   (3) ●Ruth Roosevelt LINDSLEY.
3 ●Elliott ROOSEVELT, Jr [*9669 Jourdan Way, Dallas, Texas 75230, USA*], b at Fort Worth, Texas 14 July 1936, *m* 24 Jan 1959, ●Jo Anne McFadden, and has issue,
   (1) ●David Anthony ROOSEVELT.
   (2) ●Elizabeth ROOSEVELT.
   (3) ●Elliott ROOSEVELT III.
   (4) ●Laura ROOSEVELT.
4 ●David Boynton ROOSEVELT, stockbroker [*Oyster Bay Road, Jericho, Long Island, New York 11753, USA*], b at Fort Worth, Texas 3 Jan 1942, *educ* Culver Mil Academy, and Texas Christian Univ, *m* 1st —; and 2ndly 28 April 1968, ●Michele Josephine, dau of Alexander P. Chopen (by his wife *née* O'Connor), and by her has issue,
   (1) ●Matthew Chopen ROOSEVELT, *b* at Glen Cove, New York 16 March 1972.
   (2) ●Nicholas ROOSEVELT.
Elliott Roosevelt, Sr *m* 3rdly at Grand Canyon, Colorado 3 Dec 1944 (*m* diss by div 1950), Faye Margaret Emerson, the film actress (*b* at Elizabeth, Louisiana 8 July 1917). He *m* 4thly at Miami Beach, Florida 15 March 1951 (*m* diss by div 1960), Minnewa (*b* 1911), formerly wife of Rex Ross, and dau of Alonzo Bell. He *m* 5thly at Qualicum, British Columbia Nov 1960, ●Patricia Whitehead, and by her has had issue,
5 Livingston Delano ROOSEVELT, *d* an inf.
5 ●Franklin Delano ROOSEVELT, Jr, Cmdr USNR, member of the House of Representatives, 81st-83rd Congresses, Under Sec of Commerce 1962-65, Chm Equal Employment Opportunity Commn 1965-66, Chm Fiat-Roosevelt Motors, Chm Mickelberry Corpn [*Clove Creek Farm, Poughquag, New York 12570, USA*], b at Campobello Island, New Brunswick, Canada 17 Aug 1914, *educ* Harvard (AB 1937), and Univ of Virginia (LLB 1940), *m* 1st at Wilmington, Delaware 30 June 1937 (*m* diss by div 1949), Ethel (*b* at Wilmington, Delaware 1915; *d* at Grosse Pointe, Michigan 24/25 May 1965), dau of Eugene du Pont, by his wife Ethel, and has issue,
  1 ●Franklin Delano ROOSEVELT III, teacher of economics, New School for Social Research [*404 Riverside Drive, New York, New York 10025, USA*], b at Wilmington, Delaware 19 July 1939, *educ* St Mark's Sch, Yale (BA), and Columbia Univ (MEcon), *m* at Darien, Connecticut 18 June 1962,

●Grace Ramsey (*b* at Montclair, New Jersey 1941), dau of Austin Goodyear, by his wife Louisa Robins, and has issue,
   (1) ●Phoebe Louisa ROOSEVELT.
   (2) ●Nicholas Martin ROOSEVELT.
   (3) ●Amelia ROOSEVELT.
2 ●Christopher du Pont ROOSEVELT, Assist US Attorney, Southern District [*14 Middle Patent Road, Armonk, New York 10025, USA*], b at Philadelphia 21 Dec 1940, *educ* St Paul's Sch, *m* at Concord, New Hampshire 12 June 1965, ●Rosalind, dau of Horace Havemeyer (by his wife *née* Everdell), and has issue,
   (1) ●Emily ROOSEVELT.
   (2) ●Kate ROOSEVELT.
   (3) ●Christopher Havemeyer ROOSEVELT.
Cmdr Franklin Delano Roosevelt, Jr *m* 2ndly at Manhattan, New York 31 Aug 1949 (*m* diss by div 1970), Suzanne, dau of Lee Perrin, of New York, lawyer, and by her has issue,
3 ●Nancy Suzanne ROOSEVELT [*RD1, Box 212-A, Poughquag, New York 12570, USA*], b at Manhattan, New York 11 Jan 1952, *educ* Vassar (BA 1974).
4 ●Laura D. ROOSEVELT [*3065 University Terrace, Washington, DC 20016, USA*], b at Washington, DC 26 Oct 1959.
Cmdr Franklin Delano Roosevelt, Jr *m* 3rdly at New York July 1970, ●Mrs Felicia Warburg Sarnoff.
6 ●John Aspinwall ROOSEVELT, stockbroker, Snr Vice-Pres and Dir of Bache and Coluc, served in World War II with USN (Lt-Cmdr) [*333 East 57th Street, New York, New York 10022, USA*], b at Washington, DC 13 March 1916, *educ* Groton Sch, and Harvard (AB 1938), *m* 1st at Nahant, Mass 18 June 1938 (*m* diss by div 1965), Anne Lindsay (*b* at Concord, Mass 13 July 1916; *d* at New York 28 May 1973), dau of Franklin Haven Clark, by his wife Frances Sturgis, and has had issue,
  1 ●Haven Clark ROOSEVELT, lawyer, with law firm of Cadwalader, Wickersham and Taft [*305 Millwood Road, Chappaqua, New York 10514, USA*], b at Boston 5 June 1940, *educ* Millbrook Sch, Harvard (AB 1962), and Harvard Law Sch (LLD 1966), *m* at Beverly Farm, Mass 26 Nov 1966, ●Hetty Archer (*b* April 1938), dau of John Elliott, Knowlton by his wife Hetty, and has issue,
   (1) ●Sara Delano ROOSEVELT, *b* 1968.
   (2) ●Wendy Clark ROOSEVELT, *b* 1970.
2 ●Anne Sturgis ROOSEVELT, *b* at San Diego, California 15 Dec 1942, *educ* New Sch for Social Research, *m* at Hyde Park, New York 20 June 1969, ●Douglas Sigler Luke, Jr (*b* 1 Oct 1942) [*Tower View, 3687 Kitzmiller Road, New Albany, Ohio 43054, USA*], son of Douglas Sigler Luke, by his wife Joanne, and has issue,
   (1) ●Haven Roosevelt LUKE, *b* 14 Jan 1967.
   (2) ●David Russell LUKE, *b* 12 May 1969.
   (3) ●Lindsay Anne LUKE, *b* 27 Dec 1973.
3 Sara Delano ROOSEVELT, *b* at Pasadena, California Dec 1946; *k* in a riding accident at Old Forge, Utica, New York 12 Aug 1960.
4 ●Joan Lindsay ROOSEVELT, *b* at Poughkeepsie, New York 25 Aug 1952.
Cmdr John Aspinwall Roosevelt *m* 2ndly at New York 28 Oct 1965, ●Irene E. (*b* at New York 8 March 1931), formerly wife of Benjamin Brandreth McAlpin III, and dau of James Hallam Boyd, by his wife Mary Elizabeth Watkins.

# The Half-Brother of President
# Franklin Delano Roosevelt

James Roosevelt ROOSEVELT, *b* 1854, *m* 1st 1878, Helen Schermerhorn (*d* 1893), 2nd dau of William Astor, by his wife Caroline Webster Schermerhorn (the famous society leader Mrs Astor), and had issue,

1 James Roosevelt ROOSEVELT, Jr, *b* 1879, *educ* Groton Sch, and Harvard.
2 Helen Rebecca ROOSEVELT, *b* 1881, *m* 1904, her 6th cousin Theodore Douglas Robinson (*b* 1883; *d* 1934), and had issue (*see p 424*).

# Notes

[1]  Through the Aspinwall family President Franklin D. Roosevelt was related to the wife of President Monroe, whose mother was an Aspinwall (*see p 155*).

[2]  Through the Delano family President Franklin D. Roosevelt was a fourth cousin once removed to President Grant (*see p 333*).

[3]  Through his maternal grandmother's family President Franklin D. Roosevelt was a seventh cousin once removed to his great wartime colleague Winston Churchill (*see* APPENDIX D, SOME REMARKABLE KINSHIPS).

# Harry S. Truman
## 1884-1972

———

33rd President of the
United States of America

1945-1953

HARRY S. TRUMAN, 33RD PRESIDENT

# Harry S. Truman

## 1884-1972

### 33rd President of the United States of America
### 1945-1953

VICE-PRESIDENT Truman was in the chair at a Senate session on the afternoon of 12 April 1945. He scribbled a note to his mother and sister: "I am trying to write you . . . while a windy Senator . . . is making a speech on a subject with which he is no way familiar". He advised them to switch on the radio next day: they would hear himself and President Roosevelt speak. Two hours later, in the White House, Eleanor Roosevelt put her arm round him and said gently, "Harry, the President is dead". After a pause to collect himself he asked whether there was anything he could do to help her. She replied, "Is there anything *we* can do for *you*? For you are the one in trouble now". He felt, he later remarked, as if "the moon, the stars, and all the planets had fallen on me". Roosevelt had been President for just over twelve years. It was hard to remember a period when his presence had not stretched over the American scene. The war against Germany and Japan was not over and the shape of the post-war world was barely discernible. Truman himself had spent only three months as Vice-President. Great policy decisions had not involved him. He was unaware of the vast secret program to develop the atomic bomb, though the project was already known to Russian espionage. Within three months he was conferring at Potsdam with Stalin and Churchill.

Roosevelt was an American aristocrat, the "squire of Dutchess County". Harry Truman was a little man from Missouri whose family had been too poor to send him to college. He had not felt able to marry his grade-school sweetheart Bess Wallace until 1919, when he was 34. He still had no definite career, though he had come back from service with an artillery unit in France with the rank of Major. His entry into Democratic politics was bound up with the Pendergast political machine of Kansas City. Under Boss Pendergast's auspices Truman, by now a county court judge, was successfully backed for a US Senate election in 1934. He was re-elected in 1940. During Roosevelt's third Administration he was a useful chairman of a useful Senate committee that supervised expenditure on war materials. In 1944, as Roosevelt moved toward nomination for a fourth term, his advisers persuaded him to drop Vice-President Henry Wallace. Justice William Douglas and Senator Truman were both approached and both declined. Perhaps Truman remembered the famous comment of a former Roosevelt Vice-President, John Nance Garner, that the office was "not worth a pitcher of warm spit". Pressed again, he reluctantly accepted.

Truman was a New Deal Democrat, determined to carry on with Rooseveltian policies and to show that he was nobody's fool. Problems piled upon him: increasing friction with Russia, strikes, inflation, resistance by Southern whites to his civil rights proposals. The mid-term elections of 1946 returned Republican majorities to both houses of the Eightieth Congress. Even his own party were generally hostile. The impression gained ground that he was a truculent mediocrity, the fag end of a too-long run of Democratic Administrations. His foreign policy found more favor, at least with liberal Democrats. But the Truman Doctrine and the Marshall Plan were presumed to have been the handiwork of the State Department and of General George C. Marshall. In 1948 Truman convinced the party leaders to let him try to win an election in his own right.

For almost everyone except Harry Truman the result was a foregone conclusion: a landslide victory for the Republicans. The Republican candidate, Governor Thomas E. Dewey of New York, seemed as smoothly statesmanlike as Truman was raw and strident. Southern Democrats broke away to back their own candidate, the anti-civil rights "Dixiecrat" Strom Thurmond. The left wing of the party was weakened by Henry Wallace's Progressive movement. Truman ran an old-fashioned "whistle stop" campaign, haranguing innumerable small-town audiences from the back of a train. The first returns on election night looked bad for Truman; the Chicago *Tribune* rashly put out an early edition with the banner headline "DEWEY DEFEATS TRUMAN". In fact he beat Dewey by three million votes, even though Thurmond and Wallace collected over a million votes apiece. It was an astonishing upset. Thoughtful people began to see that they had underestimated Harry Truman. They had never doubted his terrier-like tenacity: now they realized that he might also possess a considerable amount of political wisdom. In Truman's second term cartoonists and columnists tended to present him more approvingly. His piano strumming, his early morning walks, his little homilies on American history, his fierce affection for his daughter Margaret, fell into place as elements in a distinct and far from negligible personality. Truman could feel he had been vindicated, and

ELIZABETH VIRGINIA WALLACE, MRS TRUMAN

that his leadership had been instrumental in restoring Democratic control of Congress.

Nevertheless his term in office from 1949 to 1953 was full of trouble. Peace degenerated into the "cold war". China "went Communist" in 1949. In the following year war broke out in Korea. Although intervention to aid South Korea was officially carried out by the United Nations it was mainly an American operation. American predominance and the possession of the atom bomb seemed of little avail. Puzzled and angered, the American public was susceptible to the theory that democratic institutions were being undermined by subversive activities—spying, infiltration. The anti-communist "crusade" was particularly attractive to the Republicans, who could blame the Democrats for what the demagogic Senator Joseph McCarthy called "twenty years of treason". In recent years Truman has been criticized for giving way to McCarthyite pressure, or indeed for joining in the campaign.

Certainly he disliked communism as much as the average American did. The central assumption of his Administration's foreign policy, as carried out by General Marshall and Dean Acheson, was that communism was a menace which must be contained. These were honest convictions for Truman. But he detested the witch-hunters; the McCarran Internal Security Act, which obliged communists to register with the Justice Department, was passed over his veto. He defended Marshall against slanderous accusations of being a "traitor", and he risked enraging the hyperpatriots by dismissing General Douglas MacArthur for insubordination.

.Another historians' hypothesis is that it would have been better for the United States if Dewey had won in 1948. The Democrats, it is said, *had* been too long in power; anti-communist hysteria would have been less prevalent because less partisan under a Republican Administration. Possibly. But Harry Truman's own position deserves to be respected: "There is an epitaph in Boot Hill cemetery in Arizona which reads, 'Here lies Jack Williams. He done his damnedest! What more can a person do?' Well, . . . I did my damnedest, and that's all there was to it!"

# Chronology

| | |
|---|---|
| 1884 | Born at Lamar, Missouri 8 May. |
| 1885 | Family moved to a farm nr Harrisonville, Missouri. |
| 1887 | Family moved to a farm near Grandview, Missouri. |
| 1890 | Family moved to Independence, Missouri. |
| 1892-1901 | Attended school in Independence. |
| 1901-02 | Worked as timekeeper for a railroad construction contractor. |
| 1902 | Family moved to Kansas City, Missouri; worked in Kansas City *Star* mailroom. |
| 1903 | Worked as clerk with National Bank of Commerce, Kansas City. |
| 1904 | Worked as book-keeper with Union National Bank, Kansas City. |
| 1905 | Joined Missouri National Guard. |
| 1906 | Left Kansas City to manage family farm nr Grandview. |
| 1909 | Degree of Master Mason conferred by Belton Lodge No 450, Grandview. |
| 1915 | Appointed Postmaster of Grandview. |
| 1917 | Rejoined National Guard 22 May; sworn into federal military service 5 Aug; posted to Camp Doniphan, Fort Sill, Oklahoma 26 Sept. |
| 1918 | Sailed for France with regiment 30 March; landed at Brest 13 April; promoted to Captain; assumed command of Battery D, 129th Field Artillery July; took part in Battle of St Mihiel 12-16 Sept; took part in Meuse-Argonne offensive 26 Sept; Armistice signed 11 Nov. |
| 1919 | Sailed from Brest 9 April; arrived in New York 20 April; discharged from the Army with rank of Major 6 May; opened men's haberdashery shop at Independence, Missouri 29 Nov. |
| 1922 | Elected County Judge of Eastern District, Jackson County, Missouri 7 Nov. |
| 1923-25 | Attended Kansas City School of Law. |
| 1924 | Defeated for re-election as County Judge 4 Nov. |
| 1925 | Worked as membership salesman for Kansas City Automobile Club. |
| 1926 | Elected Presiding Judge of Jackson County 2 Nov. |
| 1929 | Became Democratic leader of eastern Jackson County. |
| 1930 | Re-elected Presiding Judge 4 Nov. |
| 1933 | Appointed Re-employment Director of Missouri by Harry L. Hopkins Oct. |

1934    Elected to the Senate 6 Nov.

1935    Took seat in Senate 3 Jan.

1937    Appointed Vice-Chairman of Senate sub-committee to investigate railroad financing.

1940    Re-elected to the Senate 5 Nov.

1940-41 Made 30,000 mile defense construction projects investigation trip.

1941    Denounced defense construction program in the Senate 10 Feb; appointed Chairman of Committee to investigate therein March; Truman Committee reported waste of over one hundred million dollars in military camp construction program Aug; requested military duty but was refused Dec.

1943    Made national radio broadcast on results of Truman Committee investigation 26 Nov.

1944    Nominated for Vice-President by Democratic National Convention at Chicago 21 July; election day 7 Nov.

1945    Took the oath as Vice-President at the White House 20 Jan; succeeded as 33rd President of the United States of America on the death of President Franklin Delano Roosevelt and took the oath of office in the Cabinet Room of the White House 12 April; attended the funeral of President Roosevelt at Hyde Park, New York 15 April; addressed joint session of Congress 16 April; addressed opening session of the United Nations by telephone 28 April; hostilities in Europe ended (VE Day) 8 May; sent special message to Congress outlining plans for campaign against Japan 1 June; signed Act authorizing War Department to resume acceptance of enlistments in the regular Army 2 June; witnessed signing of the United Nations Charter at San Francisco 26 June; sailed for Potsdam Conference 7 July; arrived at Antwerp, Belgium 15 July; presided at tri-partite Conference nr Potsdam 17 July-2 Aug; flew to Plymouth, England and sailed for US 2 Aug; first atomic bomb dropped on Hiroshima, Japan 5 Aug; arrived at Newport News, Virginia and travelled by train to Washington 7 Aug; signed United Nations Charter 8 Aug; second atomic bomb dropped on Nagasaki, Japan 9 Aug; Japan surrendered unconditionally 14 Aug; issued executive order ending lend-lease 21 Aug; issued executive order of seizure of Illinois Central Railroad to avert strike 23 Aug; proposed draft extension for two years 27 Aug; sent special message to Congress recommending writing-off of lend-lease debts 30 Aug; issued executive order abolishing Office of War Information 31 Aug; Japan formally surrendered to the Allies 1 Sept; V-J Day 2 Sept; sent special message to Congress asking for reduction of Army budget 25 Sept; issued executive order reorganizing the Navy Department 1 Oct; sent special message to Congress urging prompt organization of an Atomic Energy Commission 3 Oct; issued executive order abolishing War Production Board 4 Oct; sent special message to Congress urging legislation to provide one year's military training for all males between 17 and 20; signed executive order changing the design of the Presidential Flag 25 Oct; reviewed 47 warships in the Hudson River 27 Oct; conferred with the British Prime Minister Clement Attlee and the Canadian Prime Minister Mackenzie King on the atomic bomb in Washington 10 Nov; sent special message to Congress asking for legislation to avert strikes during reconversion 3 Dec; issued executive order ending War Labor Board 31 Dec.

1946    Steel strike began 20 Jan; sent first State of the Union message to Congress 21 Jan; sent special message to Congress recommending approval of $4,400,000,000 loan to Great Britain 30 Jan; steel strike ended 15 Feb; signed modified Full-Employment Act 20 Feb; issued executive order re-opening all public lands in US and Alaska to settlement, except those containing substantial deposits of fissionable materials 7 March; soft coal strike began 1 April; attended dedication of the birthplace of Franklin D. Roosevelt as a national shrine 12 April; signed Veterans Priority Act 3 May; received honorary degree of LLD from Fordham University, New York City 11 May; signed Act to continue selective service to 1 July 14 May; issued executive order of seizure of nation's railroads 17 May; issued executive order of seizure of soft coal mines 21 May; railroad strike began 23 May; ended 25 May; soft coal strike ended 29 May; received honorary degree of LLD from Washington College, Chestertown, Maryland 1 June; hard coal strike ended 7 June; signed amended Selective Service Act 29 June; attended joint session of Congress called to pay tribute to the memory of Franklin D. Roosevelt 1 July; issued proclamation recognizing the Republic of the Philippines 4 July; signed joint resolution ratifying British loan agreement 15 July; signed Act renewing Office of Price Administration 25 July; vetoed tidelands oil bill 1 Aug; signed Act increasing war pensions 8 Aug; signed Act raising salaries of Ambassadors and Ministers 13 Aug; visited Bermuda on holiday 22 Aug; returned to Washington 2 Sept; opened meeting of United Nations General Assembly in New York 23 Oct; issued executive order ending all price controls except on rent, sugar and rice 9 Nov; soft coal strike ended 7 Dec; issued executive order merging remaining wartime economic agencies into Office of Temporary Controls 12 Dec; issued proclamation officially ending hostilities of World War II 31 Dec.

1947    Delivered second State of the Union message to Congress 6 Jan; sent special message to Congress asking for extension of some of his wartime controls for an additional year 3 Feb; sent special message to Congress requesting the repeal of 24 wartime emergency laws 19 Feb; visited Mexico 3-6 March; addressed joint session of Congress outlining the so-called Truman Doctrine 12 March; 22nd Amendment to the Constitution submitted to the States for ratification 24 March; signed Act extending sugar rationing and price controls for seven months 31 March; sent special message to Congress recommending revision of the Neutrality Act of 1939 to bar sales of arms and munitions to aggressor nations 15 April; signed Act changing name of Boulder Dam to Hoover Dam 30 April; sent special message to Congress urging legislation for comprehensive public health program 19 May; signed Greek-Turkish Aid Act 22 May; sent special message to Congress requesting extension of certain wartime powers 23 May; sent special message to Congress asking for legislation for compulsory military training 5 June; visited Canada 10-12 June; formally signed peace treaties with Italy, Hungary, Rumania and Bulgaria 14 June; vetoed Income Tax Reduction Bill 16 June; sent special message to Congress asking for admission of nearly one million survivors of Nazi persecution in central Europe 7 July; signed Presidential Succession Act 18 July; signed Act accepting trusteeship of Pacific Islands formerly mandated to Japan 19 July; signed Act terminating 175 war statutes 25 July; pocket vetoed 19 Bills 30 July-8 Aug; signed Act granting Puerto Rico right to elect governor by popular vote 4 Aug; signed Act putting armed services promotion on merit basis 7 Aug; visited Brazil 1-7 Sept; ordered cancellation of all state dinners during the winter season to aid food conservation program 15 Oct; declared State of Maine a disaster area following forest fires 25 Oct; sent special message to Congress requesting financing of Marshall Plan for a four-year period; signed Act providing stop-gap aid for France, Italy, Austria and China and granted full pardons to 1,523 men convicted of violations of the Selective Service Act during World War II 23 Dec.

1948    Delivered third State of the Union message to Congress 7 Jan; submitted ten-point civil rights program to Congress 1 Feb; carried out Caribbean inspection tour 21-25 Feb; signed Act extending rent control in modified form for another year 30 March; Tax Reduction Act passed over his veto 2 April; signed Foreign Aid Act 3 April; vetoed Bill to exclude newspaper and magazine sellers from social security benefits 5 April (passed over his veto 20 April); issued executive order of seizure of nation's railroads 10 May; recognized provisional government of Israel 14 May; vetoed Bill to amend Atomic Energy Act of 1946 15 May; signed Military Aircraft Act 21 May; made transcontinental speaking tour 3-18 June; signed Peacetime Draft Act 24 June; ordered Berlin airlift 26 June; signed Foreign Aid Act 28 June; signed Housing Act 1 July; signed Federal Employee Salary Increase Act and Agricultural Act 3 July; nominated for President by Democratic National Convention at Philadelphia 15 July; dedicated Idlewild International Airport, New York City 31 July; signed United Nations Loan Act 11 Aug; made holiday cruise in Florida waters 21-29 Aug; election day 2 Nov; Presidential Electors cast their ballots (303 for Truman; 189 for Dewey; 39 for James Strom Thurmond, States' Rights Democratic party candidate) 13 Dec.

1949    Recognized Republic of Korea 1 Jan; delivered fourth State of the Union message to Congress 5 Jan; electoral votes tabulated by Congress and Truman and Barkley officially declared elected 6 Jan; sent special message to Congress asking for additional powers to reorganize executive department agencies 17 Jan; inaugurated on the east portico of the Capitol 20 Jan; sent special message to Congress proposing eight-point anti-inflation program 15 Feb; sent special message to Congress asking $5,400,000 for reconstruction of the White House 17 Feb; signed extension of Federal Rent Control Act 30 March; attended signing of North Atlantic Treaty at Washington, DC 4 April; sent special message to Congress asking for establishment of Columbia Valley Administration 13 April; signed European Recovery Act 19 April; sent special message to Congress recommending that US should join the International Trade Organization 28 April; sent special message to Congress asking for legislation to reorganize department as recommended by the Hoover Commission 9 May; signed Reorganization Act 20 June; signed North Atlantic Treaty 25 July; issued proclamation declaring North Atlantic pact in effect 24 Aug; signed extension of Reciprocal Trade Agreements Act 26 Sept; vetoed Bill to provide ten-year rehabilitation program for Navajo and Hopi Indians 16 Oct; issued executive order authorizing Atomic Energy Commission to withdraw 30 million dollars from reserve fund for new construction at Oak Ridge, Tennessee, and Hanford, Washington, atomic plants 18 Oct; attended laying of cornerstone of UN headquarters in New York 24 Oct; attended centennial of Minnesota Territory at St Paul, Minnesota 3 Nov; issued executive order authorizing Federal Housing Administration loans for low-rent housing in 27 States, District of Columbia and Puerto Rico 16 Nov; recognized United States of Indonesia 27 Dec.

1950    Delivered fifth State of the Union message to Congress 4 Jan; issued proclamation proposing Panama Canal toll increase until 1 April 1951 6 March; signed Act repealing all federal taxes on oleomargarine 16 March; issued proclamation regarding National Census 18 March; signed Act authorizing ten-year rehabilitation program for Navajo and Hopi Indians 19 April; signed Act creating National Science Foundation 10 May; reviewed first Armed Forces Day parade in Washington, DC 20 May; signed Foreign Economic Act 5 June; signed amendment to Displaced Persons Act of 1948 16 June; announced that US would support UN against North Korean invasion of South Korea 27 June;

signed Act extending selective service until 9 July 1951 30 June; vetoed Bill to amend the Hatch Act 30 June; issued executive order establishing credit controls on public housing 18 July; signed Act granting US citizenship and limited self-government to Guam 1 Aug; signed Act raising armed forces to any necessary level during national emergency 3 Aug; issued executive order to seize railroads to avert strike 25 Aug; signed new Social Security Act 28 Aug; signed Defence Production Act 8 Sept; vetoed Internal Security Bill (passed over his veto) 22 Sept; visited Hawaii 13 Oct; conferred with Gen Douglas A. MacArthur at Wake Island 15 Oct; survived assassination attempt at Blair House, Washington DC 1 Nov; conferred with British Prime Minister Clement Attlee at Washington, DC 8 Dec; issued proclamation of national emergency 16 Dec.

1951    Delivered sixth State of the Union message to Congress 8 Jan; 22nd Amendment to the Constitution ratified 26 Feb: opened fourth meeting of Foreign Ministers of 21 American Republics in Washington, DC 26 March; issued executive order reconstituting Wage Stabilization Board under Defence Production Act 17 April; signed Supplement Appropriation Acts 31 May and 2 June; signed two-year extension of Reciprocal Trade Agreements Act 16 June; signed Act extending selective service to 1 July 1955 19 June; signed Federal Flood Aid Act 18 July; signed amended Defence Production Act 31 July; issued executive order suspending tariff reductions for USSR, Communist China, and their satellites 1 Aug; issued executive order establishing Defence Materials Procurement Agency 29 Aug; signed Mutual Security Act 10 Oct; issued proclamation formally declaring that the state of war between US and Germany had terminated 19 Oct 1951 24 Oct; received HRH Princess Elizabeth and HRH The Duke of Edinburgh at the White House 31 Oct; issued executive order cancelling all tariff concessions to USSR and Poland 23 Nov.

1952    Conferred with British Prime Minister Winston Churchill at the White House 7-8 Jan; delivered seventh State of the Union message to Congress 9 Jan; authorized economic aid to Great Britain from Mutual Security program fund 5 Feb; issued executive order outlining rules for conscientious objectors 19 Feb; moved back into the White House 27 March; issued executive order to Secretary of Commerce Sawyer to seize and operate steel mills to avert national strike 8 April; signed peace treaty with Japan 15 April (ratified by the Senate 20 March; effective 28 April); signed Flood Relief Act 24 April; issued executive order returning 195 railroads to private owners 23 May; vetoed tidelands oil bill 29 May; signed compromise Arms and Military Supplies for Free Nations Act 20 June; vetoed Bill to revise laws relating to immigration, naturalization (passed over his veto) 25 June; signed Puerto Rico Constitution Act 3 July; signed Supplemental Appropriation Act 15 July; signed new GI Bill of Rights 16 July; issued executive order directing Civil Service Commission to merge all governmental loyalty programs 8 Aug.

1953    Sent eighth (and last) State of the Union message to Congress 7 Jan; retired from office and attended the inauguration of President Eisenhower 20 Jan; returned to Independence, Missouri.

1955    Appeared before Senate Foreign Relations Committee 18 April; broke ground for Harry S. Truman Library at Independence, Missouri 8 May; attended 10th anniversary meeting of UN at War Memorial Opera House, San Francisco 20 June.

1956    Visited Europe; received honorary degree of DCL from Oxford University 20 June.

1957    Attended opening of Harry S. Truman Library in Independence 6 July.

1958    Visited Spain, France and Italy.

1963    Attended the funeral of President Kennedy 25 Nov.

1964    With Mrs Lyndon B. Johnson represented US at the funeral of King Paul of the Hellenes in Athens 12 March.

1965    Witnessed signing of Medicare Act by President Johnson in Independence 30 July.

1966    Attended ceremony at the Truman Library to mark the dedication of the Harry S. Truman Center for Advancement of Peace at the Hebrew University, Jerusalem 20 Jan.

1971    Refused to accept Congressional Medal of Honor 6 May.

1972    Died at Kansas City, Missouri 26 Dec; buried in the rose garden of the Harry S. Truman Library, Independence, Missouri 28 Dec.

# The Writings of President Truman

*Years of Decisions* (1955)

*Years of Trial and Hope* (1956)

# Lineage of President Truman

WILLIAM TRUMAN, *b* in Virginia 1783, *m* in Kentucky 1807, Emma Grant Shippe, and *d* in Kentucky *ca* 1863, leaving issue,

ANDERSON SHIPPE TRUMAN, moved to Missouri 1846, *b* in Kentucky 1816, *m* at Shelbyville, Kansas 1846, Mary Jane (*b* 1821; *d* 1878), dau of Jesse Holmes, of Shelbyville, by his wife Ann Drusilla (Nancy) Tyler[1], and *d* in Missouri 1887, leaving with other issue[2],

JOHN ANDERSON TRUMAN, of Independence, Missouri, farmer and livestock salesman, *b* in Jackson County, Missouri 5 Dec 1851, *m* there 28 Dec 1881, Martha Ellen (*b* at Parish Farm (now in Kansas City), Jackson County, Missouri 25 Nov 1852; *d* at Grandview, Missouri 26 July 1947), dau of Solomon Young, by his wife Harriet Louisa Gregg, and *d* at Kansas City, Missouri 3 Nov 1914, leaving with other issue (*see* BROTHER AND SISTER OF PRESIDENT TRUMAN, *p 520*) an elder son,

HARRY S. TRUMAN[3], **33rd President of the United States of America.**

# The Descendants of President Truman

HARRY S. TRUMAN *m* at Independence, Missouri 28 June 1919, ●Elizabeth (Bess) Virginia (*b* at Independence 13 Feb 1885) [*219 North Delaware Street, Independence, Missouri, USA*], dau of David Willock Wallace, farmer, of Independence, by his wife Madge Gates, and had issue,

> ●(Mary) Margaret TRUMAN, author of biography of her father, *b* at Independence, Missouri 17 Feb 1924, *m* there 21 April 1956, ●(Elbert) Clifton Daniel, Jr, Associate Editor of *The New York Times* (*b* at Zebulon, N Carolina 19 Sept 1912), son of Elbert Clifton Daniel, by his wife Elvah Jones, and has issue,
>> 1 ●Clifton Truman DANIEL, *b* at Manhattan, New York 5 June 1957.
>> 2 ●William Wallace DANIEL, *b* at Manhattan, New York 19 May 1959.
>> 3 ●Harrison Gates DANIEL, *b* at Manhattan, New York 3 March 1963.
>> 4 ●Thomas DANIEL, *b* at Manhattan, New York 28 May 1966.

# The Brother and Sister of
# President Truman

**1** (John) Vivian TRUMAN, Dir of Federal Housing Authority in Missouri, *b* at Harrisonville, Missouri 25 April 1886, *m*, and *d* at Grandview, Missouri July 1965, leaving issue, four sons (including Mr Harry Arnold Truman, a dairy farmer and Mr Gilbert Truman) and one dau.

**2** ●Mary Jane TRUMAN, *b* at Grandview, Missouri 12 Aug 1889.

# Notes

¹ She is said to have been a cousin of President Tyler, but the relationship is not clear.

² A grandson of Anderson Shippe Truman, Ralph Emerson Truman, was a Major-Gen in the US National Guard and *d* at Kansas City in 1962.

³ His middle initial S. did not stand for anything as his parents could not decide whether to name him Solomon, after his maternal grandfather, or Shippe in honor of his paternal ancestors.

# Dwight David Eisenhower
## 1890-1969

———

34th President of the
United States of America
1953-1961

DWIGHT DAVID EISENHOWER, 34TH PRESIDENT

# Dwight David Eisenhower

## 1890-1969

## *34th President of the United States of America*
## 1953-1961

THE FATHER of President Eisenhower was born in Pennsylvania, the mother in Virginia. David Dwight Eisenhower (who later reversed his Christian names) was born in Texas and grew up in Kansas. His wife Marie (Mamie) Doud was born in Iowa. The couple were married in Colorado, where their two sons also first saw the light of day. Between the two World Wars the Eisenhowers lived variously in Panama, Washington and the Philippines. In a way such shifts were typical of American family histories—frequent movement, in a generally westward direction. For Dwight Eisenhower they were also a consequence of his career as an Army officer. Graduating from West Point in 1915, he missed the chance of service in France. With the return of peace he was confined to the Army's obscure enclave, posted hither and thither. If the United States had remained neutral in World War II he might have risen to Colonel or Brigadier but would have remained unknown to the world outside. His neat good looks, his pleasing personality, his crisp competence and his underlying ambition, which earned him a place on General MacArthur's Staff, would probably not have sufficed to win him an entry in *Who's Who*.

Instead the war came. Spotted as a likely leader by the Army Chief of Staff, General Marshall, Eisenhower was on the way up. Marshall tested him out in North Africa, Sicily and Italy. By the close of 1943 there was an urgent need to name the Allied supreme commander for the forthcoming invasion of northern Europe. Since the main weight in men and material would be provided by the United States, the appointment lay with the Americans. Roosevelt consulted Marshall, who could have secured the coveted honor for himself but dispassionately renounced it in favor of Eisenhower.

The choice seemed amply justified by results. Tact was perhaps the most important requirement for a commander who had to work with naval and air as well as ground units, with British, Canadian, French and other nationalities, and with generals as temperamental as Patton and Montgomery. Eisenhower revealed himself to be an excellent coalition general, and equally popular a few years later as commander of the NATO forces.

The political consequences were inevitable. As General Grant had once been wooed by both parties, so Eisenhower attracted attention as a potentially unbeatable presidential candidate. He resisted coaxing to run in 1948. By 1952, however, with the added civilian qualification of a period as president of Columbia University, he was heading the Republican ticket. A young California Congressman, Richard M. Nixon, was his running mate.

In 1952 and again in 1956, "I Like Ike" was an immensely appealing slogan. The Democrats and a certain number of dissidents within Eisenhower's own party remained immune to his magic. Eisenhower's amiably middlebrow tastes (golf, Wild West fiction, amateurish efforts as an artist) were contrasted with the wit and scholarly intelligence of the Democratic candidate, Adlai Stevenson. Eisenhower believed in keeping a clean desk. It was said that he had become too accustomed to military overlordship and delegated too much responsibility to his austere, peremptory assistant Sherman Adams. He was criticized for failing to stand up to McCarthyism, and for sheltering behind the Supreme Court in controversies over civil rights. His recurrent illnesses made the nation uneasy. Opponents alleged that he allowed too much power to his Secretary of State, John Foster Dulles; and that Dulles's "brinkmanship" was dangerously inconsistent. Eisenhower himself, with his belief in the efficacy of summit meetings, was attacked for naïvety. Toward the end of his second term there was an embarrassing muddle; the Russians shot down an American spy-plane, the *U-2*, whose activities the President first denied and was then compelled to admit. In sum, the charge is that Eisenhower lacked the political experience and the executive boldness to make a great President.

Since he left office in 1961, Eisenhower's reputation has risen steadily. It has been argued on his behalf that his conception of the Presidency was perfectly sound, and in keeping with the old tradition of a dignified head of state, standing somewhat above the day-to-day skirmishes of party politics. In this view, he was not unduly influenced by his Army practices. After all, he had little in common with a *prima donna* like MacArthur. He did not knuckle under to the Pentagon and he ultimately warned the nation against the dangers of the "military-industrial complex". Eisenhower had been an organizer in the Army, not a martinet or a combat soldier. His skills were in large part those of a board chairman, aware of the need to reconcile opposing views and personalities. He preferred to

MARIE (MAMIE) GENEVA DOUD, MRS EISENHOWER

govern not by edict but by persuasion. The desire to please was strong in him, and on occasion he was perhaps insufficiently firm. Nixon supporters thought him maddeningly lukewarm about his Vice-President throughout their association. The evidence suggests that Eisenhower's coolness was carefully considered. On the other hand he agreed with President Truman that Vice-Presidents in the past had been unwisely left in the dark. Eisenhower remedied this neglect by bringing Nixon into meetings of the cabinet and the National Security Council, and sending him around the world on quite taxing diplomatic assignments.

Dwight Eisenhower, unlike Truman, was not what the Scots call a bonny fighter. He had no passion for far-reaching social changes. His could be termed a businessman's Administration. His first cabinet was jokingly defined as "eight millionaires and a plumber"—the plumber being his Secretary of Labor. What he did care about most was peace. Eisenhower promised to end the Korean conflict; he kept his word so far as the United States was concerned. In his eight years America did not make any armed interventions. His love of harmony and his moderation seem in hindsight to have been sincere, worthwhile and not unproductive.

# Chronology

1890    Born at Denison, Texas 14 Oct, and named David Dwight, but later transposed his names.

1891    Family moved to Abilene, Kansas.

1910    Graduated from Abilene High School.

1915    Graduated from US Military Academy, West Point 12 June[1], assigned to 19th Infantry at Fort Sam Houston, San Antonio, Texas 5 Sept.

1916    Promoted 1st Lieut 1 July.

1917-18 Served in World War I.

1922-24 Stationed in Panama Canal Zone.

1925-26 Attended Command and General Staff School at Fort Leavenworth, Kansas.

1928    Attended Army War College at Washington, DC.

1929-32 Served on staff of Assistant Secretary of War at Washington, DC.

1932-34 Served on staff of Gen Douglas A. MacArthur, Army Chief of Staff, at Washington, DC.

1935-39   Served on staff of Gen MacArthur in the Philippine Islands.

1939   Received air pilot's licence 30 Nov.

1940   Served as Regimental Executive Officer, 15th Infantry Regt, 3rd Infantry Division at Fort Lewis, Washington; appointed Chief of Staff, 3rd Infantry Division, Fort Lewis Nov.

1941   Appointed Chief of Staff, 9th Army Corps, Fort Lewis March; Chief of Staff, 3rd Army Corps, Fort Sam Houston, San Antonio, Texas June; promoted T/Brig Sept; Japanese attacked Pearl Harbor 7 Dec.

1942   Appointed Assistant Chief of Staff, War Plans Division, War Department General Staff 16 Feb; promoted T/Major-Gen 27 March; appointed CO European Theater of Operations 11 June; promoted T/Lt-Gen 7 July; Allied C-in-C of invasion of N Africa 7 Nov.

1943   Promoted T/Gen 11 Feb; appointed Supreme Commander, Allied Expeditionary Force 24 Dec.

1944   D Day 6 June.

1945   Accepted surrender of German Army at Rheims, France 7 May.

1945-48   Army Chief of Staff.

1947   Appointed President of Columbia University, New York June.

1948   Retired from the Army 7 Feb; installed as President of Columbia University 12 Oct.

1949   Appointed Head of Joint Chiefs of Staff and principal Consultant to Secretary of Defence Forrestal by President Truman 11 Feb.

1950   Bought a farm at Gettysburg, Pennsylvania Dec; appointed Supreme Commander of European Defence by Foreign Ministers of NATO nations 19 Dec.

1951   Assumed duties of Supreme Commander NATO 2 April; conferred with President Truman in Washington, DC 3-6 Nov.

1952   Relinquished NATO Command to Gen Matthew B. Ridgway 30 May; nominated for President by the Republican National Convention at Chicago 11 July; resigned as officer in US Army 13 July; election day 4 Nov: resigned as President and Trustee of Columbia University 17 Nov (effective from 19 Jan 1953); made tour of inspection in Korea 2-4 Dec; Presidential Electors cast their ballots (442 for Eisenhower; 89 for Adlai Ewing Stevenson, the Democratic candidate).

1953   Electoral votes tabulated by Congress and Eisenhower and Nixon officially declared elected 6 Jan; inaugurated as 34th President of the United States of America on the east portico of the Capitol 20 Jan; issued executive order establishing nine-member International Information Activities Board 26 Jan; delivered first State of the Union message to Congress 2 Feb; signed Act creating post of Under-Secretary of State for Administration 7 Feb; signed Act creating Department of Health, Education and Welfare 1 April; issued executive order establishing new federal employee security program 27 April; signed Offshore Lands Act 22 May; issued executive order establishing International Organizations Employees Loyalty Board 2 June; dedicated the home of President Theodore Roosevelt, Sagamore Hill, Oyster Bay, New York, as a National Shrine 14 June; signed Act granting one million bushels of wheat to Pakistan to avert starvation 25 June; sent special message to Congress asking for authority to use surplus food supplies for emergency relief to friendly nations 30 June: Korean War ended 27 July; sent special message to Congress asking that national debt statutory ceiling be raised by $15,000,000,000; pocket vetoed Bill to repeal federal tax on motion picture admissions 6 Aug; issued executive order making refusal of Government employees to testify before congressional committees on ground of possible self-incrimination basis for dismissal 14 Oct; visited Canada 13-14 Nov; met with British Prime Minister Churchill and French Prime Minister Joseph Laniel in Bermuda 4-8 Dec; addressed General Assembly of UN in New York City 8 Dec.

1954    Delivered second State of the Union message to Congress 7 Jan; sent special message to Congress outlining 15 recommended revisions of Taft-Hartley Act 11 Jan; sent special message to Congress proposing increased social security benefits 14 Jan; declared that FBI files would not be released to congressional committees while he was President 24 March; signed Air Force Academy Act 1 April; McCarthy hearings began 22 April; signed St Lawrence Seaway Act 13 May; Supreme Court declared racial segregation in public schools unconstitutional 17 May; received Emperor Haile Selassie of Ethiopia at the White House 25 May; conferred with British Prime Minister Churchill at the White House 25-29 June; signed Communist Control Act 24 Aug; Southeast Asia Defence Treaty signed at Manila 8 Sept; dedicated Eisenhower Memorial Museum at Abilene, Kansas 11 Nov; UN General Assembly unanimously adopted his program for peaceful use of atomic energy 4 Dec.

1955    Delivered third State of the Union message to Congress 6 Jan; sent special message to Congress asking for emergency powers to defend Formosa and Pescadores 24 Jan (granted by joint resolution 28 Jan); signed Act raising salaries of Vice-President, Congressmen and the Judiciary 2 March; signed Armed Forces Pay Increase Act 31 March; signed agreement to share atomic weapon information with NATO nations 13 April; signed revised Post Office Wage Increase Act 10 June; attended tenth anniversary celebrations of the United Nations at San Francisco 20 June; attended Geneva Conference in Switzerland 18-23 July; suffered a mild heart attack at Denver, Colorado 24 Sept; addressed White House Conference on Education on 28 Nov.

1956    Sent fourth State of the Union message to Congress 5 Jan; sent special message to Congress outlining aid-to-education program 12 Jan; conferred with British Prime Minister Sir Anthony Eden at the White House 30 Jan-1 Feb; sent special message to Congress asking for revision of immigration laws 8 Feb; issued executive order exempting fathers and men of 26 and over from draft 16 Feb; vetoed bill to amend Natural Gas Act 17 Feb; announced decision to run for second term 29 Feb; sent special message on foreign aid to Congress 19 March; visited Panama 21-23 July; renominated for President by the Republican National Convention at San Francisco 22 Aug; election day 6 Nov; Presidential Electors cast their ballots (457 for Eisenhower; 73 for Stevenson; 1 for Walter Burgwyn Jones) 17 Dec.

1957    Electoral votes tabulated by Congress and Eisenhower and Nixon officially declared elected 7 Jan; sent fifth State of the Union message to Congress 10 Jan; took oath of office privately at the White House 20 Jan; inaugurated publicly on the east plaza of the Capitol 21 Jan; signed Middle East doctrine joint resolution 9 March; conferred with British Prime Minister Harold Macmillan at the White House 21-24 March; visited Gettysburg battlefield with Field Marshal Viscount Montgomery of Alamein 12 May; conferred with West German Chancellor Konrad Adenauer at Washington, DC and Gettysburg 26-28 May; issued executive order freeing young men in ready reserve programs from draft liability 13 June; signed ratification papers formalizing US membership in International Atomic Energy Agency 29 July; received HM Queen Elizabeth II and HRH The Duke of Edinburgh at Washington, DC 17 Oct; conferred with British Prime Minister Macmillan at the White House 23-25 Oct; suffered a mild stroke 25 Nov; returned to work 9 Dec; attended heads of Government NATO meeting in Paris, France 16-19 Dec.

1958 Delivered sixth State of the Union message to Congress 9 Jan; sent special message to Congress proposing National Aeronautics and Space Agency 2 April; sent special message to Congress proposing major reorganization of Defence Department 3 April; received President Theodor Heuss of West Germany at the White House 4 June; signed Alaska Statehood Act 7 July; visited Canada 8-11 July; sent special message to Congress announcing that he had ordered US Marines to Lebanon following the overthrow of the Iraq monarchy 15 July; awarded Presidential Citation to the officers and crew of *Nautilus,* nuclear submarine which made the first undersea crossing of the North Pole 8 Aug; addressed UN General Assembly in New York 13 Aug; signed Act authorizing pensions for former Presidents 25 Aug; issued executive order transferring Jet Propulsion Laboratory, Pasadena, California from Defence Department to National Aeronautics and Space Administration 3 Dec.

1959 Alaska admitted as 49th State and executive order issued adding 49th star to flag (effective from 4 July) 3 Jan; delivered seventh State of the Union message to Congress 9 Jan; visited Mexico 19-20 Feb; signed Hawaii Statehood Act 18 March; addressed North Atlantic Council in Washington, DC 4 April; dedicated Robert A. Taft Memorial Bell Tower in the Capitol grounds 14 April; conferred with "Big Four" Foreign Ministers at the White House 28 May; with Queen Elizabeth II opened the St Lawrence Seaway at St Lambert, Quebec, Canada 26 June; Hawaii admitted as 50th State and 50th star added to flag (effective from 4 July 1960) 21 Aug; visited West Germany for conference with Chancellor Adenauer 26-27 Aug; visited England and Scotland 27 Aug-2 Sept; visited France 2-4 Sept; again visited Scotland and stayed in the apartment in Culzean Castle given to him by the Scottish people after World War II 4-7 Sept; returned to US 7 Sept; received Russian Prime Minister Nikita Khrushchev at the White House 15 Sept; conferred with Khrushchev at Camp David 25-27 Sept; issued executive orders invoking Taft–Hartley Act in dock strike 6 Oct and in steel strike 9 Oct; announced transfer of Army Ballistics Missile Agency to National Aeronautics and Space Administration 21 Oct; left on "peace and goodwill" tour 3 Dec; visited Italy 4-5 Dec; visited Turkey 6-7 Dec; visited Pakistan 8 Dec; visited Afghanistan 9 Dec; visited India 9-14 Dec; visited Iran 14 Dec; visited Greece 14-15 Dec; visited Tunisia 17 Dec; visited France 18-21 Dec; visited Spain and Morocco and returned to US 22 Dec.

1960 Delivered eighth State of the Union message to Congress 7 Jan; attended signing of US-Japanese Security Treaty at the White House 19 Jan; visited Puerto Rico 22-23 Feb; visited Brazil 23-25 Feb; visited Argentina 26-28 Feb; visited Chile 29 Feb-1 March; visited Uruguay 2-3 March; again visited Puerto Rico 3-7 March; returned to Washington 7 March; conferred with President de Gaulle of France at the White House and Camp David 22-24 April; signed Civil Rights Act of 1960 6 May; signed Mutual Security Authorization Act 14 May; attended summit conference in Paris 15-17 May; visited Portugal 19-20 May; returned to US 20 May; signed Military Construction Authorization Act 8 June; visited Alaska 12-13 June; visited the Philippines 14-16 June; 23rd Amendment to the Constitution submitted to the States 16 June; visited Formosa 18-19 June;

visited Korea 19-20 June; visited Hawaii 20-25 June; returned to Washington 26 June; vetoed $7\frac{1}{2}\%$ federal employees pay increase bill 30 June (passed over his veto 1 July); addressed Republican National Convention at Chicago 26 July; signed Mutual Security Appropriation Act 2 Sept; addressed UN General Assembly in New York 22 Sept; addressed Republican rally at Chicago 29 Sept; addressed Republican rally in Philadelphia 28 Oct; issued executive order to all federal agencies to minimize foreign spending 16 Nov.

1961    Sent ninth (and last) State of the Union message to Congress 16 Jan; retired from office and attended the inauguration of President Kennedy 20 Jan; Act signed by President Kennedy restored his rank as General of the Army 22 March.

1962    Dedicated Dwight D. Eisenhower Library at Abilene, Kansas 1 May.

1963    Re-dedicated the National Cemetery at Gettysburg 19 Nov.

1965    Suffered heart attacks at Augusta, Georgia 9 and 10 Nov.

1968    Suffered further heart attacks 29 April, 15 June, 6 and 16 Aug.

1969    Operated on for intestinal obstruction 23 Feb; contracted pneumonia 28 Feb; suffered congestive heart failure 15 March; died at Walter Reed Army Medical Center, Washington, DC 28 March; buried at Abilene, Kansas.

# The Writings of President Eisenhower

*Crusade in Europe* (1948)

*Mandate for Change* (1965)

*Waging Peace* (1966)

*At Ease: Stories I Tell to Friends* (1967)

# Lineage of President Eisenhower

HANS NICHOLAS EISENHAUER, emigrated to America with his three sons, arriving in Philadelphia 17 Nov 1741, *b* in the Palatinate 1691, *m*, and had issue with two yr sons,

PETER EISENHOWER, *b* 1716, *m* Ann —, and *d* 1802, having had issue with sixteen other children, a yst son,

FREDERICK EISENHOWER, *m*, and *d* 1884 (*bur* at Belle Springs, nr Abilene), leaving issue,

JACOB FREDERICK EISENHOWER, a leader of the River Brethren of Mennonites in Kansas 1878, *b* 19 Sept 1826, *m* 25 Feb 1847, Rebecca Matter (*b* 18 March 1825; *d* June 1890), and had issue with seven other sons and six daus,

DAVID JACOB EISENHOWER, of Abilene, Kansas, gas company manager, *b* at Elizabethville, Pennsylvania 23 Sept 1863, *m* at Lecompton, Kansas 23 Sept 1885, Ida Elizabeth (*b* at Mount Sidney, Virginia 1 May 1862; *d* at Abilene, Kansas 11 Sept 1946), dau of Simon Stover, by his wife — Link, and *d* at Abilene, Kansas 10 March 1942, having had with other issue (*see* BROTHERS OF PRESIDENT EISENHOWER, *p 533*), a 3rd son,

DWIGHT DAVID EISENHOWER, **34th President of the United States of America.**

# The Descendants of President Eisenhower

DWIGHT DAVID EISENHOWER, *m* at Denver, Colorado 1 July 1916, ●Marie (Mamie) Geneva (*b* at Boone, Iowa 14 Nov 1896) [*RD2 Gettysburg, Pennsylvania, USA*], dau of John Sheldon Doud, of Denver, Colorado, by his wife Elivera Mathilda Carlson, and had issue,

**1** Doud Dwight (Icky) EISENHOWER, *b* at Denver, Colorado 24 Sept 1917; *d* at Camp Meade, Maryland 2 Jan 1921.

**2** ●John Sheldon Doud EISENHOWER, Col US Army, US Amb to Belgium 1969-71, has Legion of Merit (1961), Bronze Star (1953), and Order of the Crown of Belgium (1971), author of *The Bitter Woods*, and *Strictly Personal* [*111 White House Road, Phoenixville, Pennsylvania 19460, USA*], *b* at Denver, Colorado 3 Aug 1922, *educ* West Point (BS 1944), and Columbia Univ (MA 1950), *m* in Virginia 10 June 1947, ●Barbara Jean (*b* at Fort Knox, Kentucky 15 June 1926), dau of Col Percy W. Thompson, US Army, by his wife Beatrice Birchfield, and has issue,

   **1** ●Dwight David EISENHOWER II, *b* at West Point, New York 31 March 1948, *educ* Phillips Exeter Academy, and Amherst Coll, *m* at Marble Collegiate Church, New York City 22 Dec 1968, ●Julie (*b* at Washington, DC 5 July 1948), yr dau of Richard Milhous Nixon, 37th President of the United States of America (*qv*).

   **2** ●Barbara Anne EISENHOWER, *b* at West Point, New York 30 May 1949, *m* at Valley Forge, 17 Nov 1968, ●Fernando Echavarria Uribe [*111 East 85th Street, New York, New York, USA*], son of Hernán Echavarria, of Bogota, Colombia (by his wife *née* Uribe), and has issue,

      ●Adriana ECHAVARRIA, *b* at Bogota, Columbia 1969.

**3** ●Susan Elaine EISENHOWER, *b* at Fort Knox, Kentucky 31 Dec 1951, *m* at Gettysburg, Pennsylvania 8 Jan 1971, ●Alexander Hugh Bradshaw, Barrister-at-law (*b* at Cairo, Egypt 18 March 1941) [*23 Fitzwarren Gardens, London, N19*], eldest son of Frederick John Bradshaw, Assist Sec Gen of the Royal Commonwealth Soc, sometime British Consul in Brussels, by his wife Joan Pauline Beatrice Dagnall, and has issue,

   (1) ●Caroline Louise BRADSHAW, *b* at Middlesex Hospital, London, W1 29 March 1972.

   (2) ●Laura Madeleine BRADSHAW, *b* at 23 Fitzwarren Gardens, London, N19 29 Sept 1973.

**4** ●Mary Jean EISENHOWER, *b* at Washington, DC 21 Dec 1955.

# The Brothers of President Eisenhower

**1** Arthur B. EISENHOWER, banker, *b* at Hope, Kansas 11 Nov 1886, *m* 1st 1906 (*m* diss by div 1924), Alida B. —. He *m* 2ndly, ●Louise Grieb, and *d* at Kansas City, Missouri 26 Jan 1958, having by her had issue,
   ●Katherine EISENHOWER, *m* Berton Roneche.
**2** Edgar EISENHOWER, attorney, *b* at Denison, Texas 19 Jan 1889, *m* 1st —, and had issue,
   ●Janice EISENHOWER.
Edgar Eisenhower *m* 2ndly —; and 3rdly (*m* diss by div 1967), Lucy (*b* 1920), dau of — Dawson, and is *dec.*
**3** Roy EISENHOWER, of Kansas City, pharmacist, *b* at Abilene, Kansas 9 Aug 1892, *m* — and *d* 1942, leaving issue, three children.
**4** Paul EISENHOWER, *b* at Abilene, Kansas 12 May 1894; *d* there 16 March 1895 (*bur* Belle Springs, nr Abilene, Kansas).
**5** Earl EISENHOWER, of Charleroi, Pennsylvania, electrical engineer, *b* at Abilene, Kansas 1 Feb 1898, *m* and *d* at Scottsdale, Arizona Dec 1968, leaving issue, one son.
**6** ●Milton Stover EISENHOWER, Pres Johns Hopkins Univ 1956-67, hon LLD, apptd personal representative of his brother President Eisenhower to make fact-finding tour of Latin America 1953 [*12 East Bishops Road, Baltimore, Maryland 21218, USA*], *b* at Abilene, Kansas 15 Sept 1899, *educ* Kansas State Univ (BS, ScD), and Edinburgh Univ, *m* at Washington, DC 12 Oct 1927, Helen Elsie (*b* at Manhattan, New York 14 Aug 1904; *d* at State College, Pennsylvania 10 July 1954), dau of LeRoy Eakin, by his wife Mabel Gillespie, and has issue,
   1 ●Milton Stover EISENHOWER, Jr, IBM official [*191 Cheese Spring Road, Wilton, Conn 06897, USA*], *b* at Washington, DC 11 Dec 1930, *m* at Florala, Alabama 17 Sept 1955, ●Sally Ann (*b* at Florala 9 Aug 1932), dau of Joseph I. Booth, Jr, by his wife Aileen Casey, and has issue,
      ●Jennifer EISENHOWER, *b* at Glen Cove, New York 9 Aug 1962.
   2 ●Ruth Eakin EISENHOWER, *b* at Washington, DC 21 July 1938, *m* at Baltimore, Maryland 1962 ●Dr Thomas W. Snider (*b* at Little Rock, Arkansas 28 Dec 1933) [*1803 Indianhead Road, Ruxton, Maryland 21204, USA*], son of Harry C. Snider, by by his wife Maureen Honan, and has issue,
      (1) ●Thomas W. SNIDER, Jr, *b* at Baltimore 29 July 1963.
      (2) ●Gordon Eisenhower SNIDER, *b* at Baltimore 24 Sept 1964.
      (3) ●Michael LeRoy SNIDER, *b* at Baltimore 19 April 1967.

# Note

[1] An Act of Congress signed 25 May 1933 (amended 8 July 1937) conferred the degree of Bachelor of Science retroactively by certificate on all qualified living graduates of West Point.

# John Fitzgerald Kennedy
## 1917-1963

——

35th President of the
United States of America
1961-1963

JOHN FITZGERALD KENNEDY, 35TH PRESIDENT

# John Fitzgerald Kennedy

## 1917-1963

### 35th President of the United States of America
### 1961-1963

AT THE 1956 Democratic convention Senator John F. Kennedy of Massachusetts sought and almost won the party's vice-presidential nomination—which finally went to Senator Estes Kefauver of Tennessee. The Stevenson-Kefauver team was trounced by the Republican incumbents, Eisenhower and Nixon. But Kennedy impressed the delegates, both for his charm and for his professional flair. From that moment he was in the running for 1960—in his own eyes as the presidential candidate although others thought he should be content with the second place.

As 1960 drew near, political pundits predicted a close contest. The feeling that the Democrats had been in power too long, plus the great personal popularity of Eisenhower, had accounted for the Republican victories of 1952 and 1956. On the other hand, eight years of Republican rule were enough to disenchant the public; Eisenhower, because of the third-term amendment to the Constitution, would not again be a candidate; and on a national vote count the Democrats were the majority party. Richard Nixon, Eisenhower's heir-apparent, was a strong but not an unbeatable opponent. He had the advantage of prestige and experience, but the disadvantages of an equivocal reputation and of having to base his campaign on the previous record of the Eisenhower Government, which made him sound negative where he wished to sound statesmanlike.

John F. Kennedy's assets and weaknesses also seemed problematical. He was a war hero, he was remarkably handsome, he was the author of a Pulitzer-prize winning book about Senate leadership, *Profiles in Courage*. On the other hand his performance in the Senate was not remarkable for courage or for diligence. He had a beautiful and socially prominent young wife, Jacqueline Bouvier Kennedy. He had the clannish support of a rich, politically ambitious family, especially that of his younger brother Robert Kennedy, who had become known in Washington as a shrewd, aggressive lawyer. Family wealth enabled him to enter the Democratic primaries with a ready-made team of advisers and to campaign in a private jet aircraft. On the debit side, however, his millionaire father was said to be ruthless and cranky. In some quarters the Kennedy wealth was resented. In Massachusetts, which the Republicans had captured in 1952 and 1956, the family was associated with the machine politics of maternal grandfather "Honey Fitz". Moreover, they were Roman Catholics in a country with a traditional bias against the Catholic church. Al Smith was the only Catholic candidate previously nominated by a major party, in 1928; and conventional wisdom held that, as in Smith's case, any candidate bearing such a liability was bound to lose.

Yet the Kennedy campaign of 1960 was a dazzling success, first in the primaries, then at the party convention, then in the contest with Nixon. He had built up a fund of goodwill by speaking on behalf of the Democrats in every state of the Union. His addresses, which blended wit and serious substance, were invariably well received. Liberal intellectuals, who reluctantly abandoned Adlai Stevenson, relished a sophisticated intelligence on a par with that of their former idol. Newspapermen found him accessible, candid, amusing and quotable. Despite his youth—he was only 42 and looked 35— Kennedy displayed an impressive assurance that stopped short of pomposity. He was exceptionally photogenic: an important advantage in an election in which television was now the chief medium of communication. His four televised debates with Vice-President Nixon may have tipped the balance at the November polls, where he elbowed out his opponent by only 120,000 popular votes in a total of nearly 69 million.

With the inauguration in January 1961 Camelot began. The Kennedys arrived at the White House with a three-year-old daughter and a baby son. Harvard professors such as John Kenneth Galbraith and Arthur Schlesinger, Jr, were given posts. Writers and musicians were invited to glittering entertainments in a White House transformed by Jacqueline Kennedy's elegant taste. "What a joy", said the novelist John Steinbeck, "that literacy is no longer prima-facie evidence of treason". There was relief among men of goodwill that the old spectre of anti-Catholicism had been vanquished. There was almost universal praise for President Kennedy's inaugural address. His theme, in line with the campaign promise to "get America moving again" after the supposed torpor of the Eisenhower years, was activity, at home and abroad. The United States would "bear any burden, pay any price".

There were some early setbacks. The President was criticized for bringing his brother Bobby into the cabinet as Attorney-General. The

JACQUELINE LEE BOUVIER, MRS KENNEDY

Bay of Pigs invasion of Cuba was a disquieting fiasco. But the new Attorney-General soon revealed his mettle; and the Administration, while admitting the Cuban blunder, was able to show that the scheme was hatched before 1961. Kennedy sought to make amends by paying particular attention to Latin America. His toughness in the subsequent Cuban "missile crisis" was much admired. The Kennedy style of personal diplomacy, which took him on trips to Canada, Central America and Europe and led to a meeting with Premier Khrushchev, created an atmosphere of *détente*, symbolized by the establishment of the Peace Corps. The Kennedy space program promised spectacular results as American astronauts began to emulate the exploits of Russian spacemen. At home the President was no less conspicuous though his achievements were more modest. In a dramatic clash he compelled the steel industry to rescind a price rise as harmful to the economy. He and the Attorney-General attempted to press forward with the enforcement of civil rights. In general the response to the Kennedy Administration was enthusiastic, even adoring among the young and other sections of the public. Protest movements were still non-violent, and optimistic. Except for segregationists and a few other disgruntled groups, comment on the Kennedys was usually admiring and rarely went beyond affectionate mockery. When the President visited Dallas, Texas, in November 1963, accompanied by his wife, he had been warned that they might meet hostility. Even in his own bailiwick, Vice-President Johnson had had a bad reception. The President was as always cheerfully philosophical. His family was no stranger to calamity, and he realized that a whole army of secret servicemen could not protect a public figure against someone determined to kill. He went to Dallas in the line of duty, to help patch up a quarrel within the Democratic party, knowing that such gestures would consolidate his already almost unchallengeable claim to the party's renomination in 1964. He was killed, the columnist E. B. White wrote with a mournful irony, "in a way that he would have settled for—... with his friends and enemies all around, supporting him and shooting at him".

Disasters and disappointments—the assassination of Bobby Kennedy in 1968, the Chappaquiddick affair for Senator Edward Kennedy—have pursued the Kennedy family. The glamor of the Camelot years has faded, or at least become a distant and perhaps improbable memory. In the light of subsequent events commentators have argued that John F. Kennedy represented a phase in an excessive enlargement of presidential prerogative. He committed the nation, it has been said, to an unwholesome conception of global responsibility of which the Vietnam war was the fruit. He promised too much. Whether he will be ranked among the greatest Presidents is uncertain. But the uncertainty turns upon the definition of greatness—power, accomplishment, duration in office, wisdom, personal appeal? If he had lived he might have avoided some of the pitfalls that awaited his successor. Or he might have been trapped by them. He was only human. Nevertheless, John F. Kennedy was an Admirable Crichton among American Chief Executives, the stuff of legend, canny and clever and captivating in a mix that makes him seem unique. All deaths are sad but some are merely sad. His had a dimension of tragedy.

# Chronology

1917     Born at 83 Beals Street, Brookline, Mass 29 May.

1922-31   Attended private schools in Brookline, Riverdale, Bronx, NY, and New Milford, Mass.

1931-35   Attended Choate School, Wallingford, Conn.

1935     Attended London School of Economics; entered Princeton University 23 Sept; left college owing to ill-health 12 Dec.

1936     Entered Harvard 5 Sept.

1938     Received $1,000,000 trust fund from father on 21st birthday 29 May.

1939     Toured Europe acting as secretary to his father, then US Ambassador to Court of St James's.

1940     Graduated from Harvard as BSc *cum laude* 20 June; studied at Stanford University Graduate Sch of Business Administration, Palo Alto, California.

1941     Commissioned as Ensign, USN 5 Oct.

1942     Called up for active service and attended PT boat training school.

1943     Sailed for S Pacific March; assumed command (with rank of Lieut (junior grade)) of PT-*109* in Solomon Islands April; PT-*109* rammed and sunk by Japanese destroyer *Amagiri* 2 Aug; escaped with survivors of crew to an island from which they were rescued 8 Aug; received Purple Heart, Navy Medal and Marine Medal for this action; returned to US Dec.

1944     Underwent operation for slipped disc at Chelsea Naval Hospital, Boston.

1945     Discharged from Navy April; worked as reporter with International News Service.

1946     Elected to House of Representatives 5 Nov.

1947     Took seat 3 Jan; served in 80th, 81st and 82nd Congresses, being twice re-elected.

1952     Elected to Senate, defeating Senator Henry Cabot Lodge by 70,000 votes 4 Nov.

1953     Took seat in Senate 3 Jan.

1954    Underwent operation for spinal fusion at Hospital for Special Surgery, New York City, Oct.

1955    Underwent further operation on back Feb.

1956    Unsuccessful candidate for nomination as Vice-President, Democratic Nat Convention, Chicago.

1957    Awarded Pulitzer Prize for Biography for his book *Profiles in Courage.*

1958    Re-elected to Senate 4 Nov.

1960    Nominated for President at Democratic National Convention, Los Angeles 14 July; elected 35th President 8 Nov with 303 electoral votes against 219 for Nixon and 15 for Harry F. Byrd.

1961    Electoral vote tabulated by Congress 6 Jan and Kennedy and Johnson officially declared elected; inaugurated at Washington 20 Jan; appointed cabinet 21 Jan; gave first press conference 25 Jan; delivered first State of the Union message to Congress 30 Jan; pledged support of NATO 15 Feb; put forward Alliance for Progress program (a ten-year plan to raise living standards in Latin America) 13 March; conferred with Harold Macmillan, British Prime Minister (and uncle-by-marriage to Kennedy's late brother-in-law Lord Hartington—*see* BROTHERS AND SISTERS OF PRESIDENT KENNEDY, *p 546*) at Key West, Florida 26 March; Bay of Pigs invasion fiasco in Cuba 17-20 April, for which Kennedy accepted full responsibility; paid state visit to Canada 16-17 May; vetoed Relief Bill for William Joseph Vincent 26 May (the first of 21 vetoes); flew to Paris 31 May; met Nikita Krushchev Premier of USSR at Vienna 3-4 June; visited England 4-5 June; returned to Washington 6 June; Alliance for Progress accord signed 17 Aug; signed Peace Corps Act 22 Sept; addressed United Nations General Assembly in New York City 25 Sept; visited Puerto Rico 15 Dec; visited Caracas, Venezuela 16 Dec; visited Bogota, Colombia 17 Dec; conferred with Harold Macmillan in Bermuda 21-22 Dec.

1962    Announced increase of Army from 14 to 16 divisions 3 Jan; delivered second State of the Union message to Congress 11 Jan; opened Century 21 Exposition, Seattle, Washington 21 April by pressing a golden telegraph key in Palm Beach, Florida; visited Mexico 29 June-1 July; conferred with Harold Macmillan at Nassau, Bahamas 18-21 Dec.

1963    Delivered third and last State of the Union message to Congress 14 Jan; conferred with the Presidents of Costa Rica, El Salvador, Guatemala, Honduras, Panama and Nicaragua at San Jose, Costa Rica 18-20 March; proclaimed Sir Winston Churchill an honorary citizen of the United States 9 April; received Grand Duchess Charlotte of Luxembourg on State Visit 30 April-4 May; visited West Germany 23-26 June and following the conferment of honorary citizenship made his celebrated "Ich bin ein Berliner" speech; visited Ireland 26-29 June; visited England 29-30 June; visited Italy 1-2 July; returned to Washington 3 July; made non-political tour of 11 western states 24-29 Sept; issued proclamation declaring nuclear test ban treaty in effect 10 Oct; vetoed Relief Bill for Dr James T. Mattux 19 Nov (the last of his 21 vetoes); left for three day visit to Texas 21 Nov; flew to Dallas 22 Nov; shot in the head by an assassin while riding in an open motor-car procession through Dallas 22 Nov; rushed to Parkland Hospital, but died of his injuries at 1 pm (CST); buried at Arlington National Cemetery, Arlington, Virginia. He was the fourth President to be assassinated and the eighth to die in office.

# The Writings of President Kennedy

*Why England Slept* (1940)

*As We Remember Joe,* a tribute to his brother Joseph P. Kennedy, Jr (1945)

*Profiles in Courage* (1956)

# Lineage of President Kennedy

— KENNEDY, a tenant farmer at Dunganstown, co Wexford, Ireland, had with other issue a 3rd and yst son,

PATRICK KENNEDY, emigrated to USA 1848 and settled in Boston, Mass, where he became a cooper by trade, *b* at Dunganstown 1823, *m* Bridget Murphy (*b* 1821), and *d* of cholera at Boston 1859, leaving issue with three daus,

PATRICK JOSEPH KENNEDY, of Boston, saloon keeper, *b* at Boston 8 Jan 1858, *m* 1887, Mary Hickey, and *d* at Boston May 1929, having had issue with one other son (who *d* an inf) and two daus,

JOSEPH PATRICK KENNEDY, KM, of Boston, hon LLD Nat Univ of Ireland (1938), and Univs of Edinburgh, Manchester, Liverpool, Bristol and Camb 1939, real estate owner, financier and banker, Chm Securities Exchange Commn 1934-35 and of US Maritime Commn 1937, US Amb to the Court of St James's 1937-41, mem Commn on Orgn of Exec Branch of Fed Govt 1947 and 1953, Grand Kt of Pius IX, Kt of Equestrian Order of Holy Sepulchre and Grand Cross Order of Leopold II of Belgium, *b* at 151 Meridian Street, Boston 6 Sept 1888, *educ* Latin Sch, and Harvard (AB 1912), *m* at Boston 7 Oct 1914, •Rose, *cr* a Papal Countess by Pope Pius XII, author of *Times to Remember* (1973) (*b* at North End, Boston 22 July 1890), dau of John F. ("Honey Fitz") Fitzgerald, Mayor of Boston, by his wife Josephine Mary Hannon, and *d* at Hyannis Port, Mass 18 Nov 1969, having had with other issue (*see* BROTHERS AND SISTERS OF PRESIDENT KENNEDY, *p 546*) a 2nd son,

JOHN FITZGERALD KENNEDY, **35th President of the United States of America.**

# The Descendants of
# President Kennedy

JOHN FITZGERALD KENNEDY *m* at Newport, Rhode Island 12 Sept 1953, •Jacqueline Lee (*b* at Southampton, Long Island, New York 28 July 1929; *m* 2ndly at Skorpios, Greece 22 Oct 1968, as his 2nd wife, Aristotle Socrates Onassis, the shipowner, son of Socrates Onassis) [*1041 Fifth Avenue, New York, New York 10028, USA; Skorpios, Greece*], dau of John Vernou Bouvier III, stockbroker, by his wife Janet Lee (later Mrs Hugh Auchinloss), and had issue,

> **1** A daughter, stillborn 23 Aug 1956.
> **2** •Caroline Bouvier KENNEDY, *b* at New York 27 Nov 1957.
> **3** •John Fitzgerald KENNEDY, Jr, *b* at Washington, DC 25 Nov 1960.
> **4** Patrick Bouvier KENNEDY, *b* at Otis Air Force Base, Mass 7 Aug, *d* at Boston, Mass 9 Aug 1963.

# The Brothers and Sisters of President Kennedy

**1** Joseph Patrick KENNEDY, Jr, Lieut USN, served in World War II, *b* at Boston, Mass July 1915, *educ* Choate, London Sch of Economics, and Harvard, *k* in action over Suffolk, England 2 Aug 1944, *unm.*

**2** ●Rosemary KENNEDY, *b* at Boston Sept 1918.

**3** Kathleen ("Kick") KENNEDY, *b* at Boston 1920, *m* at Chelsea Register Office, London 6 May 1944, William John Robert Cavendish, Marquess of Hartington (*b* 10 Dec 1917; *k* in action in Belgium 10 Sept 1944), elder son of 10th Duke of Devonshire, KG, MBE (*see* BURKE'S *Peerage*), and nephew-by-marriage of Rt Hon (Maurice) Harold Macmillan, Prime Min of Great Britain 1957-63, and was *k* in a flying accident in France 13 May 1948, *sp.*

**4** ●Eunice Mary KENNEDY, *b* at Boston July 1921, *m* 23 May 1953, ●(Robert) Sargent Shriver, Jr, LLB, LLD, lawyer, Vice-Presidential candidate Nov 1972, sometime Dir Peace Corps and Office of Economic Opportunity, and US Amb to France, Lt-Cmdr USNR (*b* at Westminster, Maryland 9 Nov 1915) [*140 E Walton Place, Chicago, Illinois, USA*], son of Robert Sargent Shriver, by his wife Hilda Shriver, and has issue,

   1 ●Robert Sargent SHRIVER III, *b* 1954.
   2 ●Maria SHRIVER.
   3 ●Timothy SHRIVER.
   4 ●Mark Kennedy SHRIVER, *b* at Washington, DC Feb 1964.
   5 ●Anthony Paul SHRIVER, *b* at Boston, Mass 20 July 1965.

**5** ●Patricia KENNEDY, *b* at Boston 6 May 1924, *m* (*m* diss by div 1966), Peter Lawford, film actor (*b* 7 Sept 1923), and has issue,

   1 ●Christopher LAWFORD.
   2 ●Victoria LAWFORD.
   3 ●Sydney LAWFORD (dau).
   4 ●Robin LAWFORD (dau).

**6** Robert Francis KENNEDY, served in World War II with USNR, correspondent in Palestine for *Boston Post* 1948, admitted to Mass Bar 1951, Attorney Criminal Div, Dept of Justice 1951-52, Assist Counsel Senate Penn Cttee on Investigations 1953, Chief Counsel (and later Staff Dir) Democratic Minority 1954-59, managed election campaigns for his brother John F. Kennedy for Senate 1952 and Presidency 1960, Attorney-Gen of US 21 Jan 1961-3 Sept 1964, US Senator for New York from 1965, author of *The Enemy Within* (1960), *Just Friends and Brave Enemies* (1962), *The Pursuit of Justice* (1964), *13 Days: The Cuban Missile Crisis, October 1962* (1969), *b* at Boston, Mass 20 Nov 1925, *educ* Milton Acad, Harvard (AB), and Univ of Virginia Law Sch (LLB), *m* at Greenwich, Connecticut 17 June 1950, ●Ethel (*b* 1928), dau of George Skakel, of Chicago, Illinois, by his wife Ann Brannack, and was assassinated at Los Angeles, California 6 June 1968 (*bur* Arlington Nat Cemetery 8 June 1968), leaving issue,

   1 ●Kathleen Hartington KENNEDY, *b* 4 July 1951, *m* at Washington, DC 17 Nov 1973, ●David Lee Townsend (*b* 1948).
   2 ●Joseph Patrick KENNEDY, *b* 1952.
   3 ●Robert Francis KENNEDY, Jr, *b* 1953.
   4 ●David Anthony KENNEDY, *b* 1954.
   5 ●Mary Courtney KENNEDY, *b* 1955.
   6 ●Michael L. KENNEDY, *b* 1957.
   7 ●Mary Kerry KENNEDY, *b* 1958.
   8 ●Christopher George KENNEDY, *b* at Boston, Mass 4 June 1963.
   9 ●Matthew Maxwell Taylor KENNEDY, *b* at New York 9 Jan 1965.
   10 ●Douglas Harriman KENNEDY, *b* at Washington, DC 24 March 1967.
   11 ●Rory Elizabeth KENNEDY, *b* (posthumously) at Washington, DC 12 Dec 1968.

**7** ●Jean Ann KENNEDY, *b* at Boston Feb 1928, *m* 1956, ●Stephen Edward Smith, transport executive, and has issue,

   1 ●Stephen SMITH.
   2 ●William Kennedy SMITH, *b* at Boston, Mass Sept 1960.
   3 ●Amanda SMITH.

**8** ●Edward Moore KENNEDY, admitted to Mass Bar 1959, Assist DA of Suffolk County, Mass 1961-62, US Senator from Mass from 1962, has Italian Order of Merit [*3 Charles River Square, Boston, Mass, USA*], *b* at Brookline, Mass 22 Feb 1932, *educ* Milton Acad, Harvard (AB 1954), and Univ of Virginia Law Sch (LLB 1959), *m* 29 Nov 1958, ●(Virginia) Joan Bennett, of New York, and has issue,

   1 ●Kara Ann KENNEDY, *b* March 1960.
   2 ●Edward Moore KENNEDY, Jr, *b* 26 Sept 1961.
   3 ●Patrick Joseph KENNEDY, *b* Aug 1963.

# Lyndon Baines Johnson
## 1908-1973

———

36th President of the
United States of America
1963-1969

LYNDON BAINES JOHNSON, 36TH PRESIDENT

# Lyndon Baines Johnson

## 1908-1973

### 36th President of the United States of America
### 1963-1969

LYNDON JOHNSON had a large stock of folk tales—not all of them appropriate for a polite audience. One story he liked to tell was of a Texan applying for a job as teacher during the Depression. The interview with the local school board went smoothly. At length a member of the board pressed the anxious candidate for an answer to an important question. If he were conducting a geography class, would he teach that the earth was round or that it was flat? "I can teach it either way". The story has several possible interpretations. Lyndon Johnson was no doubt aware of all of them. As "a master of the art of the possible in politics" (Adlai Stevenson's description) he must often have pondered a central problem for the politician: how should such a man reconcile his own beliefs with the views that the voters might expect him to hold? Another political consideration, second nature to a person of "extraordinary managerial skill" (again Stevenson's phrase), was this: how could one best cajole other people into making a deal? The school teacher in the story might have offended his patrons by trying too hard to be all things to all men. Or he might have hit upon the perfect formula—exactly suited to the level of his audience.

Johnson himself came out of the barren hill country of Texas, where his parents' families had combined farming with local politics. And he was a teacher for a while before he earned a longish stay in New Deal Washington as the secretary of a Texas Congressman. He had a long political road to travel, in and out of Congress, a loyal follower of Franklin Roosevelt and a protégé of the sagacious Sam Rayburn. Squeezing through the Democratic primary by the narrowest of margins, Johnson won election to the Senate in 1948. Whether or not it was his finest hour, it was a victory of crucial importance for him. Within a few years he was a commanding figure in Washington—Democratic minority leader of the

Senate in 1953, majority leader two years later when the mid-term elections deprived the Republican administration of control of Congress. He was a power broker, revelling in the responsibility. The Eisenhower legislative program would have been paralyzed without Johnson's adroit, constructive leadership. Not only was he the complete professional politician: he shed his former Southern prejudices, especially on race relations.

By 1960 Lyndon Johnson had every right to consider himself a strong contender for the Democratic presidential nomination. Adlai Stevenson was without spirit for the contest. John F. Kennedy was a relatively new boy in the Senate, and perhaps a lightweight in Johnson's reckoning. But at the convention the nomination went to the younger man on the very first ballot. To the amazement of the party Johnson accepted Kennedy's invitation to become the vice-presidential candidate. We can only guess at his motives. He may have felt that the acceptance would stand him in good stead with the Democrats if Kennedy lost. He was also too shrewd not to realize that it was almost impossible for a Southerner, even a Western Southerner like himself, to win the nomination of a major party. The Vice-Presidency was the next best thing.

After the Kennedy–Johnson inauguration in January 1961 the Vice-President was given a respectable number of official duties. But he was in a backwater. The decisions that mattered were being taken by others. Johnson, by every instinct a man of action, was as frustrated as some of his predecessors in the second office had been. In the meantime, he could at least feel that the experience was beneficial for his family. His wife Claudia Alta Taylor ("Lady Bird") Johnson was an accomplished hostess; their two daughters Lynda Bird and Luci Baines Johnson enjoyed the Washington scene; and the Johnsons' business ventures in Texas were flourishing. If he had reached the summit of his career, so be it: retirement to the LBJ ranch was a prospect many an American would have envied him.

Then the unthinkable happened. Kennedy was gunned down in Dallas. Johnson who had accompanied him took the oath of office in the aircraft that bore him and the dead President back to the capital. A little over a year remained of the Kennedy Administration; only a few months before the election machinery started up once more. In that brief interval President Johnson brought every bit of his prodigious energy and political cunning to bear. "LBJ has been hurling himself about Washington like an elemental force", was the approving comment of the *New Republic*, a magazine that was usually quick to find fault. "To be plain about it, he has won our admiration". Kennedy's "New Frontier" visions were converted into legislation which was swiftly enacted—a civil rights Bill much in advance of previous measures, and a sweeping plan to "end poverty" in the United States. Some were reminded of the hectic atmosphere of the first

CLAUDIA ALTA (LADY BIRD) TAYLOR, MRS JOHNSON

months of Franklin Roosevelt's Presidency. Some said that Johnson's "Great Society" put the "new Frontier" to shame.

The 1964 election was a spectacular triumph for the President. A Texan was the Democratic candidate: a Texan trounced the Republicans' Barry Goldwater. It was "All The Way with LBJ". A derisive pro-Johnson campaign button said "GOLDWATER IN '64: HOT-WATER IN '65". Returned to office with a handsome mandate, LBJ maintained the pace of the Great Society. But by degrees he was the person in hot water. Sceptics began to compare the outlay on welfare programs with the enormous expenditure on the armed forces; to argue that the Great Society was a political stunt; or to suggest that it was a naïve endeavor, since by definition poverty could never be abolished—some people would always be less well off than others. There were riots in the ghettoes and campus demonstrations. The crux of the President's woes was the Vietnam war. If it had terminated as quickly as his advisers promised he might have retained his authority. But month by month the American commitment increased and opposition became more fierce. Few men could have remained cool under such a barrage of criticism. Hurt, puzzled, enraged, Johnson reacted in ways that badly damaged his reputation. He was accused of being a liar and a bully. Cartoonists drew him as a sly, coarse, vindictive creature. The sick humor of the hour produced *MacBird*, a parody of *Macbeth* insinuating that Johnson was implicated in the Dallas assassination.

LBJ had expected to offer himself again for re-election in 1968. But the pressures became too great. At the end of March in that year he announced that he was calling a halt to bombing in Vietnam, and that he would not be a candidate. In January 1969 he attended the inauguration of Richard Nixon, and then flew back to the bittersweet peace of the LBJ ranch.

# Chronology

1908    Born nr Stonewall, Texas 27 Aug.

1913    Entered school in Johnson City, Texas.

1924    Graduated from Johnson City High School.

1927    Entered Southwest Texas State Teachers College.

1930    Graduated from College with BSc degree 18 Aug.

1930-31  Taught public speaking and debate at Sam Houston High School, Houston, Texas.

1931    Appointed secretary to Representative Richard M. Kleberg 24 Nov.

1933    Elected speaker of "Little Congress" organization of congressional secretaries.

1934    Entered Georgetown University Law School 19 Sept.

1935-37  Texas Director of National Youth Administration.

1937    Elected to House of Representatives 10 April; took seat 14 May.

1938    Re-elected to the House 8 Nov.

1941    Defeated in special election for the Senate 4 Nov; commissioned Lt-Cmdr USN 9 Dec.

1942    Awarded Silver Star for gallantry in action in New Guinea 9 June; ordered back to Washington.

1948    Elected to the Senate 2 Nov.

1949    Took seat in Senate 3 Jan.

1951    Elected majority whip in Senate 2 Jan; began buying LBJ Ranch.

1953    Elected minority leader of Senate 3 Jan.

1954    Re-elected to the Senate 2 Nov.

1955    Elected majority leader of Senate 5 Jan; suffered serious heart attack 2 July.

1958    Presented US resolution calling for peaceful exploration of outer space to UN at request of President Eisenhower.

1960    Defeated for Presidential nomination at Democratic National Convention in Los Angeles 13 July; nominated for Vice-President by acclamation 14 July; elected Vice-President and re-elected to the Senate for a third term 6 Nov.

1961    Took oath of office as Senator and immediately resigned 3 Jan; took oath of office as Vice-President 20 Jan; attended independence ceremonies of the Republic of Senegal at Dakar 3 April; visited Far East and Southeast Asia May; conferred with Chancellor Adenauer and Mayor Willy Brandt in West Berlin, Germany Sept.

1962    Attended 10th anniversary celebrations of Commonwealth of Puerto Rico July; visited Middle East Aug-Sept.

1963    Attended inauguration of President Juan Bosch of Dominican Republic Feb; represented President Kennedy at the funeral of Pope John XXIII in Rome June; accompanied President Kennedy to Texas 21 Nov; succeeded as 36th President of the United States of America on the assassination of President Kennedy and took the oath of office on board the Presidential Jet *Air Force One*, at Love Field, Dallas, Texas 22 Nov; attended funeral of President Kennedy 25 Nov; addressed joint session of Congress 27 Nov; issued executive order appointing special commission to investigate Kennedy's assassination 29 Nov; ordered budget reductions in all executive departments 11 Dec; delivered first address to UN 17 Dec; conferred with West German Chancellor Erhard at Johnson City, Texas 27-28 Dec; pocket vetoed Bill to amend Tariff Act of 1930 31 Dec.

1964    Delivered first State of the Union message to Congress 8 Jan; conferred with Canadian Prime Minister Lester B. Pearson at the White House 21-22 Jan; signed Act renaming National Cultural Center as John F. Kennedy Center for the Performing Arts 23 Jan; 24th Amendment to the Constitution ratified 4 Feb; conferred with British Prime Minister Sir Alec Douglas-Home in Washington 12-13 Feb; signed Long-range Tax Reduction Act 26 Feb; signed Coast Guard Construction Program Act 11 March; sent special message to Congress on foreign aid 19 March; declared Alaska disaster area following severe earthquake 28 March; conferred with King Hussein of Jordan at the White House 14-15 April; dedicated Federal Pavilion at New York World's Fair 22 April; made flying tour of Appalachia 24 April; revisited Appalachia 7-8 May; signed Civil Rights Act of 1964 2 July; signed Mass Transit Act 6 July; signed Space Administration Appropriations Act 11 July; signed Military Construction Act 1 Aug; announced US air attacks on North Vietnamese oil depot and PT boat bases 4 Aug; signed joint resolution authorizing him to repel any armed attack against US military forces by all necessary means 7 Aug; signed Military Pay Increase Act 12 Aug; signed Highway Aid Act 13 Aug; signed Federal Employees Salary Reform Act 14 Aug; renominated for President by acclamation at Democratic National Convention in Atlantic City 26 Aug; signed Economic Opportunity Act of 1964 30 Aug; signed Housing Act 2 Sept; signed Wilderness Act 3 Sept; signed Omnibus Education Act 16 Oct; issued proclamation of 30 day mourning period for former President Hoover 20 Oct; election day 3 Nov; conferred with British Prime Minister Harold Wilson at the White House 7-8 Dec; Presidential Electors cast their ballots (486 for Johnson; 52 for Barry Morris Goldwater, the Republican candidate) 17 Dec.

1965    Delivered second State of the Union message to Congress 4 Jan; Electoral votes tabulated by Congress and Johnson and Humphrey officially declared elected 6 Jan; inaugurated on the east portico of the Capitol 20 Jan; ordered air attacks on N Vietnam 7 Feb; first US troops landed in S Vietnam 8-9 March; addressed joint session of Congress urging voting rights legislation 15 March; federalized Alabama National Guard 20 March; increased US military and economic aid to S Vietnam 2 April; sent troops to Dominican Republic to protect US lives following military coup April-May; 25th Amendment to the Constitution submitted to the States for ratification 6 July; announced additional troops to be sent to Vietnam and doubling of draft 28 July; sent special message to Congress asking for $1,700,000,000 additional defence appropriations for Vietnam War 4 Aug; recognized provisional Government of the Dominican Republic 4 Sept; signed Act establishing Department of Housing and Urban Development 9 Sept; met Pope Paul VI in New York 4 Oct; underwent gall bladder operation in Bethesda Naval Hospital, Maryland 8 Oct; returned to the White House 21 Oct; signed Highway Beautification Act 22 Oct; signed Public Works Appropriation Act 28 Oct; signed Federal Employees Salary Increase Act 29 Oct; signed Higher Education Act of 1965 8 Nov; gave dinner-dance at the White House for HRH The Princess Margaret of Great Britain and her husband the Earl of Snowdon 17 Nov.

1966     Delivered third State of the Union message to Congress 12 Jan; announced US resumption of bombing raids on N Vietnam 31 Jan; conferred with Nguyen Cao Ky, Prime Minister of S Vietnam in Honolulu, Hawaii 6-8 Feb; met with 38 State Governors and the Governors of Puerto Rico, Guam, and the Virgin Islands at the White House 12 March; visited Mexico 14-15 April; signed Supplemental Appropriation Act 13 May; anti-war demonstrators picketed the White House 15 May; signed Act creating American Revolution Bicentennial Commission 4 July; signed Space Authorization Act 5 Aug; signed Act prohibiting the use of stolen pets in medical research 24 Aug; offered to stop bombing of N Vietnam if Hanoi would agree to reciprocate 22 Sept; rejected suggestion of U Thant that US should suspend bombing of N Vietnam as first step towards a negotiated settlement 13 Oct; signed seven Conservation Acts 15 Oct; signed Act creating Department of Transportation 16 Oct; signed Act extending US exclusive fishing zone from 3 to 12 miles off coast 17 Oct; visited American Samoa, New Zealand, Australia, the Philippines, S Vietnam, Thailand, Malaysia, S Korea and Alaska Oct-Nov; returned to Washington 2 Nov; signed eight major domestic Acts 3 Nov; signed Foreign Investors Tax Act 13 Nov; underwent surgery on throat and abdomen 16 Nov.

1967     Delivered fourth State of the Union message to Congress 10 Jan; 25th Amendment to the Constitution ratified 10 Feb; conferred with S Vietnamese Prime Minister Nguyen Cao Ky and Chief of State Nguyen Van Thieu at Agana, Guam 20-21 March; signed consular convention with USSR 31 March; signed Supplementary Appropriation Act for military operations in Southeast Asia 4 April; visited Uruguay 11-14 April; visited West Germany 23-26 April; visited *Expo 67* at Montreal, Canada 25 May; conferred with British Prime Minister Harold Wilson on the Middle East crisis at the White House 2 June; proposed five-point plan for the Middle East 19 June; conferred with Soviet Premier Kosygin at Glassboro, New Jersey 23 and 25 June; signed Act extending and expanding federal mental health program 26 June; signed Act extending National Teacher Corps 29 June; signed Military Selective Service Act of 1967 and National Debt Limitation Act 30 June; signed Veterans' Benefits Act 31 Aug; issued executive order establishing New England River Basins Commission 7 Sept; signed Food Stamp Act 27 Sept; offer to halt bombing of N Vietnam if peace talks followed rejection 29 Sept; signed Vocational Rehabilitation Act of 1967 3 Oct; signed Aid to Appalachia Act 11 Oct; attended formal transfer of El Chamizal from US to Mexico 28 Oct; signed Act creating Corporation for Public Broadcasting 7 Nov; signed Equal Military Promotion for Women Act 8 Nov; signed Act creating National Commission on Product Safety 20 Nov; signed Air Quality Act 21 Nov; vetoed Bill to grant masters of certain US vessels liens on vessels for wages and other disbursements 8 Dec; signed Act extending Civil Rights Commission for five years and Wholesome Meat Act 15 Dec; visited Australia, Thailand, Pakistan, Italy and the Azores 19-24 Dec.

1968    Signed Foreign Aid Appropriation Act and Omnibus Social Security Act 2 Jan; delivered fifth State of the Union message to Congress 17 Jan; signed executive order permitting election of chief executive of the Ryukyu Islands by popular vote 1 Feb; toured military installations in US 17-18 Feb; signed Fire Research and Safety Act 1 March; visited Puerto Rico 2-4 March; signed Civil Rights Act of 1968 11 April; visited Hawaii 15-18 April; signed Organization of American States Treaty 23 April; designated Ohio and Kentucky as disaster areas following tornado 2 May; opened National Collection of Fine Arts in Washington, DC 3 May; dedicated Hall of Heroes in the Pentagon, Washington, DC 14 May; received honorary degree of LLD from Texas Christian University at Fort Worth, Texas 29 May; attended funeral of Senator Robert F. Kennedy at St Patrick's Cathedral, New York and burial at Arlington National Cemetery 8 June; signed Omnibus Safety Crime Control Act of 1968 19 June; signed Act changing dates of observance of Washington's Birthday, Memorial Day and Veterans' Day and making Columbus Day a legal holiday 28 June; signed Nuclear Non-Proliferation Treaty at the White House 1 July; visited El Salvador 6 July; visited Nicaragua, Costa Rica, Honduras and Guatamala 8 July; signed Land and Water Conservation Fund Act 15 July; visited Hawaii 18-20 July; signed Omnibus Housing Act 1 Aug; signed Act creating Flaming Gorge National Recreation Area 1 Oct; signed Acts establishing Redwood National Park, California, and National Cascades National Park, Washington 2 Oct; signed Act banning mail-order sale of rifles, shotguns and all ammunition 23 Oct; signed Act prohibiting manufacture, sale and distribution of LSD or similar drugs 25 Oct; ordered halt of air, naval and artillery bombardment of N Vietnam 31 Oct.

1969    Awarded NASA Distinguished Service Medal to *Apollo 8* astronauts 9 Jan; delivered sixth (and last) State of the Union message to Congress 14 Jan; signed Act increasing salary of President from $100,000 to $200,000 annually 17 Jan; signed executive order creating Marble Canyon National Park in Arizona and Colorado 20 Jan; retired from office and attended the inauguration of President Nixon 20 Jan; attended the funeral of former President Eisenhower in Washington, DC 1 March.

1970    Attended dedication of his birthplace and boyhood home as a National Historic Site 13 June; attended dedication of LBJ State Park, across Pedernales River from LBJ Ranch 29 Aug; attended state dinner for President Gustavo Diaz Ordaz of Mexico at Coronado, California 3 Sept.

1971    Visited Acapulco, Mexico 24 Jan-7 Feb; attended dedication of Eisenhower Museum at Abilene, Kansas 14 Oct; delivered address to New York University Graduate School of Business 15 Nov.

1972    Attended funeral of former President Truman at Independence, Missouri 28 Dec.

1973    Suffered a heart attack at LBJ Ranch and died in an ambulance helicopter *en route* to San Antonio, Texas 22 Jan; buried at LBJ Ranch, Stonewall, Texas.

# The Writings of President
# Lyndon Baines Johnson

*The Vantage Point: Perspectives of the Presidency, 1963-1969* (1971)

# Lineage of President
# Lyndon Baines Johnson

The first three generations of this lineage have been brought to light by the painstaking researches of Mr Hugh B. Johnston, Jr, of Wilson, N Carolina, and have been meticulously documented. The family is thought to be descended from the JOHNSTONS *of Annandale*, Dumfriesshire, Scotland.

JAMES JOHNSTON, of Currowaugh, in Nansemond and Isle of Wight Counties, Virginia, perhaps the son of an early colonial settler in Nansemond County (of which the oldest records have unfortunately been destroyed), *b ca* 1662, *m ante* 1690, Mary (*b ca* 1670; *d post* 1747), dau of Robert Johnson, of the Lower Parish of Isle of Wight County, planter, by his wife Katherine, and *d* in Isle of Wight County 1747 (will dated 30 Jan 1745/6, *pr* 11 June 1747), leaving issue with five other sons and five daus, a 2nd son,

JOHN JOHNSTON, of Black Creek, Southampton County, Virginia, *b* in Isle of Wight County *ca* 1696, *m* 1st, —, and had issue. He *m* 2ndly, Peninah — (*d* 1799), and *d* in Southampton County (which had been formed out of the southern part of Isle of Wight County 1752) 1783 (will dated 30 Jan, *pr* 8 May), having by her had issue. His eldest son (by his 1st marriage),

JOHN JOHNSON, settled in Franklin County, N Carolina *ca* 1767, hatter, *b* in Isle of Wight County *ca* 1724, *m* 1st, — Holland, of Nansemond County, and had issue, two or three children. He *m* 2ndly *ante* 19 June 1763, Elizabeth, dau of Robert Carr, of Nottoway Parish, Southampton County, by his wife Sarah, and by her had issue. He *m* 3rdly 28 Oct 1815, Martha (*d* 1816), widow of Elijah Denby, of Franklin County, and dau of Patewells Milner, by his wife Jacobina, and *d* in Franklin County 1829 (will dated 22 May, *pr* June), aged about 105. His son by his 1st marriage,

JOHN JOHNSON, of Oglethorpe County, Georgia, *b* in Southampton County, Virginia 28 March 1764, *m* 1st 1786, Ann (*b* in Southampton County, Virginia 14 Sept 1763; *d* in Oglethorpe County, Georgia 5 Jan 1815), dau of Samuel Eley, of Franklin County, N Carolina, by his wife Mary Hillsman, and had issue, five sons and three daus. He *m* 2ndly in Greene County, Georgia 24 May 1823, Joicy, widow of William Fears, of Greene County, and dau of — Griffin, and *d* in Oglethorpe County, Georgia 14 Feb 1828 (will dated 28 Jan, *pr* March). His 3rd son (by his 1st marriage),

JESSE JOHNSON, of Henry County, Georgia, later of Randolph County, Alabama, and finally of Caldwell County, Texas, Sheriff of Henry County 1822-31, Justice of the Peace and Judge of the Inferior Court of Henry County 1833-37, *b* in Oglethorpe County, Georgia 28 April 1795, *m* 14 Nov 1817, Lucy Webb (*b* in Greene County, Georgia 14 Jan 1798; *d* in Texas 3 March 1857), dau of Leonard Barnett, by his wife Nancy Statham, and *d* at Lockhart, Texas 15 May 1856, leaving issue with four other sons and five daus, a yst son,

SAMUEL EALY JOHNSON, cattle rancher in partnership with his brother Jesse Thomas (Tom) Johnson, established Johnson's Ranch on the Pedernales River, nr the present Johnson City (which was named after them) *ca* 1888, served in the Civil War as private in Company B, Col DeBray's Regt, CSA, and was present at the Battles of Galveston and Pleasant Hill, *b* in Randolph County, Alabama 12 Nov 1838, *m* at Lockhart, Texas 11 Dec 1867, Eliza (*b* 24 June 1849; *d* 30 Jan 1917), dau of Lieut Robert Desha Bunton, by his wife Jane McIntosh, and *d* at Stonewall, Texas 25 Feb 1915, leaving with other issue,

SAMUEL EALY JOHNSON, Jr, of Johnson City, Texas, politician, lawyer, farmer and real estate dealer, mem Texas House of Representatives 1904-09 and 1917-25, *b* at Buda, Hays County, Texas 11 Oct 1877, *m* at Fredericksburg, Texas 20 Aug 1907, Rebekah (*b* at McKinney, Texas 26 June 1881; *d* at Austin, Texas 12 Sept 1958), dau of Capt Joseph Wilson Baines, of Blanco, Texas, by his wife Ruth Ament Huffman, and *d* at Austin, Texas 23 Oct 1937, leaving with other issue (*see* BROTHER AND SISTERS OF PRESIDENT LYNDON BAINES JOHNSON, *p 560*), an elder son,

LYNDON BAINES JOHNSON, **36th President of the United States of America.**

# The Descendants of President Lyndon Baines Johnson

LYNDON BAINES JOHNSON *m* at San Antonio, Texas 17 Nov 1934, ●Claudia Alta (called Lady Bird) (*b* at Karnack, Texas 22 Dec 1912) [*LBJ Ranch, Stonewall, Texas 78761, USA*], dau of Thomas Jefferson Taylor, by his wife Minnie Pattillo, and had issue,

> **1 ●**Lynda Bird JOHNSON, *b* 19 March 1944, *m* at the White House, Washington, DC 9 Dec 1967, ●Major Charles Spittall Robb, US Marine Corps (*b* at Phoenix, Arizona) [*McLean, Virginia, USA*], son of James S. Robb, of Milwaukee, Wisconsin, by his wife Frances Woolley, and has issue,
>> 1 ●Lucinda Desha ROBB, *b* at Washington, DC 24 Oct 1968.
>> 2 ●Catherine Lewis ROBB, *b* at Washington, DC 5 June 1970.
>
> **2 ●**Lucy (Luci) Baines JOHNSON, *b* 2 July 1947, *m* at the Shrine of the Immaculate Conception, Washington, DC 6 Aug 1966, ●Patrick John Nugent (*b* 8 July 1943) [*Austin, Texas, USA*], son of Gerard P. Nugent, of Waukegan, Illinois (by his wife *née* Jocius), and has issue,
>> 1 ●Patrick Lyndon NUGENT, *b* at Austin, Texas 21 June 1967.
>> 2 ●Nicole Marie NUGENT, *b* at Austin, Texas 11 Jan 1970.
>> 3 ●Rebekah Johnson NUGENT, *b* at Austin, Texas 10 July 1974.

# The Brother and Sisters of President Lyndon Baines Johnson

**1**●Rebekah Luruth JOHNSON, *b* 1910, *m* ●O. Price Bobbitt [*Austin, Texas, USA*].

**2** Josefa Hermine JOHNSON, *b* 1912, *m* ●James B. Moss, and *d* 1961.

**3**●Sam Houston JOHNSON [*Austin, Texas, USA*], *b* 1914.

**4**●Lucia Huffman JOHNSON, *b* 1916, *m* ●Birge D. Alexander [*Fort Worth, Texas, USA*].

# Richard Milhous Nixon

## 1913-

———

37th President of the
United States of America
1969-1974

RICHARD MILHOUS NIXON, 37TH PRESIDENT and THELMA CATHERINE (PAT) RYAN, MRS NIXON (*seated*); with (*standing, left to right*) (Dwight) David Eisenhower II; Julie Nixon, Mrs Eisenhower; Patricia Nixon, Mrs Cox and Edward Ridley Finch Cox

# Richard Milhous Nixon

## 1913-

## *37th President of the United States of America*
## *1969-1974*

IT WILL be a long time before a cool verdict can be pronounced on the character and attainments of Richard Milhous Nixon, the second President to have faced impeachment and the first to have resigned. Even sharp critics, such as Garry Wills in a book called *Nixon Agonistes* (1970), agreed with admirers that Nixon made the most of his assets, at least so far as his political career was concerned. He did not have the social connections of a Franklin Roosevelt, the wealth of a Nelson Rockefeller or a John F. Kennedy, the political family tradition of a Robert A. Taft. Unlike Dwight D. Eisenhower, he had not soared to fame in the great lottery of the military profession. Unlike his rival Kennedy, he did not emerge from World War II service in the Navy as a war-hero. He had never been a successful athlete. He was not photogenic, charming or affable. He was endowed with no natural gifts as an orator. Yet he rose to the highest office in the land, and was re-elected for a second term in 1972 with one of the largest popular majorities in American history.

If he was in some ways ordinary to the point of being a nonentity, it is clear that Richard Nixon must have possessed and cultivated some extraordinary features. To some extent, like many other politicians, he was the "uncommon man with common opinions". He could hold to the received ideas of the day—for example, the menace of Communism, when he first became a member of Congress—with apparent intensity. He remained psychologically attuned to a large segment of the American electorate. This has been called the "chameleon" instinct of the politician: the capacity to assume the same coloration as that of his immediate surroundings. But the politician also needs to make himself visible, to his party and the voters, if he is ever to climb out of the ruck. Luck no doubt plays a part. Nixon came into Congress at a good moment for an aspiring young Republican. He and his colleagues could benefit from the widespread feeling that the Democrats had grown stale and slack from being too long in power. They could also capitalize on cruder allegations that the Democrats had betrayed the country during "twenty years of treason". The issue was too attractive not to be exploited. The tenacity and success with which Representative Nixon pursued Alger Hiss, in the House Un-American Activities Committee, laid a foundation for his career.

He was fortunate in being picked as Eisenhower's running mate in the 1952 election. His famous "little dog Checkers" reply to accusations of corruption, though dismissed by some as cheaply sentimental, was in its own terms extremely effective. Through eight years as Vice-President Nixon held his own with considerable skill. He revealed himself as energetic, efficient and loyal. He labored to improve his technique as a speaker. He showed courage and tenacity—and captured the headlines—when hostile mobs surrounded his car in Latin America, and when he confronted Nikita Khrushchev at an impromptu slanging-match in Moscow. He behaved with tact and some dignity in the difficult periods of President Eisenhower's illnesses. To his credit, having narrowly lost the 1960 presidential election to Kennedy, he refrained from challenging a result that may have turned upon rigging of the vote against him in Illinois. Against political probability, he survived the ignominy of further defeat in a 1962 contest for the governorship of California. Instead of disappearing into the limbo of beaten candidates, he was resilient and resourceful enough to use a well-paid position in a prominent New York law firm to build a new political base. His reward came in 1968. He had sufficient claims on his party to be picked again as their presidential nominee, in a year when the Democrats were shattered by the withdrawal of Lyndon B. Johnson and the murder of Robert Kennedy. His Administration got off to an excellent start in 1969. Nixon ended American involvement in Vietnam. The policy of rapprochement with China and Russia, and America's constructive role in restoring peace to the Middle East, were hearteningly fresh starts. Nixon was lucky again in facing a divided Democratic party in 1972; but the size of his "mandate" could seemingly not be gainsaid.

What then went wrong? Richard Nixon's followers will probably argue for many years to come that his only fault—determination to concentrate upon the nation's main tasks—was forgivable and even commendable. According to this line, he was merely following an inevitable trend toward the strengthening of executive authority in the United States. Several predecessors, most of them Democrats, had set the tone. If Eisenhower had a Sherman Adams as chief of staff, why should Nixon not have a Haldeman and an Ehrlichman? Inherited wealth brought John F. Kennedy homes in Hyannisport and Florida. Why should Nixon not use his own earnings to acquire family property in San Clemente and Key Biscayne? He was not personally extravagant. His domestic life with his wife Pat and two evidently devoted daughters was a model of propriety.

Yet Nixon was never able to live down the charge that some moral dimension was lacking in his character. His quickness and doggedness have never been in question. What causes uneasiness is a cumulative record, from the time of his first Congressional campaign, of having sought victory so single-mindedly that the means employed overshadowed the ethical ends. No successful politician is an unworldly innocent. The criticism of Nixon, calamitously documented in the Watergate affair, is that he played the political game too ruthlessly and narrowly, and that there was something hollow and synthetic about him. His political maneuvers were often an unhappy blend of the devious and the transparent, as when he tried to woo the South by making bad nominations for Supreme Court appointments. Perhaps his strongest emotions, as directed against the press and television or occasionally against Congress, were suspicion, dislike and contempt. He may have stored up resentments during his struggles for recognition that discharged themselves as spleen once he was in the White House. The isolated grandeur of that office may have reacted unfortunately upon a person of Nixon's temperament.

If so there is much irony and some pathos in his rise and fall. One of the sadder elements is that Richard Nixon tried so hard to leave positive monuments behind him: to sustain the position of the executive branch, to resolve world conflict. In leaving office in August 1974 he twice referred to the attitudes of Theodore Roosevelt—a strong Republican President, formerly a Vice-President, for whom courage was almost the supreme virtue, who won a Nobel Peace Prize, who picked his successor, and who was restlessly busy when out of office. Posterity, alas, seems likely to associate the name of Richard Milhous Nixon not with his high professed aims, but with the very things he claimed righteously to deplore: a diminished Presidency, a damaged Republican party, broken laws, tarnished faith. A final irony is that he may be damned by his own words: words which he allowed to be put on tape for the sake of the historical record. It was the disclosure of these unedifying conversations that cost him the Presidency. Not much in them provided conclusive proof of wrongdoing on the part of Nixon. Cumulatively, however, they revealed a degree of cynicism and opportunism that alienated more and more of his supporters. His mistakes would have been forgiven if only he had candidly admitted them. Instead he preferred to "tough it out". Over the dragging months of the Watergate investigations, lack of candor turned little by little into evasion, prevarication. The President was in a way too clever for his own good. He focussed his effort on holding a line until compelled to retreat to some other position. His ultimate consolation was that his opponents would not be able to muster a two-thirds vote in the Senate for a successful impeachment. The release of still more material on tape destroyed this last position. Then and only then did he admit defeat, acknowledging in his resignation speech that his "base of support" was gone. That speech cannot have been easy to write, or to have delivered. It is hard to say which feature of the address was the more remarkable, Mr Nixon's aplomb in an hour of scarifying humiliation or his apparent failure to comprehend how and why he had come to this pass.

# Chronology

1913    Born at Yorba Linda, California 9 Jan.

1919-22  Attended elementary school at Yorba Linda.

1922    Family moved to Whittier, California following failure of father's lemon grove at Yorba Linda.

1922-30  Attended elementary and secondary schools at Whittier; worked in father's grocery store.

1930    Entered Whittier College 17 Sept.

1934    Graduated from Whittier College with BA degree 9 June; entered Duke University Law School, Durham, N Carolina 18 Sept.

1937    Graduated from Duke University Law School with LLB degree 7 June; admitted to California Bar at San Francisco 9 Nov; entered law firm of Wingert and Bewley at Whittier.

1939    Taken into partnership in law firm which became Bewley, Knoop and Nixon 1 Jan; opened branch at La Habra, California; appointed Town Attorney of La Habra.

1940    Elected President of Citra-Frost Company, Whittier.

1942    Obtained post with Office of Price Administration, Washington, DC Jan; commissioned Lieut, junior grade, USN 15 June; reported for duty at Naval Reserve Aviation Base, Ottumwa, Iowa 27 Oct.

1943    Assigned to HQ Sqdn MAG5, Fleet Air Command, Noumea, New Caledonia 1 July; promoted Lieut, senior grade 1 Oct.

1943-44  Officer in charge of S Pacific Combat Air Transport Command on Bougainville and Green Islands.

1944    Returned to US and reported for duty at Fleet Air Wing 8, Alameda, California 9 Aug; transferred to Bureau of Aeronautics, Navy Department Washington, DC 30 Dec.

1945    Promoted Lt-Cmdr 3 Oct; accepted endorsement of Committee of One Hundred as candidate to run against Representative H. Jerry Voorhis to represent the Twelfth District of California 4 Dec.

1946    Discharged from active duty with USNR 10 March; elected to the House of Representatives 5 Nov.

1947    Took seat in the House of Representatives 3 Jan.

1948    Appointed Chairman of Sub-Committee of House Committee on un-American activities 5 Aug; re-elected to the House 2 Nov.

1950    Elected to the Senate 7 Nov.

1951    Took seat in the Senate 3 Jan.

1952    Nominated by acclamation for Vice-President at the Republican National Convention in Chicago 11 July; election day 4 Nov; resigned from the Senate 11 Nov (effective from 1 Jan 1953).

1953    Took the oath as Vice-President of the United States of America 20 Jan; promoted Cmdr USNR 1 June.

1955    Made Caribbean tour 6 Feb-5 March; presided at Cabinet meeting following President Eisenhower's heart attack 30 Sept.

1956    Renominated for Vice-President at the Republican National Convention in San Francisco 22 Aug; election day 6 Nov.

1957    Took oath of office privately at the White House 20 Jan, and publicly on the east plaza of the Capitol 21 Jan.

1958    Toured South America 27 April-15 May.

1959    With Queen Elizabeth II of Great Britain opened the St Lawrence Hydro-electric Project at Massena, New York 27 June; with First Deputy Premier F. R. Koslov of USSR formally opened Soviet Exhibition of Science, Technology and Culture in New York 29 June; visited Russia 23 July-2 Aug; visited Poland 3-5 Aug.

1960    Nominated for President at the Republican National Convention in Chicago 27 June; election day 8 Nov.

1961    Electoral votes tabulated by Congress and Kennedy and Johnson officially declared elected 6 Jan; retired from office as Vice-President 20 Jan; returned to California 28 Feb; joined law firm of Adams, Duque and Hazeltine, Los Angeles 13 March; consulted by President Kennedy on Cuban situation 20 April; made Midwest speaking tour 1-11 May; moved to Beverly Hills, California 15 June.

1962    Nominated for Governor of California in Republican primary 5 June; defeated in election 5 Nov.

1963    Resumed law practice in Los Angeles 14 March; moved to New York City and joined law firm of Mudge, Stern, Baldwin and Todd as general counsel 1 June; toured Europe with family 12 June-1 Aug; admitted to New York Bar at Albany 5 Dec; became general partner in law firm (re-named Nixon, Mudge, Rose, Guthrie and Alexander from 1 Jan 1964) 15 Dec.

1964    Made round-the-world business trip 22 March-15 April; campaigned for Barry Goldwater, the Republican Presidential candidate Sept-Nov.

1965    Visited Moscow 10 April; toured Asia Aug-Sept.

1966    Made round-the-world trip with family July-Aug; campaigned for Republican congressional candidates Sept-Nov.

1967    Toured Europe 6-25 March; toured Asia 3-24 April; toured South America 5-16 May; toured Middle East 5-24 June.

1968    Nominated for President at the Republican National Convention at Miami 8 Aug; election day 5 Nov; Presidential Electors cast their ballots (301 for Nixon; 191 for Hubert Horatio Humphrey the Democratic candidate; 46 for George Cosley Wallace, the American Independent party candidate) 16 Dec.

1969    Electoral votes tabulated by Congress and Nixon and Agnew officially declared elected 6 Jan; inaugurated as 37th President of the United States of America on the east plaza of the Capitol 20 Jan; issued executive order creating Urban Affairs Council 23 Jan; sent first special message to Congress requesting extension of authority to reorganize executive branch of Government 30 Jan; renamed two presidential yachts *Patricia* and *Julie* in honor of his daughters 15 Feb; sent special message to Congress requesting extension of Economic Opportunity Act 19 Feb; visited Belgium 23-24 Feb, England 24-26 Feb, West Germany 26-27 Feb, Italy 27-28 Feb, France 28 Feb-2 March, and Italy again 2 March; received Canadian Prime Minister Pierre Trudeau on official visit at the White House 24 March; signed Reorganization Act 27 March; delivered eulogy on former President Eisenhower at the Capitol 30 March; attended funeral of former President Eisenhower in Washington, DC 31 March; attended burial of former President at Abilene, Kansas 2 April; addressed Organization of American States in Washington, DC 14 April; made nationally televised report on the Vietnam War 14 May; signed executive order establishing Council on Environmental Quality 29 May; conferred with President Nguyen Van Thieu of South Vietnam at Midway Island 8 June; visited Canada 27 June; visited the Bahamas 4 July; conferred with Emperor Haile Selassie of Ethiopia at the White House 8-9 July; visited the Philippines 26-27 July, Indonesia 27-28 July, Thailand 28-30 July, South Vietnam 30 July, Thailand again 30 July, India 31 July-1 Aug, Pakistan 1-2 Aug, Rumania 2-3 Aug, and England 3 Aug; gave state dinner for the *Apollo 11* astronauts in Los Angeles 13 Aug; visited Mexico 8 Sept; signed act raising salaries of Vice-President, Speaker of the House of Representatives, President *pro tempore* of the Senate and the majority and minority leaders 15 Sept; signed Nonproliferation of Nuclear Weapons Treaty at the White House 24 Nov; signed Act extending aid to Appalachia program for two years 25 Nov; signed Draft Lottery Act 26 Nov; signed Acts establishing the home of President Taft in Cincinnati, Ohio and Johnson City, Texas, the birthplace of President Lyndon B. Johnson as national historical sites and an Act providing funds to preserve and develop the farm of President Eisenhower at Gettysburg 2 Dec; signed joint resolution providing continuing appropriations until adjournment of the 91st Congress or until enactment of pertinent Bills 8 Dec; announced further reduction of troop strength in Vietnam 15 Dec; signed Tax Reform Act of 1969 30 Dec.

1970    Signed Act creating Council on Environmental Quality 1 Jan; delivered first State of the Union message to Congress 22 Jan; signed proclamation formally placing Nonproliferation of Nuclear Weapons Treaty into effect 5 March; signed Act renaming White House police as Executive Protection Service 19 March; declared state of national emergency in postal strike and ordered regular Army and reserves to deliver mail if necessary 23 March; strike ended 24 and 25 March; signed Act prohibiting advertising of cigarettes on television and radio from 2 Jan 1971 1 April; signed Act renaming Kaysinger Bluff Dam and Reservoir, Missouri, after former President Truman 27 May; signed Act lowering voting age from 21 to 18 22 June; received TRH The Prince of Wales and The Princess Anne of Great Britain at the White House 16 July; signed District of Columbia

Crime Control Act 29 July; signed Unemployment Insurance Act of 1970 10 Aug; signed Postal Reorganization Act 12 Aug; visited Mexico 20-21 Aug; signed Act giving District of Columbia elected non-voting delegate to House of Representatives 22 Sept, visited Italy 27-30 Sept, Yugoslavia 30 Sept-2 Oct, Spain 2-3 Oct; signed Organized Crime Control Act and Urban Mass Transportation Assistance Act 15 Oct; signed Merchant Marine Act of 1970 21 Oct; signed Resource Recovery Act of 1970 and Legislative Reorganization Act of 1970 26 Oct; signed Comprehensive Drug Abuse Prevention and Control Act of 1970 27 Oct; gave reception for descendants of Presidents John Adams and John Quincy Adams at the White House 6 Nov; attended requiem mass for General de Gaulle of France at Notre Dame Cathedral, Paris 12 Nov; signed Agricultural Act of 1970 30 Nov; signed Act restoring use of 48,000 acres of Carson National Forest, New Mexico, to Taos Pueblo Indians 15 Dec; signed Family Planning Services and Population Research Act 26 Dec; signed Occupational Safety and Health Act 29 Dec; signed Securities Investor Protection Act 30 Dec; signed International Financial Institution Act and Clean Air Act of 1970 31 Dec.

1971    Signed Omnibus Crime Control Act of 1970 2 Jan; signed Acts establishing Voyageurs National Park, Minnesota, creating Chesapeake and Ohio Canal National Historic Park along the Potomac River, Federal Pay Reform Act, and act raising pensions of former Presidents and widows of Presidents 8 Jan; delivered second State of the Union message to Congress 22 Jan; visited Virgin Islands 29 Jan-1 Feb; declared California a disaster area following earthquake 9 Feb; 26th Amendment to the Constitution submitted to the States for ratification 23 March; signed Second Supplemental Appropriations Act of 1971 25 May; signed Micronesian Claims Act of 1971 1 July; signed Office of Education and Related Agencies Appropriation Act 11 July; signed Emergency Employment Act of 1971 12 July; sent Seabed Arms Control Treaty to the Senate for ratification 22 July; signed executive order establishing National Business Council for Consumer Affairs and an Act extending the Public Works and Economic Development Act of 1965 and the Appalachian Regional Development Act of 1965 5 Aug; issued proclamation declaring national emergency 15 Aug; signed Act establishing the Lincoln home at Springfield, Illinois as a national historical site 18 Aug; signed Act repealing Emergency Detention Act of 1950 25 Sept; signed Military Procurement Authorization Act of 1971 17 Nov; signed Comprehensive Health Manpower Training Act of 1971 and Nurse Training Act of 1971 18 Nov; signed Revenue Act of 1971 10 Dec; visited the Azores 12-14 Dec; signed Veterans Disability and Death Pension Act of 1971 and Veterans Dependency and Indemnity Compensation Act of 1971 15 Dec; signed Alaska Native Claims Settlement Act and Act establishing Capital Reef National park, Utah 18 Dec; signed Economic Stabilization Act Amendments of 1971 22 Dec; signed National Career Act 23 Dec.

1972    Renominated for President; burglary of Democratic National Convention HQ in Watergate Building, Washington, DC 17 June, followed by arrest of seven men; election day 7 Nov; visited China and Russia; Presidential Electors cast their ballots (517 for Nixon; 17 for George Stanley McGovern, Democratic candidate) 18 Dec; ordered resumption of bombing of N Vietnam 18 Dec.

1973    Electoral votes tabulated by Congress and Nixon and Agnew officially declared elected Jan; Watergate trial began 8 Jan; ended Wage-Price Controls 11 Jan; suspended all American offensives in N Vietnam 15 Jan; inaugurated for second term as President 21 Jan; announced that fighting would stop at midnight on 27 Jan and all troops withdrawn within 60 days and prisoners released 23 Jan;

Watergate trial ended 30 Jan after defendants had pleaded guilty on all counts; conferred with British Prime Minister Edward Heath and Foreign Secretary Sir Alec Douglas-Home at the White House 1 Feb; devalued dollar by 10% 13 Feb; mandatory price controls reimposed on 23 largest oil companies 6 March; vetoed New Funds Bill 9 March; asked for restoration of the death penalty for certain Federal crimes 10 March; Senate began hearings to investigate allegations of political espionage in the 1972 presidential election in connection with the Watergate case 17 May; held summit talks with Russian Communist Party General Secretary Leonid I. Brezhnev 16-25 June; Committee and Archibald Cox, Special Prosecutor, served *subpoenas* on the President after his refusal to release secret White House tape recordings of conversations with those allegedly involved in the affair 23 June; Select Committee went into recess 7 Aug; hearings recommenced 24 Sept; Vice-President Agnew resigned 10 Oct (*see* APPENDIX B, VICE-PRESIDENTS OF THE UNITED STATES OF AMERICA, *p 599*); Federal Appeals Court ordered the President to hand over the tapes 12 Oct; nominated Gerald R. Ford, Republican leader in the House of Representatives, as Vice-President 13 Oct; calls for impeachment of the President from members of both parties in Congress 21 Oct; formal inquiry on case for impeachment opened in House of Representatives 22 Oct; vetoed War Curb Bill 24 Oct; large Republican losses in State and local elections 7 Nov; Gulf Oil fined $5,000 for making illegal contributions to President's campaign fund 14 Nov.

1974    Rejected *subpoenas* for tapes in a letter to Senator Ervin 4 Jan; ordered to testify at trial of John Ehrlichman, but "respectfully declined" 29 Jan; House of Representatives met to consider whether grounds for impeachment existed 9 May; refused to provide further material as requested by judiciary committee 10 June; visited Egypt, Syria, Jordan and Israel with Dr Kissinger for talks with Arab and Israeli leaders in pursuit of a peaceful solution in the Middle East 12-18 June; Ehrlichman found guilty 13 July; House of Representatives voted by 27 to 11 recommending impeachment for obstruction of justice in the Watergate affair 27 July; resigned as President (the only President to do so) and flew to California 9 Aug; granted a full pardon by President Ford for all offences against US which he might have committed while in office 8 Sept; entered hospital at Long Beach, California 23 Sept; resigned as a practicing lawyer at the California Bar 25 Sept; left hospital after treatment of blood clot on lung and phlebitis in left leg 4 Oct; later revisited hospital due to lack of response to treatment.

# The Writings of President Nixon

*Six Crises* (1962)

# Lineage of President Nixon

JAMES NIXON, emigrated from Ireland and is first recorded in Delaware in 1731, *b* in Ireland *ca* 1705, *m* Mary —, and *d* at Brandywine Hundred, New Castle County, Delaware 1775, leaving issue,

GEORGE NIXON, moved from Delaware to Washington, Pennsylvania 1803, to Clinton County, Ohio 1830, and finally to Henry County, Illinois 1842, *b* in New Castle County, Delaware 1752, *m* 1st 17 Aug 1775, Sarah Seeds, and had issue. He *m* 2ndly, Martha —, and *d* at Colona Township, Henry County, Illinois 5 Aug 1842. His son by his 1st marriage,

GEORGE NIXON, moved to Pennsylvania with his father 1803, and to Ohio 1844, *b* in New Castle County, Delaware 1784, *m* 1st *ca* 1806, Hanna (*b* in Delaware *ca* 1790; *d* in Pennsylvania *ca* 1827), dau of William Wilson, by his wife Eleanor, dau of Nathan Scothorn, and had issue. He *m* 2ndly 16 Nov 1830, Christine Pence, and *d* at Richland Township, Vinton County, Ohio *ante* 1870. His son by his 1st marriage,

GEORGE NIXON, moved to Vinton County, Ohio 1853, served in the Union Army in the Civil War, *b* at Washington, Pennsylvania 1821, *m* 10 Jan 1843, Margaret Ann (*b* in Pennsylvania 1826; *d* in Ohio 18 March 1865), dau of Anthony Trimmer, by his wife Margaret, dau of William Hunt, and was *k* at Gettysburg 14 July 1863, leaving issue,

SAMUEL BRADY NIXON, *b* at Atlasburg, Washington County, Pennsylvania 9 Oct 1847, *m* 1st 10 April 1873, Sarah Ann (*b* 15 Oct 1852; *d* 18 Jan 1886), dau of Thomas Wiley Wadsworth, by his wife Mary Louise, dau of Joseph Dickinson Moore, and had issue. He *m* 2ndly, Lutheria Wyman, and *d* in Vinton County, Ohio 28 April 1914. His son by his 1st marriage,

FRANCIS (FRANK) ANTHONY NIXON, of Whittier, California, moved to California 1907, *b* at Elk Township, Vinton County, Ohio 3 Dec 1878, *m* 25 June 1908, Hannah (*b* nr Butlerville, Jennings County, Indiana 7 March 1885; *d* at Whittier, California 30 Sept 1967), dau of Franklin Milhous[1] (descended from Thomas Milhous, a Quaker, who emigrated from co Kildare, Ireland to Chester County, Pennsylvania in 1729), by his wife Almira Park, dau of Oliver Burdg[2], and *d* at La Habra, California 4 Sept 1956, having had with other issue (*see* BROTHERS OF PRESIDENT NIXON, *p* 572), a 2nd son,

RICHARD MILHOUS NIXON, **37th President of the United States of America.**

# The Descendants of President Nixon

RICHARD MILHOUS NIXON *m* at the Mission Inn, Riverside, California 21 June 1940, •Thelma Catherine (Pat) (*b* at Ely, Nevada 16 March 1912), dau of William Ryan, by his wife Kate Halberstadt Bender, and has issue,

> **1** •Patricia NIXON, *b* 21 Feb 1946, *m* in the rose garden of the White House, Washington, DC 12 June 1971, •Edward Ridley Finch Cox (*b* 2 Oct 1946), son of Col Howard Elliott Cox, by his wife Anne C. D. Finch.
> **2** •Julie NIXON, *b* at Washington, DC 5 July 1948, *m* at the Marble Collegiate Church, New York City 22 Dec 1968, •Dwight David Eisenhower II (*b* at West Point, New York 31 March 1948), only son of Col John Sheldon Doud Eisenhower, and grandson of Gen Dwight David Eisenhower, 34th President of the United States of America (*see p 532*).

# The Brothers of President Nixon

> **1** Harold Samuel NIXON, *b* at Yorba Linda 1 June 1909; *dunm* at Yorba Linda, California 7 March 1933.
> **2** •Francis Donald NIXON, storekeeper [*Whittier, California, USA*], *b* at Yorba Linda 23 Nov 1914, *m* 9 Aug 1942, •Clara Jane Lemke, and has issue,
>> **1** •Lawrene Mae NIXON, *b* 18 July 1943.
>> **2** •Donald Anthony NIXON, *b* 12 Dec 1945.
>> **3** •Richard Calvert NIXON, *b* 28 Aug 1952.
> **3** Arthur Burdg NIXON, *b* at Yorba Linda 26 May 1918; *d* at Whittier 10 Aug 1925.
> **4** •Edward Calvert NIXON, telephone manager, *b* at Whittier 3 May 1930, *m* 1 June 1957, •Gay Lynne Woods, and has issue,
>> **1** •Amelia NIXON, *b* 4 June 1958.
>> **2** •Elizabeth NIXON, *b* 14 April 1960.

# Notes

[1] Through his paternal grandfather, Franklin Milhous, President Nixon is descended from Edward III, King of England (*see* APPENDIX C, PRESIDENTS OF ROYAL DESCENT).

[2] Through his maternal grandmother President Nixon is related to two Presidents, Taft (*see p 438*) and Hoover (*see p 488*).

# Gerald Rudolph Ford

## 1913-

---

38th President of the
United States of America

1974-

GERALD RUDOLPH FORD, 38TH PRESIDENT

# Gerald Rudolph Ford

## 1913-

## *38th President of the United States of America*

## 1974-

A BOOK on the Washington scene, published in 1830, describes the White House as having an iron gate as one means of access, and also in the south-east wall enclosing the grounds a stone arch flanked by weeping willows. The book recounts an anecdote of a President's wife. Congratulated upon her installation in the White House, she "remarked with a smile, 'I don't know that there is much cause for congratulation; the President of the United States generally comes in at the iron gate, and goes out at the *weeping willows*'".

As President Nixon departed from the White House, the suddenly empty spaces on the walls were filled with pictures of another family. Vice-President Gerald R. Ford took the oath of office at a small gathering. "Congratulations, Mr President", said Chief Justice Warren Burger. The transition had been formally completed. In a brief and simple inaugural speech President Ford told the nation: "I am acutely aware that you have not elected me as your President by your ballots. So I ask you to confirm me as your President with your prayers. . . . If you have not chosen me by secret ballot, neither have I gained office by any secret promises. I have not campaigned either for the Presidency or the Vice-Presidency. I have not subscribed to any partisan platform. I am indebted to no man, and only to one woman—my dear wife—as I begin this very difficult job".

It was a well conceived speech to introduce a bizarrely unprecedented new Administration. Ford had become Vice-President only a few months earlier, in almost equally grotesque circumstances, upon the resignation of Spiro Agnew. Casting about for an acceptable replacement, Nixon turned to an old political friend. He needed to find someone who was respectable and respected, especially in Congress. Gerald Rudolph Ford—"Jerry" to his wide circle of acquaintances—perfectly fitted the bill. He had held a Michigan constituency since 1948. Since 1964 he had been Republican minority leader in the House of Representatives. He could confidently claim to have had "lots of adversaries, but no enemies that I can remember". He was securely married, with a comely wife and four attractive children. He was still remembered as a football player at the University of Michigan, and still a robust athlete at the age of 61 who kept himself trim through swimming and ski-ing. He was a solid, loyal Republican, unabashedly "Middle American" in outlook. The Speakership of the House was the summit of his ambition, but likely to elude him since the Democrats held a substantial majority. He would not in a normal situation have been considered as vice-presidential timber, let alone presidential. But the situation was far from normal. Ford's straightforward answers made a good impression at the televised Senate confirmation hearings.

The information about him produced by journalists contained a few surprises, though none of great consequence. One was that while he was linked with Grand Rapids, Michigan, he had actually been born in Omaha where his mother was living with her first husband Leslie Lynch King. The Vice-President was christened Leslie Lynch King (Jr). When his mother remarried, he took on his stepfather's name, Gerald R. Ford, as an adopted son. It was also revealed that his wife, Elizabeth Bloomer Warren, a fashion designer and former student of modern dance, had previously been married and divorced. Such disclosures hardly affected the image of Jerry Ford as an exemplary citizen and Congressman.

Weary of the Watergate imbroglio, the American public accepted him as a potential, a probable and then a *de facto* President with remarkable equanimity. People longed to believe the best of him. If he proved to be an outstanding President, he could be elected in 1976. If he proved to be of limited ability, at least he would be a refreshing change. He symbolized decent competence, and the fundamental stability of American institutions. He was even ready to laugh with an interviewer at the notorious disparagement of Lyndon Johnson, who had said that Jerry Ford played football too long without a helmet.

No matter how eager Americans were to discover merit in him, President Ford faced some difficult decisions. "Our long national nightmare is over", he said in his inaugural comments. Alas, this was not true. President Nixon had escaped impeachment but there was still a mass of unresolved business. No doubt with the best of intentions, out of compassion for the former President, Ford made his first mistake. He had every constitutional right to confer a pardon upon Nixon, and with the passage of time his gesture might come to appear sensible as well as magnanimous. But the immediate reaction was one of anger and suspicion. Problems concerning the trial of Nixon's associates, which would have been delicate in any case, now swarmed about the new

ELIZABETH BLOOMER, MRS FORD

Administration in a cloud. Inflation and the threat of a collapse in the world economy further darkened the scene. An earlier President had once called the office a "splendid misery". It remained to be seen whether Gerald Ford, undoubtedly a good American and a good Republican, could also—enveloped in controversies and crises not of his own making—pass muster as a good President.

# Chronology

1913   Born Leslie Lynch King (Jr) at Omaha, Nebraska, 14 July.

1916   Legally adopted by his stepfather and had his name changed to Gerald Rudolph Ford (Jr).

1932-33   Star player in Michigan University's national championship football teams.

1935   Graduated from Michigan University with AB degree.

1941   Graduated from Yale University Law School with LLB degree; admitted to the Michigan Bar; began to practice law at Grand Rapids as member of the law firm of Buchan and Ford.

1942-46   Served as Lt-Cmdr USNR with Pacific fleet on aircraft carrier USS *Monterey*.

1946-49   Practiced law at Grand Rapids.

1948   Received Grand Rapids Junior Chambers of Commerce Distinguished Service Award; elected member of the House of Representatives from Michigan Nov.

1949   Took seat in the House of Representatives Jan; served on Public Works Committee (until 1950).

1950   Received Distinguished Service Award as one of ten outstanding young men in US from US Junior Chamber of Commerce.

1951   Appointed to Appropriations Committee (served until 1965).

1959   Delegate to Interparliamentary Union Convention at Warsaw; received silver anniversary award (All American) of Sports Illustrated.

1961   Delegate to Interparliamentary Union convention in Belgium; received Distinguished Congressional Service Award of American Political Science Association.

1962   Delegate to Bilderberg Group Conference.

1963   Delegate to Interparliamentary Union convention at Belgrade; appointed by President Johnson a member of the Warren Commission to investigate the assassination of President Kennedy 29 Nov.

1964   Warren Commission report released 27 Sept.

1965    Elected minority leader of the House of Representatives; received honorary degrees of LLD from Michigan State University, Lansing, Michigan, Albion College, Michigan, Aquinas College, Grand Rapids, and Spring Arbor College, Michigan.

1971    Proposed impeachment of Judge William O. Douglas because excerpts from one of his books had appeared in a publication which he considered to be pornographic.

1973    Nominated Vice-President of the United States of America by President Nixon under the 25th Amendment to the Constitution Oct; appointment confirmed by Congress Dec; took the oath of office 6 Dec.

1974    Visited twice by Gen Alexander Haig (President Nixon's Chief of Staff) when Haig told Ford of contents of "damaged" tapes concerning the Watergate cover-up and asked him if he was "prepared to assume the Presidency in a very short time" 1 Aug; fulfilled speaking engagements supporting Mr Nixon in Mississippi and Louisiana 2/5 Aug; succeeded as 38th President of the United States of America on the resignation of President Nixon and took the oath of office in the East Room of the White House 9 Aug; addressed joint session of Congress 12 Aug; nominated Nelson Rockefeller as Vice-President 20 Aug; granted general pardon to former President Nixon 8 Sept; announced national program to "whip inflation" 8 Oct; appeared[1] before a House of Representatives' Sub-Committee to answer questions about the pardon granted to former President Nixon and denied "deal" ("there was no deal. Period."), though admitted "option" of pardon had been discussed with Gen Haig at their meeting before Nixon's resignation (*see above*) 17 Oct; flew to Tokyo with Dr Kissinger 18 Nov; received by Emperor Hirohito of Japan and conferred with Japanese Prime Minister Mr Tanaka 20 Nov; House of Representatives overrode the President's vetoes on a vocational rehabilitation measure Bill and a Bill to make Government information more accessible to the public 20 Nov; visited Seoul; conferred with Russian Premier Mr Brezhnev in Vladivostok and agreed on main terms of 10 year pact to control strategic arms race (to be signed on Mr Brezhnev's visit to USA summer 1975), returned to USA 24 Nov.

# The Writings of President Ford

*Portrait of an Assassin* (with John R. Stiles)

# Lineage of President Ford

CHARLES HENRY KING, of Manhattan Place and Pico Boulevard, Los Angeles, California, railroad pioneer in Wyoming, *m*, and had issue, with one other son and three daus,

LESLIE LYNCH KING, of Riverton, Wyoming, in wool, lumber and real estate, sometime wool merchant in Omaha, Nebraska, *b* 1882, *m* 1st 1912 (*m* diss by div 1915), Dorothy A. (*b* at Harvard, Illinois 1892; *m* 2ndly at Grand Rapids, Michigan 1 Feb 1916, Gerald Rudolph Ford, Pres Ford Paint and Varnish Co (*b* at Grand Rapids 9 Dec 1890; *d* 26 Jan 1962), son of George R. Ford, by his wife Zana F. Pixley, and *d* at Grand Rapids 17 Sept 1967, having had further issue—*see* HALF-BROTHERS AND SISTERS OF PRESIDENT FORD, *p 583*), dau of Levi Addison Gardner, of Harvard, Illinois, by his wife Adele Augusta, dau of George M. Ayer[2], and had issue,

LESLIE LYNCH KING, JR, adopted by his stepfather and became GERALD RUDOLPH FORD, **38th President of the United States of America.**

Leslie Lynch King *m* 2ndly at Reno, Nevada 1919, ●Margaret Atwood, of Los Angeles (*b* 1891; *m* 2ndly 1949, Roy Mather (*d* 1954), copy editor on Los Angeles *Times*) [*Balboa Island, California, USA*], and *d* at Tucson, Arizona 1941 (*bur* Forest Lawn Cemetery, Glendale, California), having by her had issue (*see* HALF-BROTHERS AND SISTERS OF PRESIDENT FORD, *p 583*).


# The Descendants of President Ford

GERALD RUDOLPH FORD *m* at Grace Episcopal Church, Grand Rapids, Michigan 15 Oct 1948, ●Elizabeth (Betty) (*b* at Chicago, Illinois 8 April 1918), formerly wife of William G. Warren, lawyer, of Michigan (to whom she was *m* 1942, and from whom she was div 1947), and dau of William Stephenson Bloomer, by his wife Hortense Nehr, and has issue,

1 ●Michael Gerald FORD [*Beverly, Mass, USA*], *b* 15 March 1950, *educ* Gordon Conwell Theological Seminary, S Hamilton, Mass, *m* in Maryland 5 July 1974, ●Gayle Ann (*b* 1951), dau of Edward A. Brumbaugh.
2 ●John (Jack) Gardner FORD, *b* 16 March 1952, *educ* Utah State Univ.
3 ●Steven Meigs FORD, *b* 19 May 1956, *educ* T. C. Williams High Sch, Alexandria, Virginia, and Duke Univ.
4 ●Susan Elizabeth FORD, *b* 6 July 1957, *educ* Holton Arms Acad, Bethesda, Maryland.

# The Half-Brothers and Half-Sisters
# of President Ford

*President Ford has no full siblings, but he has one half-brother and two half-sisters by his father's second marriage and three half-brothers by his mother's second marriage (see* LINEAGE OF PRESIDENT FORD, *p 582), all of whom are thus half-siblings of the President.*

**A:** HALF-SIBLINGS ON THE FATHER'S SIDE

**1** ●Marjorie KING, *b* 1921, *m* ●Alton Werner, of Cumberland, Maryland, Personnel Dir Kelly-Springfield Tyre Co, and has issue, two children.

**2** ●Leslie (Bud) Henry KING, Mgr Goodyear Rubber Center, Cookeville, Tennessee, *b* 1923, *m* ●Virginia —, and has issue, four children.

**3** ●Patricia KING [*Balboa Island, California, USA*], *b* 1925.

**B:** HALF-SIBLINGS ON THE MOTHER'S SIDE

**1** ●Thomas G. FORD, staff analyst for Michigan legislature, mem Michigan Legislature 1964-72, served in World War II as Lt-Cmdr USN 1940-46 [*900 Pinecrest, SE, Grand Rapids, Michigan 49506, USA*], *b* at Grand Rapids 15 July 1918, *educ* Univ of Michigan (AB 1940), *m* 12 Sept 1942, ●Janet Packer, and has issue,

> 1 ●Thomas G. FORD, Jr, *educ* Olivet Coll, Michigan (BS 1967), and Sch of Dentistry, Univ of Michigan (DDS 1971), *m*, and has issue,
> ●Cameron P. FORD, *b* 2 Oct 1973.
> 2 ●Julie G. FORD, *b* 10 March 1947, *m* 7 Aug 1971, ●Robert Vern Foster [*Berkley, Michigan, USA*].

**2** ●Richard A. FORD, Mgr Ford Paint and Varnish Co [*147 Krapp Street, NE, Grand Rapids, Michigan, USA*], *b* at Grand Rapids 3 June 1924, *educ* Univ of Michigan (ME(Chem) 1948), *m* 12 June 1947, ●Ellen Platte, and has issue,

> 1 ●Linda FORD, *b* 10 March 1948, *m* 7 Aug 1971, ●Theodore Burba [*Grand Rapids, Michigan, USA*].
> 2 ●Laurie FORD, *b* 14 June 1953.
> 3 ●Richard P. FORD, *educ* Grand Rapids High Sch.

**3** ●James F. FORD, optometrist [*1059 Idema Street, SE, Grand Rapids, Michigan, USA*], *b* at Grand Rapids 11 Aug 1927, *educ* Coll of Optometry, Chicago, *m* 28 May 1949, ●Barbara Brunner, and has issue,

> 1 ●Martha FORD, *b* 9 March 1950, *m* 15 April 1972, ●Terry Hastings [*Toledo, Ohio, USA*].
> 2 ●Emily C. FORD, *b* 13 Sept 1951.
> 3 ●Robert J. FORD, *educ* E Grand Rapids High Sch, and Central Michigan Univ.
> 4 ●John Gregory FORD, *educ* Woodcliff Sch, E Grand Rapids.

# Notes

[1] Only two other Presidents (Washington and Lincoln) have testified before a Congressional Committee. President Washington, trying out the provision in the Constitution which gives the Senate an oversight of the Executive's conduct of foreign affairs went to the Senate to ask its opinion of the Jay Treaty in 1794. His rude reception did not encourage his successors to follow suit although President Lincoln went twice, once to defend his wife against the charge that she was a Southern spy.

[2] George M. Ayer was descended from Ezra Chase, a minute man in the Massachusetts Militia, who served in the Revolutionary War. The descent is as follows:—

> Ezra Chase (*b* at Newbury, Mass 9 July 1717; *d* at Haverhill, Mass 3 March 1793) *m* at Haverhill 2 Dec 1740, Judith Davis (*b* at Haverhill 12 March 1721/2; *d* there 28 Feb 1808)
>
> |
>
> William Chase (*b* at Haverhill, 12 April 1756; *d* there 8 Dec 1838) *m* at Kensington 1 Oct 1783, Abigail Gove (*b* at Hampton Falls, New Hampshire 23 Sept 1761; *d* at Haverhill 29 Nov 1844)
>
> |
>
> Polly Chase (*b* at Haverhill 15 Aug 1784; *d* at Kenosha, Wisconsin Aug 1854) *m* at Haverhill 28 Nov 1805, Samuel Ayer (*b* at Plaistow, New Hampshire 13 Dec 1777; *d* at Kenosha 1847)
>
> |
>
> John Varnum Ayer (*b* at Haverhill 3 Jan 1812; *d* at Kenosha) *m* Elida Manney (*b* at New York 1813/14; *d* at Kenosha)
>
> |
>
> GEORGE M. AYER

# Appendices

*Appendix A*

# Jefferson Finis Davis

## 1808-1889

———

## President of the Confederate States of America

### 1862-1865

JEFFERSON FINIS DAVIS, PRESIDENT OF THE CONFEDERACY

# Jefferson Finis Davis

## 1808-1889

### *President of the Confederate States of America*
### 1862-1865

DURING THE Civil War Northerners sometimes compared President Abraham Lincoln with the Confederate President Jefferson Davis—to Lincoln's disadvantage. Lincoln, it was said, was uncouth. He knew nothing of military matters. He saw everything with the eye of a politician; the Union's war effort was therefore hindered by political interference. Davis was by contrast portrayed as a planter-aristocrat of refined tastes and appearance. He was seen as a professional soldier who had graduated from West Point, commanded a regiment in the Mexican War, and shown great ability as Franklin Pierce's Secretary of War. Instead of being a "mere politician", like Lincoln, Davis could be regarded as a "statesman". Whereas political faction engrossed and divided Washington, the Confederate Congress not far away in Richmond, Virginia, was believed to be free from party alignments. And since the South's new constitution stipulated that the President of the Confederate States should be appointed for a single term of six years, Davis did not have to turn away from the proper concerns of government to worry about votes and candidacies.

This picture was at best a half-truth. Yet the parallel lives of the two men have a certain fascinating relevance. Their two families were of obscure stock, moving inland in search of a prosperity that had so far eluded them. In 1808-09, when Davis and Lincoln were born, both families were in Kentucky—the Davises having come there from Georgia, the Lincolns from Virginia. Jefferson Davis's father headed south into the new country of Mississippi. The Lincolns drifted westward into Illinois. Fortune did not favor either father. But Jefferson Davis benefited from the talents of an ambitious elder brother, Joseph, who raised the family to wealth, respectability and even elegance within a few years. Jefferson

Davis was given a good education, where young Lincoln had to be content with the rudiments of frontier schooling. Davis emerged from four years at West Point with the stamp of an officer and gentleman—tall, erect, precise and authoritative. In the Black Hawk War he was a regular subaltern, where Lincoln was a shambling, improbable Captain of volunteers. He resigned his commission to marry Sarah Knox Taylor, the daughter of Colonel (later President) Zachary Taylor, and settle to a planter's life at "Brierfield", Mississippi. Though she died a few months later of malarial fever, Davis remained at "Brierfield". Ten years afterward he consolidated his position among the Mississippi gentry by marrying the beautiful and well-connected Varina Howell. Returning to his first profession as a Volunteer Colonel in the Mexican War, he became known as "the hero of Buena Vista". Then, as a Senator and cabinet member, Davis became a prominent spokesman for his section—a defender of slavery and state rights, and one of the Southerners who was ready to contemplate secession. He seemed an excellent choice as the Confederacy's first President. While Lincoln's qualification were scrappy, Davis was experienced alike in war and in central government, with a clear conception of the South's future as an independent nation.

Reviewing the actual course of events, historians have concluded that Lincoln nevertheless turned out to be the better President. Davis was impatient and highly strung, a prey to nervous indigestion, headaches, and acute discomfort from an eye complaint that threatened him with blindness. His apparent superiority in military sophistication proved a disadvantage. Instead of being gratified by the Presidency he was mortified, for he had hoped to command the Confederate armies. As the next best thing, Davis made the most of his constitutional authority as Commander-in-Chief. He had plenty of courage and intelligence. But he overestimated his prowess, interfering with his generals and—worst of all—revealing a sometimes petty bias. He wrongly convinced himself, for instance, that Braxton Bragg was a good general and that Joseph E. Johnston was a bad one. Davis was apt to engage in time-wasting legalistic squabbles, as he had done in a tedious quarrel with General Winfield Scott when he was Secretary of War. Robert E. Lee was idolized in the South. Davis was widely unpopular, and not even two post-war years in a Union prison or the conviction of Southern rightness he continued to express until his death in 1889 were enough to establish him properly in the hearts of the defeated Confederacy. Lincoln's flexibility, compassion and wry humor were contrasted with Davis's humorless hauteur.

The comparison, however, does scant justice to Davis. Although he himself believed until the final collapse of 1865 that the South would win, the odds against him were considerable. Quite apart from the North's superiority in men and materials, Davis had to grapple with a fundamental contradiction that the Confederacy was unable to resolve. He envisaged

VARINA ANNE HOWELL, MRS DAVIS

the South as a consolidated nation. But secession was in large part a protest against centralized government. The Governors of several states, and a great many Southerners, resisted Davis's efforts to weld a loose confederation into a single unit. The South's military efficiency was in consequence seriously impaired. Davis was resented for trying to carry out the very responsibilities that had been laid on him. The difficulties proved insuperable. Davis's presidential ordeal dwarfed even that of Lincoln. It is a credit to Jefferson Davis's inner toughness of spirit that he survived defeat, imprisonment, calumny, impoverishment, the threat of trial for treason. He would break rather than bend. To the end of his days he refused to ask for a federal pardon—preserving the fiction that he was still a citizen of a Confederate nation which now existed only as an imperfect memory.

# Chronology

1808    Born at Fairview, Christian (now Todd) County, Kentucky 3 June; family moved to Woodville, Mississippi.

1810    Father bought plantation (subsequently named Rosemont) at Woodville and began building a house there.

1815-17    Although a Baptist, attended St Thomas's College, Washington County, Kentucky, a Roman Catholic seminary.

1821    Entered Transylvania University, Lexington, Kentucky.

1824    Matriculated at West Point 1 Sept.

1828    Graduated from US Military Academy, West Point, and commissioned 2nd Lieut US Army.

1828-35    Served on frontier, including service in Black Hawk War and on staff of Col Zachary Taylor (later President and Davis's father-in-law) at Fort Crawford.

1835    Resigned commission 30 June.

1835-45    Mississippi planter.

1845-46    Member of the House of Representatives from Mississippi.

1846    Resigned from the House to fight in the Mexican War as Col of Volunteers; distinguished himself at Buena Vista; led advance regiment in attack on Monterey Sept; again resigned from Army on conclusion of war.

1847    Elected member of the US Senate from Mississippi; warmly defended the policy of the slave states and the doctrine of "States Rights".

1850    Re-elected to the Senate; against the Compromise of 1850 7 March.

1851    Retired from the Senate; unsuccessful candidate for the governorship of Mississippi.

1853    Appointed Secretary of War by President Pierce 7 March (served until 6 March 1857).

1857    Again elected to the Senate as member from Mississippi.

1860    Received "war in the streets" letter, forecasting the Civil War, from former President Pierce Jan; introduced the Davis Resolutions demanding a Federal slave code for the protection of property in slaves in the territories (passed by the Senate but rejected by the House of Representatives) May.

1861    Announced the secession of Mississippi from the Union and his consequent resignation to the Senate 21 Jan; delegates of seven seceding States (Mississippi, Florida, Alabama, Georgia, Louisiana, Texas and Virginia) met at Montgomery, Alabama, and formed a provisional government taking the name of the Confederate States of America 4 Feb; commissioned Major-General of Mississippi Militia; elected President of the Confederate States with Alexander Hamilton Stephens as Vice-President by the Provisional Congress 9 Feb; inaugurated at Montgomery 18 Feb; election confirmed by popular vote Oct.

1862    Inaugurated as President of the Confederate States of America at Richmond, Virginia 22 Feb.

1862-65  For the major events of the Civil War *see* CHRONOLOGY OF PRESIDENT LINCOLN (*pps 298-300*).

1865    President Lincoln expressed his willingness to receive peace commissioners informally 18 Jan; fled from Richmond 3 April; issued last proclamation calling for resistance to the last 4 April; held last cabinet meeting at Charlotte, N Carolina 24 April; President Andrew Johnson issued executive order for his arrest 2 May; captured by Federal Cavalry at Irwinville, Georgia 10 May; imprisoned at Fort Monroe, Virginia.

1867    Released on bond 13 May; indicted for treason.

1868    Treason trial began at Richmond 3 Dec; proclamation of amnesty to all concerned in the insurrection 25 Dec.

1869    Treason charge dropped 15 Feb.

1889    Died at New Orleans 6 Dec; buried at Hollywood Cemetery, Richmond.

# The Writings of Jefferson Finis Davis

*The Rise and Fall of the Confederate Government,* 2 vols (1878-81)

# Lineage of Jefferson Finis Davis

JOHN DAVIS, emigrated from Wales and settled in Philadelphia 1701, *m*, and had issue,

EVAN DAVIS, of Philadelphia, later moved to Augusta, Georgia, *b* at Philadelphia, *m* — Williams, a widow, and *d* at Augusta, Georgia, leaving issue,

SAMUEL EMORY DAVIS, of Fairview, Christian (now Todd) County, Kentucky, later of Rosemont, Woodville, Mississippi, served in the Revolutionary War cmdg a troop of irregular horse, *b* at Philadelphia, *m* Jane Cook (*d* at Rosemont Oct 1845, aged 85, *bur* there), of Scottish-Irish descent and said to have been a niece of the Revolutionary Gen Nathanael Greene (1742-1786), and *d* in Warren County, Mississippi 1824 (*bur* at Hurricane, Mississippi), leaving with other issue (*see* BROTHERS AND SISTERS OF JEFFERSON DAVIS, *p 598*), a yst son,

JEFFERSON (FINIS) DAVIS, **President of the Confederate States of America.**

# The Descendants of
# Jefferson Finis Davis

JEFFERSON (FINIS) DAVIS *m* 1st at Louisville, Kentucky 17 June 1835, Sarah Knox (*b* at Vincennes, Indiana 6 March 1814; *d* of malarial fever at Locust Grove, St Francisville, Louisiana 15 Sept 1835, *bur* there), 2nd dau of Zachary Taylor, 12th President of the United States of America (*see p 256*). He *m* 2ndly at her father's residence, The Briers, Natchez, Mississippi 26 Feb 1845, Varina Anne, author of a biography of her husband 1891 (*b* at Marengo, Louisiana 7 May 1826; *d* at New York 16 Oct 1906, *bur* with her husband at Hollywood Cemetery, Richmond, Virginia), eldest dau of William Burr Howell, of The Briers, Natchez (son of Richard Howell, sometime Gov of New Jersey), by his wife Margaret Louisa, dau of James Kempe (of Irish descent), and by her had issue,

**1** Samuel Emory DAVIS, *b* in Warren County, Mississippi 30 July 1852; *d* 13 June 1854 (*bur* Hollywood Cemetery, Richmond, Virginia).
**2** Margaret Howell DAVIS, *b* at Washington, DC 25 Feb 1855, *m* 1 Jan 1876, Joel Addison Hayes, Jr, of Memphis, Tennessee, and later of Colorado Springs, Colorado, banker (*b* at Holly Springs, Mississippi 4 March 1848; *d* 26 Jan 1919, *bur* Hollywood Cemetery, son of Joel Addison Hayes, and *d* 18 July 1908 (*bur* Hollywood Cemetery, Richmond, Virginia), having had issue,
 1 Jefferson Davis HAYES, *b* at Memphis, Tennessee 22 March, *d* there 24 June 1877 (*bur* there).
 2 Varina Howell Davis HAYES, *b* at Memphis, Tennessee 12 March 1878, *m* at Colorado Springs, Colorado 30 July 1904, Lt-Col Gerald Bertram Webb, MD, US Army Med Corps, tuberculosis specialist (*b* at Cheltenham, Gloucestershire, England 24 Sept 1871; *d* at Colorado Springs, Colorado 27 Jan 1948, *bur* there), son of William John Webb, by his wife Frances Suzannah Le Plastrier, and *d* at Colorado Springs, Colorado 23 Feb 1934 (*bur* there), having had issue,
  (1) ● Varina Margaret WEBB, *b* at Colorado Springs, Colorado 13 May 1905, *educ* Oldfields Sch, Glencoe, Maryland, *m* at Colorado Springs 7 Jan 1925, Gerald Webb Bennett (*b* at Colorado Springs 3 April 1900; *d* there July 1936, *bur* there), son of Charles Pattison Bennett, by his wife May Francis, and has issue,
   1*a* ● Gerald Webb BENNETT, Jr, Attorney [*2425 Ceresa Lane, Colorado Springs, Colorado 80909, USA*], *b* at Colorado Springs 11 April 1927, *educ* Fountain Valley, Yale, and Colorado Univ Sch of Law, *m* 1st at Boulder, Colorado 7 Dec 1952 (*m* diss by div 1966), Mary (*b* at Hammond, Indiana 3 Aug 1931), dau of Fred Crumpacker, by his wife Rose Turner, and has issue,
    1*b* ● Catherine Varina BENNETT, *b* at Colorado Springs 12 July 1953.
    2*b* ● Gerald Webb BENNETT III, *b* at Colorado Springs 14 March 1955.
    3*b* ● Mary Turner BENNETT, *b* at Colorado Springs 24 Aug 1956.
    4*b* ● Frederick Charles BENNETT, *b* at Colorado Springs 8 Nov 1958.
   Gerald Webb Bennett, Jr *m* 2ndly at Las Vegas, Nevada 15 June 1966, ● Olivia Jane (*b* at Denver, Colorado 4 Nov 1938), dau of John Findlay Ryland, by his wife

Lucille Olivia McCrillis, and by her has issue,
    5*b* ● Genevieve Olivia BENNETT, *b* at Colorado Springs 30 Oct 1970.
     (a) ● Joanne Kathleen BENNETT, *b* at Denver, Colorado 12 Oct 1959 (adopted).
     (b) ● Thomas John BENNETT, *b* at Denver, Colorado 22 Dec 1963 (adopted).
   2*a* ● Charles Francis BENNETT [*206 Mining Exchange Building, Colorado Springs, Colorado 80901, USA*], *b* at Colorado Springs 25 May 1932, *m* 1st (*m* diss by div 1970), Susan, dau of William Baker, by his wife Betty Jean Law, and has an adopted son and dau (*see* ADDENDUM). He *m* 2ndly 27 Dec 1973, ● Patricia Anne Mize.
  Varina Margaret Webb *m* 2ndly, ● John Wolcott Stewart (*b* at Boston, Massachusetts 12 Aug 1895) [*1520 Las Tunas Road, Santa Barbara, California 93108, USA*], son of Philip Battell Stewart, by his wife Sarah Frances Hutchinson Cowles.
  (2) Gerald Bertram WEBB, Jr, served in World War II with USAF, co-founder *Middleburg Chronicle*, Middleburg, Virginia, *b* at Colorado Springs 17 Dec 1906, *educ* St Stephen's Sch, Colorado Springs, Lawrenceville Sch, New Jersey, Deerfield Acad, Massachusetts, and Univ of Virginia, *dunm* 19 April 1947 (*bur* Hollywood Cemetery, Richmond, Virginia).
  (3) ● Frances Robine WEBB, Sec Kansas Highway Comm 1963-73 [*Apt D, 915 Menlo Avenue, Menlo Park, California 94025, USA*], *b* at Colorado Springs 11 April 1908, *educ* Steele Sch, Colorado Springs, and Oldfields Sch, Glencoe, Maryland, *m* at Colorado Springs 16 Jan 1932 (*m* diss by div), Frederick Edward Farnsworth, late US Foreign Service (*b* at Colorado Springs 8 March 1906), son of Charles Farnsworth, by his wife Edith Winslow, and has issue,
   1*a* ● Frederick Francis FARNSWORTH [*Apt 11K, 1 Emerson Place, Boston, Mass 02114, USA*], *b* at Washington, DC 6 June 1933, *educ* Harvard (AB 1961), and Harvard Law Sch.
   2*a* ● Charles Edward FARNSWORTH, lawyer, partner in law firm of Farnsworth, Denison & Sapirstein, Oakland, California [*2606 Piedmont Street, Berkeley, California 94704, USA*], *b* at Singapore 31 July 1938, *educ* Univ of Kansas (BA 1960), and Stanford Univ (LLB 1966), *m* at Topeka, Kansas 21 June 1966, ● Elizabeth (*b* at

Minneapolis, Minnesota 23 Dec 1943), dau of H. Bernard Fink, by his wife Jane Mills, and has issue,
●Jennifer Webb FARNSWORTH, *b* at El Centro, California 21 Oct 1968.

3*a*●Robert Webb FARNSWORTH, Instr of Pol Sc 1967-69 and 1972-73, mem Nat Presidential Campaign Staff of Senator George McGovern 1972 [*214 Lobes Avenue, Pacific Grove, California 93950, USA*], *b* at Montreal, Canada 24 Nov 1942, *educ* Middlebury Coll, Vermont (AB 1965), Maxwell Graduate Sch of Syracuse Univ (MA 1967), and Wayne State Univ Sch of Law (JD 1974), *m* at Bowling Green, Ohio 13 June 1966 (*m* diss by div 1972), Jennie (*b* at Washington, DC 26 March 1946), dau of William Travers Jerome III, by his wife Jean Bewkes, and has issue,
●Sara Spencer FARNSWORTH, *b* at Syracuse, New York 19 Jan 1967.

(4) ●Eleanor Leila Constance WEBB, *b* at Colorado Springs 1 Nov 1911, *educ* Miss ·Ethel Walker Sch, Simsbury, Connecticut, and Oldfields Sch, Glencoe, Maryland, *m* 1st at Harrison, New York 30 March 1935, Charles Harold Collins, Jr, airline pilot (*b* at Pelham Manor, New York 24 Dec 1910; *d* at Colorado Springs 22 June 1957, *bur* there), son of Charles Harold Collins, by his wife Alice Orr, and has issue,

1*a*●Michael Harold COLLINS [*2205 Constellation Drive, Colorado Springs, Colorado 80906, USA*], *b* at Oakland, California 12 March 1937, *m* at Colorado Springs 15 July 1961, ●Linda Corbin (*b* at Des Moines, Iowa 6 June 1939), and has issue,

1*b*●Michael Harold COLLINS, Jr, *b* at Manhattan, Kansas 1 Feb 1963.

2*b*●Edwin Corbin COLLINS, *b* at Colorado Springs 28 May 1965.

3*b*●Melissa Webb COLLINS, *b* at Colorado Springs 14 Jan 1967.

2*a*●Timothy COLLINS, Exec Vice-Pres Collins Securities Gp 1963-66, Pres from 1966, Chm Trustees, Trident Theater, Denver 1966-67, Pres and founder Denver Spurs Professional Ice Hockey Team 1967-68, Pres Mining Record (Publications, Denver) 1967-69, Dir Council on Economic Priorities, New York City 1970-72, Dir *New Democrat* (New York) 1971-72, Chm Central Park Historical Field Trips Corpn from 1974, mem Friends Council, Whitney Museum of American Art, New York City from 1974, Dir Cannon Group Inc (films), WAIF, and Planned Parenthood from 1974 [*412 East 84th Street, New York, New York 10028, USA*], *b* at Cheyenne, Wyoming 8 June 1940, *educ* Univ of Denver (BS, BA 1962), Univ of Colorado, and Cheyenne Mountain Sch, Hotchkiss Sch, *m* 1st at Denver, Colorado Nov 1957 (*m* diss by div 1964), Elizabeth (*b* at Denver 25 Dec 1939), dau of Col James Booth Berger, by his wife — Adams, and has issue,

1*b*●Timothy COLLINS, Jr, *b* at Denver, Colorado 6 May 1958.

2*b*●David COLLINS, *b* at Denver, Colorado 22 Nov 1961.

Timothy Collins *m* 2ndly at Colorado Springs 9 Oct 1964, ●Ellen Kathleen (*b* at Mexico City 24 Dec 1944), dau of Hugh Corby Fox, and by her has issue,

3*b*●Joel COLLINS, *b* at Denver, Colorado 14 Nov 1965.

Eleanor Leila Constance Webb *m* 2ndly at Colorado Springs 14 Dec 1957, ●Maxwell Starr Davidson, mechanical engr with American Crystal Sugar Co, Denver (*b* at Denver, Colorado 24 Oct 1895) [*13 Pourtales Road, Colorado Springs, Colorado 80906, USA*], son of Frank Davidson, by his wife Etta Starr.

(5) ● Joel Addison Hayes WEBB [*c/o First National Bank of Colorado Springs, Colorado, USA*], *b* at Colorado Springs 2 May 1913, *m* ●Barbara Shove Palmer, and has issue,

1*a*●Varina Marka WEBB, *b* at Colorado Springs 25 May 1940, *educ* Briarcliff Coll, Briarcliff Manor, New York, Univ of Arizona, and Univ of Colorado (BS 1968), *m* 1st 29 Nov 1959 (*m* diss by div 1965), Andrew Jerome Evans, Jr (*b* at Gary, Indiana 13 Nov 1939), son of Andrew Jerome Evans, by his wife Mary Romancheck, and has issue,

1*b*●Mary Catherine EVANS, adopted by her stepfather and now bears the name of MOSER, *b* at

Colorado Springs 1 June 1960.

2*b*●Barbara Marka EVANS, adopted by her stepfather and now bears the name of MOSER, *b* at Tucson, Arizona 13 May 1962.

Varina Marka Webb *m* 2ndly at Salina, Colorado 29 March 1969, ●Jon Kristofer Moser (*b* at Philadelphia 13 Dec 1942) [*Box 902, Vail, Colorado 81657, USA*], son of Howard Franklin Delano Moser, by his wife Hazel Williams, and has further issue,

3*b*●Michael Williams MOSER, *b* at Glenwood Springs, Colorado 24 March 1972.

4*b*●Matthew Kristopher MOSER, *b* at Glenwood Springs, Colorado 14 June 1973.

2*a*●Joel Davis WEBB, with First National Bank of Denver 1969-71, Assist Vice-Pres Nat State Bank, Boulder, Colorado from 1971 [*Deer Trail Road, Jamestown Star Route, Boulder, Colorado, USA*], *b* at Colorado Springs 20 Feb 1943, *educ* Cheyenne Mountain, Colorado Springs, The Taft Sch, Watertown, Conn, and Middlebury Coll, Vermont, *m* at Wynnewood, Pennsylvania 24 Jan 1970, ●Elizabeth Ann (*b* at Philadelphia 22 Oct 1947), dau of Robert Collins Whitmeyer, by his wife Thelma Snyder.

2 Lucy White HAYES, *b* at Memphis, Tennessee 2 Jan 1882, *m* at Colorado Springs 8 Dec 1910, George Bowyer Young, of Colorado, later of Arkansas, sheep-rancher (*b* at Naversink, Highlands, New Jersey 18 July 1874; *d* 31 Dec 1941, *bur* Colorado Springs), son of Harvey Otis Young, by his wife Josephine Bowyer, and *d* 23 March 1966 (*bur* Montrose, Colorado), leaving issue,

(1) ●Margaret Josephine YOUNG, JP (1954), *b* at Colorado Springs 13 Oct 1912, *m* at the Church of the Ascension, New York 14 May 1938, ●Richard Wadsworth Graves (*b* at Columbus, Ohio 10 May 1910) [*6401 Longwood Road, Little Rock, Arkansas 72207, USA*], son of Frank Pierrepont Graves, by his wife Helen Hope Wadsworth, and has issue,

1*a*●Jefferson Alden GRAVES [*Feddinch Mains, By St Andrews, Fife, Scotland*], *b* at Baltimore, Maryland 21 Aug 1942, *educ* Univ of Arkansas (BA 1968), and St Andrews Univ (MLH 1972), *m* at Friends' Meeting House, North Sandwich, New Hampshire 10 Nov 1972, ●Ellen Appleton (*b* 8 Sept 1945), dau of Howard Doughty, and has issue,

●Jacob Michael GRAVES, *b* at St Andrews, Fife, Scotland 21 April 1974.

2*a*●Katharine Bradford GRAVES, *b* at Baltimore, Maryland 12 May 1944, *m* at Christ Episcopal Church, Little Rock, Arkansas 5 June 1965, ●Ronald Eugene Worthen (*b* at Yuba City, California 12 Nov 1943), son of Lyndell Philip Worthen, Sr, by his wife Evelyn Knox, and has issue,

1*b*●Tamara Bliss WORTHEN, *b* at Ardmore, Oklahoma 7 Nov 1969.

2*b*●Laura Michelle WORTHEN, *b* at Ardmore, Oklahoma 16 Feb 1973.

3*a*●Varina Margaret Howell GRAVES [*3930 Guspar Drive, Dallas, Texas 75220, USA*], *b* at Baltimore, Maryland 2 May 1946, *educ* Little Rock Univ, *m* at North Little Rock, Arkansas (*m* diss by div 1965), Leslie Barton Bledsoe (*b* 17 Feb 1943), and has issue,

●Richard Carl BLEDSOE, *b* at North Little Rock, Arkansas 8 Aug 1963.

4*a*●Paul David GRAVES, *b* at Little Rock, Arkansas 9 May 1957.

(2) ●Harvey Otis YOUNG II [*1720 17th Circle, Russellville, Arkansas, USA*], *b* at Colorado Springs 25 Feb 1914, *m* at Austin, Texas 9 Nov 1952, ●Beverly Hilliard Murphy (*b* at Jeanerette, Louisiana 1 July 1913), and has issue,

●Clemence Lee YOUNG, *b* at Montrose, Colorado 11 Sept 1955.

(3) ●George Oliver YOUNG, changed his name to George Mike YOUNG [*Redvale, Colorado 81431, USA*], *b* at Colorado Springs 11 Nov 1918, *m* 1st at Montrose, Colorado 22 Dec 1939 (*m* diss by div 1959), Margaret Viola Morris (*b* at Montrose, Colorado 22 Dec 1921), and has issue,

1*a*●Carolynn Josephine YOUNG, resumed her maiden name [*Box 105, Norwood, Colorado 81423, USA*], *b* at Dry Creek Basin, Colorado 13 Oct 1941, *m* at Montrose, Colorado 7 May 1960 (*m* diss by div 1969), Allen Keith

Hovey (*b* at Montrose, Colorado 19 Dec 1938), and has issue,

1*b*●Karen Diane HOVEY, *b* at Telluride, Colorado 15 April 1961.

2*b*●Cynthia Michelle HOVEY, *b* at Montrose, Colorado 2 Sept 1962.

3*b*●Cody Lance HOVEY, *b* at Montrose, Colorado 24 March 1970.

2*a*●Jacquelynn Sara YOUNG, *b* at Telluride, Colorado 28 March 1944, *educ* Dry Creek Basin Sch, and Norwood High Sch, *m* at Norwood, Colorado 8 Dec 1961, ●James Emerson Franklin (*b* at Center, Colorado 6 Sept 1936), son of James Edgar Franklin, by his wife Mamie Elberta Bales, and has issue,

1*b*●Teresa Colleen FRANKLIN, *b* at Montrose, Colorado 1 Oct 1962.

2*b*●Pamela Amy FRANKLIN, *b* at Montrose, Colorado 11 Jan 1967.

3*b*●Matthew James FRANKLIN, *b* at Montrose, Colorado 7 Oct 1971.

3*a*●William Davis YOUNG, veterinary surg [*1890 Taylor Street, Eugene, Oregon 97405, USA*], *b* at Telluride, Colorado 26 July 1945, *educ* Norwood Public Schools, Fort Lewis Coll, and Colorado State Univ (BS 1967, DVM 1970), *m* at Norwood, Colorado 15 June 1968, ●Diana Katherine (*b* at Denver, Colorado 14 March 1946), dau of Wilbur Frank Binder, by his wife Katherine Irene Stertz, and has issue,

1*b*●Michael Todd YOUNG, *b* at Eugene, Oregon 6 Jan 1971.

2*b*●William Brad YOUNG, *b* at Eugene, Oregon 6 June 1974.

4*a*●James Morris YOUNG [*L & M Trailer Court, Space 16, Cortez, Colorado 81321, USA*], *b* at Telluride, Colorado 26 July 1945 (twin with William Davis), *m* and has issue,

1*b*●Lisa Ann YOUNG, *b* 26 April 1966.

2*b*●Jarnie Lynn YOUNG, *b* at Montrose, Colorado 23 May 1968.

3*b*●Tracy Marie YOUNG, *b* at Montrose, Colorado 12 Dec 1969.

4*b*●Jerrod Lee YOUNG, *b* at Cortez, Colorado 28 May 1972.

George Mike Young *m* 2ndly at Cortez, Colorado 15 Oct 1959, ●Vivian Marie Baer Peterson (*b* at Cortez, Colorado 2 July 1930).

(4) ●Lucinda White Hayes YOUNG [*Box 77, Redvale, Colorado 81431, USA*], *b* in San Miguel County, Colorado 28 Jan 1922, *m* at Ouray, Colorado 2 May 1941, Douglas Darrell Sullivan (*b* at Adair, Oklahoma 21 Nov 1918; *d* 23 March 1960, *bur* Grand Junction, Colorado), and has had issue,

1*a*●Michael Douglas SULLIVAN, miner [*Box 393, Norwood, Colorado 81423, USA*], *b* at Montrose, Colorado 17 Jan 1943, *educ* Norwood Grade Sch, and Norwood High Sch, *m* at Grants, New Mexico 11 Aug 1962, ●Barbara Ann (*b* at Clayton Missouri 11 Dec 1944), adopted dau of Marvin Wilborne Marshall and his wife Blanche Opal Morris, and has issue,

1*b*●Michael Douglas SULLIVAN, Jr, *b* at Montrose, Colorado 31 March 1963.

2*b*●Jefferson Wade SULLIVAN, *b* at Montrose, Colorado 8 Aug 1967.

3*b*●Stacie Liane SULLIVAN, *b* at Montrose, Colorado 2 Aug 1970.

2*a*●Sheila Lucy SULLIVAN, *b* at Grand Junction, Colorado 10 Dec 1948.

3*a* Gerald James SULLIVAN, *b* at Grand Junction, Colorado 12 Dec 1950; *d* at Montrose, Colorado 26 Dec 1965, *bur* there.

4*a*●Stephen Bowyer SULLIVAN, *b* at Montrose, Colorado 12 Dec 1954.

5*a*●Timothy SULLIVAN, *b* at Montrose, Colorado 10 Feb 1958.

6*a*●Kathleen Ann SULLIVAN, *b* at Montrose, Colorado 3 Jan 1960.

(5) ●Clemence Ann YOUNG, *b* at Colorado Springs 25 Feb 1924, *m* at Baltimore, Maryland 27 July 1946, ●Howard Earl Haller (*b* at Cleveland, Ohio 24 May 1922), and has issue,

1*a*●Howard Edward HALLER [*2914 E Chevy Chase Drive, Glendale, California 91209*], *b* at Baltimore, Maryland 30 March 1947, *m* at Canoga Park, California 20 June 1969, ●Terri Lynne Koster (*b* at Los Angeles, California 16 May 1952), and has issue,

1*b*●Jennifer Louise HALLER, *b* at Northridge, California 17 April 1970.

2*b*●Justin Douglas HALLER, *b* at Northridge, California 9 March 1973.

2*a*●John Davis HALLER [*5394 W Flying Circle Street, Tucson, Arizona 85713, USA*], *b* at Baltimore, Maryland 11 Nov 1948, *m* at Reseda, California 31 Jan 1970, ●Patricia Ann Bartley (*b* at Lewistone, Maine 28 May 1950).

3*a*●Mark Bryan HALLER, *b* at Van Nuys, California 29 April 1952.

4*a*●Deborah Colleen HALLER, *b* at Northridge, California 27 Sept 1958.

4 ●Addison Jefferson Davis HAYES, had his name legally changed to Jefferson HAYES-DAVIS 21 Feb 1890, mining engr in Utah and New Mexico 1910-14, entered First Nat Bank, Colorado 1914, served in World War I 1916-18, 1st Lieut 148th Field Arty Nov 1917, Observer with 99th Aero Sqdn 1918, Capt of Air Service 1919 (awarded Purple Heart, Silver Star, and World War I Victory Medal), ret as Pres First National Bank 1954, Dir First Nat Bank and Colorado State Highway Bd [*2 Mesa Lane, Broadmoor, Colorado Springs, Colorado 80906, USA*], *b* at Memphis, Tennessee 2 Oct 1884, *educ* Cutler Acad, Lawrenceville, Princeton Univ (BS 1907), and Columbia Univ (MS 1910), *m* 1st at Colorado Springs 28 Dec 1910 (*m* diss by div), Ruth Doreen (Doree) (*b* at Galena, Idaho 6 Aug 1886; *d* 9 Oct 1970), dau of Dr Theodore Dewitt, by his wife Harriet Matthiessen, and has had issue,

(1) Jefferson HAYES-DAVIS, Jr, *b* at Colorado Springs 2 Oct 1911; *d* there 12 July 1912 (*bur* Hollywood Cemetery, Richmond, Virginia).

(2) ●Addison HAYES-DAVIS, Assist Vice-Pres First Nat Bank, Cold Springs, ret 1973, served in World War II 1942-45 [*1318 E Monument Street, Colorado Springs, Colorado, USA*], *b* at Denver, Colorado 1 May 1913, *educ* Colorado Coll, *m* 1st at Fort Worth, Texas 5 Sept 1938, Billy Fern (*b* at Godley, Texas 17 April 1917; *d* at Fort Worth 13 April 1955, *bur* there), dau of Thomas William Sharp, and has issue,

1*a*●Jefferson HAYES-DAVIS III, *b* at Colorado Springs 6 Aug 1939.

2*a*●Bertram HAYES-DAVIS, *b* at Colorado Springs 26 Dec 1948, *educ* Univ of Alabama, and Adams State Coll, Alamosa, Colorado (BA 1975).

Addison Hayes-Davis *m* 2ndly, ●Myrtle (*b* at Jackson, Mississippi), dau of Hiram F. Cotten, by his wife Helen Lehner.

(3) ●Adele HAYES-DAVIS, Vice-Pres Colorado Springs Junior League, Vice-Pres Colorado Springs Child Nurseries Centers from 1973, received Nat Extension Homemakers Safety Awards 1960, 1961, 1963 and 1964, *b* at Colorado Springs 17 Oct 1915, *educ* Potomac Sch, Washington, DC, and Warrenton Country Sch, Warrenton, Virginia, *m* at Colorado Springs 8 Sept 1937, ●James Herbert Sinton, formerly Vice-Pres Sinton Dairy Co and Pres Sinton Farm Co and Pres Hassler-Bates Co (*b* at Colorado Springs 13 Sept 1914) [*3901 Janitell Road, Colorado Springs, Colorado, USA*], son of Herbert George Sinton, by his wife Lillian Williams, and has had issue,

1*a*●James Michael SINTON, US Army Engrg Instr 1966-69, Water Resources Engr, State of Colorado from 1973, Dir Sinton Dairy Co 1966-69, and Met Craft from 1972, Offr Fountain Valley Investment Corpn from 1971, awarded UDC Cross of Mil Service (Vietnam) 1972 [*3370 E Maplewood Ave, Littleton, Colorado 80121, USA*], *b* at Colorado Springs 28 Aug 1942, *educ* S Colorado State Coll, Pueblo County (AA 1963), and Univ of Maryland (BS 1972, MS 1974), *m* at Bethesda, Maryland 23 Aug 1969, ●Wendy Robinson (*b* at Brooklyn, New York 3 June 1944), dau of Warren Robinson Johnston, by his wife Eunice Roberta Carpen, and has issue,

●Alexandra Dewitt SINTON, *b* at Washington, DC 14 April 1972.

2*a* Alan Dewitt SINTON, in Pathology Dept, Swedish Hosp, Denver, Colorado 1965-66, *b* at Colorado Springs

13 Nov 1945, *educ* Harrison High Sch, Transylvania Coll, and Adams State Coll, Colorado, *dunm* at Colorado Springs 21 Jan 1968 (*bur* there).

Jefferson Hayes-Davis *m* 2ndly at Cheyenne, Wyoming 12 June 1941, ●Ruth Martin (*b* at Chicago, Illinois 18 Sept 1897), dau of John James McCorkell, by his wife Philippa Kent.

5 William Davis HAYES, *b* at Colorado Springs 9 June 1889, *m* (*m* diss by div), Elizabeth McKewan Davis (*b* at Philadelphia 1895), and *d* 25 May 1955 (*bur* Colorado Springs), having had issue,

(1) Elizabeth Frances Davis HAYES, *b* at Colorado Springs 20 Oct 1915; *d* 23 Aug 1916 (*bur* Hollywood Cemetery, Richmond, Virginia).

(2) ●Elise Davis HAYES, *b* at Colorado Springs 19 Feb 1917, *m* at Raton, New Mexico 31 May 1951, ●Frank Martin Train (*b* at St Anthony, Idaho 2 Aug 1914) [*RR 1, Box 321, Koloa, Kauai, Hawaii 96756, USA*], and has issue,

●Elizabeth Davis TRAIN, *b* at Colorado Springs 2 May 1952.

(3) William Davis HAYES, Jr, *b* at Colorado Springs 1 Dec 1919; *d* 1929 (*bur* Colorado Springs).

3 Jefferson DAVIS, Jr, worked in a bank in Memphis, Tennessee 1877-78, *b* at Washington, DC 16 Jan 1857; *d* of yellow fever at Memphis 16 Oct 1878 (*bur* Hollywood Cemetery, Richmond, Virginia), *unm*.

4 Joseph Evan DAVIS, *b* at Washington, DC 18 April 1859; *d* as the result of a fall at Richmond, Virginia 30 April 1864 (*bur* Hollywood Cemetery, Richmond, Virginia).

5 William Howell DAVIS, *b* at Richmond, Virginia 16 Dec 1861; *d* of diphtheria nr Biloxi, Mississippi 16 Oct 1872 (*bur* Hollywood Cemetery, Richmond, Virginia).

6 Varina Anne (Winnie) DAVIS, known as "The Daughter of the Confederacy", author of *The Veiled Doctor* (1895) and *A Romance of Summer Seas* (1898), *b* at Richmond, Virginia 27 June 1864; *dunm* at Narragansett Pier, Rhode Island 18 Sept 1898 (*bur* Hollywood Cemetery, Richmond, Virginia).

# The Brothers and Sisters of Jefferson Finis Davis

1 Joseph Emory DAVIS, of Hurricane, Mississippi, lawyer, *b* 10 Dec 1784, *m* 1st, and had issue, three daus. He *m* 2ndly 5 Oct 1827, Elizabeth Van Bethuysen (*b* 23 June 1811; *d* 24 Oct 1863), and *d* at Vicksburg, Mississippi 8 Sept 1870.

2 Benjamin DAVIS, *b* 1787 or 1788, *m* Aurelia Smith (*b* 1802; *d* 1866), and *d* 22 Oct 1827 (*bur* St Francisville, Louisiana), leaving issue, one dau.

3 Samuel A. DAVIS, *b* 1788 or 1789, *m* Lucinda Throckmorton (*b* 1795; *d* 18 Feb 1873), and *d* 1835, leaving issue, three sons and one dau.

4 Ann Eliza DAVIS, *b* 1 Sept 1791, *m* 31 March 1816, Luther L. Smith (*b* 1769 or 1770; *d* 23 Dec 1833, *bur* St Francisville, Louisiana), and *d* 13 Aug 1870 (*bur* St Francisville, Louisiana), leaving issue, four sons and two daus.

5 Isaac Williams DAVIS, *b* Oct 1792, *m* 1822, Susan Gartley, and *d* 1860, leaving issue, two sons.

6 Lucinda Farrar DAVIS, *b* 5 June 1797, *m* 1st 12 Dec 1816, Hugh Davis (*b* 1792 or 1793; *d* 12 July 1817), and had issue, one son. She *m* 2ndly 5 March 1820, William Stamps (*b* at Paris, Kentucky 3 Nov 1797; *d* 4 March 1878, *bur* at Rosemont, Woodville, Mississippi), and *d* 14 Dec 1873 (*bur* at Rosemont), having had further issue, two sons and two daus.

7 Amanda Jane DAVIS, *b* 14 Nov 1800, *m* 6 Nov 1820, David Bradford (*b* 2 Feb 1796; *d* 12 March 1844), and *d* 22 Oct 1881, leaving issue, four sons and five daus.

8 Matilda DAVIS, *d* an inf.

9 Mary Ellen DAVIS, *b* 1806, *m* 5 Feb 1820, Robert Davis (*b* 1790 or 1791; *d* 1825/30), and *d* 2 March 1824 (*bur* at Rosemont), leaving issue, two daus.

# Appendix B

# The Vice-Presidents of the United States of America

**1** 1789-1797    JOHN ADAMS, afterwards **2nd President** (*see p 65*).

**2** 1797-1801    THOMAS JEFFERSON, afterwards **3rd President** (*see p 87*).

**3** 1801-1805    AARON BURR, son of Rev Aaron Burr, President of the College of New Jersey (now Princeton Univ) [*descended from Jehu Burr, who came from England with John Winthrop 1630*], by his wife Esther, dau of Rev Jonathan Edwards, the eminent divine; *b* at Newark, New Jersey 6 Feb 1756; *educ* College of New Jersey (now Princeton); served in the Continental Army, distinguishing himself at Bunker Hill and rising to the rank of Lt-Col; resigned because of ill health 1779; admitted to the New York Bar 1782; practiced law 1783-89; Attorney-General of New York State 1789-91; US Senator from New York 1791-97; built up political machine, using the Tammany Society, which ensured victory for the Democratic-Republican faction in the 1800 Presidential Election; Vice-President of the United States of America 4 March 1801-4 March 1805; tried for treason and misdemeanor following his scheme to raise a force to conquer Texas and establish a republic there, but was finally acquitted 1806-07; went to Europe 1808; returned to US and resumed law practice 1812; *d* at Staten Island, New York 14 Sept 1836; *bur* at Princeton, New Jersey. Aaron Burr *m* 1st at Paramus, New Jersey July 1782, Theodosia (*d* 1794), widow of Col Jacques Marc Prevost, a British officer, and only dau of Theodosius Bartow, of Shrewsbury, New Jersey, by his wife Anne Stillwell (who *m* 2ndly, Philip de Visme), and had issue, one dau (Theodosia (1783-1813), a staunch supporter of her father, *m* Joseph Alston, and had issue). Aaron Burr *m* 2ndly 1 July 1833, Eliza (*b* at Providence, Rhode Island 1775), widow of Stephen Jumel, and dau of John Bowen, by his wife Phoebe Kelley. She initiated divorce proceedings the following year and the final decree was dated the day of Burr's death.

**4** 1805-1812    GEORGE CLINTON, son of Charles Clinton (who emigrated from co Longford, Ireland 1729), by his wife Elizabeth Denniston; *b* at Little Britain (now Ulster County), New York 26 July 1739; Brig-Gen in the Continental Army; a delegate from New York to the Second Continental Congress 1775; elected first Governor of New York and served for six consecutive terms 1777-95; wrote the seven *Cato* letters opposing the ratification of the Constitution, published in the New York *Journal* 1787; received three electoral votes for Vice-President 1789; defeated for Vice-President by John Adams 1792; received seven electoral votes for Vice-President 1796; again Governor of New York 1801-04; Vice-President of the United States of America 4 March 1805-20 April 1812; *d* (in office) at Washington, DC 20 April 1812; *bur* at Kingston, New York. George Clinton *m* 7 Feb 1770, Cornelia Tappan, and had issue, six children.

**5** 1813-1814    ELBRIDGE GERRY, son of Thomas Gerry (a native of Newton Abbot, Devon, who came to New England 1730), by his wife Elizabeth Greenleaf; *b* at Marblehead, Mass 17 July 1744; *educ* Harvard; elected to Massachusetts General Court 1772; a member of the Provincial Congresses and of the Committee of Safety 1774-76; a delegate to the Second Continental Congress 1776-80 and 1783-85; signed the Declaration of Independence and the Articles of Confederation; member of the House of Representatives 1789-93; appointed a member of the mission to France by President John Adams 1797; Governor of Massachusetts 1810-12; his redistribution of the Electoral districts of the State in such a manner as to give an unfair advantage to his own party originated the term "gerrymandering"; Vice-President of the United States of America 4 March 1813-23 Nov 1814; *d* (in office) at Washington, DC 23 Nov 1814; *bur* there. Elbridge Gerry *m* 12 Jan 1786, Ann Thompson, of New York (*d* 1849, the last surviving widow of a "signer" of the Declaration of Independence), and had issue, three sons and four daus.

**6** 1817-1825    DANIEL D. TOMPKINS (his middle initial did not stand for anything, but was adopted to distinguish him from another of the same name), son of Jonathan G. Tompkins [*descended from John Tompkins, who settled at Concord, Massachusetts 1640*], by his wife Sarah Hyatt; *b* at Fox Meadows (now Scarsdale), New York 21 June 1774; *educ* Columbia College, New York; admitted to the New York Bar 1797; elected to the House of Representatives, but resigned almost immediately to accept appointment as Justice of the New York Supreme Court 1804; Governor of New York 1807-17; Vice-President of the United States of America 4 March 1817-4 March 1825; *d* at Tompkinsville, Staten Island, New York 11 June 1825; *bur* at New York. Daniel D. Tompkins *m ca* 1797, Hannah, dau of Mangle Minthorne, of New York, a prominent Republican, and had issue, seven children.

**7** 1825-1832    JOHN CALDWELL CALHOUN, 3rd son of Patrick Calhoun, by his 2nd wife Martha Caldwell; *b* nr Calhoun Mills, Abbeville District, S Carolina 18 March 1782; *educ* Yale; member of S Carolina legislature 1808; member of the House of Representatives 1811-17; Secretary of War under President Monroe 1817-25; Vice-President of the United States of America 4 March 1825-28 Dec 1832; resigned on being elected to the Senate; Senator from S Carolina 1833-44; Secretary of State under President Tyler 1844-45; again Senator 1845-50; organized a series of meetings protesting against the exclusion of slavery from the new territories 1848; *d* at Washington, DC 31 March 1850; *bur* at Charleston, S Carolina. John Caldwell Calhoun *m* Jan

1811, his 2nd cousin, Floride, dau of John Ewing Calhoun, of S Carolina, by his wife Floride Bouneau (of Huguenot descent), and had issue, nine children.

**8** 1833-1837     MARTIN VAN BUREN, afterwards **8th President** (*see p 187*).

**9** 1837-1841     RICHARD MENTOR JOHNSON, son of Robert Johnson, by his wife Jemima Suggett; *b* at Beargrass (now Louisville), Kentucky 17 Oct 1780; *educ* Transylvania University, Lexington, Kentucky; admitted to the Kentucky Bar 1802; member of Kentucky legislature 1804-07; member of the House of Representatives 1807-12; resigned to command a Kentucky Regt with rank of Col under Gen William Henry Harrison (later 9th President); severely wounded at the Battle of Thames River, nr Chatham, Ontario 5 Oct 1813; credited with having killed Tecumseh, Chief of the Shawnees; again member of the House of Representatives 1814-19; Senator 1819-29; again member of the House of Representatives 1829-37; Vice-President of the United States of America 4 March 1837-4 March 1841; member of Kentucky legislature 1841-42; *dunm* at Frankfort, Kentucky 19 Nov 1850; *bur* there.

**10** 1841     JOHN TYLER, afterwards **10th President** (*see p 217*).

**11** 1845-1849     GEORGE MIFFLIN DALLAS, only son of Alexander James Dallas, Secretary of the Treasury under President Madison, by his wife Arabella Maria Smith; *b* at Philadelphia 10 July 1792; *educ* College of New Jersey (now Princeton); admitted to the Pennsylvania Bar 1813; secretary to Albert Gallatin during his mission to Russia 1813; Mayor of Philadelphia 1828; US District Attorney for E Pennsylvania 1829-31; Senator 1831-33; Attorney-General of Pennsylvania 1833-35; US Minister to Russia 1837-39; practiced law 1839-44; Vice-President of the United States of America 4 March 1845-4 March 1849; US Minister to Great Britain 1856-61; conducted negotiations leading to the Dallas-Clarendon Convention, which set the basis for the settlement of Central American difficulties; *d* at Philadelphia 31 Dec 1864; *bur* there. George Mifflin Dallas *m* at Philadelphia 23 May 1813, Sophia Nicklin.

**12** 1849-1850     MILLARD FILLMORE, afterwards **13th President** (*see p 259*).

**13** 1853     WILLIAM RUFUS DEVANE KING, son of William King (of Irish descent), by his wife Margaret Devane; *b* in Samson County, N Carolina 7 April 1786; *educ* Carolina University; member of the House of Representatives from N Carolina 1811-16; moved to Alabama 1818; Senator from Alabama 1820-44; US Minister to France 1844-46; again Senator 1848-52; Vice-President of the United States of America 24 March-18 April 1853 (the shortest term served by a Vice-President); *dunm* (in office) at Cahaba, Dallas County, Alabama 18 April 1853; *bur* at Selma, Alabama.

**14** 1857-1861     JOHN CABELL BRECKINRIDGE, only son of Joseph Cabell Breckinridge, by his wife Mary Clay Smith; *b* nr Lexington, Kentucky 21 Jan 1821; *educ* Center College, Danville, Kentucky, and Transylvania University, Lexington, Kentucky; member of Kentucky state legislature 1849-51; member of the House of Representatives 1851-55; Vice-President of the United States of America 4 March 1857-4 March 1861; nominated for President by the Southern faction of the Democrats 1860; received 79 electoral votes; Senator 1859-61; expelled from the Senate for accepting appointment as a Brig-Gen in the Confederate Army; fought at Shiloh, Vicksburg and Baton Rouge; promoted Major-Gen 1862; Confederate Secretary of War 1865; fled to Europe to escape arrest after Lee's surrender; returned to Kentucky 1868; practiced law 1869-75; *d* at Lexington, Kentucky 17 May 1875; *bur* there. John Cabell Breckinridge *m* Dec 1843, Mary C. Burch.

**15** 1861-1865    HANNIBAL HAMLIN, son of Cyrus Hamlin [*descended from James Hamlin, who settled in Barnstable County, Massachusetts ca 1639*], by his wife Anna Livermore; *b* at Paris, Maine 27 Aug 1809; admitted to the Maine Bar 1833; member of Maine state legislature, serving three times as Speaker 1836-40 and 1847; member of the House of Representatives 1843-47; Senator 1848-57; Governor of Maine (for a few weeks only) 1857; returned to the Senate 1857; Vice-President of the United States of America 4 March 1861-4 March 1865; again Senator 1869-81; US Minister to Spain 1881-82; *d* at Bangor, Maine 4 July 1891; *bur* there. Hannibal Hamlin *m* 1st 10 Dec 1833, Sarah Jane (*d* 17 April 1855), dau of Judge Stephen A. Emery, of Paris Hill, Maine, and had issue. He *m* 2ndly 25 Sept 1856, Ellen Vesta Emery, half-sister of his first wife.

**16** 1865    ANDREW JOHNSON, afterwards **17th President** (*see p 305*).

**17** 1869-1873    SCHUYLER COLFAX, son of Schuyler Colfax, by his wife Hannah Stryker (who *m* 2ndly, George W. Matthews, of Baltimore); *b* at New York 23 March 1823; founded a Whig newspaper in South Bend, Indiana; helped form Republican party in Indiana 1855; member of the House of Representatives 1855-69; Speaker of the House 1863-69; Vice-President of the United States of America 4 March 1869-4 March 1873; *d* at Mankato, Minnesota 13 Jan 1885; *bur* at South Bend, Indiana, Schuyler Colfax *m* 1st 10 Oct 1844, Evelyn Clark, of New York (*d* at Newport, Rhode Island 10 July 1863). He *m* 2ndly 18 Nov 1868, Ellen W. Wade, niece of Senator Benjamin Franklin Wade, of Ohio.

**18** 1873-1875    HENRY WILSON (born Jeremiah Jones Colbath, but legally changed his name to Henry Wilson 1832), son of Winthrop Colbath, by his wife Abigail Witham; *b* at Farmington, New Hampshire 16 Feb 1812; apprenticed to a cobbler in Natick, Massachusetts 1833; established a shoe factory 1838; member of Massachusetts state legislature, first as a whig, then as member of the Free-Soil party, which he helped to form; owner and editor of the Boston *Republican* 1848-51; Senator 1855-73; Chairman of Senate Committee on Military Affairs during the Civil War; Vice-President of the United States of America 4 March 1873-22 Nov 1875; *d* (in office) at Washington, DC 22 Nov 1875 (the only Vice-President to lie in state in the Capitol Rotunda); *bur* at Natick, Massachusetts. Henry Wilson *m* 28 Oct 1840, Harriet Malvina Howe, and had issue, one son (who *dvp*).

**19** 1877-1881    WILLIAM ALMON WHEELER, only son of Almon Wheeler, by his wife Eliza Woodworth; *b* at Malone, New York 30 June 1819; *educ* Vermont

University, Burlington, admitted to the New York Bar 1845; District Attorney of Franklin County 1846-49; Whig member of State Assembly 1850-51; Republican member and President *pro tempore* of State Senate 1858-59; member of the House of Representatives 1861-63; presided at New York Constitutional Convention 1867-68; again member of the House of Representatives 1869-77; Vice-President of the United States of America 4 March 1877-4 March 1881; *d* at Malone, New York 4 June 1887; *bur* there. William Almon Wheeler *m* 17 Sept 1845, Mary King. They had no issue.

**20** 1881     CHESTER ALAN ARTHUR, afterwards **21st President** (*see p 359*).

**21** 1885     THOMAS ANDREWS HENDRICKS, son of John Hendricks, by his wife Jane Thomson; *b* nr Zanesville, Ohio 7 Sept 1819; *educ* Hanover College, Hanover, Indiana; member of the House of Representatives 1851-55; Commissioner in General Land Office 1855-59; Senator from Indiana 1863-69; Governor of Indiana 1873-77; democratic candidate for Vice-President 1876; Vice-President of the United States of America 4 March-25 Nov 1885; *d* (in office) at Indianapolis, Indiana 25 Nov 1885; *bur* there. Thomas Andrews Hendricks *m* 26 Sept 1845, Eliza C. Morgan, of North Bend, Ohio, and had issue, one son (who *d* an infant).

**22** 1889-   LEVI PARSONS MORTON, son of Rev Daniel Oliver Morton [*descended*
     1893      *from George Morton, of Batley, Yorkshire, financial agent in London of the Mayflower Pilgrims, who arrived at Plymouth, Mass on the ship* Anna *1623*], by his wife Lucretia Parsons; *b* at Shoreham, Vermont 16 May 1824; banker; organized own banking firm 1863; formed Morton, Bliss & Co 1869; member of the House of Representatives 1879-81; US Minister to France 1881-85; Vice-President of the United States of America 4 March 1889-4 March 1893; Governor of New York 1895-97; organized the Morton Trust Co 1899; *d* at Rhinebeck, New York 16 May 1920; *bur* there. Levi Parsons Morton *m* 1st 15 Oct 1856, Lucy Young Kimball, of Long Island, New York (*d* 1871). He *m* 2ndly 12 Feb 1873, Anna Livingston Read Street (*d* 1918), and by her had issue, five daus.

**23** 1893-   ADLAI EWING STEVENSON, son of John Turner Stevenson, by his wife
     1897      Eliza Ewing; *b* in Christian County, Kentucky 25 Oct 1835; practiced law in Metamora, Illinois and later in Bloomington, Illinois; member of the House of Representatives 1875-77 and 1879-81; first Assistant Postmaster General 1885-89; Vice-President of the United States of America 4 March 1893-4 March 1897; Democratic candidate for Vice-President 1900; candidate for Governor of Illinois 1908; *d* at Chicago 14 June 1914; *bur* at Bloomington, Illinois. Adlai Ewing Stevenson *m* 20 Dec 1866, Letitia (*d* 1913), dau of Rev Lewis W. Green, President of Centre College, Danville, Kentucky, and had issue [*his grandson, Adlai E. Stevenson, was Democratic candidate for President 1952 and 1956*].

**24** 1897-   GARRET AUGUSTUS HOBART, son of Addison Willard Hobart
     1899      [*descended from Edmund Hobart, of Hingham, Norfolk, who emigrated to Massachusetts 1633*], by his wife Sophia Vanderveer; *b* Long Branch, New Jersey 3 June 1844; *educ* Rutgers Coll, New Brunswick, New Jersey; admitted to the New Jersey Bar 1866; member New Jersey State Assembly 1872-74; State Senator 1875-82; President of State Senate 1881-82;

Vice-President of the United States of America 4 March 1897-21 Nov 1899; *d* (in office) at Paterson, New Jersey 21 Nov 1899; *bur* there. Garret Augustus Hobart *m* 21 July 1869, Jennie, dau of Socrates Tuttle, of Paterson, New Jersey, and had issue, one son and one dau.

**25** 1901    THEODORE ROOSEVELT, afterwards **26th President** (*see p 411*).

**26** 1905-
1909    CHARLES WARREN FAIRBANKS, son of Loriston Monroe Fairbanks, by his wife Mary Adelaide Smith; *b* nr Unionville Center, Ohio 11 May 1852; *educ* Ohio Wesleyan University, Delaware, Ohio; admitted to the Ohio Bar 1872; practiced law in Indianapolis, Indiana 1872-97; Senator 1897-1905; Vice-President of the United States of America 4 March 1905-4 March 1909; Republican candidate for Vice-President 1916; *d* at Indianapolis, Indiana 4 June 1918; *bur* there. Charles Warren Fairbanks *m* 1874, Cornelia (*d* 1913), dau of Judge P. B. Cole, of Marysville, Ohio, and had issue, four sons and one dau.

**27** 1909-
1912    JAMES SCHOOLCRAFT SHERMAN, son of Gen Richard Updike Sherman [*descended from Philip Sherman, who emigrated to Massachusetts ca 1633 and later settled at Portsmouth, Rhode Island*], by his wife Mary Frances Sherman; *b* at Utica, New York 24 Oct 1855; *educ* Hamilton College, Clinton, New York; Mayor of Utica 1884-85; member of the House of Representatives 1887-91 and 1893-1909; Chairman of the House Committee on Indian Affairs for 14 Years; Vice-President of the United States of America 4 March 1909-30 Oct 1912; *d* (in office) at Utica, New York 30 Oct 1912; *bur* there. James Schoolcraft Sherman *m* 26 Jan 1881, Carrie Babcock, of Utica, New York, and had issue, three sons.

**28** 1913-
1921    THOMAS RILEY MARSHALL, son of Dr Daniel M. Marshall, by his wife Martha A. Patterson; *b* at North Manchester, Indiana 14 March 1854; *educ* Wabash College, Crawfordsville, Indiana; admitted to the Indiana Bar 1875; practiced law in Columbia City, Indiana; a prominent member of the Democratic party; Governor of Indiana 1909-13; Vice-President of the United States of America 4 March 1913-4 March 1921; *d* at Washington, DC 1 June 1925; *bur* at Indianapolis, Indiana. Thomas Riley Marshall *m* 2 Oct 1895, Lois I. Kimsey, of Angola, Indiana.

**29** 1921-
1923    CALVIN COOLIDGE, afterwards **30th President** (*see p 463*).

**30** 1925-
1929    CHARLES GATES DAWES, son of Gen Rufus R. Dawes, by his wife Mary Beman Gates; *b* at Marietta, Ohio 27 Aug 1865; *educ* Marietta College, Marietta, and Cincinnati Law School; admitted to the Ohio Bar 1886; practiced law in Lincoln, Nebraska 1886-94; member Republican National Executive Committee 1896; Comptroller of Currency, Treasury Department 1897-1901; organized Central Trust Co of Illinois 1902; served in World War I as member of Gen John Pershing's staff 1917-19; first Director of Bureau of the Budget 1921; Chairman of Reparations Committee to investigate German budget 1923-24 (Dawes Plan, which reduced reparations payments and stabilized German finances, adopted 20 Aug 1924); Vice-President of the United States of America 4 March 1925-4 March 1929; awarded the Nobel Peace Prize for 1925; US Ambassador to Great Britain 1929-32; President of

the Reconstruction Finance Corporation 1932-33; *d* at Evanston, Illinois 23 April 1951; *bur* at Chicago. Charles Gates Dawes *m* 24 Jan 1889, Caro D. Blymyer, and had issue, two sons and two daus.

**31** 1929-1933  CHARLES CURTIS, son of Oren A. Curtis, by his 1st wife Ellen (or Helen) Papan, and possessor of a proportion of Indian blood; *b* at N Topeka, Kansas 25 Jan 1860; admitted to the Kansas Bar 1881; practiced law in Topeka; County Attorney for Shawnee County 1884-88; member of the House of Representatives 1893-1907; Senator 1907-13 and 1915-29; Vice-President of the United States of America 4 March 1929-4 March 1933; *d* at Washington, DC 8 Feb 1936; *bur* at Topeka, Kansas. Charles Curtis *m* 27 Nov 1884, Anna E. Baird, and had issue, one son and two daus.

**32** 1933-1941  JOHN NANCE GARNER, son of John Nance Garner, by his wife Sara G.; *b* nr Detroit, Texas 22 Nov 1868; admitted to the Texas Bar 1890; member of the Texas legislature 1898-1902; member of the House of Representatives 1903-33; Speaker of the House 1931-33; Vice-President of the United States of America 4 March 1933-20 Jan 1941; *d* at Uvalde, Texas 7 Nov 1967; *bur* there. John Nance Garner *m* 25 Nov 1895, Ettie Rheiner (*d* Aug 1948).

**33** 1941-1945  HENRY AGARD WALLACE, son of Henry Cantwell Wallace, Secretary of Agriculture under Presidents Harding and Coolidge, by his wife May Brodhead; *b* in Adair County, Iowa 7 Oct 1888; *educ* Iowa State College, Ames, Iowa; Associate Editor *Wallace's Farmer* (an agricultural journal founded by his grandfather Henry Wallace) 1910-24 and Editor 1924-33; author of several books on agriculture; Secretary of Agriculture 1933-41; Vice-President of the United States of America 20 Jan 1941–20 Jan 1945; Secretary of Commerce 1945-46; Editor of the liberal weekly *New Republic* 1946-48; presidential candidate of left-wing Progressive party 1948; resigned from Progressive party 1950; *d* at Danbury, Conn 18 Nov 1965; *bur* at Des Moines, Iowa. Henry Agard Wallace *m* 20 May 1914, Ilo Browne, and had issue, two sons and one dau.

**34** 1945  HARRY S. TRUMAN, afterwards **33rd President** (*see p 507*).

**35** 1949-1953  ALBEN WILLIAM BARKLEY, son of John Wilson Barkley, by his wife Electra Smith; *b* nr Lowes, Kentucky 24 Nov 1877; *educ* Marvin College, Clinton, Kentucky, and Virginia University Law School; admitted to the Kentucky Bar 1903; Prosecuting Attorney of McCracken County, Kentucky 1905-09; County Judge 1909-13; member of the House of Representatives 1913-27; Senator 1927-49 (majority leader of the Senate 1937-46); Vice-President of the United States of America 20 Jan 1949-20 Jan 1953; again Senator 1954-56; *d* at Lexington, Virginia 30 April 1956; *bur* at Paducah, Kentucky. Alban William Barkley *m* 1st 23 June 1903, Dorothy Brower (*d* 10 March 1947), and had issue, one son and two daus. He *m* 2ndly 18 Nov 1949, Elizabeth Jane (*née* Rucker), widow of Carleton Sturtevant Hadley.

**36** 1953-1961  RICHARD MILHOUS NIXON, afterwards **37th President** (*see p 561*).

**37** 1961-1963   LYNDON BAINES JOHNSON, afterwards **36th President** (*see p 547*).

**38** 1965-1969   HUBERT HORATIO HUMPHREY, son of Hubert Horatio Humphrey, by his wife Christine Sannes; *b* at Wallace, S Dakota 27 May 1911; *educ* Minnesota University (BA 1939), and Louisiana State University (MA 1940); Mayor of Minneapolis 1945 and 1947; Senator 1948-65; Vice-President of the United States of America 20 Jan 1965-20 Jan 1969; taught at Minnesota University and Macalester Coll, St Paul, Minnesota 1969-70; re-elected Senator 1970. Hubert Horatio Humphrey *m* 3 Sept 1936, Muriel Fay Buck, and has issue, three sons and one dau.

**39** 1969-1973   SPIRO THEODORE AGNEW, son of Theodore S. Agnew (of Greek descent), by his wife Margaret Akers; *b* at Baltimore, Maryland 9 Nov 1918; *educ* Johns Hopkins University, and Baltimore University Law School (LLB 1947); County Executive of Baltimore County 1963-67; Governor of Maryland 1967-69; Vice-President of the United States of America 20 Jan 1969-10 Oct 1973; resigned office; fined and placed on probation for three years for tax evasion when Governor of Maryland. Spiro Theodore Agnew *m* 27 May 1942, Elinor Isabel, dau of W. Lee Judefind, by his wife Ruth Elinor Schafer, and has issue, one son and three daus.

**40** 1973-1974   GERALD RUDOLPH FORD, afterwards **38th President** (*see p 575*).

**41** 1974-   NELSON ALDRICH ROCKEFELLER, son of John Davison Rockefeller, Jr, FRS, by his wife Abby Greene Aldrich; *b* at Bar Harbor, Maine 8 July 1908; *educ* Lincoln Sch, New York, and Dartmouth Coll (AB 1930); banker; sometime Director, President and Chairman Rockefeller Center Inc; Trustee (and sometime President) Rockefeller Brothers Fund Inc from 1940; Co-ordinator of Inter-American Affairs 1940-44; Assistant Secretary of State under President Franklin Roosevelt 1944-45; Founder and Director (and sometime President) American International Association for Economic and Social Development (1946); Chairman President's Advisory Committee on Government Organization 1952-58; Under Secretary Department of Health, Education and Welfare under President Eisenhower 1953-54; Special Assistant to President Eisenhower 1954-55; Governor of New York State 1958-74 (re-elected 1962, 1966 and 1970); Chairman of Special Committee on Civil Defense; member Advisory Committee on Intergovernmental Relations; sometime Director, President and Chairman International Basic Economy Corporation; Chairman Human Resources Commission, Governors' Conference; nominated as Vice-President of the United States of America by President Ford 20 Aug 1974; Trustee (and sometime President and Chairman) Museum of Modern Art, New York from 1932; Founder, President and Trustee Museum of Primitive Art, New York (1954). Nelson Aldrich Rockefeller *m* 1st 23 June 1930 (*m* diss by div 1962), Mary Todhunter Clark, and has had issue, three sons (one *dec*) and two daus. He *m* 2ndly May 1963, Mrs Margaretta ("Happy") Fitler Murphy, and by her has issue, two sons.

# *Appendix C*
# Presidents of Royal Descent

NOTE: The Genealogical Tables illustrating these descents which follow, contain only brief details of the ancestors concerned. For further genealogical information on the various persons featured in the tables the reader is advised to refer to either BURKE'S *Guide to the Royal Family*, or BURKE'S *Peerage and Baronetage*, or BURKE'S *Dormant and Extinct Peerages*, or BURKE'S *Extinct and Dormant Baronetcies* or BURKE'S *Landed Gentry*, where many of them are dealt with in full.

**1  SOME ROYAL DESCENTS OF PRESIDENT WASHINGTON**

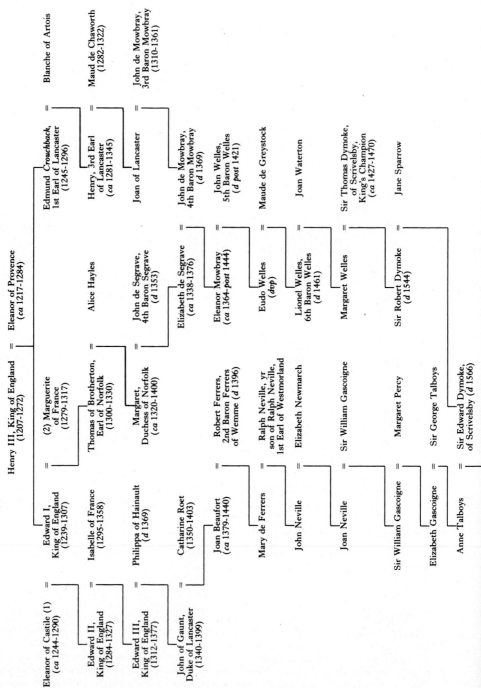

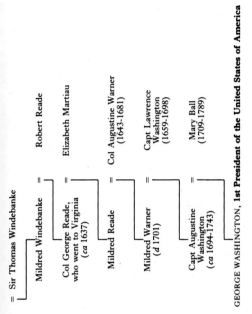

Frances Dymoke = Sir Thomas Windebanke

Mildred Windebanke = Robert Reade

Col George Reade, = Elizabeth Martiau
who went to Virginia
(ca 1637)

Mildred Reade = Col Augustine Warner
(1643-1681)

Mildred Warner = Capt Lawrence
(d 1701) Washington
(1659-1698)

Capt Augustine = Mary Ball
Washington (1709-1789)
(ca 1694-1743)

GEORGE WASHINGTON, **1st President of the United States of America**

| | | |
|---|:-:|---|
| Edward I,<br>King of England<br>(1239-1307) | = | Eleanor of Castile<br>(*ca* 1244-1290) |
| Joan of England,<br>called Joan *of Acre*<br>(1272-1307) | = | Gilbert de Clare,<br>3rd Earl of Gloucester<br>and<br>7th Earl of Hertford<br>(1243-1295) |
| Margaret de Clare | = | Hugh de Audley, 2nd<br>Baron Audley and 1st<br>Earl of Gloucester<br>(new creation) (*d* 1347) |
| Margaret de Audley,<br>Baroness Audley | = | Ralph de Stafford,<br>1st Earl of Stafford,<br>KG (*d* 1372) |
| Joan de Stafford<br>(*d* 1397) | = | John Cherleton,<br>2nd Baron Cherleton<br>(*d* 1374) |
| Edward Cherleton,<br>4th Baron Cherleton<br>(*d* 1422) | = | Eleanor Holland<br>(*d* 1405)<br>[*also a descendant<br>of Edward I*] |
| Joyce Cherleton<br>(*d* 1446) | = | John de Tibetot,<br>or Tiptoft,<br>1st Baron Tiptoft<br>(*d* 1443) |
| Joyce de Tiptoft<br>(*d* 1485) | = | Sir Edmund Sutton<br>(*d* 1483) |
| Sir John Sutton<br>(*d* 1541) | = | |
| Margaret Sutton<br>(*d* 1563) | = | John Butler |
| William Butler | = | Margaret — |
| Margaret Butler<br>(*d* 1652) | = | Lawrence Washington<br>(*d* 1616) |
| Rev Lawrence<br>Washington<br>(*ca* 1602-1653) | = | Amphyllis Twigden |
| Col John Washington<br>(1633-1677) | = | Anne Pope |
| Capt Lawrence<br>Washington<br>(1659-1698) | = | Mildred Warner<br>(*d* 1701) |
| Capt Augustine<br>Washington<br>(*ca* 1694-1743) | = | Mary Ball<br>(1709-1789) |

GEORGE WASHINGTON, **1st President of the United States of America**

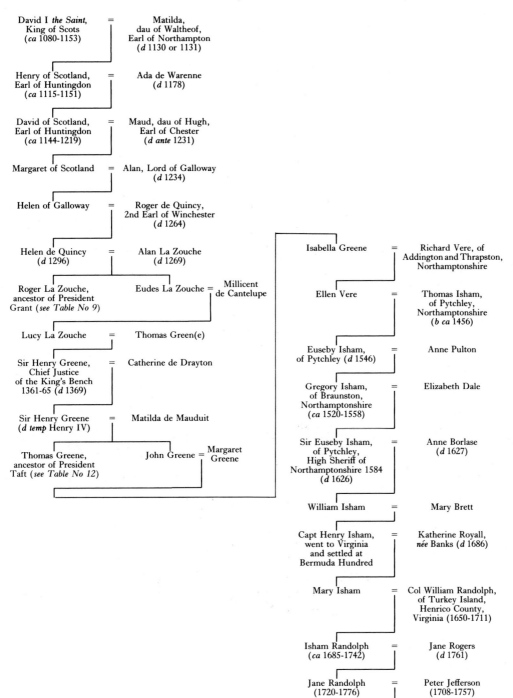

David I *the Saint*, King of Scots (*ca* 1080-1153) = Matilda, dau of Waltheof, Earl of Northampton (*d* 1130 or 1131)

Henry of Scotland, Earl of Huntingdon (*ca* 1115-1151) = Ada de Warenne (*d* 1178)

David of Scotland, Earl of Huntingdon (*ca* 1144-1219) = Maud, dau of Hugh, Earl of Chester (*d ante* 1231)

Margaret of Scotland = Alan, Lord of Galloway (*d* 1234)

Helen of Galloway = Roger de Quincy, 2nd Earl of Winchester (*d* 1264)

Helen de Quincy (*d* 1296) = Alan La Zouche (*d* 1269)

Roger La Zouche, ancestor of President Grant (*see Table No 9*) / Eudes La Zouche = Millicent de Cantelupe

Lucy La Zouche = Thomas Green(e)

Sir Henry Greene, Chief Justice of the King's Bench 1361-65 (*d* 1369) = Catherine de Drayton

Sir Henry Greene (*d temp* Henry IV) = Matilda de Mauduit

Thomas Greene, ancestor of President Taft (*see Table No 12*) / John Greene = Margaret Greene

Isabella Greene = Richard Vere, of Addington and Thrapston, Northamptonshire

Ellen Vere = Thomas Isham, of Pytchley, Northamptonshire (*b ca* 1456)

Euseby Isham, of Pytchley (*d* 1546) = Anne Pulton

Gregory Isham, of Braunston, Northamptonshire (*ca* 1520-1558) = Elizabeth Dale

Sir Euseby Isham, of Pytchley, High Sheriff of Northamptonshire 1584 (*d* 1626) = Anne Borlase (*d* 1627)

William Isham = Mary Brett

Capt Henry Isham, went to Virginia and settled at Bermuda Hundred = Katherine Royall, *née* Banks (*d* 1686)

Mary Isham = Col William Randolph, of Turkey Island, Henrico County, Virginia (1650-1711)

Isham Randolph (*ca* 1685-1742) = Jane Rogers (*d* 1761)

Jane Randolph (1720-1776) = Peter Jefferson (1708-1757)

THOMAS JEFFERSON, **3rd President of the United States of America**

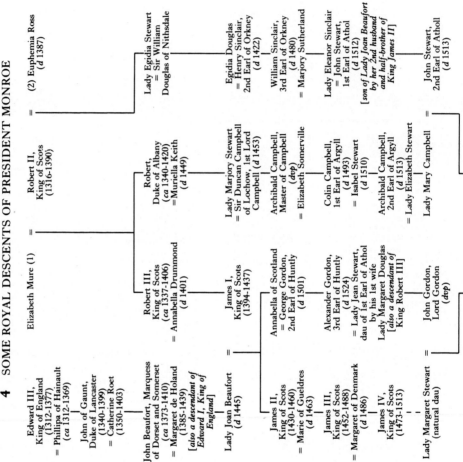

Edward III, King of England (1312-1377) = Phillipa of Hainault (ca 1312-1369)

Elizabeth Mure (1) = Robert II, King of Scots (1316-1390) = (2) Euphemia Ross (d 1387)

John of Gaunt, Duke of Lancaster (1340-1399) = Catherine Roet (1350-1403)

John Beaufort, Marquess of Dorset and Somerset (ca 1373-1410) = Margaret de Holand (1385-1439) [also a descendant of Edward I, King of England]

Robert III, King of Scots (ca 1337-1406) = Annabella Drummond (d 1401)

Robert, Duke of Albany (ca 1340-1420) = Muriella Keith (d 1449)

Lady Egidia Stewart = Sir William Douglas of Nithsdale

Lady Joan Beaufort (d 1445) = James I, King of Scots (1394-1437)

Lady Marjory Stewart = Sir Duncan Campbell of Lochow, 1st Lord Campbell (d 1453)

Egidia Douglas = Henry Sinclair, 2nd Earl of Orkney (d 1422)

James II, King of Scots (1430-1460) = Marie of Gueldres (d 1463)

Annabella of Scotland = George Gordon, 2nd Earl of Huntly (d 1501)

Archibald Campbell, Master of Campbell (dvp) = Elizabeth Somerville

William Sinclair, 3rd Earl of Orkney (d 1480) = Marjory Sutherland

James III, King of Scots (1452-1488) = Margaret of Denmark (d 1486)

Alexander Gordon, 3rd Earl of Huntly (d 1524) = Lady Jean Stewart, dau of 1st Earl of Athol by his 1st wife

Colin Campbell, 1st Earl of Argyll (d 1493) = Isabel Stewart (d 1510)

Lady Eleanor Sinclair = John Stewart, 1st Earl of Athol (d 1512) [son of Lady Joan Beaufort by her 2nd husband and half-brother of King James II]

James IV, King of Scots (1473-1513) = Margaret Douglas [also a descendant of King Robert III]

John Gordon, Lord Gordon (dvp)

Archibald Campbell, 2nd Earl of Argyll (d 1513) = Lady Elizabeth Stewart

John Stewart, 2nd Earl of Atholl (d 1513)

Lady Margaret Stewart (natural dau)

Lady Mary Campbell

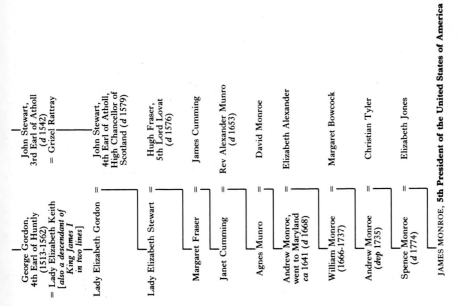

George Gordon,
4th Earl of Huntly
(1513-1562)
= Lady Elizabeth Keith
*[also a descendant of
King James I
in two lines]*

John Stewart,
3rd Earl of Atholl
(*d* 1542)
= Grizel Rattray

Lady Elizabeth Gordon =

John Stewart,
4th Earl of Atholl,
High Chancellor of
Scotland (*d* 1579)

Lady Elizabeth Stewart =

Hugh Fraser,
5th Lord Lovat
(*d* 1576)

Margaret Fraser =

James Cumming

Janet Cumming =

Rev Alexander Munro
(*d* 1653)

Agnes Munro =

David Monroe

Andrew Monroe,
went to Maryland
*ca* 1641 (*d* 1668) =

Elizabeth Alexander

William Monroe
(1666-1737) =

Margaret Bowcock

Andrew Monroe
(*dvp* 1735) =

Christian Tyler

Spence Monroe
(*d* 1774) =

Elizabeth Jones

JAMES MONROE, **5th President of the United States of America**

Edward I,
King of England
(1239-1307)
=
Eleanor of Castile
(ca 1244-1290)

Edward II,
King of England
(1284-1327)

Elizabeth of England
(1282-1316)
=
Humphrey de Bohun,
4th Earl of Hereford
and Essex (d 1321)

Edward III,
King of England
(1312-1377)

William de Bohun,
1st Earl of Northampton
(d 1360)
=
Elizabeth Badlesmere

John of Gaunt,
Duke of Lancaster
(1340-1399)
=
Catherine Roet
(1350-1403)

Elizabeth de Bohun
=
Richard Fitzalan,
4th Earl of Arundel
(d 1397)

Henry Beaufort,
Bishop of Winchester,
Lord Chancellor of
England and Cardinal
(ca 1375-1447)
×
Lady Alice Fitzalan

4th Lord Cherleton
=
Lady Elizabeth Fitzalan
(d 1425)
=
Sir Robert Goushill,
of Hoveringham, Notts

Jane (or Joan) Beaufort
(b ca 1391/2)
=
Sir Edward Stradling,
of St Donat's Castle,
Glamorgan
(ca 1389-1453)

Joan Goushill
=
Thomas Stanley,
1st Lord Stanley
(d 1459)

Sir Henry Stradling,
of St Donat's Castle
(b ca 1423)
=
Elizabeth, dau of
Sir William ap Thomas

Margaret Stanley
=
Sir William Troutbeck,
of Mobberley, Cheshire

Thomas Stradling
(ca 1454/5-1480)
=
Janet Mathew
(d 1485)

Joan Troutbeck
=
Sir William Griffith,
of Penrhyn,
Caernarvonshire
(living 1482)

Jane Stradling
(ca 1477/80-ante 1520)
=
Sir William Griffith,
of Penrhyn,
Chamberlain of N Wales

Dorothy Griffith
=
William Williams,
of Cochwillan,
Caernarvonshire,
High Sheriff of
Caernarvonshire 1570-71

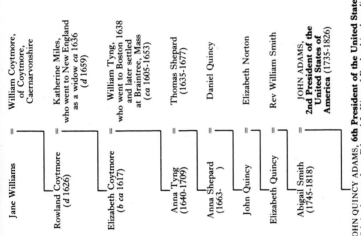

Jane Williams = William Coytmore, of Coytmore, Caernarvonshire

Rowland Coytmore (*d* 1626) = Katherine Miles, who went to New England as a widow *ca* 1636 (*d* 1659)

Elizabeth Coytmore (*b ca* 1617) = William Tyng, who went to Boston 1638 and later settled at Braintree, Mass (*ca* 1605-1653)

Anna Tyng (1640-1709) = Thomas Shepard (1635-1677)

Anna Shepard (1663- ) = Daniel Quincy

John Quincy = Elizabeth Norton

Elizabeth Quincy = Rev William Smith

Abigail Smith (1745-1818) = JOHN ADAMS, **2nd President of the United States of America** (1735-1826)

JOHN QUINCY ADAMS, **6th President of the United States of America**, 18th in descent from Edward I, King of England in three lines

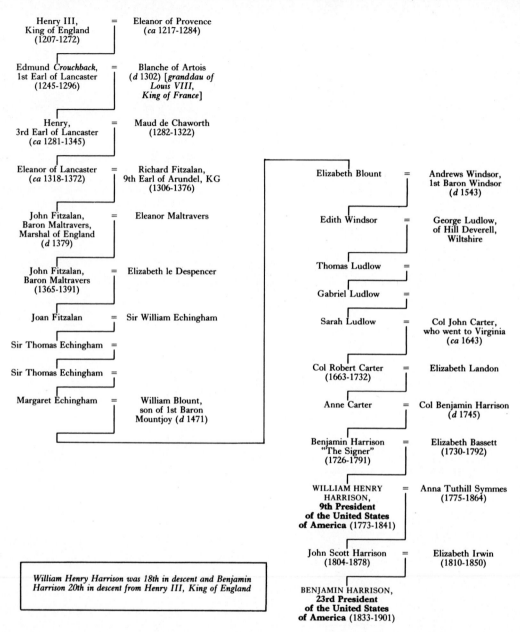

Henry III,
King of England
(1207-1272)
= Eleanor of Provence
(*ca* 1217-1284)

Edmund *Crouchback*,
1st Earl of Lancaster
(1245-1296)
= Blanche of Artois
(*d* 1302) [*granddau of
Louis VIII,
King of France*]

Henry,
3rd Earl of Lancaster
(*ca* 1281-1345)
= Maud de Chaworth
(1282-1322)

Eleanor of Lancaster
(*ca* 1318-1372)
= Richard Fitzalan,
9th Earl of Arundel, KG
(1306-1376)

John Fitzalan,
Baron Maltravers,
Marshal of England
(*d* 1379)
= Eleanor Maltravers

John Fitzalan,
Baron Maltravers
(1365-1391)
= Elizabeth le Despencer

Joan Fitzalan = Sir William Echingham

Sir Thomas Echingham =

Sir Thomas Echingham =

Margaret Echingham = William Blount,
son of 1st Baron
Mountjoy (*d* 1471)

Elizabeth Blount = Andrews Windsor,
1st Baron Windsor
(*d* 1543)

Edith Windsor = George Ludlow,
of Hill Deverell,
Wiltshire

Thomas Ludlow =

Gabriel Ludlow =

Sarah Ludlow = Col John Carter,
who went to Virginia
(*ca* 1643)

Col Robert Carter
(1663-1732)
= Elizabeth Landon

Anne Carter = Col Benjamin Harrison
(*d* 1745)

Benjamin Harrison
"The Signer"
(1726-1791)
= Elizabeth Bassett
(1730-1792)

WILLIAM HENRY
HARRISON,
**9th President
of the United States
of America** (1773-1841)
= Anna Tuthill Symmes
(1775-1864)

John Scott Harrison
(1804-1878)
= Elizabeth Irwin
(1810-1850)

BENJAMIN HARRISON,
**23rd President
of the United States
of America** (1833-1901)

*William Henry Harrison was 18th in descent and Benjamin
Harrison 20th in descent from Henry III, King of England*

---

**7** THE DESCENT OF PRESIDENT BUCHANAN FROM ROBERT II, KING OF SCOTS

*The descent of* PRESIDENT JAMES BUCHANAN, **15th President of the United States of America** *from
Robert II, King of Scots has already been indicated in his* LINEAGE (*see p 287*).

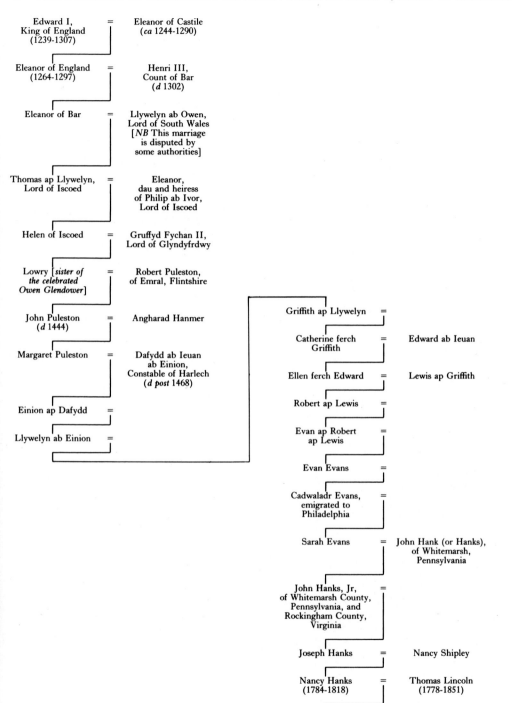

Edward I, King of England (1239-1307) = Eleanor of Castile (*ca* 1244-1290)

Eleanor of England (1264-1297) = Henri III, Count of Bar (*d* 1302)

Eleanor of Bar = Llywelyn ab Owen, Lord of South Wales [*NB* This marriage is disputed by some authorities]

Thomas ap Llywelyn, Lord of Iscoed = Eleanor, dau and heiress of Philip ab Ivor, Lord of Iscoed

Helen of Iscoed = Gruffyd Fychan II, Lord of Glyndyfrdwy

Lowry [*sister of the celebrated Owen Glendower*] = Robert Puleston, of Emral, Flintshire

John Puleston (*d* 1444) = Angharad Hanmer

Margaret Puleston = Dafydd ab Ieuan ab Einion, Constable of Harlech (*d post* 1468)

Einion ap Dafydd =

Llywelyn ab Einion =

Griffith ap Llywelyn =

Catherine ferch Griffith = Edward ab Ieuan

Ellen ferch Edward = Lewis ap Griffith

Robert ap Lewis =

Evan ap Robert ap Lewis =

Evan Evans =

Cadwaladr Evans, emigrated to Philadelphia =

Sarah Evans = John Hank (or Hanks), of Whitemarsh, Pennsylvania

John Hanks, Jr, of Whitemarsh County, Pennsylvania, and Rockingham County, Virginia =

Joseph Hanks = Nancy Shipley

Nancy Hanks (1784-1818) = Thomas Lincoln (1778-1851)

ABRAHAM LINCOLN, **16th President of the United States of America**, 21st in descent from Edward I, King of England

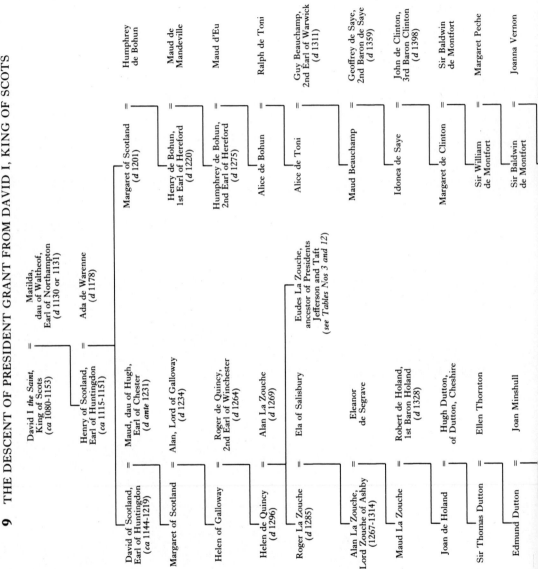

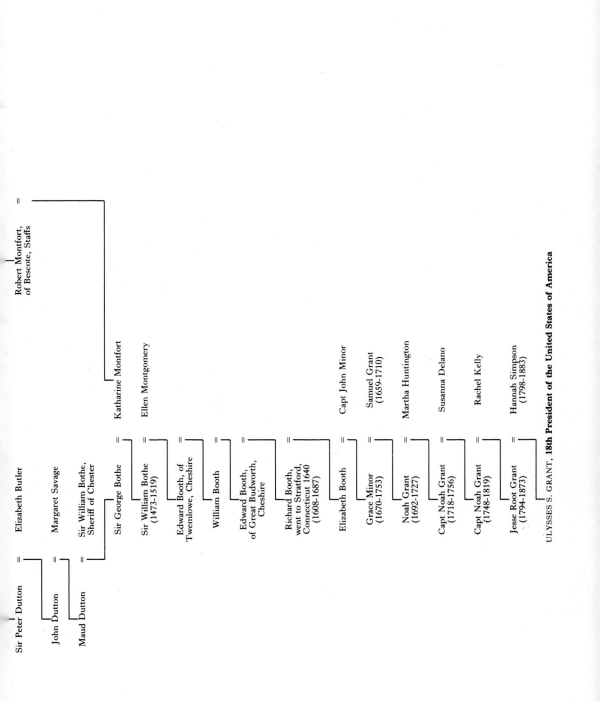

ULYSSES S. GRANT, **18th President of the United States of America**

**10 THE DESCENT OF PRESIDENT GARFIELD FROM HENRI I, KING OF FRANCE AND RHYS AP TEWDWR, KING OF DEHEUBARTH**

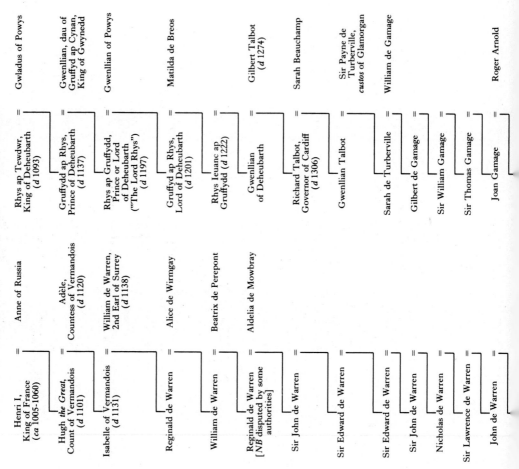

| | | |
|---|---|---|
| Henri I, King of France (*ca* 1005-1060) | = Anne of Russia | Rhys ap Tewdwr, King of Deheubarth (*d* 1093) = Gwladus of Powys |
| Hugh *the Great*, Count of Vermandois (*d* 1101) | = Adèle, Countess of Vermandois (*d* 1120) | Gruffydd ap Rhys, Prince of Deheubarth (*d* 1137) = Gwenllian, dau of Gruffyd ap Cynan, King of Gwynedd |
| Isabelle of Vermandois (*d* 1131) | = William de Warren, 2nd Earl of Surrey (*d* 1138) | Rhys ap Gruffydd, Prince or Lord of Deheubarth ("The Lord Rhys") (*d* 1197) = Gwenllian of Powys |
| Reginald de Warren | = Alice de Wirmgay | Gruffydd ap Rhys, Lord of Deheubarth (*d* 1201) = Matilda de Breos |
| William de Warren | = Beatrix de Perepont | Rhys Ieuanc ap Gruffydd (*d* 1222) |
| Reginald de Warren [*NB* disputed by some authorities] | = Aldelia de Mowbray | Gwenllian of Deheubarth |
| Sir John de Warren | | Richard Talbot, Governor of Cardiff (*d* 1306) = Gilbert Talbot (*d* 1274) Sarah Beauchamp |
| Sir Edward de Warren | | Gwenllian Talbot = Sir Payne de Turberville, *custos* of Glamorgan |
| Sir Edward de Warren | | Sarah de Turberville = William de Gamage |
| Sir John de Warren | | Gilbert de Gamage |
| Nicholas de Warren | | Sir William Gamage |
| Sir Lawrence de Warren | | Sir Thomas Gamage |
| John de Warren | | Joan Gamage = Roger Arnold |

Sir Lawrence de Warren

Thomas Arnold =

William Warren =

John Arnold =

John Warren =

Richard Arnold =

John Warren =

Nicholas Arnold =

Christian Warren =

Christian Peake = William Arnold,
who settled
in Rhode Island 1636
(1587-*ca* 1676)

Christopher Warren =

Stephen Arnold =

William Warren =

Elisha Arnold =

Susanna Carpenter =

Christopher Warren =

Katherine Arnold =

James Ballou =

John Warren,
who settled
in Watertown,
Massachusetts (*ca* 1630) =

James Ballou =

James Ballou =

Mary Warren =

John Bigelow =

James Ballou =

Tamasin Cook =

Joshua Bigelow =

Elizabeth Flagg =

James Ballou =

Mehitabel Ingalls
[*descended from
John Billington,
a Mayflower passenger*]

Mercy Bigelow
(1686-1745) =

Thomas Garfield
(1680-1752) =

Thomas Garfield
(1713-1774) =

Rebecca Johnson
(1719-1763) =

Solomon Garfield
(1743-1807) =

Sarah Stimson =

Thomas Garfield
(1773-1801) =

Asenath Hill
(1778-1851) =

Abram Garfield
(1799-1833) =

Elizabeth Ballou
(1801-1888)

JAMES ABRAM GARFIELD, **20th President of the United States of America**

Robert III,   =   Annabella Drummond
King of Scots        (*d* 1401)
(*d* 1406)

Elizabeth of Scotland   =   Sir James Douglas,
                1st Lord Dalkeith
                (*d ante* 1441)

James Douglas,   =   Elizabeth Gifford
2nd Lord Dalkeith
(*d post* 1456)

Sir John Douglas   =

David Douglas   =
of Tilquhillie

James Douglas   =

Arthur Douglas   =

John Douglas   =

John Douglas   =

James Douglas   =
(*d* 1672)

John Douglas   =

John Douglas   =   Agnes Horn
(1723-1749)

Euphemia Douglas   =   Charles Irvine
(*d* 1766)          of Cults (1696-1779)

John Irvine, MD,   =   Ann Elizabeth Baillie
emigrated to Georgia        (1749-1807)
*ca* 1765 (1742-1808)

Anne Irvine   =   Capt James Bulloch
(1770-1810)          (1765-1806)

Major James Stephens   =   Martha Elliot
Bulloch (1793-1849)         (*née* Stewart)
                (1799-1862)

Martha Bulloch   =   Theodore Roosevelt
(1834-1884)          (1831-1878)

THEODORE ROOSEVELT, **26th President of the United States
of America**, 17th in descent from Robert III, King of Scots

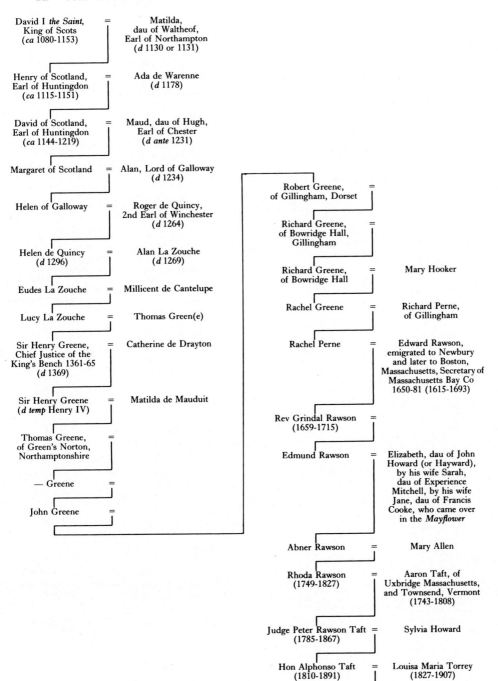

David I *the Saint*, = Matilda,
King of Scots    dau of Waltheof,
(*ca* 1080-1153)   Earl of Northampton
          (*d* 1130 or 1131)

Henry of Scotland, = Ada de Warenne
Earl of Huntingdon    (*d* 1178)
(*ca* 1115-1151)

David of Scotland, = Maud, dau of Hugh,
Earl of Huntingdon    Earl of Chester
(*ca* 1144-1219)   (*d ante* 1231)

Margaret of Scotland = Alan, Lord of Galloway
          (*d* 1234)

Helen of Galloway = Roger de Quincy,
          2nd Earl of Winchester
          (*d* 1264)

Helen de Quincy = Alan La Zouche
(*d* 1296)     (*d* 1269)

Eudes La Zouche = Millicent de Cantelupe

Lucy La Zouche = Thomas Green(e)

Sir Henry Greene, = Catherine de Drayton
Chief Justice of the
King's Bench 1361-65
(*d* 1369)

Sir Henry Greene = Matilda de Mauduit
(*d temp* Henry IV)

Thomas Greene, =
of Green's Norton,
Northamptonshire

— Greene =

John Greene =

Robert Greene, =
of Gillingham, Dorset

Richard Greene, =
of Bowridge Hall,
Gillingham

Richard Greene, = Mary Hooker
of Bowridge Hall

Rachel Greene = Richard Perne,
          of Gillingham

Rachel Perne = Edward Rawson,
          emigrated to Newbury
          and later to Boston,
          Massachusetts, Secretary of
          Massachusetts Bay Co
          1650-81 (1615-1693)

Rev Grindal Rawson =
(1659-1715)

Edmund Rawson = Elizabeth, dau of John
          Howard (or Hayward),
          by his wife Sarah,
          dau of Experience
          Mitchell, by his wife
          Jane, dau of Francis
          Cooke, who came over
          in the *Mayflower*

Abner Rawson = Mary Allen

Rhoda Rawson = Aaron Taft, of
(1749-1827)    Uxbridge Massachusetts,
          and Townsend, Vermont
          (1743-1808)

Judge Peter Rawson Taft = Sylvia Howard
(1785-1867)

Hon Alphonso Taft = Louisa Maria Torrey
(1810-1891)    (1827-1907)

WILLIAM HOWARD TAFT, **27th President of the United
States of America**, 24th in descent from David I, King of Scots

Edward III, = Philippa of Hainault
King of England (*ca* 1312-1369)
(1312-1377)

Edmund of Langley, = Isabel of Castile
Duke of York, KG (1355-1393)
1341-1402)

Constance of York × Edmund de Holand,
(*ca* 1374-1416) Earl of Kent, KG
= Thomas le Despenser, (1383-1408)
Earl of Gloucester [*descended from King Edward I*]

Alianore (or Eleanor) = James Tuchet,
Holand (*b ca* 1405), 5th Lord Audley
unsuccessfully claimed (*ca* 1398-1459)
legitimacy

Constance Tuchet = Robert Whitney, of
(or Audley) Whitney, Herefordshire
(*b post* 1430

Eleanor (or Elin) = John Puleston, of
Whitney Bers and Hafod-y-wern

Elizabeth Pugh = Rowland Owen,
Mayor of Machynlleth,
Montgomeryshire (1597),
JP (*d post* 1625)

Sir John Puleston, = Gaynor, dau of
Sheriff of Caernarvon- Robert ap Maredudd
shire and Chamberlain
of N Wales (*d* 1551)

Thomas Owen, =
of Machynlleth

Jane Puleston = Rhys Thomas, High
Sheriff of Caernarvon-
shire (1574) and
Carmarthenshire (1584)

Harry Thomas Owen, =
became a Quaker

Hugh Harry, emigrated = Elizabeth Brinton
to America on the *Vine*
(*d* 1708)

Gaynor Thomas = Richard Pugh,
of Mathafarn,
Montgomeryshire

John Harry (*d* 1763) = Frances —

Miriam Harry = Record Hussey
(*d* 1809) (*d* 1784)

Lydia Hussey = Jacob Griffith
(1757-1843) (1757-1841)

Amos Griffith = Edith Price
(*ca* 1798-1871) (1801-1873)

Elizabeth Price = Joshua Vickers Milhous
Griffith (1827-1923) (1820-1893)

Franklin Milhous = Almira Park Burdg
(1848-1919) (1849-1943)

Hannah Milhous = Francis Anthony Nixon
(1885-1967) (1878-1956)

RICHARD MILHOUS NIXON, **37th President of the United States of America**,
20th in descent from Edward III, King of England

# *Appendix D*
# Some Remarkable Kinships

1   *President Washington, Queen Elizabeth II and General Robert E. Lee*
2   *President Washington and Sir Winston Churchill*
3   *President Jefferson and Chief Justice Marshall*
4   *President Lincoln and Salmon Portland Chase*
5   *President Grant and Richard Henry Dana*
6   *President Garfield and Brigham Young*
7   *President Coolidge and General Israel Putnam*
8   *President Franklin D. Roosevelt and Sir Winston Churchill*

NOTES: (*a*) Apart from these set out here, there are several other interesting relationships illustrated in the various NOTES at the end of the chapters on the individual Presidents (*qv*). (*b*) These Genealogical Tables, as for the ones illustrating Presidents of Royal Descent (*see* APPENDIX C), only give brief details of the persons involved and reference to the other volumes in BURKE'S Genealogical Series is recommended for further study of the genealogy of some of those featured.

**1  PRESIDENT WASHINGTON, QUEEN ELIZABETH II AND GENERAL ROBERT E. LEE**

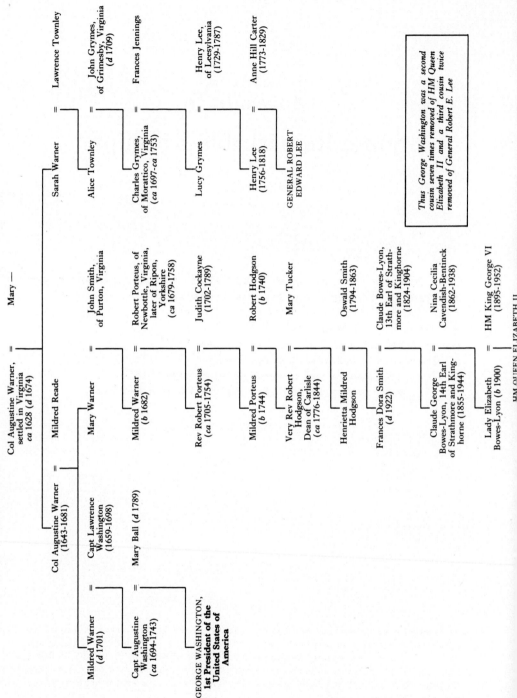

Col Augustine Warner, settled in Virginia *ca* 1628 (*d* 1674) = Mary —

Col Augustine Warner (1643-1681) = Mildred Reade

Sarah Warner = Lawrence Townley

Mildred Warner (*d* 1701) = Capt Lawrence Washington (1659-1698)

Mary Warner = John Smith, of Purton, Virginia

Alice Townley = John Grymes, of Grimesby, Virginia (*d* 1709)

Capt Augustine Washington (*ca* 1694-1743) = Mary Ball (*d* 1789)

Mildred Warner (*b* 1682) = Robert Porteus, of Newbottle, later of Ripon, Yorkshire (*ca* 1679-1758)

Charles Grymes, of Morattico, Virginia (*ca* 1697-*ca* 1753) = Frances Jennings

GEORGE WASHINGTON, 1st President of the United States of America

Rev Robert Porteus (*ca* 1705-1754) = Judith Cockayne (1702-1789)

Lucy Grymes = Henry Lee, of Leesylvania (1729-1787)

Mildred Porteus (*b* 1744) = Robert Hodgson (*b* 1740)

Henry Lee (1756-1818) = Anne Hill Carter (1773-1829)

Very Rev Robert Hodgson, Dean of Carlisle (*ca* 1776-1844) = Mary Tucker

GENERAL ROBERT EDWARD LEE

Henrietta Mildred Hodgson = Oswald Smith (1794-1863)

Frances Dora Smith (*d* 1922) = Claude Bowes-Lyon, 13th Earl of Strathmore and Kinghorne (1824-1904)

Claude George Bowes-Lyon, 14th Earl of Strathmore and Kinghorne (1855-1944) = Nina Cecilia Cavendish-Bentinck (1862-1938)

Lady Elizabeth Bowes-Lyon (*b* 1900) = HM King George VI (1895-1952)

HM QUEEN ELIZABETH II

*Thus George Washington was a second cousin seven times removed of HM Queen Elizabeth II and a third cousin twice removed of General Robert E. Lee*

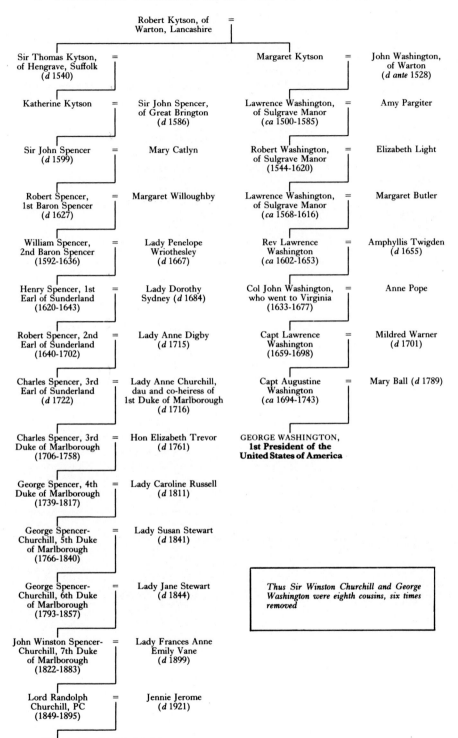

Robert Kytson, of = 
Warton, Lancashire

| Sir Thomas Kytson, = | | Margaret Kytson = | John Washington, |
| of Hengrave, Suffolk | | | of Warton |
| (*d* 1540) | | | (*d ante* 1528) |

Katherine Kytson = Sir John Spencer,    Lawrence Washington, =    Amy Pargiter
of Great Brington    of Sulgrave Manor
(*d* 1586)    (*ca* 1500-1585)

Sir John Spencer = Mary Catlyn    Robert Washington, =    Elizabeth Light
(*d* 1599)    of Sulgrave Manor
(1544-1620)

Robert Spencer, = Margaret Willoughby    Lawrence Washington, =    Margaret Butler
1st Baron Spencer    of Sulgrave Manor
(*d* 1627)    (*ca* 1568-1616)

William Spencer, = Lady Penelope    Rev Lawrence = Amphyllis Twigden
2nd Baron Spencer    Wriothesley    Washington    (*d* 1655)
(1592-1636)    (*d* 1667)    (*ca* 1602-1653)

Henry Spencer, 1st = Lady Dorothy    Col John Washington, =    Anne Pope
Earl of Sunderland    Sydney (*d* 1684)    who went to Virginia
(1620-1643)    (1633-1677)

Robert Spencer, 2nd = Lady Anne Digby    Capt Lawrence = Mildred Warner
Earl of Sunderland    (*d* 1715)    Washington    (*d* 1701)
(1640-1702)    (1659-1698)

Charles Spencer, 3rd = Lady Anne Churchill,    Capt Augustine = Mary Ball (*d* 1789)
Earl of Sunderland    dau and co-heiress of    Washington
(*d* 1722)    1st Duke of Marlborough    (*ca* 1694-1743)
   (*d* 1716)

Charles Spencer, 3rd = Hon Elizabeth Trevor    GEORGE WASHINGTON,
Duke of Marlborough    (*d* 1761)    **1st President of the**
(1706-1758)    **United States of America**

George Spencer, 4th = Lady Caroline Russell
Duke of Marlborough    (*d* 1811)
(1739-1817)

George Spencer- = Lady Susan Stewart
Churchill, 5th Duke    (*d* 1841)
of Marlborough
(1766-1840)

George Spencer- = Lady Jane Stewart
Churchill, 6th Duke    (*d* 1844)
of Marlborough
(1793-1857)

John Winston Spencer- = Lady Frances Anne
Churchill, 7th Duke    Emily Vane
of Marlborough    (*d* 1899)
(1822-1883)

Lord Randolph = Jennie Jerome
Churchill, PC    (*d* 1921)
(1849-1895)

SIR WINSTON S. CHURCHILL, KG, PC

> *Thus Sir Winston Churchill and George Washington were eighth cousins, six times removed*

## 3 PRESIDENT JEFFERSON AND CHIEF JUSTICE MARSHALL

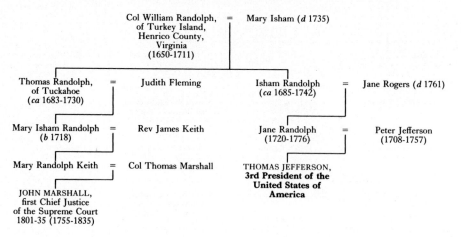

Col William Randolph, = Mary Isham (*d* 1735)
of Turkey Island,
Henrico County,
Virginia
(1650-1711)

Thomas Randolph, = Judith Fleming
of Tuckahoe
(*ca* 1683-1730)

Isham Randolph = Jane Rogers (*d* 1761)
(*ca* 1685-1742)

Mary Isham Randolph = Rev James Keith
(*b* 1718)

Jane Randolph = Peter Jefferson
(1720-1776) (1708-1757)

Mary Randolph Keith = Col Thomas Marshall

THOMAS JEFFERSON,
**3rd President of the
United States of
America**

JOHN MARSHALL,
first Chief Justice
of the Supreme Court
1801-35 (1755-1835)

## 4 PRESIDENT LINCOLN AND SALMON PORTLAND CHASE

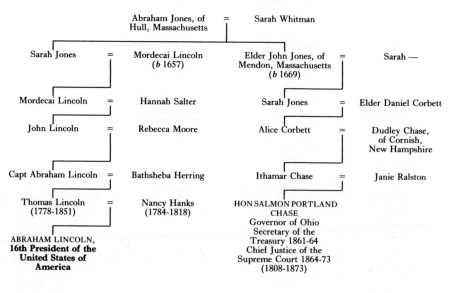

Abraham Jones, of = Sarah Whitman
Hull, Massachusetts

Sarah Jones = Mordecai Lincoln
(*b* 1657)

Elder John Jones, of = Sarah —
Mendon, Massachusetts
(*b* 1669)

Mordecai Lincoln = Hannah Salter

Sarah Jones = Elder Daniel Corbett

John Lincoln = Rebecca Moore

Alice Corbett = Dudley Chase,
of Cornish,
New Hampshire

Capt Abraham Lincoln = Bathsheba Herring

Ithamar Chase = Janie Ralston

Thomas Lincoln = Nancy Hanks
(1778-1851) (1784-1818)

HON SALMON PORTLAND
CHASE
Governor of Ohio
Secretary of the
Treasury 1861-64
Chief Justice of the
Supreme Court 1864-73
(1808-1873)

ABRAHAM LINCOLN,
**16th President of the
United States of
America**

## 5   PRESIDENT GRANT AND RICHARD HENRY DANA

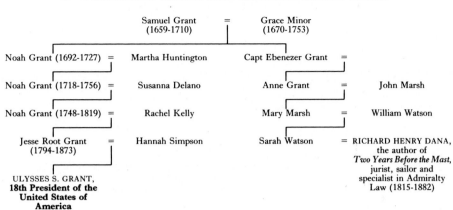

| | | | |
|---|---|---|---|
| | Samuel Grant (1659-1710) = Grace Minor (1670-1753) | | |
| Noah Grant (1692-1727) = Martha Huntington | | Capt Ebenezer Grant = | |
| Noah Grant (1718-1756) = Susanna Delano | | Anne Grant = John Marsh | |
| Noah Grant (1748-1819) = Rachel Kelly | | Mary Marsh = William Watson | |
| Jesse Root Grant (1794-1873) = Hannah Simpson | | Sarah Watson = RICHARD HENRY DANA, the author of *Two Years Before the Mast*, jurist, sailor and specialist in Admiralty Law (1815-1882) | |
| ULYSSES S. GRANT, **18th President of the United States of America** | | | |

## 6   PRESIDENT GARFIELD AND BRIGHAM YOUNG

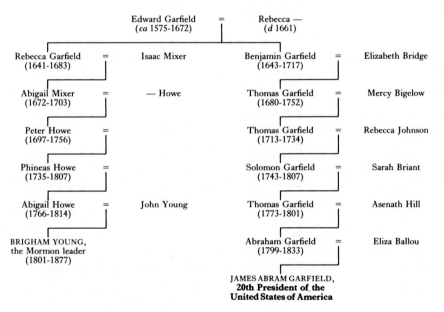

Edward Garfield (*ca* 1575-1672) = Rebecca — (*d* 1661)

Rebecca Garfield (1641-1683) = Isaac Mixer

Benjamin Garfield (1643-1717) = Elizabeth Bridge

Abigail Mixer (1672-1703) = — Howe

Thomas Garfield (1680-1752) = Mercy Bigelow

Peter Howe (1697-1756) =

Thomas Garfield (1713-1734) = Rebecca Johnson

Phineas Howe (1735-1807) =

Solomon Garfield (1743-1807) = Sarah Briant

Abigail Howe (1766-1814) = John Young

Thomas Garfield (1773-1801) = Asenath Hill

BRIGHAM YOUNG, the Mormon leader (1801-1877)

Abraham Garfield (1799-1833) = Eliza Ballou

JAMES ABRAM GARFIELD, **20th President of the United States of America**

## 7  PRESIDENT COOLIDGE AND GENERAL ISRAEL PUTNAM

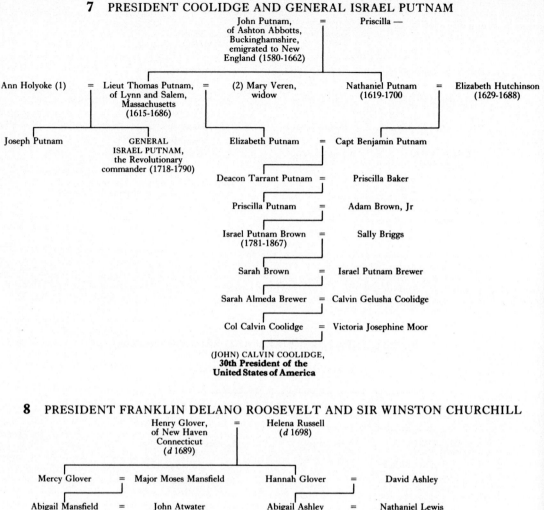

John Putnam,
of Ashton Abbotts,
Buckinghamshire,
emigrated to New
England (1580-1662)  =  Priscilla —

Ann Holyoke (1)  =  Lieut Thomas Putnam,
of Lynn and Salem,
Massachusetts
(1615-1686)  =  (2) Mary Veren,
widow

Nathaniel Putnam
(1619-1700  =  Elizabeth Hutchinson
(1629-1688)

Joseph Putnam

GENERAL
ISRAEL PUTNAM,
the Revolutionary
commander (1718-1790)

Elizabeth Putnam  =  Capt Benjamin Putnam

Deacon Tarrant Putnam  =  Priscilla Baker

Priscilla Putnam  =  Adam Brown, Jr

Israel Putnam Brown
(1781-1867)  =  Sally Briggs

Sarah Brown  =  Israel Putnam Brewer

Sarah Almeda Brewer  =  Calvin Gelusha Coolidge

Col Calvin Coolidge  =  Victoria Josephine Moor

(JOHN) CALVIN COOLIDGE,
**30th President of the
United States of America**

## 8  PRESIDENT FRANKLIN DELANO ROOSEVELT AND SIR WINSTON CHURCHILL

Henry Glover,
of New Haven
Connecticut
(*d* 1689)  =  Helena Russell
(*d* 1698)

Mercy Glover  =  Major Moses Mansfield        Hannah Glover  =  David Ashley

Abigail Mansfield  =  John Atwater              Abigail Ashley  =  Nathaniel Lewis

Abigail Atwater  =  Thomas Hall                Abigail Lewis  =  Joseph Lyman

Thomas Hall  =  Lydia Curtis                   Joseph Lyman  =  Mary Sheldon

Ambrose Hall  =  Mehitable Beach               Joseph Lyman  =  Anne Jean Robbins

Ambrose Hall  =  Clarissa Willcox              Catharine Robbins Lyman  =  Warren Delano

Clarissa Hall  =  Leonard Jerome               Sara Delano  =  James Roosevelt

Jennie Jerome  =  Lord Randolph
Churchill, PC

FRANKLIN DELANO
ROOSEVELT,
**32nd President of the
United States of America**

SIR WINSTON S.
CHURCHILL, KG, PC

*Thus the two great leaders of World War II were seventh cousins once removed. In other lines they were also eighth cousins and eighth cousins twice removed (see "Two Famous Descendants of John Cooke and Sarah Warren", by Conklin Mann in The New York Genealogical and Biographical Record, Vol LXXIII, New York, 1942)*

# Appendix E
## The Presidential Insignia

THE PRESIDENTIAL SEAL

THE PRESIDENTIAL FLAG

# *Appendix F*
# The Declaration of Independence

In CONGRESS, July 4, 1776

## THE UNANIMOUS DECLARATION of the thirteen united STATES OF AMERICA

WHEN IN the Course of human events it becomes necessary for one people to dissolve the political bands which have connected them with another, and to assume among the powers of the earth, the separate and equal station to which the Laws of Nature and of Nature's God entitle them, a decent respect to the opinions of mankind requires that they should declare the causes which impel them to the separation.

We hold these truths to be self-evident, that all men are created equal, that they are endowed by their Creator with certain unalienable Rights, that among these are Life, Liberty and the pursuit of Happiness.—That to secure these rights, Governments are instituted among Men, deriving their just powers from the consent of the governed,—That whenever any Form of Government becomes destructive of these ends, it is the Right of the People to alter or to abolish it, and to institute new Government, laying its foundation on such principles and organizing its powers in such form, as to them shall seem most likely to effect their Safety and Happiness. Prudence, indeed, will dictate that Governments long established should not be changed for light and transient causes; and accordingly all experience hath shewn that mankind are more disposed to suffer, while evils are sufferable, than to right themselves by abolishing the forms to which they are accustomed. But when a long train of abuses and usurpations, pursuing invariably the same Object evinces a design to reduce them under absolute Despotism, it is their right, it is their duty, to throw off such Government, and to provide new Guards for their future security.—Such has been the patient sufferance of these Colonies; and such is now the necessity which constrains them to alter their former Systems of Government. The history of the present King of Great Britain is a history of repeated injuries and usurpations, all having in direct object the establishment of an absolute Tyranny over these States. To prove this, let Facts be submitted to a candid world.

He has refused his Assent to Laws, the most wholesome and necessary for the public good.

He has forbidden his Governors to pass Laws of immediate and pressing importance, unless suspended in their operation till his Assent should be obtained; and when so suspended, he has utterly neglected to attend to them.

He has refused to pass other Laws for the accommodation of large districts of people, unless those people would relinquish the right of Representation in the Legislature, a right inestimable to them and formidable to tyrants only.

He has called together legislative bodies at places unusual, uncomfortable, and distant from the depository of their Public Records, for the sole purpose of fatiguing them into compliance with his measures.

He has dissolved Representative Houses repeatedly, for opposing with manly firmness his invasions on the rights of the people.

He has refused for a long time, after such dissolutions, to cause others to be elected; whereby the Legislative Powers, incapable of Annihilation, have returned to the People at large for their exercise; the State remaining in the mean time exposed to all the dangers of invasion from without, and convulsions within.

He has endeavored to prevent the population of these States; for that purpose obstructing the Laws for Naturalization of Foreigners; refusing to pass others to encourage their migrations hither, and raising the conditions of new Appropriations of Lands.

He has obstructed the Administration of Justice, by refusing his Assent to Laws for establishing Judiciary Powers.

He has made Judges dependent on his Will alone, for the tenure of their offices, and the amount and payment of their salaries.

He has erected a multitude of New Offices, and sent hither swarms of Officers to harass our people, and eat out their substance.

He has kept among us, in times of peace, Standing Armies without the Consent of our legislatures.

He has affected to render the Military independent of and superior to the Civil Power.

He has combined with others to subject us to a jurisdiction foreign to our constitution, and unacknowledged by our laws; giving his Assent to their Acts of pretended Legislation:

For quartering large bodies of armed troops among us:

For protecting them, by a mock Trial, from punishment for any Murders which they should commit on the Inhabitants of these States:

For cutting off our Trade with all parts of the world:

For imposing Taxes on us without our Consent:

For depriving us in many cases, of the benefits of Trial by Jury:

For transporting us beyond Seas to be tried for pretended offences:

For abolishing the free System of English Laws in a neighboring Province, establishing therein an Arbitrary government, and enlarging its Boundaries so as to render it at once an example and fit instrument for introducing the same absolute rule into these Colonies:

For taking away our Charters, abolishing our most valuable Laws and altering fundamentally the Forms of our Governments:

For suspending our own Legislatures, and declaring themselves invested with power to legislate for us in all cases whatsoever.

He has abdicated Government here, by declaring us out of his Protection and waging War against us.

He has plundered our seas, ravaged our Coasts, burnt our towns, and destroyed the lives of our people.

He is at this time transporting large Armies of foreign Mercenaries to compleat the works of death, desolation and tyranny, already begun with circumstances of Cruelty & Perfidy scarcely paralleled in the most barbarous ages, and totally unworthy the Head of a civilized nation.

He has constrained our fellow Citizens taken Captive on the high Seas to bear Arms against their Country, to become the executioners of their friends and Brethren, or to fall themselves by their Hands.

He has excited domestic insurrections amongst us, and has endeavoured to bring on the inhabitants of our frontiers, the merciless Indian Savages, whose known rule of warfare, is an undistinguished destruction of all ages, sexes and conditions.

In every stage of these Oppressions We have Petitioned for Redress in the most humble terms: Our repeated Petitions have been answered only by repeated injury. A Prince, whose character is thus marked by every act which may define a Tyrant, is unfit to be the ruler of a free people.

Nor have We been wanting in attentions to our Brittish brethren. We have warned them from time to time of attempts by their legislature to extend an unwarrantable jurisdiction over us. We have reminded them of the circumstances of our emigration and settlement here. We have appealed to their native justice and magnanimity, and we have conjured them by the ties of our common kindred to disavow these usurpations, which would inevitably interrupt our connections and correspondence. They too have been deaf to the voice of justice and of consanguinity. We must, therefore, acquiesce in the necessity, which denounces our Separation, and hold them, as we hold the rest of mankind, Enemies in War, in Peace, Friends.

WE, THEREFORE, the Representatives of the UNITED STATES OF AMERICA, in General Congress, Assembled, appealing to the Supreme Judge of the world for the rectitude of our intentions, do, in the Name, and by Authority of the good People of these Colonies, solemnly publish and declare, That these United Colonies are, and of Right ought to be FREE AND INDEPENDENT STATES; that they are Absolved from all Allegiance to the British Crown, and that all political connection between them and the State of Great Britain, is and ought to be totally dissolved; and that as Free and Independent States, they have full Power to levy War, conclude Peace, contract Alliances, establish Commerce, and to do all other Acts and Things which Independent States may of right do.—And for the support of this Declaration, with a firm reliance on the protection of Divine Providence, we mutually pledge to each other our Lives, our Fortunes and our sacred Honor.

JOHN HANCOCK.

*New Hampshire.*
Josiah Bartlett,
Wm. Whipple,
Matthew Thornton.

*Rhode Island.*
Step. Hopkins,
William Ellery.

*Connecticut.*
Roger Sherman,
Sam'el Huntington,
Wm. Williams,
Oliver Wolcott.

*New York.*
Wm. Floyd,
Phil. Livingston,
Frans. Lewis,
Lewis Morris.

*New Jersey.*
Richd. Stockton,
Jno. Witherspoon,
Fras. Hopkinson,
John Hart,
Abra. Clark.

*Pennsylvania.*
Robt. Morris,
Benjamin Rush,
Benja. Franklin,
John Morton,
Geo. Clymer,
Jas. Smith,
Geo. Taylor,
James Wilson,
Geo. Ross.

*Massachusetts-Bay.*
Saml. Adams,
John Adams,
Robt. Treat Paine,
Elbridge Gerry.

*Delaware.*
Ceasar Rodney,
Geo. Read,
Tho. M'Kean.

*Maryland.*
Samuel Chase,
Wm. Paca,
Thos. Stone,
Charles Carroll of
    Carrollton.

*Virginia.*
George Wythe,
Richard Henry Lee,
Th. Jefferson,
Benja. Harrison,
Ths. Nelson, Jr.,
Francis Lightfoot Lee,
Carter Braxton.

*North Carolina.*
Wm. Hooper,
Joseph Hewes,
John Penn.

*South Carolina.*
Edward Rutledge,
Thos. Heyward, Junr.,
Thomas Lynch, Junr.,
Arthur Middleton.

*Georgia.*
Button Gwinnett,
Lyman Hall,
Geo. Walton.

---

IN CONGRESS,
January, 18, 1777

**Ordered:**

That an authenticated copy of the Declaration of Independency, with the names of the Members of Congress subscribing the same, be sent to each of the United States, and that they be desired to have the same put on record.

By order of Congress.

Attest, CHAS. THOMSON, *Secy.* A true copy. JOHN HANCOCK, *Presidt.*

# Appendix G

## The Constitution of the United States of America

### THE CONSTITUTION

WE, THE People of the United States, in order to form a more perfect union, establish justice, insure domestic tranquility, provide for the common defence, promote the general welfare, and secure the blessing of liberty to ourselves and our posterity, do ordain and establish this Constitution for the United States of America.

#### ARTICLE I

*Section 1.* All legislative powers herein granted shall be vested in a Congress of the United States, which shall consist of a Senate and House of Representatives.

*Section 2.* The House of Representatives shall be composed of members chosen every second year by the people of the several states, and the electors in each state shall have the qualifications requisite for electors of the most numerous branch of the state legislature.

No person shall be a representative who shall not have attained to the age of twenty-five years, and been seven years a citizen of the United States, and who shall not, when elected, be an inhabitant of that state in which he shall be chosen.

Representatives and direct taxes shall be apportioned among the several states [which may be included within this Union, according to their respective numbers, which shall be determined by adding to the whole number of free persons, including those bound to service for a term of years, and excluding Indians not taxed, three-fifths of all other persons][1]. The actual enumeration shall be made within three years after the first meeting of the Congress of the United States, and within every subsequent term of ten years, in such manner as they shall by law direct. The number of representatives shall not exceed one for every thirty thousand, but each state shall have at least one representative; and until such enumeration shall be made, the state of New Hampshire shall be entitled to chuse three, Massachusetts eight, Rhode-Island and Providence Plantations one, Connecticut five, New-York six, New-Jersey four, Pennysylvania eight, Delaware one, Maryland six, Virginia ten, North-Carolina five, South-Carolina five, and Georgia three.

When vacancies happen in the representation from any state, the Executive authority thereof shall issue writs of election to fill such vacancies.

The House of Representatives shall chuse their Speaker and other officers; and shall have the sole power of impeachment.

*Section 3.* The Senate of the United States shall be composed of two senators from each state [chosen by the legislature thereof][2], for six years; and each senator shall have one vote.

Immediately after they shall be assembled in consequence of the first election, they shall be divided as equally as may be into three classes. The seats of the senators of the first class shall be vacated at the expiration of the second year, of the second class at the expiration of the fourth year, and of the third class at the expiration of the sixth year, so that one-third may be chosen every second year; [and if vacancies happen by resignation, or otherwise, during the recess of the Legislature of any state, the Executive thereof may make temporary appointments until the next meeting of the Legislature, which shall then fill such vacancies][3].

No person shall be a senator who shall not have attained to the age of thirty years, and been nine years a citizen of the United States, and who shall not, when elected, be an inhabitant of that state for which he shall be chosen.

The Vice-President of the United States shall be President of the Senate, but shall have no vote, unless they be equally divided.

The Senate shall chuse their other officers, and also a President *pro tempore*, in the absence of the Vice-President, or when he shall exercise the office of President of the United States.

The Senate shall have the sole power to try all impeachments. When sitting for that purpose, they shall be on oath or affirmation. When the President of the United States is tried, the Chief Justice shall preside; And no person shall be convicted without the concurrence of two-thirds of the members present.

Judgment in cases of impeachment shall not extend further than to removal from office and disqualification to hold and enjoy any office of honor, trust or profit under the United States; but the party convicted shall nevertheless be liable and subject to indictment, trial, judgment and punishment, according to law.

*Section 4.* The times, places and manner of holding elections for senators and representatives, shall be prescribed in each state by the legislature thereof; but the Congress may at any time by law make or alter such regulations, except as to the places of chusing Senators.

The Congress shall assemble at least once in every year, and such meeting [shall be on the first Monday in December][4], unless they shall by law appoint a different day.

*Section 5.* Each house shall be the judge of the elections, returns and qualifications of its own members, and a majority of each shall constitute a quorum to do business; but a smaller number may adjourn from day to day, and may be authorized to compel the attendance of absent members, in such manner, and under such penalties as each house may provide.

Each house may determine the rules of its proceedings, punish its members for disorderly behaviour, and, with the concurrence of two-thirds, expel a member.

Each house shall keep a journal of its proceedings, and from time to time publish the same, excepting such parts as may in their judgment require secrecy; and the yeas and nays of the members of either house on any question shall, at the desire of one-fifth of those present, be entered on the journal.

Neither house, during the session of Congress shall, without the consent of the other, adjourn for more than three days, nor to any other place than that in which the two houses shall be sitting.

*Section 6.* The senators and representatives shall receive a compensation for their services, to be ascertained by law, and paid out of the treasury of the United States. They shall in all cases, except treason, felony and breach of the peace, be privileged from arrest during their attendance at the session of their respective houses, and in going to and returning from the same; and for any speech or debate in either house, they shall not be questioned in any other place.

No senator or representative shall, during the time for which he was elected, be appointed to any civil office under the authority of the United States, which shall have been created, or the emoluments whereof shall have been encreased during such time; and no person holding any office under the United States, shall be a member of either house during his continuance in office.

*Section 7.* All bills for raising revenue shall originate in the house of representatives; but the senate may propose or concur with amendments as on other bills.

Every bill which shall have passed the house of representatives and the senate, shall, before it become a law, be presented to the President of the United States; if he approve he shall sign it, but if not he shall return it, with his objections to that house in which it shall have originated, who shall enter the objections at large on their journal, and proceed to reconsider it. If after such reconsideration two-thirds of that house shall agree to pass the bill, it shall be sent, together with the objections, to the other house, by which it shall likewise be reconsidered, and if approved by two-thirds of that house, it shall become a law. But in all such cases the votes of both houses shall be determined by yeas and nays, and the names of the persons voting for and against the bill shall be entered on the journal of each house respectively. If any bill shall not be returned by the President within ten days (Sundays excepted) after it shall have been presented to him, the same shall be a law, in like manner as if he had signed it, unless the Congress by their adjournment prevent its return, in which case it shall not be a law.

Every order, resolution, or vote to which the concurrence of the Senate and House of Representatives may be necessary (except on a question of adjournment) shall be presented to the President of the United States; and before the same shall take effect, shall be approved by him, or, being disapproved by him, shall be repassed by two-thirds of the Senate and House of Representatives, according to the rules and limitations prescribed in the case of a bill.

*Section 8.* The Congress shall have power

To lay and collect taxes, duties, imposts and excises, to pay the debts and provide for the common defense and general welfare of the United States; but all duties, imposts and excises shall be uniform throughout the United States;

To borrow money on the credit of the United States;

To regulate commerce with foreign nations, and among the several states, and with the Indian tribes;

To establish an uniform rule of naturalization, and uniform laws on the subject of bankruptcies throughout the United States.

To coin money, regulate the value thereof, and of foreign coin, and fix the standard of weights and measures;

To provide for the punishment of counterfeiting the securities and current coin of the United States;

To establish post offices and post roads;

To promote the progress of science and useful arts, by securing for limited times to authors and inventors the exclusive right to their respective writings and discoveries;

To constitute tribunals inferior to the supreme court;

To define and punish piracies and felonies committed on the high seas, and offences against the law of nations;

To declare war, grant letters of marque and reprisal, and make rules concerning captures on land and water;

To raise and support armies, but no appropriation of money to that use shall be for a longer term than two years;

To provide and maintain a navy;

To make rules for the government and regulation of the land and naval forces;

To provide for calling forth the militia to execute the laws of the union, suppress insurrections and repel invasions;

To provide for organizing, arming, and disciplining, the militia, and for governing such part of them as may be employed in the service of the United States, reserving to the States respectively, the appointment of the officers, and the authority of training the militia according to the discipline prescribed by Congress;

To exercise exclusive legislation in all cases whatsoever, over such district (not exceeding ten miles square) as may, by cession of particular States, and the acceptance of Congress, become the seat of the government of the United States, and to exercise like authority over all places purchased by the consent of the legislature of the states in which the same shall be, for the erection of forts, magazines, arsenals, dock-yards, and other needful buildings;—And

To make all laws which shall be necessary and proper for carrying into execution the foregoing powers, and all other powers vested by this constitution in the government of the United States, or in any department or officer thereof.

*Section 9.* The migration or importation of such persons as any of the states now existing shall think proper to admit, shall not be prohibited by the Congress prior to the year one thousand eight hundred and eight, but a tax or duty may be imposed on such importation, not exceeding ten dollars for each person.

The privilege of the writ of *habeas corpus* shall not be suspended, unless when in cases of rebellion or invasion the public safety may require it.

No bill of attainder or ex *post facto* law shall be passed.

No capitation, or other direct, tax shall be laid, unless in proportion to the census or enumeration herein before directed to be taken[5].

No tax or duty shall be laid on articles exported from any state. No preference shall be given by any regulation of commerce or revenue to the ports of one state over those of another; nor shall vessels bound to, or from, one state, be obliged to enter, clear, or pay duties in another.

No money shall be drawn from the treasury, but in consequence of appropriations made by law; and a regular statement and account of the receipts and expenditures of all public money shall be published from time to time.

No title of nobility shall be granted by the United States:—And no person holding any office of profit or trust under them, shall, without the consent of the Congress, accept of any present, emolument, office, or title, of any kind whatever, from any king, prince, or foreign state.

*Section 10.* No state shall enter into any treaty, alliance, or confederation; grant letters of marque and reprisal; coin money; emit bills of credit; make any thing but gold and silver coin a tender in payment of debts; pass any bill of attainder, ex *post facto* law, or law impairing the obligation of contracts, or grant any title of nobility.

No state shall, without the consent of the Congress, lay any imposts or duties on imports or exports, except what may be absolutely necessary for executing its inspection laws; and the net produce of all duties and imposts, laid by any state on imports or exports, shall be for the use of the Treasury of the United States; and all such laws shall be subject to the revision and control of the Congress. No state shall, without the consent of Congress, lay any duty of tonnage, keep troops, or ships of war in time of peace, enter into any agreement or compact with another state, or with a foreign power, or engage in war, unless actually invaded, or in such imminent danger as will not admit of delay.

## II

*Section 1.* The executive power shall be vested in a President of the United States of America. He shall hold his office during the term of four years[6], and, together with the vice-president, chosen for the same term, be elected as follows.

Each state shall appoint, in such manner as the legislature thereof may direct, a number of electors, equal to the whole number of senators and representatives to which the state may be entitled in the Congress: but no senator or representative, or person holding an office of trust or profit under the United States, shall be appointed an elector.

The electors shall meet in their respective states, and vote by ballot for two persons, of whom one at least shall not be an inhabitant of the same state with themselves. And they shall make a list of all the persons voted for, and of the number of votes for each; which list they shall sign and certify, and transmit sealed to the seat of the government of the United States, directed to the president of the senate. The president of the senate shall, in the presence of the senate and house of representatives, open all the certificates, and the votes shall then be counted. The person having the greatest number of votes shall be the president, if such number be a majority of the whole number of electors appointed; and if there be more than one who have such majority, and have an equal number of votes, then the house of representatives shall immediately chuse by ballot one of them for president; and if no person have a majority, then from the five highest on the list the said house shall in like manner chuse the president. But in chusing the president, the votes shall be taken by states, the representation from each state having one vote; a quorum for this purpose shall consist of a member or members from two-thirds of the states, and a majority of all the states shall be necessary to a choice. In every case, after the choice of the president, the person having the greatest number of votes of the electors shall be the vice-president. But if there should remain two or more who have equal votes, the senate shall chuse from them by ballot the vice-president[7].

The Congress may determine the time of chusing the electors, and the day on which they shall give their votes; which day shall be the same throughout the United States.

No person except a natural born citizen, or a citizen of the United States, at the time of the adoption of this constitution, shall be eligible to the office of president; neither shall any person be eligible to that office who shall not have attained to the age of thirty-five years, and been fourteen years a resident within the United States.

[In case of the removal of the president from office, or of his death, resignation, or inability to discharge the powers and duties of the said office, the same shall devolve on the vice-president, and the Congress may by law provide for the case of removal, death, resignation or inability, both of the president and vice-president, declaring what officer shall then act as president, and such officer shall act accordingly, until the disability be removed, or a president be elected][8].

The president shall, at stated times, receive for his services, a compensation, which shall neither be increased nor diminished during the period for which he shall have been elected, and he shall not receive within that period any other emolument from the United States, or any of them.

Before he enter on the execution of his office he shall take the following oath or affirmation:

"I do solemnly swear (or affirm) that I will faithfully execute the office of president of the United States, and will to the best of my ability, preserve, protect and defend the constitution of the United States".

*Section 2.* The president shall be commander in chief of the army and navy of the United States, and of the militia of the several States, when called into the actual service of the United States; he may require the opinion, in writing, of the principal officer in each of the executive departments, upon any subject relating to the duties of their respective offices, and he shall have power to grant reprieves and pardons for offences against the United States, except in cases of impeachment.

He shall have power, by and with the advice and consent of the senate, to make treaties, provided two-thirds of the senators present concur; and he shall nominate, and by and with the advice and consent of the senate, shall appoint ambassadors, other public ministers and consuls, judges of the supreme court, and all other officers of the United States, whose appointments are not herein otherwise provided for, and which shall be established by law. But the Congress may by law vest the appointment of such inferior offices, as they think proper, in the president alone, in the courts of law, or in the heads of departments.

The president shall have power to fill up all vacancies that may happen during the recess of the senate, by granting commissions which shall expire at the end of their session.

*Section 3.* He shall from time to time give to the Congress information of the state of the union, and recommend to their consideration such measures as he shall judge necessary and expedient; he may, on extraordinary occasions, convene both houses, or either of them, and in case of disagreement between them, with respect to the time of adjournment, he may adjourn them to such time as he shall think proper; he shall receive ambassadors and other public ministers; he shall take care that the laws be faithfully executed, and shall commission all the officers of the United States.

*Section 4.* The president, vice-president and all civil officers of the United States, shall be removed from office on impeachment for, and conviction of, treason, bribery, or other high crimes and misdemeanors.

## III

*Section 1.* The judicial power of the United States, shall be vested in one supreme court, and in such inferior courts as the Congress may from time to time ordain and establish. The judges, both of the supreme and inferior courts, shall hold their offices during good behavior, and shall, at stated times, receive for their services, a compensation, which shall not be diminished during their continuance in office.

*Section 2.* The judicial power shall extend to all cases, in law and equity, arising under this constitution, the laws of the United States, and treaties made, or which shall be made, under their authority; to all cases affecting ambassadors, other public ministers and consuls;—to all cases of admiralty and maritime jurisdiction; to controversies to which the United States shall be a party; to controversies between two or more States;—between a state and citizens of another state[9];—between citizens of different States;—between citizens of the same state claiming lands under grants of different States, [and between a state, or the citizens thereof, and foreign States, citizens or subjects][10].

In all cases affecting ambassadors, other public ministers and consuls, and those in which a state shall be party, the supreme court shall have original jurisdiction. In all the other cases beforementioned, the supreme court shall have appellate jurisdiction, both as to law and fact, with such exceptions, and under such regulations as the Congress shall make.

The trial of all crimes, except in cases of impeachment, shall be by jury; and such trial shall be held in the state where the said crimes shall have been committed; but when not committed within any state, the trial shall be at such place or places as the Congress may by law have directed.

*Section 3.* Treason against the United States, shall consist only in levying war against them, or in adhering to their enemies, giving them aid and comfort. No person shall be convicted of treason unless on the testimony of two witnesses to the same overt act, or on confession in open court.

The Congress shall have power to declare the punishment of treason, but no attainder of treason shall work corruption of blood, or forfeiture except during the life of the person attainted.

## IV

*Section 1.* Full faith and credit shall be given in each state to the public acts, records, and judicial proceedings of every other state. And the Congress may by general laws prescribe the manner in which such acts, records and proceedings shall be proved, and the effect thereof.

*Section 2.* The citizens of each state shall be entitled to all privileges and immunities of citizens in the several states.

A person charged in any state with treason, felony, or other crime, who shall flee from justice, and be found in another state, shall, on demand of the executive authority of the state from which he fled, be delivered up, to be removed to the state having jurisdiction of the crime.

[No person held to service or labor in one state, under the laws thereof, escaping into another, shall, in consequence of any law or regulation therein, be discharged from such service or labor, but shall be delivered up on claim of the party to whom such service or labor may be due][11].

*Section 3.* New states may be admitted by the Congress into this union; but no new state shall be formed or erected within the jurisdiction of any other state; nor any state be formed by the junction of two or more states, or parts of states, without the consent of the legislatures of the states concerned as well as of the Congress.

The Congress shall have power to dispose of and make all needful rules and regulations respecting the territory or other property belonging to the United States; and nothing in this Constitution shall be so construed as to prejudice any claims of the United States, or of any particular state.

*Section 4.* The United States shall guarantee to every state in this union a Republican form of government, and shall protect each of them against invasion; and on application of the legislature, or of the executive (when the legislature cannot be convened) against domestic violence.

## V

The Congress, whenever two-thirds of both houses shall deem it necessary, shall propose amendments to this constitution, or, on the application of the legislatures of two-thirds of the several states, shall call a convention for proposing amendments, which, in either case, shall be valid to all intents and purposes, as part of this constitution, when ratified by the legislatures of three-fourths of the several states, or by conventions in three-fourths thereof, as the one or the other mode of ratification may be proposed by Congress; Provided, that no amendment which may be made prior to the year one thousand eight hundred and eight shall in any manner affect the first and fourth clauses in the ninth section of the first article; and that no state, without its consent, shall be deprived of its equal suffrage in the senate.

## VI

All debts contracted and engagements entered into, before the adoption of this Constitution, shall be as valid against the United States under this Constitution, as under the confederation.

This constitution, and the laws of the United States which shall be made in pursuance thereof; and all treaties made, or which shall be made, under the authority of the United States, shall be the supreme law of the land; and the judges in every state shall be bound thereby, any thing in the constitution or laws of any state to the contrary notwithstanding.

The senators and representatives beforementioned, and the members of the several state legislatures, and all executive and judicial officers, both of the United States and of the several States, shall be bound by oath or affirmation, to support this constitution; but no religious test shall ever be required as a qualification to any office or public trust under the United States.

## VII

The ratification of the conventions of nine States, shall be sufficient for the establishment of this constitution between the States, so ratifying the same.

*Done in Convention by the unanimous consent of the States present the seventeenth day of September in the year of our Lord one thousand seven hundred and eighty-seven and of the Independence of the United States of America the twelfth. In witness whereof we have hereunto subscribed our Names.*

# THE AMENDMENTS

AMENDMENTS OF the Constitution of the United States of America, proposed by Congress, and ratified by the legislatures of the several states, pursuant to the fifth Article of the Constitution:

### 1ST AMENDMENT

Congress shall make no law respecting an establishment of religion, or prohibiting the free exercise thereof; or abridging the freedom of speech, or of the press; or the right of the people peaceably to assemble, and to petition the Government for a redress of grievances.

## 2ND AMENDMENT

A well regulated Militia, being necessary to the security of a free State, the right of the people to keep and bear Arms, shall not be infringed.

## 3RD AMENDMENT

No Soldier shall, in time of peace be quartered in any house, without the consent of the Owner, nor in time of war, but in a manner to be prescribed by law.

## 4TH AMENDMENT

The right of the people to be secure in their persons, houses, papers, and effects, against unreasonable searches and seizures, shall not be violated, and no Warrants shall issue, but upon probable cause, supported by Oath or affirmation, and particularly describing the place to be searched, and the persons or things to be seized.

## 5TH AMENDMENT

No person shall be held to answer for a capital, or otherwise infamous crime, unless on a presentment or indictment of a Grand Jury, except in cases arising in the land or naval forces, or in the Militia, when in actual service in time of War or public danger; nor shall any person be subject for the same offence to be twice put in jeopardy of life or limb; nor shall be compelled in any criminal case to be a witness against himself, nor be deprived of life, liberty, or property, without due process of law; nor shall private property be taken for public use, without just compensation.

## 6TH AMENDMENT

In all criminal prosecutions, the accused shall enjoy the right to a speedy and public trial, by an impartial jury of the State and district wherein the crime shall have been committed, which district shall have been previously ascertained by law, and to be informed of the nature and cause of the accusation; to be confronted with the witnesses against him; to have compulsory process for obtaining witnesses in his favor, and to have the Assistance of Counsel for his defense.

## 7TH AMENDMENT

In Suits at common law, where the value in controversy shall exceed twenty dollars, the right of trial by jury shall be preserved, and no fact tried by a jury, shall be otherwise re-examined in any Court of the United States, than according to the rules of the common law.

## 8TH AMENDMENT

Excessive bail shall not be required, nor excessive fines imposed, nor cruel and unusual punishments inflicted.

## 9TH AMENDMENT

The enumeration in the Constitution, of certain rights, shall not be construed to deny or disparage others retained by the people.

## 10TH AMENDMENT

The powers not delegated to the United States by the Constitution, nor prohibited by it to the States, are reserved to the States respectively, or to the people.

11TH AMENDMENT

The Judicial power of the United States shall not be construed to extend to any suit in law or equity, commenced or prosecuted against one of the United States by Citizens of another State, or by Citizens or Subjects of any Foreign State.

12TH AMENDMENT

The Electors shall meet in their respective states, and vote by ballot for President and Vice-President, one of whom, at least, shall not be an inhabitant of the same state with themselves; they shall name in their ballots the person voted for as President, and in distinct ballots the person voted for as Vice-President, and they shall make distinct lists of all persons voted for as Vice-President, and of the number of votes for each, which lists they shall sign and certify, and transmit sealed to the seat of the government of the United States, directed to the President of the Senate;—The President of the Senate shall, in the presence of the Senate and House of Representatives, open all the certificates and the votes shall then be counted;—The person having the greatest number of votes for president, shall be the President, if such number be a majority of the whole number of Electors appointed; and if no person have such majority, then from the persons having the highest numbers not exceeding three on the list of those voted for as President, the House of Representatives shall choose immediately, by ballot, the President. But in choosing the President, the votes shall be taken by states, the representation from each state having one vote; a quorum for this purpose shall consist of a member or members from two-thirds of the states, and a majority of all the states shall be necessary to a choice. [And if the House of Representatives shall not choose a President whenever the right of choice shall devolve upon them, before the fourth day of March next following, then the Vice-President shall act as President, as in the case of the death or other constitutional disability of the President][12]—The person having the greatest number of votes as Vice-President, shall be the Vice-President, if such number be a majority of the whole number of Electors appointed, and if no person have a majority, then from the two highest numbers on the list, the Senate shall choose the Vice-President; a quorum for the purpose shall consist of two-thirds of the whole number of Senators, and a majority of the whole number shall be necessary to a choice. But no person constitutionally ineligible to the office of President shall be eligible to that of Vice-President of the United States.

13TH AMENDMENT

*Section 1.* Neither slavery nor involuntary servitude, except as a punishment for crime whereof the party shall have been duly convicted, shall exist within the United States, or any place subject to their jurisdiction.
*Section 2.* Congress shall have power to enforce this article by appropriate legislation.

14TH AMENDMENT

*Section 1.* All persons born or naturalized in the United States, and subject to the jurisdiction thereof, are citizens of the United States and of the State wherein they reside. No State shall make or enforce any law which shall abridge the privileges or immunities of citizens of the United States; nor shall any State deprive any person of life, liberty, or property, without due process of law; nor deny to any person within its jurisdiction the equal protection of the laws.
*Section 2.* Representatives shall be apportioned among the several States according to their respective numbers, counting the whole number of persons in each State, excluding Indians not taxed. But when the right to vote at any election for the choice of electors for President and Vice-President of the United States, Representatives in Congress, the Executive and Judicial officers of a State, or the members of the Legislature thereof, is denied to any of the male inhabitants of such State, [being twenty-one years of age][13], and citizens of the United States, or in any way abridged, except for participation in rebellion, or other crime, the basis of representation therein shall be reduced in the proportion which the number of such male citizens shall bear to the whole number of [male citizens twenty-one years of age][14] in such State.
*Section 3.* No person shall be a Senator or Representative in Congress, or elector of President and Vice-President, or hold any office, civil or military, under the United States, or under any State, who, having previously taken oath, as a member of Congress, or as an officer of the United States, or as a member of any State legislature, or as an executive or judicial officer of any State, to support the Constitution of the

United States, shall have engaged in insurrection or rebellion against the same, or given aid or comfort to the enemies thereof. But Congress may by a vote of two-thirds of each House, remove such disability.

*Section 4.* The validity of the public debt of the United States, authorized by law, including debts incurred for payment of pensions and bounties for services in suppressing insurrection or rebellion, shall not be questioned. But neither the United States nor any State shall assume or pay any debt or obligation incurred in aid of insurrection or rebellion against the United States, or any claim for the loss or emancipation of any slave; but all such debts, obligations and claims shall be held illegal and void.

*Section 5.* The Congress shall have power to enforce, by appropriate legislation, the provisions of this article.

## 15TH AMENDMENT

*Section 1.* The right of citizens of the United States to vote shall not be denied or abridged by the United States or by any State on account of race, color or previous condition of servitude.

*Section 2.* The Congress shall have power to enforce this article by appropriate legislation.

## 16TH AMENDMENT

The Congress shall have power to lay and collect taxes on incomes, from whatever source derived, without apportionment among the several States, and without regard to any census or enumeration.

## 17TH AMENDMENT

The Senate of the United States shall be composed of two Senators from each State, elected by the people thereof, for six years, and each Senator shall have one vote. The electors in each State shall have the qualifications requisite for electors of the most numerous branch of the State legislatures.

When vacancies happen in the representation of any State in the Senate, the executive authority of such State shall issue writs of election to fill such vacancies: Provided, That the legislature of any State may empower the executive thereof to make temporary appointments until the people fill the vacancies by election as the legislature may direct.

This amendment shall not be so construed as to affect the election or term of any Senator chosen before it becomes valid as part of the Constitution.

## [18TH AMENDMENT[15]

*Section 1.* After one year from the ratification of this article the manufacture, sale, or transportation of intoxicating liquors within, the importation thereof into, or the exportation thereof from the United States and all territory subject to the jurisdiction thereof for beverage purposes is hereby prohibited.

*Section 2.* The Congress and the several States shall have concurrent power to enforce this article by appropriate legislation.

*Section 3.* This article shall be inoperative unless it shall have been ratified as an amendment to the Constitution by the legislatures of the several States, as provided in the Constitution, within seven years from the date of the submission hereof to the States by the Congress].

## 19TH AMENDMENT

The right of citizens of the United States to vote shall not be denied or abridged by the United States or by any State on account of sex.

Congress shall have power to enforce this article by appropriate legislation.

## 20TH AMENDMENT

*Section 1.* The terms of the President and Vice-President shall end at noon on the 20th day of January, and the terms of Senators and Representatives at noon on the 3rd day of January, of the years in which such terms would have ended if this article had not been ratified; and the terms of their successors shall then begin.

*Section 2.* The Congress shall assemble at least once in every year, and such meeting shall begin at noon on the 3rd day of January, unless they shall by law appoint a different day.

*Section 3.* If, at the time fixed for the beginning of the term of the President, the President elect shall have died, the Vice-President elect shall become President. If a President shall not have been chosen before the time fixed for the beginning of his term, or if the President elect shall have failed to qualify, then the Vice-President elect shall act as President until a President shall have qualified; and the Congress may by law provide for the case wherein neither a President elect nor a Vice-President elect shall have qualified, declaring who shall then act as President, or the manner in which one who is to act shall be selected, and such person shall act accordingly until a President or Vice-President shall have qualified.

*Section 4.* The Congress may by law provide for the case of the death of any of the persons from whom the House of Representatives may choose a President whenever the right of choice shall have devolved upon them, and for the case of the death of any of the persons, from whom the Senate may choose a Vice-President whenever the right of choice shall have devolved upon them.

*Section 5.* Sections 1 and 2 shall take effect on the 15th day of October following the ratification of this article.

*Section 6.* This article shall be inoperative unless it shall have been ratified as an amendment to the Constitution by the legislatures of three-fourths of the several States within seven years from the date of its submission.

### 21ST AMENDMENT

*Section 1.* The eighteenth article of amendment to the Constitution of the United States is hereby repealed.

*Section 2.* The transportation or importation into any State, Territory, or possession of the United States for delivery or use therein of intoxicating liquors, in violation of the laws thereof, is hereby prohibited.

*Section 3.* This article shall be inoperative unless it shall have been ratified as an amendment to the Constitution by conventions in the several States, as provided in the Constitution, within seven years from the date of submission hereof to the States by the Congress.

### 22ND AMENDMENT

*Section 1.* No person shall be elected to the office of the President more than twice, and no person who has held the office of President, or acted as President, for more than two years of a term to which some other person was elected President shall be elected to the office of the President more than once. But this Article shall not apply to any person holding the office of President when this Article was proposed by the Congress, and shall not prevent any person who may be holding the office of President, or acting as President, during the term within which this Article becomes operative from holding the office of President or acting as President during the remainder of such term.

*Section 2.* This article shall be inoperative unless it shall have been ratified as an amendment to the Constitution by the legislatures of three-fourths of the several States within seven years from the date of its submission to the States by the Congress.

### 23RD AMENDMENT

*Section 1.* The District constitution the seat of Government of the United States shall appoint in such manner as the Congress may direct:

A number of electors of President and Vice-President equal to the whole number of Senators and Representatives in Congress to which the District would be entitled if it were a State, but in no event more than the least populous State; they shall be in addition to those appointed by the States, but they shall be considered, for the purposes of the election of President and Vice-President, to be electors appointed by a State; and they shall meet in the District and perform such duties as provided by the twelfth article of amendment.

*Section 2.* The Congress shall have power to enforce this article by appropriate legislation.

### 24TH AMENDMENT

*Section 1.* The right of citizens of the United States to vote in any primary or other election for President or Vice-President, for electors for President or Vice-President, or for Senator or Representative in Congress, shall not be denied or abridged by the United States or any State by reason of failure to pay any poll tax or other tax.

*Section 2.* The Congress shall have power to enforce this article by appropriate legislation.

## 25TH AMENDMENT

*Section 1.* In case of removal of the President from office or of his death or resignation, the Vice-President shall become President.

*Section 2.* Whenever there is a vacancy in the office of the Vice-President, the President shall nominate a Vice-President who shall take office upon confirmation by a majority vote of both Houses of Congress.

*Section 3.* Whenever the President transmits to the President *pro tempore* of the Senate and the Speaker of the House of Representatives his written declaration that he is unable to discharge the powers and duties of his office, and until he transmits to them a written declaration to the contrary, such powers and duties shall be discharged by the Vice-President as Acting President.

*Section 4.* Whenever the Vice-President and a majority of either the principal officers of the executive departments or of such other body as Congress may by law provide, transmit to the President *pro tempore* of the Senate and the Speaker of the House of Representatives their written declaration that the President is unable to discharge the powers and duties of his office, the Vice-President shall immediately assume the powers and duties of the office as Acting President.

Thereafter, when the President transmits to the President *pro tempore* of the Senate and the Speaker of the House of Representatives his written declaration that no inability exists, he shall resume the powers and duties of his office unless the Vice-President and a majority of either the principal officers of the executive department or of such other body as Congress may by law provide, transmit within four days to the President *pro tempore* of the Senate and the Speaker of the House of Representatives their written declaration that the President is unable to discharge the powers and duties of his office. Thereupon Congress shall decide the issue, assembling within forty-eight hours for that purpose if not in session. If the Congress, within twenty-one days after Congress is required to assemble, determines by two-thirds vote of both Houses that the President is unable to discharge the powers and duties of his office, the Vice-President shall continue to discharge the same as Acting President; otherwise, the President shall resume the powers and duties of his office.

## 26TH AMENDMENT

*Section 1.* The right of citizens of the United States, who are eighteen years of age or older, to vote shall not be denied or abridged by the United States or by any State on account of age.

*Section 2.* The Congress shall have power to enforce this article by appropriate legislation.

Proposed 27TH AMENDMENT to the Constitution, not yet ratified by a sufficient number of States for adoption:

*Section 1.* Equality of rights under the law shall not be denied or abridged by the United States or by any State on account of sex.

*Section 2.* The Congress shall have the power to enforce, by appropriate legislation, the provisions of this article.

*Section 3.* This amendment shall take effect two years after the date of ratification.

---

# NOTES

[1] Superseded by Section 2 of the 14th Amendment.

[2] Superseded by Clause 1 of the 17th Amendment.

[3] Modified by Clause 2 of the 17th Amendment.

[4] Superseded by Section 2 of the 20th Amendment.

[5] Modified by the 16th Amendment.

[6] Modified by the 22nd Amendment.

[7] Superseded by the 12th Amendment.

[8] Modified by the 25th Amendment.

[9] Modified by the 11th Amendment.

[10] Modified by the 11th Amendment.

[11] Superseded by the 13th Amendment.

[12] Superseded by Section 3 of the 20th Amendment.

[13] Superseded by Section 1 of the 26th Amendment.

[14] Superseded by Section 1 of the 19th Amendment and Section 1 of the 26th Amendment.

[15] The "Prohibition" Amendment subsequently repealed by the 21st Amendment.

# Appendix H
# The Presidential Elections
## 1789-1972

| YEAR | CANDIDATES | RESULTS<br>(with number of *Electoral* votes received) |
|---|---|---|
| 1789 | George Washington, Virginia; John Adams, Massachusetts; John Jay, New York; Robert Hanson Harrison, Maryland; John Rutledge, S Carolina; John Hancock, Massachusetts; George Clinton, New York; Samuel Huntington, Connecticut; James Armstrong, Georgia; Edward Telfair, Georgia; Benjamin Lincoln, Georgia | 1 George Washington (69 votes)<br>2 John Adams (34)<br>3 John Jay (9)<br>4 Robert Hanson Harrison (6)<br>5 John Rutledge (6)<br>6 John Hancock (4)<br>7 George Clinton (3)<br>8 Samuel Huntington (2)<br>9 John Milton (2)<br>10 James Armstrong (one)<br>11 Edward Telfair (one)<br>12 Benjamin Lincoln (one) |
| 1792 | George Washington, Virginia; John Adams, Massachusetts; George Clinton, New York; Thomas Jefferson, Virginia; Aaron Burr, New York | 1 George Washington (132 votes)<br>2 John Adams (77)<br>3 George Clinton (50)<br>4 Thomas Jefferson (4)<br>5 Aaron Burr (one) |
| 1796 | John Adams, Massachusetts; Thomas Jefferson, Virginia; Thomas Pinckney, S Carolina; Aaron Burr, New York; Samuel Adams, Massachusetts; Oliver Ellsworth, Connecticut; George Clinton, New York; John Jay, New York; James Iredell, North Carolina; John Henry, Maryland; Samuel Johnston, N Carolina; Charles Cotesworth Pinckney, S Carolina | 1 John Adams (71 votes)<br>2 Thomas Jefferson (68)<br>3 Thomas Pinckney (59)<br>4 Aaron Burr (30)<br>5 Samuel Adams (15)<br>6 Oliver Ellsworth (11)<br>7 George Clinton (7)<br>8 John Jay (5)<br>9 James Iredell (3)<br>10 John Henry (2)<br>11 Samuel Johnston (one)<br>12 Charles Cotesworth Pinckney (one) |
| 1800 | Thomas Jefferson, Virginia (*Democratic-Republican*); Aaron Burr, New York (*Democratic-Republican*); John Adams, Massachusetts (*Federalist*); Charles Cotesworth Pinckney, S Carolina (*Federalist*); John Jay, New York | 1 Thomas Jefferson (73 votes)<br>2 Aaron Burr (73 votes)[1]<br>3 John Adams (65)<br>4 Charles Cotesworth Pinckney (64)<br>5 John Jay (one) |
| 1804 | Thomas Jefferson, Virginia (*Democratic-Republican*); Charles Cotesworth Pinckney, S Carolina (*Federalist*) | 1 Thomas Jefferson (162 votes)<br>2 Charles Cotesworth Pinckney (14) |
| 1808 | James Madison, Virginia (*Democratic-Republican*); Charles Cotesworth Pinckney, S Carolina (*Federalist*) | 1 James Madison (122 votes)<br>2 Charles Cotesworth Pinckney (47) |

| YEAR | CANDIDATES | RESULTS |
|---|---|---|
| 1812 | James Madison, Virginia (*Democratic-Republican*); De Witt Clinton, New York (*de facto Federalist*) | 1 James Madison (128 votes)<br>2 De Witt Clinton (89) |
| 1816 | James Monroe, Virginia (*Democratic-Republican*); Rufus King, New York (*Federalist*) | 1 James Monroe (183 votes)<br>2 Rufus King (34) |
| 1820 | James Monroe, Virginia (*Democratic-Republican*); John Quincy Adams, Massachusetts | 1 James Monroe (231 votes)<br>2 John Quincy Adams (one) |
| 1824 | Andrew Jackson, Tennessee (*Republican*); Henry Clay, Kentucky (*Republican*); William H. Crawford, Georgia (*Republican*); John Quincy Adams, Massachusetts (*Republican*) | 1 Andrew Jackson (99 votes)[2]<br>2 John Quincy Adams (84)<br>3 William H. Crawford (41)<br>4 Henry Clay (37) |
| 1828 | Andrew Jackson, Tennessee (*Democratic*); John Quincy Adams, Massachusetts (*Republican*) | 1 Andrew Jackson (178 votes)<br>2 John Quincy Adams (83) |
| 1832 | William Wirt, Maryland (*Anti-Masonic*); Henry Clay, Kentucky (*National Republican*); Andrew Jackson, Tennessee (*Democratic*); John Floyd, Virginia (*Independent Democratics*) | 1 Andrew Jackson (219 votes)<br>2 Henry Clay (49)<br>3 John Floyd (11)<br>4 William Wirt (7) |
| 1836 | Daniel Webster, Massachusetts (*Whig*); Hugh Lawson White, Tennessee (*Whig*); William Henry Harrison, Ohio (*Whig*); Willie Person Mangum, N Carolina (*Whig*); John McLean, Ohio (*Whig*); Martin Van Buren, New York (*Democratic*) | 1 Martin Van Buren (170 votes)<br>2 William Henry Harrison (73)<br>3 Hugh Lawson White (26)<br>4 Daniel Webster (14)<br>5 Willie Person Mangum (11) |
| 1840 | William Henry Harrison, Ohio (*Whig*); James Gillespie Birney, New York (*Liberty*); Martin Van Buren, New York (*Democratic*) | 1 William Henry Harrison (234 votes)<br>2 Martin Van Buren (60) |
| 1844 | James Gillespie Birney, Michigan (*Liberty*); Henry Clay, Kentucky (*Whig*); James Knox Polk, Tennessee (*Democratic*) | 1 James Knox Polk (170 votes)<br>2 Henry Clay (105) |
| 1848 | Lewis Cass, Michigan (*Democratic*); Zachary Taylor, Louisiana (*Whig*); Martin Van Buren, New York (*Barnburners*) | 1 Zachary Taylor (163 votes)<br>2 Lewis Cass (127) |
| 1852 | Franklin Pierce, New Hampshire (*Democratic*); Winfield Scott, New Jersey (*Whig*); John Parker Hale, New Hampshire (*Free-Soil*) | 1 Franklin Pierce (254 votes)<br>2 Winfield Scott (42) |
| 1856 | Millard Fillmore, New York (*American*); James Buchanan, Pennsylvania (*Democratic*); John Charles Fremont, California (*Republican*) | 1 James Buchanan (174 votes)<br>2 John Charles Fremont (114)<br>3 Millard Fillmore (8) |
| 1860 | Stephen Arnold Douglas, Illinois (*Democratic*); John Bell, Tennessee (*Constitutional Union*); Abraham Lincoln, Illinois (*Republican*); John Cabell Breckinridge, Kentucky (*Democratic*) | 1 Abraham Lincoln (180 votes)<br>2 John Cabel Breckinridge (72)<br>3 John Bell (39)<br>4 Stephen Arnold Douglas (12) |
| 1864 | John Charles Fremont, California (*Radical Republican*); Abraham Lincoln, Illinois (*Republican (National Union)*); George Brinton McClellan, New York (*Democratic*) | 1 Abraham Lincoln (212 votes)<br>2 George Brinton McClellan (21) |
| 1868 | Ulysses S. Grant, Illinois (*Republican*); Horatio Seymour, Indiana (*Democratic*) | 1 Ulysses S. Grant (214 votes)<br>2 Horatio Seymour (80) |
| 1872 | David Davis, Illinois (*Labor Reform*); James Black, Pennsylvania (*Prohibition*); Horace Greeley, New York (*Liberal Republican*); Ulysses S. Grant (*Workingmen's, Republican*); William Slocomb Groesbeck, Ohio (*Revenue Reformers'*) | 1 Ulysses S. Grant (286 votes)<br>2 Thomas Andrews Hendricks (for Horace Greeley who died before election) (42)<br>3 Benjamin Gratz Brown (for Horace Greeley) (2)<br>4 David Davis (one) |

| YEAR | CANDIDATES | RESULTS |
|---|---|---|
| 1876 | James B. Walker, Illinois (*American*); Green Clay Smith, Kentucky (*Prohibition*); Peter Cooper, New York (*Greenback*); Rutherford Birchard Hayes, Ohio (*Republican*); Samuel Jones Tilden, New York (*Democratic*) | 1 Rutherford Birchard Hayes (185 votes) 2 Samuel Jones Tilden (184) |
| 1880 | James Abram Garfield, Ohio (*Republican*); James Baird Weaver, Iowa (*Greenback-Labor*); Neal Dow, Maine (*Prohibition*); Winfield Scott Hancock, Pennsylvania (*Democratic*); John Wolcott Phelps, Vermont (*American*) | 1 James Abram Garfield (214 votes) 2 Winfield Scott Hancock (155) |
| 1884 | Benjamin Granklin Butler, Massachusetts (*Anti-Monopoly*); James Gillespie Blaine, Maine (*Republican*); (Stephen) Grover Cleveland, New York (*Democratic*); John Pierce St John, Kansas (*Prohibition*) | 1 (Stephen) Grover Cleveland (219 votes) 2 James Gillespie Blaine (182) |
| 1888 | Albert Redstone, California (*Industrial Reform*); Belva Ann Bennett Lockwood, Washington, DC (*Equal Rights*); Alson Jenness Streeter, Illinois (*Union Labor*); Robert Hall Cowdrey, Illinois (*United Labor*); Clinton Bowen Fisk, New Jersey (*Prohibition*); (Stephen) Grover Cleveland, New York (*Democratic*); Benjamin Harrison, Indiana (*Republican*); James Langdon Curtis, New York (*American*) | 1 Benjamin Harrison (233 votes) 2 (Stephen) Grover Cleveland (168) |
| 1892 | Benjamin Harrison, Indiana (*Republican*); (Stephen) Grover Cleveland, New York (*Democratic*); John Bidwell, California (*Prohibition*); James Baird Weaver, Iowa (*People's*); Simon Wing, Massachusetts (*Socialist Labor*) | 1 (Stephen) Grover Cleveland (277 votes) 2 Benjamin Harison (145) 3 James Baird Weaver (22) |
| 1896 | Joshua Levering, Maryand (*Prohibition*); William McKinley, Ohio (*Republican*); Charles Horatio Matchett, New York (*Socialist Labor*); William Jennings Bryan, Nebraska (*Democratic*); John McCauley Palmer, Illinois (*National Democratic*) | 1 William McKinley (271 votes) 2 William Jennings Bryan (176) |
| 1900 | Eugene Victor Debs, Indiana (*Social Democratic*); Wharton Barker, Pennsylvania (*People's*); Joseph Francis Malloney, Massachusetts (*Socialist Labor*); William McKinley, Ohio (*Republican*); John Granville Woolley, Illinois (*Prohibition*); William Jennings Bryan, Nebraska (*Democratic*); Seth Hockett Ellis, Ohio (*Union Reform*); Jonah Fitz Randolph Leonard, Iowa (*United Christian*) | 1 William McKinley (292 votes) 2 William Jennings Bryan (155) |
| 1904 | Eugene Victor Debs, Indiana (*Socialist*); Theodore Roosevelt, New York (*Republican*); Silas Comfort Swallow, Pennsylvania (*Prohibition*); Charles Hunter Corregan, New York (*Socialist Labor*); Thomas Edward Watson, Georgia (*People's*); Alton Brooks Parker, New York (*Democratic*); Austin Holcomb, Georgia (*Continental*) | 1 Theodore Roosevelt (336 votes) 2 Alton Brooks Parker (140) |
| 1908 | Thomas Edward Watson, Georgia (*People's*); Daniel Braxton Turney, Illinois (*United Christian*); Eugene Victor Debs, Indiana (*Socialist*); William Howard Taft, Ohio (*Republican*); William Jennings Bryan, Nebraska (*Democratic*); Eugene Wilder Chafin, Illinois (*Prohibition*); August Gillhaus, New York (*Socialist Labor*); Thomas Louis Hisgen, Massachusetts (*Independence*) | 1 William Howard Taft (321 votes) 2 William Jennings Bryan (162) |
| 1912 | Arthur Edward Reimer, Massachusetts (*Socialist Labor*); Eugene Victor Debs, | 1 Woodrow Wilson (435 votes) 2 Theodore Roosevelt (88) |

| YEAR | CANDIDATES | RESULTS |
|------|-----------|---------|
| | Indiana (*Socialist*); William Howard Taft, Ohio (*Republican*); Woodrow Wilson, New Jersey (*Democratic*); Eugene Wilder Chafin, Illinois (*Prohibition*); Theodore Roosevelt, New York (*Progressive*) | 3 William Howard Taft (8) |
| 1916 | Arthur Edward Reimer, Massachusetts (*Socialist Labor*); Charles Evans Hughes, New York (*Republican*); Theodore Roosevelt, New York (*Progressive*); Woodrow Wilson, New Jersey (*Democratic*); James Franklin Hanly, Indiana (*Prohibition*); Allen Louis Benson, New York (*Socialist*) | 1 Woodrow Wilson (277 votes)<br>2 Charles Evans Hughes (254) |
| 1920 | William Wesley Cox, Missouri (*Socialist Labor*); Eugene Victor Debs, Indiana (*Socialist*); Warren Gamaliel Harding, Ohio (*Republican*); James Middleton Cox, Ohio (*Democratic*); Parley Parker Christensen, Utah (*Farmer Labor*); Robert Charles Macauley, Pennsylvania (*Single Tax*); Aaron Sherman Watkins, Ohio (*Prohibition*) | 1 Warren Gamaliel Harding (404 votes)<br>2 James Middleton Cox (127) |
| 1924 | William James Wallace, New Jersey (*Commonwealth Land*); Frank Thomas Johns, Oregon (*Socialist Labor*); Gilbert O. Nations, Washington, DC (*American*); Herman P. Faris, Missouri (*Prohibition*); (John) Calvin Coolidge, Massachusetts (*Republican*); John William Davis, West Virginia (*Democratic*); Robert Marion La Follette, Wisconsin (*Progressive*); William Zebulon Foster, Illinois (*Workers'*) | 1 (John) Calvin Coolidge (332 votes)<br>2 John William Davis (136)<br>3 Robert Marion La Follette (13) |
| 1928 | Norman Thomas, New York (*Socialist*); William Zebulon Foster, Illinois (*Workers'*); Herbert Clark Hoover, California (*Republican*); Alfred Emanuel Smith, New York (*Democratic*); George William Norris, Nebraska (*Farmer Labor*); William Frederick Varney, New York (*Prohibition*); Verne L. Reynolds, New York (*Socialist Labor*). | 1 Herbert Clark Hoover (444 votes)<br>2 Alfred Emanuel Smith (87) |
| 1932 | Verne L. Reynolds, New York (*Socialist Labor*); Norman Thomas, New York (*Socialist*); William Zebulon Foster, New York (*Communist*); Herbert Clark Hoover, California (*Republican*); Franklin Delano Roosevelt, New York (*Democratic*); William David Upshaw, Georgia (*Prohibition*); Jacob Sechler Coxey, Ohio (*Farmer Labor*); William Hope Harvey, Arkansas (*Liberty*) | 1 Franklin Delano Roosevelt (531 votes)<br>2 Herbert Clark Hoover (59) |
| 1936 | John W. Aiken, Massachusetts (*Socialist Labor*); David Leigh Colvin, New York (*Prohibition*); Norman Thomas, New York (*Socialist*); Alfred Mossman Landon, Kansas (*Republican*); Franklin Delano Roosevelt, New York (*Democratic*); Earl Russell Browder, Kansas (*Communist*) | 1 Franklin Delano Roosevelt (523 votes)<br>2 Alfred Mossman Landon (8) |
| 1940 | Norman Thomas, New York (*Socialist*); John W. Aiken, Massachusetts (*Socialist Labor*); Roger Ward Babson, Massachusetts (*Prohibition*); Earl Russell Browder, Kansas (*Communist*); Wendell Lewis Willkie, Indiana (*Republican*); Franklin Delano Roosevelt (*Democratic*) | 1 Franklin Delano Roosevelt (449 votes)<br>2 Wendell Lewis Willkie (82) |
| 1944 | Claude A. Watson, California (*Prohibition*); Edward A. Teichert, Pennsylvania (*Socialist Labor*); Norman Thomas, New York (*Socialist*); Thomas Edmund Dewey, New York (*Republican*); Franklin Delano Roosevelt, New York (*Democratic*) | 1 Franklin Delano Roosevelt (432 votes)<br>2 Thomas Edmund Dewey (99) |
| 1948 | Claude A. Watson, California (*Prohibition*); Edward A. Teichert, Pennsylvania (*Socialist* | 1 Harry S. Truman (303 votes)<br>2 Thomas Edmund Dewey (189) |

*Labor*); Norman Thomas, New York (*Socialist*);
Thomas Edmund Dewey, New York (*Republican*);
Farrell Dobbs, New York (*Socialist Workers*);
Harry S. Truman, Missouri (*Democratic*);
James Strom Thurmond, S Carolina (*States
Rights Democratic*); Henry Agard Wallace, Iowa
(*Progressive*)

3 James Strom Thurmond (39)

1952   Stuart Hamblen, Oklahoma (*Prohibition*);
Eric Hass, New York (*Socialist Labor*);
Darlington Hoopes, Pennsylvania (*Socialist*);
Vincent William Hallinan, California
(*Progressive*); Dwight David Eisenhower,
New York (*Republican*); Farrell Dobbs,
New York (*Socialist Workers*); Adlai
Ewing Stevenson, Illinois (*Democratic*)

1 Dwight David Eisenhower (442 votes)
2 Adlai Ewing Stevenson (89)

1956   Enoch Arden Holtwick, Illinois (*Prohibition*);
Eric Hass, New York (*Socialist Labor*);
Darlington Hoopes, Pennsylvania (*Socialist*);
Adlai Ewing Stevenson, Illinois (*Democratic*);
Farrell Dobbs, New York (*Socialist Workers*);
Dwight David Eisenhower (*Republican*);
Thomas Coleman Andrews, Virginia (*States
Rights Party of Virginia*); William Ezra
Jenner, Indiana (*Texas Constitution*)

1 Dwight David Eisenhower (531 votes)
2 Adlai Ewing Stevenson (73)

1960   Rutherford Losey Decker, Missouri
(*Prohibition*); Orval Eugene Faubus,
Arkansas (*National States' Rights*);
Eric Hass, New York (*Socialist Labor*);
John Fitzgerald Kennedy, Massachusetts
(*Democratic*); Richard Milhous Nixon,
California (*Republican*); Farrell Dobbs,
New York (*Socialist Workers*)

1 John Fitzgerald Kennedy (303 votes)
2 Richard Milhous Nixon (219)

1964   Clifton DeBerry, New York (*Socialist
Workers*); John Kasper, Tennessee
(*National States' Rights*); Eric Hass,
New York (*Socialist Labor*); Barry Morris
Goldwater, Arizona (*Republican*); Lyndon
Baines Johnson, Texas (*Democratic*);
Earle Harold Munn, Michigan (*Prohibition*)

1 Lyndon Baines Johnson (486 votes)
2 Barry Morris Goldwater (52)

1968   Richard Milhous Nixon, California
(*Republican*); Hubert Horatio Humphrey, Minnesota
(*Democratic*); George Corley Wallace,
Alabama (*American Independent*)

1 Richard Milhous Nixon (301 votes)
2 Hubert Horatio Humphrey (191)
3 George Corley Wallace (46)

1972   Richard Milhous Nixon, California
(*Republican*); George Stanley McGovern, S Dakota
(*Democratic*)

1 Richard Milhous Nixon (517 votes)
2 George Stanley McGovern (17)

## NOTES

[1] The Jefferson-Burr tie vote necessitated an election in the House of Representatives decided on the basis of one vote for each state. On the second voting Jefferson received a majority vote of ten states.

[2] Neither Andrew Jackson nor John Quincy Adams received a majority of the 261 electoral votes. The election was submitted to the House of Representatives and the election was decided on the basis of one vote per state. John Quincy Adams received 13 states votes, one more than the required majority (also *see p 161* for comment).

# Guide to the Reader

THERE ARE basically two satisfactory ways of setting out genealogical information: in the form of a "tree" or a narrative pedigree. The tree is admirable as a vehicle for the bare bones of a *genealogy*—the names and the dates—but when used as a conveyance for a *family history*, with the character sketches and the detailed biographical material involved, it becomes cumbersome and over-loaded. As mentioned in the PREFACE a clear distinction should be made between genealogy (a cold off-putting word, usually misunderstood and mispronounced to boot) and family history (which implies greater human interest and the promise to tell one more of *what* the people were as well as *who*). If genealogy is a science, family history should be an art.

In BURKE'S *Presidential Families of the United States of America* there are examples of both genealogy and family history, and thus accordingly the former has been set out in tree form and the latter in narrative pedigree. The use of a tree in illustrating the relationship(s) between one person and another is invaluable. It clears a brain wracked by working out how many times removed its proprietor is from his sixth cousin or whatever. Trees which are kept reasonably uncluttered are simple enough to understand and it is felt that no further explanation is required here for those contained in the NOTES at the end of certain Presidential chapters in the PRESIDENTS AND THEIR FAMILIES Section; nor for those comprising APPENDICES C and D, save to mention that the sign "=" denotes marriage and "×" an extra-marital union, a broken line signifying an illegitimate descent (*e.g.* Mr Nixon's from King Edward III).

With regard to the narrative pedigrees used for the LINEAGE, DESCENDANTS, BROTHERS AND SISTERS of the Presidents, though, some general introductory remarks are called for. The BURKE'S style of setting out a family history from its earliest recorded origins down to the present day in narrative style has been gradually perfected over 150 years and is widely acknowledged as the best method of doing so. To understand how we go about it one has to grasp a new interpretation of the word "lineage". When reading a BURKE'S narrative pedigree it is a good idea to imagine that vertical parallel lines are descending down the column. These lines represent generations and each generation is progressively indented from the margin and each given a separate style of numbering (to facilitate identification). The senior line of the family, *i.e.* that dealing with (or "treating") the succession of the senior genealogical representation of the family is always on the margin. Children of the contemporary senior representative (or "head") of the family are always indented one space (a printer's "em" measure for the technically minded) from the margin and have a numeral in bold print; Grandchildren two spaces and a numeral in light print; Great-Grandchildren three spaces and a numeral enclosed in parentheses; Great-Great-Grandchildren four spaces and a numeral followed by the italicized letter "*a*"; Great-Great-Great-Grandchildren five spaces and a numeral followed by the italicized letter "*b*"—and so on and on, occasionally even to the twentieth indentation and the letter "*q*". The Diagram below might help to make this clearer:—

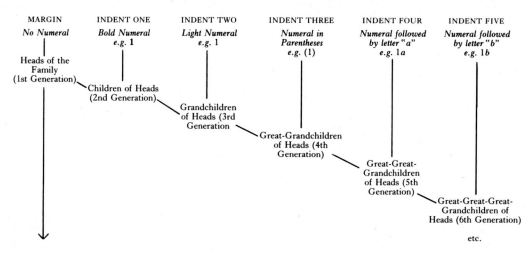

| MARGIN | INDENT ONE | INDENT TWO | INDENT THREE | INDENT FOUR | INDENT FIVE |
|---|---|---|---|---|---|
| *No Numeral* | *Bold Numeral* e.g. **1** | *Light Numeral* e.g. 1 | *Numeral in Parentheses* e.g. (1) | *Numeral followed by letter "a"* e.g. 1a | *Numeral followed by letter "b"* e.g. 1b |

Heads of the Family (1st Generation)

Children of Heads (2nd Generation)

Grandchildren of Heads (3rd Generation

Great-Grandchildren of Heads (4th Generation)

Great-Great-Grandchildren of Heads (5th Generation)

Great-Great-Great-Grandchildren of Heads (6th Generation)

etc.

All the various individual branches of the family are traced down to the present day *as one comes to them* ; and each *diagonal line* on the above Diagram is followed through to the end before reverting to the next senior line.

The style adopted for the numbering of people appearing in the pedigrees, as already explained, is based on their relative generation; but the actual numeral itself relates to their seniority amongst their brothers and sisters. Children are numbered in sequence (1, 2, 3, 4, etc.) according to their dates of birth. (This is an innovation for this book, by the way, as normally we list the boys first, *e.g.* (1), (2), (3), and then start numbering again for the girls, *e.g.* (1), (2)—even if the elder girl is in fact the oldest of the family. The reason for this method is tied in with the *primogeniture* male succession of titles and property). An only child has no numeral; and adopted children are listed (a), (b), (c), etc., without numerals.

The virtue of BURKE'S system is that the reader can see at a glance whom is related to whom by using the indentation and numbering system to find his way about the pedigree. Movement backwards (to ascertain the ancestry) and forwards (for the descendants) is as easy as travelling up and down an escalator, once the code has been "cracked". To comprehend the system fully may seem difficult at the outset—and this labored explanation, alas, could well be more of a hindrance than a help as learning oneself from practical experience through reading and referring to the pedigrees is the *only* sure way—but once it is achieved it is very much worthwhile. With one's path smoothed by the proliferating cross-references from entry to entry one is soon caught up in an intriguing network of intertangling connections as the fascination of family history establishes itself. The system is logical and never lets one down.

In this book the Presidents are the central, the all-important figures. Therefore one could say that the traditional BURKE'S narrative pedigrees have been split into three: first, the LINEAGE which covers the President's ancestry; second, the DESCENDANTS which deals with his marriage and all his descendants; and third, BROTHERS AND SISTERS which deals with the President's siblings and, sometimes, their descendants too. The general principles, however, as explained above still apply.

So much for the structure; what of the substance? Living members of the family have a circular typographical blob (*i.e.* ●) in front of their names. The basic intention is to set out the fullest possible details for each individual member of the family (of whatever age and whether living or dead). The details are usually arranged in the following sequence (if applicable):—

(i) Full Forenames and capitalized Surname at birth, with subsequent changes, other than through marriage, indicated.
(ii) Decorations, Honors and Professional Qualifications (with dates of conferment in parentheses).
(iii) Military, Civil and Business Career, with appropriate dates.
(iv) Publications, titles italicized.
(v) Foreign Honors and Awards.
(vi) Charitable Services.
(vii) Present Address(es) and Clubs (italicized in square parentheses for living people; interesting addresses of dead people are placed between *nos* (ii) and (iii) above, not in parentheses; married ladies' addresses come after their present spouse's place and date of birth—*see no* (xi) below).

(viii) Place and exact (*i.e.* day, month, year) date of Birth.
(ix) Secondary and Tertiary Education (degrees and dates in parentheses).
(x) Place and exact date of 1st Marriage (with year of Divorce in parentheses immediately after date of Marriage).
(xi) Full names and brief biographical description of Spouse (followed by place and exact dates of Birth and Death in parentheses).
(xii) Full names of Spouse's Father and Mother.
(xiii) Place and exact date of (subject's) Death. In cases of subsequent marriage *no* (xiii) comes *after* the last marriage has been dealt with in similarly full terms to the previous marriages—with each set of "issue" given under the appropriate marriage.
(xiv) Introduction to "issue". "has issue" = hereunder are given the living children of the body; "has had issue" = at least one child is dead. For issue by second and other subsequent marriages "has further issue" is used for ladies; and "by her has issue" for men.

The categories shown above are by no means divided in such a clear-cut manner in the actual individual entries for biographies. These entries are designed to flow straight on for easy readability. There is no place for purist grammar in the presentation of information in a clean, spare shorthand style. Similarly it would be a big mistake to imagine that the rules of punctuation are on speaking terms with the BURKE'S style. The only break employed is usually a comma at the end of a phrase. Dates which precede such commas help to re-inforce the termination of one "sentence" before moving on to the next. Semi-colons are used very sparingly, for example to separate one address from another inside a square parenthesis or between the dates of birth and death of an unmarried person whose education details are not given. They are also inserted to separate the details of two childless marriages from one another. Splitting up a first childless marriage from a subsequent fecund union is one of the few occasions when a full stop is used, other than at the end of an unmarried person's entry. Otherwise, if both (or more) marriages produce issue the indentations go in and out—*in* for the issue; *out* for the details of the later marriages. The numbering is *not* started afresh for the issue from different marriages of a biographee; the issue is still numbered 1-4 if the biographee had two children each by two wives. The subsequent marital career of spouses who marry a biographee and are then divorced is not recorded—their blobs are removed, though their eventual place and date of death is inserted. The remarriage of widows of biographees is given in parentheses after their places and dates of birth, with full details of their subsequent husbands and passing references to their further issue; but none of this clause applies to widowers of lady biographees. Adopted children are given, where known, with the agreement of the family concerned, but they can cannot be described as "issue".

There are naturally a thousand-and-one other small points of style which cannot all be clarified here but it is hoped that most of them are self-apparent. Liberal use is made of Abbreviations in the pedigrees and the reader is advised to refer to the LIST OF ABBREVIATIONS, which follow this GUIDE. This list is not intended as a guide to all Abbreviations generally in use but it will be found useful in connection with the pedigrees.

Finally, please rest assured there is a method to all our seeming madness, but if anything at all is not crystal clear, we shall be very happy to elucidate specific points for any reader who sends us his query.

# List of Abbreviations

| | | | | |
|---|---|---|---|---|
| AAG | Assistant Adjutant-General | | CA | Chartered Accountant |
| AB | Bachelor of Arts | | *ca* | *circa* (about) |
| ABE | American Board of Education | | Camb | Cambridge |
| AC | Air Corps (United States) | | Capt | Captain |
| Acad | Academy | | Cav | Cavalry |
| ADC | Aide-de-Camp | | CB | Companion of the Order of the Bath |
| addl | Additional | | CBE | Commander of the Order of the British Empire |
| Adjt | Adjutant | | Cdre | Commodore |
| Adm | Admiral | | CE | Civil Engineer |
| Admin | Administration/-ive | | CEF | Canadian Expeditionary Force |
| Adminr | Administrator | | Cent | Central |
| *admon* | Administration (wills) | | CF | Chaplain to the Forces |
| Adv | Advisory | | CFA | Canadian Field Artillery |
| Advr | Adviser | | Ch Ch | Christ Church |
| Agric | Agriculture,-al | | ChB | Bachelor of Surgery |
| AL | American Legion | | Chm | Chairman |
| AM | Master of Arts | | CI | Channel Islands |
| Amb | Ambassador | | CIE | Companion of the Order of the Indian Empire |
| *ante* | Before | | C-in C | Commander-in-Chief |
| apptd | Appointed | | cl | Class |
| AQMG | Assistant Quartermaster-General | | Cllr | Councillor |
| Arb | Arbitrator/-te/-ion | | Cmd | Command |
| Arch | Architect/-ure/-ural | | cmd'd | Commanded |
| Arty | Artillery | | cmdg | Commanding |
| ASCAP | American Society of Composers, Authors and Writers | | Cmdr | Commander |
| | | | Cndt | Commandant |
| ASC | Army Service Corps | | CMG | Companion of the Order of St Michael and St George |
| Assist | Assistant | | | |
| Assoc | Associate/-d/-ion | | Co | Company |
| Assocn | Association | | co | County |
| | | | Col | Colonel |
| | | | Coll | College |
| *b* | Born | | Collr | Collector |
| BA | Bachelor of Arts | | Commn | Commission |
| Bach | Bachelor | | commn'd | Commissioned |
| *bapt* | Baptized | | Commr | Commissioner |
| Batt | Battery | | Compt | Comptroller |
| BCh | Bachelor of Surgery | | Conf | Conference |
| BCL | Bachelor of Civil Law | | Conn | Connecticut |
| BD | Bachelor of Divinity | | Cons | Consultant/-ative |
| Bd | Board | | Corpn | Corporation |
| Bde | Brigade | | Corres | Correspondent/-ing |
| BEO | Board of Economic Operation | | CS | Civil Service |
| BL | Bachelor of Law | | CSA | Confederate States Army |
| Bldg | Building | | CSN | Confederate States Navy |
| Bn | Battalion | | Cttee | Committee |
| Brev | Brevet | | CVO | Commander of the Royal Victorian Order |
| BSc | Bachelor of Science | | | |
| Bt | Baronet | | | |
| *bur* | Buried | | *d* | Died |
| BURKE'S *LG* | BURKE'S *Landed Gentry* | | DAAG | Deputy Assistant Adjutant General |

| | |
|---|---|
| DAG | Deputy Adjutant General |
| DAR | Daughters of the American Revolution |
| dau | Daughter |
| DBE | Dame Commander of the Order of the British Empire |
| DC | District of Columbia (Washington) |
| DCH | Diploma in Children's Health |
| DCJ | District Court Judge |
| DCL | Doctor of Civil Law |
| DCM | Distinguished Conduct Medal |
| DD | Doctor of Divinity |
| Def | Defense |
| Deleg | Delegate/-ation |
| Dep | Deputy |
| Des | Designate |
| DFC | Distinguished Flying Cross |
| Dir | Director |
| diss | Dissolved |
| Dist | District |
| Div | Division |
| div | Divorce |
| Divnl | Divisional |
| DJAG | Deputy Judge Advocate General |
| DL | Deputy Lieutenant |
| DMus | Doctor of Music |
| DOMS | Diploma in Ophthalmic Medicine and Surgery |
| DPH | Diploma of Doctor of Public Health |
| DSC | Distinguished Service Cross |
| DSc | Doctor of Science |
| DSM | Distinguished Service Medal |
| DSO | Companion of the Distinguished Service Order |
| *dsp* | *decessit sine prole* (died without issue) |
| *dspl* | *decessit sine prole legitima* (died without legitimate issue) |
| *dspm* | *decessit sine prole mascula* (died without male issue) |
| *dspms* | *decessit sine prole mascula superstite* (died without surviving male issue) |
| *dsps* | *decessit sine prole superstite* (died without surviving issue) |
| *dunm* | Died unmarried |
| *dvp* | *decessit vita patris* (died in the lifetime of the father) |
| *dvm* | *decessit vita matris* (died in the lifetime of the mother) |
| *dvu* | *decessit vitae uxoris* (died in the lifetime of the husband/wife) |
| | |
| E | East/-ern; Earl |
| Eccles | Ecclesiastic/-al |
| ED | Efficiency Decoration |
| Edcn | Education |
| edcnalist | Educationalist |
| Edin | Edinburgh |
| *Edn* | Edition |
| *educ* | Educated at |
| Elect | Electric/-al |
| EM | Efficiency Medal |
| empd | Employed |
| engr | Engineer |
| Engrg | Engineering |
| Exam | Examiner/-ation |
| Exor | Executor |
| Expdn | Expedition |
| Expdny | Expeditionary |
| Extraord | Extraordinary |
| | |
| FAA | Fleet Air Arm |
| FAmerAcad Opt | Fellow of the American Academy of Opticians |
| FBA | Fellow of the British Academy |
| FBI | Federal Bureau of Investigation |
| Fed | Federal |
| Fedn | Federation |
| Fell | Fellow |
| FRS | Fellow of the Royal Society |
| FRSA | Fellow of the Royal Society of Arts |
| FTC | Federal Trade Commission |

| | |
|---|---|
| Fus | Fusiliers |
| F/Lt | Flight Lieutenant |
| F/O | Flying Officer |
| | |
| GBE | Knight (or Dame) Grand Cross of the Order of the British Empire |
| GC | George Cross |
| G/Capt | Group Captain |
| GCB | Knight Grand Cross of the Order of the Bath |
| Gd | Grand |
| Gen | General |
| Glas | Glasgow |
| GOC | General Officer Commanding |
| Gov | Governor |
| Gov-Gen | Governor-General |
| Govt | Government |
| Govtl | Governmental |
| Gren | Grenadier |
| Grm | Grammar (School) |
| GSO | General Staff Officer |
| | |
| HBM | His or Her Britannic Majesty |
| HG | Home Guard |
| HI and RH | His or Her Imperial and Royal Highness |
| HH | His or Her Highness |
| HIH | His or Her Imperial Highness |
| Highrs | Highlanders |
| Hist | History/-orical |
| HM | His or Her Majesty |
| HMS | His or Her Majesty's Ship |
| Hon | (The) Honourable |
| hon | Honorary |
| Hosp | Hospital |
| HRH | His or Her Royal Highness |
| HSH | His or Her Serene Highness |
| Hus | Hussars |
| Hy | Heavy |
| | |
| i/c | In charge of |
| Imp | Imperial |
| Inc | Incorporated |
| Inf | Infantry |
| inf | Infant |
| Inst | Institute |
| Instn | Institution |
| Instr | Instructor |
| Internat | International |
| | |
| JP | Justice of the Peace |
| Jr | Junior |
| Jt | Joint |
| Jtly | Jointly |
| | |
| *k* | Killed |
| *ka* | Killed in action |
| Kt | Knight |
| ktd | Knighted |
| | |
| LD | Doctor of Letters |
| Leg | Legislation |
| *LG* | *Landed Gentry* (BURKE'S) |
| LI | Light Infantry |
| Lieut | Lieutenant |
| LLB | Bachelor of Laws |
| LLD | Doctor of Laws |
| LLM | Master of Laws |
| Lond | London (not in addresses) |
| Lord-Lieut | Lord-Lieutenant |
| Lt-Col | Lieutenant-Colonel |
| Lt-Cmdr | Lieutenant-Commander |
| Lt-Gen | Lieutenant-General |
| | |
| M | Marquess |
| *m* | Married |

| | | | | |
|---|---|---|---|---|
| MA | Master of Arts | | Regd | Registered |
| Mag | Magistrate | | Regn | Region |
| Major-Gen | Major-General | | Regnl | Regional |
| Man Dir | Managing Director | | Regt | Regiment |
| Mass | Massachusetts | | Rep | Representative |
| MBE | Member of the Order of the British Empire | | Res | Reserve; Resident |
| MC | Military Cross | | ret | Retired |
| MCh | Master of Surgery | | Rev | (The) Reverend |
| MD | Doctor of Medicine | | RFC | Royal Flying Corps |
| Med | Medicine/-ical | | RI | Rhode Island |
| mem | Member | | Rly | Railway |
| Met | Metropolitan | | RM | Royal Marines |
| Mfrs | Manufacturers | | RMC | Royal Military College |
| Mgr | Manager; Monsignor | | RN | Royal Navy |
| MI | Military Intelligence | | RNR | Royal Naval Reserve |
| MIBiol | Member of the Institute of Biology | | RNVR | Royal Naval Volunteer Reserve |
| Mil | Military | | Rt | Right |
| MIME | Member of Institution of Mining Engineers | | | |
| Min | Minister/-ry | | | |
| MInstCE | Member, Institute of Civil Engineers | | S | South/-ern |
| MInstT | Member, Institute of Transport | | s | Succeeded |
| MLA | Member, Legislative Assembly | | SC | Staff Corps |
| MLC | Member, Legislative Council | | ScD | Doctor of Sciences |
| MO | Medical Officer | | Sch | School |
| MOH | Medical Officer of Health | | Scot | Scotland; Scottish |
| MP | Member of Parliament | | Sec | Secretary |
| Mtd | Mounted | | Sen | Senator |
| Munic | Municipal | | Sett | Settlement |
| MVO | Member of the Royal Victorian Order | | S/Ldr | Squadron Leader |
| | | | Soc | Society |
| | | | Sqdn | Squadron |
| N | North/-ern | | Sr | Senior |
| NAS | National Academy of Science | | SR | Supplementary (or Special) Reserve |
| Nat | National | | SS | Steamship |
| NATO | North Atlantic Treaty Organization | | surg | Surgeon |
| NI | Native Infantry | | surv | Surviving |
| nr | Near | | | |
| NY | New York State | | | |
| NZ | New Zealand | | T/ | Temporary |
| | | | TD | Territorial Decoration |
| | | | Tech | Technical |
| OBE | Officer of the Order | | *temp* | Living in time of (*tempore*) |
| | of the British Empire | | trans | Transferred |
| OCD | Office of Civilian Defense | | Treas | Treasurer/-y |
| Offg | Officiating | | Trib | Tribune |
| Offr | Officer | | Trin | Trinity |
| OM | Order of Merit | | Trop | Tropical |
| Org | Organisation | | | |
| *os* | Old Style (dates) | | | |
| OSS | Office of Strategic Service | | Univ | University |
| | | | UNO | United Nations Organisation |
| | | | USA | United States of America |
| *p* | Page | | USAF | United States Air Force |
| Parl | Parliament/-ary | | USAAF | United States Army Air Force |
| PC | Privy Councillor | | USCC | United States Chamber of Commerce |
| Perm | Permanent | | USM | United States Marines |
| Pfc | Private first class (Army) | | USMA | United States Military Academy |
| PH | Purple Heart | | USMC | United States Marine Corps |
| PhD | Doctor of Philosophy | | USN | United States Navy |
| Plen | Plenipotentiary | | USNAC | United States Naval Air Corps |
| P/O | Pilot Officer | | USNR | United States Naval Reserve |
| *post* | After | | USV | United States Volunteers |
| *pr* | Proved | | | |
| Preb | Prebendary | | | |
| Pres | President | | *v* | *versus* (against) |
| Prin | Principal | | V | Viscount |
| Priv | Private | | Visn | Visitation |
| Prob | Probate/-ion/-ionary | | Vol | Volunteer |
| Prod | Production | | | |
| Prof | Professor/-ional | | | |
| Prov | Province | | W | West/-ern |
| | | | W/Cmdr | Wing Commander |
| R | Royal | | | |
| RA | Royal Artillery; Royal Academician | | Yeo | Yeomanry |
| RAF | Royal Air Force | | yr | Younger |
| RE | Royal Engineers | | yst | Youngest |

# Index

This Index contains over 2,700 different surnames. Every surname (of living and dead people) appearing in the pedigrees (pp 27-630) has been indexed below. Surnames of Presidents are given in capitals. The page references shown in bold print are to indicate that the main entry (as opposed to a passing reference) appears there. References to surnames appearing in APPENDICES C and D (the Genealogical Tables) are given thus—"C1" signifying that the surname will be found in Table No. 1 in APPENDIX C.

# Addendum

*The information given below was received too late to be incorporated into the appropriate place in the text (which is indicated at the beginning of each item).*

**Washington** *p 59*—Mr Richard Scott Washington was *b* 13 (*not* 15) Oct, and *m* 8 (*not* 9) Nov. His 4th child, Mark Sharpe Washington was *b* 22 (*not* 24) Jan.

**Washington** *p 60, col 2*—Mr William Temple Allen Baxter is Personnel Mgr, US Civil Service Commn. He was *educ* Lafayette Coll. His dau's husband, Paul Stephen Hughes was *b* at Oneonta, New York 28 April 1949, and is son of Raymond Archie Hughes, by his wife Audrey Louise Donovan.

**Washington** *p 61, col 1*—Mrs Charles Washington Phillips (*née* Patricia June Ross) was dau of Irving Douglas Ross, by his wife Lillian Mae Fowler. Her dau-in-law, Susan Louise Buckley (*b* at Santa Monica, California 31 Oct 1951), is dau of Charles Burres Buckley, by his wife Mary Nind Lacy, and has issue, ●Kimberly Shannon PHILLIPS, *b* at Lexington Park, Maryland 26 July 1974. Mr Charles Washington Phillips, Sr's 2nd wife was formerly wife of — Blecha, and dau of Russell W. Harris, by his wife Ruth Audrey O'Dell.

**Washington** *p 62, col 2*—Mr Nathaniel Robert Williams's dau is Jacque Leanne WILLIAMS, *b* at Corpus Christi, Texas 18 Aug 1968. His adopted son is Jeffery Brian WILLIAMS, *b* at Panama City, Florida 12 May 1971.

**W. H. Harrison** *p 214, col 1*—expand entry as follows:—
●Hermione Flagler HENDRYX, *b* at Cincinnati, Ohio 17 Jan 1918, *m* at Traverse City, Michigan 2 Sept 1942, ●Dr Fred George Swartz, Jr, son of Dr Fred George Swartz, by his wife Edith Morgan, and has issue,
　1*b*●Fred George SWARTZ III, *b* at Corvallis, Oregon 10 Aug 1943.
　2*b*●Mary Ann SWARTZ, *b* at Ann Arbor, Michigan 5 June 1946.
　3*b*●Edith Myra SWARTZ, *b* at Grosse Pointe, Michigan 5 Sept 1952.

**Tyler** *p 226, col 1*—John Baytop Scott was son of Thomas Baytop Scott, by his wife Martha Gaines Marks.

**Tyler** *p 227, col 1*—expand entry as follows:—
(5) Thomas Baytop SCOTT, *b* at Mount Meigs, Montgomery, Alabama 17 May 1881, *m* at Savannah, Georgia 15 Aug 1910, Kathleen Ann Swain (*b* at Altamaha, Tattnall County, Georgia 10 Nov 1891; *d* at Atlanta, Georgia 1 March 1972), and *d* at Montgomery 3 Jan 1946, having had issue,
　1*a* Kathleen Mozelle SCOTT, *b* at Savannah, Georgia 27 June 1911, *m* at Montgomery 5 June 1935, ●Charles Hannon

Pointer (*b* at Montgomery 1908), and *dsp* at Montgomery 10 Aug 1937.
　2*a*●Grace Tyler SCOTT, *b* at Savannah, Georgia 8 April 1913, *m* at Montgomery 29 Sept 1937, ●Benjamin Watkins Lacy IV (*b* at Louisville, Kentucky 23 Oct 1912), and has issue,
　　1*b*●Benjamin Watkins LACY V, *b* at Montgomery 22 Oct 1938, *m* at Pensacola, Florida 10 Sept 1966, ●Judith Ann Vucovich (*b* at Pensacola 30 July 1944), and has issue,
　　　1*c*●Judith Ann LACY, *b* at Bunnell, Florida 4 Feb 1970.
　　　2*c*●Benjamin Watkins LACY VI, *b* at Bunnell, Florida 8 Sept 1974.
　　2*b*●Thomas Scott LACY, *b* at Montgomery 11 Aug 1942, *m* at Atlanta, Georgia 1 Sept 1965, ●Martha Elizabeth Dodd (*b* at Atlanta 24 March 1947), and has issue,
　　　1*c*●Thomas Scott LACY, Jr, *b* at Atlanta 11 July 1966.
　　　2*c*●Joseph Arthur LACY, *b* at Tallahassee, Florida 8 May 1969.
　　3*b*●Kathleen Medora LACY, *b* at Montgomery 22 Sept 1949.
　3*a*●Mary Helen SCOTT, *b* at Savannah, Georgia 22 Aug 1915, *m* at Bessemer, Alabama 29 Dec 1936, ●George Hails Foster (*b* at Montgomery 26 Dec 1914) [*321 Atwood Drive, NW, Marietta, Georgia 30060, USA*], and has issue,
　　1*b*●George Hails FOSTER, Jr, *b* at Montgomery 15 Dec 1937, *m* at Mobile, Alabama 31 July 1965, ●Alice Vivian Mighell (*b* at New Orleans 19 March 1943), and has issue,
　　　1*c*●George Hails FOSTER III, *b* at Winston Salem, N Carolina 28 Dec 1968.
　　　2*c*●Ashley Mighell FOSTER, *b* at Winston Salem 26 Dec 1971.
　　2*b*●Robert Scott FOSTER, *b* at Alhambra, Los Angeles County, California 3 April 1944, *m* 1st at San Diego, California 2 July 1966 (*m* diss by div), Lucy Ann Olsen (*b* 11 Aug 1944), and has issue,
　　　●Robert Scott FOSTER, Jr, *b* at Waukegan, Illinois 17 May 1969.
　　Robert Scott Foster *m* 2ndly at Houma, Louisiana 2 Jan 1972, ●Charlene Gayle Crawley (*b* at New Orleans 30 April 1948).
　　3*b*●Kathleen Ann FOSTER, *b* at Long Beach, California 23 Dec 1947, *m* at Montgomery 11 July 1968, ●Michael Elmore Havey (*b* at Howard AFB, Panama Canal Zone 14 Dec 1946), and has issue,
　　　●Kathleen Scott HAVEY, *b* at Fairborn, Ohio 28 April 1970.

4*b*●Mary Fairlie FOSTER, *b* at Taft, California 26 Dec 1951.

4*a*●Priscilla Cooper SCOTT, *b* at Savannah, Georgia 21 Dec 1919, *m* at Montgomery 5 May 1943, ●Quentin Claiborne Crommelin (*b* at Montgomery 1918), and has issue,

1*b*●Quentin Claiborne CROMMELIN, Jr, *b* at Montgomery 11 Oct 1944.

2*b*●Priscilla Tyler CROMMELIN, *b* at Baltimore, Maryland 21 Aug 1947.

5*a*●Robert Tyler SCOTT, *b* at Savannah, Georgia 23 Sept 1922, *m* at Mansfield, Ohio 17 March 1951, ●Margaret Van Tilburg (*b* at Mansfield 11 Oct 1928), and has issue,

1*b*●Susan Finley SCOTT, *b* at Cleveland, Ohio 25 Aug 1952.

2*b*●Kathleen Mozelle SCOTT, *b* at New Orleans 27 Aug 1957.

3*b*●Joann SCOTT, *b* at New Orleans 9 Aug 1959.

6*a*●Ann Linwood SCOTT, *b* at Montgomery 23 April 1926, *m* there 3 May 1947, ●Rev Milton LeGrand Wood III (*b* at Selma, Alabama 21 Aug 1922) [*Rt 1, Box 26, Sandersville, Georgia 31082, USA*], and has issue,

1*b*●Elizabeth Leigh WOOD, *b* at Mobile, Alabama 24 Oct 1950, *m* at Atlanta, Georgia 16 June 1973, ●Charles Bealer Pate (*b* at Darlington, S Carolina 30 Aug 1944).

2*b*●Kathleen Ann WOOD, *b* at Mobile, Alabama 15 Nov 1951.

3*b*●Milton LeGrand WOOD IV, *b* at Atlanta, Georgia 24 June 1954.

4*b*●Roberta Owen WOOD, *b* at Atlanta, Georgia 11 Jan 1960.

**Tyler** *p 227, col 2*—Charles Lewis Marks (husband of Priscilla Cooper Scott) was son of Samuel B. Marks, by his wife Laura Lewis James.

**Garfield** *p 356, col 2*—Edward Williams Garfield was *educ* Williams Coll. He *m* at Milburn, New Jersey 10 April 1928, ●Hope (*b* at Milburn 20 June 1905), dau of Frank D. Dillingham, by his wife Louise Bulkley. His sister, Mary Louise Garfield, *m* at Cleveland, Ohio 7 Oct 1931, ●William Richard Hallaran, MD (*b* at Ferozepore, India 27 Dec 1904), son of William Hallaran, RAMC, by his wife Mary Newton, and has issue,

(1) ●Sarah Newton HALLARAN, *b* at Cleveland, Ohio 1 Oct 1934, *m* there 14 June 1957, ●James Gramentine, son of James Gramentine, by his wife Helen Meier, and has issue,

1*a*●James Garfield GRAMENTINE, *b* at Cleveland 16 Aug 1960.

2*a*●Helen Elizabeth GRAMENTINE, *b* at Cleveland 12 Sept 1963.

(2) ●William Garfield HALLARAN, MD, *b* at Cleveland 2 Jan 1938, *m* there 30 March 1963, ●Elizabeth, dau of Stanley Salter, by his wife Katherine Ottesen, and has issue,

1*a*●William Patrick HALLARAN, *b* at Cleveland 16 Dec 1965.

2*a*●Timothy Richard HALLARAN, *b* at Cleveland 2 Sept 1967.

(3) ●Michael Terence HALLARAN, *b* at Cleveland 25 April 1947, *m* at N Granby, Conn 21 June 1970, ●Alice, dau of Willard Kellogg, by his wife Grace Hamilton.

**Cleveland** *p 382, col 2*—Ann Mary Cleveland's husband is Thomas Bolling Robertson III and their son is Thomas Bolling Robertson IV. Their elder dau, Elizabeth Averett Robertson, *m* at the Church of the Redeemer, Baltimore 14 Sept 1974,

●Laurence Ray Arnold, son of Clifford Emil Arnold, of St Albans, W Virginia.

**T. Roosevelt** *p 422, col 1*—Theodore Roosevelt, Jr was awarded the Congressional Medal of Honour posthumously. His grandson, Theodore Roosevelt IV, served with USN in Vietnam 1965-67 and was awarded the Navy Commendation Medal. He is Lt-Cmdr USNR, joined the Dept of State 1967, and served as 2nd Sec, US Embassy, Upper Volta. He was *b* at Jacksonville, Florida 27 Nov 1942, *educ* Groton, Harvard (AB 1965), and Harvard Business Sch (MBA 1972), *m* at Woods Hole, Mass 7 Aug 1970, ●Constance Lane (*b* at new York 5 July 1944), dau of Charles E. Rogers, by his wife Doris Draper.

**T. Roosevelt** *p 423, col 1*—Kermit Roosevelt, Jr *m* at Farmington, Conn. His wife was *b* 29 March 1917, and is dau of Houston Gaddis, by his wife Mary Avery. Their son, Kermit Roosevelt III, lawyer, was *b* at Cambridge, Mass 7 April 1938, *educ* Harvard (AB 1960), and Columbia, *m* at New Haven, Conn 7 May 1967, ●Priscilla (*b* at Baltimore, Maryland 28 Jan 1942), dau of Lloyd Reynolds, by his wife Mary Tracket, and has issue,

1*a*●Corinne Avery ROOSEVELT, *b* at New York 23 April 1969.

2*a*●Kermit ROOSEVELT IV, *b* at Washington, DC 14 July 1971.

**Taft** *p 435, col 2*—Miss Virginia Stone Taft, *b* 1950, *educ* Concord Acad, Radcliffe Coll, and Univ of Kent at Canterbury, England (MA 1973), *m* 14 Sept 1974, Keith Carabine, son of George J. Carabine, of Manchester, England.

**Davis** *p 595, col 2*—Charles Francis Bennett's 1st wife was Susan, dau of William Baker, by his wife Betty Jean Law. They had two adopted children, William Russell Bennett, *b* at Colorado Springs 21 Sept 1967, and Nina Margaret Bennett, *b* at Colorado Springs 19 Oct 1968. Charles Francis Bennett *m* 2ndly 27 Dec 1973, ●Patricia Anne Mize, and by her has issue, ●Charles Jefferson BENNETT, *b* 2 Dec 1974.

**Davis** *p 596, col 1*—Michael Howard Collins is an architect and partner in the firm of Collins & Roberts, which he formed in 1967. He was *educ* Univ of Colorado, Colorado Coll, and Kansas State Univ (B Arch 1964). His wife Linda, who founded The Children's Sch, Colorado Springs 1972, and is a mem of the Faculty of Colorado Springs Sch, is dau of Edwin Earle Corbin, by his wife Harriet Boyt.

**Davis** *p 596, col 2*—Harvey Otis Young II served in World War II as Capt USAF 1941-46 and has been a livestock rancher since 1946. He was *educ* Colorado State Univ (BSME 1941). His wife is dau of Thomas Joseph Murphy, by his wife Sophie Lee Hilliard.

**Davis** *p 597, col 1*—James Morris Young served with US Army in Vietnam 1967-69 and was awarded the Purple Heart, Bronze Star. He *m* 1st (*m* diss by div 1967), Joanne Williams, and had issue (1*b*●Lisa Ann YOUNG, *b* at Montrose, Colorado 26 April 1966). He *m* 2ndly at Norwood, Colorado 15 May 1967, ●Rosemary (*b* at Ornogu, Missouri 2 Oct 1951), dau of William Eugene Barnes, by his wife Sarah Katherine Horine, and has issue, his three yr children (*as in the text*).

**Rockefeller** *p 606*—Nelson Aldrich Rockefeller's appointment as 41st VICE-PRESIDENT was confirmed by Senate 10 Dec 1974, and he took oath of office 19 Dec 1974.